LET'S GO:

The Budget Guide to the USA

1990

Mallay B. Charters
Editor

Kimberly Chabot
Andrea Sachs
Assistant Editors

Written by Harvard Student Agencies, Inc.

PAN BOOKS
London, Sydney and Auckland

Helping Let's Go

If you have suggestions or corrections, or just want to share your discoveries, drop us a line. We read every piece of correspondence, whether a 10-page letter, a postcard, or, as in one case, a collage. All suggestions are passed along to our researcher/writers. Please note that mail received after June 1, 1990 will probably be too late for the 1991 book, but will be retained for the following edition. Address mail to: Let's Go: USA; Harvard Student Agencies, Inc.; Thayer Hall-B; Harvard University; Cambridge, MA 02138; USA.

In addition to the invaluable travel advice our readers share with us, many are kind enough to offer their services as researchers. Unfortunately, the charter of Harvard Student Agencies, Inc. enables us to employ only currently enrolled Harvard students both as researchers and editorial staff.

Published in Great Britain by Pan Books Ltd
Cavaye Place, London SW10 9PG
9 8 7 6 5 4 3 2

Published in the United States of America
by St. Martin's Press, Inc.

ISBN: 0 330 31137 9

Let's Go: USA is written by Harvard Student Agencies, Inc., Harvard University, Thayer Hall-B, Cambridge, Mass. 02138, USA.

Printed and bound in the United States of America.

Editor	Mallay Charters
Assistant Editors	Kimberly Chabot Andrea Sachs
Publishing Manager	Nathanael Joe Hayashi
Managing Editors	Allen R. Barton Helen McCracken Gould Alex MacC. Ross
Production/Communication Coordinator	Karen L. Thompson
Researcher/Writers	
Los Angeles, The Desert, Sierra Nevada, CA	Laurence W. Chang
Washington, DC; Virginia; West Virginia	William Chettle
Portland, OR; Olympic Peninsula, N. Cascade Range, San Juan Islands, WA; Vancouver, Victoria, BC	Chris Cowell
Connecticut; Maine; Massachusetts; New Hampshire; Rhode Island; Vermont	Michael B. Friemer
Florida Everglades, Florida Keys, Miami, Ft. Lauderdale, FL	Mala Goankar
San Francisco Bay Area, San Francisco, CA	Joshua B. Goldstine
Kansas City, MO; Carlsbad Caverns, National Park, NM; Texas (except Houston, Galveston Island, and East Texas); Oklahoma; Kansas; Iowa; Nebraska; South Dakota	Cherie S. Harder
Houston, Galveston Island, East Texas, TX; Memphis, TN; Arkansas; Alabama; Louisiana; Mississippi	Henry P. Harris
Northern California; Lake Tahoe, Sacramento, CA; Reno, NV	Andrew Jack
North Carolina; South Carolina; Kentucky; Tennesee (except Memphis); Georgia; Florida (except Miami, the Keys, the Everglades, and Ft. Lauderdale)	Brooke E. Jewett
Pennsylvania; Maryland; Delaware; New Jersey; New York (except NYC and	

Long Island); Ontario and Quebec, Canada	Madeline E. McIntosh
San Diego and Central Coast, CA; Arizona; New Mexico (except Carlsbad Caverns); Las Vegas, NV	Jeff Moran
Hawaii	Sean Pager
New York City and Long Island, NY	Nicole Parisier
North Dakota; Montana; Idaho; Wyoming; Colorado; Utah	Rebecca H. Rhodes
Spokane, WA; Alberta; Okanagan Valley, BC	James Rosen
St. Louis, MO; Ohio; Michigan; Indiana; Illinois; Minnesota; Wisconsin	Heberden W. Ryan
Alaska	Davis N. Schisgall
Oregon Coast and Crater Lake National Park, OR; Seattle, Mt. Saint Helens, WA	Elijah Siegler
Advertising Manager	David A. Kopp
Advertising Representatives	Kathryn L. Cahir Anthony P. Denninger Suzanne J. Kohl
Legal Counsel	Posternak, Blankstein, and Lund

ACKNOWLEDGMENTS

I was a lucky editor in that my group of researcher/writers was extremely talented and dedicated. Will Chettle wowed us with intellectual and informed coverage of Washington, DC, and won fame and glory as the 100,000th person to enter the Charlottesville visitors center. Chris Cowell trekked diligently through Oregon, Washington, and British Columbia. Mike Freimer brought his love of the outdoors and chocolate to his write-up of New England. Mala Gaonkar saved southernmost Florida from disaster by stepping in at the last minute and providing excellent coverage. Cherie Harder, the "Great Plains girl," worked her spunky way through her itinerary undeterred by bratty ten-year olds and overly persistent admirerers. Henry Harris enjoyed the requisite tour of Graceland and sent us back excellent copy of his journey through the south-central region. Andrew Jack helped us expand northern California and Reno—thanks. Brooke Jewett braved such hardships as a night on a luxury yacht/hostel in the course of her thorough and lively research of the southeast. Madeline McIntosh sailed through the Mid-Atlantic region, Ontario, Quebec, and upstate New York to provide copy so crisp and clear it was a cinch to edit. Jeff Moran, intoxicated either by the depth of the Grand Canyon or the whiteness of the full moon, braved the southwestern heat to turn in the summer's most entertaining copy. Sean Pager enthusiastically toured Hawaii, introducing us to Oahu's "other side." Niki Parisier sent us a delightfully reflective Big Apple. Rebecca Rhodes left no stone in the Rockies unturned; her diligence was truly remarkable. Jamie Rosen cheerfully delivered the goods on parts of the Pacific Northwest. Heb Ryan braved sleazy hotels and inadequate bus service to get us accurate, descriptive coverage of the Great Lakes. David Schisgall toured Alaska, "the last frontier," and wrote up his findings thoroughly and entertainingly. Thanks also to Laurence Chang, Josh Goldstine, and Elijah Siegler for their much-appreciated contributions to the book.

Whether I needed help capturing the essence of "Joisey" or verifying information on flights to Canada, my assistant editors Kim Chabot and Andrea Sachs never let me down. They consistently went above and beyond the call of duty. I can only humbly express my gratitude that they both were willing to pull so hard for our book. From that early spaghetti dinner to the pop of the champagne cork signalling the book's completion: it's been a great summer working with them.

Thanks also to Allen Barton, my eagle-eyed managing editor, and publishing manager Joe Hayashi and production/communication coordinator Karen Thompson. All three of them were instrumental in the success of *Let's Go: USA 1990.* I would also like to express my gratitude to Alex Star, Salil Kumar, and Jon Savett for their help.

Debbie, Pete, Ravi—working with you has been one of the best things about this job.

Lastly, without all the supportive people in my life, this summer wouldn't have been as wonderful. Thanks to mom, dad, and Nora. And warmest thanks to Erik, who gave me advice not only on what to include in the book but also on how to handle the demands the job imposed. His stress-relieving regimen of savory spaghetti dinners and *Jeopardy* is remembered with love.

PACIFIC STANDARD TIME
MOUNTAIN STANDARD TIME
BRITISH COLUMBIA
ALBERTA
SASKATCHEWAN
MANIT
Seattle
WASHINGTON
Olympia
Spokane
Coeur d'Alene
Portland
Salem
OREGON
NORTH DAKOT
Bismarc
MONTANA
Helena
Billings
ROCKY MOUNTAINS
Boise
IDAHO
SOUTH DAKOTA
Pierre
Missouri
Casper
WYOMING
NEBRASKA
Reno
Sacramento
Carson City
NEVADA
Salt Lake City
Provo
Cheyenne
Boulder
Denver
Linc
San Francisco
UTAH
Colorado River
COLORADO
KANSAS
CALIFORNIA
Las Vegas
PACIFIC OCEAN
Los Angeles
Santa Fe
OKLAHO
ARIZONA
Albuquerque
Phoenix
San Diego
NEW MEXICO
Tucson
El Paso
TEXAS
San Antonio
ALASKA STANDARD TIME
ALASKA
Fairbanks
YUKON TERR.
N
Anchorage
Juneau
0 kilometers 500
0 miles 300

United States
EASTERN
STANDARD
TIME
ONTARIO
QUEBEC
ATLANTIC
STANDARD
TIME
N.B.
MAINE
Augusta
Portland
Montpelier
VT.
N.H.
Concord
Boston
Provincetown
NEW
YORK
Albany
MASS.
Providence
R.I.
Hartford
New Haven
CONN.
New York
Trenton
N.J.
Atlantic City
Newark
Philadelphia
PENNSYLVANIA
Harrisburg
Wilmington
Baltimore
Dover
DELAWARE
MARYLAND
Annapolis
Washington,
D C
Chesapeake Bay
Richmond
Norfolk
VIRGINIA
WEST
VIRGINIA
Charleston
Pittsburgh
Cleveland
Columbus
OHIO
Cincinnati
Buffalo
Lake Ontario
Lake Erie
Lake Huron
Lake Michigan
Lake Superior
MICHIGAN
Detroit
ESOTA
Duluth
St. Paul
apolis
WISCONSIN
Milwaukee
Madison
Falls
IOWA
Des Moines
Chicago
Bloomington
ILLINOIS
Springfield
Indianapolis
INDIANA
Ohio
River
Kansas
City
Jefferson City
MISSOURI
St. Louis
Louisville
Frankfort
KENTUCKY
Nashville
TENNESSEE
Memphis
Mississippi
River
NORTH
CAROLINA
Raleigh
Charlotte
SOUTH
CAROLINA
Columbia
Charleston
ATLANTIC
OCEAN
ARKANSAS
Little Rock
ALABAMA
Birmingham
Montgomery
Mobile
Atlanta
GEORGIA
Savannah
Jacksonville
Jackson
MISSISSIPPI
LOUISIANA
Baton
Rouge
New Orleans
Tallahassee
FLORIDA
Tampa
Miami
Gulf of Mexico
kilometers 500
0
miles 300
0
HAWAII
STANDARD
TIME
Honolulu
HAWAII
Hilo
kilometers 200
miles 100
Capital city
Major city

CONTENTS

About Let's Go

In 1960, Harvard Student Agencies, a three-year-old nonprofit corporation established to provide employment opportunities to Harvard and Radcliffe students, was doing a booming business selling charter flights to Europe. One of the extras HSA offered passengers on these flights was a 20-page mimeographed pamphlet entitled *1960 European Guide,* a collection of tips on continental travel compiled by the staff at HSA. The following year, students traveling to Europe researched the first full-fledged edition of *Let's Go: Europe,* a pocket-sized book with a smattering of tips on budget accommodations, irreverent write-ups of sights, and a decidedly youthful slant. The first editions proclaimed themselves to be the helpmates of the "adventurous and often impecunious student."

Throughout the 60s, the series reflected its era: a section of the 1968 *Let's Go: Europe* was entitled "Street Singing in Europe on No Dollars a Day"; the 1969 guide to America led off with a feature on drug-ridden Haight-Ashbury. During the 70s, *Let's Go* gradually became a large-scale operation, adding regional European guides and expanding coverage into North Africa and Asia. In 1981, *Let's Go: USA* returned after an eight-year hiatus, and in the next year HSA joined forces with its current publisher, St. Martin's Press. Now in its 30th year, *Let's Go* publishes 11 titles covering more than 40 countries.

Each spring, over 150 Harvard/Radcliffe students compete for some 70 positions as *Let's Go* researcher/writers. Those hired possess a rare combination of budget travel sense, writing ability, stamina, and courage. Each researcher/writer travels on a shoestring budget for seven weeks, researching seven days per week, and overcoming countless obstacles in the endless quest for better bargains.

Back in a basement in Harvard Yard, an editorial staff of 28 and countless typists and proofreaders spend four months poring over more than 50,000 pages of manuscript as they push the copy through 12 stages of intensive editing. In September the efforts of summer are converted from computer diskettes to nine-track tapes and delivered to Com Com in Allentown, Pennsylvania, where their computerized typesetting equipment turns them into books in record time. And even before the books hit the stands, next year's editions are well underway.

LET'S GO: USA

General Introduction

Let's face it—the United States is a young country. Medieval historians would be bored by its tradition of relative peace and prosperity. No remnants of royal castles dot the countryside. No lost ark sits in a chamber under the soil, waiting to be discovered by intrepid archeologists and movie producers. No astronomical devices made of multi-ton granite lie in empty fields. Yet during its relatively brief history, America has played a large and influential role in international affairs, and has had its share of noteworthy domestic events. For instance, the division of America into 50 states led quite naturally to the invention of *Let's Go: USA.*

Let's Go will help you explore the mysteries of this large country without exploring the depths of your bank account. Will a visit to California leave you tanned and relaxed? Will a visit to Boston leave you wishing that you hadn't decided to drive? Is New York City actually a big apple? *Let's Go: USA* reveals all. You'll find bus schedules, directions to remote campsites and rural towns, tips on finding authentic ethnic cuisine, and hundreds of write-ups of hostels, Ys, motels, and hotels where you can save money without compromising the essentials. Whether you're wondering how to use a local transit system or who designed a skyscraper, where to go after stepping off the bus or how to buy a sleeping bag, *Let's Go* has the answers.

How To Use This Book

What exactly is covered in *Let's Go: USA?* You'll find all 50 states, and major portions of four provinces of Canada. We organize the U.S. into 15 regions, with states listed alphabetically within those regions. In the state and regional introductions, we comment on the geography, history, culture, and other outstanding or unusual characteristics of an area, and we provide tips on adjusting your travel strategies to America's regional diversity. Our maps will give you the general layout of a region, but be sure to use more detailed maps when planning your final itinerary.

As you use this book, you will become familiar with the way we organize information. **Practical Information** presents what you need to know about getting to and around a city, town, or region. For each city, we list modes of transportation, phone numbers, addresses, and visitor information. **Accomodations, Camping, and Food** sections help you take care of the necessary details. **Sights** sections let you know about the most interesting, noteworthy, and inexpensive attractions. **Nightlife, Entertainment,** and **Seasonal Events** listings suggest ways to enjoy budget-minded culture or, at times, an occasional extravagant evening.

Planning Your Trip

Budget travelers have been devising cost-effective ways to see America since Columbus fast-talked his way into Isabella's jewelry box. Riches, however, are not a prerequisite for a richly varied experience. Later budget travelers were the millions of penniless immigrants who disembarked at Ellis Island with visions of streets paved with gold. They learned to survive in the United States on much less money than a typical modern vacationer. We can't promise streets of gold, but we do promise to guide you in your quest for an affordable adventure.

You've heard that there is safety in numbers, but few people realize that there is also more money. Traveling with companions makes any trip safer, more fun, and more economical. Your address book can serve as a supplementary travel guide; staying with friends, relatives, and remote acquaintances vastly reduces accommodation costs. Off-season travel is best in May and September, when the weather is good, tourists are scarce, and prices may be lower. Sometimes, however, the season is "off" for good reason—many facilities and sights close down when the tourists go home.

Of course, many people adhere to travel tradition. Summer visitors to national parks, New England, the Pacific Northwest, and much of the Midwest will find plenty of company. Tan factories such as Florida, Hawaii, southern Arizona, and parts of Southern California attract herds of pale, cold weather refugees from mid-December through late April. Unusual tourist seasons, such as Mardi Gras in New Orleans, are noted in state, regional, and city introductions.

Travel offices, tourist information centers, chambers of commerce, and special interest organizations provide an impressive amount of free information; it's best to write with specific requests. (See our Practical Information listings for addresses of these services.) Travel agents can advise you on the cheapest transportation options, but don't rely exclusively on their information. Do some calling on your own, scan newspaper travel sections, and consult your local bulletin boards as well.

Useful Publications

Over the ages, the most popular and effective travel aids have been road maps. These can be purchased in most gas stations across the country, and are also available at local tourist information centers and public libraries. You can't do better than Rand McNally's *Road Atlas* for the U.S., Canada, and Mexico ($15).

The **U.S. Government Printing Office** prepares over 14,000 publications, many of which pertain to travel. To order the free bibliographies *Recreational and Outdoor Activities* (17) and *Travel and Tourism* (302), write to the Superintendent of Documents, U.S. Government Printing Office, Washington, DC 20402 (202-783-3238). Various national government agencies also publish brochures and books on parks, forests, and wildlife. Scan the shelves at a bookstore or library for countless specialty guides on every facet of travel in the U.S., from bed and breakfasts to beaches in the buff. *Let's Go: California & Hawaii* and *Let's Go: Pacific Northwest, Western Canada, & Alaska* are invaluable sources for those traveling in California, Oregon, Washington, Alaska, Hawaii, British Columbia, Alberta, and the Yukon.

Documents

It's a good idea for all travelers to carry two forms of identification, one of which should be a photo ID. Banks, in particular, will want to see more than one ID whenever you cash a traveler's check. Before you leave, make a photocopy of both sides of all of your important documents, such as ID and credit cards, and leave them with someone you can easily contact. If you're a student, one of your forms of ID should be proof of your student status, as there are sometimes special discounts available. (Don't expect, though, the extensive discounts on museum admission, entertainment, transportation, and accommodations found in Europe.) A current university ID card will generally suffice for Americans. Foreign students may want to purchase an **International Student Identification Card (ISIC),** available through several sources (see Information for Foreign Visitors below).

Money

Traveler's checks are accepted virtually everywhere; in most budget establishments, the "no checks" sign refers only to personal checks. All banks issue traveler's checks, some at face value, others at 1-2% commission. Members of the **American Automobile Association (AAA)** can avoid paying a commission by purchasing traveler's checks at any AAA office (see Transportation below). To buy a particular

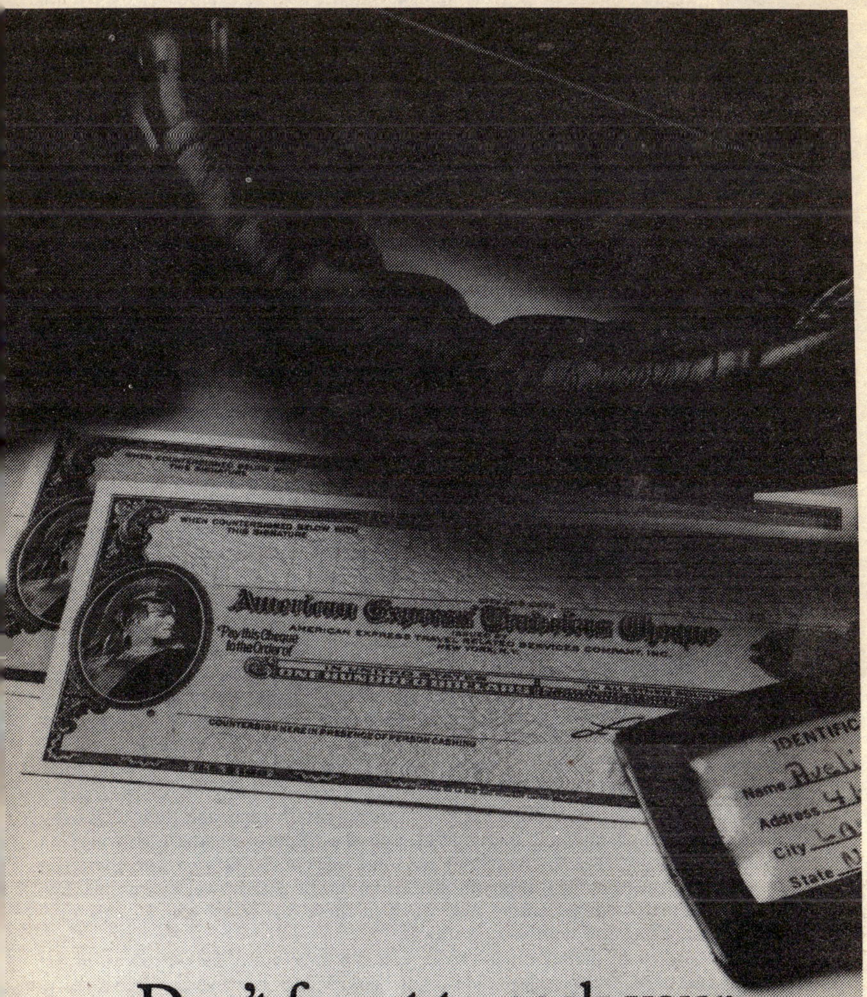
Name
Address
City
State

kind of traveler's check, consult your bank for the nearest vendor. The following is a list of well known brands and the phone numbers to call for information; additional theft or loss hotline numbers are included where applicable. American Express (800-221-7282), Bank of America (800-227-3460; hotline 800-368-7878), Barclay's (800-221-2426; hotline 800-227-6811), Citicorp (800-645-6556; hotline 800-523-1199), MasterCard (800-223-9920), Thomas Cook (800-223-7373), and Visa (800-227-6811). Most of these companies will cash and refund checks through banks and other institutions throughout the U.S. Keep at least one record of your check numbers separate from the checks to expedite replacement if they are lost or stolen. Buying traveler's checks in small denominations ($20) will allow more flexibility; some stores will not accept checks in larger denominations.

With a major **credit card** you can rent cars, make reservations, and obtain cash advances at most banks. Don't plan on relying exclusively on plastic money, as the cheapest places don't trust it. **American Express** cardholders pay a relatively steep annual fee ($55) but the card entitles them to several valuable services. Local offices will cash personal checks (including foreign checks) in any 21-day period up to $1000 ($5000 with a gold card); they pay in cash and traveler's checks depending on the office's money supply. They also cancel stolen credit cards, arrange for temporary ID, help change airline, hotel, and car rental reservations, and send mailgrams or international cables. American Express offices in the U.S. will act as a mail service if you contact them in writing beforehand and request that they hold your mail (see Keeping in Touch below). American Express also operates machines at major airports through which you can purchase traveler's checks with your card. For more information, write to American Express Card Division, 770 Broadway, New York, NY 10003 (800-528-4800). Other widely accepted credit cards are **Mastercard** and **Visa.** Visa in particular now offers many of the same travel services as American Express. Check with local banks about these services, or write to Visa, P.O. Box 5111, 1400 Union Turnpike, New Hyde Park, NY 11042 (800-227-6811).

Credit cards are also compatible with the latest form of plastic financing—**electronic banking.** At least two banking networks offer 24-hour service at automated tellers (operated by bank cards) in major cities across the country. The **Cirrus** network (800-424-7787) includes BayBanks in New England, New York Cash Exchange, First Interstate in the West, and Manufacturers Hanover in New York, among others; the **Plus** network (800-843-7587) includes Bank of America in the West, Chase Manhattan in New York, Continental in Chicago, and First City Bank of Dallas. If you're staying in major cities, a bank card may be better than traveler's checks. Be warned that the machines are sometimes out of service, and there is a limit ($500 at most banks) imposed on the amount of withdrawal in any one day. Visa and Mastercard sometimes also work in these machines. Check with local banks about these and competing services.

If you run out of money on the road, you can have more mailed to you in the form of a **certified check,** redeemable at any bank. Money can also be wired directly from bank to bank for about $6. Another alternative is a **postal money order.** Money orders can be purchased in cash at any U.S. post office for a fee of up to $1 per order, and can be cashed at another office upon display of two IDs (one with photo). The buyer should keep a receipt, as orders are refundable if lost. A generous sibling or parent can have money wired to you in minutes via **Western Union** (800-325-4176) from within the U.S. Western Union charges a wiring fee based on the amount wired and the method of payment; call for information. One must have a MasterCard or Visa to wire by phone.

The prices quoted throughout *Let's Go: USA* are the amounts before **sales tax** has been added. Tax rates vary from about five to eight percent, depending on the item and the state where it is purchased. Remember to add on this percentage to determine the real cost of whatever you are planning to buy. Most states have special hotel taxes over and above sales tax. Look on the back of your hotel room door or ask before you take the room.

Packing

First Commandment Of The Budget Traveler: Travel light.

Many travelers carry a backpack rather than a suitcase or duffel bag. Long favored by campers and hikers, backpacks use a frame to distribute their load comfortably; they also allow use of both hands. However, their tie-on design makes them more vulnerable to snagging and damage in baggage compartments. You should be able to get a good pack for around $125. Shop carefully, since poorly constructed packs are neither comfortable nor durable (see Camping and Hiking below). Talcum powder can prevent sores caused by even the most well constructed backpacks. A daypack is a good investment if you are traveling with a large pack that doesn't need to accompany you on sightseeing forays. If traveling with a backpack doesn't appeal to you, consider a small suitcase with wheels or a duffel bag with a shoulder strap. Prices vary according to quality; again, shop carefully.

Good footwear and rainwear are crucial for any traveler, and not the place to cut costs. Make sure to break in new shoes before you leave. A poncho is a logical choice for bad-weather gear since raincoats won't keep your pack dry. Most ponchos double as groundcloths and are useful for picnicking as well. Lightweight, hooded windbreakers are also excellent traveling gear. Clothing should be comfortable and should require minimal care. Darker colors can mask grime, wear and tear; lighter colors are more suitable for warmer regions. Laundromats are available in most cities. If you don't want to spend your valuable vacation time planted in front of a Maytag, consider doing laundry by hand. Pack a plastic clothesline that can be hung up in your room; your clothes can dry while you enjoy the local sights.

Travelers are sometimes separated from their luggage, temporarily or permanently. Always keep valuable items and identification on your person. Wallets (carried in front pockets), around-the-neck pouches (worn underneath your shirt), and belt pouches are good places to stash money, traveler's checks, tickets, IDs, and credit cards. Place a change of clothes, medication, and any irreplacable items in a carry-on bag.

Serious camera equipment can be expensive, fragile, and heavy. If you only want snapshots, bring a pocket camera or a small, automatic 35mm camera. Buy film in major cities at supermarkets or drugstores since tourist areas often charge ridiculous prices. Have your film hand-checked at airport X-ray machines. If your travels take you to New York City, you may want to purchase equipment there, where prices are generally the lowest in the country. (See New York City, Shopping.)

Keeping in Touch

If you plan to rely on the phone, a calling card offered by AT&T or one of its various competitors, or a Visa, Mastercard, or American Express card, can save money over calling collect. If you want to send a **telegram,** call **Western Union** (800-325-6000). A 25-word message sent from New York to Los Angeles cost $35, including delivery. Post offices offer **mailgrams,** which are the cheapest, and can be sent to any General Delivery location.

Depending on how neurotic your family is, consider making arrangements for the folks back home to get in touch with you. When planning your itinerary, include a series of mailstops where you can check for messages. Ideally these should be scheduled at least once per week. The simplest method is to rely on the **General Delivery** service of the nearest U.S. post office (same as Poste Restante in European post offices). Mail should be sent to you with the words "c/o General Delivery," the name of the town and state, and its ZIP code. To find the **ZIP code** for a particular town, consult *Let's Go* city listings or use a ZIP code directory (available at all post offices). Small towns will list only one code; larger cities have a specific ZIP code for General Delivery and may require the address of the main post office. Post offices are either closed on Saturdays or open only a half-day, and are closed on Sundays and holidays as well. Plan your mailstops for mid-week. Once a letter arrives it will be held for about a week, but may be held longer if it has an arrival date marked clearly on the front of the envelope.

If you've reserved accommodations in advance, you can usually have mail sent to their addresses, with your arrival date marked on the envelope. For emergencies, leave a few phone numbers where your family can leave messages for you.

American Express does not automatically offer a Poste Restante service as it does in Europe, but the offices in the U.S. will act as a mail service for cardholders if you contact them in writing in advance. They will hold mail for one month, forward upon request, and accept telegrams. For a complete list of offices and instructions on how to use the service, get the "Directory of Travel Service Offices" at any office or call 800-528-4800.

Health and Insurance

Common sense will cut down on aspirin and antacid consumption during your travels. Eat well and don't overexert yourself. If you know that you will require medication while you travel, obtain a full supply before you leave and carry medicine prescriptions with you. If you wear glasses or contact lenses, carry either an extra pair or a copy of your prescription.

Travelers with chronic medical conditions should wear a **Medic Alert identification tag.** In addition to indicating the nature of the condition, the tag provides the number of Medic Alert's 24-hour hotline, through which attending personnel can obtain information about the member's medical history. Lifetime membership, including a stainless steel bracelet or necklace, costs $25; write to Medic Alert Foundation International, Turlock, CA 95381-1009 (800-432-5378).

Before you leave, find out what your health insurance covers. Always have proof of insurance and policy numbers with you. If you're a student, you may be covered by your family's policy. If you have insurance through your school, find out if the policy includes summer travel. International travelers should remember that the **International Student Identification Card** provides up to $2000 in accident and illness insurance, but this is only for travel outside of the U.S. For only $11 per month, The **Council of International Education (CIEE)** (212-661-1414) offers a **Trip-Safe Plan** which will give you $2000 of medical coverage within the U.S.

A compact **first-aid kit** should suffice for minor health problems. Aspirin is an obvious essential. Other basic items include band-aids, elastic bandage, scissors, tweezers, a Swiss army knife, burn ointment, a thermometer, antiseptic, motion sickness tablets, and a medicine for diarrhea. Backpackers and bicyclists especially should pack a first-aid kit. The **American Red Cross** sells Auto First-Aid Kits through local chapters ($26.20).

If you get sick while traveling and require emergency treatment, call the police or other emergency facilities for assistance (dial 911 or 0). See our Practical Information listings, consult a telephone book for the numbers of help lines, or go directly to the emergency room of the local hospital. In general, health facilities in the U.S. are excellent, and correspondingly expensive. If the situation does not require immediate attention, look for low-cost or free clinics (e.g. public health clinics, crisis centers, or women's health centers). Hotlines can refer you to clinics where you can receive treatment without proof of insurance. Low-cost medical and dental clinics at universities and colleges may help as well. Check

Safety and Security

There are a lot of shady characters lurking around vacation spots, and even the most careful tourist can be a victim of theft or other crimes. Common sense may save your vacation from premature conclusion. After dark in large cities, avoid areas around bus and train stations, untraveled streets, and public parks. You might want to ask the manager of your hotel or hostel for advice about specific areas. Don't tempt pickpockets; carry your wallet in a front pocket and wear your purse strap diagonally like a Miss-America sash. Whenever you leave your room, take all your valuables with you, even if you are staying in a motel or hotel room. One simple tactic is to wear a money belt, even while sleeping, and bolt your door when you're in the room. While traveling, steer clear of empty train compartments, especially at night. If you want to store your gear while sight-seeing or sleeping, lock it up at a train or bus station.

Travel Assistance International (formerly Europe Assistance) operates a 24-hour-a-day hotline for emergencies and referrals (800-821-2828). You may buy a year-long travel package for $120. Included are medical and travel insurance, financial assistance, and help in replacing lost passports and visas. Write to Travel Assistance International, 1133 15th St. NW, Washington, DC 20005. Another valuable organization is **Travelers Aid International,** which provides assistance in case of theft, car failure, illness, or other "mobility-related problems." Their services are not free to all; the organization considers each case and determines need. Write to them at 1001 Connecticut Ave. NW, #504, Washington, DC 20036 (202-659-9468). See each city's section on Practical Information for local emergency, hotline, and information numbers.

Women travelers must take extra precautions; the best measure is to travel with companions, even if only temporarily. Certain cheap accommodations may entail more risks than they are worth, and hitching isn't safe alone (see Hitchhiking below). Women should also forgo genuine dives and city outskirts in favor of university accommodations, youth hostels or YWCAs. Centrally located spots are usually safest and easiest to return to after dark. Some religious organizations offer rooms only to women and are another safe option.

Accommodations

Hotels and Motels

The budget traveler typically forgoes the sumptuous rooms and doting service of luxury hotels and resorts. Never fear, however; budget accommodations are a permanent fixture on the American landscape. Flashing neon "motel" signs beckon the pennywise tourist. While nobody turns your sheets back or offers complimentary champagne, cheap and reasonably well-kept rooms are easy to find. In accommodation listings throughout this guide, "single" refers to one bed, which often sleeps two people; "double" means two beds. You should verify how many people the room accommodates, if there is a fee for extra people, and if cots are available.

Expect to pay at least $20-30 for a single in a cheap hotel. Most hotels and motels require a key deposit when you register. You will be told in advance if the bathroom is communal. Check-in is usually between 11am and 1pm and check-out is probably before 11am. You may be able to store your gear for the day even after vacating your room and returning the key, but most proprietors will not take responsibility for the safety of your belongings.

Let's Go: USA tries to determine which budget hotel or motel has the best value, based on price, safety, and location. They are ranked in order, after hostels, with the better values higher on the list. Most of the hotels listed are in downtown areas or on highways. Keep in mind that inexpensive downtown hotels are sometimes in undesirable, if not unsafe, neighborhoods. Ask the hotel owner if you can see a room before you pay for it. Hotels often have restaurants where the food is expensive but convenient. Travelers with cars should try to stay in motels outside the city limits where prices may be cheaper and parking is free.

You can reserve most hotel and motel rooms in advance, but this is often not required. Motels tend to fill up by evening, so try not to wait until nightfall to look for a room. You may receive some tips from employees at the bus or train station. If the situation looks hopeless, you can call Travelers Aid or the police (*not* the emergency telephone number) for assistance.

Various budget motels have become familiar sights on the American landscape. Budget chains offer more consistency in cleanliness and comfort than their locally operated generic competitors. Most are independently owned and operated, but will provide listings of their affiliates throughout the United States. The following is a list of chains and their information numbers: **Motel 6** (505-891-6161), **Allstar Inns**

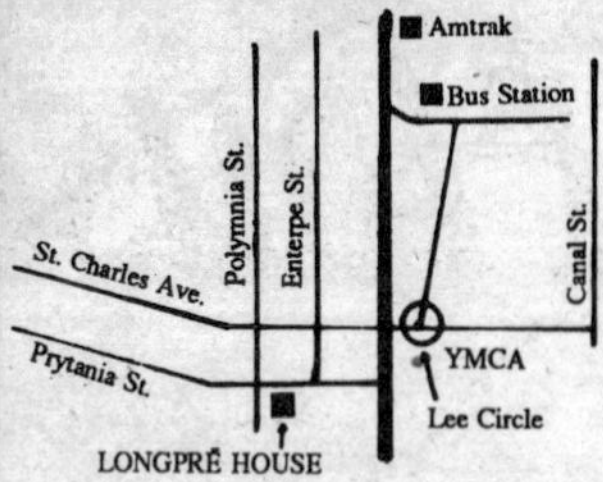

(805-687-3383), **Regal 8** (800-851-8888), **Super 8** (800-843-1991), and **Best Western** (800-528-1234). For more complete listings, consult the *National Directory of Budget Motels,* by Raymond Carlson (Pilot Books, $4.95) or Louis Bree's *State by State Guide to Budget Motels* (MarLor Press, $8.95).

Hostels

Open to everyone, regardless of age, hostels offer the least expensive ($4-12) indoor lodgings. *Let's Go: USA* always lists the nearby hostels before other lodgings in our Accommodations sections. To stay in many hostels, you must be a paid member of **American Youth Hostels, Inc. (AYH)** A one-year membership costs $20 for those 18 to 54, $10 for seniors and those under 18, and $30 for families. AYH maintains 230 U.S. hostels, ranging from simple grade, with bunk beds, cold running water, and a kitchen, to superior grade, with more room and amenities. AYH hostels are friendly, well-run, dorm-style lodgings, and are the best places to meet other budget travelers. **International Youth Hostel Federation (IYHF)** memberships are honored at all AYH hostels. The indispensable *AYH Handbook* (free with membership) includes a list of U.S. hostels, complete with their specific requirements and services. For more information write to American Youth Hostels, Inc., P.O. Box 37613, Washington, DC 20013-7613 (202-783-6161).

The network of AYH and privately run hostels in the U.S. is not nearly as comprehensive as its European counterpart. Hostels are not evenly distributed, so don't count on being able to stay in one wherever you happen to be. Most are clustered in the Northeast, the Great Lakes area, Colorado, California, and the Pacific Northwest. Many of these are in out-of-the-way locations.

The maximum length of stay at a hostel is usually three nights. Reservations (4-6 weeks in advance) are a good idea during peak traveling season, and at all times in large cities. Inconvenient hours can be a drawback at hostels. Most close their buildings from 10am to 5pm and many require check-in between 5pm and 8pm and check-out before 10am. Some have an evening curfew. Alcohol is prohibited and smoking is often restricted or prohibited. Dorm rooms are segregated by sex. Since

there is no housekeeping service, guests share domestic duties. Very few hostels have family accommodations. Hostels require that you bring or rent a sleep sack (two sheets sewn together) to cover your sleeping bag. Sleepsacks are available through **Let's Go Travel Services,** Harvard Student Agencies, Inc., Thayer Hall-B, Harvard University, Cambridge, MA 02138 (617-495-9649 or 800-5-LETS-GO) for $12.95 plus $4 shipping.

Many hostels allow nonmembers to stay for an extra $2-3. Because of local laws, some hostels, such as the YMCA hostels in Los Angeles and Boston, can't accommodate people under 18 without parental permission. City hostels often have stricter rules and higher rates.

YMCAs and YWCAs

If you're planning to stay in a city, don't overlook the **Young Men's Christian Association (YMCA).** Not all YMCAs offer overnight accommodations, but those that do are often downtown and have rates comparable to or lower than other downtown hotels. Singles average $28, doubles average $41; rooms include use of a library, pool, and other facilities. Advance reservations are recommended; a $3 reservation fee is waived for reservations made at least two months in advance. Some YMCAs accept women and families in addition to men. You may have to share a room with another sleeper and use a communal bath or shower. A refundable key deposit of about $5 is charged. Economy packages (2-8 days, $40-270) that include lodging, breakfast, dinners, and excursions are available in New York, New Orleans, Seattle, and Hollywood. The YMCA of Greater New York offers an **International Program,** 124 overnight YMCA accommodation centers in North America and abroad for students and young adults. For information and reservations, write or call **The Y's Way,** 356 W. 34th St., New York, NY 10001 (212-760-5856).

The **Young Women's Christian Association (YWCA)** also provides inexpensive housing and recreational facilities. Most YWCAs accommodate only women. Generally, facilities must be shared with others on the same floor. Nonmembers are required to pay a small membership fee in addition to the overnight fee. In well-

traveled areas, YWCAs are as popular as YMCAs, so inquire in advance about a room. Information on YWCAs with residence facilities across the country is available for $3 from the Order Department, Young Women's Christian Association of the USA, 726 Broadway, New York, NY 10003 (212-614-2700).

Bed and Breakfasts

Bed and breakfasts (B&Bs) and similar tourist homes and guest houses are private homes with spare rooms available to travelers. In some areas, they are the best bargains around; in others, a budget-busting last resort. Singles start at around $25, doubles at $45, and rates rocket upward from there. Many B&Bs are operated under the auspices of regional associations. For listings of B&Bs throughout the country, consult *Bed and Breakfast, USA* by Betty R. Rundback and Nancy Kramer. Or contact **Tourist House Associates, Inc.,** RD 2, Box 355-A, Greentown, PA 18426 (717-857-0856). Other publications include the American Bed & Breakfast Association's *Bed & Breakfast Hostlist,* which includes 1500 cities in the U.S. and Canada ($5.95) and CIEE's listings in *Where to Stay USA* ($10.95). If you order the latter from CIEE (see address below), ask them to include the Hotel Discount Plan directory. Many B&Bs aren't listed in any guidebook, so check the phonebooks and ask around as you travel.

Dormitories

Some colleges and universities open their residence halls to conferences and travelers, especially during the summer. You may have to share a bath, but rates are often low and facilities are usually clean and well-maintained. If you hope to stay at a school, contact its housing office before your vacation; recent legislation in many states has restricted or eliminated dorm room rental to individual travelers.

Alternative Accommodations

As an alternative to the more standard B&B's, contact **Servas,** an international cooperative system of hosts and travelers throughout the U.S. This non-profit organization matches travelers with hosts who provide accommodations for two to three days. You have to provide two letters of reference and arrange for an interview at least one month before your trip. Participation in the program costs $45 per year, but no money is exchanged between travelers and hosts. Contact the U.S. Servas Committee, 11 John St., #706, New York, NY 10038 (212-267-0252). If you belong to a church or synagogue, you may be able to line up similar contacts across the country.

If a night under the stars doesn't seem appealing, but you can't spare the cost of a night's lodgings, call the local Travelers Aid (see Safety and Security above) for information on places to stay in an emergency. The local crisis center hotline may have a list of persons or organizations who will give you a place to stay.

Outdoors and Camping

For hardier travelers, camping is the best way to experience the outdoors. Since campground employees are often excellent sources of information on local sights and restaurants, camping with several people is the cheapest alternative for cross-country travel.

The definitive *Woodall's Campground Directory* ($13.95; Eastern or Western edition $8.95) covers information on sites around the U.S. The smaller, regional tenting directories ($3.95) will serve adequately for most trips. Also try Woodall's Tent Camping Guide (Eastern or Western edition $7.95), campsite cookbooks, and RV-owner handbooks. Most bookstores carry the guides, but if you can't find them contact Woodall Publishing Company, 100 Corporate North, #100, Bannockburn, IL 60015-1253 (800-323-9076 or 312-295-7799). Rand McNally also publishes good camping guides.

National Parks

National parks, famous for such denizens as Ranger Rick, Yogi and Smokey the Bear, are scattered across the U.S. The U.S. Department of the Interior manages an extensive network of national parks, monuments, seashores, historic sites, and scenic rivers. Almost invariably well-organized and well-maintained, these areas attract enthusiastic campers from all over the world, some of whom stay for weeks at a time. Most national parks play an educational role through ranger talks and guided hikes. Many offer backcountry and developed tent camping in specified areas; others welcome RVs, while a few offer opulent living in grand lodges. Since each area is governed by its own rules and regulations, be sure to check at the visitors center in each park, or contact one of the 10 regional offices or the **National Park Service,** P.O. Box 37127, Washington, DC 20013-7127 (202-343-4747).

Single visit entrance fees range from $1-2 per person or $3-7.50 per carload. A **Golden Eagle Pass** ($25), available at any park entrance, entitles the bearer to one year of free entry to any part of the national park system, but does not cover use fees such as camping and parking. Travelers over 62 can obtain the free **Golden Age Passport** which entitles them and their traveling companions to free admission anywhere in the system, as well as 50% off the regular camping and user fees. The **Golden Access Passport,** also free, gives disabled persons the same privileges as the Golden Age Passport. Also available are **Park Passes,** which are annual entrance permits to a specific park or site, and **Federal Duck Stamps,** which provide one year's admission to national wildlife refuges. Contact the National Park Service for information about any of these passes.

Plan ahead when contemplating a visit to the parks. Expect crowds at most of them during the summer. Many shut down entirely in the winter, or offer only limited services. Lodges and other four-walled accommodations are in the shortest supply; reserve them months in advance. Since most campgrounds are strictly first come-first serve, plan to arrive early. In camping areas not regulated by a ranger, verify the availability of sites because the more popular parks often leave the "Campground Full" sign up throughout the high season. In a pinch, ask fellow

campers to share their site. For a booklet describing less tourist-ridden national parks, write to the **Superintendent of Documents, U.S. Government Printing Office,** Washington, DC 20402. Ask for *The National Parks: Lesser-Known Areas,* (Stock #024-005-00911-6, $1.50).

State Parks and National Forests

While most state parks may lack the grandeur of Grand Teton or Yosemite National Parks, many provide excellent camping in beautiful settings. You can crisscross the U.S. and stay at a state park almost every night. Many offer elaborate facilities and lots of room at prices much lower than those of private campgrounds. Most state parks charge a day-use fee of about 25¢ for pedestrians and $1-3 for carloads; camping is usually $5-9 per night. Some states, such as California, offer cheaper camping rates (often 50¢-$1) for hikers and bikers. Sometimes state parks will reserve a percentage (usually about half) of the sites in advance, but generally they do not fill to capacity, except on summer weekends and holidays. Quality and regulations vary from state to state. To find information on individual states, consult *Let's Go*'s Practical Information listings for each state.

National forests are a worthwhile alternative to the more heavily traveled parks. Often they border a national park, providing additional campsites and a retreat for hikers. While some have developed recreation facilities, most offer only primitive camping—no lights, no water, and no flush toilets. Few national forests are ever crowded, and the fees for entry and camping are nominal or nonexistent. Some areas of the country have few national forests (such as the Great Plains), and where they exist, they are often nearly impossible to find—one reason they're under-utilized. Do some advance research and obtain accurate and detailed maps from the forest you plan to visit. For more information and free pamphlets, contact the **U.S. Forest Service, USDA,** 12th St. and Independence Ave. SW, P.O. Box 96090, Washington, DC 20090-6090 (202-447-3957). Also, you can call 800-283-2267 to reserve a campsite at selected national forests.

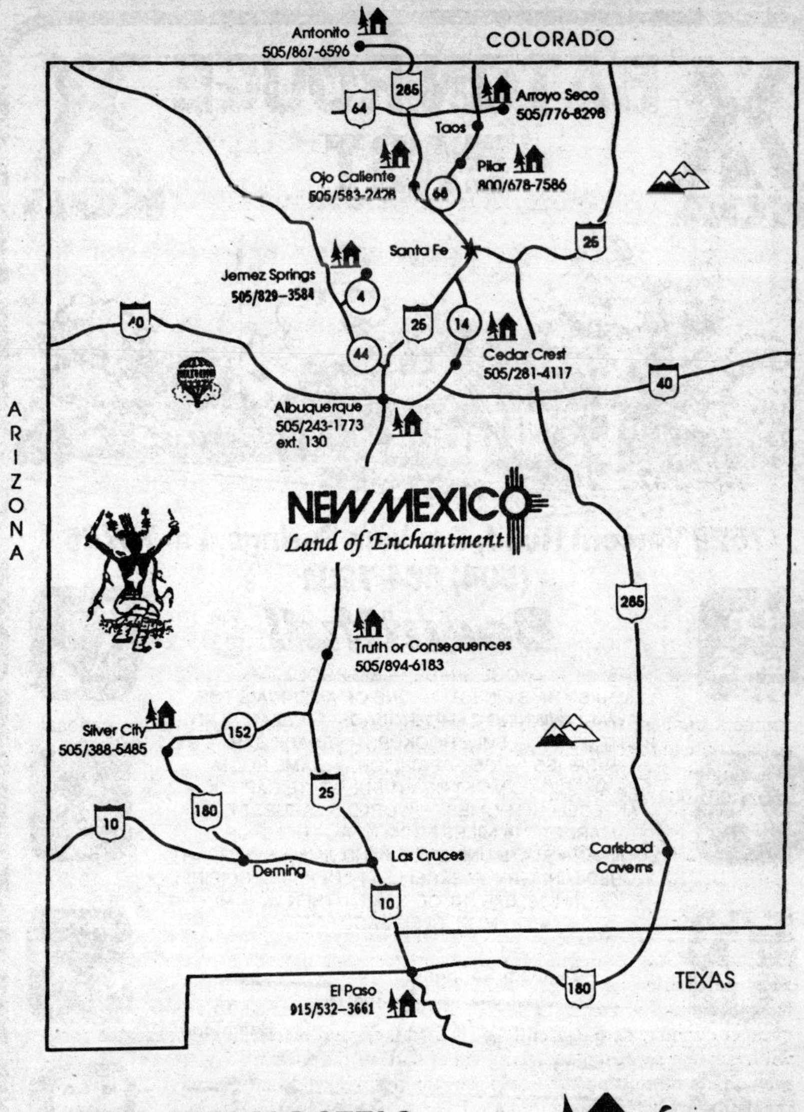

Antonito
505/867-6596
COLORADO
285
64
Arroyo Seco
505/776-8298
Taos
Pilar
800/678-7586
Ojo Caliente
505/583-2428
68
25
Santa Fe
Jemez Springs
505/829-3584
4
40
26
14
Cedar Crest
505/281-4117
44
40
Albuquerque
505/243-1773
ext. 130
ARIZONA
TEXAS
NEW MEXICO
Land of Enchantment
285
Truth or Consequences
505/894-6183
Silver City
505/388-5485
152
25
180
10
Las Cruces
Deming
Carlsbad
Caverns
10
El Paso
915/532-3661
180
TEXAS

Camping and Hiking

If you enjoy the outdoors and don't mind forgoing a few of civilization's amenities, camping may be your best budget alternative. While backcountry camping requires some special skills and can be physically demanding, tent camping in campgrounds can be pleasant even for novices. Camping is cheap, gives you more flexibility in finding a place to stay, and puts you close to some breathtaking scenery.

Equipment rental is an economical but often inconvenient alternative to buying; contact an outing club to find out what's available. Spend some time perusing catalogs and questioning knowledgeable salespeople at sporting goods stores before buying anything. Whenever possible, buy equipment from local retailers who may give you the option of "trading up" for more expensive gear after a brief trial. Many reputable mail-order firms can meet your needs and offer prices lower than those in local stores. For the best deals, look around for last year's merchandise, particularly in the fall; tents don't change much, but their prices can go down as much as 50%. **Campmor,** 810 Rte. 17 N., P.O. Box 997-P, Paramus, NJ 07653-0997 (800-526-4784), offers name-brand equipment at attractive prices. **L.L. Bean,** Freeport, ME 04033 (800-221-4221), is open 24 hours per day and has become legendary for its sturdy, high-quality equipment and dedication to customer service. Call for a free catalog. **Cabela's,** 812 13th Ave., Sidney, NE 69160 (800-237-8888) specializes in sporting goods and fishing supplies. Another source is **Recreational Equipment, Inc. (REI),** Commercial Sales, P.O. Box C-88126, Seattle, WA 98188 (800-426-4840).

If you're a novice camper, you'll need to obtain the basics: sleeping bag, pad, and tent. Choose your sleeping bag according to the weather in which you'll be camping. Most of the better bags—either down (lighter) or synthetic (cheaper, more water resistant and durable)—have ratings equal to the minimum temperature to which the bag is suitable. Anticipate the worst conditions you'll encounter, subtract a few degrees, and buy a bag. Expect to pay about $40 for a lightweight synthetic and about $135 for a down bag suitable for use in below-freezing temperatures. Sub-zero bags are more expensive at about $200. Pads to sleep on range from $10 for a simple Ensolite pad to $50 for the best air mattress or a sophisticated hybrid such as the Thermarest.

The best tents are "self-supporting" (with their own frames and suspension systems), can be set up quickly, and do not require staking. Backpackers and cyclists may wish to pay a bit more for a sophisticated lightweight tent and should get the smallest tent they can stand—some two-person tents weigh only slightly over two pounds. Expect to pay $85 for a simple two-person tent, $115 for a suitable four-person model. Eureka is one well-established and dependable brand.

Other basics include a battery-operated lantern (never gas) and a simple plastic groundcloth to protect the tent's floor. Consider purchasing fairly large water sacks and/or a solar shower if you will be staying in primitive campgrounds. Buy a canteen made of either plastic (better insulator) or metal (more leak-proof). Pack water purification pills if you don't plan to boil water before drinking it. Remember other camping essentials: Swiss army knife, toilet paper, bug repellent, calamine, first aid kit, and cooking gear. Improved campgrounds are often equipped with grills and allow you to gather firewood for cooking. Campstoves come in all sizes, weights, and fuel types. Make sure to buy brands for which accessories are easily found. Coleman's inexpensive campstove ($40) has become a classic.

Of course, you'll need a reliable backpack to hold all of this gear. If your backpack fits properly, most of the weight will rest on your hips. Packs have either internal or external frames. Internal-frame packs are best for difficult trails that require maneuvering, since they mold better to your back. For straight hiking, an external-frame pack might be better. Other features to consider are the number of compartments and whether you prefer top-loading or easy-access front-loading packs. Expect to spend at least $125.

Now that your initial investment has been made, you'll want to find a campsite to make all the hassle worthwhile. In addition to state parks and national forests, there are thousands of private campgrounds across the U.S. The quality of the conditions varies considerably, but private sites are in general more costly and crowded than public campgrounds. Private campgrounds are often the only outdoor alternative near cities. Most require a minimum stay of two nights to one week and cost $6-15 per night for two people (RVs cost more). Facilities may include water, electricity, phones, hot showers, and flush toilets. **Kampgrounds of America (KOA)** offer such luxuries as swimming pools, playgrounds, and convenience stores, but they charge you for it ($15 for 2 people).

Transportation

Air Travel

Air travel can be the most anxiety-producing element of an otherwise relaxing vacation. If you plan ahead and are patient and persistent, however, you can probably find affordable flights. Particularly on long-distance trips, air fares often dip below bus and train fares. Check the weekend travel sections of major newspapers for bargain fares. The Sunday *New York Times* has the largest travel section; other papers worth perusing include the *Chicago Tribune, L.A. Times,* and *Toronto Star.*

Special discounts abound, but generally there is no rule concerning discount air fares. Travelers invariably get the best fares by purchasing tickets at least two weeks in advance. You can save up to 60% on an advance-purchase ticket, depending on when you travel, depending when you travel. Usually, you must purchase a round-trip ticket and stay at least one Sunday and no longer than three weeks. Other restrictions to look for are pre-payment (14 days after making your reservation or 14 days before your flight) and 15-100% penalties for reservation changes or cancellation. Also ask specifically about **"red-eye"** (all-night) flights, especially on popular business travel routes. Charter flights run between some U.S. cities; they are more subject to sudden schedule changes but can save you a lot of money. Talk to a travel agent or call an airline's toll-free number.

There are a few general rules to keep in mind when booking a flight. Buy your ticket early, especially if you are traveling during the tourist season or on holidays. The day before your departure, call the airline to reconfirm your flight and to check any last-minute changes. Airlines occasionally overbook, so arrive early to ensure your seat. Being "bumped" from a flight, however, is not necessarily a bad thing. You will probably leave on the next flight and receive either a free ticket or a cash bonus. If your travel plans are flexible, try to be first in line when the airline asks for volunteers to be bumped off the flight. Traveling on a weekday (Mon.-Thurs.) is generally cheaper than traveling on the weekend.

Automobile Travel

The myth of the American traveler on the open highway has endured from pioneers in covered wagons to Jack Kerouac to the Griswold family in National Lampoon's *Vacation.* Many Americans consider their car an essential element of their personality. While traveling in the U.S. you'll probably see such statements of life-style as BMWs in Connecticut, jeeps in Denver, and Batmobiles in Gotham City. You, the budget traveler, may also express your thrifty nature by driving a less-than-glamorous model. Car travel is often the most convenient and may be the only way to reach some areas. Group travel lowers expenses; check notices on ride boards around college campuses and in student and local newspapers. The Yellow Pages may list a share-a-ride organization in your area.

For $15-70 per year (depending on where you live) the **American Automobile Association (AAA)** offers free trip-planning services, emergency road service, discounts on car rentals, and American Express traveler's checks commission-free. Your card doubles as a $5000 bail bond or $200 arrest bond certificate for almost any motor vehicle offense. For more information, contact either your local chapter or AAA, 8111 Gatehouse Rd., Falls Church, VA 22042 (800-336-4357). Many major gas companies offer similar services for drivers who have a charge account. The **Mobil Auto Club (800-621-5581) charges members $39 per year for emergency road service; Mobil either dispatches help or reimburses you later. Exxon Travel Club** (713-680-5723) offers a range of services and costs $27-42 per year. Write to Exxon Travel Club, P.O. Box 3633, Houston, TX 77253.

Bring spare change and dollar bills for tolls. Before your trip, you should tune the engine, check your tires, and buy spare fan belts. Your trunk should contain a spare tire and jack, jumper cables, extra oil, flares, and a blanket. If you know how to repair minor breakdowns and diagnose larger problems, you can avoid service stations altogether, or at least avoid being ripped off by dubious mechanics.

Renting

Almost anyone can afford to rent a car for local trips, especially if several people share the cost. Rental rates vary regionally; Florida has the lowest, northern states have the highest. Rental agencies are usually located at major airports and business districts of towns and cities. In general, automobile rental agencies fall into two categories: national companies with thousands of affiliated offices, and local companies serving only one city or area. The major rental companies usually allow cars to be picked up in one city and dropped off in another, often at considerable extra cost. Their toll-free numbers allow renters to reserve a reliable car anywhere in the country, but drawbacks include steep prices and high minimum ages for rentals (most 21, some as high as 25). Some major companies are **Alamo** (800-327-9633), **Avis** (800-331-1212), **Budget** (800-527-0700), **Dollar** (800-421-6868), **Hertz** (800-654-3131), **Holiday Payless** (800-237-2804), **National** (800-328-4567), and **Thrifty** (800-367-2277).

While many local companies observe similar age requirements, they often have more flexible policies. Some will accept a cash deposit of $50 or more in lieu of a credit card. The prices charged by a local company are often lower than those of major companies. Self-deprecating companies such as **Rent-A-Wreck** (800-421-7253) rent cars long past their prime at low daily rates. Don't go too far; these agencies usually have high mileage charges and other hidden costs. The cars are also likely to be genuine lemons.

Drivers are covered by their own insurance policies when renting a car. If you want additional coverage in case the rental car is damaged, you may obtain it through the agency. Check the price beforehand since insurance is usually expensive. Although basic rental charges run from $15-30 per day for a compact car, plus up to 20¢ per mile, most companies offer special money-saving deals. Standard transmission cars are usually a few dollars cheaper. Those planning to drive long distances should ask for unlimited mileage packages. All companies have special weekend rates. Renting by the week also entitles you to a discount.

Auto Transport Companies

If you have a driver's license but can't afford to buy or rent a car, try an auto transport company which will match you with a person who needs a car moved to another city. You give the company your destination, and they tell you when they have a car. You pay only for gas (although the first tank is usually free), food, lodging, tolls, and a refundable deposit. The transport company's insurance covers any breakdown or damage to the car. Generally, you must be 21, have a valid driver's license (an international license is fine), and agree to drive 400 miles or more per day on a fairly direct route to your destination. Stops, detours, and diversions are frowned upon—you will be given a time and distance allowance and will be charged for any extra miles on the odometer. Companies prefer couples and older travelers. Your chances are best if you're traveling from coast to coast or from New York to Miami. Both **Auto Driveaway,** 310 S. Michigan Ave., Chicago, IL 60604 (312-341-1900), and **Transporters, Inc.** (General American Shippers, Inc.), 450 7th Ave., #1804, New York, NY 10123 (212-594-2690), have over 50 offices around the country.

Bus Travel

Of all modes of public transportation, bus travel provides the best way to see the country up close. If any out-of-the-way town or park sees only one kind of public transportation, it's a bus rolling through. Depending on your viewpoint, buses have either the advantage or disadvantage of seating you next to a colorful variety of people, from seniors to students, working folk to waifs.

For extensive travel within a region, you can rely on **Greyhound** and its subsidiary **Trailways.** The nation's bus network provides the cheapest public transportation to most towns in America. Many astronauts and most of our researchers use it. In sections on specific cities, *Let's Go: USA* lists bus fares to nearby destinations, as well as the frequency and length of trips.

Greyhound sells an **Ameripass,** valid for unlimited travel in the continental U.S. on both Greyhound and Trailways. Passes are available for seven days ($189), 15 days ($249), or 30 days ($349) with optional extensions for $10 per day. The Ameripass becomes valid on your first day of travel. Discounts for children vary according to the age and number of children traveling and the number of adults paying full fares. Foreign students and faculty members are entitled to a discounted Ameripass; see the Getting Around section in Additional Information for Foreign Visitors below.

Greyhound and Trailways offer discounts for specific groups: children accompanied by an adult (ages 5-11 half-fare, 0-4 free); seniors (10% discount except on Ameripass and excursion fares); disabled travelers (companion rides free); and excursion fares (low promotional fares valid for a limited period of time). See Additional Concerns below.

Since many bus stations are in seedy areas, juggle arrival and departure times to avoid spending the night in or around the depot. Try to schedule arrivals at reasonable hours, so you can find transportation out of the bus station and a place to stay. If you are boarding at a remote "flag stop," be sure you understand where to catch the bus. Catch the driver's attention by standing roadside and flailing your arms wildly. If the bus proceeds to whiz by, it is too crowded, and the next less-crowded bus will stop for you.

You can buy your ticket at the terminal, but get there early. Ask for information on connections, schedules, and fares, then check the bus schedules and routes yourself to verify the information. Fares and discounts change seasonally. When boarding a bus, remember that the company will add a second bus when the first one is filled. If you decide not to make the trip, Greyhound and Trailways usually grant refunds. Stopovers are permitted if you want to spend time in cities along your route.

You are allowed two pieces of luggage for free, combined weight of up to 100 pounds; children are allowed half that amount. Identify your belongings clearly and retain your claim check. You can usually take a small carry-on onto the bus, as long as it fits in the overhead compartment. Always keep valuables, food, a day's supply of clothing, a Thermos, and a blanket or jacket with you inside the bus. Surprisingly efficient air conditioning sometimes brings the temperature down to arctic levels.

Green Tortoise, an "alternative" bus line, offers a friendlier budget travel option. A hostel on wheels, Green Tortoise's proprietors act as hosts and tour guides. They run renovated old coaches with foam mattresses, sofa-seats, and dinettes coast to coast, up and down the West Coast, and to national parks. All prices include transportation, use of the bus at night for sleeping, and tours of the regions you pass through. Tasty meals are prepared communally and cost $3.50 per person per meal. Tours between New York or Boston and San Francisco last 10-14 days and cost $279 in either direction. From their headquarters in San Francisco, Green Tortoise serves Seattle (2 per week, 1 day, $59) and Los Angeles (1 per week, 1 day, $30). They also offer "loops," with start and finish in San Francisco, to Yosemite National Park, Northern California, Baja, California, Grand Canyon, mainland Mexico, and Alaska. The National Park Loop hits all the biggies (12-14 days, $399). The Baja trip includes several days on the beach, with sailboats and windsurfers provided.

For specific information, write to Green Tortoise, P.O. Box 24459, San Francisco, CA 94124 (415-821-0803; 800-227-4766 outside CA).

Try to use local bus systems to travel within a town, as most cities and towns provide local transit. The largest cities have subway systems and commuter train lines as well. Americans love their cars, though, and mass transit remains limited; local buses, while invariably cheap (fares 25¢-$1), are often infrequent and unreliable. Call the city transit information number, and track down a local transit map.

Train Travel

If you're not in a particular hurry, the train can be one of the most comfortable ways to tour the country. You can walk from car to car to stretch your legs, buy overpriced edibles in the snack or dining car, and shut out the sun to sleep. It's best to travel light on the train; not all stations will check baggage and not all trains will carry it (though most long-distance ones do).

For most intercity trips, **Amtrak** is not much of a bargain compared with the bus or plane. Special services such as sleeping cars or high-speed Metroliner service cost extra. However, Amtrak offers a myriad of discounts. Watch for special holiday packages. Permanent discounts apply to: children accompanied by an adult (ages 2-11 half-fare, 2 and under free); seniors and disabled persons (25% off one-way trips); groups (15% off one way, 25% off round-trip); and circle trips (certain round trips within a region when returning on a different route). Excursion fares (round-trip travel during off-peak times) cost little more than the regular one-way tickets. They may not be combined with other discounts, except the children's fares.

The current **All-Aboard America** promotional fares offer one of the best ways to subsidize a trip encompassing several states. Round-trip travel between two cities plus two stopovers costs $189 within one region (Western, Central, or Eastern), $269 within two regions, and $309 within three. You have up to 45 days to complete the trip, and must plan an itinerary in advance. The generous Eastern region includes everything from Chicago to New Orleans, allowing, for example, a tour from New York City to Chicago to New Orleans to Miami and back to New York City on the $189 single-region ticket.

In addition to the discounts, most Amtrak tickets allow you a stopover at no extra cost. For information about rates, schedules, and discounts, call 800-USA-RAIL (800-872-7245); hearing-impaired travelers may communicate with Amtrak by means of a teletypewriter (800-523-6590; 800-562-6960 in PA).

Bicycle Travel

Aside from the initial outlay for a sturdy bicycle and requisite touring equipment, bicycle travel is about the cheapest way to go. Traveling at a relaxed pace along rural roads allows you to get to know a region more intimately than any other means of travel. Those who are less-than-athletic might try a few long rides before attempting a full-scale trip.

Gathering all the necessary equipment is perhaps the biggest hassle in preparing for a bicycle tour. While some local bike shops are helpful in providing information, the costs involved in stocking and inventory make their prices exorbitant, with few exceptions. Fortunately, mail and telephone ordering of equipment has been perfected to a fine art. Don't spend a penny before you scan the pages of *Bicycling* magazine for the lowest sale prices. **Bike Nashbar,** P.O. Box 3449, Youngstown, OH 44513-3449 (800-627-4227; 800-654-2453 in OH), is the one company that really stands out in the crowd. They almost always have the lowest prices, but if they don't, they'll cheerfully subtract 5¢ from the best nationally advertised price you can find. Parts ordered will generally be shipped on the same day. Their own line of products, including complete bicycles, is the best value. The first thing you should buy is a suitable bike helmet. It's a lot cheaper and less of a headache (literally) than CAT scans and/or funerals.

The long-distance cyclist should contact **Bikecentennial,** a national, non-profit organization that researches and maps long-distance routes across the country and organizes bike tours for members. Its best-known project is the 4450-mile TransAmerica Bicycle Trail. Bikecentennial also offers its members insurance, maps, guidebooks (including the *Cyclist's Yellow Pages*), route information service, and access to tours. Annual membership fees are $22, $19 for students, and $25 for families. For more information, write Bikecentennial, P.O. Box 8308, Missoula, MT 59807 (406-721-1776). Check out Ballantine's series of *Cyclist's Guides to Overnight Stops* ($3.95). **American Youth Hostels, Inc.** (see Accommodations above) also offers complete tours at excellent prices.

Short of building a frame or perhaps spoking a wheel, fixing a modern derailleur-equipped bike is something just about anyone can do with a few simple but specialized tools. Three useful books are *Bicycle Repair, Bicycle Touring,* and *Easy Bicycle Maintenance* ($4.95 each), all by the editors of *Bicycling* magazine. Contact Rodale Press, Inc., 33 E. Minor St., Emmaus, PA 18098 (800-441-7761; 800-441-7768 in PA).

The smartest way to protect your investment is to buy a U-shaped lock made by **Citadel** or **Kryptonite.** It's expensive ($22-49), but well worth it. Each company, for a sizeable fee, guarantees its locks against theft of your bike for one or two years.

Hiking

A hike can be as demanding as you choose; the day-hiker can embark on shorter trails of varying difficulty. Travel offices, park ranger stations, and outdoor equipment stores can help plan hikes.

The Pacific Crest Trail, stretching from the California/Mexico border to Canada, and the **Appalachian Trail,** from Georgia to Maine, are two of a long list of exciting, long-distance hiking trails. *The American Walk Book,* by Jean Craighead George, and *Off and Walking,* by Ruth Rudner, are good guides to the country's trails. Consult Dennis Look's *Joy of Backpacking* for information on proper hiking equipment and attitude.

If you're contemplating a hiking trip, good sources of information include: **American Youth Hostels** (see Accommodations above); the **Appalachian Trail Conference,** P.O. Box 807, Harper's Ferry, WV 25425 (304-535-6331); and the **Sierra Club,** 730 Polk St., San Francisco, CA 94109 (415-776-2211). The Sierra Club's *Annual Outing Catalog* will soon be available for $2. All three groups have local chapters. For topographical maps to any part of the U.S., write the **U.S. Geological Survey,** Distribution Branch, P.O. Box 25286, Denver Federal Center, Denver, CO 80225.

Hitchhiking

Everyone is taught, at an early age, the dangers of accepting either rides or candy from strangers. Your parents were right; hitching is risky at best. Although many travelers prefer it to more commercial methods, it is hardly the ideal way to travel. Women should avoid hitchhiking alone, and everyone should evaluate the driver before accepting a ride. Be especially wary if the driver opens the door quickly and offers to drive you anywhere. Make sure you'll be able to open the passenger window or door from the inside in case of an emergency. Don't sit between two people, and don't let the driver lock your belongings in the trunk. Remember that you are at the mercy of the driver.

All states prohibit hitching while standing on the roadway itself. If you try hitching on an interstate, in most states, you must limit yourself to access ramps and rest stops. Try to keep at least $20 in your wallet to prove to any suspicious police officers that you aren't destitute.

Additional Concerns

Senior Travelers

Seniors enjoy a tremendous assortment of discounts. All you need is an acceptable piece of identification proving your age and eligibility (a driver's license, Medicare card, or membership card from a recognized society of retired persons is sufficient). Travel books include: *Discount Guide for Travelers Over 55,* by Caroline and Walter Weintz (Dutton, $7.95 + $1.50 postage), *Senior Citizen's Guide to Budget Travel in the United States and Canada,* by Paige Palmer (Pilot Books, $3.95 + $1 postage), or *The International Health Guide for Senior Citizen Travelers,* by W. Robert Lange (Pilot, $4.95 + $1 postage). For information on passports, visas, and health, try *Travel Tips for Senior Citizens,* issued by the Bureau of Consular Affairs, Superintendent of Documents, U.S. Government Printing Office, Washington, DC 20402.

The **American Association of Retired Persons** offers its members a tremendous range of services and discounts, many of which aid travelers. Any U.S. resident over 50 can join for a $5 annual fee. Discounts range from 10-25% at major hotel/motel chains throughout the nation. In addition, you can get up to 40% discounts on car rental at Avis, Hertz, and National. Write to National Headquarters, Special Services Dept., 1909 K St. NW, Washington, DC 20049 (800-227-7737).

Another organization providing services to those 50 and over is the **National Council of Senior Citizens.** The NCSC offers travel programs and discounts, along with reduced medical and auto insurance rates. Annual fee is $12 per year for an individual and $16 for a couple.

Elderhostel uses the facilities of over 1000 colleges, universities, and other educational institutions worldwide. Participants spend a week or more studying subjects from music appreciation to beekeeping. Most international programs last three weeks. The $215 per week fee covers room, board, tuition, use of campus facilities, and extracurricular activities. Hostelships are available to those requiring financial assistance. You must be at least 60 to enroll and may bring a companion who is over 50. For a free catalog listing course descriptions for the current season, contact Elderhostel, 80 Boylston St., #400, Boston, MA 02116 (617-426-7788).

Days Inn operates the **September Days Club** for anyone over 50. A $12 annual fee entitles the member to 15-50% discounts at all Days Inns, discounts in restaurants and gift shops run by the chain, and a subscription to their quarterly magazine. Call 800-241-5050 or 800-344-3636.

Travelers 62 and over can obtain a free **Golden Age Passport** for lifetime free admission to all U.S. national parks, monuments, historic sites, recreation areas, and national wildlife refuges. (See National Parks above.)

Gay and Lesbian Travelers

Unfortunately, there is still a strong prejudice in many areas of the country against homosexuality. Call the national **Gay/Lesbian Crisisline** (800-767-4297) for counseling, legal or medical advice, AIDS information, and local club listings. An excellent source of books geared toward gay and lesbian travelers is **Giovanni's Room,** 345 S. 12th St., Philadelphia, PA 19107 (800-222-6996; 215-923-2960 in PA). Giovanni's Room charges $2.50 postage per book in the U.S. and $3.50 in Canada and Mexico. All of the following books are available through either Giovanni's Room or the address listed: *Gaia's Guide* ($11.95; 9-11 Kensington High St., London W8, England, $12.50, ppd.); *Spartacus International Gay Guide,* an international gay guide for men ($24.95; c/o Bruno Gmünder, Lutzowstrasse 106, P.O. Box 30 13 45, D-1000, Berlin 30, West Germany); *Bob Damron's Address Book* ($14; P.O. Box 11270, San Francisco, CA 94101 (415-777-0113)); *Places of Interest* (a series of 3 books for men ($10), women ($8), and general (with maps; $11); Ferrari Publications, P.O. Box 37887, Phoenix, AZ 85069); *Odysseus: Accommodations and Travel Guide for the Gay Community* ($14.95).

Another resource for gay and lesbian travelers is the *Gayellow Pages,* Renaissance House, P.O. Box 292, Village Station, New York, NY 10014 (212-674-0120).

Wherever possible, *Let's Go* lists local gay and lesbian information lines and community centers. Areas with large gay and lesbian populations include New York City, San Francisco, Los Angeles, Houston, Atlanta, and Montréal.

Disabled Travelers

Though facilities and services for the disabled are far from sufficient in the U.S., recent awareness has led to increased accessibility and mobility. Several books help disabled travelers plan vacations. **Twin Peaks Press** publishes three guides and also operates a worldwide nurse network: *Directory for Travel Agencies for the Disabled* ($12.95), *Travel for the Disabled* ($9.95), and, for ground travel, *Wheelchair Vagabond* ($9.95). Write to Twin Peaks Press, P.O. Box 129, Vancouver, WA 98666 (800-637-2256). Add $2 postage for the first book and $1 for each additional.

Also try *Access to the World: A Travel Guide For The Handicapped* ($12.95), by Louise Weiss; write to Facts on File, Inc., 460 Park Ave. S., New York, NY 10016 (212-683-2244) Another guide is *The Disabled Traveler's International Phrasebook,* in eight languages with three supplements available; write to Disability Press, Ltd., Applemarket House, 17 Union St., Kingston-upon-Thames, Surrey KT1 1RP, England (£1.75, supplements £0.60 each). The Government Printing Office also publishes some booklets (see Useful Publications above). If you plan to visit national parks, obtain a free Golden Access Passport at any park entrance, which entitles you and your family to free admission and a 50% reduction on campsite fees.

Most **Red Roof Inns** (800-843-7663) are accessible by wheelchair. Consult other national motel chains for information (see Hotels and Motels).

Amtrak and all airlines now serve disabled passengers if you notify them in advance. When making reservations, tell the ticket agent what services you'll need. (Ask if there are restrictions on motorized wheelchairs.) Hearing impaired travelers may use a teletypewriter to contact Amtrak (800-523-6590; 800-562-6960 in PA) and Greyhound (800-345-3109; 800-322-9537 in PA). Bus travel is a feasible and inexpensive option. Greyhound and Trailways have a **Helping Hand Service** that enables disabled travelers to bring along a companion for free. Simply show the ticket agent a doctor's letter confirming your need for assistance. Both you and your companions receive the standard two-piece, 100 pound luggage allowance, but wheelchairs, seeing-eye dogs, and oxygen tanks are not counted as part of that allowance. Major car rental agencies have a few hand-controlled cars; contact them a few days in advance to check on availability at a specific location. Try Avis (800-331-1212), Hertz (800-654-3131), or National (800-328-4567).

Wings on Wheels is absolutely the best travel organization for the disabled; they've provided information and planned tours all over the world for 25 years. They run a Seattle-based charter bus with on-board wheelchair-accessible facilities, and can arrange "anything for a group, and damn near anything for an individual" at minimal extra cost. Contact them at Evergreen Travel, 19505L 44th Ave., Lynnwood, WA 98036 (206-776-1184; 800-435-2288; 800-562-9298 in WA). For useful guides, write **Travel Information Center,** Moss Rehabilitation Hospital, 12th St. and Tabor Rd., Philadelphia, PA 19141 (215-329-5715 ext. 2233). **Mobility International USA (MIUSA),** P.O. Box 3551, Eugene, OR 97403 (503-343-1284, voice and TDD) provides information on travel programs, accommodations, and organized tours, and they publish the *Guide to International Educational Exchange* and *Community Service and Travel for Persons with Disabilities.*

Additional Information for Foreign Visitors

Orientation to the United States

The Continental U.S. is big (3100 by 1800 miles, 5000 by 2900km), and largely uninhabited. Except in the Northeast, travel between major urban centers takes long hours or even days. The American landscape is richly varied, ranging from from desert to glacier, from endless plains to glass and steel skyscrapers. No matter how much you see, there will still be plenty left for your next trip. You'll have to choose between a whirlwind, city-a-day tour and a more leisurely, meet-the-natives itinerary. In either case, you're better off concentrating your travels in two or three regions.

To preview what the different areas of the U.S. offer the traveler, scan our regional and state introductions. The regions of the United States are often as culturally distinct as two European nations; a Texan might feel as much a foreigner in New England as you would. Americans are used to diversity and most are kind to foreigners.

Although you needn't fear a terrorist attack in an American aiport, the cities of the U.S. can be more violent and crime-ridden than their European or Asian counterparts. *Let's Go: USA* lists emergency phone numbers in most cities and towns. If you're careful and alert, you will be safer during your travels.

Useful Organizations

When you begin planning your trip, you might contact the **United States Travel and Tourism Administration** (branches located in Australia, the UK, Belgium, France, Canada, W. Germany, Japan, and Mexico), which provides abundant free literature. If you can't find the address for the branch in your country, write to the U.S. Travel and Tourism Administration, Department of Commerce, 14th and Constitution Ave. NW, Washington, DC 20230 (202-377-4003 or 202-377-3811). You may also want to write to the tourist offices of the states or cities you'll be visiting. (See Practical Information listings.) Wherever you write, the more specific your inquiry, the better your chances of getting the information you need. Once you arrive, visit local tourist information centers.

Extremely useful to foreign travelers, the **Council on International Educational Exchange (CIEE)** has affiliates overseas that sell travel literature, hostel cards, and charter airline tickets. Services include issuing the ISIC (see Documents below), the *Student Travel Catalog* ($1 postage), and a publication with accommodations listings, entitled *Where to Stay USA* ($10.95). Write to CIEE at 205 E. 42nd St., New York, NY 10017 (800-223-7402 charter flights only; 212-661-1414 or 212-661-1450), or contact their other offices in Paris, Tokyo, Madrid, and W. Germany. In Canada, write to **Travel CUTS** (Canadian University Travel Services Limited), 171 College St., Toronto, Ont. M5T 1P7 (416-979-2406). In the **U.K.,** write to London Student Travel, 52 Grosvenor Gardens, London WC1 (tel. (01) 730 34 02). In **Australia,** contact SSA/STA, 220 Faraday St., Carlton, Melbourne, Victoria 3053 (tel. (03) 347 69 11).

The **International Student Travel Confederation (ISTC),** of which the CIEE is a member, is a godsend for European students. It arranges charter flights and discount air fares, provides travel insurance, issues the ISIC card in a new plastic form, and sponsors the Student Air Travel Association for European students. Write for their Student Travel Guide at ISTC, Weinbergstrasse 31, CH-8006 Zurich, Switzerland (tel. (41) 1 262 29 96).

STA Travel, based in the U.K., has over 100 offices worldwide to help you arrange discounted overseas flights. In the U.S., call 800-777-0112. Write to them at 117 Euston Rd., London NW 12SX, England, or call (01) 938 47 11 (Administration); (01) 937 99 62 (intercontinental flights); or (01) 937 99 71 (flights to North America).

If you wish to stay in a genuine American home during your vacation, there are many organizations that can help you. The **Experiment in International Living** coordinates homestay programs for international visitors wishing to join an American family for an extended period of time. Visitors of all ages live with host families long enough to receive a full dose of American culture. Homestays are arranged for all times of the year. For the appropriate address in your country, write to the U.S. Headquarters, P.O. Box 767, Kipling Rd., Brattleboro, VT 05301 (800-451-4465). The **Institute of International Education (IIE)** (see Study below) publishes their "Homestay Information Sheet" listing many homestay programs. Write to them at 809 United Nations Plaza, New York, NY 10017 (212-883-8200). See Accommodations above for information on **Servas,** a similar international travel organization.

Documents and Formalities

Almost all foreign visitors to the U.S. are required to have a **passport,** a visitor's **visa,** and proof of plans to leave the U.S. For stays of only a few days, Canadian citizens with proof of citizenship do not need a visa or passport, nor do Mexican citizens with an I-186 form who enter through a U.S. border station. To obtain a U.S. visa, contact the nearest U.S. embassy or consulate. For longer stays, international visitors usually obtain a B-2 (non-immigrant, pleasure tourist) visa valid for a maximum of six months.

If you lose your visa or passport once in the U.S., you must replace it through the embassy of your country. If you lose your I-94 form (arrival/departure certificate attached to your visa upon arrival), replace it at the nearest **U.S. Immigration and Naturalization Service** office. A list of offices can be obtained through the INS, Central Office Information Operations Unit, #5044, 425 I St. NW, Washington, DC 20536 (202-633-1900). This information does not necessarily apply for work or study in the U.S. (see Work and Study below). An I-539 form ($35) is needed to extend your length of stay in the U.S. These are obtained at the nearest Immigration and Naturalization Service. You must apply for an extension 15 to 60 days before your original departure date. In addition, your passport must be valid for at least six months past your extended deadline. You may apply to stay a maximum of six months only.

Foreign students will want to obtain an **International Student Identification Card (ISIC)** as proof of student status. These cards, now made of embossed plastic, entitle the bearer to a variety of student discounts. The ISIC is available at local travel agencies, from the International Student Travel Confederation, from CIEE, or from **Let's Go Travel Services,** Thayer Hall-B, Harvard University, Cambridge, MA 02138 (617-495-9649 or 800-5-LETS-GO). Let's Go Travel also sells American Youth Hostel memberships. The ISIC and the AYH card are available by mail.

If you are considering renting or buying a car in the U.S., you should obtain an **International Driver's License** from your national automobile association before leaving. You cannot get one in the U.S. without an American license. Driving with only a foreign (except Canadian) driver's license in the U.S. is illegal, unless your country abides by the Geneva Road Traffic Convention of 1949. Keep in mind that the usual minimum age for car rental and auto transport services is 21, but is often as high as 25.

Customs

All travelers may bring into the U.S. 200 cigarettes, $100 worth of gifts, and all personal belongings duty-free. Travelers over 21 may also bring up to one liter of alcohol duty-free. You may bring in any amount of currency without a charge, but if you carry over $10,000, you will have to fill out a report form. Travelers should carry prescription drugs in clearly labeled containers, along with a doctor's statement or prescription. Customs officials will often inquire about the amount of money you are carrying and ask your planned departure time to ensure that you will be able to support yourself while in the U.S. Officials can be stern and bullying, but do not get disgruntled; remember that not all Americans will treat you as rudely. For more information, contact the nearest U.S. Embassy or write to the **U.S. Customs Service,** 1301 Constitution Ave. NW, Washington, DC 20229 (202-566-8195). To obtain the pamphlet called *Know Before You Go,* write to U.S. Customs, P.O. Box 7407, Washington, DC 20044. Remember to check customs regulations in your country so that you will know what you may take with you on your return trip.

Currency and Exchange

U.S. currency uses a decimal system based on the **dollar ($).** Paper money ("bills") comes in six denominations, all the same size, shape, and dull-green color. The bills now issued are $1, $5, $10, $20, $50, and $100. You may occasionally see denominations of $2 and $500 which are no longer printed, but are still acceptable as currency. The dollar is divided into 100 cents (¢). Values of less than a dollar are written in two ways; 35 cents can be represented as 35¢ or $.35. U.S. currency uses six coins, all worth one dollar or less. The penny (1¢), the nickel (5¢), the dime (10¢), and the quarter (25¢) are the most common. The half-dollar (50¢) and the one-dollar coins are rare.

It is nearly impossible to use foreign currency in the U.S., and in some parts of the country, you may even have trouble exchanging your currency for U.S. dollars. Convert your currency infrequently and in large amounts to minimize exorbitant fees. It is best to buy traveler's checks in U.S. dollars so that you will not need to exchange them. Traveler's checks can be used in lieu of cash; where an establishment specifies "no checks accepted," this usually refers to personal checks drawn on a bank account. You may want to bring a credit card that is affiliated with an American company such as Interbank, affiliated with the American MasterCard; Barclay Card, affiliated with Visa; or American Express. For more information, see Money above.

Personal checks can be very difficult to cash in the U.S. Most banks require that you have an account with them before they will cash a personal check, and opening an account can be a time-consuming process.

Sales tax is the American equivalent of the Value Added Tax. Expect to pay 5-8% depending on the item. In addition, a tip of 15-20% is expected by restaurant servers and taxi drivers. The tip is sometimes included in the bill of a large dining party. Tip hairdressers 10%, and bellhops at least $1 per bag.

Sending Money

Sending money overseas is a complicated and expensive process. If you think you'll need money sent while you're in the U.S., visit your bank before you leave to get a list of its correspondent American banks. You can also arrange in advance for your bank to send money from your account to certain correspondent banks on specific dates.

Cabling money is the fastest method of transport; it usually takes 48 hours to get to a major city or a bit longer to a more remote location. You pay cabling costs plus the commission charged by your home bank; rates vary according to the amount cabled. **Western Union** (800-325-4176) offers a safe method for wiring money usually within two working days. A cheaper but slower method of sending money is by a **bank draft,** or international money order. You pay a commission (around $15-20) on the draft, plus the cost of sending it registered air mail. An **American Express** office at home can cable you up to $10,000; it costs $35 to cable $500, and the fee gets larger to cable greater amounts. Non-cardholders may also use this service for no extra charge. For some unknown reason, it is even cheaper to send money from Europe to the U.S. than the other way around. Money takes from one to three days to reach the U.S. One problem with the American Express

Moneygram (800-543-4080) is that foreigners can only cable to the U.S. from France or England—the rest of Europe and Australia only have receiving stations. Whichever method you choose, make sure that you and the sender know the exact name and address of the bank or office to which the money is being sent.

Finally, if you are stranded in the U.S. with no recourse at all, a consulate will wire home for you and deduct the cost from the money you receive. Consulates are often less than gracious about performing this service, however.

Mail and Telephones

The **United States Post Office** is a government-run monopoly, but is relatively efficient nonetheless. Individual offices are usually open weekdays from 8am to 5pm and Saturday from 8am to noon. All are closed on national holidays. A postcard mailed within the U.S. (including Alaska and Hawaii) or to Mexico costs 15¢; a letter generally costs 25¢. Canada has a special rate of 22¢ for a postcard and 30¢ for a letter. Postcards mailed overseas cost 36¢, letters 45¢; aerograms are available at the post office for 36¢. Mail within the country takes between a day and a week to arrive; to northern Europe and South America, a week to 10 days; to southern Europe, North Africa, and the Middle East, two to three weeks. Large city post offices offer **International Express Mail** service in case you need to mail something to a major European city in 40 to 72 hours.

The U.S. is divided into postal zones, each with a five-digit **ZIP code** particular to a region, city or part or a city. Some addresses have a nine-digit ZIP code, used primarily for business mailings to speed up delivery. The normal form of address is as follows:

Kim Chabot, Andrea Sachs and Mallay Charters (name)
Stellar Editors Society (name of organization optional)
5000 Waldo St. #1A (street address, apartment number)
Somerville, MA 02222 (city, state abbreviation, ZIP)
USA (country)

The telephone system, once controlled by Bell, is no longer a monopoly. **AT&T** is the leading company and competes with other long-distance phone companies such as **MCI** and **Sprint.** Telephone numbers in the U.S. consist of a three-digit area code, a three-digit exchange, and a four-digit number, written as 617-123-4567. Normally only the last seven digits are used in a **local call. Non-local calls** within the area code from which you are dialing require a "1" dialed before the last seven digits. **Long-distance calls** require a "1," then the area code, and then the seven digit number. Canada and much of Mexico share the same area code system. The area code "800" indicates a toll-free number, usually for a business. For information on specific toll-free numbers, call 800-555-1212.

The local telephone directory contains most of the information you will need about telephone usage, including area codes for the U.S., many foreign country codes, and rates. To obtain local phone numbers or area codes of other cities, call directory assistance (411 within your area code or 1-(area code)-555-1212). From any phone you can reach the **operator** by dialing "0." The operator will help you with rates and other information and give assistance in an emergency. Directory assistance and the operator can be reached without payment from any pay phone.

In order to place a call, you must first hear the dial tone, a steady tone meaning that the line is clear. After dialing, you will usually hear an intermittent, ringing noise that indicates that the call has gone through. You might also hear a "busy signal," which is a short, repetitive, buzzing tone signifying that the person you have called is on the line with someone else.

Pay phones are plentiful, most often stationed on street corners and in public areas. Be wary of private, more expensive pay phones—the rate they charge per call will be printed on the phone. Put your coins (10-25¢ for a local call) into the slot and listen for a dial tone before dialing; if there is no answer or if you get a busy signal, you will get your money back. To make a long-distance direct call, put the coins in and dial the number; an operator will tell you the cost of the first three minutes, and you must then deposit that amount. The operator will cut in after your time is up and tell you to deposit more money. Generally, long-distance rates go down after 5pm on weekdays and are further reduced between 11pm and 8am and on weekends.

If you don't have lots of change, you may want to make a **collect call** (i.e. charge the call to the recipient). To do this, first dial "0" and then the area code and number you wish to reach. An operator will cut in and ask to help you. Tell her or him that you wish to place a collect (also known as "station to station") call from (your name). You might opt for a **person-to-person** call, which is more expensive than collect. To call person-to-person, you must also give the recipient's name to the operator, but at least you will only be charged if the person you want to speak with is there. With a collect call, another party may accept the charges, and the money will be wasted if the recipient is not at that number. In some areas, particularly rural ones, you may have to tell the operator what number you wish to reach, and he or she will put the call through for you.

You can place **international calls** from any telephone. To call direct, dial the international access code (011), the country code, the city code, and the local number. Country codes may be listed with a zero in front (e.g. 033), but when using 011, drop the zero (e.g. 011-33). In some areas you will have to give the operator the number and she or he will place the call. To find out the cheapest time to call various countries in Europe or the Middle East, call the operator (dial "0"). The cheapest time to call Australia and Japan is between 3am and 2pm, New Zealand 11pm and 10am.

If a telephone call is impossible, cabling may be the only way to contact someone quickly overseas. A short message will usually reach its destination by the following day. Western Union charges about 25¢ per word, depending on the length of the message, including name and address, for overseas telegrams. Call Western Union (800-325-6000) to check rates to specific countries.

Holidays

Many listings in *Let's Go: USA* refer to holidays that may be unfamiliar to foreign travelers. **Memorial Day** falls on the last Monday of May and honors all Americans who have died in wars. The three-day weekend also signals the unofficial start of summer. Halfway through summer is **Independence Day** on July 4. Americans typically celebrate their independence from England with barbeques and fireworks. Summer ends with another long weekend at the beginning of September. **Labor Day** falls on the first Monday of September, amid a flurry of back-to-school sales. **Columbus Day** is the second Monday in October. **Thanksgiving,** the fourth Thursday of November, celebrates the Pilgrims who arrived in New England in 1620. Thanksgiving unofficially marks the start of the holiday season that runs through New Year's Day. All public agencies and offices are closed on these holidays, as well as on several others that are scattered throughout the calendar.

Measurements

The British system of weights and measures is still in use in the U.S., despite recent efforts to convert to the metric system. The following is a list of American units and their metric equivalents:

1 inch = 25 millimeters
1 foot = 0.30 meter
1 yard = 0.91 meter
1 mile = 1.61 kilometers
1 ounce = 25 grams
1 pound = 0.45 kilogram
1 quart(liquid) = 0.94 liter

12 inches equal 1 foot; 3 feet equal 1 yard; 5280 feet equal 1 mile. 16 ounces (weight) equal 1 pound (abbreviated as 1 lb.). 8 ounces (volume) equal 1 cup; 2 cups equal 1 pint; 2 pints equal 1 quart; and 4 quarts equal 1 gallon.

Electric outlets throughout the U.S., Canada, and Mexico provide current at 117 volts, 60 cycles (Hertz). European voltage is usually 220, so you might need a transformer in order to operate your non-American appliances. This is an extremely important purchase for those with electric systems for disinfecting contact lenses and other small appliances. Transformers are sold to convert specific wattages (e.g. 0-50 watt transformers for razors and radios; larger watt transformers for hair dryers and other appliances). You might also need an adapter to change the shape of the plug; American plugs usually have 2 rectangular prongs, but plugs for larger appliances often have a third prong.

The U.S. uses the Fahrenheit temperature scale rather than the Centigrade (Celsius) scale. To convert Fahrenheit to approximate Centigrade temperatures, subtract 32, then divide by 2. Or, just remember that 32° is the freezing point of water, 212°its boiling point, normal human body temperature is 98.6°, and room temperature hovers around 70°.

Time

Americans tell time on the 12-hour, not 24-hour, clock. Hours after noon are post meridiem or pm (e.g. 2pm); hours before noon are ante meridiem or am (e.g. 2am). Noon is 12pm and midnight is 12am. (To avoid confusion, *Let's Go USA* uses only "noon" and "midnight.")

The Continental U.S. is divided into 4 time zones: Eastern, Central, Mountain, and Pacific. When its noon Eastern time, it's 11am Central, 10am Mountain, 9am Pacific, and 7am central Alaskan and Hawaiian. The borders of the time zones are detailed in the map at the beginning of the book. Most areas of the country switch to daylight saving time (one hour ahead of standard) from mid-April to October.

Alcohol and Drugs

The U.S. has a long history of trying to curb its citizens' alcohol intake, adopting strict rules concerning purchase and consumption. Some areas of the country are "dry," meaning they do not permit the sale of alcohol at all, and others do not permit it to be sold on Sundays. Wherever you are, you must 21 years old to purchase alcoholic beverages legally. If you look under 30, be prepared to show a photo ID when ordering or buying alcohol. Some states go so far as to require that you possess one of their liquor licenses before you can make your purchase. Also, many drugs that are legal for either medicinal or recreational purposes in some countries may be illegal in the U.S. Possession of marijuana, cocaine, or their derivatives (among many other chemicals) is punishable by stiff fines and/or imprisonment. Check with the U.S. Customs Service before your trip (see Customs above) about any questionable drugs.

Transportation

Getting Here

The simplest and surest way to find a bargain fare is to have a reliable travel agent guide you through the jungle of travel options. In addition, check the travel sections of major newspapers for special fares, and consult CIEE (see Useful Organizations above) or your national student travel organization—they might have special deals that regular travel agents cannot offer.

From Canada and Mexico

The U.S. and Canada share the world's longest undefended border. It is easily crossed by U.S. and Canadian citizens alike. (See the Canada General Introduction for details.)

Entering the U.S. from Mexico is a bit more difficult. It is sometimes necessary for Mexicans to have a tourist visa for travel in the U.S.; contact the U.S. Embassy in Mexico City with questions. For Mexicans, as for Canadians, finding bargains on travel in the States may not be easy. Residents of the Americas may not be eligible for the discounts that airlines, bus, and train companies give to visitors from overseas.

Mexican and American carriers offer many flights between the two countries. Since air travel in the U.S. is relatively expensive, it may be cheaper to fly on a Mexican airline to one of the border towns and travel by train or bus from there. For more information regarding transportation to and from Mexico and the American west coast, see *Let's Go: Mexico* or *Let's Go: California and Hawaii.*

Amtrak, Greyhound/Trailways, or one of their subsidiaries connects with all the Mexican border towns. Most buses and trains do no more than cross the Mexico/U.S. border, but you can make connections at: San Diego, CA; Nogales, AZ; and El Paso, Eagle Pass, Laredo, or Brownsville, TX. To drive in the U.S. (see Transportation above) you need both a license and insurance; contact your local auto club or the American Automobile Association (800-336-4357) for details.

From Europe

It's very difficult to generalize about getting to the U.S. from Europe, or to offer exact fares. Prices and market conditions can fluctuate significantly from one week to the next. The best advice *Let's Go* can offer is that you have patience and begin looking for a flight as soon as you think you might be traveling to the U.S.

Flexibility is the best strategy. Direct, regularly scheduled flights are ordinarily far out of any budget traveler's range. Consider leaving from a travel hub; certain cities—such as London, Paris, Amsterdam, and Athens—have flights which are priced competitively. The money you save on a flight out of Paris, for example, might exceed the cost of getting to the airport. London is the major travel hub for trans-Atlantic budget flights. A similar flexibility in destination cities is advisable. Fares to cities only 100 miles apart may differ by that many dollars. New York is a consistently cheap travel target. Atlanta, Chicago, Los Angeles, Dallas, Seattle, and Toronto, Montréal, and Vancouver in Canada make good destinations, too.

A **charter flight** is usually the most economical option. You must choose your departure and return dates when you book, and you will lose some or all of your money if you change or cancel your ticket. Charter companies also reserve the right to change the dates of your flight or the cost of the ticket, or even to cancel your flight within 48 hours of departure. Check with a travel agent about a charter company's reliability and reputation. The most common problem with charters is delays. To be safe, get your ticket in advance, and arrive at the airport well before departure time to ensure a seat. The relatively low cost of a charter flight will usually entail fewer creature comforts.

If you decide to take a non-charter flight, you'll be purchasing greater reliability and flexibility. Major airlines offer reduced fare options. The advantage of flying **standby** is flexibility, since you can come and go as you please. Standby flights, however, are becoming increasingly difficult to find. Check with a travel agent for availability. **TWA, British Airways,** and **Pan Am** offer standby from London to most major U.S. cities. Most airlines allow you to purchase an open ticket in advance that, depending on seat availability, is confirmed the day of departure. Seat availability is known only on the day of the flight, though some airlines will issue predictions. The worst crunch leaving Europe is from mid-June to early July, while August is uniformly tight for returning flights; at no time can you count on getting a seat right away.

STA Travel is a reliable organization that arranges charter flights (see Information for Foreign Visitors above.) You might also try contacting the CIEE, which has two charter services—**Council Charter** (800-223-7402) and **Council Travel** (212-661-1450; discounts for students and teachers only). Some reliable charter companies include: **DER Tours** (800-937-1234), **Tourlite** (800-272-7600), **Travac** (800-872-8800), **Unitravel** (800-325-2222), and **Wardair** (800-237-0314).

Another reduced fare option is the **Advanced Purchase Excursion Fare (APEX).** An APEX provides you with confirmed reservations and allows you to arrive and depart from different cities. APEX requires a minimum stay of 7 to 14 days and a maximum stay of 60 to 90 days. You must purchase your ticket 21 days in advance and pay a $50-100 penalty if you change it. For summer travel, book APEX fares early; by June you may have difficulty getting the departure date you want.

Smaller, budget airlines often undercut major carriers by offering bargain fares on regularly scheduled flights. Competition for seats on these smaller carriers during peak season is fierce, so book early. Some discount transatlantic airlines include **Icelandair** (800-223-5500; New York to Luxembourg; $579-699 round trip, $448 off-season) and **Virgin Atlantic Airways** (800-862-8621; Newark, NJ to London; $608 round trip, $299 one way).

From Asia and Australia

Unfortunately, Asian and Australian travelers have few inexpensive options for air travel to the USA. Asians and Australians must make do with the APEX. There is about a $100 difference between peak and off-season flights between the U.S. and Japan. U.S. carriers offer cheaper flights than **Japan Airlines.** Seasonal fares from and to Australia are a bit more complicated, so call around to see what airlines offer the best deal. A difference of a few days can save you a good deal of money. Some of the airlines that fly between Australia and the U.S. are: **Qantas, Air New Zealand, United, Continental, UTA French Airlines,** and **Canadian Pacific Airlines.** Prices are roughly equivalent among the six, although the cities they serve vary. One compensation for the exorbitant fares is that trans-Pacific flights often allow a stopover in Honolulu, Hawaii.

Getting Around

In the 50s, President Dwight D. Eisenhower envisioned an **interstate system,** a national network of highways designed primarily to aid the military in defending precious American soil. Eisenhower's asphalt dream has been gradually realized, although Toyotas far outnumber tanks on the federally funded roads. Even-numbered roads run east-west and odd run north-south. If the interstate has a three digit number, it is a branch of another interstate (i.e., I-285 is a branch of I-85). An even digit in the hundred's place means the branch will eventually return to the main interstate; an odd digit means it won't. North-south routes begin on the West Coast with I-5 and end with I-95 on the East Coast. I-10 stretches across the entire southern border, from Los Angeles along the coast of the Gulf of Mexico to Jacksonville, FL. The northernmost east-west route is **I-94**. The national speed limit of 55 miles per hour (88km per hour) has been raised to 65 miles per hour in some areas. The main routes through most towns are **U.S. highways,** which are often locally referred to by non-numerical names. **State highways** are usually less heavily traveled and may lead travelers to down-home American farming communities. U.S. and state highway numbers don't follow any particular numbering pattern.

Airline, bus, and train companies offer discounts to foreign visitors within the U.S. **Greyhound/Trailways** offers an **International Ameripass** for foreign students and faculty members. The passes are sold primarily in foreign countries, but may be purchased for a slightly higher price in New York, Los Angeles, San Francisco, or Miami. Prices are $125 for a 7-day pass ($135 in the U.S.), $199 for a 15-day pass ($214 in the U.S.), and $279 for a 30-day pass ($299 in the U.S.). To obtain a pass, you need a valid passport and proof of eligibility; the pass cannot be extended. If you are *not* a student or a faculty member, the regular rates for passes are: $189 for seven days, $249 for 15 days, and $349 for 30 days, with optional extensions of $10 per day. Call Greyhound at 800-237-8211 for information or to request their *Visit USA Vacation Guide,* which details services for foreigners.

Amtrak's **USA Rail Pass,** similar to the Eurailpass, entitles foreigners to unlimited travel anywhere in the U.S. A 45-day pass costs $299. If you plan to travel only in one particular area, purchase a Regional Rail Pass instead. Each pass serves a single region, including Eastern ($159), Western ($239), Far Western ($159), and Florida ($45). All USA Rail Passes for children (ages 2-11) are half-fare. With a valid passport, you can purchase the USA Rail Pass outside the country or in New York, Boston, Miami, Los Angeles, or San Francisco. Check with travel agents or Amtrak representatives in Europe. If you're already in the U.S. and would like more information, call Amtrak (800-872-7245). Be smart about buying passes; they are not a bargain unless you plan to make a number of stops. Also remember that many U.S. cities are not accessible by train.

Many major U.S. airlines in America offer special **Visit USA** air passes and fares to foreign travelers. You purchase these passes outside the U.S., paying one price for a certain number of "flight coupons" good for one flight segment on an airline's domestic system within a certain time period; some cross-country trips may require two segments. "Visit USA" discount fares are available for specific flights within the U.S. if purchased in one's own country. Most airline passes can be purchased only by those living outside the Western Hemisphere, though some are available for Canadians, Mexicans, and residents of Latin America if they purchase a pass from a travel agent located at least 100 miles from the U.S. border. "Visit USA" fares are marked by a maze of restrictions and guidelines, so you should consult a travel agent concerning the logistics of these discounts.

Work

Working in the U.S. with only a B-2 visa is grounds for deportation. Before a work visa can be issued to you, you must present the U.S. Consulate in your country with a letter from an American employer stating that you have been offered a job and that you have a permanent residence in your home country. The letter must mention you by name and briefly outline the job, its salary, and its employment period. Alternatively, an American employer can obtain an H visa for you (usually an H-2, which means that qualified applicants for the position are not available in the U.S.).

Student travel organizations such as CIEE and its affiliates often assist students in securing work visas. Some have work-exchange programs, while others hire individuals who speak English fluently to act as leaders for tour groups. The **Association for International Practical Training (AIPT)** is the umbrella organization for the **International Association for the Exchange of Students for Technology Experience.** AIPT offers on-the-job training in 49 countries for students in agriculture, engineering, architecture, computer science, mathematics, and the sciences. You must apply by December 10 for summer placement, six months in advance for other placement. Contact AIPT at 320 Parkview Bldg., 10480 Little Pautuxent Parkway, Columbia, MD 21044 (301-997-2200). The government agency in your own country that handles educational exchanges and visits to other countries should be able to provide local contacts for suitable organizations.

If you are studying in the U.S., you can take any on-campus job once you have applied for a social security number. Check with your student employment office for job listings and requirements for work clearance. The government has recently begun a strict campaign to prohibit businesses from hiring employees without an H-visa, so don't expect leniency. Before being hired, all job applicants must obtain an I-9 validation by showing proof of U.S. citizenship or a work permit.

Study

Foreigners who wish to study in the U.S. must apply for either an **F-1 visa** (for exchange students) or a **J-1 visa** (for full-time students enrolled in a degree-granting program). To obtain a J-1, you must fill out an IAP 66 eligibility form, issued by the program in which you will enroll. Neither the F-1 nor J-1 visa specifies any expiration date; instead they are both valid for the "duration of stay," which includes the length of your particular program and a brief grace period thereafter. In order to extend a student visa, an I-538 form must be filled out. Requests to extend a visa must be submitted 15 to 60 days before the original departure date. Many foreign schools—and most U.S. colleges—have offices that give advice and information on study in the U.S.

Admission offices at almost all U.S. institutions accept applications directly from international students. If English is not your first language, you will generally be required to pass the **Test of English as a Foreign Language and Test of Spoken English (TOEFL/TSE)**, administered in many countries. For more information, contact the TOEFL/TSE Application Office, P.O. Box 6155, Princeton, NJ 08541 (609-921-9000).

One excellent information source is the **Institute of International Education (IIE)**, which administers many educational exchange programs in the U.S. and abroad. IIE also prints *Fields of Study at U.S. Colleges* which details courses of study and lists other resources. *Study in U.S. Colleges and Universities: A Selected Bibliography* contains information relating to your field and to U.S. education in general. If you plan a summer visit, take a look at *Summer Learning Options USA: A Guide for Foreign Nationals. English Language and Orientation Programs in the United States* describes language and cultural programs. To obtain these publications, contact IIE, 809 United Nations Plaza, New York, NY 10017 (212-883-8200). They are also available through local Fulbright Commission offices, private counseling agencies, or the U.S. International Commission Agency offices in American embassies.

The **School for International Training** offers language-training sessions, followed by three-week homestays. Write to the Experiment in International Living, Dept. of Language Services, Brattleboro, VT 05301 (800-451-4465).

Life in the United States

History and Politics

The first Europeans to wander across the Atlantic Ocean and settle in North American nearly 400 years ago were a sorry lot indeed. Primarily religious zealots, fortune hunters, and castoffs from their native countries, they settled along the East Coast. Their descendants, joined by later groups, eventually undertook an experiment known as the United States of America.

These early immigrants were by no means the first inhabitants of North America. Native Americans, whom the disoriented Christopher Columbus mistakenly dubbed "Indians," crossed a land bridge from Asia to Alaska over 37,000 years ago and fanned across North and South America. By the time Columbus claimed the "New World" for Spain in 1492, there were already about 15 million people of diverse and well-established cultures inhabiting this not-so-New World.

In the European conquest of North America, germs and viruses, not gunpowder and rifles, were crucial weapons. The Europeans infected the Native Americans' unsuspecting immune systems and decimated entire tribes. Some historians estimate that this inadvertent biological genocide killed 90% of the native population with diseases such as smallpox, typhoid, measles, and influenza.

Various nations exhibited their distinctive style of subjugation and colonization. Exploring the South on horseback, Spanish conquistadors killed and enslaved native populations and then imported slaves from Africa. These three groups eventually blended and developed into a distinctive *mestizo* culture which grew under the watchful eye of the Catholic Church and the Spanish crown. The Spaniards pushed across what is now the American Southwest into California, a region that Russia too had its eye on. Far to the North, French trappers and opportunists scavenged their way around the Great Lakes and down the Mississippi River. Dutch traders established New Amsterdam (later redubbed New York), a post at the base of the Hudson River.

Nearly all of the areas along the Atlantic coast were eventually controlled by the British crown, and England has left its mark on American culture more strongly than any other nation. Squeezed out of English society, a steady stream of roguish young men began to migrate to Jamestown, Virginia in 1607. Life was chaotic and survival was difficult for over ten years until a new, smokable crop—tobacco—was introduced to the region. With the labor of African slaves, Virginians established their fortunes and formed a stable, aristocratic, rigidly hierarchical society.

In 1630 Puritans first docked at Massachusetts Bay colony and embarked on a holy experiment to construct a theocratic society in their distinctly cerebral and conformist fashion. Governor John Winthrop reminded his earnest followers that they were to build a "city on a hill" and that the world (or at least the British monarchy) would eagerly and skeptically track their progress. The experiment worked, at least for a couple of generations, when capitalism overshadowed piety and led to widespread "declension." In 1636 the Puritans started a college to train ministers and named the new institution after its benefactor, John Harvard. No longer a seminary, Harvard College now trains politicians, doctors, investment bankers, professors, and travel guide editors.

By the mid-18th century, the colonists were irked by "taxation without representation" and exploitative policies, and became increasingly aware of the huge gap between themselves and British rulers. On July 4, 1776 colonial leaders signed the Declaration of Independence and proclaimed themselves separate from the British commonwealth. England didn't give up her colonies easily, however, and the protracted separation process known as the American Revolution ensued.

After winning the war and then stumbling through a few unstable years, the United States emerged with an innovative new Constitution, written by James Madison and ratified in 1789. The Constitution is a salute to the art of compromise; it represents the competing interests and ideologies of 18th-century leaders from the Northeast and Southern regions. Specific responsibilities are assigned to either the federal government or to individual state governments. The federal government is divided into three branches—executive, legislative, and judicial—which operate within a system of "checks and balances" in order to maintain parity and stability.

Meanwhile, the U.S. steadily grew in size. In 1803, Jefferson doubled the area of the nation after bargaining with France over a chunk of land known as the Louisiana Purchase. Immigrants from northern European nations, as well as citizens from Eastern states, settled across the Midwestern plains. White settlers carried on the American pioneer spirit as they pushed the frontier farther west. The Lewis and Clark expedition, covered wagons stumbling down the Oregon Trail, and the gold-seeking "forty-niners" all pursued opportunity, land, and money.

During the early 19th century, while tobacco and later cotton bloomed on Southern plantations, the North underwent rapid industrialization. A symbiotic and neocolonial relationship developed between North and South. Cotton from the South was shipped to Northern textile mills and was then sold in European markets. Industrialization widened the gap between North and South and made regional differences more obvious. Mid-century, differences in Northern and Southern manners, commercial habits, and demographics culminated in the debate over slavery. Led by South Carolina, 11 Southern states seceded in 1860 and formed the Confederate States of America. Secession sparked a four-year Civil War during which Yankees and Rebels tore each other apart. The war resulted in over 600,000 deaths, by far the most of any war in U.S. history. After the North won, President Abraham Lincoln liberated the slaves with an Emancipation Proclamation. Although African Americans gained emancipation, citizenship, and voting rights, U.S. government and society were scarred by racism and segregation long after the Civil War.

Famines, wars, and oppressive monarchs in Europe sent a fresh deluge of immigrants to Ellis Island, gateway to the golden land of opportunity. Settling primarily in Eastern cities, these new arrivals further enriched the already diverse population. Despite the welcome to the "huddled masses" inscribed on the Statue of Liberty, many newcomers were confronted with nativism, prejudice, and basic antagonism. The myth of America as a "melting pot" is arguable at best; many groups were quite isolated and distinct ethnic traits still endure beneath the broad, bland canopy of "American."

Rapid, groundbreaking changes marked the end of the 19th and beginning of the 20th centuries, commonly known as the Progressive Era. Railroads connected even the most remote, provincial areas to a national communication and transportation network. Big industries such as steel, oil, railroads, and shipping made the names Carnegie, Rockefeller, Vanderbilt, Morgan, and Getty synonymous with capitalism and opulence. While tycoons wallowed in cash, their employees contended with dangerous working conditions and starvation wages. The government was called upon to expand its role and pass legislation to protect the new urban working class from the health hazards of sweat shops, mills, and factories.

America's focus on domestic issues and policies shifted to a global perspective when the U.S. entered World War I ("The Great War") in Europe. Riding a crest of nationalism and victory, a confident U.S. emerged from the war in 1918 as a creditor nation in the world economy. The electorate further opened up when a magnanimous Congress finally granted women suffrage in 1920, in response to over 60 years of the courageous efforts of activists such as Susan B. Anthony and Elizabeth Cady Stanton.

While writers of the Lost Generation sulked in Parisian bars and wallowed in their post-war disillusionment, "flappers" cut their hair, shortened their hemlines, and took part in the "Roaring 20s" at home. Jazz, America's first popular indigenous music, was developed, comprising a major step in the evolution of a distinctive African-American culture. The party ended abruptly in October 1929, however, when the stock exchange crashed on Black Monday. Banks closed their doors, fortunes disappeared, thousands lost their jobs, and America entered the Great Depression.

For a confused, bitter, and impoverished nation, President Franklin D. Roosevelt was a white knight astride the New Deal. Creating a wave of legislation and countless organizations such as the Works Progress Administration, the New Deal helped put the country back to work. The bitter pill that finally cured the sick economy came in the form of another world war. Americans entered World War II on December 7, 1941 after the Japanese bombed Pearl Harbor. Patriotism again swept the nation as citizens rallied around the Allied cause. Housewives gave up nylon stockings and began to work in factories, children recycled cans and newspapers, and families huddled around their radios eager for news from the fronts. A few months after Germany surrendered in 1945, the Atomic Age commenced when the Japanese cities of Hiroshima and Nagasaki were victims of atomic bombs dropped by the U.S.

After World War II, America entered an era of prosperity and conformity. Television and mass culture emerged as a powerful unifying force. American consumers bought modern, time-saving appliances and did their darnedest to keep up with the Joneses. The rise of the middle class was accompanied by an exodus to suburbia and the sanctification of the nuclear family. Meanwhile, the Cold War and Joe

McCarthy's "Red Scare" fueled a political atmosphere of mistrust, conservatism, and isolation.

Underlying the complacency that marked the 50s, however, were seeds of the activism and protest of the 60s. In 1953 the U.S. Supreme Court's decision in *Brown v. the Board of Education* desegregated public schools. Challenging prejudice and conformism, a gay liberation movement strove to legitimize homosexuality and gain respect in the eyes of others. In California Jack Kerouac and other writers of the Beat Movement went "on the road" in search of an alternative, more expressive lifestyle. Musicians such as Elvis Presley and Buddy Holly shocked parents and thrilled teenagers with rock 'n' roll, another distinctly American sound.

When President John F. Kennedy was assassinated in Dallas in November 1963, a paralyzed nation was thrust into the 60s, a decade full of turmoil, activism, and transformation. American GIs were shipped to Vietnam to prevent communist takeover. Violence also pervaded the domestic sphere as students protested American involvement in Southeast Asia. A civil rights movement, under leaders such as Martin Luther King, Jr., gained a voice and challenged institutionalized racism and segregation. Inspired in part by Betty Friedan's groundbreaking book, **The Feminine Mystique** (1963), American women hung up their aprons, raised their consciousness, and went on the pill. The decade ended with America's "giant leap" of space exploration when the first human walked on the moon in July 1969.

The baby-boomers of the 60s abandoned their idealism to become the Me Generation of the 70s. The activists who once burned their draft cards now soaked in hot tubs, became health conscious, and boogied to the disco beat. Amid nationwide cynicism following the disgrace of the Watergate scandal, President Richard Nixon resigned in August 1974. Cars became compact as oil and gas prices reached astronomical heights, and the U.S. weathered tremendous inflation and a recession. Despite the economic down-swing, a technological boom ushered in the "Computer Age."

The 80s were the Age of Ronald Reagan. A conservative political climate and new tax laws widened the gap between rich and poor. Americans became aware of and even obsessed with exercise and health. Accompanying this body consciousness has been AIDS, the most serious health concern facing America as it enters the 90s. The Me Generation moved to a higher tax bracket and became the yuppies of the 80s. Although decidedly more subdued, American campuses were still hotbeds of protest, as apartheid, abortion, homelessness, and minority rights fueled a continuing tradition of activism. The primacy of America as *the* great economic superpower was threatened by the production and technology of Japan and South Korea. Relations with the USSR steadily improved under Mikhail Gorbachev's *glasnost.* As always, America is faced with immense choices in both the domestic and global realms and awaits the events that will mold the last decade of the 20th century.

Art

Like much of North American culture, the artistic tradition dates back to prehistoric times. Native American tribes developed art forms in a variety of media, including walrus-tusk ivory, wood, pottery, stone, and shell.

White Americans were slow to develop a fine arts tradition distinct from that of Europe. The earliest colonial artists imitated Dutch, Flemish, and Spanish masters. After the Revolution, artists such as John Singleton Copley, the first world-renowned American-trained painter, continued to adopt European models. European-American folk art, however, established itself as a vibrant and enduring tradition. Early artists put their creative energy into crafting household items that were both functional and aesthetic. From this tradition, a school known as the American Primitive emerged in the Connecticut River Valley.

Two Romantic styles of landscape painting developed in the 19th century. The Hudson River School, including Thomas Cole, celebrated the openness of the American natural environment, while the iconic lithographs of Currier and Ives typified luminism, the other Romantic style.

Visual arts changed rapidly during the period of the westward expansion and took on distinct styles in different regions. Genre paintings by artists such as George Caleb Bingham grew up in the West. In the East, James A. McNeill Whistler, Mary Cassatt, and John Singer Sargent developed their own brand of European impressionism. Winslow Homer, Grant Wood, and Norman Rockwell celebrated rural and small-town America.

Not until later in the 20th century did Americans contribute significantly to the international art community. Georgia O'Keeffe depicted abstract flowers, as well as the stark Southwestern desert landscape. Edward Hopper's modest paintings of urban scenes marked a shift in attention from the beautiful and unusual to the ugly and mundane. Pop artists Andy Warhol, Jasper Johns, and Roy Lichtenstein challenged centuries of aesthetic tradition and proved that a can of soup or a cartoon strip truly constitute art. Jackson Pollock shunned representation and turned the process of painting into the subject.

American sculpture similarly departed from traditional styles, ranging from George Segal's realistic fiberglass people to Henry Moore's abstract "reclining figures." Challenging classical monuments was the Vietnam War Memorial in Washington, DC, a simple, dignified, and understated black wall that seemed to grow out of the earth. Abstract and whimsical sculpture on a grand scale was typified by David Smith's earth art and Alexander Calder's kinetic sculpture.

Architecture

The American landscape was not always dotted with glass and steel skyscrapers. While the familiar plains tepee of the Sioux was a movable shelter of fairly simple design, many tribes developed sophisticated permanent buildings. In the Southwest, the cliffside dwellings of the early inhabitants of Grand Mesa and the pueblo apartment-like constructions of the Tiwa were constructed to protect against attack and the scorching heat.

The dwellings of the first settlers followed European models, particularly in New England. Towns and villages today still contain examples of the simple wooden houses and churches built by 17th- and 18th-century folk. Elaborate public buildings were modeled after the European Georgian style, made popular by Englishman Sir Christopher Wren. In the late colonial and early federal period, a High Georgian style, typified by Thomas Jefferson's designs, flourished.

In the West, the Spanish inspired a style of architecture that still prevails. Stucco facades, red gabled roofs, and elegant arches appear in buildings throughout California, Florida, Texas, and the Southwest. Authentic missions also survive in these regions. The French transplanted their architecture to New Orleans and other settlements along the Mississippi.

In the early 19th century, prolific New England architects Charles Bulfinch and Samuel McIntire adopted Classical elements. In the 1820s and 30s, Greek Revival designs were employed in public buildings and private homes. An eclectic approach toward mid-century signaled the rise of the Gothic Revival. The growth of U.S. cities increased the demand for large public buildings. H.H. Richardson adapted the Romanesque style in his heavy-set designs. The use of iron, and later steel, made possible an expansion upward, and the first skyscrapers were born at the close of the 19th century. The Empire State Building, completed during the Depression, was New York City's salute to modernity.

This garish aesthetic was challenged by Frank Lloyd Wright, who celebrated the midwestern landscape in his clean, low-slung "prairie houses" of the Chicago area. But the highrise would mark the future of American urban development, and the European Bauhaus School's steel-and-glass structures soon made the Empire State

Building's design obsolete. Recently, I.M. Pei took over as king of public building design; his radical, whimsical designs can be seen in Pittsburgh's PPG Place and Boston's Hancock Tower.

But perhaps the architectural fad that mostly deeply touches Americans is the mall, the increasingly gargantuan enclosed shopping center which uses fountains, plants, and even miniature amusement parks to create the "perfect" shopping environment.

NEW YORK

For almost as long as the United States has had a national consciousness, New York State has had the special power to capture the country's imagination. In the early 1800s, Thomas Cole, central figure in the coterie of American artists known as the Hudson River School, painted his glorious landscapes of the Catskills and the Hudson River Valley. The works were instantly popular; they sparked nationalistic pride by evoking images of New York as a God-given wilderness. A century later, artists were again inspired by New York. This time, however, the likes of Georgia O'Keeffe and Piet Mondrian were painting the cavernous skyscrapers and machine-like grid of Manhattan. The focus of the vision had shifted, but it was New York all the same.

To visit New York today is to see two states. The magical beauty of the wilderness portrayed by Cole still thrives upstate. While parts of it have been developed, much has remained untouched. To residents of the nation's largest metropolis, however, "The City" is the universe, and whatever lies farther north is largely irrelevant. Somehow, despite these two drastically divergent visions, New York manages to hold together as one state. Its polarity only heightens its appeal.

Practical Information

Capital: Albany.

Tourist Information: 800-225-5697 from VA north and MI east; 518-474-4116 from everywhere else. Open Mon.-Fri. 8:30am-5pm. Write to Division of Tourism, 1 Commerce Plaza, Albany 12245. Ask for the excellent, comprehensive *I Love New York Travel Guide,* which includes disabled access and resource information. **New York State Office of Parks and Recreation,** Agency Bldg. 1, Empire State Plaza, Albany 12238 (474-0456), has literature on canoeing, camping, biking, and hiking.

Time Zone: Eastern. **Postal Abbreviation:** NY.

The Catskills can entertain hikers and hang gliders for weeks, but the Adirondacks stand out as New York's natural treasure. "There are regions of the Adirondacks where no one has ever set foot," claim proud locals. New York has long worked to maintain the quality of outdoor recreation in the state. You're never a long drive from one of its 90 state parks, most of which provide excellent camping. For the nature lover, New York's Thousand Island Region is the perfect vacation spot. Muskie, walleye, and bass fishing in the "Seaway" is perhaps the best in the eastern U.S. Over 50 private campsites and parks are scattered over the 1800 islands. Call the St. Lawrence County Chamber of Commerce (315-386-4000).

US Air and **Continental** provide extensive airline services to Albany, Syracuse, Rochester, and Buffalo from Newark, NJ, near New York City. Fares vary. The cheapest rates often require a seven-day advance reservation and a Saturday night stay-over.

Amtrak sends one route up the Hudson River Valley from Penn Station to Albany and on to Niagara Falls or Montreal, and another follows I-90 from Boston to Albany and Buffalo. Buses cut across the state and stop in areas where the train does not go. **Greyhound/Trailways** has frequent service to Albany, Syracuse, Rochester, and Buffalo. Less frequent routes include the Finger Lakes area, the Catskills (including Cooperstown), the Adirondacks, the Hudson River Valley, and Niagara Falls or Montreal.

Hitchhiking is illegal in New York State. This law is enforced with particular vehemence in the New York City area, where it's not safe to begin with.

Bikers should head for the Finger Lakes region. Its gentle hills are just high enough to provide some challenge and the small farmsteads can best be explored and appreciated by bike. Moreover, the wineries of the region make for very pleasant stops. Write for the *New York Bicycle Touring Guide,* c/o William N. Hoffman, 53

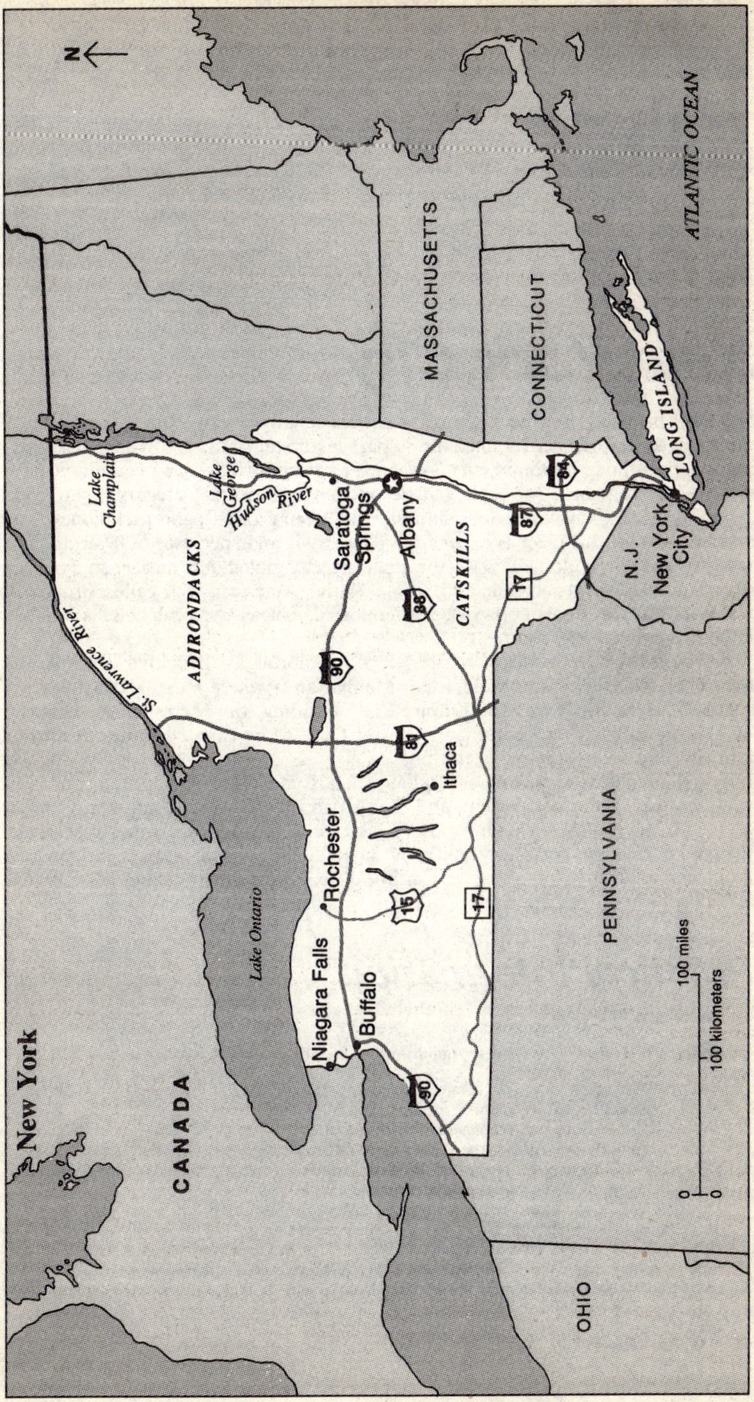
New York
N
CANADA
Lake Ontario
St. Lawrence River
ADIRONDACKS
Lake Champlain
Lake George
Hudson River
Saratoga Springs
Albany
CATSKILLS
Rochester
Niagara Falls
Buffalo
Ithaca
90
88
87
84
81
17
15
MASSACHUSETTS
CONNECTICUT
LONG ISLAND
ATLANTIC OCEAN
N.J.
New York City
PENNSYLVANIA
OHIO
0
100 miles
0
100 kilometers

Claire Ave., New Rochelle, NY 10804, or the free *Finger Lakes Bicycle Touring Guide,* Finger Lakes State Park Region, RD 3, Trumansburg 14886 (607-387-7041). For a guide to the wineries of upstate New York write to the Department of Agriculture and Markets, Capital Plaza, 1 Winner Circle, Albany 12235 (518-457-3880). Ask for the *New World of World Class Wine Making.*

Hikers will appreciate the many long trails that criss-cross the state, including the Appalachian Trail, Finger Lakes Trail, and Long Path. For information write the **NY State Department of Environmental Conservation,** 50 Wolf Rd., Albany 12233. For a general guide to outdoor recreation in New York (with extensive information on camping, hiking, and sports facilities—especially golf and tennis) write to **I Love NY Publications,** Dept. of Commerce, Albany 12245, or call the New York Division of Tourism (see Practical Information above).

New York City

New York City is a hectic, dazzling, occasionally overwhelming, and always multi-tiered experience. Its make-up is part historical sights (museums and landmarks), part modern monuments (skyscrapers, transportation and communication systems), part people (of each genetic and environmental category), part food groups (pretzels, knish, hot dogs, and Korean green grocers), and part money (lots and lots—as in, this place is expensive). The city is an experience in layering. The wealthy and the underpaid walk the same streets, gilded and mosaic-studded art deco buildings are tenements, and an old Native American trail called Broadway winds its way through an otherwise ordered grid. This is a city which tells its story in contradictions and contrast.

New York City is actually composed of five boroughs: Brooklyn, Queens, the Bronx, Staten Island, and Manhattan. Manhattan is where most of the sights are centered. Here you'll find the Empire State Building, the Metropolitan Museum of Art, the Rockefeller Center, and Central Park. More than 280 miles of subway tunnels wind around below everything.

The Big Apple is home to more Italians than Rome, more black people than Nairobi, more Jews than Jerusalem, and more Irish than Dublin. Boatloads of immigrants no longer pass through historic Ellis Island, turn-of-the-century gateway to the land of freedom and opportunity, but hopeful emigrés still flock to the concrete archipelago. Mostly from Asia, the Caribbean, and Latin America these days, immigrants constantly reshape New York.

Practical Information

Emergency: 911.

Police: 212-374-5000. Use this for inquiries that are not urgent. 24 hours.

Visitor Information: New York Convention and Visitors Bureau, 2 Columbus Circle (397-8222), 59th and Broadway. Subway: A, D, 1. Friendly, multilingual staff will help you with directions, hotel listings, entertainment ideas, safety tips, and "insider's" descriptions of New York's neighborhoods. Ask for the 3 free maps that are virtual keys to the City: *I Love New York Travel Guide* (a street map), the *MTA Manhattan Bus Map,* and the *MTA New York City Subway Map.* A visit is better than a phone call, because the lines are often busy and the maps and brochures are worth having. Open Mon.-Fri. 9am-6pm, Sat.-Sun. and holidays 10am-6pm. Branch office at **Times Square Information Center,** 158 W. 42nd St., between Broadway and Seventh Ave. Subway: A, E, N, R, D, or F. Open Wed.-Fri. 9am-6pm, Sat.-Sun. 10am-6pm. Similar information is available, but there is no telephone service. **Entertainment Information: Ticketron,** 399-4444. **Free Daily Events in the City,** 360-1333; 24 hours. **Jazz line,** 718-465-7500. **NYC Onstage,** 587-1111; updates on theatre, dance, music, children's entertainment, and other events. **Tkts.** 354-5800; at Broadway and 47th St., and at 2 World Trade Center. Half-price tickets for Broadway and Off-Broadway shows sold the day of the performance only.

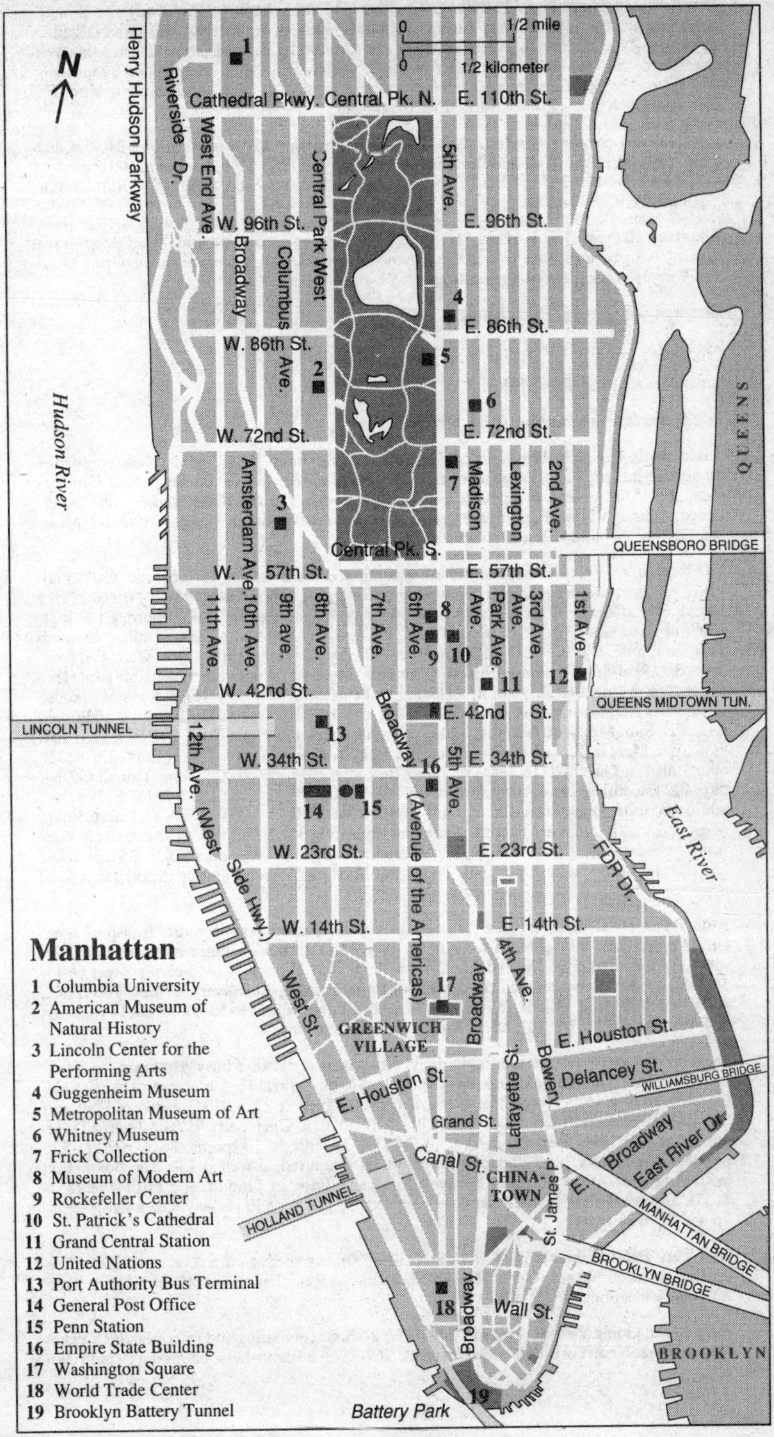
0 1/2 mile
0 1/2 kilometer
N
Henry Hudson Parkway
Riverside Dr.
West End Ave.
Cathedral Pkwy.
Central Pk. N.
E. 110th St.
Central Park West
5th Ave.
W. 96th St.
E. 96th St.
Broadway
Columbus Ave.
E. 86th St.
W. 86th St.
Hudson River
W. 72nd St.
E. 72nd St.
Amsterdam Ave.
Madison Ave.
Lexington Ave.
2nd Ave.
QUEENS
Central Pk. S.
QUEENSBORO BRIDGE
W. 57th St.
E. 57th St.
11th Ave.
10th Ave.
9th ave.
8th Ave.
7th Ave.
6th Ave.
Park Ave.
3rd Ave.
1st Ave.
W. 42nd St.
E. 42nd St.
QUEENS MIDTOWN TUN.
LINCOLN TUNNEL
12th Ave. (West Side Hwy.)
Broadway
W. 34th St.
E. 34th St.
5th Ave.
(Avenue of the Americas)
East River
W. 23rd St.
E. 23rd St.
FDR Dr.
W. 14th St.
E. 14th St.
4th Ave.
West St.
Broadway
GREENWICH VILLAGE
E. Houston St.
E. Houston St.
Bowery
Lafayette St.
Delancey St.
WILLIAMSBURG BRIDGE
Grand St.
Broadway
East River Dr.
Canal St.
CHINA-TOWN
St. James P.
E.
HOLLAND TUNNEL
MANHATTAN BRIDGE
BROOKLYN BRIDGE
Broadway
Wall St.
BROOKLYN
Battery Park
Manhattan
1 Columbia University
2 American Museum of Natural History
3 Lincoln Center for the Performing Arts
4 Guggenheim Museum
5 Metropolitan Museum of Art
6 Whitney Museum
7 Frick Collection
8 Museum of Modern Art
9 Rockefeller Center
10 St. Patrick's Cathedral
11 Grand Central Station
12 United Nations
13 Port Authority Bus Terminal
14 General Post Office
15 Penn Station
16 Empire State Building
17 Washington Square
18 World Trade Center
19 Brooklyn Battery Tunnel

Travelers Aid Society: at 158-160 W. 42nd St. (944-0013) between Broadway and Seventh Ave.; and at JFK International Airport (718-656-4870), in the International Arrivals Bldg. Subway to 42nd St. branch: A, E, N, R, D or F. 42nd St. branch specializes in crisis intervention services for the stranded traveler or crime victim. JFK office offers general counseling and referral to travelers, as well as emergency assistance. 42nd St. branch open Mon.-Fri. 9am-5pm; JFK branch open Mon.-Fri. 10am-7pm.

Consulates: Australian, 636 Fifth Ave. (245-4000). **British,** 845 Third Ave. (752-8400). **Canadian,** 1251 Sixth Ave. (768-2400). **French,** 934 Fifth Ave. (983-5660). **German,** 460 Park Ave. (308-8700). **Indian,** 3 E. 64th St. (879-8700). **Israeli,** 800 Second Ave. (351-5200). **Italian,** 320 Park Ave. (737-9100).

American Express: 150 E. 42nd St. (687-3700), between Lexington and Third Ave. Travel agency that provides traveler's checks, financial services, and other assistance. Open Mon.-Fri. 9am-5pm. Call for other locations.

Airports: see Getting There below.

Trains: see Getting There below.

Buses: see Getting There below.

Public Transit: see Getting Around below.

Taxis: Radio-dispatched taxis, Utog, 741-2000; and **Skyline,** 718-482-8686. These companies do not use meters; they charge a flat rate. To JFK, $35 with either company. **Taxi Commission,** 869-4513; general complaints and lost and found. On the street, yellow cabs can be hailed, although New Yorkers are notoriously competitive when it comes to taxi-flagging. See Getting Around below for more information.

Car Rental: All agencies have minimum age requirements and ask for deposits. Call in advance to reserve, especially near the weekend. **Goldie's Leasing Corp.,** 47-11 11th St., Long Island City, Queens (718-392-5435 or 718-392-5339), across the Queensborough Bridge, south of Astoria. $37 per day Mon.-Thurs.; $45 per day Fri.-Sun.; 100 free miles, 20¢ each additional mile. Weekly $226; 700 free miles, 20¢ per additional mile. Open Mon.-Fri. 8am-6pm, Sat. 8am-5pm. Sunday drop-off is possible. Must be 21 with a major credit card. **Discount Rent-a-Car,** 240 E. 92nd St. (410-2211), between Second and Third Ave.; offices also in Jackson Heights, Queens. Mon.-Thurs. $51 per day; 100 free miles, 20¢ each additional mile. Fri.-Sun. $162; 500 free miles, 20¢ each additional mile. Open Mon.-Fri. 8am-7pm, Sat. 9am-2pm. Must be 25 with major credit card. **Rent-a-Wreck,** 202 W. 77th St.,(800-221-8282); offices also in Queens (718-784-3302) and Brooklyn (718-998-9100). Mon.-Thurs. $39 per day; 100 free miles, 20¢ each additional mile. Fri.-Sun. $55 per day; 100 free miles, 20¢ each additional mile. Open Mon.-Fri. 7:30am-6:30pm, Sat. 8:30am-5:30pm, Sun. 8:30am-6:30pm. Must be 23 with major credit card. **American Interboro,** 403 E. 76th St. (439-9700), off York Ave. Weekdays $61; 100 free miles, 25¢ each additional mile. Weekends $163; 325 free miles, 25¢ each additional mile. Open daily 7am-7pm. Must be 21 with major credit card or a $500 deposit.

Auto Transport Companies: New York is the major departure point for auto transport agencies. Applications take about a week to process. Most agencies require more than one ID; some ask for references. **Dependable Car Services,** 1501 Broadway (840-6262). Must be 19; $50-150 deposit (depending on the model of car) returned upon delivery. **Transporters, Inc.,** 450 Seventh Ave., at 34th St. (594-2690). Must be 21 and deposit $150-300. **Auto Driveaway,** 264 W. 35th St. (967-2344), offers similar services and prices.

Bicycle Rentals: Whatever the time or day, city streets are always busy. However, on weekends from May-Oct. and on weekdays from 10am-3pm, Central Park is closed to cars, allowing bicycles to rule its roads. **Metro Bicycle,** 332 E. 14th St. (228-4344), between First and Second Ave. 3-speed bikes only, $4 per hr., $20 per day. Open daily 9:30am-6pm. I.D. required. Also at 1311 Lexington Ave., (427-4450), at 80th St. 10-speeds, $6.50 per hr., $25 per day. Same hours, but $20 deposit or credit card required, as well as I.D. **The Boathouse,** in Central Park, at the northeast corner of the Lake. Enter at 72nd St. and Fifth Ave. (861-4137). 3-speeds $6 per hr., $24 per day; 10-speeds $8 per hr., $30 per day. Open daily 10am-7pm. I.D. required.

New York Public Library: 11 W. 40th St. (930-0800), entrance at Fifth Ave. at 42nd St. Non-lending research library. Open Mon.-Wed. 10am-8:45pm, Thurs.-Sat. 10am-5:45pm. Over 80 branch locations.

Help Lines: Crime Victim's Hotline, 577-7777; 24-hour counseling and referrals. **Sex Crimes Report Line,** New York Police Department, 267-7273; 24-hour help, counseling, and referrals.

Medical Care: Walk-in Clinic, 57 E. 34th St. (683-1010), between Park and Madison Ave. Open Mon.-Fri. 8am-6pm, Sat. 10am-2pm. Affiliated with Beth Israel Hospital. **24-Hour Pharmacy: Kaufman's Pharmacy,** 557 Lexington Ave. (755-2266), at 50th St. **24-Hour Emergency Doctor,** 718-745-5900. **The Eastern's Women's Center,** 40 E. 30th St. (686-6066), between Park and Madison. Gynecological exams and surgical procedures for women. **AIDS Information,** 807-6655, 10am-10pm.

Post Office: Central branch 380 W. 33rd St., (967-8585), at Eighth Ave. across from Madison Square Garden. To pick up general delivery mail, use the entrance at 390 Ninth Ave. Open Mon.-Sat. 10am-1pm. For information call 330-3099. **ZIP code:** 10001.

Area Code: 212 (Manhattan and the Bronx); **718** (Brooklyn, Queens, and Staten Island). No extra charge for calls between these area codes, but dial "1" first. Unless otherwise specified, all telephone numbers in this chapter have a 212 area code.

Getting There

By Plane

Not only will you have to choose a carrier, but an airport as well. There are three airports servicing the New York Metropolitan Region. John F. Kennedy Airport (JFK) (718-656-4520), 12 miles from Midtown in southern Queens, handles most international flights. JFK is the largest, boasting the greatest number of flights, but intra-airport travel is time-consuming. LaGuardia Airport (718-656-4520), 6 miles from midtown in northwestern Queens, is the smallest, offering domestic flights and air shuttles (see below). Newark International Airport, 12 miles from Midtown in Newark, NJ, offers both domestic and international flights at budget fares not available at the other airports.

Many airlines offer budget flights, but the cut-rate market is always fluctutating and price wars are constant. In general, it is cheapest to fly between Monday afternoon and Thursday morning, and stay over one Saturday night. Booking at least 14 days in advance often qualifies you for a cheaper seat, subject to availability. Standby travel is a good alternative if all the budget flights are booked. Scan the *New York Times,* especially the Sunday "Travel" section, for the latest deals, or consult a travel agent with complete computer access to all airlines. Travel agents won't always direct you to the dirt-cheap flights because commissions are low, so you may have to call the airlines yourself.

The excellent "Airport Flight Guide, put out by the Port Authority, has comprehensive flight schedules as well as maps of the airports and data on airport parking and other services. It is available free by writing to: Airport Flight Guide, One World Trade Center 65N, New York 10048.

Braniff: 800-272-6433. Special deals to Florida and the Southwest.

Continental Airlines: 800-525-0280. Reduced fares with advance purchase.

Northwest Orient: 800-225-2525. Cheap in Northern states and on the West Coast.

Pan Am: 800-221-1111. Lots of international flights. The **Pan Am Air Shuttle** flies between New York and Boston or Washington every hour on the ½ hour. Runs 10:30am-2:30pm and 7:30-10:30pm on weekdays. The fare is $45 for those 24 and under. Same rate all day Sat. and Sun. until 2:30pm. No reservations necessary; just show up ½ hr. prior to departure at the Marine Air Terminal at LaGuardia.

Trump Shuttle: 800-247-8786. Similar to the Pan Am Air Shuttle, but leaves every hour on the hour. $45 for those 24 and under on weekdays between 10am-2pm and 7-9pm (until 10pm to Boston). Same fare all day Sat. and Sun. until 2pm. Leaves from LaGuardia; no reservations necessary.

U.S. Air: 800-428-4322. Budget flights all over New York State and the Northeast. Also runs **U.S. Air Express,** which is a collection of independent operators who fly small planes connecting with U.S. Air flights. Cheap fares and special deals to many U.S. port cities.

To and From the Airports

Travel between each of the airports and New York City without a car of your own becomes simpler as cost increases; you can pay in time or money. The cheapest way in dollars is public transportation. This usually involves changing mid-route from a bus to a subway or train, but service is frequent and theoretically according to a schedule. Moving up the price scale, private bus companies will charge slightly more, but will take you directly from the airport to one of three destinations: Grand Central Station (42nd St. and Park Ave.), the Port Authority Bus Terminal (41st St. and Eighth Ave.) or the World Trade Center (1 West. St.). Private companies run frequently and according to a set schedule (see below). If you want to set your own destination and schedule, however, and if you are willing to pay for this luxury, you can take one of New York's infamous yellow cabs. From JFK or Newark, this will cost at least $30; from LaGuardia at least $17. Traffic will lengthen your trip and increase its price. **Utog** (741-2000) and **Skyline** (718-482-8686) are taxi companies that charge a flat $35 for travel to JFK. For the most up-to-date information on reaching the airports, call the Airport Travel Hotline at 800-247-7433. Be warned that some services are reduced or non-existent between midnight and 6am. Finally, if you make lodging reservations ahead of time, be sure to ask about limousine services—some Ys and hostels offer door-to-door transportation from the airports for reasonable fares.

If you are renting a car the ease of your commute will vary according to the traffic conditions and your driving and navigation skills. Traffic is always heavy between 7:30-9:30am and 4:30-7pm; at other times conditions vary. Get directions from your rental agent.

There are several ways to travel between JFK and Midtown Manhattan. Public transportation offers two options. One is to take the **JFK Express Shuttle Bus** (718-330-1234) from any airport terminal to the **Howard Beach-JFK subway station,** where you can take the **IND** to a number of places in the city: 57th St. and Ave. of the Americas; 50th St. and Rockefeller Center; 42nd St. and Ave. of the Americas; 34th St. and Ave. of the Americas; Washington Square; the World Trade Center; Broadway and Nassau St.; and Borough Hall in Brooklyn. Allow at least one hour travel time. The service costs $6.50. Your second option is to take one of the city buses (the Q10, Q9, or Q3; fare $1) from the airport into Queens. The Q10 connects with the E, F, R, and A subway lines and Q3 and Q9 connect with the F and R lines, all of which will take you into Manhattan. Ask the bus driver where to get off, and make sure you know which subway line you want. Allow 90 minutes travel time. The total cost for this trip will be only $2, but it also requires some degree of caution. Some of the areas these buses service are unsafe. Those willing to pay more can take the **Carey Bus Service** (718-632-0500), a private line that runs between JFK and Grand Central Station and the Port Authority Terminal. Buses leave every 30 minutes from Kennedy during the day (1-1¼ hr., fare $9).

If your airport is LaGuardia there are two ways to get into Manhattan. If you have extra time and light luggage, take the MTA "Q 33" bus ($1 exact change or token) to the Eighth Ave. subway in Queens, and from there, take the E or F train into Manhattan ($1 token). You can catch the Q 33 from the lower level of the terminal. Allow at least 90 minutes travel time. The same word of caution applies here as with the Q buses above. The second option is the Carey Bus Service, which makes four stops in the Midtown area, the first of which is Grand Central Station. (Every 20 min., 55 min., $7.50.)

Newark Airport, in New Jersey, is as easy a commute as JFK or LaGuardia. **New Jersey Transit (NJTA)** (201-460-8444) runs a fast, efficient bus (NJTA #300) between the airport and Port Authority every 15 minutes during the day ($7). For the same fare, the **Olympia Trails Bus Service** (201-964-6233) travels between either Grand Central or the World Trade Center and the airport. (Every 20 min., 45 min.-1 hr., except in rush hour.) **NJTA Bus #107** will take you to Midtown for $2.60 (exact change required), but don't try it unless you have little luggage and lots of time. The NJTA also runs an **Air Link bus** ($4) between the airport and Newark's

Penn Station (*not* Manhattan's), and from there **PATH** trains ($1) run into Manhattan, stopping at the World Trade Center, Christopher St., Sixth Ave., 9th St., 14th St., 23rd St. and 33rd St. PATH information 212-466-7649.

From Manhattan, **Giraldo Limousine Service** (757-6840) will pick you up anywhere between 14th and 95th St. and take you to the airport of your choice for $9-17 (8am-11pm).

By Bus or Train

Getting in and out of New York can be done less expensively and more scenically by bus or train than by plane. **Port Authority,** 41st St. and Eighth Ave. (564-8484), is a tremendous modern facility with labyrinthine bus terminals. Port Authority has good information and security services, but it is in an extremely unsafe neighborhood. Be wary of pickpockets, and call a cab at night. Its bathrooms are dangerous at all times. The station is the hub of the Northeast bus network, and **Greyhound/Trailways** (971-6363 or 730-7460) is the titan here. On some routes, a 10% discount is offered to college students with ID. Purchase your tickets at least 14 days in advance for substantially reduced fares. To: Boston ($29), Philadelphia ($17), Washington, DC ($30), and Montreal ($65). (These fares offered Mon.-Thurs. only.)

Grand Central Station, 42nd St. and Park Ave., is the grandiose transportation colossus of the metropolis, with more than 550 trains running daily on its two levels of tracks. It handles **Metro-North** (532-4900) commuter lines to Connecticut and New York suburbs, and **Amtrak** (800-872-7245 or 582-6875) lines to upstate New York and Canada. From the smaller **Penn Station,** 33rd St. and Eighth Ave., Amtrak serves most major cities in the U.S., especially those in the Northeast (to Washington, DC $59, Boston $50). Penn Station also handles the **Long Island Railroad (LIRR)** (718-454-5477, see Long Island) and **PATH** service to New Jersey (432-1272).

By Car

The problem with driving to, from, or within New York City? Traffic. Rush hour, Mon.-Fri. from 7:30-9:30am and 4:30-7pm, is the worst time to drive on the city's highways. During these hours millions of commuters jam the roads; amidst the exhaust, see the American Dream at work . . . or trying to get there. Any time of day, be prepared to be terrorized by reckless cab drivers and determined jaywalkers.

The four major highways are: on the East Side, the **FDR Drive** (a.k.a. the Harlem River Drive and the East Side Highway) and the **Major Deegan;** on the West Side, the **Henry Hudson Parkway** (a.k.a. the West Side Highway, soon to be WestWay). From outside the city, I-95 leads to the Major Deegan, the FDR Drive, and the Henry Hudson. Go south on any of these roads, but be prepared for the amazing number of signs, intersecting roads and other cars separating you from your destination.

Once you are in Manhattan, traffic continues to be a problem, especially between 57th and 34th St. It is also joined by another, omnipresent, omnipotent evil: lack of parking. There are three ways to meet its challenge. **Parking lots** are the most expensive and easiest. In midtown, where lots are the only option, expect to pay at least $25 per day and up to $15 for two hours. The cheapest parking lots are downtown—try the far west end of Houston St.—but make sure you feel comfortable with the area and the lot. Is it populated? Is the lot guarded? Is it lit? Which *Honeymooners* episode is being shown tonight? Municipal parking at 53rd St. and Eighth Ave. costs $1 per half-hour.

The second alternative is short term parking. On the streets, **parking meters** cost 25¢ per 15 minutes, with a limit of one or two hours. The third is **free parking** on the crosstown streets in residential areas, but competition is ruthless. Read the signs carefully; a space is usually legal only certain days of the week. They *will* tow, and recovering your car once it's been towed will cost $100 or more. Break-ins and car theft are definite possibilities, particularly if you have a flashy radio.

Hitchhiking is illegal in New York state and the laws tend to be strictly enforced within New York City. Offenders will usually be asked to move on. It's best to take the train or bus out of the metropolitan area; hitching in and around New York City is dangerous.

Orientation

New York City is composed of five separate areas, called boroughs: Brooklyn, the Bronx, Queens, Staten Island and Manhattan. Ask most tourists, however, and they would tell you that the city is no larger than Manhattan. Not everyone, however, gives Manhattan more than its due; New York City's government was declared illegal in March 1989 because its five-person (one per borough) structure gave less-populated boroughs too much representation. Poor Manhattan. Historically, there are roots to the belief that Manhattan and New York City are one and the same. While its original inhabitants, the Algonquin, called Manhattan "Man-a-hat-ta" or "Heavenly Land," the Dutch settlers who bought the island in 1606 named it "New Amsterdam." The British later took over the island and dubbed it "New York." It was only in 1898 that the four other boroughs were encompassed into the city government. No matter how often you hear Manhattan referred to as "the City," however, each of the other boroughs has just as much right to the name.

Manhattan is actually an island flanked on the east by the East River, on the west by the Hudson River, and severed from the rest of New York by the narrow Harlem River. It is roughly 13 miles long and two and a half miles broad at its widest point. Queens and Brooklyn look on from the other side of the East River at the westernmost tip of Long Island. The Bronx is to the north of Manhattan, and Staten Island is to the south. **Queens,** the city's largest and most ethnically diverse borough, is dotted with light industry, airports, and stadiums. **Brooklyn,** south of Queens, is the city's most populous borough (2.24 million residents) and is even older than Manhattan. Founded by the Dutch in 1600, today it is home to several charming residential neighborhoods and also a dangerous slum. **Staten Island,** west of Brooklyn, is the only predominantly residential borough, similar to the suburban bedroom-communities in outer Long Island. North of Manhattan, the **Bronx** is the only borough connected by land to the rest of the U.S. Originally a Dutch estate owned by Jonas Bronck, an excursion to his family's farm was referred to as a visit to "the Bronck's." Today's Bronx accommodates both the lovely suburb of Riverdale and New York's most devastated slum, the South Bronx.

Manhattan's Districts

Because of city zoning ordinances, quirks of history, and other forces of urban evolution, Manhattan's neighborhoods often have abrupt boundaries. The harbour beginning at **Battery Park** (at the southern tip of Manhattan) is where the city began. Historic Manhattan, however, lies in the shadows of more famous monuments to the present. Today, the area is dominated by the financial office buildings around **Wall Street,** 4 blocks north of the Battery, and the civic office buildings around **City Hall,** a dozen blocks north. A little farther north, neighborhoods rich in ethnic culture rub elbows below Houston (pronounced HOW-stun) Street—**Little Italy, Chinatown,** and the southern blocks of the **Lower East Side.** To the west is the newly fashionable **TriBeCa** (Triangle Below Canal St.). **SoHo** (for "South of Houston"), a former warehouse district west of Little Italy, has been transformed into a pocket of gleaming art studios and galleries. Above SoHo is **Greenwich Village,** increasingly tawdry and increasingly nostalgic for its days as a center of intense artistic and political activity. Its tangled web of streets, neon signs, and low buildings offer sharp contrast to the nearby financial district.

A few blocks north of Greenwich Village is **Chelsea,** the late artist Andy Warhol's favorite hangout and former home of Dylan Thomas and Arthur Miller. Directly east of Chelsea near the East River is **Gramercy Park,** a pastoral collection of Victorian mansions and brownstones immortalized in Edith Wharton's *Age of Innocence.* **Midtown Manhattan** towers from 30th to 59th St., where awe-inspiring skyscrapers and controversial architecture stand side-by-side, providing office space for millions; department stores outfit New York; and the nearby **Theater District** entertains the world—or tries to.

North of Midtown, **Central Park** bisects Manhattan. On the **Upper West Side,** the gracious museums and residences of Central Park West sit next to the chic boutiques and sidewalk cafés of Columbus Ave. On the **Upper East Side,** the galleries and museums scattered among the elegant apartments of Fifth and Park Ave. create an even more rarified atmosphere.

Near 97th St., much of the Upper East Side's opulence ends with a bump where commuter trains emerge from the tunnel and the *barrio* begins. Above 110th St. on the Upper West Side is majestic **Columbia University** (founded as King's College in 1754), an urban member of the Ivy League. Some of the poorest New Yorkers live in **Harlem, East Harlem,** and **East Morningside Heights,** communities that produced the Harlem Renaissance of black artists and writers in the 1920s and the revolutionary Black Power movement in the 1960s. Although torn by crime, **Washington Heights,** just north of St. Nichols Park, is nevertheless somewhat safer and more attractive than the abandoned tenaments of Harlem, and provides a home to Fort Tryon Park, the Met's Medieval Cloisters, and a quiet community of Old-World immigrants. Still farther north, the island ends in a rural patch of wooded land.

Manhattan's Street Plan

Most of Manhattan's street plan was the result of a planned expansion. The major part of the city grew in straight lines, and at right angles. Above 14th St., the streets form a grid which even first-time visitors can quickly master. In the older Lower Manhattan area, though, most streets are named rather than numbered, and the grid pattern of the northern section disappears into a tangled web of old, narrow streets.

Above Washington Square, avenues run north-south; streets run east-west. Traffic flows east on most even-numbered streets and west on most odd-numbered ones. Exceptions are the larger streets—14th, 23rd, 34th, 42nd, 57th, 72nd, 79th, 86th, 96th, 110th, 116th, 125th, 145th, and 155th, which accommodate two-way traffic. Most avenues are also one-way. Tenth, Amsterdam, Hudson, Eighth, Avenue of the Americas, Madison, Fourth, Third, and First Avenues are northbound. Ninth, Columbus, Broadway below 59th Street, Seventh, Fifth, Lexington, and Second are southbound. York, Park, Central Park West, Broadway above 59th Street, West End, and Riverside Drive allow two-way traffic.

New York's celebrated east/west division refers to an address's location in relation to the two borders of Central Park—**Fifth Avenue** along the east side and **Central Park West** along the west. Below 59th St. where the park ends, the West Side begins at Fifth Ave. Looking for an adjective to describe your geographic position relative to something else? Uptown is anywhere north of you, downtown is south, and crosstown means to the east or the west. Want to use a noun? Uptown (above 59th St.) is the area north of Midtown. Downtown (below 34th St.) is the area south of Midtown.

A few other discrepancies in the system are worth noting. You may still hear the **Avenue of the Americas** referred to by its original name, **Sixth Avenue.** Also, Lexington, Park, and Madison Ave. lie *between* Third and Fifth Ave. Finally, above 59th St. on the West Side, Eighth Avenue becomes Central Park West, Ninth Avenue becomes Columbus Avenue, Tenth Avenue becomes Amsterdam Avenue, and Eleventh Avenue becomes West End Avenue. **Broadway** ignores the rectangular pattern and cuts diagonally across the island, veering west of Fifth Ave. above 23rd St. and east of Fifth Ave. below 23rd St.

Tracking down an address in Manhattan is not difficult. When given the street number of an address (e.g. #250 E. 52nd St.), find the avenue closest to the address by thinking of Fifth Ave. as point zero on the given street. Address numbers increase as you move east or west of Fifth Ave. On the East Side, address numbers are 1 at Fifth Ave., 100 at Park Ave., 200 at Third Ave., 300 at Second Ave., 400 at First

Ave., 500 at York Ave. (uptown) or Avenue A (in the Village). On the West Side, address numbers are 1 at Fifth Ave., 100 at the Avenue of the Americas (Sixth Ave.), 200 at Seventh Ave., 300 at Eighth Ave., 400 at Ninth Ave., 500 at Tenth Ave., and 600 at Eleventh Ave. In general, numbers increase from south to north along the avenues. The Manhattan White Pages contains a convenient "Address Locator" for addresses on numbered cross streets.

Getting Around

To be equipped for the New York City navigation experience, you will need more than an understanding of the logic underlying its streets. You will also require an ability to use the public transportation system. Get a free subway map from station token booths or the visitors bureau, which also has a free street map (see Practical Information above). Ask at the visitors bureau first, since token booth operators are usually less cooperative. For a more detailed program of interborough travel, find a Manhattan Yellow Pages, which contains detailed subway, PATH, and bus maps. Stop at a bookstore for Hagstrom's *New York City 5 Borough Atlas* ($7). For other bus or subway maps, send a self-addressed, stamped envelope about a month before you need the information to **NYC Transit Authority,** 370 Jay St. Brooklyn 11201. In the city, round-the-clock staff at the **Transit Authority Information Bureau** (718-330-1234) dispense subway and bus information.

Subways and Buses

The fare for Metropolitan Transit Authority (MTA) subways and buses is a hefty $1, so groups of four or more may find cabs cheaper for short rides. More often than not, however, the MTA provides the best way to get around New York City. Most buses are equipped with access ramps, but steep stairs make subway transit more difficult for the disabled. Call the Transit Authority Information Bureau (718-330-1234) for specific information on public transportation.

If you're near a stop and are going north-south rather than east-west, **subways** are by far the quickest means of transportation in Manhattan. East-west travelers are relegated to crosstown buses (see below), unless traversing 42nd or 14th St., which have shuttle trains. In Upper Manhattan and in Queens, Brooklyn, and the Bronx, the subways become "El" trains (for "elevated") and ride above street level to the far reaches of the city.

The New York subway system has 461 stations with 25 free transfer points where subway lines intersect. It can be extremely confusing, even with subway route map in hand. The token clerk can tell you how to get anywhere, but might be impatient and uncooperative during rush hour. Don't lose your cool, but if you're not gaining any ground turn to a transit police officer for advice. "Express" trains stop only at pre-selected busy stations; "locals" stop everywhere. Be sure to check the letter or number and the destination of each train, since trains with different destinations often use the same track. When in doubt, ask a friendly passenger or the conductor, who usually sits near the middle of the train.

The stations are slowly being rehabilitated, but some are still dirty and filled with the stench of stale urine and vintage filth. A major subway clean-up campaign, including new spray paint-resistant shiny cars, has erased much of the crude graffiti and made the atmosphere more aesthetically pleasing. However, the modernization also wiped out truly creative underground art, some of which can still be viewed on the few old cars that remain in service.

Unfortunately, crime is still a fact that cannot be erased. In stations that are crowded (most notably those around 42nd St.), pickpockets find plenty of work; in stations that are deserted, violent crimes are more possible. Always watch yourself and your belongings, and try to stay in lit areas near a transit cop or token clerk. Some stations have clearly marked "off-hours" waiting areas that are under observation and significantly safer. At any time and at any place, don't stand too close to the platform edge (people have been pushed) and keep to well-lit areas when waiting for a train. Boarding the train, make sure to pick a car with several other groups of passengers on it.

The subways run 24 hours, but at all costs avoid using them between 11pm and 7am, especially above E. 96th St. and W. 120th St. Also try to avoid rush-hour crowds, where you'll be fortunate to find air, let alone seating. If you must travel at rush hour (7:30-9:30am and 5-6:30pm on every train in every direction.), the local train is usually less crowded than the express. Buy a bunch of tokens at once: you'll not only avoid a long line, but you'll be able to use all the entrances to a station, some of which lack token clerks.

The subway network integrates once-separate systems known as the **IRT**, **IND**, and **BMT** lines. The names of these lines are still in use, and their routes remain color-coded on subway maps. Certain routes also have common, unofficial names based on where they travel, such as the "7th Ave. Line" or "Broadway" for the #1, 2, or 3; the "Lexington Line" for the #4, 5, or 6; and the "Flushing Line" for the #7. The official names are numbers and letters, but for clarity's sake, many listings in this chapter employ the alternative designations.

Because **buses** sit in traffic, during the day they often take twice as long as subways, but they are also twice as safe, are usually cleaner, and always have windows. They'll also get you closer to your destination, since they stop every 2 blocks or so and run crosstown (east-west), as well as uptown and downtown (north-south). The MTA transfer system provides north-south travelers with a slip good for a free ride east-west, or vice-versa. Just ask the driver for a transfer when you pay. Make sure you ring when you want to get off. Bus stops are indicated by a yellow-painted curb, but you're better off looking for the blue sign post announcing the bus number or for a glass-walled shelter displaying a map of the bus's route and a schedule (usually unreliable) of arrival times. Either exact change or a subway token is required; dollar bills are not accepted.

Taxis

With drivers cruising at warp speed along near-deserted avenues or dodging through bumper-to-bumper traffic with a micron or two to spare, cab rides can give you ulcers. And even if your stomach survives the ride, your budget may not. Still, it's likely that you'll have to take a taxi once in a while, in the interest of convenience or safety. Rides are fairly expensive: The meter starts at $1.15 and clicks 15¢ for each additional ninth of a mile; passengers pay all tolls and, in about half of the cabs, a 50¢ surcharge after 8pm. Finally, the underpaid cabbies expect (and really should be given) tips of around 15-20%; they won't hesitate to let you know when they're displeased. Before you leave the cab, ask for a receipt, which will have the taxi's identification number. This number is necessary to trace lost articles or to make a complaint to the Taxi Commission (869-4513). Some drivers may try to take advantage of visitors. Remember, the fare on the meter is the basic charge for the ride, not charge per person. You might also want to glance at a street map before embarking, so you'll have some clue if you're being given a personalized New York tour rather than just delivered to your destination.

Use only yellow cabs—they're licensed by the state of New York and are safe to ride in. Only the plump Checker Marathon cabs take five passengers. If you're desperate and can't find anything on the street, or if you like to plan ahead, commandeer a radio-dispatched cab (see Practical Information above). Use common sense to make rides cheaper—catch a cab going your direction and get off at a nearby street corner.

To hail a cab, stand on the curb and raise your arm. Yelling worked for Dustin Hoffman in *Tootsie,* but will attract more critical glances from real-life New Yorkers than if you too were in drag. A free cab will have the "On Call" light on its roof illuminated. During rush hour and on rainy days it is almost impossible to find an available cab.

Walking, Running, and Biking

Walking is the cheapest, the most entertaining, and often the fastest way to get around town. During rush hours the sidewalks are packed with suited and sneakered commuters. In between rush hours, the sidewalks are still full of street life. Twenty street blocks (north-south) make up a mile; the distance east-west from one avenue to the next is about triple that from block to block. For scenic strolls and educational excursions, try a walking tour of Manhattan (see Guided Tours below).

If you plan on running along the street, be prepared to dodge pedestrians and to break your stride at intersections. Women can expect cat calls and stares. The alternative to the sidewalk are paths in Central Park—most are pavement, but there is a 1.57 mile cinder loop that circles the Reservoir (between 84th and 96th St.). Joggers pack the path from 6-9am and 5-7pm on weekdays and all day on weekends. For information on running clubs, call **American Youth Hostels** (431-7100) or the **New York Roadrunner's Club** (860-4455).

Weekday biking in commuter traffic is a mortal challenge even for veteran natives. But on weekends, when the traffic thins, cyclists who use helmets and caution can tour the Big Apple on two wheels. From May-Oct., the park (except the lower loop) is closed to traffic on weekdays from 10am-3pm, and from Fri. 7pm-Mon. 6am. Otherwise, Sunday mornings are best. For a challenging and beautiful traffic-free course, try circumnavigating the 35-mile path within Central Park. If you must leave your bike unattended anywhere in Manhattan, a strong lock is a must. Avoid using the weak chain locks that theft artists specialize in snipping. If your bike is worth anything to you, invest in a **Kryptonite K-5** lock ($28.50). Don't leave any removable parts unlocked, as they will be quickly stripped from your bike.

For those who can't bring their bikes, **Metro Bicycle** (throughout Manhattan; call 228-4344) and the **Boathouse,** in Central Park (861-4137), both rent bicycles. (See Practical Information above.)

For the truly adventurous and skillful, roller skates are available at **Peck and Goodie Skates,** 917 Eighth Ave. (246-6123), between 54th and 55th St. Whiz past your favorite New York sights for $6 per 2 hr. or $10 per day. $35 deposit or credit card required. (Open Mon.-Wed. and Fri.-Sat. 10am-6pm, Thurs. 10am-7:30pm, and Sun. noon-5pm.)

Safety

Is there danger lurking around every New York street corner? It depends on what you're looking for, where you're looking, and whether you are looking at all. Danger can come in the form of the cab that barely misses you when you look the wrong way down one of the Avenues. Or danger can be the result of wandering down a dimly lit street at night.

To be safe, recognize situations in which problems might arise. Adopt a streetwise manner; be aware of your surroundings, avoid eye contact with shady types, and walk purposefully. After dark, any neighborhood in Manhattan can be unsafe. Keep to the busier, better-lit streets and sidewalks, don't walk around alone, and avoid run-down or empty sections of the city. At night, steer clear of Central Park (*especially* the northern end), the Bowery and the West Side Docks (downtown), and Morningside Park and Harlem (uptown). Use cabs instead of subways and ask the driver to watch until you get inside safely. Before you go into unknown territory, ask a cop, a cabbie, or a native New Yorker what the area is like.

Other common-sense precautions are in order at all times. Keep your wallet in the most inaccessible part of your clothing you can think of, and avoid pulling it out obviously and unnecessarily. Carrying a purse is not recommended, but if you must, hold it firmly against your body and secure all snaps and zippers. Keep identification, traveler's checks, and other valuables in a money pouch or belt, close to your body. Save flashy jewelry and expensive camera equipment for more sedate cities. Never show money to a stranger, and be wary of "travelers" who ask for too much assistance. If someone will not leave you alone, stay in a well-lit area until you can enter a store, restaurant, hotel or anywhere other people might be. When in doubt, call the police.

Finally, there is a reason that most public restrooms in subway stations are padlocked. Even the ones that are open are hardly sanitary. Ditto for the facilities at Penn Station and Grand Central. If nature calls while you're out catching the sights, try the big department stores or the better hotels, or any restaurant, bar, or café that doesn't post a sign saying "facilities for patrons only."

Accommodations

The good news is that the Big Apple has over 104,000 rooms to accommodate tourists. The bad news is that most cost upward of $60 per night. Still, you can save by advance planning—make reservations at one of the cheaper places listed below, rent by the week, share a room, or stay in an area of town that others might not stomach. Students can save by sleeping at student centers, college dormitories (in summer), and some regular hotels with special student rates. But if you have never been to New York before, note that there are certain areas to avoid after dark, and even during the day.

In general, the safest accommodations are anywhere in Upper Midtown and Midtown on the East Side and within 3 blocks of Fifth Ave. Housing listed under Columbia University is affiliated with the university and uses Columbia security. The Columbia area has a bad reputation, though, so be careful when returning after dark. Plenty of hotels are within walking distance of Penn Station and the Port Authority, but many are sleazy, most are expensive (averaging $40), and the area is crime-ridden. Generally, a solo traveler is ill-advised to stay in a hotel, since the Ys have cheaper, often more comfortable rooms. If you arrive without a reservation, call before trekking across town.

Student Accommodations

AYH has renovated a landmark building designed by Richard Morris Hunt, located on 103rd St. and Amsterdam Ave. It should be open by October 1, 1989, and beds will cost $19 per night, with a 7-day max. stay. Call 932-2300 for more information.

The accommodations below have been listed in order of safety.

Chelsea Center Hostel, 511 W. 20th St. (243-4922), at 10th Ave. Attractive bunks in a large common room, with kitchen and bath. Incredibly friendly, multilingual staff will bend over backwards for guests. Closed 11am-4pm. $16 per day includes breakfast and tea at any hour. Write or phone 2 weeks in advance and then confirm 1-2 days prior to arrival. During peak season (June-Aug.) they'll only hold your reservation until 7:30pm. If they're booked, they'll find you another place to stay.

International Student Hospice, 154 E. 33rd St. (228-7470), between Lexington and Third Ave. in East Midtown. Subway: Lexington Ave. IRT to 33rd St. Look for large colonial flag and small brass eagle above the door. Behind handsomely carved wood doors, this worn but friendly brownstone offers 22 beds for out-of-town students ages 18-25. Safe neighborhood and caring proprietor. Tiny rooms with 3 or 4 beds. Curfew midnight. $20 for the first night, $15 thereafter.

International Student Center, 38 W. 88th St. (787-7706), on the West Side. Subway: 7th Ave. IND to 86th St. Close to Central Park and Columbus Ave. Officially open only to foreigners, preferably students. Single-sex bunk rooms, no frills, in a somewhat tired brownstone. 7-day max. stay. Open daily 8am-11pm. Call after 10:30am on day of arrival. A bargain at $8. Closed June-last week in July.

International House, 500 Riverside Dr. (316-8400), by 123rd St., near Columbia University. Subway: 125th St. and Broadway. Must be over 18; students preferred. Exercise caution at all times. Available two weeks in advance for transient summer housing. Attractive facilities include gymnasium, TV lounge, cafeteria, and pub. Office open daily 8am-5pm. Singles $25. Bath included. Write or call for reservations. Housing available from the second week in May to the 3rd week in Aug.

Whittier Hall (Columbia-affiliated), 1230 Amsterdam Ave. (678-3235), across the street from campus. All rooms have access to cooking facilities. Small singles $20. Doubles with A/C, bath and kitchen $40. Make reservations in advance.

Fashion Institute of Technology, 230 W. 27th St. 10001 (760-7885), in Lower Midtown. Subway: 7th Ave. IRT to 28th St. Decent neighborhood, but adjacent to a bad one; exercise caution at night. Office open Mon.-Fri. 8am-7pm.Summer housing in standard dorm doubles (without bath) 2nd week of June-July 31; $122 per week, 1-week min. stay. Suites with kitchen and bath; $460 per month, 1-month min. stay. $6 service charge on all rooms. For couples, marriage license is necessary. Reservations and full payment required in advance.

Manhattan Hostel, 145 E. 23rd St. (979-8043), off Lexington Ave. near Gramercy Park. Subway: IRT #6 to 23rd St. A small hostel on the 3rd floor of Hotel Kenmore. A little dark, but looks safe. Double rooms with bunk bed $30, with bath $35. Single travelers can share for $15 each.

YMCAs/YWCAs

YMCA—Vanderbilt, 224 E. 47th (755-2410), between Second and Third Ave. in Midtown. Subway: Lexington Ave. IRT to 51st St. The cleanest and best of the bunch. A/C. Great gym, locker rooms, Nautilus equipment, and pool. Van service to JFK and LaGuardia ($8) and to and from 3 other Ys. 25-day max. stay. In summer singles $37. Doubles, triples, and quads $22-25 per person in bunk beds. Winter-spring and fall $34 and $19-22, respectively.

YMCA—West Side, 5 W. 63rd St. (787-4400), on the lower West Side. Subway: 59th St./Columbus Circle. Dilapidated but clean rooms in a handsome Gothic building, seconds from Lincoln Center or Central Park, with free access to 2 pools, indoor track, racquet courts, and Nautilus equipment. Singles $32, with bath $44. Doubles $46, with bath $52. Newly renovated singles with color TV and cable $38, with bath $53. A/C $3.25 additional. 10% discount for students.

CIEE New York Student Center (YMCA), William Sloan House, 356 W. 34th St. (760-5850), in West Midtown. Subway: 34th St./Penn Station. Rooms small and worn but clean and decent. This place is *big.* Laundry facilities, recreation room, and lots of helpful student travel advice. Open 24 hours. Singles $32, with bath $46. Doubles $46, with bath $60. Bunk bed doubles $40 with $12 deposit for linen. TV $1.50 per day. Discount for IYHF/AYH members. In summer book 2-3 weeks in advance.

YMCA—McBurney, 206 W. 24th St. (741-9226) in Chelsea. Subway: 7th Ave. IRT to 23rd St. Men only. Should be co-ed by fall '89. Renovations currently in progress on the 5th and 6th floors. It's a good deal if you can get past the run-down neighborhood. Small singles $26, large singles with TV $29-31. Doubles $44.

YMCA—Flushing, 138-46 N. Boulevard, Flushing, Queens (718-961-6880), in an old building close to Main St. shopping district. Subway: Flushing IRT to Main St. Safe during the day, but be careful at night. Men only. 2 pools, gym, Nautilus equipment, paddleball, and squash. Singles $25.

YWCA—Brooklyn, 30 Third Ave. (718-875-1190), near Atlantic Ave., Brooklyn. Subway: Atlantic Ave./Pacific St. Women only. The 80-year-old building is still in good shape. Plain rooms with access to kitchen facilities. Must be 18-55 and employed. Singles $68-90 per week. Application is necessary, but can be filed on the day of arrival.

Hotels

Carlton Arms Hotel, 160 E. 25th St. (679-0680), by Third Ave. Nicknamed Artbreak Hotel. Each room is a unique creation by artists from around the world. Stay inside a submarine and peer through windows at the lost city of Atlantis; travel to Renaissance Venice; or stow your clothes in a dresser suspended on an astroturf wall. The rooms are old and not luxurious, but clean. Super-friendly, slightly wacky artist staff adds to the fun. Singles $33, with bath $39. Doubles $44, with bath $50. Triples $53, with bath $61. Discounts for students and foreign tourists. Seven days for the price of 6. Reserve a month in advance.

Pickwick Arms Hotel, 230 E. 51st. St. (355-0300), in a swank East Midtown district. Subway: Lexington Ave. IRT to 51st St. The classiest of the bunch. Mirrors, brass, and real leather couches in a small, clean, well-managed hotel. TV, A/C. Singles with running water $40, with connecting shower $50, with private shower $64. Doubles and twins $86. Reserve 2 weeks in advance.

Allerton Hotel For Women, 130 E. 57th St. (753-8841), near Lexington Ave. in Midtown. Subway: Lexington Ave. IRT to 59th St. Women only. Handsome brick building with leaded glass windows in swanky, safe district. Small, angular rooms are clean. Singles with running water $53, with connecting bath $59, with private bath $70. Weekly rates $205, $228, and $239, respectively. Rooms with twin beds $75 daily. Reserve 2 weeks in advance.

Washington Square Hotel, 103 Waverly Place (777-9515), in Greenwich Village. Subway: Lexington IRT to Astor Pl. Fantastic location. Glitzy marble and brass lobby. TV, A/C, and programmed key security cards. Singles $50. Doubles $72. Twins $80. Quads $90. Reserve 1 month in advance, and send deposit 3 weeks ahead.

Malibu Studios Hotel, 2688 Broadway (222-2954) at 103rd St. Near Columbia, in an area undergoing gentrification. Bright colors and large, clean rooms with refrigerator and hot plate. Singles $40-50. Doubles $60.Weekly: singles $125-300, doubles $200-350. TV $15 per week.

Camping

Informal camping in the city's parks is not safe; those unwise enough to attempt it will be lucky to be spotted by the police before being spotted by less desirable characters.

The closest camping is across the Lincoln Tunnel from Midtown at the **New Yorker Trailer City,** 4901 Tonnelle Ave., North Bergen, NJ 07047 (201-866-0999). The park is on U.S. 1 and 9 about 20 minutes from Manhattan, and offers "camping" in the urban sense, including a laundromat, showers, and a bus direct to Port Authority (#127). (Office open daily 8am-11pm; Sept.-May 8am-3pm. For 2: tents $18, vans $20, trailers $30. Each additional person $2. Call for reservations and send 1 night deposit. Open year-round.)

For peaceful, woodland camping, you'll have to travel far from the city. New Jersey's **Cheesequake State Park,** Matawan 07747 (201-566-2161), over 30 miles from Manhattan, is 12 miles south of I-95 (the New Jersey Turnpike) off the Garden State Parkway. Sites for up to six people cost $10 per night, showers included in summer. Reservations accepted for 2 days or more; you can reserve a maximum of 14 days from Memorial Day to Labor Day by sending a $7 reservation fee, full payment, and the dates requested. (Open daily 8am-8pm; Sept.-May 8am-dusk.)

Food

While New York City's spectacular sights and entertainment captivate your other senses, the enticing smells emanating from its 25,000 restaurant kitchens will tantalize your taste buds. Although New York's delis and burger joints boast some of the best of true American fare, the Big Apple has an eclectic urban flavor stewed from diverse ethnic ingredients. New York restaurants do more than the United Nations to promote international goodwill and cross-cultural exchange. Try a *dim sum* restaurant in Chinatown or a Jewish deli on the Lower East Side; inhale espresso while dining on delicate French pastries at a café in Greenwich Village; or savor a cannoli in a sidewalk café in Little Italy.

The area between 82nd and 88th St. east of Lexington Ave. is known as Yorkville and is home to some terrific German restaurants. SoHo, in lower Manhattan, and Columbus Avenue, in the west 70s, feature outdoor cafés catering to every culinary taste. Sixth Street, between First and Third Ave., is lined with cozy Indian restaurants. MacDougal Street, south of Washington Sq., offers a multiplicity of Middle Eastern meals. Brooklyn and Queens have even greater ethnic diversity than Manhattan; restaurants in these boroughs are often less fancy and more authentic than their Manhattan counterparts.

The most consistently available and well-prepared inexpensive food in New York is pizza. (A plain slice shouldn't cost much more than $1.25.) There are vinyl-covered coffee shops every few blocks, most of which offer a frightening variety of entrees for under $6. And, in its indefatigable quest for superlatives, New York City hosts more fast-food restaurants than most American cities. While the quality and the menu at these places may remind you of home, the prices most certainly will not. A burger and fries in the city typically costs $1-2 more than it does in the suburbs.

New York's "street food"—pretzels, premium ice cream, felafel, tempura, *souvlaki,* Italian ices, sausage, fresh fruit, and more—is unparalleled in variety and quality. A big step above the street carts is take-out food, which can be even better than restaurant fare. Picnic in a park or plaza for a fraction of the price of a sit-down meal.

West Midtown

West Midtown is one of the more difficult places to find decent food at reasonable prices without stumbling onto some real emporiums of sleaze. Around Times Square and the Port Authority Bus Terminal, fast-food chains outnumber drug dealers, tourists, and prostitutes—a real achievement. The Theater District, extending along Broadway from Times Square to 52nd St., contains plenty of good but overpriced restaurants, many Japanese. West of Eighth Ave., 46th Street is "Restaurant Row," an appealing but expensive and increasingly dangerous strip.

Carnegie Delicatessen, 854 Seventh Ave. (757-2245), at 55th St. This is *the* deli—the one by which all others in the world are judged. Eat elbow-to-elbow at long tables with the regulars and celebrities, and soak up the boisterous atmosphere. The pastrami and corned beef sandwiches ($8) are incredible, enough for 2 people (but sharing will cost you $2 extra). Open daily 6:30am-4am.

Ristorante Prego, 1365 Ave. of the Americas (307-5775), between 55th and 56th St. Fast-food pasta served on marble-top tables amidst a forest of green plants. Over 25 kinds of pasta, and every dish comes with a huge bowl of marinated fresh vegetables ($7.85). Portions aren't huge, but adequate unless you're starving. Open daily 11:30am-midnight.

La Bonne Soupe, 48 W. 55th St. (586-7650), between Fifth and Sixth Ave. Excellent meals in a "bistro" that doubles as a gallery for Haitian and French paintings. Aromatic soups, served with bread, salad, dessert, and wine, designed as small meals for $7. Open Mon.-Sat. 11:30am-midnight, Sun. 11:30am-11pm.

La Fondue, 43 W. 55th St. (581-0820), between Fifth and Sixth Ave. With the dark wooden tables and chalet decor, you might begin to feel as if you're a step away from Lake Geneva. Grab some Grolsch beer and dip into the delicious cheese fondue ($9); don't miss the sublime swiss chocolate fondue with fruit ($5) for dessert. Open Mon.-Thurs. noon-midnight, Fri.-Sat. noon-12:30am, Sun. noon-11pm.

Sapporo, 152 W. 49th St. (869-8972), near Seventh Ave. This Japanese version of a coffee shop is a favorite snack spot for Broadway cast members and the lunch-time business crowd. Sweet *oyako-don* (chicken with sauteed egg patty) served on sticky rice will fuel food fantasies for weeks after your first encounter with it ($5). Open Mon.-Fri. 11:30am-midnight, Sat.-Sun. 11:30am-11pm.

East Midtown

New York has five "four-star" restaurants. Four of them are in this area, scattered amongst skyscraping office buildings, high rents, and briefcase-wielding business tycoons. But there is also food available for those without an expense account. Moreover, East Midtown houses more fast food peddlers than any other region of the city. Anyone can picnic in the area's green cloisters for free: **Greenacre Park,** 51st St. between Second and Third Ave., **Paley Park,** 53rd St. between Fifth and Madison Ave., or **United Nations Plaza,** 48th St. at First Ave.

Dosanko, 135 E. 45th St. (697-2967), and many other locations around the city. In Midtown: 423 Madison Ave., (688-8575), 10 E. 52nd St. (759-6361) and 123 W. 49th St. (245-4090). Plasticky Japanese restaurant that serves surprisingly good and reasonably priced food. The main dish here is *larmen,* a very tasty and filling soup heaped with noodles and your choice of beef, pork, chicken, and spices ($4.40). Open Mon.-Fri. 11:30am-10pm, Sat.-Sun. noon-8pm.

Horn and Hardart Co., 200 E. 42nd St. (599-1665), at Third Ave. This is the last of the automats—those places where you plunk some change in a slot and retrieve your sandwich from a hatch in the wall (just like in *Star Trek*). Additional cafeteria service offers chicken and pot roast for $4-6. Open daily 6am-10pm.

Crystal Gourmet, 422 Madison Ave. (752-2910), between 48th and 49th St. Also 666 Washington Ave. (755-2588) at 55th St. The most beautiful, bountiful salad bar in New York. Sushi, pasta vinaigrette, vegetables, and fruits in the chilled section, with lasagna, chicken, and beef dishes in the hot one—all at $4 per lb. Buffet breakfast (served Mon.-Fri. 7-10am) $2.79 per pound. Open Mon.-Sat. 7am-7pm.

Lower Midtown

Parts of Lower Midtown were once packed with small cheap eateries and corner groceries, but with the energetic sweep of gentrification, the district, especially **Chelsea,** has become a higher-priced neighborhood inhabited by deep-pocketed professionals. Overpriced and over-chic restaurants now dot the landscape, although good deals still abound. Third Avenue, between 20th and 33rd St., offers many inexpensive, if undistinguished, restaurants. Chinese restaurants are a good bet between First and Third Ave.

Empire Szechuan Restaurant, 381 Third Ave. (685-6215), between 27th and 28th St. One of a chain of tacky but reasonably priced Chinese restaurants with reliably good food. Try the broccoli with garlic sauce or the Paradise Chicken. Lunch special (served Mon.-Fri. 11:30am-3pm) under $6. Open daily 11:30am-midnight.

Shalimar, 39 E. 29th St. (889-1977), between Park and Madison Ave. White stucco walls with Indian decor and soft *sitar* music in the background. Lunch special (served daily noon-3pm) offers 6 curry choices, with rice, *dahl* (spiced lentils), and *kasundi* (onion relish) for $4.50. Open daily noon-midnight.

Peso's Mexican Grill, 102 E. 25th St. at Park Ave. S. (674-7376). One of a chain, this one with a large, slightly sterile seating area. *Quesadillas,* chili, tacos, burritos, and nachos with no added salt, lard, or artificial ingredients. Best known for its homemade salsas (free) and "Mexican pizza" (layers of tortillas filled with black beans, red sauce, scallions, dives, tomatoes and 2 kinds of cheese; $3.59). Open Mon.-Fri. 11am-9:30pm, Sat. 11am-9pm, Sun. 4-9pm.

Genroku Sushi, 366 Fifth Ave. (947-7940), between 34th and 35th St. Beats the Automat (see East Midtown) for the funkiest mechanical gimmick. A conveyor belt surrounds the oval-shaped counter and parades the food in front of you; take what you like. Pick carefully: Some of the dishes have been around the circuit one time too many. Sushi, Udon, and Ramen. Dishes $2-5. Soup $1. Open Mon.-Wed. and Fri. 11am-8pm, Thurs. 11am-8:30pm, Sat. 11am-7:30pm, Sun. noon-6pm.

Upper East Side

Luxury residences, pricey art galleries, and ritzy restaurants are the norm on Museum Mile along Fifth and Madison Ave. You'll find mediocre food at extraordinary prices in the posh and scenic museum cafés. You may want to stop in for coffee between exhibits, but head east of Park Avenue for less glamorous but more affordable dining.

East Siders swear by **Mimi's Pizza,** 1248 Lexington Ave. (861-3363), at 84th St. The ambience isn't much, but a large pie with the works ($17.50) serves three to four people (Open Mon.-Sat. 10:30am-11pm, Sun. noon-11pm.) Hot dog hounds shouldn't miss the 100% beef "better than filet mignon" $1.10 franks at **Papaya King,** 179 E. 86th St. (369-0648), off Third Ave., in business since 1933, and not to be confused with its West Side competitor, Gray's Papaya (see Upper West Side). (Open Sun.-Thurs. 8am-1am, Fri.-Sat. 9am-3am.) Or, if you want to try a real New York bagel, **H & H East,** 1551 2nd Ave. (734-7441), between 80th and 81st St., bakes them 24 hours a day (50¢). Also on the West Side, 2239 Broadway, at 80th St.

The Mad Hatter, 1485 2nd Ave. (650-9894), between 77th St. and 78th St. During the day, the glassed-in sidewalk porch lets you watch the city go by; at night, the city comes inside to party. At lunch, tuna melts $4; at dinner, open cheese steak sandwich $8. Open daily 11:30am-4am.

Jackson Hole Wyoming, 85th St. and Second Ave. (737-8788 or 737-8789) Also at 64th St. between 2nd & 3rd., and on Madison Ave. and 91st St. You probably won't be able to finish their huge, ½-pound hamburgers (37 varieties, $4-7; add $2 for fries, lettuce, and tomato). Open Mon.-Thurs. 10am-1am, Fri.-Sat. 10am-4am, Sun. 10am-11pm.

Ideal Restaurant, 238 E. 86th St. (535-0950), off Second Ave. A small, family-run restaurant, open since 1932. Delicious food, luncheonette decor, and friendly service (brush up on your German). Potato pancakes $4.50, pot roast with red cabbage and potatoes $6. Variety of German beers. Open daily 7am-11pm.

Szechuan Hunan Cottage, 1433 Second Ave. (535-1471), betwen 74th St. and 75th St. As soon as you enter this small restaurant, a glass of white wine is offered, along with a smile. Wood floors and tables, spot lighting, and a friendly crowd—but come early (6pm) to avoid waiting. Generous portions, delicious food: beef with orange flavor $8, house special *chow fun* $6. Open Sun.-Thurs. noon-11pm, Fri.-Sat. noon-11:30pm.

Fagiolini, 1393 B Second Ave. (570-5666), between 72nd and 73rd St. Walk down two steps into this narrow, sleek, quiet Italian restaurant. If the decor is New York post-modern, the food is still traditional. Try the Capellini with clams ($9) or the roast chicken with rosemary ($9.) All dishes served with a house salad. Open Sun.-Thurs. 5-10pm, Fri.-Sat. 5-11pm.

Serendipity, 225 E. 60th St. (838-3531), between Second and Third Ave. An eatery/boutique, remarkably popular with natives and tourists alike. Decorated with Tiffany lamps and vintage junk yard finds. Have a foot-long (no kidding) hot dog ($5) or an "Ultimate B.L.T." ($7.50) before moving on to a frothy tub of frozen hot chocolate ($5). Open Sun.-Thurs. 11:30am-12:30am, Fri. 11:30am-1am, Sat. 11:30am-2am.

Upper West Side

Atmosphere changes with each avenue and cross street here. The area is becoming gentrified, and to see the process in action, make your way from Columbus and 69th St. up toward Broadway and Amsterdam at 116th St. As rents in the area skyrocket, the chic cafés and bars in the 70s and 80s on Columbus Ave. are moving out and giving way to super-ritzy clothing stores of the Madison Avenue variety. Now is the time to catch this lively neighborhood before it completes its transition to sedate, overpriced elegance.

At night, **Lucy's,** 503 Columbus Ave. (787-3009), at 84th St., always draws a crowd ready to make noise and conversation. At **Cafe La Fortuna,** 69 W. 71st (724-5846), between Central Park West and Columbus Ave., you can bring a friend, a book, or both. Conversation and meditation over capuccino ($1.75) inside, or outside in their backyard garden. Open Tues.-Fri. 1pm-1am, Sat.-Sun. noon-1am. **Zabar's,** 2245 Broadway (787-2002) between 80th and 81st St., offers an entirely different food and people-watching experience. It's a deli that stretches almost an entire block, and customers are mildly fanatical in their quest for a content stomach.

Genoa, 271 Amsterdam at 73rd St. (787-1094). A tiny, family-owned restaurant with some of the very best food on the West Side. Stucco walls, wood beams, pink tablecloths, and red candlelight—Italian romance. Excellent pasta dishes from $8. Get here before 6pm or wait in line with the rest of the neighborhood. Open Tues.-Sat. 5:45-10:30pm, Sun. 5:30-9:30pm.

Museum Café, 366 Columbus Ave. (799-0150), at 77th St. In back of the Museum of Natural History, but *not* inside it, the emphasis here is on natural and fresh ingredients in elegant combinations. Smoked breast of chicken with cranberry apple compote and cheddar, $7.50. There's a glass-enclosed sidewalk area, so you can see the city as you take a break from its streets. Open daily 11:30am-midnight.

The Blue Nile, 103 W. 77th St. (580-3232), at Columbus Ave. Descend a flight of stairs and enter the world of Ethiopia. Sit on 3-legged stools to try *doro wat,* a marinated chicken billed as New York's spiciest dish ($10). All entrees served with pancake-like *injera,* an Ethopian bread. Combination dishes big enough for 2 ($12-14.50). Open Mon.-Thurs. noon-10:30pm, Fri.-Sun. noon-11pm.

Dan Tempura House, 2018 Broadway at 69th St. (877-4969). A bamboo-thatched awning hangs over a window display of Japanese trinkets, exotic plants, and fish. The clutter, continued inside the restaurant, lends a homey feel to excellent and diverse dishes. Various kinds of teriyaki, tempura, and noodles $5-7. Sushi and sashimi platter $9-12. Open Mon.-Sat. noon-2:30pm and 5-11pm, Sun. 4-11pm.

Diane's, 251 Columbus Ave. (799-6750), off 71st St. Large portions and reasonable prices make this brass-railed café a prime pick of the college crew. Spice up a 7-ounce burger ($4) with your choice of chili, chutney, or seven cheeses (85¢ per topping). Great ice cream as well. Open daily 11am-2am.

Dallas BBQ, 27 W. 72nd St. (873-2004), off Columbus Ave. Also at 21 University Place at 8th St. (674-4450). Authentic Texas-style chicken and ribs on the same bill with tasty tempura and Grandma's chicken soup. You get mountains of food, and a lot of noise in this often crowded restaurant. Early bird special (served Mon.-Sat. 4-6:30pm and Sun. 2-5pm) features soup, ½-chicken, cornbread, and potato for only $7 per dining duo. Open Sun.-Thurs. noon-midnight, Fri.-Sat. noon-1am.

The Green Tree, 111th St. and Amsterdam Ave. (864-9106). Looks like a hole in the wall, but serves the best Hungarian food west of Budapest. Try the cold cherry soup, chicken paprika, and *palacinta* (crêpe) with a bottle of *Egri Bikaver,* "Bull's Blood" (Hungarian red wine—Ravi's favorite). Lavish lunch specials $2-6 before 3pm. Open Mon.-Thurs. noon-9pm, Fri.-Sat. 10am-10pm, Sun. 5-10pm. Closed in the summer. Open Mon.-Fri. 8am-11:15pm, Sat. 9am-11:15pm, Sun. 9am-10:30pm.

La Rosita, 2809 Broadway at 108th St. (663-7804). A neighborhood joint with white formica counters, mirrors, small tables, and excellent Cuban cuisine. Tasty rice and bean dishes $3.25. Open daily 7:30am-1am.

Greenwich Village and SoHo

Here, every restaurant has a gimmick and a loyal crowd. Food awareness is high; people here know the difference bewteen quality and kitsch. Regardless, some of the best-tasting bargain-priced food in the city can be found here.

West Village

Slightly more affluent than in Emma Goldman's or even Jack Kerouac's days, the western half of Greenwich Village still draws huge crowds to its friendly pubs and neighborhood restaurants. Many of the best places have been around for ages, so don't be drawn in by trendy neon and black-tile interiors in this part of town. Bleecker Street and MacDougal Street, south of Washington Square Park, are a haven for European-style bistros which have perfected the homey "antique" look. Amidst a clutter of collectibles, **Le Figaro,** Bleecker St. (677-1100), serves personal-sized pots of exotic brews sweetly complemented by homemade pastries. (Open Mon.-Thurs. 11am-2am, Fri. 11am-4am, Sat. 10am-4am, Sun. 10am-2am.)

Late nights in the Village are crowded, but also the most fun. Explore twisting side streets and alleyways where you can join Off-Broadway theater-goers as they settle down over a burger and a beer to write their own reviews, or drop into a jazz club where top-notch music will whet your appetite. If all this sounds too "cul-cha'd," sneak down 8th St. to 6th Ave. to find some of the most respectable pizzerias in the city. The real question then becomes whether **John's** or **Ray's** makes the better pie. (See listings below.)

John's Pizzeria, 278 Bleecker St. (243-1680). Clippings on the wall commemorate various events, but the most memorable thing of all is the pizza. Cooked in a brick oven, with a crisp crust and just enough cheese, pizza for 2 $7.55. No slices, table service only. Open daily 11:30am-11:30pm.

Ray's Pizza, 465 Sixth Ave. (243-2253), at 11th St. Half of the uptown pizza joints claim to be the "Original Ray's," but any New Yorker will tell you that this is the real McCoy. The best pizza in town. Well worth braving the lines and paying $1.75 and up for a slice. Open Sun.-Thurs. 11am-2am, Fri.-Sat. 11am-3am.

Trattoria Due Torri, 99 MacDougal St. (477-6063), near Bleecker St. There are only about 8 tables here, and you can see Chef Meshel cooking in the back. Better than watching him is eating his creations. Freshly made pastas from $6-7, veal and chicken from $7-8. Try the Gnocchi Sorrentina, or *anything,* but go. Open Sun.-Thurs. 12:30am-midnight, Fri.-Sat. 12:30am-2am.

West 4th St. Saloon, 174 W. 4th St. (255-0518). Try late supper with a rowdy crowd amidst this pub's brick-walled, brass-railed decor. Salads and sandwiches $6-7.50. Catch-of-the-day priced according to season. Open daily 11am-4am.

Olive Tree Cafe, 117 MacDougal (254-3630). Middle Eastern food, and lots of stimulation. Charlie Chaplin films run continuously on the wide screen, and you can borrow chess, backgammon, and Scrabble sets, or draw with colored chalk on the slate tables. Felafel $1.75, chicken kebab platter with salad, rice pilaf, and vegetable $6. Open daily 11am-3am.

Eva's, 11 W. 8th St. (677-3496), between MacDougal and Fifth Ave. Refreshingly high quality, fast-service health food with a seating parlor. Large meatless combo plate with felafel, grape leaves, and eggplant $4. Open Sun.-Thurs. 11am-midnight, Fri.-Sat. 11:30am-1am.

Shima, 12 Waverly Place (674-1553), northeast of Washington Sq. Look for the garden and small pond through the window. Weekday combo lunch features chicken or dumpling entree, vegetable, soup, rice, and fruit for $4.75. Lavish dinners under $12. Open Mon.-Fri. noon-2:30pm and 5-11:15pm, Sat.-Sun. 5:30-11pm.

East Village and Lower East Side

There are no frills but plenty of excitement on the East Side, where pasty-faced punks and starving artists sup alongside an older generation conversing in Polish, Hungarian, or Yiddish. Here, Jewish delis and Eastern European restaurants are everywhere. The plump traditional dumplings called *knishes* make a great lunch; eat potato knishes with mustard, meat knishes with *yoich* (gravy), or *kasha* knishes (buckwheat groat) all by their delicious selves. Fill up on *pirogi,* a delicious Polish dough stuffed with potato, cheese or other ingredients; blintzes are thin pancakes rolled around cream cheese, blueberries, and other fillings. Ask for hot bagels at local bakeries. Stop at **Yonah Schimmel's Knishery,** 137 E. Houston, for a $1.50 knish or some yogurt from a 71-year-old strain. Also try the **9th Sreet Bakery,** 350 E. 9th St., and **S&W Skull Cap Corporation,** 45 Essex St., a Jewish general food store famed for its *bialys,* a tasty round onion bread.

For a change of pace, visit 6th St. between First and Second Ave., where it is lined with Indian restaurants—most of them owned by brothers. This "Little India" provides some of the most reasonably priced and delicious food in New York. Try puffy *pooris* at **Shah Bagh,** *birani* at **Panna,** or coconut soup at **Kismoth.**

Passage to India, 308 E. 6th St. (529-5770), off 2nd Ave. Newer and classier than others on the block. Dine under chandeliers and brass-framed mirrors in British Colonial style. Full *tandoori* dinner (soup, appetizer, main course, dessert, coffee) $11. Open daily noon-midnight.

Odessa, 117 Avenue A at 7th St. (473-8916). Looks like a generic coffee shop but offers terrific Ukrainian-Polish specialties. The combination dinner is a huge assortment of *pirogi,* stuffed cabbage, *kielbasa,* sauerkraut, and potato pancakes ($5.45). Open daily 7am-midnight.

Second Avenue Delicatessen, 10th St. Don't let the electronic Dow Jones tickertape fool you; the food is authentic deli. Always crowded. The waiters provide plenty of entertainment but erratic service. Try pastrami or tongue on rye ($6). Open Mon.-Fri. 8am-midnight, Sat.-Sun. 8am-2am.

Kiev, 117 Second Ave. (674-4040). Unparalleled *pirogi* and heavy foods laced with sour cream and butter. The neon sign does not signal trendiness; inside, the decor is upscale deli. Believe it or not, at 4am this is *the* punk hangout. Open 24 hours.

East Village Ukrainian Restaurant, 140 Second Ave. (529-5024), between 8th and 9th St. This authentic eatery has been recently renovated and transformed into a beautiful room with impressive chandeliers and interesting paintings. Good food cheap. Excellent hot *borscht* jammed with vegetables ($1.75). Open Mon.-Fri. noon-11pm, Sat. noon-midnight.

Ratner's Dairy Restaurant, 138 Delancey St. (677-5588). Perhaps the most famous of the authentic Jewish restaurants. Like all kosher dairy menus, only fish. Delicious soups ($3-3.50) and blintzes ($7). Open Sun.-Fri. 6am-11pm, Sat. 6am-2am.

SoHo

In between the galleries are restaurants looking themselves like works of art. Find **Dean and Deluca,** 560 Broadway, at the corner of Prince and Broadway, to see one of the gallery-gourmet grocery breed. (Open Mon.-Sat. 8am-8pm, Sun. 9am-7pm.)

Food, 127 Prince St. (no phone), off Wooster St. Popular cafeteria-style restaurant with a happy-go-lucky style. They specialize in good, natural food served in huge portions. People-watch through floor-to-ceiling windows or peruse the art while downing cold cucumber or beef barley soup ($3.50). The sandwiches ($6-8) are a light meal for 2. Open Mon.-Sat. noon-10pm. Closed last 2 weeks of Aug.

Spring Street Natural Restaurant and Bar, 62 Spring St. (966-0290), corner of Lafayette. Macrobiotic and vegetarian dishes as well as seafood and poultry. Try the vegetable tempura or eggplant tofu parmigiana, both $8.50. Open daily 11:30am-2am.

Fanelli's Cafe, 94 Prince St. (226-9412). Established in 1872. A mosaic tile floor, a grandfather clock, and a dark wood bar create atmosphere, as do the neighborhood residents who eat and drink here. Burgers $6, steamed mussels $8, beer on tap $2. Open Mon.-Sat. 10am-2am, Sun. noon-2am.

Lower Manhattan

Chinatown

Some of the best Chinese cuisine on the East Coast can be found in New York's Chinatown rice shops, which serve huge, tasty, and terrifically inexpensive portions of food. Tea shops specialize in daily *dim sum—a la carte* brunch specialties. To reach Chinatown, take the subway to the Canal St. station of the Lexington Ave. IRT, walk east 2 blocks on Canal to Mott St., go south (right) on Mott 2 blocks, then east toward the Bowery, Confucius Plaza, and E. Broadway. Explore the side streets along the way. The red and gold pagodas will tell you you're in the right place.

Fortify yourself for the trek through the crowded streets with a cup of Turtle Longevity Soup ($1.25) at **Maxim Bakery** on the corner of Canal and Mott St., or journey down Mott to Mosco St., where the proprietor of the grandly named **Hong Kong Cake Company** stand will gladly trade six coconut egg rolls or 20 bite-sized egg cakes for your single dollar.

Hee Seung Fung Teahouse (HSF), 46 Bowery (374-1319). From the subway, walk east on Canal St. to the Bowery, then take a sharp left. Large and hectic. Widely acclaimed *dim sum* dishes $1.50-1.75 (served 8am-4:30pm). Try the sesame oil and ginger crispy fish and the *jung* (sticky rice wrapped in tea leaves). Open daily 7:30am-2am.

Wohop, 17 Mott St. (962-8617). A formica decor, but one of the most popular eateries with both Chinatown natives and uptowners. Good take-out. Most dishes under $5. Open daily 11am-5am.

Chinatown Ice Cream Factory, 65 Bayard St. (608-4170), off Mott St. Some say Chinatown natives give equal business to Haägen Dazs down the street, but the homemade ice cream here comes in flavors like ginger, lichee, papaya, green tea, and red bean. Cones $1.50. Open daily noon-midnight.

Little Italy

Little Italy, north on Mulberry from Canal St., is one of the liveliest sections of town at night. To get there, take the D train to Canal St. Crammed with tiny restaurants, the neighborhood bustles with people strolling in and out of the cafés off Mulberry St. Join the crowds and stake out a table outdoors where you can enjoy cappuccino and cannoli, the perennial favorites. Try **Ferrara's,** 195 Grand St., for sweets. The **San Gennaro Festival** (226-0546) in September is a veritable orgy of food, music and laughter. Many family-owned Italian restaurants close during August, so call ahead.

Luna Restaurant, 112 Mulberry St. (226-8657). Enter through the small kitchen, where a halo of steam crowns plates of clams, to emerge in a quaint, narrow restaurant with bright blue walls. Veal *cacciatore* $8. Fresh pasta from $7.50. Open Sun.-Thurs. noon-midnight, Fri.-Sat. noon-1am.

Paolucci's, 149 Mulberry St. (226-9653). Unpretentious, family-owned restaurant. The watchful portrait of the boss hangs on the front wall. Pasta from $7. Chicken *cacciatore* with salad $9. Open Mon.-Tues. and Thurs.-Fri. noon-11pm, Sat.-Sun. noon-11:30pm.

Marionetta, 124 Mulberry St. (431-3590). Sidewalk tables let you dine without missing a single frenzied moment of Little Italy. Serves some of the most inexpensive veal dishes in the neighborhood. Veal *parmagian* $8.50, chicken *parmagian* $8. Open daily noon-2am.

Puglia Restaurant, 189 Hester St. (966-6006). Long tables make this place fun and rowdy. A favorite with New Yorkers and bold tourists. Monstrous plate of mussels $6, spaghetti $7. Entrees $4-8. Live music nightly. Open Tues.-Sun. noon-1am.

Financial District

At lunchtime and after work, brokers and lawyers crowd the **South Street Seaport,** a recently rehabilitated historic district. To get there, take train #2 or 3 to Fulton St. The central marketplace contains more gastronomic variety per square foot than anywhere else in New York. Go wild at the gourmet fast-food specialty booths—one stand serves only East Argentine dairy products; another, Southern breakfasts. Check out the Seaport on a Friday afternoon to see uptight Wall Street execs let loose over a few beers. Formal restaurants, presided over by the 142-year-old **Sweets,** 2 Fulton St. (344-9189), are very expensive and inconsistent.

Jeremy's Ale House, 254 Front St. (964-3537). A converted warehouse with sawdust floors and crumbling brick walls. Wall Street Fri. hangout; otherwise packed with a young and unpretentious crowd. Best chili around ($3.50), good seafood. Open Mon.-Sun. 10am-9pm.

Front Street Restaurant, 228 Front St. (406-1560). Two kitchens serve the long wooden tables. One has fresh seafood—squid with hot sauce $6.25, 6 oysters $6, broiled fish specials $6-7.50. The other features inexpensive "home cooking"—garnished half-pound pita burger $4, *wursts* $2, quiche and salad $5. Open Mon.-Fri. 11am-3pm and 5-9:30pm, Sat.-Sun. noon-9pm.

Wolf's Delicatessen, 42 Broadway (422-4141). There are pickles on the formica table tops, and you can order anything from Heinz over baked beans ($1.10) to corned beef and pastrami ($6.25). Open Mon.-Fri. 6am-7:45pm, Sat. 6am-3:45pm.

Brooklyn, Queens, and the Bronx

In the well-established ethnic enclaves in the other boroughs, restaurants cook for neighborhood patrons. Look for Jewish, Middle Eastern, and Eastern European restaurants in Brooklyn, Italian food in the Bronx, Greek dishes along Ditmars Boulevard in Astoria (Queens), and Indian fare in Flushing (Queens).

The culinary map of the boroughs changes constantly, as restaurants and markets reflect the growing number of immigrants from Asia, Africa, and Latin America. The Jackson Heights, Elmhurst, and adjacent Corona neighborhoods in Queens dynamically capture these diverse essences. Indian, Thai, Vietnamese, and Latin American restaurants cluster along Broadway, Roosevelt Avenue, and Junction Boulevard. (Take the subway to Roosevelt Ave./Jackson Heights, and the IRT #7 toward Flushing.)

Dominick's, 2335 Arthur Ave. (733-2807). Small, authentic Italian eatery. Vinyl tablecloths and bare walls, but great atmosphere. The waiter won't offer you a menu, or a check; he'll recite the specials of the day and then bark out what you owe at the end of the meal. Try the *linguini* dishes and the special veal and chicken *francese* dishes. A full meal will run about $9-10. Open Mon. and Wed.-Sun. 1-10pm. Get here before 6pm or after 9pm, or expect to wait at least 20 min.

Junior's, 986 Flatbush Ave. Extension, Brooklyn (718-852-5257), just across the Manhattan Bridge. Adored for roast beef, brisket, and the like. Entrees $8, complete dinner $15. Displaced New Yorkers drive for hours to satisfy cheesecake cravings here (plain slice $3). Open Sun.-Thurs. 6:30am-1am, Fri.-Sat. 6:30am-3am.

Roumely Tavern, 3304 Broadway, Astoria, Queens (718-278-7533), across the East River from the Upper East side via the Queensborough Bridge and the Astoria Line BMT. Greek accents as authentic as the food. *Spanokopita* (spinach pie; $1.75) and lamb stew ($7). Open daily noon-3am.

Pizzeria Las Americas, 40-05 Junction Blvd. (718-478-5040), under the Roosevelt "El" in Corona, Queens. Take the IRT #7 to Junction Blvd. Argentine *empanadas* and pizza. A slice with *cebollitas ralladas* $2. Open Mon.-Thurs. 10:30am-11pm, Fri.-Sun. 10:30am-midnight.

Sights

Seeing New York City is first a matter of deciding where to look. Every street corner offers something, but all street corners are not created equally. Some are interesting by accident, and some because they contain a famous monument, a museum, or architectural landmark. The best way to take in Manhattan's majesty is to explore on foot, relying on subways and buses only to cover large distances. Unfortunately, there is too much to see in a year, let alone two or three days. Whirlwind, see-it-all-from-the-seat-of-the-bus guided tours aren't a bad superficial introduction to the Big Apple. Tours will introduce various sections or themes of the city—later explore those that intrigue you on foot.

Guided Tours

Crossroads Sight-seeing Tours (581-2828) offers an eight-and-a-half-hour traditional tour, including visits to the Empire State Building, the Statue of Liberty, Wall Street, the United Nations, Greenwich Village, and Harlem ($31). Tours leave daily from 150 W. 49th St. betweeen 6th Ave. & 7th Ave. at 9am and 10am. Arrive a half-hour early to reserve a spot. Other tours available; they vary in length (2-8 hr.) and start at $13. **Short Line Tours,** 166 W. 46th St. (354-5122), runs a similar tour for the same price. **Gray Line Sight-seeing,** 900 Eighth Ave. (397-2600), between 53rd and 54th St., has 13 tours ranging from standard bus trips around Manhattan to historical explorations of upstate New York and gambling junkets to Atlantic City ($13.50-60). Arrive half-hour in advance.

Harlem Sprituals, Inc., 1457 Broadway (302-2594), between 41st and 42nd St., offers upscale tours of Upper Manhattan, including the "Sprituals and Gospel" tour, highlighted by trips to historical homes and participation in a Baptist service ($25 for 4 hr., leaves Sun. at 9am). The "Soul Food and Jazz" tour ($60) runs from 7pm to midnight and features a filling meal at a Harlem restaurant. Call 24 hours in advance for reservations. For a little less money, **Harlem, Your Way! Tours Unlimited, Inc.,** 129 W. 130th St. (690-1687), offers a similar package, without dinner, called the "Champagne Jazz Safari" ($25 on Wed., $30 Fri. and Sat. evenings). They also sponsor a three-hour walking tour of Harlem for $25. Call 24 hours in advance for reservations.

Circle Line Tours (563-3200) circumnavigates the island of Manhattan in a three-hour cruise. Twelve cruises run daily from 9:30am to 4:15pm. Cruises leave from pier 83 at the foot of W. 43rd St. (Tickets $15, seniors $13.50, under 12 $7.50.)

More specialized, neighborhood tours are offered by **Guide Service of New York,** 445 W. 45th St. (408-3332), featuring both walking and bus excursions ($10-49), and **Sidewalks of NY** (517-0201), whose unique walking tours have titles like "Famous Murder sights" and "Ghosts of the Upper West Side." All tours cost $10 and last two hours.

The **Municipal Art Society,** at the Urban Center, 457 Madison Ave. (935-3960), near 50th St., leads $12 guided walking tours; destinations change with the seasons. Their free one-hour tour of Grand Central Station meets every Wednesday at 12:30pm underneath the Kodak sign at Grand Central. Other tours follow Fifth Ave., take in the waterfront reconstruction sites, or wander through ethnic neighborhoods. In spring and early fall, the **Museum of the City of New York** (534-1672) sponsors leisurely Sunday walking tours ($15) concentrating on the city's history and architecture. The visitors bureau has free brochures with suggested outlines for touring the Big Apple by foot. An excellent, free, do-it-yourself tour of lower Manhattan is **Heritage Trail,** designated by small American flags. Pick it up in the Financial District at Broadway and Wall Street.

East Midtown

The area east of Fifth Ave. between 34th and 59th St. is the commercial center of New York, a convention of glass towers and briefcases. There are no traditional man-on-horse monuments here; instead, the celebration of 20th century accomplishments comes in the form of the corporate complex. Pre-existing these new symbols of success are older ones, still well loved, but often comparatively dwarfed in significance and magnificence.

One exception is the majestic Beaux-Arts style **Grand Central Station,** 42nd to 45th St. between Vanderbilt Pl. and Madison Ave., which is still appreciated for both its appearance and its function. Built between 1903 and 1913 by Cornelius Vanderbilt, the main concourse of this grandiloquent gateway to the metropolis services about 170,000 commuters and innumerable visitors daily. Even today, it is one of the world's largest rooms. The various vistas from the sweeping stairs off Vanderbilt Ave. as well as from the 42nd St. and Lexington Ave. entrances are worth seeing as is the vaulted ceiling covered with oakleaves, the Vanderbilt family's emblem, and constellations of the zodiac. In 1963, much of the impact of the station was drawn away from it, and up—towards Walter Gropius's imposing **Pan Am Building,** Park Ave. and 46th St., set on top of the station. Opinion on it is mixed: Some see Gropius' building as a monstrous intrusion on New York's skyline, others as a spectacular example of modernist architecture. Other Park Avenue buildings, such as the **Waldorf-Astoria Hotel,** at 50th St., recall the more subtle grandeur of pre-World War II New York.

At Lexington and 42nd St. stands the **Chrysler Building,** a seductive and absurd 1930 art-deco skyscraper, the tallest in the world when it was erected (the Empire State would steal that distinction a year later). The gargoyles on top were styled after radiator ornaments and designs copied from '29 Chrysler hubcaps. The monumental 20s **Bowery Savings Bank,** 110 E. 42nd St., built in the Romanesque style, makes capitalists feel warm all over. The **Daily News Building,** 220 E. 42nd St., is a 1919 precursor of slab architecture; the *Daily News* has its headquarters here, and a huge glass globe revolves inside. The **Ford Foundation,** 320 E. 43rd St., exemplifies both the foundation's moneyed taste and architect Kevin Roche's fusion of glass and steel in corporate modern style. Built in 1967, the lush jungle atrium was a model of mixed-use commercial buildings. (Open Mon.-Fri. 9am-5pm.)

Ceremonial capital of the political world, the **United Nations** (963-7713) overlooks the East River between 42nd and 48th St. Designed in the early 50s by an international committee including Le Corbusier, Oscar Niemeyer, and Wallace Harrison (whose ideas won out in the end), the complex itself is a diplomatic statement: part bravura, part compromise. You can take a one-hour guided tour of the **General Assembly** and the **Security Council;** tours start in the main lobby of the General Assembly every half-hour from 9:15am to 4:45pm. (Admission $4.50, students and children $2.50.) From September through December, free tickets to General Assembly meetings can be obtained in the main lobby about a half-hour before sessions, which usually begin at 10:30am and 3pm Monday through Friday.

Thanks to corporate dollars, the area a few blocks uptown is sprinkled with free atriums surrounded by potted trees, artwork, and fellow pedestrians; many atriums have free live music and almost all have clean public bathrooms. The triangle-topped **Citicorp Center,** at Lexington Ave. and 53rd St., is a larger-than-life example of New York's mixed-use buildings with atriums. Occasional free lunch-hour concerts jazz up the plaza and atrium. Pick up a free Manhattan Atrium Guide from the visitors bureau (see Practical Information above). Annexed to the Citicorp Complex is **St. Peter's Church,** a stunning, space-age chapel. (Open daily Mon.-Fri. 10am-11pm.) At 50th St. and Third Ave. is the funky **Crystal Pavillion** atrium triplex, with neon lights, dance music, water walls, and a gondola elevator. (Open Mon.-Sat. 8am-11pm.)

The **Seagrams Building,** Park Ave. between 52nd and 53rd St., pioneered modern architecture in New York. Designed in 1958 by Mies van der Rohe and Philip Johnson, the plaza and tower were set back 90 feet from the building line, and were constructed from only the finest marble, glass and bronze. Compare Johnson's new and old styles by checking out his recently completed, post-modern **AT&T Building,** 55th St. and Madison Ave. The cross-vaulted arcade (open Mon.-Fri. 8am-6pm) features scenic cafés, the AT&T Infoquest Center (see Museums below), and the ritzy, four-star **Quilted Giraffe** restaurant, which reputedly empties the deepest pockets in New York (dinner $85 *per person* if you don't drink anything and forget to tip the waiter).

At Park Ave. and 51st St. is **St. Bartholomew's Church,** a Romanesque creation by McKim, Mead & White dating from 1902. The old portico was incorporated in the 1919 rebuilding in Byzantine style; oddly enough, the parts go together beautifully. Controversy rages over the building of an office tower in the courtyard. A block east are the **Villard Houses,** also by McKim, Mead & White. Built in 1884, these graceful Italianate brownstones were incorporated into the Helmsley Palace Hotel when it was built in 1980. Helmsley was allowed to build the Palace on the condition that he preserve the incredible marble and stained glass interiors of one wing of the four-house complex.

St. Patrick's Cathedral stands at 51st St. and Fifth Ave. The Gothic Revival structure, New York's most famous church, was designed by James Renwick and opened in 1879. Today it features high society weddings and the shrine of the first American male saint, St. John Neumann. The **Olympic Tower,** across the street from St. Patrick's, has regularly scheduled free classical and jazz concerts, a reflecting waterfall pool, and seats for weary feet.

Some find it excessively opulent, but others adore the rose-pink marble, 80-foot waterfall, and gleaming bronze of the **Trump Tower,** 56th St. and Fifth Ave. The tower houses a five-story shopping mall that parades the power of New York's reigning real estate tycoon. While the stores in the complex include some of New York's most expensive, the piano and violin concerts weekdays at lunchtime are free. For a change of pace, try the cool serenity of the **IBM Atrium,** 57th St. at Madison Ave., where tall stands of bamboo and hundreds of other lush botanical specimens grace a 68-foot-high greenhouse. Just off the atrium you'll find the **IBM Gallery of Art** and the Manhattan branch of the **New York Botanical Gardens.** (Open Mon.-Fri. 8am-6pm.)

Between 48th and 50th St. and Fifth and Sixth Ave. stretches **Rockefeller Center,** a monument to the heights to which business can spur the arts. Raymond Hood and his cohorts did an admirable job of glorifying various business virtues through architecture. A wealth of art deco sculpture adorns the buildings that surround the sunken plaza, which serves as a restaurant in summer and skating rink in winter. Rockefeller Center includes **Radio City Music Hall,** at 51st St. and Ave. of the Americas (757-3100). New York's most extravagant theater has staved off bankruptcy and is still home of the leggy Rockettes. For information on daily backstage tours ($6), call 632-4000.

West Midtown

Cross 5th Ave. from the East to the West Side, and all of the control formerly in evidence vanishes. No longer do the people wear similar clothes, and walk with similar purpose. No longer do the buildings soar to approximately equal heights. The well-maintained walk next to the destitute, the purposeful next to the dilatory. The atmosphere is most visible, impressive, and oppressive in **Times Square,** at the intersection of 42nd St. and Broadway. Well-policed (and with reason), here Broadway hosts not only its famous stages but also first-run movie houses, neon lights, street performers, and porn palace after peep show after porn palace. The entire area is slated for demolition and multi-billion dollar reconstruction in the next few years, New York can no longer afford the space. The first new building, the neatly polished **Marriott Marquis** has already replaced two historic Broadway stages. Nearly all subway lines stop in Times Square (#1, 2, 3, 7, QB, N, RR, or SS).

Just west of the square, at 229 W. 43rd St., lie the offices of the **New York Times,** founded in 1857, and for which the square was named in 1904. In the 20s, the **Algonquin Hotel,** located on 44th St. between Fifth and Sixth Ave., hosted Alexander Woollcott's "Round Table," a regular gathering of the brightest luminaries of the theatrical and literary worlds, including Robert Sherwood and Dorothy Parker. The inside of the hotel has remained virtually unchanged since that time. The Oak Room still serves tea every afternoon.

A walk uptown along Broadway leads through the **Theater District,** which stretches from 41st to 57th St. At one time a solid row of marquees, some of the theaters have been converted into movie houses or simply left to rot as the cost of live productions has skyrocketed. Approximately 40 theaters are still active, mostly grouped around 45th St. Between 44th and 45 St., ½ block west off Broadway, just in front of the Shubert Theater, is a short private street reserved for pedestrians; **Shubert Alley** was originally built as a fire exit between the Booth and Shubert Theaters. Just off Shubert Alley, you may find some stars grabbing an after-show snack at **Sardi's,** a popular restaurant among high-brow theater folk.

Much farther west on 42nd St., past the seedy Port Authority Bus Terminal, lies **Theater Row,** a block of renovated Off-Broadway theaters featuring some of the best work in town.

Over on Sixth Ave., near 48th St., in the basement of the **MacGraw-Hill Building** (near Rockefeller Center) is the multi-media screen production *The New York Experience,* a sensational, sense-startling documentary of New York's history. (869-0345; shown every hr. on the hr. Mon.-Thurs. 11am-7pm, Fri.-Sat. 11am-8pm, Sun. noon-8pm. Admission $4.75, under 12 $2.90). Stop by **Little Old New York,** in the theater lobby, a charming recreation of Manhattan in the 1890s. (Free.)

Lower Midtown

The **Empire State Building,** at 34th St. and Fifth Ave. (736-3100), is the quintessential symbol of New York. The 1931 skyscraper surges 102 floors from the sidewalk with just the right combination of showiness and taste. Even though it is now only the fourth tallest building in the world, the unparalleled view from the top is well worth the pilgrimage, although you may have to wait in line to make it. The upper floors are illuminated after dark in colorful accord with the seasons or special events: red, white, and blue streaks blaze over Manhattan on Independence Day. (Open daily 9:30am-midnight. Admission to the observation deck $3.50, seniors and students $1.75.)

At 36th St. and Madison Ave., the **Morgan Library** (685-0610), housed in a beautiful Italian Renaissance building, features a large selection of medieval treasures. (Open Sept.-July Tues.-Sat. 10:30am-5pm, Sun. 1-5pm. Free.) At 34th St. and Sixth Ave. in Herald Sq. (west of the Empire State Building) is the world's largest department store, **R. H. Macy's** (736-5151), where you'll find everything from designer clothes to pianos.

Regular tours roam through the period rooms of **Theodore Roosevelt's birthplace** and childhood home at 28 E. 20th St. between Park Ave. and Broadway (260-1616; open Wed.-Sun. 9am-5pm; admission $1, over 65 and under 17 free. Take the IRT or BMT subways to stops on 14th or 23rd St.) Farther west on 23rd St. below Madison Sq. stands the wedgelike **Flatiron Building,** New York's first skyscraper, designed by Daniel Birnham in 1902. It has been immortalized in Edward Steichen's photographs. Though only 20 stories high, the building is embellished with the most elaborate stonework in the city. Today, the building houses world-famous publishing offices. It is here that your *Let's Go* evolves into its final form.

The **Chelsea Hotel,** on 23rd St., between Seventh and Eighth Ave., has sheltered many suicidal artists including, most recently, Sid Vicious of the Sex Pistols. Check out the pop-art punk lobby. Chelsea's **flower district** on 28th St. between Sixth and Seventh Ave., is most colorful during the wee hours of the morning (use caution getting there).

Upper East Side

Here you'll find some of the most expensive real estate in the world. On Park Avenue, the sidewalks are clean, and guarded by the doormen posted in each building. Penthouse gardens look out over a cityscape made homogeneous by distance.

Museums are the main attraction here for the visitor, but it's also soothing to savor the quiet elegance of **Park Avenue** and **Fifth Avenue** at night. Or, ogle the latest fashion creations in the boutiques of Madison Ave. by day.

The confident parade of the Upper East begins at 58th St. and Fifth Ave. with the **Grand Army Plaza,** a small square dominated—appropriately enough—by the huge figure of *Abundance* atop the **Pulitzer Fountain.** Surrounding Grand Army Plaza are the luxurious hotels favored by high society. Across from the Plaza, on the old site of the Savoy Hotel, stands the 50-story white marble **GM Building,** home to the world's largest toy store, **F.A.O. Schwartz.**

Central Park rolls from Grand Army Plaza all the way up to 110th between Fifth and Eighth Ave. Twenty years of construction turned these 843 acres, laid out by Frederick Law Olmsted and Calvert Vaux in 1850-60, into a compressed sequence of landscapes of nearly infinite variety. Central Park turns shabby in the northernmost stretches and is dangerous from dusk to dawn. The park contains lakes, ponds, fountains, skating rinks, ball fields, tennis courts, a castle, an outdoor theater, a bandshell, two zoos, and one of the most prestigious museums in America, the **Metropolitan Museum of Art** (see Museums below). Take a spin on the **carousel** ponies: at 75¢, one of the most exciting and least expensive whirls in the city. The **Central Park Zoo,** 5th Ave. at 64th St., has just been renovated, and once again, the monkeys are happy to ape their visitors. Kids will delight in the **children's zoo** and the pony rides. (Open Mon. and Wed.-Fri. 10am-5pm, Tues. 10am-8:30pm, Sat.-Sun. 10am-5:30pm; Sept.-May Mon. and Wed.-Fri. 10am-5pm, Sat.-Sun. 10am-5:30pm. Admission $1, seniors 50¢, under 12 25¢. Children's zoo 10¢.) The **Wollman Skating Rink** (517-4800) has been revamped by Donald Trump, and the Kong-sized new rink has good roller-skating in summer and ice-skating in winter. (Admission $5. Skate rental $2.50.) The **reservoir** is encircled by 1.6 miles of cinder track for a mélange of runners and joggers. On weekends, when most of the main roads through the park are closed to vehicles, you're guaranteed to encounter bikers, skateboarders, and skaters freewheeling to the sounds of everything from Run-DMC to Rachmaninoff. In summer, **free concerts** (360-1333) in the park are a tradition (past performers have ranged from Simon and Garfunkel to the Metropolitan Opera), as is excellent free drama during the **Shakespeare in the Park** festival (see Theater: off- and Off-Off Broadway below). The visitors center (397-3156) is located at 64th St. mid-park. (Open Tues.-Thurs. and Sat.-Sun. 11am-5pm, Fri. 1-5pm.)

Mansions once lined Fifth Avenue on the park's east side; now most have been replaced by apartment buildings. The **Frick Collection of Fine Arts,** exemplifying Fifth Avenue's turn-of-the-century opulence, was built to house Frick and his paintings in harmony (see Museums below). Glance at the old Duke house, now NYU's **Institute of Fine Art,** Fifth Ave. at 78th St., and the Harkness House, now home to the Commonwealth Fund, on Fifth at 75th St., for more examples of limestone castles.

Madison Avenue, 1 block east, is synonymous with the cutthroat advertising business, where artists, market psychologists, and salespeople conspire to manipulate America's buying habits. These Jello-Pop jingle workshops are hidden behind an unbroken facade of expensive boutiques and first-rate art galleries. Between 70th and 79th St. and all along 57th St., a gallery caps almost every block; most have free exhibits. The apotheosis of art auction houses, **Sotheby Parke Bernet Gallery,** resides at 980 Madison Ave., at 77th St. Still Farther east, visit Carl Shurz Park, at 88th St. and East End Ave., to see **Gracie Mansion** (call 570-4751 for tour information), the official residence of New York's infamous mayor, Ed Koch.

Upper West Side

Broadway leads uptown to **Columbus Circle,** 59th St. and Broadway, the symbolic entrance to the Upper West Side and the end of Midtown. Set between Central Park and the **New York Coliseum,** a convention and exhibition complex (slated for destruction in the near future), the Circle is distinguished by a statue of Christopher himself.

Three blocks north, Broadway intersects Columbus Ave. at **Lincoln Center,** the cultural hub of the city, between 62nd and 66th St. The six buildings that constitute Lincoln Center—Avery Fisher Hall, the New York State Theater, the Metropolitan Opera House, the Library and Museum of Performing Arts, the Vivian Beaumont Theater, and the Juilliard School of Music—accommodate over 13,000 spectators at a time. In daytime, the poolside benches by the Henry Moore sculpture behind the main plaza are a good spot for a picnic. At night, the Metropolitan Opera House lights up, making its chandeliers and huge Chagall murals visible to passersby through its glass panel facade. The central fountain is fabulous at any time of day. Lincoln Center's hour-long guided tours (877-1800, ext. 512) are given daily on a varying schedule. Call on the day you wish to come. (Admission $6.25, seniors and students $5.25.) From October to June, 15-minute tours of the tremendous backstage of the Metropolitan Opera are also given. (Admission $6, students $3. Reservations and schedules 582-3512.) See Entertainment below for performance information.

Cross 65th St. to reach **Central Park West,** an area of graceful old apartment buildings. As Manhattan's urbanization peaked in the late 19th century, wealthy residents sought tranquility in the elegant **Dakota,** between 72nd and 73rd St. Built in 1884, the apartment house was named for its remote location. John Lennon's streetside murder here in 1981 has made the Dakota notorious. **Strawberry Fields Forever,** in Central Park across from the Dakota, is Yoko Ono's memorial to her husband. There 25,000 plants, spread over a couple of acres, center around a simple mosaic that asks you to "Imagine." The **New York Historical Society,** 77th St. and Central Park West (873-3400), is a repository of information on the city. The friendly library staff will help you uncover obscure facts about the past or provide pop trivia. (Open Tues.-Sun. 10am-5pm. Admission $2.) Across the street, you can examine the history of the world in the enormous **American Museum of Natural History.** (See Museums and Galleries below.)

Delis usually aren't very large, but **Zabar's,** on Broadway (787-2002), between 81st and 82nd St., is a grand exception, stretching along half a city block. After navigating your way through bricks of cheese, barrels of coffee beans, racks of fresh breads, rows of exotic delicacies, and cartons of caviar, stop at the deli. Zabar's is a cultural experience no one should miss. (Open Mon.-Fri. 8am-7:30pm, Sat. 8am-midnight, Sun. 9am-6pm.)

New York City's member of the Ivy League, **Columbia University,** chartered in 1754, is tucked between Morningside Dr. and Broadway from 114th to 121st St. Columbia and **Barnard College,** the women's school across West End Ave., are in the process of merging. Diagonally across the campus at the end of 112th St. on Amsterdam Ave. is the **Cathedral of St. John the Divine** (316-7540), the world's largest Gothic cathedral, and the only one still under construction. Notice that parts are actually Romanesque. Tours start beneath the large rose window and take in the carvings, a museum of religious art, gardens, and the 13-acre grounds. (Tours Thurs.-Sat. 11am, Sun. 12:45pm; open daily 7am-5pm.)

Continue north and bear west to see **Grant's Tomb,** in Riverside Park at 122nd St. (666-1640). At one time, this used to be a popular monument, but stuck on the periphery of the city, it attracts only the brave and the few. Nevertheless, the Civil War general still rests in peace here. (Open Wed.-Sun. 9am-4:30pm.) Across the street, at beautiful **Riverside Church** (222-5900), you can hear concerts on the world's largest carillon (74 bells) twice daily and climb the tower for $1. (Open daily 9am-5pm. Tower open Mon.-Sat. 11am-3pm, Sun. 12:30-4pm. Subway: 7th Ave IRT local to 116th St., then walk 1 block west.) Stay away from this area at night and don't wander off course at any time of day.

Harlem

Although Harlem has become synonymous with urban slum, it has played a proud and vital role in black American history and culture, particularly during the Harlem Renaissance of the 20s. In those years, northern Manhattan was the posh "end of the line" for blacks fleeing prejudice and poverty in the rural south. The neighborhood has been the inspiration for major artistic movements and a magnet for jazz musicians. In the 60s, the radical Black Power movement flourished here through the Revolutionary Theater of LeRoi Jones, which performed consciousness-raising one-act plays in Harlem's streets. Nowadays, Harlem suffers from a blanket image as America's quintessential black ghetto, but the area cannot be so easily stereotyped. There are some middle-class sections of Harlem, and **Sugar Hill** is home to high-income residences. But these enclaves are often bordered by neighborhoods where crime and drugs are ever-present problems. The heart of traditional Harlem is 125th St. By the mid-140s, the neighborhood drifts into the deadly wastelands along the Harlem River, which continue over to the South Bronx. Since parts of the area are unsafe, don't plan to see Harlem on your own; go with someone who knows the area, or take a tour (see Guided Tours above).

Hidden by the noisy urban life of Harlem, vestiges of the nation's more serene colonial past have been preserved. Alexander Hamilton built his two-story, Federal-style county home, **Hamilton Grange** (283-5154), at what is now 287 Convent Ave. at 141st St. The furniture, however, has been moved to the Museum of the City of New York. (Open Wed.-Sun. 9am-4:30pm. Free.) The Georgian **Morris-Jumel Mansion,** in Roger Morris Park, at W. 160th St. and Edgecombe Ave. (923-8008), was the home of Gouverneur Morris, U.S. minister to France during the Reign of Terror, and also served as Washington's headquarters for the Battle of Harlem Heights in the autumn of 1776. (Open Tues.-Sun. 10am-4pm. Admission $2, seniors and students $1.) A little later in history, Congressman Adam Clayton Powell Jr. served as pastor of the **Abyssinian Baptist Church,** 132 W. 138th St., the oldest black church in the city.

Harlem is also home to two colleges. Gothic **City College,** 138th and Convent (690-4121), took the primarily poor children of blacks and Jewish immigrants during the first half of the century and turned them into today's national leaders. **Boricua College,** a private Hispanic liberal arts college, is one of four buildings in **Audobon Terrace,** the Beaux-Arts Complex at Broadway and 155th St. The other three buildings house the Numismatic Society Museum, the Hispanic Society of America, and the Museum of the American Indian (see Museums below). The silver dome of the **Malcolm Shabazz Masjid (Mosque),** where revolutionary leader Malcolm X was minister, still glitters on 116th St. The newly built **Harlem Third World Trade Center,** 163 W. 125th St., is working to draw new attention to the U.S.'s most famous black community.

Racial tension may have inspired beautiful and tragic love stories such as "West Side Story," but it has also fueled bitter battles between the communities of black Harlem and Spanish Harlem with violent confrontations producing all-too-real-life tragedies. Called *el barrio* ("the neighborhood"), **Spanish Harlem** borders the northeast corner of Central Park. Extending roughly from E. 97th St. north to the South Bronx, the heart of this district is busy **116th Street.** The streets of the *barrio* are alive—checkers players hang out on the stoops, and basketball players slam-dunk in chain-link courts. But again, don't venture into this neighborhood without someone familiar with it.

Washington Heights

Far above the hustle and bustle of the rest of the island, Washington Heights is an Old-World enclave. At 179th St., look for the elegant lines of the **George Washington Bridge,** the world's only 14-lane suspension bridge. Just beneath it lies **Fort Washington Park,** home of the **Little Red Lighthouse** and the remaining bastions of the original fort. For a better view of the bridge, walk west from Fort Washington Ave. to Cabrini Blvd. The journey north along Fort Washington Ave. takes you past a succession of mid-rise apartment buildings (c. 1920) to **Fort Tryon Park,** home of the **Cloisters,** where you can see New York's counterparts to the Bayeux Unicorn tapestries. (See Museums below.) One block before the park, the **St. Francis Cabrini Chapel** shelters the remains of Mother Cabrini, the first American-born saint. Her body lies in a crystal casket under the altar, but above the neck you will only see a wax mask—her head lies in Rome.

Greenwich Village and SoHo

Counter-culture still reigns supreme in the Village. Uptown past Houston to 14th St. west of Broadway, you'll find the most diverting assortment of New Yorkers. Two or three frisbees sailing through the air signal your arrival at **Washington Square Park,** the northern gateway to the Village and the focal point of **New York University.** The park is always crowded with students, musicians, professors, drug pushers, and artists; meet balding art patrons, peasant-skirted hippies, and slender, mustachioed men in designer running shorts. These are Village People.

In the late 19th and early 20th century, the Washington Square area produced more American cultural currents than any other region of the country. Stephen Crane, Theodore Dreiser, Henry James, Mark Twain, Edith Wharton, and Willa Cather all lived in the Village at one point in their life. A walk down **MacDougal Street** will take you past the ghosts of bygone social struggles and the whisperings of new ones. Louisa May Alcott, author of *Little Women,* lived at #132. Leftists such as Emma Goldman, Louise Bryant, John Reed, and Upton Sinclair regularly met in the **Liberal Club** at #137 to solve the world's problems over several stiff ones. Eugene O'Neill and Edna St. Vincent-Millay launched their careers at the **Provincetown Playhouse** across the street. (St. Vincent-Millay's home, at 75½ Bedford St., between Barrow and Grove St., is the narrowest house in the Village.) Dorothy Day, founder and leader of the Catholic Workers Movement, also lived and worked in the Village. Lost generation writers John Dos Passos and Malcolm Cowley returned from their post-World War I "exiles" to these crooked streets. Thirty years later, Beat Generation progenitors Jack Kerouac and Allen Ginsberg "howled" here in protest against post-World War II America. Today, the Village once again embraces personalities outside the mainstream, encompassing New York's largest number of Off- and Off-Off-Broadway houses as well as the city's largest gay population. Gay bars line Christopher and Gay St.

As the West Village becomes increasingly gentrified, some of the true radicals are moving away from Washington Sq. into the more run-down neighborhoods of the East Village. Stroll along colorful **St. Mark's Place** toward Tompkins Square Park, and wade through the cramped, wild clothing stores, or "participate" in a performance at one of the many experimental theaters that lurk in the old schools and church basements. **La Mama, Etc.,** 7 E. 4th St. (475-7710), is one of the first permanent experimental theaters and an early champion of Sam Shepard.Call for information about performances.

The tiny district of SoHo (an acronym for South of Houston), officially bounded by Houston, Canal, Lafayette, and W. Broadway, is the hot artists' center in town. The architecture here is American Industrial, notable for its ornate, cast-iron facades. Artists have converted factory lofts into studios, and it's impossible to walk half a block without passing a gallery, an experimental theater, or designer clothing store. High-fashioned sorts pay dearly (up to $500 for a pair of pants) to look good. Excellent galleries line W. Broadway, and although many come and go, you can count on top-quality work at **Vorpal** (165 W. Broadway) and **Leo Castelli** (420 W. Broadway).

Lower East Side, Chinatown, and Little Italy

The Lower East Side, once home for Jewish immigrants, is now a mixed Jewish and Hispanic community. This is the garment district, where you can bargain for everything from denim to silk. The quality varies from junk to jewels, although (merchants assure you) the prices are definitely unbeatable. This is also the place to buy electronic goods and appliances.

This neighborhood lies more or less between Houston and Canal St., east of Little Italy. It borders on the **Bowery,** the Skid Row of New York. The main thoroughfare is **Delancey Street,** where black-clad, bearded Hassidic shopkeepers ply various wares. Don't pass up the clothing district on Orchard St. or the Essex St. Market. Avoid the lettered avenues—"Alphabet Land"—above East Houston; Delancey Street is much safer.

Little Italy clusters around Mulberry St., several blocks south of the Village and just north of Canal St. This Italian neighborhood is an enclave of Old World cafés and restaurants. During the day, Little Italy is quieter than most districts in New York and is reminiscent of the old quarters of European cities. But by night, the sidewalks are clogged with café tables and tourists. If you're around on the second Thursday in September, you could be lapping up lasagna and *prosciutto* at the **Feast of San Gennaro,** one of the most colorful annual New York festivals. Dotted with stores selling low-cost electronics and plastics, commercial **Canal Street** divides Little Italy and **Chinatown,** the largest Asian community outside of San Francisco. Only a few steps across Canal St. from Little Italy are pagoda-topped phone booths, steaming tea shops, and firecracker vendors. During the Chinese New Year (late January or early February), the pace heightens to a level above the usual freneticism.

City Hall Area and the Financial District

The southernmost tip of Manhattan is extremely compact, and is free of threatening traffic. The narrow winding streets that discourage car travel make the area ideal for a walking tour. Wander down narrow, twisting historic lanes in between towering silver and stone skyscrapers. Five subway lines converge in the financial district, some on their way to Brooklyn Heights across the East River. Take a train to the City Hall area on Broadway at the northern fringe of the financial district, then explore south along the side streets off Broadway.

City Hall (566-5097) is a prime example of Federalist architecture and has been the scene of frenetic politicking since 1811. (Open Mon.-Fri. 10am-4pm.) From City Hall, walk down Broadway to the **Woolworth Building,** on Murray St., one of the few skyscrapers as graceful close up as from 20 blocks away. Designed by Cass Gilbert Gothic style, this 800-foot tower was the world's largest from 1913 to 1930. Inspiring mosaics and carved caricatures of Cass Gilbert and Woolworth himself decorate the lobby. A block down Broadway is **St. Paul's Chapel** (602-0874), the oldest church in Manhattan (1766). George Washington worshiped here during his presidency. (Open Mon.-Sat. 8am-4pm, Sun. 7am-3pm.)

West of Broadway, off Church St., are the city's tallest buildings, the twin towers of the **World Trade Center.** The enclosed observation deck (466-7397), on the 110th floor of #2, offers a stunning overview of Manhattan, especially at night. (Open daily 9:30am-11:30pm. Admission $3.50, seniors $1.75.)

Walk 8 short blocks down Broadway into the maw of the beast—the heavily built-up center of New York's Financial District. Sooty **Trinity Church,** at Broadway and Wall St., is dwarfed by the skyscrapers around it, and contains in its adjoining graveyard the tombs of Alexander Hamilton, Robert Fulton, and other prominent figures. Here, or nearby, pick up the **Heritage Trail,** an excellent walking tour marked by small American flags.

A short way down Wall Street, **Federal Hall** (264-8711) and the **New York Stock Exchange** (656-5168) sit diagonally across from one another. George Washington took the oath of office in Federal Hall; the building now houses historic documents. (Open Mon.-Fri. 9am-5pm. Free.) From the visitors gallery of the New York Stock Exchange (enter at 20 Broad St.), you can watch a free 15-minute movie (shown continuously Mon.-Fri.) and, from behind glass panels, view the controlled hysteria of the world's busiest commercial arena—the trading floor. Come before noon to get a ticket (free). (Open Mon.-Fri. 9:20am-3pm.)

Fraunces Tavern, a neo-Georgian construction (1719) on Broad St. at Pearl (425-1778), was yet another headquarters for Washington and is still a watering hole as well as a museum. John Jay had an office here, and in the early days of the Republic, much government business took place within its walls. (Open Mon.-Fri. 10am-4pm. Donation.) In the **Federal Reserve Bank,** 13 Liberty St. (720-6130), countries pay their debts by shifting bullion from one room to another. (Free 1-hr. tour and audio-visual display Mon.-Fri. at 10am, 11am, 1pm, and 2pm. Make appointments a week ahead by phone, and note that tickets must be mailed to you.)

New York Harbor and the Brooklyn Bridge

After its marathon journey down from Yonkers, Broadway ends in **Battery Park** on New York Harbor. A common site for political rallies, such as the No-Nukes fests of the 70s and recent anti-apartheid protests, the recently restored waterfront park commands one of the finest views of the city. New York Harbor, Brooklyn Heights, Governor's Island, the Brooklyn-Battery Tunnel, Jersey City, Ellis Island, Staten Island, and the Statue of Liberty can all be seen on a clear day. The view is a lot better, however, from the **Staten Island Ferry** (718-727-2508), which leaves from the port east of Battery Park every half-hour. A trip on the ferry is what the New York visitors bureau calls "the world's most famous, most reasonable (25¢ round-trip), and most romantic 5-mile cruise . . . " and they might very well be right.

Another ferry will take you to the renovated **Statue of Liberty** (363-3200). "The Lady," landmark of a century of immigrant crossings, is a moving, monumental sight. In 1886, Joseph Pulitzer's newspaper, *The World,* directed a private fundraising drive to erect the gift from France. The renovation of the Statue was likewise a grassroots project, funded by the contributions of schoolchildren, citizens, and corporations. The **American Museum of Immigration,** located in the statue's base, recalls the stories of the waves of immigrants who have funneled into New York Harbor. If the towering Statue enshrines the ideals of the immigrants' America, chaotic, dirty Ellis Island represents the bittersweet realities of the lives of 12 million Europeans who first experienced the U.S. through the island's people-processing facilities. **Circle Line Ferries** (269-5755) shuttle between Battery Park and Liberty Island. (Ferries leave daily every ½ hr. 9am-5pm. Fare $3.25, under 11 $1.50.) The eventual completion of Ellis Island renovations (by May 1, 1990) will bring renewed ferry service there as well.

You'll have to get up around 4am to start the day at **Fulton Fish Market.** Here on the East River, a few blocks from Wall Street, New York's store and restaurant owners have bought their fresh fish ever since the Dutch colonial period. Next door, renovations have created the **South Street Seaport** complex (669-9424). The 18th-century market, graceful galleries, and seafaring schooners will delight historians and tourists alike. An 11-block historic district along the East River and Fulton St., the seaport sprawls over two East Side piers. The decrepit but equally historic blocks on the periphery of the rehabilitated buildings are just as interesting. The **Seaport Experience** (608-7888) is an enjoyable, multi-media presentation about the area's nautical history. The **Seaport Line's** authentic paddlewheel steamboats (406-3434) offer one-and-a-half-hour day cruises departing daily on the hour at noon, 2pm and 4pm. (Fare $12, students $10), and evening cruises to the live sounds of jazz, rock, and dixie ($15-20 depending on hour and day). Cruises leave from Pier 16 at the seaport. **The Seaport Museum** (669-9424) offers tours of the area, and is open Mon.-Sun. 10am-6pm.

Uptown a few blocks, the **Brooklyn Bridge** looms. Built in 1883, the bridge was one of the greatest engineering feats of the 19th century. The 1-mile walk along the pedestrian path will show you why every New York poet feels compelled to write at least one verse about it. Photographers go wild, too, snapping the bridge's airy spider-web cables. To get to the entrance on Park Row, walk a couple of blocks west from the East River to the city hall area. Ahead of you stretch the piers and warehouses of Brooklyn's waterfront; behind you, the greatest cityscape in the universe. Plaques on the bridge towers commemorate John Augustus Roebling, its builder, who, along with 20 of his workers, died during its construction.

Brooklyn

Founded in 1600 by the Dutch, Brooklyn was the third-largest city in the U.S. by 1860. In 1898, it merged with the city of New York and became a borough, but it still maintains a strong, separate identity, with many ethnic communities and local industries. Unfortunately, Brooklyn also includes some rundown, unsafe areas—the most dangerous area is west of Prospect Park. The visitors bureau publishes an excellent free guide to Brooklyn's rich historical past that outlines 10 walking tours of the borough.

Head south on Henry St. after the bridge, then turn right on Clark St. toward the river to see one of the best imaginable views of Manhattan. Many prize-winning photographs have been taken here, from the **Brooklyn Promenade,** overlooking the southern tip of Manhattan and New York Harbor. Down from the esplanade lies the posh neighborhood of Brooklyn Heights. The headquarters of George Washington during the Battle of Long Island, **Brooklyn Heights** has attracted many authors, from Walt Whitman to Norman Mailer, with its beautiful old brownstones, tree-lined streets, and proximity to Manhattan. Continuing south, explore the area's small side streets. Soon you'll be at **Atlantic Avenue,** home to a large Arab community, with second-hand stores and inexpensive Middle Eastern bakeries and grocery stores. Atlantic runs from the river to Flatbush Ave. At the Flatbush Ave. Extension, pick up **Fulton Street,** which is the center of downtown Brooklyn, recently transformed into a pedestrian mall.

Williamsburg, several blocks north of downtown Brooklyn, has retained its Hassidic Jewish culture more overtly than Manhattan's Lower East Side. Men wear long black coats, hats, and sidelocks; women cover their shaved heads with wigs. The quarter encloses Broadway, Bedford, and Union Avenues. It closes on Saturday (*shabbat*) which is the Jewish holy day; intrusions are emphatically discouraged.

Prospect Park, designed by Frederick Law Olmsted in the mid-1800s, was supposedly his favorite creation. He was even more pleased with it than with his Manhattan project—Central Park. Because its ambiance and its reputation has been somewhat tarnished by crime, exercise caution in touring the grounds. At the corner of the park is **Grand Army Plaza,** an island in the midst of the borough's busiest thoroughfares. Olmsted designed it to shield surrounding apartment buildings from traffic. (Subway: IRT #2 or 3 to Grand Army Plaza.) The nearby **Botanic Gardens** seem more secluded, and include a lovely rose garden. They are behind the **Brooklyn Museum.** (See Museums below.)

It's hard to believe that anyone would want to celebrate the New York City subway system, but if you're in the area, make a quick stop at the **New York City Transit Exhibit,** Boerum Place and Schermerhorn St. (718-330-3060), to see the antique, graffiti-free trains. (Open Mon.-Fri. 10am-4pm, Sat. 11am-4pm. Admission $1, children 50¢. Subway: Borough Hall.)

Sheepshead Bay is on the southern edge of Brooklyn, and is both the name of a body of water, and a mass of land. The former is really part of the Atlantic Ocean. The seafood here is fresh and cheap (clams $5 per dozen along the water). Walk along **Restaurant Row** from E. 21st to E. 29th St., on Emmons Ave., and peruse menus for daily seafood specials. Nearby **Brighton Beach** has been homeland to Russian emigrés since the turn of the century. This area of Brooklyn is nicknamed "Little Odessa by the Sea" because of its pervasive Russian restaurants, newsstands, and shops. (Subway: D, M, or QB.)

Further east, the **Boardwalk,** once one of the most seductive of Brooklyn's charms, now squeaks nostalgically as tourists are jostled by roughnecks. Still, **Coney Island** is worth a visit. Enjoy a hot dog at historic **Nathan's,** Surf and Sitwell (718-266-3161; open Sun.-Thurs. 8am-4am, Fri.-Sat. 8am-5am), and ride the Cyclone roller coaster—but maybe not in that order—at **Astroland Park** (718-372-0275; open daily noon-midnight; admission $12). Be careful at night, or laser fire may not be the only thing attacking you as you play *Gauntlet* at the arcade behind the amusement park. Go meet a walrus, dolphin, sea lions, sharks, and other ocean critters in the tanks of the **New York Aquarium,** Surf and West Eighth (718-265-3400;

open Mon.-Fri. 10am-4:45pm, Sat.-Sun. 10am-5:45pm; admission $3.75, children $1.50, seniors free after 2pm Mon.-Fri.). Look for the house beneath a roller coaster, which inspired a scene in Woody Allen's *Annie Hall.*

Queens

Archie and Edith Bunker, Simon and Garfunkel, Cyndi Lauper, and Steinway pianos—all hail from Queens. The borough also houses hundreds of thousands of immigrants from around the world. Ethnic diversity is the norm here, as in the other boroughs, but Queens has a distinctive look of its own. In general, you'll see small brick, stone or clapboard houses, all with windowboxes, tiny plots of grass, and trees in front and back.

Look for them in **Astoria.** Ditmars Boulevard and Steinway Street are lined with shops and restaurants specializing in the food, clothes, and icons of Greece. The side streets are residential. (Subway: BMT's RR train from Midtown.) In northeast Queens, **Flushing's** "Little Asia" has a large population of Chinese, Korean, and Indian immigrants. Walk down Main, Prince, and Union St. in Flushing for Asian shops and restaurants. (Subway: IRT #7 to Main St.)

The beautiful **Jamaica Bay Wildlife Refuge** (718-474-0613), bordering both Brooklyn and Queens, offers over 6 miles of trails. If it's too tame for your own wild lifestyle, check out the gambling refuges of **Belmont Park,** in Elmont off the Hempstead Turnpike, and **Aqueduct Race Track** (718-641-4700; Aqueduct open late Oct.-April; Belmont open May-July and late August Wed.-Mon. 11am-5pm; grandstand admission $2).

Queens's principal attractions are concentrated in **Flushing Meadow/Corona Park,** the site of the 1964 World's Fair. A giant metal globe and twin space needles give the park a distinctive skyline. The park features the **New York Hall of Science** at the **New York State Pavilion** (718-699-0005; open Wed.-Sun. 10am-5pm; admission $3.50). Also see the **Queens Botanical Gardens** (718-886-3800; open daily 9am-dusk; free) and the **Queens Museum** (718-592-5555), with its 15,000-square-foot detailed model of the five boroughs. (See Museums below.)

Staten Island

The best part is getting there. At 25¢ (round-trip), the half-hour ferry ride from Manhattan's Battery Park to Staten Island is a third as expensive and twice as romantic as a whirl on Central Park's carousel. (See New York Harbor above for Ferry information.) Or you can drive from Brooklyn over the **Verrazano-Narrows Bridge,** one of the longest suspension span bridges in the world (4260 ft.), supported by 70-foot-high twin towers.

Once ashore, take a bus to **Richmondtown Restoration** (718-351-1611), a 100-acre restored village in Latourette Park. Among the 26 historically and architecturally intriguing 17th-century buildings is **The Vorleezer's House,** 441 Clark Ave., America's oldest elementary school, built in 1695. The **Staten Island Historical Society Museum** (718-353-1611) is in the old county clerk's office of 1848, and displays early American craftwork. (Open Wed.-Fri. 10am-5pm, Sat.-Sun. 1-5pm. Admission $3, seniors, students, and children $1.50, families $6.)

The **Snug Harbor Cultural Center,** 914 Richmond Terrace (718-448-2500), once a retirement home for sailors, overlooks New York Harbor, and features more than 20 Greek Revival buildings on 80 acres. Picnic and see some of its offerings: the **New House Gallery** of contemporary American artists (open Wed.-Sun. 1-5pm; free); the **Staten Island Children's Museum,** with participation exhibits for the 5-12 year old in you (718-273-2060; open July 5-Labor Day Tues.-Fri. 1-4pm, Sat.-Sun. 11am-5pm; Sept.-June Mon.-Fri. 1-4pm, Sat.-Sun. 11am-5pm; admission $2); and the **Staten Island Botanical Gardens** (718-273-8200, open daily dawn-dusk; tours by appointment).

Clove Lakes Park (718-390-8031), 1150 Clove Rd., in West Brighton, has picnic areas, ball fields, boating, and ice skating facilities as well as a mini yacht pond.

On Broadway and Clove Rd. is the 8½ acre **Staten Island Zoo,** which has an animal hospital with a nursery viewing area. (718-442-3100; open daily 10am-4:45pm; admission $1, seniors free, children 75¢. Free Wed.).

The Bronx

The Bronx is the toughest of the five boroughs. Scores of gutted and abandoned buildings in the **South Bronx** above the Harlem River make the area look like a war zone. But travel north, and the Bronx turns yuppie. In Riverdale small mansions and private schools create a green landscape—a suburb which contrasts starkly with the city it shares in name. **Wave Hill,** 675 W. 252 (549-2055), in Riverdale, is a beautiful pastoral estate with a majestic view of the Hudson. Samuel Clemens, Arturo Toscanini, and Teddy Roosevelt all have resided here in the Wave Hill House. The estate was finally donated to the city, and presently offers concerts and dance amidst its greenhouses and spectacular formal gardens. (Open Mon.-Tues. and Thurs.-Sat. 10am-5:30pm, Wed. 10am-dusk; Sun. 10am-7pm. Free Mon.-Fri.; Sat.-Sun. $2, seniors and students $1.)

The **Bronx Zoo** (367-1010), one of the largest menageries in America, was the first to house animals in natural surroundings. Although some animals are kept in cage-like confines, black jail bars are nowhere in evidence. On the monorail to "the Himalayas," even the cages are gone. Moats separate you from the wilder ones—or so the story goes. **Jungle World** is the zoo's indoor home for tropical, Asian wildlife. The 3-acre **Children's Zoo** features four natural environments. (Open Mon.-Sat. 10am-5pm. Sun. 10am-5:30pm. Admission Tues.-Thurs. free; Fri.-Mon $3.75, seniors free, children $1.50. Driving, take the Bronx River Parkway, or, from I-95, the Pelham Parkway. Subway: IRT #2 through the South Bronx to Pelham Parkway Station.) Across East Fordham Rd. from the zoo is the huge **New York Botanical Garden** (220-8700). Remnants of forest and untouched waterways give a glimpse of the area's original landscape. (Open Tues.-Sun. 8am-7pm. Donation required.) Don't miss the garden's recently renovated **Crystal Palace Conservatory.** (Open Tues.-Sat. 10am-4pm. Admission $3.50, students $1.25, children 75¢. Free Sat. 10am-noon.) The Metro-North Harlem line goes from Grand Central Station to the gardens (Botanical Garden Station), and includes admission (round-trip $7, seniors $5, children $3.50).

The **Hall of Fame for Great Americans,** 181st St. and University Ave. (220-6312), at Bronx Community College, features commemorative plaques and busts of national achievers. (Open daily 9am-5pm. Free.) To check out one great American in greater detail, visit **Poe Cottage** at the intersection of East Kingsbridge Road and Grand Concourse (881-8900), where Edgar Allan composed the bulk of his eerie tales. (Open Wed.-Fri. 9am-5pm, Sat. 10am-4pm, Sun. 1-5pm. Admission $1.)

Museums and Galleries

Idiosyncratic or mainstream, stuck on the distant past, or looking into the near present, there is a museum in this city for you. Even if your particular interest doesn't seem represented, be witness to a culture collecting itself. Stand under a life-size replica of a great blue whale at the **American Museum of Natural History.** Control a 900-foot aircraft carrier at the **Intrepid Sea-Air-Space Museum.** Enter the world of the 2000-year-old Egyptian Temple of Dendur or Van Gogh's 100-year-old "Cafe at Arles" at the **Metropolitan Museum of Art.** Relax alongside Monet's "Water Lilies" at the **Museum of Modern Art.**

The *New Yorker* magazine has the most extensive and most accurate listings for both museums and galleries; *New York* is also good. The Friday *New York Times* is also excellent, both for its listings (in the Weekend section) and for its reviews of major shows. Also consult the *Quarterly Calendar,* available free at any visitors bureau location (see Practical Information above). *Gallery Guide,* which can be found in local galleries, has comprehensive but often inaccurate monthly listings of gallery shows. Most museums and all galleries close on Mondays, and museums are jam-packed on the weekends. One final word: instead of demanding a flat admission fee, many museums require a "donation" (you pay what you want, but you must give something; they usually suggest a sum).

Major Collections

American Museum of Natural History, Central Park West (769-5100), at 79th to 81st St. Subway: Central Park West IND to 81st St. The largest science museum in the world, in a suitably imposing Gothic structure guarded by a statue of Teddy Roosevelt on horseback. The 45-foot-long Tyrannosaurus Rex rules over the Hall of Dinosaurs, while J.P. Morgan's Indian emeralds blaze in the Hall of Minerals and Gems. Open Sun.-Tues. and Thurs. 10am-5:45pm, Wed., Fri., and Sat. 10am-9pm. Donation; Fri.-Sat. 5-9pm free. The museum also houses **Naturemax** (769-5650), a movie extravaganza on New York's largest movie screen. Admission for museum visitors $3.50, children $1.75; Fri.-Sat. double features $5.50, children $3. The **Hayden Planetarium** (769-5920) offers outstanding multi-media presentations. Seasonal celestial light shows twinkle in the dome of the **Theater of the Stars,** accompanied by astronomy lectures. Admission $3.75, seniors and students $2.75, children $2. Electrify your senses with **Laser Rock** (769-5921) Fri.-Sat. nights, $6.

Brooklyn Museum, 200 Eastern Pkwy. at Washington Ave. (718-638-5000). Subway: IRT #2 or 3 to Eastern Pkwy. Wide-ranging collection of folk art, with everything from indigenous New York art (brownstone "sculpture" and period rooms) to items from the People's Republic of China. Changing exhibits display celebrated and unusual works, with superb painting shows. The **Botanic Garden** next door has a lovely collection of flora, including a large grove of Japanese cherry trees, a beautiful, fragrant rose garden, and the **Steinhardt Conservatory** and **Lily Pond.** Conservatory open Tues.-Sun. 10am-5:30pm. Admission $2, seniors and children $1. Museum open Mon. and Wed.-Sun. 10am-5pm. Donation; children free.

The Cloisters, Fort Tryon Park, upper Manhattan (923-3700). Subway: IND A train through Harlem to 190th St. This monastery, built from pieces of 12th- and 13th-century French and Spanish cloisters, plus a new tower, was assembled by Charles Collens in 1938 as a setting for the Met's rich collection of medieval art. Highlights include the Unicorn Tapestries, the Cuxa Cloister, and the Treasury. Open March-Oct. Tues.-Sun. 9:30am-5:15pm; Nov.-Feb. Tues.-Sun. 9:30am-4:45pm. Donation. (Includes admission to the Metropolitan Museum of Art main building.)

The Frick Collection, 1 E. 70th St. (288-0700). Subway: Lexington Ave. IRT #6 to 68th St. Robber baron Henry Clay Frick left his house and art collection to the city, and the museum retains the elegance of his French "Classic Eclectic" chateau. Its grounds will impress you, as will its setting. The Living Hall displays 17th-century furniture, Persian rugs, Holbein portraits, and paintings by El Greco, Rembrandt, Velázquez, and Titian. The courtyard is inhabited by elegant statues surrounding the garden pool and fountain. Lectures Wed. and Thurs. Open Tues.-Sat. 10am-6pm, Sun. 1-6pm. Admission $3, students $1.50. Children under 10 not allowed.

Guggenheim Museum, Fifth Ave. and 89th St. (360-3500). Subway: Lexington Ave. IRT #4, 5 or 6 to 86th St. This controversial construction has been described as a roller rink, a giant turnip, and Midwesterner Frank Lloyd Wright's joke on the Big Apple. Others hail it as the city's most brilliant architectural achievement. The Guggenheim's permanent collection, with noted works by Renoir, Manet, Kandinsky, and Miró, is in the flanking galleries. Open Wed.-Sun. 11am-4:45pm, Tues. 11am-7:45pm. Admission $4.50, seniors, students, and disabled $2.50. Free Tues. 5-7:45pm.

Metropolitan Museum of Art, Fifth Ave. (879-5500), at 82nd St. Subway: Lexington Ave. IRT #4, 5 or 6 to 86th St. If you see only one, see this. The neoclassical marble palace surrounding the original McKim, Mead & White red brick of 1874 is complemented by fountains and graceful glass barns expanding backwards and sideways into Central Park. Superb collection of almost every period through impressionism; particularly strong in Egyptian and non-Western sculpture and European painting. Take a load off your feet in the secluded Japanese Rock Garden. When blockbuster exhibits tour the world they usually stop at the Met—get tickets in advance through Ticketron. Open Tues. 9:30am-8:45pm, Wed.-Sun. 9:30am-5:15pm. Donation.

Museum of Modern Art (MOMA), 11 W. 53rd St. (708-9400), off Fifth Ave. in Midtown. Subway: IND E or F to Fifth Ave. One of the most extensive post-impressionist collections in the world, founded in 1929 by scholar Alfred Barr in response to the Met's reluctance to embrace contemporary art. Cesar Pelli's recent structural glass additions—expanded entrance hall, garden, and gallery space—flood the masterpieces with natural light. Monet's *Water Lily* room is sublime, as is Ross's *Engulfed Cathedral.* The sculpture garden is good for resting and people-watching. Open Fri.-Tues. 11am-6pm, Thurs. 11am-9pm. Admission $6, seniors $2, students $3.50, under 16 free. Donation Thurs. after 5pm.

Queens Museum, Flushing Meadow Park (718-592-5555). Subway: IRT #7 to Willets Point. Located at the site of the 1939 and 1964 World's Fairs, the museum features memorabilia from the fairs in addition to a fine collection of 20th-century art by New Yorkers. Juried exhibits of young talent and special hands-on workshops encourage the continuing development of the plastic arts. Open Tues.-Fri. 10am-5pm, Sat.-Sun. noon-5:30pm. Admission $2.

Whitney Museum of American Art, 945 Madison Ave. (570-3676), at 75th St. Subway: Lexington Ave. IRT #6 to 77th St. This futuristic fortress features a comprehensive collection of contemporary American art with works by Hopper, Soyer, de Kooning, Motherwell, Warhol, and Calder. Gallery talks Tues.-Thurs. at 2:30pm and 3:30pm, Sat.-Sun. at 2pm and 3pm. Museum open Tues. 1-8pm, Wed.-Sat. 11am-5pm, Sun. noon-6pm. Admission $4.50, seniors $2, students and under 12 free. Free Tues. 6-8pm. Three satellite branches offer small exhibits with gallery talks Mon., Wed., and Fri. at 12:30pm: **Phillip Morris Building,** at Park Ave. and 42nd St. (878-2550; open Mon.-Wed. and Fri.-Sat. 11am-6pm, Thurs. 11am-7:30pm); **The Equitable Center,** 7th Ave., between 51st and 52nd St. (554-1113; open Mon.-Wed. and Fri. 11am-6pm, Thurs. 11am-7:30pm, Sat. noon-5pm); and at **Federal Reserve Plaza,** 53 Maiden Lane (943-5655; open Mon.-Fri. 11am-6pm). Entrance to all branch galleries free.

Smaller and Specialized Collections

American Craft Museum, 40 W. 53rd St. (956-3535), across from MOMA. Subway: IND to 53rd St. American crafts presented in 5 ingenious shows per year. Open Tues. 10am-8pm, Wed.-Sun. 10am-5pm. Admission $3.50, seniors and students $1.50. Free Tues. 5-8pm.

Museum of the American Indian, at Broadway and 155th St. (283-2420), in Harlem. Subway: IRT #1 to 157th St. Exercise caution; take a friend. This 1916 *beaux arts* building houses the nation's largest collection of Native American art, including beautiful Eskimo ivory carvings. Admission $3, seniors and students $2. Open Tues.-Sat. 10am-5pm, Sun. 1-5pm.

AT&T Infoquest Center, 550 Madison Ave., at 56th St. (605-5555). High-tech, interactive exhibits help explain the tools on which our society is becoming increasingly dependent. Exhibits focus on lightwave communications, microelectronics, and computer software. Open Tues. 10am-9pm, Wed.-Sun. 10am-6pm. Free.

El Museo del Barrio, 1230 Fifth Ave. (831-7272), in East Harlem. Subway: Lexington Ave. IRT to 103rd St. Safe during the day. The only museum in the U.S. devoted exclusively to the art and culture of Puerto Rico and Latin America. Open Wed.-Sun. 11am-5pm. Admission $2, seniors and students $1.

Museum of Broadcasting, 1 E. 53rd St. (752-7684), at Fifth Ave. Subway: Lexington Ave. IRT to 53rd St. Visitors select and view tapes of classic TV and radio shows on individual consoles. Go before 1pm or expect a long wait, especially on Saturdays, despite the 1-hr. maximum viewing time. Special screenings can be arranged for groups. Monthly retrospectives focus on legendary personalities and landmark shows. Open Wed.-Sat. noon-5pm, Tues. noon-8pm. Donation.

Museum of the City of New York, 103rd St. and Fifth Ave. (534-1034), in East Harlem next door to El Museo del Barrio. Subway: Lexington Ave. IRT to 103rd St. Safe during the day. Paintings, prints, toys, and costumes present the city's humble origins and its grand evolution. The puppet exhibits are especially fun. Open Tues.-Sat. 10am-5pm, Sun. 1-5pm. Donation.

Cooper-Hewitt Museum, 91st St. and Fifth Ave. (860-6868). Subway: Lexington Ave. IRT #4, 5 or 6 to 86th St. Andrew Carnegie's majestic, Georgian mansion is now home to the Smithsonian Institute's decorative arts and design collection. All the special exhibits have considerable flair and the permanent collection of Japanese woodblocks is unique. Open Wed.-Sat. 10am-5pm, Tues. 10am-9pm, Sun. noon-5pm. Admission $3, seniors and students $1.50, under 12 free. Free Tues. 5-9pm.

Museum of Holography, 11 Mercer St. (925-0526), in SoHo. Subway: Lexington Ave. IRT to Canal St. Two fascinating floors of 3-D images from a unique collection. Free lectures and gallery tours (925-0581). Open Tues.-Sun. 11am-6pm. Admission $3.50, seniors and children $2, students $2.50.

IBM Gallery of Science and Art, Madison Ave. at 56th St. (745-6100). Small, select exhibits covering a wide range of art. Previous exhibits have featured 18th-century landscape painters and the use of computers in creating contemporary works. Open Tues.-Fri. 11am-6pm, Sat. 10am-5pm. Free.

International Center of Photography, 1130 Fifth Ave. (860-1777), at 94th St. Subway: Lexington Ave. IRT #6 to 96th St. Housed in a landmark townhouse (1914) built for *New Republic* founder Willard Straight. Historical, thematic, contemporary, and experimental works. Open Wed.-Fri. noon-5pm, Tues. noon-8pm, Sat.-Sun. 11am-6pm. Admission $3, seniors and students $1.50. Free Tues. 5-8pm. Midtown branch at 77 W. 45th St. (869-2155) is open Mon.-Fri. 11am-6pm, Sat. noon-5pm; free.

Intrepid Sea-Air-Space Museum, Pier 86 (245-0072), at 46th St. and Twelfth Ave. Bus: M16, M27, or M106 to W. 46th St. America's mostly militaristic 20th-century technological achievements celebrated in the legendary aircraft carrier. Open Wed.-Sun. 10am-5pm. Admission $6, seniors $5, children $3.25.

Jacques Marchais Center of Tibetan Art, 338 Lighthouse Ave., Staten Island (718-987-3478). Take bus S13 from Staten Island Ferry, turn right and walk up the hill. One of the finest Tibetan collections in the U.S., but the real attractions are the gardens, set on beautifully landscaped cliffs. The center itself is a replica of a Tibetan temple. Open May-Sept. Wed.-Sun. 1-5pm; April and Oct.-Nov. Fri.-Sun. 1-5pm. Admission $2.50, seniors $2, children $1.

Jewish Museum, 1109 Fifth Ave., at 92nd St. (860-1889). Subway: Lexington Ave. IRT to 96th St. A large collection of Judaica, mostly ceremonial artifacts. Open Mon., Wed., and Thurs. noon-5pm, Tues. noon-8pm, Sun. 11am-6pm. Closed Jewish holidays. Admission $4.50, seniors and students $2.50. Free Tues. 5-8pm.

Studio Museum in Harlem, 144 W. 125th St. (864-4500). Subway: Broadway IRT to 125th St. A permanent collection of avant-garde work (mostly by African-Americans) complemented by special exhibits. Open Wed.-Fri. 10am-5pm, Sat.-Sun. 1-6pm. Admission $2, seniors and students $1, seniors free on Wed.

Entertainment

Freebies

The Big Apple sponsors numerous free outdoor events and festivals. In summer, the parks of all five boroughs are graced with performances by cultural ensembles such as the New York Philharmonic, Metropolitan Opera, Shakespeare Festival, Goldman Memorial Band, and Harlem Cultural Festival. Also visible in the parks and on sidewalks are street entertainers. Jugglers, music students from Julliard and the Manhattan School of Music, comedians, breakdancers, and other struggling artists can be found on Columbus Avenue in the low 70s, at Lincoln Center, in front of the Plaza Hotel (59th and 5th Ave.), at Washington Square Park, and in many other spots.

For the scoop on free events, pick up a *Seasonal Calendar* from the visitors bureau (see Practical Information above), or call 360-1333 for a recorded listing. Check out the "Cheap Thrills" column in the *Village Voice* ($1.75) for updates on more obscure free and ultra-cheap weekly happenings (poetry readings, latino jazz, etc.).

Theater

Musicals may be in vogue right now, but drama and comedy, experimental theatre and improv also draw crowds in New York. Broadway Theater—a misnomer for 40 playhouses from 44th to 52nd St. between Broadway and Eighth Ave.—has sung, danced, and wept its way into the American imagination. But with astronomical ticket prices and a proclivity for flamboyant productions of the tried and true, it no longer monopolizes New York's dramatic spotlight. The hundreds of Off- and Off-Off-Broadway productions that highlight the experimental and the innovative are more popular than ever.

New York on Stage has a complete listing of productions, phone numbers, and prices. But you should find all the information you need in the *New York Times, New York Magazine, New Yorker,* or *Village Voice.* **Inside the Big Apple,** a booth next to the TKTS outlet at 47th and Broadway, offers free brochures about each of the current shows.

Broadway

Tickets to a Broadway show run from about $19 (2nd balcony Mon.-Fri.) to $60 (orchestra, Sat. night). When available, $10 standing room tickets (offered on the day of performance when the rest of the house is sold out) are well worth it.

Turn first to **TKTS,** which offers half-price tickets on the day of the performance, according to availability, adding a $1.50 surcharge. (Cash or traveler's checks only.) The number of tickets and plays is limited; go early for the widest choice. People start lining up at least an hour before the windows open. There are offices at 47th and Broadway (354-5800; evening performance tickets sold Mon.-Sat. 3-8pm, Wed. and Sat. matinees 10am-2pm, Sun. performances noon-8pm), and at 2 World Trade Center, on the mezzanine level, which is much less crowded (evening performance tickets sold Mon-Fri. 11am-5:30pm, Sat. 11:30am-3:30pm, matinees and Sun. performances 11am-5:30pm the day before the show).

Another source of discount seats is **Hit Shows,** 690 9th Ave., 8th floor 10036 (581-4211); they distribute coupons toward the purchase of reduced-rate tickets. (Open Mon.-Fri. 9:15am-3:45pm, or send a self-addressed, stamped envelope.) Coupons allowing you to buy two tickets for the price of one are also available at the Convention and Visitors Bureau and at the Times Square Information Center.

To reach the Broadway Theater District, take subway #1, 2, 3, or 7, or subway QB, N, or RR to Times Square, which lies 3 blocks south. The #1 train also stops at 50th St., farther up Broadway. Remember that the dirty Broadway district is crime-ridden, particularly in the late evening after the theater-goers have left the area.

Off- and Off-Off-Broadway

Tickets to the larger Off-Broadway houses are available at both TKTS booths, though the one at 2 World Trade Center only sells them Monday through Saturday 11am to 1pm. For performances at Joseph Papp's **Public Theater,** 425 Lafayette St. (598-7150), take advantage of **QUIXTIX.** The theater saves a quarter of all tickets and offers them for half-price at 6pm on the night of performance. QUIXTIX is also the place to go for free tickets to workshop rehearsals. The Public is perhaps the best, or at least the most consistent, of the Off-Broadway theaters. Even at full price, seeing most shows costs no more than $30.

The **Theater Development Fund (TDF),** 1501 Broadway, New York 10036 (221-0013), is the headquarters for a theater association that sells discount vouchers for Off-Off-Broadway plays, but you must be on their mailing list to be eligible. Two major Off-Off-Broadway theaters stage seasonal works that consistently make it to Broadway later in the season: the **Hudson Guild Theater,** 441 W. 26th St. (760-9816), and the **Playwright's Horizon,** 416 W. 42nd St. (279-4200), on Theater Row, between Ninth and Tenth Ave. Also look on Theater Row for **OFFESTIVAL,** a presentation of experimental plays, performing arts, and poetry, in early June.

The **Brooklyn Academy of Music,** 30 Lafayette Ave., Brooklyn (718-636-4100), a lavish art nouveau theater, presents revivals for just a bit less than those on Broadway ($15-35) and offers its own fall-spring season of major avant-garde-ish theater, dance, and music. The **Brooklyn Arts Cultural Association,** 200 Eastern Parkway (718-783-4469), also presents low-cost productions, and sponsors free performances in Brooklyn parks in summer.

Joseph Papp's **New York Shakespeare Festival** (598-7100) stages two free productions at the **Delacorte Theater** (861-7277) in Central Park, one late June through mid-July, and one during August. To reach the theater, enter the park from Central Park West at 81st St., or from Fifth Ave. at 79th St. Performances usually begin at 8pm Tuesday through Sunday. Tickets are distributed free at 6:15pm for the 8pm performance; be sure to get there at least four to six hours in advance. The 1989 season boasted Michelle Pfeiffer, Gregory Hines, and Jeff Goldblum in *Twelfth Night.*

Opera and Dance

The fulcrum of New York culture is **Lincoln Center,** at Broadway and 66th St. (877-1800). For a schedule of events, write Lincoln Center Calendar, 140 W. 65th St. 10023, or call the Lincoln Center Library Museum (870-1630).

The **Metropolitan Opera Company** (362-6000) is opera's highest expression. Its Lincoln Center stage is the size of a football field. The performances are excellent and its principals are among the greatest in the world. During the regular season (Sept.-May Mon.-Sat.), if you don't mind risking a nosebleed from the heights to which you'll ascend, you can get upper balcony seats for $17, but standing room in the orchestra is a steal at $10. In summer, watch for free concerts in city parks (362-6000).

At right angles to the Met, the **New York City Opera** (870-5570), under the direction of Beverly Sills, provides adequate performances of the warhorses—many in translation—and of new American works. The success of its recently-introduced English "supertitles" has led other companies to adopt them. "City" now offers a summer season and keeps its ticket prices low year-round ($12-47, standing room back row top balcony $3). Call to check the availability of rush tickets on the night before the performance you want to attend, then wait in line the next morning.

The **Light Opera of Manhattan (LOOM),** 316 E. 91st St., between First and Second Ave. (831-2000), offers Gilbert and Sullivan and other operettas. (Tickets $17.50-20, students $12.) Check the papers for performances of the **Amato Opera Company,** 319 Bowery (228-8200), and the **Bel Canto Company,** which perform in churches around the city.

The late great George Balanchine's **New York City Ballet,** the oldest in the country, alternates with the city opera for the use of the Lincoln Center's New York State Theater (877-4700), performing December through January and again in May and June. (Tickets $7-42, standing room $4.) City Ballet features works by both its founding father and current director Jerome Robbins and has maintained great success. **American Ballet Theater** (477-3030), Balanchine's greatest rival, dances at the Met during the late spring and for about two weeks in summer. Under Mikhail Baryshnikov's guidance, ABT's eclectic repertoire has ranged from the Kirov grand-style Russian ballet to experimental American post-modern choreography. The **Joffrey** ballet performs in the **City Center,** 131 W. 55th St. (581-7907), a doomed, Byzantine playhouse outside Lincoln Center.

The **Alvin Ailey American Dance Theater** (997-1980) bases its repertoire of modern dance on jazz, spirituals, and contemporary music. It is the grandest integrated company in the world, and tours internationally. The company performs at the **City Center** in December. Tickets ($15-40) are difficult to obtain. Write or call City Center weeks in advance, if possible. The **Martha Graham Dance Co.,** 316 E. 63rd St. (838-5886), performs original Graham pieces during their October New York season. She revolutionized 20th-century dance with her psychological, rather than narrative, approach to characters. (Tickets $15-40.) Look also for the seasons of the **Merce Cunningham Dance Company,** the **Dance Theater of Harlem,** and the **Paul Taylor Dance Company,** usually in spring.

Half-price tickets for many music and dance events can be purchased on the day of performance at **Bryant Park,** 42nd St. (382-2323), between Fifth and Sixth Ave.

Music

In Lincoln Center's Avery Fisher Hall (874-2424), the **New York Philharmonic,** under Zubin Mehta, plays everything from Bach to Bax, Schubert to Schoenberg. Avery Fisher's new interior, designed by Philip Johnson, is an acoustical wonder. The Philharmonic's season lasts from September through May, and jazz and classical musicians visit the rest of the year. (Tickets $7.50-35.) Senior citizen and student-rush tickets ($5) go on sale Tuesday and Thursday evenings a half-hour before the curtain rises. "Mostly Mozart" concerts are performed July through August and feature such artists as Jean Pierre Rampal. (Tickets $9-18.50.)

Carnegie Hall, Seventh Ave. at 57th St. (247-7800), one of the greatest musical auditoriums in the world, attracts opera singers, jazz singers, instrumental soloists, and symphony orchestras. (Tickets usually $15-30, but prices vary according to performance.)

Some of the best music in New York is free. In fall, call the **Cloisters** (923-3700) for scheduled concerts of medieval music. The students at the world-famous **Juilliard School** (799-5000), at Lincoln Center, give free concerts from October through June on Fridays at 8pm and often on weekdays too. In summer, free music is easy to find. **South Street Seaport** has outdoor concerts Wednesday, Thursday, Friday, and Sunday in July and August. Midtown, both **Citicorp** and **Rockefeller Center** sponsor free concerts; Citicorp's often take place at lunch hour Monday through Friday. There are free, outdoor concerts at Rockefeller Center's **Exxon Park,** between 49th and 50th, Thursdays at 12:30pm. Lastly, the **New York Philharmonic** (877-1800) gives several free performances on the **Great Lawn** in Central Park in summer.

Movies

Hollywood may make the movies, but New York popularizes them. The array of films shown in New York is incredible; even the most prestigious festivals pale by comparison. Movies tend to open in New York weeks before they're distributed across the country, and the response of Manhattan audiences and critics often shapes the success or failure of a film nationwide. Just grab a copy of any newspaper for an overview of the selection. Magazines such as *New York* and the *New Yorker* provide plot summaries and evaluations in their listings as well.

Museums like the Metropolitan and MOMA show artsy flicks downstairs, as does the New York Historical Society. The **68th Street Playhouse,** on 3rd Ave. (734-0302), and the **Paris,** 5th Ave. and 58th St. (688-2013), specialize in first-run foreign films. For cinematic exposure to Chinese culture, go to the **Sun Sing Theater,** 75 E. Broadway (619-0493). The **Thalia Soho,** 16 Vandam St. (675-0498), features classic foreign and American revivals, as does **Theatre 80 Saint Mark's,** 80 St. Mark's Place (254-7400).

For an inspiring movie-going experience, try the **Ziegfeld Theatre,** 141 W. 54th St. (765-7600). One of the last grand movie houses that hasn't been sliced up into a "multiplex," the Ziegfeld offers standard box-office attractions.

Political film festivals are hot subjects for the film room of the 92nd St. **"Y,"** 1395 Lexington Ave. (427-6000). Between LaGuardia and Thompson at 144 Bleecker St. (674-2560), you'll find **Bleecker Street Cinema,** which specializes in experimental movies. The **8th Street Playhouse** (674-6515) between MacDougal and Sixth Ave., features music films by day and cult classics by night. Its midnight series includes the *Rocky Horror Picture Show* on Friday and Saturday, a campy classic where your fellow movie goers literally put on the best show ($6).

For a real deal, check out the library. All **New York Public Libraries** show free films ranging from documentaries to classics to last year's blockbuster. Screening times may be a bit erratic, but you can't beat the price.

TV

Yes, TV. New York is the place to trade an insult with David Letterman or ask a sensitive question of Phil Donahue's guests. Several TV shows film in the Big Apple before a live audience. To join the starstruck throng, call the guest relations office at the networks about ticket availability. (NBC 664-4444; ABC 887-7777; CBS 975-4321.) Tickets for seats are often hard to come by, but are distributed by the networks without charge. Plan ahead.

Bars and Clubs

There is lots and lots to do in New York from sundown to sunup. Bars stay open until 4am, and clubs until dawn. But (there is always a but), many are expensive, and drinks' prices are outrageous. Your Gin and Tonic is going to cost you—$5 and up. Further, many bars and clubs are exclusive; if you don't have the "look," expect to wait on line indefinitely. Wearing black and/or being a single female should up your odds of getting through. On the optimistic side, there's always another place to try, whatever the hour might be. Cover charges vary during the week—Fridays and Saturdays are the most expensive (up to $20 per person). These are also the nights on which clubs will be most packed with out-of-towners. For lower covers and the most entertaining crowds, try "clubbing" early in the week, particularly on Wednesdays. The New York Convention and Visitors Bureau and Village music stores often have complimentary or reduced fare passes to clubs piled right by the register.

Although *New York* magazine, the *Village Voice,* and *After Dark* list who's playing, showtimes, locations, and sometimes cover charges, you should always call ahead to check. The most extensive listings can be found in *The Music Exchange* and *Good Times,* two pop-music newspapers, available at most stores on **Music Row,** on 48th St. between Sixth and Seventh Ave. Manhattan's nightlife isn't concentrated on a single street or strip; it spans the island from SoHo to Columbia University. For students, the New York University/Greenwich Village area is a good starting point. For those with a little more cash, First and Second Avenue in the 60s and 70s are sprinkled with chic, sleek clubs. A preponderance of gay bars and discos can be found in the West Village along Greenwich Ave. and further west.

Dance Clubs

M.K., 204 Fifth Ave. (779-1340), at 27th St. Subway: Broadway BMT to 28th St. The newest and the hottest. Four floors, each with its own decor, entice glitterati with snob appeal designed to imitate an old "gentleman's club." Small dance floor but plenty of action elsewhere. Open daily 7:30pm for dinner, 11pm-2am for dancing. Cover Sun.-Thurs. $5, Fri.-Sat. $15.

Nell's, 246 W. 14th St. (675-1567), between 7th and 8th Ave. Subway: 7th Ave. IRT to 14th St. The tacky neighborhood belies the sumptuous opulence of the huge Victorian-style sitting room inside. Overstuffed chairs, chandeliers, and bejeweled Beautiful People upstairs; angular, often-crowded dance floor downstairs. Open daily 10pm-4am. Cover Sun.-Thurs. $5, Fri.-Sat. $10.

Spo-Dee-O-Dee, 565 W. 23rd St. (206-1990). There's a long antique bar here, where you can listen to the live music or look at the most beautiful of the Beautiful People. Two sets, blues and rock, dancing in between. Cover $10, plus 2 drink minimum. Open daily 6pm-4am.

The Boy Bar, 15th St. Marks Place (674-6459), off 3rd Ave. Subway: Lexington IRT of Astor Place. Popular gay club featuring the occasional mud-wrestling competition. Long, central bar gives the club its name. Open Thurs.-Sat. 8pm-4am. Cover $5.

The Pyramid Club, Avenue A near 7th St. (420-1590). Subway: Lexington IRT to Astor Pl. Transvestite punk and 60s lighting. If you're into "unusual," you'll fit right in. Avant-garde performances nightly. Open daily 4pm-4am. Cover: Sun.-Thurs. $5 after 10:30pm, Fri.-Sat. $10.

CBGB & OMFUG, 315 Bowery (982-4052), at Bleecker. Subway: Lexington IRT to Bleecker. The initials stand for "country, bluegrass, blues, and other music for uplifting gourmandizers," but almost since its beginning in 1976, this club has been America's home for punk. It now features foreign bands and pop, in addition to hard-core. Mon. is audition night. Hard-core matinee Sun. at 3pm admits age 16 and over. Open daily 9pm-4am. Cover $5-10.

Cave Cavern, 24 First Ave. (529-9665), between 1st and 2nd St. Restaurant with dance floor in an old Roman bath. Very trendy. Open Tues.-Sun. 6pm-4am. Cover $5 on weekends.

The Works, 428 Columbus Ave. (799-7365), at 81st St. Popular gay and lesbian bar that's dark, but lit for that effect. 4 video screens and music, friendly crowd, but no dancing. Open daily 2pm-4am, no cover.

The Monster, 80 Grove St. (924-3557), near 7th Ave. Gay and lesbian dance club with 2 floors; the lower one has popular music, the upper one holds a piano bar. Open daily 4pm-4am. Cover $5 on weekends.

Limelight, 660 Sixth Ave. (807-7850), between 20th and 21st St. Subway: Broadway IRT to 23rd St. A "house of sin" located in an old church. Ms. Gulch once poured herself a man on the altar. If you can handle drinking in the pulpit, you'll have a great time. Live acts tend to be very lively. Open daily 10pm-4am. Cover Sun.-Thurs. $15, Fri.-Sat. $18.

Palladium, 126 E. 14th St. (473-7171). Subway: Lexington IRT to Union Sq. Once the No. 1 in chic, Palladium has lost its preeminent status but still draws crowds, and with good reason. Its several levels are embellished by the works of NYC artists and psychedelic bathrooms. Open Thurs.-Sat. 10pm-4am. Cover Thurs.-Sat. $20.

Music/Bars

Apollo Theater, 253 W. 125th St. (749-5838). Subway: Broadway IRT to 125th St. Use caution in the neighborhood. This historic Harlem landmark has heard the likes of Duke Ellington, Count Basie, Ella Fitzgerald, Lionel Hampton, Billie Holliday, and Sarah Vaughn. In his zoot-suit days, Malcolm X shined shoes here. Now undergoing a revival. Show tickets $5-30. Arrive at least a ½ hr. early for cheap tickets. Amateur night starts Wed. at 7:30pm. Call the theater to check what's playing.

Bottom Line, 15 W. 4th St. (228-7880), at Mercer St. in Greenwich Village. Subway: Broadway IRT to W. 4th St. Offers a mixed bag of music and entertainment—anything from jazz to country to theater. Always top-flight musicians. Shows Sun.-Thurs. at 8pm and 11pm, Fri-Sat. at 8:30pm and 11:30pm. Tickets $13-15. Double proof of age (21 and over) required, but some all-age performances.

Bradley's, 70 University Pl. (473-9700), at 11th St., in the north Village. Subway: Lexington IRT to Union Sq. Superb jazz in a wood-paneled restaurant. Usually crowded. $5 drink minimum at tables, no minimum at the bar. Music daily 9:45pm-4am.

Dan Lynch, 221 Second Ave. (677-0911), at 14th St. Subway: Lexington IRT to Union Sq. Dark smoky room with Casablanca fan, long bar, and "all blues, all the time." Pool table in back. Open daily 8am-4am; blues (and jazz) starts at 10pm. Jam session Sat.-Sun. 4:30-9pm. Cover Fri.-Sat. $5.

The Lone Star Cafe, Fifth Ave. (245-2950), at 13th St. Subway: Lexington IRT to Union Sq. The entertainment is authentic country-western, but the audience is straight out of the *New Yorker.* Lots of fun, even for Texans who didn't buy their boots at Bloomie's. Shows generally at 9:15pm and 11:30pm. Cover $10-17.

Michael's Pub, 211 E. 55th St. (758-2272), off Third Ave. Subway: Lexington IRT to 59th or 51st St. Woody Allen played his clarinet here instead of picking up his 3 Academy Awards for *Annie Hall.* He still sneaks in some Mon. nights. Sets Mon. at 9pm and 11pm, Tues.-Sat. at 9:30pm and 11:30pm. Open Mon.-Fri. noon-1am, Sat. 6pm-1am. Cover $15-25. 2-drink minimum at the tables, but no minimum at the bar.

O'Lunney's, 915 Second Ave. (751-5470), at 48th St. Subway: Lexington IRT to 51st St. Friendly neighborhood hangout featuring country music with an Irish twist. Music from 9:30pm-2:30am. Open Mon.-Sat. 11am-2am. Cover $3 at tables.

S.O.B. (Sounds of Brazil), 204 Varick St. (243-4940), at the corner of Seventh Ave. and Houston St., in the Village. Subway: Broadway IRT to Houston. Lots of Latin music and dancing until dawn. Open Tues.-Thurs. 7pm-2:30am, Fri.-Sat. 7pm-4am. Cover $15-18, or $10 with $15 dinner minimum.

Sweet Basil, 88 Seventh Ave. (242-1785), at Christopher St. Subway: Broadway IRT to Christopher St. Village hot spot frequented by jazz legends. Shows at 10pm, 11:30pm, and 1:30am. Open daily noon-2am. Cover $12 weekdays, $15 weekends during shows, plus $6 drink minimum.

Sweetwater's, 170 Amsterdam Ave. (873-4100), at 68th St. Subway: Broadway IRT to 66th St. Cool jazz blended with Columbus Ave. area chic. Shows Mon.-Fri. at 9pm and 11pm, Sat.-Sun. at 9pm and midnight, also downstairs 6pm. Open Mon.-Fri. noon-4am, Sat.-Sun. 4pm-4am. Cover $10 plus 2-drink minimum downstairs; $10 plus $10 dinner minimum upstairs.

Village Gate, 160 Bleecker St. (475-5120), near Thompson St. Subway: 6th Ave. INTS to W. 4th St. Upstairs, downstairs, and terrace offer comedy, jazz, and *salsa* to revive the dead. Jazz jams Sat.-Sun. at 2pm. Open daily 6pm-2am. Cover upstairs and downstairs $3-8; 1-2 drink minimum on the terrace.

Village Vanguard, 178 Seventh Ave. (255-4037), south of 11th St. Subway: Broadway IRT to 14th St. Features big-name performers in a dank basement where the atmosphere drips from the ceiling. Restaurant and Off-Broadway theater above ground. Shows nightly at 10pm, 11:30pm, and 1am. Cover $12, $6 drink minimum on weekdays, $7.50 on weekends.

Comedy

Catch a Rising Star, 1487 First Ave. (794-1906), near 77th St. Subway: Lexington IRT to 77th St. Local New Yorkers and West Coast comics play to a youthful crowd. Shows Sun.-Thurs. at 9pm, Fri. at 8:30pm and 11pm, Sat. at 7:30pm, 10pm, and 12:30am. Mon. is audition night. Cover $8 on weekdays, $12 on weekends. 2-drink minimum. Make reservations after 5pm the previous day.

Comedy Cellar, 117 MacDougal St. (254-3630). Subterranean annex of the artsy Olive Tree Cafe (see Food). Shows Sun.-Thurs. at 9pm, Fri. at 9pm and 11:30pm, Sat. at 8pm, 10pm, and midnight. Open daily 9pm-2am. Cover: Sun.-Thurs. $5, plus 2-drink minimum; Fri.-Sat. $10, plus $7 drink minimum. Make reservations for the weekend.

Improvisation, 358 W. 44th St. (765-8268), between Eighth and Ninth Ave. Subway: Broadway BMT to Times Square. Celebrating 25 years in the Big Apple. Shows Sun.-Thurs. at 9pm, Fri. at 9pm and 11:30pm, Sat. at 8pm, 10pm, and 12:40pm. Cover: Mon.-Thurs. $8, plus $8 drink or food minimum; Fri.-Sat. $11, plus $9 minimum.

Stand Up NY, 236 W. 78th St. (595-0850), at Broadway. Subway: Broadway IRT to 72nd St. Fun, often with a political edge. Shows Sun.-Thurs. at 9pm, Fri. at 8:30pm and 11:30pm, Sat. at 8pm, 10pm, and 12:15am. Cover: Sun.-Thurs. $7, Fri. $10, Sat. $12. 2-drink minimum.

Shopping

On every New York street corner there's something to buy. Peddlers sell earrings, stockings, elixers, and gimmicks that can best be labeled "etc."; department stores sell designer gold brooches and Calvin Klein underwear. As a rule, most things will be expensive, but shopping successfully is fortunately less a question of luck than of knowing where to hunt for what.

In Soho, huge **Canal Jean,** the funkiest and one of the cheapest stores in New York, 504 Broadway (226-1130), is stuffed with neon ties, baggy pants, and silk smoking jackets. Poke around the bargain bins out front. (Open Sun.-Thurs. 10am-8pm, Fri.-Sat. 10am-9pm.) On weekends, check out the flea market at the western end of Canal for honest-to-god antiques along with the usual funky junk. Back up Broadway, in Greenwich Villge, the **Antique Boutique,** 712 Broadway near Astor Place (460-8830), sells both stunning vintage clothing and interesting new designs. (10% discount for students with ID. Open Mon.-Sat. 10:30am-midnight, Sun. noon-8pm).

Greenwich Village is full of little boutiques. The best values are leather goods. Try the shoe stores along 8th St. between Fifth and Sixth Ave., the saddlebag shops on W. 4th St., and the handmade sandal stores off Bleecker St. in the West Village. For mainstream fashion with a funky flair and antique clothing, check out **Reminiscence,** 74 Fifth Ave. near 13th St. (243-2292, open Mon.-Sat. 11:30am-8pm, Sun. 1-6pm). **Forty-Seventh Street Photo,** 45th St. (260-4410), between Fifth Ave. and Ave. of the Americas, usually has the best prices for electronic gadgets of all kinds. (Open Mon.-Thurs. 9am-6pm, Fri. 9am-2pm, Sun. 9am-5pm.)

New York's selection of books and records is outstanding. **Barnes and Noble,** 105 Fifth Ave., at 18th St. (807-0099; open Mon.-Fri. 9:30am-8pm, Sat. 9:30am-6:30pm, Sun. 11am-6pm) and at other locations, has an enormous, comprehensive selection of books and classical records at discount prices. The downtown branch also has the widest selection of textbooks in New York and has a sale annex across the street with four floors of bargain bestsellers and "books for a buck." The monarch of used bookstores is the gargantuan **Strand,** 828 Broadway at 12th St. (473-1452), with its surrounding smaller establishments. Strand stocks rare and out-of-print books and will search out obscure titles for you if they're not on hand in the store. (Open Mon.-Fri. 9:30am-9:20pm, Sat. 9:30am-6:30pm, Sun. 11am-6pm.) The largest record store in New York is **Tower Records,** 1961 Broadway at 66th St. (799-2500), and 692 Broadway at 4th St. (505-1500; open daily 9am-midnight); near the latter branch are superb used record dealers who also sell bootlegs and imports, such as **Bleecker Bob's Golden Oldies,** 118 W. 3rd St. (475-9677, open Sun.-Thurs.

noon-1am, Fri.-Sat. noon-3am), and **CBGB Record Canteen,** 313 Bowery (677-0455; open daily noon-2am.)

Buy designer clothes second-hand at **Encore,** Madison at 82nd St. (879-2850; open Mon.-Wed. and Fri.-Sat. 10:30am-6pm, Thurs. 10:30am-7pm, Sun. 12:30-6pm), or at **Michael's,** on Madison between 79th and 80th (737-7273; open in summer Mon.-Fri. 9:30am-6pm; rest of the year Tues.-Sat.). In the elegant old department stores such as **Gucci's, Saks, Bergdorf's,** and **Bonwit Teller,** all on Fifth Avenue in the fifties, the price of an umbrella may be twice the cost of your vacation, but the ambiance is free. Wonder at the window displays of **Tiffany's, Van Cleef and Arpels,** and **F.A.O. Schwartz,** the Disneyland of toy stores, all in the same chic Fifth Avenue region. During the holiday seasons shoppers stand in line between Thanksgiving and New Year's to marvel at the spectacular window displays in Fifth Avenue stores. At 60th St. and Third Ave. is **Bloomingdale's,** ("Bloomies"), a crowded department store which mass-markets expensive chic.

No shopping spree is complete without a visit to the world's largest department store, **Macy's,** 151 W. 34th St. (695-4400). Covering a square city block, Macy's not only sells everything under the sun, but also offers free exhibits and special events. Winter brings on an entire floor of magic in Santaland, and late August heralds the Tap-o-Mania, a parade down 34th St. of almost 4000 simultaneously tapping pairs of feet.

Long Island

Three million people live in Long Island's many communities—urban Hempstead, rural Holtsville, impoverished Roosevelt, and haughty Locust Valley. The suburbs sprawl over an astonishing 40 miles, clear to the middle of Suffolk county, but beyond them are rural towns that seem to belong in New England. Beautiful beaches lie on the south side, while luxurious mansions dot the landscape to the north. The former have long been public property, and in recent years, many of the latter have been made accessible to the general public. Both are worth seeing—the natural and the cultivated—you need only choose your beauty.

Although Queens and Brooklyn are contiguous with "The Island," the Queens-Nassau line marks a shift in landscape that emphasizes the boundary. Out here people read *Newsday,* not the *Times* or *Daily News;* their hockey team is the Islanders, not the Rangers; and they revel in their privileged position as a neighbor to, not a component of, the great metropolis. Fortunately for the visitor, the Island is cheaply and easily accessible from Manhattan. Nearly all your transit needs will be served by some combination of the **Long Island Rail Road (LIRR)** (516-794-5477), which operates out of Penn Station in Manhattan, and the **Metropolitan Suburban Bus Authority (MSBA)** (516-222-1000), which operates daytime buses in eastern Queens, Nassau, and Western Suffolk. Depending on where you go and what time you leave, train fare will vary from $7 round-trip (for nearby suburbs in non-rush hour times) to $25 round-trip (for the more distant spots, during rush-hour). **Suffolk Transit** (516-360-5700) takes over farther east. Bikes may be carried on LIRR by permit only.

Long Island's **area code** is 516.

Suburban Long Island: Nassau and Western Suffolk Counties

The North Shore of Long Island was once known as the "Gold Coast" because of the string of mansions built by 19th-century industrialists in the hills overlooking Long Island Sound. Many of these houses have been turned into museums, and the grounds that have been spared from developers are now gardens, arboretums, or nature preserves open to the public.

From west to east, some principal North Shore sites are: **Falaise** (883-1612), in Sands Point Park and Preserve, the former Guggenheim estate (1-hr. guided tour every ½ hr; admission $2, children under 12 not allowed; open Sat.-Wed. 10am-3:30pm); **Old Westbury Gardens,** on Old Westbury Rd. (333-0048), where the splendor of the main house and its collection of painting and sculpture is matched only by that of the formal English gardens outside (open late April-late Oct. Wed.-Sun. 10am-5pm; tours available; admission to the house $3, to the garden and parking $4.50, combined tickets for seniors $3.50); **Sagamore Hill,** on Cove Neck Rd. near Oyster Bay (922-4447), the summer home of Theodore Roosevelt, now jammed with Teddy memorabilia (open daily 9:30am-5pm; admission $1, seniors and children free); the **Vanderbilt Museum** (262-7858) and the **Vanderbilt Planetarium,** on Little Neck Rd. (262-7800), in Centerport, in the Hispano-Moroccan Vanderbilt mansion (museum open Tues.-Sat. 10am-4pm, Sun. noon-5pm; admission $4, seniors and students $3, children $2); and the **Museums at Stony Brook,** at Main St. and State 25A (751-0066), which include works by William Sidney Mount, a carriage museum, and period buildings (open Wed.-Sat. 10am-5pm, Sun. noon-5pm; admission $4, seniors $3, students $2.75, children $2).

In Central Nassau, near Nassau Community College, the **Cradle of Aviation Museum** (222-1190) documents Long Island's role in the history of aviation from Lindbergh (who took off from Roosevelt Field, Garden City) to the Lunar Module (which was built at Calverton by Grumman). There are two hangars filled with planes. (Free guided tours. Open April-Oct. Fri.-Sun. noon-5pm.) Take Meadowbrook Parkway to Stewart Ave. W., and follow signs to Nassau Community College. Or take MSBA #16 or 35 to the College from Hempstead Station for $1. (LIRR $3.50 to Hempstead from Penn Station.)

The south shore of Long Island is protected by barrier islands that constitute some of the finest white sand beaches in the northeast. **Jones Beach** (785-1600) is the most famous of these and closest to the city—therefore it is also the most crowded. Take the Long Island Expressway to Grand Central/Northern State Pkwy. and then either Meadowbrook Pkwy. or Wantagh Pkwy. to the beach. Wantagh Parkway is farther east but less congested on beach days. (Memorial Day-Labor Day parking $4.) The south shore is also home to three large contiguous state parks in Bay Shore and Oakdale. **Heckscher State Park,** on Heckscher Pkwy. (581-2100), has swimming, winter sports, and camping. ($4 per car.) **Bayard Cutting Arboretum,** on Montauk Hwy. in Oakdale (581-1002), offers hours of nature walks. (Open Wed.-Sun. 10am-5pm. Admission $3 per car.) The **Connetquot River Preserve** (581-1005), still farther north, has nearly 4000 acres of hiking and riding trails. (Admission $1. Call 1 day ahead to make a reservation, or obtain a permit by writing to the Long Island State Parks and Recreation Commission, Administration Headquarters Permit Dept., P.O. Box 247, Babylon 11702.) The staff leads guided nature walks on weekends and cross-country skiing in winter. (Open Tues.-Sun. 6am-4:30pm.) These three parks form the southern end of the 34-mile **Greenbelt Trail** that runs all the way across Long Island to **Sunken Meadow State Park** on the Sound. Call 234-3112 for information on hiking or camping along the trail. For bicycling information, contact the **Long Island Bicycle Club** (628-2590; 7:30-8:30am and 4-5:30pm), which leads informal rides and can direct you to local clubs.

Heckscher, across from the Bay Shore LIRR Station (from Penn Station 70 min., off-peak $5.25), is convenient to **Fire Island Ferries** (665-5045), which run to the affluent communities on the west end of **Fire Island,** the largest and most famous of the barrier islands. (Round-trip $9.50, under 11 $4.75. Pedestrians only; bikes go on the freight boat.) Farther west are two more ferries. **Sayville Ferry Company** (589-0810) runs to **Sailor's Haven Visitor Center** ($7.50 round-trip) on Fire Island National Seashore, and to the predominantly gay summer communities of Cherry Grove and The Pines ($9 round-trip). Follow the signs from Rte. 27 or the Sayville LIRR ($5.25). From Patchogue, the **Davis Park Ferry Company** (475-1665), directly opposite the Patchogue LIRR station ($5.75), will take you and your bike to the campground at **Watch Hill Visitors Center.** (One way $4.25, seniors $4, children $2.50, bikes $2 extra.) Reservations are taken Fridays from 9am to 11am, and are recommended in the summer. (Campground open May 15-Oct. 15. Free.)

Since the LIRR runs all night from most major suburban stations, there is little reason to sleep in suburbia. Lodging starts at $70-80 for a double.

Some generic advice on Long Island dining—**delis** are always a good, cheap take-out option; and Long Island **diners** bear little resemblance to their greasy, classic cousins, offering an astonishing variety of good, home-cooked food. Meals start at $4, and menus often run several pages.

The North Fork

The North Fork, center of the oyster and whaling industries at the turn of the century, is now a mixture of farmland, pebbled beaches, and idyllic small towns. Only accessible by ferry (8 minute-ride), Shelter Island recreates New England in a lush woodland setting and is a perfect place for an afternoon drive. The beaches on Long Island Sound, less crowded than the South Shore, are wonderful places to swim, sail, and fish. Many of the towns have historical societies and maintain one or two small museums or restorations.

East along the North Fork, several wineries take advantage of the fact that local climate and soil conditions rival Napa Valley's. Their wines are the real thing, too—not "New York State" wine, that fruity grape juice which fills wine coolers. Local winery tours and wine tastings give you a chance to be the judge. Technically, you must be 21 or over to try the wine but carding is on a very casual basis. **Hargrave Vineyards** (734-5111), on the North Rd. (Rte. 48) in Cutchogue, is the oldest (founded in the 70s) and, some say, the best of the wineries, though overpriced. (Free tours May-Dec. Sat.-Sun. at 2pm. Open daily 10am-5:30pm.) **Pindar** (734-6200) on the Main Rd. (Rte. 25) in Peconic, produced two of the wines chosen for George Bush's Inauguration. It's also friendlier and more down-home than Hargrave. (Free tours every hr. Open April 1-Dec. 31 daily 11am-6pm.)

You have to look hard during the summer to find reasonably priced accommodations in North Fork. Most comfortable doubles start at $60 and can rise to an outlandish $140. The best option is the **Vineyard Motor Inn,** on Main Rd. in Jamesport, 5 miles from Riverhead or Mattituck. (Doubles $55-75.) The cheapest choice on Shelter Island is the **Chequit Inn,** on Grand St. (749-0018), a run-down, 150-year-old inn that overlooks the bay with 44 old-fashioned singles from $45, doubles from $53. **Camping** remains the cheapest choice in summer, but you must be 21, married, or accompanied by parents or guardians to use New York State Campgrounds. **Wildwood State Park,** P.O. Box 518, Wading River 11792 (929-4314), on Long Island Sound, is convenient to the North Shore and rarely fills, but come early on Friday for summer weekends. It's located on Rte. 25A, 5 miles northwest of Riverhead, within 25 miles of most east end attractions. (Campsites $9-10.) **Eastern Long Island Kampgrounds,** P.O. Box 89, Greenport 11944 (477-0022), on the North Rd. in Greenport, offers tent sites, pool, and organized activity nightly. (Open April-Oct. Sites $17. Reservations required.) Crashers should be alert to the local hunting season (usually late fall to winter).

Dining on the east end need not deplete your wallet if you exercise a little resourcefulness. **Bob's Fish Market and Restaurant,** Rte. 114 (749-0830), 2 miles south of the North Ferry, serves hearty dinners of fresh-caught fish ($7-12). (Open daily 5-9pm.) The **Hellenic Snack Bar,** on North Rd. (477-0138), at the Greenport/East Marion line, 3 miles east of Sound Beach, is a popular Greek family restaurant. (Sandwiches from $5. Dinners $8.50-12. Open daily 8am-10pm.) On Shelter Island, the **Chequit,** in the Chequit Inn (see above), is good for breakfast ($6-10; served Mon.-Fri. 8-11am, Sat.-Sun. 8am-noon), but dinner is too expensive.

Bike rentals are available on the North Fork at **Country Time Cycles,** on Main Rd. (298-8700), in Mattituck. (10-speeds $15 1st day, $10 each additional day, $50 per week. Credit card deposit required.) Or try **Piccozzi's Service Station,** Bridge St. (Rte. 114) (749-0045), Shelter Island Heights, a 10-minute walk from the North

Ferry. (For 8 hr.: 3-speeds $18, 12-speeds $19; either $70 per week. $250 deposit or credit card imprint.)

The LIRR serves Riverhead and the North Fork two to four times per day (fare $12.25, off-peak $8.25). **Suffolk Transit's** (360-5700) S-92 bus runs from Greenport to E. Hampton and back, once in the morning and five times every afternoon; it connects with the LIRR at Riverhead at noon and 5pm each day. The 9A bus, a North Fork local, makes connections with the Orient Point Ferry (323-2743) to New London, CT. (Fares on the S-92 and 9A 90¢.) **Sunrise Express** provides summer bus service to the North Fork from New York City and Queens. (Call 477-1200; 800-527-7709 outside Suffolk County. Fare $15 one way, $28 round-trip.)

The South Fork

The sandy peninsula of the South Fork is more popular than the North Fork in summer. The spectacular oceanfront homes of New York's elite, resort hotels, and parklands await the droves of Manhattanites and other wealthy tourists who descend on the Hamptons and Montauk in July and August. Consequently, the area becomes emphatically chic and crowded. Check *The Hamptons* magazine (free) for information on art exhibits, nightlife, and music on the bustling South Fork; Westhampton and Southampton are particularly lively.

As on the North Fork, fascinating museums and historical sites can be found in almost every town. One of the best of these museums is the **Long Island Whaling Museum,** on Main St. (725-0770), 2 blocks south of **Sag Harbor,** on the first floor of the Masonic Temple. (Open May-Sept. Mon.-Sat. 10am-5pm, Sun. 1-5pm. Admission $2, seniors and children 75¢.) Tiny Sag Harbor once rivaled New York as an international port. Around the corner on Garden St., you'll find the **Custom House** (941-9444), the restored 1791 private home of Thomas Dering, First Collector of the port of Sag Harbor. (Open Memorial Day-Labor Day Tues.-Sun. 10am-5pm. Admission $1.50, children $1.) For a taste of modern culture, **Guild Hall,** 158 Main St. (324-0806), in **East Hampton,** a few blocks west of town, offers contemporary art exhibits, lectures, and panel series. (Open daily 10am-5pm. Donation.) The **Parrish Art Museum,** 25 Job's Lane (283-2118), in **Southampton,** ½ mile south of the railroad station in the heart of town, offers first-rate contemporary art exhibits, films, and jazz concerts. (Open Mon. and Thurs.-Sat. 10am-5pm, Sun. 1-5pm. Donation.)

Vineyards on the South Fork are beginning to achieve recognition. Of these, **Bridgehampton Winery** (537-3155), off the main road in Bridgehampton, is one of the most successful; it has garnered several awards since its first harvest in 1982. (Tours given on the hr. complete with wine tastings; $1. Open Sun.-Fri. noon-5pm, Sat. 11am-5pm.)

In summer, you'll have to compete with many wealthy New Yorkers for even the most modest lodgings; and from November to April, almost everything is closed. There are some low-season deals, though, especially in Montauk Village. The absolute best deal on the east end is the **Montauket,** on Tuthill Rd., (668-5992), 1 mile north of Montauk Village. (Go north on Edgemere Ave. and turn left on Tuthill Rd.) This place has a friendly staff and a location close to the railroad station. Dilapidated, but not unhygienic doubles cost $40. This small hotel fills up quickly. (Open June-Sept.) The **Royal Oaks Hotel,** on Rte. 114 (725-0714), just south of Sag Harbor, offers simple, clean doubles for $45 from April to late September. Camp in summer at **Hither Hills State Park** (668-2461), right on the ocean between Montauk and East Hampton. You can't beat the location. The 150 campsites are available in July and August by lottery (at other times, by reservation); to enter, send a self-addressed stamped enveloped to Camping, P.O. Box 247, Babylon, 11702, before the January drawing. (1-week max. stay. Sites $10. Open April 15-Sept.)

You can always get good, cheap take-out food from a deli, and you'll find two or three in every East End village. Line up at any deli or diner at 7am with half the local work force for breakfast specials. West of Hither Hills before East Hampton on the Montauk Hwy., you'll find the **Clam Bar at Napeague** (267-6348). This highway pit stop serves clams, oysters, shrimp, and half a cold lobster for $5. (Open daily in summer noon-8pm.) Dinner on the South Fork is expensive or it's pizza.

You'll find many possibilities for hiking in state and county parks. Call 669-1000 (state parks) or 567-1700 (county parks) for details. One of the more unusual places to hike is at **Mashomack Preserve,** Rte. 114, on Shelter Island, 1 mile north of the South Ferry. Part of the Nature Conservancy's national chain of open lands, this preserve boasts 2000 acres of hiking trails and miles of bay-shore beaches. You can explore by reservation only. A permit is not necessary—simply phone the manager the day before you show up (749-1001).

You can often see as far as 40 miles from the **Montauk Point Lighthouse,** on the easternmost tip of Long Island (on the end of the Montauk Hwy.). First, however you must climb the 137 steps to the viewing tower. (Open Memorial Day-Sept. daily 10:30am-6pm. Admission $2, children $1; parking $3, free after 4pm.)

The East End is served several times daily by the **LIRR.** Trains roll through the Hamptons and Montauk three times per day (9 on summer weekends). The three-and-a-half-hour ride to Penn Station makes daytripping a little rough (one way, peak $12.25, off-peak $8.25). **Suffolk Transit's** S-92 bus also serves parts of the South Fork (see the North Fork for details). **Hampton Jitney** is a private bus company that runs 15-25 buses per day to and from the Hamptons. (In Manhattan 212-936-0440; on Long Island 516-283-4600). Fare between Manhattan and South Fork is $15, with stops in almost all the villages and towns from Westhampton to Montauk. Pick-up the bus in Manhattan at 41st St. at 3rd Ave., and 70th St. at Lexington Ave. Call for schedule information.

Upstate New York

In the language of New Yorkers, "upstate" may refer to anything from the craggy peaks of the Adirondacks to the rushing waters of Niagara Falls. The area as a whole often has to brace itself against losing its identity to "The City" down south. Yet, once surrounded by the natural beauty and diversity of the state's landscape and the richness of its history, you may find it easy to forget that such things as metropolis, smog, and traffic even exist. Villages dot the mountainous strip which begins just north of the city and stretches to Canada. The terrain around the Finger Lakes is lush, hilly, and verdant. Historic Albany is an important inland port at the end of the Hudson River. And, of course, Niagara Falls roar majestically at the Canadian border.

Syracuse

During your upstate ramblings, you'll probably pass through Syracuse, a transportation hub and a pleasant place to live, but not a city worth an extended stay. For just 10¢, you can board one of the green **"Salt City" trolleys.** Schedules are available at the chamber of commerce, or wait by one of the green signs on Salina and W. Water St. A 15-minute ride takes you by most downtown sights. Architecture buffs should note the spectacular 30s art deco style of the **Niagara Mohawk Power Co.,** 300 Erie Blvd. W., and the **New York Telephone** building, at the corner of S. State and W. Washington St. The **Erie Canal Museum,** 318 Erie Blvd. E. (471-0593), is in the historic **Weighlock Building.** (Open Tues.-Sun. 10am-5pm. Admission $1, ages 5-13 50¢, Tues. free.)

Grab a bite to eat at **Xristou's Deli,** 116 E. Fayette St. (422-2581), where Greek specialties include hot lunch dishes, salads, sandwiches, and pastries. Don't miss your complimentary shot of ouzo. Friendly atmosphere, moderate prices. (Open Mon.-Fri. 7am-4pm, Sat. 11am-2pm.) **Charlie Bubbles Restaurant,** in the Sedgwick Inn, 1100 James St. (472-6966), has a 65-item, arguably oxymoronic "Fantasy Salad

Bar." Dinners $6-10. (Open Mon.-Thurs. 7am-9pm, Fri.-Sat. 7am-10pm, Sun. 8am-9pm.) Look in the area around the campus of **Syracuse University** for nightlife and cheap restaurants.

Downing International Hostel (AYH) is at 459 Westcott St. (472-5788; check-in 5-9pm, check-out 9:30am; $7). Travel to and from Syracuse by **Greyhound,** 815 E. Erie Blvd. (471-7171) or **Trailways,** 200 W. Jefferson (471-7709). **Amtrak** (463-1135) is an inconvenient 12 miles east of town on E. Manlius Center Rd. in East Syracuse. The enthusiastic staff of the **Greater Syracuse Chamber of Commerce,** 100 E. Onondaga St. (470-1343), downtown at S. Salina St., are exceedingly happy to tell you anything else you might like to know. Syracuse's **ZIP code** is 13210; the **area code** is 315.

Albany

With millions of dollars spent on urban renewal and the celebration of its 1986 Tricentennial, Albany is now undergoing what many residents term a "renaissance." This is an overstatement, but recent efforts to increase tourism have helped to make the state capital more than just a place to make a quick bus or a train connection.

Founded by Dutch settlers in 1614, Albany (then called Beverwyck) was taken by the English in 1664, and was part of the land grant given by King Charles II to his brother James, Duke of York and Albany. During the Revolutionary War, Albany was the objective of the British General John Burgoyne's invasion from Canada, but that endeavor ended with an American victory in Saratoga in late 1777. Albany maintained its prominence during the 1800s as an inland port on the Hudson River. The state capitol and the bells of city hall's tower recall Albany's history, as does the **Schuyler** (pronounced SKY-ler) **Mansion,** 32 Catherine St. (434-0834). Built in 1761, the elegant Georgian home was owned by prominent colonial businessman and general Philip Schuyler. Here George Washington and Benjamin Franklin dined, Alexander Hamilton married Schuyler's daughter in the drawing room, and Gen. Burgoyne was "incarcerated" for several weeks after Saratoga. (Open Wed.-Sat. 10am-5pm, Sun. 1-5pm; Jan.-March Sat. 10am-5pm, Sun. 1-5pm. Free.)

Besides the Schuyler, Albany offers a rather limited menu of sight-seeing activity. The most outstanding feature of the entire downtown area is the **Rockefeller Empire State Plaza,** State St., a $1.9 billion architectural marvel. The plaza houses the **New York State Museum** (474-5877; open daily 10am-5pm; free), and the **New York State Performing Arts Center** (473-3750). The museum's exhibits show the history and development of the state's different regions, including Manhattan, and range from Native American arrowheads to an original set for "Sesame Street." For a bird's-eye view of Albany, visit the observation deck on the 44th floor of the tallest skyscraper in the plaza. (Open Mon.-Fri. 9am-4pm.)

The modern plaza provides a striking contrast to the more traditional architectural landscape of the rest of the city. Within walking distance, on Washington Avenue, are **City Hall,** by H.H. Richardson, an earthy Romanesque; and the **capitol building** (also worked on by Richardson), a Gothic marvel.

Most of the accommodations in Albany are expensive and even motels tend to be pricey. Luckily, there is a small, but clean and comfortable, hostel right in town. The **Mansion Home Hostel** is at 46 Elm St. (434-4963; members only, $7). There are only three beds, so be sure to reserve in advance. The **State University of New York** dorms (442-5902) require a bus ride to the Western Ave. campus. Standard dorm rooms include linen. (Open Mon.-Fri. 9am-10pm. Singles $30. Doubles $40. June-Aug. only.) Another option is the friendly **Fort Crailo Motel,** 110 Columbia Turnpike, Rensselaer 12144 (472-1360), in a safe area 1½ miles from downtown, near the Amtrak station. (Singles $32. Doubles $36.) Men can try their luck at the **YMCA,** 274 Washington Ave. (479-7196; singles $22). For women, the closest **YWCA** with rooms is a half-hour bus ride away at 44 Washington Ave. (374-3394;

open Mon.-Fri. 8:30am-8:30pm. Singles $22. Call for availability.) Reservations are recommended at both Ys.

Albany's best features may be its convenient transportation terminals, by which you leave the city. **Amtrak,** East St., Rensselaer (465-9971 or 800-872-7245), across the Hudson from downtown Albany, runs to New York City (7-9 per day, 2½ hr., $37). Station open daily 10:30am-midnight. **Greyhound,** 34 Hamilton Ave. (434-0121), also offers service to New York City (9 per day, 3 hr., $27). Station open daily 6am-12:30am. **Trailways,** 1 block away at 360 Broadway (436-9651), connects to points in the Adirondacks. To: Lake George (6 per day, in winter 3 per day, 1 hr., $9); Lake Placid (6 per day; in winter 3 per day, 3¾ hr., $20.50); and Tupper Lake (1 per day, 4 hr., $25.80). (Open Mon.-Fri. 5:30am-11pm, Sat.-Sun. 7:30am-11pm.) For local travel, the **Capitol District Transit Authority (CDTA)** (482-8822) serves Albany, Troy, and Schenectady. The schedule is confusing and coverage in some areas is spotty, but a quick call to the main office will set you straight. (Fare 60¢).

Albany's **ZIP code** is 12201; the **area code** is 518.

Catskills

In 1820, New York City author and historian Washington Irving recounted the seductive and soothing qualities of the Catskills in the tale of *Rip Van Winkle.* In the story, Rip joins the mountain party of a group of gnomes and falls asleep for 20 years. These lovely mountains continue to captivate city-dwellers, who migrate up the highways of the Hudson and Mohawk River Valleys in search of unpolluted air and the tranquility of the dense hemlock forests. Beyond the lakeside resorts, visitors can find peace and natural beauty in the state-managed Catskill Preserve, home to quiet villages, sparkling streams, and miles of hiking and skiing trails.

Trailways provides excellent service through the Catskills. The two main stops are at **Kingston,** 400 Washington Ave. (914-331-0744), and **Oneonta,** 47 Market St. (607-432-2661 or 613-238-6668). At least seven other stops in the area, including Woodstock, Pine Hill, Saugerties, and Hunter, connect with New York City, Albany, and Utica. Road conditions are consistently good.

Catskill Preserve

The 250,000-acre, state-run Catskill Preserve is the area's real attraction. The **Esopus River,** just to the west, is great for trout fishing and for late-summer inner-tubing in the **Phoenicia** area. Rent tubes at **The Town Tinker,** on Bridge St. (688-5553), in Phoenicia. (Inner tubes $6.50 per day; must have $15 or a driver's licence as a deposit. Life jackets available, but not required. Open May-Sept. daily 9am-6pm.) Throughout the preserve, hundreds of trails lead to lovely mountain brooks, hidden lakes, deep forests, and Batman's summer retreat. Hikes range from half-day jaunts to the top of a mountain to longer backpack trips traversing the entire region. Some trails are crowded in summer, especially those in the eastern section of the park. To camp in the backcountry for more than three days, you must obtain a permit from the nearest ranger station (518-255-5453). Trails are maintained year-round, and lean-tos are available, although they are sometimes dilapidated and crowded. Treat water with chemical or boil it, and pack your garbage. To reach the head of your chosen trail, take a Trailways bus from Kingston—drivers will let you out anywhere along the park's main routes. (Call 914-331-0744 for information on routes and fares.) For more information, pick up Bennet and Maisa's *Walks in the Catskills* or the American Geographical Society's *The New York Walk Book.*

The only hostel in the region is located near Belleayre Mountain in **Pine Hill.** (914-254-4200. Mailing address: Bonnie View Ave., P.O. Box 665, Pine Hill, 12465.) It is easily accessible since Trailways stops at Rte. 28 in Pine Hill. Turn right to Elm St., left on Main St., left on Bonnie View Ave., and walk ¼ mile. The 4-person rooms are bright and clean. Kitchen facilities available. ($7, winter weekends $10. Open May-March.)

One of the many well-run **state campgrounds** can serve as a base for your hiking, fishing, or tubing adventures. (Open May-Sept. Sites $8, $9.50 on weekends. Reservations necessary on holiday weekends.) Try one of the following: **North Lake,** Rte. 23A (518-589-5058), 3 miles northeast of Haines Falls; **Devil's Tombstone,** Rte. 214 (518-688-7160), 3 miles south of Hunter; **Woodland Valley** (914-688-7647), 5 miles southwest of Phoenicia; **Kenneth L. Wilson** (914-679-7020), 5 miles east of Mt. Tremper, off Rte. 28; **Little Pond** (914-439-5480), 14 miles northwest of Livingston Manor, off Rte. 17; **Beaverkill** (914-439-4281), 7 miles northwest of Livingston Manor; **Mongaup Pond** (914-439-4233), 10 miles northeast of Livingston Manor, off Rte. 17, exit 96; or **Morningside Park,** Loch Sheldrake, on City Rte. 52 (914-434-8230).

Adirondacks

The Adirondacks, New York's last bastion of backwoods wilderness, are the largest natural preserve in the East. Large portions of the mountain forests are still undeveloped, but modern expansion has not spared the area. The Adirondacks' trees, lakes, and wildlife are victims of pollution from urban areas far to the south. More than 200 lakes in the area have become stagnant, and acid rain has left its mark on many tree and fish populations, especially in the fragile high-altitude environments. But despite these warning signs, much of the Adirondacks remains as it was over a century ago.

Of the six million acres in the Adirondacks Park, 40% is fully open to the public. Two thousand miles of hiking and skiing trails criss-cross the forest and mountain scenery. An interlocking network of lakes and streams makes the gentle Adirondack wilds a perennial favorite of canoeists. Mountain climbers may wish to tackle **Mt. Marcy,** the state's highest peak (5344 ft.), at the base of the Adirondacks.

The Adirondacks are famous for sports resorts and encompass a dozen well-known alpine ski centers. **Lake Placid** has twice hosted the winter Olympics and is frequently the site of national sports competitions (see Lake Placid below). **Saranac Lake** is another center for winter activity, including the **International Dog Sledding Championship** at the end of January. **Tupper Lake** and **Lake George** also have celebrations every January and February. Hiking trails covered in snow are great for snowshoeing, and plenty of cross-country ski trails wind through forest preserves and state parks.

The Adirondacks have extra appeal for the budget traveler, since cheap accommodations are plentiful. Lake Placid and nearby towns are home to many inexpensive hotels and campgrounds (see Lake Placid below). The region's youth hostel is located in the basement of **St. James Episcopal Church Hall** (518-668-2634), Montcalm and Ottawa St., 1 block from bus terminal in Lake George, only a block from the lake. (Check-in until 8pm, later only with reservations; $7.25; open May 26-Sept. 5.) Probably the best deal in the area is the **Adirondack Loj,** P.O. Box 867, Lake Placid 12946 (523-3441), 8 miles east of Lake Placid off Rte. 73. The lodge is a beautiful log cabin right on Heart Lake, with comfortable bunk facilities and a family atmosphere. (B&B $18.50, with dinner $28. Linen provided. Campsites $6. Lean-tos $10.) Guests can swim, fish, canoe, and use rowboats free of charge. In winter, explore the wilderness trails on rented snowshoes ($6 per day) or cross-country skis ($10 per day; call ahead for weekends and during peak holiday seasons.) The **Johns Brook Lodge,** in Keene Valley, 20 miles southeast of Lake Placid off Rte. 73, offers an even more rustic experience; it's located at the end of a 3½-mile hike. The lodge has mixed-sex bunks and lean-tos and is famous for its great food. Bring linen or a sleeping bag. (Beds $7. B&B $14, with dinner $22. Open for full service late June-Labor Day. Only a caretaker available Memorial Day-late June and Labor Day-Columbus Day.)

Those with a car can get to the **High Peaks Base Camp,** P.O. Box 91, Upper Jay (946-2133). The site isn't picturesque and there are no lounge facilities for residents, but the $15 B&B package is a bargain. The adjacent restaurant has good food and live music. From Lake Placid, take 86N to Wilmington, turn right at the Mobil station, right on Springfield Rd, then go 3½ miles.

In the forest, there are free shelters by the trails. Always inquire about their location before you plan a hike. You can camp for free in the backcountry anywhere on public land, as long as you are at least 150 feet away from a trail, road, water source, or campground and stay below 4000 feet altitude.

The Adirondacks are served best by **Adirondacks Trailways,** with frequent stops along I-87. You can take a bus to Lake Placid, Tupper Lake, and Lake George from Albany. The Lake George bus stop is at the Mobil station, 320 Canada St. (668-9511). **Greyhound** also serves Lake George ($9), Plattsburgh ($21.75), and Groverskill from Albany. Hitchhiking in the Adirondacks is not difficult along the main routes, especially near Lake Placid. Traveling in the backwoods is tough during the muddy spring thaw (March-April).

Contact the State Office of Parks and Recreation (see New York Practical Information) in Albany for information on the Adirondacks. The best information on hiking, outdoor life, and the mountains is provided by the **Adirondack Mountain Clubs (ADK),** 17 Ridge St., Glens Falls 12801 (518-793-7737; open Mon.-Fri. 8:30am-4:30pm).

The Adirondacks' **area code** is 518.

Lake Placid

Lake Placid was first promoted as a summer resort in 1850 by Melvil Dewey (creator of the Dewey Decimal library classification system), who began the exclusive Lake Placid Club. The town's fame was cemented by the Winter Olympic Games, which were held here in 1932 and 1980. Currently the Adirondacks' premier tourist spot, Lake Placid attracts crowds of casual visitors and world-class athletes. The international flags and stores that fill Main Street don't impair the inviting, old-village atmosphere. The town's facilities are unmatched in the U.S. Temperatures can plummet to -40°F and more than 200 inches of snow may fall in an Adirondack winter, but well-plowed main roads keep the region open. Ice fishing on the lakes is popular, especially with locals, as is ice skating ($3 to skate on the Olympic speed-skating rink; open late Nov. to mid-March daily 3-5pm and 7-9pm).

Just out of town on Rte. 73, you can't miss the 70- and 90-meter ski jumps of the **Intervale Complex** (523-2202) that loom above the alpine landscape. Admire the airborne ski jumpers from the spectator towers. (Elevators $5, ages 4-12 $4. Open daily 9am-5pm. Disabled access.) Three miles farther along Rte. 73, the **Olympic Sports Complex** (523-4436) recreation area offers a pleasant trolley-car ride in summer and luge and bobsled runs to the daring in December. The bobsled-run ride, made to international specifications for competition, costs $12. (Open Tues.-Sun. 1-3pm; mid-December to mid-March Tues.-Sat. 9am-4pm. A parent must sign a waiver for those under 18.) The Olympic recreation area also offers 35 miles of well-groomed cross-country ski trails. (Open daily 9am-4pm. $6 fee in winter.)

In addition to its fantastic ski slopes, **Whiteface Mountain,** near Lake Placid, provides a panoramic view of the Adirondacks. You can get up to the summit via the **Whiteface Memorial Highway** ($3.50 toll, cars only), a chairlift ($3.50, seniors and children $2.50), or an elevator ($2.50). The extensive **Whiteface Mountain Ski Center** (946-2223) has the largest vertical drop in the East (3216 ft.). Don't bother with the $3.50 tour of the waterfalls at **High Falls Gorge** (946-2278) on Rte. 86 near Whiteface. Hike below the road to see the same scenery for free.

History buffs will enjoy a quick visit to the farm and grave of abolitionist John Brown, off Rte. 73, 3 miles southeast of Lake Placid (523-3900; open May to mid-Oct. Wed.-Sat. 10am-5pm, Sun. 1-5pm; free). The west branch of the **Ausable River,** just east of the town of Lake Placid, lures anglers to its shores. Fishing licenses for nonresidents are $9 for 3 days, $25 for the season. Call the "Fishing Hotline" at 518-891-5413. The **Lake Placid Center for the Arts,** on Saranac Ave. at Farm Ridge (523-2512), hosts a local art gallery and theater, dance, and musical performances. (Open daily 1-5pm; in winter Mon.-Fri. 1-5pm. Free.) Just 15 minutes from the city is **Santa's Workshop** (946-7838), America's oldest theme park. (Open Memorial Day-Columbus Day daily 9:30am-4:30pm. Admission $9, ages 3-17 $7, under 3 free.)

For spring and fall breakfasts, try the **Hilton Hotel,** 1 Mirror Lake Dr. (523-4411), right at the beginning of Main St. At the Hilton's lunch buffet, $4.75 buys a sandwich and all-you-can-eat soup and salad (served noon-2:30pm). **The Cottage,** 5 Mirror Lake Dr. (523-9845), has relatively inexpensive meals (sandwiches and salads $4-6) with views of the lake and many, many athletes. (Lunch served daily 11:30am-3:30pm. Bar open noon-1am). **Mud Puddles,** 3 School St. (523-4446), below the speed skating rink, is popular with disco throwbacks and the pop music crowd. (Open Wed.-Sun. 9pm-3am. Cover $1.50.)

Most accommodations in the area are expensive. The **St. Moritz Hotel,** 31 Saranac Ave. (523-9240), is off the northern end of Main St., past the Hilton Hotel. (Clean and comfortable doubles $30, with breakfast $32.) Try the **Highland House,** 3 Highland Place (523-2377), up the hill from Main St. ($28.50; breakfast included.) The High Peaks Base Camp, Adirondack Loj, and Johns Brook Lodge (see Adirondacks above) are all within several miles of Lake Placid. Campers have many options, including backcountry camping (free), the Adirondack Loj's campgrounds, and the numerous developed state sites near Lake Placid and Saranac Lake. The closest one is **Meadowbrook State Park** (891-4351), located 4½ miles west of Lake Placid on Rte. 86 in Raybrook. (Sites $6. Open mid-April to mid-Oct.)

To explore Lake Placid by bike, rent 10-speeds at **Sundog Ski & Sport,** 90 Main St. (523-2752; $3 per hour, $12 per day). The shop also rents cross-country skis ($10 per day) and downhill skis ($14 per day; open Mon.-Fri. 9am-7pm, Sat.-Sun. 9am-9pm. Must have ID, but no deposit is necessary.) The **State Tourist Office,** 90 Main St. (523-2412), will give you brochures on the area and the entire state. (Open Mon.-Fri. 9am-5pm.) Browse the local outdoors shops for hiking and canoe guides to the Adirondacks.

Trailways has extensive service in the Adirondacks, stopping at the **326 Main St. Deli** in Lake Placid (523-1527; open daily 6:30am-10pm). **Greyhound** has a flag stop at the same deli, which lies on the route to Saranac Lake and to Montréal via Keeseville. By car, Lake Placid is at the intersection of Rte. 86 and 73.

Emergency is 911. **Weather** is 792-1050. The Lake Placid **post office,** 201 Main St. (523-3071), is open Mon.-Fri. 8:30am-5pm, Sat. 8:30am-noon. Lake Placid's **ZIP code** is 12946; the **area code** is 518.

Ithaca

Ithaca combines the best of urban and rural living. The deep river gorges in and around Ithaca and the beauty of the surrounding Finger Lakes region make the town as relaxed—and relaxing—as any countryside. However, Ithaca is also an active educational and cultural center, with Ivy-League Cornell University perched atop the hills.

Within a 10-mile radius of Ithaca there are 150 waterfalls, plus many paths, bridges, and gardens that offer spectacular views. In **Buttermilk Falls State Park,** Buttermilk Falls descend more than 500 feet and end in a clear pool. Within the park, **Pinnacle Rock** towers 40 feet above the water. The same bus that runs south to Buttermilk Falls also runs north to **Stewart Park** (272-8535), with swimming in Lake Cayuga, a playground, picnic area, tennis courts, and a restored carousel. A bike trail runs from the Ithaca Commons to Stewart Park.

Perched on Ithaca's hills, Cornell University is home to 18,000 students, 100 departments, and 4000 courses. To take a tour led by a Cornell student, go to Day Hall, 1st floor, University Campus (255-6200). Go up the 164 steps of **Sage Chapel** for a breathtaking view. (Open Mon.-Fri. 8am-5pm.) The **Herbert F. Johnson Museum of Art** (255-6464), on the corner of Central and University Ave., displays Asian and graphic art, as well as 19th- and 20th-century paintings. Designed by I.M. Pei, the oddly-shaped building is known as "the sewing machine." Its lobby is currently guarded by the enormous *Herakles in Ithaka,* sculpted entirely of car bumpers. (Open Tues.-Sun. 10am-5pm. Free.)

South of the campus you'll find the small, energetic neighborhood of **Collegetown,** a popular spot after dark. **The Nine's,** 311 College Ave. (272-1888), features live bands, beer, and pizza. (Open Mon.-Sat. 11:30am-1am, Sun. 3:30pm-1am.) **The Haunt,** 114 W. Green St. (273-3355), diagonally across from Woolworth's, near the corner of S. Geneva St., plays Motown, funk, and classic rock music. (Live bands most nights. Open daily 8pm-1:30am.)

Ithaca is known for **Brown Cow Yogurt,** bagel wars, and an impressive variety of fine restaurants. One of the original owners of the **Moosewood Restaurant,** at Seneca and Cayuga St. (273-9610), downtown, wrote the *Moosewood Cookbook* and *The Enchanted Broccoli Forest.* The restaurant serves different gourmet vegetarian and fish dishes each day. (Lunch $3-4, dinner $6-9. Open Mon.-Sat. 11:30am-2pm and 6-9pm.) **Heart's Content,** 156 State St. (272-0185), on the Commons, serves sandwiches ($1-6), soup, salads, and great cheesecake. (Open Mon.-Wed. 8am-7:30pm, Thurs-Fri. 8am-9pm, Sat. 8am-7:30pm, Sun. 8am-5pm.)

Collegetown Bagels, 413 College Ave. (273-9655), has a variety of bagels, cheap ice cream, and lines of students. For outdoor seating and great coffee, try **Cafe Decadence,** 114 Dryden Rd. (272-8490), downhill from the intersection of Dryden and College Ave.

The only youth hostel in the area is in Trumansburg (see the Finger Lakes below). The **Elmshade Guest House,** 402 S. Albany St. at Center St. (273-1707), charges $20 per person. Just 4 miles from downtown, the **Historic Cook House,** 167 Main St., Newfield (564-9926), has doubles with a full country breakfast for $35. Take the Newfield bus out of town. Each place has pleasant (and similar) rooms. Near Cornell University, the **Hillside Inn,** 518 Stewart Ave. (272-9507), has rooms from $29 to 40. For a complete listing of hotels, motels, and B&Bs, contact Ithaca's chamber of commerce. Nearby state parks with camping facilities include **Robert H. Treman State Park** (273-3440), 4 miles south on Rte. 13, and **Buttermilk Falls State Park** (273-5761), 1 mile south on Rte. 13. (Sites $9. Open May-Oct.) To reach **Willowwood Camp** (272-6087), take Rte. 13 south out of Ithaca, and pick up Rte. 327 north; turn left on Hines Rd., then right onto Rockwell. (Sites $10, with electricity and water $12.)

Ithaca's **Greyhound** station is at W. State and N. Fulton St. (272-7930), west of the mall. (Open 6am-9pm.) **Ithaca Transit** (273-7348) provides bus service to Cornell University, Ithaca College, Stewart Park, and Buttermilk Falls. (Operates Mon.-Sat. 6am-6pm. Fare 50¢. Transfer valid for 1 hr.) In addition, **Cornell University Transit** (255-3782) supplies bus service around Cornell. (Operates 5am-6:30pm. Fare 25-50¢.) **Tomtran (Tompkins County Transportation Services Project** (274-5370) covers a wider area than Ithaca Transit, including Trumansburg and Ulysses, both northwest of Ithaca on Rte. 96, and Cayuga Heights and Lansing Village, both due north of Ithaca on Rte. 13. All buses stop at the Ithaca Commons, westbound on Seneca St. and eastbound on Green. (Fare 60¢.)

For bike rental, try **Black Star Bicycles,** 12 Judd Falls Rd. (272-4170). From the Commons, walk up State and turn to Mitchell. (Bikes $10 per day, $25 per week; open Fri.-Mon. 10am-5:30pm, Thurs. 10am-8pm. Deposit equal to rental fee.) **Bike Rack,** 404 College Ave. (272-1010) (near Dryden Rd. in Collegetown) also rents bikes for $10-15 per day.

Ithaca sits at the south end of Cayuga Lake, the longest of the Finger Lakes. It is 60 miles southwest of Syracuse on I-81 and Rte. 13 and 220 miles northwest of New York City. Once you get to the town, you will notice the two Ithacas: the flat downtown area by the lake, and the hilly Cornell campus.

The **Ithaca Chamber of Commerce** is inconveniently located at 904 E. Shore Drive (272-1313). From the bus station, turn left on State St., then left on Cayuga all the way to E. Shore Dr. (about a 30-min. walk). (Open Mon.-Fri. 9am-5pm.) They also operate a **tourist booth** at the entrance to Stewart Park on Rte. 13 (272-9432). Take bus #4 in front of Woolworth's, near the intersection of Green and Cayuga St. (Open Memorial Day-Labor Day daily 9am-6pm.)

The **Post Office** is at 213 N. Tioga St. E. Buffalo (272-5454), 2 blocks north of the center of town on the Commons. (Open Mon.-Fri. 8:30am-5pm., Sat. 8:30am-noon.) Ithaca's **ZIP code** is 14850; the **area code** is 607.

The Finger Lakes

Broken up by gentle hills, the slender waterways of the Finger Lakes—Canandaigua, Keuka, Seneca, Cayuga, Owasco, Skaneateles, and others—are steeped in Iroquois lore. According to legend, the Great Spirit laid his hands upon the earth, and the impression of his fingers became lakes. A more geological explanation attributes the lakes' shapes to the expansion of ice sheets in pre-existing valleys during the glacial age.

Traveling by bus is possible but difficult, as routes are few. Some connections are available from Ithaca (see Ithaca), but most places can't be reached by public transportation. The easiest way to get around is by car, but biking and hiking allow a closer view of this beautiful country. Contact the **Finger Lakes State Park Region** (see New York Practical Information) for free maps and tips. You might also want to examine the booklet *20 Bicycle Tours in the Finger Lakes* ($6.95), prepared by Backcountry Publications, P.O. Box 175, Woodstock, VT 15091. Also try the *Finger Lakes Bicycle Touring Map* (see New York Practical Information).

The **Finger Lakes Trail Conference,** P.O. Box 18048, Rochester 14618-0048 (716-288-7191), is responsible for the **Finger Lakes Trail,** an east-west footpath from the Catskills westward to the Allegheny Mountains. This 350-mile trail and its 300 miles of branch trails link several state parks, most with camping facilities. Write for free maps.

Fifteen of the 20 state parks in the Finger Lakes region have **campsites** and nine have cabins. The brochure *Finger Lakes State Parks* contains a description of the park location, services, and environs; pick it up in any park or from the Finger Lakes State Park Region (see above). The **New York State Parks Office,** Albany 12238 (518-474-0456), is also helpful.

Trumansburg, 13 miles north of Ithaca on Rte. 96, is a good base for exploring the area. **Taughannock Falls** are a spectacular sight, as the water cascades from a height of 215 feet. Walk about 1 mile along the ravine leading from Cayuga Lake to the falls, where powerful flow has cut through the solid cliffs over the course of 9000 years. The cheapest place to stay in Trumansburg is the **Podunk International Hostel,** on Podunk Rd. (387-9277). The mattresses are on the top of a barn on a Finnish homestead farm. A bathroom is across the yard, but there is no kitchen. Sauna use in winter. (Members only, $5 in summer, $7 in winter. Call ahead.) The **Taughannock State Park** has cabins and camping facilities (607-387-6739; open 8am-10pm; cabins $20 for 4, $80 per week; sites $8, with electricity $9. Open April-Oct.).

The fertile soil of the Finger Lakes area makes the region the heart of New York's wine industry. Wine tasting and touring one of the small local vineyards is a relaxing way to spend a day. Unfortunately only a couple of the wineries (those by Cayuga) are accessible by bus. **Americana Vineyards,** East Covert Rd., Interlaken (607-387-6801), is 2 miles north from Trumansburg (3-4 Greyhound buses per day to Ithaca; tours and tasting Mon.-Sat. 10am-8pm, Sun. noon-8pm. Free). Also in Interlaken is **Lucas Winery,** 150 County Rd. (607-532-4825; open July-Aug. daily 11am-5pm; June and Sept.-Nov. Sat.-Sun. only). On the eastern side of Seneca Lake, visit **Wagner Winery,** Rte. 414 (607-582-6450), in Lodi, one of the best. (Free tours and tasting Mon.-Sat. 10am-4:30pm, Sun. 10am-5pm.)

Corning, at the southern reaches of the Finger Lakes area, is the renowned glass-making center where Corningware and Steuben Glass originated. Plan to spend an afternoon at the overwhelming **Corning Glass Center** (607-974-8271). There is a *lot* of glass here—cut, molded, blown, stamped, painted, etched, engraved, and oven-resistant. (Open daily 9am-5pm. Admission $3, seniors $2, ages 6-17 $1.50.)

Seneca Falls is considered the birthplace of the women's rights movement, since the 1848 Seneca Falls Convention was held here. The town was home to Elizabeth Cady Stanton and Amelia Bloomer, two leading suffragists. Visit the **National Women's Hall of Fame,** 76 Fall St. (315-568-8060), where 38 outstanding American women are commemorated through photographs and biographies (Open Sun. 1-5pm, Mon.-Sat. 10am-4pm. Admission $3, seniors $2, under 12 free).

Niagara Falls and Buffalo

The beauty and the sheer magnitude of Niagara Falls consistently inspire awe in visitors. Despite the considerable commercialization and tourism of the region, the falls are truly majestic, with 200,000 cubic feet of water per second rushing over this natural wonder on the Niagara River. As immortalized by the Three Stooges, the falls are a perennial summer vacation spot for American families. For years, newlyweds have come to the "Honeymoon Capital of the World" for waterfalls and waterbeds. Others have been lured to Niagara for its danger. In 1901, schoolteacher Annie Taylor was the first to successfully go over the falls in a barrel. Unluckier daredevils have failed such death-defying stunts, all of which were outlawed in 1961.

Practical Information

Emergency: 911.

Visitor Information: Niagara Falls Convention and Visitors Bureau, 345 3rd St. (285-2400), next to the city bus station. Also runs an information center in the bus station and at other locations scattered across the city. Pick up the free *Niagara USA,* which has a good map of Niagara and the surrounding area, as well as helpful practical information. Open May-Sept. daily 8:30am-8:30pm; Oct.-April Mon.-Fri. 9am-5pm. **Buffalo Area Chamber of Commerce,** 107 Delaware Ave., Buffalo (852-7100), next to City Hall on the 2nd floor of the Statler Tower. Pick up the free *Official Visitor's Guide to Buffalo,* which describes attractions and visitor services in Buffalo and includes an adequate map of the downtown area. Open Mon.-Fri. 8:30am-5pm.

Amtrak: 55 Dick Rd., Niagara Falls (683-8440 or 800-872-7245), 2 miles down Lockport St. Dangerous at night. Open daily 6:30am-3pm. In Buffalo, 75 Exchange St. (856-2075). Open 24 hours.

Greyhound/Trailways: 4th St. at Wendell Way, Niagara Falls, NY (282-1331), downtown. The only intercity bus terminal in Niagara Falls, NY. Ticket office open Mon.-Fri. 8am-6pm, Sat. 8am-4pm. In downtown Buffalo, Greyhound/Trailways buses (855-7511) depart from the **Buffalo Transportation Center,** 181 Ellicott St. (855-7211). From City Hall, walk down Niagara St. and follow Eagle St. to your left. To: New York City (8 per day, 8 hr., $61); Boston (5 per day, 12 hr., $80); Chicago (6 per day, 12 hr., $83). Ameripass valid on Canadian Greyhound, Gray Coach, and Canada Coach lines. Ticket office open 3am-1am.

Niagara Frontier Metro Transit System: 855-7211. Provides local city transit. Bus #40 is the only transportation to Niagara Falls, NY (17 per day, 1 hr., $1.60).

Post Office: 1615 Main St. (285-7561), Niagara Falls, NY. Open Mon.-Fri. 8:30am-5pm, Sat. 8:30am-noon. **ZIP code:** 14302.

Area Codes: 716 (New York), 416 (Ontario).

Niagara Falls, NY, faces the Canadian town of the same name across the Niagara River. The river runs north from Lake Erie to Lake Ontario. Buffalo lies 20 miles south where the Niagara River leaves Lake Erie. The falls are 90 miles from Rochester, and nearly 400 miles from New York City.

Accommodations and Camping

Niagara Falls Frontier Hostel (AYH), 1101 Ferry Ave., Niagara Falls, NY 14301 (282-3700 or 285-9203), a few blocks from the Falls, just east of the intersection of Niagara and 10th St. Convivial, international atmosphere. Excellent facilities, including a kitchen and a lounge with TV. 44 beds. Travelers without cars given first priority if space is short. Parking available. Bike rental $4 per day. Open 5-11pm. Check-out 9:30am. Members only, $9. Reservations recommended. Closed Dec. 10-Jan. 2.

Niagara Falls International Hostel (CHA), 4699 Zimmerman Ave., Niagara Falls, Ont. L2E 3M7 (416-357-0770), in a pleasant, brick Tudor building 5 miles from the Falls, between Morrison and Queen St. off River Rd., near the train station. Kitchen, dining room, lounge, 38 beds. Open 8-10am and 5-11pm, lights-out 11:30pm. CDN$8, non-members CDN$12. Linen $1. Sleeping bags not allowed. Make reservations in summer.

Young's Guest House, 574 3rd St., Niagara Falls, NY (282-0919), downtown. Very clean, run by a nice little old lady. 9 rooms. Singles $18. Doubles $25. Try to call ahead.

Norton's Motel and Campsite, 2405 Niagara Falls Blvd., Wheatfield 14304 (731-3434), 1 mile from downtown Niagara Falls, NY, on Rte. 62, off I-90. The hostel itself is fine, but you may not like its strip-like location. Singles $30. Campsites $11. Open May-Oct.

Sights and Entertainment

The **Cave of the Wind Tour** takes you to the foot of the American falls by elevator. (Open May 15-Oct. 20 10am-8pm. Admission $3, ages 5-11 $2.50. Raincoats provided.) The **Maid of the Mist Tour** (284-8897) takes you to the foot of Horseshoe Falls by boat. (Tours every 15 min. May-June 20 Mon.-Fri. 10am-5pm, Sat.-Sun. 10am-6pm; June 21-Labor Day daily 9:15am-8pm; Labor Day-late Oct. Mon.-Fri. 10am-5pm, Sat.-Sun. 10am-6pm. Tickets $5, ages 6-12 $2.90.)

Away from the falls, for some history of the region, browse through an impressive collection of Iroquois arts and crafts at **The Turtle,** 25 Rainbow Mall, Niagara Falls, NY (284-2427), between Winter Garden and the river. (Open May-Sept. daily 9am-6pm; Oct-April Tues.-Fri. 9am-5pm, Sat.-Sun. noon-5pm. Admission $3, seniors $2.50, children $1.50.) **Schoellkopf's Niagara Falls Museum** (278-1780) depicts the birth of the falls. (Open Memorial Day-Labor Day daily 9:30am-7pm; Labor Day-early Nov. 10am-5pm; mid-Nov. to Memorial Day Wed.-Sun. 10am-5pm. Nominal fee. Take the pedestrian overpass from Whirlpool St. near the aquarium.)

Visitors can walk between the American and Canadian sides by crossing the **Rainbow Bridge.** On the Ontario side, **Queen Victoria Park** provides a good view of the water. Niagara Falls, Ontario served as a home and haven for W.E.B. DuBois's 1905 "Niagara Movement," the forerunner of the National Association for the Advancement of Colored People (NAACP). Just minutes from the Falls, **Clifton Hill** (356-2299) has a multitude of gift shops, streetside cafes, and motels. "The Hill" is also home to **Ripley's Believe It or Not Museum, The Guinness Museum of World Records, The Super Star Recording Studio,** and many other pop-culture attractions. Each attraction charges its own admission (average CDN$5).

Buffalo, New York State's second largest city, offers high culture and streetside fun. The **Albright-Knox Art Gallery,** 1285 Elmwood Ave. (882-8700), enjoys a worldwide reputation as an outstanding center of contemporary art. Its extensive modern collection will please anyone interested in American and European art of the past 30 years. If you plan to be in Buffalo in mid-June, catch the annual **Allentown Arts Festival** that takes place along Delaware and Elmwood Ave. and Allen St. The intersection of **Elmwood and Allen** is also the core of an active after-dark scene. Free noontime concerts take place at the plaza downtown. People-watchers will find a good vantage point by climbing to the top of **City Hall** (open Mon.-Fri. 9am-3:30pm, Sat. 9am-5pm). City and county parks are centers for winter activities such as tobogganing, skating, and skiing. Pick up a list of parks at the chamber of commerce (see Practical Information above) or write to the Parks Department, Niagara Sq., Buffalo, NY 14202.

Food

The touristy atmosphere of Niagara Falls makes it nearly impossible to find food that isn't vastly overpriced. If you want to avoid the fast food in the **Rainbow Centre,** try some of the tavern-like spots near the intersection of Niagara and 4th St. The oddly named **Arterial Restaurant,** right at the intersection, offers twelve "wings" fur $2.75 or a burger $1.50.

Buffalo's great contribution to contemporary cuisine is the "Buffalo-style" spicy chicken wing. Try your wings where they originated, at the **Anchor Bar,** 1047 Main St. (886-8920; single portion $3.50; open daily 10:30am-2am), or at any local restaurant. Another local specialty, found on almost any menu, is "beef on a weck," a pile of thinly sliced roast beef on a caraway and salt roll. For fresh produce, try the **Broadway Market,** 999 Broadway.

NEW ENGLAND

As its older towns proudly remind, New England has been an intellectual, political, and cultural center for the entire nation since before the "United States" was even officially born. Yankee spirit has forged strong regional traditions here, among them a centuries-old commitment to education and a fascination with government. Students and scholars from across the country pour into New England's colleges each fall, reinvigorating the old towns and cities. Town meetings still take place in many rural hamlets, and local and state politics dominate conversations.

Yet New England is an unlikely cradle for any sort of civilization—the soil is barren, the coast is rocky and treacherous, and the land is wrinkled with mountains. Early white settlers found a threatening wilderness and a difficult life on this edge of the Atlantic. However, modern travelers approach a less menacing landscape. Their goal is often to abandon the larger cities and towns for more isolated places: the region's dramatic coastline, the fall foliage and rolling hills of western Massachusetts and Connecticut, the weathered Green and White Mountains of Vermont and New Hampshire, and especially Maine's backcountry wilderness.

Travel

Distances are small in this corner of the U.S., and an excellent network of roads makes even the most remote corner of New England accessible in a day's drive from "the Hub," Boston. New England also has the greatest regional system of public transportation in the country. Smaller companies such as **Vermont Transit,** throughout Vermont, and **Bonanza** and **Plymouth & Brockton** on Cape Cod, take you where **Greyhound/Trailways** cannot.

Amtrak is useful for getting to Boston or Providence via the Connecticut coast or for reaching western Massachusetts; New Hampshire and Maine are not served and Vermont has only late-night service on the "Montrealer." Hitchhiking, while not recommended in or near Boston (take a commuter train to the outskirts), is safer and more accepted in rural New England than in many areas of the U.S. People are accustomed to students, young travelers, and foreign visitors.

Flying to New England from New York City or Newark, NJ via inexpensive shuttles can be a good alternative to the bus or train. If you're a student or under 26, ask about special rates to Boston at Pan Am and Trump.

A breathtaking way to explore rural New England is by unmotorized locomotion. Try the bike trails in coastal areas, such as Cape Cod and the North Shore in Massachusetts, and the more challenging routes in the White and Green Mountains. Southern New Hampshire is ideal for a cyclist: rolling hills, old towns, and farm houses line the way. AYH provides help in planning bike trips, giving tips for those on the road, and sponsoring several regional tours. Contact the **Greater Boston Council of AYH,** 1020 Commonwealth Ave. 02215 (617-731-5430), or write for the *World Adventure Catalogue,* available from the **AYH National Administration,** P.O. Box 37613, Washington DC 20013-7613 (202-783-6161).

Visitor information is a cinch to come by in New England. Chambers of commerce and regional travel bureaus are extraordinarily helpful, and can inform you about fairs, music festivals, and local celebrations. Browse local bookstores for regional travel guides with details on sights and activities.

The **accommodations** situation is a mixed bag. Boston groans with some of the highest hotel rates in the nation, budget motel chains are scarce, and most rural inns cater to wealthy, vacationing urbanites. Yet New England supports no fewer than 29 well-spaced **AYH hostels.** Hostel-like ski lodges in Vermont and Appalachian Mountain Club (AMC) huts (see below) in the White Mountains provide more deals. During fall foliage season (Sept.-Oct.), accommodations prices escalate in Vermont, New Hampshire, and western Massachusetts. You might want to head

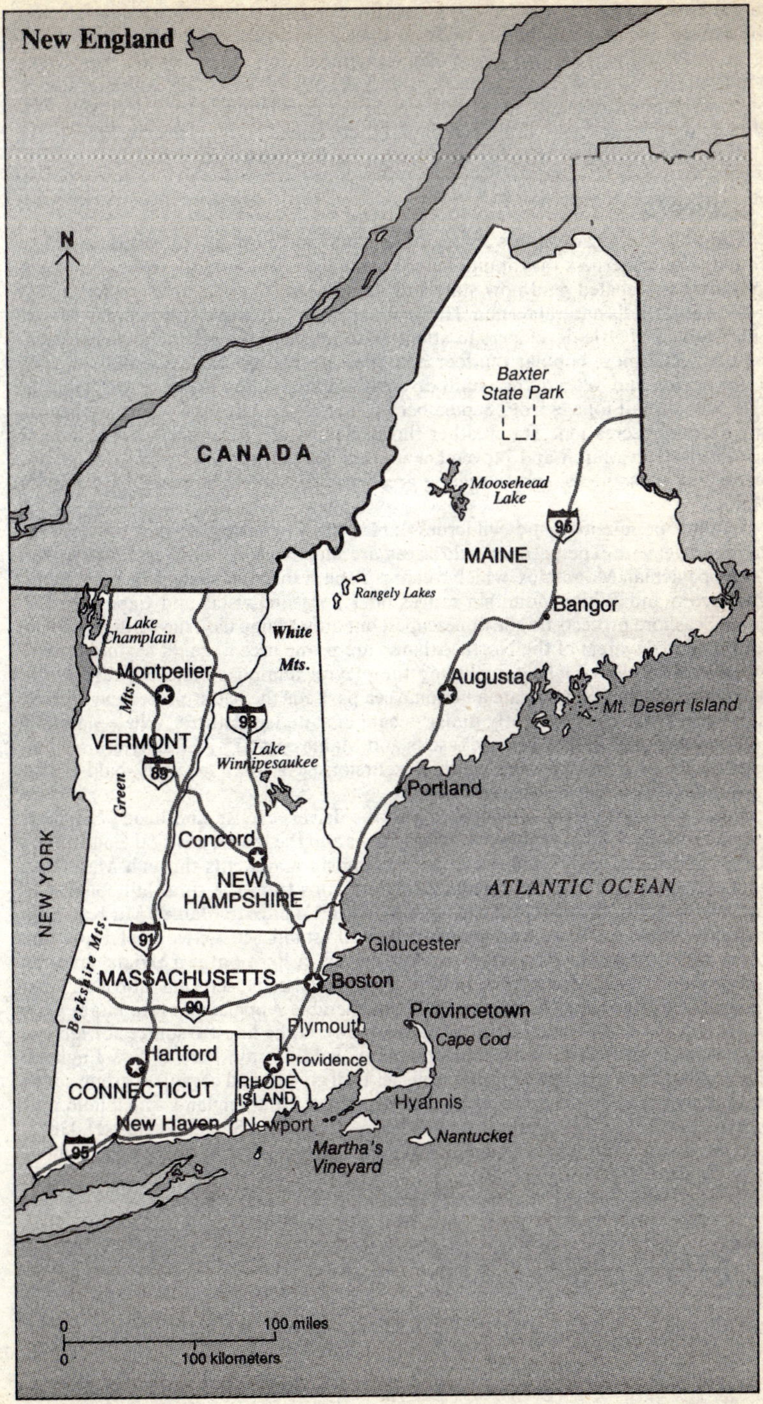
New England
N
CANADA
Baxter
State Park
Moosehead
Lake
MAINE
95
Rangely Lakes
Bangor
Augusta
Mt. Desert Island
Portland
Lake
Champlain
White
Mts.
Montpelier
Green
Mts.
VERMONT
89
93
Lake
Winnipesaukee
Concord
NEW
HAMPSHIRE
NEW YORK
ATLANTIC OCEAN
91
Berkshire Mts.
Gloucester
MASSACHUSETTS
Boston
90
Provincetown
Plymouth
Cape Cod
Hartford
Providence
CONNECTICUT
RHODE
ISLAND
Hyannis
New Haven
Newport
Nantucket
95
Martha's
Vineyard
0
100 miles
0
100 kilometers

to the less colorful coast then. Cape Cod, for example, is less touristed in fall than in summer, and accommodation prices drop by a fifth. State parks and forests proliferate in New England, and many offer **camping** at low rates ($6-10). The **Green Mountain National Forest** in Vermont and the **White Mountain National Forest** of New Hampshire create many more camping opportunities for the traveler, including both inexpensive developed sites and free backcountry camping. State parks and national forests slow down or close up during the winter months.

Outdoors

The first European settlers struggled to tame and in many cases proceeded to destroy the wilderness they found here. Fortunately, the settlers' zeal to beat back the forest has abated, and now state and national parks and forests protect much of New England's natural terrain. However, groups such as the Appalachian Mountain Club still battle developers in attempts to preserve the privately owned backcountry. The most popular outdoor activities are hiking, bicycling and canoeing in the spring and fall, and downhill or cross-country skiing in the winter months. The brilliant fall foliage from September to November heightens the enjoyment of any outdoor recreation. The weather through most of the region is unpredictable at best, though March and November may be particulary dreary. Watch out for black flies, mosquitoes, and swarming greenhead flies in the summer, especially in Maine.

Wildlife populations and wilderness areas are increasing despite the region's dense settlement. The premier wild areas are along the Atlantic seashore and in the Appalachian Mountains, which roll north-south through western New England. The Green and White Mountain ranges offer gorgeous vistas and Cape Cod National Seashore protects fragile dunescapes, but only Maine has true wilderness. The cold, polluted waters of the North Atlantic are prime breeding and feeding ground for several species of whale, including the playful humpback and the rare Right. A landmark proposal to create a national sea park for the better protection of these endangered whales is currently under debate in state legislatures. Whale-watching cruises along the coast of Massachusetts and Maine cost $15-25. Many cruise companies offer other worthwhile wildlife excursions; you may see seals, bald eagles, cormorants, and many other seabirds.

All of these wild areas are accessible to the driver, cyclist, and hiker. Canoeists are particularly fond of Maine's Allagash River and the tamer, pastoral Connecticut River, which divides Vermont and New Hampshire and cuts through Massachusetts and Connecticut. The **Appalachian Trail** runs from the rural hill country of northwestern Connecticut over the Greens and the Whites to Maine's Mt. Katahdin in Baxter State Park. A well-maintained, well-established network of trails link lesser hills throughout the region: the Long Trail in Vermont is a Scouts' favorite, and the Metacomet-Monadnock Trail in western Massachusetts and northern Connecticut is exhilarating in any season. The venerable Appalachian Mountain Club (AMC), 5 Joy St., Boston 02108 (617-523-0636), is the finest resource for anyone who wants to backpack, camp, canoe, or enjoy wildlife anywhere in New England. The club maintains trails and huts, publishes trail guides, and organizes group canoe and hiking trips. You can find chapters throughout New England which hold outings and meetings. New Hampshire Publishing Company, Somerworth, NH 03878, puts out an excellent series of guides to hiking, canoeing, and ski touring throughout New England.

Connecticut

Although it's hard to imagine, Connecticut was once a rugged frontier. Settlement of the Connecticut Valley by Puritans from Massachusetts in the 1630s was the beginning of the colonists' westward movement. Today, Connecticut clearly has two faces; the old Yankee tradition mingles with an urban one brought by the flood of commuters to New York City. Traveling northeast from New York, New England officially begins where Red Sox fans predominate over Yankees partisans. Sophisticated research has placed the divider near New Haven.

Hartford, Connecticut's state capital and the nation's insurance headquarters, takes no risks and offers nothing unexpected. As you pass Hartford en route to more diverting New England destinations, take a gander at the flashy new glass skyscrapers and the white-domed **Old State House.** Get off at the State St. exit to see this colonial, red-brick masterpiece for yourself. Designed by Charles Bullfinch in 1796, the State House features a beautiful senate chamber and a free-standing spiral staircase. Fans of American literature won't want to miss the Mark Twain and Harriet Beecher Stowe houses, located just west of the city center on Rte. 4. The Victorian **Mark Twain Mansion,** 77 Forest St. (525-9317), housed the Missouri-born author for 17 years. Twain composed his masterpiece *Huckleberry Finn* here. **Harriet Beecher Stowe** lived next door on Nook Farm shortly before her death and well after the publication of *Uncle Tom's Cabin.* (Both houses open June to mid-Oct. Mon.-Sat. 9:30am-4pm, Sun. noon-4pm; mid-Oct. to May Tues.-Sat. 9:30am-4pm, Sun. noon-4pm. Admission $6.50 for both houses, seniors $5.50, ages 6-16 $2.75.) Also in Hartford is the small but absorbing **Hartford Atheneum,** 600 Main St. (278-2670; 247-9111 for recorded information), a museum of fine and decorative arts that features a rambling collection of Americana. (Open Tues.-Sun. 11am-5pm. Admission $3, seniors and students $1.50, under 13 free. Free Thurs., and Sat. from 11am-1pm.) About 45 minutes east of Hartford struts **Storrs,** whose E. O. Smith high school has nourished talents as diverse as those of jet-setter "Lili" Charters and publishing magnate M. Barclay C.

Connecticut's coastal towns along the Long Island Sound were busy seaports in the nation's early days. The bustle and adventure that Melville found in towns like these—the dark, musty inns filled with tattooed sailors swapping stories of their journeys, and ships passing in the night—are history. Today, the coast is important mainly as a resort and sailing base, but maritime enthusiasts will enjoy two former whaling ports, New London and nearby Mystic Seaport. **New London** sits proudly on a hillside overlooking the majestic **Thames River.** Behind stately **Union Station** (designed by H. H. Richardson) lies a **visitors center,** which offers free maps and directions for a "historic walk" through downtown. The **Coast Guard Academy** (444-8270; open May-Oct. 9am-5pm) is a five-minute drive up Rte. 32. The free tour takes you through the Coast Guard Museum and the beautiful cadet-training vessel **U.S.S. Eagle** (when it is in port). **Mystic Seaport** (572-0711) is a restored 19th-century whaling port. The main attraction here is the **Charles W. Morgan,** a fully restored, three-masted whaling ship. (Seaport open daily 9am-5pm. Admission $12.50, ages 5-18 $6.25. Take I-95 5 miles east from New London and follow signs to Mystic Seaport or take SEAT bus #2 or 3 from Union Station to Anderson Little ($1), then bus #10 to Mystic ($1).)

Practical Information

Capital: Hartford.

Tourist Information: Department of Environmental Protection, 165 Capitol Ave., #265, Hartford 06106 (566-2304). Supervises over 100 state parks and forests, many with camping. Dispenses topographical maps. Camping reservations through this office recommended for July and summer weekends. **Connecticut Forest and Park Association,** P.O. Box 389, East Hartford 06108. Hiking and outdoor activities information. **Connecticut Coalition of Bicyclists,** P.O. Box 121, Middletown 06457. Write for a state bike map and *Connecticut Bicycle Directory.* **Department of Transportation,** (566-4954). **State Information Bureau,** 165 Capitol Ave., Hartford 06106 (842-2200).

Time Zone: Eastern. **Postal Abbreviation:** CT.

New Haven

You know you're in the right place when you see a T-shirt that reads "Harvard's a disease—Yale's the cure." Obscured by the now centuries-old rivalry between the two Ivy League institutions is the oh-so-God-awful truth: Yale was founded in 1638 by a group of New England clergymen who left decadent Harvard to create a commercial city with the scriptures as its fundamental law. New Haven is now a university town with academic types and a working class population living somewhat uneasily side by side (the university has been plagued by long strikes in recent years). As with most old New England cities, urban renovation is running rampant, and you may find it difficult to find a quiet spot out of earshot of jackhammers and construction companies.

New Haven is laid out in nine squares; the central one is the Green, a convenient focal point for sightseeing. The small business district and the **Yale University** campus surround the Green. The campus draws visitors with its striking architecture and rich history. Neo-Gothic spires and ivy-covered buildings set the tone for serious Yalies shuffling between classroom and library. The adjacent downtown area consists mostly of bookstores, boutiques, cheap sandwich places, and other services catering to students and their professors.

New Haven, and particularly the Yale campus, is full of distinctive and attractive buildings. The omnipresence of American Collegiate Gothic on campus lends a sobriety that its Cambridge cousin lacks. **Sterling Memorial Library,** 120 High St. (432-2798), was designed by James Gambel Rodgers, a firm believer in the sanctity of printed material: the building looks so much like a monastery that even the telephone booths are shaped like confessionals. Rodgers spared no expense to make Yale's library look authentic—the figurines on the library's exterior were decapitated to replicate those at Oxford, which, because of decay, often fall to the ground and shatter. (Open in summer Mon.-Wed. and Fri. 8:30am-5pm, Thurs. 8:30am-10pm, Sat. 10am-5pm; during the academic year Mon.-Fri. 8:30am-midnight, Sat. 10am-5am, Sun. 2-10pm.)

The massive **Beinecke Rare Book and Manuscript Library,** 121 Wall St. (432-2977), is built entirely from Vermont marble. Don't miss the intriguing windowless construction; light filters through the marble walls. (Open Mon.-Fri. 8:30am-5pm, Sat. 10am-5pm.) Notice the neo-Gothic cops-and-robbers motif on the **Law School's** facade along Wall St. between High and York St.

Most of New Haven's museums are on the Yale Campus. The **Yale University Art Gallery,** 1111 Chapel St. (432-0600), claims to be the oldest university art museum in the Western Hemisphere (opened in 1832). Especially notable are its collection of John Trumbull paintings and Italian Renaissance works. (Open in summer Tues.-Sat. 10am-5pm, Sun. 2-5pm; during the academic year Tues.-Wed. and Fri.-Sat. 10am-5pm, Thurs. 10am-8pm, Sun. 2-5pm. Free.) The **Yale Center for British Art,** 1080 Chapel St. (432-4594), contains the finest such collection outside England. (Open Tues.-Sat. 10am-5pm, Sun. 2-5pm. Free.) The **Peabody Museum of Natural History,** 170 Whitney Ave. (436-0850; 432-5050 for recorded message), houses Rudolph F. Zallinger's Pulitzer Prize-winning mural, portraying the North American continent as it appeared 70 to 350 million years ago. Other exhibits range from Central American cultures to the dinosaur hall displaying the skeleton of a Brontosaurus. (Open Mon.-Sat. 9am-4:45pm, Sun. 1-4:45pm. Admission $2, seniors $1.50, ages 5-15 $1. Free after 3pm.)

The **Wooster Square** area, a 10-minute walk from downtown, is a good neighborhood for a stroll, with charming brownstones and a quiet park. Walk down Chapel St. away from Yale with the Green on your left and cross State St.

Food in New Haven is reasonably cheap, catering to the student population.

Yankee Doodle Coffee Shop, 258 Elm St. (865-1074). A tiny, diner-like place, squeezed into a 12-foot-wide slice just across the street from the Yale Boola-Boola Shop. $1.35 gets you eggs, toast, and coffee. Open Mon.-Sat. 6:30am-2:30pm.

Clark's, 68 Whitney Ave. (776-8465), ½ mile from the Yale campus. Students, professors, and office workers all crowd in for tasty lasagna, good soups, and gyros and *souvlaki* ($3-6). Open Mon.-Sat. 11am-12:30am, Sun. 11am-midnight.

Louis Lunch, 263 Crown St. (562-5507). The wife-and-husband team serves the best flame-broiled burger on the East Coast for $1.65. Established in 1895, the wooden shack the restaurant is housed in looks at least that old. Open Mon.-Fri. 9am-4:30pm.

Pepe's, 157 Wooster St. (865-5762), in the old Italian Wooster Square neighborhood. Their white clam pizza ($8) is outstanding. Open Mon. and Wed.-Thurs. 4-10:30pm, Fri.-Sat. 11:30am-midnight, Sun. 2:30-10:30pm.

Ashley's Ice Cream, 278 York St. (865-3661). The best locally owned store, with creamy ice cream and a myriad of sinful dessert options. Wins the battle for the après-pizza crowd. Open Sun.-Thurs. noon-midnight, Fri.-Sat. noon-1am.

New Haven offers plenty of late-night entertainment. You might want to check **Toad's Place,** 300 York St. (777-7431, recording of live music schedule; 562-5589 for specific questions), to see if one of your favorite bands is in town. (Box office open daily 11am-6pm; bar open Sun.-Thurs. 8pm-1am, Fri.-Sat. 8pm-2am.) **Partner's,** 365 Crown St. (624-5510), is a favorite gay hangout. (Open Sun.-Thurs. 7pm-1am, Fri.-Sat. 7pm-2am.) One of the several seedy, friendly nightspots is the **Anchor Bar,** 272 College St. (865-1512), just off the Green. (Open Mon.-Thurs. 11am-1am, Fri.-Sat. 10am-2am.) The **Yale Repertory Theater** (432-1234) has produced such illustrious alums as Meryl Streep and Henry "the Fonz" Winkler. (Half-price student tickets. Season September to May.) Not to be outdone, New Haven's **Long Wharf Theater** (787-4282) received a special Tony Award in 1978. (Tickets $21-26, student rush $5.)

In summer, the Green is the site of free **New Haven Symphony** concerts (865-0831), the **New Haven Jazz Festival** (787-6343, or 669-1662), and other free musical series. The Department of Cultural Affairs (787-8956), 770 Chapel St., prints a sheet describing free summer events.

Inexpensive accommodations are extremely hard to find in New Haven. The hunt is especially difficult around Yale Parents weekend (mid-Oct.) and graduation (early June). **Hotel Duncan,** 1151 Chapel St. (787-1273), has decent singles for $38 and doubles for $52, both with bath. The **Nutmeg Bed & Breakfast,** 222 Girard Ave., Hartford 06105 (236-6698), can make you reservations for doubles in B&B's in New Haven at $35-45. The nearest parks for camping are **Cattletown** (264-5678) and **Hammonasset,** (245-2785) both at least 20 minutes by car.

On the banks of the Housatonic River south of New Haven, the smaller town of **Stratford** is home to the **American Shakespeare Theater,** 1850 Elm St. (375-5000), exit 32 off I-95. (Tickets $19-29.) During the summer Shakespeare Festival, some of the country's most able actors and directors stage the Bard's plays while strolling minstrels, musicians, and artists grace the grounds.

To obtain free bus and street maps, and information about current events in town, stop in at the **New Haven Visitors and Convention Bureau,** 900 Chapel St. (787-8822), on the Green. (Open Mon.-Fri. 9am-5pm.) **Yale Information Center,** Phelps Gateway, 344 College St. (432-2300), also facing the Green, gives organized tours and free maps of the Yale campus. Pick up a 50¢ walking guide and *The Yale,* a guide to undergraduate life ($2). (Free Harvard-bashing 1-hr. tours Mon.-Fri. at 10:30am and 2pm, Sat.-Sun. at 1:30pm. Office open daily 10am-3:30pm.) To get to New Haven, you might consider **Amtrak,** Union Station, Union Ave. (777-4002 or 800-872-7245), with its newly renovated station, but it's not a safe area at night. To or from Yale, take city bus A ("Orange St."), J, or U ("Waterbury"), or walk 6 blocks northeast to the Green. To: Boston ($29-32.50), Washington, DC ($64), and New York ($18-21). **Metro-North Commuter Railroad,** Union Station (497-2089 or 800-223-6052), runs trains to New York's Grand Central Station for half of Amtrak's fare ($8-10.75). Ticket counter open daily 6am-10:30pm.New Haven's **Greyhound** station is located at 45 George St. (772-2470). Frequent service to: New York ($14.50), Boston ($26.40), Providence ($23), Cape Cod/Hyannis ($32), and

New London ($9). Open Mon.-Sat. 7:45am-8:30pm, Sun. 7:45am-9:30pm. **Peter Pan Bus Lines,** Union Station (467-8777), offers buses to Boston ($29).

Connecticut Transit serves New Haven and the surrounding area from 470 James St. (624-0151). Most buses depart from the Green. (Open Mon.-Fri. 8am-4:30pm. Information booth at 200 Orange St. open Mon.-Fri. 9am-5pm.)**Thrifty Rent a Car,** 37 Union St. (562-3191 or 800-367-2277), offers economy cars starting at $31.25 per day ($22.75 on the weekend, 2-day minimum), with 150 free miles. Open Mon.-Fri. 8am-6pm, Sat. 8am-4pm, Sun. 10am-4pm. You must be 25. **Carolyn's Checker Cab,** (468-2678) can take you from downtown to the aiport for $8-9.

New Haven (unlike Yale) is a cinch to get into. The city lies at the intersection of I-95 (110 miles from Providence) and I-91 (40 miles from Hartford). At night, don't wander too freely out of the immediate downtown area and the campus, as some surrounding sections are notably less safe. The Yale area is well patrolled by campus police. Keep in mind that the downtown area is also kept under constant surveillance by the police on the lookout for illegally parked cars. Around 4pm on weekdays the tow trucks are out in full force, so be sure to read parking signs carefully.

Area Code: 203.

Maine

From the grassy slopes of Mt. Desert Island to the gloomy forests surrounding Mt. Katahdin, Maine has something for every wilderness buff. The rapids of the Allagash Waterway will challenge the most expert of canoeists, while hikers, campers, and bicyclists may find bliss in Maine's backwoods lakes, the most remote in New England, and coastal Acadia National Park, unparalleled for windswept wildness. Tourists and "Down-Easters" alike savor lobsters in the many fishing ports along Rte. 1. But Maine is not all imposing countryside. Portland, through an aggressive program of civic renewal, is taking its place among the cultural centers of the Eastern seaboard, and three small liberal-arts colleges—Bowdoin, Bates, and Colby—lie within 60 miles of the city.

Practical Information

Capital: Augusta.

Tourist Information: Maine Publicity Bureau, 97 Winthrop St., Hallowell 04347-2300 (289-2423). **Bureau of Parks and Recreation,** State House Station #22 (1st floor Harlow Bldg.), Augusta 04333 (289-3821). **Maine Forest Service,** Bureau of Forestry, State House Station #22 (2nd floor Harlow Bldg.), Augusta 04333 (289-2791).

Time Zone: Eastern. **Postal Abbreviation:** ME.

Maine Coast

Boat-builders, lobster-fishers, Right whales, and other rare breeds feel at home in Maine. Fishing was the earliest industry here, but the proximity of harbors and forests fostered a vigorous trade in shipbuilding; both continue strongly today. On the puny scale of New England, the state of Maine looms large, and its celebrated coastline is the most interesting in the region.

The length of the coast due northeast from Kittery to Lubec is a mere 228 miles, but the jagged inlets and mountainous peninsulas give the entire shoreline a length of 3478 miles. Anglers appreciate the generous coastline year-round. Lobstering is a major industry here, and eating a day's catch is the highlight of many a traveler's visit. Lobsters are always cheap, but they're better before July, when most start to molt. Be forewarned that lobster-poaching is treated very seriously—people have been shot at for this illegal pastime. The color codings and designs on the buoy markers are registered with the state and are as distinct as a cattle rancher's brand.

U.S. 1 hugs the coastline, stringing together the port towns. Lesser roads or small ferry lines connect to the remoter villages and offshore islands. The best place for information is the Maine Information Center in Kittery (439-1319; P.O. Box 396, Kittery 03904), 3 miles north of the Maine-New Hampshire bridge. (Open Mon.-Fri. 9am-5pm; in summer Mon.-Sat. 8am-9pm, Sun. 8am-6pm.) **Greyhound** is the only form of public transportation along the Maine coast, offering sporadic service to Biddeford, Portland, Camden, and numerous small towns from Portsmouth, NH and Boston. A car or bike is necessary to reach some points of interest. Hitching is fairly easy along the coast, especially along the 20 miles of Rte. 3 between Ellsworth and Bar Harbor on Mt. Desert Island.

Portland

For a virtually tourist-free taste of New England coast, go to Portland. Destroyed by a fire in 1866, the city was rebuilt only to decline in the late 1960s. An effort to revitalize the downtown area is underway, and the results thus far are promising. The attractive Old Port Exchange, lined with restaurants, taverns, and craft shops occupying former warehouses, lends a 19th-century air to the waterfront. The location and low prices in Maine's largest city make it an ideal base for sight-seeing and daytrips to the surrounding coastal areas, such as Casco Bay and the Casco Bay Islands. Nearby Sebago Lake provides great opportunities for sunning and waterskiing.

Practical Information

Emergency: 911.

Visitor Information: Chamber of Commerce: 142 Free St. (772-2811), next to the intersection of Congress and High St. Open Mon.-Fri. 9am-5pm. Pick up a self-guiding walking tour of the city for 25¢.

Greyhound, 950 Congress St. (772-6587), on the eastern outskirts of town. Office open daily 7:30am-5:45pm and 7:30-8:15pm. To: Boston (9 per day, $14-20); Bangor (5 per day, $22); and some points north.

Metro Bus Company, 114 Valley St. (774-0351), ½ mile south of Greyhound. Buses operate 5:30am-11:30pm. Information available 24 hours. Fare 80¢, seniors and disabled 40¢, under 5 free. Exact change required.

Prince of Fundy Cruises, P.O. Box 4216, Station A, Portland 04101 (800-341-7540). Ferries to Yarmouth in southern Nova Scotia leave from Commercial St. near Million Dollar Bridge June 23-Sept. 19 at 9pm, from May 4-June 22 and Sept. 20-Oct. 22 at 9:30pm. $65 per person, ages 5-14 $32.50. Off-season $45 and $22.50, respectively. Cars $90, motorcycles $30, bikes $10. Off-season $70, $20, and $7 respectively. Reservations required.

Taxi: ABC Taxis, 772-8685. About $2 from the bus station to downtown.

Haggets Cycle Shop, 34 Vannah Ave. (773-5117), 1 mile north on Forest Ave. 10-speeds $15 per day. Open Mon.-Fri. 9am-5:30pm, Sat. 9am-4:30pm. $25 cash deposit.

Help Line: Rape Crisis, 774-3613. 24 hours.

Post Office: 125 Forest Ave. (871-8410), exit off I-295. Open Mon.-Fri. 7:30am-5pm, Sat. 9am-noon. **ZIP code:** 04101.

Area Code: 207.

Portland is 110 miles up the coast from Boston on I-95, about a 2½-hour drive; a much prettier route follows U.S. 1. Bangor is 145 miles farther north. Most of the city's sights and attractions cluster around the old port on Commercial and Fore Streets. The downtown area is along Congress Street toward the bay. I-295 detours from I-95 to form the western boundary of the downtown area. Several offshore islands are served by regular ferries.

Accommodations and Camping

Portland has several inexpensive accommodations, and exit 8 off I-95 is a budget hotel center.

YWCA, 87 Spring St. (874-1130), up the street from the Civic Center. Women only. Clean and friendly, though the rooms are small and have cement-block walls. Lounge, kitchen, and pool. Singles $25. Doubles $20.

YMCA, 70 Forest Ave. (874-1111), south side of Congress St., 1 block from the post office. Men only. Pool. Singles $18, $60 per week. $5 key deposit.

Hotel Everett, 51A Oak St. (773-7882), off Congress St., downtown. Clean and orderly though a bit drab. No visitors. Singles and doubles $30-34, off-season $26-32. Weekly rates available. Reservations required.

Wassamki Springs, 855 Saco St. (839-4276), in Westbrook. Closest campground (15 min.) to Portland. Drive west down Congress St. about 6 miles. Full facilities with its own sandy beach; you'll be surrounded by flocks of migrant Winnebagos. Sites $14 for 2, $6 each additional person. Shower and electricity extra. Open May to mid-Oct. Reservations requested, especially for July and August.

Food

Diners, delis, and cafés abound in Portland. Check out the active port on Commercial Street, lined with sheds selling fresh clams, fish, and lobsters daily.

Carbur's, 123 Middle St. (772-7794). Take Spring St. to Old Port, where it becomes Middle St. If you try the quintuple sandwich ($9), the servers and cooks will parade around the dining room chanting "Down East Feast." The Beggar's Banquet is just that—soup, salad, and bread ($3.25). Open Sun.-Thurs. 11:30am-10pm, Fri.-Sat. 11:30am-11pm.

Hu-Shang, 33 Exchange St. (733-0300). Good Chinese food served in a slightly Western atmosphere. Lunch $3.75-7, dinner $5-14. Open Mon.-Thurs. 11:30am-10pm, Fri.-Sat. 11:30am-11pm, Sun. noon-10pm; Nov.-May Mon.-Thurs. 11:30am-9:30pm, Fri.-Sat. 11:30am-10:30pm, Sun. noon-9:30pm.

Raffle's Café Bookstore, 555 Congress St. (761-3930). Near downtown. Enjoy a light lunch while doing a little heavy reading. Has salads, sandwiches, bagels, croissants, and desserts. Cheese and fruit board $4.25-5.25. Open Mon.-Wed. 8am-5:30pm, Thurs.-Fri. 8:30am-8:30pm, Sat. 9:30am-4:30pm, Sun. 4-9pm.

Tree Café, 45 Danforth St. (774-1441). Two levels of tables around a small, central stage. Dinner $7-12 with rice and salad. Live reggae, jazz, folk, rock or cabaret nightly. Open daily 5pm-2am.

Three Dollar Dewey's, 446 Fore St. (772-3310), in the old Port. Dewey's re-creates the atmosphere of an old English pub, serving over 65 varieties of beer and ale. The clientele wears everything from tie-dye to L.L. Bean. Great chili, free popcorn. Open Mon.-Sat. 11:30am-1am, Sun. 11:30am-midnight.

Sights

You can walk to most sights in Portland, others are accessible only by blimp. The **Portland Museum of Art,** 7 Congress Square (775-6148), at the intersection of Congress, High, and Free St., has a worthwhile collection of Winslow Homer watercolors. (Open Tues.-Wed. and Fri.-Sat. 10am-5pm, Thurs. 10am-9pm, Sun. noon-5pm. Admission $3, seniors and students $2.50, ages 6-16 $1, under 6 free. Free Thurs. night.) Down the street stands the **Wadsworth Longfellow House,** 485 Congress St. (772-1807). The well-run tour concerns local Portland history and the Wadsworth and Longfellow families but focuses on the poet's life and personal belongings. Skip it if you're short on time or cash. (Tours every ½ hr. June to mid-Oct. Tues.-Sat. 10am-4pm. Admission $2.50, under 12 $1.)

While the history of Portland's **Old Port Exchange** begins in the 17th century, the area's shops, stores, and homes were rebuilt in Victorian style after the fire of 1866. The **Portland Observatory,** 138 Congress St. (774-5561), was built in 1807. Climb the 102 steps for the view of Casco Bay and downtown Portland. (Open in June Fri.-Sun. 1-5pm; July-Labor Day Wed. and Fri.-Sun. 1-5pm, Thurs. 1-8pm; Labor Day-Oct. open weekends. Admission $1, children 35¢.) Call **Casco Bay**

Lines, on Customs House Wharf (774-7871), for a different view of the bay (2½-hr. sunset cruise $8; 5½-hr. cruise to Bailey Island $10.75, leaving at 10am; special fares for seniors and children). **Eagle Boat Tours,** 170 Commercial St. (774-6498), and **Longfellow Cruise Lines,** 1 Long Wharf (774-3578), also offer a variety of inexpensive cruises.

South of Portland

Kennebunkport and Kennebunkport Beach are popular hideaways for wealthy authors and artists. It's also the vacation home of President Bush. In high season, the town center is crammed with strolling tourists. A walk along Ocean Ave. to Cape Arundel and Walkers Point offers beautiful vistas of the rocky coast and a close-up of the graceful mansions. **Yankeeland Campground** (985-7576) will put you up for the night. For more information, contact the **Kennebunk-Kennebunkport Chamber of Commerce,** P.O. Box 740 04043 (967-0857), located at Coopers corner (Rte. 35 and 9).

Ogunquit, as the town proudly advertises, means "beautiful place by the sea" in the Abenaki language. It's hard to find fault with the name after taking in the fine ocean panorama from atop Bald Head Cliff, just south of Perkins Cove, off Shore Road, or walking the Marginal Way toward Perkins Cove. Just north of York, the town is now a popular summer resort for the wealthy and a breeding ground for starving artists. The **Ogunquit Playhouse** (646-5511; P.O. Box 915, Ogunquit 03907) has the best summer theater on the coast. (Plays and musicals $16. Season runs mid-June to Aug.) You can spend the night at **Dixon's Campground** (363-2131) on Rte. 1, 2 miles south of Ogunquit. (Sites $19 for 2 people, with water and electricity $23. Open May 26-Sept. 12.) Up the coast from Ogunquit and a mile east on Rte. 9 from Wells is the **Rachel Carson National Wildlife Refuge** (646-9226), home to numerous rare birds. This quiet spot is a moving tribute to the naturalist and author of *Silent Spring.* Information on accommodations and restaurants is available at the **chamber of commerce** (646-2939) or the **information bureau,** on Main St. (646-5533).

To get a better feel for these small coastal towns, take Rte. 1 south from Portland, rather than I-95. Rte. 9A, off Rte. 1, offers a lovely, winding drive around the peninsula below Portland.

From Portland to Mt. Desert Island

Many of the coastal towns north and south of Portland are ideal for a few hours stay. Unfortunately, many are unserved by public transportation. **Greyhound's** U.S. 1 route serves Biddeford and Saco south of Portland and Freeport, Brunswick, Camden, Bangor, and Ellsworth, among other towns, to the north of Portland.

Less than 20 miles north of Portland on I-95 lies **Freeport,** often called the "birthplace of Maine." It was here that documents proclaiming Maine's independence from Massachusetts were signed in 1820. More significantly—to the rest of the world—Freeport is the birthplace of the enormously successful outdoor and sporting goods store **L.L. Bean** (865-4761). What started in the 1920s as a humble manufacturer of a waterproof hunting shoe went on to market everything from sturdy tents to men's and women's wear that epitomizes preppy style. This operation is right in the middle of Freeport—follow the signs. It's open 365 days per year, 24 hours per day.

As U.S. 1 turns up along **Penobscot Bay,** the heart of the Maine coast appears. Small, rugged islands covered with fir rise abruptly out of the sea. Finding inexpensive accommodations in the coastal hamlets can be difficult, so you might want to press northward to Mt. Desert unless you are equipped with camping gear. There is one place on U.S. 1 that you should not miss: **Moody's Diner,** in Waldoboro, 20 miles southwest of Camden. In business since 1927, this popular eatery hasn't changed much since then. Famous in several states for its good, inexpensive meals and old-fashioned setting, it has great home-made pies ($1); try strawberry-rhubarb *a la mode.* Sandwiches cost $1.50-3.50. (Open Mon.-Thurs. midnight-midnight, Fri.-Sat. midnight-11:30pm, Sat. 5am-11:30pm, Sun. 5am-midnight.)

Eight tall-masted schooners grace the harbor in **Camden,** 1 mile north of Rockport. The **Camden Hills State Park,** 1¼ miles north of Camden on U.S. 1 (236-3109), is often full in July and August, but if you come before 1pm, you're almost certain to get a site. This coastal retreat offers over 40 miles of trails; one leads up to Mt. Battie. The park also has information on local private campgrounds. (Maine residents $6.50, nonresidents $8; $4 in off-season. Open May 15-Oct. 15.) The **Camden Area Chamber of Commerce,** in Camden Town Landing (236-4404), has information on area attractions and on rooms in local private homes ($12-30). (Reservations 289-3824; open June 25-Sept. 15 Mon.-Fri. 9am-5pm, Sat.-Sun. 10am-4pm; Sept. 16-June 24 Mon.-Fri. 9am-5pm.)

Several coastal towns serve as bases for explorations of nearby islands. From **Lincolnville,** 5 miles north of Camden near the state park, you can take a **Maine State ferry** (800-521-3939 or 789-5611) to Islesboro on Warren Island in Penobscot Bay. (5-9 per day, depending on the season, 8am-5pm, last ferry returns at 4:30pm, 20 min., one way $1-1.75, ages 5-11 75¢-$1, cars $4-6.25.)

South of Blue Hill on the other side of Penobscot Bay is **Deer Isle,** a picturesque forested island with rocky coasts accessible by bridge from the mainland. From Stonington, at the southern tip of Deer Isle, a mailboat (367-5193) leaves three times daily (except Sun.) for **Isle au Haut,** part of Acadia National Park ($7). The boat stops at the town landing. From there, exploration is by foot or bike (no rental bikes available on the island). The only accommodations are three sites at **Duck Harbor Campground** ($7; reservations necessary). Call Acadia Park Headquarters (288-3338) or write to P.O. Box 177, Bar Harbor 04609. (Open mid-May to mid-Oct.)

Mount Desert Island

In spite of its name, Mt. Desert (pronounced de-ZERT) is not barren. Spruce and birch forests, rough, rocky beaches, cliffs, and mountains create a rugged landscape. The waters of the Atlantic—calm in summer, but often stormy in winter—are too cold for all but the hardiest of souls, but the beauty of the ocean and its scattered islands is there for everybody. Wind-swept **Acadia National Park,** the only national park in the Northeast, features rugged headlands, fine beaches, plenty of tidal-pool critters, and activities such as whale-watching cruises. **Bar Harbor** is a lively town with inexpensive places to eat and sleep. Come here in winter if you can stand the cold wind and rain—you'll have the dramatic scenery all to yourself.

Practical Information

Emergency: Acadia National Park, 288-3360 or 288-3369. **Bar Harbor Police,** 288-3391 (outside park and late hours).

Visitor Information: Acadia National Park Visitors Center, (288-3338), 3 miles north of Bar Harbor on Rte. 3. Information on the park and over 100 weekly naturalist programs conducted by park rangers. Browse through *Beaver Log,* the park's information newspaper. Open June 15-Aug. daily 8am-6pm; May-June 14 and Sept.-Oct. 8am-4:30pm. **Park Headquarters** (288-3338), 3 miles west of Bar Harbor on Rte. 233. Information Mon.-Fri. 8am-4:30pm. **Bar Harbor Chamber of Commerce** (288-3393), at the Harbor. Open June 23-Sept. 24 daily 9am-11pm; May 14-June 22 and Sept. 25-Oct. 21 daily 9am-5pm. Also in Cottage St. Municipal Bldg. (288-5103). Open Mon.-Fri. 8am-4pm.

Ferries: Beal & Bunker, Cranberry Isles (244-3575; 244-7485 after 4:30pm). Boats to Cranberry Islands from Northeast Harbor (1-6 per day, 15-25 min. $2.50 one way, under 12 $1.50.) **Canadian National Marine (CNM),** Bar Harbor (288-3395 or 800-432-7344; 800-341-7981 outside ME). Ferry to Yarmouth, Nova Scotia. (June 23-Sept. 24, one way $34, ages 5-12 $17, car $63, bike $7.50; Jan. 1-June 22 and Sept. 25-Dec. 31, one way $25.50, ages 5-12 $12.75, car $47.25, bike $5.75. Cabins $30.50.)

Bike and Boat Rental: Acadia Bike/Canoe, 48 Cottage St. (288-5483), next to the post office. Mountain bikes $15 per day, tandems $25 per day, canoes $22, and kayaks $35-55 per day. Guided kayak half-day tours $29, including equipment. Open May 1-Oct. 15 daily 8am-6pm. **Bar Harbor Bicycle Shop,** 141 Cottage St. (288-3886). Mountain bikes $14 per day, $9 per

½-day, helmets, locks and maps included. Open early May-Sept. daily 8am-8pm. **Latitude 44,** 39 Cottage St. (288-5805). Intro-level sailboard $30 per day, composite boards $39 per day, wetsuits $10 per day. Roof racks and information on nearby lakes included. Group introductory lessons $30. Open May-Oct. daily 10:30am-5pm.

ZIP code: 04609

Area Code: 207.

Accommodations and Camping

Use Bar Harbor as a base for explorations. On Mt. Desert or on one of the outer islands, you might get an excellent site by asking the owners of private land for permission to pitch a tent.

Mt. Desert Island Youth Hostel (AYH), Kennebec St., Bar Harbor (288-5587), behind the Episcopal Church on Mt. Desert St. Friendly managers; two large dorm rooms, common room, and kitchen. Curfew 11pm. Lockout 9:30am-4:30pm. $8, nonmembers $11. Open June 16-Aug. 31.

YWCA, 36 Mt. Desert St., Bar Harbor (288-5008). Women only. Singles $18, $70 per week. Bed in double room $15, $60 per week. Bed in 8-bed dorm room $12, $50 per week.

McKay Lodging, 243 Main St., Bar Harbor (288-3531). Very clean, homey, and comfortable. Doubles $40, with private bath $60. Breakfast included.

The Cadillac Motor Inn, 336 Main St. Bar Harbor (288-3831). Adequate rooms, each with private bath, cable TV and telephone. Singles $28-31. Doubles $39-65. Cheaper off-season.

Acadia Motel-Hotel, 20 Mt. Desert St., Bar Harbor (288-5721), across from the Youth Hostel. Rooms are clean if a bit utilitarian. Doubles $42.

Acadia National Park Campgrounds: Blackwoods, Rte. 3 (288-3274), 4 miles south of Bar Harbor, 2½ miles east of Seal Harbor. Amphitheater slide programs. Over 300 sites at $10 each, seniors $5. Open year-round. Reservations through Ticketron only. Formally June 15-Aug. 15 by reservation only, but cancellations filled on a first come-first serve basis. Arrive around 10am. **Seawall,** Rte. 102A (244-3600), near the Bar Harbor Lighthouse, 2 miles south of Southwest Harbor. Amphitheater programs. Walk-in sites $5, drive-up $8, seniors $4. First come-first serve.

Food and Entertainment

Seafood is the natural way to go here. Unfortunately, you generally won't find lobster in a restaurant for under $8-9. Clamming, picking mussels, and crabbing are free and fun—spend an afternoon in the low tide mud pool.

Beals's, at Southwest Harbor (no phone), at the end of Clark Point Rd. The best price for lobster in the most authentic setting, and you get to pick your own live lobsters from a tank. About $6.50 for a cooked lobster; eat outside and bring your own alcohol. Open Mon.-Sat. 9am-8pm, Sun. noon-8pm; off-season Mon.-Sat. 9am-6pm, Sun. noon-6pm.

The Lighthouse Restaurant, in Seal Harbor (276-3958), right in the center of town. Special fish fry on Fri. nights November to Christmas. Sandwiches $2-5, lobster roll $8, entrees $10-13. Open May-June 15 daily 8am-9pm; June 15-Labor Day daily 8am-10pm; Labor Day-Nov. hours vary.

Chances, Main St. (276-5045), in Northeast Harbor. Plain and simple. Sandwiches $3-4, entrees $9-15, catch of the day $10. Open Mon.-Sat. 11am-11pm.

Rosalie's, 46 Cottage St. (288-5666), in downtown Bar Harbor. Standard Italian fare: spaghetti dinners $5-6, extra large (19-inch) pizzas $10. Open April-Oct. daily 11am-midnight.

Geddy's, 19 Main St, Bar Harbor (288-5077), just up the hill from the water. Excellent blues, jazz, reggae, and rock. Live entertainment ($1-2) half the week, dancing the rest. Concerts $8-15. Open April-Oct. daily 2pm-1am.

Sights

Formerly a playground for the very wealthy, **Bar Harbor** is now a tourist magnet. With the increase in tourism and the fire of 1947, the famous and wealthy have moved to more secluded Northeast Harbor and Seal Harbor; armadas of sailboats flying the burgees of New England yacht clubs still make it up to this part of the island every summer. The "real" towns where fishing and boat building have not yet been replaced by tourism are to be found in the western part of the Island and include Southwest Harbor.**Little Cranberry Island** offers the most spectacular view of Acadia, as well as the cheapest uncooked lobster around at the fishers' co-op.

From Northeast Harbor, the **Sea Princess Islesford Historical and Naturalist Cruise** (276-5352) brings you to an osprey nesting site and past lobster buoys. You might be lucky enough to see harbor seals, cormorants, or pilot whales on the cruise. **Islesford Historical Museum** on Little Cranberry Island is in sight of the fjord-like Somes Sound. (Two cruises per day May weekends and June 6-Oct. 14 daily; fare $7, ages 4-12 $5.) The **Isleford Ferry Company** (276-3717; 422-6815 off-season) offers a shorter two-hour cruise, visiting only the osprey and seal communities and the town of Islesford on Cranberry Island (1 per day, $6, under 12 $4), and a tour guided by a National Park Ranger to Baker Island (1 per day, 4½ hr., $10, under 12 $6).

If you're a whale-lover, try the **Acadian Whale Watcher,** 55 West St., Bar Harbor (288-9794), offering one or two trips daily June-Oct. ($25, seniors and ages 9-14 $20, ages 3-8 $15.) The **Frenchman Bay Co.,** 1 West St. (288-3322) in Bar Harbor also offers whale watching aboard schooner *Bay Lady.*

Acadia National Park offers some of the best hikes and most intimate explorations of Mt. Desert Island. The only national park in New England, Acadia was established in 1916 to preserve this particularly inspiring portion of Maine's rocky coast, islands, and mountains. Thirty-three thousand acres of the park sit on Mt. Desert, and it spills over onto **Schroodic Peninsula** to the east and **Isle au Haut** to the west. On Mt. Desert, the mountains rise directly out of the sea, culminating in Cadillac Mountain, the highest Atlantic headland north of Brazil.

From the visitors center, 5 miles north of Bar Harbor on Rte. 3, take the **Loop Road** veering left along the shore of the island. Here, Mt. Desert Island faces the open sea and great waves roll up against steep granite cliffs. The sea comes into **Thunder Hole** at half-tide with a bang, sending a plume of spray high into the air and onto the tourists. To the right just before the Loop Rd. turns back to the visitors center is **Cadillac Mountain.** Only for cars and bikes; mopeds are not allowed on the ride up. A 5-mile hiking trail to the summit starts at Blackwoods campground, 2 miles east of Seal Harbor. The top of Mt. Cadillac, where sunlight first reaches the U.S., makes a great place for a picnic—on a clear day you can see Mount Katahdin, 150 miles to the north.

The **Wildwood Stables** (276-3622), along the Park Loop Rd., runs one-hour carriage tours ($8, seniors $7, ages 6-12 $5, ages 2-5 $3.50) through the park, as well as 1¼-hr. horseback tours ($20). Reservations are strongly suggested.

You can also explore Acadia by bike. At the visitors center, you can pick up the *Bicycle Guide to Acadia,* which includes information on the 50 miles of carriage paths in the park, 15 designed exclusively for cyclists. The brochure also gives invaluable safety precautions. Note that many of the paths in the park are accessible only to mountain bikes.

Inland Maine

Northeast from the White Mountains of New Hampshire to Presque Isle lies the largest wilderness area east of the Mississippi River—miles of splendid, forested mountains dotted with hundreds of lakes, disturbed only by an occasional logger, canoeist, or angler. The few roads through the region are owned by huge paper companies, as is most of the land. By agreement with the state, nearly all of the roads are open to the public, sometimes for a small fee. If at all possible, pull to the side of the road when you see the loaded logging trucks approaching. It is difficult for them to stop, and they don't like to try.

Baxter State Park and the Allagash

"Greatest Mountain," in local Indian dialect, **Mount Katahdin** looms as the northern terminus of the **Appalachian Trail,** the ancient 2020-mile footpath that follows the Appalachian ridge from Georgia to Maine. The Maine portion of the trail is the most rugged and remote, at one point meandering 100 miles without crossing any public roads or villages. Ponds and streams support a large moose population and an increasing number of bears.

The closest town to the park is **Millinocket.** Home of the Great Northern Paper Co., Millinocket is the largest producer of newsprint in the U.S. Stock up on food here before entering the park, and get a complete list of trails with accompanying detailed maps at the **Baxter State Park Headquarters,** 64 Balsam Dr., Millinocket 04462 (723-5140; open Memorial Day-Labor Day Mon.-Fri. 8am-6pm, Sat.-Sun. 8am-5pm; June-Aug. Mon.-Fri. 8am-5pm).

The main entrance to the park is 20 miles north of Millinocket. There is no bus service, but hitching is fairly easy in summer. There is a motor vehicle charge of $8 per day (free for Maine residents). During high season, competition is fierce for sites at one of the park's nine official **campgrounds.** Reservations are a good idea; Maine residents are guaranteed at least 30% of the sites. (Sites $8 for 2. Open May 15-Oct. 15.) There are also bunkhouse accommodations available for $5, and lean-tos for $4. The most popular site, at the foot of Mt. Katahdin, is **Chimney Pond.** For emptier, quieter sites, choose the northern end of the park. Only Abol, Katahdin Stream, Nesowadnehunk Stream, and Daicey Pond campgrounds are accessible by car. None of the sites has hookups. Park authorities recommend treating lake or stream water with iodine, or boiling it for a minimum of five minutes.

Millinocket is also a popular base for expeditions to the **Allagash Wilderness Waterway,** an untamed river that winds through thick forests. There are numerous outfitters in town. The logistics of an Allagash trip can be challenging—plan ahead. The 85-mile run from **Telos Lake** north to the Canadian border is a popular and challenging trip that crosses only two private logging roads. Camping is permitted only at one of the 66 designated campsites along the waterway (May-Nov. sites $4, residents $3). Write the Bureau of Parks and Recreation, Maine Dept. of Conservation, State House, Station #22, Augusta 04333 (207-289-3821), for information and maps. The waterway is a long drive past Baxter Park from Millinocket.

Moosehead Lakes Region

This remote part of Maine is still truly wild; the native bears, moose, mosquitos, forests, and ponds remain almost unsubdued by humans. The looping road from Ripogenus Dam near Baxter State Park through Greenville to Rockwood leads past lakes and ponds frequently visited by moose in search of grass in the water. Today, **whitewater rafting** enthusiasts frequent this premier region of fast water. Most of the trips are on the Kennebec, Penobscot, and Dead Rivers. No experience is required except for the most technical runs, but all the trips are expensive. **Eastern River Expeditions,** P.O. Box 1173, Greenville 04441 (695-2411 or 695-2248; 800-634-7238 outside ME), has guided trips from April-Oct. ($32-365), and also offer canoe and kayak instruction. **Wilderness Rafting Expeditions,** is in Rockwood in the heart of Moosehead Lake Country, 20 miles north of Greenville (534-2242 or 534-7305; P.O. Box 41-MP, Rockwood 04478). This outfit has similar trips and price ranges. You might also try **Northern Outdoors,** P.O. Box 100, Rte. 201, the Forks 04985 (663-4466; 800-553-7238 outside ME). Reservations are required for any expedition—try to go on a weekday or anytime before July, when the river is much less crowded. The adrenaline-pumping adventure can be well worth the money, especially when the water is high and the dams are released.

Buy food and spend the night in **Greenville,** at the southern tip of Moosehead Lake. The **chamber of commerce** (695-2702), in the center of town, will give you a list of local campgrounds and a map of the area. (Open daily 9am-5pm; Nov.-April Thurs.-Sat. 10am-2pm; 24-hour recording gives accommodation information.)

Sandy Bay Camps (695-2512) has cabins right on the lake ($37.45 for 2), and tent sites ($3). **Rockwood** has cabin accommodations at **Rockwood Cottages** (534-7725; doubles from $40 per night, $240 per week). From Rockwood, take a boat ride to the **Mt. Kineo Hotel,** an abandoned monument of the past, and climb **Mount Kineo,** a 1000-foot peak with 700-foot cliffs plummeting to the lake.

Rangeley Lakes Region

This region is only beginning to develop its tourist industry, but it does contain Maine's two largest ski areas. **Sugarloaf** and **Saddleback** sit on the state's second highest mountain, the only one in the East with true alpine skiing on an exposed summit cone. The area's large lakes— **Rangeley, Mooselookmeguntic, Flagstaff,** and **Umbagog**—are crowded with boaters and anglers in summer. Lake canoeing is made easier with numerous campsites along the lake shores and islands. Whitewater raft trips are possible on the **Androscoggin River.** The Appalachian Trail crosses over several summits in the region. The **Bigelow Range,** which has escaped the recreational development that scarred its mountain neighbors, remains a wild mountain ridge. Its stretch of trail is especially well maintained.

There are several inexpensive places to stay in the area. The **Farmhouse Inn** (864-5805), on Rte. 4, 1½ miles south of Rangeley, offers bunkrooms for $18 a night. Camping at **Rangeley State Park** is permitted May 15-Oct. 1. (Sites $10, residents $8, $1 day-use fee.) For a list of campgrounds, including those in the state park, and for other information, contact the **chamber of commerce,** P.O. Box 317, Rangeley 04970 (864-5571; open Mon.-Sat. 9am-5pm, Sun. 10am-2pm).

Massachusetts

Richard Nixon, when asked if he had ever visited a communist country, replied, "Massachusetts." Despite its modest proportions, this iconoclastic commonwealth has carved a large niche for itself in American history. In a state that takes ideas seriously, politics have often assumed a life of their own. Massachusetts's favorite family, The Kennedys, clambered over local turbulence to attain national prominence, and it is the source of no small pride that this was the lone state to cast its votes for George McGovern in 1972.

In many ways, Massachusetts considers itself the cerebral cortex of the national body. The oldest university in America, Harvard, was founded in Cambridge in 1636, and the nation's first public schools established in 1635. Countless literati have hocked their wares in this intellectual marketplace, including Hawthorne, Emerson, Thoreau, Melville, Howells, Wharton, and William and Henry James—to say nothing of the diligent *Let's Go* staff.

But Massachusetts is not merely a state of snooty idea-mongerers, for workers since the early 19th century have sweated in the textile mills and factories of towns like Lowell, Lawrence, Worcester, Springfield, and Fall River. A salty atmosphere pervades the coast where fishing villages such as Gloucester and New Bedford retain a nautical charm, while the Berkshires are full of farms, fall foliage, and forested hills. Cape Cod is a major tourist magnet, famous for its beautiful beaches and quaint, shingled coastal towns. Boston, "the Hub," is the economic and cultural overlord of the state and indeed much of New England.

Practical Information

Capital: Boston.

Tourist Information: Massachusetts Division of Tourism, Department of Commerce and Development, 100 Cambridge St., Boston 02202 (727-3201; 800-632-8038 for *Spirit of Massachusetts* guides). Open Mon.-Fri. 9am-5pm.

Time Zone: Eastern. **Postal Abbreviation:** MA.

Boston

In the Revolutionary era, Boston, today the oldest major city in the U.S. (1630), was at the forefront of American politics and commerce. Since that moment of glory, this attractive, compact port-town has receded somewhat from national prominence. At moments, Boston behaves as little more than a shrine to its days of Puritans and patriots. However, the city also has a youthful quality which keeps its venerable past from overwhelming it. This is due in part to its long committment to academic and cultural excellence—the city boasts more than 400 institutions of higher learning. The concentration of students fosters a vigorously intellectual atmosphere, further supporting a vibrant visual and performing arts scene. Diversity also contributes to this city's freshness. Boston encompasses significant Irish, Italian, Hispanic, Asian and African-American communities. It is also a mix architecturally, since a recent invasion of yuppies has sparked a downtown building boom. If Boston lacks raw excitement, it offers a gracious mix of the historic and the contemporary that ensures the city timeless charm.

Practical Information

Emergency: 911.

Visitor Information: National Historic Park Tourist Bureau, 15 State St. (242-5642). Information on historical sights and 8-min. slide shows on the Freedom Trail. Some rangers speak foreign languages (Chinese, Dutch, French, German, and Lithuanian). Open daily 9am-5pm, except holidays. **Boston Visitors Information Center,** on Tremont St. at Park, near the Boston Common and the beginning of the Freedom Trail. Free information packet includes *Boston by Week.* Official guide to Boston, city map and Freedom Trail map $2. Open daily 9am-5pm. **Greater Boston Convention and Tourist Bureau,** Prudential Plaza West, P.O. Box 490, Boston 02199 (536-4100). Open Mon.-Fri. 9am-5pm.

Logan International Airport: 567-5400, east Boston. Easily accessible by mass transit. The free **Massport Shuttle** connects all terminals with the "Airport" T-stop. A taxi to downtown Boston costs $10, to Cambridge $12-17. **Airways Transportation Company** (267-2981) runs shuttle buses between Logan and major downtown hotels (service daily on the hr. and ½ hr. 7a,-7pm, 7-11pm on the hr. only. $5.50.)

Travelers Aid: 711 Atlantic Ave. (542-7286). Open Mon.-Fri. 8:45am-4:45pm. Other locations: Logan Airport Terminals E (567-5385) and A (569-6284), and the desk in Greyhound stationk (542-9875); hours vary for each.

Amtrak: South Station, Atlantic Ave. (482-3660 or 1-800-USA-RAIL). T: South Station. To: New York City (12 per day, 4½ hr., $49.50; before 8am, after 6pm, and all day Sat. $38.50) and Washington, DC (8 per day, 8½ hr., $88).

Greyhound/Trailways: 10 St. James Ave. (423-5810). T: Arlington. 2 blocks southwest of the Public Gardens. To: New York City (17 per day, 5 hr., Mon.-Thurs. $29, Fri.-Sun. $31) and Washington, DC (12 per day, 11 hr., Mon.-Thurs. $61, Fri.-Sun. $69). Also the station for **Vermont Transit** and **Bonanza** lines. Open 24 hours. **Peter Pan Lines** (426-7838), across from South Station on Atlantic Ave. T: South Station. Serves Western Massachusetts and Albany, NY. Connections to New York City via Springfield ($29). Open daily 5am-midnight.

Massachusetts Bay Transportation Authority (MBTA): 722-3200, or 800-392-6100; Mon-Fri. 8:30am-4:30pm. The subway system, known as the "T," consists of the Red, Green, Blue, and Orange lines. Green and Red Lines run 5:30am-12:30am. Fare 75¢, transfers free; beware of exit fares in outlying areas. Bus service reaches more of the city and suburbs; fare one token or 75¢, but may vary depending on destination. Bus schedules available at Park St. subway station. A "T passport" offers discounts at local businesses and unlimited travel on all subway and bus lines and some commuter rail zones. 3-day pass $8, ages 5-11 $4; 7-day pass $16, ages 5-11 $8. **MBTA Commuter Rail:** 227-5070, 800-392-6099. Lines to suburbs and North Shore leave from North Station, Porter Square, and South Station T stops. The **Boston and Maine Railroad** (227-5070) also runs out of North Station.

Taxi: Red Cab, 734-5000. **Checker Taxi,** 536-7000. **Cambridge Taxi,** 876-5000.

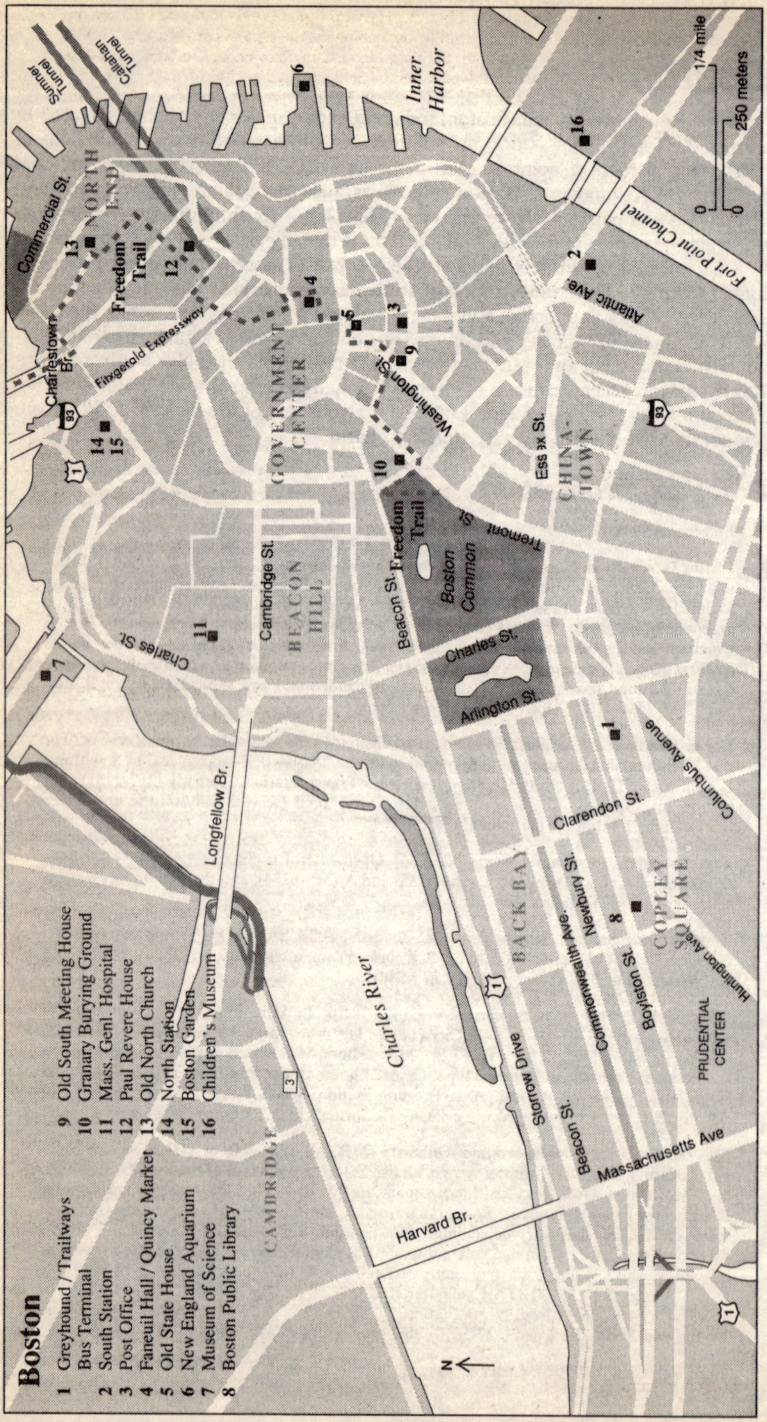
Boston
1 Greyhound / Trailways Bus Terminal
2 South Station
3 Post Office
4 Faneuil Hall / Quincy Market
5 Old State House
6 New England Aquarium
7 Museum of Science
8 Boston Public Library
9 Old South Meeting House
10 Granary Burying Ground
11 Mass. Genl. Hospital
12 Paul Revere House
13 Old North Church
14 North Station
15 Boston Garden
16 Children's Museum
Sumner Tunnel
Callahan Tunnel
Inner Harbor
Commercial St.
NORTH END
Freedom Trail
Charlestown Br.
Fitzgerald Expressway
GOVERNMENT CENTER
Washington St.
Atlantic Ave.
Fort Point Channel
1/4 mile
250 meters
Essex St.
CHINA-TOWN
Tremont St.
Boston Common
Beacon St.
Cambridge St.
BEACON HILL
Charles St.
Arlington St.
Columbus Avenue
Clarendon St.
Longfellow Br.
BACK BAY
Newbury St.
Commonwealth Ave.
COPLEY SQUARE
Huntington Ave.
Boylston St.
PRUDENTIAL CENTER
Charles River
Storrow Drive
Beacon St.
Massachusetts Ave
Harvard Br.
CAMBRIDGE
N

Car Rental: Brodie Auto Rentals, 24 Eliot St., Harvard Square (491-7600). $21-27 per day for sub-compact plus 15, 16 or 17¢ per mile, depending on the type of car. Must be 21 with credit card. Open Mon.-Fri. 8am-6pm, Sat. 8am-noon, Sun. 9am-noon. **Dollar Rent-a-Car,** 1651 Mass Ave., Harvard Square (354-6410). Sub-compact staying within New England $39 per day. Must be 21 with credit card. Open Mon.-Fri. 7:30am-6pm, Sat.-Sun. 8am-4pm. There are other offices at many locations in Boston, including the Sheraton Hotel (523-5098) and Logan Airport (569-5300).

Bike Rental: Community Bike Shop, 490 Tremont St. (542-8623), near the Common. $15 per day. Driver's license and credit card deposit required. Open Mon.-Fri. 10am-7pm, Sat. 10am-6pm.

Weather: recorded forecast, 936-1234.

Help Lines: Rape Crisis Center, 492-7273. **Gay and Lesbian Helpline,** 267-9001.

Post Office: McCormack Station, Milk St., Post Office Sq. (654-5686), in the Financial District. Open Mon.-Fri. 8am-5pm. **ZIP code:** 02109.

Area Code: 617.

About 240 miles north of New York, Boston is easy to reach from anywhere in New England. I-93 (going south it's called the Southeast Expressway) passes through Boston and by Cambridge while the Massachusetts Turnpike (I-90) from the west terminates in Boston. I-95/Rte. 128 skirts the city to the west, connecting the other major highways.

Abandon your car near your lodgings and take to the sidewalks and subways, because Boston drivers come in two styles: homicidal and suicidal. If you do choose to drive around the city, be defensive; Boston's pedestrians can be as aggressive as the drivers. Also, don't become a casualty of the Boston police department's war on illegal parking.

Boston was not a planned city. The intricate layout lacks any logic. Many street names (e.g. Cambridge St.) are repeated throughout the city as well as in neighboring towns. Get a map at the visitors center and ask for detailed directions wherever you go. The hub of the Hub is the 48-acre **Boston Common,** bounded by Tremont, Boylston, Charles, Beacon, and Park St. From the Common the **Freedom Trail** wanders north and east past **Beacon Hill,** the financial district around **Goverment Center, Quincy Market,** and the **North End.** East of the Common is the commercial shopping district around the **Downtown Crossing** and Washington Street pedestrian mall; new highrise shopping and office complexes threaten to extinguish the nearby **Combat Zone,** the red light district. To the south and east of the shopping district lie the crowded streets of **Chinatown,** and the upwardly mobile **South End.** The **Public Gardens** are directly across Charles St. to the west of the Common, and from it Beacon, Commonwealth, Newbury, and Boylston Streets run west through **Back Bay** to the **Fenway** and **Brookline.**

Accommodations and Camping

Cheap accommodations are hard to come by in Boston. Early September, when students and their parents arrive for the beginning of the school year, is a tight time, as is the first week of June, when families of graduating seniors pack into hotel rooms reserved six months to a year in advance. Those with cars should investigate the motels along highways in outlying areas. **Boston Bed and Breakfast,** 16 Ballard St., Newton (332-4199), is a residential service that organizes over 100 accommodations around the Boston area. Singles go for $55-70, doubles for $70-95. (Open Mon.-Fri. 9am-5pm.)

Boston International Youth Hostel (AYH), 12 Hemenway St. (536-9455), in the Fenway. T: Auditorium. Clean but barren rooms containing several beds. Hall bathrooms, though some rooms have sinks. Lockers, common rooms, and two kitchens. 186 beds in summer, 100 in winter. Lockout 10am-5pm. Cafeteria and kitchen facilities. Registration 5-11pm. Lockout 10am-5pm. Midnight curfew. $12, nonmembers $15. Linens $2. Reservations recommended in summer.

Garden Hall Dormitories, 164 Marlborough St. (267-0079), Back Bay. T: Copley. Excellent location. Spartan dorms with bed, dresser, and desk. Some rooms with private bath. Singles, doubles, triples, and quads available. No cooking, no meals served. 3-day min. stay. Open Mon.-Fri. 9am-1pm (no weekend admissions.) Check-out 11am. $22 per person. Must bring own linen. Key deposit $10. Reservations required. Open June 1-Aug. 15.

Longwood Inn, 123 Longwood Ave. (566-8615), Brookline. T: Longwood Ave. Quiet neighborhood. A Victorian mansion with a kitchen, dining room, TV room, laundry, sun room and parking. The management is friendly and the rooms comfortable. Check-in Mon.-Fri. 9am-5pm, Sat. and Sun. 9am-1pm, though these are flexible. Singles $38-47. Doubles $41-49. Each additional adult $8, child $5. Reservations recommended.

Anthony's Town House,1085 Beacon St. (566-3972), Brookline. T: between Carlton and Hawes St. (Green Line C train). A bit far from downtown but very convenient to the T stop. Nicely furnished. Every room has a TV and some have A/C or cable TV. 14 rooms for 20 guests, who range from trim professionals to scruffy backpackers. Noon check-out. Singles $45. Doubles $55. Reservations not required.

Greater Boston YMCA, 316 Huntington Ave. (536-7800), down the street from Symphony Hall on Mass. Ave. T: Northeastern. Women accepted. Hall bathrooms. Clean but battered. Friendly atmosphere; partially used as overflow housing for Northeastern students. Cafeteria. Use of pool and recreational facilities. 10-day max. stay. Renewal and check-out before 11am. Singles $28. Doubles $41. Hot breakfast included. Key deposit $5. I.D. and luggage required for check-in; must be 18 yrs.

Berkeley Residence Club (YWCA), 40 Berkeley St. (482-8850). T:Copley. Great location. Men not allowed above the lobby. Hall baths, some doubles have sinks. Cafeteria, TV room, sundeck. Check-out 11am. Singles $32, weekly $160. Doubles $40, weekly $200. Nonmembers $2 extra. Towel deposit $2.

Susse Chalet Motor Lodge, Morrissey Blvd. (287-9200), in Dorchester, off the Southeast Expressway exits 17, 19, and 20. Good basic accommodations with restaurant next door (entrees $4-10). Check-out 11am; check-in 2pm. Singles $46.70. Doubles $50.70. Reservations recommended.

Food

There are several distinct regions where budget travelers can find food in Boston. Watched over by the historic gilded grasshopper, **Faneuil Hall Marketplace** and **Quincy Market** (T: Government Center) are frequented by natives and tourists alike. An astonishing number of cafés, restaurants, and food stands are jumbled among equal numbers of souvenir and specialty gift shops; almost any kind of fast food from peanut butter to pizza can be found somewhere under the market's long roofs. Just up Congress St., **Haymarket** attracts both budget-conscious shoppers and sightseers to its open-air stalls. Pick up fresh fish, produce, meats, and cheeses here for well below supermarket prices. Indoor stores open daily dawn-dusk; outdoor stalls Fri.-Sat. only. (T: Government Center or Haymarket.) Nearby, the **North End** features great food in the heart of Little Italy (T: Haymarket), while the restaurants in Chinatown are almost as numerous as the people (T:Chinatown).

Durgin Park, 340 Faneuil Hall (227-2038). T: Government Center or Haymarket. Sit at long tables elbow-to-elbow in this bustling Boston institution and let the famous surly servers entertain you. Traditional Irish boiled dinner of corned beef and cabbage $7. Seafood, ribs, or steak served with cornbread $4.25-15. Open Mon.-Sat. 11:30am-10pm, Sun. noon-9pm.

Ruby's, 280 Cambridge St. (523-9036). T:Government Center. Two eggs, toast, and coffee for a truly anachronistic $1 (served Mon.-Fri. until 11am, Sat.-Sun. until 10am). Sandwiches and lunch platters mostly $3-5. Open Mon.-Fri. 7am-9pm, Sat.-Sun. 8am-9pm.

No Name Restaurant, 15½ Fish Pier (338-7539). T: South Station. Follow Sumner St. over the bridge, left on Viaduct St., right on Northern Ave. The best seafood at the best prices in Boston ($6-9). Very informal, fast service—the line moves quickly because the servers rush you through your meal. Huge servings of award-winning chowder chock full o' clams (cup $1.15, bowl $2.50). Open daily 11am-10pm.

Imperial Teahouse, 70 Beach St. (426-8543), in Chinatown. T: Chinatown. Brilliant carved dragons and their companions overlook the way to the spacious second floor and a good view of the streets of Chinatown. Smaller room downstairs. Sweet and sour pork $7. Butterfly shrimp with vegetables $9.50. Open daily 9am-2am.

Bangkok Cuisine, 177a Massachusetts Ave. (262-5377), across the street from the Christian Science Church complex. T: Auditorium. Delicious food and friendly service make this one of the best Thai restaurants in Boston. Large quantities of food at bargain prices. Lunch $4-6, dinner $7-10. Open Mon.-Thurs. 11:30am-3pm and 5-10:30pm, Fri.-Sat. 11:30am-3pm and 5-11pm, Sun. noon-3:30pm and 5-10:30pm.

Kebab-N-Kurry, 30 Massachusetts Ave. (536-9835). T: Auditorium. One of Boston's most delicious secrets, its best advertisement is the tangy aroma of spices emanating from the door. North Indian cuisine with a few dishes from Bombay and southern India. Entrees $8-12. Open Mon.-Sat. noon-3pm and 5-10:30pm, Sun. 5-10:30pm.

Tim's Tavern, 329 Columbus Ave. (247-7894), in the South End. A small place at the back of a narrow bar, crowded at lunchtime with workers from around Copley Sq. Serves large portions of American and spicy Cajun cuisine ($4.50-7). Open Mon.-Sat. 11am-10pm.

The European, 218 Hanover St. (523-5694), in the North End. T: Haymarket. Massachusetts' oldest Italian restaurant is a Boston tradition. Generous portions and friendly service. However, don't expect a romantic night out. The long elbow-to-elbow tables in one room and the small juke boxes in another seem more appropriate for a roadside diner. Expect a wait of up to 1 hr. on weekends. Entrees $6.25-16.50. Open daily 11:30am-12:30am.

Sights

The **Freedom Trail** (536-4100) is a simple and cheap way to see historic Boston's places of interest. Marked by a red brick or painted line on the sidewalks, the trail makes two loops: the Downtown Loop takes you by the **Old South Meeting House,** the **Old State House,** and the **Granary Burial Ground;** the North End Loop passes **Old North Church, Paul Revere's House,** and **Copp's Hill Burial Ground.** If you meet up with a guided tour, don't hesitate to join. The *U.S.S. Constitution* and **Bunker Hill Monument** in Charlestown are a bit farther off the beaten track, but worth visiting. For a map and information about the sights, stop at the visitors information center on the Boston Common. Allow yourself a full day to do both loops. The sights are more crowded on weekends and in summer; some charge a small admission fee.

The **Black Heritage Trail's** 14 stops are marked with a special red, black, and green logo. The trail covers sites of particular importance to the development of Boston's Afro-American community including: the **African Meeting House** (1805), the earliest black church in North America; the **Robert Gould Shaw and 54th Regiment Memorial** to black soldiers who fought in the Union Army and their white Boston leader; and the **Lewis and Harriet Hayden House,** a station on the underground railroad. Pick up a map from the National Historic Park Tourist Bureau. Guided tours available (742-1854).

At two places you can climb above Boston's maze of streets and see the entire city at once. The Hancock Building, 200 Clarendon St., Trinity Place and St. James Ave. (572-6492), is New England's tallest building (740 ft.). The **John Hancock Observatory** at its 60th floor offers colorful exhibits about the landmarks in view. (Open Mon.-Sat. 9am-11pm, Sun. 10am-11pm. Nov.-April daily noon-11pm. Admission $2.75, seniors and ages 5-15 $2, students with ID $2.25. T: Copley.) The **Prudential Skywalk,** on the 50th floor observation deck of the Prudential Center, Back Bay (236-3318), provides a 360° view. (Open Mon.-Sat. 10am-10pm, Sun. noon-10pm. Admission $2.50, seniors, students with ID, and ages 5-15 $1.50.)

Beacon Hill, the Common, Chinatown, and Back Bay

Beacon Hill is almost the same today as it was when Louisa May Alcott lived at 10 Louisburg Square. Residential since its settlement by the Puritans, the neighborhood has always been well stocked by blue-bloods. Several buildings designed by architect Charles Bulfinch welcome visitors, including the State House and the Harrision Gray Otis House. The gold-domed **State House** offers exhibits on Massachusetts and colonial history, government, and artwork. Free tours include the Hall of Flags, House of Representatives, and the Senate Chamber. (Visitor information: Doric Hall, 2nd floor (727-3676). Open Mon.-Fri. 9am-5pm with tours Mon.-Fri. 10am-4pm.) The **Harrison Gray Otis House,** 141 Cambridge St. (227-3956), is the headquarters for the Society for the Preservation of New England Antiquities. (Open for tours on the hour Tues.-Fri. noon-5pm, Sat. 10am-5pm. Admission $3, children $1.50.) The Society can give you information on various other New England historical sites. The nearby **Boston Athenaeum,** 10½ Beacon St. (227-0270), houses over 700,000 books, and offers tours of its library, art gallery, and print room. (Open Mon.-Fri. 9am-5:30pm. Tours Tues. and Thurs 3pm; reservations required.)

Charles Street, Beacon Hill's front door, is less forbidding than the mews and heavily curtained windows of the residential areas on high. Boston Brahmins, at the pinnacle of American high society, share the brick sidewalks with the fashionable contingent of Boston's gay community. The art galleries, cafés, antique stores, and other small shops with hanging wooden signs make this a good spot for an afternoon stroll.

The **Boston Common,** at the base of the hill, was established in 1634, making it the oldest public park in the U.S. Scattered around the green, **Boston Massacre Monument,** the **Lafayette Monument,** the **Declaration of Independence Monument,** and St. Gauden's bas-relief **Civil War Monument** stand as reminders of the somber lessons of history. However, the atmosphere here is anything but sober and reverent. In warm weather, the Common is thick with frisbee players, street musicians, drug dealers, government employees, and families out for the afternoon. Don't walk here at night.

Across Charles St. from the Common, bronze characters from the children's book *Make Way for Ducklings* point the way to the Swan boats in the **Public Gardens.** The pedal-powered boats glide around a quiet pond lined with big shade trees and brightly hued flower beds. (Swan boats (522-1966) open Apr. 19-June 20 10am-4pm, June 21-Labor Day 10am-5pm, Labor Day-Sept. 17 noon-4pm. Admission $1, under 12 75¢.)

Pagoda-like telephone booths mark Boston's **Chinatown.** Clustered within this small area are many restaurants, food stores, and novelty shops where you can buy Chinese slippers and 1000-year-old eggs. Chinatown has two big celebrations each year. The first is **New Year,** usually celebrated on a Sunday in February. The festivities include lion dances, other traditional dance performances, and Kung Fu exhibitions. The **August Moon Festival** honors a mythological pair of lovers at the time of the full moon. Watch for listings in "Boston by Week."

In the **Back Bay,** west of the Public Gardens, serene three-story row houses line the only logically laid-out streets in Boston. The thoroughfares running east-west (Boylston and Newbury St., Commonwealth Ave., and Marlborough and Beacon St.) are crossed by north-south streets ordered alphabetically, from Arlington St. to Hereford St. Originally this was the "back bay" of Boston Harbor. Landfill and elegant folk moved in about 150 years ago. **Commonwealth Avenue** ("Comm. Ave.") is a European-style boulevard whose grassy median is punctuated with statuary and benches, but the more interesting stroll is along chi-chi **Newbury Street,** past dozens of small galleries and unusual boutiques. T: Arlington, Copley, or Auditorium.

The handsome **Copley Square** area extends the whole length of Back Bay on commercial Boylston St. Recently renovated and officially reopened in June 1989, the square may soon have a range of seasonal activities including a farmers market, folk dancing, and a food pavilion. A permanent feature is the **Boston Public Library,** 666 Boylston St. (536-5400), a massive, classic baroque building, liberally inscribed with the names of hundreds of authors. Inside is a tranquil courtyard with fountain and garden, overlooked by benches and window seats. Relax here or in the vaulted reading room, side by side with Brahmins, street people, and starving artists. A program of lectures and films is given in the auditorium. (Open Mon.-Thurs. 9am-9pm, Fri. 9am-5pm. Sat. and Sun. in winter.) Across the square H. H. Richardson's Romanesque fantasy, **Trinity Church,** is dwarfed by I. M. Pei's mirrored **Hancock Tower. Copley Place,** a complex containing a hotel and a ritzy mall in the corner next to the library, is most popular with the local high school students.

Back Bay loses some of its formality on the riverside **Esplanade,** a park that extends all the way from the Longfellow Bridge to the Harvard Bridge. Boston's very own pseudo-beach on the Charles, the Esplanade fills with summer sun-seekers. However, don't go in the water unless you are immune to hepatitis. Bikers and roller skaters, upholding Boston's rules of the road, try to mow down pedestrians on the walkway. The bike path follows the river all the way to Wellesley and makes a nice afternoon's ride. The Esplanade is also the site of one of Boston's best-loved cultural events, the concerts of the **Boston Pops Orchestra** (266-1492) at the **Hatch Shell.** Led by John Williams, the Pops play there during the first week of July at 8pm. Admission is free; make sure to arrive early, before the crowds get unmanageable. On July Fourth, nearly 100,000 Boston patriots throng the Esplanade to hear the Pops concert (broadcast by loudspeaker throughout the area) and to watch the terrific fireworks display following it. Arrive before noon for a seat on the Esplanade, but you can also watch the fireworks from basically anywhere in the immediate vicinity no matter how late you get there. The regular Pops season at **Symphony Hall** runs May 9-July 2 and July 11-15. Tickets $9.50-27.50.

At the far eastern end of the Esplanade on the Charles River Dam, the **Museum of Science,** Science Park (723-2500; T: Science Park), contains, among other wonders, the largest "lightning machine" in the world and a multi-story roller coaster for small metal balls that purports to explain energy states. Within the museum, the **Hayden Planetarium** features models, lectures, films, laser and star shows, and the **Mugar Omni Theatre** runs films of popular scientific interest on a four-story domed screen. (Open Tues.-Thurs. and Sat.-Sun. 9am-5pm, Fri. 9am-9pm; Labor Day-May 1 Sat.-Thurs. 9am-5pm, Fri. 9am-9pm. Admission $6, seniors and ages 4-14 $4. Combined admission and Omni tickets $9, $12, or $15. Free Wed. afternoons Labor Day-May 1.)

Quincy Market, Government Center, and the Waterfront

Upon completion, Boston's red-brick and cobblestone **Quincy Market** received nationwide praise as an example of urban revitalization. The pretty buildings that house souvenir shops and trendy boutiques were architecturally significant but decrepit warehouses not long ago. The market is overpriced and often crowded, but it is still fun for browsing. At night, come for the lively bar scene. **Faneuil** (FAN-yul) **Hall**, the gateway to the market, was donated to the city to serve as a marketplace and community hall in 1742 by Peter Faneuil. Sometimes called the "cradle of American Liberty," it was the gathering spot for townspeople angry with King George. (Hall open daily 9am-5pm.) The red-brick plaza just above Quincy Market, **Government Center,** is not quite as picturesque, nor is monstrous **City Hall** (725-4000), open to the public. (T: Government Center.)

Boston's wharf area is on the other side of the expressway near Haymarket and the North End. (T: Aquarium.) At the excellent **New England Aquarium** (973-5200), Central Wharf on the Waterfront, giant sea turtles, sharks, and their companions swim tranquilly as visitors peer into their 187,000 gallon tank. Around the base of the tank penguins cavort in a mini-archipelago all their own. The museum also has numerous more "conventional" exhibitions, and offers free short films. Dolphins and seals perform in the ship *Discovery,* moored alongside. On weekends lines tend to be long. (Open Sept.-June Mon.-Thurs. 9am-5pm, Fri. 9am-8pm, Sat.-Sun. and holidays 9am-6pm; July-Aug. Mon.-Tues. and Thurs. 9am-6pm, Wed. and Fri. 9am-8pm, Sat.-Sun. and holidays 9am-7pm. Admission $7, students $6, ages 4-15 $3.50. Fri. and summer Wednesdays after 4pm $1 off.)**Boston Harbor Cruises** (227-4320) leave from Long Wharf, adjacent to the aquarium, for one-and-a-half-hour tours of the harbor. The season runs roughly from March-late Sept. (Departures at 11am, 1pm, and 3pm. Admission $8, seniors $6, under 12 $4. Sunset cruises, at 7pm, $8.)

Walk south to Congress Street Bridge and Museum Wharf to board the **Boston Tea Party Ship and Museum** (338-1773), which manages to convey little of the drama of the event it commemorates. Trying your hand at heaving tea chests overboard is fun, though. (Open daily 9am-6pm. Admission $5, ages 5-14 $3.75.) At the **Children's Museum,** 300 Congress St. (426-8855), also on Museum Wharf, kids of all ages play with the hands-on exhibits. Don't miss the Kyo No Machiya, an authentic two-story house from Kyoto, Japan. (Open July 1-Labor Day Mon.-Thurs. and Sat.-Sun. 10am-5pm, Fri. 10am-9pm; in off-season closed Mon. Admission $6, seniors and ages 2-15 $5; Fri. 5-9pm $1. T: South Station; follow the signs with the milk bottles on them.) Slightly north of Quincy Market, but also on the waterfront, is the historic **North End,** the city's oldest residential district, and currently an Italian enclave. (T: Haymarket.)Part of the Freedom Trail, this is the ideal place to sip cappuccino and indulge in pastries.

The Fenway and Museums

The **Fens** is a smallish park named for the fen at its center, a marshy patch of public land where Bostonians staked out victory gardens years ago and residents still work vegetable patches. It is pleasant enough during the day, but avoid it at night. The **Fenway** is a larger area that is home to some of Boston's major cultural institutions, the best of the area's rowdy nightlife, and **Fenway Park,** the home of the 1988 American League Eastern Division Champion **Boston Red Sox.** (Box Office 267-8661. Open Mon.-Fri. 9am-5pm, Sat. 9:30am-2pm. T: Fenway (Green line D Train) or Kenmore.)

Boston's small but high-quality **Institute of Contemporary Art (ICA),** 955 Boylston St. (266-5151), attracts major contemporary artists to Boston. Exhibits change every eight weeks. The museum also offers music, dance, and film presentations. Discussions with art authorities: Sat. 2pm, with artists: Sun 10am. (Open Wed., Sun. 11am-5pm, Thurs.-Sat. 11am-8pm. Admission $4, seniors and under 16 $1.50, students with ID $3. Free Thurs. 5-8pm. T: Auditorium.)

Two blocks down Massachusetts Ave. from Boylston is the Mother Church of the **First Church of Christ, Scientist,** One Norway St. (262-2300), founded in Boston by Mary Baker Eddy. The **Mother Church** is the world headquarters of the Christian Science movement, and its complex of buildings is appropriately vast and imposing. Both the Mother Church, which seats thousands, and the smaller, older church behind it can be seen only by guided tour; the guides do not proselytize. (Tours Mon.-Sat. 9:30am-3:30pm, Sun. 11:15am-2pm.) In the Christian Science Publishing Society next door, use the catwalk to pass through the **Mapparium,** a 40-foot-wide stained-glass globe. (Tours Mon.-Sat. 9:30am-3:30pm.)

The **Museum of Fine Arts (MFA),** 465 Huntington Ave. (267-9300), near the intersection with Massachusetts Ave., displays outstanding Egyptian and Asian collections, a good showing of impressionists, and superb Americana. Don't miss John Singleton Copley's fascinating portraits of his contemporaries Paul Revere and Samuel Adams, or his dramatic *Watson and the Shark.* Also on display are the two famous unfinished portraits of George and Martha Washington, painted by Gilbert Stuart from life in 1796. (Open Tues.-Sun. 10am-5pm, Wed. 10am-10pm. West Wing only open Thurs.-Fri. 5-10pm. Admission $5, West Wing only $4, seniors $4. Sat. free to all 10am-noon. T: Museum, Green line E train.)

A few hundred yards from the MFA is the beautiful **Isabella Stewart Gardner Museum,** 280 The Fenway (566-1401; 734-1359 for recorded events information). The small, Venetian-style palace was originally the home of "Mrs. Jack" Gardner, a woman whose eccentricities scandalized Boston in her day, but whose impeccable, if eclectic, taste eventually left the city a superb art collection. A stunning courtyard occupies the center, and centuries-old architectural fragments litter the corridors. (Chamber music on 1st floor Sept.-June Tues. at 6pm, Thurs. at 12:15pm, and Sun. at 3pm. Open Tues.-Sun. noon-5pm; Sept.-June Tues. noon-6:30pm, Wed.-Sun. noon-5pm. Admission $5, seniors and students $2.50, children free.)

The **John F. Kennedy Presidential Library** (929-4523), designed by I.M. Pei, is a bit out of the way on Morrissey Blvd., Columbia Point, Dorchester. Inside this white cuboid oceanside building is a fascinating, if sometimes trivia-bound, museum that uses photographs, documents, audio-visual exhibits, and mementos to document the career of John and Robert Kennedy. (Open daily 9am-5pm. Admission $3.50, seniors $2, under 16 free. T: JFK/UMass on the Ashmont branch; free MBTA shuttle to the U Mass campus, a short walk from the library.)

Nightlife and Entertainment

At night the buzz of activity in Boston doesn't fade just because the sunlight has; for many the dinner hour marks only the starting point. Folk, jazz, rock, comedy and other more liquid inebriants are all easily found here. Check the *Phoenix* "Boston After Dark" listings for up-to-date information. Expect to have your ID checked, although a few clubs in Boston have under-21 nights, and other bars may admit you if you don't drink.

Certain bars cater to a gay and lesbian clientele on specific nights or at all times. **Campus/Manray,** 21 Brookline St., Central Sq. (864-0406; T: Central), features Top-40 and progressive music for women on Sundays and is open to a mixed crowd the rest of the week. (Open Wed.-Sun. 8pm-1am.) **Chaps,** 27 Huntington Ave., (266-7778; T: Copley), is primarily a gay male bar with a blend of older and younger patrons. (Open daily 10am-2am. Cover $1-3).

The Black Rose, 160 State St., Faneuil Hall (742-2286). T: Government Center. Irish pub and Boston fish market food served with an authentic accent. Live traditional Irish music Sat., Sun. 4-8pm and daily at 9pm. Open daily 11:30am-1:30am. Cover Fri.-Sat. nights $5.

Cantab Lounge, 738 Mass Ave., Central Sq. (354-2658). T: Central. Every Fri. and Sat. night, the **Mystery Cafe** downtairs features jazz from 10pm-2am. The upstairs bar has live music and dancing Thurs.-Sat. Lively college crowd. Open Mon.-Thurs. 8am-1am, Fri.-Sat. 8am-2am, Sun. noon-1am.

The Channel Club, 25 Necco St., South Boston (451-1050). T: South Station. A forum for the best reggae, new wave, and heavy metal, featuring national and local bands. Huge dance floor, 8 bars, game room, concession stand. Capacity 1500. Occasional 18-and-over nights. (Open daily, hours vary. Cover $3-10.)

Metro/Axis, 13-15 Lansdowne St., Kenmore Sq. (262-2424). T: Kenmore. A spacious dance club with loyal regulars. Some 18-and-over nights. Open Wed.-Sat. 10pm-2am. Cover varies.

Rathskeller ("Rat" for short), 528 Commonwealth Ave., Kenmore Sq. (536-2750). T: Kenmore. Showcases exciting new bands; performances start around 9:30pm. Cover $4-8.

Those with a taste for more dignified, highbrow pursuits will not be disappointed. Boston is full of musicians, dancers, actors, and *artistes* of every description. The *Boston Phoenix* and the "Calendar" section of the Thursday *Boston Globe* list activities for the coming week. Also check the "Boston by Week" pamphlet available at the visitors center. **Bostix,** Faneuil Hall (723-5181), sells half-price tickets to sporting events and performing arts on the day of performance. Service charge of $1-2 per ticket. (Cash only. Open Tues.-Sat. 11am-6pm, Sun. 11am-4pm.)

The Boston "theater district" is near the Boylston T-stop and the **Wang Center for the Performing Arts,** 268 Tremont St. (482-9393), but you can uncover top-quality drama throughout the metropolitan area. The **Shubert Theater,** 265 Tremont St. (426-4520), and the **Wilbur Theater,** 246 Tremont St. (426-1988), host Broadway hits calling in Boston. Tickets for these and for shows at the **Charles Playhouse,** 74 Warrenton St. (426-6912), are costly (around $30). The area's professional companies are cheaper, and may provide a more interesting evening. The **Boston Shakespeare Company,** 52 St. Botolph's St., Back Bay (267-5600), the **American Repertory Theater (ART),** at Harvard's Loeb Theater, 64 Brattle St. (547-8300), the **New Ehrlich Theater,** 539 Tremont St. (482-6316), and **Huntington Theater Co.,** 264 Huntington Ave. (266-3913) at Boston University are well-established artistic institutions. (Tickets $10-24.) College theater is also plentiful and affordable. During term-time, investigate the **Loeb Drama Center** (864-2630), the **Tufts Theater-Arena** (381-3493), the **Boston University Theatre** (266-3913), the **MIT Drama Shop** (253-2877) and **Shakespeare Ensemble** (253-2903), and **Hasty Pudding Theatricals,** 12 Holyoke St. (495-5205), Harvard's all-male review, the oldest theatrical organization in the world. The Pudding is well known as the finest college entertainment in the country—alumni include Jack Lemmon and Fred Barton—and 1990 will see *GQ* cover models and Las Vegas club entertainment duo Michael Starr and Jon Blackstone leading the list of HPT performers.

The **Boston Symphony Orchestra,** 201 Mass. Ave. (266-1492), at Huntington, holds its concert season from October to April. Rush seats go on sale three hours before Thurs. and Sat. concerts. Open rehearsals on Wednesdays cost under $10, and bargain tickets are available Friday at noon for that day's show. In summer, when the BSO retreats to Tanglewood, the **Boston Pops Orchestra** sets up at Symphony Hall or the Esplanade and plays programs of classics and pop on weekend evenings.

In October the big event is the **Head of the Charles** regatta, the largest single-day regatta in the U.S., attracting crew teams from across the country. The 3-mile races begin at Boston University Bridge and the best vantage points are on the Weeks footbridge and Kennedy St. Bridge near Harvard. On April 19, memories of the "Head" are trodden underfoot by the 10,000 runners competing in the **Boston Marathon.** Call the Massachusetts Division of Tourism for details (617-727-3201).

For other special events, such as the **St. Patrick's Day Parade** in South Boston (March 17), **Patriot's Day** celebrations (April 19), the week-long **Boston Common Dairy Festival** (June), the **Boston Harbor Fest** (early July), and the North End's **Festival of St. Anthony** (mid-August), see thc Boston *Phoenix* or *Globe* calendars.

Cambridge

Separated from Boston only by the Charles River, Cambridge is an independent city in the eyes of the law and its residents. Balding professors, tie-died hippies, street punks, and construction workers turn Cambridge into a socioeconomic Babel, with eccentric liberal politics to boot. Even more than Boston, Cambridge is a student town, home to both Harvard University and the Massachusetts Institute of Technology (MIT).

Practical Information

See Boston Practical Information above for more complete and detailed listings.

Emergency: 911

Visitor Information: Harvard University Information Center, 1352 Massachusetts Ave., Harvard Sq. (495-1573). The best information source in Cambridge, with maps, guides, and cultural information about Harvard Sq. and the university. Tours of the university given several times per day. The **Cambridge Discovery Booth** (497-1630), in Harvard Sq., provides information about both Cambridge and Boston, as well as MBTA bus and train schedules. Tours of the university and surrounding area are given in the summer. (Open daily 9am-6pm; in off-season Mon.-Sat. 9am-5pm, Sun. 1-5pm.) *The Unofficial Guide to Life and Harvard* ($5.95), 275 pages of comprehensive, up-to-date listings of Boston and Cambridge restaurants, entertainment, sights and activities, transportation, and services, is available at Harvard Student Agencies, Thayer Hall Basement-B, Harvard Yard (495-3030; open Mon.-Fri. 9am-5pm).

Massachusetts Bay Transportation Authority (MBTA): 722-3200, or 800-392-6100; Mon.-Fri. 8:30am-4:30pm. Subway operates 5:30am-12:30am.

Taxi: Cambridge Taxi, 876-5000.

Post Office: 125 Mt. Auburn St. (876-6483), Harvard Sq. Open Mon.-Fri. 8am-5:30pm, Sat. 9am-1pm. **ZIP code:** 02138.

Area Code: 617.

Massachusetts Avenue ("Mass. Ave.") is Cambridge's major artery. Most of the action takes place in squares (that is, commercial areas—none is actually square) along Mass. Ave. and the Red Line. **MIT** is just across the Mass. Ave. Bridge at **Kendall Square,** on the Red Line; **Central Square** is the heart of urban Cambridge; and frenetic, eclectic **Harvard Square** is one T-stop away from Central.

Accommodations

Cambridge YMCA, 820 Massachusetts Ave. (876-3860). T: Central. Men only. Sometimes full. Hall bathrooms. 7-day max. stay. 11am checkout. Singles only, $26. Key deposit $10. Reservations recommended, or try to get there by 11am. 2 forms of ID (one picture) required.

Cambridge YWCA, 7 Temple St. (491-6050), just off Mass. Ave. near the Central T-stop. Women only. Kitchen and laundry facilities. Check-out 11am. Singles only, $30, nonmembers $35. Additional cot $8. Key deposit $10. Reservations recommended.

The Kirkland, 67 Kirkland St. (547-4600), near Harvard Sq. T: Harvard. This small hotel's motto reads: "for lean-pocket transients since 1945"; the emphasis is on transients. The management is friendly enough, but their 44 rooms need renovating badly. The decor consists of peeling paint, uncarpeted halls, and mismatched wallpaper. No phones, no TV. Singles $25-45. Doubles $45-55. Reservations not accepted.

Susse Chalet Inn, 211 Concord Turnpike (Rte. 2), Fresh Pond (661-7800), ½ mile from the Alewife T-stop. Standard chain-type lodgings just outside Cambridge. Check-out 11am. Singles $46.70. Doubles $50.70. Reservations suggested.

Food

Thousands of college students flee cafeteria fare to the restaurants of Harvard Square nightly, and for good reason. An enormous selection of funky eateries is packed into the tiny area. A 15-minute walk around should uncover offerings to satisfy even the most esoteric tastebuds. Don't be afraid, though, to wander beyond the Square if you start feeling as if you've seen one kid too many in a crimson sweatshirt. Explore Massachusetts Ave. where it slopes down into Central Sq., it's lined with great Indian restaurants, and even has a decent Ethiopian restaurant, **Asmara.**

For cheap grub, try **Elsie's,** 71 Mt. Auburn St. (354-8362; sandwiches $2.30-3.50; open Mon.-Fri. 7am-midnight, Sat. 8am-4pm, Sun. 11am-7pm); **Charlie's Kitchen,** 10 Eliot St. (492-9646; $4-8; open Mon.-Sat. 11:30am-11pm, Sun. noon-11pm); **Café Avventura,** 36 Kennedy St. in the Garage, (491-5311; pizza: small $3.75-6.25, large $6.50-9.50, open Mon.-Thurs. 11:45am-11pm, Fri.-Sat. 11:45am-midnight, Sun. noon-6pm); or **Tommy's Lunch,** Mt. Auburn St. Tommy's is something of a Harvard institution—surly service, sneering Tommy, and lots of greasy onion rings.

Bangkok House, 50 JFK St. (547-6666). The large portions of delicious Thai food come in three categories: mild, spicy, and very spicy. If you get a three-starred dish be prepared to sweat. Entrees $7.25-12.The coconut soup is deliciously aromatic. Open Sun.-Thurs. noon-3pm and 5-10pm, Fri.-Sat. noon-3pm and 5-10:30pm.

Dolphin Seafood, 1105 Mass. Ave. (354-9332), between Harvard and Central Sq. Crowded and friendly. Huge portions of fresh seafood $5.25-9.50. Cheap lunch specials. Open Mon.-Sat. 11am-10pm, Sun. 4-10pm. Come early on weekends.

Oh! Calcutta!, 468 Massachusetts Ave. (576-2111). Immensely successful Indian restaurant. Atmosphere needs a little work, but service is great. Large portions of delicious food, from the fiery pickled vegetables to sweet rice pudding. Lunch $4-5, dinner entrees $7-10.45. Open daily noon-10:30pm.

Pizzeria Uno, 22 John F. Kennedy St. (497-1530), Harvard Sq. One of the wooden signs reads "If we're busy try our place in Chicago." On weekends you'd better have an airline ticket handy because the wait can be over an hour, and the service is slow. Worth it for th rich, delicious food though. Individual pizza $4.25-5.45, regular $8-9.50. Express lunch Mon.-Fri. 11am-3pm, 5 minutes, $4. Open Sun.-Wed. 11am-1am, Thurs.-Sat. 11am-2am.

The Skewers, 92 Mt. Auburn St. (491-3079), Harvard Sq. Large servings of tasty Middle Eastern food at bargain prices. Sandwiches $4.25-4.75, dinner entrees $6.50-7.25. Open Mon.-Sat. 11am-11pm, Sun. noon-10pm.

Stock Pot, 57 John F. Kennedy St. (492-9058), in the Galleria Mall. Great salad bar ($4.30), hearty soups ($2.50-3.20), and pocket sandwiches ($3.75) in a relaxed atmosphere. Open Mon.-Sat. 11:30am-8:30pm, Sun. 4-8:30pm.

Ching Hua Garden, 24 Holyoke St. (547-4969). Mozart and Beethoven tunes relax patrons. Mandarin, Szechuan, and Hunan cuisine. Lunch $4-4.50, dinner $5-9.75. Open Mon.-Thurs. 11:30am-3pm, 5-10pm, Fri.-Sat. 11:30am-3pm and 5-11pm.

Bruegger's Bagel Bakery, 83 Mt. Auburn St. (661-4464), Harvard Sq. Great sandwiches, but don't expect to be able to sit down in this tiny place to enjoy yours. Fresh bagels 35¢, ½ dozen $1.85, 1 dozen $3.50. Cream cheeses $1.50-3.15. Bagel sandwiches $2.25-3.30. Open Mon.-Sat. 7am-9pm, Sun. 8am-5pm.

Herrell's, 15 Dunster St. (497-2179), Harvard Sq. Current holder of the "Best Chocolate Ice Cream in Boston" title, Herrell's makes their ice cream on the premises, unlike the main competition, **Emack & Bolio's,** 1310 Mass. Ave. At Herrells, lap up some of their sinfully rich "chocolate pudding" ice cream inside a vault, painted to resemble the ocean depths. Open daily 11am-1am; off-season noon-midnight. For frozen yogurt fans, the *in* place to pick up your fix is **Luscious Licks,** on Eliot St.

Nightlife and Entertainment

In warm weather the entertainment is free as the songs of jazz and folk musicians float (and sometimes flop) through the streets around Harvard Square. The numerous cafés are crowded at all times of year for lunch or after-hours coffee. Try the outdoor tables at **Café Pamplona,** 12 Bow St. (open Mon.-Sat. 11am-1am, Sun. 2pm-1am), or the relaxed **Café Algiers,** 40 Brattle St. (492-1557; open Sun.-Thurs. 10am-12:30am, Fri.-Sat. 10am-1:30am). The **Blacksmith House,** 56 Brattle St. (354-3036), serves up more than just café and bakery items; here the Cambridge Center for Adult Education presents various poetry readings throughout the year (admission varies) and also musical programs on summer Thursdays at 8pm. Jazz, broadway, classical piano, and Sondheim all cost $3.50 (limited seating). The **Coffee Connection** (492-4881) on Dunster St. in the Garage Mall has a fine selection of coffees and teas as well as an array of delightful desserts. (Open Mon.-Thurs. 8am-11pm, Fri. 8am-midnight, Sat. 9am-midnight, Sun. 9am-11pm.) But if your idea of nightlife is a little louder than coffee and a heavy discussion of the modern novel, Cambridge can accommodate you well.

The Boathouse Bar, 56 JFK St., Harvard Sq. (491-6476). Usually populated by the Harvard Business School set and Kirkland House society. On weekend nights and after hockey and football games, the college crowd fills the bar. Sometimes the line stretches out the door. Open Sun.-Thurs. noon-1am, Fri.-Sat. noon-2am.

The Bow and Arrow Pub, Bow St. and Mass Ave., Harvard Sq. Decidedly non-college-kid clientele; usually an impressive assortment of motorcycles outside. One of the cheapest beers in town. Good juke box. Open Sun.-Thurs. 11am-1am, Fri.-Sat, noon-1am.

Catch a Rising Star, 30b Joh F. Kennedy St. (661-9887), Harvard Sq. All ages, but you must be 21 to drink. "Open mike" comedy Sun. and Mon. Comedy shows: Sun.-Thurs. at 8:30pm, Fri. at 8:30pm and 11pm, Sat. at 7:30pm, 9:45pm, and midnight. Cover $5-12.50.

Hong Kong, 1236 Mass Ave. (864-5311), Harvard Sq. The scorpion bowls are a Harvard tradition. The food here is not acclaimed, but the bar upstairs is popular, crowded, and rowdy. Open Sun.-Thurs. 11:30am-1am, Fri.-Sat. 11:30am-2am.

T.T. The Bear's Place, 10 Brookline St. (492-0082), Central Sq. Best club in Cambridge for hard rock. Open Tues.-Sat. 6pm-1am (8pm-1am for music). Cover $3-6.

Sights

According to Cotton Mather, **Harvard University** got its name in 1638 when "Mr. John Harvard, a reverend, and excellent minister of the gospel," dying of consumption, "quickly after his arrival here, bequeathed the sum of *seven hundred, seventy nine pounds, seventeen shillings and two pence,* towards the pious work of building a *Colledge.*" Then the school was only two years old; today it's a lot more expensive to get your name placed on the rolls. Visiting is cheaper, and quicker. Ask at the information center about guided tours of the campus (see Practical Information above).

The university's "heart" is **Harvard Yard,** of which the western half ("The Old Yard") was the site of the school's first buildings. The Yard is where all Harvard students live in their first year of study. John F. Kennedy was housed in Weld, and Emerson and Thoreau in Hollis. The Yard's eastern half is the site of classroom buildings, **Memorial Church,** and **Widener Library** (495-2413). Widener is the centerpiece of the Harvard University Library, the largest academic library in the world with 10.5 million volumes total. While visitors can't browse among Widener's shelves, they are welcome to examine Harvard's copy of the Gutenberg Bible and other rare books in the Treasure Room and to take in the beautiful Sargent murals.

Harvard of the late 20th century extends well beyond Harvard Yard down to the Charles River. The **Harvard Houses**—the university's attempt to duplicate the learning environment of Oxford and Cambridge—cover an area that extend from Massachusetts. Ave. to Memorial Dr. They are the centers of undergraduate life; each has a distinct identity. Across the river lies the **Business School** and the university's athletic facilities. North of Harvard Yard are the **Law School, Divinity School,** and **Radcliffe Quadrangle,** and west the **School of Education** and **Radcliffe Yard.**

The university has a number of small but entertaining museums worth visiting. The **Fogg Art Museum,** 32 Quincy St. (495-2387, 495-9400 for recorded information), is well endowed with works from virtually every major period and culture. The **Sackler Museum,** 485 Broadway, across the street, focuses on ancient, Asian, and Islamic art. (Both open Tues.-Sat. 10am-5pm, Thurs. 10am-9pm, Sun. 1-5pm. Admission to both $3, seniors and students $1.50, Sat. mornings free to all.) Next door, Le Corbusier's "machine for living," the **Carpenter Center,** 24 Quincy St. (495-3251), shows student and professional work with especially strong photo exhibits, not to mention great film series. (Open Mon.-Fri. 9am-11pm, Sat. 9am-6pm, Sun. noon-10pm.) Included in the Museums of Natural History (495-3045) are the **Peabody Museum of Anthropology and Ethnology,** which has large collections from North, Central, and South American Indian cultures, and the **Mineralogical and Geological Museums,** containing gems, minerals, ores, and meteorites. The most famous exhibit is that of the "glass flowers" at the **Botanical Museum** (495-1910), astoundingly accurate models of 780 species of plants that were used in the teaching of basic botany, but the **Museum of Comparative Zoology** is really more fun. Among the dinosaur bones are a Triceratops head and the Nothosaur, a 42-foot sea monster with six-inch teeth. Also on display are whale skeletons and stuffed birds and mammals. (All open Mon.-Sat. 9am-4:30pm, Sun. 1-4:30pm. Admission $2, seniors and students $1.50, children 50¢. Free Mon. 9-11am.)

For a less academic view of Cambridge, walk up dappled **Brattle Street** toward the 18th-century homes once occupied by wealthy Tories; #101 (Hastings House), and #113 and #115, which belonged to the Longfellows, are typical examples of old Cambridge. The **Longfellow House** (876-4491) is a National Historic Site and well worth visiting for the glimpse of the writer's life it affords. (Admission $2, seniors and ages under 17 free. Open daily 10am-4:30pm for tours only.) The National Park service rangers can provide information on other historical sights in Cambridge, as well as a walking guide to old Cambridge.

At the end of Brattle St. lies the **Mt. Auburn Cemetery** (547-7105). The first botanical-garden cemetery in the U.S., it has 170 acres of beautifully landscaped grounds. Famous people buried here include Louis Agassiz, Nathaniel Bowditch, Charles Bulfinch, Dorothea Dix, Mary Baker Eddy, Winslow Homer, and H.W. Longfellow.

Lexington and Concord

On the 18th of April in 1775, Paul Revere *et al.* rode from Boston to the town of **Lexington** to warn Revolutionary leaders of the approaching British troops. The next morning, a handful of Minutemen gathered, prepared to battle with the British. The first shots of the Revolutionary War were fired, and the first blood shed on

Lexington Green. The **Minuteman Statue** of Captain John Parker now stands on the corner of the Green and looks back to Boston, still watching for the invader.

The **Hancock-Clarke House,** 36 Hancock St. (861-0928), where Samuel Adams and John Hancock were sleeping that fateful night, is today a museum of the American Revolution. The Lexington Historical Society also maintains the **Buckman Tavern** opposite the Green (862-5598), where Minutemen gathered before the battle, and the **Munroe Tavern,** 1332 Massachusetts Ave. (862-1703), which served as the British headquarters and field hospital. (All 3 open mid-April to Oct. 31 Mon.-Sat. 10am-5pm, Sun. 1-5pm. Admission $2, ages 6-16 50¢. Combined ticket $4.50.)

The **visitors center,** 1875 Massachusetts Ave. (862-1450), at the corner of the Village Green, has a diorama outlining and explaining the Battle of Lexington and Concord. (Open 9am-5pm, Nov.-June daily 10am-4pm.)

The five-mile **Battle Road** leads from the Lexington Green to the town of **Concord.** After the initial confrontation in Lexington, Minutemen gathered in Concord to await the British. The **Old North Bridge** over the Concord River, where the first real skirmish took place, witnessed "the shot heard 'round the world." In the summer, from the nearby **North Bridge Visitor Center,** 174 Liberty St. (369-6993), rangers present interpretive talks at the Bridge, ½ mile from Concord Center. (Open daily 9am-6pm; off-season 9am-5pm.) Take a short walk from the Bridge to the visitors center and **Minuteman National Historic Park** to see several dioramas of the battle and a splendid garden reaching down to the river.

Not enthralled by military history? The area also has its share of attractions for the more literary minded. One of Concord's most famous sons, Henry David Thoreau, retreated to **Walden Pond,** 1½ miles south on Rte. 126, in 1845 "to live deliberately, to front only the essential facts of life." His book *Walden* contains some of the thoughts and observations from his two years there. Questions about this naturalist philosopher can be answered at the **Thoreau Lyceum,** 156 Belknap St. (369-5912; open April 1-Dec. 1 Mon.-Fri. 10am-5pm, Sun. 2-5pm; Jan. 1-Feb. 15 Thurs.-Sun.; Feb. 16-March 31 Tues.-Sun. Admission $2, students $1, children 50¢.) Walden Pond (369-3254) is today a state reservation, popular with picnickers, swimmers, and boaters. The site of the cabin Thoreau built is marked by granite posts at the far end of the pond. (Open daily dawn to dusk. Parking $3.) If Walden Pond is too crowded, head down Rte. 62 east from Concord center to **Great Meadows National Wildlife Refuge** (443-4661), another of Thoreau's favorite haunts. (Open dawn-dusk.) Thoreau, Ralph Waldo Emerson, Nathaniel Hawthorne, and Louisa May Alcott are buried at bucolic **Sleepy Hollow Cemetery,** Rte. 62, 3 blocks from the center of town.

Canoe rentals for the Concord and Sudbury Rivers are available at the **South Bridge Boat House,** 496 Main St. (369-3998 or 371-2465. Open April-Oct. daily 9am-7:30pm. Mon.-Fri. $5.70 per hr., $25 per day. Students $5 per hr., $22 per day. Sat.-Sun. $7 per hr., $36 per day.)

An excellent local map and information on events and sites in Concord are available in a rack outside the **chamber of commerce,** in Wright Tavern on Main St., or at the **information booth,** just outside the town center on Heywood St. off Lexington Rd. (Open May 30-Oct. 31 daily 9:30am-4:30pm; April 19-May 30 weekends only 9:30am-4:30pm.) Concord, just 20 miles north of Boston, is served by MBTA "Commuter Rail" trains leaving from North Station ($2.75). MBTA buses from Alewife Station in Boston run several times a day to Lexington (50¢).

Salem

Salem has built a thriving tourist trade on the town's history of "witch persecution" in the 17th century. However, many of the historical offerings here pertain to Salem's 19th-century maritime trade and hometown literary figure, Nathaniel Hawthorne. It's worth your while to wander the town's less traveled streets on your own, but you can also take a **trolley tour** (744-5463; $6, ages 5-12 $2; ticket allows you to get on and off the trolley and see the sights at your own pace). A 1.3-mile foot trail, delineated by a red line painted on the pavement, will take you past the town's most famous sights.

Where the town hits the Atlantic, you'll find multicolored **Pickering Wharf,** enjoyable for window-shopping, and useful for its public restrooms. Across the street is the **Custom House,** 178 Derby St. (744-4323), where Hawthorne dreamed up *The Scarlet Letter,* one of the earliest great American literary works. (Open daily 8:30am-6pm, off-season 8:30am-5pm. Free.) The Custom House is part of the **Salem Maritime National Historic Site.** Farther along the waterfront, the **House of the Seven Gables,** 54 Turner St. (744-0991), runs tours presenting more Hawthornalia. (Open daily 9:30am-5:30pm; Sept.-June 10am-4:30pm. Admission $4, ages 6-17 $2.)

Cut by the red line trail, **Salem Common** lies between Hawthorne Blvd. and Washington Square E. On the southwest side of the Common, the **Salem Witch Museum,** 19½ Washington Square N. (744-1692), at Hawthorne Blvd. and Brown St., presents a reenactment of the notorious trials with dramatic lighting, sound, and 13 stage sets. Might offer a bit *too* much drama for the youngest set. (Open 10am-7pm; Sept.-June 10am-5pm. Admission $3, seniors $2.50, ages 6-14 $1.75.)

Salem's most substantial sight, the **Peabody Museum,** in East India Sq., recalls the town's former role as the leading Atlantic whaling and merchant shipping port. Enjoy wide-ranging exhibits on maritime history, art, and whaling, along with samples of unusual goods imported from international ports. (Open Mon-Wed. and Fri.-Sat. 10am-5pm, Thurs. 10am-9pm, Sun. and holidays noon-5pm. Admission $4, seniors and students $3, ages 6-16 $1.50.) Two blocks past the museum, ethnic music, dance, and food fill the Salem marketplace in summer weekly street festivals. Also near the museum is the **Essex Institute,** at 132 Essex St. (744-3390). An important archive of materials relating to New England history, it also contains a museum crammed to the rafters with silver, furniture, portraits, toys, and other oddities. Don't miss the 15-minute slide show. Four old houses on the same block are under the institute's care and are open to visitors. (Museum and houses open June-Oct. Mon.-Wed. and Fri.-Sat 9am-5pm, Thurs. 9am-9pm, Sun. 1-5pm; Nov.-May museum galleries Tues.-Wed. and Fri.-Sat. 9am-5pm, Thurs. 9am-9pm, Sun. 1-5pm; Nov.-May Gardner-Pingree House Tues.-Sun. 1-5pm. Admission to museum and houses $5, seniors $4, ages 6-16 $2.50.)

Red's Sandwich Shop, 15 Central St. (745-3527), offers breakfast ($1-2.50) and lunch ($1.50-5) at small tables and a crowded counter. (Open Mon.-Sat. 5am-3pm, Sun. 6am-1pm.) Just down the street try the large open-faced sandwiches ($3-4) at **Soup du Jour,** 7 Central St. (744-9608). Entrees $5-16, Chicago pizza $5-6.25. (Open Mon.-Wed. 11:30am-9pm, Thurs.-Sat. 11:30am-10pm.) Close to the Customs House and waterfront, **Tammany Hall Restaurant** serves fish, veal, chicken, and beef ($8-12) in a Victorian atmosphere. (Open Mon.-Sat. 11am-11pm, Sun. 11am-3pm and 4-11pm.)

The most reasonable accommodations in Salem are at **Hotel Lafayette,** 116 Lafayette St. (745-5503), near the train station. (Singles $55. Doubles $65.) Certainly nothing special, but you can get a smaller room for $35-40. The nearest campsite is **Winter Island,** 51 Winter Island Road (745-9430), about 1.5 miles from the center of Salem. Bathrooms with showers. Two-week max. stay. $10 per tent, max. of 4 people per tent.

The **visitors information booth** at Riley Plaza (open April-Oct. daily 9:30am-4pm) and the Salem **Chamber of Commerce,** 32 Derby Sq. (774-0004; open Mon.-Fri. 9am-5pm) will help you find your way around.

Salem is 20 miles northeast of Boston, accessible by train from North Station (½ hr., $2.25) or by bus from Haymarket (45 min., $2). By car, take Rte. 128 north to Rte. 114 (exit 25E).

Cape Ann

Cape Ann comprises the rocky peninsula at the end of Rte. 128, and the coastline immediately south. Here are some of the area's prettiest beaches. Pack a picnic and hike along the seashore as gulls wheel overhead and wild roses turn their windblown faces skyward. The Cape Ann fishing towns are where Europeans first settled in the region; if the main action has long since moved inland, the quaint streets of these modern-day villages still possess a unique New England charm.

The most extensive tourist information on the area is available at the **Cape Ann Chamber of Commerce** 33 Commercial St. (283-1601), in Gloucester. (Open Mon.-Fri. 8am-6pm, Sat. 10am-6pm, Sun. 10am-4pm.) Pick up the *Cape Ann Guide,* a free publication, with information on sights, special events, and beaches. The *North Shore Guide,* also free, contains similar information about towns on the coast from Boston to New Hampshire.

While Route 128 is the most direct way to Cape Ann, the secondary roads (Rte. 127 from Boston, or Rte. 133 from points north) are much more scenic. You can also take the commuter rail out of North Station. Route 127 hugs the coast, presenting views of rocky harbors from Beverly to the cape.

Hammond Castle Museum

The town of Magnolia is home to **Hammond Castle Museum,** 80 Hesperus Ave. (283-2080 or 283-7673), built in the late 20s by inventor and professional eccentric John Hayes Hammond Jr. to house his collection of medieval relics acquired in raids on Europe. Hammond was a friend and rival of Isabella Gardner, and his strange home, though less outrageously eclectic, is reminiscent of Boston's Gardner Museum. There are Friday evening recitals in the Great Hall on a huge organ, and concerts ranging from Bach to reggae usually on weekend nights (tickets $10). (Open daily 9am-5pm. Admission and tour $4, seniors and students with ID $3.50, ages 6-12 $2.50.)

Magnolia is accessible from Boston by train from North Station. By car, turn off Rte. 127 (Summer St.) at Raymond St., which becomes Hesperus Ave.

Gloucester

The nation's oldest seaport, **Gloucester** was settled in 1623 by English colonists who came "to praise God and catch fish." Today, sight-seeing may have eclipsed God-praising, but Gloucester remains one of the world's foremost fishing ports. Visit Gloucester toward the end of June to see the bishop perform the annual **Blessing of the Fleet,** Cape Ann's biggest summer event, complete with carnival, parade, and dancing in the streets. The tumult takes place near the **Fishermen's Memorial** on Western Ave., a bronze representation of a helmsman.

Gloucester is the **whale-watching** capital of New England. Half a dozen companies will take you to see the minke, right, finback, and humpback whales that play off the coast. Try the **Cape Ann Whale Watch** (283-5110), **Yankee Whale Watch** (281-0313, 800-942-5464), **Seven Seas Whale Watch** (283-1776), or **Cap't. Bill & Sons Whale Watch Cruises** (283-6995). If you'd rather look at something that doesn't stare back, try the **Rocky Neck Art Colony** along Rocky Neck Ave. in E. Gloucester (283-4319). With about 20 galleries, it is the oldest working art colony in America and has had such distinguished alumni as Winslow Homer and Fitz Hugh Lane. (Most galleries open spring-fall 10am-10pm.) Painters aren't the only ones to have been inspired by the area, however. Gloucester was the long-time residence of Beat poet Charles Olsen; Olsen attempted to capture the town's spirit in his epic *Maximus Poems.*

Inexpensive food is available at **Chick's Roast Beef and Seafood** diner, 218 Main St. (283-1405). Sandwiches and subs $1.35-3.50. (Open Sun.-Wed. 11am-12:30am, Thurs. 11am-1:30am, Fri.-Sat. 11am-2am.) The **Down East Oyster House,** 116 E. Main St., E. Gloucester (283-2057), is well worth the few extra dollars. Try any of the seafood, lobster, or chicken dinners ($8-12).

Unfortunately, there are no budget accommodations in Gloucester. Camping is the only alternative if you're determined to spend the night. The **Cape Ann Campsite,** off Rte. 128 and 133 in W. Gloucester (283-8683), consists of 100 tent sites

1 mile from the beach. Two- to three-day min. stay on weekends. (Sites $12 for 2. Open May-Oct.) The **Camp Annisquam Campground,** on Stanwood Ave. off Rte. 133 (283-2992), has sites for $14 a night.

The **Cape Ann Chamber of Commerce,** 33 Commercial St. (283-1601), has extensive information on the area as well as accommodations listings. (Open Mon.-Fri. 8am-6pm, Sat. 10am-6pm, Sun. 10am-4pm.) The **information booth** on Western Ave. (Rte. 127) (283-2651) can also help you find your way around. (Open mid-June to Aug. daily 10am-6pm.) Gloucester is accessible from Boston by Rte. 128 and 127, from the north by Rte. 133, and from the MBTA Commuter Rail at North Station.

Rockport

Just 5 miles east of Gloucester, **Rockport** is a small seaside town that refuses to lose its leafy charm despite the annual onslaught of tourists. After you've had your fill of the tacky souvenir shops on the main pier, browse in one of the galleries or take a refreshing stroll along one of the coastal roads.

Generations of artists have found inspiration in Rockport, and today about every other building on Main St. is a small gallery. The **Rockport Art Association,** 12 Main St. (546-6604), with a membership of over 250 artists who have all lived and worked in the area, shows art works in a small gallery. (Open Mon.-Sat. 9:30am-5pm, Sun. 1-5pm; Nov.-April Mon.-Fri. 10am-4pm, Sat. 10am-5pm, Sun. 1-5pm.) In June the Art Association hosts the **Rockport Chamber Music Festival** (546-7391).

The galleries, together with the shops and cafés, tumble out along the narrow streets of **Bearskin Neck. Back** and **Front Beaches** reach out from one side of the Neck; **Rockport Harbor** is on the other. The waterfront is, not surprisingly, the place to look for good seafood. **Lobster in the Ruff** on South Rd. has sandwiches for $1.50-4, baked stuffed scrod for $7, and sauteed scallops for $9. (Open Sun.-Thurs. 11am-8pm, Fri.-Sat. 11am-9pm.)

The **Information Center** on Upper Main St., Rte. 127, is part of the Rockport Chamber of Commerce (546-6575). It's a bit of a walk from the harbor, but offers a free placement service for rooms. To get to Rockport from Boston, take Rte. 128 or 127 north. Also accessible by commuter rail from North Station, Rockport is the next stop after Gloucester.

Plymouth

Every American elementary school kid learns the story of how the Pilgrims stepped ashore onto Plymouth Rock in the winter of 1620 to be greeted by friendly Indians and fat turkeys. Historical significance aside, the rock itself (on Water St.) is unimpressive; two-thirds of it are underground. However, if the town's central attraction is an anti-climax, there is another sight that more than compensates. This is **Plimoth Plantation,** Warren Ave. (746-1622), a "living museum" that superbly recreates the early settlement. In the **Pilgrim Village** costumed actors impersonate actual villagers, and you can help them in daily routines such as tending the garden. Nothing in the village can be traced to the modern era, and the actors feign ignorance of all events after the 1630s. The nearby **Wampanoag Summer Encampment** recreates an Indian village of the same period, presenting the culture of the original New Englanders. The **Mayflower II,** built in England and docked in Plymouth Harbor, attempts to capture the atmosphere of the original ship. (Village open April-Nov. daily 9am-5pm. Encampment open May-Oct. daily 9am-5pm. Admission for both the village and encampment $12, children $8. Mayflower open July-Aug. 9am-7pm, Sept.-Nov. and April-June daily 9am-5pm. Admission $5 and $3.25, respectively. Combination tickets $15 and $10, respectively. To get to Plimouth Plantation, take Rte. 3 south to exit 4 and follow the signs, or follow Main St. 3 miles out of the center of town. Across the street from the public beach.)

Inexpensive food abounds in Plymouth—just stay away from the restaurants around Plymouth Rock. **Go-Go's Sub Shop,** 46 Main St. Ext. (746-3395), 1 block from the post office, serves subs and burgers for $3-4. Take your provisions to the nearby **Brewster Gardens,** a quiet public park with a brook meandering through it, and have a picnic. **Souza's Seafood** (746-5354), on the Wharf, serves great lobster rolls ($5.70) and other seafood sandwiches ($2.45-4.60). (Open daily 11am-8pm.) For free cranberry refreshments, visit the **Cranberry World Visitors Center** (747-1000), located on the waterfront just past the Town Wharf. A self-guided exhibit demonstrates how cranberry products are made; it's worth a quick visit if only to sample the varieties of cranberry drinks. Cooking demonstrations are given daily at 11am. (Open July-Aug. Mon.-Fri. 9:30am-9pm; April-Nov. daily 9:30am-5pm. Free.)

Camping is the best bet for overnight stays around Plymouth, as local motels and guest houses tend to be expensive and the beach is technically off-limits. **Myles Standish Forest** (866-2526), 7 miles south of Plymouth via Rte. 3 to Long Pond Rd., offers 450 campsites for two for $10 ($12 with showers). Hiking trails and bike paths add to this peaceful park's attraction. **Ellis Haven Campground,** Federal Furnace Rd. (746-0803), charges $15 for two (with 2 kids free; each additional person $2).

Find out more about Plymouth, Cape Cod and the rest of New England at the **tourist information center** (746-1150), 2 miles from Plymouth Center on Rte. 3, exit 5, Long Pond Rd. (Open Sat.-Thurs. 9am-5pm, Fri. 9am-8pm; fall and winter daily 8:45am-4:30pm.) Near the town wharf on N. Park St., the **Plymouth Information Center** (746-4779) is run by the chamber of commerce and arranges local accommodations. You can also pick up a free map of Plymouth and a self-guided walking tour there. (Open Sat.-Thurs. 9am-5pm, Fri. 9am-8pm.)

Plymouth is tucked into the south shore of Massachusetts Bay, 35 miles south of Boston and 32 miles northwest of Hyannis on Rte. 3. The **Plymouth and Brockton Street Railway Company** (actually a bus), 8 Industrial Park Rd. (746-0378; 800-328-9997 in MA), handles service to Plymouth from Boston's central Greyhound Terminal (Mon.-Fri. 6:40am-12:15am, 15 per day, $6). The bus takes only an hour, but stops at the Industrial Park Terminal, 3 miles from Plymouth Center. From the Hyannis terminal (775-5524), 15-19 buses per day run between 10:15am and 9:15pm. (To Hyannis $4.25, 1 hr.) The **Plymouth Rock Trolley,** 20 Main St. (747-3419), operates daily from 8am to 8pm every 15 to 20 minutes. (Fare $3, under 12 $1.) Trolleys run around town and out to Plimoth Plantation.

The **post office** is at 6 Main St. Ext. (746-4028), in Plymouth Center. (Open Mon.-Fri. 8:30am-5pm, Sat. 8:30am-noon.) Plymouth's **ZIP code** is 02360; the **area code** is 508.

Cape Cod

In 1602, when Bartholomew Gosnold first landed on this peninsula in southeastern Massachusetts, he named it Cape Cod in honor of all the codfish he caught in the waters around it. It was by hook and net that the towns on the Cape used to survive, but in recent decades tourism, not fishing, has sustained the Cape. Mindful of the fragility of the ecosystem, President Kennedy established the Cape Cod National Seashore in 1961 to protect the less-developed areas of the Cape from commercialism. The national seashore protects much of the "forearm," including the Cape's most dramatic ocean beaches. Wide white beaches are Cape Cod's trademark. No matter where or how long you stay, you can enjoy the miles of sandy shore. But don't disturb the fragile dunes; stay on the designated trails. Consult the **National Seashore's Visitors Centers,** at **Salt Pond,** U.S. 6 in Eastham (255-3421), just north of the "elbow," and **Province Lands,** on Race Point Rd. to the right off U.S. 6 near Provincetown (487-1256; open in summer daily 9am-6pm; in spring and fall 9am-4:30pm). Both provide maps, information on the park, and frequent, ranger-led free walks and discussions about the dunes, cranberry bogs, and beaches.

To get to and around Cape Cod, take a bus, boat, train, or bring your bike. The **Cape Cod & Hyannis Railroad** is a delightful way to get from Hyannis to Sandwich through the "backyard of the Cape," and uses only old-fashioned train cars. **Bonanza Bus Lines** connects Boston with Falmouth and Woods Hole, and Hyannis with New York City. **Plymouth and Brockton Street Railway** serves Hyannis ($5) and the Cape out to Provincetown. The 135-mile-long **Boston-Cape Cod Bikeway** connects Boston with Bourne on the Cape Cod Canal and extends to Provincetown, at land's end. Among the most scenic bike trails in the country are those on either side of the **Cape Cod Canal,** in the Cape Cod National Seashore, and the 14-mile **Cape Cod Rail Trail** from Dennis to Eastham.

Contact the **Cape Cod Chamber of Commerce,** at the junction of Rte. 6 and 132 in Hyannis (362-3225), for comprehensive information about the Cape. See the Martha's Vineyard section for information on ferries from Woods Hole and Hyannis to this off-Cape island.

The **ZIP code** for Woods Hole is 02543, for Falmouth 02541. The General Delivery ZIP code is 02540. The **area code** for Cape Cod is 508.

Sandwich

The oldest town on the Cape, Sandwich has quiet shady streets lined with white clapboard and weathered-grey shingled houses. Here you'll find none of the bustle of the tourist strips in Hyannis or Provincetown.

The combination of timber, a small harbor, and sea grass for packing made Sandwich an ideal spot for glassmaking in the 19th century, when the town was famous for its "lacy" pressed glass. The **Sandwich Glass Museum,** 129 Main St. (888-0251), explains the techniques that were used, and displays a beautiful collection of pressed and blown glassware. (Open daily 9:30am-4:30pm. Admission $2.50, ages 6-12 50¢.)

The nearby **Thornton W. Burgess Museum,** 4 Water St. (888-4668) is an entertaining tribute to the Sandwich-born naturalist and storyteller whose most famous character is Reddy Fox. (Open Mon.-Sat. 10am-4pm, Sun. 1-4pm.) The tiny museum and the nearby **Dexter Grist Mill** stand by the serene **Shawme Pond** and are frequented by flocks of ducks, geese, and swans.

The **Heritage Plantation,** on Grove and Pine St. (888-3300), is about a mile from the center of town and is a great place to spend an afternoon. The museums are unusual; one is full of antique cars and another has a working 1912 carousel. The plantation is ensconced in 76 acres of gardens, criss-crossed by paths. (Open mid-May to Oct. daily 10am-5pm. Admission $7, seniors $6, ages 5-12 $3.)

Sandwich provides its guests with unadulterated nature. At **Sandwich Beach,** Town Neck Rd., off Tupper Rd., off Rte. 6A, and **Scusset Beach,** at Sagamore and Sandwich on the Cape Cod Canal, near the junction of Rte. 3 and 6, relax on an uncrowded stretch of Cape Cod shore.

The **Shawme-Crowell State Forest** (888-0351), on Rte. 130 and 6, has 240 camping sites July-Oct. at $12 per night. **Peters Pond Park Campground,** Cotuit Rd. (477-1775), in south Sandwich, offers swimming, fishing, boating, a grocery store, and showers. (140 sites. $13-14 per night. Open mid-April to mid-Oct.)

If you don't have a car you'll have to take the scenic **Cape Cod and Hyannis Railroad** (866-4526) to get to Sandwich. Starting from Center St. across from the Hyannis bus station, the train makes one stop in Sandwich and goes as far as Sagamore, though you can't get off there (round-trip $10.50). From the depot in Sandwich follow Jarves St. into the center of town.

Hyannis

Often called the "hub of Cape Cod," Hyannis is the region's commercial center. The Pilgrims might have settled in Hyannisport instead of Plymouth in 1620, but the difficult navigation forced them to move on. Now the town is famous for its nearby beaches and the Kennedy family's compound of summer houses. If you like honky-tonk resort towns, with plenty of mini-golf and souvenir shops, then Hyannis is for you. It's also a good base from which to visit other spots on the Cape, including Barnstable, Falmouth, and Martha's Vineyard.

Set aside an afternoon for a picnic or swim at **Hathaway's Pond** in nearby Barnstable, on the Bay side of the Cape. (Parking fee for nonresidents $4.) Daily expeditions in pursuit of humpback whales are run by the Hyannis **Whale Watcher Cruises.** Their 100-foot cruiser launches from Barnstable Harbor, 3 miles from Hyannis, from April to November. (775-1622, 362-6088. Reservations suggested, taken 7am-9pm. Fare $13.50-21.50.)

You'll find plenty of good eateries at the **West End Marketplace,** 615 Main St. (Open daily 11am-1am.) **Guido Murphy's** (775-7242) has creative lunch specials such as the "Rube Goldburger," and a build-it-yourself burger. Live music nightly. Sun. comedy night (cover $3), Wed. college night (free with college ID), Thurs. Beach Party (cover $3). (Open Mon.-Sat. 11:30am-1am, Sun. noon-1am.) For seafood on the harbor, try **Baxter's Fish n' Chips,** 177 Pleasant St. Order one of their good-sized meals at the front counter and then sit with a view of the fishing boats. (775-4490; $5-9; open Tues.-Sun. 11:30am-8pm). The **Hearth 'n Kettle Restaurant,** 412 Main St. (771-3737), tries for a colonial tavern atmosphere with dark wood paneling and costumed servers. (Breakfast $2-5, lunch $3-6, dinner $10-12. Open Sun.-Thurs. 7am-10pm, Fri.-Sat. 7am-midnight.)

The best place to stay in Hyannis is the **HyLand Youth Hostel (AYH),** 465 Falmouth Rd. (775-2970), in a pine grove off Rte. 28. Kitchen facilities. Dorms have 42 bunk-beds total. (Open 7-9:30am and 5-10:30pm. $9, nonmembers $13. Family rooms available. Sheets $1. Reservations suggested June-Aug.) From Main St. toward Hyannisport, Sea St. has some decently priced inns and guest houses. Try the **Sea Beach Inn,** 388 Sea St. (775-4612), close to the beach, at the intersection with Gosnold St. It gives you a comfortable double bed with shared bath plus continental breakfast for $45 ($55 with private bath. In off-season $35, with private bath $45.) The **Sea Witch Inn,** 363 Sea St. (771-4261), also has decent doubles for $30-55, discounted in the off-season. (Open according to the owner's whims.)

Hyannis is midway across the Cape's upper arm, 3 miles south of U.S. 6 on Nantucket Sound. The **Hyannis Bus Station,** 17 Elm St. (775-5524), sends off the buses of **Plymouth & Brockton** and **Bonanza Lines** (open Mon.-Fri. 4:45am-8:30pm, Sat.-Sun. 5am-8:30pm). Buses go to Provincetown (in summer 7 per day; in winter 3 per day, 1½ hr., $7); Providence, RI (6 per day, 2 hr., $12.50); New York (6 per day, 6½ hr., $31.50); Boston (15-24 per day, 2 hr., $8); and Plymouth (11-15 per day, 1 hr., $4.25). Shuttle buses are sent to Falmouth and Woods Hole Mon.-Sat. 3-5 times daily. **Amtrak** sends a direct train from New York to Hyannis on Fridays and one from Hyannis to New York on Sundays (6 hr., $53). Other days you will have to take the bus to Boston to catch the train.

Ferries to Martha's Vineyard and Nantucket are run by **Hy-Line Cruises** (778-2600) from mid-May to Oct. and leave from the Ocean St. Dock. (Fare $9.50, under 12 $4.75.)**Bike rentals** are available at Cascade Motor Lodge, 201 Main St. (775-9717), near the bus and train stations. (Bikes $10-12 per day. $30-36 per wk.)

The **Hyannis Area Chamber of Commerce,** 319 Barnstable Rd. (775-2201), about a mile up the road from the bus station, can help you plan a visit to Hyannis. (Open Mon.-Sat. 9am-5pm, Sun. 11am-3pm; Sept.-May Mon.-Sat. 9am-5pm.) If you're planning a day at the beach, call to find out the **weather** (771-0500 or 771-5522).

Hyannis's **ZIP code** is 02601; the **area code** is 508.

Provincetown

At the tip of the Cape, Provincetown is known for its old clapboard houses, narrow streets, large gay community, clusters of artists, and whaleboats, whose occupants now carry cameras instead of harpoons. The dunes, scruffy expanses of sand and hardy brush, surround the town. If you tire of the Commercial Street parade, solitude in the wilds of the national seashore is never far away.

Practical Information

Police: 911.

Visitor Information: Provincetown Chamber of Commerce, 307 Commercial St. (487-3424), MacMillan Wharf. Open in summer daily 9am-5pm; in fall and spring Mon.-Sat. 10am-4pm. **Province Lands Visitor Center,** Race Point Rd. (487-1256). Information on the national seashore; free guides to the nature and bike trails. Open July and Aug. daily 9am-6pm; mid-April to Nov. daily 9am-4:30pm.

Plymouth and Brockton St. Railway: in the chamber of commerce (800-328-9997). Six buses per day to and from Hyannis ($7).

Bay State Spray and Provincetown Steamship: 20 Long Wharf, Boston (723-7800). In the Provincetown Chamber of Commerce (487-1741). Ferries to Boston (3 hr.) $15 one way, same-day round-trip $25, ordinary round-trip $30. Daily in summer and some weekends from Labor Day-Memorial Day.

Provincetown Shuttle Bus: 487-3353. Serves Provincetown and Fleming Cove Beach. Operates late June-early Sept. daily 8am-midnight, 8am-6pm for the beach. Pick up a schedule at the Chamber of Commerce. Fare $1, seniors 50¢.

Bike Rental: Arnold's, 329 Commercial St. (487-0844). $1.50-3.50 per hr., $5-15 per day, $30-72 per wk. Credit cards accepted. Open 8:30am-5:30pm. Deposit and ID required.

Post Office: 211 Commercial St. (487-0163). Open Mon.-Fri. 8:30am-5pm, Sat. 9:30-11:30am. **ZIP code:** 02657.

Area Code: 508.

Provincetown is tucked into the cupped hand at the end of the Cape Cod arm. Boston is 120 miles by land via U.S. 6 and Rte. 3, Boston's "Southeast Expressway," but much closer by sea across Cape Cod and Massachusetts Bay. The Cape Cod Canal lies 66 miles "down Cape." The duneland surrounding this little town is protected by the national seashore.

Accommodations, Camping, and Food

Get a free list of personable little guest houses from the chamber of commerce. The **Joshua Paine Guest House,** 15 Tremont St. (487-1551), has four bright rooms with handsome furniture. (Singles $30. Doubles $35. Open mid-June to mid-Sept.) In the quiet east end of town is the **Cape Codder,** 570 Commercial St. (487-0131), which has a small private beach with a wooden deck. Continental breakfast. (Singles $20-25. Doubles $33-41. Open mid-April to Oct.)

Parking for the National Seashore property is closed from midnight to 6am, but you can't camp legally on the public lands anyway. The visitors center can provide a list of private campgrounds within the seashore; for all of them reservations are recommended in the summer. In the western part of town, **Coastal Acres Camping Court,** West Vine St. Ext. (487-1700), is usually full, so reserve early. (3-night min. stay. Sites $14. Open April-Oct.) About 7 miles southeast of P-town on U.S. 6, the villages of **North Truro** and **Truro** have several popular campgrounds nestled among the dwarf pines by the dunelands. The only one open year-round is **North Truro Camping Area,** Highland Rd., North Truro (487-1847), ¼ mile east of U.S. 6. (Sites $6.50 per person, $13 minimum per day; $20 deposit required with reservation.) The **Little America Youth Hostel,** at the far end of North Pamet Rd., Truro 02666 (349-3889), rests on park service land 1½ miles east of U.S. 6. The popular hostel has 48 bunks and sees a steady traffic of bikers all summer. ($9, nonmembers $12. Open early June-early Sept. Reservations recommended.)

Eating out is usually expensive in Provincetown. You could settle for the fried seafood shacks on MacMillan Wharf, but a much better selection lies on Commercial St. The wait at the **Mayflower Cafe,** 300 Commercial St. (487-0121), is definitely worth it. The place is friendly and unpretentious; Portuguese and seafood specialties go for $4-8. (Open daily 11:30am-10pm.) **Stormy Harbor,** 277 Commercial St. (487-1680), serves breakfast from 7:30 to 11:30am ($1.70-5.25).

Sights, Activities, and Entertainment

Commercial Street is Provincetown's main drag. In high season, pedestrians take over from the automobiles. The street festival goes on every day and night—often until 3am. The fervor of activity heightens in late June with the annual **blessing of the fleet,** a three-day celebration.

The **Provincetown Heritage Museum,** 356 Commercial St., holds a half-scale model of the fishing schooner *Rose Dorothea.* This version is 63 feet long and is the world's largest indoor model of its kind. (487-0666; open daily 10am-6pm. Admission $2, under 12 free.) If you're interested in art, try the galleries on Commercial Street. Most prominent is the **Provincetown Art Association,** 460 Commercial St. (487-1750), which houses exhibits of paintings, prints, and sculptures by old and new P-town artists. (Open Sun.-Thurs. noon-4pm, Fri.-Sat. noon-4pm and 7-10pm. Admission $2, seniors, students, and children $1.)

From anywhere that you might wander you'll see the **Pilgrim Monument** on Town Hill, a 352-foot stone tower commemorating the landfall of the Pilgrims on Nov. 11, 1620. From the 252-foot observation platform you can behold the entire tip of Cape Cod. (487-1313; monument and museum admission $2, ages 4-12 $1. Open daily 9am-5pm; July-Sept. 9am-9pm.)

During the spring and fall, great whales parade by Provincetown on their annual migrations from the North Atlantic to the Caribbean. **Whale Watching Cruises** take you out to the fertile shoals where humpback, fin, mincke and rare right whales feed. May and September are the best months for cetacean-sighting. Naturalist guides enhance the three- to four-hour tours offered by the three P-town operations: **Dolphin Fleet** (255-3857; 800-826-9300 in MA); **Portuguese Princess** (487-2651; 800-442-3188 in MA); and **Provincetown Whale-Watch** (487-3322; 800-992-9333 in MA). All leave from and operate ticket booths on MacMillan Wharf. Look for the discount coupons in chamber of commerce brochures available throughout Cape Cod.

Back on *terra firma,* you can roam the wide, sandy beaches that surround Provincetown on foot or bike. If you rent a bike from **Arnold's** (see Practical Information), you get a free map of the trails. The friendly manager of the little-known **Provincetown Horse and Carriage Co.,** 27 West Vine St. (487-1112), can help both novice and experienced riders explore on the back of a horse or pony. One-hour trail rides cost $20. You must be at least 12 years old.

Martha's Vineyard

Although Martha's Vineyard and nearby Nantucket are often referred to in a single breath, there is a world of difference, not to mention a fair amount of water, between them. Whereas life on Nantucket revolves pretty much around one town, larger Martha's Vineyard has several centers of activity: Edgartown, Vineyard Haven, Oak Bluffs, and smaller towns including Chilmark, West Tisbury, and Menemsha. Although both islands lure visitors with miles of pristine sandy beaches and dunes, the Vineyard is more hospitable to the budget traveler. From protected waters like Katama Bay, Menemsha Pond, and Lake Tashmoo to the high cliffs of Gay Head, this island offers landscape guaranteed to captivate even the frequent visitor. Be warned, though; much of the Vineyard has been taken over by private landowners, who carefully guard their private beaches.

The time to visit the Vineyard is fall, when the tourist season starts to die down, the weather turns crisp, the leaves turn color, and prices drop. If summer is your only chance to visit the islands, avoid weekends.

Separated from Cape Cod by Vineyard Sound, Martha's Vineyard requires its visitors to come either by air or sea. Air travel is prohibitively expensive, but the ferry ride is agreeable and takes less than an hour from Woods Hole or Falmouth. All ferries land in either **Vineyard Haven** or **Oak Bluffs,** two towns 3 miles apart on the island's north shore. Once on the island, biking between **Edgartown,** Vineyard Haven, and Oak Bluffs is fairly easy along flat bike paths. Three bike rental places are **Martha's Vineyard Scooter and Bike,** in Vineyard Haven (693-0782; 10-speeds $10 per day; $20 deposit); **Oak Bluffs Bike Rental,** Circuit Ave. Ext. (693-7543; 10-speeds $10 per day); and **R.W. Cutler,** Main St., Edgartown (627-4052; $8 per day; $10 deposit). Inexperienced riders may find the trek to Gay Head or Menemsha a bit strenuous. Taxis are expensive, but there is a shuttle bus. (693-0058, 693-1555, 693-4681. Vineyard Haven-Oak Bluffs-Edgartown: late May to mid-June 8am-7pm; mid-June to early Sept. 8am-12:30am. For up-island service call the numbers above.) Hitching is fairly easy along inland roads.

The chamber of commerce puts out a free yearly publication called *Martha's Vineyard,* which describes everything you might want to see or do on the island. Also pick up free copies of the *Best Read Guide to Martha's Vineyard,* which contains self-guided walking tours of the three largest towns, Vineyard Haven, Oak Bluffs, and Edgartown. Each of these has a few historic homes or small museums devoted to local history, but the real attraction of the Vineyard lies outdoors. **Felix Neck Wildlife Sanctuary, Cedar Tree Neck, Long Point,** and the **Cape Pogue Wildlife Refuge and Wasque Reservation** are all open for exploring. Miles of bike trails crisscross the island, and of course there are eight public beaches scattered all around the shore. (Movie buffs will probably recognize the one along Beach Rd. from the thriller *Jaws.*) The best one of all is **South Beach,** directly south of Edgartown; its big waves and fine sand are worth a day's visit.

Cheap sandwich and lunch places are not too hard to find on the Vineyard. Fried-food shacks all over the island sell clams, shrimp, and fries (meals $5-7). Sit-down dinners, however, generally cost at least $15. A glorious and greasy exception is **Louis',** State Rd., Vineyard Haven (693-3255), where lunch is $4-5 and dinner is about $9-15, with unlimited bread and salad bar included. (Open Mon.-Sat. 11:30am-9pm, Sun. 4-9pm.) If the ferry ride from Woods Hole has made you hungry, try **A.J.'s Seafood and Steak,** Main St. (693-4480), near the docks in downtown Vineyard Haven. Breakfast $1.50-4.70, entrees $4.50-7. (Open daily 7:30am-9pm.) Stock up on good bread and delicious pastries at the friendly **Black Dog Tavern and Bakery,** on Beach St. Ext. (693-9223), at the harbor. (Open daily 6am-9pm.) In Oak Bluffs, **Veg-out** (693-9357), at the corner of Kennebec and Lake Ave., has a 34-item salad bar ($5 per pound). (Open Memorial Day-Labor Day daily 7am-11pm.) **Mad Martha's** (693-9151) is an island ice cream institution, with stores in Vineyard Haven, Edgartown, Oak Bluffs, and Gay Head. (Open daily 11am-midnight.) The **Morning Glory Farm,** at the corner of Machacket and Tisbury Rd. (627-9003), sells produce right from the field. (Open May-Thanksgiving Mon.-Sat. 9am-5:30pm.)

The cheapest place to stay on the island is the **Manter Memorial Youth Hostel (AYH),** Edgartown Rd., West Tisbury (693-2665), 5 miles inland from Edgartown on the bike route. The hostel gets very crowded in summer, but almost never turns anybody away. (Registration 5pm. Curfew 10pm. Members $9, nonmembers $12. Sheets $1. Reservations required. Open April-Nov.) **Martha's Vineyard Reservations,** P.O. Box 1322, Vineyard Haven 02568 (693-7200), **Dukes County Reservations Service,** P.O. Box 2370, Oak Bluffs 02557 (693-6505), and **Accommodations Plus,** RFD 273, Edgartown 02539 (627-8590), will make reservations for you three months in advance. You can also get a free list of inns and guest houses from the Chamber of Commerce. Oak Bluffs is the best place to look for relatively inexpensive rooms. The century-old **Nashua House,** (693-0043) on Kennebec Ave. in Oak Bluffs, is across from the post office. The walls are unfinished, but the rooms are brightly painted and cheerful. (Doubles $29-39.) The more polished **Narragansett House,** 62 Narragansett Ave. (693-3627), is in a quiet residential area south of downtown Oak Bluffs. (Doubles $45-65 from Memorial Day to mid-Sept.; off-season $30-50. Breakfast included.) **The Towers,** 32 Pequot Ave. (693-9894), is in the same neighborhood. (Singles $23. Doubles $46. Open mid-June to mid-Sept.)

There are two campgrounds on the island. **Martha's Vineyard Family Campground,** Edgartown Rd., Vineyard Haven (693-3772), has 150 sites. Groceries are available nearby. A reservation deposit is required. (Open mid-May to mid-Oct. Sites $19 for 2, each additional person $8.) **Webb's Camping Area,** Barnes Rd., Oak

Bluffs (693-0233), 4 miles from Edgartown, is more spacious, with 150 shaded sites. (Sites $19-21 for 2, each additional person $8. Open mid-May to mid-Sept.)

The **Martha's Vineyard Chamber of Commerce** is located on Beach Rd., Vineyard Haven (693-0085; open Memorial Day-Labor Day Mon.-Fri. 9am-5pm, Sat. 10am-2pm.) Prospective revelers should note that Edgartown and Oak Bluffs are the only "wet" towns on the Vineyard. Bar owners are notoriously strict about carding.

Ferries to the island leave from Woods Hole, Falmouth, Hyannis and New Bedford. The **Woods Hole, Martha's Vineyard, and Nantucket Steamship Authority** (693-0367 in Vineyard Haven; 693-0125 in Oak Bluffs; 228-0262 Nantucket; 540-2022 or 548-3788 in Woods Hole; 771-4000 in Hyannis) leaves from Woods Hole. (Round-trip Woods Hole $8; mid-May to mid-Oct. $7.50; ages 5-15 $3.80; automobiles mid-Oct. to mid-May $28; mid-May to mid-Oct $53; bikers $5.) From Falmouth, you can take the **Island Queen Ferry,** (548-4800), across from the town dock, which runs from late May to early Oct. (Round-trip pedestrians $8, children $4, bikers $5.) In Hyannis, take the **Hyline** ferry (778-2600 in Hyannis; 693-0112 in Oak Bluffs. Pedestrians and bikers only. One way $9.50, children $4.75.) **Martha's Vineyard Schamonchi Ferry,** Pier 44 (997-1688), leaves from New Bedford's Lennard Wharf. (One way $7, children $4. Same-day round-trip $14, children $6, bikers one way $4.)

The **ZIP code** is 02539 for Edgartown; 02568 for Vineyard Haven; and 02557 for Oak Bluffs. The **area code** for Martha's Vineyard is 508.

The Berkshires

Equidistant from Boston and New York, the Berkshires have long attracted escapees from city life. Today's budget travelers need not be disturbed by the spectre of the Berkshires' exclusively upper-class past; good roads, B&Bs, and campgrounds have made these mountains accessible to all.

Just about everything in Berkshire County runs north-south: the mountain range giving the county its name (a southern extension of the Green Mountains of VT); the 80 miles of winding **Appalachian Trail;** the **Hoosac** and the **Housatonic rivers;** and U.S. 7, the region's main artery, on its way from Connecticut to Vermont. **Berkshire Regional Transit** (499-2782), known as "the B," spans the Berkshires from Williamstown to Great Barrington. Buses run every hour (Mon.-Sat.); fares are 75¢-$2.25. System schedules are available on the bus. To see sights located far from the town centers, you'll have to drive. The county has more than 100,000 acres held as **state forests** and parks, offering numerous improved and semi-improved camping sites for $10. For information about the parks, contact Region 5 Headquarters, P.O. Box 1433, Pittsfield 01202 (442-8928).

The Berkshires's **area code** is 413.

Northern Berkshires

Take off into the Northern Berkshires on the **Mohawk Trail** (Rte. 2). Perhaps the most famous highway in the state, it's crowded during the fall foliage weekends, but the panorama is tremendous. Five miles south of Greenfield, on the Mohawk Trail lies **Historic Deerfield,** off Rte. 5. This completely restored, idyllic village boasts a main drag of 12 18th- and 19th-century homes. Learn about the village's history, including many massacres by Native American tribes, at the visitors center (774-5581; tours available). **Williamstown** lies at the end of the Mohawk Trail. The Board of Trade at Williamstown sponsors an **information booth** (458-9077) at the junction of Rte. 2 and 7, at the end of Main St. (Open daily 24 hours, staffed by volunteers in summer.)

At **Williams College,** second oldest in Massachusetts, lecturers compete with the beautiful scenery for their students' attention. Skip the tour and head for cultural resources: **Chapin Library** (597-2462; open Mon.-Fri. 9am-noon, 1-5pm) has a number of rare American manuscripts, including a display of original copies of the Declaration of Independence, Articles of Confederation, Constitution, and Bill of Rights. The **Williams College Museum of Art** (597-2429), which emphasizes American and non-Western art, is also worth a visit. (Open Mon.-Sat. 10am-5pm, Sun. 1-5pm. Free.)

Try not to spend too much time indoors in Williamstown; the surrounding wooded hills will be calling you the moment you arrive. The **Hopkins Memorial Forest** (597-2346), on Northwest Hill Rd., is about 1½ miles from the college. Owned and run by Williams' Center for Enviromental Study, it has over 2,000 acres open to the public for hiking and cross-country skiing. **Spoke Bicycles and Repairs,** 408 Main St. (458-3456), rents bikes in a variety of speeds for $8 per day and can give you advice on good rides in the area.

Leave Williamstown by Rte. 7; once you've arrived in Lanesboro, look for North Main St. on your left. This is the access road to **Mount Greylock,** the highest peak in Massachusetts (3491 ft.). You can also enter from Rte. 2, near North Adams. Hiking trails begin from the neighboring towns of Lanesboro, Williamstown, North Adams, Adams, and Cheshire; get maps at the **Mount Greylock Visitors Information Center,** Rockwell Rd. (499-4262), along the pleasantly winding road from Lanesboro to the summit. (Open Mon.-Fri. 9am-4pm, Sat.-Sun. 9am-5pm.) Once at the top, climb the hideous **War Memorial** for a breathtaking (and annotated) view. Sleep high in rugged **Bascom Lodge** (743-1591; May-June bunks $18, under 10 $9; July-Oct. Fri.-Sat. $20 and $10, Sun.-Thurs. $18 and $9 respectively. Breakfast $5, trail lunch $2.50.). Farther south, at **Tanglewood,** you will find the summer home of the **Boston Symphony Orchestra** (1½miles west of Lenox on Rte. 183). The season runs from June 30-Sept. 2. Tickets range from $7-46. Saturday open rehearsals are $9. For information call 637-1666 or 637-1940.

New Hampshire

New Hampshire farmers have struggled for over two centuries with the rugged landscape and severe weather, but their frustration is the outdoors persons elation. The White Mountains dominate the central and northern regions, so that nearly every part of the state identifies with some tall peak. Rising above all, Mt. Washington (6,288 ft.) is the highest point in the Appalachians. On clear days you can see five states and the Atlantic Ocean from its summit. Three great notches create narrow passageways between Washington and other monster Whites. South of the mountains you'll find beautiful lakes where dark forest marches right down to stony shores and the state's modest coastline. Much of southeastern New Hampshire has been engulfed by the Boston metropolis, but a few traditional, sleepy settlements remain within 75 miles of the Hub.

Practical Information

Capital: Concord.

Tourist Information: Office of Vacation Travel, 105 Loudon Rd., P.O. Box 856, Concord 03301 (271-2343 or 271-2666). Open Mon.-Fri. 8am-4pm. **U.S. Forest Service,** P.O. Box 638, 719 Main St., Laconia 03247 (528-8721). Open Mon.-Fri. 8am-4:30pm. **Events and Information Hotline,** 224-2525; 800-258-3608 from New England and NY. Includes skiing and fall foliage.

Help Lines: Winter Ski Conditions, 224-2525, 224-2526, or 800-258-3608 (in NY or New England). For **cross-country** conditions, call 224-6363 or 800-262-6660 (in New England).

Time Zone: Eastern. **Postal abbreviation:** NH.

White Mountains

New Hampshire's gnarled granite peaks and forested slopes and valleys are its biggest tourist attraction. On any given weekend, carloads of vacationers stream into northern New Hampshire, choking the narrow highways and spewing exhaust into the mountain breezes. Gullible travelers succumb to the lure of roadside pseudo-attractions such as Santa's Village ("electronimated Jingle Jamboree"), but the Whites sing a subtler melody. The wind-swept crags and forested valleys lure nature-lovers back year after year. Hikers take to the hills in spring and summer and all enjoy the rich hues of the fall foliage. In the winter, cross-country skiers glide silently down the paths they hiked in the months before.

The beauty of the mountains is peaceful, yet these peaks are treacherous. Every year, Mt. Washington claims at least one life. The weather here is some of the worst on earth; a gorgeous day can suddenly turn into a chilling storm when the wind kicks up over 100mph and the thunderclouds rumble through. The average temperature on the summit is 26.7°F and the average wind speed is 35 miles per hour.

There is an excellent visitor information and transportation network in the mountains. The friendly, experienced **Appalachian Mountain Club (AMC)** and **U.S. Forest Service** provide reliable information. The information facilities of the AMC are in Pinkham Notch, on Rte. 16, midway between Gorham and Jackson (466-2725; open in summer Sat.-Thurs. 6:45am-10pm, Fri. 6:45am-midnight, varies fall-spring), and Crawford Notch, U.S. 302, Carroll (846-7773; open in summer daily 8:30am-4:30pm; mid-May to June and Sept.-Dec. hours vary. Closed Jan. to mid-May). Any AMC hut can give you information. The U.S. Forest Service's main information center is south of the mountains at 719 Main St., Laconia 03247 (528-8721; open Mon.-Fri. 8am-4:30pm). There are several regional ranger stations at important gateways to the National Forest: Ammonoosuc, on Trudeau Rd., Bethlehem (869-2626), 1 mile north of U.S. 3 (open Mon.-Fri. 7am-4:30pm); Androscoggin, at 80 Glen Rd., Gorham (466-2713; open Mon.-Fri. 7am-4:30pm); Saco, Kancamagus Hwy., Conway (447-5448), 100 yards off U.S. 16 (open daily 8am-4:30pm); and Pemigewassett, Rte. 175, Holderness (536-1310; open Mon.-Fri. 8am-4:30pm). There are plenty of state and locally operated visitor information centers as well. The main **visitors center,** P.O. Box 10, North Woodstock 03262 (745-8720), is in Lincoln on Rte. 112 east off I-93 at exit 32. (Open Sat.-Thurs. 8:30am-6pm, Fri. 8:30am-10pm.) Information centers dot the White Mountains. The following are open late May to mid-October: Conway (Rte. 16); Franconia (Rte. 18); Glen (Rte. 16 and 302); Gorham (Rte. 16 and 2); Lincoln (I-93); and Twin Mountain (Rte. 302 and 3). Intervale (Rte. 16 and 302), Jackson (Rte. 16A), and North Conway (Rte. 16 and 302) are open year-round.

If you plan to do much hiking invest in the *AMC White Mountain Guide,* available in most bookstores ($13). It has invaluable descriptions of trails, trailheads, and general hiking, as well as seven maps. The AMC also offers 21 two- to eight-night guided hikes (466-2727) through the Whites, at three different skill levels.

The AMC provides the best **accommodations** in the Whites. It operates eight huts, with bunks for 36-90 people, spaced 1½-5½ hours average hiking time apart on the Appalachian Trail. During the summer, these full-service facilities offer family-style breakfasts and dinners, bunks, blankets, and pillows. From October through May, certain huts are open on a caretaker basis, with shelter and cooking equipment provided. (In summer $42 with 2 meals, $32 with breakfast; rates can drop steeply depending on the season and on the hut.) Reservations are necessary at least one month in advance in the summer to guarantee a place, but you have a decent chance of getting a bunk if you phone later. The AMC **Pinkham Notch Camp** (466-2727) and **Crawford Notch Hotel** (846-7773) offer similar accommodations, but are right off the main highways (Rte. 16 and 302). At any of the AMC facilities, you can ask about working in exchange for food and lodging; in August, maintenance work is steady.

Not only are there inexpensive hotels (see Pinkham Notch below) and plenty of campgrounds, but free or cheap camping is allowed in most of the extensive **White Mountain National Forest.** No camping is allowed above the tree line, within 200 feet of a trail, or within ¼ mile of roads, huts, shelters, tent platforms, lakes, or streams; the same rules apply to building a wood or charcoal fire. The **U.S. Forest Service** also runs 22 different designated campgrounds (sites $7-9, bathrooms and firewood usually available). Call to find out which is closest to your destination. Be sure to inquire about the special restrictions enforced in some areas, including all of the designated Wilderness Areas.

The White Mountains area is well-served by bus. **Concord Trailways** (228-3300; 800-852-3317 in NH; 800-258-3722 in New England) runs north-south and connects Boston with Concord, Conway, Franconia, and the AMC Pinkham Notch Camp. **Vermont Transit** (800-451-3292, 356-5858 in North Conway) makes daily runs between Portland, ME, and Burlington, VT, that stop at North Conway, AMC Crawford Notch Hostel, and Bretton Woods.

The **AMC shuttle** system (466-2727) supplements the bus networks from June 3 to September 4, providing a great way to move quickly from one trailhead to another. There is a morning shuttle from Crawford to and from Lafayette Place in Franconia Notch. Another leaves Pinkham Notch for Webster Cliff and Crawford. The shuttle is quite inexpensive (Crawford to Pinkham $6.50, Lafayette to Crawford $5.50). Other stops are made only by reservation. Pick up the brochure *AMC Hiker Shuttle Service* at any AMC hut or ask for rates and timetable.

Next to hiking, bicycling is the best way to see the mountains close up. Of course, it's strenuous (less so if you approach the mountains from the north, according to some bikers). Check the guide/map *New Hampshire Bicycle,* available at many information centers. You might also consult *25 Bicycle Tours in New Hampshire,* available in local bookstores and outdoor equipment stores. (For bike rental suggestions, see North Conway.)

For **trail and weather information,** call the Pinkham Notch Camp (466-2725) or the WMWV-WBNC weather phone (447-5252). Regional **ZIP codes** include: North Conway, 03860; Jackson 03846; Franconia, 03580; and Gorham, 03581. The White Mountains' **area code** is 603.

Franconia Notch

The westernmost of the three great notches, Franconia is best known for the **Old Man of the Mountains.** Hawthorne addressed this massive granite visage in his 1850 story "The Great Stone Face," and P.T. Barnum once offered to buy it. A 40-foot-high human profile formed by three ledges of rock atop a 1200-foot cliff, the Old Man is supported by rivets these days, and can be best viewed between 10am and sunset from the east shore of **Profile Lake** (I-93).

To the north, **Great Cannon Cliff,** a 1000-foot sheer drop into the cleft between **Mount Lafayette** and **Cannon Mountain,** challenges climbers. It takes considerable technical skill to go up the "Sticky Fingers" or the "Meat Grinder" route; they do all the work for you at the 80-passenger **Cannon Mountain Aerial Tramway** (823-5563; open May 25-Oct. and Dec. to mid-April daily 9am-4:30pm; tickets $6.50, ages 6-12 $3. $5.50 for one-way hikers).

To the south, **The Flume** (823-5563) is a White Mountain rarity: a well-developed tourist "sight" that's worth your time and money. Free movies are given at the new visitors center every half hour. From there, walk the 2-mile nature trail or take the bus to the mouth of the gorge. A boardwalk leads straight through, beneath sheer granite walls up to 90 feet high, and past pools and waterfalls. (Open mid-May to Oct. daily 9am-4:30pm; limited operations Oct. 27-Nov. 2. Tickets $5, ages 6-12 $2.50)Close to the Flume, you can cool off at the **Basin,** a 20-foot pothole beneath a waterfall. **Echo Lake,** farther along on I-93, is a popular picnic and swimming spot.

Myriad trails lead up into the mountains on both sides of the Notch, providing excellent dayhikes and spectacular views. Be prepared for severe weather, especially above treeline. The **Lake Trail** from **Lafayette Place** in Franconia Notch State Park winds 1½ miles to **Lonesome Lake.** (The AMC operates a hut here in the summer.) The **Greenleaf Trail** (2½ miles), which starts at the Old Man parking lot, and the **Old Bridle Path** (3 miles), which starts at Lafayette Place, are only a bit more ambitious. Both lead up to the the AMC's Greenleaf Hut near the summit of Mt. Lafayette, overlooking Eagle Lake, a favorite destination for sunset photographers. From Greenleaf, you can trudge the next 7½ miles east up and along **Garfield Ridge** to the AMC's most remote hut, the **Galehead.** Dayhikes from this base can keep you occupied for days. Sites at the Garfield Ridge campsite are $4.

Back at normal altitudes, you can camp at the **Lafayette Campground,** in Franconia Notch State Park (823-5563; open May 10-Oct. 10. $10 per night, Fri.-Sat. $12, seniors $8). If Lafayette is full, try the friendly **Fransted Campground** (823-5675), 1 mile south of the village and 3 miles north of the notch. (Sites $12 for 2, $1 each additional adult, children free. Bike rentals available for $1.50 per hr. Open year-round.) From Lincoln, the Kancamagus Highway (NH Rte. 112) branches east for a scenic 35 miles through the **Pemigewassett Wilderness** to Conway. The large basin rimmed by 4000-foot peaks is a popular backpacking and skiing area. South of the highway, trails lead into the **Sandwich Ranges,** a secluded series of lesser peaks, including **Mount Chocorua,** whose picturesque rocky cone you've probably seen on postcards and placemats.

Pinkham Notch

Hunched below Mt. Washington, Pinkham Notch and Rte. 16 cut the White Mountains from Gorham south to Jackson. Near Gorham, there is an **AYH hostel** (466-5130), part of the Bowman Base Camp in **Randolph.** (Members $10. Open May 30-Oct. 12.) The hostel is at the foot of Lowes Path, which climbs Mt. Adams. It's a strenuous hike, but mercifully far away from Mt. Washington's freeway-like trails. Stay at the **Madison Springs** AMC hut below the summit, and be prepared for nasty weather. The view is sensational, especially the sunrise over the Carter Range. In Gorham, you can also stay overnight in the **Berkshire Manor,** 133 Main St. (466-9418), which has kitchen facilities. (Singles $18. Doubles $25.)

Pinkham Notch Camp, run by the AMC (466-2727), at the height of the notch, is the definitive source for local information. You'll find advice on weather and trail conditions as well as hiking guides and maps to the area. Bed and breakfast cost $27, with buffet dinner $36. You can also buy meals here (breakfast and lunch $5, dinner $9, trail lunch $3.50; reservations are essential July-Aug.). Hitchhiking from nearby **North Conway** is not usually much of a problem, and lodging can be cheaper there. You can pitch a tent as long as it's more than ¼ mile from the AMC camp. A tough 4½-mile hike leads up to the **Lakes of the Clouds** AMC hut, just 1½ miles from Mt. Washington's summit. Be prepared for very high winds and even snowfall in late August. This is the most popular of the AMC's huts, so reserve early. An easier 6½-mile trail leads into the Carter Range to the **Carter Notch** AMC hut. There are two trout-stocked mountain lakes up here, and a maze of caves to explore. If you prefer to camp without making any great ascents, go a few miles further north up Rte. 16 to **Dolly Cap Campground** (603-466-3984), 5 miles south of Gorham. (191 tentsites, with bathrooms $9. Open year-round.)

The real challenge is, of course, the ascent of Mt. Washington. The most popular hiking trail is the 4-mile **Tuckerman's Ravine,** which offers a strenuous climb over steep glacial cirques. If you're in good shape you can easily make the round-trip in a day (in summer). If you feel less energetic there's the **Mount Washington Auto Road** (466-3988), a spectacle-packed 8-mile dirt road that winds to the summit. ($11 per driver, $4 per passenger, ages 5-12 $3. Weather permitting road open mid-May to mid-Oct. 7:30am-7:30pm; shorter hours early and late in the season.) The road begins at the **Glen House** on Rte. 16 and features a steady stream of fumes and families in mid-summer. If you're car-less but need transportation, make the trip with the **van service** ($15, ages 5-12 $10).

On the overbuilt summit, you'll find a snack bar, an information center, a museum, and the **Mount Washington Observatory,** where the highest wind speeds ever recorded on earth (231mph in 1934) were registered. The **Summit Museum** details the mountain's infamous weather (466-3347; open daily May 25-Oct. 12 9am-6pm weather permitting; tickets $1).

North Conway

North Conway, centrally located to many skiing centers, offers a collection of factory outlet stores at the intersection of Crawford and Pinkham gaps (U.S. 302 and Rte. 16). The White Mountains' major city, its equipment stores are the finest in the area. **Eastern Mountain Sports (EMS),** on Main St. (356-5433), on the premises of the Eastern Slope Inn, sells clothing and excellent books on the area. EMS offers cross-country ski rentals ($10-12 per day), tents, sleeping bags, and other camping equipment. **Joe Jones,** on Main St. (356-9411), at the corner of Mechanic St., rents bikes for $15 per half-day, $20 per day. (Open in summer Sun.-Wed. 9am-6pm, Thurs.-Sat. 9am-8pm; off-season hours vary.) The **information booth** (356-3171) on Rte. 16 in the center of town hands out a comprehensive list of accommodations in the area. (Open Sun.-Thurs. 8:30am-6pm, Fri.-Sat. 8:30am-7pm; off-season daily 9am-5pm.)

Skiing

New Hampshire has excellent cross-country and downhill skiing. It's expensive, but you can cut costs by watching for package deals and skiing on weekdays. All three cross-country centers offer close to 100 miles of trails—marked and unmarked, flat and mountain—along with rentals and lessons. For a one-day excursion on marked trails (as opposed to roughing it through the wilderness), count on $6-9 for a trail fee and $10-15 per day for rentals. **Jackson Ski Touring Foundation,** in Jackson (383-9355), 12 miles north of North Conway, provides the quintessential New England experience. Its trails wind past beaver dams, a covered bridge, and country inns. Visit **Waterville Valley X-C Ski Center** (236-8311; 800-258-8988 outside NH), 13 miles east of I-93's Campton exit, and trek through wilderness trails in adjacent White Mountain National Forest, **Bretton Woods Ski Touring Center** (278-5000), several miles north of Crawford Notch, which boasts an elaborate trail system. Not as well known as the mega-resorts of Vermont, downhill ski centers in New Hampshire usually offer well-groomed, slightly less expensive skiing that is no less exhilarating. Skiing on weekdays will enable you to beat the crowds, and the pass will be $5 less. Resorts cluster along I-93 in the west and in Mt. Washington Valley in the east. Those off I-93, collectively known as **Ski 93,** in Lincoln, P.O. Box 517 03251 (745-8101), offer easier access. **Loon Mountain** (745-8111), 3 miles east of I-93 at Lincoln, avoids overcrowding by limiting lift ticket sales, and also has a free beginners' tow (7 lifts, 41 trails). **Waterville Valley** (236-8311) offers great downhill as well as cross-country skiing (8 lifts, 46 trails). **Cannon Mountain** (823-5563; 800-552-1234 in New England), north of Franconia Notch, offers some good skiing off a large tram. For information on all Mount Washington Valley packages, contact the **Valley Chamber of Commerce,** P.O. Box 385, North Conway 03860 (356-3171). **Wildcat Mountain** (446-3326), in Jackson, has scenic vistas of Mt. Washington (5 lifts, 30 trails). Some of New England's best-groomed trails are at **Attitash** (800-258-0316) in Bartlett (6 lifts, 25 trails). Experts can head for **Tuckerman's Ravine,** a steep, treacherous glacial wall; hike to the top in late spring to conquer the most challenging slope in the East.

Rhode Island

Rhode Island is tiny (Texas is more than 200 times its size), but it has a full measure of exciting diversions. Unassuming Providence presents many surprises to be unearthed among its colleges, ethnic communities, and colonial neighborhoods. Newport, which shared capital status until 1900, has beautiful beaches, a bustling waterfront, even more colonial houses, and grandiose mansions. Most of the "Ocean State" derives its life-blood from Narragansett Bay, and anyone who doesn't eat quahogs (pronounced KOH-hog), a large, chewy clam variety, is considered a social outcast.

Practical Information

Capital: Providence.

Tourist Information: Rhode Island Division of Tourism, 7 Jackson Walkway, Providence 02903 (800-556-2484 or 277-2601). **Department of Environmental Management** (State Parks), 9 Hayes St., Providence 02903 (277-2771).

Time Zone: Eastern. **Postal Abbreviation:** RI.

Providence

Like Rome, Providence sits aloft seven hills. Unlike Rome, its residents are a combination of Ivy League types, starving artists, housewives in green Plymouth Belvederes, and smartly suited business types. Despite the construction downtown, Providence is a very walkable city. Visitors should begin with the extensive colonial neighborhood on **College Hill,** east of downtown (one of the best-preserved in the country), and shouldn't neglect the colorful ethnic neighborhoods around town. Only an hour from Boston and 3½ hours from New York, this small sleepy city lacks the driving intensity of its bigger cousins yet has an underground vitality.

Practical Information

Emergency: 272-1111, 0, or 911.

Visitor Information: Greater Providence Convention and Visitors Bureau, 30 Exchange Terrace (274-1636). Near the bus and train stations, next to City Hall. Among the usual maps and tourist literature is a self-guided walking tour. Open Mon.-Fri. 9am-5pm. **Roger Williams National Memorial Visitors Center,** 282 N. Main St. (528-5385), in between the Brown campus and downtown. Open daily 9am-5pm; mid-Oct. to mid-May daily 8:30am-4:30pm. **Providence Preservation Society,** 21 Meeting St. (831-7440), at the foot of College Hill, off Main St. Housed in the 1772 Shakespeare's Head, originally a post office, book shop, and printing shop. Detailed information on historic Providence. Pick up instructions on self-guided tours of the city's historic neighborhoods (80¢ each) or rent a $3 audio cassette tour. Open Mon.-Fri. 9am-5pm.

Travelers Aid: Bonanza Bus Station, 1 Sabin St. (521-2255. 24 hours.) Desk staffed Mon.-Fri. 8:30am-5pm.

Amtrak: 100 Gaspee St. (800-872-7245). A new, gleaming white concrete structure behind the State Capitol. A 10-min. walk to Brown or downtown. Station open daily 5am-11:15pm. To Boston ($12) and New York ($39).

Greyhound and Bonanza Buses: 1 Sabin St. (751-8800). Very frequent service to Boston (1 hr., $7.50) and New York (4 hr., $29). Open daily 4:45am-10:30pm.

Rhode Island Public Transit Authority (RIPTA): On Sabin St. (781-9400 or 800-662-5088, from Newport 847-0209. Office open Mon.-Sat. 7am-7pm). **Information booth** on Kennedy Plaza, across from the visitors center, provides in-person route and schedule assistance. Open Mon.-Fri. 8am-4:30pm. Buses operate daily 5:30am-9:30pm. Intercity connections and service to points south and Newport. Fares 25¢-$1.75. In Providence, fares are generally 60¢. Senior citizens with photo ID ride free Mon.-Fri. 9am-3pm, Sat.-Sun. all day.

Bike Rental: Rainbow Bicycles, 144 Brook St. (861-6176), at the corner of Brook and Transit St., near the southern end of Thayer St. 3-speeds. $2.50 per hr., $15 per day. Personal check, driver's license, or credit card accepted as a deposit. Open Mon.-Wed. and Fri.-Sat. 10am-6pm, Thurs. 10am-8pm.

Post Office: 24 Corliss St. (276-6800). Open Mon.-Fri. 7am-9pm, Sat. 8am-6pm. **ZIP code:** 02904.

Area Code: 401.

Metropolitan Providence sprawls over a good fraction of "Little Rhody." I-95 connects Rhode Island's capital city to Boston, 50 miles to the north, and New York City, 185 miles to the southwest. The city lies at the confluence of the mighty Seekonk, Moshassuck, and Woonasquatucket rivers with Narragansett Bay. The state capitol and the downtown business district cluster just to the east of the intersection of I-95 and I-195. **Brown University** and the **Rhode Island School of Design (RISD)** (pronounced "RIZZ-dee") pose on top of a steep hill east of downtown. **Providence College** is tucked into the northwestern corner of town, about 2 miles from the city center out Douglas Pike.

Accommodations

Rooms are especially difficult to uncover in late May and early June, graduation time at Providence's many colleges and universities. The **YMCA,** 160 Broad St. (456-0100), west of downtown overlooking I-95, is the cheapest place around, but it's poorly run and the neighborhood is questionable at best. Women accepted. Check-in and check-out at noon. ($30 per day, $70 per wk. ID required. Must be 18 or over.) You would do much better to find a place closer to College Hill; the friendly **International House,** 8 Stimson Ave. (421-7181), near the Brown campus, has two comfortable rooms that are usually booked. (Singles $45, students $25. Doubles $50, students $30. Reservations, taken Mon.-Fri. 9:30am-3pm, are usually essential.) The **Susse Chalet Motor Lodge,** 36 Jefferson Blvd., Warwick (941-6600 or 800-258-1980), a 15-minute drive on I-95 south, is convenient only if you have a car. (Singles $40.70. Doubles $44.70.) There's another Susse Chalet on Rte. 6, just off Rte. 195 a few miles east (336-7900).

Bed and Breakfasts of Rhode Island, Inc. will reserve a room in a private house or inn at an average price of $65 for a double, including breakfast. They represent over 100 B&Bs throughout the state. Outside Providence, the average price is $55. (941-0444; open Mon.-Fri. 9am-8pm, Sat. 10am-2pm; Labor Day-Memorial Day Mon.-Fri. 9am-5pm.) You can try making reservations at some of the in-town B&Bs yourself. **Mrs. Dorothy James,** 5 Medway (331-4293), rents singles for $45 and doubles for $55 in a house located a few blocks off Thayer St. **Mrs. Helen Meier,** 196 Butler Ave. (751-5914), rents singles for $40 and doubles for $50.

Unfortunately, there's no camping anywhere near Providence.

Food and Entertainment

For cheap food, visit the Italian district on Federal Hill just west of downtown, the student hangouts on College Hill to the east, or the city's beautiful old diners.

Angelo's Civita Farnese, 141 Atwells Ave. (621-8171), on Federal Hill. Walk west on Broadway from downtown, then turn right near the Holiday Inn and cross the highway overpass; or, take bus #26 ("Atwells"). The large acorn marks Federal Hill. Eggplant parmesan $2.75, spaghetti with garlic and oil $2.25. Open Mon.-Sat. 11am-8:30pm.

Loui's Family Restaurant, 286 Brook St. (861-5225), near the Brown campus. The students on the hill swear by it. Try the famous #1 special (2 eggs, homefries, toast, coffee for $2.12). Bacon cheeseburger $1.85. Open daily 6am-3pm.

Mutt's Pizza, 167 Benefit St. (351-6888). King of the College Hill for pizza, a deep dish costs $5.80. Watch for the 2-for-1 special. Sandwiches $2-4. Open Mon.-Thurs. 11am-11pm, Fri.-Sat. 11am-midnight, Sun. 1-10pm. Next door is **Geoff's,** with great sandwiches for $3-6.

Luke's Luau Hut, 59 Eddy St. (331-4265), behind City Hall. Ask to be seated in the psychedelic basement room with the blowfish lantern, and feast there on Duck Mona-Mona, Beeg Luau, or the incomparable pu-pu platter ($5-15 per person). Upstairs open Sun.-Thurs. 11:30am-9:30pm, Fri.-Sat. 11:30am-10pm. Basement open Mon.-Fri. 11:30am-3pm, Sun.-Thurs. 5-9:30pm, Fri.-Sat. 5-10:30pm.

Spat's Pub Restaurant, 230 Thayer St. (331-3435), on College Hill. A restaurant with a classy feel: dark wood tables, shining brass, and background jazz. Lunch $3-5.50. Dinner entrees $5-13. Open Mon.-Thurs. 11am-1am, Fri. 11am-2am, Sat. 9am-2am, Sun. 9am-1am.

Providence has a lively music scene and great bars. **The Rocket,** 73 Richmond St. (273-9619) downtown, is a fun place to see local bands, and **The Living Room,** 273 Promenade St. (521-2520), brings up-and-coming national and local acts into a friendly club atmosphere. Read the *New Paper,* distributed free on Wednesdays, or check the "Weekend" section of the Friday *Providence Journal* to find out more. Exciting distractions include the nationally acclaimed **Trinity Repertory Company,** 201 Washington St. (351-4242); the AAA-level **Pawtucket Red Sox,** who play at McCoy Stadium in Pawtucket (724-7300); the stock car races at the **Seekonk Speedway** (336-8488), a few miles east on Rte. 6, and the **Providence Performing Arts Center,** 230 Weybosset St. (421-2787), which hosts a variety of concerts and Broadway musicals. The **Cable Car Cinema,** 204 S. Main St. (272-3970) with an attached café shows art and foreign films in an unusual setting; you sit on couches instead of regular seats. The **Avon Repertory Cinema,** 260 Thayer St. (421-3315), is a favorite with the Brown crowd and shows first-run intellectual films and classics.

Sights

Providence's most notable historic sights cluster on **College Hill,** a 350-year-old neighborhood. **Brown University** claims several 18th-century structures, including **University, Wilson,** and **Sayles Halls,** and lamp-lined **Benefit Street** has a concentration of beautiful houses and historic buildings. Tours are given by the Brown Admissions Department (863-2378). Edgar Allan Poe courted Sarah Helen Whitman, the inspiration for Annabel Lee, at the **Providence Athaeneum,** 251 Benefit St. (421-6970), a Greek Revival structure that houses a private library. (Open Mon.-Fri. 8:30am-5:30pm; off-season also Sat. 9:30am-5:30pm. Free.) In addition to founding Rhode Island, Roger Williams created the Baptist Church as well; the **First Baptist Church of America,** built in 1775, stands at 75 N. Main St. Looking down from the hill, you'll see the **Rhode Island State Capitol** (277-2311). Its enormous unsupported marble dome is second only in size to St. Peter's in Rome. (Free guided tours Mon.-Fri. 8:30am-5pm. Building open Mon.-Fri. 8:30am-4:30pm.)

Nearby at the **RISD Museum of Art,** 224 Benefit St. (331-3511), you can view a first-rate collection of Greek, Roman, Asian, and impressionist art. Don't miss the gigantic, 10th-century Japanese Buddha. (Open Wed.-Sat. noon-5pm; in winter Tues.-Wed. and Fri.-Sat. 10:30am-5pm, Thurs. noon-8pm, Sun. 2-5pm. Admission $1, seniors 50¢, ages 5-18 25¢.) Student art is displayed during term time at the **Waterman Gallery,** in the Waterman Building. The **Woods-Gerry Gallery,** 62 Prospect St. (331-3511), shows both student and faculty artwork. (Open Mon.-Sat. 11am-4pm, Sun. 2-5pm.) A handsome mansion at 110 Benevolent St., the **Museum of Rhode Island History** (331-8575) has four rooms of interesting exhibits from the Rhode Island Historical Society's collections. (Open Mon.-Sat. 11am-4pm, Sun. 1-4pm. Admission $1.50, seniors and students $1, ages 7-17 50¢.) Also maintained by the Historical Society is the 1786 **John Brown House,** 52 Power St. (331-8575), an impressive residence built by the wealthy China trade merchant. (Open Tues.-Sat. 11am-4pm, Sun. 1-4pm; Jan.-Feb. weekends by appointment. Admission $2.50, seniors and students $1.)

Thayer Street is a popular student hangout and shopping spot. Built in 1828, the **Arcade,** 65 Weybosset St. (456-5403), on downtown's busiest commercial street, is the nation's oldest shopping mall. While the mall itself was built in the Greek Revival style, current proprietors tend to the trendy, vending yogurt cones with pride.

The **Blithewood Gardens and Arboretum,** on Ferry Rd. (Rte. 114), Bristol (253-2707), has 33 acres of lovely manicured grounds and gardens. (Grounds open Tues.-Sun. 10am-4pm. Admission $2, children 50¢. Mansion tours mid-April to Oct. $4, seniors $3, children $1.) **Slater Mill Historic Site,** on Roosevelt Ave., Pawtucket (725-8638), built in 1793, was the nation's first water-powered textile mill. (Open June-Sept. Tues.-Sat. 10am-5pm, Sun. 1-5pm; March-May and Sept. 6-Dec. 22 Sat.-Sun. 1-5pm. Admission $3, ages 6-14 $2.)

If you're interested in a quiet walk or jog, head over to the spacious grounds of **Roger Williams Park,** with their carousel and zoo, on the Cranston-Providence line; the lovely **Butler Hospital** (456-3700) estate; **Colt State Park,** in Bristol, where many local and national bands perform in summer; or the rolling green of **Swan Point Cemetery,** on Blackstone Blvd., where you can see the less-than-grotesque grave of horror writer H.P. Lovecraft.

Newport

Newport represented the escape from duty into an atmosphere of unmitigated holiday-making.
—*Edith Wharton,* The Age of Innocence

Before the American Revolution, Newport was one of the five largest towns in America and a thriving seaport, participating in the triangle trade in rum, slaves, and molasses. Occupation by the British thwarted development, and the town lost momentum until it was targeted as the ideal retreat by affluent vacationers in the mid-19th century. In the "Gilded Age," Newport emerged unrivaled as the most popular American resort. The "summer cottages" built by the elite were colossal mansions designed—without regard for cost—by America's best architects, in imitation of Neoclassical and baroque models. Crammed to the rafters with *objets d'art,* these "white elephants," as Henry James called them, testified to the determination of the *arrivistes* to purchase as much culture as possible. Today, however, the toys of the rich are racing and cruising yachts instead of gilded tea sets. You will see several 12-meter yachts with *Newport* emblazoned across their sterns, and regattas for many classes are held here. Former host to the America's Cup international sailing race, Newport's sailing industry still booms.

Newport is no longer a quiet town with freshly-caught fish on the wharves and roving packs of sailors; today the only way you'll find fish on the wharves is wrapped in a sauce with a soupçon of something, and the ambient scents come mainly from small French bottles. A lot of money is being made in Newport. By the end of your visit—if you're not careful—too much of it will have been yours. The off-season is a good time to visit. In chillier days, the restaurants downtown offer fireplaces, hot cider and grog, and a softer sell.

Practical Information

Emergency: 911.

Visitor Information: Newport County Convention and Visitors Bureau, 23 America's Cup Ave. (849-8048 or 800-458-4843). Free map. Open daily 8am-8pm, off-season 9am-5pm. Pamphlets and public restrooms are also available at the **Newport Harbor Center,** 365 Thames St. For more information on Newport call 800-242-1510 or 800-242-1520.

Bonanza Buses: Newport Gateway Center, 23 America's Cup Ave., next to the Convention and Visitors Bureau (846-1820). To Boston (8 per day, 1½ hr., $10).

Rhode Island Public Transit Authority (RIPTA): 1547 W. Main Rd. (847-0209 or 800-662-5088). Very frequent service to Providence (1 hr., $2) and points between on Rte. 114. Buses leave from the Newport Gateway Center. Free Newport Loop bus (Memorial Day-Labor Day daily 10am-7pm) to main sights, shopping areas, and at the chamber of commerce. Office open Mon.-Fri 4:30am-8pm, Sat. 6am-7pm.

Car Rental: Newport Ford, 310 W. Main Rd. (846-1411). Compact Escort $30 per day with 100 free miles, 15¢ each additional mile. Open Mon.-Fri. 8am-5pm. Must be 21. Credit card deposit $200.

Bike Rental: Ten Speed Spokes, 18 Elm St. (847-5609). Rents 1-, 3-, and 10-speeds. 10-speed $15 per day. Tandems $5 per day. Open Mon.-Sat. 9:30am-5:30pm, Sun. noon-5pm. Must have credit card and photo ID.

Post Office: 320 Thames St., opposite Perry Hill Market. Window service Mon.-Fri. 7:30am-5:30pm, Sat. 9am-noon; lobby Mon.-Fri. 6am-7pm, Sat. 6am-5pm, Sun. 10am-5pm. **ZIP code:** 02840.

Area Code: 401.

Newport commands a boot-shaped peninsula on the southwest corner of the Aquidneck Island in Narragansett Bay. The long span of the Newport Bridge (Rte. 138) connects the town to the smaller Conanicut Island to the west, which is in turn connected to the mainland by the Jamestown Bridge. From Providence, take I-195 east to Rte. 114 south via Mt. Hope Bridge (¾ hr.). From Boston, take Rte. 128 south to Rte. 24 south to Rte. 114 south (called the West Main Rd. near Newport) or Rte. 138 south (the East Main Rd.). On summer weekends, beat the traffic by taking the back door into town: on Rte. 138 south, turn left onto Valley Rd. and continue past Newport Beach onto Memorial Blvd. (1½ hr.).

West Main Road becomes Broadway in town. **Thames Street** is the main drag on the waterfront, and is pronounced as it looks, not like the river through London. The best way to get around in Newport is to walk or take the free RIPTA loop bus.

Accommodations

Newport is known for its Great Gatsby mansions and million-dollar yachts; lodging here is expensive. Head for the convention and visitors bureau for guest house brochures and free phones from which to call them. Guest houses offer bed and continental breakfast with colonial-style intimacy. If you're not fussy about sharing a bathroom or missing out on a sea view, you might find a double for $50. Singles are practically nonexistent. Avoid summer weekends, when many hotels and guest houses are booked solid two months in advance and rates are $10-$20 higher. Also, be warned that many of Newport's cheaper accommodations close for the winter. **Bed and Breakfasts of Rhode Island, Inc.** can make a reservation for you in Newport at an average of $65 per night.

If you arrive in town after the visitors bureau closes, there are some larger guest houses to try. The **Brinley Victorian,** 23 Brinley St. (849-7645), has 17 fantastic rooms with antique furniture in a quiet neighborhood. Doubles May-Oct. $75-80, Nov.-April $55-60. Prices cheaper if you come with 4-6 people; a suite for 4 is $135. At the **Queen Anne Inn,** 16 Clarke St. (846-5676), near Washington Sq., rooms are attractive with handsome wallpaper, bedspreads and wooden furniture. No private baths are available. (Singles $35. Doubles $45-70. Closed Nov.-April.) **Melville Ponds Campground,** 181 Bradford Ave., Portsmouth (849-8212), is the best in the area. Offers ice, firewood, clean washrooms with free hot showers, pay phones, small playground, full hookups. Open April-Oct. daily 8am-11pm. If you arrive after 11pm, set up and pay in the morning. Free beach nearby. Two adults and 2 children with tent $12 per night. Trailer hookup $14, full hookup $17.) Reservations recommended for summer weekends.

Food

For a picnic along romantic Cliff Walk or on the sands of nearby Fort Adams State Park, stop at the **Corner Store and Deli,** 372 Thames St. (847-1978), a restaurant-deli-grocery store with sandwiches ($2.50-4), plus salads and Italian specialties to go. (Open Sun.-Fri. 7am-9pm, Sat. 7am-10pm.) If you eat downtown, you'll help restaurant owners meet their high rents. Along the waterfront and wharves, sandwiches, salads, and pasta dishes are the best deals. Walk a few blocks away from downtown and you'll go through a time warp to true 1950s diners and New England seafood shacks. Sit at a booth and try Linda's Chili or Tish's Pea Soup at the funky **Franklin Spa,** 229 Franklin St. (847-3540, open Mon.-Sat. 6:30am-5pm, Sun. 6:30am-1pm).

Dry Dock Seafood Restaurant, 448 Thames St. (847-3974), a few blocks south of the wharves. Small, cheap, homey place frequented by locals. Big, crispy portion of fish and chips $4.75, lobster special $9.50, good stuffed quahogs $1.25. Burgers and fish sandwiches run $1-4. Open daily 11am-10pm.

The Island Omelette Shoppe, 1 Farewell St. (847-9389), a family-run diner popular with local working people. Best breakfast in town, fast and cheap ($1-5). Open daily 6am-2pm.

Salas, 343 Thames St. (846-8772). Italian and "oriental" pasta with 8 sauces, in ¼, ½, or 1 lb. servings (½ lb. spaghetti with red clam sauce $4). Seafood $7-10; raw bar cheaper than most. (Open daily 4-10pm.) The **Brasserie** downstairs has a similar menu. Open June-Sept. 25 Tues.-Sun. 5-10pm.

Sights

Several private companies offer bus, trolley, or watercraft tours, but don't bother, since everything in Newport is easily accessible on foot or bicycle. The **Newport Historical Society,** 82 Touro St. (846-0813), offers two-hour walking tours led by knowledgeable guides for small groups (June 15-Sept. Fri-Sat. at 10am. Tour $3, under 12 free). The building on Touro St. also houses exhibits from the society's collection of odds and ends from Newport's past. (Free.) For a self-guided walking tour pick up a free copy of the *Best Read Guide—Newport.*

Most tourists come to see the mansions, seven of which are now owned by the Preservation Society of Newport County, 118 Mill St. (847-1000). Unless you want to go on a serious gilt trip, tours of the interiors are not necessary. Instead, walk the length of **Bellevue Avenue** or stroll by the sea along the spectacular **Cliff Walk** (take a right off the east end of Memorial Blvd.) and enjoy the architecture. If you must venture inside, start at the **Breakers,** on Ochre Point Ave. Built for Cornelius Vanderbilt II in 1895, this mansion is the most famous and the most lavish of all. The **Marble House** and **Rosecliff,** both on Bellevue Ave., furnished settings for the movie *The Great Gatsby.* (All mansions open May-Oct. daily 10am-5pm, with limited hours in April. Some open longer on particular days July to mid-Sept.) Several private palaces also open their doors to the public. Antiques crowd the rooms of **Belcourt Castle,** on Bellevue Ave. (846-0669; open June 19-Nov. 5 daily 9am-5pm; March 18-June 18 and Nov. 6-Jan. 1 daily 10am-5pm; limited hours rest of the year. Admission $4.50, seniors $3.50, students $3, ages 6-12 $1.50.) The **Astor's Beechwood,** on Bellevue Ave. (846-3772), between Rosecliff and Marble House, belonged to Caroline Astor, the Queen of the Newport *nouveau riche.* Mrs. Astor's "servants" (Beechwood Theater Company) will welcome you as her personal guests. (Admission $4.50, ages 6-11 $2.50.) Cycle the 10-mile loop along **Ocean Drive** for breathtaking scenery. On the way you'll pass **Hammersmith Farm** (846-0420), the childhood home of Jackie Bouvier Kennedy Onassis and the "summer White House" 1961-63. (Open Memorial Day-Labor Day daily 10am-7pm; April-May and Sept.-Oct. 10am-5pm; Nov. and March Sat.-Sun. only. Admission $5, children $2.)

Though not as spectacular as the mansions, Newport's collection of colonial and Victorian buildings is enormous. Visit the Historical Society for suggestions on do-it-yourself walking tours. Most of the famous revolutionary luminaries at one time or another passed through the **Old Colony House** (846-2980), in the middle of

Washington Sq. Each of the three rooms appears as it did during one of the buiding's major periods of construction since 1743. (Free tours on weekends. Open Tues.-Sat. 10am-4pm, Sun. noon-4pm; limited hours off-season.) The **White Horse Tavern,** on Marlborough St. (849-3600), is the oldest drinking establishment in the country. The building dates to 1673, but it was first opened as a tavern in 1687 by the father of William Mayes, a notorious Red Sea pirate.

Since Rhode Island was founded as a haven of religious freedom for colonists fleeing Puritan Massachusetts, it is no surprise that the most interesting colonial buildings in town are houses of worship. The **Quaker Meeting House,** built in 1700, on the corner of Marlborough and Farewell St. (847-2481), is Quaker plain inside and out. The original steeple, criticized as too "papist," was torn down in 1807. The **Touro Synagogue,** 83 Touro St. (847-4794), a beautifully restored Georgian building, is the oldest synagogue in the U.S., dating back to 1763. It was to the Newport congregation that George Washington wrote the famous letter that describes the U.S. as giving "to bigotry no sanction, to persecution no assistance." (Free tours every ½ .hr. in summer. Open late June-Labor Day Sun.-Fri. 10am-noon, 1-5pm; Labor Day-Nov. and May-June Sun.-Thurs. 2-4pm; Dec.-April Sun. 2-4pm.) Towering **Trinity Church,** facing Thames St. in Queen Anne Sq., boasts a pew reserved for George Washington back in the days when Newport was a revolutionary army stronghold.

The Redwood Library and Athenaeum, on Bellevue Ave. and Old Beach Rd. (847-8720), built in 1748-1750, is the oldest library in continuous use in the country. 141 portraits watch you from all sides as you enter. (Open daily 9:30am-5pm.) The **Wanton-Lyman Hazard House,** 17 Broadway (846-3622), is the oldest standing house in Newport (1675) and was the site of the Stamp Act riot of 1765. (Open June 15-Aug. 31 Tues.-Sat. 10am-5pm. Admission $2, under 12 free.)

No racqueteer should miss the **Tennis Hall of Fame,** 194 Bellevue Ave. (849-3990), in the Newport Casino. The first U.S. national championships were held here in 1881. The Casino has one of the few facilities in the world for the ancient and arcane game of court tennis. A Virginia Slims tennis tournament is held here in the late summer. (Open daily 10am-5pm, Nov.-April 11am-4pm. Admission $4, under 16 $2.)

May through September, hardly a day passes without some race or regatta on Narragansett Bay or Rhode Island Sound. The annual **Fools' Rules Regatta** takes place in late August (423-1492), in which contestants create a sailing vessel from non-standard materials and then race them on a 500-yard course. If you don't sail, at least take some time to walk the plank onto vessels available for visits. The Bannister's Wharf Marina is open to the public and has been home port for the 12-meter yachts *Clipper, Independence, Courageous,* and *Gleam.* Check out the free *Newport This Week's Yachting & Recreation Guide* for a description of regattas and a calendar of events.

Enter through Gate 1 of the U.S. Navy's training center on Coasters Harbor Island to view a different sort of sea power. Appearances to the contrary, tourism is not Newport's largest industry. The U.S. Navy is the town's largest employer, and second only to the Rhode Island state government. On special occasions, you can tour the successors to the wooden ships and iron men from the time of John Paul Jones. You can also sit in on the ceremonies and full dress parades, or visit the **Naval War College Museum** (841-4052; open June-Sept. Mon.-Fri. 10am-4pm, Sat.-Sun. noon-4pm; Oct.-May Mon.-Fri. 10am-4pm).

The closest place to swim, body surf, or lay on the sand is Newport Beach (known to Newporters as First Beach or Easton's Beach), at the north end of Cliff Walk. Watch for the windsurfers (even in the middle of winter). Second Beach, in Middletown, is second closest, but it costs about $10 to park in summertime. Other good beaches can be found in Little Compton, Narragansett, and along the shore between Watch Hill and Point Judith. If you like cliff-diving or hiking over sand dunes, head for Brenton Point or Fort Adams State Parks, south of town, accessible by Ocean Drive.

Entertainment

Lovers of classical, folk, and jazz each have a festival to call their own. The **Newport Music Festival** (849-0700), attracts pianists, violinists, and other classical musicians from around the world, presenting them in the ballrooms and lawns of the mansions in July. Tickets and information are available at the Convention and Visitors Bureau. (Dates and prices vary.) Also in late July you might chorus with folksingers such as Pete Seeger at the **Newport Folk Festival** (847-3710). The festival runs two days, noon-6:30pm, rain or shine. Three weeks later the **Newport Jazz Festival** (847-3710) comes to town. The setting for both festivals is a grassy field at Fort Adams State Park, overlooking the ocean. Purchase tickets in advance through the visitors center (folk $20, jazz $25), or buy them at the gate (folk $22.50, jazz $27.50). **Christmas in Newport,** a non-profit organization, sponsors a stockingfull of classy little concerts, readings, teas, and other events in December, many free or with nominal admission. (Write P.O. Box 716, Newport 12840; 849-6454; open 5-7pm in Nov.-Dec.)

Newport's nightlife is active and predictably trendy. Local and out-of-state musicians play at the **Blue Pelican Jazz Club,** 40 W. Broadway (847-5675), a famous hotspot with a diverse roster of performers. (Open daily 6pm-1am. Cover $4-5.) Chic travelers may want to visit **Maximillian's,** 108 William St. 2nd floor (849-4747), across the street from the Tennis Hall of Fame, one of the city's most popular discos. (Open Tues.-Sat. 8:30pm-1am. Cover Tues.-Thurs. $3, Fri.-Sat. $5.) Better yet, if you just sailed into town, saunter down Bannister's Wharf and stop in at the **Black Pearl Pub** (and café in good weather). (Open daily 11:30am-3pm, Sun.-Thurs. 5:30-10pm, Fri.-Sat. 5:30-11pm.)

Some of Newport's best theater struts upon the stage at the **Rhode Island Shakespeare Theater** (849-7892), on Webster St., off Bellevue Ave. (Performances Thurs.-Sun. 8pm. Tickets $10, student rush $5.) The **Newport Playhouse** (849-4618), next to Jeremiah's Restaurant on Connell Highway, puts on light comedies. (Performances usually Fri.-Sun. Tickets $8, seniors and students $6. Take Harrison Ave. bus from the YMCA.) Newport also has a resident modern dance group, the **Island Moving Company** (847-4470), which hosts a short summer season.

Balls whiz by at 188 miles per hour, athletes somewhat more slowly, at the **Jai Alai Fronton,** 150 Admiral Kalbfus Rd. (849-5000 or 800-451-2500; 800-556-6900 outside RI), at the base of the Newport Bridge. (Games May 5-Oct. 9 Mon.-Sat. 7:30pm, matinees Mon. and Sat. at noon. Seats $2-3.50, standing room $1.) Read the weekly *Newport This Week* for more entertainment information.

Near Newport: Block Island

Once a barren hideaway of small treeless hills, Block Island has become an increasingly popular daytrip as Nantucket and Martha's Vineyard become saturated with tourists. Weathered shingles, quaint buildings, and serenity give the island its old New England charm. It's almost as if life stands still here. Bring a picnic, head due south from Old Harbor where the ferry lets you off, and hike to the Mohegan Bluffs. If you're adventurous and careful, wind your way down to the Atlantic waters 70 yards below. The **Southeast Lighthouse,** high in the cliffs, has warned sailors since 1875; its beacon is the brightest on the Atlantic coast.

The **Block Island Chamber of Commerce** (466-2982 or 466-2436), is at the ferry dock in Old Harbor Drawer D, Block Island 02807. (Open Mon.-Fri. 10am-4pm, Sat. 10am-noon; mid-Oct. to mid-May Mon.-Fri. approximately 10am-2pm.) You can also ask for the free *Block Island Chamber of Commerce Directory* at the Newport Chamber of Commerce.

Cycling is an ideal way to explore the island. Try the **Old Harbor Bike Shop,** to the left of where you exit from the ferry (466-2029). (10 speeds $2.50 per hr., $12.50 per day; single mopeds $10-12 per hr., $35-45 per day; double mopeds $18-20 per hr., $50-65 per day. Car rentals: $35 per 4 hr., $55 per day, 20¢ each additional mile. Open daily 8:30am-7:30pm. You must be 21 with a credit card or leave a $100 deposit.)

Interstate Navigation Co., Galilee State Pier, Point Judith 02882 (401-789-3502; on Block Island 401-466-2261) runs one ferry per day (July 1-Sept. 10) between Providence and Block Island (at 8:30am, 3½ hr. One way $5.25, round-trip $7.75; bicycle $1.70. Stops at Ft. Adams at 10:30am, 1½ hr. One way $4.75, round-trip $7; bicycle $1.25). Year-round service to Block Island leaves only from Point Judith, near the town of Galilee, across Rhode Island Sound west of Newport. An interstate ferry leaves from Point Judith (frequency varies between 8-10 per day in summer, to 1 per day Dec.-Feb.; 1 hr., one way $5, same day round-trip $8, bicycle $1.40 each way; car $32.40 round-trip).

The **police** can be reached at 466-2622 and the **Coast Guard** at 466-2086. The post office is on Ocean Ave. Block Island's **ZIP code** is 02807. Since all phones are on the 466 exchange, you need only dial the last four digits while on the island.

Vermont

There's a story about a Texas rancher who goes to Vermont to study the dairy farming industry. After spending the day touring pastures, barns, and farmhouses with his Vermont-born host, the Texan remarks, "You know, down in Texas, I can hop in my car and drive all day and still not reach the other side of my ranch."

"Ay-uh," says the Vermonter, "Had a car like that once myself."

Known for their dry wit and laconic provincialism, Vermonters have more recently earned a reputation for their progressive, liberal politics. Common interests have resulted in some interesting political reforms: Vermont led the way with anti-litter legislation several years ago and, more recently, town meetings across the state passed a nuclear-freeze referendum. Burlington's Bernie Sanders was the first socialist mayor of a major city in the U.S.

In the late 60s and early 70s, many dissatisfied young urbanites headed for a simpler, more peaceful life in Vermont, setting up communes in Putney, the Northeast Kingdom, and elsewhere. Today one often finds hippies and long-time residents discussing organic farming techniques or the latest in wood stoves. Vermont's park system emphasizes rural tranquility, and includes many excellent streamside retreats. The state parks fill only on September and October weekends.

Practical Information

Capital: Montpelier.

Tourist Information: For lodging, events, attractions, dining, and camping, try either the **Vermont Travel Division,** 134 State St., Montpelier 05602 (828-3236; open Mon.-Fri. 7:45am-5:30pm, Sat. 9am-5:30pm, Sun. 11:30am-3pm; off-season Mon.-Fri. 7:45am-4:30pm), or the **Chamber of Commerce,** P.O. Box 37, Montpelier 05601-0037, Granger Rd., I-89 exit 7, (223-3443; open Mon.-Fri. 8:30am-5pm). For the scoop on hiking, camping, and the great outdoors, try the **Department of Forests, Parks, and Recreation,** 103 S. Main St., Waterbury (244-8711; open Mon.-Fri. 7am-4:30pm). **U.S. Forest Supervisor,** Green Mountains National Forest, 151 West St., Rutland 05701 (775-2579; open Mon.-Fri. 8am-4:30pm). **District Ranger,** Green Mountains National Forest RD#3, Middlebury 05753 (388-4362), RD#1, P.O. Box 108, Rochester 05767 (767-4261).

Public Transportation: Vermont Transit Lines, 135 St. Paul Street, Burlington, VT 05401 (864-6811 for information).

Time Zone: Eastern. **Postal Abbreviation:** VT.

Skiing

Twenty-six downhill resorts and 50 cross-country trail networks are packed into Vermont. For a free winter attractions packet, call the Vermont Travel Division (see Practical Information), or write **Ski Vermont,** 134 State St., Montpelier 05602.

Vermont's famous downhill ski resorts offer a choice of terrain from easy "bunny" slopes to steep and mogul-covered runs, and a great variety of accommodations, including cheap dorms. The best known resorts are: **Killington** (422-3333 or 422-3261; 107 trails, 18 lifts, 6 mountains); **Sugarbush** (583-2381; lodging 800-537-8427; 71 trails, 16 lifts, 2 mountains); **Stowe** (253-7311; lodging 800-253-4754; 44 trails, 10 lifts; see Stowe for more details); and **Jay Peak** (800-451-4449; 32 trails, 6 lifts). Vermont's big cross-country resorts mean you don't have to backtrack. Try: the **Trapp Family Lodge,** Stowe (253-8511; lodging 800-247-8693; 60 miles of trails); **Mountain Meadows,** Killington (757-7077; 25 miles); **Woodstock** (457-2114; 47 miles); and **Sugarbush-Rossignol** (583-2301 or 800-451-4320; 40 miles).

Brattleboro

Southeastern Vermont enjoys a rare mix of deep-rooted farming traditions and New Age creativity. One of the largest towns in Vermont, energetic, commercial Brattleboro is a good base for exploring the surrounding countryside. In the village of Putney, 5 miles to the north, alternative lifestyles are much in evidence; craft cooperatives are a prime example. This section of the Connecticut River valley is especially popular during the stunning fall foliage season.

Brattleboro is right on the Connecticut River, which you can explore by canoe. Rentals are available at **Connecticut River Safari,** 257-5008, 603-363-4724) onPutney Rd. (Rte. 5). ($12 per ½-day, $18 per day; longer packages available.) They also run a touring and guiding service on the Connecticut and other New England rivers. The **Brattleboro Outing Club** also rents canoes (257-0296) and runs skiing and bicycling programs. (Secretary: Box 335, Brattleboro, 05301; 603-399-4963.)

Inexpensive places to eat are easy to come by. The **Common Ground Community Restaurant,** 25 Eliot St. (257-0855), a collectively run workers' cooperative, serves a wide range of affordable vegetarian cuisine in a relaxed, informal atmosphere. You can get soup, salad, bread and beverage for $3.60. (Open Mon. and Wed.-Sat. 11:30am-9pm, Sun. 10:30am-1:30pm and 5:30-9pm; Dec.-May Fri.-Sat. 11:30am-9pm, Sun.-Thurs. 11:30am-8pm.) For locally grown fresh fruits, vegetables, and cider, go to the **farmers' markets** on the Town Common, Main St. (June 14-Sept. 13 Wed. 10am-2pm) or on Mink Farm, Rte. 9 west of town (May 13-Oct. 14 Sat. 9am-2pm). The **Spring Tree Chocolate Factory Outlet,** on Rte. 5 (Putney Rd.) (254-8784), offers mouthwatering chocolate at discount prices. The milk almond bar ($7.75 per lb.) and dark chocolate mint truffles ($7.60 per lb.) will storm your senses. (Open Mon.-Sat. 10am-5:30pm, Sun. noon-5pm.)

The renovated **Latchis Hotel,** 2 Flat St. (254-6300), downtown, is the best lodging bargain, though the cheaper rooms can be dreary. (Singles $34-52. Doubles $40-62.) The neighborhood around Flat St. and Eliot St. can be rough at night. The **West Village,** 480 Western Ave. (254-5610), is in West Brattleboro about 3 miles out of town on Rte. 9. (Singles $30. Doubles $35.) **Fort Dummer State Park,** Old Guildford Rd. (254-2610), on U.S. 5, just ½ mile south, has campsites with fireplaces, picnic tables, hot showers, and bathroom facilities. (51 tentsites $7 each. 10 lean-tos $10 each. Firewood $1 per armload. Open Memorial Day-Labor Day.) **Molly Stark State Park** (464-5460) is 15 miles west of town on Rte. 9. (24 tentsites $7 each, 10 lean-tos $10 each. Hot showers 25¢. Open May 25-Oct. 10.)

The nightlife of Brattleboro has two faces: one for jazz and reggae crowds, the other for locals driving pick-ups. **Mole's Eye Cafe,** 4 High St. at Main St. (257-0771), has jazz, reggae, and rock bands on Wednesday, Friday and Saturday nights. (Light meals about $5). (Open daily 11:30am to 1 or 2am. Cover $3, free Wed.) **Colors,** 20 Elliot St. (254-8646), is a fun, relaxing place popular with both gay and straight people. (Open Sun.-Fri. 8pm-2am, Sat. 8pm-1am. DJ Wed.-Sun. Cover Thurs.-Sat. $2.) Contact the **Arts Council of Windham County,** (387-4114), for their calendar of upcoming events, or call their 24-hour events recording (257-1234).

The **chamber of commerce,** 180 Main St. (254-4565), is open Mon.-Fri. 8am-5pm. In summer, an information booth (257-1112) on the commons brings you up to date.

(Open Memorial Day-Labor Day daily 9am-5:30pm; Labor Day-Columbus Day Sat.-Sun. only.)

Amtrak's "Montrealer" from New York City and Springfield stops in Brattleboro behind the museum once daily to Montreal and once daily south to New York City. Arrange tickets and reservations at **Lyon Travel,** 10 Elliot St. (254-6033. Open Mon.-Fri. 9am-5pm, Sat. 10am-2pm.) **Greyhound** and **Vermont Transit** stop in the parking lot behind the Howard Johnson's at I-91 exit 2 (254-6066). Brattleboro is on Vermont Transit's Burlington-New York City route (4-5 per day, $31). Other destinations include Springfield, MA (4 per day, $10) and White River Junction (4 per day, $11), with connections to Montpelier, Waterbury, Burlington, and Montreal.

Brattleboro's **ZIP code** is 05301; The **area code** is 802.

Bennington

A minor industrial center, Bennington is also the state's third largest town (pop. 16,000). Bennington trumpets its status as the first chartered town in Vermont, and historical sites abound. Pick up a map and a brochure describing **Historic Bennington Walking Tours** at the **chamber of commerce** at Veteran's Memorial Dr. (447-3311. From the bus terminal, turn right and walk up the street less than a mile behind the deer park. (Open Mon. 9am-5pm, Tues.-Fri. 9am-7pm, Sat. 9am-6pm, Sun. 10am-4pm.)

The town is mostly built up around the intersection of Rte. 9 (E. and W. Main St.) and Rte. 7 (N. and S. streets). Walking through it, you will pass many old buildings, although the only one you can glance into is the **Old First Church** (First Congregational Church). The church was not only the home of the oldest Protestant religious organization in Vermont, but it was also the first place in the U.S. to separate church and state. The church is still used for services, but is open to the public late June-Oct. daily 10am-noon and 1-4pm. Down the street is the **Bennington Museum,** W. Main St. (447-1571), with the world's largest collection of folk artist Grandma Moses's paintings and the oldest Stars and Stripes in existence. (Open mid-Jan. to mid-Dec. daily and some other winter weekends 9am-5pm. Admission $4.50, seniors and students $3.50, under 12 free.) Up the hill, the **Bennington Battle Monument,** a 306-foot obelisk at the end of Monument Ave., commemorates General John Stark's victory over the British. (Museum shop 447-0550. Open daily April 1-Oct. 31 9am-5pm. Admission $1, ages 6-12 50¢.) The **Norman Rockwell Exhibition,** Rte. 7A (375-6423), Arlington, 14 miles north, displays over a thousand Rockwell *Saturday Evening Post* covers. (Open daily 9am-5pm; off-season 9am-4pm. Admission $1.)

To escape from the steady stream of traffic through the center of Bennington try **Back-Road Country Tours** (442-3878). For $12.50 per person you get a one-hour jeep ride through the back roads of Bennington County with commentary on the local farms, covered bridges, wildlife, and folklore. (Trips daily year-round.)

Geannelis' Restaurant, 520 Main St. (442-9778), is very popular and serves tasty sandwiches ($2-3), dinner ($4-7), and fine ice cream ($1.25). (Open Mon.-Sat. 6am-8pm, Sun. 7am-8pm.) Down the street, **Occasionally Yoghurt,** 604 Main St. (442-2526), has big salads ($2-5) and other natural vegetarian foods. (Open daily 11am-9pm.)

Greenwood Lodge and Tentsites, P.O. Box 246, Bennington (442-2547), is an 8-mile trip east on Rte. 9 in Woodford Valley. The Long Trail is just 3 miles away. (Open July 1-Sept. 7, fall weekends, and some winter months. Dorms $10 with AYH card. Camping $10. Private family rooms from $25, slightly higher rates for fall foliage season. Linen, towels, and soap $2. Hot showers in lodge. Canoeing free.) In town, try the comfortable **Bennington Motor Inn,** 143 W. Main St. (442-5479; singles $44; doubles $44-56). The chamber of commerce can provide you with a list of places to stay, most of which are at least $35-40 for a double. Camping is cheaper: Stay at **Woodford State Park** (447-7169), 10 miles east on Rte. 9. (Open

Memorial Day-Columbus Day Sites $8.50.) **Pine Hollow Camping Area,** Old Military Rd., off Barker's Pond Rd. off U.S. 7 (823-5569), is 2 miles east of Pownal Center, 6 miles from Bennington, and offers swimming and tranquility. (Open May 15-Oct. 15. Sites $8.)

Bennington pins down the southwestern corner of Vermont, 39 miles across the Green Mountains from Brattleboro, and 60 miles south of Rutland on U.S. 7/7A. **Vermont Transit,** 126 Washington Ave. (442-4808), takes you to Middlebury, Rutland, Burlington, Montreal, and Albany, NY. (Open daily 7am-11:30pm.)

Bennington's **ZIP code** is 05201; the **area code** is 802.

White River Junction and West

Central Vermont is graced with the subtle pleasures of quiet winding back roads and the sight of grazing cows in quiet green pastures. If you enjoy rural rubbernecking, plan an east-west trip along U.S. 4, or a north-south trip on Rte. 100. The roads are best reached from U.S. 5 or I-89, where they intersect with the Connecticut River at White River Junction. This unremarkable town serves as **Vermont Transit's** (295-3011) major bus center for eastern and central Vermont, with connections across New Hampshire, Burlington, and up and down the Connecticut River. (Office open Mon.-Fri. 6am-8:30pm, Sat. 6am-5pm, Sun. 7:45am-9:30pm.)

An information booth across the street from the bus station can fill your pockets with brochures on Vermont. (Open Memorial Day-Oct. 15, daily 10am-5pm.) Also in the Junction you'll find the **Catamount Brewery,** 58 S. Main St. (296-2248), where delicious, unpasteurized, amber ale is produced in strict accordance with the brewing methods of British ale. (Tours Tues. at 11am, Fri. at 1pm, Sat. at 1am and 1pm. Store open Mon.-Sat. 9am-5pm. Free samples.)

For a quick bite to eat, stop at the **Polkadot Restaurant,** 1 N. Main St. (295-9722), a classic diner resting next to a retired Boston & Maine steam engine. (Two pork chops with applesauce $5.25. Open daily 5am-9pm.) There are a few motels around, but the best bet for lodging is the **Hotel Coolidge,** 17 S. Main St. (295-3118 or 800-622-1124), right in the middle of town. The rooms are clean but go down in quality with the price. (June-Oct. singles $27-49, doubles $32.50-55. Rates slightly lower in winter.)

Six miles west of White River Junction on U.S. 4 is **Woodstock,** a town which is part Vermont country village and part wealthy vacation resort. Visitors park their Saabs, Porsches, and BMWs along the quaint village streets between gift and craft shops. The **information booth** (457-1042) in the middle of the village green, dispenses all the information you need. (Walking tours, starting from the green, are offered mid-June to Oct. Mon., Wed. and Sat. at 10:30am ($2.50), daily in foliage season. Office open June 20-Oct. 31 daily 10am-6pm.) The **Woodstock Historical Society,** 26 Elm St. (457-1822), is in **Dana House,** which contains a rich collection of antique furniture and artifacts. (Open May-Oct. Mon.-Sat. 10am-5pm, Sun. 2-5pm. Admission $2.50, seniors $1, children 50¢.) The **Vermont Raptor Center,** part of the **Vermont Institute of Natural Sciences,** Church Hill Rd. (457-2779), is a "living museum" introducing visitors to the owls and hawks of northern New England. (Open May-Oct. Wed.-Mon. 10am-4pm; Sept.-April Mon. and Wed.-Sat. 10am-4pm. Admission $3.50, ages 5-15 $1.)

Eat in the jungle beneath the gaze of a stone lion at **Bentley's Greenhouse,** 7 Elm St. (457-3400). This is a combination soda fountain, sandwich and florist shop (sandwiches $2.75). (Open Mon.-Wed. 8:30am-5:30pm, Thurs.-Sat. 8:30am-8pm, Sun. 8:30am-5pm.) The best ice cream in town is served at the **Mountain Creamery,** 33 Central St. (457-1715). Notable flavors include Myers rum raisin and Vermont maple walnut. (Open daily 7am-6pm.) Spend the night in the beautifully remodeled **1826 House,** 57 River St. (457-1335, single $40; doubles $40-45), with its wide wooden floorboards and quiet back porch. The **Silver Lake Campground** (234-9974) is 9 miles north of town on Rte. 12 near Barnard, with no public transportation available. (Open Memorial Day-Columbus Day. Sites $12.75 per family, $2 each additional adult.)

To rent a quality bike and explore the scenery around Woodstock on wheels, go to **The Cyclery Plus,** on U.S. 4 (457-3377), in West Woodstock. ($12 per half-day, $18 per day, $60 for 5 days. Open Mon.-Fri. 9am-6pm, Sat. 9am-5pm.) **Wilderness Trails** at the Quechee Inn, Clubhouse Rd., in Quechee will rent you a bike or canoe for the day. (295-7620; 1 person $14, 2 people $25, half days and additional days $9.) The information booth on the green has maps of trails for nearby Mountains Tom and Peg, as well as local bike routes. A 25-minute walk up Mt. Tom will afford a good view of the town. **Vermont Transit** stops at Whippletree Shop, Central St. (457-1325) in Woodstock. (To White River Junction 3 per day, $2.70; to Rutland 3 per day, $4.85.) **Gilbert's Hill,** 2 miles north of town on Rte. 12, is the site of the first ski town in the U.S., and an annual reenactment complete with huge wooden skis is held every February. Join the local families throughout the winter at **Suicide Six Ski Area** (457-1666), 3 miles north of town. Six miles east on U.S. 4 is **Quechee Gorge,** a 165-foot drop from the road to the Ottaquechee River below.

Genuine Vermont sharp cheddar cheese is made only in certain counties. One authentic producer is the **Plymouth Cheese Factory,** Rte. 100A (672-3650), 6 miles south of U.S. 4 and Killington. (Open daily 8am-5:30pm; off-season 8am-5pm; closed Sundays Christmas-April.) Another big cheese from Plymouth, **Calvin Coolidge,** was born in this tiny village. Next door to his birthplace is the old homestead where his father swore him in as president in 1923 after learning of the sudden death of Warren G. Harding. (Open May 22-Oct. 18 daily 9:30am-5:30pm. Admission $1, children free.) Five miles south on Rte. 100 lies glistening **Echo Lake,** a great place for a picnic and a swim. (Rent a canoe or paddle boat for $2 per hr. Admission $1.)

Middlebury

Middlebury is a pleasant stopover between Bennington and destinations north. Its small-town charm is supplemented by wealth brought in by students and tourists. **Main Street** (what else?) is the town's spine. It eventually winds north to Middlebury College, where stores, fine cafés, and restaurants give way to dorms. The **University of Vermont** (388-2011) breeds sturdy Morgan horses nearby. Take Rte. 125 west, then right on Rte. 23 2½ miles. Guided tours are available. (Stables open May 1-Nov. 1 daily 9am-4pm. Admission $2.50, teenagers $1, under 12 free.) If you meet groups of Americans all speaking anything but English, don't be alarmed. **Middlebury College** (388-3711) conducts rigorous summer immersion programs where students speak only the language they are learning.

Biking is not too strenuous in the gentle hills around the town. Spend a day at **Lake Dunmore,** and from there bike up to **Silver Lake** with its canopy of birch trees and pines. On the way, you'll pass by the beautiful **Falls of Lhana.** The north side of the lake is the place for an invigorating, if chilly, dip without the encumbrance of a swimsuit.

Visit the studios of the **Vermont State Craft Center** at Frog Hollow, which produces an eclectic, though expensive, array of glass, pottery, carvings, and textiles. (388-3177. Open Mon.-Sat. 9:30am-5pm, and Sun. 11am-4pm; Jan.-May Mon.-Sat. 9:30am-5pm.) Nearby, the **Sheldon Museum,** 1 Park St. (388-2117), has a collection of antiques including furniture, glass, china, books, newspapers, and documents that provide a good picture of rural New England in the 1800s. (Open June-Oct. 31 10am-5pm. Admission $2.50, seniors and students $2, under 12 50¢.)

Middlebury's many fine restaurants cater primarily to those with larger expense accounts, but the year-round presence of students assures the survived of places with cheaper fare. **Calvi's,** 42 Main St. (388-9038 or 388-9338), is an old-fashioned soda fountain with old-fashioned prices. (Open Mon.-Sat. 8am-10pm). Students flock to the more upscale **Mister Up's,** Bakery Lane (388-6724), just off Main St. and overlooking Otter Creek, for exotic appetizers and alcoholic concoctions. Beer batter mushrooms ($4), escargot florentine ($5.50). (Open Mon.-Sat. 11:30am-midnight, Sun. 11am-midnight.)

Information on Middlebury and its environs can be gathered at the friendly **Addison County Chamber of Commerce,** 2 Court St. (388-7951), just 50 yards from the bus stop. (Open Mon.-Sun. 9am-5pm; off-season Mon.-Fri. 9am-5pm.) Unfortunately, the area's cheapest accommodations are mostly the farthest away. **Homestead Bed and Breakfast** (545-2263), on Lemmon Fair Rd., 2½ miles from town, has cheery rooms in an almost-new ranch style house. (Singles $28. Doubles $35.) **Branbury State Park** (247-5925), 7 miles south on U.S. 7, then 4 miles south on Hwy. 53, will make a smaller hole in your pocket. (Open Memorial Day-Columbus Day. Sites $8.50. Reservations recommended July 4-Aug. 15.) **Lake Dunmore Kampersville** (352-4501), 8 miles south on U.S. 7, then 2 miles east on 53, is a pleasantly kool setting. (Open year-round. Sites $15.50 for 2 adults, children free, $5 per extra family on the same site. Reservations recommended, especially in July.)

Nightlife in Middlebury hops, thanks to collegiate proximity. On the banks of Otter Creek, the trendy **Woody's,** 5 Bakery Lane (388-4182), off Main St., has upscale dishes and drinks. (Open Mon.-Sat. 11:30am-midnight, Sun. 10:30am-3pm and 5-9:30pm.) Across the street, **Amigos,** 4 Merchants Row (388-3624), serves up Mexican food ($2.50-9) and live local music Fridays from 10pm-1am. (Open Mon.-Sat. 1:30am-10pm, Sun. 4-10pm. Bar open nightly until midnight.)

Middlebury is on U.S. 7, at the base of the Green Mountains, 42 miles south of Burlington. The **Long Trail** passes by along the ridges in the **Green Mountain National Forest,** a few miles east. **Vermont Transit** buses stop at Keeler's Gulf, 16 Court St. (388-4373), west of Main St. Buses serve Albany, New York City, Boston, and Burlington. You can ask to be let off on the Middlebury College campus, a few minutes' ride from the station. You can rent bikes and cross-country skis at the **Bike & Ski Touring Center,** 74 Main St. (388-6666) Waxless cross-country skis $7.50 per day, waxable $5 per day; 3-speeds $1.50 per hr., $5 per day, $7.50 per weekend. Open Mon.-Thurs. and Sat. 9:30am-5:30pm, Fri. 9:30am-8pm.)

Middlebury's **ZIP code** is 05753; the **area code** is 802.

Montpelier

Crowded in by the surrounding mountains, Montpelier (pop. 8000), is an unassuming small New England town. Its identity as Vermont's capital is evident only when you see the proud **State House,** State St. (828-2228), topped with its shining gold dome. (Tours July to mid-Oct. 10am-3:30pm, Sat. 11am-2:30pm. Open Mon.-Fri. 8am-4pm.)

Trace the history of the Green Mountain state at the Vermont Historical Society's **Vermont Museum,** 109 State St. (828-2291). Permanent and changing exhibits encompass a range of furniture, documents, photographs, and other artifacts. (Open Nov.-June Mon.-Fri. 9am-4:30pm; July-Oct. Sat.-Sun. 9:30am-4pm. Donation required.)

From Montpelier, you can explore the nearby **"Northeast Kingdom,"** three Vermont counties famous for their fall foliage. The town of **Craftsbury Commons,** in the Kingdom, is home to the **Craftsbury Center (AYH),** Hosmer Pond on Lost Nation Rd. (586-7767; $10 per night. Reservations required: write to P.O. Box 31, Craftsbury Common 05827).

Montpelier is the home of the **New England Culinary Institute,** 250 Main St. (223-6324), and thus a fine place for a budget-blasting binge. The **Elm Street Cafe,** 38 Elm St. (223-3188), run by the institutes' first-year students, has mostly American cuisine. (Lunch specials under $5. Open Mon.-Fri. 7-10am, 11:30am-1:30pm and 5:30-9pm.) **Tubbs Restaurant,** 24 Elm St. (229-9202), is operated by second-year students and features French cuisine. (Lunch entrees $4.75-5; dinner entrees $11-16. Open Mon.-Fri. 11:30am-2pm and 6-9:30pm, Sat. 6-9:30pm.) The school's bakery, **La Brioche** (229-0443), is in the same building and has delicious pastries and cakes. Vermont cheese and produce are used to prepare vegetarian dishes at the **Horn of the Moon Café,** 8 Langdon St. (223-2895). Salads $1.75-3.50, breakfasts and lunches under $5. (Open Mon. 7am-3pm, Tues.-Fri. 7am-9pm, Sat. 8am-9pm; off-season Mon. 7am-3pm, Tues.-Sat. 7am-9pm, Sun. 10am-2pm.)

The **Vermont Travel Division,** 134 State St. (828-3236; open June to mid-Oct. Mon.-Fri. 7:45am-5:30pm, Sat. 9am-5:30pm, Sun. 11:30am-3pm; mid-Oct. to May Mon.-Fri. 7:45am-4:30pm), can provide you with a list of restaurants and accommodations in the area, and tourist information about the whole state. Try the **Montpelier Bed and Breakfast,** 22 North St. (229-0878), about a ½ mile from the capitol. Very comfortable singles are $23-28, doubles $35-39, all non-smoking. The cheaper rooms do not come with breakfast. The **Green Valley Campground** (223-6217) is six miles east of town on Rte. 2 and offers swimming and showers. (Open May-Oct., sites $9, with water and electricity $11.) The **Capitol Home Hostel,** RD #1, Box 2750 (223-2104), offers 6 beds at $8 per night. Reservations by phone required.

Montpelier rests just off I-89, 4 miles northwest of Barre, 40 miles southeast of Burlington and 50 miles northwest of White River Junction. **Vermont Transit** is behind Chittenden Bank at 112 State St. (223-7112). The well-run company sends out buses to Burlington, White River Junction, Montreal, and Portland, with connections to the rest of Vermont and other New England states.

Montpelier's **ZIP code** is 05602; the **area code** is 802.

Stowe

Between Montpelier and Burlington lie Vermont's prime ski areas. From November until April, **Stowe** (253-7311 or 800-253-4754) is the focal point for all sorts of winter activities and one of the ski capitals of the East. Its trails spread out across the slopes of **Mount Mansfield** and neighboring **Spruce Peak.** Farther up Rte. 108 is **Smugglers' Notch** (644-8851 or 800-451-8752), another high-priced resort, named for the illicit activities that went on here in the 19th century. Cross-country skiing centered on Stowe's **Trapp Family Lodge,** Trapp Hill Rd. (253-8511 or 800-826-7000), is some of the finest in the country.

Stowe has much to offer the summer visitor in addition to wonderful hiking opportunities. Rent bikes (1- or 10-speeds $5 per hr., $15 per day; mountain bikes $18.50 per day) at **Stowe Mountain Sports,** Mountain Rd. (253-4896, open Mon.-Sat. 10am-6pm), or at the **Mountain Bike Shop,** Mountain Rd. (253-7919; mountain and road bikes $6 per hr., $20 per day). **Buccaneer Country Lodge,** 1390 Mountain Rd. (253-4772) rents flat water canoes for $25 a day. Horseback riding is available at **Edson Hill Manor,** Edson Hill Rd. (253-8954 or 888-5137), and **Topnotch at Stowe,** Rte. 108 (253-8585; guided tours $20, private lessons available.)

The alpine slide down Spruce Peak is a concrete, gutter-shaped slide doused with streaming water, which descends through beautiful woods and meadows. (Open mid-June to Labor Day daily 10am-5pm; weekends only Memorial Day to mid-June and Labor Day-Columbus Day. Admission $5, children $3.50.) You can take the gondola to the top of Cliff House just below the summit of Mt. Mansfield (open mid-June to Columbus Day daily 10am-5pm; weekends only Memorial Day to mid-June; fare $8, children $4); or for $8 you can burn out your brakes by driving the 4½ miles up and down Mt. Mansfield. (Open Memorial Day-Columbus daily 10am-5pm. For all, call 253-7311, ext. 2288.) If you're looking for a good daytrip, hike the **Long Trail** ascending Mount Mansfield. There are a few lean-tos on this trail for overnight camping. Contact the **Stowe Area Association** on Main St. (253-7321 or 800-247-8693), right in the center of the village, for free booking service and summer information on the area's lodging, restaurants, and activities, including skiing. (Open winter Mon.-Fri. 9am-8pm, Sat.-Sun. 9am-6pm; in summer Mon.-Fri. 9am-6pm, Sat. 10am-4pm, Sun. 11am-5pm.)

Lodging in Stowe covers a wide price range. Most places are off Rte. 100 (Main St.) or along Rte. 108 (Mountain Rd.) up to the ski areas. The **Vermont State Ski Dorm,** (253-4010) is open as an AYH hostel June 15-Oct. 15, $6 per night.**Godin's Lodge,** on Rte. 100 (253-8969), will put you up for $10, $35 for the week. (Open

Dec. 1-May 15.) The **Golden Kitz,** Mountain Rd. (253-4217), is relaxed and informal, if a bit crowded with odd bric-a-brac. (Singles with shared bath are $20-40 in peak ski season, $15-28 in summer. Doubles range from $38-68 in the peak ski season, $34-50 in the early and late ski seasons, and $28-50 in summer. Breakfast included.) The **Gold Brook Campground** (253-7683) is 2 miles from the town center on Rte. 100. (Sites $10.50.) **Smuggler's Notch Recreation Area** (253-4014) offers lean-tos ($10.60) and tent sites ($7). (Open May 19-Oct. 14; reservations suggested.) Visit the Stowe Area Association on Main St. for a more complete list of accommodations.

Stowe is 12 miles north of I-89's exit 10, which is 27 miles southwest of Burlington. **Vermont Transit** runs one bus each day from Stowe to Newport and one to Burlington.

Ben and Jerry's Ice Cream Factory, Rte. 100 (244-5641), is a couple miles off I-89 in Waterbury. Starting in 1978 in a converted gas station, Ben and Jerry have gone on to develop some of the best ice cream in the world. Celebrated flavors include Heath Bar Crunch, Raspberry, and White Russian. ($1 tours daily 9am-5pm every ¼ hr.) You can indulge at their store daily 9am-9pm.

Stowe's **ZIP code** is 05672; the **area code** is 802.

Burlington

Burlington is Vermont's only city, with a population of 40,000. After a few weeks elsewhere in Vermont, this humble figure sure looks big. Five local schools, including the University of Vermont, vitalize this isolated burg, and the cool waters of Lake Champlain remind the visitor that this is still, after all, Vermont.

Practical Information

Emergency: 911.

Tourist Information: Lake Champlain Regional Chamber of Commerce, 209 Battery St. (863-3489), right next to the ferry pier. Open Mon.-Fri. 8:30am-5pm, Sat. 10am-2pm and Sun. 11am-2am.; late Sept.-late June Mon.-Fri. 8:30am-5pm.

Amtrak: 29 Railroad Ave., Essex Jct. (879-7298), 5 miles from the center of Burlington. Trains head north in the morning, south in the evening. To New York (1 per day, 9 hr., $62). Open 5:45am-noon, 1-6pm, and 7-11pm. Bus to downtown every ½ hr., 75¢.

Buses: Vermont Transit, 135 St. Paul St. (864-6811), at the corner of Main St. Connections include Boston ($37), Montreal ($15), White River Junction ($12.35), Middlebury ($6.10), Bennington ($15.75), and Montpelier ($6.30). Open daily 7am-8pm.

Chittenden County Transit Authority (CCTA): 135 St. Paul St., 864-0211. Frequent, reliable service. Downtown hub at Cherry and Church St. Connections with Shelburne and other outlying areas. Buses operate Mon.-Sat. 5:45am-10:30pm depending on routes. Fare 75¢, seniors and disabled 35¢, under 18 50¢.

Taxi: Yellow Cab, 864-7411.

Bike Rental: Ski Rack, 81-85 Main St. (658-3313). Bikes $15-25 per day, tandems $35 per day. Open Mon.-Thurs. 9am-7pm, Fri. 9am-9pm, Sat. 9am-6pm, Sun. noon-5pm. The chamber of commerce provides maps of the Burlington Bike Path and parks.

Post Office: 11 Elmwood Ave. (863-6033), at the corner of Pearl St. Open Mon.-Fri. 8am-5pm, Sat. 9am-noon. **ZIP code:** 05401.

Area Code: 802.

Burlington is on the eastern shore of long, narrow Lake Champlain, 225 miles northwest of Boston, 100 miles south of Montreal. The central part of Burlington is quite compact and there is an active pedestrian mall downtown. The city's hills and the expansion of its outskirts may make it necessary to take the local transit system to reach the suburbs.

Accommodations, Camping, and Food

The **YWCA,** 278 Main St. (862-7520), for women only, has dorm rooms in a big old house. (Laundry and kitchen facilities. 12 beds only. $5 membership required. Singles $16, $44-52 per week. Doubles $28. Triples $39.) **Howden Cottage,** 32 N. Champlain St. (864-7198), has two clean and cozy rooms with shared bath. Non-smoking only. (Singles $35. Doubles $50. Off-season $30 and $40 respectively. Continental breakfast included.) The ugly orange **Mid-Town Motel,** 230 Main St. (862-9686), is the only cheap place right in the middle of Burlington. Rooms are not too clean and bathrooms unpleasant. (Singles $30. Doubles $35-40. Just up the hill from the bus station.) Three miles out from downtown, **Mrs. Farrell's Home Hostel,** 27 Arlington Court (865-3730), has six beds for $9 a night. Reservations required. **Burlington Beach Campsite,** Institute Rd. (862-0942), is only 1½ miles north of town on Rte. 127, along Lake Champlain. (Open May 15-Oct. 1. Sites $10-15. Showers and beach.) Take the CCTA North Ave. bus leaving from the main city terminal on St. Paul Street. **Shelburne Campground,** Shelburne Rd. (985-2540), is 1 mile north of the center of Shelburne and 4 miles south of Burlington. Buses stop right next to the campground. (Open April-early Oct. Sites $12 for 2 people, $1 each additional person.)

Henry's Diner, 155 Bank St. (862-9010), has been the place to meet the locals and eat good, inexpensive food since 1925. (Sandwiches $1.75-4, full meals $5-10. Open Tues.-Sat. 6:30am-8pm, Sun. 8am-2pm.) The **Oasis Diner,** 189 Bank St. (864-5308), is Henry's competition down the block. They offer similar nouvelle diner cuisine at similar prices in an aluminum art deco setting. (Open Mon.-Sat. 5:30am-4:30pm.) **Carbur's,** 115 St. Paul Street (862-4106), close by Main St., has the famous quint-decker Queen Lily special sandwiches ($8.88), and the world's zaniest menu. (Open daily Sun.-Thurs. 11am-midnight, Fri.-Sat. 11am-1am.) Try the **Vt. Pasta Company,** 156 Church St. (658-2575), at the end of the pedestrian area for a variety of pasta dishes ($3.50-5) and sandwiches ($2-4.50). Finish off any meal with a trip to **Ben and Jerry's Ice Cream,** 169 Cherry St. (862-9620; open Mon.-Thurs. 10:30am-midnight, Fri.-Sat. 10:30am-1am, Sun. 11am-midnight). Good luck polishing off their "Vermonster," a meal in itself—it includes 20 scoops of ice cream, 10 scoops of chopped walnuts, 7 scoops of strawberries, and 5 scoops of whipped cream. Taste a sample here and then head to B&J's factory tour in Waterbury (see Stowe). **Sha-na-na's,** 101 Main St. (865-2596), has nightly DJ's playing 50s and 60s music. Jitterbug lessons Tues. nights. (Open Mon.-Fri. 11:30am-2am, Sat. 7pm-1am, Sun. 7pm-2am. Cover Thurs. $2, Fri.-Sat. $3.)

Sights

Burlington preserves a historic center, cultivates a healthy cultural life, and enjoys a scenic setting. Spend some time window-shopping and people-watching in the **Church Street Marketplace,** in the Church Street Historic District. The brick-lined street has plenty of small shops and cafés to explore. **South Willard Street, City Hall Park,** and **Battery Street** are other interesting historic areas to stroll through.

You don't have to be a history buff to enjoy the following two tours. **New England Dairy Foods,** 398 Pine St. (863-3968), will lead you around the largest quiche and cheesecake factory in New England. (Free samples. Tours Mon.-Fri. at 10am, 11am and noon. Store open Mon.-Thurs. 9am-5:30pm, Fri. 9am-6:30pm, Sat. 9:30am-5pm.) Then, head to the nearby **Champlain Chocolate Company,** 431 Pine St. (864-1807; open Mon.-Sat. 9:30am-5:30pm). Summertime culture vultures shouldn't miss the **Champlain Shakespeare Festival** and **Vermont Mozart Festival** held in July and August. For more works from the Bard, go to the University of Vermont's Royall Tyler Theatre, on campus (656-2094; box office open Mon.-Fri. 10am-5:30pm, Sat. 10am-1pm; tickets $10-12.50, seniors and students $8, matinees $6). The Flynn Theatre Box Office, 153 Main St. (863-5966), handles Mozart performances. (Open Mon.-Fri. 10am-4:30pm, Sat. 10am-1pm. Tickets $7-50.) The **Flynn**

Theatre, an art deco movie house built in 1930, hosts and sponsors a broad range of performances, including free folk concerts at Battery Park (mid-late summer) and free jazz concerts, part of the **Discover Jazz Festival,** in mid-June. (Flynn Theatre Box Office handles tickets.)

Near Burlington

Seven miles south of Burlington in **Shelburne** is the **Shelburne Museum** (985-3344), which houses a large collection of Americana. The entire town is a museum sprawling across 45 acres. Many of the 35 buildings have been transported from other New England towns. A double covered bridge from Cambridge, the paddlewheeler *Ticonderoga* from Lake Champlain, and a schoolhouse from Vergennes are also featured. (Open mid-May to mid-Oct. daily 9am-5pm. Admission $12, children $4.) Five miles farther south on Rte. 7, the **Vermont Wildflower Farm** (425-3500), has a seed shop and acres of wildflower gardens to wander through. (Open May to mid-Oct. daily 10am-5pm. Admission $2, seniors $1.50, under 12 free.)

Burlington and Shelburne both lie on the shore of **Lake Champlain,** a 100-mile inland body of water that drains into the St. Lawrence River in Canada. Ferries crisscross the lake, nestled in a broad valley between the Green Mountains and New York's Adirondacks. The **Lake Champlain Ferry** (864-9804) will take you across the lake from Burlington's King Street Dock to Port Kent, NY, and back. (June 22-Sept. 4 7:30am-7:30pm 14 per day; May 18-June 21 8am-5:30pm 8 per day; Sept. 5-Oct. 15 8am-5:30pm 8-11 per day. One way $3, ages 6-12 $1, with car $11.50.) You can also take a ferry from Grand Isle to Plattsburg, NY, or go 14 miles south of Burlington and take one from Charlotte, VT, to Essex, NY (fare for either: one way $1.50, ages 6-12 50¢, with car $6.50). You get a great view of the environs from the top of nearby **Mt. Philo State Park.** (425-2390. Campsites $7, lean-tos $10.) Take the **Vermont Transit** bus from Burlington heading south along Rte. 7 to Vergennes. Twisting U.S. 2 cuts through the center of the lake by hopping from the mainland to **Grand Isle** to **North Hero Island** and then to Québec, Canada.

There are several state campgrounds on the islands, and much of the surrounding land is wilderness. The marsh to the north is protected in the **Missiquoi National Wildlife Refuge.** Camp at **Burton Island State Park** (524-6353), which is accessible only by ferry (8:30am-6:30pm) from Kamp Kill Kare State Park, off U.S. 7, 50 miles north of Burlington and 3½ miles southwest of St. Albans. **Grand Isle** has its own state park with camping (372-4300), just off U.S. 2 north of Keeler Bay. All state campground sites in the Lake Champlain area cost $8.50.

THE MID-ATLANTIC

The diverse and densely populated states along the Eastern Seaboard tell the story of a nation's creation and development. American capitalism began in Jameston, VA, where early colonists came in search of wealth. Constitutional democracy and free speech are celebrated in Philadelphia, the nation's first capital. The right to religious freedom is cherished by Mennonites and Amish. Tremendous factories, bustling harbors, and large rural areas all testify to an earnest work ethic.

It is often difficult to view the Mid-Atlantic as a unified region. There is no common heritage. Perhaps the most cohesive elements lie in the the cold and convincing facts of economic success, political power, and urban growth. From the ivy-covered brick of Philadelphia to the Federal grandeur of Washington, DC, it is here that the payoffs of the American dream vaunt themselves.

Travel

Competition is fierce among **airlines** for the traffic moving up and down the northeast corridor. Look for bargains in the big-city newspapers. **New York Air** offers low fares, and **Pan Am** has a cheap shuttle between Washington, DC and New York.

Train travel has been well established in the mid-Atlantic longer than in most regions of the U.S. **Amtrak** runs frequent "Northeast Corridor" trains that run north-south and connect Washington, Baltimore, Philadelphia, and New York. The east-west routes in Pennsylvania and West Virginia provide better service to remote areas than the bus companies. In larger cities such as Philadelphia and Washington, DC, Amtrak connects directly with city commuter-rail lines and bus lines.

Greyhound/Trailways covers the mid-Atlantic states, including the Chesapeake Bay area. Large cities' local transit systems tend to be excellent. The efficient **New Jersey Transit System** links New York City and Philadelphia with Atlantic City and most New Jersey towns.

If you're **hitchhiking,** look for ride boards at local colleges and universities instead of thumbing road-side. In all but the most rural areas, the frontier spirit of neighborliness vanished generations ago.

Finding reasonably priced **accommodations** in the cities becomes more difficult each year. The unfortunate flip side of gentrification is a marked increase in downtown hotel prices as older hotels give way to luxury conventioneers' inns. Regional Ys are closing residential facilities in many places. Budget hotel chains are often at the edge of town. **Bed and breakfasts** are sometimes cheaper for longer stays. Philadelphia has the most B&B budget options. In beach areas, look for cottages available on a weekly basis. If you're in the mood to pamper yourself, consider going to a popular area in the off-season, when rates sometimes drop to one-half to one-third the seasonal cost. In Washington, DC, where "off-season" means every weekend, tickets to area attractions are often included with room rental. **Youth hostels** shine bright in an otherwise dismal regional accommodations scene. AYH maintains an excellent chain of hostels in the big cities and a fair smattering on the coastlines.

Outdoors

There is plenty of outdoor fun in the Mid-Atlantic states. The celebrated **Appalachian Trail** crosses the area. For information, contact the Appalachian Trail Conference, P.O. Box 807, Harper's Ferry, WV 25425 (304-535-6331). In Virginia, the **Blue Ridge Parkway** traverses the Shenandoah and Great Smoky Mountains. Other major outdoor areas are the national seashores along the coast, and the national forests in the Appalachians. Raft or backpack in the wilds of Pennsylvania and West

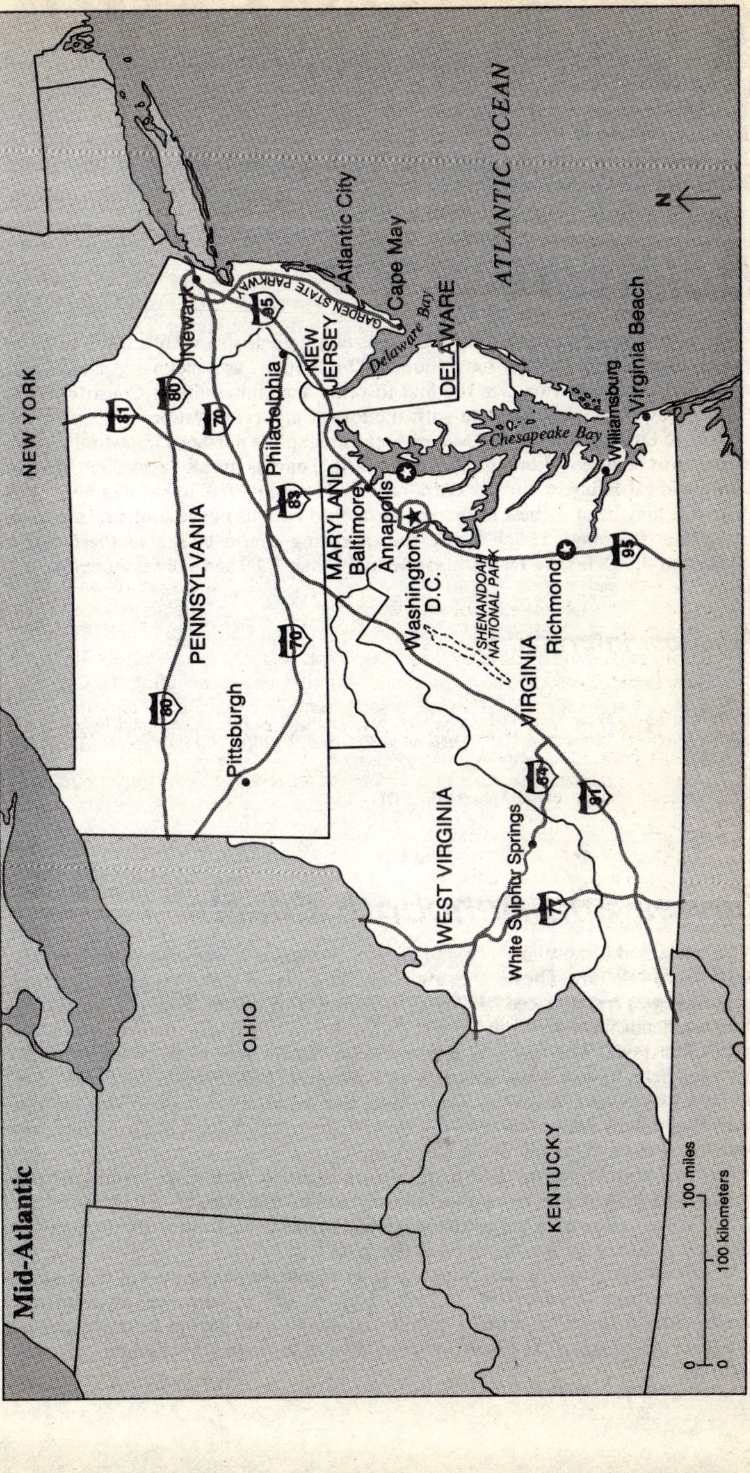
Mid-Atlantic
NEW YORK
PENNSYLVANIA
Pittsburgh
Philadelphia
Newark
NEW JERSEY
GARDEN STATE PARKWAY
Atlantic City
Cape May
Delaware Bay
DELAWARE
MARYLAND
Baltimore
Annapolis
Washington, D.C.
Chesapeake Bay
Williamsburg
Virginia Beach
Richmond
VIRGINIA
SHENANDOAH NATIONAL PARK
WEST VIRGINIA
White Sulphur Springs
OHIO
KENTUCKY
ATLANTIC OCEAN
N
0 100 miles
0 100 kilometers

Virginia's Allegheny Mountains. Wildlife refuges scattered along the Atlantic Ocean and its bays protect birds and wild ponies alike.

Bikers can choose between roads along flat beaches, through sloping valleys and gentle, rolling hills, or up arduous mountains. Biking is possible year-round, but the ideal times are April, May, and mid-September to mid-October. For information, contact one of the bicycle clubs that offer a variety of group tours, such as Bike VA, P.O. Box 203, Williamsburg, VA 23187 (804-253-2985), or Blue Ridge Biking, Inc., P.O. Box 504, Montezuma, NC 28653 (704-733-5566).

Delaware

Delawareans seek to make up for their state's small size with a fierce pride in its rich historical past. They have adopted "First State" as a nickname, a reference to the fact that Delaware was the first to ratify the United States Constitution in 1787. Delaware is also the state with the lowest highest elevation.

Most of Delaware's population is concentrated in the northern industrial region, on the strip between Wilmington and Newark. Tourists usually associate the state with chemical industry and big corporations. Here, in 1938, nylon was born. But Delaware may be at its best in the less developed regions of the southern seacoast; Lewes and Rehoboth Beach typify the easygoing charm of the southern resort towns, and the Delaware Dunes preserve more than 2000 acres of seashore for public use.

Practical Information

Capital: Dover.

Tourist Information: State Visitors Service, 630 State College Rd., Dover 19901 (800-282-8667; 800-441-8846 outside DE). **Division of Fish and Wildlife,** William Penn St., Dover 19901.

Time Zone: Eastern. **Postal Abbreviation:** DE.

Area Code: 302.

Lewes and Rehoboth Beach

The reserved atmosphere of these seaside retreats is a welcome relief from the usual boardwalk fare. The beaches are clean, the air is salty, and the people, particularly in Lewes (pronounced "LOO-iss"), keep to themselves. Founded in 1613 by the Zwaanendael colony from Hoorn, Holland, Lewes proudly touts itself as Delaware's first town. The best way to learn about Lewes is to walk around town. If you need help, try the **Lewes Chamber of Commerce** (645-8073), in the Fisher Martin House on King's Highway. (Open Mon.-Sat. 10am-3pm.) A good idea for food is the **Lighthouse Restaurant** (645-6271), on Fisherman's Wharf, just over the drawbridge in Lewes. (Open daily 7am-9:30pm.)

Due east from Lewes, on the Atlantic Ocean, is the secluded **Cape Henlopen State Park** (645-8983), home to a seabird nesting colony and popular for its sparkling-white "walking dunes." Campsites (645-2103) are available from April through October on a first come-first serve basis (from $12).

With a minimum of advance planning, you can join the committees of vacationing bureaucrats from Washington, DC who convene at the sand reefs of Rehoboth Beach on hot summer weekends—to mix and mingle with anyone who may donate to a future campaign. The beach is a popular spot for high school graduation celebrations.

The **chamber of commerce,** Rehoboth Ave. (800-441-1329 or 227-2233), in the restored train station, provides brochures, but can't help much with budget accommodations. (Open Mon.-Fri. 9am-4:30pm.) For inexpensive lodging, walk 1 block from the boardwalk to the **Lord Baltimore,** 16 Baltimore Ave. (227-2855), which has clean, comfortable, practically beachfront rooms. Try to get a porch room facing the ocean. (Singles and doubles from $40.) Or walk a little further from the beach to the cluster of guest houses on the side lanes off 1st St., just north of Rehoboth Ave. The family-run **Abbey,** 31 Maryland Ave. (227-7023), is a good bet. (2-day min. stay. Doubles from $34.) The **Three Seasons Camping Resort** (277-2564), 1 mile west of Rte. 1 on Rte. 273, provides RV campers (no tents) with a pool, store, and snack bar. (Sites from $15. Reservations taken only by mail; write to P.O. Box 156, Rehoboth Beach 19971.) The **Big Oaks Family Campground,** P.O. Box 53, Rte. 1 (645-6838), is at the intersection of Rte. 1 and 24. (Recreation room, playground, and TV room. Sites $15.)

At the **Country Squire,** 17 Rehoboth Ave. (227-3985), you can sit at the bar and talk with natives over one of the Squire's complete dinner specials (about $6). On Tuesdays (3-11pm), join the "Brown Collar" Gaming club—a rag-tag collection of tourists and townies who gulp down 95¢ beers over a game of poker, darts, backgammon, blackjack, bumper pool, or Trivial Pursuit. This is also the best place for breakfast (specials $3; open daily 7am-1am). Another good bet for the hungry is barbecue fare at **Camby's,** 7 Rehoboth Ave. (227-3334).

Greyhound/Trailways serves Lewes (flag stop at the parking lot for Tom Best's on Rte. 1; no phone) and Rehoboth Beach (227-7223; small station at the dry cleaners on Rehoboth Ave.). Buses run to: Washington (3½ hr., $25); Baltimore (3¼ hr., $23); and Philadelphia (4 hr., $24). Lewes is on one end of the 70-minute **Cape May, NJ/Lewes, DE Ferry** route (Lewes terminal 645-6313; for schedule and fare information, see Cape May above). **Webb Transportation** (645-5000) operates shuttle bus service between the ferry terminal and Rehoboth (mid-June to Labor Day $9; in off-season cab service $15). To get around within Rehoboth, use the free trolley transportation run by the **Ruddertowne Complex** (227-3888; Memorial Day-Labor Day daily noon-1am every hr.), which serves points between Rehoboth and Dewey Beaches. The trolley stops at the Boardwalk and Rehoboth Ave. The **Jolly Trolly,** which gives a 10-mile narrated tour of the Rehoboth area ($3.50), also runs from Boardwalk and Rehoboth Ave.

The **post office** in Rehoboth is at 59 Rehoboth Ave. (227-8406). (Open Mon.-Fri. 8:30am-5pm, Sat. 8:30am-noon.) The **ZIP code** for Lewes and Rehoboth Beach is 19971; the **area code** is 302.

Maryland

The Chesapeake Bay has been at the core of life in Maryland since the 17th century. Today, countless oysters and crabs are pulled out of the bay, and its shipping lanes serve many mid-Atlantic cities. Beaches and tributaries provide a playground for recreational boaters. Yachts, Navy vessels, tankers, and trawlers alike anchor at the gleaming cities of Baltimore and Annapolis. Washington, DC and the Potomac River are critical to Maryland as well, as workers in both the public and private sectors commute into DC from the suburbs of the "Old Line State."

Practical Information

Capital: Annapolis.

Tourist Information: Office of Tourist Development, 1748 Forest Dr., Annapolis 21401 (269-3517). **Forest and Parks Service,** Tawes State Office Bldg., Annapolis 21404 (269-3776).

Time Zone: Eastern. **Postal Abbreviation:** MD.

Baltimore

Baltimore's character is part stevedore, part steel worker, and part society snob. The city is energetically trying to make the transition from a past, when the three parts clashed abrasively, to a more integrated future when the city will once again boom economically. Historic stone and the run-down warehouses of the once-dominant Baltimore & Ohio Railroad stand beside new glass-sided office towers. The gleaming reconstruction of the Inner Harbor, complete with ultracommercial Harborplace, symbolizes Baltimore's largely successful efforts to renovate and revitalize itself.

Practical Information

Emergency: 911.

Visitor Information: Office of Promotion and Tourism, 34 Marketplace, The Brokerage Building, #310 (837-4636), off Pratt St., 2 blocks north of the World Trade Center. Take buses #7, 10, or 27, or hop on the Inner Harbor trolley from any point along the water. Ask for *Baltimore Scene,* a monthly publication with excellent maps, lodging and eating hints, and schedules of events. Open Mon.-Fri. 9am-5pm. Information also at 600 Water St., in the Brokerage Building (open Mon.-Fri. 10am-6pm); and in a booth at Harborplace on the downtown waterfront (open daily 10am-6pm). A satellite booth is located at Penn Station. Usually open late Fri. evenings, weekday mornings, and all day Sun.

Travelers Aid: 685-3569; 685-5874 24-hour hotline. Offices at Penn Station (open Mon.-Thurs. 9am-noon, Fri. 9am-9pm, Sat. 9am-1pm, Sun. 10am-5pm) and the Baltimore-Washington Airport (open Mon.-Fri. 9am-9pm, Sat.-Sun. 9am-5pm).

Baltimore-Washington International Airport (BWI): 859-7111, on Rte. 46 off the Baltimore-Washington Expressway, about 8 miles south of the city center. Use BWI as your gateway to Baltimore or Washington, DC. Get downtown by Amtrak ($6), MTA bus #16. **Airport limousines** (859-3000) run daily every ½ hr. 5am-midnight ($5). Hilton Hotel shuttle buses run every hr. ($14).

Amtrak: Penn Station, 1515 N. Charles St. (539-2112). Outside the city center but easily accessible by buses #3, 11, and 18 to Charles Station, downtown. Or take the Charles St. trolley to the Inner Harbor. Trains run approximately every hr. to: New York ($54); Washington, DC ($13); and Philadelphia ($25.50). Open daily 6am-10pm. Amtrak also serves Baltimore ($6) and Washington, DC ($10.50) from the Baltimore-Washington International Airport.

Greyhound/Trailways, (931-4000), has 2 locations in Baltimore: one downtown at 210 W. Fayette St. (near Howard), the other 3 miles east of downtown at 5625 O'Donnell St., near I-95. Frequent connections to: New York ($30); Washington, DC ($9); and Philadelphia ($13). Open 24 hours.

Local Transit: Mass Transit Administration (MTA), 109 E. Redwood St. (539-5000; 760-4554 toll-free from Annapolis; both lines answered Mon.-Sat. 6am-11pm, Sun. 2:30-11pm; 659-2700 24-hour recording). A bus and rapid-rail system. Reliable service to most major sights within the city; service to outlying areas more complicated. Bus #16 serves the airport. Pick up a free *MTA Ride Guide,* available at any visitor information center. Some buses operate 24 hours. Fare 90¢, transfers 10¢. 1-day **tourist pass** for unlimited travel anywhere in the city on any form of public transportation $2.25. Available at most visitor information centers and hotels. **Baltimore Trolley Works:** 501 Key Hwy. (396-4259), operates two trolley routes downtown. The "Charles St." trolley runs north on Charles St. from the Inner Harbor to Penn Station and south along Maryland Ave. and Cathedral St. (Mon.-Sat. 11am-7pm.) The "Inner Harbor" trolley runs along the length of the harbor from Little Italy to Key Highway (Mon.-Sat. 11am-10pm, Sun. 11am-7pm.) Fare 25¢; no transfers.

Taxi: Yellow Cab, 685-1212.

Car Rental: Thrifty Rent-A-Car (768-4900 or 800-367-2277). Economy cars from $27 per day with 150 free miles. Must be 21, with credit card or a deposit of $60-100 per day.

Water Taxi: Pier 1, Inner Harbor. Continuous shuttle serving Harbor Place, the Science Center, the Rusty Skupper, Little Italy, Pier 5, and the Aquarium. Open Sun.-Thurs. 11am-11pm, Fri.-Sat. 11am-midnight. Crosses from the northeast to the southeast sides of the harbor, covering a distance that can be walked in about a ½ hr. Fare $1.25, daily pass $2.75.

Help Lines: Sexual Assault, 366-7273. 24 hours. **Gay Hotline,** 837-8888. Sun.-Thurs. 7:30-10pm, Wed.-Sat. 4:30-10:30pm.

Post Office: On the 900 block of Fayette St. (347-4425). **ZIP code:** 21233.

Area Code: 301.

Baltimore lies in central Maryland, 100 miles south of Philadelphia and about 150 miles up the Chesapeake Bay from where it joins the Atlantic Ocean. The **Jones Falls Expressway (I-83)** bisects the city, and ends at the Inner Harbor. **I-95** and the **Baltimore-Washington Expressway (I-295)** brush the southwest corner of the city and lead directly to Washington. Drivers should expect delays when passing Baltimore on any route. Many of the tourist sites are concentrated within a mile west of I-83. The Baltimore Beltway, I-695, makes a loop around the city. Baltimore is a conglomeration of several centuries of decentralized growth, with Old Baltimore roughly at the hub. Since the streets are not numbered logically, a bus and road map (available at most bookstores and hotels) is essential.

Accommodations and Camping

There are few reasonable lodging options near downtown. **Amanda's Bed and Breakfast Reservation Service,** 1428 Park Ave. (225-0001), is an alternative to budget hotels. (Singles from $32. Doubles from $40.)

Baltimore International Youth Hostel (AYH), 17 W. Mulberry St. (576-8880), near the downtown bus and Amtrak terminals. Take the "Charles St." trolley or MTA bus #3, 11, or 18. An elegant 3-story townhouse with kitchen and lounge. Curfew 11pm. Check-in 5-9pm. Closed 9am-5pm. Chores required. $9; off-season $10.

Abbey-Schaefer Hotel, 723 St. Paul St. at Madison (332-0405). Take bus #3 or 9. Clean and comfortable. Singles with hall bath $40. Doubles with private bath $40, with king-size bed $45. Deposit $10.

Christien Motel, 8733 Pulaski Hwy. (687-1740), on Rte. 40E, east of Baltimore, across the beltway from downtown. Rooms furnished with antiques. Singles $30-35. Doubles $34-38.

Capitol KOA, Hog Farm Rd., P.O. Box 149, Millersville (923-2771), 10 miles from the Baltimore Beltway, 16 miles from DC, 11 miles from Annapolis. Full facilities, including pool. Take MD's commuter train (Marc) to Odenton, MD (leaves from DC's Union Station, $7.60 round-trip) and then hitch 3 miles to the campground or catch the campground's free shuttle bus from the Odenton station (leaves campground at 7:15am, returns from Odenton at 6:30pm). Sites $14. Open April-Nov.

Food

Crabs are Baltimore's specialty. In many restaurants, steamed, hard-shelled crabs are served by the dozen with a wooden mallet to break them open.

Harborplace, at Pratt and Lombard St., has a beautiful view of the harbor and food both fast and fancy. For enough money, some interesting Baltimore specialties can be obtained from the chain stores: **Phillips'** crab cakes are among the finest in Maryland, **Thrasher's** fries with vinegar are an Eastern Shore tradition, **Gourmet Chips** dips potato chips into chocolate, and no place makes better Polish sausage than **Ostrowski's Polish Kielbasa.** (Harborplace open Mon.-Sat. 10am-9:30pm, Sun. noon-8pm.) Baltimore also has several enclosed markets. The largest and most famous is **Lexington Market** (685-6169), on Lexington at Eutaw St., northwest of the harbor. Besides an endless variety of produce, fresh meat, and seafood, it serves most of the same food as Harborplace, often at cheaper prices. (Open Mon.-Sat. 8:30am-6pm. Take bus #7.)

No Da Gi, 2126 Maryland Ave. (547-1106), at 22nd St. Take bus #3, 9, or 11. Excellent Korean cuisine and a few Chinese and Japanese dishes. Goldfish stare at diners from their huge tank in the middle of the dining room. Lunch specials $6-7. Dinners $8-15.

Ikaros, 4805 Eastern Ave. (633-3750), 2 miles east of downtown. Take bus #10. A romantic hideaway in the heart of East Baltimore's Greek community. The *avgolemono* soup, with egg, lemon, beef, and rice ($1), is an ideal opener for the spinach and feta pies ($2). Open Sun.-Mon. and Wed.-Thurs. 11am-10pm, Fri.-Sat. 11am-11pm.

Haussner's, 3242 Eastern Ave. (327-8365), at the corner of Clinton St. and Eastern Ave. Take bus #10. An East Baltimore institution. Huge dining room is full of impressive artwork. German cuisine. Lunch specials $5-7, sandwiches $2-4. Open Tues.-Sat. 11am-11pm.

Bertha's Dining Room, 734 S. Broadway (327-5795), at S. Broadway and Lancaster St. in Fells Point. Plate of mussels $6.15. Also has *paella* and fresh fish dishes. Jazz Tues. and Fri.-Sat. Dixieland Wed. 9pm-midnight. Open Sun.-Thurs. 11:30am-11pm, Fri.-Sat. 11:30am-midnight.

Buddy's, 313 N. Charles St. (332-4200). Good salad bar $5.25. Wed. is Grateful Dead night. Live jazz Thurs.-Sat. Open Mon.-Fri. 11am-1am, Sat. 2pm-1am.

Thompson's Sea Girt House, 5919 York Rd. (435-1800). Eat crab cakes here or have them shipped anywhere in the U.S. Open Mon.-Thurs. 11:30am-11pm, Fri. and Sat. 11:30am-midnight, Sun. 12:30pm-10pm.

Bo Brooks, 5415 Belair Rd. (488-8144). Complete seafood menu includes "Baltimore's Best Steamed Crabs." Family atmosphere. Open Mon.-Fri. 11:30am-2:30pm and 5pm-midnight, Sat. 5pm-midnight, Sun. 3:30-9:30pm.

Sights

Baltimore's growth has not hindered its rich heritage. Shakespeare, Thames, and Fleet Street maintain their mid-18th century names and **Federal Hill,** overlooking Baltimore's harbor, celebrates Maryland's ratification of the U.S. Constitution in 1788. At the same time, Baltimore is dressing up all over, with the **Inner Harbor** as the focal point of the transformation. Most museums and attractions within walking distance from this enormous port. Buses #7, 8, 10, 11, and most others will take you to or near the harbor.

The **Top of the World** observation deck of the pentagonal **World Trade Center** (837-4515) affords a fine, five-sided view of the city. (Open Mon-Fri. 10am-5pm, Sat. 10am-8pm, Sun. noon-7pm. Admission $2, ages 5-15 $1.)

The U.S. frigate *Constellation* dominates the west side of the harbor. The first commissioned ship of the U.S. Navy, it sailed from 1797 until 1945, serving in the War of 1812, the Civil War, and as flagship of the Pacific Fleet during World War II. (Open daily 10am-8pm; off-season 10am-4pm. Admission $2, seniors $1.50, children $1.) Also moored in the harbor are the U.S.S *Torsk* submarine and the lightship *Chesapeake.* These two vessels make up the **Baltimore Maritime Museum** at Pier III (396-9304. Open daily until dark. Admission $2.50, seniors $2, children $1.)

Continue down the west side of the harbor to Harborplace, Baltimore's trendy wharfside mall. (Open Mon.-Sat. 10am-9:30pm, Sun. noon-8pm.) Also at this edge of the harbor, the **Maryland Science Center,** 601 Light St. (685-2370), offers science films, a planetarium, and an exhibit on computer technology. Don't miss the IMAX Theater's 5-story screen and dazzling sound system. (Open daily 10am-8pm. Admission $6.50, seniors and under 13 $5.50.) Special mention goes to the Baltimore branch of the **National Aquarium,** on Pratt St. (576-3810), back on the west side of the harbor. This imposing, geometrically unique structure houses seven levels of aquatic life, featuring a shark tank, a reef tank, and a simulated Amazon tropical forest. Plan to wait in line. (Open Mon.-Thurs. 9am-5pm, Fri.-Sun. 9am-8pm; mid-Sept. to mid-May Sat.-Thurs. 10am-5pm, Fri. 10am-8pm. Admission $7.75, seniors, students, and ages 12-18 $6, ages 4-11 $4.75.)

To get a feel for Baltimore's historic districts, take bus #10 from Pratt St. to Broadway, and walk 2 blocks to **Fells Point,** passing through **Little Italy** on the way. This is authentic old Baltimore, with cobblestone streets, quaint shops, and historic pubs set against a backdrop of tug boats in the harbor. Stop in at the **Society for the Preservation of Federal Hill and Fells Point,** 812 S. Ann St. (675-6750), for an informative discussion of the area. (Open Mon.-Fri. 9am-4:30pm.)

Farther from the heart of town, the **Baltimore Museum of Art,** at Charles and 32nd St. (396-7101), next to the Johns Hopkins University campus, houses the Isabel and Etta Cone collection of impressionist paintings. The **Wurtzberger Sculpture Garden** features works by Rodin, Manzu, Giacometti, and Epstein. (Open Sept.-Aug. 17 Tues.-Fri. 10am-4pm, Sat.-Sun. 11am-6pm. Admission $2, under 18 free. Thurs. free. Take bus #3 or 11.)

The **Maryland Historical Society,** 201 W. Monument St. (685-3750), has Francis Scott Key's original manuscript for *The Star Spangled Banner,* as well as 19th-century period rooms, American portraiture, and silver. (Open Tues.-Fri. 11am 4:30pm, Sat. 9am-4:30pm, Sun. 1-5pm. Admission $2.50, seniors $1, ages 4-12 75¢.) The **Peale Museum,** 225 Holliday St. (396-1149), lies 7 blocks north of Inner Harbor, just off I-83. Built in 1814, it served as Baltimore's first City Hall. It has a garden, sculptures, paintings, and an exhibit on Baltimore's rowhouses. (Open Tues.-Sat. 10am-5pm, Sun. noon-5pm. Free.) The **Walters Art Gallery** (547-2787), at Charles and Centre St. in the historic Mt. Vernon Place, houses a large and impressive collection. (Open Tues.-Sun. 11am-5pm. Admission $2, seniors $1, under 18 or students with ID free. Wed. free.)

Druid Hill Park (396-6106) contains the **Baltimore Zoo** (366-5466), a spectacular conservatory, and a lake surrounded by lots of greenery. (Take bus #4, 7, or 22 from Fayette St.) **Fort McHenry National Monument** (962-4290), located at the foot of E. Fort Ave., off Rte. 2 and Lawrence Ave., where captive Francis Scott Key wrote the "Star Spangled Banner." (Open daily 9am-8pm; Labor Day-Memorial Day 9am-5pm.)

Entertainment and Nightlife

Outdoor entertainment animates the Inner Harbor during the summer. The **Showcase of Nations,** a weekly series of outdoor fairs, celebrates a different culture each week. The fairs tend to be similar, but they're always fun. Sold along with the international fare are the ever-present crab cakes and beer.

Pier 6, at the Inner Harbor, has popular, jazz, and classical concerts. If you sit out on Pier 5, you can hear the music without paying the (occasionally hefty) admission. (625-1400; 800-638-2444 outside MD; tickets $10-22). Free concerts of all types of music take place every Sunday (7-8:30pm) April through Labor Day at the Harborplace Amphitheatre. The **Left Bank Jazz Society,** in the famous Ballroom at 1717 N. Charles St. (945-2266), has a Sunday show at 5pm. The **Baltimore Folk Music Society** (366-0808) sponsors Wednesday-night dances in the fall at the historic Lovely Lane Church at 2200 St. Paul St.

Chesapeake Bay

The Chesapeake Bay is a long scraggly arm of the Atlantic Ocean that reaches from the coast of Virginia up through Maryland, nearly cleaving the state in two. For thousands of years, the bay was worshipped by Native Americans as the "Great Salt River." The water's varying salinity and its shallowness made it one of the world's best breeding grounds for oysters and blue crabs. Unfortunately, the centuries of development have taken their toll on these waters. Despite recent conservation measures, fish, oysters, and crabs are slowly disappearing, and sedimentation has already filled and shortened many of the bay's tributaries. Within 10,000 years, the Chesapeake Bay may be a flat piece of oceanfront land.

Bay tourism is split by the three states and one district that share its waters. For pamphlets, write or call the Virginia Division of Tourism, the Maryland Office of Tourist Development, the Delaware State Visitors Center, or the Washington, DC Convention and Visitors Association. (All addresses and phone numbers in respective state or district introductions.)

The region's public transportation system is underdeveloped. Greyhound/Trailways bus #122, originating in New York City, goes to Salisbury, Princess Anne, Westover Junction, and Pocomoke City. Make connections with Washington, DC, Baltimore, or Philadelphia via Greyhound bus #127.

Greyhound/Trailways also covers the eastern shores of the Chesapeake and Annapolis. The bay is bounded on the west by I-95, on the south by I-64, on the east by U.S. 9, 13, and 50, and on the north by U.S. 40.

Annapolis

Maryland's capital is an artistically renovated colonial port with narrow streets, 16 miles of waterfront, and one of the country's highest concentrations of 18th-century Georgian architecture. Its present rustic charm stands beside Annapolis's considerable historical contributions to the nation. Settled in 1649, Annapolis functioned as a temporary national capital and the meeting place of the Continental Congress from November, 1783 to August, 1784. In 1786, the Annapolis Convention met here to consider inter-state commercial disputes such as navigation rights of the Potomac. This convention was a precursor to the Philadelphia Constitutional Convention, which was instrumental in the ratification of the U.S. Constitution. In 1845 the U.S. Naval Academy was founded here, and its beautiful campus is still a major point of interest.

Annapolis's city plan features interconnecting circles with streets extending out like rays. **Anne's Episcopal Church** stands in **Church Circle.** In the heart of Annapolis, in **State Circle,** is the **Maryland State House** (974-3400), where the Continental Congress met to ratify the Treaty of Paris in 1784, thus ending the American Revolution. (Tours leave from the information desk at 10am, 11am, 2pm, 3pm, and 4pm. Open daily 9am-5pm. Free.) From State Circle, two arms stretch through the city: Main Street to the dock and Maryland Avenue to the naval academy. Follow Main Street for food and entertainment, Maryland Avenue for history.

A walk down Maryland Ave. will take you past the **Paca House and Gardens,** 186 Prince George St. (263-5553). Governor William Paca, who designed the house himself, was a signer of the Declaration of Independence. The estate has been beautifully restored and appears much as it did before the American Revolution. (Last tour at 3pm. Open Tues.-Sat. 10am-4pm, Sun. and holidays noon-4pm. Admission $5.)

Further down Maryland Ave., the prestigious **U.S. Naval Academy** is home to harried, short-haired "plebes" (freshmen) in official sailor dress desperately trying to remember the words of the navy fight songs. **Bancroft Hall,** the world's largest dormitory, is an imposing Georgian structure that houses the entire student body. In the yard outside Bancroft Hall you can witness the noon lineup and formations of the disciplined students. **King Hall,** the academy's gargantuan dining hall, is a madhouse at lunchtime, when the entire brigade is served in under four minutes. King Hall even has its own brand of ketchup. For good luck, try to toss a penny into the quiver of the bronze statue of Tecumseh that stands in front of King Hall.

The **Naval Museum** in Preble Hall has a simple collection of naval artifacts, including uniforms, swords, model ships, and paintings. (Open Mon.-Sat. 9am-4:45pm, Sun. 11am-4:45pm. Free.) **John Paul Jones's Crypt** is decorated with bronze dolphins and seaweed. Jones was the Revolutionary War naval hero who quipped, "I have not yet begun to fight." Walking tours of the academy begin at the **Ricketts Hall** visitors center, directly inside the gates of the Academy at the end of Maryland Ave. (267-6100; March-May 10am-2pm on the hr.; June-Labor Day 9:30am-4pm every ½ hr.; Labor Day-Thanksgiving 10am-3pm on the hr. Admission $2, under 12 $1.)

Those who are into politics should grab a quick bite to eat at **Chic and Ruth's Delly,** on Main St., a popular hangout for local and state politicians. Try the (Senator) "Barbara Mikulski" sandwich ($3.50) or one of 22 kinds of donuts (35¢) (Open 24 hours.) For something a bit more refined, head to **Truffles,** 50 West St. (626-1038), where you can cool down on a hot day with excellent salads, soups, and sandwiches. (Soup and salad lunch special $5.50; open Mon.-Thurs. 11:30am-8:30pm, Fri.-Sun. 11:30am-9:30pm.) Back at the dock, visit the **Market House,** an indoor market with great seafood, chicken, candy, fruits, and vegetables. (Open Mon.-Thurs. 9am-6pm, Fri.-Sat. 9am-7pm, Sun. 10am-7pm.)

Locals swear by **Marmaduke's Pub,** at the corner of Severn and 3rd St. in Eastport. Sailors flock here at night to watch videos of their races. Crabcakes, burgers, and other entrees are reasonably priced. Wet your whistle with a "dark and stormy" (dark rum, ginger beer, and lime). Spend a happy hour at **Uncle Harry's Outdoor Café,** 62 State Circle, behind Harry Browne's. Beer is $1.75, and free steamers are served with your drinks. Later on, stroll down **Ego Alley,** right next to the dock, where the tan and fit parade and preen. Grab an ice cream cone and people-watch, or head into one of the many bars clustered in this section of town.

At the top of Main St., over the water, the **Maryland Inn,** elegant Georgian home of the **King of France Tavern** (269-0990), features live jazz nearly every weekend. On Tuesday nights in July and August (7-9pm), the free **Starlight Concert Series** is held at the end of the dock past the Harbor Master's House.

If you decide to stay the night, be prepared to shell out big bucks. **Haidi Zech,** 1315 Colony Dr. (268-8437), is a friendly bed and breakfast in the area. (Singles $30-40. Doubles $40-55. No smoking.) The **Prince George Inn,** 232 Prince George St. (263-6418), in the heart of the historic district, is a charming, century-old townhouse. (Singles $42. Doubles $52.50.) For cheaper accommodations, find your way to the **Capitol KOA,** Hog Farm Rd., P.O. Box 149, Millersville, MD (923-2771), 11 miles from Annapolis, near Odenton. (For information and directions, see Baltimore.)

Annapolis is on Rte. 2, off U.S. 50/301, 50 miles east of Washington, DC, and 30 miles southeast of Baltimore. From Washington, take U.S. 50 east to exit 70 (Rowe Blvd.) and follow signs to the historic district. From Baltimore, follow Rte. 2 south to U.S. 50 west, cross Severn River Bridge, then take exit 70. Baltimore's excellent **Mass Transit Authority** (760-4554) makes hourly runs from downtown Baltimore to Annapolis. (Express bus #210 Mon.-Fri. 6am-8pm, 1 hr., $2.05 one-way. Local bus #14 Mon.-Fri. 5am-midnight, Sat.-Sun. 6am-9pm, 90 min., $1.85.) **Greyhound/Trailways** connects Annapolis with Washington, DC (4 per day, 40 min., $11) and with towns on the far side of the Chesapeake Bay. Call the Baltimore or Washington Greyhound/Trailways stations for schedules (931-4000). **Annapolis Transit,** 160 Duke of Gloucester St. (263-7964), operates a web of city buses connecting the historic district with the rest of town (Mon.-Sat. 6am-10pm). The free, efficient **Annapolis Trolley Shuttle** (267-7790) provides a park-and-ride service from the Navy/Marine Stadium parking lot, off Rte. 70, to the historic district (Mon.-Sat. every 20 min.).

For tourist information and orientation, stop by the **Tourism Council,** 152 Main St. (268-8687; open Mon.-Fri. 8:30am-5pm), or the dockside information booth (open April-Oct. daily 10am-5pm). The council's *Rambling Through Annapolis* is well worth 75¢. Organized walking tours ($1.50) start from **Historic Annapolis,** old treasury building, State Circle (267-8149). The colonially-dressed guides of **Three Centuries Tours,** 48 Maryland Ave. (263-5401), lead daily two-hour walking tours ($5) at 9:30am from the Annapolis Hilton, and at 1:30pm from the city dock.

Annapolis's **ZIP code** is 21401; the **area code** is 301.

Assateague and Chincoteague Islands

Sometime in the 1820s, the Spanish galleon *San Lorenzo* foundered off Maryland's short stretch of Atlantic coast. All human passengers were lost, but a few horses managed to swim ashore. More than a century and a half later, the Chincoteague ponies, descendants of those original survivors, still roam the unspoiled beaches of Assateague Island.

Assateague Island is divided into 3 parts. The **Assateague State Park** (301-641-2120), off U.S. 113 in southeastern Maryland, is a 2-mile stretch with picnic areas, beaches, and hot-water bathhouses. (Campsites $15.) Also in Maryland, the **Assateague Island National Seashore** (301-641-1441) claims most of the long sandbar both north and south of the state park. The national park has its own campground, beaches, and ranger station (301-641-3030; sites with cold water only $5). Free backcountry camping permits are available at the ranger station. Fire rings are set up along 4 to 13-mile hikes; otherwise it's just you and nature. The third part of the Assateague Island is the **Chincoteague National Wildlife Refuge** (804-336-6122), which stretches along the south of the island on the Virginia side of the Maryland/Virginia border. The refuge is a temporary home for the threatened migratory peregrine falcon, a half million Canada and snow geese, and the beautiful Chincoteague ponies. If you're nearby in late July, stick around for the annual "pony penning" festival. At low tide, on the last Thursday in July, the wild ponies are herded together and made to swim from Assateague, MD to Chincoteague, VA, where they are auctioned off. The lucky unpurchased ponies swim back to Assateague. But whenever you visit, bring plenty of insect repellent, since the island is a haven for six-legged nuisances.

To get to Assateague Island, take **Greyhound/Trailways** to **Ocean City,** with daily express and local routes from Baltimore ($21), Washington, DC ($25), Norfolk, VA ($31), and Philadelphia ($30). The station in Ocean City is at Philadelphia and 2nd St. (301-289-9307). The **Ocean City Chamber of Commerce** (289-8559) has information on accommodations. (Open Mon.-Sat. 10am-5pm, Sun. noon-6pm.) The **Sunrise Motor Inn,** P.O. Box 185, Chincoteague, (336-3434), off Maddox Blvd., north of Main St., has standard rooms. (Singles from $31. Doubles from $34.) To get to Assateague Island from Ocean City, take a taxi (about $12). It's also possible to get there from the town of Chincoteague, which lies on Chincoteague Island, 10 miles east of U.S. 13. **Greyhound/Trailways** makes a stop on U.S. 13 at Oak Hall Exxon Service Station (804-824-5935). The stop, 11 miles from town, is called T's Corner; it's served from Salisbury, MD and Norfolk, VA. For more information on the area, call or write to Chincoteague Chamber of Commerce, P.O. Box 258, Chincoteague, VA 23336 (804-336-6161; on Beach Rd., across from Park's Market; open daily 9am-5pm).

New Jersey

You from Joisey? I'm from Joisey. What exit?
—Joe Piscopo

New Jersey is more than just miles of asphalt set against a background of smokestacks and oil drums. It's also more than the decaying industrial and resort towns delineated by artists such as William Carlos Williams in his poem *Paterson* and Bruce Springsteen in his numerous albums. Just off the exit ramps is a thriving shopping mall culture, enthusiastically embraced by denizens of the Bargain State. Here the shaggy, overprocessed hairdos and white fringed leather outfits of local boys Bon Jovi reign. The state also offers tranquil natural beauty and friendly towns. Peace and quiet imbue comfortable outposts such as Princeton in the center of the state. Or try one of the state's enticing beaches, such as those of Ocean City and Cape May.

Practical Information

Capital: Trenton.

Tourist Information: State Division of Tourism, CN 826, Trenton 08625 (609-292-2470).

Gambling: Legal age 21.

State Song: "Born to Run," by Bruce Springsteen.

Time Zone: Eastern. **Postal Abbreviation:** NJ.

Newark Airport

New Jersey's largest city and the fourth-largest metropolitan region in the U.S. is consistently associated exclusively with its airport. However, Newark has its own Broad Street lined with tall, new office buildings and an active port area. The airport is nevertheless the town's main attraction, with daily overseas flights and a better reputation for on-time flights than either La Guardia or Kennedy Airports in New York.

If you absolutely, positively have to stay in Newark overnight, try the **Airway Motor Inn,** 853 Rte. 1 and 9N, Elizabeth (354-3840), which has small, dark, but clean rooms. Ask for a room away from the highway and the parking lot. (Singles $30. Doubles $32. No reservations accepted. Take the Sheraton courtesy van—it's right around the corner.)

There are no lockers in Newark Airport, but to store luggage during a layover, use **Unique Delivery,** Bldg. 51 (961-2250), next to North Terminal. Look for the unmarked gray door. They will pick up your luggage at the airport ($3) and store it for $1 per bag, per day (backpacks $1.50). (Open daily 7:30am-midnight.)

Princeton

Princeton rests peacefully off Rte. 1, 50 miles southwest of New York City and 11 miles north of Trenton. The main attraction of this quietly charming town is Ivy-League **Princeton University.** Princeton has turned out presidents (James Madison and Woodrow Wilson), tycoons (J.P. Morgan), and movie stars (Jimmy Stewart and Brooke Shields). But no travel guides.

Practical Information

Emergency: 911.

Visitor Information: Princeton University General Information (452-3000). Open daily 8am-11pm. **Princeton University Communication/Publication Office,** Stanhope Hall (452-3600). Campus maps, current information, including the *Princeton Weekly Bulletin,* with a calendar of events. Open during the term Mon.-Fri. 8:45am-5pm. **Orange Key Guide Service,** 73 Nassau St. (452-3603), in the back entrance of MacLean House. Free campus tours, pamphlets, and maps. Tours Mon.-Sat. at 10am, 11am, 1:30pm, and 3:30pm, Sun. at 1:30pm and 3:30pm. Office open Mon.-Sat. 9am-5pm, Sun. 1-5pm.

Trains: Amtrak (800-872-7245) connects Princeton Junction, 3 miles south of Princeton on Rte. 571, to New York City ($20.50) and Philadelphia ($17.50). Stops at Princeton only in the early morning and evening. **New Jersey Transit** (201-460-8444, 800-772-2222 in NJ; 6am-midnight). Serves Princeton Junction. To New York City (1 hr., $9.20). Prices include a 5-min. ride on the "dinky," a small train connecting the town and campus to the outlying station.

Buses: New Jersey Transit (800-772-2222, 6am-midnight). Buses leave from Princeton University and Palmer Sq. for Trenton 6am-10pm at 18 and 48 min. after the hr. ($1.25, exact change). Bus K links Princeton to the hotels and motels on Rte. 1 (every hr., 8:50am-9:40pm). **Suburban Transit** (249-1100; 8:30am-5:30pm). Three Princeton locations: Nassau Pharmacy, 80 Nassau St. (921-7400; open Mon.-Sat. 9am-7pm, occasional Sun.); Cox's Store, 182 Nassau St.; and Amoco Station, in Princeton Shopping Center. To New York every ½ hr., $6.90 one way, $13 round-trip.

Taxi: Associated Taxi Stand, 924-1222; 7am-midnight.

Post Office: 921-9563, in Palmer Sq., behind Tiger Park. (Open Mon.-Fri. 8am-4:30pm, Sat. 8:30am-noon.) **ZIP code:** 08540.

Area Code: 609.

Located in the green heart of the "Garden State," Princeton is within commuting distance of both New York City and Philadelphia. Driving from New York City, take the Holland Tunnel to the New Jersey Turnpike and exit at Hightstown. From

Philadelphia, take I-95 north to Rte. 206, which leads to Nassau St., Princeton's main strip, with shops clustered on one side, and the university set back on the other side.

Accommodations, Food, and Entertainment

There are no budget accommodations in the town of Princeton. Budget motels are located along Rte. 1 and near the giant Quaker Bridge Mall, 4 miles south of Princeton, served by local bus (see Practical Information above).

Sleep-E-Hollow Motel, 3000 U.S. 1, Lawrenceville (609-896-0900), 5 miles south of Princeton, offers beds in small, well-worn rooms. Singles $28.50. Doubles $32.50.

McIntosh Inn, U.S. 1 and Quaker Bridge Mall, Lawrenceville (609-896-3700), 4 miles south of Princeton. Clean, large, modern rooms. Singles $34. Doubles $41. Extra cot $3.

Most of Princeton's reasonably priced restaurants line Witherspoon Sreet and Nassau Street. You can't miss Witherspoon St.—it intersects Nassau just across from the main gates of the university.

P.J.'s Pancake House, 154 Nassau St. (924-1353). Loud and crowded, with old wooden tables filled with students' grafitti. Good food, most meals $5-7. Open Mon.-Thurs. 7:30am-10pm, Fri. 7:30am-3am, Sat. 8am-3am, Sun. 8am-10pm.

Marita's Cantina, 134 Nassau St. (924-7855). Standard Mexican dishes in a fun atmosphere. A la carte items $2-4.25, lunch buffet $6. Open Sun. 11:30am-11pm, Mon.-Sat. 11:30-2:30am.

The Annex, 128½ Nassau St. (921-9520). A popular student hangout and bar, darker and often less noisy than P.J.'s. Italian and American entrees ($5-7), and omelettes and sandwiches ($2-3.50). Open Mon.-Sat. 11am-1am.

Thomas Sweet's Ice Cream, 183 Nassau St. (924-0454). Also at Palmer Sq., across from the Nassau Inn. The perfect end to any meal. Have them blend a topping into their homemade ice cream ($2-3). Open Sun.-Thurs. 11am-11pm, Fri.-Sat. 11am-midnight.

On May 17, 1955, Princeton students held the first pro-rock 'n' roll demonstration in history by blaring Bill Haley and the Comets's "Rock Around the Clock" until 1am (when the Dean woke up and told them to turn it off). Students mix with locals in the basement pub of **Nassau Inn,** a beautiful, expensive hotel in operation since 1757. Check Princeton's *Weekly Bulletin* for the scoop on films, concerts, and special events. Students and professional actors perform at **McCarter Theater,** on campus in the **Kresge Auditorium** (452-5200; box office open Mon.-Sat. noon-5pm).

Sights

Orange Key Guide Service (see Practical Information above) provides free tours of the university. The school is the fourth oldest in the Ivy League (started in 1746), but the campus was the first of its kind in this country. Many of the buildings are Gothic, but the 2500-acre campus has other architectural styles as well. Don't miss **Nassau Hall,** which, when completed in 1756, was the largest stone building in colonial America. Each graduating class places a commemorative plaque and a patch of ivy on the outer wall. The two magnificent bronze tigers represent the school's mascot. **Whig** and **Clio Hall,** named and modeled after a Greek temple, are home to the oldest college literary and debating club in the U.S. **Firestone Library** is the largest open-stack library in the world.

The sculptures scattered throughout the university come from the $11 million **Putnam Collection.** A piece of a distorted human face stands in front of the **University Art Museum** (452-3762). Tours of the outdoors sculptures (works by Alexander Calder, Henry Moore, Pablo Picasso, and David Smith) or of the museum's permanent indoor collection can be arranged through the university. (Open Tues.-Sat. 10am-4pm, Sun. 1-5pm. Free.)

The town of Princeton is not entirely dominated by the university. Visit **Bainbridge House,** 158 Nassau St. (921-6748), the Georgian home and birthplace of Commodore William Bainbridge, commander of "Old Ironsides," the U.S.S. *Consti-*

tution. Now, it's the headquarters of the **historical society,** where visitors can pick up free maps for self-guided walking tours through Princeton. One of the highlights is the row of mansions on **Library Place.**

Atlantic City

The riches-to-rags-to-riches tale of Atlantic City began over 50 years ago when it reigned as the monarch of resort towns. Vanderbilts and Girards graced the legendary boardwalk of the town whose opulence inspired the depression-era board game for would-be-high-rollers, *Monopoly.* Unfortunately, with the rise of competition from Florida resorts, the jewel of the East began to dull. Atlantic City suffered through decades of decline, unemployment, and virtual abandonment.

But in 1976, state voters gave Atlantic City a reprieve by legalizing gambling. One quarter of the U.S. population lives within 300 miles of Atlantic City, and fortune-seeking pilgrims flock to the shore to throw dice and maybe get a suntan. The glamour is superficial at best, and the seedy areas stand as an inevitable by-product of the city's obsession with gambling. The dirt and dank, however, are quickly forgotten as you enter the gloriously tacky, velvet-soaked casino lobbies. Atlantic City is a magnet for everyone, from high-rolling millionaires, to senior citizens desperate for that one last chance, to students cautiously sampling the fare. "Profit" is the city's (unofficial) motto.

Practical Information

Emergency: 911.

Visitor Information: Visitors Bureau of Atlantic City, 2310 Pacific Ave. (348-7044), conveniently located near Mississippi Ave. Open Mon.-Fri. 9am-4:30pm. Next door is the **Atlantic City Convention Bureau,** 2314 Pacific Ave. (348-7100 or 800-262-7395). Open Mon.-Fri. 9am-5pm.

Bader Field Airport: 345-6402. Serves New York/La Guardia, Philadelphia, Washington, DC, Newark, and other destinations. Buses run between Bader Field and the Boardwalk.

Buses: Greyhound/Trailways, 345-5403 or 344-4449. Frequent service to New York (2½ hr., $18) and Philadelphia (1¼ hr., $15). **New Jersey Transit,** 344-8181 or 800-582-5946 (6am-10pm). Extensive service to New York and Philadelphia, with connections to Ocean City ($2), Cape May ($3.25), and Hammonton ($3). Open 24 hours.

Atlantic City Municipal Bus Terminal: Arkansas and Arctic Ave. (347-5413). Main terminal for all inter-city buses, and one of the bus industry's hottest destinations.

Help Lines: Rape and Abuse Hotline, 646-6767.

Post Office: Illinois and Pacific Ave. (345-4212). **ZIP code:** 08401.

Area Code: 609.

Gamblers specials make bus travel a cheap, efficient way to get to Atlantic City. Many casinos will give the bearer of a bus ticket receipt about $10 in cash and sometimes a free meal as well. The deals are well advertised in the yellow pages under "Bus Charters" in New Jersey, New York, Pennsylvania, Delaware, and Washington, DC. Also, Greyhound/Trailways has same-day round-trip specials to Atlantic City.

Atlantic City lies just past midway down New Jersey's coast. It is accessible by the **Garden State Parkway.** A railway center is promised by 1990 to connect Atlantic City with New York City, Philadelphia, and Washington, DC. Hitching is not recommended.

Walking and buses are good ways to get around Atlantic City. For across-town service 'round the clock, take a $1 ride in one of the famous **jitneys.** For Boardwalk transportation, try the **Rolling Chair**—it's a bit of an investment ($2.50 per person, per mile), but Atlantic City locals chat with you while they push. Hail a chair on the Boardwalk, or call 347-7148. (In summer only, daily 9am-4am.) Less exotic and less expensive, the yellow tram runs continuously ($1). Also, **New Jersey Transit** (344-8181) runs local buses ($1) along Atlantic Ave.

Accommodations and Camping

Large, red-carpeted, beachfront hotels have replaced four green houses, and have bumped smaller operators out of the game. A hundred bucks for a single is standard. Smaller hotels along **Pacific Avenue,** a block away from the Boardwalk, have rooms for less than $60, and rooms in Ocean City's guest houses are reasonably priced. Be sure to reserve ahead, especially on weekends. Many hotels lower their rates during the middle of the week. Winter is slow in Atlantic City, when water temperature, gambling fervor, and hotel rates all drop significantly. Campsites closest to the action are the most expensive, and most close September through April. Reservations may be necessary for a room or a site in July and August.

Irish Pub and Inn, 164 St. James Place (344-9063), near the intersection of St. James Place and the Boardwalk. Cheap and close to the action. Singles $30. Doubles $35-50. Key and towel deposit $5. Open May-Oct. Good Irish food served 24 hours, year-round.

Hotel Casino, 28 Georgia Ave. (344-0747), just off Pacific Ave. Adequate rooms Mon.-Fri. $30, Sat.-Sun. $40.

Birch Grove Park Campground, Mill Rd. Northfield (641-3778). 300 acres. Attractive and secluded but still near the casinos. 2-day min. stay in summer.

Casino KOA, 1997 Black Horse Pike, Pleasantville (641-3085). The closest campsite to the casinos, with its own bus service to the gambling strip. Sites $18.75 for 2.

Food

Whether or not you actually gamble, take advantage of the cheap **casino buffets** intended to lure you in. Most offer daily lunch and dinner all-you-can-eat deals for $10-12. If you're looking for a friendly diner, try the **Coffee Mill,** (345-6432), at Pacific and Kentucky Ave. (Dinner platters from $8. Pasta $5; open daily 11am-midnight.) Since 1946, the **White House Sub Shop,** Mississippi and Arctic Ave. (345-8599), has served world-famous subs and sandwiches. This place is a favorite of Bill Cosby, Johnny Mathis, and Frank Sinatra—who is rumored to have subs flown to him while he's on tour ($4-6.50, half-subs $2-3.70). (Open Mon.-Sat. 10am-midnight, Sun. 11am-midnight.) For renowned Italian food, hit **Tony's Baltimore Grille,** 2800 Atlantic Ave. (345-5766), at the corner of Atlantic and Iowa Ave. They serve the best pizza in town, plus spaghetti dishes ($4), seafood ($7.50), and more. (Open 24 hours.)

Entertainment

Casinos

You have to see the casinos to believe them. Inside, thousands of square feet of flashing lights, plush carpet, and milling people are reflected by one-way ceiling mirrors that conceal the big-brother gambling monitors. People in dressy clothes can still be found, glimpses of Atlantic City's more glamorous past, but the t-shirt-and-jeans gamblers now outnumber their flashy cohorts. The rattle of chips and clicking of slot machines are incessant and seductive. Each casino has its own personality. The biggest are **Bally's Park Place,** Park Place and the Boardwalk (340-2000), and **Resorts International,** North Carolina Ave. and the Boardwalk (344-6000). Posh spots include the **Golden Nugget,** Boston Ave. and the Boardwalk (347-7111), and **Caesar's Boardwalk Regency,** Arkansas Ave. and the Boardwalk (348-4411). **Harrah's Marina Hotel,** Brigantine Blvd. and Absecon Inlet (441-5000), and the **Atlantis,** Florida Ave. and the Boardwalk (344-4000), are hot clubs. Rounding out the list are the **Claridge,** Indiana Ave. and the Boardwalk (340-3400), the **Trump Hotel Casino,** Mississippi Ave. and the Boardwalk (441-6000), **Trump's Castle Casino,**

Huron Ave. and Brigantine Blvd. (441-2000), and **Showboat,** States Ave. and the Boardwalk (343-4000). The **Sands,** Indiana Ave. and the Boardwalk (441-4000), and **TropWorld Casino,** Iowa Ave. and the Boardwalk (340-4000), have extensive facilities that include golf and tennis. You may be amused by the two "moving sidewalks" that carry customers from the Boardwalk to the only two casinos without a Boardwalk entrance. Not surprisingly, these sidewalks move in only one direction.

Casinos are open nearly all the time (Mon.-Fri. 10am-4am, Sat.-Sun. 10am-6am). They ply you with alcohol as long as you are gambling (you must be 21 to get in), and many don't have windows or clocks so you won't notice the hours slip away. To curb your (almost inevitable) losses, stick to the cheaper games: blackjack, slot machines, and the low bets in roulette and craps. A book like John Scarne's *New Complete Guide to Gambling* will help you plan an intelligent strategy, but keep your eyes on your watch or you'll have spent five hours and five digits before you know it.

Beaches and Boardwalk

The ocean is never more than a throw of the dice away. Atlantic City squats on the northern end of long, narrow **Absecon Island,** which has 7 miles of beaches—some pure white, some lumpy gray. The **Atlantic City Beach** is free, and often crowded. Adjacent **Ventnor City's** sands are nicer. The legendary **Boardwalk** of Atlantic City has been given over to the purveyors of the quick fix, and is packed with junk-food stands, arcades, souvenir shops, and carnival amusements. In Ventnor City, the Boardwalk's development tapers off, and it becomes a pleasant place to take a walk, jog, or bike.

Cape May

A walk along Cape May's tree-lined boulevards, past flower beds and verandas, is wonderfully evocative. It's not hard to conjure up turn-of-the-century ladies and gentlemen sipping afternoon tea. After fire ravaged the town in 1876, the city was rebuilt entirely in the then-current architectural style, an effort rewarded in 1976 when Cape May was designated a national historic landmark. The 5000 permanent residents (who constitute the highest concentration of Mayflower descendants in the country) take their legacy seriously, and cultivate Cape May's image as a Victorian anachronism.

Tourists are the life-blood of Cape May, and the town gladly caters to visitors. Visit the **Welcome Center,** 405 Lafayette St. (884-9562). Free courtesy phones are available for reserving space at participating guest houses and motels. (Open Mon.-Sat. 9am-4pm, Sun. 1-3pm.) For a detailed introduction to Cape May's history and architecture, try a guided walking tour ($4) from the **Mid-Atlantic Center for the Arts,** 1048 Washington St. (884-5404).

The entire shore of New Jersey was plagued by tremendous pollution during the summer of 1988, after which the state launched a vigorous campaign to clean up the beaches. Thanks to this the sand at Cape May is once again immaculate. It actually glistens, still dotted with some of the famous Cape May diamonds (actually quartz pebbles that glow when cut and polished). If you unroll your beach towel on a city-protected beach (off Beach Ave.), make sure you have a **beach tag.** Beachgoers over 12 must wear one June to September from 10am to 5pm. Pick up a tag at any of the numerous beachside booths (daily $2, weekly $5, seasonal $10). The **Cape May Light House** and **Cape May Point State Park** (884-2159), just west of town, are other tourist attractions. The light house was built in 1859 and, if you can manage the 183-step climb, its balcony offers a magnificant panorama of the New Jersey and Delaware coasts.

Many of the well-preserved seaside mansions now take in nightly guests, although most cater to the well-heeled *New York Times* B&B set. Truly cheap rooms don't exist in Cape May, and even reasonable rates are hard to find. The **Clinton Hotel,** 202 Perry St. (844-3993), is at the center of Cape May's scenic business district,

3 blocks from the beach. Rooms are clean and comfortable. (Open late June-Labor Day. Singles from $38. Doubles from $47. Call 516-799-8889 for pre-season reservations.) Also splendid is the centrally located **Congress Hall,** Beach Ave., between Perry and Congress St. This beautiful, weathered establishment (built in 1879) has a sweeping veranda and lawn and a pool. (Singles from $42. Doubles from $48.) For reservations, call 884-8421 (May-Oct.) or 858-0670 (Nov.-April). **Cold Spring Campground,** 541 New England Rd. (884-8717), is several miles from town. (Sites $12 for 2.) Campgrounds line Rte. 9 from Atlantic City to the cape. The closest to the Cape May beach is the **Cape Island Campground,** 709 Rte. 9 (884-5777; sites $17). For general information, contact the **Cape May County Campground Association,** P.O. Box 175, Cape May Court House, Cape May 08210 (884-5314).

Cozy, romantic, but expensive restaurants are readily available in Cape May. For reasonably priced steamed clams and local color, try **Kahn's Ugly Mug** (884-3450), on the mall (12 clams for $6; open Mon.-Sat. 11am-2am, Sun. noon-2am). The **Ocean View Restaurant,** at Beach and Grant Ave. (884-3772), on the southern end of Beach Ave., is a local choice for fresh seafood. It offers generous servings of fish ($3) and marine panoramas. (Open daily 7am-10pm.) **Carney's,** 401 Beach Ave. (884-4424), features nightly bands in a lively atmosphere. (Open Mon.-Sat. 9:30am-2am, Sun. noon-2am.) There are free summer concerts at the town's bandstand.

Despite its small size and geographic isolation, Cape May is well served by public transportation. By car, from the north it's literally the end of the road—follow the Garden State Parkway south as far as it goes. From the south by car, take the **Cape May, NJ/Lewes, DE ferry.** (Cape May Terminal 886-2718; Lewes Terminal 302-645-6313, Nov. 10-April 9 4 ferries per day; April 10-June 18 6 ferries per day; June 19-Sept. 14-15 ferries per day; extra runs on holidays. Vehicle and driver $17, other passengers $4, pedestrians $4; motorcyclists $13.50.) The ferry takes 70 minutes. **New Jersey Transit,** Victorian Village Plaza (884-5689 or 800-582-5946 in NJ, or 201-460-8444; 6am-10pm), runs buses to Cape May from Atlantic City ($3.05) and New York City (3½ hr., $21.60). Bus #102 runs between the town of Cape May and the Cape May/Lewes ferry terminal, a few miles north of town (7 trips per day, $1), as well as to nearby Wildwood and its boardwalk rides. You can rent bikes to tour Cape May at **Village Bike Shop** (884-8500), in Victorian Plaza ($3 per hr., $8 per day; open daily 8am-5pm).

Cape May's **ZIP code** is 08204; the **area code** is 609.

Wildwood

The relentless glare of the sun parches your throat as your legs buckle from exhaustion. Just when you think that you cannot stagger along any further, something glimmers off in the distance—not a mirage, but the Atlantic Ocean. Your journey across one of the widest beaches on the New Jersey shore has finally ended.

If the trek to the ocean is not for you, sate yourself at Wildwood's 2½-mile-long boardwalk, with its multitude of arcades, food stands, and amusement parks—which collectively boast more rides than Disney World. When your brain is fried and your fifth soft-serve ice cream cone has melted on your shirt, head 2 blocks inland to **Pacific Avenue.** This pear-tree-lined strip is the heart of Wildwood's shopping district and also hosts many nightclubs and theaters. A word to the faint-hearted: Visiting Wildwood in June may well spoil the fun, since legions of graduates from nearby high schools swarm the beach and boardwalk, intent on satisfying their various adolescent cravings.

Wildwood's eating establishments typically have outrageous prices, but bargains aren't scarce. The **Ocean Terrace,** 3616 Boardwalk (729-0550), near the Boardwalk and Lincoln Ave., serves all-you-can-eat breakfasts ($4.50; from 8am) and sandwich or pasta dinners ($6; from 4:30pm). Some of the best seafood in the area is served at **Johnson's Seafood Restaurant,** Burk and Pacific Ave. (522-1976), where an all-you-can-eat fish fry is $8. **Pompeo's Restaurant,** 17th Ave. and Boardwalk, N. Wildwood (522-7029), has children's meals (under $5), pasta ($8), and deep-fried Chesapeake oysters ($10.15). For lunch or a quick dinner, don't miss **Luigi's Famous Cheesesteaks,** at Pacific Ave. and Burk St. The self-proclaimed King of Steaks, Luigi serves cheesesteaks and hoagies ($3.50).

Accommodations at Wildwood range from expensive to not-quite-so-expensive. **Sea Tag Lodge,** 226 E. Glenwood Ave. (522-6484), has a refrigerator and fan in every room. (Singles $25 mid-week, $30 weekends.) The **Rosemont Hotel,** 230 E. Glenwood Ave. (522-6204), offers singles with shared bath for $26, doubles with shared bath for $40. Various independently run establishments rent "apartments and rooms" with more character than the local hotels. Try **Barletto's,** 132 E. Rio Grande (552-5885), for old but clean rooms (from $35). On the other side of town, **Trio's Apartments and Rooms,** at 221 E. Glenwood (522-6996), has comfortable rooms for $37.

Wildwood is a 40-minute drive south from Atlantic City and three hours from New York City via the Garden State Parkway. From the south, take I-95 to the Delaware Memorial Bridge, follow Rte. 49, and finally Rte. 47. New Jersey Transit, New Jersey and Oak Ave. (522-2491 or 800-582-5946), has daily connections to Atlantic City ($2.90), Cape May ($1.70), and Philadelphia ($12.40).

Pennsylvania

While Pennsylvania currently most often is associated with historic Philadelphia or industrial Pittsburgh, it was founded as a haven of religious freedom. Driven by the persecution of his fellow Quakers, William Penn, Jr. petitioned the British Crown for a tract of land in North America in 1680. He arrived in 1682, named his colony after his father, and embarked on an experiment in religious tolerance that immediately attracted a widely diverse population. Around the time of the American Revolution, Pennsylvania seemed destined to become the most prominent state in the emerging nation. The Declaration of Independence was signed in Philadelphia, which was also the country's original capital and the site of the First Continental Congress. However, the state was soon overshadowed. New York City rapidly grew larger than Philadelphia, becoming the nation's most important center of commerce, and Washington, DC was chosen as the nation's capital.

When a second revolution, the Industrial Revolution, hit America, Pennsylvania again made a strong start but again was soon superseded. While Pittsburgh became the center of the nation's steel production, America's largest industry, automobile manufacture, eventually made its home in Detroit. Oil was first discovered in Titusville, but just as the industry began to flourish, larger deposits were discovered in Texas and Oklahoma. Now Pennsylvania's steel industry is stagnant, and oil barely trickles from a few remaining wells. Most recently, Three Mile Island helped Pennsylvania to claim an unfortunate superlative: the worst nuclear power plant accident in the U.S.

But Pennsylvania rallies in the face of adversity. In 1976, Philadelphia groomed its historic shrines for the Bicentennial celebration, and the tourist trade continues to boom. Even beleaguered Pittsburgh is experiencing a renaissance. And between the two cities, the Pennsylvania countryside retains most of the natural charm it had when Penn first settled there. From the rolling farmland of Lancaster county, home of the Amish, to the deep river gorges of the Allegheny Plateau, Pennsylvania's landscape is beautiful and varied. The state is especially suited to budget travelers, with a chain of a dozen or so hostels spaced no more than a day's bike ride apart, from Philadelphia through Lancaster County to near Gettysburg and on to Ohiopyle and the Pittsburgh area.

Practical Information

Capital: Harrisburg.

Tourist Information: Bureau of Travel Development, 416 Forum Bldg., Harrisburg 17120 (787-5453). Information on hotels, restaurants, and sights. **Bureau of State Parks,** P.O. Box 1467, Harrisburg 17120 (787-8800). The detailed, free *Recreational Guide* is available at all visitor information centers.

Time Zone: Eastern. **Postal Abbreviation:** PA.

Philadelphia

Most visitors come to Philadelphia to see its historic shrines: a statue of founder William Penn, Independence Hall, the Liberty Bell, Christ Church. The culturally inclined visitor should stop by the Philadelphia Museum of Art, the Ben Franklin Institute, and the Academy of Music. The city is also home to a slew of campuses: The University of Pennsylvania, Villanova, Haverford, Swarthmore, Temple, Drexel, and Bryn Mawr.

But what many travelers overlook in their visit to the "city of brotherly love" is the people. Scions of old families inhabit the Main Line, while young professionals dominate the downtown areas of Center City, Society Hill, and South Street. And throughout the city a varied ethnic population clings to tradition in distinctive enclaves.

Practical Information

Emergency: 911.

Visitor Information: Visitors Center, 1525 John F. Kennedy Blvd. at 16th St. (636-1666). Pick up a free *Philadelphia Visitor's Guide* and the *Philadelphia Quarterly Calendar of Events.* The film *Independence* is shown 9:30am-4:15pm. Open daily 9am-6pm; off-season 9am-5pm. **Greater Philadelphia Cultural Alliance (GPCA),** 1718 Locust St. (735-0570). Information about diverse cultural communities. Open Mon.-Fri. 9am-5pm. **Philly Fun Phone,** 568-7255. 24-hour recorded information line on current sports, music, dance, and theater. **National Park Service Visitor Center,** 3rd and Chestnut (597-8974; 627-1776 for recording). Information on Independence Park, including orientation film. Also has the *Visitor's Guide* and the *Quarterly Calendar of Events.* Open Sept.-June daily 9am-5pm; July-Aug. 9am-6pm. Film shown 9:30am-4:15pm. Tour assistance for non-English-speaking and the disabled.

Philadelphia International Airport: (492-3181; 6am-11pm), 8 miles southwest of Center City on I-76. The SEPTA Airport Rail Line runs from Center City to Philadelphia International Airport in 27 min. Trains leave daily 5:30am-11:25pm from 30th St. Station, Suburban Station, and Market East ($4). Cab fare downtown is $21, but you can take one of the frequent limousines that serve Center City hotels (about $7).

Amtrak: 30th St. Station at 30th and Market St. (824-1600 or 800-872-7245). To New York ($28), Washington, DC ($32), and points in western PA. Station open 24 hours. A cheap way to go between Philadelphia and New York City is train service: Take the SEPTA commuter train to Trenton, NJ ($3.50), then hop on a New Jersey Transit train to NYC through Newark ($7.51).

Buses: Greyhound/Trailways, 10th and Filbert St. (931-4000), 1 block north of Market, near the 10th and Market St. subway stop in the heart of Philadelphia. To: New York City ($18), Washington, DC ($21), and Atlantic City ($8). Station open 24 hours. **New Jersey Transit,** 569-3782, at the Greyhound Terminal (569-3752). To: Atlantic City ($9.25), Ocean City ($10), and other points on the Jersey Shore.

Southeastern Pennsylvania Transportation Authority (SEPTA): 574-7800. Most buses operate 6:30am-1am, some all night. Extensive bus and rail service to suburbs. Two major subway routes: east-west (including 30th St. Station and the historic area) and north-south (including the stadium complex in south Philadelphia). The subway is unsafe after dark. Buses serve the 5-county area. Subway connects with commuter rails: the Main Line Local runs through the western suburb of Paoli ($3.50), and SEPTA runs north as far as Trenton, NJ ($3.50). Pick up a SEPTA **system map** ($1.50), also a good street map, at any subway stop. Fare $1.25, transfers 25¢.

Taxi: Yellow Cab, 922-8400.

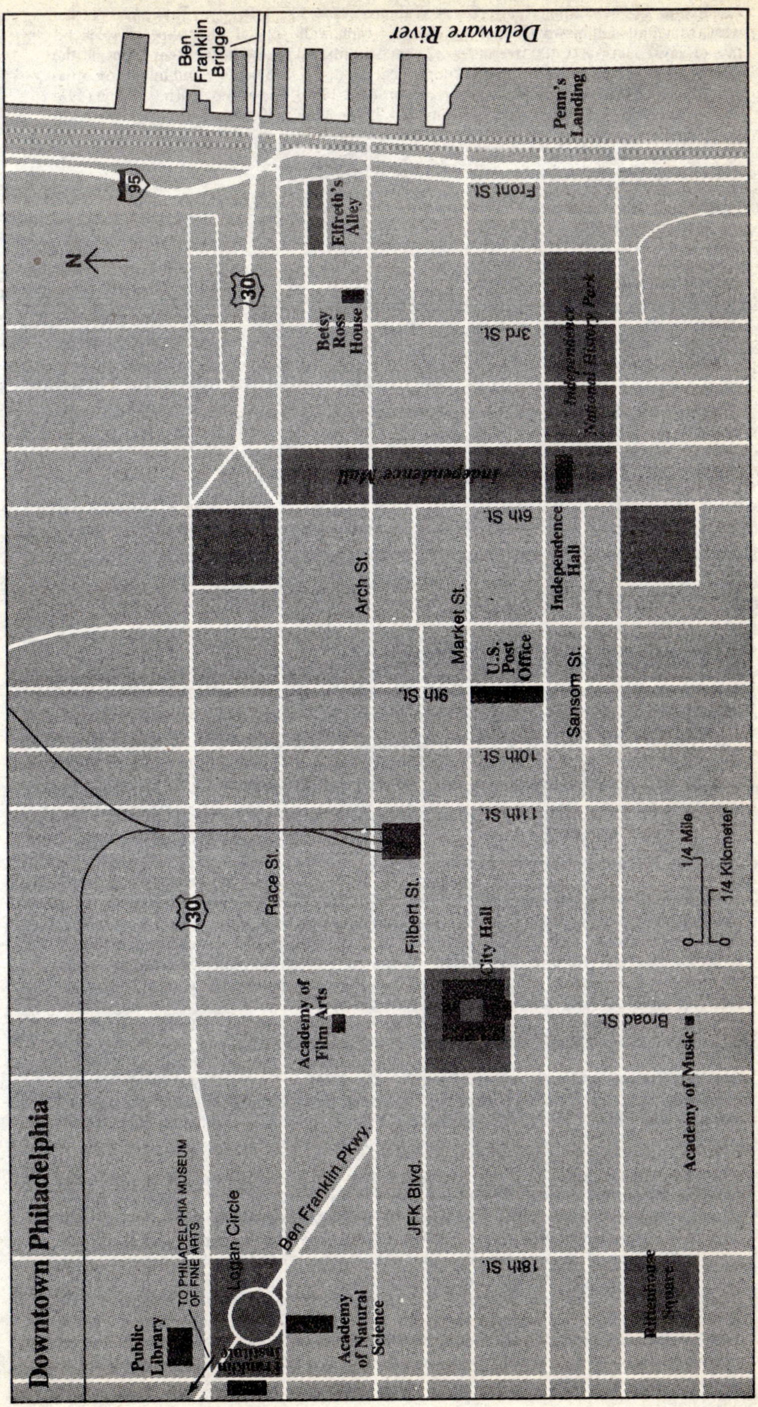
Downtown Philadelphia
Delaware River
Ben Franklin Bridge
Penn's Landing
95
Front St.
Elfreth's Alley
N
30
Betsy Ross House
3rd St.
Independence National History Park
Independence Mall
6th St.
Independence Hall
Arch St.
Market St.
U.S. Post Office
Sansom St.
9th St.
10th St.
11th St.
Race St.
Filbert St.
City Hall
1/4 Mile
1/4 Kilometer
0
Academy of Film Arts
Broad St.
Academy of Music
JFK Blvd.
Ben Franklin Pkwy.
Logan Circle
TO PHILADELPHIA MUSEUM OF FINE ARTS
18th St.
Rittenhouse Square
Public Library
Franklin Institute
Academy of Natural Science

Car Rental: Ugly Duckling Rent-a-Car, 4 Walnut St. (296-7177), Berwyn. Take SEPTA train west from Philadelphia to Daylesford, then a 5-min. walk to Walnut St. Special weekend rate (3 days) about $60, 100 free miles, 12¢ each additional mile. **Thrifty Rent-a-Car,** at the airport and 509 N. 22nd (365-3900). Compact car Mon.-Fri. $38 per day, unlimited free mileage. **American International Rent-a-Car,** airport (492-1750), and at the Amtrak station (492-0555). Mon.-Fri. $32.75 per day, Fri.-Sun. $64.75 for 3 days; 100 free miles, 23¢ each additional mile.

Help Lines: Gay Switchboard, 547-7100. Answered 6-11pm.

Post Office: 30th and Market St. (596-5316). Open 24 hours. **ZIP code:** 19104.

Area Code: 215.

Philadelphia is 100 miles from New York City, 133 miles from Washington, DC, and 296 miles from Boston. Founder William Penn, Jr., a survivor of London's great fire in the 1600s, planned his city as a logical and easily accessible grid pattern of wide streets. The north-south streets are numbered from the **Delaware River,** flowing near Penn's Landing and Independence Hall on the east side, to the **Schuylkill River** (pronounced "school-kill") on the west. The first street is **Front,** the others are numbered consecutively from 2 to 69. **Center City** runs from 8th Street to the Schuylkill River. From north to south, the primary streets are Race, Arch, JFK, Market, Sansom, and South. The intersection of Broad (14th St.) and Market, the location of City Hall, marks the focal point of Center City. The **Historic District** stretches from Front to 8th Street and from Vine to South Street. The sprawling, historic **University of Pennsylvania** rests on the far side of the Schuylkill River, about 1 mile west of Center City. **University City** includes the Penn/Drexel area west of the Schuylkill River.

Accommodations and Camping

Downtown Philadelphia is full of luxury hotels, so anything inexpensive is popular. But if you make arrangements even a few days in advance, you should be able to find comfortable lodging close to Center City for under $30. **Philadelphia Bed & Breakfast Service,** P.O. Box 4755, Philadelphia 19134 (634-4444) and **Bed and Breakfast, Center City,** 1804 Pine St., Philadelphia 19103 (735-1137; open Mon.-Fri. 10am-6pm, Sat. 10am-4pm) can find you a room in a private home. (Singles $10-45. Doubles $20-70.) Camping is available to the north and west of the city, but you must travel at least 15 miles.

Chamounix Mansion International Youth Hostel (AYH), West Fairmount Park (878-3676). Take bus #38 from JFK Blvd. to Ford and Cranston Rd., walk in the direction of the bus until Chamounix St., then turn left and follow until the road ends at hostel (about a 20-min. walk). Or, from the visitors center, take the Fairmount Park Trolley directly to the door (trolley leaves visitors center at 4pm). Built in 1802, this former country estate is clean and beautifully furnished. 50 beds, showers, kitchen, and coin-operated laundry. Some basic groceries for sale. Extraordinarily friendly and helpful staff. Call 4:30-8pm for reservations or check-in. Closed 9:30am-4:30pm; lock-out 11pm. $8, nonmembers $12. Linen $2.

Old First Reformed Church, 4th and Race St. (922-4566), in Center City, 1 block from the Independence Mall and 4 blocks from Penn's Landing. Historic church that converts its social hall to a youth hostel for 20. Mattresses on the floor, showers. 3-night max. stay. Call or drop by 5pm-10pm. $5. Breakfast included. Open July 5-Aug 28.

The Divine Tracy Hotel, 20 S. 36th St. (382-4310), near Market St., in a safe area across from the Sheraton/University City. Impeccably clean, quiet, and well-maintained rooms. Hotel run on a volunteer basis by members of the Peace Mission, a religious movement dedicated to the achievement of world peace. Women must wear skirts and stockings at all times in the public areas of the hotel; men must not wear shorts or have their shirts untucked. Men and women live on separate floors and are permitted to visit only in the lobby. No smoking allowed. Check-in 7am-11pm. Singles $20-22. Doubles $15-17 per person with shared bath, $35 with private bath. Fans and TVs for rent. The management does not permit alcohol or food (except small snacks) in the rooms, but the **Keyflower Dining Room** (386-2207) offers incredibly cheap and healthful, if bland, food. Entrees $1.65-2. Open to the public Mon.-Fri. 11:30am-2pm and 5-8pm.

International House, 3701 Chestnut St. (387-5125). Take bus D to 37th and Walnut, or bus #12 to 34th and Walnut. Clean dorms in an attractive, modern complex. Cafeteria-style restaurant open daily 11:30am-midnight. Must have a student ID or be affiliated with university or exchange programs. Only a few rooms available during school year. 1-night min. stay. Singles in a 10-room suite with shared bath $42, plus deposit. Doubles $50. No reservations accepted.

YWCA, 2027 Chestnut St (564-3430). Take bus #42 or D to 20th and Chestnut. Women only, must be over 18. Nonmembers must join ($35) if staying longer than a week. Rooms are a bit dark and unpleasant. Be careful in the neighborhood after dark. Private baths. Singles $25, $150 per week. $25 deposit. Reservations essential.

Timberlane Campground, 117 Timber Lane, Clarksboro, NJ 08020 (609-423-6677), 15 miles from Center City. 35 sites; $11, with full hookup $13.50.

Phoenixville Area YMCA Campground, P.O. Box 310, Phoenixville 19460 (933-5865), on Rte. 29, about 25 miles west of city. Trails by a creek (no fishing), tennis courts, swimming pool. Sites $13, with electricity $15. Open May-Oct.

Tohickon Family Campground, RD #3 Covered Bridge Rd. (536-7951), Quakerstown, 40 miles north of the city. On a well-stocked creek; rowboats available. Pool, general store, showers, laundry facilities. Sites $16, with electricity and water $18, with full hookup $19. Open April-Oct.

Food

More than 500 new restaurants have opened their doors in Philadelphia in the past decade, making the city one of America's most exciting dining spots. Inexpensive food abounds on Sansom St. between 17th and 18th; on South St. between 2nd and 7th; and on 2nd St. between Chestnut and Market. Lots of new places are opening up on **Penn's Landing,** on the Delaware River between Locust and Market St. Try the famous hoagie or cheesesteak, two local specialties. You may become addicted to the renowned Philly soft pretzel.

To stock up on staples, visit the **Italian Market** at 9th and Christian St. (Open daily dawn-dusk.) The **Reading Terminal Market,** at 12th and Arch St. (922-2317), is the place to go for picnic-packing. A Philadelphia tradition since 1893, it offers many food stands where you can buy fresh produce, or find delicious and cheap alternatives to fast-food courts, such as a huge serving of ice cream for $1. (Open Mon.-Sat. 8am-6pm.)

Historic District

Jim's Steaks, 4th and South (928-1911). Take the 4th St. trolley or bus #10 down Locust St. A Philadelphia institution since 1939, serving some of the best steak sandwiches in town ($3.35-3.70). Eat to beat Jim's current record holder—11 steaks in 90 minutes. Open Mon.-Thurs. 10am-1am, Fri.-Sat. 10am-3am, Sun. noon-10pm.

Lee's Hoagies, 220 South St. (925-6667), near South and 2nd St. Authentic hoagies ($2.90-4.50) since 1953. The 3-foot hoagie is a taunting challenge to gluttonous tourists. Hours vary.

Fu Wing House, 639 South St. at 6th St. (922-3170), down the street from Jim's. Serves a great hot-and-sour soup ($1.60). Open Mon.-Thurs. 5-11pm, Fri. 5pm-midnight, Sat. 4pm-midnight, Sun. 4-11pm.

Dickens Inn, Head House Sq., 2nd St. (928-9307), between Pine and Lombard. British country cooking. Try the shepherd's pie ($4), Cornish pasty ($3), or soup of the day with bread ($2.50). Open daily 11:30am-9:30pm.

Center City

Charlie's Famous Waterwheel Restaurant, downstairs at 1526 Samson St., between 15th and 16th St. The cheesesteaks will fill you up for days. Munch on free meatballs, pickles and fried mushrooms at the counter while you wait. Open daily 10am-8pm.

Saladalley, 1720 Samson St. between 17th and 18th Sts. A good alternative to Charlie's. Huge salad bar featuring truly innovative combinations of fresh fruits, vegetables, and light sauces. Salad sold by weight. Open Mon.-Sat. 11am-10pm, Sun. 11am-9pm (brunch until 4pm).

University City

Audrey's Pit Barbecue, 113 S. 40th St. (386-5125). Considered the best barbecue restaurant in town. Jack Nicholson eats here. Try the half-chicken ($3.50) or the barbecued beef sandwiches ($3.25). Customers rave about the potato pie (89¢). Few seats, mostly take-out. Open Mon. 4-10pm, Tues.-Thurs. 11:30am-10pm, Fri.-Sat. 11:30am-1am, Sun. 2pm-10pm.

Sweet Basil, 4000 Chestnut St. (387-2727) at 40th St. Cool and sophisticated. Eclectic menu with Indonesian, Cajun, and vegetarian entrees. Lunches $4-6.25, dinners $7-13. Open Mon.-Thurs. 11am-10pm, Fri.-Sat. 11am-11pm.

Ohara's, 3925 Walnut St. (382-5195). Students swarm here for a respite from dining hall food. Good burgers ($3-5) and sandwiches ($3.50-4). After 5pm on Tuesdays, all-the-chicken-wings-you-can-eat $4.50. Open daily 11am-2am.

Eden, 3721 Chestnut St., at 38th St. Wholesome and satisfying grilled fish and chicken specialties served on a garden terrace. Deviled crab cake with potatoes and salad $5.15. Salads, quiche, and pizza, too. Open Mon.-Sat. 11am-10pm.

Sights

Still smarting from W.C. Field's devastating quip, "I went to Philadelphia—and it was closed," the city goes all out to present its best side to visitors. A convenient way to see the sights is on **Fairmount Park Trolley Tours** (879-4044 for recorded information). Sponsored by the city's park commission, the tours pass by all the major sights, and you may board or get off at your leisure. (Tours leave every ½ hr. from the tourist center, 16th and JFK, or at the Independence Park Visitors Center. April-Nov. Wed.-Sun. 10am-4pm. Admission $3; includes discounts at attractions.)

Independence Hall and the Historic District

The buildings of the **Independence National Historic Park** (open daily 9am-5pm; in summer hours extended) witnessed events that have since passed into American folklore. In **Independence Hall,** between 5th and 6th St. on Chestnut, the *Declaration of Independence* was signed in 1776, and the *United States Constitution* was drafted and signed in 1787. George Washington's chair, at the head of the assembly room, is engraved with a half-sun, which was the subject of Ben Franklin's remark after the ratification of the Constitution: "Now at length I have the happiness to know that it is a rising and not a setting sun." (Free guided tours daily every 15-20 min.) The U.S. Congress first assembled in nearby **Congress Hall** (free self-guided tour), while its predecessor, the First Continental Congress, convened in **Carpenters' Hall,** 2 blocks away at 4th and Chestnut St. (Open Tues.-Sun. 10am-4pm.) North of Independence Hall lies the **Liberty Bell Pavilion.** The cracked Liberty Bell itself, one of the U.S.'s most famous national symbols, refuses to toll even when vigorously prodded.

Slightly out of the way, at 532 N. 7th St., is the **Edgar Allan Poe House,** one of America's many (597-8780). Here the American literary giant wrote some of his most macabre poems and stories, including *The Raven* and *The Tell-Tale Heart.* (Open daily 9am-5pm. Free.) The **Library Company of Philadelphia,** 1314 Locust St., near 13th St., was founded by Ben Franklin over 250 years ago, originally existing as a club whose members' dues purchased books from England. Outside of its present headquarters stands a weather-worn Statue of Franklin.

Just south of **Rittenhouse Square,** 2010 DeLancey St., is the **Rosenbach Museum and Library** (732-1600), which houses rare manuscripts and paintings, including the earliest-known copy of Cervantes' *Don Quixote.* (open Tues.-Sun. 11am-4pm. Guided tours $2.50.) Also near Rittenhouse Sq., the **Mütter Museum** (567-3737) of Philadelphia's College of Physicians displays gory medical paraphernalia. (Call before visiting. Open Mon.-Fri. 9am-5pm.)

West Philadelphia (University City)

West Philly is home to both the **University of Pennsylvania** and **Drexel University,** located across the Schuylkill from Center City, within easy walking distance of the 30th St. Station. Penn was founded in 1740 by Benjamin Franklin. Here in 1765 the country's first medical school was founded, and it continues to thrive today. The Penn campus is a haven of green lawns and red-brick quadrangles. Shops line Chestnut St. and fraternities line Spruce; warm weather brings out a varied collection of street vendors along the Drexel and Penn borders.

The **University Museum of Archeology and Anthropology,** 33rd and Spruce St. (898-4000), is home to one of the finest archeological collections in the world. (Open Sept.-June Tues.-Sat. 10am-4:30pm, Sun. 1-5pm. Admission $3, seniors and students $1.50.) In 1965, Andy Warhol had his first one-man show at the **Institute of Contemporary Art,** 34th and Walnut St. The gallery is still on the art scene's cutting edge. (Open Sat.-Tues. and Thurs. 10am-5pm.)

The remainder of the park contains preserved residential and commercial buildings of the Revolutionary era. **Franklin Court** to the north, on Market between 3rd and 4th St., is the site of Ben Franklin's home, and includes an underground museum and an architectural-archeological exhibit. (Open daily 9am-5pm.) Nearby is **Washington Square** and an eternal flame commemorating the **Tomb of the Unknown Soldier.** Across from Independence Hall is Philadelphia's branch of the **U.S. Mint,** 5th and Arch St. (Open daily in summer 9am-4:30pm; in spring and fall Mon.-Sat. 9am-4:30pm. Free.) A self-paced guided tour explains the mechanized coin-making procedure.

Tucked away near 2nd and Arch St. is the quiet, residential **Elfreth's Alley,** allegedly "the oldest street in America," along which a penniless Ben Franklin walked when he arrived in town in 1723. On Arch near 3rd St. is the tiny **Betsy Ross House,** where legend has it that the first flag of the original 13 states was sewn. **Christ Church,** on 2nd near Market, was the fashionable Quaker church of colonial Philadelphia. Ben Franklin is buried in the nearby Christ Church cemetery at 5th and Arch St. On Spruce near 8th St. is the burial ground of **Mikveh Israel,** the first Jewish congregation of Philadelphia. Also see the Quaker meeting houses: the original **Free Quaker Meeting House** at 5th and Arch St, and a new and large one at 4th and Arch St.

Society Hill proper begins where the park ends, on Walnut St. between Front and 7th St. Now Philadelphia's most distinguished residential neighborhood, housing both old-timers and a new yuppie crowd, the area was originally a tract of land owned by the Free Society of Traders, a company formed to help William Penn, Jr. consolidate Pennsylvania. Three-hundred-year-old Federal-style townhouses line picturesque cobblestone walks, illuminated by old-fashioned streetlamps. **Head House Square,** 2nd and Pine St., was a marketplace in 1745 and now houses restaurants, boutiques, and craft shops. An outdoor flea market is held here on weekends in summer.

Located on the Delaware River, **Penn's Landing** (923-8181) is the largest freshwater port in the world. It holds the *Gazela,* a three-masted, 178-foot Portuguese square rigger built in 1883 (923-9030; tours daily noon-5pm; admission $1); the *Moshulu,* the world's largest steel sailing ship (925-3237; tours Mon.-Sat. 11am-6pm, Sun. 1-6pm; admission $1); the U.S.S. *Olympia,* Commodore Dewey's flagship during the Spanish-American War (922-1898; tours daily 10am-4:30pm; admission $3, children $1.50); and the U.S.S. *Becuna,* a World War II submarine (tours in conjunction with the *Olympia*).

Benjamin Franklin Parkway

Nicknamed "America's Champs-Elysées," the Benjamin Franklin Parkway is a wide, diagonal deviation from William Penn's original grid pattern of city streets. Built in the 20s, this tree- and flag-lined street connects Center City with Fairmount Park and the Schuylkill River. Admire the elegant architecture of the twin buildings at Logan Square, 19th and Parkway, that house the **Free Library of Philadelphia** and the **Municipal Court.**

At 20th and Parkway you'll find the **Franklin Institute** (448-1200), which amazes visitors with four floors of gadgets and games depicting the intricacies of space, time, motion, and the human body. (Open Mon.-Sat. 10am-5pm, Sun. noon-5pm. Admission $5.50, seniors $3.50, ages 4-11 $4.50, under 4 free. Disabled access.) The **Fels Planetarium** inside offers a glimpse of the reaches of the universe. (Shows Mon. at 12:30pm, Tues.-Fri. at 12:30 and 2pm, additional shows on weekends. Admission $1.50.) The planetarium features a spectacular laser show ($6) on Thursday, Friday, and Saturday evenings.

A casting of the *Gates of Hell* stands outside the **Rodin Museum,** at 22nd St. and the Parkway (787-5476). The museum houses the most complete collection of Rodin's works outside Paris. (Open Tues.-Sun. 10am-5pm. Free. Disabled access.)

The exhibit of precious gems and the 65-million-year-old dinosaur skeleton at the **Academy of Natural Sciences,** 19th and Parkway (299-1000), are truly awesome. (Open Mon.-Fri. 10am-4pm, Sat.-Sun. 10am-4:30pm. Admission $4.50, children $3.50.) Farther down 26th St. is one of the world's major art collections, the **Philadelphia Museum of Art** (763-8100). Here you'll find Rubens' *Prometheus Bound,* Picasso's *Three Musicians,* and Duchamp's *Nude Descending a Staircase,* as well as extensive Asian, Egyptian and decorative arts collections. (Open Tues.-Sun. 10am-5pm. Admission $5, seniors and under 18 with student ID $2. Free Sun. 10am-1pm.)

Fairmont Park sprawls behind the Philadelphia Museum of Art on both sides of the Schuylkill River. Bike trails and picnic areas abound, and the famous old **Philadelphia Zoo** occupies one corner of the park. **Boathouse Row,** which houses the shells of local crew teams, is especially beautiful when lit at night. During the day, hikers may wish to venture out to the northernmost arm of Fairmont Park, where trails leave the Schuylkill River and wind along the secluded Wissahickon Creek for 5 miles.

Center City

Center City, the area between 12th St. and 23rd St. and between Vine St. and Pine St., is a whirlwind of activity. **City Hall,** Broad and Market (686-4546), an ornate structure of granite and marble with 20-foot-thick foundation walls, is the nation's largest public municipal building, even bigger than the U.S. Capitol. Until 1908, it was the highest building in the U.S., helped by the 37-foot statue of William Penn, Jr. on top. (Guided tours available. Open Mon.-Fri. 9am-5pm.)

The **Afro-American Historical and Cultural Museum,** 7th and Arch St. (574-0380), was America's first museum devoted solely to the history of African-Americans. (Open Tues.-Sat. 10am-5pm, Sun. noon-6pm. Admission $1.50, seniors and children 75¢.) Try your hand at the sensual **Please Touch Museum,** 210 N. 21st St. (963-0666), designed specifically for children seven and under. (Open Tues.-Sun. 10am-4:30pm. Admission $4.) The **Pennsylvania Academy of Fine Arts,** Broad and Cherry St. (972-7600), the country's first art school and one of its first museums, has an extensive collection of American and British art. Of particular note are the works by Charles Wilson Peale, Thomas Eakins, Winslow Homer, William Russ and Gilbert Stuart, but there are also more contemporary pieces. (Tours Tues.-Fri. at 11am and 2pm, Sat.-Sun. at 2pm. Open Tues.-Sat. 10am-5pm, Sun. 11am-5pm. Admission $2, seniors and students $1, under 12 free. Free Sat. 10am-1pm.)

The **Wistar Institute,** 36th and Spruce St. (898-3708), has a gruesome collection of anatomical specimens. Built in 1892, the walls of the oldest independent research institute in the U.S. are lined with skeletons, mutant limbs, and giant tumors. A 45-minute tape describes the exhibits. (Open Mon.-Fri. 10am-4pm. Free.)

Entertainment

Check Friday's weekend magazine section in the Philadelphia *Inquirer* for entertainment listings. *Au Courant,* a gay and lesbian weekly newspaper, lists and advertises events throughout the Delaware Valley region. The bar scene is lively in University City and along South Street. The latter area usually has a wide variety of live music on weekends.

Philadelphia Academy of Music, Broad and Locust St. (893-1930). Formerly under the direction of the late Eugene Ormandy, and now under Ricardo Muti. Many critics rate the Philadelphia Orchestra the best in America. Its winter home was modeled artistically after Milan's *La Scala* and acoustically after a perfect vacuum. The season runs from September through May. General admission tickets ($2) for seats in the amphitheater go on sale at the Locust St. entrance 45 minutes before Friday and Saturday concerts. Check with the box office for availability.

Mann Music Center, George's Hill, near 52nd St. and Parkside Ave., Fairmount Park (567-0707). 5000 seats under cover, 10,000 on outdoor benches and lawns. Summer home for Philadelphia Orchestra, ballet, jazz, and rock. Pick up free lawn tickets June-Aug. on the day of performance from the visitors center at 16th St. and John F. Kennedy Blvd. (See Practical Information above).

Robin Hood Dell East, Strawberry Mansion Dr. (686-1776 or 477-8810 in summer), in Fairmount Park. Top names in pop, jazz, gospel, and ethnic dance perform nightly July-Aug. The Philadelphia Orchestra holds several free performances here in summer, and as many as 30,000 people gather on the lawn. Inquire at the visitors center (636-1666) for upcoming events.

Shubert Theater, 250 S. Broad St., Center City (732-5446). Various dance, musical, and comedy performances keep this attractive theater active all year.

Cutter's Grand Café amd Bar, Commerce Sq. at 21st and Market St. (242-8991), in Center City. The beer menu was designed according to the specifications of Michael Jackson (a world expert on beer, not music), right down to the temperature at which each selection should be served ($2-3.50). Open Mon.-Sat. 11am-3am, Sun. 11am-1am.

Dobb's, 304 South St. (928-1943). A mixed-menu restaurant (entrees $6-8.50) with live rock nightly. Half-price burgers on Mondays; Wednesday all-you-can-eat crab with corn on the cob $8. Open daily 6pm-2am.

Near Philadelphia

Valley Forge

Neither battles nor artillery bombardments took place here, but during the winter of 1777-78, 11,000 men quartered at Valley Forge under George Washington's leadership spent agonizing months fighting starvation and disease. Only 8000 survived. Nonetheless, inspired by the enthusiasm of General Washington and by the news of an American alliance with France, and drilled into efficiency by Inspector General Baron Von Steuben, the American troops left Valley Forge stronger and better trained. They went on to victories in New Jersey and eventually reoccupied Philadelphia.

The park today consists of 2033 acres. (Open 6am-10pm.) Self-guided tours begin at the **visitors center** (783-7700), where there is also a free museum and a 15-minute audio-visual program played daily twice per hour from 9am to 5:30pm. (Open daily 8:30am-6pm; Labor Day-Memorial Day 9am-5pm.) The tour features Washington's headquarters, reconstructed soldier huts and fortifications, and the Grand Parade Ground where the army drilled. It costs $1 to enter Washington's headquarters, but most other exhibits and buildings in the park are free. Auto tapes rent for $6.40. The park has three picnic areas and, although there is no camping within the park, there are campgrounds nearby. A 5-mile bike trail winds up and down the hills of the park. Bikes can be rented daily 9am to 4:30pm ($4 per hour, $11 per day). If you don't mind the hike, the **Mount Joy Observatory Tower,** at a corner of the park, offers a great view of the Pennsylvania countryside.

To get to Valley Forge, take the Schuylkill Expressway westbound from Philadelphia for about 12 miles. Get off at the Valley Forge exit, then take Rte. 202 South for 1 mile and Rte. 422 West for 3 miles to the Valley Forge exit. Or take SEPTA bus #45 from 16th and John F. Kennedy (JFK) Blvd. in Center City to King of Prussia Plaza, then bus #99 (to Royers Ford or Phoenixville, *not* to Norristown), which stops at the Valley Forge visitors center ($3).

Lancaster County

Lancaster County is home to one of the most closely knit and least assimilated immigrant groups in America, the **Pennsylvania Dutch.** Not Dutch at all, they are actually immigrants from the Rhineland of Germany and Switzerland. While several different religious groups come under the heading of Pennsylvania Dutch, all are united by their simple lifestyles. The best-known are the **Amish,** who interpret the Bible literally, emphatically reject modern technology, and live secluded from the rest of society. They're friendly and willing to converse with respectful tourists. Enjoy home-grown food and home-baked goods from the many small roadside market stands operated by Amish families. One traditional food is chow-chow, a delightful jarful of vegetables, vinegar, and sugar.The Amish are the most orthodox of the **Mennonite** sects. The **Moravians,** called "fancy Dutch," are mostly German Lutherans and Reformed Church members. They produce the colorful six-pointed hex signs gracing the sides of barns.

It's best to see this area by car. The **Mennonite Information Center,** 2209 Millstream Rd. (299-0954; open Mon.-Sat. 8am-5pm), just off Rte. 30, offers a film and arranges tours with local Mennonite guides. The **People's Place,** on Main St. in Intercourse (768-7171), 11 miles east of Lancaster, was created to help Mennonites and visitors learn more about each other on a personal basis. Here, among other things, you'll find the movie *Who Are the Amish?* (Open Mon.-Sat. 9:30am-9:30pm. Movie shown Mon.-Sat. 9:30am-5pm every ½ hr. Admission $2.50, children $1.10.)

In the middle of Amish country is **Lancaster City,** with its clean, red-brick row houses. This city, which was the U.S. capital for one day back in 1777, boasts graceful Georgian architecture, an opera house, lovely small parks, an eye-catching Vietnam memorial in the center of the city, and the home of James Buchanan, 15th U.S. President. The **Lancaster Association of Commerce and Industry,** 100 Queen St. (397-3531), offers guided walking tours of Lancaster City. (Leave from 100 S. Queen St. April-Oct. Mon.-Sat. at 10am and 1:30pm, Sun. at 1:30pm; in summer also Mon. at 6:30pm. Call 392-1776 for reservations.) For assistance with accommodations and attractions, try the **Pennsylvania Dutch Visitors Bureau Information Center,** 501 Greenfield Rd. (299-8901), on the east side of Lancaster City just off Rte. 30. B&Bs in the Lancaster area usually start at $35 for a double, and the people at the bureau will help you find vacancies. Their movie, *The Lancaster Experience,* provides a good introduction to the area.

The best places to eat require at least a day's advance notice; contact the owners of the Bowmansville Youth Hostel for a list of names of local Amish and Mennonite families who don't mind having supper guests. Call one of these families the day before, and they will feed you a home-grown feast. (Pay whatever you feel is appropriate.) If you don't have a day, several area restaurants, mostly scattered along Rte. 30 and 340, offer hearty German-style food (usually all-you-can-eat about $8). Look for dishes such as chicken pot pie, *snitz, knepp,* and shoo-fly pie. **The Family Style** is 4½ miles east of Lancaster City on U.S. 30; 3 miles farther down the road is **Millers Smorgasbord** (687-6621). The **Amish Barn,** on Rte. 340 (768-8886), between Bird-In-Hand and Intercourse, offers specialties such as scrapple or fried corn meal mush for $2.85.

Three **youth hostels** fringe the western side of the Lancaster County area ($7, nonmembers $11). All are rather difficult to get to without a car or bike, but call ahead to ask about rides. The **Bowmansville Youth Hostel (AYH),** P.O. Box 157, Bowmansville 17507 (215-445-4831; open Jan. to mid-Dec.), is about 26 miles from Lancaster on Rte. 625 near I-76. It has a kitchen, and the owners are friendly. (Take bus #12 to New Holland, last bus at 5:20pm, then walk or hitch the remaining 6 miles.) Fifteen miles east, the **Geigertown Youth Hostel (AYH),** P.O. Box 49, Geigertown 19523 (215-286-9537; open March 2-Nov. 30), lies near French Creek State Park off Rte. 82. There's always extra room in the "snoring building" and you can sometimes arrange transportation from Reading, which is served by bus. A little farther out is the **Marsh Creek Youth Hostel (AYH),** P.O. Box 262, E.

Reeds Rd., Lyndel 19354 (215-458-5881), in Marsh Creek State Park. The hostel rests off Rte. 282 near I-76. Downington, 5 miles south, is on Greyhound's Philadelphia-Lancaster route (#325).

There seem to be as many campgrounds as cows in this lush countryside. (Sites $11-15.) The closest year-round facility is **Old Millstream Camping Manor,** 2249 U.S. 30 E. (299-2314), 4 miles east of Lancaster City. **Roamers Retreat,** 5005 Lincoln Hwy. (442-4287 or 872-8994), is open only from April to October. (For reservations, call or write RD #1, P.O. Box 41B, Kinzers 17535.) **Shady Grove,** RD #2, Rte. 897, Reinholds 17569 (484-4225) has sites for $8.50.

Greyhound/Trailways runs one bus per day between Lancaster and Philadelphia ($9). The bus terminal in Lancaster is at 22 West Clay St. (397-4861). **Amtrak,** 53 McGovern Ave. (800-872-7245), also makes the trip between Lancaster and Philadelphia ($10.50). Lancaster City has its own bus system, **Red Rose Transit,** 47 N. Queen St. (397-4246; open Mon.-Fri. 5am-8pm, Sat. 6am-6pm, Sun. 10am-6pm), serving the city and the immediate countryside. Except to the shopping center, buses don't operate on Sunday. The base fare is 75¢; seniors ride free on off-peak hours. Rent bikes in Lancaster or in Ephrata, at **Martin's Bike Shop,** Rte. 322, R.D. 3 (354-9127), for $5 per day. (Open Mon.-Tues. and Thurs.-Fri. 9am-9pm, Sat. 9am-4pm.)

Just across the northwest border of Lancaster County, is the "brown" town of **Hershey,** famous for its milk chocolate products. Here the street lights are shaped like candy kisses and streets are named Chocolate and Cocoa. East of town at **Hershey Park** (534-3005), the **Chocolate World Visitors Center** presents a free, automated tour through a simulated chocolate factory. After viewing the processing of the cacao bean of from tropical forests through final packaging, visitors emerge into a pavilion full of chocolate cookies, chocolate candy, chocolate milk, and chocolate Christmas ornaments—all for sale, of course. (Open daily 9am-6:45pm.) At the Hershey Park amusement center, you can stand in line for the various rides and meet walking, talking Reese's cups. (Admission $18, ages 4-8 $15; prices drop after 5pm.)

Camp between Lancaster and Hershey at **Ridge Run Campground,** 867 Schwanger Rd., Elizabethtown 17022 (367-3454). Schwanger Rd. connects Rte. 230 and 283; the campground lies 8 miles from Hershey and 15 miles from Lancaster (sites $14). **Greyhound/Trailways** goes to Hershey from Philadelphia ($21) once daily, stopping at 337 W. Chocolate St. (397-4861). Pick up a free **Map of Amish Farmlands** at any tourist spot in Lancaster County, or write to 340-23 Club, P.O. Box 239, Intercourse 17534.

The **ZIP code** in Lancaster City is 17604, in Hershey 17033; the **area code** in Lancaster County and Hershey is 717.

Gettysburg

"The world will little note, nor long remember what we say here, but it can never forget what they did here." So ran Abraham Lincoln's *Gettysburg Address,* delivered in 1863 to those gathered to mourn the Union soldiers who fell in the Civil War's bloodiest battle. (He was only half right, of course.) Each year, thousands of visitors come to these peaceful Pennsylvania fields to relive those three dark days during which more than 7000 people died. Fields such as Valley of Death, Devil's Den, Bloody Run, and Cemetery Hill sprout a forest of monuments to those who fought.

Unfortunately, the park entrances swarm with tacky collections of commercial establishments. Bypass them by taking U.S. 15 south to the Taneytown Rd. exit. This will lead you directly to the park and the **National Park Service Visitors Information Center** (334-1124; open daily 8am-6pm; in off-season hours vary). With the visitors center's free map, you can bike, drive, or walk the roads and trails within the park. (Roads open daily 6am-10pm, weather permitting.) The **Electrical Map** presentation, also in the visitors center, is an excellent way to orient yourself in the park. (½-hr. program shown every 45 min. 8:15am-5:15pm. Admission $2, seniors $1.50, under 16 free.) Next to the visitors center is **Cyclorama Center,** where you can see an original draft of the Gettysburg Address manuscript and the film *Gettysburg 1863,* shown periodically throughout the day.

Near the national cemetery is the **National Tower** (334-6754), whose high-speed elevators whisk you 300 feet above *terra firma* to a spectacular view. Also in Gettysburg is a **National Civil War Wax Museum,** on Steinwehr Ave. (334-6245).

Adjoining the park's west side is the **Eisenhower Farm,** where the 34th U.S. President spent his retirement years. Donated by the Eisenhower family, it is now a national historic site. (Shuttle bus runs every 15 min. 9am-4:15pm. Admission $2.25, children 70¢.)

There is no shortage of eateries either near the park or in Lincoln Sq. The **Dutch Cupboard,** 523 Baltimore (334-6227), serves dishes such as *schnitz un knepp* ($8), *schmeir kaes,* and shoo-fly pie ($1.20). (Open daily 8am-9pm.) The **Springhouse Tavern,** 89 Steinwehr Ave. (334-2100), in Dobben's Rest near the park headquarters, was built in 1774, is still owned by the same family, and has the same oak bartop. Try a salamagundi or an "ordinary"—soup, salad, homemade bread and a glass of wine—all for $4.30.

The best place to sleep in Gettysburg is the roomy and cheerful **Gettysburg Youth Hostel,** 27 Chambersburg St. (334-1020), on U.S. 30 just past U.S. 15. (Kitchen, stereo, living room; curfew 11pm, check-out 9:30am. $7, nonmembers $10.) Otherwise, you can try the **Holland Tourist Court,** 2700 York Rd. (334-4380), 5 miles east of town on U.S. 30. (Singles and doubles $30.) There are several **campgrounds** in the area. Just a mile south on Rte. 134 is **Artillery Ridge,** 610 Taneytown Rd. (334-1288), which has a riding stable. (Sites $13.) **Moyers Mountain Retreat,** in the delta of U.S. 15 and 30, has a heated outdoor pool and trails that connect to the **Appalachian Trail** (800-231-2267; 800-233-7546 outside PA; base fee $10).

Gettysburg is in south-central Pennsylvania, off U.S. 15, about 30 miles south of Harrisburg. **Greyhound/Trailways** (334-7064) serves Gettysburg from Philadelphia (1 per day, $18). The city of Gettysburg is nearly surrounded by the battlefield. The **Gettysburg Travel Council** at the old train depot, 35 Carlisle St., Lincoln Sq. (334-6274), has information on local accommodations and regional attractions. (Open daily 9am-6pm; off-season hours vary.) The **chamber of commerce** is at 33 York St. (334-8151; open Mon.-Fri. 9am-5pm.)

Gettysburg's **area code** is 717.

Ohiopyle State Park

Hidden away in the forgotten and unpronounceable landscapes of southwestern Pennsylvania are some of the loveliest forests in the East, lifted by steep hills and cut by cascading rivers. The area's first inhabitants dubbed this part of the state "Ohiopehhle" ("white frothy water"), because of the grand Youghiogheny River Gorge (pronounced "yock-a-gay-nee"; locals call it "The Yock"), which provides the focal point of Pennsylvania's Ohiopyle State Park. The park's 18,000 acres have hiking, fishing, hunting, and a complete range of winter activities, but the most popular activity is whitewater rafting along the river.

Within the park, but not too near the campgrounds, are four raft and canoe outfitters: **White Water Adventures** (329-8850; $18 special Wed.-Thurs.); **Wilderness Voyageurs** (329-4752); **Laurel Highlands Tours** (329-8531); and **Mountain Streams and Trails** (329-8810). Prices are roughly the same, and all include transportation to the nearby Yough River. Guided raft trips cost about $25 on weekdays, $45 on Saturdays, $37 on Sundays. Wear a swimsuit, loose shorts, and a wool sweater and wool socks if it's cold. If you are experienced enough to try the river on your own, rent a raft from one of the four outfitters listed above or from **Youghiogheny Raft Rentals,** P.O. Box 31, Ohiopyle 15470 (329-8372. Rafts and equipment for 4 people $31 on weekdays, $41 on weekends. 2-person canoes $30, inflatable kayak $25. $30 cash or credit deposit.) **Fishing licenses** are available at the park service or the **Falls Market,** on Main St. ($20, PA residents $12).

Back on U.S. 40 toward Harrisburg, you'll come across the site of **Fort Necessity,** an American/British stronghold dating from the French and Indian War. (Visitors information center open daily 9am-4:30pm.) Upon his defeat at Fort Necessity, Washington moved his men 60 miles north to Ligonier, where the beautiful and austere **Fort Ligonier** stands. Finally, from Fort Ligonier, Washington and his reinforced army defeated the French in 1758. (Open April-Oct. daily 9am-5pm. Admission $3, children $1.) The **Royal Welsh Fusiliers in America** re-enact battles and camp life of the 1750s on some summer weekends.

The Ohiopyle State Park has the **Ohiopyle Youth Hostel (AYH),** P.O. Box 99, Ohiopyle 15470 (329-4476; 24 bunks, kitchen. $6). Also within the park are over 200 **campsites** with sanitary facilities ($7; call ahead on weekends). For reservations or more information on camping, contact Ohiopyle State Park, P.O. Box 105, Ohiopyle 15470 (329-8591).

Ohiopyle is on Rte. 381, 64 miles southeast of Pittsburgh via Rte. 51 and U.S. 41. The closest public transportation is to Uniontown, a large town about 20 miles to the west on U.S. 40. **Greyhound/Trailways** serves **Uniontown** from Pittsburgh (3 per day, 1½ hr., $9).The **area code** in Ohiopyle and the surrounding area is 412.

Allegheny National Forest

The Allegheny National Forest, which contains a half-million acres of woodland stretching south of the New York border for 40 miles, offers year-round recreational opportunities including hunting, fishing, and trail biking. The forest makes an excellent detour on a cross-state jaunt on I-80, as its southern border is only 20 miles from the interstate. The forest is divided into four quadrants, each with its own ranger station to provide maps and information about activities and facilities within its area. (Southwest: Marienville Ranger District (927-6628; open Mon.-Sat. 7am-5pm). Northwest: Sheffield Ranger District (968-3233; open Mon.-Fri. 8am-4pm). Northeast: Bradford Ranger District (362-4613; open daily 8am-4:30pm). Southeast: Ridgway Ranger District (776-6172; open Mon.-Fri. 7:30am-4pm).) Swimming and beach passes for the park are available at the ranger stations ($3 per car, $1 per person). There is no charge for picnic sites or boat launches.

Camping facilities in the park are abundant and generally open from March to October first come-first serve. A "host" is available at most sights to assist campers and answer questions. (Sites $5-12, depending on the location and the time of year.) **Tracy Ridge** in the Bradford district and **Heart's Content,** in the Sheffield district are particularly pretty.

From whatever direction you approach the Allegheny Forest, you'll find a small, rustic community near the park where you can buy groceries or find accommodations. **Ridgway,** 25 miles from I-80 (exit 16) at the southeastern corner, is particulary scenic. Entering the **Bogert House,** 140 Main St. (773-7185), you'll feel as if you're stepping back into the golden age of railroads. The building's staircase, pressed-tin ceilings, ancient elevator, and mirror-backed bar (in the adjoining **Tap Room)** have earned it a spot in the National Register of Historic Places. The rooms themselves are a bit gloomy, but they're clean, the sheets are real linen, and the proprietor is incredibly friendly. (Singles $17, with kitchen $18. Doubles $20. Try to call a few days ahead.) **The Original,** 161 Main St. (752-7576), has great "baked" subs for $2.50-3 and burgers with fries for $2. Complete with jukebox. (Open daily 11am-9pm.) You can eat in the old train depot, now **Crispy's Fried Chicken,** at the intersection of Main St. and Montmorenci Rd. (773-7305). Two eggs with homefries and toast $1.39. (Open daily 7am-9pm.)

The **Kinzua Point Information Center** (726-1291), at a dramatic riverbend on Rte. 59 in the northeast portion of the forest, provides information on forest recreation, including camping. (Open Memorial Day-Labor Day Sun.-Thurs. 9:30am-5:30pm, Fri.-Sat. 9:30am-8pm.) To get to Ridgway and the national forest by public transportation, take **Greyhound/Trailways** from Harrisburg through Dubois ($26.75), or from Philadelphia, Pittsburgh, or Buffalo, NY. To hitch up to the forest, try to catch a ride at the bus station. Fortunately, U.S. 219 is a busy country road with lots of truck traffic. If you plan to drive inside the forest yourself, be careful during wet weather. About half of the region is served only by dirt roads.

The **area code** for this region is 814.

Pittsburgh

When Rand McNally named Pittsburgh the nation's "#1 most liveable city" in 1985, many Americans, Pittsburgh residents included, were surprised. This was, after all, the city that Charles Dickens called "Hell with the lid off" a century ago. Although its status as number one is debatable, Pittsburgh now has a lot more to offer than steel mills belching smoke. Climb **Duquesne Incline** to the top of Mt. Washington for a perfect view of a surprisingly beautiful city. The factories have been replaced by serene skyscrapers and colorful city parks. The bridges cast geometric patterns on Pittsburgh's three famous rivers (the Monongahela, Allegheny, and Ohio), and the skyline stretches from the awe-inspiring **Cathedral of Learning** to the **PPG Place,** a startling glass tower whose array of spires oddly imitates the cathedral's Gothic architecture.

Practical Information

Emergency: 911.

Visitor Information: Gateway Center, 4 Gateway Ctr. (281-7711), downtown, in a little glass building on Liberty Ave., across from the Hilton. Open May-Oct. Mon.-Fri. 9:30am-5pm, Sat.-Sun. 9:30am-3pm; Nov.-March 9:30am-5pm, Sat. 9:30am-3pm. **Greater Pittsburgh Chamber of Commerce,** 3 Gateway Ctr. (392-4500). Open Mon.-Fri. 9am-5pm. **Events Hotline,** 391-6840. 24 hours.

Travelers Aid: Two locations: Greyhound Bus Terminal, 11th St. and Liberty Ave. (281-5474), and the airport (264-7110). **Foreign Language Aid,** 624-7800.

Greater Pittsburgh International Airport: 778-2500, in Moon Township, 15 miles west of downtown by I-279 and Rte. 60. Serves most major airlines. **Airport Limousine Service** (471-2250). To downtown (Hilton Hotel or Westin William Penn) $8.

Amtrak: Liberty and Grant Ave. (621-4850 or 800-872-7245 for reservations; 471-8752 for information), on the northern edge of downtown, next to Greyhound and the post office. Station open 24 hours. Ticket office open 8:30am-1pm, 2-5:15pm, 10:30pm-3am, 4-7:15am. Safe and very clean inside, but be cautious about walking from here to central downtown at night. To: Philadelphia (2 per day, 7¼ hr., $57) and New York (2 per day, 9 hr., $79).

Greyhound/Trailways: 11th St. and Liberty Ave. (391-2300), on the northern outskirts of downtown. Station open 24 hours. Large and fairly clean with police on duty. Home of Joyce Warner, top Greyhound ticket agent. To: Philadelphia (7 hr., Mon.-Thurs. $40, Fri.-Sun. $44); New York (9 per day, 9-11 hr., Mon.-Thurs. $68, Fri.-Sun. $75); and Chicago (4 per day, 9-11 hr., Mon.-Thurs. $59, Fri.-Sun. $65).

Port Authority of Allegheny County (PAT): 231-5707. Operates city bus and fledgling 1¼-mile subway. Schedules and maps at most department stores and in the Community Interest Showcase section of the yellow pages. Base fare $1.

Taxi: Yellow Cab Company, 665-8100. **People's Cab Company,** 681-3131. **Diamond Cab,** 824-0984.

Car Rental: Rent-A-Wreck, 1200 Liberty Ave. (461-1409). $20 per day; insurance $6. Must be 21 with major credit card or a $150 cash deposit. **Alamo,** 930 Broadway Rd., airport area (800-327-9633). $31 per day. Extra $6.25 charge if under 25 and/or out-of-state. **Thrifty,** 1432 Beers School Rd. (264-1775), near airport or 3501 Forbes Ave. (682-5454), Oakland. $35 per day. 150 free miles. Must be 25 or over. **Budget,** 700 5th Ave. (261-3320), downtown; also at airport (262-1500). $39 per day Mon.-Thurs., $22 Fri.-Sun. Must be 21 or over.

Help Lines: General Help Line, 255-1155. 24 hours. **Rape Action Hotline,** 765-2731. 24 hours. **Center for Victims of Violent Crime,** 1520 Penn Ave. (392-8582). 24 hours. **Persad Center, Inc.,** 441-0857, emergencies 392-2472. A counseling service for the gay community.

Post Office: 7th and Grant St. (644-4570). Open Mon.-Fri. 7am-6pm, Sat. 7am-4:30pm. **ZIP code:** 15230.

Area Code: 412.

Pittsburgh lies in southwestern Pennsylvania on I-79, 386 miles from New York, 308 miles from Philadelphia, and 247 miles from Washington, DC. The downtown area is a triangle, formed by two rivers—the Allegheny on the north and the Monongahela to the south—coming together to form a third, the Ohio. Beginning at the Monongahela, streets parallel to it in the downtown area triangle are numbered 1 through 7.

Accommodations and Camping

Reasonable accommodations are easy to find in Pittsburgh. Downtown is fairly safe, even at night; Pittsburgh has the lowest crime rate for a city of its size in the country.

Point Park College Youth Hostel (AYH), 201 Wood St. (392-3824), 8 blocks from Greyhound/Trailways. Catch a bus on Liberty Ave. or walk 5 blocks downtown on Grant St., take a right on Forbes Ave., and walk 3 blocks until Wood St., then turn left and walk 2 blocks. Clean dorm singles with bath and a magnificent view. Check-in until 11pm. After 5pm ask security guard for the R.A. on duty. Members only, $7.50. Reservations recommended. Open Sept.-May.

St. Regis Residence for Women, 50 Congress St. (281-9888), in the red brick church directly opposite the Civic Arena on Wylie St. past the Chatham Center. A 10-min. walk from the bus terminal, but take a cab at night. A Catholic-run home for women working and studying in the Pittsburgh area. Singles $10. Give them a day's notice.

Red Roof Inn, 6404 Stubenville Pike on Rte. 60 (787-7870), east of the Rte. 22/Rte. 30 junction near the airport. From Greyhound, take bus #26E. Singles $30. Doubles $36.

The nearest campsite is the **Pittsburgh KOA,** R.D. #1, P.O. Box 280 A, Evans City 16033 (776-1150), 20 miles from downtown. Take I-79 to Mars exit. Facilities include tents and swimming. (Sites $15.) **Bethany Christian Campground,** R.D #1, P.O. Box 217, Washington 15301 (483-6235) is 20 miles south of Pittsburgh on I-79.

Food

In Pittsburgh's inner triangle, restaurants are elegant and expensive. Those in the South Side's **Station Square** are chic, while those in **Allegheny Square** to the north provide standard overpriced fast food of new urban malls. On the East Side, Walnut Street in Shadyside is where the golf club set "does" lunch, while Oakland is filled with collegiate watering holes. Many of Pittsburgh's ethnic groups have stayed in the pockets where they originally settled, giving each neighborhood its own distinctive cuisine.

Original Hot Dog Shops, Inc., 3901 Forbes Ave., Oakland (621-7388), at Bouquet St. A rowdy, greasy Pittsburgh institution with the best dogs in town. Call it "the O" and they'll think you're a native. Sells "thousands of pounds of fries" each week and has 50 different kinds of beer. Hot dogs start at $1.91. Open daily 9am-4:30am.

Star of India, 412 S. Craig St., Oakland (681-5700). Classic Indian cuisine in a no-frills setting. Vegetarian entrees available. Luncheon specials $6-7, dinners slightly more. Open Mon.-Sat. 11:30am-2:30pm and 5-10pm, Sun. 5-10pm.

Pace's Ice Creamery and Deli, 420 S. Craig St., Oakland (683-2780), at the intersection of Craig St. and Forbes Ave., across from the Carnegie Museum. Cafe-style indoor and outdoor seating. Sit and watch students and yuppies go by. Large gourmet salad $3.25, one scoop of ice cream $1.04, espresso 94¢. Open Sun.-Thurs. 11am-11pm, Fri.-Sat. 11am-midnight.

Anna's Place and Chang's Place, 410 1st Ave., downtown (261-4166), near Smithfield St. The 2 proprietors use the same address yet keep separate identities. Anna offers Korean, Japanese, and American cuisine, including some of the least expensive sushi around ($2-6 for 6 pieces). Chang serves standard oriental dishes. Sesame chicken with soup or salad $3.55. Open Mon.-Fri. 11am-3pm and 5-9pm, Sat. 5-9pm.

Suzie's Greek Specialties, 130 6th St., downtown (261-6443). Specializes in homemade Greek dishes, bread, and pastries ($6-8). Open Mon.-Fri. 11am-9pm, Sat. 4-11pm.

Alexander's Pasta Express, 5104 S. Liberty Ave., Bloomfield (687-8741 or 682-9824). Take bus #86A ("East Hills") to Liberty and S. Aiken Ave. An unpretentious and cozy Italian-American restaurant and bar. Great spinach and cheese ravioli with a meatball $5.50, New York Strip Steak $7. Open Mon.-Sat. 11am-12:30am, Sun. 11am-10:30pm.

Grand Slam Bar and Grill, 5520 Walnut St. (683-2582), in the Theater Mall. Take bus #71B or D down 5th Ave., get off at Aiken, and walk 2 blocks to Walnut. Calzones, subs, salads, and pizzas with a baseball theme. "Fowl Ball" chicken pizza $7. Nightly specials include 2-for-1 pizza on "Tequila Tuesday" and Wed. "Vodka and Wing" night. A good stop before going upstairs for jazz at the **Balcony** (see Nightlife below). Open Mon.-Thurs. 11:30am-10pm, Fri.-Sat. 11:30am-2am.

Georgetown Inn, 1230 Grandview Ave. (481-4424), at the top of the Duquesne Incline on Mt. Washington. Good fare and an amazing view. Dinners $6-8.

Sights

The **Golden Triangle,** formed by the **Allegheny** and **Monongahela River,** is home to **Point State Park** and its famous 200-foot fountain. The **Fort Pitt Blockhouse and Museum** (281-9285), in the park, is a relic from the French and Indian War. (Open Wed.-Sat. 9am-5pm, Sun. noon-5pm. Admission $1.50, seniors $1, children 50¢.) **PPG Place,** on Stanwix St., is a high-rise complex with glass towers pointed like church spires. (Open Mon.-Fri. 10am-6pm, Sat. 10am-5pm.) The square in front features a musical fountain. Check the outdoor message board for times of free performances, ranging from Scottish Brass Bands to jazz. About 3 miles east along the Blvd. of the Allies, in **Schenley Park,** the **Phipps Conservatory** (622-6914 or 622-6915) is 2½ acres of happiness for the flower fanatic. (Open June-Aug. Mon.-Fri. 9am-5pm, Sept.-May Mon.-Fri. 9am-5pm and 7-9pm. Admission $1.) The park is bounded by Edwardian homes. To the north are **Carnegie-Mellon University,** the **University of Pittsburgh,** and a collection of ethnic neighborhoods. The 42-story **Cathedral of Learning,** between Forbes and 5th Ave. (624-6000), dominates the city's diverse architecture.

Other city sights are across the three rivers from the Golden Triangle. Northward, across the Allegheny, steal a look at **Three Rivers Stadium,** where the Steelers and Pirates play. Visit the **Buhl Science Center** (237-3333), in **Allegheny Square,** where the special hands-on exhibits and sky shows are entertaining both for children and adults. (Open Sun.-Thurs. 1-5pm, Fri. 1-9:30pm, Sat. 10am-5pm. Admission $4, under 18 $2.) To the west of Allegheny Sq. is the tropical **Pittsburgh Aviary** (323-7234; open daily 9am-4:30pm; free. Take bus #16D or the Ft. Duquesne bridge.)

The **Pittsburgh Zoo** in Highland Park (441-6262; take bus #71A "Negley" or 71B "Highland") has a children's zoo, a reptile building, an aquarium, an Asian forest, and an African savanna. (Open Mon.-Fri. 9am-5pm, Sat.-Sun. 10am-5pm. Admission $3, children $1. Parking $1.)

To get to the **South Side,** take the Smithfield Street Bridge across the Monongahela River. The star attraction here is **Station Square,** a cleverly renovated railway terminal featuring shops and restaurants. Sharing the riverbank is the **Gateway Clipper Fleet** (355-7979), which offers narrated sight-seeing cruises on the three rivers. (Fare $3.75 and up.) Towering behind Station Sq. is **Mount Washington;** the **Duquesne** and **Monongahela Inclines** (trolleys) ascend the slope to an observation platform. (Open Mon.-Sat. 5:30am-12:45am, Sun. and holidays 8:45am-midnight. Fare 75¢.)

Two of America's greatest financial legends, Andrew Carnegie and Henry Clay Frick, made their fortunes in Pittsburgh. Their bequests to the city have greatly enriched its cultural scene. The most spectacular of Carnegie's gifts are the art and natural history museums, together called **The Carnegie** at 4400 Forbes Ave. (622-

3131; take any bus to Oakland and get off at the Cathedral of Learning.) The natural history section is famous for its 500 dinosaur specimens. The art museum's modern extension houses a collection strong in impressionist, post-impressionist, and 20th-century works. Every three years, The Carnegie hosts "The International," one of the country's oldest recurring contemporary art exhibits. (Open Tues.-Sat. 10am-5pm, Sun. 1-5pm.)

While Henry Clay Frick is best known for his art collection in New York, his early acquisitions are displayed at the **Frick Art Museum,** 7227 Reynolds St., Point Breeze (371-0600). The permanent collection contains Italian, Flemish, and French works from the 13th through 18th centuries. (Open Wed.-Sat. 10am-5:30pm, Sun. noon-6pm. Free. Take bus #67A, F, E, C, or 71C.) **Clayton,** the Frick family mansion next door, is scheduled to open in the fall of 1990.

Entertainment and Nightlife

A happy result of Pittsburgh's metamorphosis from industrial to corporate town is the revitalization of its artistic life. The internationally acclaimed **Pittsburgh Symphony Orchestra** (392-4821) performs October through May at **Heinz Hall,** 600 Penn Ave., downtown, but has free summer evening outdoor concerts at Point State Park. The **Pittsburgh Public Theater** is widely renowned, but visitors with thin wallets should check out the **Three Rivers Shakespeare Festival** (624-4101), at University of Pittsburgh's Steven Foster Memorial Theater, near Forbes Ave. and Bigelow Blvd., downtown. (Tickets Tues.-Thurs. $14.50, Fri.-Sat. $18.) The **Three Rivers Arts Festival** (687-7614) is held during three weeks in June, in Gateway Center, Point State Park, Allegheny Courthouse, and Station Square. Exhibitions and demonstrations of painting, sculpture, and crafts, and live performances of plays and music are all free.

You can wet your whistle or flex your dancing muscles at one of Pittsburgh's many nightspots. **Peter's Pub,** 116 Oakland Ave. (692-9288), is a raucous hangout frequented by U. Pitt's athletic teams. Also near the university is **C.J. Barney's Wooden Key,** 3907 Forbes Ave. (621-2149), absolutely jammed on Thursday, when $3 buys all-you-can-drink from 9pm to midnight. (Open Mon.-Sat. 11am-2am.) The jazz scene is very much alive in Pittsburgh. Hear it nightly at Shadyside's **Balcony,** Theater Mall, 5520 Walnut St. (687-0110). (Open Wed.-Thurs. until midnight, Fri.-Sat. until 1am. No cover. Take bus #71B or D down 5th Ave. to Aiken and walk to Walnut St.) Or, if you don't mind the distance, head to the **James Street Tavern,** 422 Foreland Ave., North Side (323-2222). The restaurant upstairs is pricey, but after 8pm, especially on Thursdays, the jazz downstairs is simply amazing. (No cover.)

Virginia

Every state has its point of pride: Virginia's is its history. Virginia played an important role in colonial times with the settlements of Jamestown and Williamsburg. Along with Massachusetts, it led the revolt against England, and it was here at Yorktown that the British finally surrendered. Virginia has also been important to the U.S. in another way; nicknamed the "Mother of the Presidency," Virginia is the birthplace of eight U.S. presidents, including the first, George Washington. These "patriotic" contributions cohabit uneasily with Virginia's ambiguous role in the Civil War. The centerpiece of the Confederacy, Virginia supplied the most soldiers and money and suffered the greatest damage. Today, the War has not been forgotten as plaques, shrines, and statues commemorating the heroes and battles crowd the landscape. A remarkable number of streets are named after Jefferson Davis and Robert E. Lee.

Despite its nostalgia for the past, Virginia has integrated itself well into the present, and it has much to offer the visitor. Richmond, the capital, is a thriving, exciting city, while northern Virginia is enjoying an economic boom. The Blue Ridge Mountains to the west offer spectacular views—especially in fall—as well as hiking, camping, and canoeing. Charlottesville, home to the University of Virginia, offers an intellectual atmosphere and a strong taste of the south's famed gentility. And for fun and sun, Virginia Beach to the east can't be beaten.

Practical Information

Capital: Richmond.

Tourist Information: Virginia Division of Tourism, Bell Tower, Capitol Sq., 101 N. 9th St., Richmond 23219 (800-847-4882 or 786-4484). **Division of State Parks,** 1201 State Office Bldg., Richmond 23219 (226-1981). For the free **Virginia Accommodations Directory,** write to Virginia Travel Council, 7415 Brook Rd., P.O. Box 15067, Richmond, VA 23227.

Time Zone: Eastern. **Postal Abbreviation:** VA.

Shenandoah National Park

Before 1926 when Congress authorized the establishment of Shenandoah National Park, the area was a series of rocky, threadbare farms along the Blue Ridge Mountains. Thirteen years later, the farmers and their families had been booted off their lands and the area was left to return to its "natural" state. Fields were replaced by forests, cows and pigs by wild deer and bears, and rugged dirt roads by an ultra-modern highway, Skyline Drive.

As a result, today Shenandoah National Park is an extremely scenic place. In summer, the cool mountain air offers a respite from the region's usual heat and humidity. Go early in June to see mountain laurel blooming in the highlands. In the fall vast numbers of tourists drive through to look at the magnificent fall foliage.

Practical Information

Emergency (in park): 999-2227, or contact the nearest ranger. Collect calls accepted.

Park Information: 999-2266 (daily 9am-5pm); recorded message 999-2229. Mailing address: Superintendent, Shenandoah National Park, Luray, VA 22835.

Visitor Information: Dickey Ridge Visitors Center (mile 4.6; 635-3566), closest to the north entrance. Offers daily interpretative programs. Open April-Oct. 9am-5pm. **Byrd Visitors Center** (mile 50; 999-2243, ext. 281), in the center of the park. Has a movie and museum explaining the history of the Blue Ridge Range and the culture of its mountain folk. Open 9am-5pm. Both stations also offer changing exhibits on the park, free pamphlets detailing short hikes, daily posted weather updates, and ranger-led nature hikes.

Area Code: 703.

From its northern entrance at Front Royal to Rockfish Gap, 105 miles further south and just 25 miles west of Charlottesville, **Skyline Drive** (entrance $5 per vehicle; $2 per hiker, biker, or bus passenger (pass good for 7 days); seniors and disabled free) hugs the spine of the Blue Ridge, and winds through Shenandoah National Park. The posted speed limit is 35 m.p.h., which gets tedious. The drive is closed immediately following periods of bad weather. Most of the facilities hibernate from November through March.

Miles along Skyline Dr. are measured north to south, beginning at Front Royal. There is no public transportation. Within the park, hitching opportunities are rare; outside the park, it's illegal.

If you plan to stay more than a day, purchase the *Park Guide* ($1), a booklet containing all the park regulations, trail lists, and a description of the area's geological history. The *Guide to Skyline Drive* ($4.50) is also packed with information on accommodations and activities. Both books are available at the visitors centers.

Accommodations and Camping

The park maintains rustic cabins with hot showers, outdoor grills, and picnic facilities, as well as more expensive motels at: **Skyland** (mile 42; 999-2211; March-Sept. cabins $32-62 double occupancy, motel rooms $64 for 2 people, $5 each additional person; in Oct. cabins $37-67, motel rooms $65-67. While the cabins are relatively sparse, the motel rooms are quaint and comfortable. The ones with views cost more); **Big Meadows** (mile 51; 999-2221; mid-May to Sept. cabins $53-55 double occupancy, motel rooms $64 for 2 people, $5 each additional person; in Oct. cabins $58-60, motel rooms $68. Rooms are the same as at Skyland.); and **Lewis Mountain** (mile 58; 999-2255; mid-May to Sept. Cabins $47, in Oct. cabins $48.). Reservations are usually necessary for all these accommodations, up to six months in advance for the fall season. Call the lodges or write **ARA Virginia Sky-Line,** P.O. Box 727, Luray 22835. All the lodges and cabins close from November through March. For cheaper accommodations, stay in Front Royal, right at the gateway to the park. A particularly good bargain is the **Cool Harbor Motel,** 15th and Shenandoah Ave. (635-4114). Cable TV, swimming pool. (All rooms $32.)

The park service also maintains four major campgrounds: **Matthews Arm** (mile 22); **Big Meadows** (mile 51); **Lewis Mountain** (mile 58); and **Loft Mountain** (mile 80). All have stores, laundry facilities, and showers (no hookups). Big Meadows (992-2221) is one of the larger sites and offers a wide range of activities such as films and hikes; it is especially popular and reservations are required (visit your local Ticketron outlet or write: Ticketron, Dept. R., 401 Hackensack Ave., Hackensack, NJ 07601). The others are on a first come-first serve basis. Lewis Mountain is probably the nicest for tenters. All cost $8 except Big Meadows ($10).

Hikers on the **Appalachian Trail** can make use of primitive open shelters, the three-sided structures with stone fireplaces that are strewn along the trail at approximately 7-mile intervals. Even if a shelter is full, campers will often move over to make room for a new arrival. You can also camp in the open anywhere along the trail, as long as you are out of sight of the trail itself and 25 yards from a water supply. Free camping permits (required) can be obtained from the ranger station at any entrance to the park, the vistors centers, or Park Headquarters (halfway between Thornton Gap and Luray on U.S. 211). The **Potomac Appalachian Trail Club** maintains seven primitive cabins along the trail ($1), and six cabins in backcountry areas of the park. You must reserve in advance by writing to the club at 1718 N St. NW, Washington, DC 20036 (202-638-5306).

Sights and Activities

Shenandoah is criss-crossed by trails. The **Appalachian Trail** runs the park's length. When your feet will take you no farther, saddle up a horse at the **stables** about a mile south of Skyland (mile 42.6; reservations at Skyland Lodge, 999-2211; $11 per hr.). Horse trails are marked with a yellow blaze.

One of the most strenuous hiking trails goes up **Old Rag Mountain** at mile 45. The 3-mile hike takes you through a tunnel and narrow splits in the rock where you must remove your pack to squirm through. (It's wise to bring a friend along. A thin one, though.) The stupendous view from the rocky summit makes every step of the hike worthwhile. This area, called **Whiteoak Canyon,** contains six spectacular waterfalls. The 5-mile trail connecting these falls leads to **Limberlost,** a virgin hemlock forest. Trout fishing is excellent in the rushing waters of **Whiteoak Canyon.** Try to come in the spring when the water is at its fullest and there are still relatively few campers.For an easier hike try the **Dark Hollow Trail** at mile 51. This 7-mile hike takes you to a gorgeous set of falls—the closest falls to Skyline Drive in the entire park.

Drivers will enjoy **Mary's Rock Tunnel** (mile 32), where the road goes straight through almost 700 feet of solid rock. One mile farther north is **Thornton Gap** and a magnificent panorama. From the Matthews Arm campground (mile 22), you can hike up Hogback Mountain or stick to the road and view the twisting Shenandoah River from the **Hogback Overlook** (mile 21).

Take a break from hiking or driving at one of Shenandoah's seven **picnic areas** located at Dickey Ridge (mile 5), Elkwallow (mile 24), Pinnacles (mile 37), Big Meadows (mile 51), Lewis Mountain (mile 58), South River (mile 63), and Loft Mountain (mile 80). All have tables, fireplaces, water fountains, and comfort stations. If you forget to pack a picnic basket, swing by the **Panorama Restaurant** (mile 31.5) for a meal with a view. (Sandwiches $2-4. Dinner $4-12. Open April-Nov. daily 9am-7pm.) The dining rooms at Skyland Lodge (mile 42) and Big Meadows Lodge (mile 51) also welcome hungry visitors.

Blue Ridge Parkway

If you don't believe that the best things in life are free, this could change your mind. The 469 miles of the Blue Ridge Parkway run through Virginia and North Carolina connecting the **Shenandoah** and **Great Smoky Mountains National Parks.** (See Tennessee chapter.) Administered by the National Park Service, the parkway adjoins hiking trails, campsites and picnic grounds. It is every bit as scenic as Skyline Drive, but much wilder and less crowded. From Shenandoah National Park, the parkway winds through Virginia's **George Washington National Forest** from Waynesboro southwest to Roanoke. The forest offers spacious campgrounds, canoes for rent, and swimming in cold, clear mountain water at **Shenandoah Lake** (mile 16).

Self-guided nature trails range from the **Mountain Farm Trail** (mile 5.9), a 20-minute hike to a pleasant reconstructed homestead, to the **Hardwood Cove Natural Trail** (mile 167), a three-hour excursion. Of course, real devotees tackle the **Appalachian Trail,** which runs the length of the parkway. The Park Service hosts a variety of ranger-led interpretive activities.

Some of the more spectacular sights on and near the parkway include a 215-foot-high, 90-foot-long limestone arch called **Natural Bridge.** It now supports an unnatural highway and hosts unnatural nightly music, sound, and light shows (800-533-1410, 800-336-5727 outside VA; open daily 7am-dusk; admission $4, children $2). The arch was once owned by Thomas Jefferson, who bought the site from King George III for 20 shillings; it was also initialed by George Washington. These initials are still visible today. At **Mabry Mill** (mile 176.1), and **Humpback Rocks** (mile 5.8), you can see what pioneer life was like, and at **Crabtree Meadows** (mile 339), you can purchase local crafts.

For general information on the parkway, call **visitor information** in North Carolina (704-298-3202 or 704-259-0701). For more information, call the park service in Roanoke, VA (703-937-6458 or 703-937-6213), or in Montebello, VA (703-377-2377). There are ten **visitors centers** along the parkway, plus seven stands where you can pick up brochures. Located at entry points where major highways intersect the Blue Ridge, the centers offer various exhibits, programs, and information facilities. Pick up a free copy of the helpful *Milepost* guide.

There are nine **campgrounds** along the parkway, each with water and restrooms, located at miles 61, 86, 120, 169, 241, 297, 316, 339, and 409. The fee is $6; reservations are not accepted. Contact the parkway for information on backcountry and winter camping. Camping in the backcountry of the George Washington National Forest is free.

The cities and villages along the parkway offer a range of accommodations. For a complete listing, pick up a *Blue Ridge Parkway Directory* at one of the visitors centers, or the *Virginia Accommodations Directory.* The communities listed have easy access to the parkway and many, such as **Asheville** and **Boone,** NC, and **Charlottesville,** VA, have historic and cultural attractions of their own.

Greyhound/Trailways provides access to the major towns around the Blue Ridge. Buses run to and from Richmond, Roanoke, Waynesboro, and Lexington; a bus serves Buchanan and Natural Bridge between Roanoke and Lexington once per day. For information, contact the station in Charlottesville (see Charlottesville Practical

Information) or in Roanoke: **Greyhound/Trailways,** 26 Salem Ave. SW (703-342-6761; open 24 hours).

In case of an **emergency,** call 703-982-6491 in VA; 704-259-0701 or 704-298-9612 in NC, evenings and weekends 704-298-0453. Be sure to give your location to the nearest mile.

Charlottesville

Never say "Thomas" Jefferson here. This genteel college town, set in the foothills of the Blue Ridge Mountains, cherishes a special relationship with the third U.S. President—their own Mr. Jefferson. The President's lofty home, Monticello, and prototype university, the University of Virginia, are lasting architectural monuments to his many accomplishments. As can be expected from a college town, there are lots of bookstores to browse in as well as countless cheap eateries.

Practical Information

Emergency: 911.

Visitor Information: Chamber of Commerce, 415 E. Market St. (295-3141), within walking distance of Amtrak, Greyhound/Trailways, and historic downtown. Open Mon.-Fri. 9am-5pm. **Thomas Jefferson Visitors Bureau,** Rte. 20 near I-64 (293-6789 or 977-1783). Take bus #8 ("Piedmont Community College") from 5th and Market St. Same information as chamber of commerce, plus state-wide brochures. Staff makes lodging inquiries and reservations. Free museum on Monticello and the Jefferson family. Good place to hitch a ride to Monticello, Ash Lawn, and Michie Tavern. Open daily 9am-5pm. **University of Virginia,** at the rotunda in the center of campus (924-1019). There is a larger University visitors center off U.S. 250 west—follow the signs (924-7116). Here there are a wide selections of campus maps, transit schedules, entertainment guides, and hints on budget accommodations. Open daily 9am-4:45pm.

Amtrak: 810 W. Main St. (800-872-7245 or 296-4559). To: Washington, DC ($20.50) and New York ($76).Open daily 5:30am-9pm.

Greyhound/Trailways: 310 W. Main St. (295-5131), within walking distance of historic downtown. To: Richmond ($9.65), Virginia Beach ($31), Washington, DC ($18.50), Norfolk ($24.70), and Lynchburg ($12). Open daily 6am-midnight.

Charlottesville Transit Service: 296-7433. Bus service within city limits, including most hotels and UVA campus locations. Buses operate Mon.-Sat. 6:20am-7pm. Maps available at both information centers, City Hall, and the UVA student center. Fare 60¢, seniors and disabled 30¢, 5 and under free.

Yellow Cab: 295-4131. To Monticello approximately $10.

Post Office: Main office, 1155 Seminole Trail (Rte. 29). Open Mon.-Fri. 8am-5:30pm, Sat. 8am-2pm. **ZIP code:** 22906.

Area Code: 804.

Charlottesville rests in a delta formed by Rte. 29, Rte. 250, and I-64. It is a city with two downtowns: one on the west side near the university, and "Historic Downtown" about a mile east. The two are connected by **University Avenue,** running east-west, which becomes **Main Street.** Hitchhiking within town is fairly easy.

Accommodations, Camping, and Food

Reasonably priced accommodations are concentrated near the university and at the junction of Rte. 29 north and the Rte. 250 bypass, also known as the Barracks Road area. **Guest House Bed and Breakfast** (979-7264; open noon-5pm) arranges rooms from $45 for a double. Because of the proximity of the Blue Ridge Mountains, camping facilities are readily available. For clean, standard motel rooms with TV, take bus #2 or 7 from the bus station or downtown to the **University Lodge,** 140 Emmet St. (295-5141. Singles $32. Doubles $37. Each additional person $5.)

For slightly more upscale accommodations and a swimming pool, try the **Econo Lodge,** 400 Emmet St. (296-2104. Singles $33. Doubles $38.) Above Chancellor's Drug Store near the campus, **Chancellor Apartments,** 1413½ University Ave. (295-5457), offers old but comfortable quarters. (11pm curfew. No alcohol. Shared baths; sink in each room. Singles $12. Doubles $15. Each additional person $2. Call ahead.) You can camp close to town at **Lake Reynovia,** 1770 Avon St. (296-1910). Take bus #3 to Avon St. at Altavista; from there it's a 1½-mile hike or hitch. Sites are spread around the lake. (Sites $12. Hookups $2. $1 per person over 2 people.)

You'll find good Southern cooking in Charlottesville's unpretentious diners and family restaurants. **City Market,** 4th St. SW, at Carver Recreation Center (971-3260), sells local produce, other foods, and homemade crafts. (Open mid-April through Oct. Sat. 7am-noon; June-July Tues. 7am-11am and Sat. 7am-noon.) For a homemade meal in a fun 50s atmosphere, complete with aqua-tiled walls and a rocking jukebox, pop into the **Blue Moon Diner,** 512 W. Main St. (293-3408), 2 blocks from the bus station. The great staff, large portions, and low prices will keep you smiling. (Breakfast anytime, omelettes, sandwiches, and burgers $1-4. Open Mon.-Fri. 7am-10pm, Sat.-Sun. 8am-4pm.) For a light, heathful meal, try the **Garden Gourmet,** 811 W. Main St. (295-9991), an all-natural eatery with international gourmet and vegetarian fare. You can't go wrong with the fresh salads (homemade dressing) or tofu sub ($2-4). They play live folk, jazz, and rock music at dinner (6-10pm). (Open Mon.-Thurs. 11:30am-2:30pm and 5:30-9:30pm, Fri. 11:30am-2:30pm and 5:30-10pm, Sat. noon-3pm and 5:30-10pm.) Closer to the university, try **Armands Chicago Pizzeria,** 1517 University Ave. (971-5533). Their deep-dish pizza is as good as it gets. Try their daily $4.49 all-you-can-eat pizza/salad lunch special. A large pizza costs about $11. The ambiance is upscale collegiate. (Open Sun.-Thurs. 11:30am-10:30pm, Fri.-Sat. 11:30am-closing.)

Sights and Entertainment

Monticello, on Rte. 53 (295-8181 or 295-2657), is the house that took Mr. Jefferson 40 years to design and build. From the classical lines of the famous dome to the manicured lawns and gardens, it's a place of beauty; from the automatic doors to the dumbwaiter, it's both an ingenious and functional structure. (Open March-Oct. daily 8am-5pm; Nov.-Feb. 9am-4:30pm. Admission $7, seniors $6, ages 6-11 $2.) A ½-mile away on Rte. 53, historic **Michie Tavern** (977-1234) still offers hospitality to travelers after 200 years. As one of Virginia's oldest remaining homesteads, the Tavern offers a glimpse of 18th-century social life, a general store, and an operating grist mill. Experience colonial cuisine in "The Ordinary," a converted slave house. (Lunch buffet $7.65, ages 6-11 $2.75. Open daily 11:30am-3pm. Tavern-museum open daily 9am-5pm. Admission $4, ages 6-11 $1. Admission $2 if you eat lunch at The Ordinary.)

Mr. Jefferson's "academical village" has become the gorgeous **University of Virginia,** rated in 1976 as "*the* outstanding achievement" of American architecture since 1776. The **Rotunda** (924-0311) was inspired by the Roman Pantheon. (Open daily 9am-4:45pm. Free tours from the Rotunda daily at 10am, 11am, 2pm, 3pm, and 4pm.) Stop by the **Fayerweather Gallery,** on Rugby St. to look at displays of student art. A few hundred feet on is the University **Bayly Art Museum,** also on Rugby Rd. A permanent display of small masterpieces from the Renaissance and 19th and 20th centuries, as well as a good collection of colonial art and constantly changing exhibitions. (Free. Open Tues.-Sun. 1-5pm.)

Today the university catches most of the limelight, but in colonial times the downtown area was the center of action. Now known as **Historic Downtown,** it includes **Court Square,** the original commercial center, and **Swan Tavern** (now the Red Land Club; 296-6442), where early legislators gathered. Stop by the **Albermarle County Historical Society Museum** and pick up the *Guide to Historic Downtown Charlottesville,* a self-guided, walking tour of the city. And don't forget to glance at their exhibitions on local history. (All city buses go to historic downtown.) The wine connoisseur might fancy a visit to **Oakencraft Vineyard and Winery,** Rte. 5

(298-4188). This is one of many wineries that dot the region. It offers free tours and wine tastings. (Open daily April-Dec. 11am-4pm.)

Charlottesville loves blues, rock and roll, and all combinations thereof. Bars open their doors around 8pm, and all close at 2am. The **Virginian,** 1521 University Ave. (293-2606), has been a university tradition since the 20s. The **Blue Ridge Restaurant and Brewing Co.,** 709 W. Main St. (977-0017), across from the Amtrak station, has its own brewery right next door. The **Court Square Tavern,** 500 Court Sq. (296-6111), lets you drink your way around the world, with over 100 imported beers. **Ash Lawn,** on Rte. 6 (293-9539; open March.-Oct. daily 9am-6pm; Nov.-Feb. 10am-5pm), is the 19th-century plantation home of President James Monroe. It hosts a **Summer Music Festival** (box office 293-8000, open daily noon-6:30pm), featuring comic opera from mid-June to mid-August. (Tickets $10, seniors $9, students $7.) Also check the offerings of the **Heritage Theatre** (924-3376) for their summer festival of plays. (Tickets $7, available 10am-6pm at the box office at Culberth Theatre on the university campus. Performances June-Aug. Mon.-Sat. at 8pm.)

Richmond

The former capital of the Confederacy, Richmond was almost completely destroyed by fire in 1865 during the last days of the Civil War. Now, after extensive restoration, it has regained its antebellum charm, with a modern flair. Capital of Virginia, it is the social and economic hub of the state.

Practical Information

Emergency: 911.

Visitor Information: Richmond Visitors Center, 1700 Robin Hood Rd. (358-5511), exit 14 off I-95/64, in a converted grain depot. Shows a helpful 6-min. video of the city's various attractions. Can reserve accommodations, as well as arrange walking tours and provide quality maps. (Open Memorial Day-Labor Day daily 9am-7pm, Labor Day-Memorial Day 9am-5pm.) Also located inside the 6th St. Marketplace (788-6829; open Mon.-Fri. 10am-3pm, Sat. 10am-8pm, Sun. noon-6pm). The state of Virginia operates their own visitors center in the Bell Tower, 101 N. 9th St. (786-4484), near the State Capitol. (Open Mon.-Fri. 8:15am-5pm, Sat.-Sun. 9:30am-4:30pm.)

Amtrak: 7519 Staple Mills Rd. (264-9194 or 800-872-7245), miles out of town. Taxi fare to downtown $12. Station open daily 8am-7pm.

Greyhound/Trailways: 2910 N. Boulevard (353-8903). Take bus #24 to the visitors center. To: Washington, DC ($16.70), Charlottesville ($9.65), and Charleston, WV ($68). Open 24 hours.

Greater Richmond Transit Co: 101 S. Davis St. (358-4782). Maps available in the basement of city hall, 900 E. Broad St., and are reproduced in the Yellow Pages. Fare 75¢, exact change. Transfers available. There are also trolleys which serve downtown and various historic sights. Fare 25¢.

Post Office: 1801 Brook Rd. (775-6292). Take bus #22 or 37. Open Mon.-Fri. 8:30am-6pm. **ZIP code:** 23232. **Area code:** 804.

Accommodations and Camping

Budget motels around Richmond are scarce. There is **Motel 6,** 5704 Williamsburg Rd., Sandston (222-7600), about 6 miles east on Rte. 60, across from the airport. The rooms are spare but clean. (Singles $25.51. Doubles $28.70. Take the "Seven Pines" bus.) Three miles from the center of town, the **Executive Inn,** 5215 W. Broad St. (288-4011), offers grand (by motel standards) but slightly faded rooms. Pool. (Singles $32. Doubles $35. Breakfast included.) Nearer town, the **Massad House Hotel,** 11 N. 4th St. (648-2893), 4 blocks from the Capitol, has charming and comfortable rooms. (Singles $29. Doubles $36.) Across the river in the south side of Richmond, try the **Cloverleaf Inn,** 5456 Midlothian Turnpike (231-6281), accessible by bus #63. (Singles $25. Doubles $30.) Most of Richmond's **B&Bs** are converted mansions lining Monument Ave. (rooms $45-70). Call Lyn M. Benson at **Bensonhouse of Richmond** (648-7560 or 780-1522; 10am-6pm), or **Abbey Hill Bed and Breakfast** (353-4656 or 355-5855) for more information.

The closest campground is at **Pocahontas State Park,** 10300 Beach Rd. (796-4255), about 15 miles southwest on Rte. 10 and Rte. 655. It offers showers, biking, lakes, and huge pool (Pool $1.75, ages 3-12 $1.25. No hookups. Sites $7.) Reserve a site by phone through Ticketron (499-0853; Virginia Beach office open April-Nov.).

Food

Richmond offers a variety of good cheap eats as well as more upscale restaurants in areas such as the restored **Shockoe Slip Historic District** (Main, Canal, and Cary St. between 10th and 14th St.) and in the diverse community called **The Fan** (bordered by Monument Ave., Main St., Laurel St., and Boulevard). In the Fan, try **Joe's Inn,** 205 N. Shields Ave. (355-2282), which serves huge portions of spaghetti in a casual setting. (Lunch $2-3, dinner $7-8. Open daily 9am-2am.) The **Texas-Wisconsin Border Cafe,** 1501 W. Main St. (355-2907), features chili, potato pancakes, and *chalupas.* Stuffed wild game stare at you from the walls. (Lunch $2-5. Open daily 11am-2am.)

Closer to the Capitol, **Gus' Corner Restaurant,** 100 N. 8th St. (788-1484), is a sandwich shop popular with Virginia politicians. Try the Lebanese marinated beef served in a pita with onions and 12 seasonings ($3.75). (Open Mon.-Fri. 7am-7pm.) Down the street from the Greyhound Terminal and visitors center is the original **Bill's Barbecue,** 3100 N. Boulevard (355-9745). Chow down on a beef barbecue sandwich ($1.79). This is glorified fast food, but it's cheap. (Open Mon.-Thurs. 7am-11pm, Fri.-Sat. 7am-midnight, Sun. 10am-11pm.)

In the Shockoe Slip district, try the **Peking Pavilion,** 1302 E. Cary St. (649-8888). Excellent service, elegant decor, and gourmet Chinese food are all yours for a very reasonable price. Their *Kung Pao* chicken is particularly noteworthy. Dinners $7-10. (Open Sun.-Fri. 10:30am-2:30pm and 5-10:30pm, Sat. 10:30am-2:30pm and 5pm-midnight.)

Sights

Ever since Patrick Henry declared "Give me liberty or give me death" in Richmond's **St. John's Church,** 2401 E. Broad St. (648-5015), the river city has been quoting, memorializing, and bronzing its historical heroes. (Church open Mon.-Sat. 10am-3:30pm, Sun. 1-3:30pm. Sundays at 2pm an actor recreates the famous 1775 speech, given when the church served as the site of a Revolutionary Convention.) Larger-than-life statues of George Washington, Thomas Jefferson, and other revolutionaries grace the **State Capitol** grounds (786-4344). The building was designed by Jefferson and is a masterpiece of neo-classical architecture, as well as home to the oldest legislative body in the Western hemisphere. Inside the building, look for the statues of the eight presidents and Jefferson Davis, all born in Virginia. Attendants arrange free tours. (Open daily 9am-5pm.) For more sculpture, follow Franklin Ave. from the Capitol until it becomes **Monument Avenue,** which is lined with trees, gracious old houses, and towering statues of Confederate heroes. Note how Robert E. Lee, who survived the War, faces towards his beloved South, and Stonewall Jackson, who didn't, glares recriminantly to the North.

Other reminders of the past can be found in the world's largest collection of Civil War artifacts at the **Confederate Museum and White House of the Confederacy,** 1201 E. Clay St. (649-1861; open Mon.-Sat. 10am-5pm, Sun. 1-5pm. Admission $3, seniors $2.50, ages 7-12 $1.25; both museum and house $5, seniors $4.50, ages 7-12 $2.) Historic homes and plantations are plentiful in the Richmond area. Built in 1790, the **John Marshall House,** 818 E. Marshall St. (648-7998), home of the deeply influential Chief Justice, has been restored with authentic period and Marshall family furnishings. (Open Tues.-Sat. 10am-5pm, Sun. 1-5pm. Admission $3.) Nearby is the **Valentine Museum,** 1015 E. Clay St. (649-0711). Changing exhibits trace the life and history of Richmond, and there is also a large collection of period costumes. (Open Mon.-Sat. 10am-5pm, Sun. noon-5pm. Admission $3.50, seniors $3, ages 7-12 $1.50.) Combination ticket to the Confederate Museum and White House of the Confederacy, John Marshall House, and Valentine Museum (all within easy walking distance of each other) are $4, seniors $3, ages 7-12 $2.

The **Hollywood Cemetery** (648-8501), at the south end of Laurel St., is the final resting-place of U.S. Presidents Monroe and Tyler, 18,000 Confederate soldiers, and the Confederate president, Jefferson Davis. (Take bus #11; enter at Albemarle and Cherry St. Open daily 8am-6pm.)

Virginia's capital does have a few sights unadorned by bronze plaques, battle dates, or bird droppings. The Southeast's largest art museum, the **Virginia Museum of Fine Arts,** Grove Ave. and North Blvd. (367-0844), downtown, has an outstanding art nouveau gallery, a gorgeous collection (the largest outside the USSR) of Fabergé jewelry and Easter eggs made for the Russian Czars, and a fine showing of impressionist and contemporary art. (Open Tues.-Wed. and Fri.-Sat. 11am-5pm, Thurs. 11am-10pm, Sun. 1-5pm.) The **Maggie L. Walker National Historic Site,** 110-A E. Leigh St. (780-1380 or 226-1981), commemorates the life of an ex-slave's gifted daughter. Physically handicapped, Maggie Walker advocated black women's rights and succeeded as founder and president of a bank. (Park rangers conduct house tours Thurs.-Sun. 9am-5pm. Free.)

Stop by **Maymont House and Park,** 1700 Hampton St. (house 358-9756, park 358-7166), to wander through the opulent Dooley mansion, and the variegated grounds. Check the current edition of *Style Weekly* magazine (free), available at the visitors center and stands around town, to see what free entertainment is being staged in **Dogwood Dell,** an outdoor theater below the **Carillon World War I Memorial,** also on the 100-acre Maymont grounds. (Grounds open daily 10am-7pm, Nov.-March 10am-5pm. House tours Tues.-Sat. 10am-4:30pm, Sun. noon-4:30pm. Donation required.)

The **Science Museum of Virginia,** 2500 W. Broad St. (367-0000 or 367-1013), has hands-on exhibits, a cosmic laser planetarium show, and an Imax film projector. It's located in a grand, now-defunct train station. (Open Mon.-Fri. 9:30am-8pm, Sat.-Sun. 11:30am-8pm. Admission $3, seniors and ages 4-17 $2.50. Call 367-8277 for planetarium show times.)

East of the capitol, follow your tell-tale heart to the **Edgar Allan Poe Museum,** 1914-16 E. Main St. (648-5523). Poe first gained national recognition working on the staff of Richmond's *Southern Literary Messenger,* and spent more time here than any other city; he was raised and married here, though you'll find him in town never more. The building is stuffed with Poe memorabilia and is the oldest stone building in Richmond. (Open Tues.-Sat. 10am-4pm, Sun.-Mon. 1:30-4pm. Admission $3, students $1.)

Take in a panoramic view of Richmond's eclectic mix of historic and modern buildings from either the top floor **City Hall Skydeck,** 9th and Broad St. (open Mon.-Fri. 8am-5pm), or **Church Hill,** a 19th-century neighborhood with St. John's Church at its center.

Civil War buffs should pay a visit to the outskirts of Richmond to the **Richmond National Battlefield Park,** 3215 E. Broad St. (225-1981). The visitors center has extensive exhibits on the Civil War, as well as maps detailing the battlefields and fortifications surrounding the city. (Open daily 9am-5pm. Free.)

Williamsburg, Yorktown, and Jamestown

Williamsburg, Yorktown, and Jamestown are pleasant towns that feed tourists history with a wee spoonful of sugar. Williamsburg, for example, a former colonial capital, claims to be a faithfully restored version of its 18th century self, right down to costumed actors. But don't look for dirt roads, open sewers, or slaves. Cynicism aside, the towns are beautiful and quite interesting historically if you overlook the hokum.

The **Colonial Parkway,** which connects Williamsburg, Jamestown, and Yorktown, does not support commercial enterprise and thus also helps to preserve an unspoiled atmosphere. Travelers should visit in late fall or early spring to avoid the crowds, temperature, and humidity in summer. The visitor should also be aware that all the signs pointing to Colonial Williamsburg do not actually get one there, but to the visitor center instead. To drive to the restored area proper, take the Lafayette St. exit off the Colonial Pkwy. Parking is surprisingly easy to find.

Practical Information

Emergency: 911.

Visitor Information: Williamsburg Area Tourism and Conference Bureau, 201 Penniman Rd. (253-0192), about ½ mile northwest of the transportation center. Ask for the free *Visitors Guide to Virginia's Historic Triangle.* Open Mon.-Fri. 8:30am-5pm. **Tourist Visitor Center,** Rte. 132-132y, Williamsburg (229-1000, ext. 7645), about a mile northeast of the train station. Tickets and transportation to Colonial Williamsburg. Basic admission ticket to bus service and your choice of 12 buildings $17, ages 6-12 $9. The "Royal Governor's Pass" provides admission for up to 4 consecutive days ($21, children $10.75). A "Patriot's Pass" provides unlimited admission to all colonial Williamsburg properties for up to 1 year ($25, children $12.50). Open Feb.-Dec. daily 8:30am-8pm; Jan. 9am-5pm. **Yorktown Visitors Center,** at the end of Colonial Parkway (898-3400). National Park Service information center for Yorktown Battlefield. Open June 19-Labor Day daily 9am-6:30pm; Labor Day-June 18 8:30am-5pm. **Jamestown National Park Visitors Center** (229-1733), the 2nd stop after you enter Jamestown Island. Has a 15-min. orientation film and a museum. Open daily 8:30am-7:30pm, but park gates close at 6:45pm. Off-season hours vary.

Transportation Center: At the end of N. Boundary St., across from the fire station. **Amtrak,** 229-8750 or 800-872-7245. Direct service to: New York ($54), Washington, DC ($22.50), Philadelphia ($26), and Baltimore ($49.50). Open Mon.-Tues. and Fri. 7:30am-8:30pm, Wed.-Thurs. and Sat. 7:30am-2:30pm, Sun. 2-9pm. **Greyhound,** 229-1460. Open Mon.-Fri. 8am-6pm, Sat.-Sun. 8am-5pm. To Washington, DC ($20). **James City County Transit (JCCT),** 220-1621. Service along Rte. 60, from Merchants Sq. in the Historic District, west to Williamsburg Pottery, or east past Busch Gardens. Does not go to Yorktown or Jamestown. Service Mon.-Fri. 6:15am-6:20pm. Fare 75¢ each, plus 25¢ per zone change; exact change required.

Williamsburg Limousine Service: 877-0279. To Busch Gardens and Carter's Grove (at 9am, 10am and 1:30pm. $5 round-trip). Guided tours to: Jamestown (daily 9am, $17); to Yorktown (1:30pm, $15); and both towns ($30, includes museum admission). The limousines will pick you up and return you to your Williamsburg lodgings. Make reservations.

ZIP Codes: 23185 (Williamsburg), 23490 (Yorktown), and 23081 (Jamestown).

Area Code: 804.

Williamsburg lies some 50 miles southeast of Richmond between Jamestown (10 miles) and Yorktown (14 miles).

Accommodations and Camping

The few bargains in the Williamsburg area lie along Rte. 60 west or along Rte. 31 south toward Jamestown. From Memorial Day to Labor Day, rooms are scarce and prices higher, so try to call at least two weeks in advance. Centrally located, family-run guest houses are clean, comfortable, cheap, and friendly alternatives to hotels. For a complete listing of accommodations, pick up a copy of the free *Visitors Guide to Virginia's Historic Triangle* (see Practical Information above).

The closest hostel, **Sangraal-by-the-Sea Youth Hostel (AYH),** Rte. 626 (776-6500), near Urbanna, is 30 miles away. Hotels close to town, right next to the historic district, are not cheap. One marginal bargain is the **Bassett Motel,** 800 York St. (229-5175). Just 3 blocks from Colonial Williamsburg. Large, clean rooms. (Singles $40. Doubles $45.) Five minutes from the historic district is **Mrs. H. J. Carter,** 903 Lafayette St. (229-1117). Dust mice would not dare hide under the four-poster beds in these large, airy rooms. (Singles and doubles $22. Reservations suggested. **Motel 6,** Rte. 60 W. (565-3433), 2½ miles from Colonial Williamsburg, offers standard motel fare, with a pool. (Singles $26. Doubles $32.)

Smaller guest houses include the **Thompson Guest House,** 1007 Lafayette St. (229-3455; singles $25-30), and **Holland's Sleepy Lodge,** 211 Harrison Ave. (229-6321; rooms $21-27). There are also several campsites in the area. **Anvil Campgrounds,** P.O. Box 1774, Williamsburg (565-2300), 3 miles west of Colonial Williamsburg Information Center on Rte. 60, offers a swimming pool, bathhouse, recreational hall, miniature golf, and store. (Sites $11-15.) **Indian Village Campground,** 1811 Jamestown Rd., 2¼ miles south on Rte. 31 from Rte. 199, has similar facilities and also rents cabins. (Sites $10-15.) Nearby is **Brass Lantern Campsites,** 1782 Jamestown Rd. (229-4320 or 229-9089; sites $8-12.)

Food

If you want to eat where the colonials did, you have to dress for their approval; semi-formal dress and reservations are required for most places in the historic district. For less pomp and more rustic circumstance, pack a picnic from one of the supermarkets clustered around the **Williamsburg Shopping Center,** at the intersection of Richmond Rd. and Lafayette St., or try the fast-food strip along Rte. 60.

The Old Chickahominy House, 1211 Jamestown Rd. (229-4689), is over a mile from the historic district but worth the trip. Share the antique and dried-flowers decor with pewter-haired locals whose ancestors survived "Starvation Winter" in Jamestown. Miss Melinda's "complete luncheon" is Virginia ham served on hot biscuits, fruit salad, a slice of buttermilk pie, and iced tea or coffee ($4.75). (Open daily 8:30-10:30am and 11:30am-2:30pm. No reservations, so get there early or expect to wait.) At **Paul's Delly Restaurant and Pizza,** 761 Scotland St. (229-8976), strike up a conversation with a William and Mary student over crisp *strombolis* ($5.50-7) and filling subs ($2.80-4.50). (Open daily 11am-2am.)

Sights and Activities

At the end of the 17th century, when English aristocrats wore brocades and wigs, Williamsburg was the capital of Virginia. During the Revolutionary War, the capital moved to Richmond, taking with it much of Williamsburg's grandeur. In 1926, John D. Rockefeller, Jr., came to the financial aid of the distressed city and faithfully restored part of the town as a colonial village. As a result, today in **Colonial Williamsburg** fife and drum corps parade while cobblers, bookbinders, blacksmiths, and candle and clockmakers go about their tasks using 200-year-old methods. The place is also stocked with events; on any given day there might be a Punch and Judy show, an evening of 18th-century theater, or a militia review.

Of course, there is a price for all this—if you want to see it all. The tourist visitors center (see Practical Information above) offers several admission packages. However, if the packages aren't your ticket, for no charge, you can walk the streets, ogle the buildings, browse in the shops, march behind the fife and drum corps, lock yourself in the stockade, and even use the restrooms. For pre-Revolutionary festivities without a cover charge, stop by **Chowning's Tavern** after 9:30pm and join in the "colonial diversions." Patrons down mugs of ale, consume barrels of complimentary peanuts, and play colonial board games, while enjoying the ribald strains of the local balladeer.

The other focal point of Williamsburg, **William and Mary,** is the second oldest college in the United States. Chartered in 1693, the college has educated Presidents Jefferson, Monroe, and Tyler. The **Sir Christopher Wren building,** which was also restored with Rockefeller money, is the oldest classroom building in the country. Behind the union building are the beautiful and elegant **Sunken Gardens,** the centerpiece of the old campus. (Tours Mon.-Fri. at 10am and 2:30pm.)

Nearby, in the historic district, are the shops at **Merchant Square,** a series of elegant boutiques and eateries in colonial houses. Park here and walk straight into Williamsburg.

When you tire of American history, head to **Busch Gardens,** 3 miles east of Williamsburg on Rte. 60 (253-3350). Rides, shows, and shops come together under a European theme, "The Old Country." Join in on the raucous year-round Octoberfest in the German pavilion. Take a free self-guided tour of the **Anheuser Busch Brewery.** (Open daily May 13-Sept. 3. Hours vary. Admission $20.) Williamsburg Limousine serves Busch Gardens twice per day (see Practical Information above). You can also cool off at **Water Country USA** on Rte. 199 E. (229-9300), ¼ mile east of I-64. The new water theme park features a wave tank and water rides as well as variety shows. (Open June 17-Aug. 20 daily 10am-8pm; Aug. 21-Sept. 4 and May 26-June 16 10am-7pm. Admission $15.)

Jamestown and **Yorktown** are both important parts of the American Colonial story. The National Park System provides free, well-administered visitor's guides to both areas. At the **Jamestown National Historic Site** you'll see remains from the first permanent English settlement of 1607, glassblowers at work, and exhibits explaining colonial life. At the visitors center, see the 15-minute film *Jamestown, A Beginning.* Rangers lead tours through the town every half-hour. (Historic area open in summer daily 8:30am-6:45pm. Off-season hours vary. Admission $5 per car, $2 for bikers and pedestrians.)Also see the nearby **Jamestown Festival Park** (229-1607), a museum commemorating the Jamestown settlement. Here you'll find changing exhibits, a reconstruction of James Fort, an Indian village, and full scale replicas of the 3 ships which brought the original settlers to Jamestown in 1607. (Open daily 9am-5pm. Admission $5, ages 6-12 $3.)

Yorktown was the site of the American Revolution's last significant battle. British General Charles Lord Cornwallis and his men seized the town for use as a port in 1781. Surrounded and stormed by the Americans and French, the British were forced to surrender. Stop in at the national park's **visitors center** for a short movie explaining the surrender. Guided tours of the British inner defense line (a series of mounds and moats) are available throughout the day. If you have a car, take a 7-mile self-guided tour of the battlefield, or rent a tape cassette and recorder for $2 in the visitors center. (Open daily 8:30am-6:30pm, last tape rented at 5pm.) Across town, the **Yorktown Victory Center** (887-1776), on Rte. 238 1 block from Rte. 17, offers a museum filled with items from the Revolutionary War, as well as an intriguing "living history" exhibit. In an encampment in front of the center, a troop of soldiers from the Continental Army of 1772 take a well-deserved break from active combat. Feel free to ask them about tomorrow's march or last week's massacre. (Open daily 9am-7pm. Admission $5, children $2.50. Combination tickets to Jamestown Festival Park $7, ages 6-12 $5.)

The **James River plantations** were the bastions of the slave-holding Virginia aristocracy. The mansions were built near the river to facilitate the planters' commercial and social life. **Carter's Grove Plantation,** 6 miles east of Williamsburg on Rte. 60, is a masterpiece of Georgian architecture. Williamsburg Limousine (see Practical Information above) offers two daily round-trip tours from Colonial Williamsburg ($4). Admission includes a self-guided tour of the still-active **Wolstenholme Town** archeology site (in front of the house), an early British settlement even more short-lived than nearby Jamestown. (Plantation and town open March-Nov. and Christmas week daily 9am-5pm. Admission $7, free with Colonial Williamsburg Patriot's Pass.)

Berkeley Plantation, (795-2453) halfway between Richmond and Williamsburg on Rte. 5, was the site of the first Thanksgiving in 1619, and later the birthplace of U.S. presidents Benjamin and William Henry Harrison. Be sure to pause and enjoy the terraced boxwood gardens. (Open daily 8am-5pm. Admission $6.) **Shirley Plantation** (795-2385), west on Rte. 5, is a beautiful Queen Anne mansion which survived colonial wars, and, incredibly, Reconstruction. The Carter family still owns the land it began to develop in 1613. (Open daily 9am-5pm, last tour at 4:30pm. Admission $5, students $4, children $2.) **Sherwood Forest Plantation** (829-

5377), about 10 miles from the Berkeley Plantation on Rte. 5, was the home of U.S. Presidents William Henry Harrison and John Tyler. It is the largest frame house in America. (Grounds open daily 9am-5pm. Admission $2, children 50¢. Mansion open for tours by appointment. Tours $6.75 for 4.)

Virginia Beach

Utopian idealists will be gratified to find that the workers' paradise already exists—it is Virginia Beach. But no one thought it would be so expensive. The main attraction here is the beach; this is not a place for the sensitive or the aesthete. Emphasis is on contemporary hedonism, not colonial history, and an excess of fast-food joints, arcades, and T-shirt shops along Atlantic Avenue cater to the summer-long party. At night, Virginia Beach's flotsam and jetsam frequent the boardwalks; women should walk with a friend or wear earplugs.

Virginia Beach's crazy diversions don't stop at the beachfront. Test your psychic ability at the visitors center of the **Edgar Cayce Association for Research and Enlightenment,** 67th St. and Atlantic Ave. (428-3588), which is dedicated to the development of psychic potential and holistic health. (Open Mon.-Sat. 9am-10pm, Sun 1-10pm; Sept.-May Mon.-Sat. 9am-5:30pm, Sun. 1-6pm. Free.) There are few public parks like **Mount Trashmore,** adjacent to the Norfolk-Virginia Beach Expressway, about 6 miles out of town. Constructed from alternating layers of soil and trash, Mt. Trashmore contains a soap box derby ramp and man-made lakes. The beach's more traditional sights are also worth seeing. Explore the depths of the Atlantic Ocean, make waves, or get to know the inhabitants in the touch tank at the new **Virginia Marine Science Museum,** 717 General Booth Blvd. (425-3476; open daily 9am-5pm, extended hours in summer. Admission $3.50, seniors and children $2.75. Take the South Rudee Trolley.)

Arts are alive on the beach at the **Virginia Beach Arts Center,** on the right of the entrance of the westbound Virginia Beach-Norfolk Expressway, across from the Pavilian Convention Center (425-0000). This new facility features a peaceful sculpture garden and exhibitions of 20th-century art. The center also sponsors the annual Boardwalk Art Show in mid-June, the largest outdoor art show on the East Coast. History was made at **The First Landing Cross,** at Cape Henry, where America's first permanent English setters, the Jamestown colonists, touched the New World's shores on April 26, 1607.

Junk-food junkies will love Virginia Beach, thanks to the proliferation of fast-food joints that litter the boardwalk and main drags. However, there are also a number of inexpensive restaurants with local flavor hidden in the neon glare. **The Jewish Mother,** 3108 Pacific Ave. (422-5430), dotes on her customers with quiche, omelettes, crêpes ($4-9), deli sandwiches ($4-5), and desserts ($2-3). One of the most popular eateries in town. (Entertainment nightly. Open daily 9am-3am.) **The Raven,** 1200 Atlantic Ave. (425-9556), lays out well-prepared seafood, steaks, and salad in a tinted-glass greenhouse setting. Outdoor dining in season. (Sandwiches and burgers $4-6, dinners $9-15. Open Mon.-Fri. noon-2am, Sat. and Sun. 8am-2am.) **Giovanni's Pasta Pizza Palace,** 20th St. and Atlantic Ave. (425-1575), serves tasty Italian pastas, pizzas, and hot grinders. (Lunches and dinners $5-7. Open daily noon-11pm.) Prospective picnickers should head for the **Virginia Beach Farmer's Market,** 1989 Landstown Rd. (427-4395; open daily 8:30am-dark.) At 31st St. and Baltic Ave., the **Farm Fresh** supermarket salad bar, stocked with fresh fruit, pastas, and frozen yogurt, is a bargain at $2 per pound. (Open 24 hours.)

Finding a cheap place to stay in Virginia Beach is difficult. Atlantic Avenue and Pacific Avenue run parallel to the oceanfront, buzz with activity during the summer, and claim the most desirable hotels. September and May offer the best rates. Ideally situated within sight of the ocean, bus station, laundry, post office, and market, **Angie's Guest Cottage-Bed and Breakfast and AYH Hostel,** 302 24th St. (428-4690), still ranks as the best place to stay on the entire Virginia Coast. The Yates mother and daughter team welcome guests with unbelievable warmth; they won't turn anyone away. They'll even go out of their way to help guests with job- and house-hunting. (Kitchen and lockers available. Memorial Day-Labor Day $10, nonmembers $14. Off-season $7.85, nonmembers $10. Linens $2.) If you stay in the guest cottage, breakfast is included. (Doubles $38-52. Quads $48-60. Call 10am-10pm.) Two other clean lodging options are the **Ocean Palms Motel,** 30th St. and Arctic Ave. (428-8362 or 428-5357; singles $40), and the **Viking Motel,** 2700 Atlantic Ave. (428-7116), just a block from the beach. (Rooms from $45, off-season $20.)

Camping on the beach is illegal, and the number of campgrounds around make it unnecessary. The **Seashore State Park,** about 8 miles north of town on U.S. 60 (481-2131), has camping spots ($10). Because of its excellent location amid sand dunes and cypress trees, the park is very popular, so call two to three weeks ahead for reservations (490-3939; Mon.-Fri. 10am-4pm; open 8am-dusk; take the North Seashore Trolley). **KOA,** 1240 General Booth Blvd. (428-1444), runs a quiet campground with free bus service to the beach and boardwalk. (Sites $14-20 for 2. Komfortable and kapacious 1-room Kamping Kabins $36.)

The **Virginia Beach Visitors Center,** 19th St. and Pacific Ave. (425-7511 or 800-446-8038), provides assistance in finding budget accommodations and dispenses information on area sights. Skip the slide show. (Open Mon.-Sat. 9am-8pm, Sun. 9am-5pm.)

Virginia Beach is about 16 miles southeast of Norfolk, just north of the Outer Banks of North Carolina. **Greyhound,** 1017 Laskin Rd. (422-2998), connects with Norfolk, Williamsburg, and Richmond, and with Maryland via the Bridge Tunnel. The **Virginia Beach Transit/Trolley Information Center,** 20 Pacific Ave. (428-3388), next to the visitors center, provides complete information on area transportation and tours, including trolleys, buses, and ferries. (Open 9am-6pm daily.) In summer, the **Atlantic Avenue Trolley** runs from Rudee Inlet to 42nd St. (Daily 10am-2am; fare 50¢, seniors and disabled 25¢.) Other trolleys run along the boardwalk, the North Seashore, and to Lynnhaven Mall. Bus #32 connects Virginia Beach's oceanfront with its sprawling inland shopping malls. (Service to the Lynnhaven Mall and Hilltop Shopping Center from 19th St. and Pacific Ave. Mon.-Sat. 9am-10pm. $1.)

To get around in Virginia Beach at high speed, rent a bike or moped from **Moped City Rentals, Inc.,** 21st St. and Pacific Ave. (Bikes $6 for 1½ hr. Mopeds $20 for 1½ hr.)

Virginia Beach's **ZIP code** is 23458; the **area code** is 804.

Washington, DC

Drawing its models from the Greeks and Romans, Washington, DC was old before it began, born in a series of vast and domineering buildings. To borrow a phrase once applied to St. Petersburg, it is the most "abstract and intentional of cities." The monuments and museums ringing the center of town look like geometric shapes plunked down to conform to some strange notion of symmmetry—although hardly that of the city's grand architect, Pierre L'Enfant. The careful grid that L'Enfant laid down in 1791 has been so fractured and dissected that it remains honored largely in the breach.

The politics and machinery of the city always seem incidental when compared to its edifices. The capitol lilliputs even the most important of senators; the White House reduces presidents to lodgers. Nevertheless, politics *is* the profession of this town. Aspirants to culture may go to Los Angeles or New York, but most power-seekers come here, making Washington, DC the Ellis Island of ambitions.

Mild in winter and glorious in autumn, only in summer does the city reclaim its southern heritage with endless days of high humidity and temperatures of 90°. There is even a rumor that the Republic's founding fathers, in their infinite wisdom, chose Washington as a capital precisely because they hoped the heat would prevent

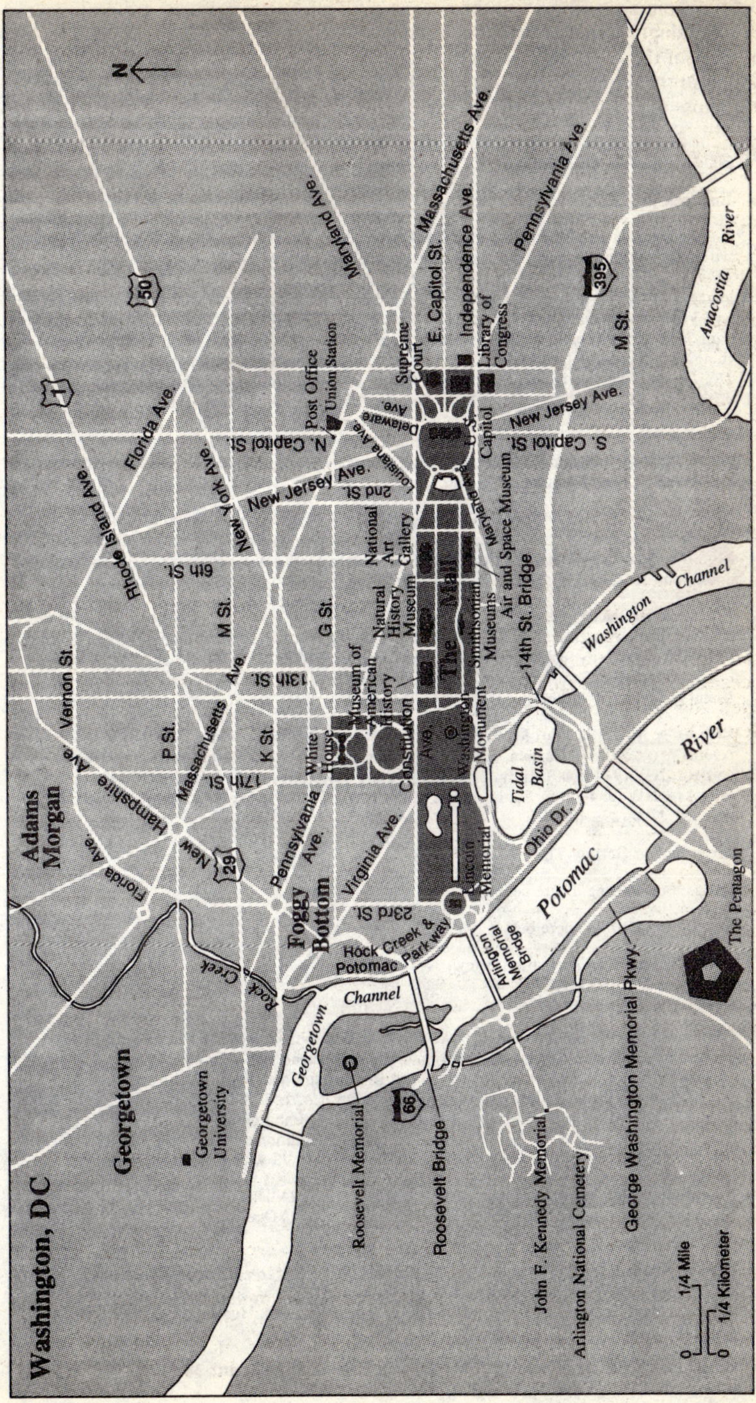
Washington, DC
N
Georgetown
Georgetown University
Adams Morgan
Foggy Bottom
Florida Ave.
New Hampshire Ave.
Vernon St.
P St.
17th St.
Massachusetts Ave.
K St.
13th St.
M St.
6th St.
Rhode Island Ave.
New York Ave.
Florida Ave.
N. Capitol St.
Post Office
Union Station
Maryland Ave.
Massachusetts Ave.
E. Capitol St.
Independence Ave.
Pennsylvania Ave.
Supreme Court
Library of Congress
Delaware Ave.
Louisiana Ave.
U.S. Capitol
New Jersey Ave.
S. Capitol St.
M St.
Anacostia River
New Jersey Ave.
2nd St.
National Art Gallery
Maryland Ave.
Air and Space Museum
Smithsonian Museums
The Mall
Natural History Museum
G St.
Museum of American History
White House
Constitution Ave.
Washington Monument
14th St. Bridge
Washington Channel
Tidal Basin
River
Potomac
Ohio Dr.
Lincoln Memorial
Virginia Ave.
Pennsylvania Ave.
23rd St.
Hock Creek & Potomac Parkway
Rock Creek
Georgetown Channel
Roosevelt Memorial
Roosevelt Bridge
Arlington Memorial Bridge
The Pentagon
George Washington Memorial Pkwy.
John F. Kennedy Memorial
Arlington National Cemetery
1/4 Mile
1/4 Kilometer
1
50
29
66
395

politics from becoming a full time obsession. Unfortunately, someone invented air conditioning. No matter what the weather, Washington offers the visitor a limitless number of things to do: sight-seeing, dancing at avant-garde nightclubs, taking in a show at the Kennedy Center, and perhaps, just at the limits of one's field of visions, a glimpse of the meaning of America.

Practical Information

Emergency: 911.

Visitor Information: Visitor Information Center, 1455 Pennsylvania Ave. NW (789-7000), within the "Willard collection" of shops. A very helpful first stop. Ask for *Washington Visitors Map,* which shows metro stops near points of interest, and *Washington's Attractions.* Language bank service in over 20 languages. Open Mon.-Sat. 9am-5pm. **Washington Convention and Visitors Association (WCVA),** 1212 New York Ave. NW (789-7000). Open Mon.-Fri. 9am-5pm. Write or call for copies of *Washington, DC: A Capital City* (information on everything from museum hours and exhibits to car rentals and accommodations) and *Washington, DC, Dining/Shopping Guide.* **Information Center at Union Station,** Massachusetts and Delaware Ave. NE (289-1908). Open Mon.-Sat. 9am-5pm. Seasonal events are recorded in the free weekly *City Paper,* the "Weekend" section of the Fri. **Washington Post,** the "Washington Weekend" section of the Thurs. **Washington Times,** the monthly *Washingtonian* magazine, or the free city magazines *Go, Where,* and *This Week in the Nation's Capital,* available at area hotels. **Events Hotline:** 737-8866.

International Visitors Information Service (IVIS): 733 15th St. NW, #300 (783-6540). 24-hour language bank in over 50 languages (after 11pm, emergency calls only). Office open Mon.-Fri. 9am-5pm. Desk at International Arrivals in Dulles Airport (661-8747) open daily noon-7pm. In summer, also staffs a desk at Union Station.

Travelers Aid: Main office at 1015 12th St. NW (347-0101). Helpful for orientation to the city and in emergencies. Open Mon.-Fri. 9am-5pm. Desks at Union Station (347-0101; TDD 371-1937; open daily 9:30am-6pm); National Airport (684-3472; TDD 684-7886; open Sun.-Fri. 9am-9pm, Sat. 9am-6pm); and Dulles Airport (661-8636; TDD 471-9776; open Sun.-Fri. 10am-9pm, Sat. 10am-6pm).

Embassies: Australia, 1601 Massachusetts Ave. NW (797-3000). **Britain,** 3100 Massachusetts Ave. NW (462-1340). **Canada,** 501 Pennsylvania Ave. NW (682-1740). **France,** 4101 Reservoir Rd. NW (944-6000). **Italy,** 2110 Leroy Place NW (265-3570). **Japan,** 2520 Massachusetts Ave. NW (234-2266). **Spain,** 2700 15th St. NW (265-0190). **West Germany,** 4645 Reservoir Rd. NW (298-4000).

Airports: See Getting There below.

Trains: See Getting There below.

Buses: See Getting There below.

Local Transit: See Orientation below.

Taxis: See Orientation below.

Car Rental: Thrifty Rent-a-Car, 4714 Miller Ave., Bethesda (986-0922). Weekday rates $31-46; 100 free miles, 25¢ each additional mile. 3-day weekend rate $79; 450 free miles. Must be 25 with major credit card. **Northeast Ford Rental Cars and Vans,** 1720 New York Ave. NE (636-8470). Weekday rates $27-43; 100 free miles, 15-20¢ each additional mile; weekend rates $70-120. Must be 21 with major credit card. **MPG Car Rental,** 1522 K St. NW (289-0283). Weekday rates $28-40; 150 free miles, 20¢ each additional mile. 3-day weekend rate $59-89; 200 free miles, 20¢ each additional mile. Must be 23 with major credit card.

Bike Rental: Fletcher Boat House, 4940 Canal Rd. NW (244-0461). $4 for 2 hr., $7 per day. They also rent canoes and rowboats ($6 per hr., $10 per day.) Open daily 9am-6pm. No rentals after 5pm.

Foreign Newspapers: Periodicals Plus, 1825 I St. NW (223-2526). **Editorial El Mundo,** 1796 Columbia Rd. NW (387-2831). **Key Bridge Newsstand,** 3323 M St. NW (338-2626). **Newsroom Farragut Square,** 1001 Connecticut Ave. NW (872-0190). **Hudson News,** 529 14th St. NW (783-1720).

Help Lines: Crisis Hotline, 628-3228. **Gay and Lesbian Switchboard,** 387-4348.

Post Office: N. Capitol St. and Massachusetts Ave. NE (682-9595), across from Union Station. Open Mon.-Fri. 7am-8pm, Sat. 8am-2pm, Sun. 10am-4pm. **ZIP code:** 20002.

Area Code: 202.

Getting There

Unless you sail into Washington on the Potomac, you're sure to hit gridlock as you approach the city. You can miss the major traffic snarls if you avoid arriving during commuter rush hours (Mon.-Fri. 7-10am and 3:30-6:30pm).

Road signs on all the interstates are highly confusing. The two main roads from Baltimore and the North are the **Baltimore-Washington (B-W) Parkway** and **I-95.** To go downtown, take the Parkway and follow signs for New York Ave. To get to the upper northwest quadrant, take I-95 to the Silver Spring exit onto the Capitol Beltway (I-495), then exit 20 (marked Chevy Chase) onto Connecticut Ave. and take a left. From the south, take I-95 (which becomes I-395) directly to the 14th Street Bridge or the Memorial Bridge. Both lead downtown. From the west, take I-66 East over the Roosevelt Bridge and follow signs for Constitution Ave. I-66 is a simpler, faster way to get to the heart of Washington than I-495. But beware: To encourage car-pooling and fuel conservation, vehicles on I-66 East (7-9am) and I-66 West (4-6pm) must carry at least three people Mon.-Fri. Even out-of-towners have to pay the $50 fine if they break this law.

Washington is served by three airports. **National** (685-8000), 15 minutes from downtown, is closest to the District and handles domestic flights only. Washington's Metrorail subway system can whisk you from National to several downtown stops for 80¢, or you can take a bus to the Capitol Hilton at 16th and K St. (Buses $7, vans every ½ hr., $5.) Cab fare downtown is about $8. **Dulles** (661-8020), 35 minutes from downtown, handles mostly international, transcontinental, and bargain flights. Buses, every half hour, are $14; taxi fare downtown is $35-40. **Baltimore-Washington International** (261-1000) is about 45 minutes from downtown. Buses, every half hour, are $14; taxi fare downtown is $40-45. Call the **Washington Flyer** (685-1400) for complete information on airport bus service to and from all three airports. Pan Am Airlines (845-8000) offers frequent shuttle service from National to LaGuardia ($69 one-way, $45 for those under 21). Continental Airlines (478-9700) offers shuttle service from National to Newark ($89 one-way, $45 for under 21).

Amtrak's **Metroliner** service (484-7540 or 800-872-7245) may be the fastest, although not necessarily the cheapest ($47 one way), way to travel between New York and Washington. The trip between Penn Station and Union Station takes just over 3 hours. The Red Line subway will take you from Union Station to other parts of the city.

Greyhound/Trailways, 1005 1st St. NE (565-2662), at L St. station, is in a slightly unsafe area. Disabled facilities. Provides frequent daily direct service to: Atlantic City (every 1-1½ hr., $21); Philadelphia (every 2-3 hr., $25); New York City (every ½-1 hr., $36); and Baltimore (every ½-1 hr., $9). Open 24 hours.

Orientation

The Capitol is the geographic center of DC's street layout. The four **quadrants** of the city—Northwest (NW), Northeast (NE), Southwest (SW), and Southeast (SE)—are defined by the four streets radiating from the Capitol Building: N. Capitol, S. Capitol, E. Capitol, and the Mall. North-south streets are numbered, and run perpendicular to the east-west lettered streets. On either side of E. Capitol St. and the Mall, parallel streets run alphabetically from A-W. (Note: I and K are often written Eye St. and Kay St.) Once the letters of the alphabet are exhausted, two-syllable street names follow in alphabetical order. Next come three syllable names, then names of trees and flowers. Before setting out for your destination, be sure to check the quadrant indicator (NW, NE, SW, SE) of the address. Blocks are numbered in increments of 100, making street addresses easy to locate. For example, 1350 Q St. is between 13th St. and 14th St.

Washington's neighborhoods showcase American cultural diversity. The **Mall** lies at the heart of the city, dotted with various memorials, the Capitol, the Smithsonian museums, and numerous government buildings. Off the Mall to the north is **Chinatown,** on G and H St. between 6th and 8th St. NW. **Georgetown,** centered around Wisconsin Ave. and M St. NW, is across the river from Rosslyn, Virginia. It has a frenetic pace, set largely by its sizeable student population. **Adams Morgan,** a hip, colorful, multi-ethnic community with a Soho feel sits between 18th St. and Kalorama Park on Columbia Rd. To the south, down Connecticut Ave., is **Dupont Circle,** a popular gay hangout, as well as a home to upscale eateries and cafés. On the west side of the National Zoological Park, between Observatory and Sheridan Circles, is the **Embassy District.** The area bounded by Pennsylvania and Constitution Ave. and 18th and 26th St. NW, once a swamp, is now known as **Foggy Bottom** and is home to George Washington University, the Kennedy Center, and the State Department.

John F. Kennedy once wryly commented about his adopted city, "It's a mixture of Northern charm and Southern efficiency." Despite its elegant design, Washington is a nightmare of one-way streets and tangled traffic. Further, finding a parking space is a nearly impossible task. Parking garages are exorbitant and metered spaces simply are not available during much of the day. Traffic police are strict about parking violations, and fines are steep. If, as on most of Constitution Ave., the signs read "No Parking 4-6:30pm, Mon.-Fri." do not saunter happily to your vehicle at 4:15; it probably won't be there. A right turn on a red light is permitted.

Metrorail (637-7000), the Washington subway system, is a sight in its own right. (Main office is at 600 5th St. NW. Open daily 6am-11:30pm.) The Dupont Circle Station has the longest escalator in the Western Hemisphere (204 ft.), and the architecture throughout the system is futuristic though a little sterile. The trains are clean, quiet, crime-free, and air-conditioned, and Metro maps are easy to understand. Trains run every 10 or 15 minutes Mon.-Fri. 6am to midnight, Sat. 8am to midnight, and Sun. 10am to midnight. Rush-hour fares vary from 80¢ to $2.40, according to the distance you travel. At all other times, fares vary from 80¢ to $1.10. Station attendants in glass booths are on hand to answer questions, but the computerized fare cards must be bought from machines in the station before you enter the subway, and must be carried until you reach your destination. If you plan to connect with a bus after your ride, get a transfer pass before boarding the train. To use the subway several times, buy a fare card for $5; a $10 fare card is discounted 50¢. The $5 weekend family tour pass allows a group of four unlimited travel on the Metrorail. (Avaliable at the Metro Center Stop and from some hotel concierges.)

The extensive **Metrobus** (same phone, address, and hours as Metrorail) system serves Georgetown, downtown, and the suburbs. Service is relatively reliable. Downtown, the bus stops every four blocks. Regular fare is 75¢, but again, rush-hour fares vary. Senior citizens and disabled people are eligible for reduced fares at all times with a valid WMATA ID card, and children under 5 ride free when accompanied by a paying passenger.

Two types of people use the Washington, DC **taxi** system: Those who understand the zone system (cabbies and residents) and those who don't (you and millions of tourists). Fares are determined by the number of zones you cross. Washington's many zone boundaries are rather arbitrary, but zone maps are posted in cabs. Bring a pen and a simple map of DC on your ride and sketch away. Taxi drivers have a penchant for stuffing their cabs full of riders heading for the same part of the city; this practice reduces the fare considerably, but may be catastrophic for travelers who are late for a train or bus connection. The only way to prevent this delay is to offer extra money.

Accommodations and Camping

Washington hotels are notoriously expensive, but there are a few bargains to be had. Look for package deals and call the 800 numbers of the major national chains. The **Holiday Inn Capitol Mall** (479-4000 or 800-465-4329) usually offers bargains.

Another option is a bed and breakfast. Although B&B's in the area are not cheap, many provide deluxe rooms for a moderate price. **Bed and Breakfast, Ltd.** (328-3510) will make reservations for you at participating establishments. (Singles $30-65. Doubles $45-75. Call Mon.-Fri. 10am-5pm., Sat. 10am-1pm.) Or try the **Bed and Breakfast League, Ltd.** (363-7767). (Singles $30-55. Doubles $45-65. Call Mon.-Fri. 9am-5pm.)

Campers have few options. For information on nearby parks in Maryland and northern Virginia, call the **National Park Service,** (1100 Ohio Dr. SW, 485-9666; open Mon.-Fri. 8am-4pm), or **Dial-a-Park** (485-7275). See the Baltimore, MD, Accommodations for more camping listings.

Washington International Youth Hostel (AYH), 1009 11th St. NW (737-2333), at K St. Metro: Metro Ctr., exit at G and 11th St. Clean and attractive bunks, bath, and kitchen in a recently renovated hostel. Friendly management. Separate facilities for men and women. 250 bed capacity. Secure storage area, lounges, laundry facilities, and linen rental ($2). Disabled access. 3-day max. stay flexible. Curfew midnight. Check-in 5-11pm, check-out 9:30am. Members only, $13.

University Dorms: Catholic University, 620 Michigan Ave. NE (635-5277). Metro: Brookland CUA. A/C, kitchen facilities; cafeteria nearby. Singles $12, with A/C $16. Doubles $10 per person, with A/C $12. Requires mail application and 20% deposit. Mailing address: Office of Resident Life, 108 St. Bonaventure Hall, Catholic University, WDC, 20064. Rooms available mid-May to Aug. **American University,** Leonard Hall (885-3373), or McDowell Hall (885-3375), Housing Office (885-2599). Metro: Tenley Town. Kitchen facilities, cafeteria. Unmarried students and government interns only. Shuttle bus runs from Metro stop to dorms Mon.-Fri. 7:30am-midnight. 2-week min. stay. Doubles only, $73 per person per week. Linens $5 per night. Rooms available June-Aug. **Georgetown University,** P.O. Box 2214, WDC, 20057 (687-3999). Kitchen facilities and cafeteria. 3-week min. stay. Singles $14 with A/C. Doubles $10, with A/C $11. Bring your own linens. Requires mail application and 20% deposit. Rooms available June to mid-Aug.

Swiss Inn, 1204 Massachusetts Ave. NW (371-1816). Metro: Metro Ctr., 12th St. Friendly townhouse in a safe area. Spare, clean rooms include private bath and kitchen. Rent TVs for $2 per day, color $4. 2-day min. stay. Singles $48, $248 per week. Doubles $58, $278 per week. Call for reservations.

Allen Lee Hotel, 2224 F St. NW (331-1224), near George Washington University and Kennedy Center, within walking distance of the Mall and Georgetown. Metro: Foggy Bottom. Great price and location, but you'll sacrifice cleanliness for the convenience. Color TV. Singles $26, with bath $33. Doubles $32, with bath $40. Cash and traveler's checks only. Reservations essential in summer.

Adams Inn, 1744 Lanier Place NW (745-3600). Metro: Woodley Park-National Zoo. Pleasant residential neighborhood within easy walking distance of the zoo and Adams Morgan. Victorian furnishings. Laundromat nearby. Check-in 3-9pm. Singles $35, with bath $50. Doubles $40, with bath $55. Each additional person $5. Full breakfast included. Reservations necessary.

University Inn, 2134 G St. NW (342-8020). Metro: Foggy Bottom. Conveniently located in the heart of the George Washington University campus. Aging but clean rooms; slightly noisy neighborhood. Color TV. Laundry facilities. No private baths. Singles $42. Doubles $47.

The Reeds, P.O. Box 12011, WDC, 20005 (328-3510; open Mon.-Fri. 10am-5pm). Metro: McPherson Sq. or Dupont Circle. Marginal neighborhood. Victorian mansion with sumptuous antique furnishings and formal gardens. Spacious, comfortable, and beautifully decorated rooms. Laundry facilities. Shared bath. Singles $45. Doubles $55. $5 extra during peak season (March 15-June 15; Sept 1-Thanksgiving). Continental breakfast included. Reserve 3 weeks in advance.

Kalorama Guest House at Kalorama Park, 1854 Mintwood Place NW (667-6369), and at **Woodley Park,** 2700 Cathedral Ave. NW (328-0860). Metro: Woodley Park-National Zoo. Friendly staff manages several Victorian townhouses in nice neighborhoods. Enjoy Continental breakfast in the backyard garden and afternoon sherry in the Oriental-carpeted living room. Laundry facilities. Singles $40-65, with bath $55-85. Doubles $45-75, with bath $60-95. Each additional person $10. Reservations with full prepayment required.

Greenbelt Park, Greenbelt, MD (344-3948), 8-10 miles from town off the B-W Pkwy. Metro: from Metro Ctr. take Orange line to New Carrollton, then bus T-16 to Crescent and Ridge Rd. (bus leaves hourly); $1.65 total fare. By car: take Greenbelt exit off B-W Pkwy., keep right, pass light, and turn left after 1 mile. A green gem, run by the Feds. Quiet, spacious camping. Hiking trails. No hook-up. $6 per site. First come-first serve, but seldom fills.

Capital KOA Campground, Millersville, MD. (923-2771). Located half-way between Washington and Baltimore. By car: take Rte. 50E to Rte. 3N, 11 miles to Rte. 178. Free shuttle to Washington. Just like summer camp. Swimming pool. Recreation room. Free games and movies. Hook-ups available. $15.50 per site. Cabins $23. Open April-Oct.

Food

Washington's ethnic eateries please the palates of foreign nationals from all over the globe. The best places are filled with compatriots dining on authentic food.

If you get hungry in the Capitol Hill area, take the free Senator Subway from the Capitol to the cafeteria under the Dirksen side of the Senate Office Building. (Open Mon.-Fri. noon-2:30pm.) Sometimes the political stars deign to eat with mere mortals. The food is plain, but the government cafeterias offer some of the cheapest fare in the District. Most of the Smithsonian buildings also have reasonably priced cafeterias. **Union Station,** Massachusetts and Delaware Ave. NE (298-1908), has recently been remodeled to its former 1907 Beaux Arts glory. Not only is it a train station, but it also has a number of shops and eclectic eateries. The best bargain restaurants, however, are concentrated in **Dupont Circle** and **Adams Morgan.** Choices range from down-home southern to Cuban and Ethiopian.

Another Washington special is the open-air market at the wharves on Maine Ave. and 9th St. SW. You can buy low-priced seafood straight from the Chesapeake Bay, or just go for the sights and smells. The food stands at **Eastern Market,** Independence Ave. and 9th St., on Capitol Hill, sell fresh produce, baked goods, meat, and seafood. Metro: Eastern Market. Nearby **Montrose Park** on R St. NW is a good picnic site.

Near Capitol Hill

Tune Inn, 331½ Pennsylvania Ave. SE (543-2725). A real dive with 20-yr. veteran staff. No pretense here: Blue and white collars alike talk over the country & western oldies on the jukebox. Very basic menu includes omelettes, sandwiches, roast beef and chicken; nothing over $4. Beer 80¢ a glass. Open daily 8am-2am.

Hawk 'n' Dove, 329 Pennsylvania Ave. SE (543-3300). A very popular student pub and café. Enjoy hearty sandwiches and burgers as wild game stare at you from the wall. Dinners $6-13, sandwiches $4-8, midnight breakfast $5.50. Sun.-Thurs. 10am-2am, Fri.-Sat. 10am-3am.

Hunan on Capitol Hill, 201 D St. NE (544-0102), at the Capitol's backdoor. $5.50 lunch specials include egg roll, fried rice, and entree. Dinner $5-9. Open Sun.-Thurs. 11:30am-10pm, Fri.-Sat. 11:30am-11pm. Happy hour 4-7pm.

The Dubliner, 4 F St. NW (737-3773). Roomy red-and-green Irish pub serving big plates of fish and chips ($6.50). Sandwiches $5-7; lunch specials $8-9; dinner $11-14. Irish entertainment and crowds on the weekends. Open daily 11am-2am.

Armand's Chicago Pizzeria, 226 Massachusetts Ave. NE (547-6600), also located at 4231 Wisconsin Ave. NW (686-9450). Delivery 363-5500. A long-time favorite for deep-dish pizza. All-you-can-eat lunch pizza and salad bar a deal for $5; subs and ice cream drinks, too. This is simply the best pizza in Washington. Open Sun.-Thurs. 11:30am-11pm, Fri.-Sat. 11:30am-midnight.

Dupont Circle

Sholl's Colonial Cafeteria, 1990 K St. NW (296-3065), in the Esplanade Mall. Good American cooking at extraordinarily low prices: spaghetti ($1.75), chopped steak ($2), and roast beef ($2.75). Fresh food and generous portions, as well as daily specials. Try the homemade pies for dessert. Open Mon.-Sat. 7am-2:30pm, and 4-8pm.

Food for Thought, 1738 Connecticut Ave. NW (797-1095), 2 blocks from Dupont Circle. Good, healthful food in a 60s atmosphere. Ten different vegetable and fruit salads, plus sandwiches and daily hot specials. Local musicians play in the evenings. Lunch $5-8, dinner $6-11. Open Mon. 11:30am-3pm and 5pm-midnight, Tues.-Fri. 11:30am-midnight, Sat. noon-midnight, Sun. 5pm-midnight.

Café Petitto, 1724 Connecticut Ave. NW (462-8771). Excellent Italian regional cooking in an understated atmosphere. Try the aesthetic antipasto buffet ($6) and fried Calabrian pizza. Dinner $6-10. Open daily 11:30am-midnight.

Kramer Books and Afterwards Café, 1517 Connecticut Ave. NW (387-1462). Dine in a bookshop. The food is standard fare tending to *nouvelle,* but the desserts are worth a special stop. Try their Kahlua Walnut Pie. Live music after 10pm. This is where a good number of Washington's slender literary population goes. Open Sun.-Thurs. 10am-1am, Fri.-Sat. 10am-whenever.

Georgetown

Georgetown Café, 1623 Wisconsin Ave. NW (333-0215). Offers solid and delicious greasy American food with Middle Eastern dishes on the side (hummus and felafel $3). Breakfast anytime $1-3, lunch $2-4, dinner $4-7. Open 24 hours.

Vietnam-Georgetown Restaurant, 2934 M St. NW (333-0215). An excellent restaurant next to another great place, the **Viet Huong,** 2928 M St. NW (337-5588). Both serve fine crispy roll appetizers, and gold-coin pork and chicken with lemon grass entrees. Bank machines in lobby rarely work. Lunch at Vietnam-Georgetown $4-5, dinner $6-11. Open Sun.-Thurs. 11am-11pm, Fri.-Sat. noon-midnight. Lunch special at the Viet Huong (soup and entree) $4.25, dinner $6-11. At happy hour (5-7pm), free drink with your meal. Open Sun.-Thurs. 11am-3pm and 5-10:30pm, Fri.-Sat. 11am-10:30pm.

Tandoor, 3315 M St. NW (333-3376). Some of the finest Northern Indian cuisine in Washington. Wonderful batik draperies on the walls. Try their Murgh Tandoor Chicken cooked in an authentic clay oven. Dinners $6-10. Open Mon.-Fri. noon-2:30pm and 5:30-11pm, Sat. noon-2:30pm and 5pm-midnight, Sun. noon-10:30pm.

Enriqueta's, 2811 M St. NW (338-7772). High prices and low decor, but still the best authentic Mexican cuisine in DC. Try their signature dish—pork-stuffed baked peppers with sweet spicy fruit glaze ($11). Lunch $7-10. Dinner $10-13. Open Mon.-Thurs. 11:30am-2:30pm and 5-10pm, Fri. 11:30am-2:30pm and 5-11pm, Sat. 5-11pm, Sun. 5-10pm.

Hamburger Hamlet, 3125 M St. NW (965-6970). Vast array of burgers topped with everything from guacamole to caviar ($5-6). These are some of the best burgers in DC. Sandwiches, salads, chili, and seafood $6-12. Open Sun.-Thurs. 11am-2am, Fri.-Sat. 11am-3am.

Adams Morgan

The Red Sea, 2463 18th St. NW (483-5000), and **Meskerem,** 2434 18th St. NW (462-4100). The consistent favorites among DC's rapidly growing crop of Ethiopian restaurants. Use the traditional pancake bread, *injera,* to eat the spicy lamb, beef, chicken, and vegetable *wats* (stews). Red Sea has live music on Fri. and Sat. amidst modest decor; Meskerem offers a more attractive setting complete with skylight and dining loft. Dinner $5-9. Red Sea open daily 11:30am-2am. Meskerem open Mon.-Thurs. 5pm-midnight, Fri.-Sun. noon-midnight.

Thai Taste, 2606 Connecticut Ave. NW (387-8876). Metro: Woodley Park-National Zoo. DC's black and neon magnet for Thai food lovers. Try the fried beef with chili paste and coconut milk. Dinner $6-13. Open Mon.-Thurs. 11:30am-10:30pm, Fri.-Sat. 11:30am-11pm, Sun. 5-10:30pm.

Mixtec, 1792 Columbia Rd. NW (332-1011). Fantastic Mexican cuisine in a café setting. Rightly famous for their *tacos al carbón* ($2.75). Dinner $3-9. Open Sun.-Thurs. 9:30am-9pm, Fri.-Sat. 9:30am-10pm.

New Orleans Café, 1790 Columbia Rd. NW (234-5111). Creole, gumbo, and jambalaya in real Cajun style. *Beignets,* New Orleans style doughnuts, 3 for $1.25. Lunch $4-6, dinner $6-13. Breakfast, lunch, and dinner served all day. Open Sun.-Thurs. 8:30am-10pm, Fri.-Sat. 8:30am-11pm.

Farther Out

Florida Avenue Grill, 1100 Florida Ave. NW (265-1586), at 11th St., 2½ miles north of the Mall. Metrobus: 11th St. or 16th St. to Florida Ave. A small diner overflowing with locals. Framed faces of boxers and entertainers beam down at you from the back wall. Awesome soul food: breakfast with salmon cakes or spicy half-smoked sausage, eggs, satisfying grits, hotcakes, or southern biscuits ($3-4.50); lunch and dinner with meat, vegetables, and bread ($4.25-7). Open Mon.-Sat. 6am-9pm.

Thai Flavor, 3709 MaComb St. NW (966-0200). Authentic and cheap Thai food. Try their *phad thai* or their chicken with red basil. They also deliver orders over $12. Dinner $6-12. Open Mon.-Sat. 11:30am-midnight, Sun. 5pm-midnight.

Sights

Politics may be the business of Washington, but the city has cultural aspirations as well. It sports a truly wide array of museums, monuments, historic sites, parks, and libraries. An after-dark tour of the monuments is a romantic way to escape the daytime heat and crowds.

Organized bus tours of Washington are operated by **Tourmobile,** 1000 Ohio Dr. SW, (554-7950 or 554-7020), and **Gray Line,** at 4th and E St. SW. (479-5900). Tourmobile, a concession of the National Park Service, stops at 18 major points of interest in the city. Ride all day for $7.50, under 12 $3.75. (Operates daily 9am-6:30pm; Labor Day-June 15 daily 9:30am-4:30pm.) They also have frequent trips to the Arlington Cemetery (daily 9am-6:30pm; $2.50, children $1.25), three daily tours to Mt. Vernon ($13, children $6.25), and two-day combined tours ($21, children $10). Buy tickets at one of the booths near eight major toursites or from the driver, and board at any stop on the Mall. For the same prices, a fully equipped van for the disabled is available (make reservations at least 24 hours in advance, 554-7020). Gray Line offers a variety of tours in and around Washington, including an all-day tour (leaves 9am, $34, children $17) and an evening tour (leaves 8pm; Oct. 30-March 28 7:30pm; $15, children $7). Seniors with an AARP card get a 10% discount.

For a comprehensive two-hour narrated tour of the city aboard a trackless trolley, try **Old Town Trolley Tours,** 3150 V St. NE (269-3020). Buy tickets at the Old Post Office Pavilion, 1100 Pennsylvania Ave. NW or from a hotel concierge, and catch a trolley at one of 17 stops (mostly major hotels). Operates daily 9am-8pm; Labor Day-Memorial Day 9am-4pm; $11, seniors, students, and active military $9, children $5. You can reboard free. Connoisseurs of the offbeat should try **Scandal Tours** (387-2259), a tour of the more sensational side of Washington. See, among other things, the Pentagon, Watergate, and Gary Hart's townhouse. Tour guides are Reagan, Bush, Nixon, and Ollie North imitators. Tours leave from the Ritz Carlton Hotel, 2100 Massachusetts Ave. NW, Sat. and Sun. at 10am, noon, 2pm, and 4:30pm. Tickets are $20; to purchase, call 800-233-4050.

Capitol Hill

The beautiful, Renaissance-style **Capitol Building** is a must-see. Walk by at night, and if a lantern is lit high in the central dome, then congress is in session. Free tours from the east side doors take you through the main halls of the building. (Tours every 15 min. 9am-3:45 pm; 225-6827 or 224-3121; for disabled tour information 224-4048.) To enter the visitors' galleries on your own, write your Representative or Senator for a pass. Visitors interested in seeing an actual congressional committee hearing should consult the *Washington Post's* daily "Today in Congress" column, which is usually placed in the front section. (Capitol open daily 9am-4:30pm. Metro: Capitol S. or Union Station.)

Behind the Capitol at 1st St. and Maryland Ave. NE is the **Supreme Court Building** (479-3000). There are various exhibits on the Court and Constitution in the basement. Check the "Court Calendar" of the *Washington Post* to see if the Court is in session. (Oct.-April the court hears oral arguments (10am-3pm); decisions are handed down May-June (10am). Lecture tours every hour Mon.-Fri. 9:30am-3:30pm when court is not in session. Building open Mon.-Fri. 9am-4:30pm. Metro: Capitol South.)

Next to the Supreme Court is the world's most comprehensive library, the **Library of Congress,** 1st St. and Independence Ave. SE (287-5000 or 287-5458). The architecture inside is breathtaking, and most library services are available to the public. Check out the circular reading room from the second floor visitors' gallery, the Gutenberg Bible, and the library's copies of Shakespeare's First Folio. (Free

45-min. tours Mon.-Fri. every hr. 9am-4pm. Open Mon.-Fri. 8:30am-9:30pm, Sat.-Sun. and holidays 8:30am-5pm. Call for hours of exhibit rooms.)

Shakespeare buffs will enjoy the **Folger Shakespeare Library and Theater,** 201 E. Capitol St. SE (544-7077). The Elizabethan theater resembles the Globe Theater in London and stages performances regularly; Renaissance books and manuscripts are on display. (Open Mon.-Sat. 10am-4pm. Evening performances at 8pm, Sat. matinees at noon and 2pm. Tickets $16-35, ½-price tickets for seniors and students with ID ½ hr. before showtime. Box Office: 546-4000. Metro: Capitol S.)

The **Capital Children's Museum,** 800 3rd St. NE (543-8600 recorded message or 638-5437) is a "hands on" museum. Make tortillas, step inside an Indian burial ground, wander through a maze, or build a log cabin; there are enough activities here to occupy an army of children for several hours. All children must be accompanied by an adult. (Admission $4, seniors and under 2 $1. Open daily 10am-5pm. Metro: Union Station.)

On the Mall side of the capitol, the free **U.S. Botanical Gardens Conservatory,** at 1st St. and Maryland Ave. SW (225-8333), houses tropical, sub-tropical, and desert plants. The affiliated park across the street on Independence Ave. contains summer flowers, perennials, trees, and shrubs. The indoor collection of orchids is especially worth seeing. (Open daily 9am-9pm; in winter daily 9am-5pm. Metro: Capitol S. or Federal Center, SW.)

Museums on the Mall

The **Smithsonian Institution** is a glorious conglomeration of 14 galleries and museums, most of which are on or near the Mall. (Open daily 9am-5pm; 357-2700, recording 357-2020, TDD 357-1729.) All are free, of high quality, wheelchair accessible, and offer written guides in French, German, Spanish, and Japanese. Nearly 140 years ago, the Smithsonian was founded as the National Museum of the U.S. with money from the bequest of an Englishman, James Smithson. All of the Smithsonian's museums are open daily, generally from 10am to 5:30pm; in summer some extend their hours, and in winter some are closed on weekends. Exceptions are indicated below. (For further information on disabled facilities, pick up a free copy of *Smithsonian: A Guide for Disabled Visitors* at any Smithsonian location or write to Office of Public Affairs, Smithsonian Institution, WDC 20560. Cassette (free) and braille ($2) editions available.) The administrative offices are housed in **The Castle,** 1000 Jefferson Dr. SW, on the center of the Mall. The outstanding **Smithsonian Folklife Festival** (287-3424), usually held in late June and early July, celebrates the arts and crafts of a different culture each year.

The **National Air and Space Museum,** 6th St. and Independence Ave. (357-2700), near the Capitol on the south side of the Mall, is the world's most-visited museum. Touch moon rocks and gawk at airplanes—the Wright brothers' *Kitty Hawk,* Lindbergh's *Spirit of St. Louis*—and the spacecraft. Try to catch one of the astonishing 70mm movies shown on their five-story screen. (Movie $2, seniors, students with ID, and children $1; double features at 5:35 and 6:50pm $3.75 and $2.50. Tours of museum highlights daily at 10:15am and 1pm. Recorded tours available in English, French, Spanish, German, Japanese, Portuguese, and Italian for $2.50, seniors and students $2. Museum open daily 9:30am-7:30pm, off-season 10am-5:30pm. Metro: L'Enfant Plaza.)

The **Hirshhorn Museum and Sculpture Garden,** next door at 7th St. and Independence Ave. SW (357-4080), contains the most comprehensive collection of 19th- and 20th-century European and American sculpture in the world. The gift shop sells art books and incomparable jazz and folklore records issued solely by the Smithsonian. The **Sculpture Garden,** on the Mall across from the main building, is a quiet oasis in the bustle of downtown DC, with works by sculptors such as David Smith, Alexander Calder, and Aristide Maillol. (Tours Mon.-Sat. at 10:30am, noon, and 1:30pm, Sun. at 12:30, 1:30, and 2:30pm. Open daily 10am-5:30pm.)

The **Arts and Industries Museum,** 900 Jefferson Dr. SW (357-2700), is next to the Castle on the south side of the Mall. This museum recreates the 1876 Centennial exhibition in Philadelphia and looks like a huge, multinational flea market. Look for the *Baldwin* locomotive and the Liberty Bells made from sugar, tobacco, and cotton. (Free tours by appointment. Open daily 10am-5:30pm.)

The **Museum of African Art,** 950 Independence Ave. SW (357-4600; 357-2700 on weekends), is in the Quadrangle beside the Castle. Housed in an innovative, three-level, underground building, the museum displays a varied collection of ceremonial masks and figures, textiles, sculpture, and functional objects, including works in wood, metal, ceramics, and ivory. (1-hr. tours leave from the information desk Mon.-Fri. at 10:30am and 1:30pm, Sat.-Sun. at 11am, 1pm, and 3pm. Open daily 10am-5:30pm.)

The Smithsonian's newest museum, the **Arthur M. Sackler Gallery,** 1050 Independence Ave. SW (357-2700), shares the unique granite and glass building with the Museum of African Art. The Sackler's array of Asian and Near-Eastern art includes jade, gold, silver, and bronze artifacts, ancient ritual objects, manuscripts, and 20th-century scrolls. Take a break in the Victorian *parterre* surrounding the museum. (Tours leave from the information desk Mon.-Fri. at 11:30am and 2:30pm, Sat.-Sun. at 11:30am. Open daily 10am-5:30pm.)

Journey through the seven seas (well, almost) at the Washington branch of the **National Aquarium,** 14th St. between Constitution Ave. and E St. NW (377-2825), in the lower level of the Commerce Department Building. The nation's oldest public aquarium showcases over 1,000 specimens of freshwater and marine animals. Added attractions include the Touch Tank, shark feeding (Mon., Wed., Sat. at 2pm), and piranha feeding (Tues., Thurs., Sun. at 2pm). (Open daily 9am-5pm. Admission $1.50, seniors and children 75¢. Metro: Federal Triangle.)

Sitting diagonally across the Mall from the Castle, the **National Museum of American History,** 14th St. and Constitution Ave. (357-1300), is like an attic of the American past. Among its many exhibits are the original star-spangled banner, an exhibit called *Life After the Revolution 1780-1800,* the gowns of America's First Ladies, and Horatio Greenough's infamous "topless" sculpture of George Washington. "We the People" and "A Nation of Nations" offer thought-provoking looks at America's cultural heritage. Visit the 1910-style ice cream parlor on the first floor for a deliciously grandiose banana split. (Tours Mon.-Thurs. at 10am, 11am, and 1pm, Fri.-Sun. at 11am and 1pm. Open daily 9:30am-7pm, off-season 10am-5:30pm.)

You'll recognize the **National Museum of Natural History,** 10th St. and Constitution Ave. (357-2700), directly opposite the Castle, by the triceratops—popular with the playground set—standing outside. High points are the Hope Diamond, the Blue Whale, dinosaur skeletons, and an insect zoo. For kids, there's the *Discovery Room* and *Naturalist Center.* (Tours daily from the Rotunda at 10:30am and 1:30pm. Self-guided recorded tours in English and Spanish $2, senior citizens $1.75, children $1. Open daily 9:30am-7pm, off-season 10am-5:30pm.)

The spectacular interior space of the East Wing of the **National Gallery,** 6th St. and Constitution Ave. NW (737-4215), close to the capitol, is architect I.M. Pei's celebration of light and triangles. Look for the immense Calder mobile. The knife-edge corner of the building is one of the sharpest corners in modern architecture; according to legend, if you touch it, or even better, kiss it, you'll have good luck. The East Wing houses the more modern part of the National Gallery painting collection as well as first-rate, international traveling shows. The West Wing holds one of the world's greatest collections of European paintings in a serene pseudo-19th-century setting (the building was constructed in 1940). (Free East Wing tours Mon.-Sat. at 11:30am, Sun. at 12:30pm; West Wing introductory tours Mon.-Sat. at 1pm, Sun. at 4pm; guided tours in French, Spanish, German, and Italian given intermittently—call 842-6246 for details. Museums open Mon.-Sat. 10am-5pm, Sun. noon-9pm. Metro: Archives or Judiciary Square.)

Off the Mall

Among the fascinating permanent exhibits at the **National Archives,** at 7th St. and Constitution Ave. NW, just north of the Mall, are the Magna Carta, the Bill of Rights, the Declaration of Independence, and the Constitution. From the 7th

St. bus shelter beside the Archives, a shuttle leaves at 8am, 9:30am, 11:30am, 1:45pm, and 3:15pm for 845 S. Picket St., Alexandria, where you can hear the infamous Watergate tapes; call the Archives at 756-6498 for information. (Open daily 10am-9pm; off-season 10am-5:30pm. 523-3183; recording 523-3000. Free.)

Also behind the line of museums on the North Mall, the **Federal Bureau of Investigation (FBI)**, between 9th and 10th St. and Pennsylvania Ave. NW (324-3447), gives the most entertaining tour in Washington. Thrill to the anti-communist exhibit, mementos of notorious criminals captured by the FBI, a laboratory of agents examining forensic specimens used to identify criminals, and a live firearms demonstration. It's better than prime time TV. Get there early in the morning or call to make reservations. The tour has become hugely popular and lines are enormous. (Free 1-hr. tours every 15 min. Open Mon.-Fri. 8:45am-4:15pm. Metro: Federal Triangle or Metro Center.)

The **Bureau of Engraving and Printing,** 14th and C St. SW (447-9709), just south of the Washington Monument, offers continuous tours of the presses that annually print over 20 billion dollars worth of money and stamps. (Self-guided tours. Open Mon.-Fri. 9am-2pm. Free.)

Ford's Theater, 511 10th St. NW (426-6924), contains the Presidential Box, frozen in time on April 15, 1865, the night Lincoln was shot. The Lincoln Museum is downstairs. Across the street from Ford's Theater is the morbid **House Where Lincoln Died,** 526 10th St. NW (426-6380). The house is worth a stop, if only for the furnishings and carefully restored rooms. (Open daily 9am-5pm. Free. Metro: Metro Center.)

The Smithsonian's **National Portrait Gallery,** 8th and F St. NW (357-2700), displays portraits of Americans from all walks of life. See Gilbert Stuart's famous unfinished portraits of George and Martha Washington, the Hall of the Presidents, and the *Time* magazine cover collection. (Tours Mon.-Fri. 10am-3pm, Sat.-Sun. and holidays 11am-2pm. Open daily 10am-5:30pm. Metro: Gallery Place.) The **National Museum of American Art,** 8th and G St. NW (357-2700), shares the building with the National Portrait Gallery. It's often deserted, despite its excellent sampling of American art from the classical to the modern abstract. (Tours Mon.-Fri. at noon, Sun. at 1:45pm. Open daily 10am-5:30pm.)

The **National Building Museum,** F St. NW (272-2448), between 4th and 5th St., exhibits displays of achievements in American building arts and architecture. The museum building itself is stunning: Look 150 feet up at the 244 busts tucked in niches around the Old Pension Building's Great Hall. (Tours Tues. at 11am and 12:30pm, Wed.-Fri. at 12:30pm, Sat.-Sun. 1pm. Open Mon.-Fri. 10am-4pm, Sat.-Sun. and holidays noon-4pm. Metro: Judiciary Sq., F St. exit.)

The White House Area

For a summer visit to the **White House,** 1600 Pennsylvania Ave. NW (456-2200 or 456-7041), try to have the office of your Senator or Representative arrange a tour. Otherwise, you'll have to suffer through a one- or two-hour wait for the regular, abbreviated tour, which takes you only through five public rooms used for receptions. (Open Tues.-Sat. 10am-noon. Free tour tickets available at booth on the Ellipse, 755-7798; open 8am-noon. Metro: McPherson Sq. or Farragut W.) In a stately 19th-century building at 17th St. between E St. and New York Ave. NW, the **Corcoran Gallery of Art** (638-3211), DC's largest and oldest private gallery, has a permanent collection of American and European art. (Free tours at 12:30pm, Thurs. at 6:30pm. Open Tues.-Wed. and Fri.-Sun. 10am-4:30pm, Thurs. 10am-9pm. Metro: Farragut W.) The **Renwick Gallery,** 17th St. and Pennsylvania Ave. (357-2531), features fascinating exhibits of design, crafts, and decorative arts. (Tours by appointment 10am-2pm. Open daily 10am-5:30pm. Metro: Farragut W.) The **National Museum for Women in the Arts,** 1250 New York Ave. NW (783-5000), celebrates women's artistic contributions in its permanent collection and traveling exhibits. The beautifully renovated Renaissance Revival building is home to works in a multitude of media—fresco to photography, ceramics to silver, nylon to neon. Collection includes pieces by Georgia O'Keeffe, Mary Cassatt, Helen Frankenthaler, and over

200 others from around the world. (Tours by appointment. Open Tues.-Sat. 10am-5pm, Sun. noon-5pm. Free.)

Memorials

If you're willing to stand in a long line to take the elevator 555 feet to the top, the **Washington Monument,** on the National Mall (426-6839), at 15th St. NW, will reward you with a perfect view down Constitution Ave. to the Capitol and across the Potomac River. The monument is the tallest building in Washington. Originally, it was to have a large baroque base, but money ran out, resulting in its present obelisk simplicity. (Stairs closed.) Spectacular **Fourth of July** festivities are held here, and during the rest of the summer the Washington Monument alternates with the Capitol building as the site of **free outdoor concerts** by the U.S. Military bands (June-Labor Day at 8pm). Call the National Park Service (485-7275) for concert information. (Monument open April 1-Labor Day daily 8am-midnight, last elevator 11:45pm; Labor Day-March 31 9am-5pm. Metro: Smithsonian.)

A visit to the **Lincoln Memorial,** West Potomac Park at 23rd St. NW (426-6842), is most memorable at twilight, when the image of the Washington Monument ripples in the long reflecting pool. The Gettysburg and the Second Inaugural Addresses are carved into the wall. Here, Martin Luther King, Jr., delivered his "I Have a Dream" speech, and black operatic singer Marion Anderson sang from the steps when the Daughters of the American Revolution barred her entrance to Constitution Hall. Call ahead to tour the memorial's underground supports. (Tours on request 8am-midnight. Open 24 hours.) Walk around to the south side of the Tidal Basin, past the cherry trees, to the **Jefferson Memorial** (426-6822). Jefferson's imposing figure stands prominently in an open building adorned with excerpts of his famous writings. (Tours 8am-midnight. Open 24 hours.) Cruise around the Tidal Basin in front of the memorial in a two-person paddleboat ($5.50 per hr.; 484-0206; daily 10am-7pm.)

The names of over 58,000 war casualties are carved into the haunting black granite **Vietnam Veterans War Memorial** (426-6700), sunken into the ground on the north side of the reflecting pool at Constitution Ave. and 21st St. NW, like "a rift in the earth." Designer Maya Ying Lin's eloquent design provokes violent and powerful emotions. Its eye-level simplicity and spare presentation confront the confusion and complexity of the war, and the nighttime reflections of the Capitol, the Washington Monument, and the Lincoln Memorial symbolize the ideals these soldiers gave their lives to uphold. After a bitter controversy over the aptness of such an abstract construction, a remarkably realistic statue of three veterans, by Frederick Hart, was built close to Lin's masterpiece.

The unforgettable World War II photograph of weary Marines triumphantly hoisting an American flag on Mt. Suribachi has been immortalized in the largest bronze statue ever cast, the 78-foot **Iwo Jima Statue Marine Corps Memorial,** which commemorates all Marines lost since 1775. (On Rte. 50, near Arlington Cemetery. Open 24 hours. Metro: Arlington Cemetery.)

Dupont Circle/Adams Morgan

Dupont Circle and Adams Morgan are the twin hubs of Washington's ethnic, intellectual, and gay communities. Massachusetts and New Hampshire Avenues intersect in Dupont Circle about 10 blocks north of the White House. The Circle's grassy island is popular with chess players, lunching office workers, and drug dealers. Colorful and increasingly popular Adams Morgan is off upper Connecticut Ave., along Columbia Rd. **Farragut Square,** 3 blocks south of Connecticut Ave., on 17th St. between I and K St. NW, is a pretty place to picnic to the summer sounds of flute duets and jazz sax players.

The **Phillips Collection,** 1600-1612 21st St. NW (387-0961) was America's first museum of modern art. In addition to Renoir's masterpiece, *Luncheon of the Boating Party,* this intimate museum houses a connoisseur's choice of 19th- and 20th-century French painting and the work of American modernists such as Georgia O'Keeffe and Arthur Dove. (Free concerts Sept.-May Sun. at 5pm; check the *Wash-*

ington Post's "Weekend" for information. Free tours Wed. and Sat. at 2pm. Disabled access. Open Tues.-Sat. 10am-5pm, Sun. 2-7pm. Metro: Dupont Circle, Q St. exit.)

The **National Geographic Explorer's Hall,** 17th and M St. NW (857-7588; N.G. Society 857-7000), displays the world's largest free-standing globe and features fascinating exhibits on early humanity, Colorado cliff dwellers, and accounts of Arctic and underwater expeditions. Temporary exhibits have included Spanish treasure salvaged from sunken galleons and displays on the development of holography. (Open Mon.-Sat. and holidays 9am-5pm, Sun. 10am-5pm. Disabled access. Metro: Farragut North.)

The **Woodrow Wilson House,** 2340 S St. NW (387-4062), was the President's home from 1921 until his death in 1924. Washington's only public presidential home is filled with artifacts from World War I, Wilson's administration, and the 1920s. (1-hr. tours on request given by friendly, knowledgeable guides. Make reservations for tours for the blind and the hearing-impaired. Open Tues.-Sat. 10am-4pm, Sun. noon-4pm. Admission $3.50, seniors and students $2. Metro: Dupont Circle.)

The **Textile Museum,** 2320 S St. NW (667-0441), houses a colorful display of new and antique carpets and cloths from Asia, the Middle East, and South America. (Tours Wed. 1:30pm and Sun. 2pm. Open Tues.-Sat. 10am-5pm, Sun. 1-5pm. Donation. Metro: Dupont Circle.) The **National Rifle Association Museum,** 1600 Rhode Island Ave. NW (828-6255), features Guns! Guns! Guns! Over 1,000 firearms are on display including Teddy Roosevelt's pistol and Ronald Reagan's flintlock. (Open Mon.-Fri. 10am-4pm. Free.)

Take in the spectacular view of Washington and the surrounding area from the Pilgrim Observation Gallery at **Washington National Cathedral,** Massachusetts and Wisconsin Ave. NW (537-6200). The sixth largest in the world and the second largest in the U.S., this impressive 14th-century Gothic cathedral features intricate stained glass windows, stone carvings, Woodrow Wilson's tomb, and the London Brass Rubbing Center. (Continuous tours Mon.-Sat. 10am-3:15pm, Sun. 12:30pm and 2:45pm. Open Mon.-Fri. 10am-7:30pm, Sat.-Sun. 10am-4:30pm; Sept. 8-May 3 daily 10am-4:30pm. Metro: Tenleytown, then bus #36 "Hillcrest.")

Georgetown

The settling of Georgetown preceded the construction of the District of Columbia, and some streets retain their original names. Today, Georgetown buzzes with constant activity. **M Street** and **Wisconsin Avenue,** the main streets running through Georgetown, overflow with unusual stores, fashionable clubs, and expensive restaurants. If what you're looking for is slightly offbeat, Georgetown probably has it. But it won't be cheap. Some of DC's most beautiful townhouses are on the winding streets off the main drags. A warning: On weekend nights, gridlock is the norm here.

Georgetown is, not surprisingly, the home of **Georgetown University,** 3800 Reservoir Rd. NW, a Jesuit school known for fine academics and a stellar basketball team. The shady campus displays a wide variety of architectural styles including some good examples of collegiate Gothic. Daily tours are given by the admissions office. (687-3600; general information 687-3634; student activities 687-3704.)

Dumbarton Oaks Museum and Garden, 1703 32nd St. NW (342-3233), is a country estate nestled in the heart of one of Washington's busiest districts. The mansion houses a rare collection of Pre-Columbian and Byzantine art, and the gardens vie with the best in Europe. (Open Tues.-Sat. 2-5pm. Gardens open 2-6pm. Admission $2, seniors and children $1. Wed. seniors free. Free to all Oct. 31-April 1. Disabled access. Metro: Dupont Circle, transfer to Q St., bus up Wisconsin Ave.)

Hillwood, 4155 Linnean Ave. NW (686-5807), is the former mansion of General Foods' heiress Marjorie Meriweather Post. Hillwood contains the largest collection of Russian decorative art outside of Russia. (Tours daily at 9am, 10:30am, noon, and 1:30pm by appointment only; $7. Reserve well in advance. Gardens open Mon. and Wed.-Sat. 11am-4pm. Admission $2. Minimum age 12.)

Parks

If the Mall seems too bleak a place to spend a hot summer afternoon, ride the Metro out to the **National Zoological Park,** on the 3000 block of Connecticut Ave. NW (673-4800 or 673-4717). One of the largest and best-run zoos in the country, highlights include two giant pandas, bald eagles, kangaroos, and exotic birds. (Tours by special arrangement; call 673-4955. Grounds open daily 8am-8pm, buildings 9am-6pm; Sept. 16-April 30 daily 8am-6pm, buildings 9am-4:30pm. Metro: Woodley Park-National Zoo.)

The **Potomac Park** lies north and south of the Jefferson Memorial and Tidal Basin. Look for a metal giant emerging from the earth. It's a sculpture called *The Awakening.* Golf, swimming, and paddleboating are available. (For paddleboats, call 484-3475; open daily 9am-9pm. $5.50 per hour. Those under 18 must be accompanied by an adult.) **Lafayette Square,** on Pennsylvania Ave. and 16th St., is a meticulous little park named after the French general who helped the U.S. win the Revolution. The **U.S. National Arboretum,** 3501 New York Ave. NE (475-4815), spreads across 444 acres of magnificently landscaped grounds. The special bonsai collection will make you feel tall. (Open Mon.-Fri. 8am-5pm, Sat.-Sun. 10am-5pm. Bonsai collection open daily 10am-2:30 pm. Call about facilities for the disabled. Metro: Stadium Armory, walk to 24th and R St. NE.)

George Washington was counted among the engineers and architects of the **Chesapeake and Ohio Canal,** one of the country's first "think-big" schemes. The plan foresaw the Potomac River as the chief trade route between Europe and the Midwest. Now a national historic park (653-5844), the Georgetown portion of the canal is a charming park and the setting for free jazz concerts on Sunday afternoons. The park runs parallel to the Potomac River all the way to Cumberland, MD, with 185 miles of biking and hiking trails. You can rent boats and canoes for the canal ($4.50 per hr., $10 per day), or bikes ($7 per day) for the towpath at **Fletcher's Boat House,** 4940 Canal Rd. NW (244-0461; open daily 9am-7:30pm). The park service offers 1½-hour rides on a 19th-century, mule-drawn canal boat, *The Georgetown,* accompanied by commentary. (Call 472-4376. Rides April 10-Oct. 20 Wed.-Sun. at 10:30am, 1pm, and 3pm, Fri.-Sat. 10:30am, 1pm, 3pm, and 5pm. Admission $4, seniors $3, under 12 $2.50.)

Seasonal Events

Martin Luther King, Jr.'s Birthday, 3rd Monday in Jan. (727-1186). Dancing, singing, and a parade down Constitution Ave.

Black History Month, in Feb. (357-2700). Special exhibits at the Museum of African Art; programs in the Baird Auditorium.

Lincoln's Birthday, Feb. 12 (485-9666). Wreaths laid at his grave at noon; speeches given, including a reading of the Gettysburg Address at the Lincoln Memorial.

George Washington's Birthday, the Mon. before Feb. 22 (426-6700). Open house at Mount Vernon and wreath-laying ceremony at the Washington Monument at 11:30am. Alexandria, VA, celebrates with the Old Homes Tour (549-0205); a reenactment of Revolutionary War Camp, Fort Ward Park, 4301 W. Braddock Rd., Sun. before the holiday; and a huge parade, complete with drums, bagpipes, and military bands.

Chinese New Year, in Feb. (638-1044 or 660-6986). The mayor sets off the first firecracker as dragon dancers parade through the streets of Chinatown.

St. Patrick's Day Parade, March 17 (or the Sunday before), down Constitution Ave., between 7th and 17th St. (424-2200). Floats, dancers, and Irish music from 1-3:30pm.

Smithsonian Kite Festival, late March (357-3030). Go fly a kite or watch designers of all ages at the Washington Monument compete for prizes and trophies.

The National Cherry Blossom Festival, late March or early April (789-7000). Cherry Blossom Parade on Constitution Ave. from 7th to 17th St. Celebration of spring, the cherry blossoms, and Japanese-American friendship (the trees were given to the U.S. by Japan in 1912). Other events include fireworks, a fashion show, music, the Japanese Lantern Lighting ceremony, and a marathon.

Easter Egg Roll, Easter, White House Lawn (456-2200). Kids under 8 only; must be accompanied by an adult. Eggs and entertainment provided.

Imagination Celebration, early April at the Kennedy Center (254-3600). Performing arts festival for young people hosts some of the best National Children's Theatre Companies.

White House Spring Garden Tour, one weekend in mid-April (456-2200). Includes West Lawn and Jacqueline Kennedy Rose Garden. **Fall Tour** (426 6700) in mid-Oct.

Greek Spring Festival, late May (829-2916). Ste. Constantine and Helen Greek Orthodox Church, 4115 16th St. NW. Greek food, music, dancing, games, arts and crafts. **Fall Bazaar** (829-2910) in mid-Sept.

Memorial Day, last Mon. in May (485-9666). More wreath-laying at Arlington and the Vietnam Memorial. The National Symphony Orchestra plays on the West Lawn of the Capitol. Bring a blanket.

Potomac Riverfest, 2 weekends in June (387-8292). Free entertainment, fireworks, boat rides, exotic food, and water events along the river at various locations in southwest DC.

Festival of American Folk Life, late June (357-2700). On the Mall. A display of American arts and crafts such as clogging and whittling.

Gay Pride Day, June 18 (833-3234 or 387-4348). An annual rally and march in support of gay rights.

Fourth of July, (guess when). Festivities begin with a parade along the Mall and the DC Free Jazz Festival (783-0360), with free concerts at Western Plaza. The National Symphony Orchestra performs on the Capitol steps, while crowds rock 'n' roll at the Washington Monument. Fireworks at 9:15pm. This is Washington's biggest blow-out of the year, so expect massive and sometimes rowdy crowds. Take the subway and *not* a car.

Bastille Day Race, July 14 (452-1132). Dominique's Restaurant sponsors the 12-block race, in which waiters carry champagne glasses on trays and demonstrate their juggling ability for the prize: a free trip to Paris. Race starts at 20th St. and Pennsylvania Ave. NW at noon.

National Frisbee Festival, Labor Day Sunday (301-843-2634). The largest non-competitive frisbee festival with world-class champions and disc-catching dogs. On the Mall near the Air and Space Museum.

Add Arts Festival, Labor Day Weekend (783-0360). All DC's a stage during 2 days of music, dance, film, family entertainment, and food along Vendors' Mall (700 F St.) and Western Plaza (1300 Pennsylvania Ave.).

Adams Morgan Day, 2nd Sun. in Sept. (745-0179). A Latino *fiesta,* complete with food, arts, crafts, and music in DC's Hispanic Adams-Morgan area near 18th St. and Columbia Rd.

Veteran's Day, Nov. 11 (475-0843). The president lays a wreath at Arlington's Tomb of the Unknown Soldier and at the Vietnam Veteran's Memorial.

Candlelight Tour of the White House, in Dec. (426-6700). See the White House by candles set in 6-foot-high teak candlesticks. You can also take the **Candlelight Tour of Alexandria,** Virginia's stately homes (549-0205).

Hannukah Festival, in Dec. (857-6583), B'nai B'rith Center. Traditional music and food.

U.S. Capitol Tree Lighting, mid-Dec. (224-3069). The tree at the Capitol is lit the day before the "Pageant of Peace," as military bands perform.

National Christmas Tree, lit by the president the Thurs. before Christmas (485-9666), in the Ellipse. Choruses sing traditional music. Until New Year's Day, the Mall and the Ellipse host choral performances, a nativity scene, and a burning Yule log. *Tannenbaum* maniacs will love the **Smithsonian Trees of Christmas** (357-2700), outside the Museum of American History, which are bedecked with ornaments from all over the world.

New Year's Eve at the Old Post Office (673-7663). Tens of thousands bid farewell to days of Auld Lang Syne amidst food, drink, live entertainment, and merriment at the city's largest party. Watch as the postage stamp drops from the Post Office Tower at midnight.

Outside the District

Great Falls Park (759-2925), 10 miles outside the district on MacArthur Blvd., affords an excellent view of the falls and is a great place for a picnic. Take advantage of hiking and riding trails, rock climbing, nature walks, and guided tours, and, for the more adventurous, excellent class-three rapids for kayaking, canoeing or rafting.

At the **Arlington National Cemetery,** located across Memorial Bridge in Arlington (703-692-0931), the 175,000 graves include those of Robert Kennedy, Joe Louis, Oliver Wendell Holmes, and the simple, but moving, grave of unknown casualties of war. The inscription on the **Tomb of the Unknown Soldier** reads, "Here rests in honored glory an American soldier known but to God." Watch for the changing of the Honor Guard every hour. An eternal flame burns next to the grave of John F. Kennedy. (Open April-Sept. daily 8am-7pm; Oct.-March 8am-5pm. Metro: Blue to Arlington Cemetery, or take the Tourmobile.)

Need a parking space? Try the **Pentagon** (695-1776), across Memorial Bridge. The Pentagon is the world's largest office building (23,000 employees), and its mammoth parking lot blots out a good chunk of Arlington, VA. Hour-long tours of the Defense Department and Armed Forces' Headquarters include the Time-Life Collection of World War II art, Hall of Heroes, Flag Corridors, and more. (Tours every ½ hr. after security check at Tourbooth in Pentagon Metro stop. Open Mon.-Fri. 9:30am-3:30pm. Free.)

In **Alexandria's Old Town,** (VA), over 1000 18th-century buildings have been completely restored. Major sights include the Torpedo Factory Art Center, where nearly 200 artists have their studios, Christ Church, George Washington's Masonic Memorial, and the Gadsby's Tavern Museum. There are also a series of fine boutiques and restaurants. To get to **Alexandria,** cross the 14th St. Bridge and go south on the George Washington Pkwy.; by Metro, take the yellow line to King St. Station and catch DASH bus #2 or 5 (60¢). For more information, call Alexandria Visitors Center (703-549-0205).

Eight miles south of Alexandria at the end of the parkway, **Mount Vernon** (703-780-2000) is a delight. George Washington chose the loveliest spot on the whole length of the Potomac River for his house. A tour of the gardens and the small buildings surrounding the entry drive will give you a good idea of how a Southern tobacco plantation operated. Washington's tomb is also on the 30-acre grounds. (Open daily 9am-5pm; Nov.-Feb. 9am-4pm. Admission $5, seniors $4, children $2. Most buildings and grounds are wheelchair-accessible.) Take the Yellow or Blue Metroline to National Airport, then bus #11H ("Fort Belvoire"). Gray Line Sightseeing Tourmobiles (301-386-8300) can also transport you here. (Tours daily at 9am, 4 hr., $18, children $9.) **Washington Boat Lines** (554-8000) runs trips Tues.-Sun. that are usually crowded. (March-Nov. at 9am and 2pm, 4¾ hr. Buy tickets 1 hr. before departure. Fare $16.25, ages 6-11 $9. Cruise leaves from Pier 4, 6th and Water St.)

Entertainment

Keep up with the whirl of events and club listings with the free weekly *City Paper,* the "Washington Weekend" section of every Thursday's *Washington Times,* the "Weekend" section of every Friday's *Washington Post,* the monthly *Washingtonian* magazine ($2), or the free city magazines *Go* (monthly), *Where* (monthly), and *This Week in the Nation's Capital* (weekly).

Performing Arts

Washington is now the nation's fourth-largest theater city (as rated by *Variety* magazine). The **National Theater,** 1321 Pennsylvania Ave. NW (800-233-3123 or 628-6161; Metro: Metro Center), one of America's oldest, presents Broadway shows. Tickets run from $25-40. Same-day, half-price tickets and advance tickets are available for this and other theaters at **TICKETplace,** 12th and F St. NW (call 842-5387), at Metro Center, 12th St. exit. The **Arena Stage,** 6th St. and Maine Ave. SW (488-3300; Metro: L'Enfant Plaza), has one of the best repertory companies in the nation.

The **John F. Kennedy Center for the Performing Arts,** 2700 F St. NW (254-3600), is a dazzlingly white multi-theater complex that hosts performances by the Washington Opera, internationally renowned ballet troupes, Broadway shows, and screenings for the American Film Institute. Take in the view of the Potomac from the roof terrace. At Christmas, a *Messiah* sing-along is held in the Opera House. (Tickets $5.75, students half-price; standing-room tickets available before performances. Free tours 10am-1pm. Open daily 10am-9pm. Metro: Foggy Bottom.)

The **Wolf Trap Farm Park**, 1624 Trap Rd., Vienna, VA (255-1860), offers summer performances by famous ballet and dance companies, top-name musicians, symphonies, and sometimes even ice skaters. Audiences sit indoors or lounge on the lawn outside the open-walled Filene Center.

Nightlife

During the summer, Washington comes alive with music. The cozy amphitheater at the **Meriweather Post Pavilion** (982-1800) attracts big-name rock bands. (Take Rte. 270 to Columbia, MD, and follow the signs.) A series of summer concerts is held within the city as well. Every evening at 8pm, catch one of the **U.S. Military Bands** at either the West Terrace of the Capitol, or Sylvan Theatre on the Washington Monument grounds. (Information: Navy Band 433-2525, Army Band 696-3399, Marine Band 433-4011, Air Force Band 767-5658.) Museums are often the sites of free concerts as well (check the National Gallery of Art and the Air and Space Museum). If jazz and soul are more your thing, try the **Carter Barron Amphitheater,** at 16th St. and Colorado Ave. NW (829-3200), which offer concerts every weekend. (Tickets $5.)

One of the liveliest sections of the city, **Georgetown** is a great place to experience Washington nightlife. On Friday and Saturday evenings, the streets are crowded with musicians, flower sellers, Hare Krishna devotees, rowdy students, and stylish socialites. Drinkers should beware of inflated prices; try the **Tombs,** 1226 36th St. NW (337-6668; open Mon.-Thurs. 11am-2am, Fri.-Sat. 11am-3am, Sun. 10am-2am), near the Georgetown campus; the **American Café,** 1211 Wisconsin Ave. NW (944-9464; open Mon.-Thurs. 11am-3am, Fri.-Sat. 11am-4am, Sun. 10:30am-3am), which is a good inexpensive restaurant; or the **Bayou,** 3135 K St. NW (333-2897; open Mon.-Thurs. and Sun. 8pm-2am, Fri.-Sat. 8pm-3am), which features nightly big-name rock 'n' roll. Cover ranges from $2-15.

Badlands, 1415 22nd at P St. NW (296-0505). Popular gay bar. Mixed ages, small dance floor, video room. Open Tues. and Thurs. 9pm-2am, Fri.-Sat. 9pm-3am, Sun. 5pm-2am. Cover: Tues. $1, Thurs. $2, Fri.-Sat. $4, Sun. $1 (after 7pm).

Blues Alley, 1073 Rear Wisconsin Ave. NW (337-4141). World-class jazz artists and Creole cuisine have starred at this Georgetown jazz supper club—located in an actual alley behind Wisconsin Ave.—for over 20 years. Dinner $12-16 served from 6pm. Shows Sun.-Thurs. at 8pm and 10pm, Fri.-Sat. at 8pm, 10pm, and midnight. Call for schedule, prices, and reservations.

Brickskeller, 1523 22nd St. NW (293-1885). Metro: Dupont Circle. Steaks and buffalo burgers ($4-14), but the real attraction is their enormous selection of beer—over 500 brands. Mon.-Thurs. 11:30am-2am, Fri. 11:30am-3am, Sat. 6pm-3am, Sun. 6pm-2am.

Cities, 2424 18th St. NW (328-7194). Hot spot for eclectic dining and dancing crowd. Stays "in" by completely changing its menu and decor every 4 months to highlight a new city. Dinner $12-16. Nightclub upstairs features contemporary disco, long bar, and lounge. Restaurant open Sun.-Thurs. 6-11:30pm, Fri.-Sat. 6pm-midnight. Dancing Wed.-Thurs. 10pm-2am, Fri.-Sat. 10pm-3am. Cover: Wed.-Thurs. $5, Fri.-Sat. $7.

Comedy Cafe, 1520 K St. NW (638-5653). Metro: Farragut North. The best comedy club in town. Cover varies, usually $8 on weekends, $16 with dinner. Open mike night Thurs. Cover $2.49. Drink and dance to oldies downstairs at Jonathan's (open Mon.-Fri. 11:30am-2am). Café open Wed.-Fri. 11:30am-2:30pm, Thurs.-Sat. 7pm-2am. Shows Fri. at 8:30 and 10:30pm, Sat. at 7:30, 9:30, and 11:30pm. Call for reservations.

Dakota, 1777 Columbia Rd. NW (265-6600). Filled with young urban hipsters, this sleek place has a roomy, lighted dance floor, mezzanine for people-watching, and 2 bars. Top-40 and progressive music. **Montana Café** in back has new American cuisine (dinner $6-10). Café open Tues.-Sun. 6:30-11pm. Dancing Tues. 6:30pm-1am, Wed.-Thurs. 6:30pm-2am, Fri.-Sat.

6:30pm-3am, Sun. (gay night) 6:30pm-2am. Cover: after 9:30pm, Tues. $3, Wed. $4, Fri.-Sat. $7, Sun. $2.

D.C. Space, 433 7th St. NW (347-4960 or 347-1445), at E St. Space is the place for cabaret dinner theater, live bands, films, poetry readings, and art shows. Cabaret shows Wed.-Thurs. at 7pm, Fri.-Sat. at 7:30pm. Rock, jazz, and new wave bands Wed.-Thurs. at 10:30pm, Fri.-Sat. at 11pm.

Fifth Column, 915 F St. NW (393-3632). Dance on 3 levels of a converted downtown bank amidst fishtanks, sculptures, photography, and paintings by local artists. Progressive music on main floor, lounge upstairs, harder rock downstairs. Artsy crowd. Open Wed.-Thurs. and Sun. 9pm-2am, Fri.-Sat. 9pm-3am. Cover Fri.-Sat. $7.

Kilamanjaro, 1724 California St. NW (328-3838). International disco club features African, Latin, and Caribbean disco, plus calypso and reggae. Also serves lunch and dinner. Happy hour 4-8pm. Open Mon.-Thurs. and Sun. noon-2am, Fri. noon-4am, Sat. 3pm-4am. Cover: after 9pm, Thurs. and Sun. $3, Fri.-Sat, $6.

930 Club, 930 F St. NW (393-0930 or 638-2008). Metro: Metro Center. A star among DC nightclubs featuring hot new alternative and progressive rock bands. Box office open Tues.-Fri. after 1 pm. Cover $7-9. Under 18 can get in with hand stamped. Happy hour video cabaret Wed.-Fri., doors open at 4pm.

One Step Down, 2517 Pennsylvania Ave. NW (331-8863), near George Washington University. Metro: Foggy Bottom-GWU. Great local and out-of-town groups, usually from New York. All-jazz jukebox; free jam sessions Sat.-Sun. 3:30-7:30pm. Open Sun.-Thurs. 10am-2am, Fri.-Sat. 10am-3am. Happy hour 3-7pm. Cover: Sun.-Mon. and Thurs. $5, Fri.-Sat. $7.50-10.

West Virginia

The boundary line between the Virginias was drawn during the Civil War era, when most of Virginia seceded from the Union. The westernmost counties, choosing to keep their ties with the north, became a separate state in 1863, thus formalizing the longstanding rift between the mountainous and coastal regions.

West Virginia at last appears to be economically rising from the dust of its coal-mining history. Although cities such as Charleston still have colossal manufacturing plants, many towns have redirected their energies toward tourism. An example is the recent attempt to attract visitors to the majestic Allegheny Mountains. While years of neglect are still obvious in the poor roads and occasional barren areas (from previous strip-mining), now an excellent state park system enables visitors to hike, raft, and explore caverns throughout the rugged peaks.

Practical Information

Capital: Charleston.

Tourist Information: Travel Development Division, 1900 Washington St., Charleston 25305 (348-2286 or 800-225-5982). **Division of Parks and Recreation,** 1800 Washington St., Charleston 25305. **U.S. Forest Service Supervisor's Office,** Sycamore St., Elkins 26241 (636-1800).

Time Zone: Eastern. **Postal Abbreviation:** WV.

Area Code: 304.

Harpers Ferry

Lying at the confluence of the Shenandoah and Potomac Rivers and ringed by the Blue Ridge Mountains, tiny Harpers Ferry's main interest is historical. In October of 1859, the radical abolitionist John Brown led his 22-man "army of liberation" into the town to seize the U.S. arsenal here and its large store of weapons. Brown hoped his actions would incite a large-scale slave insurrection, but he was mistaken. In two days, troops under the command of Robert E. Lee regained control of the town, and Brown was eventually hung. Though the raid was a failure, it was an indicator of the increasing emotional heat that surrounding the slavery issue. Less than two years later, the nation slid into civil war.

The best place to begin a tour of the town is at the **visitors information center,** on Shenandoah St. in the park (535-6371). There, you will find orientation films, exhibits, and a host of activities explaining the historical significance of the area. (Park Service office and historic buildings are open daily 9am-5pm; in summer 8am-5pm.) The park itself consists of restored buildings, including a general store, tavern, and blacksmith's shop as well as the building where John Brown made his final stand. Costumed and uniformed members of the National Park Service are on hand to talk about daily life in the 19th century, the story of John Brown's raid, and the town's destruction during the Civil War. History buffs should head to the **Park Service Book Store** on High St. with its excellent collection of Civil War literature.

If the Park Service's various displays are not enough to satisfy your curiosity about the raid, pay a visit to the **John Brown Wax Museum,** at the corner of High and Potomac St. (536-6321). Here the life of John Brown and the story of his raid are replayed in a series of vignettes about as hot as wax can get. (Open March-Dec. daily 9am-5pm.)

But Harpers Ferry offers more than a look at the past. Nearby **Jefferson's Rock** provides a view that the statesman once declared "worth a trip across the Atlantic." The vista includes two rivers and three states. The old campus of **Storer University,** one of the first black colleges in the United States, is also nearby. Harper's Ferry offers easy access to the **Appalachian Trail** and the **Chesapeake and Ohio Towpath. Appalachian Trail Conference Headquarters** can be contacted by writing P.O. Box 807. (535-6331; open Mon.-Fri. 9am-5pm.) **Blue Ridge Outfitters** (725-3444), a few miles west of Harpers Ferry on Rte. 340 N. arranges several excursions, from two-hour canoe trips on the Shenandoah to three-day whitewater rafting on Virginia's toughest waterways. Prices range accordingly, starting at $27. (Open daily 8am-7pm.)

For accommodations try the **Harpers Ferry Hostel,** Rte. 2, P.O. Box 248E (301-834-7652), located across the C&O canal in Knoxville, MD. ($7; in winter $8.) Call about a ride from the Harpers Ferry train station. From the front porch of the **Hill-top House,** on Ridge St. (535-2132 or 800-338-8319), you can see the sun set on the Blue Ridge Mountains as you overlook Maryland, Virginia, and West Virginia. Only five minutes from the center of town, this hotel has extremely quiet and comfortable rooms. (Singles $54. Doubles $59.) For cheaper accommodations try the **Comfort Inn,** Rte. 340 and Union St. (535-6391). A 10-minute walk from town. (Singles $42. Doubles $48. Continental Breakfast included.) Nearby Martinsburg, WV offers several motels, but little else. The rooms at the **Wheatland Motel,** 1193 Winchester Ave. (267-2994), have TV and A/C. (Rooms from $25, some with disabled access and facilities.)

You can **camp** along the C&O Canal, where sites are spaced 5 miles apart, or in one of the five Maryland state park campgrounds that lie within 30 miles of Harpers Ferry. The nearest are **Washington Monument State Park** (301-432-8065), 15 miles north on Rte. 67 near Boonsboro (sites $4), and **Greenbrier State Park** (301-791-4767), a few miles north of Boonsboro on Rte. 66 between exits 35 and 42 on I-70 ($10).

Make Harpers Ferry a stop on the C&O Canal, or a daytrip out of Washington, D.C. **Amtrak** (800-872-7245) serves Harpers Ferry directly from DC (1 per day, 1½ hr., $11.50; reservations required). The **Greyhound/Trailways** station there, on E. All Saints' St. (301-663-3311), has connections to DC ($10), Baltimore ($8), and Cumberland, MD ($15.40).

Harpers Ferry's **ZIP code** is 25425; the **area code** is 304.

Monongahela National Forest

Mammoth **Monongahela National Forest,** popular with white-water rafters, is home to deer, bear, and wild turkeys, and spelunkers prowling around below ground in magnificent limestone caverns. But camping is the main attraction here, with 600 miles of prize hiking trails and over 500 campsites to lure the traveler. Camp in an established site ($10 or less), or sleep in the backcountry for free. Twenty-five miles north on Rte. 92, the forest's **Lake Sherwood Area** (536-3660) offers fishing, hunting, swimming, hiking and boating, as well as several campgrounds. The campground fills only on major holidays. (2-week max. stay. Sites $8-9.) A three-hour drive north will bring you to **Blackwater Falls State Park** (800-225-5982), ¼ mile southwest of Rte. 32. This dazzling waterfall is the most popular in West Virginia. (Campgrounds available, with hiking and swimming, April-Oct. Sites $8-9.) For advice and information on exploring Monongahela, visit the White Sulphur Springs **Forest Service Office** in the Federal Building (536-2144), at the corner of E. Main and Mountain Ave. (Open Mon.-Fri. 8am-4:45pm.) For information on the whole forest, which encompasses much of West Virginia's most scenic mountain country, contact the Supervisor's Office, Monongahela National Forest, P.O. Box 1548, Elkins 26241 (636-1800; Mon.-Fri. 9am-5pm).

SOUTHEAST

To the uninitiated, the Southeast looks like a glorious, endless beach. The Atlantic seaboard and Gulf Coast have some of the country's best and most popular oceanfront playgrounds. A long string of cities such as North Carolina's Nag's Head, South Carolina's Myrtle Beach, and Florida's Daytona Beach, Ft. Lauderdale, and Miami Beach stretch along the coast, seeming to exist only for sunbathers. To these add Disney World, the world's most popular attraction, and you get Vacationland, USA.

But the reputation as a beacher's paradise can be very misleading. Apart from these vacation communities, and such thriving areas as Atlanta and the Research Triangle, the Southeast possesses a pace and culture distinct from the rest of the country. Hard-hit by economic depression, the residents of this agriculture-dependent region continue to view the wealthier and more industrialized north almost as a foreign country. They cling defiantly to the religion and patriotism (no flag-burning here) that they feel has always been the country's backbone.

Perhaps the greatest and most unifying element of the Southeast is that nearly everyone has a porch—from Georgia's poorest farmers to Charleston's *grandes dames.* Most natives like to pass an evening there, swinging and sipping iced tea, chatting with neighbors or even with passing strangers. Outside the vacation and business centers, you will rarely find someone in the Southeast who doesn't have time to talk.

Travel

In the winter months, waves of northern tourists flood the Southeastern beaches. Florida's collegiate spring break phenomenon, corresponding with school calendars, begins in February, peaks in mid-March, and tapers off into mid-April. Although the crowds of December to April may make finding rooms difficult, this tourist activity can be a blessing for the budget traveler. Look for advertisements of special deals on accommodations and transportation in northern newspapers and college publications. Summer brings crowds to Orlando, Myrtle Beach, the Outer Banks, and other amusement hot spots.

Atlanta's Hartsfield Airport, the world's second busiest, is the region's major air terminal. **Delta, Eastern,** and **Southern Airlines** are major carriers throughout the South. **U.S. Air** can fly you conveniently and inexpensively through Pittsburgh to most major Southern cities.

Amtrak trains begin in Boston and travel down the southeastern coast in two branches. One connects the middle part of North Carolina, western South Carolina, and Atlanta, then goes west to Alabama and eventually to New Orleans. The other travels down eastern North Carolina, South Carolina, and Georgia, and finishes up in Florida where, thanks to Henry Flagler, service is excellent. Unfortunately, there are no routes connecting the two branches. However, Amtrak does have service connecting Florida with New Orleans.

Bus travelers should have few problems getting to most of the region's cities and towns. Atlanta is a central terminus for **Greyhound/Trailways,** and even the Great Smokies are brought within range by an infrequent schedule out of Asheville, NC. The most poorly served areas are North Carolina's Outer Banks and Georgia's low country.

Car rental rates in Florida are consistently lower than anywhere else in the U.S. National companies drop their rates to $99 per week, and **Alamo** (800-327-9633) frequently offers $60 per week specials with low ($30) or non-existent drop-off fees. Find more good deals at **General** (800-327-7607), a regional company; **Value** (800-327-2501); **Holiday Pay-Less** (800-237-2804); and **Thrifty** (800-367-2277). **Na-**

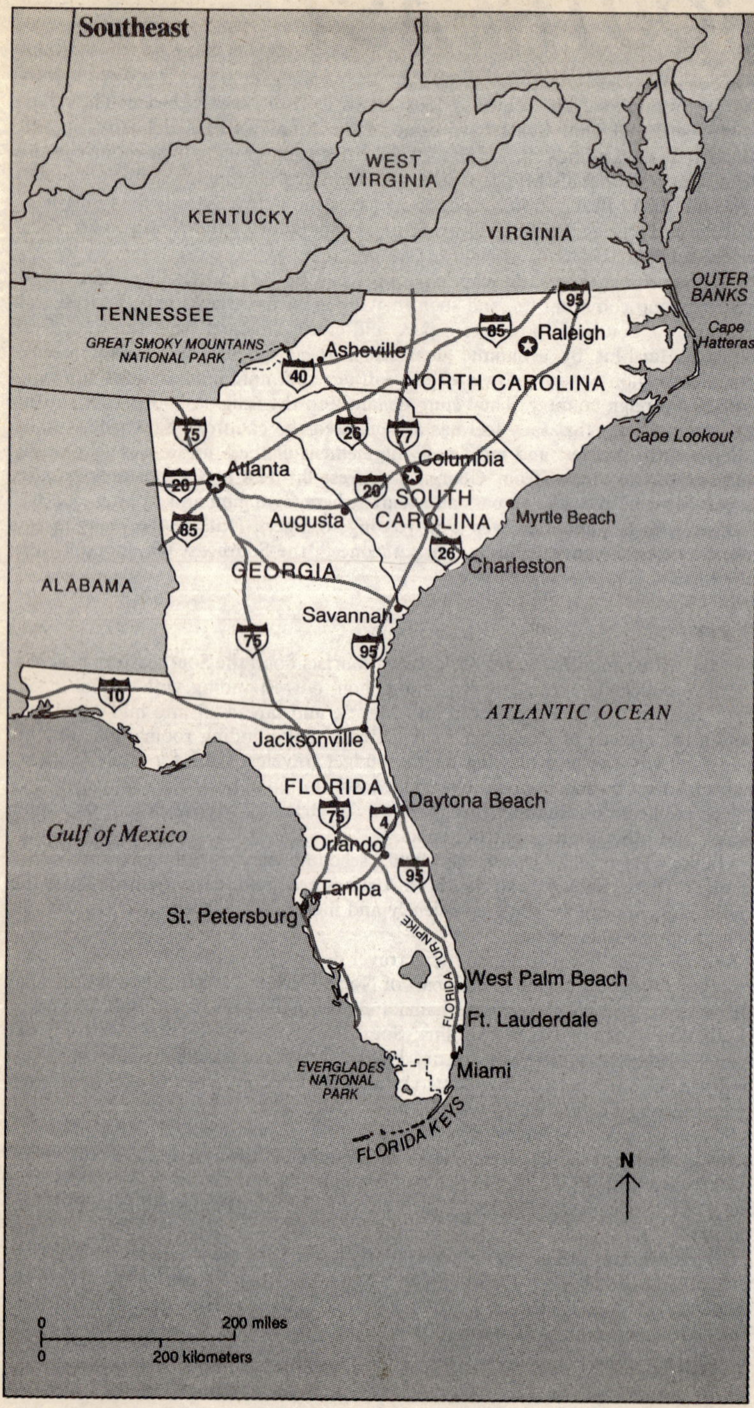
Southeast
WEST VIRGINIA
KENTUCKY
VIRGINIA
TENNESSEE
OUTER BANKS
Cape Hatteras
GREAT SMOKY MOUNTAINS NATIONAL PARK
Asheville
Raleigh
NORTH CAROLINA
Cape Lookout
Atlanta
Columbia
SOUTH CAROLINA
Augusta
Myrtle Beach
Charleston
GEORGIA
ALABAMA
Savannah
ATLANTIC OCEAN
Jacksonville
FLORIDA
Daytona Beach
Gulf of Mexico
Orlando
Tampa
St. Petersburg
FLORIDA TURNPIKE
West Palm Beach
Ft. Lauderdale
Miami
EVERGLADES NATIONAL PARK
FLORIDA KEYS
N
0
200 miles
0
200 kilometers
95
85
40
75
26
77
20
85
26
75
95
10
75
4
95

tional (800-227-7368) sometimes has special discounts and regulations for students and foreigners. Be sure to call around before you make reservations.

There are youth hostels scattered throughout the Appalachians and Florida, but aside from camping, there are few other bargain accommodations. Look for budget hotel chains, such as **Motel 6** (505-891-6161) and **Econo Lodge** (800-446-6900) on the outskirts of cities. Winter is the high season here; the sweltering sun and high humidity of June, July, and August often result summertime bargains. **State parks** with campsites are plentiful throughout the region, and many **national forests** offer free primitive camping.

Florida

In 1513 Ponce de León landed on the Florida coast near what would soon be St. Augustine, in a quest for the elusive Fountain of Youth. Multitudes continue to be seduced by the Sunshine State's promise: the elderly seek a retirement haven, immigrants come in hope of greater opportunity, students are lured by the promise of a deep tan and a cold beer, and adults and children alike are drawn by the fantasy of Disney World. You will never meet an "average" Floridian—Cuban immigrants mingle with rednecks, retirees, and reveling students.

An uglier side emerges from this land of illusion. Florida's booming population is putting an increasing strain on the state's resources. Burgeoning commercial strips and tremendous development have created a long string of neon eyesores on the state's once pristine beaches. A steady flow of often unemployed illegal aliens flood into southern Florida, exacerbating already volatile and fear-ridden race relations. Most of the illegal drugs that eventually reach northern cities enter through Florida, creating an overwhelming enforcement problem. All of these factors mingle in the crucible of Miami, an immensely rich, wonderful, and frightening city.

Illusions and disillusionment aside, there is hardly a place in the world that caters to visitors as well as Florida. The beaches are beautiful, the amusement parks are wonderful, and the weather is nearly perfect.

Practical Information

Capital: Tallahassee.

Tourist Information: Florida Division of Tourism, 126 Van Buren St., Tallahassee 32301 (487-1462). **Department of Natural Resources—Division of Recreation and Parks,** 3900 Commonwealth Blvd., #613, Tallahassee 32303 (488-7326). **U.S. Forest Service,** 227 N. Bruro St., P.O. Box 1050, Tallahassee 32302 (681-7265).

Time Zones: Eastern and Central (westernmost part of panhandle is 1 hr. behind Eastern).
Postal Abbreviation: FL.

Jacksonville and the North Coast

Jacksonville promotes itself as the second-largest city (in terms of square mileage) in the U.S., succumbing only to Los Angeles. Its airport and bus and train terminals make it a good starting point for excursions to the dunelands of the northern coast. Jacksonville is a tourism vacuum, but it is good natured and tries hard to please visitors. Nearby Fort Clinch State Park and Little Talbot Island State Park preserve the best uncrowded and undeveloped beaches between South Carolina and Cuba.

Practical Information

Emergency: 911.

Visitors Center: Jacksonville Convention and Visitors Bureau, 6 E. Bay St., #200 (353-9736), 1½ blocks from the Jacksonville Landing. Free map of Duval County, necessary in this sprawling town. Pick up coupons for local hotels. Open Mon.-Fri. 7:30am-5pm.

Airport: Jacksonville International Airport, Airport Rd. (757-1902), 20 miles north of downtown off I-95. The **Greyhound Airport Express** leaves the airport at 10am, 3:55pm, and 7:55pm; leaves downtown daily at 5:45pm and 9:40pm. Fare $3.50, $4.20 if you buy your ticket at the airport.

Amtrak: 3570 Clifford Lane (locally 768-1553 or 800-872-7245), 6 miles northwest of downtown, off U.S. 1. To: Miami ($67), Washington, DC ($124), and Savannah ($32). Open 24 hours.

Greyhound/Trailways: 10 Pearl St. (356-1841), downtown. To: Miami ($51), St. Augustine ($6), New Orleans ($82), and Washington, DC ($105). Open 24 hours.

Local Transit: Jacksonville Transportation Authority, 100 N. Myrtle St. (630-3100), downtown. Information kiosk at the intersection of W. Forsyth and N. Hogan St. Open Mon.-Fri. 6am-6pm. Ferry across St. John's River (251-3331) operates daily 6:20am-10:15pm, every ½ hr. Leaves you on Rte. A1A, a few miles south of Little Talbot State Park on Little Talbot Island. Cars $1.50, pedestrians 10¢.

Taxi: Yellow Cab, 354-5511. Base fare $1.25, $1.25 per mile.

Car Rental: Alamo, 1735 Airport Rd. (800-327-9633), 5 min. from terminal by free Alamo Shuttle. Sub-compacts $23 per day, $67 per week. Free dropoff in FL cities. Open 24 hours. Must be 21, extra $5 charge if under 25. Must have credit card or a $100 deposit through a travel agent, or a $50 deposit if you prepay 14 days in advance.

Post Office: 1100 King's Rd. (359-2840), downtown. Open Mon.-Fri. 8:30am-5pm, Sat. 9am-1pm. **ZIP Code:** 32202.

Area Code: 904.

Jacksonville has three distinct areas, each a half-hour to an hour drive from each other, separated by miles of anonymous urban expanse. The first two are the beaches south of St. John's River, known collectively as Jacksonville's Beaches, and those north, including **Fort Clinch State Park** and **Little Talbot State Park.** The third, and by far the least worthwhile, is Jacksonville proper, sprawling 20 miles east from the coast. **Atlantic Boulevard** and **Beach Boulevard** are the major thoroughfares that run through the dead zone between Jacksonville and its beaches. Once in the beach region, **3rd Street** is the main drag, running parallel to the shore. Downtown is bisected by **Main Street,** which runs north from the north bank of the St. John's River.

Accommodations and Camping

The biggest problem with Jacksonville accommodations is getting to them. Long distances and bad public transportation can be frustrating. If you arrive at the airport after the last Greyhound shuttle leaves at 7:55pm, and you don't want to rent a car, stay at **Motel 6,** 10885 Hark Rd. (757-8600), Dunn Ave./Busch Dr. exit off I-95 (singles $22), or the **Econo Lodge,** 1351 Aiport Rd. (741-4844; singles $24). The **Salt Air Motel,** 425 Atlantic Blvd. (246-6465), often fills by early evening. (Singles from $25. Doubles from $33. Call ahead in summer.) The **Ocean View Motel,** 60 Ocean View Dr. (246-9514), mostly rents rooms by the week. (All rooms $35 with kitchenette.) The only campground accessible by public transportation is **Kathryn Abbey Hanna Park,** on Wonderwood Rd., Mayport (249-4700), south of Mayport Naval Base and north of Atlantic Beach. (Tent sites $10, campers $13.26. Park admission 50¢.) If that's full, try **Fort Clinch,** Rte. A1A (261-4212), on the coast of the St. John's River (sites $19, with electricity $21). **Little Talbot Island State Park** (251-3231) is 15 miles south of Fort Clinch (tent sites $17, with electricity $19).

Food

Rapid urban growth and summer tourist crowds have encouraged the proliferation of slick roadside seafood restaurants. Local favorite **Patti's,** 7300 Beach Blvd. (725-1662), has good Italian food. Also, check out **Bono's Barbeque,** on Beach Blvd. (398-4248), 2-3 miles east of downtown. The **Ritespot Restaurant** has two locations: 665 Atlantic Blvd. (249-8666; open Mon.-Sat. 7am-10pm) and 4683 Ocean St., Mayport (246-2484; open Tues.-Thurs. and Sun. 11am-9pm, Fri.-Sat. 11am-10pm). The small, homey Ritespots serve catch o' the day for $8.50 and all-you-can-eat shrimp for $7. Across the street is **Damnifino,** 4536 Ocean St. (247-1466), which serves only fresh, local fish and white Mayport shrimp. (Shrimp dinner $9, fish dinner $8, fish sandwich $4. Open Mon.-Sat. 11am-10pm, Sun. noon-9pm.)

Sights

There are virtually no sights of historic interest in Jacksonville because the entire city burned to the ground early in the century. To compensate, the city has built a flashy new mall called the **Jacksonville Landing** on the downtown waterfront, and created the **Riverwalk** on the opposite bank. By far the best way to kill an afternoon in town is the **Cummer Gallery,** 829 Riverside Ave. (336-6857), 1 block from the river. The small gallery has an excellent art collection and gorgeous Italian-style gardens. (Open Tues.-Fri. 10am-4pm, Sat. 1-5pm, Sun. 2-5pm. Donation.) The **Jacksonville Art Museum,** 4160 Boulevard Center Dr. (398-8336), has Chinese porcelain, pre-Columbian, and modern art, and works by contemporary regional artists. (Open Tues.-Fri. 10am-4pm, Thurs. 10am-10pm, Sat.-Sun. 1-5pm.)

The beaches, of course, are Jacksonville's main attraction. Golden seashores extend almost continuously from Pointe Vedra in the south to Fernandina in the north. To the south, Neptune and Atlantic, the "Jacksonville Beaches," are the most crowded, but still large and beautiful.

Saint Augustine

Founded by the Spanish in 1565, St. Augustine is the oldest city in the U.S. Aging swashbuckler Juan Ponce de León heard that the waters of a particular spring in Florida would bring perpetual youth, and his quest led him to St. Augustine. Contrary to the claims of tourism bigwigs in St. Augustine and condominium peddlers throughout the state, Ponce de León never did find the Fountain of Youth. The Spanish flavor of the elegantly preserved old town makes St. Augustine a welcome respite from its garish southern neighbors, and a friendly, compact contrast to Jacksonville's urban void.

Practical Information

Emergency: 911.

Visitors Information: Visitors Center, 10 Castillo at San Marco Ave. (824-3334). From the Greyhound station, walk north on Ribeira, then right on Orange. Pick up hotel coupons and the free *Chamber of Commerce Map,* a comprehensive city guide. The ½-hr. movie, *St. Augustine Adventure,* is a clever introduction to the city (every ½ hr., $2). Open daily 8:30am-5:30pm.

Greyhound/Trailways: 100 Malaga St. at King St. (829-6401). To: Jacksonville (5 per day, 50 min., $9.15) and Daytona Beach (7 per day, 1 hr., $6). Open Mon.-Fri. 7:45am-7:45pm, Sat. 7:45am-4pm.

Taxi: Ancient City Taxi, 824-8161. From the bus station to motels on San Marco about $2.

Bike Rental: Buddy Larson's Bike Rental, 130 King St. (824-2402). $3 per hr. Open Mon.-Sat. 9am-5:30pm.

Help Lines: Rape Crisis, 1-355-7273 or 1-350-6808.

Post Office: King St. at Martin Luther King Ave. (829-8716). Open Mon.-Fri. 8:30am-5pm, Sat. 10am-1pm. **ZIP code:** 32084.

Area Code: 904.

St. Augustine is on the northeast coast of Florida, about 40 miles south of Jacksonville and 47 miles north of Daytona Beach. The bus station, tourist office, budget motels, and tourist district are all within walking distance of one another. Historic St. Augustine is concentrated in the area between the **San Sebastian River** and the **Matanzas Bay** to the east and is easily covered on foot. **King Street,** running along the river, is the major east-west axis and crosses the bay to the beaches. **St. George Street,** also east-west, contains most of the shops and many sights in St. Augustine. Most of it is closed to vehicular traffic. **San Marco Avenue** and **Cordova Street** travel north-south. Winter brings a surge of activity to **Vilano Beach,** northeast of the city, and to **Anastasia** and **St. Augustine Beach,** south and east of the city.

Unfortunately, St. Augustine has no public transportation.

Accommodations and Camping

There are several clusters of cheap motels: one a short walk north of town on San Marco Avenue; another directly to the east of the historic district, over the Bridge at Lions, along Anastasia Boulevard; and a third near Vilano Beach. Several inns in the historic district are worth a splash of cash. Those traveling by automobile should consider the excellent seaside camping facilities at **Anastasia State Park** or a beach motel on Rte. A1A several miles south of the city.

The St. Francis Inn, 279 St. George St. (824-6068), at St. Francis St., 2 doors down from the Oldest House. A charming 10-room inn with a jungle of flowers and a tucked-away pool. Built in 1791, the inn preserves much of its original interior. Iced tea and juice served all day. Free bike use. Room with 1 double bed $40, with twin beds $43. Cottage on premises with full kitchen and living room $92 for 4, about $108 for 6. Continental breakfast included.

American Motel, 42 San Marco Ave. (829-2292), near the visitors center. Owner won't take your money until you've inspected your room. He'll also provide transportation to and from the bus station when a car is available. Big, clean singles or doubles $26, weekends $35-43. Check visitors center for coupons.

The Palms Motor Inn, 137 San Marco Ave. (824-6181), ½ mile from the visitors center. Old but clean rooms. Pool. A few singles $12-15. Singles by the road (only marginally noisier) $22, others $28. Doubles $32. Each additional person $4. Ask about discounts for *Let's Go* users.

Seabreeze Court, 208 Anastasia Blvd. (829-8122), just over the Bridge of Lions east of historic district. Clean rooms with A/C, TV, pool. Near good restaurants. Singles $18. Doubles $24. Each additional person $4. Kitchenette $5 extra.

Anastasia State Recreation Area, on Rte. A1A (471-3033), 4 miles south of the historic district. From town, cross the Bridge of Lions, and bear left just beyond the Alligator Farm. Open 8am-sundown. Sites $20, with electricity $22, $18 after the first night. Make reservations for weekends.

Food

The flood of daytime tourists in St. Augustine's historic district and the abundance of budget eateries make lunch here a delight. Stroll St. George Street and check the daily specials scrawled on blackboards outside each eatery. Locals prefer the restaurants clustered at the southern end of St. George near King Street. Finding a budget dinner in St. Augustine is trickier, since downtown is deserted after 5pm. However, if you venture onto Anastasia Boulevard, you can find good meals for under $6. Those interested in mass quantities of food should try the all-you-can-eat buffet at the **Quincey Family Steakhouse** (797-5677), 2 miles south of town on A1A at Ponce de León Mall. (Open daily 11am-10pm.) **Barrancotto's Roma Restaurant,** 208 Vilano Rd. (829-5719), on Vilano Beach, has Italian entrees ($6-8). The seafood-wise will seek out the surf 'n' turf dinners ($6) at **Captain Jack's,** 410 Anastasia (829-6846), across from O'Steens (open Mon.-Sat. 4:30-9pm).

O'Steen's, 205 Anastasia Blvd. (829-6974), 1½ miles from downtown and 4 blocks from the Bridge of Lions. Across from Seabreeze Court Motel. A lively local gathering place with great prices. Go before 5pm to beat the dinner crowd. Daily special includes entree, salad or soup, and choice of 2 vegetables ($3.50, seafood $4.50). Open Mon.-Sat. 11am-8:30pm. No reservations accepted.

El Toro Con Sombrero, 10 Anastasia Blvd. (842-8852), just over the Bridge of Lions from downtown, on the left. Look carefully because the sign is hidden by a sign for the sports bar. If you like Mexican food and 50s jukebox music, this is your place. Tacos $1.15. Open daily 7am-1am.

Café Camacho, 11-C Aviles St. (824-7030), at Charlotte St., 1 block from St. George St. in the historic district. Part vintage clothes shop, part café. Serves up delicious fruit shakes, cuban specials, sandwiches, soups, and vegetarian dishes. Lunches $1.75-4. Open Wed.-Mon. 7:30am-5pm.

A New Dawn, 110 Anastasia Blvd. (824-1337). A health-conscious grocery store with a sandwich and juice counter. Delicious vegetarian sandwiches ($2-3) and fruit shakes and sodas ($1-2). Open 8am-6pm.

Sights and Entertainment

The historic district centers around St. George Street and begins at the City Gate near the visitors center. Go to **San Agustín Antiguo,** Gallegos House, St. George Street (824-3355), St. Augustine's authentically restored 18th-century Spanish neighborhood. "Artisans" and "villagers" describe to visitors the highlights of the Spaniards' rather spartan New World existence. (Open daily 9am-5pm. Admission $2.50, seniors $2.25, students and ages 6-18 $1.35.) A drawbridge marks the only entrance to the 17th-century **Castillo de San Marcos,** 1 Castillo Dr. (829-6506), off San Marco Ave. This fort, the oldest masonry fortification in the country, contains a large courtyard surrounded by guardrooms, livery quarters for the garrison, storerooms, a jail, and a chapel. (Open daily 9am-5:45pm; Nov.-April 8:30am-5:15pm. Admission $1, over 62 and under 12 free.)

St. Augustine has several old stores and museums open for inspection. The self-descriptive **Oldest House,** 14 St. Francis St. (824-2872), dates from the early 1700s. The walls, like those of Castillo de San Marcos, are built of a local shellrock, coguina. (Open daily 9am-5pm. Admission $3, seniors $2.75, students $1.50.) The **Oldest Store Museum,** 4 Artillery Lane (829-9729), has over 100,000 odds and ends from the 18th and 19th centuries. (Open Mon.-Sat. 9am-5pm, Sun. noon-5pm. Admission $2.50.) Also in the old part of the city is the coguina **Cathedral of St. Augustine,** begun in 1793. Although several fires destroyed parts of the cathedral, the walls and facade are original.

Henry Flagler, patron saint of Florida, built two resorts in St. Augustine in 1888. Frequented by the rich and well-manicured, the hotels were once *the* luxury vacation spot. The former Ponce de León Hotel, at King and Cordova St., is now **Flagler College.** In 1947, Chicago publisher and lover of large objects Otto Lightner converted the Alcazar Hotel into the **Lightner Museum.** (Open daily 9am-5pm. Admission $3, ages 12-18 $1.)

Six blocks north of the information center is the **Mission of Nombre de Dios,** Ocean St. (824-2809), a moss- and vine-covered structure that was the site of the first Catholic service in the U.S. on September 8, 1565. Looming over the mission is a 208-foot steel cross commemorating the city's founding. (Open Mon.-Fri. 8am-8pm, Sat.-Sun. 9am-8pm. Mass Mon.-Fri. at 8:30am, Sat. at 6pm, Sun. at 8am. Donation.) Rejuvenate yourself in the company of hordes of tourists at a replica of the **Fountain of Youth** that Ponce de León never found at 155 Magnolia Ave. (829-3168; open daily 9am-5pm. Admission $3.50, seniors $2.50, ages 6-12 $1.50. Go right on Williams St. from San Marco Ave. and continue a few blocks past Nombre de Dios.)

Visitors can tour St. Augustine by land or by sea. **St. Augustine Sight-seeing Trains,** 170 S. Marcos Ave. (829-6545), offers a variety of city tours lasting from one to eight hours. (Open 8am-5pm.) The one-hour tour ($7, ages 6-12 $2) is a good introduction to the city and starts at the front of the visitors center. **Coleé Sight-**

seeing **Carriage Tours** (829-2818) begin near the entrance to the fort ($5 per hr.; open daily 8:30am-5pm). The **Victory II Scenic Cruise** (824-1806) navigates the mighty Matanzas River. Catch the boat at the City Yacht Pier, 1 block south of the Bridge of Lions (1¼ hr., leaves at 1, 2:45, 4:30, 6:45, and 8:30pm; $6, under 12 $2).

St. Augustine has an impressive array of bars. **Scarlett O'Hara's,** 70 Hypolita St. (824-6535), at Cordova St., is popular after dark. Its barbecue chicken sandwiches ($3.60) are filling and juicy; its drinks are hefty and cool. Live entertainment begins at 9pm every night. (Open daily 11:30am-1am.) Try the **Milltop,** 19½ St. George Street (829-2329), a tiny bar situated above an old mill in the restored area. Local string musicians play on the tiny stage (daily 1pm-midnight). On St. Augustine Beach, **Panama Hattie's** (471-2255) caters to the post-college crowd.

Daytona Beach

Daytona Beach changes with the seasons. Fall and winter bring senior citizens south to the sunshine. Each spring thaw, pale northern college refugees flood the miles of hard-packed beaches and indulge in decadent fun. In summer, families romp the length of the beach and race car fans flock for the annual International Speedway road race, just a few miles from the shore. During any season, hundreds of cars roll along the beach, within feet of sunbathers. With cheaper accommodations than Ft. Lauderdale and almost as many activities, Daytona proves an economical option for the agoraphile traveler.

Practical Information

Emergency: 911.

Visitor Information: Destination Daytona!, at the chamber of commerce, 126 E. Orange Ave., on City Island (255-0415 or 800-845-1234). Teleguide coupons. Open Mon.-Fri. 9am-5pm.

Travelers Aid: 771 Briarwood Dr. (252-4752, 24 hours). Open Mon.-Fri. 8:30am-4:30pm.

Daytona Beach Regional Airport: 189 Midway Ave. (255-8441). The Daytona-Orlando Transit Service (DOTS) shuttle (257-5411) runs between Orlando's airport and Daytona. Runs 4:30am-9pm, every 1½ hr., $15. Call ahead for reservations.

Amtrak: 2491 Old New York Ave., Deland (800-872-7245), 24 miles west on Rte. 92. To: Orlando (2 per day, 1 hr., $6); Tampa (2 per day, 3 hr., $22); Ft. Lauderdale (1 per day, 6 hr., $49); and Miami (1 per day, 7 hr., $53).

Greyhound: 138 S. Ridgewood Ave. (253-6576), 4 miles west of the beach. Catch any of the several different routes to the beach at the Volusia County Terminal. To: Orlando (9 per day, 1 hr., $10.50); St. Augustine (5 per day, 1 hr., $9.50); Tampa (7 per day, 4 hr., $26); Ft. Lauderdale (8 per day, 6 hr., $30); Miami (11 per day, 8½ hr., $40). Open Mon.-Sat. 5am-1:30am, Sun. 5-8am and 10:30am-1:30am.

Local Transit: Votran Transit Company, 761-7700, at the corner of Palmetto and Bay, on the mainland. Bus service operates Mon.-Sat. 5:30am-6:30pm. Fare 60¢, transfers free. Free system maps available at hotels.

Taxi: AAA Cab Co., 253-2522. $1.25 per mile.

Car Rental: Alamo, at the airport (255-1511 or 800-327-9633). Sub-compact $19 per day, $67 per week with unlimited mileage. Free drop-off in Jacksonville or Ft. Lauderdale. Must be 21 with credit card or a $50 deposit through travel agent.

Help Lines: Rape Crisis and Sexual Abuse, 258-7273.

Post Office: 55 Granada Blvd., Ormond Beach (677-0333). Open Mon.-Fri. 8:30am-5pm, Sat. 9am-1pm. **ZIP code:** 32074.

Area Code: 904.

Daytona is 53 miles northeast of Orlando and 90 miles south of Jacksonville on Florida's northeast coast. The city of Daytona Beach is surrounded by water, with the Halifax River (Intracoastal Waterway) slicing through its middle and the Atlantic Ocean to the east. Central Artery **Route A1A,** also known as **Atlantic Avenue,** pulses with enough motels, tanning oil shops, t-shirt shops, and fast-food eateries. **Broadway (U.S. 92)** divides Atlantic north-south. The beach, 23 miles of hard-packed sand, encompasses four towns: quiet **Ormond Beach** to the north, rowdy **Daytona Beach** to the south, family-friendly **Daytona Beach Shores** farther south, and **Ponce Inlet** at the very southern tip. Pay attention when hunting down street addresses, as the north-south streets often change numbering systems as they pass through the various small towns that line the ocean.

Accommodations and Camping

Almost all of Daytona's accommodations are on Rte. A1A, on the beach or across the street. During spring break prices may triple; try the cheaper and quieter hotels on the mainland along Ridgewood Ave. Make reservations well in advance if you plan to be in Daytona any time December through May. During the off-season (summer and fall), cheap rooms are easy to find. Cars are generally allowed on the beach from sunrise to sunset, with evening parking permitted in a few areas, but don't plan to sleep on the well-patrolled beach.

Daytona Beach International Youth Hostel (AYH), 140 S. Atlantic Ave. (258-6937), 1 block north of Broadway (U.S. 92). A big hostel 1 block from the beach with clean kitchen facilities and recreation room. Usually full of fun-loving international students. All rooms have A/C or fans, most have TVs. The owner takes hostelers on waterskiing trips to a freshwater lake ($5). Lockers available. $10, nonmembers $13. Members $65 per week. Key deposit $5.

Camelia Hotel, 1055 N. Atlantic Ave. (252-9963). Neither luxurious nor on the beach, but clean and friendly. All rooms have cable TV. *Let's Go* users warmly welcomed. May-Feb. singles $18, doubles $22. Spring break singles $60, doubles $70. Each additional person $4. Kitchen use $4.

Mil-Mark Motel, 1717 N. Atlantic Ave. (AIA) (258-6238). Clean rooms with cable TV and A/C. Singles $18, each additional person $5. Spring break rooms $80-120.

Nova Family Campground, 1190 Herbert St. (767-0095), in Port Orange, south of Daytona Beach. 10 min. from the beach. Take bus #7 or 15 from downtown or the beach. Shady sites, pool, grocery store. Open 9am-8pm. Sites $13. Open sites posted after hours, just register next day.

Tomoka State Park, 2099 N. Beach St. (677-3931), is 6 miles north of Daytona, north of Ormond. Take bus #3 ("North Ridgewood") to Domicilio and walk 1 mile north. The park has nature trails, a museum, and lots of shade. **Flagler Beach State Park,** Flagler Beach (439-3931), off A1A, 14 miles farther north, also offers a recreation area and a beach. (Sites for both $10, with hookup $12. Reserve 2 months in advance during peak seasons.)

Food

Triple S Supermarket, 167 S. Atlantic Ave. (252-8431), across the street from the youth hostel, features deli sandwiches and subs ($1-3.50). For the freshest seafood, go down to Ponce Inlet; in the late afternoon you and the pelicans can watch the local fishers bring back your dinner. Local resorts often serve buffets in their bars, and you can usually eat as much as you want for the price of one drink. Try the **Holiday Inn,** 400 N. Atlantic, which serves free, mediocre food every night in its roof-top bar. Hostel managers can direct you to to the right resort each day of the week.

Manor Buffet, 101 Seabreeze Blvd. (253-3359). A fantastic place to stuff your face without draining your wallet. Dinners come with soup and salad bar. Mostly frequented by seniors—don't show up in a wet swimsuit and Daisy Duke cut-offs. Menu is low-sodium and low-fat. Lunch $3.25, dinner $4.25, drinks included. Open Mon.-Sat. 11am-3pm and 4-8pm, Sun. 11am-8pm.

Oyster Pub, 555 Seabreeze Blvd. (255-6348). More bar than restaurant, patrons eat at the bar or at tiny tables. Hearty sandwiches ($2-4) and 20¢ oysters all day. Open daily 11:30am-3am.

Gringo's Mexican Restaurant, 701 N. Atlantic Ave. (258-0610). Cozy place with *comidas excelentes* (good grub) for the *hombre con hambre* (hungry guy). Try the combination platters (from $4.45). Open daily 5-10pm.

B & B Fisheries, 715 Broadway (252-6542). Family-owned business almost lives up to its motto, "If it swims . . . we have it." Take-out broiled flounder or sea trout lunches under $4. Sit-down meals quite a bit pricier. Open Mon.-Sat. 11am-9:30pm. Take-out service Mon.-Sat. 11:30am-8:30pm.

Sights and Events

The beach is Daytona's *raison d'être.* During spring break, students from practically every college in the country come here to get a head start on summer. The beach in Daytona proper resembles a highway, as dozens of cars crawl along it. To avoid the inevitable traffic jams, you'll have to arrive early (6 or 7am) and leave early (3pm or so). It costs $3 to go onto the beach, and police strictly enforce the 10 mph limit. Agoraphobes should head north of Ormond to the undeveloped, uncrowded stretch between Ormond and Flagler Beach. **New Smyrna Beach,** 15 miles south of Daytona Beach, is also less tourist-saturated. (Parking Mon.-Fri. $1, Sat.-Sun. $2.)

Throughout spring break, concerts, hotel-sponsored parties, and other hype aid students in their fevered search for fun. Although the best information travels by mouth, check the box office at the west end of **Ocean Center,** on Wild Olive Ave. (254-4545 or 800-858-6444), a concert site. Buy tickets here or at the outlets in various malls and record stores throughout Daytona and Ormond.

The **Daytona International Speedway,** 1801 Speedway Blvd. (254-6767), just off I-95 on U.S. 92, has racing events from July through March, with most taking place in February and July. (General admission to most races $20-25.) Events during Speed Week (Feb. 11-19) include the **Daytona 500** (Feb. 19), the **Goody's 300** (Feb. 18), and the **ARCA 200 World Championship Race** (Feb. 12). Tickets for these events run $20-45. The **Pepsi Firecracker 400 NASCAR Race** takes place on the first Saturday in July. For information, contact the Ticket Office, Drawer S, Daytona Beach 32015 (254-6767).

Daytona's streets are blocked off when the annual **Motorcycle Week** revs up on the first weekend in March, culminating with the international **Daytona 200 Motorcycle Classic.** (Tickets $10.)

Entertainment

A myriad of night spots try unsuccessfully to imitate **Penrod's on the Beach,** 600 N. Atlantic Ave. (255-4471). Undoubtedly the hottest club during spring break, Penrod's hosts poolside parties, taco buffets, and daiquiri days. The $9 cover includes admission to **Plantation,** the neighboring bar. **T.C.'s Top Dog** is a hot-dog eatery at 425 N. Atlantic Ave. (257-7766), 1 block off Seabreeze Blvd. Photos of revelry past line the inside walls of this little funhouse. For other fun clubs and bars, check out **Finky's Showplace,** 640 N. Grandview (255-5059), off A1A (cover $3); **Razzle's,** 611 Seabreeze Blvd. (257-6236); and the **Ocean Deck,** 127 S. Ocean Ave. (253-5224), on the beach behind the Mayan Hotel, with live reggae.

Orlando and Disney World

Though Orlando likes to tout itself as "the world's vacation center" and one of the country's fastest-growing cities, millions annually descend on this central Floridian city for just one reason: Disney World, the world's most popular tourist attraction. Walt Disney chose the area south of Orlando as the place for his expanded version of California's Disneyland. Disney has since complemented the Magic Kingdom with the Epcot Center and brand new Disney-MGM Studios theme parks.

A number of parasitic attractions have sprouted nearby to cash in on Disney tourism. Be warned: There are many ways to blow your dough in this land of illusions, but you are best off spending your time and money first at Disney.

There is little else to see in downtown Orlando other than pretty lakes and parks. For a change of pace, visit nearby Winter Park, home of Rollins College and an appealing college town that is miraculously unaffected by the frenzied "entertainment" biz of its neighbor.

Practical Information

Emergency: 911.

Visitor Information: Orlando-Orange County Visitors and Convention Bureau, 8445 International Dr. (351-0412), several miles southwest of downtown at the Mercado (Spanish-style mall). Take bus #8, 21, 27, 28, and 29 from downtown. Maps and information on nearly all of the amusement park attractions in the area. Pick up a free bus system map. Open daily 8am-8pm.

Amtrak: 1400 Sligh Blvd. (843-7611 or 800-872-7245). Take S. Orange Ave., turn west on Columbia, then right on Sligh. 3 blocks east of I-4. To: Tampa (2 per day, 2 hr., $16); Jacksonville (2 per day, 3½ hr., $26); Miami (1 per day, 5½ hr., $46). Open daily 7am-9pm.

Greyhound/Trailways, 300 W. Amelia St. at Hughy Ave. (843-7720 for 24-hour fare and ticket information), downtown near Sunshine Park, 1 block east of I-4. One bus per day leaves at 10:15am for Sea World, Epcot Center, and the Magic Kingdom (Mon.-Fri. $7.50 round-trip, Sat.-Sun. $9.50), and leaves Disney at 7pm. One bus per day leaves at 10:30am for Cypress Gardens and leaves the Gardens at 6:20pm (one way $13; round-trip $24). To: Tampa (9 per day, 2½ hr., $17); Jacksonville (13 per day, 3 hr., $25); and Miami (7 per day, 7 hr., $38). Open 24 hours.

Local Transit: Tri-County Transit, 438 Woods Ave. (841-8240 for information Mon.-Fri. 6:30am-6:30pm, Sat. 7:30am-5pm, Sun. 8am-4pm). Downtown terminal between Central and Pine St., 1 block west of Orange Ave. and 1 block east of I-4. Schedules available at most shopping malls, banks, and at the downtown terminal. Serves the airport and Sea World. Buses operate daily 6am-9pm. Fare 75¢, transfers 10¢.

Taxi: Yellowcab, 422-4455. $2.25 first mile, $1.30 each additional mile.

Car Rental: Alamo, 8200 McCoy Rd. (857-8200 or 800-327-9633), near the airport. $25 per day, $78 per week, $6 extra per day if under 25. Mandatory $12 refueling charge (don't fill the tank up before you turn it in). $40 drop-off fee to Jacksonville or Miami. Open 24 hours. Must have major credit card or a $50 deposit through travel agent.

Orlando Airport Limousine: 324 W. Gore St. (859-4667). Operates a booth at the airport for transportation to most hotels, including the Airport Hostel ($3). The cheapest transportation besides the bus if you're alone. (A group of 3 or more can split a taxi fare between hotels and airport.) Also runs from most hotels to Disney ($11 round-trip). Open 24 hours. Call a day in advance to reserve seat to Disney.

Help Lines: Rape Hotline, 847-8811.

Post Office: 46 E. Robinson St. (843-5673), at Magnolia, downtown. Open Mon. 7am-5pm, Tues.-Fri. 8am-5pm. Sat. 9am-noon. **ZIP code:** 32802.

Area Code: 407.

At the center of the hundreds of small lakes and amusement parks that dot the region is Orlando proper. Downtown centers around Lake Eola, east of I-4 and south of Colonial Drive. Streets are divided north-south by **Route 17-92 (Mills Avenue)** and east-west by **Colonial Drive.** I-4 runs through the center of everything, with "east" meaning north, and "west" meaning south.

Unlike other Florida vacation spots, the Orlando area is landlocked. Daytona is 55 miles to the northeast, St. Petersburg 100 miles southwest, and Miami 230 miles southeast. **Disney World** and **Sea World** are 15 to 20 miles south of downtown on I-4; **Cypress Gardens** is four times farther away down the interstate in Winter

Haven. Transportation out to the parks is a cinch. Most hotels have a shuttle service to Disney, otherwise take the bus or call a limousine. All options cost about $12.

Accommodations and Camping

Orlando does not cater to the budget traveler. Prices for hotel rooms rise exponentially as you approach Disney World, so plan to stay in a hostel or in downtown Orlando. Reservations are a good idea in December, January, March, and April, and on holidays. The cheapest places to **camp** are in Kissimmee, a few miles east of Disney World, along U.S. 192. There are no federal or state parks around the area, but one city park and six Orange County parks have campsites ($7, with hookup $10). Contact **Orange County Parks & Recreation Department,** 118 W. Kaley St. (420-4290), and **Orlando Parks Department,** 1206 W. Columbia (849-2283), for more information. (Both open Mon.-Fri. 9am-4:30pm.)

Orlando International Youth Hostel at Plantation Manor (AAIH), 227 N. Eola Dr. (843-8888), at E. Robinson, downtown on the east shore of Lake Eola. Porch, TV room, kitchen facilities. Rooms sleep 4-6. A/C in some rooms. To Disney $10 round-trip; they also buy and sell tickets to Disney for $22. Hostel beds $12. Private rooms $26.

Airport Hostel, 3500 McCoy Rd. (859-3165 or 851-1612), off Daetwiler Rd., behind the La Quinta Motel. Take bus #11 ("Airport") from the airport or downtown. Kitchen facilities, fans in every room, and tropical fruit trees out back. Airport Limo to Disney ($10 round-trip). $9. Breakfast included.

Young Women's Community Club (AYH), 107 E. Hillcrest St. (425-2502), at Magnolia, 4 blocks from Plantation Manor, right behind the Orlando Sentinel. Take bus #10 or 12; staff recommends a taxi. Women aged 16-44 only. Clean, safe, and friendly. Pool. $10. Flexible 3-night max. stay. Good breakfast $2, dinner $4. No reservations accepted.

Travelodge (AYH), 409 Magnolia (423-1671), downtown. Fancy motel that takes in hostelers. Color TV, A/C. Adjoining 24-hour restaurant. Members only; bed in double $13. Continental breakfast included.

Sun Motel, 5020 W. Irlo Bronson Memorial Hwy., Kissimmee (396-6666). Very reasonable considering proximity to Disney World (4 miles). Color TV, phone, pool. Singles $50. Doubles $55. Off-season $25 and $28, respectively.

KOA, U.S. 192 (396-2400 or 800-247-2728; 800-331-1453 outside FL), down the road from Twin Lakes. Kind of kute Kamping Kabins $21.75. Pool, tennis, store (open 7am-11pm). So large that even in season you're bound to get a site due to cancellations, but get there early. Free buses twice per day to Disney. Office open 24 hours. Tent sites $17.75, with hookup $24.75. Each additional person $2.

Stage Stop Campground, 700 W. Rte. 50 (656-8000), 8 miles north of Disney in Winter Garden. Take exit 80 off the Florida Turnpike N., then left on Rte. 50. Office open daily 8am-8:30pm. Sites with full hookup $13, $72 per week.

Food

Orlando has plenty of good, cheap eateries. If you need to save money, avoid eating on Church Street and in the touristy International Drive area southwest of town on I-4.

Lilia's Grilled Delight, 3150 S. Orange Ave. (851-9087), 2 blocks south of Michigan St., 5 min. from the downtown business district. This small, modestly decorated Philippine restaurant is one of the best-kept secrets in town. Don't pass up the *lumpia,* a tantalizing combination of sauteed meat, shrimp, vegetables, and peanut butter in a fried dough, or the *adobo,* the Philippine national dish. Lunch $3-5, dinner $4-7. Open Mon.-Sat. 11am-7pm

Numero Uno, 2499 S. Orange Ave. A local favorite serving tasty Cuban specialties in a casual setting. Roast pork dinner with rice, plantains, and salad about $7. Open Mon.-Thurs. 11am-9:30pm, Fri. 11am-10pm, Sat. 1-10pm.

Malcolm's Hungry Bear, 924 W. Colonial Dr. (422-3135), downtown Orlando, 5 blocks west of I-4, across from the Holiday Inn. Bring a church bulletin any Sun. for up to $1 off. Every meal is all-you-can-eat. Breakfast $3, lunch $4, dinner $5. Cubs under 10 ½-price. Open daily 7am-9:30pm.

Old Munich Bavarian Inn, 61 E. Church St. (425-4060 or 425-4444), between Magnolia and Orange. German goulash soup, homemade liverwurst, and schnitzels. Live entertainment. Lunch $4-7, dinner $7-10. Open Mon.-Fri. 11am-10pm, Sat. 5-10pm.

Nature's Table, 331 N. Orange Ave. (648-1841), downtown. Vegetarian and healthful specialties. Delicious fruit and protein powder shakes ($1-2), yogurt, juice. Open Mon.-Fri. 9am-5pm.

Ronnie's Restaurant, 2702 Colonial Plaza (894-2943) at Bumby St. Unintentionally vintage 50s deco. Delicious mix of Jewish and Cuban food. Famous for the breakfast special ($5) that may tide you over for a week.

East India Ice Cream, 327 Park Ave., S. Winter Park. Breezy, quiet ice cream parlor that's a favorite hangout for Rollins students. Delicious ice cream dishes ($1-3).

Entertainment

The **Church Street Station,** 129 W. Church St. (422-2434), downtown, between South and Garland St. is a slick, overpriced, block-long entertainment complex with five huge bar-restaurants, all variations on the theme of Orlando's early days. From 5pm, a $5 cover admits you to all of the bars. For more interesting, less expensive nightlife, explore Orange Avenue downtown. Several good bars and clubs have live music and dancing, at very reasonable prices. The **Orange Quarter,** 70 N. Orange Ave. at Washington St. (841-7246), hosts live reggae nightly.

Disney World

Admit it: You came here to see Disney World. The reigning monarch of amusement parks, with its sprawling labyrinth of kiddie rides and Disney movie sets with cash registers, has captured you. So relax, forget reality, and pretend you're five years old. Maybe six.

If bigger is better, Disney World is certainly the best park in the U.S. The World (824-4321 for information daily 8am-10pm) is now divided into three continents: the **Magic Kingdom,** with its six theme parks; the **Epcot Center,** part science fair, part World's Fair; and the brand new **Disney-MGM Studios,** a real movie and TV studio combined with Magic Kingdom-style rides. They are located a few miles from each other, in the town of Lake Buena Vista, 20 miles west of Orlando via I-4.

A one-day entrance fee of $29 (ages 3-9 $23) admits you to *one* of the three parks. It allows you to leave and return to the same park later in the day. A four-day **passport** ($97, ages 3-9 $77) admits you to all three and includes unlimited transportation on the Disney monorail, boats, buses, and trains. You can also opt for a five-day pass ($112, ages 3-9 $90). The multi-day passes need not be used on consecutive days, and they are good forever. Disney attractions that charge separate admissions are **River Country** ($11.75, ages 3-9 $9.25) and **Discovery Island** ($7.50, ages 3-9 $4; combination for the two $15, ages 3-9 $11); **Typhoon Lagoon** ($17.50, ages 3-9 $14.50); and **Pleasure Island,** whose prices vary. (For descriptions, see Other Disney Attractions below).

Gray Line Tours (422-0744) and **Airport Limo** offer transportation from most hotels to Disney World, (leaves hotel about 9am, leaves Disney about 7pm; about $10 round-trip). Major hotels and some campgrounds provide their own shuttles for guests. **Bikers** are stopped at the main gate and driven by security guards to the inner entrance where they can stash their bikes free of charge.

Disney World opens its gates 365 days per year, but hours fluctuate according to season. The busiest season is during the summer when school is out, but Christmas, Thanksgiving, Spring Break, and the month around Easter are the "peak" times when the park is packed. The week between Christmas and New Year is the busiest of the year. The crowd hits the main gates beginning at 10am, so to enjoy a less crowded fantasy land, arrive as close to 9am as possible and seek out your favorite rides or exhibits before noon. You'll wait from 15 minutes to an hour, sometimes even longer, at big attractions.

Magic Kingdom

Seven "lands" make up the Magic Kingdom. You enter on **Main Street, USA,** which is meant to capture the essence of turn-of-the-century hometown America. Architects have employed "forced perspective" here: the ground floor of the shops are 9/10 the size they would be in real life, and the second and third stories are progressively smaller. Walt describes his vision in the "Walt Disney Movie" at the Hospitality House, to the right as you emerge from under the railroad station. The Main Street Cinema shows some great old silents. Late afternoons on Main Street turn gruesome, when the "All America Parade" marches through at 3pm. Near the entrance, you'll find a steam train that tours the seven different lands.

Tomorrowland imagines space travel and future lifestyles. The indoor roller coaster **Space Mountain** is the high point of this section, definitely an E-ticket. Lines are very, very long. The golden-spired Cinderella Castle is the gateway to **Fantasyland,** where you'll find twirling teacups, flying elephants, and other imagination-stretching attractions. **20,000 Leagues Under the Sea** is a highpoint, as well as the beloved but repetitive **It's A Small World.** (You may never get the tune out of your head.) Catch **Magic Journeys,** a plotless 3-D movie with excellent effects.

Liberty Square and **Frontierland** are devoted to U.S. history and a celebration of Mark Twain. History buffs will enjoy the Hall of Presidents, and adventurers should catch the rickety, runaway Big Thunder Mountain Railroad. The Haunted Mansion is a hilariously ghoulish spectacle. A steamboat ride past Tom Sawyer Island is a good way to relax from the endless walking, and be sure to stop in at the **Country Bear Jamboree.**

Adventureland, the last park in the Magic Kingdom, is devoted to tropical islands. The Jungle Cruise is a tongue-in-cheek tour through tropical waterways populated by not-so-authentic-looking wildlife. Pirates of the Caribbean explores caves where animated buccaneers battle, drink, and sing.

Epcot Center

In 1966, Walt Disney dreamed up an "Experimental Prototype Community Of Tomorrow" (EPCOT) that would evolve constantly, never to be completed. It was to incorporate new ideas and industries from American technology, functioning as a self-sufficient, futuristic utopia. Walt's vision was not completely realized—no humans live there—and you may be put off by the not-so-subtle advertising that leaks into its corporate-sponsored attractions. Nevertheless, it's still impressive and can be terrific fun.

Epcot is divided into **Future World** and **World Showcase.** For smaller crowds, visit the former in the evening and the latter in the morning. The large trademark geosphere forms the entrance to **Future World and Spaceship Earth,** where visitors board a "time machine" for a somewhat interesting tour through the evolution of communication. A highlight of Future World is the **Journey Into Imagination,** which features the ever-popular 3-D **Captain Eo,** starring one-gloved oddity Michael Jackson.

The rest of Epcot is the **World Showcase**—a series of international pavilions surrounding an artificial lake. Epcot opened Norway in the summer of 1988, and is currently negotiating with Israel and Africa for new pavilions. Each country is represented by a clichéed architectural style or monument, as well as typical national food. Citizens of the various countries perform dances, theatrical skits, and other forms of cultural entertainment at each pavilion. Before setting out around the lake, pick up a schedule of events at Epcot Center Information in Earth Station. At best you can see a gorgeous 360° film made in China or a 180° film from France, featuring spectacular landscapes and stirring music, or take an exciting ride at Norway's **Maelstrom.** At worst you may find yourself insulted by the simplistic, Mickey-Mouse (so to speak) approach to culture, or by the incessant souvenir-vending.

Every night at 10pm in summer, Epcot has a magnificent show called **Illuminations,** which features music from the represented nations accompanied by dancing lights and fireworks. During other seasons, it is only shown on Saturdays. The best vantage point is the porch of the **Cantina de San Angel** in the Mexican pavilion.

Orlando residents often buy season passes to Disney World just to eat at the pavilions in the World Showcase. Rumor has it that many Floridians pay Epcot's hefty admission price solely to eat at the **Restaurant Marrakesh** in the Moroccan Pavilion. Head chef Lahsen Abrache cooks delicious *brewat* (spicy minced beef fried in pastry) and *bastilla* (sweet and slightly spicy pie). A belly dancer performs in the restaurant every evening. (Lunch $8-12. Dinner $10-14. Make reservations early in the day at the World Key Terminals in Earth Station.) The Mexican, French, and Italian pavillions also serve up excellent food at similar prices.

Disney-MGM Studios

Disney-MGM Studios have successfully created a "living movie set." Strolling through the park are many of the familiar Disney characters dressed in Hollywood theme costumes, as well as a host of "streetmosphere" characters dressed as directors, starlets, gossip columnists, and fans. A different real live star leads a parade across **Hollywood Boulevard** every day. Events such as stunt shows and mini-theatricals take place continually throughout the park.

Your visit will divide into two parts. The first, the theme park, centers around Epcot-style rides and attractions, exploring the history of film and various elements of TV and film-making. The second and more interesting part of the studios is the two-hour **Backstage Studio Tour** through Disney's working studio. The animation section is a high point, and is shown on a separate tour (10am-7pm), covering all stages of cartoon production.

Other Disney Attractions

As if those three attractions were not enough fun and money, Disney also offers several other parks with different themes and separate admissions (see Disney World above). The newest is **Typhoon Lagoon,** a 50-acre water park, centered around the world's largest wave-making pool. You can actually surf the 7-foot waves that appear out of nowhere every 90 seconds. There is also a salt water coral reef stocked with tropical fish and harmless sharks, six water slides, and a wonderful creek on which you can take a ride of relaxation, an anomaly at Disney.

The other new addition is **Pleasure Island,** a dining and entertainment complex with shops, restaurants, food carts, and entertainment for all ages. Built to resemble a swimming hole, **River Country** offers water slides, rope swings, and plenty of room to swim. Across Bay Lake from River Country is **Discovery Island,** a zoological park.

Near Orlando: Sea World and Cypress Gardens

Sea World, west of Orlando, off I-4 at Rte. 528 (407-351-3600 for operator; 407-351-0021 for recording), 19 miles southwest of Orlando, is one of the country's largest marine parks—you need about six hours to see it all. Shows feature mammals such as whales, dolphins and humans. **Baby Shamu,** a three-ton orca, is the big star, but the Seal and Otter Show, with Sir Clyde and Sir Seamore, and the water ski show are equally entertaining. Shows are popular, so arrive early to get a seat. If the sun gets unbearable, visit the air-conditioned building housing the Fantasy Theater, an educational show with live characters in costume. (Open daily 8:30am-10pm; off-season 9am-7pm. Admission $23.30, ages 3-11 $19. Sky Tower ride $2.50 extra. Guided tours $5.50, children $4.50. Take Greyhound from Orlando or bus #8. Smallest crowds in Feb. and Sept.-Oct.)

Cypress Gardens (813-324-2111; 407-351-6606 in Orlando), in Winter Haven, is a botanical garden with over 8000 varieties of plants and flowers. The "Gardens of the World" feature plants, flowers, and sculptured mini-gardens depicting the gardening styles of many countries and periods. Winding walkways and electric boat rides take you through the foliage. The main attraction is a water-ski show given daily at 10am, noon, 2pm, and 4pm. Take I-4 southwest to Rte. 27 south, then Rte. 540 west. Greyhound stops once per day on its Tampa-West Palm Beach schedule ($20 from Tampa to Cypress Gardens; open daily 8am-9:30pm; in winter 9am-7pm. Admission $17, ages 6-11 $11.50.) Look for $3 off coupons at motels and visitors centers.

Cocoa Beach/Cape Canaveral

Known for its cosmic surfing, the Cocoa Beach area is also the blast-off site for moon voyages and shuttle flights. The "Space Coast" is one of Florida's less-cluttered beaches, and most of the sunbathers, even during spring break, are actually natives.

The **Kennedy Space Center** (800-432-2153 recorded information, in FL only), 8 miles north of Cocoa Beach, is the site for all of NASA's blast-offs. The Kennedy Center's **Spaceport USA** (452-2121 for reservations) is a huge welcoming center for visitors. The main attractions are the two-hour bus tours of the complex and the IMAX film about the space shuttle, *The Dream is Alive,* projected on a five-and-a-half story screen. (Tours depart from Spaceport USA daily 9:20am-6pm. $4, under 12 $1.75. Movie tickets $2.75, under 12 $1.75.) Buy tickets to both immediately upon arrival—there is often a long wait. Admission to the center itself is free, as are the five movies in the Galaxy Theater and half-hour walking tours of the exhibits. The NASA Parkway, site of the visitors center, is accessible only by car, via State Rd. 405. From Cocoa Beach, take Rte. A1A north until it turns west into Rte. 528, then follow Rte. 3 north to the Spaceport.

The NASA complex is surrounded by the **Merritt Island Wildlife Refuge** (867-8667). The large marshy area is a haven for deer, sea turtles, alligators, and eagles. (Open 8am-sunset.) Just north of Merritt Island is **Canaveral National Seashore** (867-2805; open 6:30am-sunset), 67,000 acres of undeveloped beach and dunes. (Take Rte. 406 east off U.S. 1 in Titusville.) There is a nude beach at the northernmost point, accessible to the public.

For a bite to eat, try **Herbie K's** diner, 2080 N. Atlantic Ave., south of Motel 6. A shiny chrome reproduction of a 50s diner, Herbie serves macaroni and cheese, chicken pot pie, and happy haw (apple sauce). Hamburgers are $2. At the beach, **Motel 6,** 3701 N. Atlantic Ave. (783-3103), has a pool and large, clean rooms with TV and A/C. (Singles $30. Each additional person $8. Reservations necessary.) If Motel 6 is full, try the **Gateway to the Stars Motel,** 8701 Astronaut Blvd. (Rte. A1A) (783-0361), in Cape Canaveral. Big, old rooms sleep up to four people. (Rooms $30; Jan.-April $40.) Pitch your tent at scenic **Jetty Park Campgrounds,** 400 East Jetty Rd. (783-7222), Cape Canaveral. (Sites $9.72, with hookup $14.57. Reservations necessary Jan.-May.)

The Cocoa Beach area, 50 miles east of Orlando, consists of the mainland towns Cocoa and Rockledge, oceanfront towns Cocoa Beach and Cape Canaveral, and Merritt Island in between. **Route A1A** runs through Cocoa Beach and Cape Canaveral, and **North Atlantic Avenue** runs parallel to the beach. Cocoa Beach is inaccessible by bus, and has no local public transportation. Cocoa, 8 miles inland, is served by **Greyhound,** 302 Main St. (636-3917), from Orlando ($12). From the bus station, taxi fare to Cocoa Beach is about $10 (call 783-8294), but hitching is fairly easy, especially if you move with the crowds along Rte. 520 from Orlando. A **shuttle** service (784-3831) connects Cocoa Beach with Orlando International Airport, Disney World ($25), and the Kennedy Space Center ($12). Make reservations a day in advance and ask about special rates for groups of five or more.

The **Cocoa Beach Chamber of Commerce,** 1300 N. Atlantic Ave. (783-3650), in the Holiday Inn, has information on special events and can provide suggestions on cheap, temporary housing. (Open Mon.-Fri. 9am-5pm). The main office is at 400 Fortenberry Rd. (459-2200), Merritt Island. (Open Mon.-Fri. 8:30am-5pm.) For a comprehensive list of restaurants and all kinds of information about the area, ask at the **Broward County Tourist Development Council** (453-0823 or 800-872-1969), at the Kennedy Space Center.

Cocoa Beach's **ZIP code** is 32922; the **area code** is 407.

Fort Lauderdale

Fort Lauderdale is the official spring break capital of the world. Every year, pale, lust-crazed flocks descend on the city and trade their No-Doze for Budweiser. Lately, however, the spring break crowds are beginning to thin out, in response to: an open-container law prohibiting partiers from drinking east of the Intercoastal Waterway; a 36-inch-high wall between the sand and A1A, compelling drunken revelers to cross at streetlights; and crack-downs on drunk driving, fake IDs, and indecent exposure.

In off-season, tourists less preoccupied with carnal fulfillment and more appreciative of the land and ocean's beauty stroll the wide beach. Broad-sailed boats and luxury yachts cruise up and down the coast or anchor at the city's canals and ports. When the spring break parties finally end, Fort Lauderdale breathes a huge sigh of relief.

Practical Information

Emergency: 911.

Visitor Information: Chamber of Commerce, 208 SE 3rd Ave. (527-8755), downtown, between Las Olas and Broward Blvd. Well equipped. Open Mon.-Fri. 8am-5pm.

Fort Lauderdale/Hollywood International Airport: 3½ miles south of downtown on U.S. 1 (Federal Hwy.), at exits 26 and 27 on I-95. Scheduled for expansions through 1990.

Amtrak: 200 SW 21st Terrace (463-8251 or 800-872-7245), just west of I-95, ¼ mile south of Broward Blvd. Take bus #9, 10, or 81 from downtown. Daily service on "The Floridian" to: Miami (2 per day, 1½ hr., $6); Orlando (1 per day, 4 hr., $40); and Jacksonville (1 per day, 6 hr., $60). Open daily 7:30am-6:45pm.

Greyhound: 513 NE 3rd St. (764-6551), 3 blocks north of Broward Blvd. at Federal Hwy., downtown. Unsavory location, especially at night. To: Orlando (2 per day, 3 hr., $35); Daytona Beach (2 per day, 3 hr., $36); and Tampa (2 per day, 2½ hr., $40). Open 24 hours.

Broward County Transit (BCT): 357-8400 (call Mon.-Fri. 7am-7pm, Sat. 8am-5pm, Sun. 8am-4pm). Extensive regional coverage. Most routes go to the terminal at the corner of 1st St. NW and 1st Ave. NW, downtown. Operates daily 6am-9pm every ½ hr. on most routes. Fare 75¢, seniors 35¢, transfers 10¢. 7-day passes $8, available at beachfront hotels. Pick up a handy system map at the **Broward County Office Plaza,** 115 S. Andrews Ave., 1 block south of Broward Blvd.

Car Rental: Alamo, 2601 S. Federal Hwy. (525-4715 or 800-327-9633). Cheapest cars $23 per day, $68 per week, unlimited mileage, free drop-off in Daytona and Miami. Free shuttle to airport. Must be 21 with credit card or a $50 deposit, through travel agent.

Moped and Bike Rentals: Avoid the expensive joints on the beach, and Nick Mopeds of Syros Island. **International Bicycle Shop,** 1900 E. Sunrise Blvd. at N. Federal Hwy. (764-8800). Take bus #10 from downtown or bus #36 from A1A north of Sunrise. $10 per day, $35 per week. $100 deposit. Open Mon.-Fri. 10am-9pm, Sat. 9am-9pm, Sun. 11am-5pm. No minimum age.

Taxi: Yellow Cab, 565-5400. **Public Service Taxi,** 587-9090, 7am-1am.

Help Lines: Crisis Hotline, 467-6333. 24 hours.

Post Office: 1900 W. Oakland Park Blvd. (527-2028). Open Mon.-Fri. 7:30am-5pm, Sat. 8:30am-2pm. **ZIP code:** 33319.

Area Code: 305.

Ft. Lauderdale lies 27 miles north of Miami and 43 miles south of West Palm Beach on I-95. I-95 is undergoing reconstruction through 1992, making congestion on this highway commonplace. **Alligator Alley** (Rte. 84/I-75) slithers 100 miles west from Ft. Lauderdale across the swamps to Naples on the Gulf Coast of Florida.

The city spreads back from its sun-soaked, sandy stretch of Atlantic beach. **Broward Boulevard** divides the city north-south, **Andrews Avenue** east-west. Streets and boulevards (east-west) and avenues (north-south) are labeled NW, NE, SW, or SE according to the quadrant. The built-up, unpleasant downtown centers around the intersection of **Federal Highway** (U.S. 1) and **Las Olas Boulevard,** about 2 miles west of the oceanfront. Between downtown and the waterfront, yachts fill the ritzy, Venice-like inlets of the **Intracoastal Waterway.** The strip (variously called Rte. A1A, N. Atlantic Blvd., 17th St. Causeway, Ocean Blvd., and Seabreeze Blvd.) runs along the beach for 4 miles between **Oakland Park Boulevard** to the north and Las Olas Boulevard to the south. Las Olas Boulevard is the pricey shopping street; **Sunrise Boulevard** has most shopping malls. The Boulevards degenerate into criminally ugly commercial strips west of downtown.

Accommodations and Camping

Hotel prices vary from slightly unreasonable to absolutely ridiculous, increasing exponentially as you approach prime beachfront. High season runs from mid-February to early April. Investigate package deals at the slightly-worse-for-wear strip hotels in Ft. Lauderdale.

Small motels crowd each other one or two blocks off the beach area, many of which offer efficiencies. Look along Birch Road, one block back from Rte. A1A. **The Broward County Hotel and Motel Association,** 1212 NE 4th Ave. (462-0409), provides a free directory of area hotels. (Open Mon.-Fri. 9am-4:30pm.) Scan the *Ft. Lauderdale News* and the Broward Section of the *Miami Herald* for occasional listings of local residents who rent rooms to tourists in spring. Call 357-8100 for general information on camping in Broward County. Crashing on the well-patrolled beaches is impossible.

Sol Y Mar Youth Hostel (AYH), 2839 Vistamar St. (566-1023), 2 blocks west of Rte. A1A, 1 block south of Sunrise Blvd. From downtown, take bus #40 to the intersection of Birch and Vista Mar. Will pick you up at the bus station for $3.50. Nice, clean, and new. Two-room apartments with 6-8 beds, A/C, and shower. Recreation room, BBQ, and nice pool. 5-min. walk to beach. Office open 9-11am and 5-7pm. $12, nonmembers $15.

International Youth Hostel (AYH), 905 NE 17th Terrace (467-0452). From downtown, take bus #30 to NE 15th Ave. and Sunrise Blvd. Walk east on Sunrise to NE 17th Terrace. Will pick you up at the bus station. Somewhat dank, cramped rooms, each with 7 beds and a shower. $7, members only. Fills quickly; call ahead.

Estoril Apartments, 2648 NE 32nd St. 33306 (563-3840), 2 blocks west of the Intracoastal Waterway and 1 block north of Oakland Park Blvd. From downtown, take bus #20 to Coral Ridge Shopping Center and walk 2 blocks east on Oakland. If you're a student, you can probably persuade the family who runs the apartments to pick you up from the bus station or airport. A 10-min. walk to the beach, but quiet and nice. Very clean rooms with A/C, TV, and a small kitchenette. Pool and BBQ. *Let's Go* users warmly welcomed. Office closes about 11pm. May-Dec. 15 singles $25, doubles $28; Jan.-April singles $40-45. Reserve in Feb.-March with 25% deposit.

Motel 6, 1801 State Rd. 84 (760-7999), 3 blocks east of I-95 and 3 miles southwest of downtown. Take bus #14 to Rte. 84 and SW 15th Ave. and walk 3 blocks west. Far from the action. Clean, no-frills rooms. Singles $29.38. Doubles $35.92. Reserve far in advance for Sept.-May.

Ocean Lodge, 200-300 S. Ocean Blvd., Pompano Beach (442-2030), near the Ft. Lauderdale border on A1A. From downtown, take bus #11 north up A1A. Clean, attractive rooms. Singles $26, with kitchenette $30. Open May-Oct.

Easterlin County Park, 1000 NW 38th St. Oakland Park (776-4466), northwest of the intersection of Oakland Park Rd. and I-95, less than 4 miles west of the strip and 3 miles north of downtown. Take bus #14 from downtown to NW 38th St. or #72 along Oakland Park Ave. to Powerline Rd. By car take Sample exit from I-95. 2-week max. stay. Registration open 24 hours. Sites with electricity, BBQ pits, and picnic table $15.

Quiet Waters County Park, 6601 N. Powerline Rd. (NW 9th Ave.), Pompano Beach (360-1315), 10 miles north of Oakland Park Blvd. I-95 exit 37. From downtown, take bus #14. Cramped, commercialized, but friendly. Bizarre 8-person "boatless water skiing" and other water sports. No electricity. Check-in 2-7pm. Fully equipped campsites (tent, mattresses, cooler, grill, canoe) for up to 6 people, Sun.-Thurs. $12, Fri.-Sat. $25 plus $20 refundable deposit.

Food

The clubs along the strip offer massive quantities of free grub during happy hour: surfboard-sized platters of wieners, chips, and hors d'oeuvres, or all-you-can-eat pizza and buffets. However, these bars have hefty cover charges (from $5) and expect you to buy a drink once you're there (from $2). Further, these bars are nightclubs, not restaurants, and the quality of their cuisine shows it. The restaurants below serve "real" food.

Old Florida Bar-B-Q, 1388 E. Oakland Park Blvd. (561-1877). Take bus #10 or 20. Thumbnail-sized rib eatery with great beans and slaw ($13), snappy, friendly service and the wit and wisdom of owner Bill Claus. Open for lunch and dinner.

Southport Raw Bar, 1536 Cordova Rd. (525-2526), by the 17th St. Causeway behind the Southport Mall on the Intracoastal Waterway. Take bus #40 from the strip or #30 from downtown. Aggressively marine decor. Spicy conch chowder $2, fried shrimp $4.75. Open Mon.-Sat. 11am-2am, Sun. noon-midnight.

Tina's Spaghetti House, 2110 S. Federal Hwy. (522-9943), just north of 17th St. Take bus #10 from downtown. Authentic red checked tablecloths and hefty furniture. Popular with the locals since 1952. Lunch specials $4-5. Spaghetti dinner $6-7. Open Mon.-Thurs. 11:30am-10pm, Fri. 11:30am-11pm, Sat. 4-11pm, Sun. 4-9pm.

Scalley's Saloon, 2925 E. Commercial Blvd. (771-7808). Take bus #30 from downtown. Every sandwich ($3) weighs 10 oz., whether roast beef, flounder, or a burger. Free buffet with happy hour (drink purchase required) Mon.-Fri. 4-8pm. Open daily 11am-2am.

The Laughing Yak, 3024 E. Commercial Blvd. (491-7582), across from Scalley's. Take bus #30 from downtown. For something wild, try the Mongolian lunch buffet ($7.25), which includes 4 raw vegetables, 3 raw meats, rice, and a cooking surface at your table where you finish the job. Open Sun.-Tues. and Thurs. 11:30am-2pm and 5:30-10:30pm, Fri.-Sat. 11:30am-2pm and 5:30-11pm.

Grandma's Ice Cream, 3354 N. Ocean Blvd. (564-3671), just north of Oakland Park Blvd. Take bus #11 from downtown. Easily recognizable by the bright red 1901 Oldsmobile truck outside. Known for its cinnamon ice cream. Open daily noon-11pm.

Nightlife

If the beach by day doesn't provide enough action, Ft. Lauderdale offers all kinds of licit and illicit entertainment by night. Planes flying over the strip often hawk hedonistic happy hours at local watering spots. The drinking age in Florida is 21, and make sure you bring a passport or a driver's license, not a college ID, as proof of age. Be sure not to confine yourself to night spots on the strip, and remember that buses only run until 9pm.

Durty Nelly's, 3051 NE 32nd Ave. (564-0720), 1 block south of Oakland Park Blvd. and 2 blocks west of the beach. Take bus #72 or 11 from downtown. Live jazz, country, and rock. The inside bar is overcrowded, but the lounge area beside the Intracoastal Waterway is cozy. Free hot dogs, but drink purchase required. Open Mon.-Sat. 11am-2am, Sun. noon-2am.

Art Stock's Playpen, 3411 N. Federal Hwy. (565-2996), between Oakland Park and Commercial Blvd. Take bus #10 from downtown. Attracts the 2-fisted beer-drinking crowd to its famous wet T-shirt contests and Battle of the Bands. Known for heavy metal on Mon. ("metal-madness") nights. Open Mon.-Fri. 8pm-2am, Sat. 8pm-3am. Cover $5.

Backstreets, 200 W. Broward Blvd. (467-8990). The best dancing in Ft. Lauderdale; also features female swimsuit "competitions" and male strippers. Swimming pool and jacuzzi in back. Open Mon.-Sat. 9pm-5am. Cover $9 for members, $11 for nonmembers. Membership $10 at door.

The Candy Store, 1 N. Atlantic Blvd. (761-1888 or 761-3511). Take bus #11 from downtown. Many a callipygian young woman shows up for the Miss Cheeks contest and portly lads participate in the belly-flop contests. Free all-you-can-eat pizza in the afternoon. Open Mon.-Fri. 11am-2am, Sat. 11am-3am. Cover $5.

Penrod's on the Beach, 303 N. Atlantic Blvd. (763-1359). Take bus #11 from downtown. Spring break beer specials, feed-your-face extravaganzas, best legs contests, and raw bar. Seven entertainment rooms. Open daily 11am-2am. Cover $9.

Club Pink Pussycat, 1440 SE 17th Causeway (523-0402). Take bus #40 from the strip or #30 from downtown. "Beer, booze, and babes," screams a sign outside. All-nude dance revue. Open Mon.-Fri. 11am-2am, Sat 11am-3am, Sun. 1pm-2am. Cover $4.

Sights and Activities

Ft. Lauderdale is low on things to see for those uninterested in sun and sin. To see why Ft. Lauderdale is called the "Venice of America," take a tour of its waterways aboard the **Jungle Queen,** located at the **Bahia Mar Yacht Center** on Rte. A1A 3 blocks south of Las Olas Blvd. (3-hr. tours daily 10am and 2pm, $6.50, children $4.50.) For those desiring more intimate acquaintance with the ocean, **Bill's Sunrise Boat Rental,** 2025 E. Sunrise Blvd. (462-8962), offers equipment for a variety of water sports. On the beach, at 301 Seabreeze Blvd. (467-1316), Bill's charges $5 more for jet skis and boats but also offers snorkeling trips (1½ hr., $25), windsurfer rentals ($30 for 3 hr., $50 per day; $300 deposit), and waterskiing boats and drivers ($75 per hr., up to 6 people).

Six Flags Atlantis, 2700 Stirling Rd. (926-1000), is the largest water theme park in the world. Admission includes unlimited use of the Slidewinder water slides and the Raging Rampage. If rain interrupts your day at Atlantis for 59 consecutive minutes or more, you receive a free raincheck to return another day. (Open daily 10am-10pm. Admission $12, seniors $7, ages 3-11 $10, under 2 free. Head south on I-95, exit at Stirling Rd., and turn left under the overpass.)

Miami

Barely 100 years ago, a wealthy Ohio matron named Julia Tuttle bought herself some Biscayne Bay swampland and decided to start a city. Only after convincing Florida patron saint Henry Flagler to build a railroad to the place, and then a hotel, did she manage to instigate the development of a major urban and cultural center. Today Miami is a complicated, international city. There is Little Havana, a well-established Cuban community; Coconut Grove, with its village-in-the-swampland bohemianism; placid, well-to-do Coral Gables, one of America's early planned cities; and the black communities of Liberty City and Overtown.

Practical Information

Emergency: 911.

Visitor Information: Greater Miami Convention and Visitors Bureau, 4770 Biscayne Blvd. (539-3000; 800-641-1111 outside of Miami), a few blocks north of Rte. 195, on the 14th floor of County Bank Bldg. Pick up a "Map Manual," essential for negotiating the different forms of public transit. Open Mon.-Fri. 8:30am-6pm, Sat. 9am-noon. **Coconut Grove Chamber of Commerce,** 2820 McFarlane Rd. (444-7270). Lots of maps and advice. Open Mon.-Fri. 9am-5pm. The **Miami Beach Resort Hotel Association,** 407 Lincoln Rd., #10G (531-3553), can help you find a place on the beach. Open Mon.-Fri. 9am-5pm.

Miami International Airport: 7 miles northwest of downtown (871-7515). Bus #20 is the most direct public transportation into downtown (bus #3 is also usable); from there, take bus C or K to south Miami Beach.

Amtrak: 8303 NW 37th Ave. (835-1221-3 or 800-872-7245), not far from the Northside station of Metrorail. Bus L goes directly to Lincoln Rd. Mall in south Miami Beach. Open 7am-7:45pm. To: Orlando (1 per day, 5½ hr., $46); Jacksonville (2 per day, 8 hr., $67); and Washington, DC (2 per day, 22 hr., $142).

Greyhound/Trailways: 99 NE 4th St. (374-7222 for fare and schedule information.) To: Orlando (10 per day, 6½ hr., $38); Jacksonville (8-10 per day, 11 hr., $51); and Atlanta (7 per day, 15½ hr., $92). Ticket window open 5am-midnight.

Metro Dade Transportation: (638-6700; 6am-11pm for information). The city's transit system is complex and the buses tend to be tardy. The extensive **Metrobus** network converges downtown; most long bus trips transfer in this area. Lettered bus routes A through X serve Miami Beach. After dark, some stops are patrolled (indicated with a sign). Service daily 6am-8pm; major routes until 11pm or midnight. Fare 75¢. Pick up a *Map Manual* at the Convention and Visitors Bureau or at information stands at the corner of W. Flagler and NW 1st Ave. and on the Lincoln Road Mall in Miami Beach. Both open Mon.-Fri. 8am-5pm. Futuristic **Metrorail** service downtown. Fare $1, no bills; rail-bus transfers 25¢. The **Metromover** loop downtown, which runs 6:30am-7pm, is linked to Metrorail.

Taxis: Yellow Cab, 444-4444. **Metro Taxi,** 888-8888. **Central Taxi,** 532-5555.

Car Rental: Value Rent-a-Car, 1620 Collins Ave., Miami Beach (532-8257). $18 per day, $99 per week. Open daily 8am-4pm. Must be 21 with credit card or a $225 deposit. **Way-Lo,** 1701 Collins Ave. (871-4561), in the Ritz Plaza. $25 per day, $119 per week plus insurance. Open 8am-6pm. Must be 25 with credit card.

Auto Transport Company: Dependable Car Travel, 162 Sunny Isles Blvd. (945-4104). $21 per day, $89 per week. Open Mon.-Fri. 9am-5pm, Sat. 9am-noon. Must be 21 with a credit card or passport and foreign license.

Bike Rental: Miami Beach Cycle Center, 923 W. 39th St., Miami Beach (531-4161). $3 per hr., $12 per day, $32 per week, 2-hr. minimum. Open Mon.-Fri. 9:30am-6pm, Sat. 9:30am-5pm. Must be 18 with credit card or a $40 deposit. **Dade Cycle Shop,** 3216 Grand Ave., Coconut Grove (443-6075). $3-6 per hr., $15-22 per day. Open daily 9am-6pm. Must have $10 deposit and driver's license or credit card.

Help Lines: Crisis Hotline, 358-4357. **Rape Treatment Center and Hotline,** 1611 NW 12th Ave. (549-7273). **Gay Community Hotline,** 759-3661. **Center for Survival and Independent Living (C-SAIL),** 1310 NW 16th St. (547-5444). Offers information on services for the disabled. Lines open Mon.-Fri. 8am-6pm.

Post Office: 500 NW 2nd Ave. (371-2911). Open Mon.-Fri. 8:30am-5pm, Sat. 8:30am-12:30pm. **ZIP code:** 33101.

Area Code: 305.

Miami faces the Bahamas across the Strait of Florida, close to the southern tip of the Sunshine State. The most dazzling of Florida's many east coast cities, Miami is 350 miles from Jacksonville, 660 miles southeast of Atlanta, and 860 miles from New Orleans.

Three highways criss-cross the Miami area. I-95 is the most direct route north-south. Just south of downtown, I-95 runs into U.S. 1, known as the **Dixie Highway.** U.S. 1 goes as far as the Everglades entrance at Florida City and then all the way out to Key West. **Route 836,** a major east-west artery through town, connnects I-95 with the **Florida Turnpike,** passing the airport in between. Take Rte. 836 and the Turnpike to Florida City to avoid the traffic on Rte. 1.

Pay careful attention to the systematic street layout. Do not confuse Miami Beach street addresses with those of Miami. Streets in Miami run east-west, avenues north-south, and both are referred to by number—into the hundreds. All of Miami is divided into NE, NW, SE, and SW sections: the dividing lines (downtown) are **Flagler Street** (east-west) and **Miami Avenue** (north-south). Some numbered streets and avenues also have names—i.e., Le Jeune Rd. is SW 42nd Ave., and SW 40th St. is called Bird Rd.

Several causeways connect Miami to Miami Beach. The most useful is **MacArthur Causeway,** which feeds onto 5th St. in Miami Beach. Numbered streets run across the island, with numbers increasing as you go north; the main north-south drag is **Collins Avenue.** In south Miami Beach, **Washington Avenue,** 1 block to the west, is the main commercial strip, while **Ocean Avenue,** actually on the waterfront, lies 1 block east. The **Rickenbacker Causeway** is the only connection to Key Biscayne.

Accommodations and Camping

Finding a cheap room should never be a problem in Miami. Several hundred flea-bag art deco hotels in South Miami Beach stand at your service. (For safety and security, do not go south of 5th St.) A "pullmanette" (40s lingo) is a room with kitchen facilities; and in South Florida, any hotel room short of the Fontainebleau Hilton is likely to have cockroaches ("palmetto bugs"), so try not to take them as indicators of quality. In general, the peak season for Miami Beach runs late December to mid-March.

Camping is not allowed in Miami and the nearest campgrounds are north or west of the city. If you are serious about camping, go straight to one of the nearby National Parks.

The Clay Hotel (AYH), 406 Española Way, Miami Beach (534-2988), on Washington Ave. between 14th and 15th St. Take bus C or K from downtown. Cheerful chaos reigns in the 7 buildings. Kitchen, laundry facilities and ride boards. A very international crowd. Most rooms have 4 beds; 2 rooms share a bathroom. No curfew. $9, nonmembers $11. A/C $1. Hotel singles $17-20, doubles $25-28. Key deposit $5.

Waves Hotel, 1060 Ocean Ave., Miami Beach (531-5835), on the beach at 11th St. Renovated, with friendly atmosphere. A/C, HBO, washer and dryer in basement. *Let's Go* users welcomed. Singles and doubles April 1-Dec. 15 $40; 10% student discount in summer, and you can probably bargain down to $30. Pullmanette rates start $5 higher. Ocean views $10 higher. Key deposit $10, for pullmanettes $20.

San Juan Hotel, 1680 Collins Ave. (538-7531). Small, clean, old pullmanettes. Singles and doubles $24.

The New Coronado Hotel, 9501 Collins Ave., Miami Beach (866-1625). Directly on the ocean, near the fading pastel palaces of Miami Beach. Spare but clean rooms with refrigerator and TV. Singles $49. Doubles $54. Off-season $30 and $35, respectively.

Miami Airways Motel, 5001 36th St. (883-4700), near the airport. Clean rooms, A/C, pool, HBO. They'll pick you up at the airport. Singles $32. Doubles $37. 6% discount for stays of 5 or more days.

Palmer House Hotel, 1119 Collins Ave., Miami Beach (538-7725), 3 blocks west of the beach. A nice, clean, venerable art deco establishment with air conditioned pullmanettes. Singles $29, off-season $25. Each additional person (up to 3) $4. $125 per week, off-season $100.

Larry & Penny Thompson Memorial Campground, 12451 SW 184th St. (232-1049), a long way from anywhere. By car, drive 20-30 min. south along Dixie Hwy. Pretty grounds in a grove of mango trees; laundry, store, and all facilities, plus artificial lake with swimming beach, beautiful park, and even water slides. Office open 8am-5pm, but late arrival OK. Lake open 10am-5pm. Sites $11 ($67 per week), with hookup $17 ($100 per week).

Food

If you eat nothing else in Miami, be sure to try Cuban food. Specialties include *media noche* sandwiches (a sort of Cuban club sandwich on a soft roll, heated and compressed); *mamey* ice cream, a bright red concoction; rich *frijoles negros* (black beans); and *picadillo* (shredded beef and peas in tomato sauce, served with white rice). For Cuban sweets, seek out a *dulcería,* and punctuate your rambles around town with thimble-sized swallows of strong, sweet *cafe cubano* (25¢).

In Miami Beach, cheap restaurants are not common, but an array of fresh bakeries and fruit stands can sustain you for the day for under $3.

La Rumba, 2008 Collins Ave., Miami Beach (538-8998), between 21st and 20th St. Good, cheap Cuban food and noisy fun. Try their *arroz con pollo* ($6). Open daily 7:30am-midnight.

Versailles, 3555 SW 8th St. (444-0240 or 444-9660), just west of Little Havana on Calle Ocho. Not the cheapest, but you won't find a better or larger Cuban menu around. 4-oz. palomilla steak with plantains and rice $7.50. Open Mon.-Thurs. 8am-2am, Fri. 8am-3:30am, Sat. 8am-4:30am, Sun. 9am-2am.

Wolfie's, 2038 Collins Ave., Miami Beach (538-6626), at corner of 21st St. Giant, extremely popular New York-style deli, famous for its cheesecake. Lunch $3-7, dinner $5-10. Open 24 hours. A 2nd Wolfie's is at **Rascal House,** 17190 Collins Ave., near Hallandale (947-4581). Open daily 7am-1:45am.

Canton Too, 2614 Ponce de Leon Blvd., in Coral Gables (448-3736). Indisputably the best Chinese food in Miami. The honey chicken ($4.70) is out of this world. Open Mon.-Thurs. 11am-11pm, Fri.-Sat. 11am-midnight, Sun. 2-11pm.

Olympic Flame Greek Restaurant, 904 Lincoln Road Mall at Jefferson, Miami Beach (538-2745). Authentic, delicious Greek meals ($7). Open Mon.-Sat. 11am-8pm.

Our Place Natural Foods Eatery, 830 Washington Ave., Miami Beach (674-1322). Natural foods—juices, salads, pita, tofutti, etc. Lunch $3-5, dinner $4-10. Also a New Age books section, and live folk music on weekends. Open Mon.-Thurs. 11am-7pm, Fri.-Sat. 11am-11pm.

King's Ice Cream, 1831 SW 8th St. (643-1842), on Calle Ocho. Tropical fruit flavor *helados* (ice cream) like coconut (served in its own shell), *mamey,* and banana. Also try *churros* (thin Spanish donuts) or *café cubano* (10¢). Open daily 10am-11pm.

Sights

South Miami Beach, the swath of town between 6th and 23rd St., is filled with hundreds of hotels and apartments whose sun-faded pastel facades recall what sun-thirsty northerners of the 20s thought a tropical paradise should look like. The art deco palaces comprise the country's largest national historic district, and the only one to preserve 20th-century buildings. The **Miami Design Preservation League,** 1201 Washington Ave. (672-1836), offers guided and self-guided walking tours (1½ hr. guided tours Sat. 10:30am, $5; office open Mon.-Fri. 10am-6pm, Sat. 10am-1pm). The area is populated with a fascinating mixture of people, including large retired and Latin immigrant communities. Recently a group called the **South Florida Art Center** (674-8278) has been trying, with some success, to revive the fading Lincoln Road Mall as the center of a new art district. Their **cooperative gallery,** 942 Lincoln Road Mall, between Meridian and Lenox, exhibits the work of unknown artists, and they have also helped others open their own galleries on the mall. (Gallery open Tues.-Thurs. and Sat. noon-6pm, Fri. noon-6pm and 7-11pm.)

On the waterfront downtown is Miami's newest attraction, the **Bayside** shopping complex, with fancy shops, exotic food booths, and live reggae or *salsa* on Friday and Saturday nights. If you're interested in cinema's nautical leftovers, at Bayside you'll also find MGM's *Bounty,* used in the filming of *Mutiny on the Bounty.* Tours are given by guides in "authentic" (i.e. ripped) nautical clothing ($3.50, under 12 $1.50; tickets sold Sun.-Thurs. noon-8pm, Fri. noon-10pm, Sat. 10am-10pm).

Little Havana lies between SW 12th and SW 27th Ave. (take bus #3, 11, 14, 15, 17, 25, or 37). **Calle Ocho** (SW 8th St.), is at the heart of this district and the corresponding section of W. Flager St. is a center of Cuban business and activity. The **Little Havana Development Authority,** 970 SW 1st St., #407 (324-8127), arranges free walking tours that start from Domino Park, given one day's notice. You'll visit a cigar factory and some of the city's best shops and food stands. The works at the **Cuban Museum of Arts and Culture,** 1300 SW 12th Ave. (858-8006), reflect the bright colors and rhythms of the best Cuban art, providing a thoughtful counterpart to the street scenes of the nearby Calle Ocho. (Open Mon.-Fri. 10am-4:30pm, Sat.-Sun. 1-5pm. Donation. Take bus #27.)

An entirely different atmosphere prevails on the bay south of downtown in self-consciously rustic **Coconut Grove** (take bus #1 or Metrorail from downtown). The center of the grove is the area around the intersection of Grand Ave. and Main Hwy. Drop into a watering hole like **Señor Frog's,** 3008 Grand Ave. (448-0999), with its bang-up tables and phenomenal salsa. (Open Sun.-Thurs. 10:30am-1am, Fri.-Sat. 10:30am-2am.) If you ever wondered what the hanging gardens of Babylon would have looked like as a shopping mall, stroll through **Mayfair-in-the-Grove,** at the head of Grand Ave. This complex is a whimsical, waterfall-studded mix of Gaudi, Watts Towers, and sheer inventiveness.

On the bayfront between the Grove and downtown stands **Vizcaya** (recorded information 579-4813; also 579-2708 and 579-2808), set in acres of elaborately landscaped grounds. Built in 1916 by International Harvester heir James Deering, the four facades of this impressive 70-room Italianate mansion hide a hodgepodge of European antiques. (Open daily 9:30am-5pm, last admission 4:30pm. Admission $4.50. Take bus #1 to 3251 S. Miami Ave., or Metrorail to Vizcaya.) Across the street from Vizcaya, both the **Museum of Science** and its **Planetarium,** 3280 S. Miami Ave. (854-4247; show information 854-2222), offer laser shows and their ilk and are jam-packed with children. (Open daily 10am-6pm. Admission $5, children $3.50. Planetarium shows extra.)

Among Miami's commercial attractions is the popular **Seaquarium,** 4400 Rickenbacker Causeway, Virginia Key (361-5703), just minutes from downtown. The Seaquarium offers an array of shows with trained killer whales, man-eating sharks, and scads of dolphins. (Open daily 9:30am-6:30pm; ticket office closes 5pm. Admission $14, children $10.) **Planet Ocean,** 3979 Rickenbacker Causeway (361-9455), across the street, offers a more educational atmosphere for learning the secrets of the deep. (Open daily 10am-6pm; ticket office closes 4:30pm. Admission $7.50, ages 4-12 $4.)

Near Miami, the **Everglades National Park** teems with exotic life. Visit the park in winter or spring, when heat, humidity, storms, and bugs are at a minimum, and the wildlife congregates around the water. The park is accessible on the north via the Tamiami Trail (U.S. 41) or by the main park road (Rte. 9336) out of Florida City. The best way to tour the largely inaccessible park is to take Rte. 997 40 miles through the flat grasslands to Flamingo, on Florida Bay, stopping at the various nature trails and pullouts along the way. Stop at the **visitors center,** P.O. Box 279, Homestead 33030 (247-6211), by the park headquarters just outside the entrance, to see a film on the Everglades and to pick up maps and information. (Open daily 8am-5pm.) The visitors center also sponsors a variety of hikes, canoe trips, and amphitheater programs. To get face-to-snout with an alligator, try the **Anhinga Trail,** 2 miles beyond the entrance.

Entertainment

Miami nights are so pleasant year-round that the city never needs to sleep. **Woodies** (538-5401), at Ocean Ave and 4th St., Miami Beach, run by Rolling Stone Ron Woods, is definitely the hottest nightspot in town. (Cover $5-12.) The beach also provides an array of good alternatives like **Club Nu,** with its bopsy pop music, on Collins Ave. at 21st St. (Cover around $10.) For blues, try the **Peacock Cafe,** 2977 McFarlane Rd., Coconut Grove (445-0550; open Mon. 8pm-midnight, Tues.-Thurs. and Sun. 9pm-1am, Fri.-Sat. 10pm-2am). If you're broke, **Friday Night Live,** at **South Point Park,** at the very southern tip of Miami Beach, features free concerts sponsored by the city. (Information 579-6040.) Down Washington Ave. at the corner of Española Way, the **Cameo Theater** (532-6212) hosts live punk and other kinds of rock bands about once a week. For gay nightlife, check out **Uncle Charlie's,** 3673 Bird Ave. (442-8687), just off Dixie Hwy. (Cover $1.)

P.A.C.E. (Performing Arts and Community Education) (856-1966) offers more than a thousand concerts each year (jazz, rock, soul, dixieland, reggae, salsa, bluegrass), most of which are free. For more information on what's happening in Miami, check *Miami-South Florida Magazine,* or the "Living Today," "Lively Arts," and Friday "Weekend" sections of the *Miami Herald,* which also publishes a Spanish edition.

The Florida Keys

Whether you drive through the Keys or fly above them in an airplane, you'll be dazzled by their silvery coral islets, golden bars of sand, and emerald mangrove trees. Sheltered by coral reefs, bathed in the warm currents of the Gulf Stream, and cooled by the breezes of the Atlantic, the Keys enjoy sun and settings more Caribbean than Floridian. The barrier reefs lie approximately 6 miles offshore, a glorious 100 yards or so in width. Adored by divers, the reefs harbour the oceans' most diverse and colorful life as well as hundreds of wrecked ships and legends of lost treasure.

The Keys run more east-west than north-south. **Mile markers** divide U.S. 1, a.k.a. the Overseas Highway. They begin with mile 126 in Florida City and end with zero on the corner of Whitehead and Fleming Streets in Key West. Mile markers are used instead of street addresses to indicate the location of homes and businesses.

Greyhound runs three buses per day to Key West from Miami, stopping in Coral Gables, Perrine, Homestead, Key Largo (451-3664), Marathon (743-3488), Big Pine Key, and Key West (296-9072). Biking along U.S. 1 across the swamps between Florida City and Key Largo is made impossible by the lack of road shoulders, so bring your bikes on the bus. Hitchhiking, though illegal in Monroe County, is a cinch since there is only one road.

The **area code** on the Keys is 305.

Key Largo

When a traveler crosses the mangrove swamps and crocodile pools of upper Florida Bay, Key Largo sounds the first welcome to the Keys. Largo's **John Pennecamp State Park,** mile 102.5 (451-1202), 60 miles from Miami, provides the casual visitor with a rare chance to explore the living reef off the Keys, although the view is somewhat murky from the glass-bottomed boats ($10-11). The **Coral Reef Company** (451-1621, 248-4300, or 800-432-2871) sails visitors 6 miles past mangrove swamps to the reef. (Snorkeling tours daily at 9am, noon, and 3pm. 1½ hr. of water time and a quickie lesson including gear for $17 at 9am, otherwise $19 per person.)

Key Largo locals get away from the touristy bake shops and cafés at the **Captain's Cabin,** 45 Garden Cove Dr. (451-2720). This colorful waterfront restaurant is a few blocks southeast of the intersection of U.S. 1 and Rte. 905, about a mile north of the state park. Tasty seafood dinners run $4-6. (Open Mon.-Thurs. 11am-midnight, Fri.-Sat. 11am-1am.) **The Italian Fisherman,** mile 104 (451-4471), is the ideal dinner place with fine food and a spectacular view of Florida Bay. This restaurant was a former illegal gambling casino and the locale of scenes from Bogart's movie *Key Largo.* (Lunch $4-5, dinner $6-13. Open daily 11am-11pm.) **Perry's,** mile 102 (451-1834), serves fresh local seafood and charbroiled steaks. They also offer a "you hook 'em, we cook 'em" service for $2.50. (Perry's is also at Islamorada, mile 82.5 (664-5066); Marathon, mile 52 (743-3108); and, the original and most famous Key West location, 3800 N. Roosevelt Blvd. (294-8472). (Lunch $4-9, dinner $6-15. Open daily 11am-11pm.)

Gilbert's Mini Resort, Jewfish Creek, mile 108 (451-1133), has a clean motel with decent rates (Sun.-Thurs. doubles $55, Fri.-Sat. $65), a restaurant, marina, fishing boat rentals ($59-89 per ½-day), and airboat tours. If the state park's campsites are full, try crowded but well-run **Kings Kamp Marina,** mile 103.5 (451-0010; sites by the ocean $14). Look for the concealed entrance on the northwest (Gulf) side of U.S. 1. The cheapest motel in Key Largo is **Sea Trails** (852-8001), mile 88.5, on the bayside. (Large, plain rooms with 1 double bed and 1 twin bed $35.) The **Hungry Pelican,** mile 99.5 (451-3576) is nicer and friendlier. (Clean, cozy trailers with a double bed $35.)

The **Florida Upper Keys Chamber of Commerce,** mile 105.5 (451-1414), at Rte. 905, has maps and brochures on local attractions. (Open Mon.-Fri. 9am-5pm.) The Key Largo **post office** is at mile 100 (451-3155, open Mon.-Fri. 8am-4:30pm, Sat. 8am-noon). Key Largo's **ZIP code** is 33037; the **area code** is 305.

Key West

This is the end of the road. If you're searching for a tropical paradise, you can do no better in the U.S. than Key West. The island's pastel clapboard houses, hibiscus and bougainvillea plants, year-round tropical climate, and gin-clear waters make it a seductive spot for any traveler.

Settled by English, Bahamanians, Cubans, New Englanders, and Southerners, Key West inhabitants have made their living salvaging wrecked ships, making cigars, gathering sponges, and fishing for turtle and shrimp. After 1912, when Florida's patron saint Henry Flagler built a railroad over land and water to Key West, the industry of lodging, feeding, and overcharging tourists has also employed more than a few "conchs" (locals). Nonetheless, it's still a salty small town with a carefree, relaxed atmosphere that has attracted Tennessee Williams and Ernest Hemingway among the hordes of tourists. Today, an easygoing tolerance of diversity still attracts those outside the mainstream—a new generation of writers and artists, gay people (who own or manage more than half of Key West's businesses), recluses, adventurers, and eccentrics.

Practical Information

Emergency: 911.

Visitor Information: Key West Chamber of Commerce, 402 Wall St. (294-2587), in old Mallory Sq. Useful Humm's *Guide to the Florida Keys and Key West* available here. Also have an accommodations list which notes guest houses popular with gay people. Open daily 9am-5pm. **Key West Visitors Bureau,** P.O. Box 1147, Key West 33041 (296-3811 or 800-352-5397), produces a detailed guide to accommodations. Open Mon.-Fri. 9am-5pm. **Key West Welcome Center,** 3840 N. Roosevelt Blvd. (296-4444), just north of the intersection of U.S. 1 and N. and S. Roosevelt Blvd. Open daily 9am-5pm.

Key West International Airport: on the southeast corner of the island. Serviced by Eastern and Piedmont airlines. No public bus service.

Greyhound: 615½ Duval St. (296-9072). Obscure location in an alley behind Antonio's restaurant. Open Mon.-Sat. 7am-12:45pm and 2:30-5:30pm. To Miami (3 per day, 5 hr. stopping along all the keys, $32).

Key West Port and Transit Authority: City Hall (292-8159 or 292-8164). One bus (Old Town) runs clockwise around the island and Stock Island the other (Mallory St.) runs counterclockwise. Pick up a clear and helpful free map from the chamber of commerce or any bus driver. Service about once every 15 min. except hourly service Mon.-Sat. 6:30-10pm. Service Mon.-Sat. 6am-10pm, Sun. 6:40am-6:40pm. Fare 75¢, seniors and students 35¢.

Taxi: Key West Independent, 294-7277.

Car Rental: Alamo, Key Wester Inn, 975 S. Roosevelt Blvd. (294-6675 or 800-327-9633), near the airport. $33 per day, $132 per week. Under 25 $5 per day extra. Must be 21 with major credit card or a $50 deposit through a travel agent. Drop-off in Miami a prohibitive $60.

Bike Rental: Key West Hostel, 718 South St. (296-5719). $6 per day, $30 per week; for hostel residents only. Open daily 8am-noon and 5-8pm. $20 deposit. **Bubba's Bike Rental,** 705 Duval St. (294-2618). $5 per day, $25 per week. Open daily 10am-5pm. Must have credit card or a $50 deposit.

Help Lines: 296-4357. **Handicapped Transportation,** 294-8468 (Key West Port and Transit Authority).

Post Office: 400 Whitehead St. (294-2257), 1 street west of Duval, at Eaton. Open Mon.-Fri. 8:30am-5pm. **ZIP code:** 33040.

Area Code: 305.

Just 5 miles long and 3 miles wide, Key West lies at the end of Rte. 1, 160 miles southwest of Miami. Only 90 miles north of Havana, Cuba, Key West is farther south than many islands in the Bahamas.

Key West is divided into two sectors. The eastern part of the island, called "Des Moines" or "America" by some, harbors the tract houses, chain motels, shopping malls, and the airport. **Old Town,** the west side of town, below White St., is cluttered with beautiful old conch houses. **Duval Street** is the main north-south thoroughfare in Old Town, **Truman Avenue** the major east-west route. Key West is cooler than mainland Florida in summer, and much warmer in winter.

Driving is slow; most of the highway is a two-lane road with only an occasional passing lane. Bikers be warned: police enforce traffic laws. Use hand signals, stop at signs, and watch for one-way streets.

Accommodations and Camping

Beautiful weather resides year-round in Key West, and so do tourists. As a result, good rooms at the nicer hotels go for up to $400 per day, especially during the winter holidays. There is no "off-season." Key West is packed except from mid-September to mid-December, and even then, don't expect any room to go for less than $40.

Try to bed down in Old Key West; the beautiful, 19th-century clapboard houses here lend charm to any sojourn. Some of the guest houses in the Old Town are for gay men exclusively, and quite a few offer complimentary breakfasts. During the busy spring months, police tend to look the other way when people park overnight at the pullouts by the Keys' bridges.

Key West Hostel (AYH), 718 South St. (296-5719), at Sea Shell Motel in Old Key West, 6 blocks west of Duval St. Take any bus to the corner of South and Reynolds St. Rooms with 4 beds, shared bath. A/C comes on at night. Kitchen open until 9:30pm. No curfew. Office open daily 8am-noon and 5-8pm. $11, nonmembers $14. Key deposit $5. Motel rooms in summer $36, in winter $55. Call ahead to check availability; also call for late arrival.

Island House, 1129 Fleming St. (294-6284), at the corner of Fleming and White St. Take any bus to corner of White and Fleming. For gay men only. Rooms with A/C, fans, and radio; slick, ritzy atmosphere and decoration. Sauna, pool, jacuzzi, and weight room. Singles in summer with shared bath $50; in winter $80.

Tilton Hilton, 511 Angela St. (294-8697), next to Greyhound station. Plain rooms, as cheap as you'll find. Singles in summer $28.

Jabour's Trailer Court, 223 Elizabeth St. (294-5723), 3 blocks from North Duval St., between Greene and Caroline St. Cramped trailer lots, but the only game in Old Town. Run by family of humorous conchs who aren't on the make. Tents seldom turned away. Tents $15 for 2, vans $15 for 2, hookup $24 for 2. Each additional person $3.

Boyd's Campground, 6401 Maloney Ave. (294-1465), on Stock Island. Take bus to Maloney Ave. from Stock Island. 12 acres on the ocean. All facilities, including showers. Primitive sites $18, water and electric $2 extra, air/heat $2 extra. Waterfront sites $3 extra.

Food

Expensive restaurants line festive Duval Street. Side streets offer lower prices and fewer crowds. **Fausto's Food Palace,** 522 Fleming St. (296-5663), the grocery store in Old Town, is the best place to pick up supplies. (Open Mon.-Sat. 8am-8pm, Sun. 8am-6pm.) Just about no one leaves the Keys without slurping down a piece or three of **key lime pie,** although the genuine article (look for a tangy yellow filling) is hard to find. Don't let anyone tell you that key limes are green. Pick up a copy of *The Masked Gourmet* ($1) at the Key West Welcome Center for reviews.

La Cubanita Restaurant, 601 Duval St., #3 (294-4246 or 294-3023), off Duval on a shady side street. Noisy and fun. The best-priced Cuban food around. Try the Cuban sandwich ($3) or a palomilla steak dinner ($7.50).

La Bodega, 829 Simonton St. (294-6544), 1 block east of Duval, at the corner of Olivia. Cluttered, with dozens of caged parakeets and the upper balcony of an old, unpainted conch house. Sandwiches ($3-4) and fresh soups ($2.25). Open Mon.-Sat. 8am-11pm, Sun. 10am-11pm.

Half-Shell Fish Market, Land's End Village (294-5028), at the foot of Margaret St. on the waterfront 5 blocks east of Duval. Rowdy and popular with tourists. Great variety of seafood dinners $8-10. Famed for its spring conch chowder ($2.50). Open daily 11am-11pm. Turtle Kraals next door (see Sights below).

El Cacique, 125 Duval St. (294-4000). Cuban food at reasonable prices. Homey and colorful. Filling lunch and dinner specials, with pork or local fish, black beans, and rice under $6. Try fried plantains, conch chowder, or bread pudding as side dishes, and flan ($1.25) as dessert. Open daily 8am-9pm.

Hercules Bar-B-Q, 3332 N. Roosevelt Blvd. (296-3846), just behind the Searstown Laundry, 1½ miles west of Old Town. Take any bus to the Searstown Mall. A local secret, this tiny shack serves juicy, thick barbecue pork and beef sandwiches ($3). Take-out only. Open Mon.-Sat. 10:30am-9pm, Sun. 10:30am-7pm.

Sights

Biking is a good way to see the sights in Key West, but first you might want to take the **Conch Tour Train** (294-5161), a narrated ride through Old Town, leaving from Mallory Sq. The touristy one-and-a-half-hour trip costs $10, children $3, but the guide provides you with a fascinating history of the area. (Operates daily 9am-4:30pm.) **Old Town Trolley** runs a similar tour, but you can get on and off throughout the day.

For many years a beacon for artists and writers, **Hemingway House,** 907 Whitehead St. (294-1575), on Olivia St., is where Papa wrote *For Whom the Bell Tolls* and *A Farewell to Arms.* Tour guides at the houses are notoriously awful; grin and bear it or walk through the house on your own. About 50 cats (supposedly descendants of Hemingway's cats) make their home on the grounds. (Open daily 9am-5pm. Admission $5, children $1.) The glass-bottomed boat *Fireball* takes two-hour cruises to the reefs and back (296-6293; 3-4 per day; tickets $12, ages 3-12 $6). The **Coral Princess Fleet,** 700 Front St. (296-3287), offers snorkeling trips with free instruction for beginners. (2 per day, $24; open daily 8:30am-7:15pm). Similar boat trips on the **Admiral's Fleet,** Greene St. at Duval (294-8383), or **Reef Raiders,** 109 Duval St. (294-3635), take you out to various parts of the living coral reefs off Key West. These companies also offer glass-bottom boat trips. The **Audubon House,** 205 Whitehead St. (294-2116), built in the early 1800s, houses some fine antiques and a private collection of the works of ornithologist John James Audubon, including his *Birds of America* folio. (Open daily 9:30am-5pm. Admission $4.50, ages 6-12 $1.)

The **San Carlos Institute,** 516 Duval St., was built in 1871. This freshly restored paragon of Cuban architecture, shining with majorca tiles from Spain, is now home to a research center for Hispanic studies. The **Haitian Art Company,** 600 Frances St. (296-8932), 6 blocks east of Duval St., is crammed full of vivid Caribbean artworks. (Open Mon.-Sat. 9am-5pm.)

Down Whitehead St., past Hemingway House, you'll come to the **Southernmost Point** in the continental U.S. and the adjacent Southernmost Beach. A small, cone-shaped monument and a few conchshell hawkers mark the spot. The **Monroe County Beach,** off Atlantic Ave., has an old pier allowing access past the weed line. The **Old U.S. Naval Air Station** offers deep water swimming on Truman Beach. **Mel Fisher's Treasure Exhibit,** 200 Greene St. (296-9936), will dazzle you with glorious gold. Fisher discovered the sunken treasures from the shipwrecked Spanish vessel, the Atocha. The National Geographic film is included in the $5 admission (children $1). (Open daily 10am-6pm, doors close 5:15pm.)

After Duval Street, watch a sunset from the **Mallory Square Dock.** Magicians, street entertainers, and hawkers of tacky wares work the crowd, swimmers and speedboaters show off, and the crowd always cheers when the sun slips into the Gulf with a blazing red farewell. Keep a lookout for the Iguana Man.

Every October, Key West holds a week-long celebration known as **Fantasy Fest,** which culminates in an extravagant parade. The entire population of the area turns out for the event in costumes that stretch the imagination. In April, the Conch Republic celebration is highlighted by a bed race, and the January through March Old Island Days feature art exhibits, a conch shell-blowing contest, and the blessing of the shrimp fleet.

Entertainment

The daily *Key West Citizen* (sold in front of the post office) and monthly *Solares Hill* and *The Conch Republic* (available at the Key West Chamber of Commerce, lobbies, and waiting rooms) all cover events on the island. Nightlife in Key West starts at 11pm, and goes on until very late. Many establishments are situated on or off Duval Street. Gay travelers can expect a little heckling from out-of-town cruisers at night, but violence is rare and hassles can be avoided by staying away from the straight bars at the far north end of Duval.

Sloppy Joe's, 201 Duval St., at Greene (294-5717). Reputedly one of Papa Hemingway's preferred watering holes; the decor and rowdy tourists would probably now send him packing. The original bar was in Havana but moved to "Cayo Hueso" (i.e. Key West) when Castro rose to power. The frenzy heightens during the Hemingway Days Festival in mid-July. Reasonable draft prices. Open daily 9am-whenever the action stops.

Captain Tony's Saloon, 428 Greene St. (294-1838). The oldest bar in Key West. In 1967, owner Tony Tarracino campaigned barefoot for mayor of Key West and lost by only 86 votes. He's also a confessed gunrunner, gambler, adulterer, and small-time hustler. Open daily noon-very, very late. Tony is usually at the bar at 9pm.

The Bull Bar, 224 Duval St. Not a place to nurse wine coolers; don't enter unless your prepared to poison your esophagus with $1 schnapps shots. Live music nightly. Open Mon.-Sat. 10am-2am, Sun. noon-2am. The **Whistle Bar** upstairs opens at 5pm and closes at the same time as the Bull. The balcony overlooks Duval St., thereby allowing you to whistle at unsuspecting tourists—hence the name. 2-for-1 drinks 5-9pm.

La Terraza de Martí (also called **La Te Da**), 1125 Duval (294-8435). Some of the best (albeit expensive) food in town. The front balcony is where José Martí, the Cuban rebel, made incendiary speeches to raise money for the Cuban revolution in the 1890s. Open daily 10am-2am.

Tampa and St. Petersburg

The Gulf Coast communities of Tampa and St. Petersburg have a style distinct from that of most east coast vacation magnets. Far less raucous and touristy than the east coast, Tampa and St. Petersburg offer quiet beaches, beautiful harbors, and perfect weather. Tampa is both one of the nation's fastest-growing cities and largest ports, and boasts a thriving financial, industrial, and artistic community. Across the bay, St. Petersburg is a relaxed, attractive retirement community, that braces itself each spring when the rumble of approaching spring breakers is heard from the north. The high season on the Gulf Coast lasts from October to April.

Practical Information

Emergency: 911.

Visitor Information: Tampa/Hillsborough Convention and Visitors Association, 100 S. Ashley Dr., #850 (223-1111 or 800-826-8358). Teleguide coupons and some brochures. Open Mon.-Fri. 8am-4:45pm. **West Tampa Chamber of Commerce,** 3005 W. Columbus Dr. (879-2866). Open Mon.-Fri. 9am-5pm. **Ybor City Chamber of Commerce,** 1513 8th Ave. (248-3712). Open Mon.-Fri. 11am-3pm. **St. Petersburg Chamber of Commerce,** 401 3rd Ave. S. (821-4069). Open Mon.-Fri. 8:30am-5pm.

Travelers Aid: In Tampa, 253-5936. Open Mon.-Fri. 8:30am-4:30pm. In St. Pete, 823-4891.

Tampa International Airport: 276-3400, 5 miles west of downtown. HARTline bus #30 runs between the airport and downtown Tampa. **St. Petersburg Clearwater International Airport** is right across the bay. **The Limo** (822-3333) offers 24-hour service from both airports to Tampa, St. Pete, and the beaches from Ft. Desoto to Clearwater ($9.75). Make reservations 12 hours in advance.

Amtrak: In Tampa, 601 Nebraska Ave. (229-2473 or 800-872-7245), at Twiggs St., 1 block north of Kennedy. To: Orlando (2 per day, 2 hr., $16); Jacksonville (2 per day, 5 hr., $40); Savannah (2 per day, 8 hr., $70). Open 7:30am-8pm. No trains go south of Tampa (i.e. no service to St. Pete). In St. Pete, 3601 31st St. N. (522-9475). Amtrak will run you over to Tampa by bus ($5).

Greyhound/Trailways: In Tampa, 610 E. Polk St. (229-1501 or 229-2112), next to Burger King, downtown. To Miami (5 per day, 10 hr., $40) and Orlando (7 per day, 1½ hr., $17). In St. Pete, 180 9th St. N., downtown.

Local Transit: In Tampa, **Hillsborough Area Regional Transit (HARTline),** 254-4278. Fare 60¢, transfers 10¢. To get to St. Pete, take bus #100 express service from downtown to the

Gateway Mall ($1). In St. Pete, **St. Petersburg Municipal Transit System,** 530-9911. Most routes depart form Williams Park at 1st Ave. N. and 3rd St. N. Ask for directions at the information booth there. Base fare 60¢, transfers 10¢.

Help Lines: Rape Crisis, 530-7233. **Gay/Lesbian Crisis Line,** 1-586-4297.

ZIP Codes: Tampa 33602, St. Pete 33713.

Area Code: 813.

Tampa is at the corner of a bay in the middle of Florida's west coast, 85 miles west of Orlando. The city is laid out on a quadrant. **Florida Avenue** divides the city east-west, **Kennedy Boulevard,** which becomes **Frank Adams Drive** (Rte. 60), divides it north-south. Numbered avenues run east-west and numbered streets run north-south. You can reach Tampa on I-75 from the north, or I-4 from the east.

St. Petersburg is 22 miles to the southwest of Tampa, on the tip of the peninsula between the Gulf of Mexico and Tampa Bay. **Central Avenue** divides St. Petersburg north-south. Avenues run east-west, streets north-south. The St. Pete beachfront includes the towns of **St. Petersburg Beach, Treasure Island, Madeira Beach,** and **Indian Rocks Beach,** all connected by U.S. 699. Extending from Clearwater Beach in the north to Pass-a-Grille Beach in the south, a chain of barrier islands separates St. Petersburg from the Gulf of Mexico. The stretch past the Don CeSar Hotel (a pink montrosity recently declared a historical landmark) in St. Petersburg Beach and Pass-a-Grille Beach has the best sand, a devoted following, and the least pedestrian and motor traffic.

Tampa and St. Pete are connected by three causeways.

Accommodations and Camping

It is hard to find inexpensive, convenient lodgings in Tampa, but St. Petersburg has a youth hostel and many cheap motels along 4th Street North and U.S. 19. Some advertise singles for as little as $16, but these tend to be old and dirty. To avoid the worst neighborhoods, stay on the north end of 4th Street and the south end of U.S. 19. Fortunately, there also several inexpensive motels on the St. Pete beach. In Tampa, you can try to contact the Overseas Information Center at the **University of South Florida** (974-3104) for help in finding accommodations. **Florida Suncoast Bed and Breakfast,** P.O. Box 12, Palm Harbor 33563 (784-5118), can arrange private lodgings in the area, as well as in Clearwater, Saratoga, and Bradenton (from $28). Write for an application.

Tampa

Motel 6, 333 E. Fowler Ave. (932-4948), near Busch Gardens. From I-275, take the Fowler Ave. exit. On the northern outskirts of Tampa, 30 miles from the beach. Singles $25, each additional person $6.

St. Petersburg

St. Petersburg International Hostel (AAIH), 215 Central Ave. (822-4095), at the Detroit Hotel, downtown. Big, clean rooms with 2-4 beds, some with private bath. Kitchen and laundry facilities. Bike rentals ($3 per hr.). Call for pick-up at Greyhound or Amtrak. In the same building, the **Club Detroit** offers live music five nights a week. $10, $50 per week. Private rooms from $18. Key deposit $5.

YMCA, 116 5th St. S. (822-3911), at 2nd Ave. S. Men only. Small rooms with hall showers. $16.58. Key deposit $20.

AAA Motel, 6345 4th St. N. (525-5900). Small, clean rooms with A/C and cable TV. Ask for a room in back to escape highway noise. Singles $18, each additional person $2.

Kentucky Motel, 4246 4th St. N. (526-7373). Large, clean rooms. Singles $20. Doubles $22-25. Dec.-April rooms $10 more.

Grant Motel, 9046 4th St. N. (576-1369), 4 miles north of town on U.S. 92. Pool. Clean rooms. Most have fridge, all have A/C. Ask about the single for $21. Otherwise, singles $26, doubles $28. Jan 1-April 15 singles $36, doubles $38.

Buccaneer, 10800 and 10836 Gulf Blvd. (367-1908 or 800-826-2120), on Treasure Island. Great beachfront rooms. *Not* a party den. Will lend grills for cookouts. Doubles $29-38, with fridge $38-41. High season $45-62 and $65, respectively. Breakfast included. Each additional person $6. Key deposit $5.

Windjammer, 10450 Gulf Blvd., St. Pete Beach (360-4940). Down the street from the Buccaneer. Large, clean rooms. Doubles $40-42, with kitchen $42-46. High season $50 and $52, respectively. Each additional person $5.

Camping is best at **Fort DeSoto State Park** (866-2662), composed of five islands at the southern end of a long chain of keys and islands. The park is a wildlife sanctuary and makes a good daytrip or oceanside picnic spot. (Sites $12.) Disregard the "no vacancy" sign at the toll booth (75¢) at the Pinellas Bayway exit. However, from January to April, you may want to make a reservation in person at the St. Petersburg County Building, 150 5th St. N., #63, or at least call ahead. (2-day min. stay; curfew 10pm; no alcohol allowed in the park.) In Tampa, try the **Busch Travel Park,** 10001 Malcolm McKinley Dr. (971-0008), ¼ mile north of Busch Gardens, with pool, store, recreation room, and train service to Busch Gardens and Adventure Island. (Tent sites $8.30, RV sites $14.75.)

Food

Prices are high in yuppie Tampa, but there are cheap Cuban and Spanish restaurants. Black bean soup, Gazpacho, and Cuban bread are served up everywhere. Ybor City definitely has the best Cuban food and the most reasonable prices.

St. Petersburg's restaurants cater to its retired population—they're cheap, good, and low-sodium, but generally close by 8 or 9pm. Those eating later should try St. Pete Beach or 4th Street. The beach has several forgettable surf 'n' turf spots, but there are a few places that serve excellent, cheap seafood.

Tampa

JD's, 2029 E. 7th Ave. (247-9683), in Ybor City. Take bus #12. Soups, sandwiches, and Cuban food in a roomy, low key restaurant. Breakfast $2.50. Lunch $3-5. Open Mon.-Sat. 9am-3pm.

The Columbia, 2117 E. 7th Ave. (248-4961), in Ybor City. This elegant block-long Spanish restaurant is the oldest in the Sunshine State. Meal is accompanied by violinists and Flamenco dancers. Lunch $5-7. Dinners $9-25 plus $5 per person for entertainment. Open daily 11am-11pm.

St. Pete

Goody Goody, 1119 Florida Ave. N. (223-4230). The best burgers ($2-2.30) in town. Decor is straight out of *Lost in Space.* Open Mon.-Sat. 7:30am-7:30pm.

Crabby Bills, 402 Gulf Blvd., Indian Rocks Beach (595-4825). Cheap, extensive menu. Ultra-casual atmosphere. Serves blue crabs (6 for $5.50). Open Mon.-Thurs. 11am-10pm, Fri.-Sat. 11am-11pm. Arrive before 5pm to avoid a 20-min. wait.

The Scandia, 19829 Gulf Blvd., Indian Shores (595-5525 or 595-4928). Danish theme pervades. Small dining rooms, pleasant atmosphere. Dinners $6-11. Open Tues.-Sat. 11:30am-9pm, Sun. noon-8pm.

Ollie O's, 101 1st Ave. NE, St. Pete (822-6200), in the Old Soreno Hotel, 2 blocks from the youth hostel. It only *looks* expensive. Huge steaks with fries $6, sandwiches about $4. Open Mon.-Thurs. 7am-5:30pm, Fri. 7am-6pm, Sat. 7am-5:30pm.

Sights and Activities

Tampa

Bounded roughly by 22nd Street, Nebraska Avenue, 5th Avenue, and Columbus Drive, **Ybor City** is Tampa's Latin Quarter. The area expanded rapidly after Vincent Martínez Ybor moved his cigar factories here from Key West in 1886. Although cigar manufacturing has been mechanized, some people still roll cigars by hand and sell them for $1 in **Ybor Square,** a 19th-century cigar factory converted into an upscale retail complex. (Open Mon.-Sat. 10am-9pm, Sun. noon-6pm. Free.) **Ybor City State Museum,** 1818 9th Ave. at 21st St. (247-6323), traces the development of Ybor City, Tampa, the Cigar Industry, and Cuban migration. (Open Tues.-Sat. 9am-noon and 1-5pm. Admission 50¢.) At **Three Birds Bookstore and Coffee Room,** 1518 7th Ave. (247-7041), you can enjoy cappucino or fruit punch over a slice of cheesecake as you read the latest issue of the *Paris Review.* Fortunately, aside from the square itself, the area has remained relatively unspoiled by urban gentrification. East 7th Avenue still resembles an old neighborhood. Keep an ear out for jazz and a nose out for Spanish cuisine. Don't stray too far off the main drag, however—the area becomes increasingly dangerous. Bus #5, 12, and 18 run to Ybor City from downtown.

Now part of the University of Tampa, the Moorish **Tampa Bay Hotel,** 401 W. Kennedy Blvd., was the most fashionable Florida coast resort hotel in 1889. Teddy Roosevelt trained his Rough Riders in the back yard before the Spanish-American War. The small **Henry B. Plant Museum** (253-3333), in a wing of the University of Tampa building, is an orgy of rococco craftsmanship and architecture. The exhibits themselves, which include Victorian furniture, oriental art, and Wedgewood pottery, pale in comparison. (Guided tours 1:30pm. Open Tues.-Sat. 10am-4pm. Donation.)

The **waterfront** provides much of Tampa's atmosphere. Banana boats from South and Central America unload and tally their cargo every day-oh at the docks, 139 Twiggs St., near 13th St. and Kennedy Blvd. Every year in February the *Jose Gasparilla,* a fully rigged pirate ship, loaded with hundreds of exuberant "pirates," "invades" Tampa, and kicks off a month of parades and festivals, such as the **Gasparilla Sidewalk Art Festival.**

Downtown, the **Tampa Museum of Art,** 601 Doyle Carlton Dr. (223-8128), houses the Joseph Veach Nobre collection of classical and modern works. (Open Tues.-Sat. 10am-5pm, Wed. 10am-9pm and Sun. 1-5pm. Free.) Across from the University of South Florida, north of downtown, the **Museum of Science and Industry,** 4801 E. Fowler Ave. (985-5531), features a simulated hurricane. (Open daily 10am-4:30pm. Admission $2, ages 5-15 $1.)

If you insist on going to all the major amusement parks in Florida, your next stop is **Busch Gardens—The Dark Continent,** 3000 Busch Blvd. at NE 40th (971-8282; take I-275 to Busch Blvd., or take bus #5 from downtown). Busch Gardens has the usual rides, as well as an enormous zoo. In an interesting switch, people are confined to trains and boats, as giraffes, zebras, ostriches, and antelope roam freely across a 60-acre plain. (The lions and tigers live on their own islands.) (Open daily 9am-8pm; off-season 9:30am-6pm. Admission $20, under 2 free, 5-8pm $15. Parking $2.) A morning visit to the **Anheuser-Busch Hospitality House** inside the park is a surefire way of making your afternoon more enjoyable. There is a three-drink limit, and you must stand in line for each beer, but you can sip whatever they have on tap.

St. Petersburg

St. Petersburg's main attraction is its coastline. **Pass-a-Grille Beach** is the nicest, but the **municipal beach,** at Treasure Island, accessible from Rte. 699 via Treasure Island Causeway, is free.

If you're too sunburned to spend another day on the beach, head for **Sunken Gardens,** 1825 4th St. N. (896-3187), with over 7000 varieties of exotic flowers and plants. (Open daily 9am-5:30pm. Admission $6, ages 3-11 $3.) A private collector with appropriately surreal sensibilities opened the **Salvador Dalí Museum,** 1000 3rd St. S. (823-3767), in Poynter Park, on the Bayboro harbor waterfront. The museum contains the world's largest collection of Dalí works and memorabilia, including some of his most important paintings. As Dalí himself said "Never a dully moment avec Dalí." (One-hr. tours. Open Tues.-Sat. 10am-5pm, Sun. noon-5pm. Admission $3.50, seniors and students $2.50, under 8 free.) The **Museum of Fine Arts,** 255 Beach Dr. N. at 2nd Ave. (896-2667), has an eclectic permanent collection. The

Palladian-style building is a work of art in itself. (Open Tues.-Sat. 10am-5pm, Sun. 1-5pm, 3rd Thurs. of every month 10am-9pm. Donation.)

Georgia

The residents of the South's largest state are beginning to prosper. Atlanta has been dubbed the capital of the New South, and Savannah's stately antebellum homes are undergoing restoration. However, it is unlikely that economic success will disrupt Georgia's southern lifestyle—the state remains largely agrarian and sultry days keep bustling activity in check. Even in cosmopolitan Atlanta, genuine hospitality is the rule, making Georgia the perfect place for a long, neighborly visit.

Practical Information

Capital: Atlanta.

Tourist Information: Department of Industry and Trade, Tourist Division, 230 Peachtree St., Atlanta 30301 (656-3590), across from Atlanta Convention and Visitors Bureau. **Department of Natural Resources,** 270 Washington St., SW, Atlanta 30334 (800-542-7275; 800-342-7275 in GA). **U.S. Forest Service,** 1720 Peachtree Rd., NW, Atlanta 30367 (347-2385). Information on the Chattahoochee and Oconee National Forests.

Time Zone: Eastern. **Postal Abbreviation:** GA.

Atlanta

Atlanta's seal, a Phoenix and the motto *Resurgens,* sums up the city's fabulous recovery since 1864, when it was burned to the ground by General Sherman. Today, Atlanta is the largest metropolitan area in the Southeast and an economic powerhouse. It has the world's second busiest airport, the headquarters of Coca-Cola, and offices of over 400 of the Fortune 500 corporations. Nineteen institutions of higher learning, including Georgia Tech and Emory University, call Atlanta home.

Not surprisingly, fame and prosperity have diffused Atlanta's old-south flavor. The influx of transplanted Yankees and Californians, the third-largest gay population in the U.S., and the presence of a host of ethnic groups have lent the city a cosmopolitan air. This air is enhanced by Atlanta's progressivism in race relations. Atlanta has played a vital role in the struggle for civil rights. It is the birthplace of Martin Luther King, Jr. and witnessed considerable unrest and activism during the 60s. In 1974, the city elected one of the nation's first African-American mayors, Maynard Jackson, who was succeeded by Andrew Young, also black, who is the current mayor. Sleek and upbeat, Georgia's capital is regarded as an anomaly by many residents of the state's more rural counties.

Practical Information

Emergency: 911.

Visitor Information: Atlanta Convention and Visitors Bureau, 233 Peachtree St., #200 (659-4270), Peachtree Center, Harris Tower, downtown. The staff is not particularly interested in budget travelers, but stop by to pick up a free copy of *Atlanta and Georgia Visitors' Guide* ($3 on newsstands). Open Mon.-Fri. 9am-5pm. Satellite information centers are at **Peachtree Center Mall** (521-6633), **Lenox Square Shopping Center** (266-1398), and **Hartsfield International Airport** (767-3231). All open Mon.-Fri. 10am-5pm.

Travelers Aid: 81 International Blvd. (527-7400), in Greyhound building. Limited information on accommodations. Open Mon.-Fri. 8am-8pm., Sat. 10am-6pm. After hours, call 522-7370 for assistance.

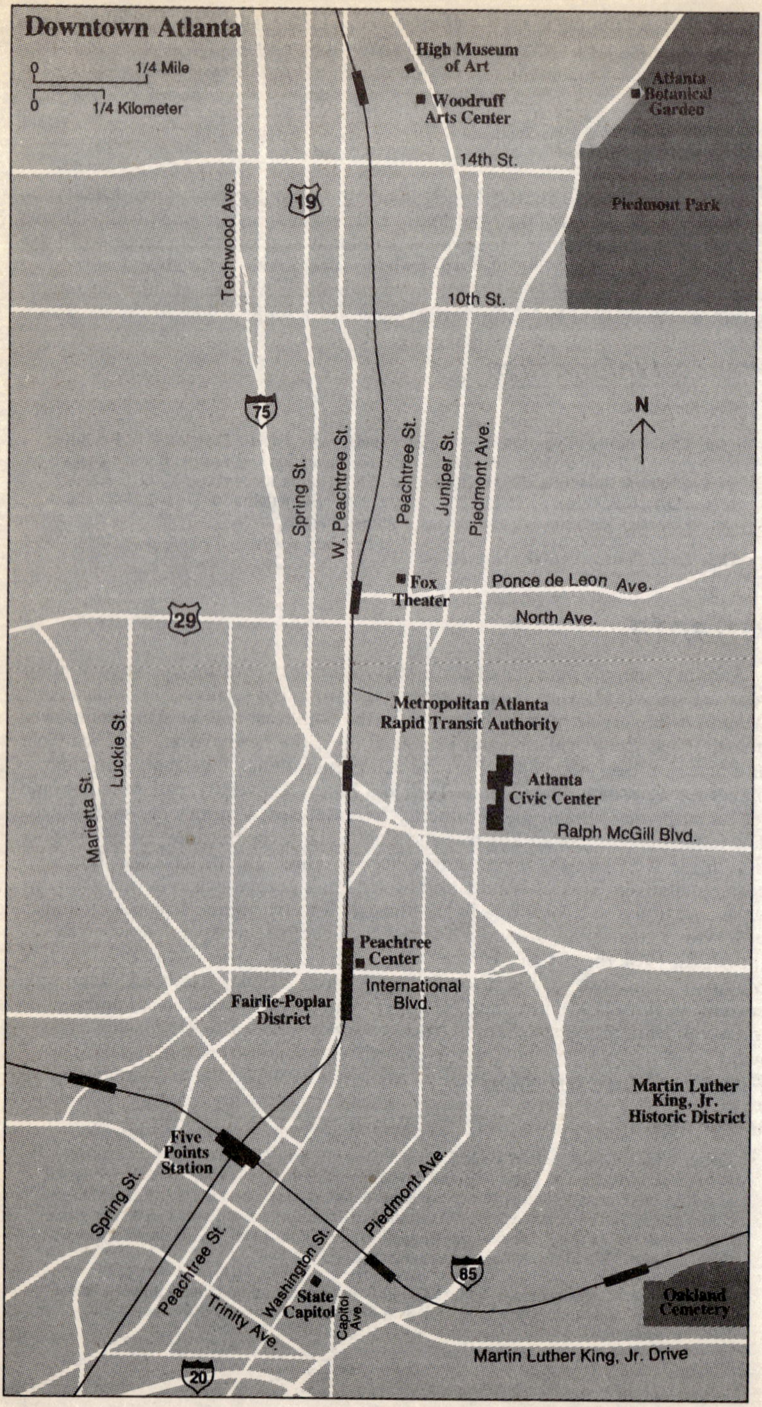
Downtown Atlanta
0 1/4 Mile
0 1/4 Kilometer
High Museum of Art
Woodruff Arts Center
Atlanta Botanical Garden
14th St.
19
Piedmont Park
Techwood Ave.
10th St.
75
N
Spring St.
W. Peachtree St.
Peachtree St.
Juniper St.
Piedmont Ave.
Fox Theater
Ponce de Leon Ave.
29
North Ave.
Metropolitan Atlanta Rapid Transit Authority
Atlanta Civic Center
Luckie St.
Marietta St.
Ralph McGill Blvd.
Peachtree Center
International Blvd.
Fairlie-Poplar District
Martin Luther King, Jr. Historic District
Five Points Station
Spring St.
Piedmont Ave.
Peachtree St.
Washington St.
Trinity Ave.
State Capitol
Capitol Ave.
85
Oakland Cemetery
Martin Luther King, Jr. Drive
20

Hartsfield International Airport: South of the city, bounded by I-75, I-85, and I-285. General information 530-6600; international services and flight information 530-2081. Headquarters of **Delta Airlines** (756-5000 or 800-523-7777). International travelers can get phone assistance in 6 languages at the **Calling Assistance Center** in the international terminal. The subway is the easiest way to get downtown. The **Atlanta Airport Shuttle** (525-2177) runs vans from the airport to downtown, Emory, and Lenox Sq. ($11). **Northside Airport Express** (455-1600) serves Stone Mountain, Marietta, and Dunwoody. Buses run daily 5am-midnight ($12-15).

Amtrak: 1688 Peachtree St., NW (872-9815), at I-85, 3 miles north of downtown. Take bus #23 to and from the "Arts Center" subway station. To: New Orleans (2 per day, 11hr., $88); Washington, DC (2 per day, 14 hr., $106); and Charlotte (1 per day, 5 hr., $43). Open daily 6:30am-9:30pm.

Greyhound/Trailways: 81 International Blvd. (522-6300), 1 block from Peachtree Center. MARTA: Peachtree Center. To: New Orleans (7 per day, 9 hr., $74); Washington, DC (8 per day, 16 hr., $93); and Chatanooga (8 per day, 2½ hr., $21). Open 24 hours.

Metropolitan Atlanta Rapid Transit Authority (MARTA): 522-4711; schedule information Mon.-Fri. 6am-10pm, Sat.-Sun. 8am-4pm. Combined rail and bus system serves virtually all area attractions and hotels. Operates Mon.-Sat. 5am-1am, Sun. 6am-midnight in most areas. Fare 85¢, transfers free. $7 weekly pass gives unlimited access. Pick up a system map at the **MARTA Ride Store,** Five Points Station downtown, or at one of the satellite visitor information centers. If you get confused, just find the nearest MARTA courtesy phone in each rail station.

Taxi: Checker, 351-1111. **London,** 688-5658. Base fare $1, $1 per mile.

Car Rental: Atlanta Rent-a-Car, 3185 Camp Creek Pkwy. (763-1160), just inside I-285, 3 miles east of airport. Nine other locations in the area including one at Cheshire Bridge Rd. and I-85, 1 mile west of the Liddberg Center Railstop. Rates from $20 per day with 100 free miles, 15¢ each additional mile. Must be 21 with major credit card.

Help Lines: Rape Crisis Counseling, 659-7273. 24 hours. **Gay/Lesbian Center Help Line,** 892-0661. Answered 6-11pm. Center located at 63 12th St. (876-5372).

Post Office: 39 Crown Rd. (765-7266). Open Mon.-Fri. 9am-5pm. **ZIP code:** 30321.

Area Code: 404.

Atlanta is in the northwest quadrant of the state, 150 miles east of Birmingham, AL and 113 miles south of Chattanooga, TN. The city lies on north-south I-75 and I-85 and on east-west I-20. It is circumscribed by **I-285** ("the perimeter").

Getting around is confusing at first because everything seems to be named Peachtree. However, of the 26 roads bearing that name, only one, **Peachtree Street,** is a major north-south thoroughfare, as are **Spring Street** and **Piedmont Avenue. Ponce De Leon Avenue** and **North Avenue** are major east-west routes. In the heart of downtown, where angled streets and shopping plazas run amok, there is no easily navigable plan.

Accommodations and Camping

If you plan to stay in Atlanta for more than a few days, check with the **International Youth Travel Program (IYTP).** The convention and visitors bureau (see Practical Information above), will try to locate a single for $18. Unfortunately, there are no hostels in Atlanta, so the IYTP is your cheapest bet besides the YMCA. **Bed and Breakfast Atlanta,** 1801 Piedmont Avenue NE (875-0525; call Mon.-Fri. 9am-noon or 2-5pm), offers singles from $35. **Atlanta Hospitality,** 2472 Lauderdale Dr. NE (493-1930), has singles for $28, doubles for $45, and a $10 membership fee good for one year. (Make reservations 2 weeks ahead.)

YMCA, 22 Butler St. (659-8085), between Edgewood and Auburn, 3 blocks from downtown. Men only, and usually full of semi-permanent residents. Community shower. Singles $16.22. Key deposit $5. Hard to find space here, and they don't take reservations.

Best Way Inn, 144 14th St. NW (873-4171), near the highway. Tidy rooms and friendly management. Singles $31. Doubles $36. Key deposit $5.

Motel 6, 6 locations in the Atlanta area, all just outside the perimeter. Marietta, 2360 Delk Rd., exit 11 from I-75 (952-8161), has large rooms and a pool. Singles $23, each additional person $6. Norcross, 6015 Oakbrook Pkwy. (446-2311), exit 37 onto Jimmy Carter Blvd. from I-85, is newer. Singles $26, each additional person $6.

Travelodge, 1641 Peachtree St. NE (873-5731), in sight of the Amtrak Station. Clean, attractive rooms. Complimentary coffee and jumbo danish. Singles from $39. Doubles from $44.

Arrowhead Campsites, I-20W and Six Flags Rd. (948-7302), 10 miles west of downtown. Subway to Hightower, then bus to Six Flags. Excellent facilities, including pool and laundry. Tent sites $11.75, RV sites $14.75.

Stone Mountain Family Campground, on U.S. 78 (498-5710), 16 miles east of town. Exit 30-B off I-285 or subway to Avondale then "Stone Mountain" bus. Part of state park system. Tent sites $9. RV sites $9.50. Make reservations 2 weeks ahead.

Food

Soul food and home-style Southern cooking are Atlanta's specialties. Favorite dishes include fried chicken, black-eyed peas, okra, sweet potato pie, and mustard greens. "Pot likker" is water that has been used to cook greens—dip in a hunk of cornbread and enjoy. If your heart is not into soul food, however, Atlanta offers plenty of options. Do-it-yourselfers can procure produce at one of the South's largest outdoor markets, the **Georgia State Farmers Market,** 16 Forest Pkwy. (366-6910), exit 78 off I-75 south. (No MARTA service.) The grocery in building K is open daily from 8am to 5pm. Fresh fruits, vegetables, eggs, and smoked meats are on sale 'round the clock in 80 acres of open-air, drive-through stalls. Travelers without a car may find the **Dekalb County Farmers Market,** 3000 E. Ponce De Leon St. (377-6400), more accessible. (Open Tues.-Sun. 10am-9pm. Take the subway to Avondale and then the "Stone Mountain" bus.)

Mary Mac's Tea Room, 224 Ponce De Leon Ave. NE (876-6604). Take the "Georgia Tech" bus north. One of Atlanta's best budget restaurants. Famous for its amazing array of fresh vegetables, homemade bread, and fried foods. Waiters tend to rush you. Lunch $3-5, dinner $4-10. 10% discount at dinner with student ID. Open Mon.-Fri. 11am-4pm and 5-8pm.

The Varsity, 61 North Ave. NW at I-85 (881-1706). Take the subway to North Ave. station. Order at the world's largest drive-in or brave the masses to eat inside. Unique sandwiches about $2, but best known for chili dogs and the greasiest onion rings in the South. Eat in one of the giant TV rooms—1 room for each channel. Open Sun.-Thurs. 7am-12:30am, Fri.-Sat. 7am-2am.

Tortilla's, 725 Ponce De Leon (892-3493). A tiny, neon-lit Mexican eatery. Cheap, good tacos and burritos $1.75, enormous super burrito $2.90. Open Mon.-Fri. 11am-10pm, Sat. noon-10pm.

Cha Gio Vietnamese Restaurant, 996 Peachtree St. NE at 10th St. (885-9387), near the Arts Center subway stop. Three locations, all of which offer cheap, filling dinners ($4-6). Open Mon.-Fri. 11am-3pm and 4-10pm, Sat. 11am-10pm, Sun. 11am-9pm.

Touch of India, 962 Peachtree St. (876-7777). Three-course lunch specials $3-3.50. Popular with locals. Atmosphere and service are worthy of a much more expensive restaurant. Open Mon.-Sat. 11:30am-2:30pm and 5:30-10:30pm, Sun. 5-10:30pm.

Eat Your Vegetables Cafe, 438 Moreland Ave. NE (523-2671), in the Five Points area. Vegetarian foods (hummus, soyburgers, and salads) in a friendly atmosphere. Dinners $6-9. Open Mon.-Fri. 11:30am-2pm and 6-10:30pm, Sat. 6-10:30pm, Sun. 11am-3:30pm.

Huey's, 1816 Peachtree St. (873-2037). An open-air café acclaimed for its New-Orleans-style *beignets* (12 for $4). Open Mon.-Thurs. 7am-midnight, Fri. 7am-1am, Sat. 9am-1am, Sun. 9am-11pm.

Sights

Atlanta's sights are scattered, but the effort it takes to find them usually pays off. Redeveloped **Underground Atlanta** is actually 6 blocks of shops, restaurants, and nightspots all below the street. The entrance to Underground Atlanta is beside the "5 points" subway stop. To appreciate the downtown area, take one of the six walking tours offered April through October by the **Atlanta Preservation Center,** 84 Peachtree St. NW (522-4345). Volunteers guide you through: the **capitol** area (Wed. and Sat. at 10am, 1½ hr., $3); the **Fairlie-Poplar** area (Tues. at 10am and Sun. at 2pm, 2 hr., $3) with the city's earliest high-rises; the **Fox Theater District** (Mon. and Thurs. at 10am, Sat. at 10am and 11:30am, 2 hr., $3), where preservation work began; **Inman Park** (Thurs. at 10am and Sun. at 2pm, 1½ hr., $3), a nationally celebrated preserve of the city's first garden suburb, including the home of Coca Cola magnates Asa Chandler and Ernest Woodruff; **Oakland Cemetery,** where Margaret Mitchell, author of *Gone With The Wind,* is buried (Sat.-Sun. at 2pm, 1½ hr., $3); and the **West End,** where Victorian houses include the **Wren's Nest,** 1050 Gordon St. SW (753-8535), former home of Joel Chandler Harris (creator of Br'er Rabbit *et al*). The house still contains Harris's original furnishings, books, photos, and typewriter. (Open Tues.-Sat. 10am-5pm, Sun. 2-5pm. Admission $3, ages 13-19.) Take bus #71 ("Cascade") from the West End subway station. *Gone with the Wind* fans can visit the Margaret Mitchell Room in the **Atlanta Public Library,** Carnegie Way and Forsythe St. Here you'll find autographed copies of her famous book, as well as other memorabilia. (Open Mon. and Fri. 9am-6pm, Tues.-Thurs. 9am-8pm, Sat. 10am-6pm, Sun. 2-6pm.)

More recent history can be explored in the **Martin Luther King Jr. National Historic Site.** The 23½-acre area includes the restored house where King was born, 501 Auburn Ave. (331-3919; open daily 10am-4:30pm, off-season 10am-3:30pm. Free.) King is buried at the **Martin Luther King Center for Nonviolent Social Change,** 449 Auburn Ave. (524-1956). There is also a collection of King's personal effects and a film about his life. (Open Mon.-Fri. 9am-5:30pm, Sat.-Sun. 10am-5:30pm. Admission $1. Take bus #3 from Peachtree/Alabama.)

At the **Peachtree Center** and the surrounding downtown area visitors can find elegant shops, restaurants, office buildings, and spectacular hotels. The **Woodruff Arts Center,** 1280 Peachtree St. (892-3600; take the subway to Arts Center), houses the **High Museum** (892-4444), which is in Richard Meir's award-winning building, made of glass, steel, and white porcelain. Its collection includes European decorative arts, European and American paintings, photography, and temporary exhibits of contemporary art. (Open Tues.-Sat. 10am-5pm. Wed. 10am-9pm, Sun. noon-5pm. Admission $4, seniors and students with ID $2, children $1.) The museum branch at Georgia-Pacific Center (577-6939) is free (open Mon.-Fri. 11am-6pm).

In **Grant Park,** between Cherokee Ave. and Boulevard, the 40-acre **Zoo Atlanta** is undergoing a $25 million renovation. Among the new exhibits is the Masai Mara, a re-creation of an African savannah. (Open Mon.-Fri. 10am-5pm, Sat.-Sun. 10am-6pm.; Sept.-June daily 10am-5pm. Ticket office closes 4:30pm. Admission $5.75, ages 3-11 $3.) Next door to Zoo Atlanta is **Cyclorama,** the world's largest painting in the round. Completed in 1885, the 50-foot high, 900-foot work depicts the 1864 Civil War Battle of Atlanta, complete with 3-D features and lighting and sound effects. (Open daily 9:30am-5pm; Sept.-April 9:30am-4:30pm. Admission $3.50, seniors $3, children $2. Take bus #31 "Grant Park.") The 60-acre **Atlanta Botanical Garden,** Piedmont Ave. at the Prado (876-5858), has five acres of landscaped gardens, a 15-acre hardwood forest with walking trails and an exhibition hall. The **Dorothy Chapman Fugua Conservatory** holds hundreds of species of rare tropical plants. (Open Tues.-Sat. 9am-6pm, Sun. noon-6pm. Admission $4.50, seniors and children $2.25. Free Thurs. 1:30-6pm. Take bus #36 "North Decatur" from the arts center.)

West Paces Ferry Road cuts through **Buckhead,** one of the most beautiful residential districts in the southeast. The Greek Revival **Governor's Mansion,** 391 West Paces Ferry Rd. (261-1776), has elaborate gardens and furniture from the Federal period. (Tours Tues.-Thurs. 10-11:30am. Free.) In the same neighborhood, discover the **Atlanta Historical Society,** 3101 Andrew Dr. NW (261-1837). On the grounds are the **Swan House,** a lavish Anglo-Palladian Revival home; and the **Tullie Smith House,** an antebellum farmhouse. Don't miss the intriguing *Atlanta Resurgens* exhibit, in which famous and not-so-famous Atlantans praise the city. (Tours every ½ hr. Open Mon.-Sat. 9:30am-4:30pm, Sun. noon-5pm. Admission $4.50, seniors and students $4, ages 6-12 $2. Take bus #40 "West Paces Ferry" from Lenox Station.)

The eclectic **Little Five Points Business District,** at the intersection of Moreland and Euclid Ave. NE, is the center of Atlanta's bohemian community. The fortunate may catch a glimpse of the psychedelic "Magic Bus" driven by the band YUR ("Your Universal Reality"), whose headquarters are in the neighborhood. Stroll through the second-hand clothing and record stores. Frisbee-flyers should be sure to stop at **Identified Flying Objects,** 1164 Euclid Ave. NE, a Frisbee department store. (Open Tues.-Fri. noon-7pm, Sat.-Sun. noon-6pm.)

A respite from the city is available at **Stone Mountain Park** (498-5600), 16 miles east on U.S. 78. Here, a fabulous bas-relief monument to the Confederacy was carved into the world's largest mass of granite. The "Mount Rushmore of the South" features Jefferson Davis, Robert E. Lee, and Stonewall Jackson and measures 90 by 190 feet. The enormous statue is dwarfed by the mountain, which is surrounded by a 3200-acre recreational area. Check out the dazzling laser show on the side of the mountain each summer night at 9:30pm. (Admission $4 per car. Park open 6am-midnight. Take bus #120 "Stone Mountain" from the Avondale subway stop. Buses leave only Mon.-Fri. at 4:40pm and 7:50pm.)

Six Flags, 7561 Six Flags Rd. SW (948-9290), at I-20 W., at 331 acres, is one of the largest theme amusement parks in the nation, and includes several roller-costers, a free-fall machine, live shows, and whitewater rides. On summer weekends, the park is packed solid. (Open in summer roughly 10am-10pm. One-day admission $17.50, 2 days $19, seniors and children under 42 inches $12. Take bus #201 "Six Flags" from Hightower Station.)

Entertainment

The cheapest way to have fun in Atlanta is with a MARTA pass ($5) and a copy of *Creative Loafing,* available free at hotels, newsstands, and stores. Other listings are in *Weekend,* a supplement to the Friday *Atlanta Journal.* Look for free summer concerts in Atlanta's parks. The outstanding **Woodruff Arts Center,** 1280 Peachtree St. NE (892-2414), houses the Atlanta Symphony and the Alliance Theater Company. For more theater, check the **Fox,** 660 Peachtree (881-1977), or the **Atlanta Civic Center,** 395 Piedmont (523-6275).

Atlanta's nightlife is frenetic, varied, and inexpensive. Night spots are concentrated in **Buckhead** and in **Virginia Highlands,** a neighborhood east of downtown with trendy shops and a friendly, hip atmosphere. For Chicago-style blues, go to **Blind Willie's,** 828 N. Highland Ave. (873-2583). The poorly lit, run-down club is a fitting home for its emphatic blues, Cajun food, and ever-present crowd. Live music starts at 10pm. Open daily at 6pm. Cover Mon.-Fri. $3, Sat.-Sun. $5.) In Buckhead, **Blues Harbor,** 3179 Peachtree Rd. (261-6717), is a saloon/blues night club/restaurant. The $10 fresh lobster special is flown in from Maine every other day. The **Metroplex,** 388 Marietta St. NW (523-1468), features punk and heavy metal. **Confetti,** 3906 Roswell Rd. (237-4328), is popular for dancing. **Jack and Jill's,** 112 10th St. NE (873-5405), is a downtown gay bar.

Check out one of the $1 movies at the **Excelsior Mill,** 695 North Ave. (577-6455). Housed in an original turn-of-the century mill, the Excelsior serves pizza, beer, and sandwiches in its downstairs cinema pub ($3-5). Upstairs in its rock club, the Excelsior displays its Kentuckian—the "smoothest and largest" Wurlitzer pipe-organ in the Southeast (2000 pipes).

Savannah

Anyone who tells you that Savannah is not the most beautiful city in the South must be from Charleston, SC, because only that city can challenge the splendor of Savannah's serene parks lined with Spanish-moss-hung oaks, swaying palmetto trees, and elegant antebellum townhouses.

A fire in 1820 destroyed more than 460 of Savannah's gracious homes. Later, when the price of cotton crashed at the turn of the century, many of the homes and warehouses along River Street fell into disrepair, and the Federalist townhouses and English Regency mansions that lined Savannah's boulevards became boarding houses or were razed. But when Sherman captured the city on December 22, 1864, he spared the prominent Confederate seaport from destruction. In the mid-1950s, the Group of Concerned Citizens mobilized to restore and preserve the downtown area—it's done an amazing job.

Practical Information

Emergency: 911.

Visitor Information: Savannah Visitors Center, 301 W. Broad St. at Liberty St. (944-0456), in a lavish former train station. Excellent free maps and guides. Open Mon.-Fri. 8:30am-5pm, Sat.-Sun. 9am-5pm. The **Savannah Exposition,** in the same building, has photographs, exhibits, and 2 brief films that depict the city's history. Open daily 9am-4pm. Admission $2.25, seniors $2, teens $1.25, children 75¢.

Amtrak: 2611 Seaboard Coastline Dr. (234-2611 or 800-872-7245), 4 miles outside the city. Taxi fare to city about $6. To: Charleston, SC (3 per day, 1¾ hr., $22) and Washington, DC (5 per day, 11 hr., $108). Open Sun.-Thurs. 4pm-8am, Fri. 8am-Sat. midnight.

Greyhound: 610 E. Oglethorpe Ave. (232-2135), convenient to downtown. Bad neighborhood. To: Jacksonville (11 per day, 3 hr., $20); Charleston, SC (3 per day, 2½ hr., $21); and Washington, DC (8 per day, 17 hr., $85). Open 24 hours.

Local Transit: Chatham Area Transit (CAT), 233-5767. Buses operate 6am-11pm. Fare 75¢, transfers 5¢. **C&H Bus,** 530 Montgomery St. (232-7099). The only public transportation to Tybee Beach. Buses leave from the civic center in summer at 8:15am, 1:30pm, and 3:30pm, returning from the beach at 9:25am, 2:30pm, and 4:30pm. Fare $1.35.

Bike Rental: Historic Savannah Foundation, at the Hyatt Regency, 2 W. Bay St. (233-3957), and the Desoto Hilton, 15 E. Liberty St. (232-4624). $3 per hr., $5 for 2 hr., $10 per day.

Help Lines: Rape Crisis Center, 233-7273.

Post Office: 2 N. Fahm St. (235-4646). Open Mon.-Fri. 8:30am-5pm. **ZIP code:** 31402.

Area Code: 912.

Savannah lies on the coast of Georgia at the mouth of the **Savannah River,** which runs along the border with South Carolina. Charleston, SC, is 100 miles up the coast; Brunswick, GA is 90 miles to the south. The city stretches south from bluffs overlooking the river. The restored 2½-square-mile **downtown historic district** is bordered by **East Broad** and **West Broad,** and on the north and south by the river and **Gaston Street.** This area is best explored on foot. **Tybee Island,** Savannah's beach, is 18 miles east on Hwy. 80 and 26. Spring is the busiest and most beautiful season in Savannah.

Accommodations and Camping

Before you get a room anywhere in Savannah, go to the visitors center and peruse their selection of coupons. The downtown motels are near the historic area, visitors center, and Greyhound station. The neighborhood is neither charming nor clean, but it's fairly safe. Do not, however, stray south. For those with cars, Ogeechee Road (U.S. 17) has several independently owned budget options. Those who are willing to spend a little extra should try the **Bed and Breakfast Inn,** 117 W. Gordon St. (238-0518), on Chatham Sq. in the historic district. Rooms have TV, A/C, and shared bath. (Singles $30. Doubles $38; reservations required.)

Thunderbird Inn, 611 W. Oglethorpe Ave. (232-2661), opposite the Greyhound station, a few blocks from the historic district. Cinder-block walls and a charmless neighborhood, but the rooms are clean and cheap. Singles $26. Doubles $28. Off-season $23 and $25, respectively.

Quality Inn, 231 W. Boundary St. (232-3200), just west of the Greyhound station, near the historic district. Fairly luxurious. Cable TV and in-room movies. Ask about free transportation to the airport and bus stations. Singles $38. Doubles $43. Get a coupon for $30 per room (up to 4 people) at the visitors center.

Budget Inn, 3702 Ogeechee Rd. (233-3633), about a 15-min. drive from the historic district. Take bus #25B ("Towers and Ogeechee"). Comfortable rooms with TV and A/C. Pool. Rooms $27. Pick up a coupon ($22 per room) at the visitors center. Reservations recommended; call collect.

Sanddollar Motel, 11 16th St. (786-5362), Tybee Island. 1½ miles south on Butler Ave. A small, family-run motel practically on the beach. Most rooms rented weekly, but singles may be available for $25 (less in winter). On summer weekends, the motel rents out completely for large parties.

Camping: Skidaway Island State Park, Skidaway Rd. (356-2523). No public transportation. Follow Liberty St. east out of downtown; soon after it becomes Wheaton St., turn right on Waters Ave. and follow it to the Diamond Causeway, then look for signs. **Richmond Hill State Park,** off Rte. 144 (727-2339), ½ hr. south of downtown, exit 15 off I-95 (take I-16 west from downtown). Quieter than Skidaway and usually less crowded. Both registration offices open daily 8am-5pm; sites $10.

Food

Savannah is a budget gourmand's paradise, but the price is tired legs. There's little good food downtown and, except for Mrs. Wilkes, the best budget meals are along the waterfront. Try the early-bird dinner specials at **Corky's,** 407 E. River St. (234-0113), and the happy-hour discounts at **Kevin Barry's Irish Pub,** 117 W. River St. (233-9626), with live Irish folk music Wednesday through Sunday after 9pm.

Mrs. Wilkes Boarding House, 107 W. Jones St. (232-5997)—no sign. Home-style restaurant in the basement of a townhouse. A Savannah institution where patrons gather at tables for 12. All-you-can-eat lunch of meat, vegetables, breads, and iced tea $6.50. Mrs. Wilkes still works the small dining room and Mr. Wilkes collects your money after you bring your dish to the sink. Go before 11:15am or after 2pm to avoid the wait, or go around back for a generous take-out picnic. Open Mon.-Fri. 8-9am and 11:30am-3pm.

Bill Hilliard's, 3005 Victory Dr., Thunderbolt (354-5430), 4 miles east of the historic district. Take the "Henry St." bus. Fresh seafood dinners with salad, hushpuppies, and fries from $7. Renowned buffets served Mon.-Sat. 11am-3pm ($5), Sun. 11am-9pm ($6). Open daily 11am-midnight.

Mammy's Kitchen, 5794 Ogeechee Rd. (925-6007), on U.S. 17, 8 miles south of downtown. Excellent, cheap barbecue. $5.50 specials include bread and iced tea, $2.75 sandwiches include beans and fries. Open Mon.-Thurs. 10:30am-9pm, Fri.-Sat. 10:30am-10pm.

Sights

In addition to restored antebellum houses, the downtown area includes over 20 small parks and gardens. The **Historic Savannah Foundation,** 41 W. Broad St. (233-7703; 233-3597 for 24-hour reservations), offers a variety of guided one- and two-hour tours ($6-10). You can also catch any number of bus and van tours, leaving about every 10-15 minutes from outside the visitors center ($6-9). Ask inside for details.

The best-known historic houses in Savannah are the **Owens-Thomas House,** 124 Abercorn St. (233-9743), on Oglethorpe Sq. and the **Davenport House,** 324 E. State St. (236-8097), a block away on Columbia Sq. The Owens-Thomas House is one of the best examples of English Regency architecture in America. (Last tour at 4:30pm. Open Oct.-Aug. Tues.-Sat. 10am-5pm, Sun.-Mon. 2-5pm. Admission $3, students $2, children $1.) The Davenport typifies the Federalist style and contains an excellent collection of Davenport china. The house had become a tenement by the 30s, slated to be razed for a parking lot. Its salvation in 1955 marked the birth of the Historical Savannah Foundation and the effort to restore Savannah. There are guided tours of the first floor every 15 minutes; explore the second and third floors at your leisure. (Last tour at 3:30pm. Open Mon.-Sat. 10am-4pm, Sun. 1:30-4pm. Admission $2.50, children $1.25.)

Lovers of Thin Mints, Scot-teas, and, of course, Savannahs may want to make a pilgrimage to the **Juliette Gordon Low Girl Scout National Center,** 142 Bull St. (233-4501), at the corner of Oglethorpe, the birthplace of the association's founder. The first troop of young women in green was begun here in 1912. The "cookie shrine" contains an interesting collection of Girl Scout memorabilia and is also one of the most beautiful houses in Savannah. (Open Feb.-Nov. Mon.-Sat. 10am-4pm, Sun. 12:30-4:30pm; Dec.-Jan. Mon.-Tues. and Thurs.-Sat. 10am-4pm. Admission $3, under 18 $2.)

For a less conventional view of Savannah's history, arrange to tour the **Negro Heritage Trail.** Tours are offered on request by the Savannah branch of the Association for the Study of Afro-American Life and History, King-Tisdell Cottage, Negro Heritage Trail, 514 E. Huntington St., Savannah 31405 (234-8000; open Mon.-Fri. noon-9pm). One day's notice is necessary; donations are encouraged.

Savannah's violent past is displayed at **Fort Pulaski National Monument** (786-5787), 15 miles east of Savannah on Hwy. 80 and 26. (Open 8:30am-6:45pm. In summer admission $1 per person, max. $3 per carload; free rest of year.) Fort Pulaski marks the battle site where rifled cannonry was introduced in the Civil War, making Pulaski and all forts obsolete. **Fort Jackson** (232-3945), also along Hwy. 80 and 26, was built in the early 1800s and contains exhibits on the Revolution, the War of 1812, and the Civil War. Together with Fort Pulaski, it makes a quick detour on a daytrip to Tybee Beach. (Open Tues.-Sun. 9am-5pm; off-season Sat.-Sun. 9am-5pm. Admission $1.75, seniors and students $1.25.)

Brunswick and Environs

Brunswick, 79 miles south of Savannah, is of zero interest to the traveler beyond its **Greyhound** station at 1101 Gloucester St. (265-2800; open Mon.-Sat. 7am-noon and 2-11pm, Sun. 7-9am and 4-11pm). **The Hostel in the Forest (AYH),** however, is the best reason to visit coastal Georgia. This paradise-in-the-pines, 9 miles west of Brunswick on U.S. 82 (your maps and the AYH guide may say U.S. 84, but the road signs all say 82), ½ mile from the road, is every budget traveler's dream. There is no lock-out, no curfew, and few rules, and the low-key manager shuttles to the Brunswick Greyhound station for $2. (Call 264-9738, 265-0220, or 638-2623 usually after 5pm.) The manager can usually be convinced to use the pickup to make daytrips to Savannah, the Okefenokee Swamp, and the coastal islands. If possible, arrange to stay in one of the two treehouses at the hostel, each complete with a 25-square-foot picture window and a spacious double bed. (Ordinarily reserved for couples.) $6. Take I-95 to exit 6 and travel west on U.S. 82 (a.k.a. 84) until you see the easy-to-miss sign for the hostel in the eastbound lane (about 1½ miles from the interchange), and make a U-turn ½ mile farther along at Myer Hill Rd.

For the second-best reason to visit the region, and a traditional Southern specialty, try **Twin Oaks Pit Barbecue,** 2618 Norwich St. (265-3131), 8 blocks from downtown Brunswick, across from the Southern Bell Building. With $2 barbecue sandwiches and $4.50 plates, it's hard to beat. Also try the breaded french fries.

Cumberland Island National Seashore's 16 miles of salt marsh, live-oak forest, and sand dunes are laced with a network of trails and interrupted by a few decaying mansions. Reservations are necessary for overnight visits. (882-4335; reservations by phone only. Call daily 10:30am-4pm, no more than 8 weeks in advance. Sites on a standby basis 15 min. before the twice-daily ferry departures to Cumberland Island.) The **ferry** (¾ hr., $7.88) leaves from St. Mary's on the mainland at the terminus of Rte. 40, on the Florida border (daily at 9 and 11:45am, returning at 10:15am and 4:45pm, extra trip Fri.-Sun. at 3:40pm; off-season Thurs.-Mon. only). **Greyhound** buses from Brunswick and Jacksonville, FL serve the Navy base on a spur off Rte. 40, 10 miles from the dock.

The **area code** for this region is 912.

North Carolina

England's first attempt to colonize North America took place on the shores of North Carolina. This ill-fated episode ended when Sir Walter Raleigh's 1587 Roanoke Island settlement vanished inexplicably. Since then, however, pirates, patriots, and secessionists have brought adventure to the North Carolina coast. Today, this historic area is best known for the Outer Banks' oceanfront playground, most of which is administered by the Cape Hatteras National Seashore.

The coast's mercenary streak contrasts sharply with both the mellow sophistication of the Raleigh, Durham, and Chapel Hill Research Triangle, in the center of the state, and with the west's down-to-earth mountain culture. As long as people still smoke cigarettes, North Carolina's agriculture will thrive. The natural beauty of the Blue Ridge Parkway and the Great Smoky Mountains rounds out the western border of this quietly grand and ever-gracious state.

Practical Information

Capital: Raleigh.

Tourist Information: Travel and Tourism Division, 430 N. Salisbury St., Raleigh 27611 (919-733-4171 or 800-847-4862) **Department of Natural Resources and Community Development,** Division of Parks and Recreation, P.O. Box 27287, Raleigh 27611.

Time Zone: Eastern. **Postal Abbreviation:** NC.

Outer Banks

Cape Hatteras National Seashore preserves the Outer Banks's white sand beaches and shifting dunes for public use. The waters surrounding the islands have been less kind to navigators past than they are to present-day visitors; over 600 ships have wrecked on the shoals offshore, bringing legends of ghostly affairs to the region. Roanoke Island, for example, hides America's oldest mystery. An entire English colony settled here only to disappear in less than three years. No trace of it was ever found.

The area is a mix of unpleasant beach towns and idyllic wilderness. Narrow **Bodie Island,** on the Outer Banks' northern end, where the towns of Nags Head, Kitty Hawk, and Kill Devil Hills lie, is overwhelmed by high-density development and terrible traffic. To escape this mess, travel south on Rte. 12 through the magnificent wildlife preserves, across Hatteras Inlet, to the remote town of **Ocracoke,** where you will find some of the Outer Banks' many beautiful and empty beaches.

Practical Information

Emergency: 911. **Ocracoke park rangers:** 928-5111.

Visitor Information: Aycock Brown Visitors Center, off Rte. 158, after the Wright Memorial Bridge, Bodie Island. Information on accommodations and picnic areas plus National Park Service schedules. Open in summer Mon.-Thurs. 8:30am-6:30pm, Fri.-Sun. 8:30am-7:30pm; in winter Mon.-Fri. 9am-5pm. **Cape Hatteras National Seashore Information Centers: Bodie Island,** Rte. 12 at Bodie Island Light House (441-5711; special programs, guided walks, and information; open daily 9am-6pm); **Hatteras Island,** Rte. 12 at Cape Hatteras (995-4474; camping information, demonstrations, and special programs; open daily 9am-6pm); and **Ocracoke Island,** next to the ferry terminal at the south end of the island (928-4531; information on ferries, camping, lighthouses, and wild ponies; open daily 9am-5pm).

Ferries: Toll ferries operate to Ocracoke from **Cedar Island,** north of Morehead City on U.S. 70 (2¼ hr.) and **Swan Quarter,** on the northern side of Pamlico Sound off U.S. 264/Rte. 45 (2½ hr.), both on the mainland. $10 per car (reserve in advance), $1 per pedestrian, $2 per biker. (Cedar Island 225-3551, Swan Quarter 926-1111, Ocracoke 928-3841. All open daily 6am-9pm; off-season 6am-9pm.) Free ferry across Hatteras Inlet between Hatteras and Ockracoke (until 11pm; every 40 min., off-season every hr.)

Taxi: Beach Cab, 441-2500. Serves Bodie Island and Manteo. Base fare $1.50, each additional mile $1.20. $2 extra for trips to Manteo.

Car Rental: National, (mile 5½; 441-5488 or 800-328-4567), Kill Devil Hills. $40 per day. 50 free miles, 22¢ each additional mile. Open Mon.-Sat. 9am-5pm. Must be 21 with major credit card.

Bike Rental: Pony Island Motel (928-4411) and the **Shushy Stand** on Rte. 12, both on Ocracoke Island. $1 per hr. Open daily 8am-dusk.

Weather Line: 995-5610, or tune your radio to 1530 AM.

ZIP Codes: Manteo 27954, Nags Head 27959, Ocracoke 27960.

Area Code: 919.

Four long, narrow islands strung north-to-south along half the length of the North Carolina coast comprise the Outer Banks. **Bodie Island** includes the towns of **Kitty Hawk, Kill Devil Hills,** and **Nags Head** and is connected to Elizabeth, NC, and Norfolk, VA, by U.S. 158. **Roanoke Island** is between Bodie and the mainland on U.S. 64, and includes the town of **Manteo. Hatteras Island** stretches like a great sandy elbow and is connected to Bodie by a bridge. **Ocracoke Island,** the southernmost, is linked by free ferry to Hatteras Island, and by toll ferry to towns on the mainland. **Cape Hatteras National Seashore** encompasses Hatteras, Ocracoke, and the southern end of Bodie Island. On Bodie Island U.S. 158 and Rte. 12 run parallel to each other until the beginning of the preserve. After that Rte. 12 (also called the Beach Rd.) continues, stringing Bodie, Hatteras, and Ocracoke together with free bridges and ferries. Addresses on Bodie Island are determined by their distance in miles from the Wright Memorial Bridge.

Nags Head and Ocracoke are 76 miles apart and public transportation is minimal, so it's easiest to get around by car. Hitching is relatively safe and fairly common, but you'll have to wait for a ride. The flat terrain makes hiking and biking pleasant, but bikers and walkers should be extra cautious in the Outer Banks' ferocious traffic; stick to Hatteras and Ocracoke for quieter routes.

Accommodations and Camping

All of the motels are on Rte. 12, mostly in the town of Nags Head, and they'll cost you plenty. For budget accommodations, try the town of Ocracoke. On all three islands the "in season" usually runs June 16 to Labor Day, when rates are much higher and reservations are necessary. Reserve seven to ten days ahead for weekday stays and up to a month for weekends. Rangers advise campers to bring extra-long tent spikes because of the loose dirt, and tents with extra-fine screens to keep out the flea-sized, biting "no-see-ums." Strong insect repellent is also helpful. Crashing on the beach is illegal and, worse yet, rambling drivers occasionally run over sleeping campers.

Nags Head/Kill Devil Hills

Olde London Inn, Mile 12, Beach Rd. (441-7115), Nags Head oceanfront. Golf privileges and recreational facilities. Clean, spacious rooms whose drab color is offset by huge picture windows. Cable TV, A/C. Doubles $46.45. Off-season singles $26.

Traveler's Inn Motor Lodge, Mile 16½ (441-5242). In summer, rooms with 1 double bed and 1 single bed $47, with kitchenette $57; after Labor Day $18 and $29, respectively. Cottages $70, with A/C $80; after Labor Day $60 and $70, respectively.

Nettlewood Motel, Mile 7, Beach Rd. (441-5039), Kill Devil Hills, on both sides of the highway. Private beach access. Don't let the uninviting exterior and small rooms prevent you from enjoying this clean, comfortable motel. 4-day min. stay on weekends. Singles with refrigerator $34, with efficiencies $49; Jan. 1-June 16 and Oct. 3-Dec. 31 $28 and $32, respectively. Oceanfront unit for 6 $75. Free day for week-long stays.

Ebb Tide Motel, Mile 10, Beach Rd. (441-4913), Kill Devil Hills. A family type of place with the standard motel repertoire of rooms. A/C, cable TV, and use of pool and hot tub. Rooms $45-67, Labor Day-Thanksgiving $26-44. Continental breakfast included.

Ocracoke

Sand Dollar Motel, off Rte. 12 (928-5571), ½ block from Back Porch Restaurant. Go south on Rte. 12 and turn right at the Pony Island Inn. Turn right at the end of the road; the motel is on the left. Wayne and Celia Isbrecht will make you feel at home in this breezy, quiet motel. Singles $35. Doubles $44. After Labor Day $28 and $32, respectively.

Beach House, on Rte. 12 (928-4271). B&B in a pleasant neighborhood. The antique-filled rooms are very clean and charming. Rooms $35.

Oscar's House (928-1311), 1 block from Silver Lake harbor, 1 mile from the ocean. Quaint B&B with 4 rooms, shared baths. Memorial Day-June singles $40, doubles $50. July-Labor Day singles $45, doubles $55. Off-season singles $35, doubles $45. Full vegetarian breakfast included.

Edwards Motel and Cottages, off Rte. 12 (928-4801). Next to the Sand Dollar Motel. 4-day min. stay. Rooms with A/C, TV, and 2 double beds $39, with 2 double beds and 1 single bed $43. Off-season $32 and $37, respectively.

There are five **campgrounds** on Cape Hatteras National Seashore, all open mid-April to mid-October. **Oregon Inlet** is on the southern tip of Bodie Island, **Salvo, Cape Point** (in Buxton), and **Frisco** are near the elbow of Hatteras Island, and **Okracoke** is in the middle of Ocracoke Island. All have restrooms and cold running water. All sites (except Ocracoke's) are $8, first come-first serve. Reserve Ocracoke sites ($10) through **Ticketron Reservation Office,** P.O. Box 2715, San Francisco, CA 94126, or stop by the Ocracoke Ticketron terminal. For information, contact Cape Hatteras National Seashore, Rte. 1, P.O. Box 675, Manteo, NC 27954 (473-2111).

Food

Food on the Outer Banks consists primarily of very expenive seafood and steak restaurants. There are, however, low-budget alternatives to surf 'n' turf entrees. **Sam and Omie's,** Mile 16, Beach Rd. (441-7366), near Whalebone junction, offers dinners ($6-12) and sandwiches ($2-5). (Open Mon.-Sat. 7am-11pm, Sun. 7am-9pm.) The **Mex-Econo,** Mile 8½, Beach Rd. (441-8226), is in Kill Devil Hills. Dorm-room decor, punk servers, and alternative music create an off-beat atmosphere in this former town hall. Large, delicious Mexican meals $4-5. If a gourmet dinner overlooking the Atlantic is more your fancy, drop by **Papagayo** (mile 7½; 441-7232), Kill Devil Hills. Savor the Mexican seafood and homemade desserts in the relaxed atmosphere of the 51-year-old inn's pine-paneled dining room. (Dinners $6-10. Open daily 5-10:30pm.) In Okracoke, the **Trolley Stop** (928-4041) has salads, subs ($3-4.50), sandwiches ($2-3.25), and the cheapest burgers on the island. The fresh fish sandwich is a good catch for $2.50; reel in a complete dinner for $5.50. (Open daily 9am-6pm.) Go by **Maria's Restaurant and Tavern** (928-6891), just to see this charming old dance hall. The 40-item salad bar, seafood, and Italian dinners will fill you up for $9-16. (Open daily noon-10pm.) Near the Wright Brothers' National Memorial, try popular **Kelly's Outer Banks Restaurant and Tavern,** Mile 10½ (441-4116; open daily 4:30pm-1:30am). **RV's** (441-4888) on the causeway offers sandwiches ($5-6), dinner ($9-14), music, and an incredible view of the sunset over the sound. (Open daily 11:30am-10:30pm.) Pick up staples under the ceiling fans at the **Community Store,** near the ferry slip. (Open daily 7am-7pm.)

Sights and Activities

Many sights throughout the Outer Banks detail the region's colorful history and often provide respite from the flurry of discos, fast-food joints, and water parks which draw pop-culture pilgrims each summer.

In Kill Devil Hills, visit the **Wright Brothers National Memorial,** Mile 8, U.S. 158 (441-7430), where Orville and Wilbur Wright made the world's first sustained, controlled power flight in 1903. At the park you can see models of their planes and shacks, hear a detailed account of the day of the first flight, and view the dramatic monument which the U.S. government dedicated to the Wrights in 1932. (Open daily 9am-7pm; in winter 9am-5pm. Presentations every hour 10am-4pm. Admission $1, $3 per carload, free if party includes seniors.) In nearby **Jockey's Ridge State Park,** home of the East Coast's largest sand dunes, hang-gliders float in the wind that Orville and Wilbur left.

On **Roanoke Island,** the **Fort Raleigh National Historic Site,** off Rte. 64, offers three separately run attractions in one park. The **Elizabeth Gardens** (473-3234) are a beautiful display of flowers, herbs, and trees punctuated by antique statues and fountains. (Open daily 9am-5pm; in summer 9am-8pm. Admission $2, under 12 free.) Next door is the theater where *The Lost Colony,* America's oldest outdoor drama, is performed. Written by Pulitzer Prize-winning author Paul Green, the play was first performed in 1937 and has been produced here for 49 consecutive seasons. (473-3414; performed Mon.-Sat. mid-June to late Aug. 8:30pm; tickets $10, seniors and disabled $9, under 12 $4.) **Fort Raleigh** (473-5772) is a reconstructed 1585 battery, where a museum and performance of Elizabethan music recall the earliest days of English activity in North America. (Visitors center open Mon.-Sat. 9am-8pm, Sun. 9am-6pm.)

On Ocracoke Island, surf and sun are the main attractions. With the exception of the town of Ocracoke on the southern tip, the island is a completely undeveloped national seashore. **Trolley Tours** (928-1111), available in summer, begin at **Trolley Stop One,** Rte. 12, and take you past a British cemetery, the Okracoke lighthouse, and various other points of interest. (Tours Mon.-Sat. at 10:30am, 2:30pm, 5pm; Sun. at 1pm and 6pm. Call about schedules after Labor Day. Admission $3.50, seniors $3, children $1.75.) At the national seashore, you can swim in the surf, fish, hike, bike, and take long walks on the beaches. Park rangers lead nature walks, give demonstrations, and offer interpretive talks. At the **Soundside Snorkel,** rangers teach visitors to snorkel. Bring tennis shoes and a swimsuit. (Sun. and Fri. at 3pm. Equipment rental $1. Make reservations at the Okracoke Visitors Center any time from 9am the day before until 2:30pm the day of the program.)

Raleigh, Durham, and Chapel Hill

The infusion of more PhDs per capita than any other part of the nation into this sleepy Southern atmosphere gives the Research Triangle its hybrid flavor. Raleigh, the state capital, is an inviting, easygoing town. The former tobacco capital of the world, Durham is now, ironically, a city devoted to medicine, with many medical schools, hospitals, and research centers. These facilities, along with prestigious Duke University, contrast sharply with some of Durham's decaying neighborhoods. Twenty miles down the road, much smaller Chapel Hill, home of the nation's first state university, is a cozy college town.

Practical Information

Emergency: 911.

Visitor Information: Raleigh Capitol Area Visitor Center, 301 N. Blount St. (733-3456). Focuses on buildings in the capitol area. Open Mon.-Fri. 8am-5pm, Sat. 9am-5pm, Sun. 1-5pm. **Durham Chamber of Commerce,** Northwestern Bank Building, 3rd floor, 201 N. Roxboro St. (682-2133). Not geared toward the budget traveler. Open Mon.-Fri. 8:30am-5pm. **Chapel Hill Chamber of Commerce,** 104 S. Estes Dr. (967-7075). Open Mon.-Fri. 8:30am-5pm.

Raleigh-Durham Airport: 15 miles northwest of Raleigh on U.S. 70. Many hotels and rental car agencies provide free airport limousine service.

Amtrak: 320 W. Cabarrus, Raleigh (833-7594 or 800-872-7245). To Miami (1 per day, 16 hr., $151) and Washington, DC (2 per day, 6 hr., $41.50). Open Mon.-Fri. 8am-9pm, Sat.-Sun. 8:30-11:30am and 6:30-9pm.

Greyhound/Trailways: Raleigh: 314 W. Jones St. (828-2567). To: Durham (6 per day, 40 min., $6) and Chapel Hill (5 per day, 80 min., $7). Good north-south coverage of NC, to: Greensboro (3 per day, 3 hr., $13); Richmond (7 per day, 3½ hr., $27); Charleston (1 per day, 8 hr., $37). Open 24 hours. Durham: 101 S. LaSalle St. (383-0774), 2 miles northeast of Duke University. To: Chapel Hill (8 per day, 30 min.); Charlotte (4 per day, 4 hr.); Winston-Salem (5 per day, 3 hr.). Open daily 6:30am-11pm. Chapel Hill: 311 W. Franklin St. (942-3356), 3 blocks west of the center of town. Open Mon.-Fri. 9am-8pm, Sat.-Sun. 8am-8pm.

Local Transit: Raleigh: **Capital Area Transit,** 833-5701. Operates Mon.-Fri., reduced service Sat. Fare 50¢ off-peak, 60¢ during peak hours. Durham: **Duke Power Company Transit Service,** 688-4587. Most routes leave from the 1st Federal Building at Main St. on the loop, downtown. Buses operate 6am-6pm; some routes have service until 10pm. Fare 50¢, transfers 10¢.

Taxi: Safety Taxi, 832-8800. $1.20 per mile. **Shared Ride Taxi Service,** (822-5522). Gives lifts to seniors and the disabled ($1-2).

Help Lines: Rape Crisis, 755-6661.

Post Office: Raleigh: 310 New Bern Ave. (831-3661). Open Mon.-Fri. 8:30am-4:30pm, Sat. 8:30am-noon. Durham: 323 E. Chapel Hill St. (541-5466). Open Mon.-Fri. 8:30am-5pm. Chapel Hill: Franklin St., at the center of town. Open Mon.-Fri. 8:30am-5:30pm. **ZIP codes:** Raleigh 27611, Durham 27701, Chapel Hill 27514.

Area Code: 919.

Raleigh and Durham are 20 miles apart, connected by U.S. 70; Durham and Chapel Hill are 10 miles apart, connected by by U.S. 15-501; and Chapel Hill and Raleigh are 25 miles apart, connected by I-40. They are between I-85 and I-95 in north-central North Carolina.

Accommodations and Camping

Hotels in downtown Raleigh are of average quality, with standard prices and seascape paintings. If you have a car, stay in Durham, where lodgings are cheaper and more pleasant than those in the triangle's other two points.

Friendship Inn, 309 Hillsborough St., Raleigh (833-5771), 3 blocks west of the capitol, 3½ blocks from Greyhound. Clean, ordinary motel rooms in a decent but humdrum part of Raleigh. Singles $29. Doubles $32.

YWCA, 1012 Oberlin Rd., Raleigh (828-3205), ½ mile east of Cameron Village Shopping Center. Women only. Large, luxurious, and mostly residential facility. Hall bath. Singles $15. "Transient" guests must have an informal interview with the director.

Umstead State Park, U.S. 70 (787-3033), northwest of Raleigh. Tent and trailer sites. Large lake for fishing; hiking trails. Open June.-Aug. 8am-9pm; shorter hours Sept.-May. Sites $5.

Motel 6, 2101 Holloway St., Durham (682-5100). Take the Wake Forest exit from U.S. 70. The bus goes to Wellons Village Shopping Center, 3 blocks away. Clean, small, dark rooms. Near the highway but far from downtown Durham. Singles $19. $6 each additional person.

Carolina-Duke Motor Inn, I-85 at Guess Rd., Durham (286-0771). Large, clean rooms with plush extras such as phone and a movie channel (movies $6). Free bus service to the middle of Durham. Pick up a coupon in the lobby for the **Wabash Express** restaurant next door (breakfast $2).

Food

It is not surprising that the best budget restaurants in the triangle area are near the universities. In Raleigh, **Hillsborough Street,** across from North Carolina State University, has a wide array of friendly, inexpensive restaurants. The same can be said of **9th Street** in Durham and **Franklin Street** in Chapel Hill.

Clyde Cooper's Barbeque, 109 E. Davie, Raleigh (832-7614), 1 block east of the Fayetteville Street Mall, downtown. A large crowd of locals chows down on the barbecued pork ribs. Dinners $4. Open Mon.-Sat. 10am-6pm.

Side Street, 225 N. Bloodworth St., Raleigh (828-4927), 3 blocks from the Capitol on N. Bloodworth and E. Lane St. Don't let the run-down exterior fool you—this is a classy place right down to the antique furniture and fresh flowers on the tables. Huge, somewhat exotic sandwiches $4. Open Mon.-Sat. 11am-3pm and 5-9pm.

Two Guys, 2504 Hillsborough St., Raleigh (832-2324), near campus. Spicy pizza ($6.25), large spaghetti portions ($3). Open Mon.-Wed. 11am-10pm, Thurs.-Sat. 11am-11pm, Sun. noon-10pm.

The Ninth Street Bakery Shop, 754 9th St., Durham (286-0303). More than a bakery; sandwiches from $2. Try the huge, honey-drenched cinnamon rolls. Live music nightly. Open Mon.-Thurs. 7am-7pm, Fri.-Sat. 8am-11pm, Sun. 8am-3pm.

Well Spring Grocery, 1002 9th St., Durham (286-2290). Cheaper than the city's other natural food stores. Open daily 8am-6pm.

Ramshead Rath-Skellar, 157-A E. Franklin St., Chapel Hill (942-5158), 1 block from downtown. This venerable subterranean bistro offers classic roast beef sandwiches and legendary cheesecake. Meals $4-6. Open Mon.-Thurs. 11am-2:30pm and 5-9:30pm, Fri.-Sat. 11am-2:30pm and 5-10:30pm, Sun. 11am-2:30pm and 5-9pm.

Skylight Exchange, 405½ W. Rosemary St., Chapel Hill (933-5550). A sandwich counter and used book and record store featuring live music on the weekends. Sandwiches $2-3. Open Mon.-Thurs. 10am-11pm, Fri.-Sat. 10am-1am, Sun. 1-9pm.

Mariakakis Restaurant and Bakery, 15-501 Bypass, Chapel Hill (942-1453), a 3-mile drive from campus. Addictive Arabic bread. Large cheese pizza $6. Open Mon.-Sat. 11am-9pm.

Sights

While the main focus is on the three universities, the triangle has its share of intriguing historical sights as well.In Raleigh you can see the **capitol grounds** and tour the **capitol building,** built in 1840. (Open Mon.-Fri. 8am-5pm, Sat. 9am-5pm, Sun. 1-5pm.) Across the street is the **Museum of Natural Sciences** at Bicentennial Plaza (733-7450), which has exhibits on animals, fossils, gems, and stars "George," a live 17-foot Burmese Python. (Open Mon.-Sat. 9am-5pm, Sun. 1-5pm. Free.) Also across from the capitol at 109 E. Jones St. is the **Museum of History** (733-3894). Exhibits cover the history of North Carolina Roanoke days to the present. (Open Tues.-Fri. 9am-4:30pm, Sun. 1-6pm. Free.)Pick up a brochure at the visitors center for a self-guided tour of the renovated 19th-century homes of **Historic Oakwood.** The **North Carolina Museum of Art,** 2110 Blue Ridge Blvd. (833-1935), off I-40 (Wade Ave. exit), has eight galleries with works from ancient Egypt and by Raphael, Botticelli, Rubens, Monet, Homer, Wyeth, and O'Keeffe. (Tours Tues.-Sat. 1:30pm. Open Tues.-Sat. 9am-5pm, Fri. 9am-9pm, Sun. noon-5pm. Free.) A tour of **North Carolina State University** on Hillsborough St. (737-2437) includes the **Pulstar Nuclear Reactor.** (Tours leave from the Bell Tower on Hillsborough St. Mon.-Fri. at noon during the semester.)

The **University of North Carolina** at Chapel Hill (962-0045) is the oldest state university in the country, and its Georgian architecture wears the years well. Astronauts practiced celestial navigation at the university's **Morehead Planetarium** (962-1248)—you, on the other hand, may only stargaze there. (Open Sun.-Fri. 12:30-5pm and 6:30-9:30pm, Sat. 10am-5pm and 6:30-9:30pm. Admission $3, seniors and students $2.50, children $2.) Over the next two years there will be many special events all over campus as the university celebrates its bicentennial. Call for details.

In Durham, **Duke University** is the major attraction. The admissions office at 2138 Campus Dr. (684-3214) serves as a visitors center. The **Duke Chapel** (tours and information 684-2572) is the center of the university and sparkles with its splendid Gothic architecture and seven beautiful stained glass windows. If you're lucky you may hear music streaming out of the 5000 pipes of **Memorial Organ.** (Open 8am-5pm during the school year.)

Two buildings to the left of the chapel is the walkway to the **Bryan Center,** Duke's maze-like student center, with a gift shop, a café, a small art gallery, and information on activities. Near West Campus on Anderson St. are the **Sara Duke Gardens** (684-3698), with over 15 acres of landscaped gardens. (Open daily 8am-dusk.) Duke's Georgian-style East Campus houses the **Duke Museum of Art** (684-5135), with its small but impressive collection. The six galleries are quiet and uncongested so you can relax and enjoy the works. (Free.)

On the other side of Durham, up Guess Rd., is the **Duke Homestead,** 2828 Duke Homestead Rd. (477-5498). Washington Duke first started in the tobacco business here, and the beautiful homestead is still a small working farm. (Open April-Oct. Mon.-Sat. 9am-5pm, Sun. 1-5pm; Nov.-March Tues.-Sat. 10am-4pm, Sun. 1-4pm.)

The three major universities and a total student population larger than that of many small countries ensure a plethora of campus plays, concerts, guest lectures, exhibits, workshops, and athletic events. For a complete listing of entertainment all over the triangle area, pick up a copy of the weekly *Spectator Magazine,* available at most restaurants, bookstores, and hotels.

The Carolina Mountains

The sharp ridges and rolling slopes of the Southern Appalachian mountain ranges create some of the East's most magnificent scenery. At one time, North Carolina's edenic highlands were an exclusive enclave of America's rich and famous. The Vanderbilts, for example, once owned a large portion of the nearly 500,000-acre **Pisgah National Forest,** which they subsequently willed to the U.S. government. Today the **Blue Ridge, Great Smoky, Black, Craggy, Pisgah,** and **Balsam Mountains** that comprise the western half of North Carolina are a budget traveler's paradise. Campsites blanket the region, coexisting with elusive but inexpensive youth hostels and ski lodges. Enjoy the area's rugged wilderness backpacking, canoeing, whitewater rafting, or cross-country skiing. Motorists and cyclists can follow the **Blue Ridge Parkway** (see Blue Ridge Parkway, VA).

The Blue Ridge Mountains are divided into two areas. The first, more northern area is the High Country, which includes the territory between the town of Boone and the town of Asheville, 100 miles to the southwest. The second area comprises the Great Smoky Mountains National Park and Nanatahala National Forest.

Boone

Named for famous frontiersman Daniel Boone, this mountain town has a variety of year-round outdoor activities such as hiking, rock climbing, whitewater rafting, and skiing. However, because of the presence of **Appalachian State University,** Boone also enjoys a large selection of cultural activities, many of which draw upon the area's rich folk heritage.

Practical Information

Emergency: 911. **National Park Service/Blue Ridge Parkway Emergency,** 259-0701 or 800-727-5929.

Visitor Information: Boone Area Chamber of Commerce, 350 Blowing Rock Rd. (264-2225), at the intersection of Rte. 321 and 105 in the center of Boone, nearly 7 miles north of the Blue Ridge Pkwy. Information on accommodations and sights. Open daily 9am-5pm. **North Carolina High Country Host,** 701 Blowing Rock Rd. (264-1299; 800-438-7500; 800-222-7515 in NC). Pick up copies of the *North Carolina High Country Host Area Travel Guide,* an informative and detailed map of the area, and the *Blue Ridge Parkway Directory,* a mile-by-mile description of all services and attractions located on or near the Blue Ridge Pkwy. Open daily 9am-5pm.

Greyhound/Trailways: At the AppalCART station on Winkler's Creek Rd. (264-2920). Take a left from Rte. 321 at Wendy's—it's on the right. Flag stop in Blowing Rock. One per day to Hickory and most points east, south, and west. Obtain schedule information in Hickory.

To: Hickory ($9) and Charlotte (2½ hr., $19). Open Mon.-Fri. 8am-5pm, Sat. 10am-2pm, Sun. 10am-2pm.

Local Transit: Boone AppalCART, on Winkler's Creek Rd. (264-2278). Local bus and van service, 3 routes. The Red Route links downtown Boone with ASU and the motels and restaurants on Blowing Rock Rd. The Green Route services Rte. 421. The crosstown route runs between the campus and the new marketplace. The Red Route operates Mon.-Fri. every hr. 7am-7pm, Sat. 8am-6pm. The Green Route operates Mon.-Fri. every hr. 7am-6pm. The crosstown route operates 7am-11pm. Fare 50¢ in town, charged by zones in the rest of the county.

Post Office: 637 Blowing Rock Rd. (264-3813), and 103 W. King St. (262-1171). Open Mon.-Fri. 9am-5pm, Sat. 9am-noon. **ZIP code:** 28607.

Area Code: 704.

Boone is located in the northwest corner of the state, by the Pisgah National Forest, about 22 miles from Tennessee. Most of Boone's motels and businesses are on Rte. 321 (Blowing Rock Rd.) and on Rte. 321-421 (King St.), which runs perpendicular to it. Appalachian State University stands at their junction.

Coming from other points on the East Coast, use **Charlotte** as your gateway city to the mountains. **Piedmont Airlines** (800-251-5720) has established a hub at Charlotte's **Douglas Airport.**

Accommodations and Camping

Boone area's decent motels tend to be very pricey. On the other hand, the hostels and campgrounds are lively, well-run, and inexpensive.

Blowing Rock Assembly Grounds (AYH), P.O. Box 974, Blowing Rock (295-7813), near the Blue Ridge Parkway. Ask the bus driver to let you off at Blowing Rock Town Hall or at the Rte. 321 bypass and Sunset Dr. depending on the direction you're traveling—it's about 2 miles from both points. Call the hostel for a pick-up. Turn at the first left onto Possum Hollow Rd; at the road's end turn left onto Sunset Dr. Where Sunset ends turn left 300 yards, and the hostel will be on your right. The rooms are fairly primitive, but clean and generally uncrowded. Communal bathrooms. Sports facilities and cheap cafeteria. Gorgeous setting, access to hiking trails. Primarily used by religious groups on retreat, so be prepared for a friendly but conservative atmosphere. $6, nonmembers $8; off-season $8 and $10, respectively.

Trailridge Mountain Camp (AYH), Rte. 2, Hughes Gap Rd., Bakersville (688-3879), 25 miles west of the Blue Ridge Pkwy., within walking distance of the Appalachian Trail. Call for a pick-up. Take Rte. 226 west to the community of Buladean; at the gas station, turn right on Hughes Gap Rd. Get off the Appalachian Trail at Hughes Gap Rd. and walk 2 miles south (towards NC). A fun, albeit noisy place—chiefly a summer camp for boys ages 6-16. The open-air cabin sleeps about 16 and has no electricity (it's a long, dark walk to the latrine). Swimming, sports, hiking, and evening entertainment. Shuttle for hikers and bikers to nearby trailheads. All hikers may use shower and toilet facilities ($1). $6, nonmembers $8. Meals must generally be taken with the campers June 12-Aug. 20. Breakfast $2.50, lunch $2, dinner $3. Open Jun-Aug.

The Longvue Motel, 716 Blowing Rock Rd., Boone (264-2920), at the southern end of Rte. 321 in the heart of Boone. Motel serves as the Boone Trailways terminal. Small, shabby, clean rooms; this is nothing special. Weekdays $22. Weekends $32. Off-season $18.

The Elk Motel, 321 S. Blowing Rock Rd., Boone (264-6191). Dilapidated building, gloomy but clean rooms. Singles $32. Doubles $43. Off-season $20 and $24, respectively.

Choose between developed **campsites** and free primitive camping in the Boone area and the Pisgah National Forest. Along the parkway, spectacular sites without hookups are available for $7 at the **Julian Price Campground,** Mile 297 (963-5911), 130 sites; **Linville Falls,** Mile 316 (963-5911), 55 sites; and **Crabtree Meadows,** Mile 340 (675-4444), 71 sites (open May-Oct. only). Cabins in **Roan Mountain State Park** (800-421-6683) comfortably sleep six and are furnished with linens and cooking utensils. (Sun.-Thurs. $45.50, Fri.-Sat. $58, $290 per week.) The state park offers pool and tennis facilities and tends to be less crowded than the campgrounds on the parkway.

Food

Most of the country kitchens perched on the sides of the careening mountain roads have been in business for decades and offer good, solid fare for under $5.

Woodland's, Rte. 321 bypass, Blowing Rock (295-3651), offers live entertainment nightly and authentic Carolina mountains barbecued pork and beef ($4-5). (Open Mon.-Fri. 11am-midnight; kitchen closes at 10pm.)

Dan'l Boone Inn, 105 Hardin St. (264-8657), at the junction of Rte. 321 and 421. Family style meals with ham biscuits and plates heaped high with vegetables and meat. All-you-can-eat $9. Open Mon.-Fri. 11am-9pm, Sat.-Sun. 7am-9pm.

Shadrack's Bar-B-Q and Seafood Barn, 729 Blowing Rock Rd. (264-1737), in an old roller skating rink, behind the Peddlar Steak House. All-you-can-eat BBQ pork, chicken, and ribs or fried catfish, accompanied by live bluegrass and clogging ($9). Buffet Thurs. 5:30-9pm, Fri. 5:30-10pm, Sat. 5:30-11pm. Music begins at 7pm. Sun. lunch 11:30am-2pm ($7). Music begins at 12:30pm.

Sights and Activities

An Appalachian Summer (262-6084) is a three-month, high-caliber festival of music, art, theater, and dance. **Horn in the West** (264-2120), located near Boone off Rte. 105, presents the saga of the American Revolution as it was fought in the Southern Appalachians. (Tues.-Sun. 8:30pm. Admission $8-12.) Use Boone as a base from which to explore the mountain towns to the west and south. The community of **Blowing Rock,** 7 miles south at the entrance to the Blue Ridge Pkwy., is a folk artists' colony. Its namesake is a rock overhanging Johns River Gorge; chuck a piece of paper over the edge and the wind will blow it back into your face. AppalCART goes to the Blowing Rock Town Hall from Boone twice daily. Stop by **Parkway Craft Center,** Mile 294 (295-7938), 2 miles south of Blowing Rock Village, where members of the Southern Highland Handicraft Guild demonstrate their skills and sell their crafts. (Open May-Oct. daily 9am-5:30pm.)

Hiking, biking, whitewater rafting, and skiing are popular ways to enjoy the mountains. Hikers should arm themselves with the invaluable large-scale map *100 Favorite Trails* ($2). If you're interested in rock climbing, check out **Appalachian Mountain Sports** (264-3170), on Hwy. 105 S., in Boone. They offer professional instruction, mostly for small groups (1-3 people). The guides will meet you on the trail for a half-day of instruction, or a 2 to 3-day trip. (Rates from $65 per person for a 3-person group. The store rents backpacking gear and can help you plan your own expedition on the trails.) Consider joining one of the guided expeditions led by the staff of **Edge of the World,** P.O. Box 1137, Banner Elk (898-9550), on Rte. 184 downtown. A complete outdoor equipment and clothing store, Edge of the World leads many day-long backpacking, whitewater canoeing, rafting, and rock climbing trips all over the High Country for under $40. One of their most popular is a two-day summer backpacking trip across the Roan Mountain Balds ($75, including transportation, all equipment, 4 meals, instruction, and guide). Edge of the World also rents equipment. (4-person tents $7 the 1st night, $6 the 2nd, $4 each additional night; 2-person tents $1 less each night. Sleeping bags $4 for the 1st night, $3 the 2nd, $2 each additional night. Sleeping pads $1 per day, cook stoves $2 per day, backpacks $4 per day.)

Downhill skiers can enjoy the Southeast's largest concentration of alpine resorts. Four are concentrated in the Boone/Blowing Rock/Banner Elk area: **Appalachian Ski Mountain,** P.O. Box 106, Blowing Rock (800-322-2373; lift tickets weekends $24, weekdays $16, with full rental $27); **Ski Beech,** P.O. Box 1118, Beech Mountain (387-2011; lift tickets weekends $26, weekdays $21, with rentals $38 and $28, respectively); **Ski Hawknest,** Town of Seven Devils, 1605 Skyland Dr., Banner Elk (963-6561; lift tickets weekends $20, weekdays $10, full rental $10 and $6, respectively); **Sugar Mountain,** P.O. Box 369, Banner Elk (898-4521; lift tickets weekends $33, weekdays $24, rentals $12 and $10, respectively). AppalCART (262-0501) runs a daily shuttle in winter to Sugar Mountain and four times per week to Ski Beech. Call the High Country Host (264-1299) for ski reports.

If you have a car, the 5-mile access road to **Grandfather Mountain** will lead you to unparalleled views of the entire High Country area. At the top you'll find a private park featuring a suspension bridge and a small zoo ($6). To hike or camp on Grandfather Mountain, you must get a permit ($3 per day), available at the Grandfather Mountain County Store on Rte. 221, Appalachian Mountain Sports, Edge of the World, or the Scotchman store at the Shanty Spring Trail at the junction of Rte. 105 and 184. (Contact the Backcountry Manager, Grandfather Mountain, Linville, NC 28646 for more information.) North Carolina Rte. 194, 226, 261, and 80 near the towns of Banner Elk, Beech, Elk Park, Bakersville, and Bandana meander through verdant mountainsides and narrow valleys; by day, they're a sportscar driver's dream, but by night the absence of guardrails makes them a hair-raising experience.

Asheville

Asheville's setting embodies classic Appalachian beauty, with its hazy blue mountains, deep valleys, spectacular waterfalls, and plunging gorges. The city's diversions include novelist Thomas Wolfe's childhood home, and a series of summer folk festivals. A recent infusion of capital has provided Asheville with the sumptuous Haywood Park Hotel and shops.

Practical Information

Emergency: Police and fire, 252-1110.

Visitors Information: Chamber of Commerce, 151 Haywood St. (258-3858, 800-548-1300 in NC), off I-240, on the northwest end of downtown. Ask at the desk for the detailed city street map, city transit route map, and comprehensive sight-seeing guide. Open Mon.-Fri. 8:30am-5:30pm, Sat.-Sun. 9:30am-5pm.

Greyhound/Trailways: 2 Tunnel Rd. (253-5353), 2 miles east of downtown, near the Beaucatcher Tunnel. Bus #13 ("Oteen/Beverly Hills") or 14 ("Haw Creek/Tunnel Rd.") runs to and from downtown every ½ hr. Last bus 5:50pm. To: Charlotte (3 per day, 3 hr., $16); Knoxville (7 per day, 3 hr., $21); Atlanta ($36). Station open daily 6:30am-10pm.

Asheville Transit: 360 W. Haywood (253-5691). Service within city limits. All routes converge on Pritchard Park downtown. Buses operate Mon.-Sat. 5:30am-7:30pm, most at ½-hr. intervals. Fare 60¢, transfers 30¢.

Post Office: 33 Coxe Ave. (257-4113), at Patton Ave. Open Mon.-Fri. 8:30am-5pm, Sat. 9am-noon. **ZIP code:** 28802.

Area Code: 704.

Asheville hugs the hills of the Blue Ridge Mountains in western North Carolina. Knoxville, TN, is 100 miles to the northwest across Great Smoky Mountains National Park, and Winston-Salem is 144 miles east on I-40. Downtown Asheville is bordered by I-240 on the north and I-40 on the south. The Blue Ridge Pkwy. is accessible by I-40 east.

Accommodations and Camping

Asheville's independently owned motels tend to be cheaper than budget chains. Many are concentrated on **Merrimon Avenue,** north of the city (take bus #2 "Merrimon Avenue"), and on **Tunnel Road.** Make reservations early around folk and craft festivals and holidays.

American Court Motel, 85 Merrimon Ave. (253-4427), 1 block past the Downtown Motel. Clean, surprisingly pretty rooms, friendly manager. Cable TV, A/C, pool, and laundromat. Non-smoking rooms available. Singles $28-32. Doubles $32-39.

Interstate Motel, 37 Hiawassee St. (254-0945), off I-240 at U.S. 25. Behind the Civic Center in the heart of downtown. Clean but smoky rooms. Ask for one away from the highway. Cable TV and A/C. Singles $26.

Downtown Motel, 65 Merrimon Ave. (253-9841), on Merrimon St. just north of the I-240 expressway. A 10-min. walk from downtown or take bus #2. Old, dark rooms. Pool. Singles $25. Doubles $28.

Red Carpet Inn, 120 Patton Ave. (254-9661). Rooms are being remodeled, and prices may go up when construction is finished. Low rates, great location. Singles $26. Key deposit $5.

With the Blue Ridge Pkwy., Pisgah National Forest, and the Great Smokies all within easy driving distance, you're bound to find a campsite you like. Close to town is **Bear Creek RV Park and Campground,** 81 S. Bear Creek Rd. (253-0798). Take I-40 exit 47, and look for the sign at the top of the hill. (Pool, laundry, groceries, and jacuzzi. Tent sites $12. RV sites with full hookup $16.50.) In Pisgah National Forest, the nearest campground is **Powhatan,** off Rte. 191, 12 miles southwest of Asheville. (Open May-Sept.)

Food

You'll find nearly every fast-food chain on **Tunnel Road** and **Biltmore Avenue.** Downtown Asheville offers some reasonable alternatives to the hamburger and frozen custard monarchs. The **Western North Carolina Farmers Market** (253-1691), at the intersection of I-240 and Rte. 191, near I-26, has plenty of fresh produce, as well as crafts. (Open Mon.-Sat. 8am-6pm, Sun. 1-6pm. Take bus #16 to I-40, then walk ½ mile.)

Bill Stanley's Barbeque and Bluegrass, 20 South Spruce St. (253-4871), in the rear corner of a building adjacent to the police station. Hickory-cooked barbecue and fried chicken. Bluegrass and cloggers on the side. All-you-can-eat buffet dinner $8.59. Open Tues.-Thurs. 11am-2pm and 6-11pm, Fri. 11am-2pm and 6pm-midnight, Sat. 6pm-midnight.

Johnny O's Sandwich Shop, 36 Battery Park Ave. Stand-up lunch counter. Cheeseburger 70¢. Open daily 6:30am-2:30pm.

Stone Soup, at Broadway and Walnut St. (255-7687). Also on Wall St., downtown. A cooperative that makes fresh bread and serves nitrate-free sausage. Soup and sandwiches from $1.50. Packed from noon-2pm and for Sun. brunch. Open Mon.-Fri. 7am-4pm, Sat. 8am-4pm, Sun. 9:30am-1:30pm.

Malaprops Bookstore/Café, 61 Haywood St. (254-6734), downtown, in the basement of the bookstore. Gourmet coffees, Atlanta bagels, tofu. Sandwiches $3-4. Poetry readings and live music every night. Open daily 10am-8pm.

Sights and Festivals

The **Thomas Wolfe Memorial,** 48 Spruce St. (253-8304), between Woodfin and Walnut St., was the novelist's boyhood home, a boarding house run by his mother. Wolfe depicted the "Old Kentucky Home" as "Dixieland" in his first novel, *Look Homeward, Angel.* The house contains original furnishings. (Open Mon.-Sat. 9am-5pm, Sun. 1-5pm; hours vary in winter. Admission $1, students 50¢.)

It's rare that a summer day goes by in Asheville when there is *not* a festival taking place. In June, the **Cullowhee Music Festival** (227-7608) features a series of performances in classical music. (Tickets $5-15 per performance. Series ticket $42, seniors and students $30.) The **Mountain Dance and Folk Festival** (800-548-1300), now in its 62nd season, has a 3-day competition in clog and square dancing, mountain traditional and bluegrass music, and individual musicianship. It takes place in August at the Civic Center. (Tickets $5-7). The **Swannanoa Chamber Festival** (298-3325) in July has weekly chamber music concerts. ($8 per performance, $35 for a series ticket.) The **Southern Highland Crafts Fair** takes place in mid-July at the Civic Center and has crafts demonstrations, folk music, and dancing. Call the chamber of commerce for information.

South Carolina

In 1860, South Carolina became the first state to secede from the Union, only to be decimated throughout the next 17 years by northern occupation and a collapsed economy. The state has had a long, slow climb back to prosperity and has seen little of the growth or success that now characterizes Georgia's Atlanta or North Carolina's Research Triangle. The lowland farmers continue to eke out a living, and the Piedmont "up-country" is largely accessible only by two-lane country roads. Charlestonians sit out on the porches of their beautiful antebellum houses and talk about the War Between the States, "the late unpleasantness," as if it were the Vietnam War. Except for trashy Myrtle Beach, a classic Atlantic hotspot, you will find southern pace, culture, and charm predominant here.

Practical Information

Capital: Columbia.

Tourist Information: Department of Parks, Recreation and Tourism, Edgar A. Brown Bldg., 1205 Pendleton St., #110, Columbia 29201 (734-0122). **U.S. Forest Service,** P.O. Box 970, Columbia 29202 (765-5222).

Time Zone: Eastern. **Postal Abbreviation:** SC.

Columbia

The capital is a quiet, unassuming city whose pervasive college-town flavor overshadows state politics. The University of South Carolina provides most of the city's excitement and nightlife. The city began in 1786, when colonial bureaucrats in nearby Charleston decided that their territory needed a proper capital city. Virtually overnight, surveyors found some land near the Congaree River and supervised its clearing. They laid out each street 100 feet wide to insure the settlers' health and safety. Within two decades, over 1000 people had poured into one of America's first planned cities. Stop by for a pleasant refuge from the high-powered sight-seeing of Charleston and the honky-tonk of Myrtle Beach.

Columbia's 18th-century aristocratic elegance has been preserved by the **Historic Columbia Foundation,** in the **Robert Mills House,** 1616 Blanding St. (252-7742), 3 blocks east of Sumter St. (Tours Tues.-Sun.) Mills, one of America's first federal architects, designed the Washington Monument and 30 of South Carolina's public buildings. Across the street, at 1615 Blanding, is the **Hampton-Preston Mansion,** once used by Union forces as a Civil War headquarters. (Open Tues.-Sat. 10am-4pm, Sun. 1-5pm. Tours $3, students $1.50, under 6 free.) Stroll through USC's **Horseshoe,** at the junction of College and Sumter St., which holds the university's oldest buildings, dating from the beginning of the 19th century. The **McKissick Museum** (777-7251), at the top of the Horseshoe, offers intriguing changing exhibits based on the university's extensive collection of Twentieth Century-Fox Movietonenews Newsreels. (Open Mon.-Fri. 9am-4pm, Sat. 10am-5pm, Sun. 1-5pm. Free.) Columbia's award-winning **Riverbanks Zoo** is on I-26 at Greystone Blvd., northwest of downtown. The 800 animals are displayed in natural-looking mini-habitats. (Open Mon.-Fri. 9am-4pm, Sat.-Sun. 9am-5pm; off-season daily 9am-4pm. Admission $3.50, seniors $2, students $2.75, ages 3-12 $1.50.)

The Five Points business district, at the junction of Harden, Devine, and Blossom St., caters to Columbia's large student population. (From downtown, take the "Veterans Hospital" bus.) **Groucho's,** 611 Harden St. (799-5708), in the heart of Five Points, is a Columbia institution—a New York-style Jewish deli serving large sandwiches at rock-bottom prices ($3-5). (Open Mon.-Fri. 10am-6pm, Sat. 11am-4pm.) **Yesterday's Restaurant and Tavern,** 2030 Devine St. (799-0196), is another Five Points institution. Enjoy complete dinner specials ($4) or vegetarian and dinner pies. (Open Sun.-Tues. 11:30am-1am, Wed.-Sat. 11:30am-2am.) **The Lizard's Thicket,** a local chain, offers country-style dinners (meat with vegetable and cornbread muffins $3-4). **The Columbia State Farmers Market,** Bluff Rd. (737-3016), across from the USC Football Stadium, is a good place to stock up on fresh produce shipped in from all corners of South Carolina.

The **Off-Campus Housing Office,** 1407 Blossom St. (777-4174), may be able to link you up with owners of private homes in the university community who rent rooms. Otherwise, the only budget option downtown is the **Heart of Columbia,** 1011 Assembly St. (799-1140). Shabby-looking exterior, but clean rooms, a safe neighborhood, and friendly management. (Singles $24. Doubles $26.) Just west of downtown, across the Congaree River, a number of inexpensive motels line Knox Abbot Dr. **Motel 6,** 1144 Bush River Rd., off exit 108 at I-20 and I-26, has 124 rooms. (Singles $23, additional guests $6 each.) **Sesquicentennial State Park** (788-2706) has sites with electricity and water ($8). (Take "State Park" bus from downtown. By car, take I-20 to Two Notch Road (Rte. 1) exit, and head northeast 4 miles on Two Notch Rd.)**The Greater Columbia Convention and Visitors Bureau,** at 301 Gervais St. (254-0479), is not budget-oriented. (Open Mon.-Fri. 8:30am-5pm, Sat. 10am-5pm, Sun. 1-5pm.) Get the low-down on campus life and events at the **University of South Carolina Information Desk,** Russell House Student Center, 2nd floor (777-3196), on Green St. at Main St., across from the Horseshoe. They'll provide you with campus maps, shuttle schedules, and advice on nearby budget accommodations. (Take any "Owens Field" bus headed south on Sumter St. and get off at Green St.) **Travelers Aid** is at 1800 Main St. (733-5450; open Mon.-Fri. 9am-5pm).

Columbia is in the heart of South Carolina, at the junction of I-20, 26, and 77. It is 112 miles from Charleston, 92 miles from Charlotte, NC, 143 miles from Myrtle Beach, and 215 miles from Atlanta. Most buses running along the East Coast stop here. The **Congaree River** marks the western edge of the city. **Assembly Street** and **Sumter Street** are downtown's major north-south arteries; **Gervais Street** and **Calhoun Street** cut east-west. The **Amtrak** station is at 903 Gervais St. (252-8246 or 800-872-7245). Trains leave once per day to: Washington, DC (9½ hr., $79); Miami (12 hr., $112); and Savannah (2 hr., $29). The station is open Mon.-Sat. 8:30am-4:30pm and 10:30pm-6:30am, Sun. 10:30pm-6:30am. Lockers are 50¢ for 24 hours. The **Greyhound/Trailways** station is at 2015 Gervais St. (779-0650), near the intersection of Harden and Gervais St., about a mile east of the capitol. Buses serve Charlotte, NC (4 per day, 2 hr., $19); Charleston, SC (5 per day, 2½ hr., $18); and Atlanta (8 per day, 4½ hr., $38). The station is open 24 hours. **South Carolina Electric and Gas** (748-3019) operates local buses daily; most routes start from the transfer depot at the corner of Assembly and Gervais St. (Fare 50¢, transfers free.) The **Post Office** is at 1601 Assembly St. (733-4647; open Mon. and Fri. 7:30am-6pm, Tues.-Thurs. 7:30am-5pm). The General Delivery **ZIP code** is 29202; the **area code** is 803.

Myrtle Beach

Myrtle Beach is a living museum of American pop culture. More than a beach, it's a phenomenon—the third most popular destination on the East Coast (after Disney World and Atlantic City). The beach is the grand attraction of Myrtle Beach, and the concession area is its grand distraction. The streets of Myrtle Beach are lined with t-shirt shops, fireworks warehouses, all-you-can-eat smorgasbords, fast-food franchises, and gift shops. There are 15 miniature golf courses in the area, such as **Grand Prix Golf,** at the southern end of the strip (open 9am-midnight; $5), and several waterparks, such as **Wild Rapids Waterslide,** 301 S. Ocean Blvd. (448-4647). The length of the beach and boulevard is called the **Grand Strand.**

If the activities on the street aren't incredible enough, head toward the flashing lights and schlocky museums at the beach center, Ocean Blvd. between 5th and 12th St. Or launch into shopping ecstasy at the **Waccamaw Pottery and Outlet**

Park, west of the beach on U.S. 501 between Myrtle Beach and Conway, a 500-acre complex of over 100 factory outlet stores. (Open in summer daily 9am-10pm.)

The restaurants in Myrtle Beach are largely predictable and overpriced steak and seafood places. You won't find any interesting budget cuisine here—look instead for local hangouts that serve burgers, sandwiches, and beer. **River City Cafe,** 21st Ave. N. (448-1990), serves huge juicy hamburgers, homemade fries, beer, wine, and free peanuts in a fun, collegiate atmosphere. Wade through the peanut shells on the floor to tell Donna, the owner, chef, and hostess, that you're a *Let's Go* reader and she might slip you some crispy, fresh onion rings. (Open Mon.-Sat. 11am-10pm, Sun. noon-9pm.) **Angelo's Steak and Pasta,** 203 King's Hwy., has "all-you-care-to-eat" pasta specials, with salad and garlic bread, for $6. For a good, square meal under $5, join the loyal, budget-conscious fans of **K and W Cafeteria** (448-1669), locations at both ends of town, on Business 17. At dinner expect a 20-minute wait. **Olympic Flame Restaurant and Pancake House,** 14th Ave. N. and Ocean Blvd. (448-2756), 1 block from the beach, starts the day right with fluffy pancakes ($2.25) and omelettes ($2.60). (Open daily 6:30am-10pm.)

All of the motels in Myrtle Beach are expensive and many are unaffordable in summer. The most inexpensive places are just west of the beach property in the 3rd St. area or on U.S. 17. You can often bargain for a lower hotel rate. Off-season prices plunge. The **Sun Villa Motel,** 302 2nd Ave. S. (626-3037), has shabby, dingy, but fairly tidy rooms 3 blocks from the beach. Most have stove and refrigerator. Owner will pick guests up at Greyhound (no charge). (Rooms with one double and one single bed $35, each additional person $3-10. Special rates for foreign students. Key deposit $10.) **Ocean West Motel,** 204 N. King's Hwy., has old but clean rooms with cable TV ($35). The **Bon-Air,** 1401 S. King's Hwy., has slightly run-down rooms. (Singles $35. Doubles $39. Weekdays $10 less.)

To enjoy the outdoors and distance yourself from the frenzied beach, camp at the **Myrtle Beach State Park** (238-5325). Just south of town off U.S. 17, across from the air force base, the park encloses a stretch of non-commercial and relatively uncrowded shoreline. (Gates open 6am-midnight; off-season 6am-dark. Sites $12.) There are also several private campgrounds, but some have rules against single campers, so call ahead if you're alone. **KOA Kampgrounds,** King's Hwy. and 5th Ave. S. (448-3421), is less than 1 mile outside of town. (Sites with water and electricity $17, with full hookup $19.50. Make reservations.) **Apache Family Campground,** 9700 King's Hwy. N. (449-7323), is slightly farther away. Some sites are on the beach, some in pine groves. (Families only. Sites $20-23.) Sleeping on the beach is illegal, as are parties, and the beaches are all heavily patrolled.

Myrtle Beach reclines at the center of the Grand Strand, a stretch of coastline that extends for 60 miles from the North Carolina border to Georgetown. **U.S. 17,** also called **King's Highway,** runs north-south along the coastline and provides access to most points of interest. **Route 501** west in the direction of Conway leads to the popular factory outlet stores. Myrtle Beach's **Greyhound** terminal, at 9th Ave. N. and U.S. 17 (448-2471), has connections to: Charleston (3 per day, 2 hr., $17); Florence (2 per day, 45 min., $13); and Wilmington (3 per day, 2 hr., $12). (Station open Mon.-Fri. 8am-2:30pm and 7-8:45pm, Sat. 8am-2:30pm, Sun. 8-9am, noon-2:30pm, and 7-8:45pm.) To get around Myrtle Beach and Conway, use **Coastal Rapid Public Transit (CRPTA).** (626-9138 in Myrtle Beach; 248-7277 in Conway. Local fare 75¢; Conway to Myrtle Beach $1.25.) You can rent a bike at **The Bike Shoppe,** 711 Broadway (448-5103; $5 per hr. for sturdy 1-speeds; leave license or credit card as deposit).

Stop at the **Chamber of Commerce,** 13th Ave. N. and King's Hwy. (626-7444), for a free copy of *Beachcomber* and information on current activities. (Open Mon.-Fri. 8:30am-5pm, Sat. 9am-noon, Sun. noon-5pm.) The **post office** is at 505 N. King's Hwy. (626-9533, open Mon.-Fri. 8:30am-5pm, Sat. 9am-noon). Myrtle Beach's **ZIP code** is 29577; the **area code** is 803.

Charleston

The story goes that a Charlestonian, when asked if he'd lived there all his life, replied, "Not yet." Such is the loyalty to the only American city founded by nobility, where dukes, barons, and earls once presided over great coastal plantations. Although this oligarchy lasted less than 50 years, the city still presents a refined and aristocratic face. Charleston's antebellum homes, old churches, hidden gardens, winding cobblestone streets, and iron gateways exude southern charm and romance. The Charleston area offers the resources of its Atlantic coastal islands as well. Whether in the bounds of the old walled city or out by the ocean, visitors will find this hospitable town well worth a stay.

Practical Information

Emergency: 911.

Visitor Information Center: 85 Calhoun St. (722-8338), in front of the Municipal Auditorium. Walking tour map (50¢) has lots of historical information and good directions. The ½-hr. slide show, *The Charleston Adventure,* should not be confused with the remarkable *Dear Charleston,* but it is a respectable overview of Charleston's past and present. Tickets $3, children $1.50. Open Mon.-Fri. 8:30am-5:30pm, Sat.-Sun. 8:30am-5pm.

Amtrak: 4565 Gaynor Ave. (744-8264), 8 miles west of downtown. "Durant Ave." bus will take you from the station to the historic district. To: Richmond (3 per day, 7 hr., $46); Savannah (3 per day, 2 hr., $22); and Washington, DC (3 per day, 14 hr., $95). Open daily 4am-noon and 12:30-10pm.

Greyhound: 89 Society St. (722-7721), between King and Meeting St., a short walk from the historic district. To: Myrtle Beach (3 per day, 2 hr., $17); Savannah (3 per day, 3 hr., $21); and Washington, DC (2 per day, 11 hr., $73). Open daily 7am-6pm.

Local Transit: South Carolina Electric and Gas Company (SCE&G City Bus Service), 2469 Leeds Ave. (747-0922). Operates Mon.-Sat. 5:10am-1am. Fare 50¢. Also operates **Downtown Area Shuttle (DASH)** Mon.-Fri. 8am-5pm. Fare 50¢, transfers to other SCE&G buses free.

Car Rental: Thrifty Car Rental (552-7531 or 800-367-2277). $30 per day; 200 free miles, 20¢ each additional mile. Must be 25 with major credit card.

Bike Rental: The Bicycle Shoppe, 283 Meeting St. (722-8168). $3 per hr., $12 per day. Open daily 10am-5:30pm. Must have ID.

Taxi: Yellow Cab, 577-6565. Base fare $1, $1 per mile.

Help Lines: Hotline, 744-4357. 24 hours. General counseling and comprehensive information on transient accommodations. **People Against Rape,** 722-7273. 24 hours.

Post Office: 11 Broad St. Open Mon.-Fri. 8am-5pm, Sat. 8am-noon. **ZIP code:** 29401.

Area Code: 803.

About 100 miles north of Savannah and the same distance south of Myrtle Beach, Charleston sits midway along the South Carolina coastline. The city dominates an ocean-facing peninsula bathed by rivers on both sides. **Old Charleston** is confined to the southernmost point of the mile-wide peninsula below **Calhoun Street. Meeting Street, King Street,** and **East Bay Street** are major north-south routes through the city.

Accommodations and Camping

Motel rooms in regal Charleston cost a princely sum. Investigate the rooms for rent just across the Ashley River, on U.S. 17 South. Several tiny establishments offer $12-15 rooms. Cheap motels are all a good distance from downtown and are not a practical option for those without cars. **Charleston East Bed and Breakfast,** 1031 Tall Pine Rd., Mt. Pleasant (884-8208), east of Charleston off U.S. 701, will try to place you in one of their 16 private homes. Rooms are $30 to 50, $5 to 10 less if you're alone.)

Rutledge-Museum Guest House, 114 Rutledge Ave. (722-7551). Rooms in beautiful Victorian houses in the heart of downtown. Manager is laid back, friendly, and will not let you step foot in Charleston before she's given you a full orientation. Most rooms sleep 2 or more. Singles $35. Shared rooms $15 per person. Rates are lower if you stay more than a few days.

Motel 6, 2058 Savannah Hwy. (556-5144), 4 miles out at 7th Ave. Clean and pleasant, but far from downtown. Fills frequently. Singles $26, each additional person $6.

There are several inexpensive campgrounds in the Charleston area, but they are not close to downtown. Eight miles south on U.S. 17, **Oak Plantation Campground** (766-5936; sites $10.70 for 3). Also look for **Pelican's Cove,** 77 Center St., Folly Beach (588-2072; sites $17, with full hookup).

Food and Nightlife

There's more to Charleston cuisine than that famous South Carolina rice. Tourists are faced with many eating options, unfortunately most very expensive. In the historic district you can lunch at a number of elegant places for about $5. Dinner will lighten your wallet considerably. If you don't mind busting your budget for a night, go for a traditional seafood dinner.

Marina Variety Store/City Marina, Lockwood Blvd. (723-6325). Pleasant view of the Ashley River from an otherwise unremarkable dining room. Good shellfish and great nightly specials under $7. Open Mon.-Sat. 6:30am-3pm and 5-10pm, Sun. 6:30am-3pm.

Henry's, 54 N. Market St. (723-4363), at Anson. A local favorite. Not cheap, but the food is good. Try the curried shrimp ($8.50). On the weekends, live jazz upstairs starts at 9pm and there is a late-night breakfast. Open Mon.-Wed. 11:30am-10:30pm, Thurs.-Sun. 11:30am-1am.

Alice's Restaurant, 973½ King St., at Cleveland, north of downtown, near Hampton Park and the Citadel. Serves anything you want. Southern cooking and reasonable burgers. Open Mon.-Thurs. 7:30am-10pm, Fri. 7:30am-12:30am, Sat. 11am-12:30am, Sun. 11am-7pm.

Poogan's Porch, 72 Queen St. (577-2337), between King and Meeting St. Cajun cooking served in a tastefully restored city mansion. Sip iced tea on the veranda—you'll feel like an authentic Charlestonian. Lunch is the only affordable meal ($6-8). Open daily 11:30am-2pm.

Before you go out in Charleston, pick up a free copy of Poor Richard's *Omnibus,* available at grocery stores and street corners all over town. It lists local concerts and other events. Locals rarely dance the *Charleston* anymore, but night spots are anything but stodgy. The ban on Sunday drinking has even been lifted. Most nightlife is in the **Market Street** area. **Cafe 99,** 99 S. Meeting St. (577-4499), has deliciously strong drinks ($2-4) and live music nightly on the porch. (Open daily 3:30pm-12:30am.)

Sights and Seasonal Events

Saturated with ancient homes, historical monuments, churches, galleries, and gardens, Charleston is a tourist's delight. Many organized tours allow you to see the city by foot, car, bus, boat, trolley, or carriage. Several have information and ticket centers near the visitors information center on Calhoun St. Others begin on Market St. near the historic district or along the waterfront. **Gray Line Water Tours** (722-1112) gives you your money's worth. (2-hr. boat rides leave daily at 10am, 12:30pm, and 3pm. Fare $7.50. Reservations recommended.) For an appropriately old-fashioned view of the city, **Charleston Carriage,** 96 N. Market St. (577-0042), provides 50-minute horse-drawn tours of the city ($9, children $4.50), starting from Buggy Whip Gift Shop (9am-sunset). There is a free shuttle service from the visitors information center and downtown hotels. Before you start touring, though, see *Dear Charleston,* an internationally acclaimed documentary on the city's history as recounted through the musings of long-time residents. *Dear Charleston* is a fast-paced, quirky, and offbeat glimpse behind Charleston's architectural facades. The film is shown daily on the hour (10am-4pm, except 1pm) at the **Preservation Society Visitor Center,** 147 King St. (723-4381), and also shown hourly at **Dear Charleston**

Theater & Gifts, 52 N. Market St. (577-4743; admission at both places $3.25, children $1.75).

The **Nathanial Russell House,** 51 Meeting St. (723-3646), features a magnificent flying staircase that spirals without support from floor to floor, as well as elliptical rooms. The **Edmonston-Allston House,** 21 E. Battery St. (722-3405), looks out over Charleston Harbor. (Both open Mon.-Sat. 10am-5pm, Sun. 2-5pm. Admission to 1 house $4, to both $6.) Two other houses noted for their architecture are the 18th-century **Heyward-Washington House,** 87 Church St. (722-0354), and the **Joseph Manigault House,** 350 Meeting St. (722-2996), built in 1802. The Washington House includes the only 18th-century kitchen open to the public in Charleston. (Both open daily 10am-4:30pm. Admission to 1 house $3, to both $5.) The **Calhoun Mansion** is one of Charleston's most detailed and costly restorations. The largest privately owned residence in the city, it was built around 1876. The woodwork, furniture, and garden are ornate and beautiful.

Founded in 1773, the **Charleston Museum,** 360 Meeting St. (722-2996), has a collection that ranges from natural history specimens to old sheet music, most connected in some way with the city. (Open Mon.-Sat. 9am-5pm, Sun. 1-5pm. Admission $3, ages 3-12 $1.50.) The **Gibbes Gallery,** 135 Meeting St. (722-2706), has a fine collection of portraits by prominent American artists. (Open Sun. and Mon. 1-5pm, Tues.-Sat. 10am-5pm. Admission $2, seniors and students $1, children 50¢.)

No visit to Charleston would be complete without a jaunt to **Fort Sumter** (722-1691) in Charleston Harbor. The first state to secede from the Union, South Carolina has the dubious honor of having started the Civil War by attacking this Union stronghold on April 12, 1861. From mid-March to Labor Day, two-hour tours leave several times daily from the Municipal Marina, at the foot of Calhoun St. and Lockwood Blvd. ($7.50, ages 6-12 $3.75). A museum at the fort explains its role in the Revolutionary and Civil Wars. (Free.)

From mid-March to mid-April, the **Festival of Houses** (723-1623) celebrates Charleston's architecture and tradition, as many private homes open their doors to the public. Music, theater, dance, and opera converge on the city during **Spoleto Festival USA** (722-2764; late May and early June), the "world's most comprehensive arts festival." During **Christmas in Charleston** (723-7641), tours of many private homes and buildings are given. Many motels offer special reduced rates at this time.

Magnolia Gardens, (571-1266), 10 miles out of town on Hwy. 61, off Rte. 17, treats visitors to 50 acres of gorgeous gardens with 900 varieties of camelia and 250 varieties of azalea. Get lost in the hedge maze. You'll probably want to skip the manor house, but consider renting bicycles ($3 per hr.) to explore the neighboring swamp and bird sanctuary. (Open Sun.-Wed. 8am-6:30pm, Thurs.-Sat. 8am-8pm. Admission $7, seniors $6, teens $5, children $3.)

SOUTH CENTRAL

You know you're in Dixie when strangers greet you with "howdy" when you pass by on the street. Hospitality is still the trademark of the South Central States. There's also a corresponding lack of hustle and bustle, even in urban centers Memphis and New Orleans. The region is overwhelmingly rural and agricultural. As a result, it is one of the poorest areas in the country, but also one of the most beautiful.

To experience the South is to experience those who live there. More than most areas, this is a place truly characterized by the people who make it their home, and who have done so for generations. Be sure to take the opportunity to drive through the back roads of rural Arkansas, to attend Sunday mass in northern Alabama, or to chat with Acadians in the depth of Louisiana's bayous.

Travel

Seasonal fluctuations in travel in the South mean you can plan your trip either to join or avoid the crowds. Besides extraordinary Mardi Gras, many festivals and special events liven the area from March through September.

Greyhound/Trailways serves the region fairly comprehensively. However, many of the more remote locations, in Mississippi and Alabama especially, are served only once daily.

Amtrak is less reliable; many of the less populated areas are not served at all and several of the routes between larger towns and cities run only three times per week. Once-daily schedules cut through central Alabama to Atlanta, GA, north through central Mississippi to Memphis, TN, and Chicago, IL, and west along the Gulf Coast of Louisiana to Houston, TX. Arkansas is served on a St. Louis, MO to Dallas, TX , run, and Northern Kentucky has service, too. Only central and southern Georgia are unserved.

It's well worth the money to rent a car, even for only a few days, to see the heartland. Take every opportunity to drive through the countryside on the (often poorly maintained) state and country roads. Farms are gradually being consolidated by large corporate owners, making the landscape appear curiously devoid of residents. However, this slow erosion of the traditional way of life may be hard for the outside observer to spot. To those accustomed to a more developed America, it often looks as if the lush rural hamlets haven't changed in decades. If you're behind your own steering wheel, don't try to make time near small towns since speed traps are not uncommon here.

Hitchhiking is generally good throughout the South. Information centers and wayside parking areas are good places to test your luck. However, long-haired men draw more comments and stares than rides, even from their contemporaries.

Apart from camping, there are few bargains in accommodations. The only hostels worthy of note are near the Smokies (Gatlinburg, TN) and in New Orleans. Look for budget hotel chains such as Days Inn (800-325-2525) and Econo Lodges (800-446-6900) on the outskirts of cities. **State parks** with campsites are fairly plentiful throughout the South; **national forests** are sprinkled through the region, offering remote campgrounds and free primitive camping in unspectacular surroundings. Be sure to make room or campsite reservations if you're planning to visit betweeen March and September, since local festivals held then often draw huge crowds.

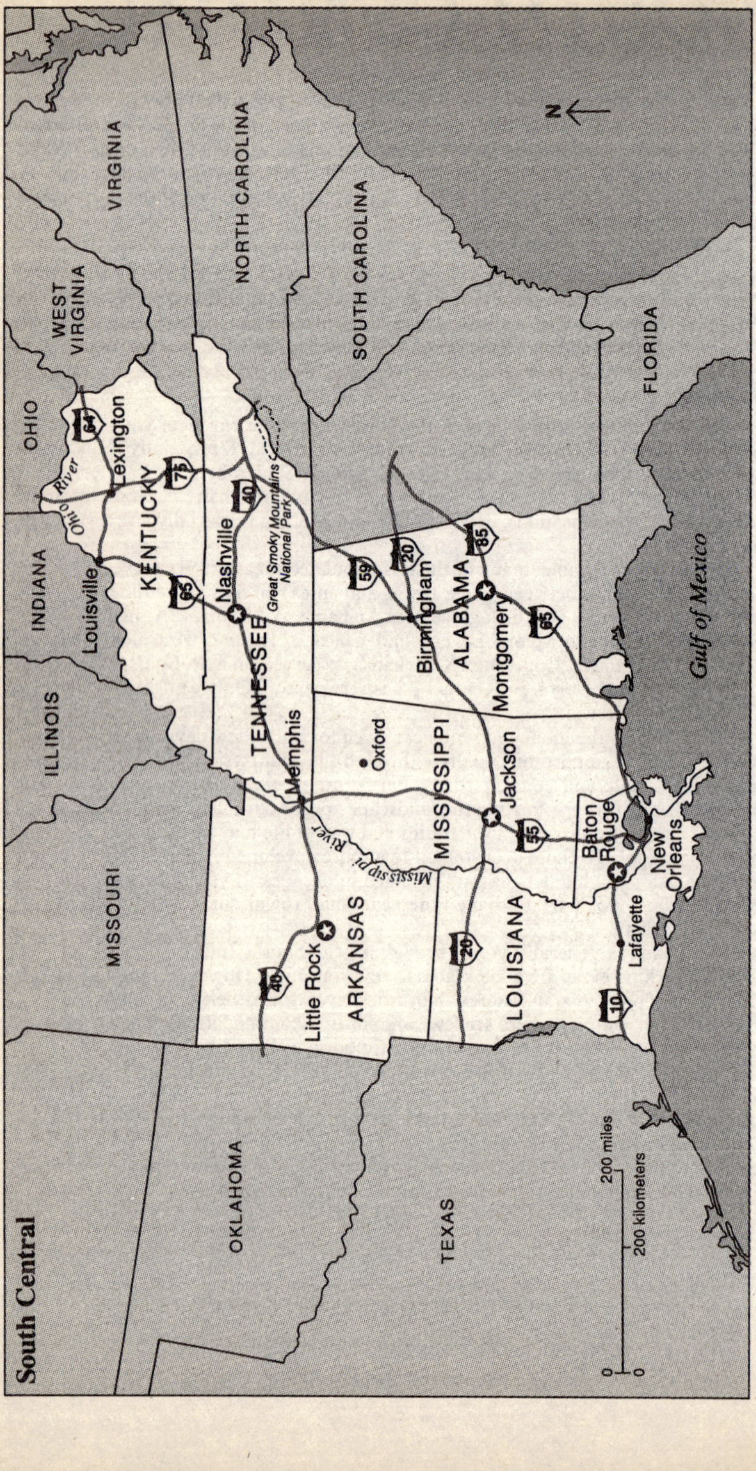
South Central
OHIO
INDIANA
ILLINOIS
MISSOURI
OKLAHOMA
TEXAS
WEST VIRGINIA
VIRGINIA
NORTH CAROLINA
SOUTH CAROLINA
FLORIDA
KENTUCKY
TENNESSEE
ARKANSAS
MISSISSIPPI
ALABAMA
LOUISIANA
Ohio River
Mississippi River
Gulf of Mexico
Lexington
Louisville
Nashville
Memphis
Little Rock
Oxford
Jackson
Birmingham
Montgomery
Baton Rouge
New Orleans
Lafayette
Great Smoky Mountains National Park
64
75
65
40
59
20
85
55
10
N
200 miles
200 kilometers
0
0

Alabama

Change comes slowly to Alabama, but this is no longer a backwards-looking state. Alabamans are becoming more prosperous as their economy transforms from an agricultural to an industrial base. The "Alabama Reunion" is the state's current campaign to retrieve Alabama's expatriates. Boasting about social change, development, and a new awareness in a state that has formerly lagged behind, Alabama is on the move.

Visit Mobile and Montgomery if you need convincing. Three-and-a-half turbulent decades after Rosa Parks refused to relinquish her seat at the front of a Montgomery bus, urban Alabama has matured into an appropriate cultural center for a state proud of its history. These cities have revitalized themselves into fitting showpieces of a truly scenic and multifaceted state, in which white sand beaches line the Gulf Coast and the fertile southern lowlands rise gently to the plateaus and peaks of the Appalachian north.

Practical Information

Capital: Montgomery.

Tourist Information: Alabama Bureau of Tourism and Travel, (261-4169, 800-252-2262 outside AL). Open Mon.-Fri. 8am-5pm. **Travel Council,** 600 Adams Ave., #254, Montgomery 36104 (263-3407). **Division of Parks,** 64 N. Union St., Montgomery 36130.

Time Zone: Central (1 hr. behind Eastern). **Postal Abbreviation:** AL.

Montgomery

The stars and bars of the Confederate flag grace Montgomery as often as do the more familiar stars and stripes. This is a proud city, rich in history and Southern heritage and politically prominent. While its industry and agriculture have always played second fiddle to Birmingham's, the expansive metropolis to the north, Montgomery has grown as a result of its position as the state's center of government and culture.

The capital of the Confederacy in 1861, this former slave-holding town became the focus of the nationwide civil rights effort a century later, culminating in Martin Luther King's 1965 march from Selma to the state capitol's steps. Today, progress has been made in addressing Montgomery's legacy of racial tensions. The scheduled erection of a civil rights memorial is symbolic of the direction in which this state capitol heads.

Practical Information

Emergency: 911.

Visitor Information: Visitor Information Center, 220 N. Hull St. (262-0013). Open Mon.-Fri. 8:30am-4:30pm, Sat.-Sun. 10am-4pm. **Chamber of Commerce,** 41 Commerce St. (834-5200). Open Mon.-Fri. 8:30am-5pm.

Travelers Aid: 265-0568. 24 hours. Operated by Salvation Army.

Greyhound/Trailways: 210 S. Court St. (264-4518). To: Birmingham (7 per day, 3 hr., $14); Mobile ($7 per day, 4 hr., $25); and Tuskegee (8 per day, 1 hr., $6).Open 24 hours.

Montgomery Area Transit System (MATS): 701 N. McDonough St. (262-7321). Operates throughout the metropolitan area Mon.-Sat. 5 or 6am-5pm. Fare 80¢, transfers 10¢.

Taxi: Yellow Cab, 262-5225. $1 first 1/5 mile; $1 each additional mile.

Help Lines: Council Against Rape, 264-7273. **Help-A-Crisis,** 279-7837.

Post Office: 135 Catoma St. (284-7576). Open Mon.-Fri. 8am-5pm, Sat. 8am-noon. **ZIP code:** 36104.

Area Code: 205.

Montgomery is located at the intersection of I-65 and I-85, in south central Alabama, 91 miles south of Birmingham, 192 miles north of Mobile and the Gulf Coast. The downtown follows a grid pattern: **Madison Avenue** and **Dexter Avenue** are the major east-west routes; **Perry Street** and **Lawrence Street** run north-south.

Accommodations

Accommodations are not hard to find for those with a car; I-65 at the Southern Blvd. exit overflows with cheap beds. The **Capitol Inn** and **Town Plaza** are well-kept budget motels centrally located in the downtown historic district.

Capitol Inn, 205 N. Goldthwaite St. at Heron St. (265-0541), downtown, on a hill overlooking the city. Near the bus station. Immaculately kept. Pool. Singles $25. Doubles $30.

Town Plaza, 743 Madison Ave. (269-1561) at N. Ripley St. Venerable, with somewhat comfortable rooms. Bring your own blanket as they provide only a sheet and a bedspread, and bring your own A/C as there are fans only. Adults only. Singles $18. Doubles $22.

The Inn South, 4243 Inn South Ave. (288-7999). Nice rooms, but way out. Rooms under $25.

Whitley Hotel, 231 Montgomery St. (262-6461), between Molton and Lee St., downtown. Respectable rooms in a once-grand hotel. Only a handful of rooms are rented out. Singles $31. Doubles $38.

KOA Campground, ¼ mile south of Hope Hull exit (288-0728), 4 miles from town. Swimming pool. Tent sites $9.50, with water and electricity $13.

Food

The Farmer's Market Cafeteria, 315 N. McDonough St. (262-9163). Half of Montgomery lunches here on buffet-style meals, where there are dozens of tables and hardly an empty seat. Two meat dishes and 4 vegetables $4. Open Mon.-Fri. 5am-2pm.

Chris's Hot Dogs, 138 Dexter Ave. (265-6850). A Montgomery institution with 60 years under its belt. This is where the other half of Montgomery eats lunch. Gourmet hot dogs ($1.20-2) and thick Brunswick stew ($1). Open Mon.-Thurs. 7:30am-8pm, Fri. 7:30am-9pm, Sat. 10am-8pm.

The China House, 701 Madison Ave. (832-4004), 2 blocks from the Town Plaza Motel. Chinese fast food cooked in 2 giant woks 5 feet from your nose. The chef prepares egg drop soup (85¢) with a flamboyance that rivals that of the greatest Asian culinary masters. The *lo mein* dishes prompt equally fiery displays ($3.75). Open Mon.-Thurs. 11am-9pm, Fri. 11am-8pm, Sat. 11am-7pm.

Sights

The Reverend Martin Luther King, Jr. and other civil rights leaders organized the 1955 Montgomery bus boycott from the **Dexter Avenue King Memorial Baptist Church,** 454 Dexter Ave. (263-3970), where King was pastor. Ten years later, King led the civil rights march from Selma, Alabama, past this church to the Montgomery apitol. The basement mural chronicles the movement's struggle during the 1960s. (Open Mon.-Fri. 8:30am-4:30pm. Free. Call ahead.)

Three blocks north, at Hull and Madison, is **Old Alabama Town,** a historic district on North Hull St. The district is an artfully maintained complex of 19th-century buildings including a pioneer homestead, an 1892 grocery, a schoolhouse, an early African-American church, and a freed slave's house. Open Mon.-Sat. 9:30am-3:30pm, Sun. 1:30-3:30pm. Admission $5, ages 5-18 $1.50.) Begin your tour at the **Information Center,** 310 North Hull St. (263-4355).

Behind the **State Capitol** (presently closed to the public due to restoration) stands the elegant **First White House of the Confederacy,** 644 Washington Ave. (261-

4624), Jefferson Davis's home when he was president of the Confederacy. (Open Mon.-Fri. 8am-4:30pm, Sat.-Sun. 9am-4:30pm. Free.)

The **Wynton M. Blount Cultural Park,** located southeast of the city off Woodmere Blvd., is the city's impressive new center for the humanities. **The Alabama Shakespeare Festival,** 1 Festival Dr. (277-2273), is one of the most remarkable sights in the South. This $22 million professional complex attracts some of the best Shakespearean actors and scholars in the world. The Festival, set in an English country park, stages a variety of plays, including Broadway shows. Adjacent to the Shakespeare Festival, the **Montgomery Museum of Fine Arts** houses a substantial collection of 19th- and 20th-century paintings and graphics, and a unique interactive children's exhibit, "Artworks." (Open Tues.-Wed. and Fri.-Sat. 10am-5pm, Thurs. 10am-9pm, and Sun. noon-5pm. Free.) For further information on events in the city, call the chamber of commerce's **FunPhone** (265-2783), a 24-hour recording.

Tuskegee

In the post-Reconstruction Era, when the former Confederate states were beginning to encode segregation with Jim Crow laws, the status of African-Americans virtually returned to that of the days of slavery. Booker T. Washington, a former slave, believed that African-Americans could best combat repression through self-education and an acceptance of the limits on the possibility of black emancipation. The curriculum at Washington's college, now **Tuskegee University,** revolved around practical endeavors such as agriculture and carpentry. Almost all of the campus buildings were built by students. George Washington Carver, an agricultural scientist who became head of the U.S. Agricultural Department, researched and taught at Tuskegee, discovering that he could prepare a full, varied meal using only one ingredient: the peanut.

Now more academically oriented, Tuskegee covers over 160 acres, and the buildings of Washington's original institute comprise a national historical site. A walking tour of the campus begins at the **Carver Museum.** Inside the museum is the Visitor Orientation Center (727-6390). (Both open daily 9am-4:30pm. Museum is free.) **The Oaks,** Old Montgomery Rd., is a restored version of Washington's home. (Free.)

Stay on campus in **Dorothy Hall** 1212 Old Montgomery Rd. (727-8753; singles $23.54; doubles $27.89). Some rooms are available for $11 with shared bath and no A/C. Reservations advisable. The **Dorothy Hall Cafeteria** serves breakfast Mon.-Fri. 7:30-9am and lunch Mon.-Fri. 11:30am-1pm. The **University Cafeteria** serves breakfast, lunch, and dinner.

To get to Tuskegee, take I-85 toward Atlanta and exit at Rte. 81 south. Turn right at the intersection of Rte. 81 and Old Montgomery Rd. (Rte. 126). **Greyhound** also has frequent service from Montgomery (1 hr., $6).

Tuskegee's **ZIP code** is 36083. The **area code** is 205.

Mobile

Mobilians call their hometown the "South's finest city." And they just may be right. Mobile (pronounced mo-BEEL) is a well-kept secret; the splendor of its antebellum mansions, the serenity of its azalea-lined streets, and the warmth of both its climate and its people are enticing. And for the budget traveler, the low prices only add to the charm. Mobile is not another sleepy Southern city, but an energetic and thriving port. It is a city that has protected the South since the colonial days, and its preeminence in the Gulf Coast region is as marked today as it was in the 18th century.

Practical Information

Emergency: 911.

Visitor Information: Fort Condé Information Center, 150 S. Royal St. (434-7304), in a reconstructed French fort near Government St. Open daily 8am-5pm.**Mobile Convention and Visitors Bureau,** 1 St. Louis Center, #2002 (433-5100; 800-662-6282 outside AL). Open Mon.-Fri. 8am-5pm.

Travelers Aid: 438-1625. Lines open Mon.-Fri. 9am-4:30pm. Operated by the Salvation Army; ask for Travelers Services.

Greyhound/Trailways: 201 Government Blvd. (432-1861), at S. Conception, downtown. To: New Orleans ($24), Montgomery ($25), and Birmingham ($34). Open 24 hours.

Mobile Transit Authority (MTA): 344-5656. Operates Mon.-Sat. 6am-7pm. Fare 50¢. Major depot is at Bienville Sq., St. Joseph, and Dauphin St.

Taxi: Yellow Cab, 432-7711.

Help Lines: Rape Crisis, 473-7273. **Crisis Counseling,** 666-7900. 24 hours.

Post Office: 250 St. Joseph St. (694-5917). Open Mon.-Fri. 8am-4:30pm, Sat. 8am-noon. **ZIP code:** 36601.

Area Code: 205.

Mobile Bay, on the Gulf of Mexico, is about 135 miles east of New Orleans. The downtown district fronts the Mobile River. **Dauphin ("Doffin") Street** and **Government Boulevard** are the major east-west routes. **Royal Street** and **St. Joseph Street** are the north-south byways. Some of Mobile's major attractions are outside of downtown. The *U.S.S. Alabama* is off the causeway leading out of the city; Dauphin Island is 30 miles south.

Accommodations and Camping

Accommodations are both reasonable and accessible, but stop at the Fort Condé Information Center first; they'll make reservations for you and get you a 10 to 15 percent discount. The MTA runs a "Government St." bus regularly which reaches the Government St. motels listed below, but they are all within a 15-minute walk from downtown. For information on the area's many B&B's, contact **Bed and Breakfast Mobile,** P.O. Box 66261, Mobile, 36606 (205-473-2939).

Economy Inn, 1119 Government St. (433-8800), in the Church St. historic district. Nice, comfortable rooms. Pool. A 15-minute walk to downtown, less to the museums. Singles $18. Doubles $25. $2 extra for a ground floor room.

Park Inn Downtown, 255 Church St. (433-6923). Between the bus station and Fort Condé. Rooms are typically motelish, but comfortable. Pool. This motel has a habit of changing its name, so check with Fort Condé's first; there they'll also bring the rates down to $25 for a single. Singles $32. Doubles $36.

Towne House Inn, 1061 Government St. (438-4653). Adequate rooms at a very affordable price. Not terribly well kept. Pool. Singles $17. Doubles $27.

Heart of Mobile Inn, 559 Government St. (433-0590). Fair rooms at a fair price, close to downtown. On the dingy side. Singles $22. Doubles $28. (Tax included.)

Admiral Semmes, 250 Government St. (432-4441), across the street from the bus station. Large, venerable, somewhat shabby rooms with a balcony overlooking the pool. Singles $30. Doubles $35.

I-10 Kampground, 400 Theodore Dawes Rd. E. (653-9816), 7½ miles west on I-10 (exit 13). Pool and laundry facilities. No public transportation. Sites $12.

Food

Unfortunately, Mobile has few inexpensive restaurants outside the fast food strips along Government St. and Airport Blvd. **Wintzels,** 605 Dauphin St. (433-1004),

6 blocks west of downtown, has famous seafood at good prices (crab omelette sandwich $4) and an excellent salad bar. (Open Mon.-Sat. 11am-9pm.) **Argiro's**, Battleship Pkwy. (626-1060), next to the *U.S.S. Alabama,* provides both cheap sandwiches ($2-3) and local color; businessmen and sailors frequent this small shop. (Open Mon.-Thurs. 8am-9pm, Fri.-Sat. 8am-10pm, Sun. 10am-6pm.) An incredible bargain downtown, in the basement of the First National Bank building, is **Zitsos Cafeteria,** 31 N. Royal St. (438-3233). Open for breakfast and lunch weekdays, entrees range from 50¢ to $2 and there is no ambience whatsoever.

Sights and Entertainment

Mobile encompasses four historic districts: **Church Street, DeToni Square, Oakleigh Garden,** and **Old Dauphin Way.** Each offers a unique array of architectural styles. The information center can give you maps for walking or driving tours of the former residences of cotton brokers and river pilots as well as the "shot-gun cottages" of their servants.

The **Church Street East District** (Church St. is divided into east and west subdistricts) is closest to downtown and is the second-oldest of the districts. The homes and buildings all date from after the 1839 fire, and therefore showcase the popular American architectural styles of the mid- to late 19th century, including Federal, Greek Revival, Queen Anne, and Victorian.

In the **DeToni Historical District,** north of downtown, tour the **Richards-DAR House,** 256 North Joachim St. (434-7320), an award-winning example of America's antebellum Italianate architectural style. The house has been tastefully restored. On slow days the staff will invite you in for tea and cookies. (Open Tues.-Sat. 10am-4pm, Sun. 1-4pm. Tours $2, children 50¢.) **Christ Church,** 115 S. Conception St. (433-1842), lies opposite the tourist office at Fort Condé. Dedicated in 1842, the church contains beautiful German, Italian, and Tiffany stained glass windows.

One of the most elegant buildings in the historic collection is **Oakleigh,** 350 Oakleigh Place (432-1281), with its cantilevered staircase and enormous windows that open onto all the balconies upstairs. Inside, a museum contains furnishings of the early Victorian, Empire, and Regency periods. (Tours every ½ hr., last tour leaves at 3:30pm. Open Mon.-Sat. 10am-4pm, Sun. 2-4pm. Admission $4, seniors $3, college students with ID $2, children $1.)

Two downtown museums are worth visiting. The **Museum of the City of Mobile,** 355 Government St. (438-7569), displays artifacts representative of the different eras of Mobile's history, including the Mardi Gras presentation, a reminder that it was not New Orleans but Mobile that started this traditional festival on the Gulf Coast.

The battleship *U.S.S. Alabama,* permanently moored at **Battleship Park** (433-2703), was involved in every major World War II battle in the Pacific. The park is at the entrance of the Bankhead Tunnel, 2½ miles east of town on I-10. Berthed along its port side is one of the most famous submarines of the war, the *U.S.S. Drum.* (Open daily 8am-sunset. Admission $5, ages 6-11 $2.50. Parking $1.)

Gray Line of Mobile (432-2229) leads interesting sightseeing tours of the downtown historic areas twice daily. (Tours Mon.-Sat. 10:30am and 2pm, Sun. 2pm. 1 hr-long. Fare $7, children $3.)

For nighttime entertainment, stop in at **Trinity's Downtown,** 465 Auditorium Dr. (432-0000), where bands play rock and reggae Wednesday through Saturday nights. (Open Mon.-Thurs. 11am-midnight, Fri.-Sat. 11am-2am.) **Adam's,** at the Ramada Inn, 600 S. Beltline Hwy, (344-8030), is the up-and-coming hotspot of Mobile nightlife. (Open nightly until 1am.)

For information on events and specific dates, call the 24-hour recording **Tel-Events** (342-0133).

Arkansas

The smallest state (except for Hawaii) west of the Mississippi, Arkansas stubbornly resists categorization. Only the southeastern portion of the state resembles the flat, agricultural land of the Deep South. The rest of Arkansas has a little bit of everything: culturally autonomous Little Rock, a friendly community without all the grit and grime of most big cities; Hot Springs and Eureka Springs, convenient respites from the relentless southern summer heat; the rivers and hills of the Ozark Mountains, some of the most scenic areas of the country; and the mountains of the northwest.

For outdoors-folk, this state offers ideal camping, fishing, and the like. The numerous national and state parks are among the country's less frequented and most scenic.

Practical Information

Capital: Little Rock.

Tourist Information: Arkansas Dept. of Parks and Tourism, 1 Capitol Mall, Little Rock 72201 (800-643-8383 or 501-682-7777).

Time Zone: Central (1 hr. behind Eastern). **Postal Abbreviation:** AR.

Little Rock

Little Rock straddles the Arkansas River and serves as the political and geographical center of the state. An immaculate city, surrounded by green, rolling hills, Little Rock has begun to revitalize its downtown area. The new pedestrian mall on Main St. has begun a "yuppification" of this sleepy southern city. Unfortunately, as in other towns that cater primarily to a three-piece-suit crowd, there is a limited amount of entertainment for the budget traveler. After exhausting Little Rock's historic sites and homes, you'll find that the city's next best feature is its central location; the hot springs beckon to the west, the Ozark Mountains to the northwest.

Practical Information

Emergency: 911.

Visitor Information: Arkansas Dept. of Parks and Tourism, 1 Capitol Mall (800-643-8383 out-of-state or 800-482-8989 in-state), directly behind the capitol building. **Little Rock Bureau for Conventions and Visitors,** corner of Markham and Main St. (376-4781), near the Greyhound station. Open Mon.-Fri. 9am-3:30pm, closed for lunch. Call **Telefun** (372-3399) for listing of activities in Little Rock.

Amtrak: Markham and Victory St. (372-6841 or 800-872-7245), near downtown. To: St. Louis (3 per week, 7 hr., $65) and Dallas (3 per week, 7 hr., $72).

Greyhound/Trailways, 118 E. Washington St. (372-1861), across the river in North Little Rock. Use the walkway over the bridge to get downtown. Cab fare should run less than $4. To: St. Louis ($54), New Orleans ($65), and Memphis ($23).

Central Arkansas Transit (CAT): 614 Center St. (375-1163). Regular buses every ½-hr. Mon.-Sat. 6am-6pm. Very reliable service. Fare 75¢.

Taxi: Black and White Cab, (374-0333). Base fare 90¢, then 90¢ per mile.

Help Lines: Rape Crisis: 375-5181, 24 hours. **Weather line:** 834-0316.

Post Office: 600 W. Capitol and 5th St. (377-6470). Open Mon.-Fri. 7am-5:15pm. **ZIP code:** 72201.

Area Code: 501.

Little Rock is situated in the middle of Arkansas, on I-40 140 miles west of Memphis, TN, and 335 miles east of Oklahoma City, OK. **I-30** also passes through Little Rock, 320 miles northeast of Dallas, TX. Most of Little Rock's streets were "planned" with no apparent pattern in mind. **Broadway** and **Main** are the major north-south arteries. **Markham** and all streets numbered 1-36 run east-west.

Accommodations and Camping

The Quapaw Inn Bed and Breakfast, 1868 S. Gaines St. (376-6873), 2 blocks west of 17th and Broadway. This quaint Victorian house is pricey for 1 person, but for 2, it's *the* place to stay in Little Rock. Extremely friendly proprietor. Breakfast is huge and delicious. (Rooms $40-50, $10 less for one person.) Call in advance and ask for the **Let's Go** discount.

Econolodge, 322 E. Capitol (376-3661). Downtown. Clean, comfortable, econo-like. Pool. Unsafe area at night. Singles $25. Doubles $32.

Little Rock Inn, 6th and Center St. (376-8301), downtown. Rooms are attractive and fairly clean. Saloon and pool. Not the greatest bunch of transients, but safe. Often full. Singles $27.77. Doubles $33.12.

Deluxe Inn, 308 E. Capitol (375-6411), downtown. Clean rooms, but the place is somewhat seedy and the area is unsafe at night. Pool and cable TV. Singles $20. Doubles $26.

KOA Campground, North Little Rock, Crystal Hill Rd. (758-4598), between exit 12 on I-430 and exit 148 on I-48, 7 miles from downtown. From $14, hookups extra.

Sands RV Park, on Chicot Rd. S. (565-7491), at I-30 junction. RVs only. $10 for 2, each additional person $2.

Food

Little distinguishes Little Rock's local cuisine, although several eateries do offer decent bargains.

Juanita's, 1300 S. Main St. (372-1228). The city's best Mexican food in a fun, loud, cantina atmosphere. Reasonable prices (entrees $6-10), nightly entertainment, and a hoppin' bar. Try Marguerita night on Monday ($1.25), or Sat. champagne brunch ($1 a glass). Open Mon.-Fri. 11:30am,-2:30pm and 5:30-10pm, Sat. noon-10:30pm, and Sun. 5-9pm.

Hungry's Cafe, 1001 W. 7th St. (372-9720). Loud and fun, serving solid breakfast and lunch specials ranging from shrimp to enchiladas, along with 2 vegetables and bread for under $4. Open Mon.-Fri. 6am-2pm.

The Oyster Bar, 3003 W. Markham St. (666-9954). Seafood and "Po' Boy" sandwiches at reasonable prices ($5-7). Big screen TV, pool tables, entertainment, cheap draft beer, and a decidedly laid-back atmosphere where paper towel rolls take the place of napkins. A lot of fun for eating or just mingling. Open Mon.-Thurs. 11am-10pm, Fri.-Sat. 11am-10:30pm, happy hour Mon.-Fri. 3-6:30pm.

White Water Tavern, 2500 7th St. (374-3801). Popular gathering place and watering hole, serving Southern cooking (full meal under $5). Try a foot-long hotdog ($2.50). Full of local color. Open Mon.-Sat. 11am-2am.

Jimmy's Serious Sandwiches, 5116 W. Markham St. (666-3354), across from War Memorial Stadium. Delicious sandwiches, including "The Garden," a national award-winner. Very serious sandwiches with order of soup or fruit salad under $5. Open Mon.-Fri. 11am-9pm, Sat. 11am-3pm.

Center Street Cafe, 612 Center St. (372-9485). The business luncheon spot frequented by the blue-suit crowd. Home-cooked specialties like chicken-fried steak ($4.45), as well as sandwiches and salads. Entrees (which includes two veggies and warm biscuits) under $5. Open Mon.-Fri. 11am-2pm.

Sights

Little Rock's historic downtown district is known as the **Quapaw Quarter.** It includes the **Governor's Mansion,** 1800 Center St., and the **State Capitol** (682-5080) at the west end of Capitol St. (Free 45-min. tours on the hr., Mon.-Fri. 9am-4pm, Sat. 10am-5pm, and Sun. 1-5pm. Call in advance on weekends.) The **Old State**

House, 300 W. Markham St. (371-1749), boasts a large collection of 19th-century Arkansas memorabilia. (Open Mon.-Sat. 9am-5pm, Sun. 1-5pm. Free.) The worthwhile **Arkansas Territorial Restoration,** 214 E. Third St. (371-2348) is also a step into the state's past, featuring three restored, previously prominent Little Rock residences from the mid-19th century. (Open Mon.-Sat. 9-11am and 1-4pm, Sun. 1-5pm. 50-min. tours every hr. on the hr. Free first Sun. of the month.) The **War Memorial Park,** just northwest of the State Capitol, has a small amusement park on the grounds.

A mile south of downtown is **MacArthur Park,** elegant grounds home to two interesting museums. The **Museum of Science and History** (628-3521) is housed in the old arsenal building where General Douglas MacArthur was born. The museum is dedicated to explaining "Arkansas, Its Land and People," and is particulary suited for children. (Open Mon.-Sat. 9am-4:30pm, Sun. 1-4:30pm. Admission $1. Mon. free.)

The **Old Mill Park,** (682-7777) in North Little Rock, features an old mill house and several bridges covered with twining tree branches and vines. All of these structures were constructed in the Depression era as part of the Works Progress Administration program for artisans. This site was a setting for the opening scenes of *Gone With the Wind.*

Closer to home, along the banks of the Arkansas River, you'll find **Riverfront Park,** a pleasant place for a walk, home to the legendary "Little Rock" itself. Access is best through the back of the Excelsior Hotel at Markham and Center St. If you like riverboats, take a ride on the paddle wheeler **Spirit** (376-4150; 1-hr. cruises $5, children $2.75). Departs from the North Little Rock side of the Arkansas River Tues.-Sat. at 2pm.) Natives of the town celebrate their waterway every year at **Riverfest.**

About 15 miles east on Rte. 165 is the **Toltec Mounds State Park** (961-9442), where visitors can see the remains of an ancient Native American religious shrine. (Open Tues.-Sat. 8am-5pm, Sun. noon-5pm. Admission $1.50, ages 6-15 50¢.) Thirteen miles west of Little Rock on Rte. 10 and then 2 miles north on Rte. 300 is **Pinnacle Mountain State Park,** a fairly tame "wilderness park." The 1000-foot climb to the top is moderately steep, but the summit view is superb. Look for the fossils, and bring water with you on the hike. Information is available from the Superintendent at Pinnacle Mountain State Park, R 1, Roland Rd., P.O. Box 34, Roland 72135 (868-5806). It's worth visiting, but make it a daytrip only; there are no camping facilities.

Entertainment and Nightlife

Little Rock has an active cultural life, including a symphony, an opera theater, and community theaters. Conducted by Robert Henderson, the **Arkansas Symphony,** 2500 N. Tyler (666-1761), performs in Robinson Auditorium from October to March. (Tickets $3-9; student rush tickets available 10 min. before performance $2.)

The **Arkansas Opera Theatre** (666-1761), 1011 W. 6th St., performs in September, December, and April at the Arkansas Art Center. (Tickets $8.50 and $12.50.) **Ballet Arkansas,** at the Tanglewood Center (666-0756), performs in the spring and fall. The Arts Center (372-4000) also sponsors free summer theatrical and musical performances. The **Arkansas Repertory Theatre,** at 6th and Main St. (378-0405), and the **Community Theatre of Little Rock,** 1501 Maryland (376-4582), turn out quality dramatic productions.

You can also spend an evening watching Little Rock's winning minor league baseball team, the **Arkansas Travelers** (an AA affiliate of the St. Louis Cardinals), at their splendid 1930s ballpark, Ray Winder Field. (664-1555. Tickets $1.)

Other forms of nightlife are limited. There's dancing at **Bennigan's,** 104 South University (664-8160), at Markham; the crowd is young and lively. (Open Mon.-Sat. 11am-2pm. $2 cover on weekends.) The **Oyster Bar** (see Food above) has great bands on Fridays and Saturdays. **Gabriels on Main Street,** 501 Main St. (376-6113), draws a professional crowd to hear music of the 50s, 60s and 70s and live bands on weekends. (Open Mon.-Sat. 11am-1am.) For further information about what's happening in Little Rock, consult the free bi-weekly guide *Spectrum* or the monthly *Today.*

Hot Springs

Get out of Little Rock and come to Hot Springs, an old-fashioned spa town enmeshed in a national park established to preserve the natural springs. The water bubbles up from the oak- and hickory-covered Hot Springs Mountain. When it reaches the surface, it is 143°F and totally pure—NASA used the water to protect the Apollo mission moon rocks from bacteria. Famous visitors to the waters have included Hernando de Soto, who discovered the springs in 1541, Franklin D. Roosevelt, and Al Capone.

Hot Springs had its heyday in the 1920s, when the medicinal properties and healing powers of the springs made it one of the country's most popular resorts. The town has been in decline since the 1940s, however, and today seems like a city that was on its way to becoming a ghost town but changed its mind halfway through. There are some signs of revitalization, however, and the national park, the springs, and old-fashioned town are still worth visiting. Furthermore, it is one of the least expensive resort towns in the nation.

On Bathhouse Row, the **Fordyce** functions as the information center for the national park. During the summer it runs hourly 45-minute **Thermal Features Tours,** from 10:15am-4:15pm, at 15 minutes past each hour. The free tour provides a fascinating introduction to the springs. The **Buckstaff** (623-2308) is the only still functioning bathhouse along the row. Baths are $9.50, massages $10. Open Mon.-Fri. 7-11:45am and 1:30-3pm, Sat. 7-11:45am. Less expensive is the **Hot Springs Health Spa,** N. 500 Reserve. Bath $8, massage $10. Open daily 9am-9pm.

When you're not bathing in the springs or hiking in the park, try cruising Lake Hamilton on the **Belle of Hot Springs,** with one-hour narrated tours alongside the Ouachita Mountains and Lake Hamilton mansions. (Fare $7, children $3. Call 525-4438 for more information.) In town, the **Mountain Valley Spring Water Company,** 150 Central Ave. (623-6671), offers free samples and tours of its national headquarters. The **Magic Springs** amusement park is at 2001 Hwy. 70 E. (624-5411 in Hot Springs; 800-643-1212 outside AR. Open in summer Sun.-Fri. 10am-6pm, Sat. 10am-11pm. Admission $10, ages 3-11 $9).

The **Bathhouse Show,** 701 Central Ave., (623-1415) is a must see. A two-hour comedy-musical-variety show, the show is a hilarious and fun-filled spectacle for the whole family, tracing the history of Hot Springs musically, from the "boogie-woogie" years to the rock 'n' roll era. Performances Tues.-Sun. 8pm. Call ahead for reservations.

Most of the town shuts down by dusk, but for late evening entertainment try **Dad's Place,** 218 Park St. (623-3311) at the Ramada Inn. Live country and pop bands perform nightly until 2am. The **Saw Mill Depot,** at Broadway and Market St. (623-3082), draws a local crowd and stays open even later, Mon.-Fri. 11am-3am, Sat. 5:30pm-3am. Farther out, **Pope's 270 Club,** 4824 Malvern Rd. (262-9974), is an old-fashioned place where you can kill time over a few beers and tune out to the jukebox. Try a game of pool or shuffleboard—you may end up in one of the tournaments. (Open Mon.-Sat. 10am-2am.)

Hot Springs has a number of small restaurants and watering holes worth visiting. Snack on *beignets* (doughnuts without a hole) and *café au lait* at **Café New Orleans,** 210 Central Ave. (624-3200; open daily until 11:30pm. Live entertainment Fri. and Sat. nights.) **Rod's Pizza Cellar,** at Spring and Broadway, serves delicious Italian specialties for under $7. **Martin's Recreation Center,** 831 Central Ave. (623-5791), is really friendly and serves inexpensive breakfasts (under $3) and plate lunches (under $4; open Mon.-Sat. 5:30am-5:30pm).

For the budget traveler who has a little bit extra to spend, the **Arlington Hotel,** at Fountain and Central St. (623-7771), is a world-class resort—of yesteryear—at very reasonable rates. Singles from $38, family rates from $56. For the less extravagant, the **Best Motel,** 630 Ouachita (624-5736), has small, cabin-like rooms just south of downtown. Singles $20. Doubles $30. The **Perry Plaza Motel,** 1007 Park Ave. on Hwy. 7 (623-9814), offers air-conditioned suites with a bedroom, bathroom, and kitchen. (Sept.-Dec. and May $20; Feb.-April $40; rest of year $25. Each additional person $5.) The motels clustered along Hwy. 7 and 88 are similarly priced, although rates go up during the tourist season (Feb.-April). Camping is cheaper (see State Parks below).

Before touring Hot Springs, you should stop by the **Visitors Center,** downtown at the corner of Central and Reserve St. (624-3383). Visitors should remember that Hot Springs becomes especially crowded during the horse racing season at nearby **Oaklawn** racetrack (Feb.-April).

Hot Springs's **ZIP code** is 71901. The **area code** is 501.

State Parks Nearby

Lake Catherine Park is readily accessible by car from Hot Springs. The park covers over 2000 acres of Ouachita Mountain, on the shores of beautiful Lake Catherine. Camping starts at $5 per day (844-4176). Take exit 97 off I-30 and go 12 miles north on Rte. 171. (Canoe rentals $10 per day, power boats $14 per ½-day, $21 per day.)

Lake Ouachita Park is situated on the largest of three artificial lakes near Hot Springs. The EPA considers it the second-cleanest lake in the nation. Travel 3 miles west of Hot Springs on U.S. 270, then 12 miles north on Rte. 227. Numerous islands lie just offshore where you can escape civilization and enjoy the quiet coves and rocky beaches. Fishing is plentiful, and camping is available from $5 per day (767-9366); fishing boats rent for $5 per day.

Ozarks

Beaten and worn by ages of weathering, one of the world's oldest mountain ranges now barely surpasses hill status in height. The terrain, though, is something more than hilly: Twisting switchback roads, steep scenic bluffs, and lush woods make for a challenging vacationland. Settling the land in northern Arkansas and southern Missouri required self-relaince and stubbornness, and the Ozark folk culture today is marked by reclusiveness and a fierce concern for preserving their traditional way of life.

Today's traveler should find things a bit tamer than they were a century ago. The Ozarks have become a major resort area for Missouri, Arkansas, and neighboring states, so there are plenty of tacky gift shops around. The scenery, however, remains outstandingly rugged; this area was made for hiking. Arkansas folk love to canoe, fish, and float down the Ozarks' rivers, especially the Buffalo; likeminded travelers should arrive before mid-summer, when the rivers begin to run too low for sport.

Hitching is good, and generally safe. Few buses go into the area; drivers should follow Rte. 7, 71, or 23 for best access and views. The **Arkansas Department of Parks and Tourism** (800-643-8383; see Arkansas Practical Information) can also help out. If you want to paddle a portion of the **Buffalo National River,** contact the Buffalo Point Concessions, Rte. A, P.O. Box 214, Yellville 72687 (449-6206), or the Superintendent, P.O. Box 1173, Harrison 72601 (741-5443; canoe rental $20 per day, cabin $40 per day). The **Arkansas Bikeways Commission,** 1200 Worthen Bank Bldg., Little Rock 72201, dispenses a bike trail map for the Ozark region. Also, the **Eureka Springs Chamber of Commerce,** (800-643-3546 outside Arkansas; 253-8737 in-state) has excellent vacation planning material.

Eureka Springs

Opinions about Eureka Springs vary; Ozark locals abhor its tourism while many central Arkansans will drive five hours every weekend to enjoy its friendly, Victorian charm, and many erstwhile tourists have become permanent residents. Although Eureka Springs may be the most touristy of the Ozark towns, it offers unique architecture and great entertainment. **The Great Passion Play** (253-9200) has brought fame to Eureka Springs. Modeled after Germany's Oberammergau Passion Play, which depicts Christ's last days, it is staged in a huge amphitheater atop a hill, and draws up to 4000 visitors to each show. (Performances from April-Oct. every evening except Mon. and Thurs. Tickets $7, $8, and $10. Ages 4-11 half-price. For reservations, write to the Great Passion Play, Eureka Springs 72632.) The amphitheater is off Rte. 62, within a mile of town. **Gray Line Bus Tours** (253-9540) provides transportation to and from the play ($2.50 per person round-trip). They pick you up and drop you off at your hotel, motel, or campground. The play is wheelchair-accessible.

If you want outdoor amusement, the **Alpine Hiking Club** (253-9868) sponsors Sunday hikes into the surrounding area. The hikes visit places inaccessible by car. Hikers meet at the **New Orleans Hotel,** 63 Spring St. (spring-fall at 7:15am; winter at 1:15pm.) There are about 80 different hikes and all levels of ability are welcome.

The town is filled with tourist-oriented restaurants. The **Gazebo** (253-9551), at the junction of Rte. 62 and 23 north in the Best Western Eureka Inn, is a popular dining spot with 1890s décor. The **Wagon Wheel,** 84 S. Main St. (253-9934) is a country-western bar decorated with antiques. Get away from the usual tourist glitz and try their ½-pound burgers and huge steak fries ($4). (Open Mon.-Fri. and Sun. 10am-2am).

Accommodations in Eureka Springs are not difficult to find, but prices are impossible to predict. They vary daily according to the crowds, from as low as $18 for singles in August to $45 during April. The **King's Highway Hotel,** 96 King's Hwy. (253-7311), is friendly and generally reasonable. (Singles $26. Doubles $29. $6 extra on weekends. Off-season singles and doubles $20.) The best package deal in town is **Keller's Country Dorm,** Rte. 62 (253-8418), 5 miles east of town. You get a dorm bed, breakfast, dinner, and a reserved ticket to the Passion Play, all for $24 (additional nights $9). You must call Richard Keller ahead of time to get this rate.

There are several **campgrounds** near Eureka Springs. Prices range from $5-10. **Pinehaven Campsites,** on Hwy. 62 (253-9052), 2 miles east of town, charges $9 per tent, $14 for a full RV hookup. Farther, but more picturesque, **Lake Leatherwood,** 2 miles west on Rte. 62 (253-8624), sees more anglers than tourists. Rates begin at $5 per tent. The **KOA** (253-8036) is 3 miles farther on Rte. 62, then ¾ mile south on Rte. 187. (Open April-Oct.) Rates start at $8-10.

For extra help in planning your time here, call the **chamber of commerce** on Rte. 62, just north of Rte. 23 (800-643-3546 or 253-8737; open May-Oct. daily; Nov.-April Mon.-Fri. 9am-5pm.)

Gray Line Bus Company (253-9540) runs two-hour city tours at 9am, 11:30am, and 2:30pm from May 4 to early November. ($8.50, youths $4.50.) The buses will pick you up and take you back to any motel or campground in Eureka Springs. (Pick-up times approximately 15 min. before tour departure time. Out-of-town pickup approximately 30 min. before departure time.) The town is also accessible by trolley. Check schedules with the chamber of commerce.

Eureka Springs's **ZIP code** is 72632. The **area code** is 501.

Near Eureka Springs

Go southeast of Eureka Springs on Rte. 62 and then on Rte. 14 to get to the **Ozark Folk Center** (269-3851), near **Mountain View.** The center is a living museum of the cabin crafts, music, and lore of the Ozarks. Among the craftspeople practicing their trades in the **Crafts Forum** are a blacksmith, a basket maker, a potter, a gunsmith, and a furniture maker. Trams transport guests to the Crafts Forum from the visitors center. (Admission $4.50, children $2.50. Open daily 10am-5pm; Nov.-March open weekends only). Musicians give traditional concerts in the auditorium nightly at 8pm. The audience is invited to participate in the jigs. (Admission $5, children $3.) Seasonal events include the **Arkansas Folk Festival** and the **Mountain and Hammered Dulcimer Championships** (late April), the **Banjo Weekend** (mid-May), and the **Arkansas Old-Time Fiddlers Association State Championship** (late Sept.). The Fiddlers Championship is quite a sight. Hundreds of locals, old pros, and young apprentices play authentic music of the Ozarks. Many of the people in this area are of Scottish or Irish descent, and the music shows clear signs of its Celtic roots.

Blanchard Spring Caverns are 15 miles northwest of Mountain View on Rte. 14 and on the way from (or to) Eureka Springs. Two trails leave from the **visitors center** (757-2211; open daily 9:30am-5pm). The **Dripstone Trail** (almost ½ mile) is a heavily-traveled, paved trackway through an underground water-carved passage. Hardier souls will enjoy the **Discovery Trail** (1.2 miles), which passes the cave's natural entrance and the stream. (Tours $5.) Camping and swimming are allowed.

Kentucky

Native folks say that even if you've never been to Kentucky, you feel as if you're coming home. It's the place to hang up the Home Sweet Home sampler, settle into a comfortable, hand-made rocking chair, and watch the clouds roll over the bluegrass hills. But make no mistake—Kentucky's genteel, down-home style has a sophisticated, cosmopolitan edge. The state that produced frontiersman Daniel Boone and "Honest Abe" Lincoln also reared statesman Henry Clay and the pioneer movie director D.W. Griffith. The thoroughbreds exemplify this best of all. They frolic in the bluegrass pastures, but come Derby Week, the bets are on as they race furiously in the Run for the Roses.

Practical Information

Capital: Frankfort.

Tourist Information: Kentucky Department of Travel Development, Capital Plaza Tower, 22nd floor, Frankfort 40601 (502-564-4930 or 800-225-8747). **Department of Parks,** Capital Plaza Tower, Frankfort 40601 (800-255-7275).

Time Zones: Central (1 hr. behind Eastern) and Eastern. **Postal Abbreviation:** KY.

Louisville

Perched on the Ohio River, just between the North and the South, Louisville (pronounced "LOU-uh-vul") has its own way of doing things. It's an immigrants' town imbued with Southern grace and architecture. Beautiful Victorian neighborhoods surround skyscrapers, smokestacks, and the enormous meat-packing district of Butchertown.

One of Louisville's biggest draws is its plethora of arts offerings. The city boasts a symphony, an opera, ballet, and modern dance troupes, as well as an excellent art museum. Of course, its star feature is the Kentucky Derby. Every year on the first Saturday in May, well-mannered Louisville pulls out all the stops and pours the mint juleps for this week-long gala. The Run for the Roses ends an extravaganza that lures over half a million visitors to a combination carnival, fashion display, and horse show. Kentuckians are deadly serious about their horse racing—the prize for the race is incredible prestige and almost a million bucks.

Practical Information

Emergency: 911.

Visitor Information: Louisville Convention and Visitor Bureau, 400 S. 1st St. (582-3732), at Liberty, downtown. The standard goodies, including some bus schedules. Open Mon.-Fri. 8:30am-5pm, Sat.-Sun. 8:30am-4pm. Visitor centers also at 6th and Jefferson St., and at I-71 as you enter the city. **Information Line,** 800-633-3384; 800-626-5646 outside KY. **Concert Line,** 584-7655. Information on rock, jazz, and country concerts.

Travelers Aid: 585-5961.

Airport: Standiford Field, 367-4636, 15 min. south of downtown on I-65. Take bus #2 into the city.

Greyhound/Trailways: 720 W. Muhammad Ali Blvd. (585-3331), at 7th St. To: Indianapolis (7 per day, 1½ hr., $26.25); Cincinnati (10 per day, 2 hr., $20); Chicago (8 per day, 5 hr., $54); and Nashville (16 per day, 2 hr., $36.50). Storage lockers cost $1 for 24 hours, $3 for each additional day. Open 24 hours.

Transit Authority River City (TARC): 585-1234. Major routes are on the main intersecting streets off Broadway, running east-west, and off 4th St., running north-south. Operates daily 6am-midnight, but varies with bus route. 60¢ during peak hours, 35¢ all other times. Disabled access. Also runs a trolley on 4th Ave. from River Rd. to Broadway (10¢).

Taxi: Yellow Cab, 636-5511. Base rate $1, $1.20 per mile.

Car Rental: Rent-a-Heap-Cheap, 2901 Preston Hwy. (636-9146). $20 per day. Travel limited to a 30-mile radius. Open Mon.-Fri. 9am-5:30pm, Sat. 9am-5pm. Must be 25 and have liability insurance and major credit card or a $110 deposit.

Help Lines: Rape Hot Line, 581-7273. 24 hours. **Crisis Center,** 589-4313. 24 hours. **We Speak Your Language,** 589-4450. Help in 41 languages.

Time Zone: Eastern.

Post Office: Gardner Lane (454-1602). Take the Louisville Zoo exit off Rte. 264, follow Gardner Lane 1 mile. Open Mon.-Fri., 7:30am-7pm, Sat. 7:30am-1pm. **ZIP code:** 40232.

Area Code: 502.

Louisville sits 72 miles west of Lexington, 101 miles southwest of Cincinnati, OH, and 260 miles east of St. Louis, MO. Major highways through the city include I-65 (north-south expressway), I-71, and I-64. The Henry Watterson Expressway, also called I-264, rings the city. The central downtown area is defined north-south by Main Street and Broadway, and east-west by Preston and 19th Street.

Aside from theater and riverfront attractions, much activity in Louisville takes place outside the central city, but the bus system is fairly extensive and goes to all major areas.

Accommodations

Accommodations are easy to find in Louisville, but not particularly cheap. If you want a bed during Derby Week you should make a reservation at least six months to a year in advance, and be prepared to pay high prices. The visitors center (800-626-5646) will help after March 13. During Derby Weekend, the **University of Lousiville** allows camping (tents only) on their Belknap Campus soccer fields, about a mile from the track ($5 per tent). At other times, if you don't choose one of the few affordable options downtown, try one of the many cheap motels that line the roads just outside of town. Newburg and Bardstown are likely spots for budget accommodations.

Motel 6, 3304 Bardstown Rd. (456-2861), about 6 miles southeast of downtown. Take Jefferson St. east from downtown, turn right on Baxter Ave., then bear left on Bardstown Rd., 3 miles down; or take bus #17 from Liberty and 7th St. Pool. Singles $23, each additional person $6. Watch for weekend specials.

San Antonio Inn, 927 S. Second St. (582-3741). The cheapest downtown and looks it. Rough and shabby; women should not stay here. Singles $24. Doubles $29.50. Must be 21 with a photo ID.

Thrifty Dutchman Budget Motel, 3357 Fern Valley Rd. (968-8124), just off I-65. A hike from downtown. Very clean, large rooms. Pool. Singles $24. Doubles $28.

Travelodge, 2nd and Liberty St. (583-2841), downtown, behind the visitors center. Big, clean rooms. Singles $39. Doubles $42. Local calls 50¢.

KOA, 900 Marriot Dr., Clarksville, IN (812-282-4474), across the bridge from downtown, beside I-65; take the Stansifer Ave. exit. Grocery and playground; miniature golf and a fishing lake at the Sheraton across the street. Sites $12.50 for 2, each additional camper $3, under 17 $2. Kozy, kute Kamping Kabins $20.

Food

Louisville's chefs whip up a wide variety of cuisines, but prices can be steep. Butchertown and the Churchill Downs area have several cheap delis and pizza places. Otherwise, you must venture away from downtown for inexpensive, interesting food.

Kienle's, Shelbyville Rd. (897-3920), 3 blocks north of I-264, in the Shelbyville Rd. Plaza. Take bus #19 or #31 from downtown. Gourmet German delicatessen serves lunch (from $4) and dinner ($14-15). Sample Louisville's own Derby Pie, a patented chocolate-nut concoction. Open Tues.-Sat. 10am-9pm. Reservations required for dinner.

Mom's East Side Cafe, 1605 Story Ave. (583-2625), at Frankfort and Ohio St., 1 block from Hadley Pottery. Take bus #15 or 31 from downtown. Just like home—walk through the kitchen on the way to the dining room. Dinners under $4. Sandwiches $2-3. Open Sun.-Thurs. 6am-9pm, Fri.-Sat. 6am-10pm.

Kaelin's, 1801 Newburg Rd. (451-1801), at Speed Ave., 2 miles southwest of downtown. Take bus #21. Now *this* is Kentucky Fried Chicken. Lunch from $4.25, dinner from $5.15. Special smaller portions for seniors, mini-cheeseburgers for kids. Carry-out chicken by the bucket or barrel, chili or condiments by the pint. Open Mon.-Thurs. 11am-11pm, Fri.-Sat. 11am-midnight, Sun. 10am-10pm.

The Old Spaghetti Factory, 235 W. Market St. (581-1070), at 3rd St., downtown. Part of a national chain. Big helpings of spaghetti in a gorgeous remodeled turn-of-the-century department store. Full dinner with salad, bread, and ice cream $4-6. Popular with families—you may have to wait. Open Mon.-Thurs. 5-10pm, Fri.-Sat. 5-11pm, Sun. 4-10pm.

Tumbleweed Mexican Food and Mesquite Grill, 1900 Mellwood Ave. (895-8800). Take Story Ave. east, go a few blocks south on Brownsboro, turn left and go a mile on Mellwood. Huge portions of Tex-Mex favorites in a lively barroom atmosphere. Entrees $4-12. Open Mon.-Thurs. 11am-11pm, Fri.-Sat. 11am-midnight, Sun. noon-11pm.

Horses and Such

Even if you miss the Kentucky Derby, try to catch **Churchill Downs,** 700 Central Ave. (636-3541), 3 miles south of downtown. Take bus #4 (4th St.) to Central Ave. Although horses race here for only three months out of the year, the beautiful grounds and famous twin spires merit a visit on their own. The famous twin spires that tower over the race track lend the place some glamor. (Grounds open in racing season daily 10am-4pm. During racing April 26-June 28, post time Tues.-Fri. 3:30pm, Sat.-Sun. 1:00pm. During racing Oct. 26-Nov. 29, post time Tues.-Sun. 1pm. Grandstand seats $1.50, clubhouse $3, reserved clubhouse $5. Parking $2-3.) The **Kentucky Derby Festival** starts the week before the Derby and culminates with the Run for the Roses (the first Saturday in May). Balloon and steamboat races, music, and all manner of hullabaloo are featured during the week. (Seats for the derby cost $35-over $5,000. Admission to the infield or grandstand $20.)

The **Kentucky Derby Museum** (637-1111), at Churchill Downs, provides the historic context essential for a true appreciation of the significance of the race. The museum offers a slide presentation on a 360° screen, tours of the stadium, profiles of famous stables and trainers, a simulated horse-race for betting practice, and tips on what makes a horse a "sure thing." (Open daily 9am-5pm. Admission $3, seniors $2.50, ages 5-12 $1.50.) The **Louisville Downs** (964-6415), 4520 Poplar Level Rd., south of I-264, hosts harness racing during most of the year. There are three meets: July 4-Sept. 12 Mon.-Sat., and Sept. 27-Oct. 29 and Dec. 26-April 28 Tues.-Sat. Post time is 7:30pm and there are 10-12 races per night. (General admission $2, clubhouse $3. Minimum bet $2. Parking $2.)

If you're tired of being a spectator, go on a trail ride at **Iroquois Riding Stable,** 5216 New Cut Rd. (363-9159; $8 per hr.)

Sights and Entertainment

For an excellent and entertaining introduction to Louisville and Kentucky, see **Kentuckyshow,** 651 4th Ave. at Broadway (561-1111), which covers the state's history and culture. (Shows April-Aug. daily 11am-2pm on the hr.; Sept.-March 11am and 2pm. Admission $3, seniors and children $2.)

Just south of downtown and Oak St., especially on 2nd through 4th St., beautifully maintained Victorian homes comprise part of **Old Louisville.** Farther south, in University of Louisville territory, the **J.B. Speed Art Museum,** 2035 S. 3rd St. (636-2893), has an impressive collection of Dutch paintings and tapestries, as well as Renaissance, modern, and contemporary art, and a sculpture court. The museum also has a touch-and-see gallery for visually impaired visitors. (Open Tues.-Sat. 10am-4pm, Sun. 1-5pm. Admission $2, students free. Take bus #4.)

The **Riverfront Plaza,** a landscape park overlooking the Ohio River, serves as a focal point for downtown Louisville. In the summer, the Riverfront Plaza hosts four **Heritage Weekends** with live bands and dancing and plenty of food (call 566-5065 for information). The **Belle of Louisville** (582-2547), an authentic sternwheeler, cruises the Ohio, leaving from Riverfront Plaza at the foot of 4th St. (In summer Tues.-Sun. at 2pm. Sunset cruises Tues. and Thurs. 7-9pm; nighttime dance cruise Sat. 8:30-11:30pm. Fare $6.50, seniors $5.50, under 12 $3. Night cruise $10.)

The **Museum of History and Science,** 727 W. Main St. (561-6100), downtown, emphasizes hands-on exhibits, where you can press your face against the window of an Apollo space capsule. You can also settle back and enjoy the new IMAX theater with its four-story screen. (Open daily 9am-5pm. Admission $3, seniors and children $2. IMAX tickets $2.50 extra.) At the **Louisville Zoo,** 1100 Trevilian Way (459-2181), between Newbury and Poplar Level Rd., across I-264 from Louisville Downs, the animals are exhibited in almost natural settings. The ostriches come close enough to the rails to freak out even the hardiest zoo-goer. Ride on an elephant's back or on the tiny train that circles the zoo. (Open daily 10am-5pm; Sept.-April Tues.-Sun. 10am-4pm. Gate closes 1 hr. before zoo. Admission $4, seniors $1.75, children $2.)

Hillerich and Bradsby Co., 1525 Charleston-New Albany Rd., Jeffersonville, IN (812-288-6611), 6 miles north of Louisville, manufactures the famous "Louisville Slugger" bat. Tours are conducted weekdays at 11am and 2pm throughout the year, except the last three days in June and first two weeks in July. (Go north on I-65 to exit for Rte. 131, then turn east. Free.) **Hadley Pottery,** 1570 Story Ave. (584-2171), near Ohio St., just east of downtown, has been producing Mary Alice Hadley's gorgeous, unconventional pottery since 1940. (Free 30-min. tours Mon.-Fri. at 2pm. Shop open Mon.-Fri. 8:30am-4:30pm, Sat. 9am-12:30pm. Take bus #15 or 31.)

Louisville's thriving nightlife offers everything from bluegrass and Beethoven to Brecht and Beckett. The **Kentucky Center for the Arts,** 5 Riverfront Plaza (584-7777), off Main St., is Louisville's newest entertainment complex, and hosts major performing arts groups. The **Actors Theater,** 316 W. Main St. (584-1205), between 3rd and 4th St., a Tony award-winning repertory company, gives performances at 8pm and some matinees. The **Phoenix Hill Tavern,** 644 Baxter Ave. (589-4957; take bus #17), is the place to go for live music in Louisville. Two bands play every night, with energetic country-rock on the first floor and cozy easy-listening on the second. Retreat to the roof-top bar or fresh-air patio. (Open Mon.-Sat. 4pm-2am. Dinner buffet Tues.-Fri. 4:30-7:30pm. Cover $1-2.50, $6 for patio entertainment.) Escort service to your car or to the bus stop after hours. The **Butchertown Pub,** at Story and Webster St., also has live bands and a dance floor; take bus #15 ("Market St."). Bands play in University of Louisville's **Red Barn** (588-7332 or 588-6691) on Friday and Saturday nights in the summer. Bring a picnic dinner to **Shakespeare in the Park,** Central Park (634-8237), Wednesdays to Sundays between June 19th and August 9th. (Performances at 8:45pm.)

Near Louisville

The country's (and perhaps the world's) finest bourbon whiskey comes from Kentucky, and the smoothest of Kentucky bourbons hails from 22 miles southeast of Louisville, around Bardstown. At **Jim Beam's American Outpost** (543-9877) in Clermont, 15 miles west of Bardstown, Booker Noe, Jim Beam's grandson and current "master distiller," helps narrate a film about bourbon. Don't miss the free lemonade. From Louisville, take I-65 south to exit 112, then Rte. 245 south for 2½ miles. From Bardstown, take Rte. 245 north. (Museum open Mon.-Sat. 9am-4:30pm, Sun. 1-4pm. Free.) For more good spirits, tour of the **Maker's Mark Distillery** (865-2881), Loretto, 19 miles southeast of Bardstown. Take Rte. 49 down to Rte. 52. The site is a historic landmark that shows how alcohol was made in the 19th century. (Tours Mon.-Fri. every hr. on the ½ hr. 10:30am-3:30pm. Free.) The **Oscar Gatz Whiskey History Museum,** at 5th and Flaget (348-2999), in Bardstown, depicts the history of distilling. (Open Mon.-Sat. 9am-5pm, Sun. 1-5pm. Free.) Greyhound leaves Louisville at 5pm every night for Bardstown. By car, take I-65 south, then Rte. 245.

Abraham Lincoln's birthplace (358-3874) is now a national historic site 45 miles south of Louisville near Hodgenville on U.S. 31E, Rte. 61. From Louisville, take I-65 down to Rte. 61. Fifty-six steps representing the 56 years on Lincoln's life lead up to the stone monument that shelters the small log cabin. Only a few of the Lincoln logs that you see are believed to be original. A rather slow-moving film describes Lincoln's ties to Kentucky. (Open Memorial Day-Labor Day daily 8am-6:45pm; Labor Day-Oct. 8am-5:45pm, Oct.-April 8am-4:45pm, April-Memorial Day 8am-5:45pm. Free.) There is no public transportation, but **Gray Line** (637-6511) gives tours of Lincoln's birthplace and Mammoth Cave (reservations required).

Hundreds of enormous caves and narrow passageways wind through **Mammoth Cave National Park,** 80 miles south of Louisville off I-65, west on Rte. 70. Mammoth Cave is the world's longest network of cavern corridors—over 325 miles in length. Devoted spelunkers will want to try the six-hour "Wild Cave Tour" (in summer only, ages 16 and up $15), but there are also 2-hour, 2-mile historic tours ($3.50, seniors and children under 16 $1.75) and 1½-hour tours for the disabled ($2). The caves are at 54°F year-round, so bring a sweater. The **visitors center** (758-2328) is open 7:30am to 6:30pm, off-season 8am to 5:30pm. Greyhound serves **Cave City,** just east of I-65 on Rte. 70.

The **area code** for the Mammoth Caves area is 502.

Lexington

In 1775, an exploring party camping in Kentucky heard news of the Battle of Lexington far off in Massachusetts, and so named the spot. Since then, Lexington has grown in size to become Kentucky's second-largest city and the world's largest burley tobacco center. The downtown area has recently been rehabilitated and expanded. However, the town has managed its urban renewal with remarkable style and has managed to retain its charming original neighborhoods.

The inhabitants of this gracious city in the heart of the bluegrass are most famous for their dedication to horse breeding and training. Instead of suburbs Lexington has thousand-acre farms of blue grass and white fences. Over 150 horse farms grace the Lexington area, and have nurtured such greats as Citation, Lucky Debonair, and Majestic Prince. These pure-bred equines fetch royal prices as well; a thoroughbred yearling recently sold for a record $13.1 million at the annual Keeneland sale. A local horse-buying guide is called *How to spend a million dollars.*

Practical Information

Emergency: 911.

Visitor Information: Greater Lexington Convention and Visitors Bureau, #363, 430 W. Vine St. (233-1221), in the convention center. Brochures, maps, and bus schedules. Open Mon.-Fri. 8:30am-5pm, Sat. 10am-5pm. There are also information centers on I-75 just north and south of Lexington.

Greyhound: 477 New Circle Rd. (255-4261). Lets passengers off 4 blocks north of Main St. Open 6:45am-11:30pm. To: Louisville (11 per day, 1½ hr., $15); Cincinnati, OH (9 per day, 1½ hr., $15); Knoxville, TN (9 per day, 3 hr., $38.50).

Lex-Tran: 109 W. London Ave. (252-4936). A good public transportation system serving the university and city outskirts. Most buses leave from Vine or Main St. Free trolley serves downtown area. Operates 6am-6:30pm. Fare 60¢, transfers 10¢.

Taxi: Lexington Yellow Cab, 231-8294. Base fare $1.90, $1.15 per mile.

Weather Line: 293-9999.

Help Lines: Rape Crisis, 253-2511.

Time Zone: Eastern.

Post Office: 1088 Nandino Blvd. (231-6700). Open Mon.-Fri. 8:30am-4:30pm, Sat. 9-11am. **ZIP code:** 40511.

Area Code: 606.

Lexington rises out of the rolling pasturelands of central Kentucky, 72 miles east of Louisville. Lexington is also convenient to Cincinnati, 80 miles to the north on I-75. The city is surrounded by **New Circle Road** highway, which is intersected by many roads that connect the downtown district to the surrounding towns. **High Street, Vine Street,** and **Main Street** are the major east-west routes downtown; **Limestone Street** and **Broadway** are the north-south thoroughfares.

Accommodations and Camping

The concentration of horse-related wealth in the Lexington area tends to push accommodation prices up. The cheapest places are located out of the city on roads beyond New Circle Rd. If you're having trouble on your own, **Dial-A-Accommodations** (233-7299) will locate and reserve a room free of charge in a requested area of town and within a specific price range. (Open Mon.-Fri. 9:30am-5pm.)

Kimball House Motel, 267 S. Limestone St. (252-9565), downtown. Gives new definition to the word "charm." You'll feel as if you're in a turn-of-the-century boarding house in these clean, antique-filled rooms. Friendly, helpful management. Some singles, 4th floor, no A/C, with shared bath are just $16. Ask about them specifically; they often fill by late afternoon. Otherwise, the cheapest singles are $22. Doubles $28. $5 key deposit.

University of Kentucky, Apartment Housing (257-3721). Full kitchen and private bathroom. Fold-out sleeper. Rooms also available during the school year if there is space. 5-day max. stay. $20. Call ahead on a weekday. Available May 15-Aug. 15.

YMCA, 239 E. High St. (255-9622), downtown. Men only. Rooms with bed and dresser. If the Y is full, they will offer you space in the Salvation Army's homeless shelter on W. Main St. Singles $20, $30 with private bath. $5 key deposit. Call at least a few days ahead.

Bryan Station Inn, 273 New Circle Rd. (299-4162); take Limestone St. north from downtown and turn right onto Rte. 4. Clean, pleasant rooms in the middle of a motel/fast-food strip. Singles $26. Doubles $28. Rates decrease commensurate with the length of your stay.

Princess Motel, 3061 Lexington Rd. (Rte. 27) (885-6808), 5 miles from downtown. Shabby and awfully smelly, but it's cheap. Singles $21.75. Doubles $25.75.

There are many good, cheap campgrounds near Lexington; unfortunately, a car is necessary to reach them. The **Kentucky Horse Park Campground,** 4089 Iron Works Pike (233-4303), 10 miles north off I-75, has 160 sites and offers a free shuttle to the KY Horse Park and Museum. (2-week max. stay. Tent sites $8, $10 with hookup.) **Clay's Ferry Campground,** Rte. 7 (623-1569), offers swimming in the Kentucky River and a recreation hall. (Sites $8. Open April-Nov.)

Food and Nightlife

Good, down-home bluegrass food is Lexington's specialty. The few distinctive restaurants—anomalies, really—are near the university. Downtown, avoid the chic new retail area and explore the surrounding streets for hidden delis and sandwich shops.

Hall's on the River (255-8105), on Boonesboro Rd., 30 min. southwest of downtown. Follow Richmond Rd., which turns into Athens Boonesboro Rd. Pass the I-75 interchange—Hall's is exactly 8 miles away. Sample the "hot brown" (the Kentuckian version of an open-faced turkey sandwich with ham and a special sauce) and other local dishes. Entrees with 2 side dishes (new potatoes, veggies, biscuits, or beans) $8-12. Open Mon.-Thurs. noon-10pm, Fri.-Sat. noon-11pm. Also downtown at **Hall's on Main,** 735 E. Main St. (269-3269), take bus #4A. Open Mon.-Thurs. 11am-2pm and 4-10pm, Fri.-Sat. 11am-11pm, Sun. noon-4pm.

Central Christian Church Cafeteria, 219 E. Short St. (255-3087), 1 block north of Main St. Decent country food—greens and cornbread, fried fish, homemade pies—for under $3. Open Mon.-Fri. 6:30am-2:30pm.

Alfalfa Restaurant, 557 S. Limestone St. (253-0014), across from Memorial Hall at the University of Kentucky; take bus #2A. Fantastic home-cooked international and vegetarian meals. Complete dinners with salad, bread, and entree under $10. Live music nightly. Open Tues.-Thurs. 5:30-9pm (in summer until 9:30pm), Fri. 5:30-10pm, Sat. 10am-2pm and 5:30-10pm, Sun. 10am-2pm.

Joe Bologna's, 103 W. Maxwell St. (252-4933) at S. Limestone, 5 blocks south of Main. A popular college hang-out for pizza ($4-10). You'll need extra napkins for the juicy beef sub, a gourmet cheesesteak. Open Mon.-Thurs. 11am-midnight, Fri.-Sat. 11am-2am, Sun. noon-11pm.

High Rose on Cantina, 301 E. High St. (252-9498). Hearty Mexican dishes (all entrees with beans, chips, and salsa) $4-7. Cheap beer and rowdy rock and country music. Open Mon.-Sat. 11am-1am, Sun. 11am-11pm.

Sights

To escape the stifling swamp conditions farther south, plantation owners built beautiful summer retreats in milder Lexington. The most attractive of these stately houses are only a few blocks northeast of the town center, in the Gratz Park area behind the public library. Wrap-around porches, wooden minarets, stone foundations, and rose-covered trellises distinguish these from the neighborhood's newer homes.

At the end of the park across from the library is the **Hunt Morgan House,** 201 N. Mill St. (253-0362). Built in 1814 by John Wesley Hunt, the first millionaire west of the Alleghenies, the house was later home to Thomas Hunt Morgan, who won a Nobel Prize in 1933 for proving the existence of the gene. The house's most colorful inhabitant was the confederate general John Hunt Morgan. Chased by Union troops, the general once rode his horse up the front steps and into the house, leaned down to kiss his mother, and rode out the back door. What a guy. (Tours $3, ages 6-12 $1.50, Tues.-Sat. 10am-4pm, Sun. 2-5pm.)

Kentucky's loyalties were sharply divided in the Civil War. Five blocks from the Hunt-Morgan House is the childhood home of Mary Todd, who later married Abraham Lincoln. The **Mary Todd Lincoln House** is at 578 W. Main St. (233-6666). (Last tour at 3:15. Open April 1-Dec. 15 Tues.-Sat. 10am-4pm. Admission $3.)

Transylvania University, west of Broadway, north of 3rd St. (233-8242), was the first college west of the Alleghenies. It has a stately array of Greek Revival buildings and an impressive alumni list—two vice-presidents, 50 Senators, 100 Representatives, 36 governors, and 34 ambassadors. Legend has it, however, that it long suffered under a curse that caused various freak accidents. The spell was broken only when the corpse of the man supposedly responsible, an eccentric professor named Rafinesque, was brought back and buried on university grounds. His crypt is behind a classroom door in Old Morrison Hall. Ask to see it at your own risk; many believe the curse only lies dormant. (Guided tours upon request Mon.-Fri. 9am-4pm.) On Richmond Rd. at E. Main St. you can admire **Ashland** (266-8581), the 20-acre homestead of statesman Henry Clay. The mansion's carved ash interior came from trees that grew on the property. (Open in summer Mon.-Sat. 9:30am-4:30pm, Sun. 1-4:30pm; in winter 10am-4pm. Admission $4, children $1.50. Take bus #4A on Main St.)

Horses and Seasonal Events

Horse farms, for the most part, no longer permit tourists to come and gawk. One exception is **Spendthrift Farm** (299-5271), 8 miles northeast of downtown. (Tours from the training center, 3380 Paris Pike, given Mon.-Sat. at 9, 10, and 10:30am. Make an appointment through the visitors center.)

The touristy but pretty **Kentucky Horse Park,** 4089 Iron Works Pike (233-4303), exit 120, 10 miles north on I-75, is a state park with full facilities for equestrians, a museum, two films, and the Man O' War Monument. (2-hr. tours given all day. Open in summer 9am-7pm; times vary the rest of the year. Admission $8, ages 7-12 $4. Horse-drawn vehicle tours $4, ages 7-12 $2.50.)

If horse racing is more your style, visit the **Keeneland Race Track,** 4201 Versailles Rd. (254-3412), west on U.S. 60. (Races Oct. and April; post time 1:30pm.) The public is welcome at morning workouts. (April-Oct. 6-10am.) The final prep race for the Kentucky Derby is held here in April. The **Red Mile Harness Track,** 847 S. Broadway (255-0752; take bus #3 on S. Broadway), has racing April to June and also in September. (Post time 7:30pm.) It is worth a visit just to see the crowds—a mix of wholesome families and seasoned gamblers. (Admission $1.50, reserved seating $3, programs $2, parking $1.50, women free Thurs., seniors free Fri.) The public is welcome to watch morning workouts during racing season (7:30am-noon).

In June, the **Festival of the Bluegrass** (846-4995), at Masterson Station Park, attracts thousands for a Kentucky-style hootenanny. Camping at the festival grounds is free. The **Lexington Junior League Horse Show** (mid-July), the largest outdoor show in the nation, unfolds its pageantry at the Red Mile (see above).

Near Lexington

Outside Lexington, in Richmond, exit 95 off I-70, is **White Hall** (623-9178), home of the abolitionist Cassins Clay, Henry's cousin. The elegant mansion is really two houses, one Georgian and one Italianate. The one-hour tour covers seven different living levels. (Admission $2, ages 6-12 $1.75.) **Fort Boonesborough** (527-3328), a re-creation of one of Daniel Boone's forts, is also in Richmond. The park has films about the pioneers, samples of 18th-century crafts, and a small museum. (Open April-Aug. daily 9am-5:30pm; Sept.-Oct. Wed.-Sun. 9am-5:30pm. Admission $3, ages 6-12 $1.75. Combination White Hall/Boonesborough tickets cost $4.)

Ten miles south of Richmond and 30 miles south of Lexington, where the bluegrass meets the mountains, is **Berea,** home of the world-renowned **Berea College** (986-9341), a tuition-free school founded in 1855. Many of the 1500 students, most from Appalachia, pay for their expenses by operating the school's crafts center. (Campus tours leave from the corner of **Boone Tavern** Mon.-Fri. at 9am, 1:30pm, and 3pm, Sat. at 9am.) The Art Department's galleries display the students' ceramics, weaving, and furniture, along with visiting exhibits and photographs documenting the history of southern Appalachia. (Open Mon.-Fri. 9am-noon and 1-4pm.) The **Appalachian Museum** (986-9341, ext. 5530), Jackson St., on campus, charts regional history through arts and crafts. (Open Mon.-Sat. 9am-6pm, Sun. 1-6pm.)

Because of the emphasis on craft skills at Berea College, the town has a concentration of galleries, gift shops, and workshops. Of particular interest is **Churchill Weavers,** Lorraine Court (986-3127), off I-75 and U.S. 25, north of town, the largest handweaving firm in the country. (Tours Mon.-Fri. 9am-noon and 1-4pm. Free. Gift shop open Mon.-Sat. 9am-6pm, Sun. noon-6pm.) The student-run crafts center has two locations: the **Boone Tavern Gift Shop,** in the hotel (986-9341, ext. 5233; open Mon.-Sat. 8am-8pm, Sun. noon-8pm), and the **Log House Sales Room** on Estill St. (986-9341, ext. 5225; open Mon.-Sat. 8am-5pm). During May and early fall, the town is flooded with tourists for the **Kentucky Guild of Artists' and Craftsmen's Fair,** at the Indian Fort Theater. The fair features good folk music and food. In mid-August, the local **McClain Family Band** holds their annual bluegrass festival (986-8111) on their Big Hill Farm. To reach Berea, take Greyhound bus #360 (3 per day), on the Lexington-Knoxville route; the bus will leave you at the B & B Grocery in town.

Between Harrodsburg and Lexington, about 25 miles southwest on U.S. 68, is **Shaker Village** (734-5411), at Pleasant Hill. The 5000-acre farm features 27 restored Shaker buildings. A tour of the entire farm includes demonstrations of everything from apple-butter-making to coopering. (Open daily 9am-6pm. Admission $6, ages 12-17 $2.50, ages 6-11 $1.) You can enjoy Shaker hospitality and eat and sleep in original Shaker buildings. (Dinner $12-14. Singles $30-55. Doubles $45-65. Reservations required.) Greyhound #350 runs to Harrodsburg, 7 miles from the village.

The **Red River Valley,** in the northern section of the Daniel Boone National Forest, approximately 50 miles southeast of Lexington, beckons visitors from around the country. Immortalized in song and square dance, this spacious land of sandstone cliffs and stone arches is an ideal day's outing from Lexington. **Natural Bridge State Park** (663-2214), 2 miles south of Slade, is the major attraction of the upper valley. The Red River Gorge highlights the lower valley. Greyhound #296 will get you as close as Stanton (10 miles west of Slade), where there is a U.S. Forest Service Office (663-2853). If you're driving, take the Mountain Parkway (south off I-64) straight to Slade, and explore the region bounded by the scenic loop road, Rte. 715. Camp at **Natural Bridge State Resort Park** (800-325-1710; 800-633-2170 in KY). The campground has a pool, facilities for the disabled, boat rental, and organized square dances. In mid-June, it is the site of the **National Mountain Style Square Dance and Clogging Festival.** (Tent sites $8.50, with hookup $10.)

Cumberland Gap

Cumberland Gap National Historical Park is an almost completely uncommercialized area. It's home to Daniel Boone's **Wilderness Trail,** a natural passage through an 800-foot break in the Appalachian Mountains. The park surrounds the route that Boone and 30 axemen blazed along an ancient Native American Buffalo trail in 1775.

Today the park provides 50 miles of trails of varying length. Some features such as the White Rocks are accessible only by trail. Atop Brush Mountain lies the **Hensley Settlement.** This collection of 12 farms was worked for 50 years until it was abandoned in the 1940s. The settlers lived in an isolated encamplment of rough-hewn chestnut log houses. Since 1965, the park service has restored five farmsteads, the schoolhouse, and cemetery. Two farmers maintain the buildings and fields using Hensley family techniques. You can reach the settlement by a one-day hike or in a 4-wheel-drive vehicle. (3-hr. tours offered several times per day. Tours $4, children $2.)

You can canoe, kayak, and whitewater raft on rapids year-round. The Cumberland River can be reached from the **Cumberland Falls State Resort Park** (800-325-0063), southwest of Corbin on KY Rte. 90 off U.S. 25W. Raft from Rte. 90, 5 miles east of the enormous falls. By a full moon the falls show the only known moonbow in the Western Hemisphere. (Tent sites at the park $8.50. Buffet lunch at the lodge $5, dinner $8.) **Sheltowee Trace Outfitters** (679-5026) offers rafting trips on the river, as does **Cumberland Outdoor Adventures,** on KY Rte. 90, 5 miles east of Cumberland Falls.

There is a **campground** on Rte. 58 in Virginia (10pm-6am quiet rule. Sites $8. Free firewood.) Permits are required for backcountry camping. (Free; available at the visitors center.) Make reservations if you want to stay at one of the group sites or shelters. ($1 per person.) For non-campers, there is a string of uninspiring but cheap motels along U.S. 25E in Middlesboro. The **Parkview Motel** (606-248-4516) has spotlessly clean, albeit dark, rooms and is very convenient to the park. (Singles $22. Doubles $27. $5 key deposit.)

The park **headquarters and visitors center** (606-248-2817) is about ⅛-mile from Middlesboro, KY, off U.S. 25E. There rangers offer a series of free walking tours, educational and historical programs, and exhibits in the summer. (Open daily mid-June to Aug. 8am-6pm; Sept. to mid-June 8am-5pm.)

Louisiana

Thomas Jefferson struck quite a bargain when he purchased the Louisiana Territory from Napoleon for $15 million in 1803. Not only did he gain a region of tremendous natural wealth, he considerably increased the social diversity of young America. The richness of the alluvial soil in Louisiana is matched only by that of its cultural heritage. Each successive wave of settlers has left its layer of ethnic sediment. The original French population of the early 18th century was augmented by the arrival of the Acadians, French settlers expelled from Nova Scotia by the British in 1755. These Cajuns (a corruption of "Acadians") retreated to the swampy Louisiana hinterland, creating distinctive dialects, music, folklore, and fashionable cuisine. Their influence combined with that of Spanish, African, Native American, and Caribbean elements to create a gumbo of settlers.

Today's visitor to Louisiana will find this mix's unusual spice still very much in evidence. French terms tend to creep into the local dialect, and Cajun and zydeco tunes, the region's distinctive brand of hot dance music, are often sung entirely in patois. The famous cuisine, needless to say, is as regionally unique as it is delicious. While Louisiana has suffered severely from the regional oil depression, it has regrouped behind the tourist industry. As a result, it offers plenty of inexpensive activities.

Practical Information

Capital: Baton Rouge.

Tourist Information: State Travel Office, P.O. Box 94291, Capitol Station, Baton Rouge 70804 (342-7317 or 800-334-8626). Open daily 8am-4pm. **Office of State Parks,** P.O. Box 1111, Baton Rouge 70821. Open Mon.-Fri. 9am-5pm.

Time Zone: Central (1 hr. behind Eastern). **Postal Abbreviation:** LA.

New Orleans

Founded around 1718 by the French, ceded to the Spanish and then reacquired by the French, New Orleans had already existed quite happily for almost a century before it became a U.S. territory in 1803. Known as "the city that care forgot," New Orleans ("N'awlins" to natives) seems Mediterranean or Caribbean in contrast to the more straight-laced Anglo-Saxon cities on the East Coast. New Orleans loves to party. In the 19th century, in the red-light district known as "Storyville," its atmosphere of revelry simmered together with elements from African and European popular music to form the exuberant language of jazz. Today, it's still a city that loves to party.

The climax of the year's bacchanalia is reached during the Mardi Gras celebrations held the week before Ash Wednesday (usually in late Feb.). Anxious to have as much fun as their religion and bodies will allow before Lent, the townspeople parade, dance, sing, and drink until midnight of Mardi Gras itself, the "Fat Tuesday" before Ash Wednesday.

Practical Information

Emergency: 911.

Visitor Information: If you like to plan your vacation before you leave home, write to the **Greater New Orleans Tourist and Convention Commission** (566-5011), 1520 Sugar Bowl Dr. Once there, try the **New Orleans/Louisiana Tourist Center,** 527 St. Ann, Jackson Square (568-5661), in the French Quarter. Free city and walking tour maps. Open daily 9am-5pm. **Infocall,** 837-4344.

Travelers Aid: 211 Camp St. (525-8726), at the YMCA. Provides aid to stranded people—temporary shelter, food, and money, if necessary. Open Mon.-Fri. 8am-4:30pm.

Moisant International Airport: 15 miles west of the city. Served by the major domestic airlines as well as by larger Latin American carriers. **Louisiana Transit Authority** (737-9611) runs between the airport and downtown at Elk and Tulane every 30-45 min. for $1.10. Pickup in front of Hertz. Airport limousine shuttles to downtown hotels $8, cabs $18.

Union Passenger Terminal: 1001 Loyola Ave., a 10-min. walk to Canal St. via Elk. Terminus for statewide interstate bus and train systems. Open 24 hours for tickets and information. **Amtrak,** 528-1610 or 800-872-7245. To: Memphis (1 per day, 8 hr., $69) and Houston (3 per wk., 8 hr., $67). **Greyhound/Trailways,** 525-9371. To: Baton Rouge (16 per day, 2 hr. $19); Memphis (5 per day, 11 hr., $56); and Houston (9 per day, 9 hr., $39).

Regional Transit Authority: Plaza Tower, 101 Dauphin St., 4th floor (569-2700), at Canal. Bus schedules and transit information. Office open Mon.-Fri. 8:30am-5pm. Phone line provides route information 24 hours a day. All buses pass by Canal St., at the edge of the Quarter. Fare 60¢.

Taxi: United Cabs, 522-9771. **Checker Yellow Cabs,** 525-3311. **Liberty Bell Cabs,** 822-5974. Base rate $1.10, each additional mile $1.

Car Rental: Budget Car Rental, 1317 St. Charles (525-9417), plus 6 more locations. $32 per day, $19 on weekends. 150 free miles. Add $5 per day if under 25. Open daily, 7am-midnight. Must be 21 with credit card or 25 with a cash deposit.

Auto Transport Company: Auto Driveaway, 201 Kent Ave., Metaire (885-9292).

Bike Rental: Bicycle Michael's, 618 Frenchman (945-9505), a few blocks west of the Quarter. $3.50 per hr., $12.50 per day. Open Mon.-Sat. 10am-7pm.

Help Lines: Gay Counseling Line, 522-5815. Usually operates nightly 5-11pm.

Post Office: 701 Loyola Ave. (589-2201), near Union Passenger Terminal, a 10-min. walk from Canal St. Open Mon.-Fri. 8:30am-4:30pm, Sat. 8:30am-noon. **ZIP code:** 70140.

Area Code: 504.

Although part of the Mississippi Delta, New Orleans is not actually on the Gulf of Mexico. The city is tucked between a bend in the **Mississippi River** and the southern shore of **Lake Pontchartrain.** Jackson is 210 miles north; Atlanta is 480 miles to the northeast; Houston is 350 miles west along the Gulf. Keep in mind that the main streets of the city follow the curve in the river; it's easy to get lost even though New Orleans is a fairly small city. The major tourist area is the small **French Quarter (Vieux Carré),** bounded by the **Mississippi River, Canal Street, Esplanade Avenue,** and **Rampart Street.** Streets in the French Quarter follow a grid pattern, and traveling on foot is not difficult. The **Garden District** is west of downtown. Buses to all parts of the city pass by Canal St. at the edge of the Quarter.

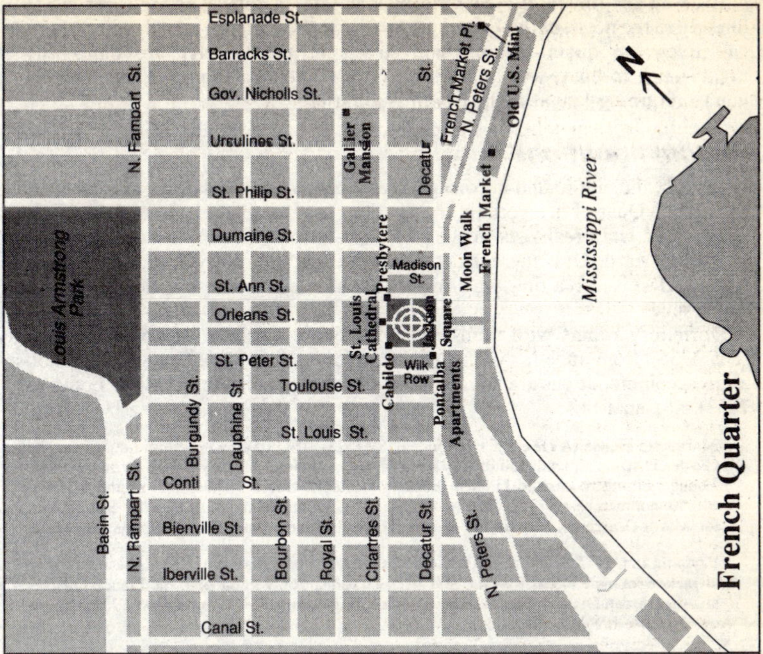
French Quarter
Esplanade St.
Barracks St.
Gov. Nicholls St.
Ursulines St.
St. Philip St.
Dumaine St.
St. Ann St.
Orleans St.
St. Peter St.
Toulouse St.
St. Louis St.
Conti St.
Bienville St.
Iberville St.
Canal St.
Basin St.
N. Rampart St.
Burgundy St.
Dauphine St.
Bourbon St.
Royal St.
Chartres St.
Decatur St.
N. Peters St.
Louis Armstrong Park
Gallier Mansion
Presbytere
St. Louis Cathedral
Cabildo
Madison St.
Jackson Square
Wilk Row
Pontalba Apartments
Moon Walk
French Market
French Market Pl.
Old U.S. Mint
Mississippi River
N

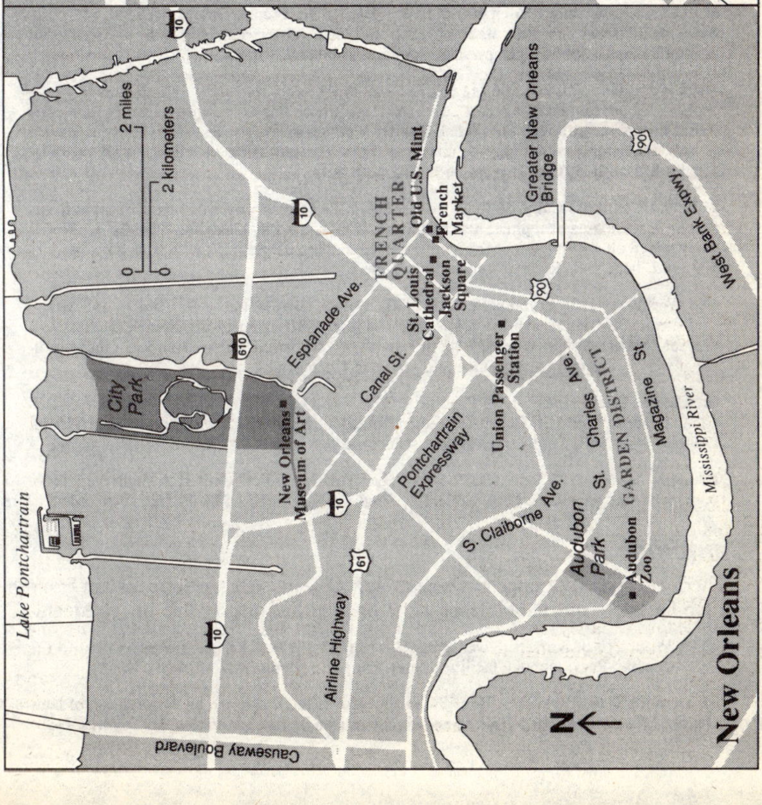
New Orleans
Lake Pontchartrain
Causeway Boulevard
Airline Highway
City Park
New Orleans Museum of Art
Esplanade Ave.
Canal St.
Pontchartrain Expressway
S. Claiborne Ave.
Audubon Park
Audubon Zoo
St. Charles Ave.
Magazine St.
GARDEN DISTRICT
Union Passenger Station
St. Louis Cathedral
Jackson Square
FRENCH QUARTER
French Market
Old U.S. Mint
Greater New Orleans Bridge
West Bank Expwy.
Mississippi River
2 miles
2 kilometers
0
10
610
61
90
N

Even by day, much of New Orleans is unsafe, in particular the tenement areas directly to the north of the French Quarter and those directly northwest of Lee Circle. Even the quaint-looking side streets of the Quarter are dangerous at night—stick to busy, well-lit thoroughfares. Take a cab back to your lodgings if you're returning late at night from the Quarter.

Accommodations

It's very difficult to find inexpensive yet decent accommodations in New Orleans; the French Quarter is especially trying. Your best bet might be one of the few inexpensive **bed and breakfasts** in the city, the best of which are listed below.

During Mardi Gras there is not a vacant room in the city and prices invariably rise. Jazzfest is also a time when rooms are scarce; make reservations as far ahead as possible.

Dormitory rooms with semi-private baths are available at **Loyola University** (865-3735), from June to August (singles $25; doubles $31). Cramped and not-so-clean accommodations are yours for only $6 at the **India Hotel,** 124 S. Lopez (822-7833), at Canal St.

Marquette House (AYH), 2253 Carondelet St. (523-3014), in an antebellum house near the Garden District, and only minutes by streetcar to the Quarter. Usually teeming with travelers. Lounge, dining room, and kitchen. Lockers available. Check-in 7:30am-1pm and 3-11pm. $10.50, nonmembers $13.50. Private doubles $22, nonmembers $25. Linen $1. Reservation for Mardi Gras must be paid in full in advance; include self-addressed, stamped envelope.

Prytania Inn, 1415 Prytania St. (566-1515). One of the best deals in the city. Clean and very attractive rooms 1 block from the St. Charles streetcar, only minutes to the French Quarter and the Garden District. Free laundry facilities. Singles from $29. Doubles from $33. Sumptuous 2-course breakfast included.

Hotel Villa Convento, 616 Ursulines (522-1793), in the French Quarter. An elegant, clean boarding house with friendly staff. Singles from $39. Doubles from $49. There is 1 room that accommodates 4 for $20 per person. Continental breakfast included.

906 Mazant Guest House, 906 Mazant St. (944-2662), southeast of the French Quarter. Take St. Claude bus from Rampart and Canal. A friendly boarding house with a European, hostel-like atmosphere. Although the French Quarter is not far away (2 miles) and is easily accessible by bus, the neighborhood may be unsafe at night. Pleasant rooms furnished with antiques. Singles $15 with A/C or private bath, $25 with both.

LaSalle Hotel, 1113 Canal St. (523-5831 or 800-521-9450), downtown, 4 blocks east of Bourbon St. Unsafe area at night. This small hotel is unexpectedly clean and friendly. Coffee always served on antique sideboard in lobby. Free movies. Singles $27, with bath $39. Doubles $30, with bath $45. Reservations recommended.

Old World Inn, 1330 Prytania St. (566-1330), 1 block away from the St. Charles Ave. streetcar. Clean and friendly, with a homey atmosphere. Convenient to the French Quarter and Garden District. Singles from $27.50, more with private bath. Doubles from $35. One quintuplet for $75. Complimentary juice and coffee in the morning.

St. Charles Guest House, 1748 Prytania (523-6556). Quiet neighborhood near Garden District, restaurants, and St. Charles streetcar. Nice pool. Singles $25, with private bath $35-38. Doubles from $40. Continental breakfast included.

Economy Motel, 1725 Tulane (529-5411), near Tulane Medical Center. A slight step above your basic budget motel. Pool, cable TV. Singles $37. Doubles $43. Breakfast included.

Camping

There are several campgrounds near New Orleans. All are quite distant from the French Quarter, and public transportation is either unavailable or infrequent.

KOA West, 219 S. Starrett, River Ridge 70123 (467-1792). RTA bus transportation to the city available. Pool, laundry facilities. Sites $20 for 2 people.

St. Bernard State Park, P.O. Box 534 Violet, 70092 (682-2101), 18 miles southeast of New Orleans. Take I-10 to Rte. 47 south and go left on Rte. 39 through Violet and Poydras. Nearest public transportation to New Orleans ½ mile away. Pool. Registration until 10pm. Sites $9, seniors $7.

Fontainebleau State Park, P.O. Box 152, Mandeville 70448 (626-8052), southeast of Mandeville on U.S. 190., on the shores of Lake Ponchartrain. Sites $9.

Parc d'Orleans II, 10910 Chef Menteur Hwy. (242-6176 or 800-535-2598 outside LA), 3 miles east of the junction of I-10 and U.S. 90 (Chef Menteur Hwy.). Near public transporation into the city. Pool, laundry facilities. Sites from $10 for 1 person, each additional person $2.

Food

Acadian refugees, Spaniards, Italians, African-Americans, and Native Americans have all influenced New Orleans's distinctive culinary style. Hot, spicy, and delicious, Creole cooking appears in some form on almost all menus. Big eaters will be satisfied by the Southern breakfast of grits, eggs, bacon, and corn bread. For lunch, try a seafood po'boy (a long french-bread sandwich filled with fried oysters or shrimp) or red beans and rice. Other New Orleans specialties are gumbo (a spicy soup made with okra and seafood or chicken) and jambalaya (rice with meat, vegetables, sometimes fish or shrimp, and a piquant red pepper sauce). Sample the tiny fresh crawfish, the southern cousin of the Maine lobster. Famous restaurants such as **Antoine's,** 725 St. Louis St. (581-4422; open Mon.-Sat. noon-2pm and 5:30-9:30pm), and **Le Ruth's,** 636 Franklin St. (362-4929), serve excellent food in relatively relaxed surroundings, but don't bust your budget here. The small, traditional local places lend New Orleans its charm.

Cool off in the summer months with a "snow ball" (sno-cone); the best are sold at **Hansen's,** 4801 Tchoupitoulas St. (891-9788). Expect a line. (Open Tues.-Fri. and Sun. 3-9pm.) Indulge yourself with some Creole pralines; some of the best and cheapest are at **Laura's Candies,** 600 Conti and 155 Royal St. (525-3880; open daily 9am-10pm). The **French Market,** between Decatur and N. Peters St. on the east side of the French Quarter, sells fresh vegetables. The grocery stores on Decatur St. have the rest of the fixings you'll need for a picnic.

French Quarter

Acme Oyster House, 724 Iberville (522-5973). Fresh oysters shucked before your eyes; 6 for $2.75, 12 for $4.50. Also good po'boys. No-frills decor but friendly service. Open Mon.-Sat. 11am-10pm, Sun. noon-7pm.

Quarter Scene Restaurant, 900 Dumaine (522-6533). This still undiscovered cornerside café serves delicious salads and seafood and pasta entrees ($4-7). A tasty surprise is the *Dumaine* ($4), a peanut butter and banana sandwich topped with nuts and honey. Open 24 hours.

Croissant d'Or, 617 Ursuline St. (524-4663). Delicious French pastries at reasonable prices in a historic building that was the first ice cream parlor in New Orleans. Open daily 7am-5pm.

Mama Rosa's, 616 N. Rampart (523-5546), on the edge of the French Quarter. The best pizza in New Orleans (small cheese $7). Also serves heaping salads and gumbo ($3). Open Tues.-Thurs. 10:30am-10:30pm, Fri.-Sun. 10:30am-11:30pm.

Port Orleans, 228 Bourbon St. (528-9315). Very touristy, but good seafood at prices lower than most other French Quarter restaurants. Oyster and shrimp platter $4.25. Kitchen open Mon.-Fri. 11am-1am, Sat.-Sun. 11am-3am. Bar usually open until 4am.

Café du Monde, French Market (561-9235) at the intersection of Decatur and St. Ann St. A people-watcher's paradise since the 1860s. Drink *café au lait* and eat perfectly prepared hot *beignets* with powdered sugar (3 for $1.65). Open 24 hours.

Outside the Quarter

St. Charles Tavern, 1433 St. Charles Ave. (523-9823). Have a blast at this neighborhood gathering spot, frequented by friendly cops and cabbies. Enjoy their salad bar and pizza ($3 each) and a Dixie beer. Open 24 hours.

Franky and Johnny's, 321 Arabella, off Tchoupitoulas southwest of downtown. Good seafood and po'boys served in a fun and lively atmosphere. Try the turtle soup ($2.50). Open Sun.-Thurs. 11am-11pm, Fri.-Sat. 11am-midnight.

Camellia Grill, 626 S. Carrollton Ave. (866-9573). Take the St. Charles streetcar away from the Quarter to one of the finest diners in America, complete with cloth napkins and servers who put on a great performance. Try the chef's special omelette ($5.50) or partake in the amazing pecan pie. Expect a wait on weekend mornings. Open Sun.-Wed. 8am-1am, Thurs.-Sat. 8am-2am.

Domilise's, 5240 Annunciation (899-9126). Also uptown. This neighborhood restaurant serves the best po'boys in New Orleans, huge and cheap (around $3.50). Open Mon.-Sat. 9am-7pm.

Mais Oui, 5908 Magazine Ave. (897-1540). Home cooking at its best. Delicious corn bread and gumbo. Entrees run from $5-8 and the menu changes daily. Bring your own wine. Open Mon.-Fri. 11:30am-2:45pm and 5:30-8:45pm, Sat. 5:30-8:45pm.

Mother's Restaurant, 401 Poydras, (523-9656), 4 blocks north of Bourbon St. Mother's has been serving up unparalleled crawfish *etouffé* ($5.25) and seafood po'boys to locals for almost half a century. Entrees from $4.25. Open daily 5am-10pm.

Joey K's, 3001 Magazine St. (891-0997). This comfortable neighborhood restaurant serves great Southern breakfasts as well as good seafood, Italian food ($5-7), and po'boys ($3-4.25). Open Mon.-Thurs. 6am-9pm, Fri. 6am-10pm, Sat. 6am-9pm.

Sights

French Quarter

Allow yourself at least a full day to take in the Quarter at leisure. The oldest section of the city, it is justly famous for its ornate wrought-iron balconies, French architecture, and joyous atmosphere. Known as the **Vieux Carré,** the historic district of New Orleans remains unexploited by commercialism. There's a large gay community here. Walk through the residential section down **Dumaine Street** toward **Rampart Street** to escape the more crowded area near the river. Stop in at a neighborhood bar; tourists are taken in stride here and you'll feel welcome.

Jackson Square is the heart of the Quarter. Centered around a bronze equestrian statue of General Andrew Jackson, the victor of the Battle of New Orleans, the square is alive with artists, mimes, musicians, breakdancers, and magicians. Across the street, the **Moonwalk** offers a scenic view of the river and shipping wharves. The **Louisiana State Museum** is in four different buildings, three of which (the **Cabildo, Presbytère,** and **1850 House**) are in Jackson Square. The fourth, the **Old U.S. Mint,** 400 Esplanade (568-6968), is outside the Quarter, and houses interesting collections on the history of African-Americans, jazz, and the Mardi Gras. All buildings, except for the Cabildo, are open for touring. (All open Wed.-Sun. 10am-5pm. Admission $3, seniors and students $1.50, under 12 free.)

Be sure to make use of the free tours offered by the **Jean Lafitte National Historical Park,** 916-918 North Peters (589-2636) in the French Market. Six excellent tours run daily including those of the Quarter itself and of the popular "City of the Dead" cemetery (reservations required).

Several of the Quarter's historical homes open their doors to the public. One of the most interesting is the **Hermann-Grima House,** 820 St. Louis St. (525-5661; tours every ½ hr.; open Mon.-Sat. 10am-3:30pm; admission $3, seniors $2.50, students $2). Creole cooking demonstrations are offered October through May on Thursdays. The **Gallier House,** 1132 Royal St. (523-6722; see Museums below) is considered one of the best small museums in the country. Visitors are given free refreshments after the tours.

Outside the Quarter

Much of New Orleans outside the Vieux Carré is also attractive, with elegant, spacious boulevards that bear little resemblance to the cramped blocks of the old quarter. **St. Charles Avenue** has some of the city's finest buildings, including elegant 19th-century homes, still in perfect condition.

The streetcar named "Desire" was derailed long ago, but the **St. Charles Streetcar** should be back in operation (by Oct., 1989), after a year-long overhaul. This old-fashioned train takes you through some of New Orleans's most beautiful neighborhoods at a leisurely pace for a mere 60¢, but keep in mind that the best of New Orleans can be seen by just strolling around. Be sure to get off the train at the **Garden District,** an opulent neighborhood between Jackson and Louisiana Ave. The many different influences of French, Italian, Spanish, and American architecture are at work here, creating an extraordinary compilation of magnificent structures, rich colors, lacy ironworks, and of course, exquisite gardens. Notice that many have no basements and are raised several feet above the ground, affording protection from the swamp on which New Orleans was built. The wet foundations of the city even trouble the dead—all the city's cemeteries must be elevated so that the deceased may rest in peace above water. The **Jean Lafitte National Historical Park** (see above) leads a daily walking tour of this district. You can also pick up a copy of a self-guided tour at their office.

City Park, at the corner of City Park Ave. and Marconi Dr. (482-4888), is a 10-minute drive north of the Quarter, and is one of the five largest city parks in the U.S.—even bigger than New York City's Central Park. Besides the **Museum of Art** (see Museums below), it encompasses a botanical garden, golf courses, tennis courts, 800-year-old oak trees, lagoons, and a miniature train.

As impressive as **City Park** is **Audubon Park,** across from Tulane University. Designed by the same architects who planned Central Park in New York City, it contains lagoons, statues, stables, and the delightful **Audubon Zoo** (861-2537). In the zoo a re-created Louisiana swamp, which includes numerous alligators, is just one of the many excellent exhibits. A free museum shuttle takes you from the Audubon Park entrance (streetcar stop #36) to the zoo for free. (Zoo open Mon.-Fri. 9:30am-5pm, Sat.-Sun. 9:30am-6pm. Admission $5.50, seniors and children $2.75.) You can get back to the old quarter from Audubon Park by steamboat; the *Cotton Blossom* (586-8777) sails the Mississippi daily from Canal St. to the zoo and back. It costs more than the streetcar ($5.50, children $4.50) but is a good way to see the port. (Trips at 11am, 1:45pm, and 4:30pm from the zoo landing.)

Back downtown, the "foot of Canal St.," where the riverboats dock, is dominated by the **World Trade Center,** the **Old Customs House,** and **Riverwalk,** a multi-million dollar conglomeration of overpriced shops overlooking the port. Invest $2 to elevator up to the 31st floor observation deck for a superb view of the city, or better yet, buy an expensive drink at the **Top of the Mart,** a revolving bar on the 33rd floor. It's a rip-off, of course, but it's particularly enchanting at sunset. (Open Sun.-Thurs. noon-midnight, Fri.-Sat. noon-1am. $4.25 minimum.)

If you have spare time and money, you may want to take a **riverboat cruise.** The *Cajun Queen* and *Creole Queen* (524-0814) offer various cruises (1½-5 hr., $10-14). Tours offer interesting history and anecdotes about New Orleans and Cajun and Creole life, but the boat ride from Audubon Zoo is an adequate and less expensive substitute. Swamp tours, while expensive, are a better deal. The best ones are in Western Louisiana, but if your travels don't take you into the Louisiana hinterland, see bayou country and the Beauregard Plantation aboard **The Voyageur** (523-5555). Tours leave the ferry landing at the foot of Canal St. daily at 10am and return at around 3pm. (Tickets $9.50, children $4.75.)

Museums

Gallier House Museum, 1118-1132 Royal St. (523-6722). This elegant restored French Quarter residence brings alive the taste and lifestyle of mid-19th century New Orleans. Tours every ½-hr. Open Mon.-Sat. 10am-3:45 pm. Admission $3, seniors and students $2.50.

New Orleans Historic Voodoo Museum, 724 Dumaine (523-7685). Exciting occult displays and artifacts. Not for the faint-hearted. Buy *gris-gris* potion in the gift shop. Open daily 10am-dusk. Admission $3, seniors and students $2, children $1.

Musée Conti Wax Museum, 917 Conti St. (525-2605). One of the world's finest houses of wax. The voodoo display and haunted dungeon are perennial favorites. Open daily 10am-5pm except during Mardi Gras. Admission $4, ages 13-18 $3, under 13 $2.

New Orleans Museum of Art, City Park (488-2631). Take the Esplanade bus from Canal and Rampart. The collection of New Orleans's small but pleasant fine arts museum includes local decorative arts, paintings of area subjects, opulent works by the jeweler Fabergé, and a small number of paintings by European and American masters. Open Tues.-Sun. 10am-5pm. Admission $4, seniors and children $2.

Confederate Museum, 929 Camp St. (523-4522). An extensive collection of Civil War records and artifacts. Located just west of Lee Circle, in an ivy-covered stone building. Open Mon.-Sat. 10am-4pm. Admission $2, seniors $1, children 50¢.

Louisiana Nature and Science Center, 11000 Lake Forest Blvd., (246-5672), in Joe Brown Memorial Park, Eastern New Orleans. Hard to reach without a car, but a wonderful escape from the frivolity of the French Quarter. Trail walks, exhibits, planetarium shows, and 86 acres of natural wildlife preserve. Open Mon.-Fri. 9am-5pm, Sat.-Sun. noon-5pm. Admission $3 seniors $2, children $1, families $7.

Entertainment

You've come to the right place. Any night of the week, any time of year, multitudes of people join the constant festival of the French Quarter. And that's only the beginning. After exploring the more traditional jazz, blues, and brass sound of the Quarter, assay the rest of the city for less tourist-oriented music and more local clientele. Check *OffBeat* or *Gambit,* the free weekly entertainment newspapers, or the Friday edition of the Times-Picayune's entertainment guide "Lagniappe" to find out who's playing in the clubs.

ew Orleans jazz, born here at the turn of the century in the red-light district, is no longer the cutting edge of this musical idiom. But outstanding traditional jazz can still be enjoyed at tiny, dimly-lit historic **Preservation Hall,** 726 St. Peter St. (523-8939). When the **Preservation Hall Jazz Band** is away touring the world, other classic groups perform here. If you don't get there when the doors open, be prepared for a lengthy wait in line, and, once inside, poor visibility (but fine acoustics) and sweaty standing-room only. (Admission $2; no drinks are sold, although you can bring your own soft drinks. Doors open at 8pm; music begins at 8:30pm and goes on until midnight.)

Keep your ears open for **Cajun** and **zydeco** bands, a local specialty. Using accordions, washboards, triangles and drums, they perform hot dance tunes (to which locals expertly two-step) and exuberantly sappy waltzes. Their traditional venue is the *fais do-do,* lengthy, wonderfully sweaty dances. Anyone who thinks couple-dancing went out in the 50s should try one of these; just grab a partner and throw yourself into the rhythm.

The annual **New Orleans Jazz Festival** (522-4786), held at the fairgrounds, features music played simultaneously from six stages. The festival also includes a Cajun food and crafts festival. It's a lot of fun and has great music, but it gets more like a zoo each year. The 1990 festival will be held in late April. Book your room early.

French Quarter

New Orleans bars stay open late, and few bars follow a strict schedule. In general, they open around 11am and close around 3am. If you want to take your drink outside, simply ask for a "Go Cup." (Most American cities prohibit the consumption of alcohol in public areas.)

Old Absinthe House, 240 Bourbon St. (523-3181). The marble absinthe fountain inside has been dry since absinthe was outlawed. The Absinthe Frappe is a recreation of the drink with anisette or Pernod liqueur ($3.75). Reputed to be the oldest bar in America.

The Napoleon House, 500 Chartres St. (524-9752). One of the world's great watering holes and less touristy than Bourbon St. bars. Located on the ground floor of the Old Girod House, which was built as an exile home for Napoleon as part of a plan to spirit him away from St. Helena. The "Fenwick Love Potion" is delicious, especially when chased with Dixie beer. Food served. Open daily roughly 11am-2am.

The Old Absinthe Bar, 400 Bourbon St. (525-8108). Drinks reasonable (for the French Quarter), and they often have a blues band there led by Bryan Lee. This bar has seen the likes of Mark Twain, Franklin D. Roosevelt, the Rolling Stones, and Humphrey Bogart. Check out their business cards up on the wall. Open Sun.-Thurs. 9:30pm-2am, Fri.-Sat. 5pm-3am.

Pat O'Brien's, 718 St. Peter St. (525-4823). The busiest bar in the French Quarter, and probably the most touristed. You can listen to the pianos in one room, mix with local students in another, or sit beneath huge fans in the courtyard. Open Sun.-Thurs. 10am-4am, Fri.-Sat. 10am-5am.

Storyville Jazz Hall, 1104 Decatur (525-8199). This large music hall opens onto the street and plays a variety of bands from Southern metal to cool jazz. Stand outside and listen before you pay the cover charge. Open Tues.-Fri. 8pm-whenever, Sat.-Sun. 1pm-whenever.

Bourbon Pub/Parade, 801 Bourbon St. (529-2107). Everyone welcome at this gay dance bar. "Tea dance" on Sunday evenings with all the beer you can drink for $5. Bar open 24 hours. Dancing nightly 9pm-whenever.

Outside the Quarter

Tyler's Beer Garden, 5234 Magazine St. (891-4989). Take the Magazine St. bus. Popular student bar. Good progressive jazz. The food is good, too—happy-hour oysters, 12 for $2. Cover: Mon.-Sat. $2-4.

Maple Leaf Bar, 8316 Oak St. (866-5323). The best local dance bar, offering zydeco and Cajun music where everyone does the two-step. The party begins Sun.-Thurs. at 10pm, Fri.-Sat. 10:30pm.

Benny's Bar, 938 Valence St. (895-4905), uptown. A trendy local spot with an interesting mix of patrons who come for the fine blues, reggae, and R&B. Music starts at 11pm. Open daily.

Igor's, 2133 St. Charles Ave. (522-7913). Take the St. Charles streetcar. This laundromat, pool room, bar and restaurant is the hot spot for lodgers at the Marquette House. Cheap food (10-inch pizza $3.75). Doing laundry will never be the same again. Open 24 hours.

The F&M Patio Bar, 4841 Tchoupitoulas (895-6784). This is where all the uptowners go for late-night fun. Two excellent juke boxes and a patio bar add to the entertainment. This place starts really rocking around 1am and keeps on rocking until morning.

Tipitina's, 501 Napoleon Ave. (897-3943). This locally renowned establishment attracts the best local bands and even some big names. Keep your eyes open for one of their fantastic *fais-do-dos.* A wide variety of music styles, best to call ahead. Cover $3-10.

Snug Harbor, 626 Frenchman (949-0696), just east of the Quarter near Decatur. Blues vocalists Charmaine Neville and Amasa Miller sing here regularly. The cover is no bargain, but Monday evening with Ms. Neville is not bad for $8.

Jimmy's, 8200 Willow St. (866-9549), off Carrollton Ave. Popular bar featuring many punk and new wave bands.

Plantations

Before the Civil War, slave plantations were the lifeblood of the rural Louisiana economy. The banks of the Mississippi between New Orleans and Baton Rouge are dotted with relics of the oldest aristocratic society. The best way to see the plantations is to rent a car for a day and drive along the Mississippi toward Baton Rouge along Hwy. 18 and 1. Frequent and free ferries across the Mississippi operate at Plaquemine, White Castle, and between Lutcher and Vacherie. The visitor information centers in New Orleans and Baton Rouge provide information on tours.

Nottoway, Rte. 405 (545-2730), between Bayou Goula and White Castle, 20 miles south of Baton Rouge on the southern bank of the Mississippi. Often called the "White Castle of Louisiana," this is the largest plantation home in the South, an incredible 64-room mansion with 22 columns, large ballroom, and a 3-story stairway. This was the first choice of David O. Selznick for filming *Gone with the Wind* (the owners wouldn't allow it). Open daily 9am-5pm. Admission and 1-hr. guided tour $8, children $4.

San Francisco Plantation House, Rte. 44 (535-2341), 2 miles north of Reserve, 23 miles from New Orleans on the north bank of the Mississippi. Built in 1856, this beautifully restored plantation is galleried in the old Creole style with the main living room on the 2nd floor. The exterior, painted 3 different colors, is reminiscent of the decorations on the elegant Mississippi River steamboats in the 19th century. (Open daily 10am-4pm. Admission $5, students $2.50, children $1.50.)

Houmas House, River Rd., Burnside (473-7841), a little more then halfway to Baton Rouge on the northern bank of the Mississippi. The setting for the movie **Hush, Hush, Sweet Charlotte,** starring Bette Davis and Olivia DeHavilland, this house was built in 2 sections. The rear was constructed in the last quarter of the 18th century; the Greek Revival mansion in front was built in 1840. Beautiful gardens and furnishings. Open Feb.-Oct. daily 10am-5pm; Nov.-Jan 10am-4pm. Admission $5, students $3, children $2.

Baton Rouge

Small and secluded, in the heart of Louisiana's plantation country, Baton Rouge provides a quiet retreat after the revelry of New Orleans. Today, the city is curiously uncrowded and devoid of traffic, but it was not always so peaceful. Until he was felled by an assassin's bullet in 1935, the controversial but always colorful Louisiana governor, Huey Long, held court in the state's capital city. Nicknamed the "Kingfisher" after his successful political overthrow of the Louisiana aristocracy, Long was famous for his populist political machine. While unquestionably corrupt, Long was unquestionably one of the city's greatest benefactors, and a huge statue of him stands guard in front of the capitol he built, the tallest in the U.S. Long might have been the last exciting thing to happen to this lethargic city. Everything closes by 2pm downtown and the area is vacant by 5pm sharp. Only the round-the-clock partying at Louisiana State University rescues Baton Rouge from perpetual sleep.

Practical Information

Emergency: 911.

Visitor Information: Baton Rouge Convention and Visitors Bureau, 838 N. Boulevard (383-1825). Pick up the visitors guide and don't expect too much from the staff. Open daily 8am-5pm.

Greyhound/Trailways: 1253 Florida Blvd. (343-4891), at 13th St. A 15-min. walk from downtown. Unsafe area at night. To: New Orleans (11 per day, 2 hr., $13) and Lafayette (6 per day, 1 hr., $8). Open 24 hours.

Capital City Transportation: 336-0821. Main terminal at 22nd and Florida Blvd. Buses run Mon.-Sat. approximately 6:30am-6:30pm. Service to LSU decent, otherwise unreliable and/or infrequent. Fare 75¢.

Help Lines: Crisis Intervention/Suicide Prevention Center, 924-3900. **Rape Crisis,** 383-7273. Both open 24 hours.

Post Office: 750 Florida Blvd. (381-0713), off River Rd. **ZIP code:** 70821.

Area Code: 504.

Baton Rouge is 80 miles northwest of New Orleans up I-10 and the meandering Mississippi. I-10 connects Baton Rouge with Lafayette and Acadiana on the west. The state capitol is on the east bank of the river; the city spreads eastward.

Accommodations, Camping, and Food

Most budget accommodations are out of town along east-west Florida Boulevard, (U.S. 190), or north-south Airline Highway (U.S. 61). Try the **Alamo Plaza Hotel Courts,** 4243 Florida Blvd. (924-7231). Take bus #6 ("Sherwood Forest") east on Florida Blvd. from the Greyhound station. The clean, spacious rooms have cable TV. (Singles $22. Doubles $26.) **Louisiana State University** provides cheap accommodations at their on-campus hotel run out of Pleasant Hall (387-0297). Flat rate of $38 for as many as you can fit. Take bus #7 ("University") from North Blvd. behind the Old State Capitol. **The Budgetel Inn,** 10555 Rieger Rd. (291-6600 or

800-428-3438), has clean, adequate rooms. (Singles $28. Doubles $35.) The **General Lafayette** is downtown, and offers very mediocre rooms for $35 and up. It should be used only as a last resort.

The **KOA Campground** (664-7281), is 12 miles east of Baton Rouge (Denham Springs exit off I-12). Well-maintained sites, with clean facilities and an accommodating staff, cost $12.50 for two people, $14 with water and electricity.

The best places to eat in Baton Rouge are near Louisiana State University (LSU) on **Highland Avenue.** Try **The Chimes,** 3357 Highland (383-1754), across the street from LSU, for burgers, po'boys, seafood, fried alligator ($5.50), live entertainment, and a selection of 70 different beers. (Open Mon.-Fri. 11:30am-2am, Sat. 4pm-midnight, Sun. noon-midnight.) Nearby, **Louie's Café,** 209 W. State (346-8221) is a 24-hour grill famous for its omelettes (around $4). Right behind Louie's is **The Bayou,** 124 W. Chimes (346-1765), one of the locals' favorite bars, where you can play free pool from 5-8pm and drink select longnecks for 99¢. Downtown, the **Frostop Drive-In,** 402 Government (344-1179), is a fun 50s-style burger place. (Open Mon.-Fri. 9:30am-8:30pm, Sat. 10:30am-8:30pm, Sun. 11am-8pm.)

Sights

The most prominent building in Baton Rouge is also the first one you should visit. The unique **Louisiana State Capitol** (342-7317) is a magnificent *art moderne* skyscraper built in a mere 14 months between 1931 and 1932. The front lobby alone is worth a visit, but visitors may also go to the 27th floor observation deck for free. (Open Mon.-Sat. 8am-4:30pm.) One of the most interesting buildings in the U.S., it continues to attest the power of Long's personality. Look for the plaque in a back corridor indicating the spot where he was assassinated. (He is buried in front under the statue.) The **Old State Capitol,** at River Rd. and North Blvd., an eccentric Gothic Revival castle, offers free tours. (Open Tues.-Sat. 9am-4:30pm.) Just south of downtown, the **Beauregard District** boasts typically ornate antebellum homes. Walk down North Boulevard from the Old State Capitol to the Visitor's Center to take in the beauty of this neighborhood.

Just a block away from the Old Capitol on River Rd. is the **Riverside Museum** of the **Louisiana Arts and Science Center** (344-9463). Climb on the old steam engine and train cars parked next door. The museum has a good collection of sculpture, photographs, and paintings by contemporary Louisiana artists. (Open Tues.-Fri. 10am-3pm, Sat. 10am-4pm, Sun. 1-4pm. Admission $1.50.) The museum runs the **Old Governor's Mansion,** at North Blvd. and St. Charles St. The governor's residence from 1930 to 1963, this was once Huey Long's mansion. (Open Sat. 10am-4pm and Sun. 1-4pm. Admission $2.)

Those who don't have a car to visit outlying plantations (see Plantations under New Orleans) can visit **Magnolia Mound Plantation,** 2161 Nicholson Dr. (343-4955), the only plantation on the regular bus line. A late-18th-century wooden home, Magnolia has been well restored and furnished with antiques. (Open Tues.-Sat. 10am-4pm, Sun. 1-4pm, last tour at 3:30pm. Admission $3.50, seniors $2.50, students $1.50.)

Tour the harbor in the *Samuel Clemens* steamboat (381-9606), which departs from Florida Blvd. at the river for one-hour cruises. (Tours March-Sept. daily at 10am, noon, and 2pm; Oct.-March Wed.-Sun. at 10am, noon, and 2pm. Admission $5, children $3.) The *U.S.S. Kidd* (342-1942), a World War II destroyer, is open for inspection on the river just outside the Louisiana Naval War Memorial Museum. (Open daily 9am-5pm. Admission to ship and museum $3.50, children $2. Ship only $1, children 50¢.)

Acadiana

Originally French settlers in Nova Scotia, the Acadian people were expelled from their homes in 1755 by the English government. Their ships came ashore all down the Atlantic coastline and in the Caribbean, and the people were given a hostile reception in most places; in Massachusetts, Georgia, and South Carolina they were made indentured servants. It soon became clear to the Acadians that their only hope for freedom lay in reaching French territory: Louisiana. On their arrival, they settled on the Gulf Slope. Many of the present-day inhabitants of St. Martin, Lafayette, Iberia, and St. Mary parishes are descendants of the original settlers.

Since the 18th century, Acadian or "Cajun" culture has been threatened with extinction. Louisiana passed laws in the 20s forcing Acadian schoolchildren to speak English. More recently, the oil boom of the past few decades has endangered the Acadian identity's survival. Lafayette, a center of Acadian culture, was seen by oil executives and developers as the Houston of Louisiana, and mass culture recklessly assaulted this small town and its neighbors. However, the proud people of southern Louisiana have resisted homogenization—the state has been declared bilingual, and a state agency, the **Conseil pour le developpement du français en Louisiane,** was established to preserve Acadian French in schools and in the media.

"Cajun Country" spans the southern portion of the state, from Houma in the east to the Texas border. Much of it bayou and swampland, the unique natural environment has become intertwined with Cajun culture. The music and the cuisine, especially, are symbolic of the ruggedness of this traditional, family-centered society.

Lafayette

Lafayette makes a fine base for exploring Acadiana, although there's not much to do here. The town was a center for oil businesses in southern Louisiana in the 70s and 80s, but growth was stalled by the drop in crude prices.

The town depicts "true" Cajun life in its interesting reconstructed **Acadian village** (981-2364), 10 miles from the tourist center. The 19th-century buildings include a general store, a chapel, a garden, and some private residences. (Open daily 10am-5pm. Admission $4, seniors $3, students $1.50. Take U.S. 167 north, turn right on Ridge Rd., left on Mouton, and then follow signs.) The **Lafayette Museum,** 1122 Lafayette St. (234-2208), contains heirlooms, antiques, and Mardi Gras costumes. (Open Tues.-Sat. 9am-5pm, Sun. 3-5pm. Admission $3, seniors $2, children $1.)

Lafayette is built on the edge of the Atchafalaya Swamp, and from Baton Rouge it's reached by the Atchafalaya Freeway, a 32- mile bridge over the bayous that is a triumph of modern engineering. Get closer to the elements by embarking upon one of the **Atchafalaya Basin Swamp Tours** (228-8567), in the nearby town of Henderson. The captain explains how crawfish are harvested and how the interstate highway was built on the unstable swamp mud. (Tours (1¾ hr.) leave at 8am, 10am, 1pm and 3pm. Fare $7, children $4.)

For Cajun food and live Cajun music and dancing, go to **Mulates,** 325 Mills Ave., Breaux Bridge (332-4648). In downtown Lafayette, visit **Les Café des Artistes,** 537 Jefferson St. (234-2030), a chic gathering place. Innovative sandwiches ($3.75-4.25) are served in a gallery of modern art. (Open Tues.-Thurs. 7am-10pm, Fri. 7am-midnight, Sat. 8am-2am, Sun. 8am-8pm.) Down the road is **Chris' Poboys,** 631 Jefferson St. (234-1696), which offers po'boys ($4-5) and seafood platters ($5). (Open Mon.-Fri. 11am-8pm.)

Several motels are a $3 cabfare from the bus station. The closest and most appealing is the **Travelodge,** 1101 Pinhook Rd. (234-7402). Newly renovated, this motel has large, attractive rooms, cable TV, a pool, and an accommodating staff at a great price. (Singles $23. Doubles $26.) The **Super 8,** 2224 N. Evangeline Thruway (232-8826), just off I-10, has spacious, clean rooms, a pool, and friendly management. (Singles $26. Doubles $32.) Evangeline Highway is lined with other inexpensive chain motels, including **La Quinta** (233-5610) and **Motel 6,** (233-2055). Avoid motels on Cameron Street; this area is unsafe. If you're traveling alone or have a little extra cash, treat yourself to bed and breakfast at **Til Frere's House,** 1905 Verot School Rd. (984-9347), which has rooms decorated with antiques, plus private baths, Turkish towel robes, large breakfasts and complimentary drinks (mint juleps always on hand) and snacks. (Singles $45. Doubles $55. Mention *Let's Go* and you may get a 15% discount.) Campgrounds are few and far between. The closest is **KOA Lafayette** (235-2739), 50 miles west of town on I-10, exit 97. (Sites $14.)

Pick up a copy of *The Times* (available at restaurants and gas stations all over town) to get informed about what's going down this week. Considering its size and location, Lafayette has a surprising amount of after-hours entertainment, including the **Cajun Dance,** a world-class concert hall that regularly brings in acts and concerts of national prominence. On Fridays during spring and fall, Lafayette kicks off the weekend with **Downtown Alive!,** a series of free concerts featuring everything from new wave to Cajun and zydeco. (All concerts 5:30-8pm. Call 268-5566 for information.) If you visit in April, the **Festival International de Louisiane** blends the music, visual arts, and cooking of this region into a francophone festival, drawing hundreds of visitors of all ages and nationalities to Lafayette to pay tribute to the influence of the French upon Southwestern Louisiana.

Lafayette is at Louisiana's major crossroad. I-10 leads east to New Orleans (130 miles) and west to Lake Charles (76 miles); U.S. 90 heads south to New Iberia (20 miles) and the bayou country; U.S. 167 runs north into central Louisiana. Lafayette is also a railroad stop for Amtrak's *Sunset Limited,* linking New Orleans with Houston and Los Angeles. Lafayette to: New Orleans (1 per day, 3 hr. $26); Houston (3 per wk., 5 hr., $47); and New Iberia (3 per wk., 20 min., $6). The station is at 133 E. Grant St., near the bus station, but it is unstaffed. There is no phone and tickets must be purchased in advance through a travel agent. **Greyhound,** 315 Lee Ave. (235-1541), connects Lafayette to New Orleans (7 per day, 2½ hr., $19) and Baton Rouge (9 per day, 1 hr., $8), as well as to small towns such as New Iberia (2 per day, 1 hr., $3). The **Lafayette Bus System** runs infrequently, and not on Sundays (fare 45¢); its headquarters are at 400 Dorset (261-8570). But you'll need a car or a lucky thumb to really explore Acadiana and the Gulf Coast bayou country. **Thrifty Rent-a-Car,** 401 E. Pinhook (237-1282), usually has the best deals. (Must be 21 with major credit card.)

The **post office** is at 1105 Moss (232-4800). Lafayette's **ZIP code** is 70501; the **area code** is 318.

New Iberia and Southcentral Louisiana

New Iberia is home to a host of traditional southern plantations. Most are in private hands, but **Shadows on the Teche,** 317 E. Main St. (369-6446), is open to the public. Built in 1831, it was neglected after the Civil War until a Southern aristocrat refurbished the crumbling mansion. (Open daily 9am-4:30pm. Admission $4, children $2.)

Seven miles away, the beautiful **Avery Island,** on Rte. 329 off Rte. 90, is home to the world- famous **Tabasco Pepper Sauce** factory. This is where the McIlhenny family has produced the famous sauce for nearly a century. Guided tours complete with a sample taste are included. (Open Mon.-Fri. 9-11:45am and 1-3:45pm, Sat. 9-11:45am. Free. A 50¢ toll is charged to enter the island.) Nearby are the **Jungle Gardens** (369-6243), 250 acres which were developed in the 19th century by E. A. McIlhenny. The gardens include a sanctuary for herons and egrets, waterways, a lovely wisteria arch, camelia gardens, Chinese bamboo, alligators, and an 800-year-old statue of the Buddha. The sanctuary helped save the snowy egret from extinction. This elegant bird, once hunted for the long plumes it grows during mating season, now nests in the gardens from February to mid-summer. (Open daily 9am-5pm. Admission $4.25, children $3.25).

For a unique look at swamp and bayou wildlife, take an **Airboat Tour** (229-4457) of Lake Fausse Point and the surrounding area. (Tickets $40 for 4. Tours 1-3 hr.)

New Iberia is 21 miles southeast of Lafayette on U.S. 90. **Amtrak** (800-872-7245) serves New Iberia between New Orleans and Lafayette. **Greyhound** (364-8571) pulls into town at 101 Perry St. Buses head to Morgan City ($6), New Orleans, and Lafayette three times a day.

The **Tourist Information Center** is at 2690 Center St. (365-1540), at the intersection of Hwy. 14. (Open daily 9am-5pm.) The **post office** is at 817 E. Dale St. (364-4568). The **ZIP code:** is 70560. The **area code** is 318.

Acadian Wildlife

Much of lush Acadiana has been turned over to wildlife. The subtropical environment supports many species in a mixture of marsh, bottomland hardwoods and backwater areas, called "bayous." Explore this bayou country to fish, see wildlife, or enjoy the jungle-like terrain, about 40 miles southeast of New Iberia near Bayou Vista. **Atchafalaya Delta Wildlife Area,** rich in birdlife, lies at the mouth of the Atchafalaya River in St. Mary Parish. The preserve encompasses bayous, potholes, low and high marsh, and dry ground. Rails, snipes, coot, and gallinules thrive here. Access is by boat launches from Morgan City near the Bayou Boeuf locks. Primitive campsites are available in the area.

Visit the **Attakapas Wildlife Area,** in Southern St. Martin and Iberia Parishes. The area center lies 20 miles northwest of Morgan city and 10 miles northeast of Franklin. This hauntingly beautiful area is composed mainly of flat swampland, but includes a large amount of raised land used as a refuge by animals during flooding. In Attakapas cypress-tupelo, oak, maple, and hackberry grow on the high ground, and a variety of swamp plants such as alligator weed flourishes in the wetlands. Hunting is popular here—mostly for squirrels, deer, and rabbits. Local residents you may want to encounter include beavers, otters, muskrats, raccoons, bobcats, hawks, and alligators. The area can be reached by boat; public launches leave from Morgan City on Rte. 70. Watch for signposts. No camping is allowed.

Mississippi

In the heart of the South Central region lies Mississippi, multifaceted and quintessentially Deep South. Overwhelmingly rural, and almost entirely dependent on agriculture, it is the poorest of states, continually last in the United States in almost every category from economic growth to per capita income to quality of health care. It's important to get off the interstates and explore the "real" Mississippi; take the Natchez Trace, which slices through the state, or stick to the back roads. The views from the major highways fail to do justice to this beautiful country.

Practical Information

Capital: Jackson.

Tourist Information: Division of Tourism, 1301 Walter Siller's Bldg., 550 High St. (359-3414 or 800-647-2290). Open Mon.-Fri. 8am-5pm. **Bureau of Parks and Recreation,** P.O. Box 10600, Jackson 39209.

Time Zone: Central (1 hr. behind Eastern). **Postal Abbreviation:** MS.

Jackson

Jackson is the state capital and the only major urban area of Mississippi. A combination of a briskly growing sunbelt city and sleepy Deep South town, it's full of 20th-century activity, but without the thronging crowds of most major cities. It also keeps the hours of a smaller town—even the historic and business districts barely come to life during working hours. After 5:30pm on weeknights and all day Saturday and Sunday, Jackson sleeps. Lastly, it has none of the tense atmosphere of a big metropolis; come here if you want to experience the warmth and traditional beauty of the South's most hospitable city.

Practical Information

Emergency: 911.

Visitor Information: Tourist Information Center, 1100 Lakeland Dr. (960-1800). Open Mon.-Fri. 8:30am-5pm, Sat. 8:30am-4:30pm. The **Convention and Visitors Bureau,** 921 N. President St. (960-1891), is more conveniently located. Open Mon.-Fri. 8:30am-5pm.

Allen C. Thompson Municipal Airport: To the east of downtown, off I-20. Cab fare to downtown runs approximately $13.

Amtrak: 300 W. Capitol St. (355-6350). To: Memphis (1 per day, $42) and New Orleans (1 per day, $39). Open daily 7:30-10:30am and 5-7:30pm.

Greyhound/Trailways: 201 S. Jefferson St. (353-6342). Unsafe area at night. To: Dallas (4 per day, 10 hr., $65); Montgomery (7 per day, 6 hr., $40); and Memphis (1 per day, 4 hr., $32). Open 24 hours.

Jackson Transit System (JATRAN): (948-3560), in the Federal Bldg., downtown. Limited areas. Bus schedules and maps are posted at most bus stops. Buses operate Mon.-Fri. 6am-5:30pm, Sat. 7am-6pm. Fare 60¢.

Help Line: First Call for Help, 352-4357. Information referral service.

Taxi: Veterans Cab, 355-8319. $1.10 base fare, $1 per mile.

Post Office: 401 E. South St. (968-0572). Open Mon.-Fri. 7am-7pm., Sat. 8am-noon. **ZIP code:** 39201.

Area Code: 601.

Jackson is at the intersection of I-55 (north to Memphis, south to New Orleans) and I-20 (east-west). Highways 49, 51, and 80, as well as the scenic **Natchez Trace,** which stretches 550 miles from Natchez to Nashville, TN, can get you there. **State Street** runs north-south through downtown, **High Street** runs east-west.

Accommodations

The accommodations scene is pretty grim, as there are few motels downtown. However, if you have a car, you will have no problem finding lodging along I-20 and I-55.

Sun 'n' Sand Motel, 401 N. Lamar St. (354-2501), downtown. Very friendly. Large, clean rooms with cable TV, and free local phone calls. Pool. Singles $30. Doubles $35.

Admiral Benbow Inn, 905 N. State St. (948-4161), near downtown. Comfortable, clean rooms and a nice pool. Singles $35. Doubles $40.

Red Roof Inn, 700 Larson St. (969-5006), by the fairgrounds. Singles $28. Doubles $37.

Motel 6, 970 I-20 Frontage Rd. (948-3692), off the highway. Pool. Rooms start at $20.

Food

Jackson specializes in Southern food, catfish, and plate lunch specials. The restaurants cater to the young, professional crowd; most spots are inexpensive and lively.

Primo's, 1016 N. State St. (948-4343). A Jackson tradition. Excellent, cheap Southern food (burgers and sandwiches $3-5); breakfasts with creamy grits and huge omelettes under $3. Open Mon.-Sat. 7am-10pm, Sun. 8am-10pm.

The Elite Cafe, 141 E. Capitol (352-5606). Friendly lunch spot with great corn bread and veal cutlets. Plate lunch specials with 2 vegetables and bread under $4.50. Be prepared to wait in line during lunch rush—this place is very popular. Open Mon.-Fri. 7am-9:30pm, Sat. 5-9:30pm.

The Iron Horse Grill, 320 W. Pearl St. (355-8419). Airy, comfortable restaurant in a huge converted smoke house. Primarily Tex-Mex ($5-8); steak and seafood entrees more expensive. A pianist accompanies lunch and dinner. Open Mon.-Sat. 11am-10pm.

Sights and Entertainment

The old and the new compete everywhere in Jackson; the city has two capitol buildings. Built in 1840, the **Old State Capitol** (354-6222), at the intersection of Capitol and State St., now houses an excellent museum of Mississippi's long, often dramatic history. (Open Mon.-Fri. 8am-5pm, Sat. 9:30am-4:30pm, Sun. 12:30-4:30pm. Free.) The state legislature's current home is the beautiful **New State Capitol** (359-3114), at Mississippi and Congress St., completed in 1903. The beaux arts grandeur of the building has been preserved by a huge restoration project in 1979, and the building gleams in all its original glory. (Guided tours Mon.-Fri. 9am, 10am, 11am, 1:30pm, 2:30pm, and 3:30pm. Open Mon.-Fri. 8am-5pm, Sat. 10am-4pm, Sun. 1-4pm. Free.) Several other museums in the downtown area are well maintained and worth a visit. **The Mississippi Museum of Art** at Pascagoula and Lamar St. (960-1515), has a fabulous collection of Americana and a fun participatory Impression Gallery for kids. (Open Tues.-Fri. 10am-5pm, Sat.-Sun. noon-4pm. Admission $2, children $1.) Next door to the museum is the **Russell C. Davis Planetarium** (960-1550), considered one of the best in the world. (Galactic and musical shows Tues.-Fri. 8pm; Sat. at 2, 4, 8pm; Sun. 2 and 4pm. Admission $3, seniors and children $2.) A terrific presentation of nature and wildlife for the whole family can be seen at the **Mississippi Museum of Natural Science** on Jefferson St. (354-7303), across from the fairground. (Open Mon.-Fri. 8am-5pm, Sat. 9:30am-4:30pm.) And don't miss the **Governor's Mansion** (359-3175), a national historic landmark. This Greek Revival antebellum mansion is fully restored and the hourly tours are an enlightening introduction to Mississippian politics. (Open Tues.-Fri. 9:30am-11am.)

For a more in-depth look at some fine architecture, visit the **Manship House,** 420 E. Fortification (961-4724), just a short walk north from the New Capitol. Charles Henry Manship, the Civil War mayor of Jackson, built this Gothic Revival "cottage villa," which has been restored to its 19th-century condition. (Open Tues.-Fri. 9am-4pm, Sat.- Sun. 1-4pm.) **The Oaks,** 823 N. Jefferson St. (353-9339), is Jackson's oldest house (1746) and was occupied by Sherman during the siege of the city in 1863. (Open Mon.-Fri. 10am-4pm, Sat.-Sun. 1:30-4pm. Admission $2, students $1.)

Finally, the **Smith-Robertson Museum and Cultural Center,** 528 Bloom St. (960-1457), directly behind the Sun 'n' Sand, is dedicated to preserving the culture of African-American Mississippi. It portrays the struggle of African-Americans through artifacts and pictures from the African past to the present. (Open Mon.-Fri. 9am-5pm. Free.)

After a sweaty day of sightseeing, stop in at **Hal & Mal's Restaurant and Oyster Bar,** 200 Commerce St. (948-0888), which provides nighttime entertainment in a converted warehouse; bands play Thursday through Saturday nights. (Restaurant open Mon.-Sat. 11am-10pm; bar open until 1am.) The hottest bar in town is **Poets,** 1885 Lakeland Dr. (982-9711), usually packed with a young, fun crowd. (Open Mon.-Sat. noon-12:30am.)

Oxford

The approach to Oxford—flat farmland and long dirt roads—gives no hint of the cultured college town that awaits. If you were expecting another sleepy Mississippi community, you'll be surprised by BMWs, polo shirts, khaki pants, and—yes—oxfords, all due to the presence of the **University of Mississippi** (affectionately known as Ole Miss). The university is also the source of several art shows, concerts, and writers' conferences.

Home of the late writer William Faulkner, and familiar to his readers as the inspiration for his Yoknapatawpha County, Oxford retains many of the qualities described in his novels—large Southern homes, shady magnolia trees, and deep-rooted tradition. This, combined with the cosmopolitan charm of the university, results in a town of both traditional beauty and modern culture.

Oxford lies 130 miles southeast of Memphis, TN, on Rte. 6, 23 miles east of I-55. For the most part, the town is small enough to cover easily on foot. **University Avenue** is the major east-west thoroughfare, intersecting with **Lamar** a few blocks south of the town square. **Van Buren Avenue** and **Jackson Avenue** cross the square parallel to University Ave.

In Oxford, as in most southern towns, everyday life revolves around the town square. The white sandstone county courthouse, featured in Faulkner's works, is an impressive centerpiece for the old business district. About 5 blocks west on University Ave. is the **University of Mississippi,** which once stood as a monument to Southern tradition but has been integrated since 1962. The **Center for the Study of Southern Culture** at the Barnard Observatory (232-5993), founded in 1977, researches all facets of Southern life. It sponsors the **Blues Archive** across the street at 340 Farley Hall (232-7753), an immense repository of blues recordings including 9000 records from B.B. King's private collection. (Open Mon.-Fri. 8:30am-noon.)

A walk down South Lamar and along Old Taylor Rd., or better yet, through Bailey's woods along a path from behind the Skipworth Museum on Museum Ave., leads to **Rowan Oak** (234-3284 or 232-7318), the home of William Faulkner, which is tucked in the woods at a bend in Old Taylor Rd. The house remains as Faulkner left it when he died. (Open Mon.-Fri. 10am-noon and 2-4pm, Sat. 10am-noon, Sun. 2-4pm.) Afterwards, inspired visitors can head to **Square Books** (see Food below) for a Barq's root beer and terrific browsing through an impressive collection of Southern writing.

Catfish is the local delicacy, but you'll also find a few restaurants which cater to the fun-loving and budget-conscious students of Ole Miss. **The Gin,** 201 Harrison St. (234-0024), 1 block southeast of Oxford Sq., is a converted cotton warehouse where you'll always find a lively crowd. (Sandwiches and burgers under $6. Open Mon.-Wed. and Sat. 11am-midnight, Thurs.-Fri. 11am-1am.) **The Hoka,** right next door at 304 S. 14th St. (234-3057), is best known for its carpeted ceilings and its cheesecake, but also serves sandwiches and catfish ($3-6). (Open daily 11am-"whenever, but usually by 2am.") These two neighboring watering holes are most crowded on weekend nights when Ole Miss students are ready to party. **Square Books,** 200 S. Lamar St. (236-2262), in the square, serves sandwiches ($2-4) and killer sweets (brandy bread pudding and pecan squares) in a café upstairs from the bookstore. (Open Mon.-Sat. 9am-9pm, Sun. noon-5pm.) **Cafe Olé,** 1612 University Ave. (234-1707), ¼ mile east of the town square, serves incredible Mexican food including vegetarian specialties like spinach enchiladas and vegetable fajitas. (Entrees $3-8. Open Mon.-Fri. 11am-2pm and 5-10pm, Sat. 5-10pm.)

Nightlife largely centers on the Gin and the Hoka, but **Syd and Harry's,** 118 Van Buren Ave. (236-3193) in the square has the best music in town. Dance five nights a week to a mixture of blues, rock, and progressive music, or just relax with your favorite beer. (Open Mon. and Wed. 4pm-midnight, Thurs.-Fri 4pm-1am, Sat. 5pm-midnight.)

Lodging is inexpensive in Oxford, but it can be impossible to get a room during football games, graduation, and the Faulkner Festival in late July. **The Ole Miss Motel,** 1517 E. University Ave. (234-2424), provides comfortable, clean rooms with A/C, telephone, and color TV. Some rooms have refrigerators. (Singles $21. Doubles $28. Prices increase on the weekends.) **The University Inn,** 2201 Jackson Ave. (234-7013), about 1 mile from the university, is more luxurious, offering steamrooms, whirlpools, and a pool. (Singles $33. Doubles $39. Use of pool $2 extra.) A last resort is **Johnson's Motor Inn,** 2305 Jackson Ave. (234-3611), right next door. (Singles $23. Doubles $27.)

Before touring Oxford, you might stop by the **Oxford Tourism Council,** 229 W. Jackson Ave. (234-4651), near Ole Miss (open Mon.-Thurs. 9am-5pm, Fri. 9am-4pm), or the **Tourist Information Center** (232-2149), in Oxford. (Open Mon.-Sat. 8am-noon and 1-5pm.) At the **Greyhound station** 925 Van Buren Ave. (234-1424), you can make connections to Memphis (1 per day, 2 hr., $15) and Birmingham

(1 per day, 4 hr., $31). Mississippi is notorious for its infrequent and inconvenient Greyhound schedules.

Oxford's **post office** is located at 911 Jackson Ave. (234-5615). The city's **ZIP code** is 38655.

Vicksburg

The death knell for the Old South sounded at Vicksburg. On July 4, 1863, the same day that Gettysburg fell, the "Gibraltar of the South" surrendered to the Union forces. Today, the federal government keeps the peace at the **Vicksburg National Military Park,** which surrounds the town. It's best to drive to the battlefield, museums, and cemetery east of town at exit 4B on I-20, on Clay St. (Admission $3 per car, $1 per person if entering by bus, seniors and children free.) The **visitors center** (636-0583 or 636-9421; 800-221-3536 outside MS), at the entrance, provides maps. A two-hour guided tour of the town leaves from the center ($15). (Open daily 8am-6pm; off-season 8am-5pm.) For more information about Vicksburg, visit the **Tourist Information Center** (636-9421), directly across the street from the park. (Open Mon.-Fri. 8am-5pm, Sat. and Sun. 9am-4pm.) Unfortunately, you'll need a car to visit most of Vicksburg. Although it is a small city, the bus station, the information center, downtown, and the far end of the sprawling military park are at the four extremes of the city.

Within the park, visit the **National Cemetery** and the **U.S.S. Cairo Museum** (636-2199). The museum's centerpiece is the restored iron clad gunboat *Cairo,* the first vessel ever sunk by a remotely detonated mine. The museum displays a fascinating array of artifacts that were preserved for over a century after the ship sunk in the waters of the Yazoo River. (Open daily 8am-9:30pm; off-season 8am-5pm. Free.)

The **Old Court House Museum,** 1008 Cherry St. (636-0741), presides over Vicksburg's town center, 3 miles from the park's entrance. It was used as a prison for captured Union soldiers during the Siege of Vicksburg. Today it is considered one of the South's finest Civil War museums, housing an impressive collection of relics and artifacts from the "War Between the States." (Open Mon.-Sat. 8:30am-4:30pm, Sun. 1:30-4:30pm. Admission $1.50, seniors $1, under 18 75¢.)

Next door, continuing the martial theme, is **Toys and Soldiers, A Museum,** 1100 Cherry St. (638-1986), where 25,000 toy soldiers await you. (Open Mon.-Sat. 9am-4:30pm, Sun. 1:30-4:30pm. Tours $2, under 18 $1.50, families $5.) Two blocks away is the **Biedenharn Candy Museum,** 1107 Washington St. (638-6514), where Coca-Cola was born. The museum displays Coke memorabilia from as far back as 1894, and you can snag a Coke for 40¢. (Open Mon.-Sat. 9am-5pm, Sun. 1:30-4:30pm. Admission $1.75, children $1.25. Disabled access.)

For a fascinating and informative introduction to Vicksburg's history, be sure to catch **"Vanishing Glory,"** 717 Clay St. (634-1863), a multi-media theatrical panorama. (Shows on the hour daily 10am-5pm; admission $3, students $2.)

Scattered across Vicksburg are several fine antebellum homes. **Balfour House,** 1002 Crawford St. (638-3690), is downtown. The Greek Revival home served as local headquarters for the Union Army after they took Vicksburg. (Open daily 9am-5pm. Admission $4, children $2.) The **Martha Vick House,** 1300 Grove St. (638-7036), was the home of the last of the Vicks in Vicksburg. The restored building contains many elegant French paintings. (Open daily 9am-5pm. Admission $4, age 12-18 $2.) The latter, like many of the restored Vicksburg estates, doubles as a B&B (ask at the Vicksburg Convention and Visitors Bureau).

While downtown, chow down at **Burger Village,** 1220 Washington St. (638-0202), which serves inexpensive burgers (under $3) and seafood in a friendly atmosphere. (Open Mon.-Thurs. 9am-6pm, Fri.-Sat. 9am-7pm.) The **New Orleans Café,** 1100 Washington St. (638-8182), provides decent seafood, sandwiches, and salads for under $6 and also provides weekend entertainment in its **Other Side Lounge.** (Open Sun.-Thurs. 11am-10pm, Fri.-Sat. 11am-11:30pm.) Across the street is **Miller's Still Lounge,** a real Southern watering hole with live entertainment and the smell of popcorn nightly. (Open Sun.-Thurs. 11am-10pm, Fri.-Sat. 11am-11:30pm.) A mile south of downtown you'll find **Giani's,** 3421 Washington St. (638-0105), Vicksburg's only "complete Italian restaurant." Tasty pasta entrees $5-9. (Open Mon.-Fri. 11:30am-2pm and 5-9pm, Sat.-Sun. 5-9pm.) From there take a short drive south on Washington St. to the **Louisiana Circle.** This secluded overview offers truly breathtaking vistas of the great Mississippi River.

Cheap accommodations in Vicksburg are not hard to find, except around the July 4th weekend; the military park's reenactment draws thousands of tourists, and hotel rates tend to rise. Most hotels are located by the park, so don't expect to stay in town. The **Hillcrest Motel,** 4503 Hwy. 80 E. (638-1491), has clean and comfortable singles for $19.90 and doubles for $22.90. The **Scottish Inn,** I-20 at Highway 80 E. (638-5511), provides singles for $23 and doubles for $26. **The Vicksburg Battlefield Kampground,** 4407 I-20 Frontage Rd. (636-9946), has a pool and laundromat. ($9-11 for 2 people.)

Vicksburg lies 30 miles west of Jackson on I-20, and 200 miles north of New Orleans. The **Greyhound/Trailways** station is inconveniently located at 3324 Halspear Rd., off Frontage Rd. (To Jackson: 8 per day, 1hr., $8). Vicksburg's **ZIP code** is 39180; the **area code** is 601.

Mississippi Coast

Billed as the South's Riviera, **Biloxi** and its neighbors Gulfport and Pascagoula have tossed aside their tranquil origins to become hyped-up resorts. Biloxi once served as the centerpiece of the Old Spanish Trail from Florida to the California missions; today, known as Highway 90 or Beach Boulevard, the "trail" is lined with fast food operations, drive-through liquor stores, gimmicky hotels, and new condominiums. Less tacky than the coastline in Florida's Panhandle, Mississippi's Gulf shores are partially redeemed by the subtropical scenery, the white sandy beaches, and the presence of the **Gulf Islands National Seashore,** 10 miles offshore. Get away from it all with the herons, snakes, and alligators on one of the remote islands. The **Biloxi Chamber of Commerce,** 1036 Fred Haise Blvd. (374-2717), across from the lighthouse, eagerly offers aid to tourists. (Open Mon.-Fri. 8:30am-5pm.) The **Biloxi Tourist Information Center,** 710 E. Beach Blvd. (374-3105), down the street from the bus station, is not particularly geared to the budget traveler. (Open Mon.-Fri. 8am-6pm, Sat. 9am-6pm, Sun. noon-5pm.)

Within Biloxi, the unofficial capital of the coast, attractions away from the beach are sparse. Between Biloxi and Gulfport you'll find the mansions, pavilions, and grounds of **Beauvoir,** W. Beach Blvd. and Beauvoir Rd. (388-1313), the last home and present shrine of Confederate President Jefferson Davis. (Open daily 9am-5pm. Admission $4, children $2.) Also along the shoreline is the **Biloxi Lighthouse,** which, according to legend, was painted black after President Lincoln's assassination. Actually, it was painted because it had rusted. Today it's snowy white, and open seasonally for viewing the Gulf and the town. (Open March-Oct. 9am-sunset. Admission 50¢.)

The water is warm on Biloxi's beaches and swimming goes on until well past Labor Day, but the shore is frequently a bit unsightly. Hurricane Camille devastated this area 20 years ago and the coast has never fully recovered. Crystal blue waters can be found nearby on **Ship Island,** in the national seashore, which served as the North's command center for the pivotal Battle of New Orleans. *USA Today* has called this one of the nation's 10 best beaches. Hiking is also fabulous, but beware of alligators and wear plenty of sunscreen. Boats to the island depart from Biloxi's Buena Vista Motel, Central Beach Blvd. (432-2197; 6-hr. trips mid-May to Sept. daily 9am and noon; April to mid-May Sat.-Sun. 9am and noon; admission $11, children $5). You can camp overnight on **Horn Island** or **East Ship Island;** call Davis Bayou (875-9057) to charter a boat (approximately $25). Campers should remember to pack insect repellent.

Accommodations on the coast can be very costly; the cheapest places are located beyond the reach of public transportation. Several motels offer singles and doubles for about $25-35 midweek in summer, with even higher rates on weekends. The **Biloxi Hilton** is surrounded by half a dozen mediocre motels with good prices, sometimes as low as $15 for a single in the off-season. Among them is the **Economy Inn,** 100 Brady Dr. at W. Beach Blvd. (388-7321). Camping is also a cheap alternative; rates vary from $10-15 depending on the season. The most convenient site is the **Biloxi Beach Campground,** U.S. 90 at 3162 W. Beach Blvd. (432-2755). Farther from town are **Martin's Lake and Campground,** 14601 Parker Rd., 1 mile north of I-10 at exit 50, Ocean Springs (875-9157), and the campground at **Gulf Islands National Seashore,** Hanley Rd., off U.S. 90 also in Ocean Springs.

Biloxi is 90 miles east of New Orleans and 70 miles west of Mobile. Jackson is 170 miles inland. Getting into and out of Biloxi is rarely problematic as the town is well-served by intercity buses. **Greyhound/Trailways,** 322 Main St. (436-4366), offers frequent service to New Orleans (9 per day, 2½ hr., $16) and Jackson (4 per day, 4 hr., $18).

Coast Area Transit (896-8080) operates buses along the beach on Hwy. 90 from Biloxi to Gulfport (buses marked "Beach"). (Buses supposedly operate Mon.-Sat. every 70 min. Board at any intersection. Fare 75¢.)

The **post office** is on Main St., near the bus station. Biloxi's **ZIP code** is 39530; the **area code** is 601.

Tennessee

Tennessee encompasses three distinct regions that correspond roughly to the great loops in the Tennessee River. East Tennessee is hillbilly country, home to the beautiful Great Smoky Mountains. The rolling farmlands of central Tennessee surround the rhinestone glitter of Nashville. The western portion of the state looks to Memphis and the Mississippi River for the maintenance of a more "southern" way of life. Tennessee's geographic distinctions crystallized culturally during the Civil War, when a ferocious rift developed between the pro-Union eastern section and the Confederate west. This divided state has offered the legendary Davy Crockett and Andrew Jackson to American history, but it has also earned a measure of notoriety for its backwoods mentality. The Scopes "Monkey Trial" took place in Dayton in 1925, and the teaching of evolution was forbidden here until 1967. Aided by FDR's Tennessee Valley Authority (TVA) dams and a host of other New Deal initials, however, Tennessee today appears to be coming out of the woods. Knoxville was the site of the 1982 World's Fair, and Nashville and Memphis attract millions of visitors each year to their musical shrines.

Practical Information

Capital: Nashville.

Tourist Information: Tennessee Dept. of Tourist Development, P.O. Box 23170, Nashville 37202 (741-2158). Open Mon.-Fri. 8am-4:30pm. **Tennessee State Parks Information,** 701 Broadway, Nashville 37203 (742-6667).

Time Zone: Central (Memphis and Nashville; 1 hr. behind Eastern) and Eastern (Chattanooga, Knoxville). **Postal Abbreviation:** TN.

Memphis

Memphis prides itself on being the "heart of America," and it literally is. Memphis is the commercial center for a huge region that includes Western Tennessee, Arkansas, Missouri, Alabama, and Mississippi. From anywhere in the country, each and every package sent through Federal Express widns up at their Memphis headquarters for sorting. It is the city that gave America two of its most deeply-loved musical styles—W.C. Handy's blues originated here, on the legendary Beale Street, and it was here that Elvis Presley and others fused gospel, rhythm-and-blues and country into the explosive new sounds of rock 'n' roll.

Memphis also has more than a trace of the traditionalism that is quintessentially middle-American. Although it is the nation's 15th-largest city, it has a small-town charm, a traditional southern hospitality. While other cities have grown upward, Memphis has grown outward. Therefore, it has managed to keep its downtown small and neighborly, while the city extends for miles eastward.

Memphis enters the 1990s as a city of promise. Racial tensions and the decline of the inner city in the 1960s and 1970s have prompted the city to make concerted efforts to improve living conditions for the large black community and to create a new self-image. There has been an economic resurgence over the last several years, and as Memphis begins to plan for its 175th anniversary in 1993, it is a city truly on the rise.

Practical Information

Emergency: 911.

Visitors Information Center: 207 Beale St. (526-4880), 2 blocks south on 2nd St. and 2 blocks east on Beale from Greyhound downtown. Quite helpful—everything from bus maps to restaurant guides. Open Mon.-Sat. 9am-5pm, Sun. noon-5pm.

Memphis International Airport: just south of the southern loop of I-240. Taxi fare to the city ranges from $12-13—it is best to negotiate in advance. Public transportation to and from the airport is only $1.25, but it's a long and difficult trip for a traveler unfamiliar with the area.

Amtrak: 545 Main St. S. (526-0052 or 800-872-7245), at Calhoun, on the southern edge of downtown. Unsafe area in the day, dangerous at night. To: New Orleans (1 per day, 7½ hr., $69, round-trip from $76) and Houston (3 per week, 14 hr., $136). Open Mon.-Sat. 8am-12:30pm, 1:30-5pm, 9pm-6am, Sun. 9pm-6am.

Greyhound/Trailways: 203 Union Ave. (523-9253), at 4th St., downtown. Unsafe area at night. To: Nashville ($34) and New Orleans ($57). Open 24 hours.

Memphis Area Transit Authority (MATA): 61 S. Main St. (274-6282). Bus routes are extensive and cover most suburbs. If you're in a hurry, forget it; buses take their time and do not run frequently. Downtown's 2 major stops are at Front and Jefferson St., and at 2nd St. and Madison Ave. Operates Mon.-Fri. 8am-5pm, major lines until 11pm, Sat.-Sun. less frequent service. Fare 85¢.

Taxi: Yellow Cab, 526-2121. 95¢ 1st 1/9 mile, 10¢ each additional mile.

Crisis Line: 247-7477. 24 hours. Also refers to other numbers.

Weather line: 756-4141.

Time Zone: Central (1 hr. behind Eastern).

Post Office: 555 S. 3rd St. (521-2140), at Calhoun St. Take bus #13. Open Mon.-Fri. 8:30am-5:30pm, Sat. 10am-noon. **ZIP code:** 38101.

Area Code: 901.

Memphis spreads out from the east bank of the **Mississippi River** in the southwest corner of Tennessee, 200 miles southwest of Nashville and 300 miles south of St. Louis, MO. The city is circled by **I-240.** Downtown, named avenues run east-west and numbered ones north-south. **Madison Avenue** divides north and south addresses. Poplar and Union Avenues are two main thoroughfares that lead to the heart of the city from the east; 2nd and 3rd Streets arrive from the south.

Accommodations

The accommodations outlook in Memphis is fair if you have a car; otherwise you will have to take one of the unreliable buses to reach the reasonable places. Downtown is more expensive, but the difference in price might well be made up in cab fare. Less pricey but less comfortable motels can be found on Elvis Presley Blvd. near Graceland. Book ahead if you are coming between August 12-16, when Elvis fans from around the world gather to pay tribute. The visitors information center has a thorough listing of places. Contact **Bed and Breakfast in Memphis,** P.O. Box 41621, Memphis 38174 (726-5920), for guest rooms in Memphis homes. French-, and Spanish-speaking hosts are available. (Singles $27-55. Doubles $32-55.)

Lowenstein-Long House/Castle Hostelry (AYH), 1084 Poplar and 217 N. Waldran (527-7174). Convenient location—a long but not impossible walk from downtown, or accessible by bus #50 from 3rd St. Beautiful accommodations in an elegant Victorian mansion. Laundry facilities. $10, nonmembers $13.

Days Inn—Downtown, 147 Union Ave. (527-4100). Across from the Peabody Hotel. Central location. If discounts are in effect (check first with the Visitors Travel Center) this is the best bargain downtown at $30 for 1-4 people.

Regal 8 Inn, 1360 Springbrook Rd. (396-3620), just east of intersection of Elvis and Brooks Rd. Near Graceland. Pool. Free coffee and doughnuts in the morning. Free shuttle to and from airport. Singles $25.88. Doubles $35.88.

Food

Memphis abounds with cheap soul-food restaurants that serve chitlins (crunchy fried pigskin), hamhocks, fried catfish, collard greens, and the like. It's also the barbecue capitol of the world (Pizza Hut even barbecues its pizza). Every May, the city hosts an annual barbecue contest. Be sure to try southern barbecue, which in Memphis means pork.

The Rendezvous, Downtown Alley (523-2746), in the alley across from the Peabody Hotel, off of Union St. between the Ramada Inn and the Days Inn. A Memphis legend, serving large portions of ribs. Open Tues.-Thurs. 4:30pm-midnight, Fri.-Sat. noon-midnight.

Spaghetti Warehouse, 40 W. Huling St. (521-0907), off S. Front St. Great family restaurant. Get a beautiful plate of pasta for under $5 as you dine in a restored trolley car or on a carousel. Friendly staff. Open Mon.-Thurs. 11am-10pm, Fri. 11am-11pm, Sat. noon-11pm, Sun. noon-10pm.

Mike's Barbeque Pit, 73 Monroe (527-4773), near the river, downtown. Serves barbecue, grill food, and tamales. Homey for a pit. Full meal under $5. Open Mon.-Fri. 6am-3pm, Sat. 7am-2pm.

Front St. Delicatessen, 77 S. Front St. (522-8943). Lunchtime streetside deli, popular with Memphis-style yuppies. Patio dining in sunny weather. Open Mon.-Fri. 8am-4pm, Sat. 11am-3pm.

Arcade Restaurant, 540 Main St. S. (526-5757), across the street from the train station. This classic diner offers a great meal ($2-6) at all hours of the day and night. Fried catfish steak $4.

Leonard's Barbecue Pit, 1140 Bellevue Blvd. S. (948-1581). An old Elvis haunt serving good barbecue ($3-5). Open Mon.-Sat. 10am-5pm, Sun. 11am-5pm.

P and H Café, (for Poor and Hungry) 1532 Madison Ave. (274-9794). Run by the matronly Wanda, this local favorite serves huge burgers and grill food ($3-5). Local bands play on Sat. night. Open Mon.-Sat. 11am-3am.

The North End, 346 N. Main St. (526-0319), downtown. Dark but cozy. Extensive menu including tamales, wild rice, and creole dishes ($3-8). Try the great Hot Fudge Pie ($2.35). Happy hour 4-7pm. Live entertainment on weekends. Open daily 11am-3am.

Sights

It is the moral imperative of every red-blooded American rock 'n' roll fan to pay homage to Elvis Presley's legacy at his mansion, **Graceland,** 10 miles south of downtown at 3794 Elvis Presley Blvd. (332-3322; 1-800-238-2000 outside TN). The house and its neo-baroque furnishings were purchased in 1957 by the man who was then the nation's only "pelvis-gyrating singer." The mansion is the central part of the tour, and includes the exuberantly-designed TV Room, Pool Room, Jungle Room, Music Room, and more. The King and his family are buried next door in the Meditation Gardens, where hordes of teary-eyed women pray over Elvis's grave. Across the street, you can visit several Elvis museums, the centerpiece of which (you can't miss it) is the **Lisa Marie,** Elvis's personal 96-passenger airplane (named after his daughter), casually parked next to the parking lot. Say hello to Elvis's Uncle Vester, who still works here and dispenses witticisms for free. Don't come to Graceland looking for a glimpse into the reality of the King's world. The complex is so built up and commercialized that it resembles an amusement park, and the tour guides paint white-washed portraits of Elvis, glorifying him as a born-again-Christian. However, this atmosphere attracts some interesting tourists; sitting on the tour bus with this particular slice of America is at least half the Graceland "experience." (Open May daily 8am-5pm; June 1-14 and Aug. 12-31 daily 8am-6pm; June 15-Aug. 11 daily 8am-7pm; Sept.-Oct. and March-April daily 9am-5pm; Nov.-Feb. Wed.-Mon. 9am-5pm. Tickets to the Versailles of pop star dwellings are sold at 3797 Elvis Presley Blvd. and cost $7.50, seniors $6.50, ages 4-12 $4.75. The entire package, including the *Lisa Marie* and Elvis's private bus costs $13, seniors $12, children $8.75. Take bus #13 ("Lauderdale/Elvis Presley") from 3rd and Union.)

Memphis' other sights are downtown and midtown. Most famous in downtown is **Beale Street,** billed, rather apocryphally, as the birthplace of the blues. After a long period of neglect, it is now being reborn through careful restoration by the city, perhaps to the detriment of its former character. Take an evening stroll, visit W.C. Handy's one-room house and listen to blues bands in the local bars. A five-and-dime store run by the same family since 1876, **A. Schwab,** 163 Beale St. (523-9782), still offers old-fashioned bargains. A "museum" of relics-never-sold gathers dust on the mezzanine floor, including an array of voodoo potions and powders.

On April 4, 1968, the **Lorraine Motel,** 406 Mulberry St., was the site of the assassination of Martin Luther King, Jr. The second-floor motel room outside which King was shot is being renovated into a museum and civil rights center (to be completed in 1991).

In the heart of downtown is the **Peabody Hotel,** 149 Union St. This luxurious hotel was the social center of Memphis society in the first half of this century, and folklore had it that the Mississippi Delta began in its lobby. Now the hotel keeps ducks in its indoor fountain; every day at 11am and 5pm the management cracks out the red carpet and the ducks waddle to and from the elevator with piano accompaniment. Get there early because sometimes the ducks are impatient—the spoiled brats.

Mud Island, 125 N. Front St. (526-7241), is downtown's newest attraction. See the entire Mississippi River in miniature, a Civil War Museum, and a B-17 bomber. Catch a "Sunset Party" Wed. evenings from early May-Labor Day. (Open daily April-Thanksgiving, hours change seasonally. Pick up a calendar of events at the Visitors Information Center. Admission $4, seniors and children $2.50.)

Hard-core music buffs might want to visit tiny **Sun Studio,** 706 Union Ave. (521-0664), where Elvis, Jerry Lee Lewis, Johnny Cash, and Carl Perkins first ventilated their vocal chords for producer Sam Phillips. (30-min. tours every hr. on the ½-hr. Open daily 10:30am-5:30pm. Admission $4, children $2.)

The "Showboat" bus takes you to all the sights of midtown. Buy an all-day ticket for $2. A major sight is the **Victorian Village,** which consists of 18 mansions in various stages of restoration and preservation. The **Mallory-Neeley House,** 652 Adams St. (523-1484), one of the village's two mansions open to the public, was built in the mid-19th century. (Open Tues.-Sat. 10am-4pm, Sunday 1-4pm. Admission $4, seniors and students $3.) The French Victorian **Fontaine House,** 680 Adams (526-1469), was built in 1870. (Open Mon.-Sat. 10am-4pm, Sun. 1-4pm. Admission $4, students and children $2.)

The **Memphis Brooks Museum of Art** is set in attractive Overton Park (722-3500) and houses a mid-sized collection of Impressionist art and sculpture. Major renovations will be completed by the 1990 season. (Open Tues.-Sat. 10am-5pm and Sun. 1-5pm. Free.) Next door is the **Memphis Zoo and Aquarium,** (726-4775; open daily 9am-4:30pm. Admission $3.25, seniors and children $1.50. Free on Mon. after 3:30pm.) Many Memphians also visit **Libertyland,** 940 Early Maxwell Blvd. (274-1776), a large amusement park near MSU. (Open June-Oct. Tues.-Thurs. 10am-7pm, Fri.-Sat. 10am-9pm, Sun. noon-7pm. April-June Sat. 10am-7pm, Sun. noon-10pm. Admission $11, seniors $3, after 4pm $8. Children must be at least 42 inches tall.)

Your budget may not accommodate the expensive restaurants along the river, but a stroll along the Mississippi is free. The river runs clear where it passes Memphis, making the sunsets especially memorable.

Entertainment

Key magazine, distributed by the visitors information center, or the "Playbook" section of the Friday morning *Memphis Commercial Appeal* will give you an idea of what's going down around town. The **Antenna Club,** 1588 Madison Ave. (725-9812), is the city's chic rock revue. Nightly blues can be found, although usually with a cover charge, on **Beale Street;** get down at the **Rum Boogie Cafe,** 182 Beale St. (528-0150). Monday night is Modern Music night at **Night Moves,** 3659 S. Mendenhall Rd. (794-4555), at Winchester. Worth the trek only if you have a car, and be prepared for a rougher crowd if you don't go on Monday. (Cover $1.) **GDI's on the River,** 287 S. Front St. (526-1086), is a popular gay bar with a mixed clientele on Tues. nights. (Open Sun.-Thurs. 8am-3am, Fri.-Sat. 8pm-5am. Cover $2.50.) Also try **Hernando's Hide-a-Way,** 3210 Hernando Rd. (398-7496), near the intersection of Elvis Presley Blvd. and Brooks. The black, box-like building looks closed from the outside. (Open daily noon-4:30am; bands begin at 9:30 pm. Take bus #13 ("Lauderdale") from downtown.)

The majestic **Orpheum Theater,** 89 Beale St. (525-7800), is a classic movie palace, complete with 15-foot high Czechoslovakian chandeliers and an organ. The theater shows classic movies on the weekends along with an organ prelude, a cartoon, and a Buck Rogers episode. The **Memphis Chicks,** 800 Home Run Lane (272-2687), near Libertyland, are a big hit with fans of Southern League baseball.

Nashville

Newcomers may find that Nashville, founded in 1779 and Tennessee's capital since 1843, is a city of only uneasily reconcilable elements. The beating heart of country music is also the "Wall Street of the South," a slick, thriving financial hub. The same Nashvillle that is headquarters to the Southern Baptists and a hotbed of fundamentalism is also a center of the fine arts and home to **Vanderbilt** and **Fisk University.** Don't get hung up on trying to make sense of it all. Nashville is a crazy, eclectic, unapologetically glitzy place with a terrific symphony, more churches per capita than anywhere else in the U.S., and an air of perpetual celebration.

Practical Information

Emergency: 911 or 327-1300.

Visitor Information: Nashville Area Chamber of Commerce, 161 4th Ave. N. (259-3900), between Commerce and Union St. downtown. Ask for the *Hotel/Motel Guide,* the *Nashville Dining & Entertainment Guide,* and a *Calendar of Events.* Information booth in main lobby open Mon.-Fri. 8am-4:30pm. **Nashville Tourist Information Center,** I-65 at James Robertson Pkwy. (242-5606), exit 85, a little over ½ mile east of the state capitol, just over the bridge.

Take bus #3 ("Meridian") east on Broadway. Open daily until sunset. *Spotlight on the Arts* ($3.50) is available at the **Metro Arts Commission,** 111 4th Ave. S. (259-6374).

Travelers Aid: 256-3168.

Metropolitan Airport: Eight miles south of downtown. Limos $7 one way, taxis $12-14, MTA buses 75¢ (½-hr. ride).

Greyhound: 200 8th Ave. S. (256-6141), at Demonbreun St., 2 blocks south of Broadway, downtown. Borders on a rough neighborhood. To: Memphis (9 per day, 4 hr., $34); Montgomery, AL (7 per day, 6 hr., $43); Washington, DC (7 per day, 16 hr., $91); Atlanta, GA (7 per day, 7½ hr., $43); Louisville, KY (14 per day, 4 hr., $35.50). Open 24 hours.

Metropolitan Transit Authority (MTA): 242-4433. Buses operate Mon.-Fri. 5am-midnight, less frequent service Sat.-Sun. Fare 75¢, zone crossing or transfers 10¢.

Taxi: Nashville Cab, 242-7070. 90¢ for first mile, $1.30 each additional mile.

Weather Line: 361-6417

Help Lines: Crisis Line, 244-7444. **Rape Hotline,** 327-1110. **Handicapped Information,** 259-6676.

Time Zone: Central (1 hr. behind Eastern).

Post Office: 921 Broadway (251-5321), downtown, across from the Sheraton and next to Union Station. Open Mon.-Fri. 8am-6pm, Sat. 8am-noon. **ZIP code:** 37202.

Area Code: 615.

Nashville is located on the **Cumberland River** smack in the middle of Tennessee, 178 miles west of Knoxville, and 209 miles northeast of Memphis. Take I-40 or I-24 from the east or west and I-65 from the north or south.

The names of Nashville's streets are undeniably fickle. **Broadway,** the main east-west thoroughfare, becomes **West End Avenue** just outside downtown, at I-40, and later becomes **Harding Road.** Downtown, numbered avenues run north-south, parallel to the Cumberland River. The curve of **James Robertson Parkway** encloses the north end, becoming **Main Street** on the other side of the river (later Gallatin Pike), and **McGavock Street** is at the south end. The area between 2nd and 7th Ave., south of Broadway, is unsafe at night.

Accommodations and Camping

Finding a room in Nashville is not difficult, just expensive. Most places are within 20 miles of downtown. It's best to make reservations well in advance, especially for weekend stays. A dense concentration of budget motels line W. Trinity Lane and Brick Church Pike at I-65, north of downtown. Even cheaper hotels inhabit the area around Dickerson Rd. and Murfreesboro, but the neighborhood is seedy at best and not recommended for women. If you're traveling in a small group, an efficiency suite is an economical option: **Lexington Hotel Suites,** 2425 Atrium Way, off Briley Pkwy., behind Holiday Inn, east of downtown, offers a queen-size bed with hide-a-bed for $64. If you know your plans in advance, contact **Bed and Breakfast of Middle Tennessee** (297-0883; singles $20-50; doubles $25-60), or **Bed and Breakfast Host Homes,** P.O. Box 110227, Nashville 37222 (331-5244; singles $26-50; doubles from $32). **Hallmark Inns,** part of a local chain, are cheaper than the national chains.

Motel 6, 311 W. Trinity Lane (227-9696), at exit 87B off I-24/I-65; 323 Cartwright St., Goodlettsville (859-9674), take the Long Hollow Pike west, off I-65, then turn right onto Cartwright; and 95 Wallace Rd. (333-9933), take exit 56 from I-24, go west on Harding Pl. 1 block, left at Traveler's Inn Lane, and left on Largo. Clean and friendly. All have singles for $26, $6 each additional person.

Tudor Inn-Downtown, 750 James Robertson Pkwy. (244-8970), at 8th Ave. N. Take bus #8 on 8th Ave. from the Greyhound station. A little dark, but near town. Singles $28, $32 on weekends. Doubles $38.

The Cumberland Inn, I-65 N. and Trinity Ln. (226-1600), on the other side of the interstate from Motel 6. Large, clean rooms. Singles $29. Doubles $39. On weekends $39 and $49, respectively.

Brick Church Inn, 2403 Brick Church Pike (226-7490), at I-24/65, just off Trinity Ln. In a luxurious new building. In summer singles $42, doubles $49; in winter singles $28. Rates fluctuate on a daily basis.

There are three campgrounds within walking distance of Opryland USA, which you can reach by public transportation from 5th St. For the **Fiddler's Inn North Campground** (885-1440), the **Nashville Travel Park** (889-4225), and the **Two Rivers Campground** (883-8559), take the Briley Pkwy. north to McGavock Pike, exit West, then go west on Music Valley Dr. (Sites $15-17 for 2.)

Food

Mercifully, you don't need to sample the fast-food emporia that litter Nashville; eat at the inexpensive native restaurants instead. Barbecue and fried chicken are local favorites; pecan pie or goo-goo clusters (peanuts, chocolate, caramel, and marshmallow) keep the town's dentists in business. The 2000 block of Elliston Place, near Vanderbilt, is crammed with restaurants that cater to collegiate tastes and budgets. The **Farmer's Market,** north of the capitol between 3rd and 7th Ave., is open until sunset.

Loveless Motel Restaurant, Hwy. 100 (646-9700), at Rte. 5, 15 miles southwest of town. Accessible by car only. True country-style cooking at its best. Famous for its preserves, fried chicken, and hickory-smoked ham. Try the homemade biscuits with red-eye gravy, a special blend of ham drippings and coffee ($3-8). Open Tues.-Sat. 8am-2pm and 5-9pm, Sun. 8am-9pm. Reservations recommended.

Brown's Diner, 2102 Blair Blvd. (269-5509), near Vanderbilt. In front is a bar in an incredibly dilapidated old diner. Behind it is a dining room in a large addition. The music and college crowds fill the diner at lunchtime. Burgers $4-5. Open Mon.-Sat. 11am-10:30pm. Bar is open until midnight.

The Old Spaghetti Factory, 160 2nd Ave. N. (254-9010), downtown. An Italian chain restaurant in a turn-of-the-century antique shop that serves only spaghetti dinners ($4-6). Arrive early, make reservations, or wait up to an hour in the beautiful rosewood bank boardroom that serves as a lobby. Open Mon.-Thurs. 5-10pm, Fri.-Sat. 5-11pm, Sun. 4-10pm.

Bienvenidos, 160 8th Ave. N. (255-2250). Large portions of hearty Mexican and Texan favorites. Lunches are a steal at only $4 (dinners slightly more). Try the combo dishes ($5-10). Open daily 9am-9pm.

Sights

Fast-food chains and fast paths to the grace of God set a brisk pace for Nashville. **Music Row,** the home of Nashville's most famous industry, is along Division and Demonbreun Street from 16th to 19th Avenue South, bounded on the south by Grand Avenue. (Take bus #3 to 17th Ave. and walk south.) If you can survive the mobs outside the **Country Music Hall of Fame,** 4 Music Sq. E. (256-1639), at Division St., you can gawk at Elvis's "solid gold" Cadillac and other country music memorabilia. Included in the admission is a tour of RCA's historic **Studio B.** (Open Sept.-May daily 9am-5pm; June-Aug. daily 8am-8pm. Admission $6.50, ages 6-11 $1.75, under 6 free.) If you want to record your own hit, the **Recording Studio of America,** 1510 Division St. (254-1282), underneath the **Barbara Mandrell Country Museum,** lets you do your own vocals on pre-recorded, high-quality 24-track backgrounds to popular country and pop tunes. Choose a set and make a video, too. (Audio recording $12.88, video $20. Open daily June-Aug. 8am-8pm; Sept.-May 9am-5pm.)

A 15-minute walk west from Music Row along West End Ave. to **Centennial Park** will soon explain why Nashville calls itself the "Athens of the South." In the park stands an exact-size replica of the **Parthenon.** Originally built as a temporary exhibit for the Tennessee Centennial in 1897, the Parthenon was such a hit that the model was rebuilt in more durable form. The Cowan Collection of American Paintings is housed in the basement galleries in April, August, and December. Greek theater is performed on the steps in mid-July and August. (Open Tues.-Sat. 9am-5pm, Sun. 1-5pm. Free.)

A walk through the downtown area reveals more of Nashville's eclectic architecture. **Union Station Hotel,** 1001 Broadway (726-1001), is a towering restored turn-of-the-century train station and one of the best known landmarks in Nashville. The **Ryman Auditorium** (254-1445), off Broadway at 5th, originally built as a tabernacle, housed the Grand Ole Opry from 1943 to 1974. (Guided tours 8:30am-4:30pm. Admission $2, ages 6-12 $1.) Turn up 2nd Ave. from Broadway to study the cast-iron and masonry facades of the handsome commercial buildings from the 1870s and 1880s, many of which have been converted into restaurants and nightspots. The **Tennessee State Capitol,** Charlotte Ave. (741-1621), a handsome Greek Revival structure atop the hill next to downtown, offers free guided tours. (Open Mon.-Fri. 9am-4:30pm.) Across the street is the **Tennessee State Museum,** 505 Deaderick (741-2692), whose exhibits chronicle Tennessee's history. (Open Mon.-Sat. 10am-5pm, Sun. 1-5pm. Free.)

If you tire of the downtown area, rest at the **Cheekwood Botanical Gardens and Fine Arts Center,** Forest Park Dr. (356-8000), 7 miles southwest of town; the well-kept, leisurely, English-style gardens are a welcome change from Nashville's glitz. (Open Tues.-Sat. 9am-5pm, Sun. 1-5pm. Admission $2.50, ages 7-17 $1. Take bus #3 ("West End/Belle Meade") from downtown to Belle Meade Blvd. and Page Rd.) Nearby is the **Belle Meade Mansion,** 110 Leake Ave. (356-0501), at Harding Rd., displays Southern antebellum opulence at the site of the nation's first thoroughbred breeding farm. (2 tours per hr., last tour at 4pm. Open Mon.-Sat. 9am-5pm, Sun. 1-5pm. Admission $4, students $3.50, ages 13-18 $2, ages 6-12 $1.50. Take bus #3 to Harding and Leake.)

Thirteen miles east of town is the **Hermitage,** 4580 Rachel's Lane (889-2941); take exit 221 off I-40. Andrew Jackson's beautiful manor house sits on 625 acres and is an ideal spot for a picnic. Be prepared for crowds during the summer months. (Open daily 9am-5pm. Admission $3.75, ages 6-13 $1.25.)

Fisk University's **Van Vechten Gallery** exhibits a distinguished collection of American art. The gallery owns a portion of the **Alfred Steiglitz Collection,** donated to Fisk by Georgia O'Keeffe, Steiglitz's widow.

Entertainment

Nashville offers a wide array of expensive nightspots. Many feature the country tunes for which the town is known; others cater to jazz, rock, bluegrass, or folk music fans. Fridays and Sundays the *Tennessean* has entertainment listings; the *Nashville Banner's* listings come out on Thursday afternoon. The Nashville *Key,* available at the chamber of commerce, is also a good source of information.

Once the bar district for Nashville's printing industry, **Printer's Alley,** downtown off Union St. between 3rd and 4th St., now appeals to the conventioneer crowd. Though somewhat above the go-go dancer mentality, the white, plastic neon signs and flashing arrows and light bulbs clearly mark the alley as the hot spot of show sleaze. Cramped within these close quarters are six or seven clubs with floor shows nightly except Sunday. All serve dinner and charge a cover of $3, more if big-name performers are playing.

If you want more sleaze for your buck, the affordable side of the downtown area nightlife is on lower Broadway from 6th Ave. to the river. Until the Grand Ole Opry moved out of town, this was where the stars boozed it up. At night the area is exciting but potentially dangerous. Women should not venture here alone. Try **Tootsie's Orchid Lounge,** 422 Broadway (251-9725), for good country and western music and affordable drinks. Many stars got started here; for years it was operated by Tootsie Bess, a kind-hearted woman who lent money to struggling musicians until they could get on the Ole Opry. (Open Mon.-Sat. 10am-3am, Sun. noon-3am.)

West of downtown, the **Bluegrass Inn,** 1914 Broadway (329-1112), at the rear, has beer, chips, and bluegrass music with a cinderblock-and-cement motif. A good-natured sort of place. The cover depends on who is playing (normally around $4). (Open Wed.-Thurs. 9pm-midnight, Fri.-Sat. 9pm-1am.) The more genteel **Blue Bird Cafe,** 4104 Hillsboro Rd. (383-1461), in Green Hills, plays blues, folk, soft rock, and a little bit of jazz. Women traveling solo will feel comfortable in this mellow, clean-cut establishment. Dinner, served until 8:30pm, consists of salads and sandwiches ($4-6.50). Music begins at 9:30pm. (Open Mon.-Sat. 5:30pm-3am; cover $5. Go west on Broadway, then south on 21st, which turns into Hillsboro Rd.) The **Station Inn,** 402 12th Ave. S. (255-3307), offers serious bluegrass. (Open Tues.-Sun. 7pm-whenever, music starts at 9pm. Cover $4. Mon. night jam session free.)

A cross between Las Vegas glitz and Disneyland wholesomeness, with the best in country music thrown in, **Opryland USA** (889-6700) is still Nashville's largest draw. The amusement park part contains all the requisite family attractions from roller coasters to cotton candy. But it also has over 10 live music shows, each performed several times in different areas throughout the day. At other times, country music is piped throughout the entire park. (Open March 28-May 24 Sat.-Sun.; May 25-Sept. 7 daily; Sept. 11-Nov. 1 Sat.-Sun. until sunset. Admission $20.42 for 1 day, $23.42 for 2-3 days.) The **Grand Ole Opry** moved here from the town center in 1976. *The* place to hear country music, the Opry is held every Friday and Saturday night. Matinees are added during peak tourist season (March-Sept.). Tickets cost $10-11.50 Friday and Saturday nights, $8-9.50 for matinees. Reserve tickets from Grand Ole Opry, 2804 Opryland Dr., Nashville 37214. Enclose a check or money order, or call 615-889-3060. General admission tickets can be purchased at the box office only, starting at 9am on Tuesday for weekend shows. Check the Friday morning *Tennessean* for the performers.

There's more to entertainment in Nashville than country music, especially if you're willing to hunt for it. Rock bands play at the **Exit/In,** 2208 Elliston Place (321-4400; cover $4), and across the street at **Elliston Square,** near the Vanderbilt campus. Minors should head to the gleaming, neon-lit **Heartthrob Cafe and Philadelphia Bandstand,** 2200 Metrocenter Blvd., at Fountain Sq., featuring Top-40 dance hits and mobs of teens—no alcohol is served and only those under 21 are admitted. (Open Sun. and Thurs. 7pm-midnight, Fri.-Sat. 7pm-1am. Cover $5.) **The World's End,** 1713 Church St. (329-3480), is a popular gay hangout with a restaurant and dance club. Weekly rock publications listing concerts are available at **Mosko's Market,** 2204-B Elliston Place (327-3562). Cheap watering holes include **Springwater,** 115 27th Ave N. (320-9512), with pool tables, near the Parthenon, and **The Villager,** 1719 21st Ave. S. (269-9148), near Vanderbilt.

Great Smoky Mountain National Park

The largest wilderness area in the eastern U.S., Great Smoky Mountain National Park encompasses a half-million acres of gray-green Appalachian peaks, bounded on either side by misty North Carolina and Tennessee valleys. The Smokies are home to bears, wild hogs, white-tailed deer, groundhogs, and wild turkeys, and more than 1500 species of flowering plants. Whispering conifer forests line the mountain ridges at elevations of over 6000 feet, rhododendrons burst into their full glory in June and July, and by mid-October, the sloping mountain flanks have become a giant crazy-quilt of color.

Nine hundred miles of hiking trails and 170 miles of road criss-cross the park. The **Appalachian Trail** is the park's central north-south boulevard (hikers only). For information, contact the **Appalachian Trail Conference,** P.O. Box 807, Harper's Ferry, WV 25425. **Newfound Gap Road** (U.S. 441), connecting Gatlinburg, TN, with Cherokee, NC, may seem like a busy California freeway on a warm summer afternoon. A spur goes all the way up to **Elingman's Dome,** the highest point in the park. **Little River Road** works its way through the southwest quadrant of the park, out to the 11-mile Cades Cove loop. This drive and numerous overlooks along Newfound Gap Rd. offer truly magnificent scenery.

Start any exploration of the area with a visit to one of the park's three visitors centers. **Sugarlands,** on Newfound Gap Rd. 2 miles south of Gatlinburg, is the park's headquarters. (Open in summer 8am-6pm; in spring and fall 8am-5pm; in winter 8am-4:30pm.) **Cades Cove** (436-1275) is in the park's western valley, 22 miles southwest of Sugarlands on Little River Rd., 15 miles southwest of Townsend, TN. (Open daily in summer 9:30am-7pm; in fall 8:30am-5:30pm; in spring 9:30am-5:30pm.) The **Oconaluftee Visitors Center,** 4 miles north of Cherokee, NC (497-9147), serves travelers entering the park from the Blue Ridge Parkway and all points south and east (open same hours as Sugarlands). The park **information line** (615-436-1200; open daily 8:30am-4:30pm) connects all three visitors centers. The rangers can answer travel questions, field emergency message calls, and trace lost and found equipment.

At each visitors center you'll find displays amplifying the park's natural and cultural resources, bulletin boards displaying emergency messages or public information, brochures and films, and comfort stations. Be sure to ask for *The Smokies Guide,* a newspaper tabloid with a comprehensive explanation of the park's changing natural resources and all the park's practical information. The standard park service brochure, *Great Smoky Mountains,* provides the best driving map in the region. Hikers should be sure to ask the visitors center staff for assistance in locating an appropriately detailed backcountry map. You can also tune your car radio to 1610 AM at various marked points for information.

Accommodations and Camping

A free permit is required for backcountry camping at the park's many primitive sites. Just follow the simple self-registration procedures posted at outlying ranger stations and at the three visitors centers. If your trip's itinerary calls for a stop at one of the "rationed" primitive campgrounds, you'll have to obtain in-person or telephone authorization from the park's headquarters. (All sites $5-7, each with picnic table and fireplace. Toilet and sink facilities, no showers.) Sites at three (**Smokemont, Elkmont,** and **Cades Cove**) of the Smokies' 10 developed campgrounds are available for reservations; the remainder are first come-first serve. (Sites $10.) If you're hauling a trailer or staying at one of the park's more accessible campgrounds during the summer, reservations are a must. Obtain them not more than eight weeks in advance by writing to Ticketron, Dept. R, 401 Hackensack Ave., Hackensack, NJ 07601 (804-456-2267).

There are three youth hostels in the area around the park. The closest is **Bell's Wa-Floy Mountain Village (AYH),** Rte. 3, P.O. Box 611 (615-436-7700), 10 miles east of Gatlinburg on Rte. 321. From the center of Gatlinburg catch the east-bound trolley (25¢) to the end of the line. From there, it's a 5-mile walk to Wa-Floy. Trolley service also runs past Wa-Floy from Gatlinburg three times per day—ask in town or call for times. The semi-private apartment rooms are equipped with kitchenettes. On the beautifully landscaped grounds, you'll find a swimming pool, tennis courts, a meditation area, and walking trails leading into the heart of the national park. ($10. Call for reservations.) On the other side of the park, in North Carolina, you can unwind after a hike or river ride in the spacious communal living room of Louise Phillip's **Smokeseege Lodge (AYH),** P.O. Box 179, Dillsboro (704-586-8658), on Rte. 441, 11 miles south of Cherokee. Hitch a ride from Cherokee or walk from the nearest Greyhound/Trailways stop, nearly 3 miles away in Sylva, NC. If you're driving from the Smokies, watch carefully on the right-hand side of Rte. 441 for a small, triangular AYH logo—the hostel is at the end of the wagon-wheeled road. Kitchen facilities are available. No smoking or drinking permitted. (11pm curfew. $7, extra $10 AYH fee for nonmembers. Call ahead for availability. Open April-Oct.) Pitch a tent by the river or sleep in the loft of an open barn for $2. Further south, near Wesser, the bustling **Nantahala Outdoor Center (NOC),** U.S. 19 W., P.O. Box 41, Bryson City (704-488-2175), welcomes both seasoned hikers and inexperienced adventurers. Although no longer an official AYH, the NOC continues to offer hostelers cheap beds. There are bunks in simple wooden cabins at "base camp" on the far side of the river and in fairly large-sized motel rooms with kitchenettes. Showers, kitchen, linen, and laundry facilities included. ($6. Call ahead for reservations.) Next to the NOC's general store and equipment sales department, their riverfront restaurant serves hearty, affordable country-style food ($3-5).

The NOC's rates for 2½-hour whitewater rafting expeditions are pricey, but you can rent your own raft for a self-designed trip down the Nantahala River (Mon.-Fri. $12, Sat.-Sun. $15. One-person inflatable "duckies" $20 per day.) The NOC also rents canoes and kayaks and offers instruction for the novice. Most trips have minimum age or weight limits; day care service is available at the center. Trip prices include transportation to the put-in site and all equipment.

Hike on the Appalachian Trail or rent a bike to explore some of the old forest service roads. (Rental $2 per hr. Must have major credit card or $50 deposit.) The NOC staff will gladly assist if you need help charting an appropriate daytrip.

The NOC also maintains seasonal "outposts" on the **Ocoee, Nolichucky, Chattoga,** and **French Broad Rivers,** all within 100 miles of its Bryson City headquarters. Although these do not have overnight facilities, a rafting expedition on any of these rivers makes a satisfying daytrip if you have a car. Be sure to check into NOC's 20% discounts during March and April. You can also rent 1-speed and children's bikes at the Cades Cove campground ($2 per hr.) for a ride of 4 to 11 miles, manageable by even a novice.

GREAT LAKES

The Great Lakes change mood with considerable speed. One day they're as smooth as a backyard fish pond, the next as choppy and black as the North Atlantic, sending 20-foot swells over seawalls and sucking down 50,000-ton freighters. Lake Superior, the largest and deepest, has the least populated and most scenic coasts. Lake Michigan is a sports-lover's paradise, with deep-water fishing, swimming, sailing, and dunes for hang gliding. Lake Erie has suffered the most from industry, but thanks to vigilant citizens and strict regulations this shallowest lake is regaining its former beauty.

In contrast to the lakes, the dark forests and rural farmlands sheathed in fields of wheat and corn seem tame. The only motion for miles may be a red-tailed hawk winging overhead. In the 19th and early 20th century, immigrants came by the millions—some farmers in search of rich soil, others hoping to tap the land's supplies of iron and copper. Cities like Milwaukee and Cincinnati sprang up as commercial hubs for transporting the region's raw materials.

Long gone is the era of the "New Frontier," which brought the meteoric growth of the railroads and auto industries so pivotal to the nation's development. Though hard hit by inflation and changes in the economy in the mid-70s, urban centers around the Great Lakes have battled back and maintain their traditional blend of urban energy and heartland charm. Minneapolis and St. Paul are a sophisticated center for the arts; Indianapolis is a mecca for U.S. sports activity; and Cleveland and Detroit, most devastated by the industrial slump, are revamping their cityscapes with innovative developments. Chicago sits at the heart of the region. Its world-class music, architecture, and restaurants join hands with a gritty brand of politics and a relaxed, unpretentious sensibility.

Travel

Small regional airlines serve major Great Lakes cities best. Operating out of Chicago's Midway Airport, **Midway Airlines** (800-621-5700) offers cheap flights and many specials to East Coast and Midwest cities. (New York to Chicago $129 on Sat.-Sun., $238 otherwise; Chicago to Detroit $29.) **Northwest Airlines** (800-225-2525) flies mainly to northern cities and the West Coast, using Minneapolis and Detroit as hubs. Book one month in advance for discount fares. **United** (800-241-6522) is not always as cheap but is certainly convenient, with a Chicago hub serving most Midwestern cities nonstop.

Amtrak's national hub is Chicago, and routes radiate throughout the southern Great Lakes region. Only one route serves Wisconsin and Minnesota, with a branch from the Twin Cities to Duluth; northern Michigan is unserved. But you'll have no trouble getting around by bus in the more populous areas of the Great Lakes states. **Greyhound** provides the most extensive coverage, particularly in Wisconsin and Minnesota. Greyhound buses and connecting lines completely encircle Lake Michigan, following shoreside highways the entire route, but the Upper Peninsula (U.P.) is served only in the middle of the night. Regional bus companies include **Indian Trails** and **North Star** lines in Michigan, **Badger Bus** in Wisconsin, and **Indiana Motor Bus.**

The Great Lakes region stands out as the only area in the central U.S. that is well served by **youth hostels.** Conveniently, these hostels tend to lie near established bike trails and access points to canoe routes. Approximately 20 hostels stretch across Michigan from Detroit northwest to the central Lake Michigan shore. Ohio has a well-spaced smattering of hostels, while Minnesota has a cluster around the Twin Cities. Southern Wisconsin has several more. Indiana and Illinois, except for Chicago, are hostel wastelands. Look for a room or an extra bed at one of the many college campuses. State universities often have huge numbers of dorm rooms for

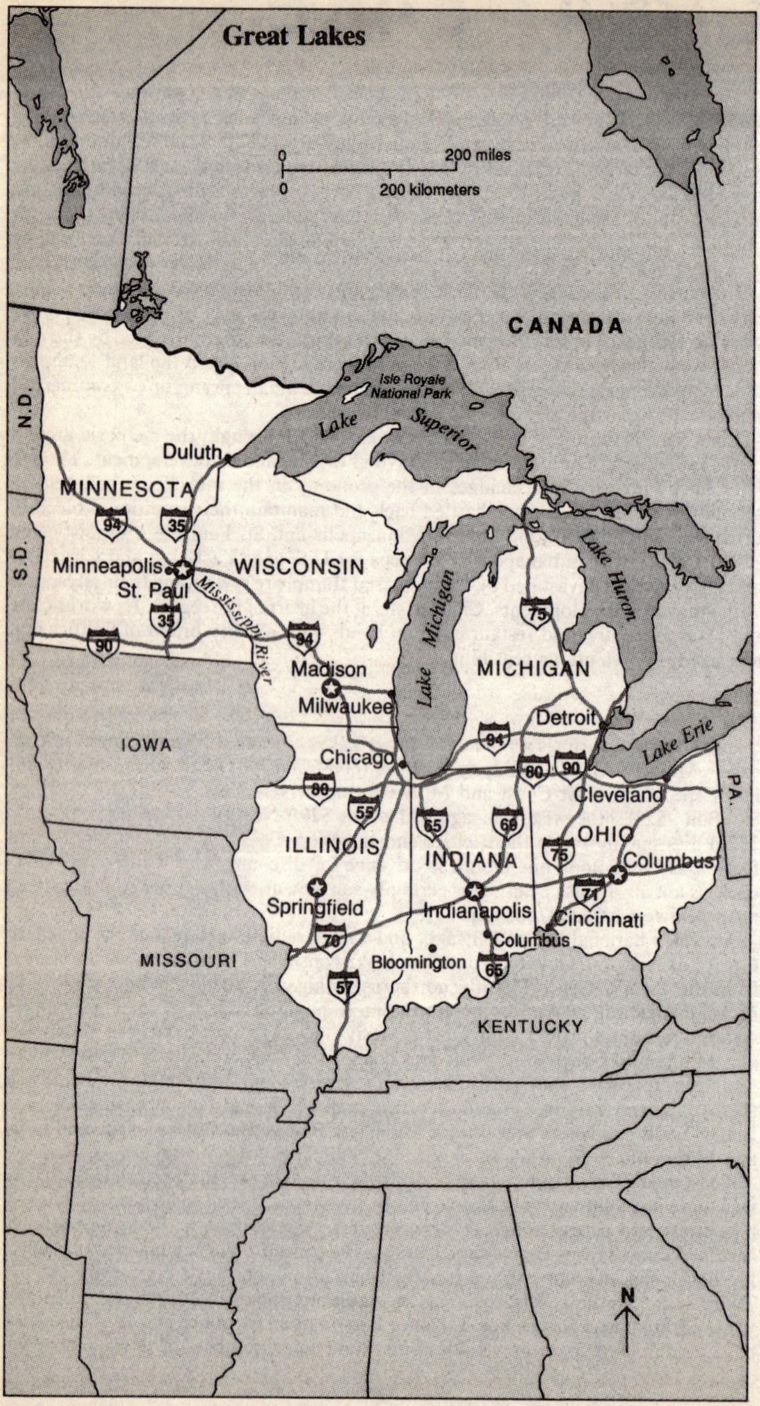
Great Lakes
0
200 miles
0
200 kilometers
CANADA
Isle Royale National Park
Lake Superior
N.D.
S.D.
Duluth
MINNESOTA
94
35
Minneapolis
St. Paul
35
90
WISCONSIN
Mississippi River
94
Madison
Milwaukee
Lake Michigan
Lake Huron
75
MICHIGAN
Detroit
94
Lake Erie
IOWA
Chicago
80
80
90
Cleveland
PA.
55
65
69
ILLINOIS
INDIANA
OHIO
75
Columbus
Springfield
Indianapolis
71
Cincinnati
70
Columbus
MISSOURI
Bloomington
65
57
KENTUCKY
N

sharing or renting. In summer, motels in popular tourist areas double and even triple their prices. Illinois, Indiana, and Wisconsin have an ample supply of **Motel 6's** and slightly more expensive **Red Roof Inns** (800-848-7878).

Outdoors

The most scenic routes in the southern Great Lakes states for driving and biking are, surprisingly, not along the lake coasts, but in the southern parts of Indiana and Ohio. Rugged cliffs, deep valleys, and lush forests stand in contrast to the flatlands of the north. Hoosier and Wayne National Forests are in Indiana and Ohio, respectively. Minnesota's Boundary Waters and the forests and craggy coasts of Michigan's Upper Peninsula challenge the intrepid nature lover with untamed wilderness. For general information on the National Park Service properties, contact the Midwest Regional Office, 1709 Jackson St., Omaha, NB 68102 (402-221-3471). Contact the National Forest Service's Regional Office at 310 W. Wisconsin Ave., Milwaukee, WI 53203.

Illinois

Several years ago, *Chicago Sun Times* columnist Mike Royko lambasted downstaters as "Chicago-hating bumpkins and rubes," "gopher chasers," "boobs, yahoos, and boobkins," and the legislature erupted for a day as the "hayseed" representatives marched through the assembly chamber in protest. The event was an exaggerated demonstration of the contradictions that mark this state. Politically, the division is most clear. Jesse Jackson's home, Chicago, is a Democratic town, while southern Illinois is conservative, Republican territory, home to Phyllis Schlafly. Chicagoans take justifiable pride in their vibrant economy and lively culture, but downstaters know that their farms provide much of the fuel for the north's economic furnaces. Even within that metropolis, Illinois's dual nature is played out daily. Inside the steel-and-glass towers, the pinstripe-clad workforce trades corn futures, pork bellies, and soybeans. Not surprisingly, one of Chicago's most impressive skyscrapers looks like a corn cob. Despite the distinct split among Illinoisans, they share the values of the American Midwest: hard work and a sense of identity that seems to grow out of the soil.

Practical Information

Capital: Springfield.

Tourist Information: Office of Tourism, 620 E. Adams St., Springfield 62706 (782-7139). **Travel Center,** 310 S. Michigan Ave., Chicago 60604 (793-4732).

Time Zone: Central (1 hr. behind Eastern). **Postal Abbreviation:** IL.

Chicago

Carl Sandburg's "City of the Big Shoulders" is huge, a metropolis of seven million people resting at the base of Lake Michigan. Between machine maneuvers and racial rhetoric, Chicago politics are as stormy as the lake. As a cultural center, the city is considerably more subdued and sophisticated. No longer the hog butcher of the world, Chicago is a music lover's paradise, with top-notch blues clubs and a world-class symphony orchestra. After the Great Fire of 1871, Chicago was rebuilt and became a hotbed of modern architectural design, a movement led by Frank Lloyd Wright and Louis Sullivan.

Today, three of the world's tallest buildings rise above the Midwestern flatlands, overlooking factories, international art galleries, working-class neighborhoods, af-

Downtown Chicago
N
0 1/4 Mile
0 1/4 Kilometer
Lincoln Ave.
Lincoln Park
Eugenie St.
North Ave.
N. Larrabee St.
Lake Shore Drive
Gold Coast
Lake Michigan
Division St.
Chicago River
Oak St.
Hancock Building
Chicago Ave.
Old Water Tower
Museum of Contemporary Art
Clark St.
Dearborn St.
State St.
Ontario St.
Ohio St.
Grand Ave.
Kinzie St.
Lake St.
Randolph St.
Washington Blvd.
Madison St.
Monroe St.
Adams St.
Jackson Blvd.
Van Buren St.
Franklin St.
Wells St.
La Salle St.
First National Bank
Wabash Ave.
Michigan Ave.
Chicago Art Institute
Sears Tower
Chicago Harbor
Grant Park
JFK Expressway
Eisenhower Expressway
Congress Parkway
Polk St.
Columbus Dr.
Roosevelt Rd.
Field Museum Of National History
Shedd Aquarium
Adler Planetarium
Bernham Park Yacht Harbor
Soldier Field
Ryan Expressway
Jefferson St.
South Branch

fluent suburbs, and urban blight. Behind the citadels on the lakefront, ethnic communities rival a United Nations quorum for variety, and include German, Irish, and large Polish enclaves, as well as one of the most politically powerful black communities in the U.S.

Practical Information

Emergency: 911.

Visitor Information: Chicago Tourism Council Visitors Information Center, 163 E. Pearson (280-5741), in the Water Tower Pumping Station. Open 9:30am-5pm. Pick up a copy of the *Chicago Visitors Guide.* **Chicago Chamber of Commerce,** 200 N. LaSalle (580-6900), at Lake St. Open Mon.-Fri. 8:30am-5pm. **Tourist Information Center,** 310 S. Michigan Ave. (793-2094), across from the Art Institute. Open Mon.-Fri. 7am-5pm. **Visitor Eventline,** 225-2323. 24-hour recording of concerts, plays, and sports events.

Travelers and Immigrants Aid: 327 S. LaSalle St. (435-4500; after hours 222-0265). Other locations at O'Hare Airport (686-7562), Greyhound (435-4500), and Union Station (435-4500). The main office provides language assistance, legal aid, and information for the disabled.

Consulates: Australia, 111 E. Wacker Dr. (329-1740); **Canada,** 310 S. Michigan Ave. (427-1031); **France,** 444 N. Michigan Ave. (787-5359); **West Germany,** 104 S. Michigan Ave. (263-0850); **Ireland,** 400 N. Michigan Ave. (337-1868); **Israel,** 111 E. Wacker Dr. (565-3300); **Italy,** 500 N. Michigan Ave. (467-1550); **Mexico,** 540 N. LaSalle St. 3rd floor (670-0240); **United Kingdom,** 33 N. Dearborn St. (346-1810). Most open Mon.-Fri. 9am-5pm.

O'Hare International Airport, off I-90. Depending on traffic, a trip between downtown and O'Hare can take up to 2 hr. The **Rapid Train** runs between the Airport el station and downtown. **Continental Air Transport** (454-7800) connects the airport to selected downtown and suburban locations. Runs every 30 min. 6am-11:30pm; fare $9.75. **Midway Airport,** on the western edge of the South Side. To get downtown, take CTA bus #54B to Archer, then ride bus #49, 62, or 162 to State St. For an extra 20¢, the 99M express runs from Midway downtown 6:30am-8:15am and from downtown to Midway during the afternoon rush hour. Continental Air Transport costs $7.50. For limousine service to either airport, call **C.W. Limousine Service** (493-2700).

Amtrak: Union Station (558-1075 or 800-872-7245), Canal and Adams St. downtown. Take the el to State and Adams, then walk up Adams 7 blocks to Union Station. Amtrak's main hub. Station open 24 hours; tickets sold 9am-9:30pm.

Greyhound: Clark and Randolph St. (781-2900). Take the el to State and Washington. The hub in central U.S. Also serves as home base for several smaller companies covering the Midwest. To: Milwaukee ($13), Detroit ($47), and St. Louis ($35). Open 24 hours.

Local Transit: See Transportation below.

Car Rental: Fender Benders Rent-a-Car, 1545 N. Wells St. (280-8554), 1½ blocks from the Sedgwick el stop. $20 per day. 100 free miles the first day, 50 the 2nd; 15¢ each additional mile. From $119 per week. Open Mon.-Fri. 8:30am-6:30pm. Must be 21 with major credit card.

Auto Transport Company: National U-Drive, 2116 N. Cicero Ave. (889-7737).

Help Lines: Metro Help, 929-5150. 24-hour crisis line. **Rape Crisis Line,** 872-7799. 24 hours. **Gay Horizon Hotline,** 929-4357.

Medical Emergency: Cook County Hospital, 633-6000. Take the Congress A train to the Medical Center Stop.

Post Office: 433 W. Van Buren St. (765-3200 or 765-3210), 3 blocks from Union Station. Open 24 hours. **ZIP code:** 60607.

Area Code: 312.

Orientation

Chicago runs north-south along 29 miles of southwest Lake Michigan lakefront, with a slight western tilt. The city and its suburbs sprawl across the entire northeastern corner of Illinois. Most cross-country road, rail, and airplane trips in the northern U.S. pass through Chicago.

Despite its vast size, Chicago is neatly organized. The center of the grid-like pattern of streets is at **State Street,** the east-west axis, and **Madison Street,** the north-south axis. State and Madison also mark a busy commercial area called the **State Street Mall.** If you need to determine the location of a given address, find out what "hundred" N, S, E, or W the street is numbered. Each block increases by 100 in number (with a few exceptions) as the distance from State and Madison increases. There are very few east numbers because the lake gets in the way. South streets are usually numbered (not named), with the exception of 1200 S., which is known as Roosevelt.

Chicago's other neighborhoods are diverse and frequently polarized. If you arrive by bus or train, you'll be in Chicago's **Loop,** the skyscraper-studded downtown area surrounded by elevated train (el) tracks. This neighborhood is safe during the business day, but not after dark. Just south of the Loop and southwest of the natural history museum lies **Pilsen,** a center of Chicago's Latino community. **Chinatown** is just south of Pilsen. Avoid the **Near South Side,** in the south 30s, and the wastelands of the **Near West Side,** west of I-90/94; these are two of the most dangerous urban slums in America. Ritzy business and residential districts extend north of the Loop along Michigan Avenue into the affluent north lakeshore. They culminate in the wealthy suburbs on the northern edge of Cook County.

Working and middle-class neighborhoods extend outward from the core city area. The western and northern districts have mixed ethnic neighborhoods. Poles are concentrated near Oak Park. **Uptown** is home to Greeks (on Lawrence Ave., in the 4600-4800 blocks especially); Vietnamese and other Southeast Asians (in Argyle); and clusters of Haitians and Native Americans. Irish neighborhoods lie throughout the western portion of the city. The northern suburb of **Skokie** is well known for its Jewish community. Just southeast of Chicago, blue-collar workers of all creeds labor in **Gary,** Indiana, a languishing steel giant.

Transportation

The **Chicago Transit Authority,** part of the **Regional Transit Authority** (836-7000 in the city, 800-972-7000 in the suburbs), runs rapid transit trains, subways, and buses. The CTA runs 24 hours, but late-night service is infrequent and unsafe in some areas. Maps are available at many stations, the Water Tower Information Center, the Convention and Tourist Bureau, and the RTA Office. The **elevated rapid transit train** system, called the **el,** bounds the major downtown section of the city, the Loop. Trains marked "A," "B," or "all stops" may run on the same tracks along different routes. Subway and bus fare is $1, and transfers are 25¢, plus 10¢ to transfer to the subway. Supertransfers (good Sun.-Mon. 3am-3am and all day on major holidays) go for $1.75. Fourteen-day passes ($25) are sold each week on Thursdays and are good starting the following Sunday. On Sundays and holidays from Memorial Day weekend to the end of September, you can tour Chicago's cultural attractions on CTA's **Culture Buses** (10:30am-4:55pm, $2.50, seniors and children $1.25). Three routes serve the North, South, and West Sides. Many sights and museums described below are on a Culture Bus route, and some offer a discount upon presentation of a Culture Bus Supertransfer.

Several major highways crisscross the city and urban area. The **Eisenhower (I-290)** cuts west from the Loop. **I-90** pivots around the Eisenhower; to the northwest it's called the **Kennedy,** to the south, the **Dan Ryan.** The **Edens (I-94)** splits off from the Kennedy and heads north to the suburbs.

Accommodations

With budget lodgings in Chicago, you get what you pay for, and sometimes not even that. Women especially might want to play it safe and stay in less thrifty hotels.

Weekend specials ($64-69) are offered at the **Allerton Hotel,** 701 N. Michigan Ave. (440-1500 or 800-621-8311), the **Executive House Hotel,** 71 E. Wacker Dr.

(346-7100 or 800-621-4005), the **Lenox House,** 616 N. Rush St. (337-1000 or 800-445-3669), and the **Midland Hotel,** 172 W. Adams (332-1200 or 800-621-2360). **Oxford House,** 225 N. Wabash (346-6585 or 800-344-4111), at Wacker Dr., has a $39-per-night weekend special. Another option is **Chicago Bed and Breakfast,** 1704 Crilly Court 60014 (951-0085), a referral service that offers over 60 rooms of varying prices throughout the city and outlying areas. Daily rates start at $40 per person. Cooking facilities are often available.

Chicago International Hostel (AYH and IYH), 6318 N. Winthrop (262-1011). Take Howard St. northbound train to Loyola Station. Walk south and east on Sheridan Rd. to Winthrop, then ½ block south. Clean rooms, safe and convenient neighborhood. Kitchen. Linen included. $10, nonmembers $13, each additional night $9.

International House (AYH), 1414 E. 59th St., Hyde Park (753-2270), off Lake Shore Dr. Take the Illinois Central Railroad to 59th St. and walk ½ block west. Part of the University of Chicago. 200 comfortable dorm-style rooms. Shared bath. Cheap cafeteria. $14, nonmembers $23. Open June 15-Sept. 1. Reservations required.

Baker Hall, National College of Education, 2808 Sheridan Rd. (475-1100, ext. 3177), between the Baha'i Temple and Evanston Hospital. Take the northbound train from Howard to Central St. Very nice dormitory with shared bath; cafeteria. $15 per person (all rooms have 2 beds). Open June-Aug. Reserve at least a week in advance.

Hotel Cass, 640 N. Wabash (787-4030), just north of the Loop. Take subway to Grand St. Pleasant place, clean rooms. Singles $35. Doubles $40. $5 key deposit. A/C $5.

Hotel Walker, 111 W. Huron (787-1386), Near North Side. Lumpy mattresses. Small, clean rooms. Singles $35. Doubles $50. Weekly $80-85. $5 key and linen deposit. $10 phone service deposit.

Leaning Tower YMCA, 6300 W. Touhy (647-1122), Niles. From Jefferson Park subway, take bus #85A. Look for ¼-scale replica of the leaning tower of Pisa. Private bath, housekeeping. Singles $27. Doubles $30. Off-season $4-5 less. Key deposit $5.

YMCA, 3333 N. Marshfield Ave. (248-3333), near North Side, near Lincoln Ave. district. Men only, minimum age 19. Much less attractive than the hostels for the short-term visitor, but low weekly rates ($55-60). $14.42 per day. All singles.

YMCA and YWCA, 33 W. Chicago Ave. (944-6211). Good security, bare rooms. Singles $24. Doubles $32. Students $65 per week, $228 per month.

Pioneer Motel, 8835 Ogden Ave., Brookfield (485-9686), on U.S. 34, 3 miles east of I-294 in the city's western suburbs. Accessible only by car. Clean, spacious, comfortable rooms. Singles $27, $2 each additional person. $5 key deposit.

Food

The "city that works" is also a city that eats—very well. Like many urban dwellers, Chicagoans flee downtown come dusk, and most of the best food finds are far away from the Loop, in busy nightlife districts or tiny neighborhoods. One of Chitown's favorite fillers is its renowned pizza, which features a thick crust covered with melted cheese, fresh sausage, sauteed onions and peppers, and a spicy sauce made from fresh whole tomatoes. Besides pizza, however, you can sample especially good Southeast Asian, Mexican, and Greek food. Dig into anything from Thai noodles to sizzling ribs at the city's **Taste of Chicago Festival,** where 80 vendors tempt your tastebuds in late June and early July. *Chicago* Magazine ($2) offers a comprehensive guide with honest and thorough listings cross-indexed by price, cuisine, and location.

Pizza

Pizzeria Uno, 29 E. Ohio (321-1000), and **Due,** 619 N. Wabash (943-2400). Uno is where it all began. In 1943, owner Ike Sewall introduced Chicago-style deep dish pizza, and though the graffiti-stained walls have been painted over and the restaurant is franchised across the nation, the pizza is still damn good. **Due** is right up the street, but the atmosphere and consistency—as well as the legend—are lacking. Pizzas $5-15. Both open Mon.-Thurs. 11:30am-1:30am, Fri. 11:30am-2:30am, Sat. noon-2:30am, Sun. noon-11:30pm.

Aurelio's, 18162 Harwood St., Homewood (798-8050). Lots of delicious pizza ($3-19.25) served in a colorful and slightly chaotic atmosphere. Open Mon.-Thurs. 11:30am-11pm, Fri.-Sat. 11:30am-12:30am, Sun. 4-11pm.

Edwardo's, 10 locations include: 1212 N. Dearborn (337-4490), Near North Side; 521 S. Dearborn (939-3366), downtown; and 1321 E. 57th St. (241-7960), in Hyde Park. Vegetable-fanciers will love the spinach or broccoli souffle pizza ($11). Hours vary by location.

Gino's East, 160 E. Superior (943-1124). Wait 30-40 min. while they make your "pizza de résistance." Small pan pizza ($6) serves 2. Open Mon.-Sat. 11am-midnight, Sun. 11am-10pm.

Loop

For a cheaper alternative to most Loop dining, try the surprisingly good fast-food joints in the basement of the State of Illinois Building at Randolph and Clarke St.

The Berghoff, 17 W. Adams (427-3170), offers moderately priced German and American fare, including terrific strudel and home-brewed beer. German pot roast $6.50. Open Mon.-Thurs. 11am-9:30pm, Fri.-Sat. 11am-10pm.

Near North

Billy Goat's Tavern, 430 N. Michigan Ave. (222-1525), hidden on lower Michigan Ave. Inspiration for Saturday Night Live's legendary "Cheezborger, cheezborger—no Pepsi, Coke" greasy spoon. Ask for a nifty goat hat. Cheezborgers $1.80. Open Sun.-Fri. 7am-2am, Sat. 7am-3am.

Ed Debevic's, 640 N. Wells (664-1707), and 660 Lake Cook, Deerfield (945-3242). A legend. Burgers, chicken pot pie, and other all-American dishes. Full dinners $5. Packed on weekend nights. N. Wells location open Mon.-Fri. 11am-11pm, Sat. 10am-1am, Sun. 11am-midnight. Deerfield location closes a bit earlier.

John Barleycorn Memorial Pub, 658 W. Belden Ave. (348-8899), at Lincoln Ave. This English-style pub has long attracted an artsy, intellectual crowd by playing classical music and showing art slides on 3 large screens. Reasonably priced menu, burgers $5. Kitchen open until 1am. Open Sun.-Fri. 11am-2am, Sat. 11am-3am.

North Side

Cafe Phoenicia, 2814 N. Halsted St., 549-7088. A tribute to the (Phoenician) alphabet and nautical tableaux spice up the walls of this little Lebanese outfit. Outstanding hummus $3, lamb kebab $8. Open Mon.-Sat. 11:30am-2pm and 5-10:30pm, Sun. 4-9:30pm. Reservations required on weekends.

Heartland Cafe, 7000 N. Glenwood (465-8005), at Lunt Ave. Cheap, delicious vegetarian food, complete with live folk and jazz Fri. and Sat. evenings (cover $2.50), outdoor café, and a hip bookstore. Dinner entrees $7.25-$9.50. Open Mon.-Thurs. 9am-1am, Fri.-Sat. 9am-3am, Sun. 9am-2am.

Mekong, 4953 N. Broadway (271-0206), at Argyle St. A busy, spotless Vietnamese restaurant. Tasty soups $3.50-4, fried noodles $4.50-$10. Open Sun.-Tues. and Thurs. 10am-10pm, Wed. 4-10pm, Fri.-Sat. 10am-11pm.

Launa Thai, 5951-5 N. Broadway (878-1155), between Thorndale and Elmdale Ave. Attractive family-run restaurant. Curry dishes $3.75-4.50. Open Tues.-Fri. 11am-10pm, Sat.-Sun. noon-10pm.

Marco's Paradise, 3358 N. Sheffield (281-4848), down the street from Wrigley Field. The downstairs is private and claustrophobic, but the first floor is open and airy. Try the enchiladas mexicanas ($5.75) or the *carne asada* (skirt steak; $9). Open Sun.-Fri. noon-midnight, Sat. noon-2am. Reservations suggested on weekends.

North Shore

La Choza, 7630 N. Paulina (761-8020), Evanston, 1 block west of Howard el stop. The seedy, broken neon storefront conceals a vine-covered canopied terrace in the back. Chow down on the "Mexico City"—enchilada, tostada, beans, and rice ($5.35). Open Tues.-Thurs. 11am-11pm, Fri. 11am-11:30pm, Sat. 11am-midnight, Sun. noon-10:30pm.

Walker Bros. Original Pancake House, 153 Green Bay Rd. (251-6000), Wilmette, between Central and Lake. Stunning collection of stained glass and Tiffany lamps. Heavenly apple pancakes ($6) at this family restaurant chain. Huge lines for Sunday brunch. Open Sun.-Thurs. 7am-10:30pm, Fri.-Sat. 7am-midnight.

South Side

Casino Restaurant, 9706 S. Commercial (221-5189), in steel-mill slag valley neighborhood. A pool table, a multilingual juke-box, and outstanding Serbo-Croatian food. Spicy *cevapcići* (Serbian sausages), huge Serbian hamburgers ($3.75), and soup (50-75¢). Open Tues.-Sat. 11am-9pm.

Medici on 57th, 1327 E. 57th St. (667-7394), Hyde Park. University of Chicago students flock here for custom-made burgers ($4-5). Open Sun.-Thurs. 9am-12:30am, Fri.-Sat. 9am-1:30am.

Three Happiness, 2130 S. Wentworth Ave. (791-1228), in Chinatown. Expect long lines Sunday for Chicago's best *dim sum* (items $1.55), served around noon. Reinforce your wallet if you plan to stay for dinner ($10-12). Open Mon.-Thurs. 10am-midnight, Fri.-Sat. 10am-1am, Sun. 10am-10pm.

Near West Side and Oak Park

Al's Italian Beef, 1079 W. Taylor St. (226-4017), at Aberdeen, near Little Italy. Take a number and don't be bashful about standing and eating at the counter—there are no tables or chairs. Great Italian beef sandwiches ($2.45) and fries. Wash your meal down at the Italian lemonade stand across the street. Open Mon.-Sat. 9am-1am.

La Majada, 226 W. Harrison, Oak Park (848-8838). Superb Mexican food—try the *chiles rellenos* ($8). Dinners $9-11. Open Sun.-Thurs. 11:30am-11:30pm, Fri.-Sat. 11:30am-12:30am.

The Parthenon, 314 S. Halsted St. (726-2407), in Greektown. Enjoy anything from gyros ($5.25) to *saganaki* (cheese flamed in brandy; $2.75). Dinners $4.25-13.50. Open Sun.-Thurs. 11am-1am, Fri.-Sat. 11am-2am.

Sights

While public transportation and your feet will serve you well around town, guided tours are a less demanding alternative. Tours start near major hotels; you must make reservations. **American Sight-seeing Tours-Chicago,** 520 S. Michigan Ave. (427-3100), has two- to eight-hour tours ($12-37). **Gray Line of Chicago,** 33 E. Monroe St. (346-9506), has two- ($14) to seven-hour tours and three-hour cruises ($19). **Mercury Sight-seeing Boats** (332-1353) and **Shoreline Marine Sight-seeing Boat** (673-3399) charter cruises ($4.50-9).

Museums

Admission to each of Chicago's major museums is free at least one day per week. The "Big Five" allow exploration of everything from the ocean to landscape painting to the stars, while a handful of smaller collections represent diverse ethnic groups and professional interests. For more information, call the **Chicago Council on Fine Arts Hotline** at 346-3278 (24 hours).

The Art Institute of Chicago, Michigan Ave. and Adams St. (443-3500). The city's premier art museum houses the finest collection of French impressionist paintings west of Paris. Also contains works by El Greco, Chagall, Van Gogh, Picasso, and Rembrandt. Open Mon. and Wed.-Fri. 10:30am-4:30pm, Tues. 10:30am-8pm, Sat. 10am-5pm, Sun. and holidays noon-5pm. Donation $5, seniors and students $2.50. Free Tues.

The Adler Planetarium, 1300 S. Lake Shore Dr. (322-0300). Features astronomy exhibits and a sophisticated skyshow. Don't overlook the Astro-Center, a $4 million subterranean addition. Skyshow 5 times per day in the summer, less frequently in the winter. Admission $3, seniors free, ages 6-17 $1.50. Planetarium open Sat.-Thurs. 9:30am-5pm, Fri. 9:30am-9pm. Free.

Shedd Aquarium, 1200 S. Lake Shore Dr. (939-2438). The world's largest indoor aquarium houses over 5000 species of fresh and saltwater fish in 206 exhibition tanks. The Oceanarium, scheduled for completion in 1990, will feature small whales, dolphins, seals, and other marine mammals. Open daily May-Aug. 9am-5pm; Sept.-Oct. and March-April 10am-5pm; Nov.-Feb. 10am-4pm. Admission $3, seniors and ages 6-17 $2. Free Thurs.

Field Museum of Natural History, Roosevelt Rd. at Lake Shore Dr. (922-9410), across the street from the aquarium. Geological, anthropological, botanical, and zoological exhibits. Don't miss the Egyptian mummies, the Native American Halls, the Hall of Gems, and the dinosaur display. Watch out for rhinos in the elevators. Open daily 9am-5pm. Admission $3, families $10, seniors and students $2, ages 6-17 $1. Free Thurs.

Museum of Science and Industry, 5700 S. Lake Shore Dr. (684-1414). Hands-on exhibits ensure a crowd of children, overgrown and otherwise. Highlights include the Apollo 8 command module, a German submarine, a life-size replica of a coal mine, and a 16-ft. human heart. Open Mon.-Fri. 9:30am-5:30pm; Labor Day-Memorial Day 9:30am-4pm. Free.

DuSable Museum of African-American History, 740 E. 56th Place and Cottage Grove (947-0600), Washington Park. Illuminating exhibit on everything from ancient African sculpture to the 60s black arts movement. Open Mon.-Fri. 9am-5pm, Sat.-Sun. noon-5pm. Admission $2, seniors and students $1, under 13 50¢. Free Thurs.

Peace Museum, 430 W. Erie (440-1860). Daring, multimedia exhibits that may turn even the most bellicose visitor from hawk to dove. Open Tues.-Sun. noon-5pm, Thurs. noon-8pm. Admission $3.50, seniors and students $2.

The Oriental Institute, 1155 E. 58th St. (702-9520), on the University of Chicago campus. An extraordinary collection of ancient Near Eastern art and archeological treasures. Open Tues.-Sat. 10am-4pm, Sun. noon-4pm. Free.

The Museum of Contemporary Art, 237 E. Ontario (280-2660), within walking distance of the Water Tower. Exhibits change often. One gallery devoted to local artists. Open Tues.-Sat. 10am-5pm, Sun. noon-5pm. Admission $4, seniors and students $2. Free Tues.

Outdoors

Chicago's string of lovely lakefront parks fringe the area between the city proper and Lake Michigan. On a sunny afternoon you'll see a cavalcade of sunbathers, dog walkers, roller skaters, and skateboard artists, yet everyone still has room to stake out a private little piece of the paradise. Lincoln, Grant, Burnham, and Jackson Parks are operated by the Recreation Department (294-2200).

Lake Michigan lures swimmers to the **Lincoln Park Beach** and the **Oak Street Beach,** on the North Side. Both are crowded, popular places to swim and soak in the sun. The smaller and rockier beaches between 49th and 57th St. on the South Side are also clean, accessible, and equipped with changing houses. (Open mid-June to Labor Day daily 9am-9:30pm.) Call the Chicago Parks District for further information (294-2333).

Lincoln Park, 2021 N. Stockton Dr. (871-3999), rents paddleboats by the hour ($7, with $2 deposit) and the half-hour ($4, with $1 deposit). The Park District maintains jurisdiction over eight harbors from May 15 to October 15 for powerboats and sailboats. Great apes, farm animals, and snow leopards are just a few of the inhabitants of **Lincoln Park Zoo,** 2045 N. Lincoln Park W. (294-4660). Also in the park, you can walk among the cactus in the **Lincoln Park Conservatory** (294-4770). (Both open daily 9am-5pm. Free.) Be warned that muggers haunt the park after dark.

Spend a relaxing summer day at **Grant Park,** on the waterfront between Roosevelt Rd. and Monroe St., east of Michigan Ave. If you hang around until 9pm, watch the hour-long, computer-operated light display at **Buckingham Fountain.** Jets of water spray 90 feet into the air, illuminated by colored lights hidden in the fountain base. You can also rent ice skates in the winter ($1.50-2.50) or bring your own roller skates to the **Richard J. Daley Bicentennial Plaza** (294-4792), in Grant Park. The **Garfield Park Conservatory,** 300 N. Central Park (533-1281), has palms, cacti, ferns, and tropical plants enclosed in its 4½ acres. (Open daily 9am-5pm. Free.)

The Loop

After the Great Fire of 1871 left the city a *tabula rasa,* Chicago became a workshop for leading architects such as Daniel Burnham, Louis Sullivan, and later Mies Van der Rohe, whose Chicago school transformed urban design throughout the world. The Loop is a mecca for architecture buffs. A one-and-a-half-hour walking tour takes you past pioneer skyscrapers; dazzling masterworks of art deco, international style, and postmodern architecture; impressive modern sculpture; and the world's tallest building.

The best place to start is the **ArchiCenter,** 330 S. Dearborn (782-1776). Volunteers lead excellent walking tours (about $5, often less for seniors and students), and the center offers lectures, photograph exhibits, and a bookstore. The center is appropriately located, since the **Monadnock Building** was the last of the important wall-bearing constructions before Chicago's architects gave the world the skyscraper's revolutionary steel-frame skeleton.

From the ArchiCenter, go west on Jackson Blvd. to LaSalle St. Here at the **Board of Trade Building,** designed by Holabird and Root just before the 1929 crash, you'll see the real forces that drive Chicago. Cosmopolitan art deco ornament goes head-to-head with a huge monument to Ceres, the Greek goddess of grain, that stands 609 feet above street level. At the fifth-floor vistors gallery (open 9:30am-2pm), you can watch the frantic trading of Midwestern farm goods at the world's oldest and largest commodity futures exchange.

If you continue west on Jackson to Franklin St., you can't miss the looming 110-story **Sears Tower** (875-9696). The best thing about the world's tallest building is the skydeck—on a clear day you can see four states. (Open daily 9am-midnight. Admission $3.75, under 15 $2.25.)

The First National Bank Building and Plaza (732-6037) stands about 2 blocks northeast at the corner of Clark and Munroe St. The world's largest bank building sweeps the eye to the sky with its diagonal slope. Marc Chagall's vivid mosaic, *The Four Seasons,* lines the block and sets off a public space often used for concerts and lunchtime entertainment.

One street over is State and Madison, the most famous block of "State Street that great street" and the focal point of the Chicago street grid. Exquisite ironwork and the famous extra-large Chicago window mark Louis Sullivan's Carson Pirie Scott store. If you have a chance, visit Sullivan's other masterpiece, the **Auditorium Building,** several blocks south, at the corner of Congress and Michigan. Beautiful design and flawless acoustics highlight this Chicago landmark.

No one knows exactly what the Picasso sculpture at the foot of **Daley Center Plaza** is supposed to represent, although it has marked this public space at the corner of Dearborn and Washington since 1967. Across the street is Joan Miró's *Chicago,* the sculptor's gift to the city.

One block north to Randolph and Clark takes you to the controversial and visually stunning **State of Illinois Building,** designed by Helmut Jalm in 1985. A hypermodern version of the town square, it features a sloping atrium, circular floors that allow full view of hundreds of employees, and elevators and escalators with their guts exposed.

Near North

The city's ritziest district lies above the Loop along the lake, just past the Michigan Avenue Bridge. Overlooking the stretch is the **Tribune Tower,** 435 N. Michigan Ave., a Gothic skyscraper that was the subject of a hotly-contested international design competition in the 20s. The building is home to one of Chicago's major newspapers, and the inside lobby is studded with quotations celebrating freedom of the press.

Chicago's **Magnificent Mile,** along Michigan Avenue north of the Chicago River, is a conglomeration of ritzy shops and galleries. En route you'll pass the **Chicago Water Tower and Pumping Station,** at the corner of Michigan and Pearson Ave. (467-7114). Built in 1867, these were the only public structures to survive the Great Chicago Fire. The pumping station, which still supplies water to nearly 400,000 people on the North Side, now houses the multimedia production *Here's Chicago.* For $4.75 (seniors and students $3.50, under 12 $2.50), you can go on a brief narrated tour through the pumping station, watch a 45-minute slide portrayal of Chicago, and see a slick 10-minute aerial view of the city. (Open Sun.-Thurs. 10am-5pm, Fri.-Sat. 10am-5:30pm.) A short walk north on Michigan Ave. leads to the

John Hancock Center, 875 N. Michigan (751-3681), a towering office building with observation decks.

Beautiful old mansions and apartment buildings fill the streets between the Water Tower and Lincoln Park. Known as the **Gold Coast,** the area has long been the elite residential section of the city. The early industrialists and city founders made their homes here and, lately, many families have decided to move back in from the suburbs. If you walk a few more blocks east, you come upon Lake Michigan and the Oak St. Beach.

Urban renewal has made **Lincoln Park** the popular choice for upscale yuppies. Bounded by Armitage to the south and Diversey Ave. to the north, lakeside Lincoln Park is also a center for recreation and nightlife, with beautiful harbors and parks, and some of the city's liveliest clubs and restaurants along North Halsted and Lincoln Avenue.

If you hear the bells of St. Michael's Church, you're in **Old Town.** This neighborhood is crowded with eclectic galleries, shops, and nightspots on gentrified streets. Absorb some of the architectural atmosphere while strolling the W. Menomonee and W. Eugenie St. area. In early June, the Old Town Art Fair attracts artists and craftspeople from across the country. Many residents open their restored homes to the public. (Take bus #151 to Lincoln Park and walk south down Clark or Wells St.)

North Side and North Shore

Extending from Diversey Ave. to Howard St., the North Side is a mix of ethnically diverse residential neighborhoods. **Graceland Cemetery** runs through the heart of the area along Clark St. Elaborate tombs and monuments designed by the likes of Louis Sullivan and Lorado Taft make the burial ground one of Chicago's most interesting sights and a posthumous status symbol. The ArchiCenter (922-3432; see The Loop above) offers tours, and the cemetery office at the northeast corner of Clark St. and Irving Park Rd. has guidebooks for sightseers.

Though they finally lost their battle against night baseball in 1988, **Wrigleyville** residents remain, like much of the North Side, fiercely loyal to the **Chicago Cubs.** Just east of Graceland Cemetery, at the corner of Clark St. and Addison, tiny, ivy-covered **Wrigley Field** is the North Side's most famous institution. After a game, walk along Clark St. in one of the city's busiest nightlife districts, where restaurants, sportsbars, and music clubs abound.

South Side

A hodgepodge of neighborhoods with distinct boundaries, the South Side is not uniformly safe for the blithe out-of-towner. But if you exercise caution, a visit here is truly rewarding. The South Side is home to some of Chicago's most vital ethnic communities, beautiful buildings, and points of historical interest.

Seven miles south of the Loop along the lake is **Hyde Park,** an uneasy ivory tower of intellectualism. The **University of Chicago's** beautiful, Neo-Gothic campus dominates the neighborhood. A former haven for the city's artists and musicians, Hyde Park became the first American community to undergo urban renewal in the 50s. The artists return in June for the **57th Street Art Fair.** The neighborhood also features Frank Lloyd Wright's famous **Robie House,** at the corner of Woodlawn Ave. and 58th St. (Unfortunately, the original furniture was removed to the nearby **Smart Gallery,** at 5550 S. Greenwood Ave.) From the Loop, take bus #6 ("Jefferson Express") or the Illinois Central Railroad from the Randolph St. Station south to 57th St. Be careful after dark.

Neighboring **Kenwood** is the home of Jesse Jackson's Operation PUSH headquarters at 50th and Drexel, as well as the Middle Eastern "Castle" of Elijah Muhammad, one-time mentor of activist Malcolm X and boxer Muhammad Ali. Although this eclectic area is far safer than its neighbor to the north, the untutored traveler should beware.

Once considered the nation's most perfect community, **Pullman Historic District** on the southeast side began in 1885, when George Pullman, the inventor of the sleeping car, hired British architect Solon S. Beman to design a model working town so that his Palace Car Company employees would be "healthier, happier, and more productive." Unfortunately, the earliest of suburbs was troubled by worker resentment over Pullman's power. For local flavor and a chat with some serious history buffs, try the **Hotel Florence,** 11111 Forrestville Ave. (785-8900), which, in the 19th century, was the center of the community. It now houses a restaurant and the **Historic Pullman Foundation** (785-8181; guided tours leave from the hotel the first Sun. of each month May-Oct. Admission $3.50, seniors $3, students $2. By car, take I-94 to W. 111th St. By train, take the Illinois Central Gulf Railroad to 111th St./Pullman).

Home of the Democratic machine, **Bridgeport** is considered by many a symbol of the Old Chicago. The Irish neighborhood at 37th and Halsted has given Chicago four of its mayors, including Richard Daley.

Near West Side and Oak Park

The Near West Side, bounded by Wacker St. to the east and Odgen Ave. to the west, is a fascinating group of tiny ethnic enclaves. Farther out, however, is the West Side, one of the most dismal slums in the U.S.

Greektown might not be as Greek as it once was, but what remains is several blocks of authentic restaurants (north of the Eisenhower on Halsted) that continue to draw people from all over the city.

A few blocks down Halsted, the historic **Hull House** stands as a reminder of Chicago's role in turn-of-the-century reform movements. It was here that Jane Addams devoted her life to her settlement house and earned her reputation as a champion of social justice and welfare. Hull House has been relocated to 800 S. Halsted, but painstaking restoration and thoughtful exhibits about Near West Side history make the **Hull House Museum** (413-5353), at the same location, a fascinating part of a visit to Chicago.

Little Italy, along Taylor St., remains a tighter residential area than its Greek neighbor. Charming storefront restaurants, delis, and bakeries serve this relatively self-contained community. Nearby, the **University of Illinois at Chicago** rises above area neighborhoods, a striking monument to austere, high modern architecture.

Ten miles west of downtown on the Eisenhower (I-290) lands you in **Oak Park.** Ernest Hemingway lived here, as did Frank Lloyd Wright, who endowed the community with 25 of his spectacular homes and buildings. The **visitors center,** 158 Forest Ave. (848-1500) has maps and guidebooks. (Open daily 10am-5pm.) Don't miss the **Frank Lloyd Wright House and Studio** (same telephone number), with his beautiful 1898 workplace and original furniture. Admission and tickets for 10 different tours ($3-25) can be purchased at the visitors center, although a visit on your own is much cheaper. (By car, exit north from the Eisenhower on Harlem Ave. and follow markers. By train, take the Lake St./Dan Ryan el to Harlem/Marion stop.)

Entertainment

To stay on top of Chicago events, grab a copy of the free weekly *Chicago Reader,* or tune in to **WXRT** 93.1FM. *Chicago* magazine has exhaustive club listings. The Chicago **Bears** play football at Soldier's Field, the **White Sox** swing in the South Side at Comiskey Park, and the **Cubs** play ball at gorgeous Wrigley Field. For current sports events, call **Sports Information** (976-1313).

Theater

Chicago is one of the great theater centers of North America. Unfortunately, most tickets are expensive. One budget option is to buy half-price tickets on the day of performance at **Hot Tix Booths,** 24 S. State St., downtown. (Open Mon. noon-6pm, Tues.-Fri. 10am-6pm, Sat. 10am-5pm. Tickets for Sun. shows on sale Sat.) There are also booths in Oak Park Mall and Evanston (1616 Sherman). Phone **Curtain Call** (977-1755) for information on ticket availability, schedules, and Hot

Tix booths. Also check with theaters to see if they offer half-price student rush tickets 30 minutes before showtime.

Over the last decade, Chicago has fostered a number of smaller theaters similar to the off-off-Broadway houses in New York City. Mostly located on the North Side and known as "Off-Loop" theaters, these houses specialize in original contemporary drama. David Mamet got his start at **Steppenwolf Theater,** 2851 N. Halsted (472-4141; tickets $16-23, Sun.-Thurs. $2 senior and student discount). Major theaters for Broadway-bound productions are located in the downtown area. The **Shubert Theater,** 22 W. Monroe St. (977-1700), and the **Blackstone Theater,** 60 E. Balbo St. (341-8455), near State St., both stage Broadway productions. The Shubert is better known, and more expensive ($16-42). Blackstone's shows start at $6-7. (Showtimes Tues.-Sat. 7:30pm, Wed. and Sat. at 2pm, Sun. at 3pm.) Several suburban playhouses also offer the works of major playwrights. Complete listings are in the free *Chicago Theater Guide,* available at Hot Tix booths.

Body Politic Theater (871-3000) and **Victory Gardens Theater,** both at 2261 N. Lincoln Ave. Various genres; often hosts touring companies. Downstairs, the Victory Gardens presents drama by Chicago playwrights. Tickets for both $15-25.

Organic Theater Co., 3319 N. Clark St. (327-5588). Original works and avant-garde adaptations. Showtimes Tues.-Fri. at 8pm, Sat. at 6:30pm and 9:30pm, Sun. at 3pm and 8pm. Tickets $10-28.

Wisdom Bridge Theater, 1559 W. Howard St. (743-6442). Mostly new material or creative postmodern productions, such as a Kabuki *Macbeth.* Showtimes vary. Tickets $18-24.

Kuumba Professional Theater, 343 S. Dearborn (461-9000). The most established of the city's many black theater groups. Showtime usually 8pm. Tickets $12-15.

Apollo Theatre, 2540 N. Lincoln (935-6100). Launched *A Soldier's Play.* Tickets $22.50-28.50, $2 student discount.

Comedy

Chicago boasts a plethora of comedy clubs, the most famous of which is the **Second City Comedy Revue,** 1616 N. Wells St. (337-3992). Second City has been busting guts for nearly 30 years with its satirical spoofs of Chicago life and politics. John Candy, Bill Murray, and the late John Belushi and Gilda Radner are among its most accomplished alumni. (Shows Tues.-Thurs. and Sun. at 9pm, Fri.-Sat. at 8:30 and 11pm. Tickets $7.50-9.50. Reservations recommended, but during the week you can often get in if you show up 1 hr. early.) A free improvisation session follows the show.

Dance, Classical Music, and Opera

Many topnotch international dance companies, including ballet, ethnic, and modern troupes, perform in the **Auditorium Theater,** 50 E. Congress Parkway (922-2110). **FINEART** (346-3278) is a cultural events hotline sponsored by the Chicago Office of Fine Arts. The **Chicago City Ballet** performs at the auditorium under the direction of Maria Tallchief. (Tickets $25-47.50.) **MoMing,** 1034 W. Barry (472-9894), celebrates avant-garde dance in a warehouse building on the North Side. On two weekends in mid-July, you can watch for just $1.98. (Performances usually cost $8-10.)

The **Chicago Symphony Orchestra (CSO),** conducted by Sir George Solti, performs in **Orchestra Hall,** 220 S. Michigan Ave. (435-8111). Renowned guest artists highlight the season (Sept. 28 to June 9, $12-42). Tickets are hard to come by, but there are regularly scheduled non-subscription and university nights. The CSO has a summer season at **Ravinia Festival** in suburban Highland Park (see Seasonal Events below). In summer every Wednesday at noon, the **Chicago Public Library Cultural Center,** 78 E. Washington St. (346-3278), features free outdoor concerts.

The **Lyric Opera of Chicago,** Civic Opera House, 20 N. Wacker Dr. (332-2240 or 332-2244), still puts on some of the most popular shows in town. The season runs from September to January (tickets $15-75).

Seasonal Events

Like Chicago's architecture, the city's summer celebrations are done on a grand scale. City dwellers head for the lakefront beaches and parks, or they jam the outdoor cafés and beer gardens. The **Ravinia Festival** (728-4642), in Highland Park, a northern suburb, is famous throughout the Midwest and runs from late June to late September. The Chicago Symphony Orchestra, ballet troupes, folk and jazz musicians, and comedians perform throughout the festival's 14-week season. (Shows start between 7:30 and 8:30pm. Admission $20-35. $5 buys you a patch of ground for a blanket and picnic. To reach Ravinia Park, take the Chicago and Northwestern Commuter Railway to the main gate ($3.75), or the Ravinia bus service from the Loop ($6 round-trip).

The **Fourth of July Celebration** (744-3315) in Grant Park draws huge crowds for its fireworks display and performance of Tchaikovsky's *1812 Overture.* Prime your buds for the **Taste of Chicago** festival around July 4th. Chicago's best chefs set out samples at bargain prices on endless tables; you can stuff yourself for $10. In mid-July, Lake Shore Park, Lake Shore Drive, and Chicago Avenue are the scene of the **Air and Water Show,** featuring several days of boat races, parades, hang gliding events, and stunt flying, as well as a performance by the Blue Angels precision fliers.

Chicago's **Blues Festival** (744-3315), in early June, presents homegrown music to the thousands who turn out at the **Petrillo Music Shell** in Grant Park. Even more of a spectacle are the **Chicago Gospel Festival,** in July, and the **Chicago Jazz Festival,** at the end of August. On a smaller scale, Chicago also has over 75 ethnic and neighborhood festivals. Call the 24-hour hotline (744-3315) for information.

Nightlife

Chicago's eclectic nightlife is a grab bag of music, clubs, bars, and more music. "Sweet home Chicago" is proud of the innumerable blues perfomers who played there (a strip of 43rd St. was recently renamed Muddy Waters Drive). For other tastes, jazz, folk, reggae, and punk clubs rock people all over the North Side. Aspiring pick-up artists swing over to **Rush and Division,** an intersection that has replaced the stockyards as one of the great meat markets of the world. To get away from the crowds, head to a little neighborhood spot for a lot of atmosphere. Call the **Jazz Hotline** (666-1881).

Blues

B.L.U.E.S., 2519 N. Halsted St. (528-1012), el to Fullerton, then westbound Fullerton bus. Slightly cramped, but the music is unbeatable. Its sister location, **B.L.U.E.S. etcetera,** 1124 W. Belmont (549-9436), has a spacious dance floor and is, in general, a more energetic blues bar. Music starts at 9pm. Open Sun.-Fri. 8pm-2am, Sat. 8pm-3am. Cover Sun.-Thurs. $5, Fri.-Sat. $7.

Kingston Mines, 2548 N. Halsted St. (477-4646), just north of B.L.U.E.S. Shows 6 nights per week. Watch for the "Blue Monday" jam session. Music starts at 9:30pm. Open Sun.-Fri. until 4am, Sat. until 5am. Cover Mon. $5, Tues.-Thurs. and Sun. $7, Fri.-Sat. $8.

New Checkerboard Lounge, 423 Muddy Waters Dr. (624-3240). Chicago's oldest blues club is the last authentic remnant of the old days. In a shady, unsafe South Side neighborhood, but a worthwhile pilgrimage for the serious fan. Music starts Mon.-Fri. at 9:30pm., Sat. at 10pm, Sun. at 8pm. Closing time varies. Cover $3-5.

Wise Fools Pub, 2270 N. Lincoln St. (929-1510); take the el to Fullerton, go south on Lincoln. Intimate Lincoln Park setting for top blues artists. Mon. night's Big Band Jazz series is great fun, too. Bar open daily 4pm-2am. Music 9:30pm-1:30am. Cover $4-8.

Other

Butch McGuires, 20 W. Division St. (337-9080), at Rush St. Father of the singles bar. The owner estimates that "over 2400 couples have met here and gotten married" since 1961—he's a little fuzzier on divorce statistics. Drinks cost $1.75-4.25. Open Mon.-Thurs. 10:30am-2am, Fri. 10:30am-4am, Sat. 9:30am-5am, Sun. 9:30am-midnight.

Cabaret Metro, 3730 N. Clark (549-3604). Cutting-edge concerts ($4-20) and Wed. night "Rock Against Depression" extravaganzas ($4 for men, women free) entertain a hip, younger crowd. Open Sun.-Fri. 9:30pm-4am, Sat. 6:30pm-5am.

Christopher Street, 3458 N. Halsted (975-9244). Lots of guppies (gay urban professionals) swim in this attractive, upscale fishbowl with 3 bars, a huge dance floor, and aquarium wallpaper. Drinks $2-4. Open Sun.-Fri. 4pm-4am, Sat. 4pm-5am. Cover Fri. $2, Sat. $3 ($1 goes to AIDS research).

Danny's, 1951 W. Dickens Ave. (489-6457), Bucktown. Zebratone walls, Elvis memorabilia, and a jukebox with everything from the Ramones to Tammy Wynette. Favorite with artsy locals. Not in the greatest neighborhood, but great fun once you get there. Draft beer $1.50. Open daily 3pm-2am.

Jazz Showcase, 636 S. Michigan (427-4300), in the Blackstone Hotel. Number-one choice for serious jazz fans. During the jazz festival, big names heat up the elegant surroundings with impromptu jam sessions. Music Tues.-Sun. at 8:30pm and 10:30pm, Fri.-Sat. at 9pm and 11pm. Closing time and cover vary.

No Exit, 6970 N. Glenwood (743-3355), in Rogers Park. This North Side coffeehouse has live nightly jazz. While the musicians warm up, you can warm down by reading or playing chess. Sandwiches $3.24. Cover $3-5.

Sluggers World Class Sports Bar, Inc., 3540 N. Clark (248-0055), near Wrigley Field. Take the el to Addison. If TV monitors tuned to every sporting event imaginable don't turn you on, maybe the game room with ski ball, trampoline hoop, and the city's only indoor batting cage will. Drinks go up 50¢ during Cubs games, but on Wed. nights beer is only 25¢. Hours depend entirely on the current sports scene.

Tania's, 2659 N. Milwaukee Ave. (235-7120). Exotic dinner and dancing adventure with hot *salsa cumbia* and *merengue* bands. No jeans. Music Sun. 8pm-2am, Wed.-Thurs. 9:30pm-2am, Fri.-Sat. 10pm-3am. No cover, but a 2-drink minimum.

Wild Hare & Singing Armadillo Frog Sanctuary, 3350 N. Clark (327-0800). Take the el to Addison. Live rastafarian bands play nightly to a packed house. Open daily until 2-3am. Cover $3-5.

Springfield

Springfield poet Vachel Lindsay wrote, "in our little town a mourning figure walks, and will not rest." That figure is Abraham Lincoln, who settled in Springfield in 1837 to practice law. The capital of Illinois has the final word on Abe memorabilia. Rest assured, however, that despite a deluge of tourists, the city never stoops to kitsch. Springfield's version of "The Lincoln Story" is commendably tasteful.

Practical Information

Emergency: 911.

Visitor Information: Springfield Convention and Visitors Bureau, 109 N. 7th St. (789-2360 or 800-545-7300). Open Mon.-Fri. 8am-5pm. **Lincoln Home Visitors Center,** 426 S. 7th (789-2357). Open daily 8:30am-5pm. Both locations have useful brochures on restaurants, hotels, camping, events, recreation, and services for senior citizens and the disabled.

Amtrak: 3rd and Washington St. (753-3651 or 800-872-7245). Near downtown. To: Chicago (2-4 per day, 3½-4 hr., $31) and St. Louis (2-3 per day, 2½ hr., $19). Open daily 6am-9:30pm.

Greyhound: 110 N. 9th St. (544-8466), near downtown. To: Chicago ($25) and St. Louis ($12). Open 7:30am-10:30pm.

Springfield Mass Transit District, 928 S. 9th St. (522-5531). Pick up maps at headquarters or at the tourist office on Adams. All 12 lines serve the downtown area along 5th, 6th, or Monroe St., near the Old State Capitol Plaza. Fare 50¢, free transfers. Buses operate Mon.-Sat. 6am-6pm. **Access Illinois Transit Service (AITS)** buses for seniors and the disabled. Call 24 hours in advance to arrange trip (522-8594).

Post Office: 2105 E. Cook St. (788-7200), at the corner of Weir St. Open Mon.-Fri. 7:45am-6pm, Sat. 8am-noon. **ZIP code:** 62703.

Area Code: 217.

I-55 connects Springfield with Chicago (200 miles) and St. Louis (90 miles). I-72 passes through from the east, and U.S. 36 from the west. Numbered streets in Springfield run north-south, but only on the east side of the city. All other streets have names, with **Washington Street** dividing north-south addresses.

Accommodations and Camping

Most inexpensive places are located in the eastern and southern parts of the city, off I-55 and U.S. 36. Bus service to the outlying areas from downtown is limited. Downtown rooms are $10-30 more. Make sure you have reservations on holiday weekends and during the state fair in mid-August. Check with the visitors bureau about finding very reasonable weekend packages offered by slightly more upscale hotels. All accommodations listed here have color TV and air conditioning.

Best Inns of America, 500 N. 1st St. (522-1100). Clean, bright, comfortable rooms. Pool. Singles $33.88. Doubles $35.88-41.88. Continental breakfast included. Key deposit $1.

Best Rest Inn, 700 N. Dirksen Pkwy. (522-7961). Take the "Bergen Park-Grandview" bus to the 700 block of Milton, then go 3 blocks east. Shabby rooms. Singles $21. Doubles $32.

Motel 6, 3125 Wide Track Dr. (789-1063), has standard motel room fare and a pool. Singles $22. Doubles $28.

Super 8, 1330 S. Dirksen Pkwy. (528-8889) or 3675 S. 6th St. (529-8898). Clean, well-maintained. Singles $27.88. Doubles $35.88.

Travel Inn, 500 S. 9th St. (528-4341), downtown. Very tempting pool—a haven from land sharks. Clean, somewhat shabby rooms. Singles $28. Doubles $35. Weekly $100.

For camping, try **Lake Victoria Campground,** 3151 Stanton Rd. (529-8206), 4 miles southeast of downtown. Take bus #10 ("Laketown"). Tent sites $6, with electricity $14, each additional person $6.

Food

Horseshoe sandwiches are a Springfield culinary specialty. Looking more like ripe meadow muffins than horseshoes, these tasty concoctions consist of ham on prairie toast covered by a tangy cheese sauce and french fries. In and around the **Vinegar Hill Mall,** at 1st and Cook St., a number of moderately priced restaurants serve horseshoes, barbecued ribs, Mexican and Italian food, and seafood.

Saputo's, 801 E. Munroe (544-2523), at 8th St., 2 blocks from Lincoln's home. Family-owned and operated for 40 years. Red lighting, red table cloths, red chairs, and—of course—red tomato sauce. Tasty Southern Italian cuisine. Large baked lasagna $4.25. Open Mon.-Fri. 10:30am-1pm, Sat. 5pm-1am, Sun 5-10pm.

Norb-Andy's, 518 E. Capitol (523-7777), 2½ blocks east of the state capitol. Emphatically nautical theme. Oars, ships, and a backward-running clock all decorate this politicians' hangout. Horseshoes $4.75-6. All-American dinner entrees $7-19. Bar open 11am-11pm. Open Mon.-Sat. 11am-10pm.

Feedstore, 528 E. Adams St. (528-3355), across from the Old State Capitol. Nothing fancy inside, just good food. Sandwiches $2.60-3.60. No-choice special $4.25. Open 11am-3pm.

Sights

The Lincoln Home Visitors Center shows an 18-minute film on "Mr. Lincoln's Springfield." The **Lincoln Home** (492-4150), the only one Abe ever owned, is at 8th and Jackson, in a restored 19th-century neighborhood. (Open daily 8:30am-5pm; hours may be reduced in winter due to bad weather. 10-min. tours every 5-10 min. from the front of the home. Free, but you must pick up passes at the Lincoln Home Visitors Center.) A few blocks northwest, at 6th and Adams, you'll find the **Lincoln-Herndon Law Offices** (782-4836), where Honest Abe practiced before ascending the political ranks. (Open for tours only daily 9am-5pm; last tour at 4:15.

Free.) Around the corner to your left is the **Old State Capitol** (782-7691), across fom the Downtown Mall, a weathered limestone edifice with a majesty that rivals its Greek models. Here, Lincoln delivered his stirring and prophetic "House Divided" speech in 1858, warning that the nation's half pro-slavery and half abolitionist government could be a volatile source of disunion. Lincoln's Gettysburg Address is on display. (Open daily 9am-5pm. Guided tours throughout the day. Free.)

Springfield has more to offer than Lincolnalia. Don't miss the **Dana-Thomas House,** 301 E. Lawrence Ave. (782-6776), 6 blocks south of the Old State Capitol. This stunning and well-preserved 1902 home is one of Frank Lloyd Wright's early experiments in design and a wonderful example of the Prairie School style. Furniture and fixtures are Wright orginals as well. (Open Thurs.-Mon. 9am-4pm. One-hr. tours every ½ hr. Free.)

Indiana

The difference between the popular explanations for Indiana's nickname of "Hoosier" symbolizes the competition between the state's rural and industrial traditions. One explanation holds that the name is a corruption of the pioneer's call to visitors at the door, "who's there?"; the other claims that its use spread from Louisville where the labor contractor Samuel Hoosier employed Indiana workers who later became known as Hoosiers. Today, more than a half century later, visitors still find two Indianas: the heavily industrialized northern cities and the slower-paced southern counties.

In this competition between the rural and the urban Indiana, the latter wins out unfairly. Too many people think only of Gary's smokestacks and the Indianapolis 500 when Indiana comes to mind. Visit the athletic, urban mecca of Indianapolis, but don't miss the rolling green hills and rural beauty downstate. The state that produced TV celebrities David Letterman and Jane Pauley also features beautiful scenery, especially during the fall when the foliage around Columbus and other rural areas puts on a spectacular show.

Practical Information

Capital: Indianapolis.

Tourist Information: Indiana Division of Tourism, 1 N. Capitol, #700, Indianapolis 46204 (232-8860; 800-289-6646 in-state). **Division of State Parks,** 616 State Office Bldg., Indianapolis 46204 (232-4124).

Time Zones: Eastern and Central (1 hr. behind Eastern). **Postal Abbreviation:** IN.

Indianapolis

Legend has it that when David Letterman was a weathercaster in Indianapolis, he was run out of town for warning of hail "the size of canned hams." The city has, perhaps, become hipper since then; certainly it has become slicker. A revitalization of the downtown area (spurred by hosting the 1987 Pan Am Games) has made Indianapolis cosmopolitan and eminently likable. The city is now banking on its new, world-class sports facilities to boosts its number of cultural and recreational activities. "Naptown" is awakening.

Practical Information

Emergency: 911 or 632-7575.

Visitor Information: Indianapolis City Center, 201 S. Capital St. (237-5200), in the Pan Am Plaza, across from the Hoosierdome. Open Mon.-Fri. 10am-5:30pm, Sat. 10am-4pm. **Fun Fone,** 237-5210. 24-hour recording listing of the week's events sports, theater, and other areas.

Indianapolis International Airport: 7 miles southwest of downtown near I-465. To get to the city center, take bus #9 ("West Washington").

Amtrak: 350 S. Illinois (263 0550 or 800-872-7245), behind Union Station. Somewhat deserted, but the area is relatively safe. Trains to Chicago ($38) only. Open Mon.-Fri. 7am-3pm, Sat. 5:15-9:15am and 8:30-11:45pm, Sun. 7-11am and 8:30-10pm.

Greyhound: 127 N. Capital Ave. (635-4501), downtown at E. Ohio St., 1 block from Monument Circle. Fairly safe area. To Chicago ($25.25), Columbus, ($24), and Louisville ($25.25). Open 24 hours. **United Limo** operates out of the same station at Door 2 and serves cities within the state.

Metro Bus: 14 E. Washington St. (632-1900 or 635-3344), 1 block from Monument Circle. Open Mon.-Fri. 7:30am-5:30pm. Fare 75¢, rush hour $1. Transfers 25¢.

Taxi: Yellow Cab, 637-5421.

Car Rental: Rent-a-Bent, 2233 E. Washington St. (632-4429), 2½ miles east of downtown. Daily rates from $11 plus 10¢ per mile; weekly $99 with unlimited mileage. Car must not leave the state. Open Mon.-Fri. 9am-6pm, Sat. 9am-5pm. $150 deposit required.

Weather/Time Line: 222-2222.

Time Zone: Eastern. **Post Office:** 125 W. South St. (464-6000), across the street from Amtrak. Open Mon.-Wed. and Fri. 7am-5:30pm, Thurs. 7am-6pm. **ZIP code:** 46206.

Area Code: 317.

Indianapolis lies about 183 miles south of Chicago, and 113 miles north of Louisville. **I-465** rings the city and provides access to all points downtown. The center of Indianapolis is located just south of **Monument Circle** at the intersection of **Washington Street** (U.S. 40) and **Meridian Street.** Washington is the north-south dividing line; Meridian is the east-west dividing line.

Accommodations and Camping

Indianapolis offers plenty of budget motels. Most, however, are about 5 miles from downtown, off I-465, and there is very limited bus service to these areas. If you come in May for the Indy 500, motels are more expensive, especially on weekends; you must make reservations a year in advance.

Ace Motel, 7201 E. Washington St. (356-7227), between Shadeland Ave. and I-465. Take bus #8 from downtown. Stained carpets and musty smell. Singles $20. Doubles $28.

Inn Towner Motor Inn, 401 E. Washington St. (637-6464), opposite the arena downtown. Dark elevator and hallways, but rooms are comfortable and clean. Singles $36. Doubles $45.

Dollar Inn, 4630 Lafayette Ave. (293-9060), at I-65. Convenient to the Speedway and Eagle Creek Park. Small, clean rooms. Singles $22. Doubles $27.

Tower Inn, 1633 N. Capitol Ave. (925-9831), across from the Methodist Hospital. Very clean and well-maintained. Singles $38, with student ID $30. Doubles $48.

Kamper Korner, 1951 W. Edgewood Ave. (788-1488), 1 mile south of I-465 on Rte. 37. No bus service. Open area with no shade. Laundry, grocery, showers, free fishing, and swimming. 11pm-7am quiet hours enforced. Tents $14, $15 for water and hookup. Limited services Nov. to mid-March.

Food and Entertainment

Indianapolis greets visitors with a variety of restaurants that range from ethnic holes-in-the-wall to trendy locales decked out in vintage American kitsch.

Tourists and residents alike head for **Union Station,** 39 Jackson Place (266-8740), 4 blocks south of Monument Circle, a 13-acre maze of restaurants, shops, dance clubs, bars, and hotels. Nearly every edible substance imaginable is sold in this beautifully and authentically refurbished rail depot. The second level is an oval of moderately priced ethnic eateries. (Entrees average $2.50-5. Open Mon.-Thurs. 10am-9pm, Fri.-Sat. 10am-10pm, Sun. 11am-6pm.)

Acapulco Joe's, 365 N. Illinois Ave. (637-5160), downtown. The hot, spicy food will sear your tastebuds. For the gringo, they offer peanut butter and jelly sandwiches. 3 tacos $4. Open Mon.-Thurs. 7am-9pm, Fri.-Sat. 7am-10pm.

Athaneum Turner's Rathskeller, 401 E. Michigan St. (849-3972), downtown. Located in the basement of Indianapolis's historic "German House." Huge outfit high on character, low on price. *Wiener schnitzel* with vegetables $4.50, "Farmer Plate" of sausages, cheese, and soup $5. Open for lunch daily 11am-1:30pm, for dinner Wed. and Fri. 5:30-8:30pm.

Laria's, 317 S. College Ave. (638-7706), about 10 blocks from downtown. A 50s throwback, with shiny vinyl furniture and chrome chairs. Award-winning food. Spaghetti and meatball dinner $9. Open Mon.-Thurs. 11am-9:30pm, Fri. 11am-11pm, Sat. 3-11pm.

Nightlife makes waves 6 miles north of the downtown area at **Broad Ripple,** at College Ave. and 62nd St., typically swamped with students and yuppies. The area has charming ethnic restaurants and art studios in original frame houses, as well as some artsy bars. **The Patio Lounge,** 6308 Guilford Ave. (253-0799), sponsors underground bands for $1-3 cover. (Open Mon.-Fri. 5pm-3am, Sat. 8pm-3am. Take bus #17 "College-Broad Ripple" north from central downtown.)

The City Market, 222 E. Market St. (634-9266), 2 blocks east of Monument Circle in a renovated 19th-century building, has produce stands and 15 ethnic markets. Prices are reasonable but not rock-bottom. (Open Mon.-Sat. 6am-6pm.)

Sights

Often obscured by the hubbub surrounding the Indy 500, Indianapolis's cultural attractions promise a pleasant afternoon. "Please touch" is the motto of the **Children's Museum,** 3000 N. Meridian St. (293-6923). Kids help run hands-on exhibits, which include a turn-of-the-century carousel, a huge train collection, petting zoos, and high-tech electronic wizardry. (Open Tues.-Sat. 10am-5pm, Sun. noon-5pm. Free.) The **Indianapolis Museum of Art,** 1200 W. 38th (923-1331), houses a large collection of Turner paintings and watercolors as well as Robert Indiana's LOVE sculpture. The museum sits in a beautifully landscaped 154-acre park with gardens and nature trails. (Open Tues.-Sun. 11am-5pm. Free, except for special exhibits.) The **Eiteljorg Museum,** 334 N. Senate Ave. (636-9378), west of downtown, features Native American and Western art. (Open Tues.-Sat. 10am-5pm, Sun. noon-5pm. Admission $2, seniors $1.50, under 12 $1.) Stunning African and Egyptian decor graces the **Walker Theatre,** 617 Indiana Ave. (635-6915). Erected in 1927, the theatre is a symbol of the Indianapolis black community's spirit and has hosted such jazz greats as Louis Armstrong and Dinah Washington. The Walker complex sponsors plays, dance performances, and a week-long black film festival in late October. Even if you can't make one of the shows, go just to see the splendid interior. Upstairs in the ballroom, the **Jazz on the Avenue** series offers live music every Friday night.

The Indianapolis 500

When in Indianapolis, do as the natives do and visit the **Indianapolis Motor Speedway,** 4790 W. 16th St. (241-2500). Take Speedway exit off I-465 or bus #25 ("West 16th."). A shrine dedicated to the automobile, this 1909 behemoth encloses an entire 18-hole golf course. Except in May, you can take a bus ride around the 2½ mile track for $1. Adjacent is the **Speedway Museum** (Indy Hall of Fame), which houses a collection of Indy race cars and antique autos, as well as racing memorabilia and videotapes highlighting historic Indy moments. (Open 9am-5pm. Admission $1, under 16 free.)

America's passion for the automobile reaches a frenzy during the **500 Festival** when 33 aerodynamic, turbocharged, 2½-mile-to-the-gallon race cars circle the asphalt track at speeds over 225 mph. Beginning with the time trials for two weekends in mid-May preceding the race, the party culminates with the big blowout on the

Sunday of Memorial Day weekend (weather permitting). Book hotel reservations early and buy tickets in advance. For ticket information, call 248-6700; open daily 9am-5pm.

Bloomington

Bloomington is most famous for the "Hoosier Hysteria," a condition characterized by reverence for Bobby Knight and his basketball team. **Indiana University,** the proud home of this deeply loved team, is also the site of the town's only other attractions.

Although the I.U. campus is vast, it is best explored on foot. Expect a blister or two. The university has a superb rare book collection at the **Lilly Library,** E. 7th St. (855-2452; open Mon.-Thurs. 8am-8pm, Fri. 8am-5pm, Sat. 9am-5pm, Sun. 1-5pm. Free). Across the street, the **University Art Museum** (855-4826), a triangular structure designed by I.M. Pei, houses exhibits of ancient Mediterranean, Asian, and African art. (Open Tues.-Sat. 9am-5pm, Sun. 1-5pm. Free.) Indiana University also has a superb music department; visit the **Musical Arts Center** (885-9053), on Jordan Ave. During term-time, there are terrific opera performances, symphony concerts, musicals, and free popular concerts Wednesdays. (Tickets $8-12, students $3-6.) If you crave food or information, visit the huge **Indiana Memorial Union** (856-6381), on 7th St., which has a deli (open 9:30am-4pm) on the mezzanine floor and a campus information booth on the first floor.

The Hoosier basketball team is ever popular, and tickets are hard to come by unless you know a friendly student. Other sporting events include the **Little 500** bike race held in the university stadium on the third Saturday in April. The movie *Breaking Away* portrayed this event as a town-gown duel; in reality it's just an opportunity for students and alumni to party it up.

As in many large university towns, the campus blends in with the town streets. The shops and restaurants in Bloomington are concentrated in the block bordered by **4th** and **7th Street** running east-west, and **College** and **Walnut Street** traveling south and north, respectively. **Kirkwood Avenue** is lined with student hangouts. **Nick's English Hut,** 423 E. Kirkwood Ave. (332-4040), serving burgers ($2.50-3.35), and beer (pound jars 90¢, pitchers $4) combines the atmosphere of a traditional tavern with the energy of a college hot-spot. (Open Mon.-Sat. 11am-2am, Sun. noon-midnight.) For delicious Greek fare, a safe bet is the **Trojan Horse,** 100 E. Kirkwood (332-1101), for a gyros sandwich ($2.85). (Open Mon.-Thurs. 11am-11pm, Fri.-Sat. 11am-midnight, Sun. 3-9pm.) Slightly removed from the college scene, **The Snow Lion,** 113 S. Grant St. (336-0835), serves Tibetan food in quiet and elegant surroundings. Seafood entrees $7-10. (Open daily 5-10pm.)

If you intend to stay overnight, try to avoid home game weekends, "Little 500" day in April, and graduation week, when rates are higher and hotels are booked solid. If garish floral patterns and a seedy neighborhood don't bother you, the **Downtown Motel,** 509 N. College Ave. (336-6881), right around the corner from the Greyhound station, has clean rooms. (Singles and doubles $22.63. $1 key deposit.) The **Stony Crest Motel,** farther north at 1300 N. Walnut St. (332-9491), at 17th St., has clean rooms and a swimming pool. (Singles $24. Doubles $29.) Campers should try the **Harding Ridge Federal Campground** (837-9453), 7 miles south on Rte. 446, on the shore of Lake Monroe. (Primitive sites $7, $9 with hookup.) Also on the lake is the **Paynetown-Monroe Reservoir** (837-9490), 4 miles south on Rte. 446 (primitive sites $3, $8 with hookup).

The **Bloomington/Monroe County Visitors Bureau,** 2855 N. Walnut St. (334-8900 or 800-678-9828), off Rte. 37, has information on sights, restaurants, and lodging in and around Bloomington and Monroe County. The **Greyhound** station, 535 N. Walnut St. (332-1522), at the corner of 10th St., is about 8 blocks away from campus, and serves Indianapolis ($9.50). (Open Mon.-Fri. 4:30am-5:30pm, Sat. 4:30am-4pm, Sun. bus times only.)

The **ZIP code** for Bloomington is 47401; the **area code** is 812.

Columbus

After World War II, the Cummins Engine Company decided that Columbus's educational facilities were behind the times. The company set up a fund to pay architect fees for school buildings, stipulating that the architect must be of world stature. Since then, churches, fire stations, and everything in between have sprung up under this innovative program. Today, Columbus is home to 50 public and private buildings that make up the most concentrated collection of contemporary architecture in the world.

The first stop on your tour should be the helpful **visitors center,** 506 5th St. (372-1954), at Franklin. Check out the extension of the Indianapolis Museum of Art on the second floor. (Visitors center open March-Nov. Mon.-Sat. 9am-5pm, Sun. 10am-2pm; Nov.-March Mon.-Sat. 9am-5pm.)

A walking tour of downtown takes about 1½ hours. A block away from the visitors center, the **Cleo Rogers Library** by I.M. Pei, complete with Henry Moore sculpture, and the **First Christian Church** by Eliel Saarinen (designer of the St. Louis Gateway Arch), are set off by the well-preserved Victorian homes that make up the rest of downtown. Of the other specially commissioned buildings, must-sees are Eero Saarinen's stunning **North Christian Church,** whose futuristic exterior has been copied all over the world; Harry Weese's **Otter Creek Clubhouse,** which sits atop what some consider the nation's finest golf course; and the ultramodern **Commons,** designed by César Pelli, a shopping mall that houses a performance center, art gallery, and an indoor playground.

The Commons contains a couple of casual eateries, but it's a better idea to head across the street to **Zaharako's** (known locally as **The Greeks**), 329 Washington St. (379-9329). Established in 1900, the restaurant features onyx soda fountains, a 50-foot mahogany bar, Tiffany lamps, and marble counters. Come for ice cream, candy, or hearty sandwiches ($1.10-2.20). The **Imperial 400 Motor Inn,** 101 W. 3rd St. (372-2835), offers reasonable, comfortable rooms, a heated pool, and a convenient location. (Singles $30-36. Doubles $30-40.) **KOA** (342-6229) is 6 miles south on I-65 at Ogleville. (Sites with hookup and water $15, each additional person $3. Primitive sites $12.) **Greyhound** is at 204 E. 8th St. (376-3821) and sends four buses daily to Indianapolis ($10.25). (Open Mon.-Fri 9am-5:45pm, Sat. 8:45am-12:45pm.)

The **ZIP code** for Columbus is 47401; the **area code** is 812.

Michigan

Gerald Ford, Malcolm X, and Madonna: not the most likely trio. But all three grew up in Michigan, and it's no suprise they come from the state that offers more variety than any other in the Midwest. A nationwide magnet for liberals and intellectuals, Michigan's natural beauty also stands out, from the rugged, unpeopled forests on the Upper Peninsula to beautiful lakeside resorts on the magnificent fresh water shoreline. The state is still recovering from a slump that struck the auto industry in the early 80s, but manufacturing giants have rebounded and still supply the nation with three-quarters of its cars. Meanwhile, Detroit is in the midst of an ambitious and promising facelift. From Hemingway's "Big Two-Hearted River" to the Motor City, Michigan shifts into any gear with ease.

Practical Information

Capital: Lansing.

Tourist Information: Michigan Travel Bureau, 333 S. Capitol Ave., Lansing 48933 (800-543-2937). **Department of Natural Resources,** Information Services Center, Steven T. Mason Bldg., P.O. Box 30028, Lansing 48909 (373-1220). Detailed information on state parks, forests, campsites, and other public facilities.

Time Zones: Central (1 hr. behind Eastern) and Eastern. **Postal Abbreviation:** MI.

Detroit

Detroit is urban America in microcosm—industrial might and blight. The black towers of Renaissance Center, beside the emerald-hued Detroit River, illustrate the successful redevelopment of the river area. The neighborhood has new hotels, shopping centers, and office buildings and resembles other rehabilitated urban centers. Much of downtown, however, remains a dismal zone of chronic unemployment and crime. In poor neighborhoods, children play barefoot while bulletproof glass, attack dogs, and barred windows protect shops and homes. More depressing are the deserted neighborhoods, wastelands of gutted buildings and glass-strewn streets.

Detroit's condition, however, is not terminal. Still the car capital of the world, Motor City's hopes rise with the renewed vigor of the American automotive industry. The same working class energy and diversity that once made Detroit famous as home of the Motown sound flourishes today in the ethnic festivals held every summer weekend. There is much to see and do in Detroit, but perhaps most fascinating is the city itself. It is a living, breathing industrial giant, which, while crippled by unemployment and violence, nevertheless lumbers on.

Practical Information

Emergency: 911.

Visitor Information: Detroit Convention and Visitors Bureau, on Hart Plaza at 2 E. Jefferson St. (567-1170). From Greyhound terminal, turn right at Randolph St., then right onto Jefferson. Pick up the free *Detroit Visitors Guide.* Open daily 9am-5pm. Also at 100 Renaissance Center, #1950 (259-4333). **What's Line,** 298-6262, is a recorded listing of entertainment events. **Ticketmaster,** 645-6666.

Travelers Aid: 211 W. Congress, 3rd floor (962-6740).

Detroit Metropolitan Airport: 942-3550. 21 miles west of downtown off I-94. **Commuter Transportation Company** and **Kirby Tours** (963-8585; 800-521-0711 outside MI; 800-345-6237 in MI) have shuttles to downtown $10. Taxi fare downtown is a steep $25-27.

Amtrak: 2601 Rose St. (964-5335 or 800-872-7245), on 17th St., 1½ blocks south of Michigan Ave. To: Chicago ($24) and Cleveland ($33). Open daily 6:30am-midnight.

Greyhound: 130 E. Congress at Randolph St. (961-8502), downtown. For connections to city buses, walk ½ block west on Congress St. to Woodward Ave., then north to Cadillac Sq. To: Chicago ($47), Toronto ($36.20), and New York ($95.50). Open 24 hours; ticket office open 5:45am-1:15am.

Public Transit: Detroit Department of Transportation (DOT), Cadillac Sq. Dept. of Transportation, 1301 E. Warren (833-7692). Carefully policed public transport system. Serves the downtown area, with limited service to the suburbs. Most buses operate until 1am. Fare $1, transfers 10¢. **People Mover,** Detroit Transportation Corporation, 150 Michigan Ave (224-2160). Ultramodern facility circles the Central Business District with 13 stops. Fare 50¢. **Southeastern Michigan Area Regional Transit (SMART),** 962-5515. Bus service to the suburbs. Fare $1-2.50, transfers 10¢.

Taxi: Unity Cab, 834-3300. 24 hours.

Car Rental: Call-a-Car, 877 E. Eight Mile Rd. (541-2700), in Hazel Park at I-75. Car must not leave MI. From $10 per day; 100 free miles, 14¢ each additional mile. Must be 21 with credit card and insurance.

Help Lines: Crisis Hotline, 224-7000. **Gay and Lesbian Community Information Center,** 940 W. McNichols (345-2722).

Time Zone: Eastern.

Post Office: 1401 W. Fort (226-8440), at 8th St. Open Mon.-Fri. 8:30am-5pm, Sat. 8am-noon. **ZIP Code:** 48200.

Area Code: 313.

Detroit faces Windsor, Ontario, across the Detroit River. Detroit is 275 miles east of Chicago, above Lake Erie on the banks of the Detroit River. The suburban area is huge and sprawling. Years of mass exodus from downtown have created a ring of affluent suburbs and ethnic neighborhoods.

One-way streets and punctual parking meter personnel carefully monitor the Motor City's well-maintained and surprisingly uncrowded road system. Detroit's streets form a grid, with the major east-west arteries, known as the "Mile Roads," marked out in 1-mile segments north of downtown. I-94 heads east from the airport as the **Detroit Industrial Parkway** to downtown, where it becomes the **Ford Freeway.** South of downtown, I-75 is known as the **Fisher Freeway;** north of downtown, it turns into the **Chrysler Freeway.** I-96 is called **Jeffries Freeway,** and Route 10 is the **Lodge Highway.**

If you plan to stay for more than a few days, get a copy of *Monthly Detroit* ($1.50) at area newsstands. It gives a detailed listing of events, nightspots, restaurants, theater, dance, tours, and sports.

Accommodations and Camping

Although weekend specials are available at many downtown hotels, few other options are both cheap *and* safe. If you opt for cheap, be sure to arrive in daylight and be willing to forgo nightlife. The area around the Amtrak station is unsafe. The Greyhound station, near the gentrified riverfront, attracts a varied crowd—don't leave alone on foot after dark. It's best to take a bus or cab to reach other parts of the city.

Teahouse of the Golden Dragon Home Hostel, 8585 Harding Ave. (756-2676), in Centerline, north of 10 Mile Rd. off Kyle. Take SMART bus #510 or 515. Rooms double as personal space for housemother. Chorus of clocks chime through the night. $5.

Country Grandma's Home Hostel (AYH), 22330 Bell Rd. (753-4901), in New Boston, midway between Detroit and Ann Arbor. Close to Metro Parks. $7, nonmembers $10 (includes temporary membership); additional nights $8.

Motor City Home Hostel (AYH), 16901 Burgess (533-9597). On Grand River bus line, 12 miles from downtown. Large brick home run by an avid bicyclist. 2 beds. $6, reservations required.

Americana Motel, 1999 E. Jefferson Ave. (567-8888). Close to safe Renaissance Center area. Clean but dark rooms. Singles $30. Doubles $40. Key deposit $5. Look for Sun.-Thurs. summer specials at $23.80.

Red Roof Inn, 2350 Rochester Rd. (689-4391), in Troy, ½ hr. from downtown. Exit 67 off I-75. Singles $34. Doubles $36.

Roadway Inn, 8230 Merriman Rd. (729-7600), just outside the Detroit Metro airport. Accessible only by car; take I-94 to Merriman Rd. Free shuttle service to and from airport. Singles $32. Doubles $38.

Mercy College of Detroit, 8200 W. Outer Dr. (592-6170), 11 miles from downtown off the Lodge Freeway (Rte. 10). Campus secure, but surrounding area shaky. Sinks in rooms, shared bath. Kitchen and laundry facilities. Singles $15, students $12. Doubles $26, students $20.

University of Windsor, Vanier Hall, Wyandotte St. W. and Huron Church Rd. (519-973-7074), in Windsor, Canada, near the USA Bridge. Take the Tunnel Bus, then bus #1C. Less convenient, but much safer and more pleasant than comparable accommodations. Clean, spacious rooms with A/C. Singles CDN$22. Doubles CDN$36. Student rate CDN$13.50. Will accept the face value in American money. Open May-Aug.

You'll have to trek some distance if you want to camp. A dozen state parks with campgrounds lie about 40 miles out, off I-75, 96, and 94. **Sterling State Park** (289-2715) is 37 miles south of Detroit, ½ mile off of I-75, just north of the city of Monroe. (Open 24 hours. Sites $8, including electricity.) The **Detroit-Greenfield KOA,** 6680 Bunton Rd., Ypsilanti (482-7722), is about 30 miles from downtown Detroit and 3 miles east of Ypsilanti. From I-94 (exit 187), go 1 mile south onto Rawsonville

Rd., turn right onto Textile Rd., then go 1 mile and turn left onto Bunton—the campground is ½ mile farther. (216 sites. $17 for 2, with water and hookup $20. Each additional person $3, ages 4-17 $2. Open March 30-Nov. 18.) The **Windsor South Resort Kampground** (519-726-5200) offers comparable rates and facilities, with discounts for U.S. dollars. Take the tunnel or bridge to Hwy. 3, then go south on Howard Ave. to Texas Rd.

Food and Nightlife

Ethnic food is the best budget option in Detroit. From late April to mid-September, Hart Plaza is the scene of a series of weekend ethnic festivals: Afro-American, Arabic, German, Irish, Mexican, Ukrainian, and others. The *Do it in Detroit* brochure, available at the visitors bureau, lists ethnic festivals held at Hart Plaza (224-1184). To savor the essence of **Greektown,** munch on *baklava* as you stroll down Monroe Ave., about 4 blocks northeast of the Ren Cen. **Trappers Alley,** 508 Monroe St. (963-5445), houses 90 food and retail shops. (Open Mon.-Thurs. 10am-9pm, Fri.-Sat. 10am-11pm, Sun. noon-7pm.) **Eastern Market** (833-1560), at Gratiot and Russell Ave., just north of Fisher Freeway, is an outdoor meat and produce market. Another popular area for eating, drinking, and listening to music is the **Rivertown** area in the renovated **Warehouse District,** 1 mile east of the Ren Cen off E. Jefferson Ave. **Mexican Town,** a lively neighborhood south of Tiger Stadium, is just being discovered.

Niki's Taverna, 735 Beaubien St. (961-4303), just south of Monroe St., close to the Ren Cen, in Greektown. White-collar lunch crowd. Gyros with fries $4.45. Open daily 10am-4am.

Jacoby's, 624 Brush St. (962-7067), near Greyhound station, 2 blocks north of Ren Cen. 85 years of beer and *sauerbraten* have earned this old German restaurant landmark status. Great drinks, fantastic fresh perch, and small but delicious sandwiches all under $5. Jazz Fri. nights. Open Mon.-Tues. 11am-10pm, Wed.-Thurs. 11am-11pm, Fri.-Sat. 11am-midnight, Sun. noon-3pm.

Alvin's Finer Delicatessen and Detroit Bar, 5756 Cass (832-2355), across the street from Wayne State University. Deli Sandwiches $2.25-3.45. Open Mon.-Fri. 11am-6pm, Sat.-Sun. 9am-2am. Bar open until 2am every night. Live Music Thurs.-Mon. in the back room ranges from acoustic to dance to jazz. Cover $2-4.

Woodbridge Tavern, 289 St. Aubin St. (259-0578), at Woodbridge, in Rivertown. Comfortable old-style bar, restored to its 20s character, complete with a honky-tonk piano and an outdoor terrace known as Marcia's Vineyard. Sandwiches and burgers $3.50-5. Open Mon.-Sat. 11am-2am, Sun. noon-10pm. Live classic rock 'n' roll Thurs.-Sun. Cover Mon.-Sat. $1-2.

Soup Kitchen Saloon, 1585 Franklin (259-1374), at Orleans, in Rivertown. Try a taste of Nantucket for dinner (cornmeal-fried oysters, $9). Open Mon.-Thurs. 11am-1am, Fri. 11am-2:30am, Sat. 4pm-2am, Sun. 4pm-1am. Top blues and jazz performers Wed.-Sun. at 9pm. Cover varies, but usually $2-6.

Xochimilco Restaurant, 3409 Bagley (843-0179), in Mexican Town. People come from all over Michigan to enjoy the *botanes* (chips smothered with refried beans), Mexican sausages, and other goodies ($4.75-6.75). Huge servings. Open daily 11am-4am. Extremely popular, so plan to wait 20-30 min.

St. Andrew's Hall, 431 E. Congress (961-6358), 2 blocks in front of the Ren Cen. Remodeled church offers no salvation, but instead cutting-edge entertainment on several dance floors and stages. DJs, unknown bands, and big name acts. Cover $3-10.

Sights

The sparkling waterfront district is quite small and takes no more than a day to explore. The **Civic Center** and **Renaissance Center (Ren Cen)** between E. Jefferson St. and the waterfront, display striking modern architecture. Tours of the Ren Cen are given regularly. (For general Ren Cen information call 446-7800; tour information 591-3611; 9am-5pm.)

The civic center includes the **Philip A. Hart Plaza** (224-1185), a 10-acre "people place" that accommodates ethnic festivals on summer weekends (afternoons and evenings), free concerts in summer, and ice skating in the winter. Look for the computerized fountain and spiraling pylon of the **Dodge Fountain,** known as the "flying donut," designed by Noguchi. Across the street is the striking **Joe Louis Monument,** a huge black arm and fist suspended on cables and designed by Robert Graham. The civic center also includes the new **Joe Louis Arena** and Cobo Hall (567-6000) one of the nation's largest convention centers, and **Arena,** where rock bands blast at night.

Just north of downtown, the magnificent **Fox Theatre,** 2211 Woodward Ave. (567-6000), has been painstakingly renovated. Now, as in 1929, it is a gilt picture palace of impressive dimensions and gaudy decorations. **The Detroit Institute of Arts (DIA),** 5200 Woodward Ave. (833-7900), 2½ miles north of downtown, has one of the nation's most comprehensive fine arts collections. Diego Rivera's spectacular 1932 *Detroit Industry* frescoes alone merit a visit. (Open Tues.-Sun. 9:30am-5:30pm. Donation.) The institute sits in Detroit's **Cultural Center,** a 40-block cluster of public and private cultural institutions bordered by Wayne State University (take bus #53). A quick walk from the DIA takes you into the "Streets of Old Detroit" at the **Detroit Historical Museum,** 5401 Woodland (833-1805; Open Wed.-Sun. 9:30am-5pm. Donation). Right next door, you can conduct experiments at the **Detroit Science Center,** 5020 John R. St. (577-8400; open Tues.-Fri. 9am-4pm, Sat. 10am-7pm, Sun. noon-7pm. Admission $4, seniors and ages 6-12 $3, ages 4-5 $1.) Explore the technical and social ramifications of the Underground Railroad at the **Museum of African American History,** 301 Frederick Douglass (833-9800; open Wed.-Sat. 9:30-5pm, Sun. 1-5pm. Donation.). Barry Gordy's Motown Record Company has moved to Los Angeles, but the humble **Motown Records Museum,** 2648 W. Grand Blvd. (875-2264), preserves the memories. Downstairs, see the primitive studio which recorded the tunes that shot the Jackson Five, Marvin Gaye, Smokey Robinson, and Diana Ross to fame. (Open Mon.-Sat. 10am-5pm, Sun. 2-5pm. Admission $3, under 12 $2. The museum lies east of Rosa Parks Blvd., about 1 mile west of the John C. Lodge Freeway. By bus, take the "Dexter Avenue" right to the museum from downtown.)

The colossal **Henry Ford Museum,** 20900 Oakwood Blvd., and **Greenfield Village,** Michigan Ave., Dearborn (271-1620 or 271-1976; 24 hours), off I-94, definitely warrant a foray into the suburbs. The 12-acre museum has more than the expected parade of antique cars. It also displays more sensational items, such as the chair Lincoln sat in and the car Kennedy rode in when they were shot. Greenfield Village is a collection of 80 transplanted historic buildings, including a turn-of-the-century amusement park, the Wright brothers' bicycle shop, the courtroom where Lincoln practiced law, Puritan homes, and various shops, houses, taverns, and a mill, all set in a beautiful 240-acre park. (Open daily 9am-5pm. Admission to museum and village $9.50 each, seniors $8.50, ages 5-12 $4.75. 2-day combination tickets $16, children $8. Take SMART bus #200 and 250.)

If you're looking for a safe, quiet refuge away from the city bustle, head to **Belle Isle Park** (267-7115), a 985-acre island in the Detroit River. (Open daily 10am-5pm. Free.) Pick up DOT Jefferson bus #25 (eastbound) at the corner of Jefferson and Randolf (in front of the Ren Cen) to MacArthur Bridge, then transfer to Belle Isle bus #4. Designed by Frederick Law Olmsted, Belle Isle has a variety of recreational facilities and fishing spots, as well as a conservatory, an aquarium, and a small zoo. Ask the driver for a brochure detailing a walking and bus tour of the island.

Events

America's Motor City turns into the Monte Carlo of the Midwest for one great week a year. The **Detroit Grand Prix** (259-5400), the only Formula One World Championship race in the U.S., takes place the third week in June. The time trials are held the Friday before the race from 10am to 6pm. The course follows the city streets by the Ren Cen. (Tickets about $10 for Sat., $25 for Sun. 3-day reserved grandstand seat $95-120.)

Jazz fans should visit Detroit during Labor Day weekend for the **Montreux-Detroit Kool Jazz Festival** (259-5400), the U.S. half of the Swiss Montreux International Jazz Festival. Most concerts are free, except for headliners such as Dizzy Gillespie.

Ann Arbor

Dominated by the University of Michigan, Ann Arbor is among the most progressive, cultured, and lively university towns in America. It combines a relaxed small town atmosphere with world-class art, music, theater, dance, and film. Smoking grass brings only a $5 fine, an anomaly anywhere in the U.S., but especially in the conservative Midwest.

Ann Arbor is basically a laid back college town, but when the students leave, locals indulge in a little celebrating. Besides the world-famous **Summer Art Fair** in late July, which packs hundreds of thousands into the city and clogs the streets, the **Ethnic Fair** in early September celebrates food, culture, and crafts from around the world. The **German Festival,** on the last Saturdays of June, July, and August, highlights the German heritage that is common to most of the upper Midwest. The summer begins, however, with the **Ya'soo Festival** on the first weekend in June, where participants dance in the streets and enjoy Greek festivities. The visitors bureau, U of M information, and kiosks will give you more ideas.

For inanimate culture, the university features some top-notch free museums. Art buffs should head for the **University of Michigan Art Museum (UMAM),** at the corner of State and University, in the Diag. The museum houses a choice but quickly perused collection of works from around the world. Paths for biking, jogging, or just walking crisscross town and lead through the **Nichols Arboretum** and **Gallup Park** (662-9319), next to the **Huron River** on the city's northeastern edge. A string of small, artificial islands connected by arched bridges forms ponds for water sports and fishing. (Parks open daily 6am-10pm.) In summer, you can rent bikes and canoes at the park. (662-6319. Bike rentals $4 for 2 hr. Canoes $6 for 2 hr., Sat. and Sun, $7 extra. Open Mon.-Fri. 11am-9pm, Sat.-Sun. 9am-9pm. Must have a $10 cash deposit and drivers license.) On warm afternoons, the **Mathaei Botanical Gardens** becomes a favorite haunt of students. Call the Ann Arbor Recreation Department (994-2326) or the Park and Recreation Department (994-2780) for information.

During the academic year you can get cheap food at the **U of M Cafeteria,** West Quad, 541 Thompson St., Center Campus, or at the **Michigan League,** 911 N. University Ave. (764-0446; open Mon.-Sat. 7:15am-7:30pm). The **U of M Union** also offers a mélange of restaurants, as well as specialty shops and bookstores. If you don't mind shelling out more than $5, you'll find lots of nice places playing Simon and Garfunkel songs. Most student hangouts are on **Main Street** downtown, **State Street** close to Central Campus, and in the **South University** "Village" uptown.

Drink your beer from pint jars on the outdoor balcony at **Casa Dominick's,** 812 Monroe (662-5414), across from the law quad. (Tasty pasta, pizza, and Italian dishes $4-5; pints of beer $1.60. Open Mon.-Sat. 7:30am-10pm, Sun. 4-8pm. Bar open Mon.-Fri. 4-10pm.) **Park Avenue Delicatessen,** 211 S. State St. (665-9535), doubles as an amateur art gallery. Try a Bell of the Ball sandwich (bell peppers, onions, salami, mustard on french bread; $4.75). (Open Mon.-Sat. 11am-7pm, Sun. 11am-6pm.) For more wholesome homecookin', try **Grandma Lee's,** 120 E. Liberty (665-8299)—don't miss the freshly baked raisin bread ($1.79) and thick-sliced toast (99¢; open daily 6:30am-7pm.) Pack a picnic at the **farmers market** that springs up every Saturday and Wednesday (7am-3pm), outside the Kernytown Mall on N. 5th Ave.

Ann Arbor has excellent nightspots that cater to its fun-seeking college population. Look for blues, reggae, and rock 'n' roll at **Rick's American Café,** 611 Church

St. (996-2747; open Mon.-Sat. 3pm-2am; cover $2-5, more for big acts). **The Blind Pig,** 208 S. 1st St. (996-8555), also has live blues performers. (Open Mon.-Sat. 1pm-2am. Cover $3-15.) **Del Rio,** 122 W. Washington (761-2530), at Ashley, is managed cooperatively by its employees—a vestige of a fast-dying Ann Arbor tradition. It's also a pleasant restaurant and bar with free jazz Sunday nights. (Open Mon.-Fri. 11:30am-2am, Sat. noon-2am, Sun. 5:30pm-2am.)

For information on current classical performances, contact the **University Musical Society** (764-2538; open Mon.-Fri. 9am-4:30pm) or the **Ann Arbor Symphony Orchestra** (994-4801), 527 E. Liberty (994-4801). You can hear live jazz every night in this town; for information, call **Eclipse Jazz** (763-0046) or ask around.

Despite the predominance of expensive hotels and motels in Ann Arbor, it is possible to find reasonable prices. Book way ahead if you plan to stay during commencement in early May, during any home-game weekend in the fall, or during the Summer Art Fair in late July. **University of Michigan,** West Quad, 541 Thompson St., Center Campus; Baits Dorm, Hubbard Rd., North Campus; and Mary Markley, 1503 Washington Heights (764-5325), near the hospital, has immaculate, comfortable rooms. Dorm singles $18. Doubles $26. **Red Roof Inn,** 3621 Plymouth Rd. (996-5800), U.S. 23 (exit 41), has singles for $36, doubles for $38. The **Ann Arbor YMCA** is at 350 S. 5th Ave. at William St. (663-0536), in downtown Ann Arbor. Women allowed. Clean, dorm-style rooms have shared bath. Laundry facilities available. (Singles $20, $73 per week.) **Embassy Hotel,** 200 E. Huron (662-7100), has a convenient location that compensates for small, musty and slightly shabby rooms. (Singles $26. Doubles $32.)

Ann Arbor lies 40 miles west of Detroit on I-94 and is approximately 20 miles from **Detroit Metro Airport. Commuter Transportation Company** and **Kirby Tours** (963-8585 or 800-345-6237; outside MI 800-527-0711) run frequent shuttles between the airport and the U of M Union (around $12). Ann Arbor's layout is a well-planned grid. **Main Street** divides the town east-west and **Huron Street** divides it north-south. The central campus of the university lies 5-6 blocks east of Main St., south of E. Huron St. (about a 15-min. walk from the center of town).

The **Ann Arbor Convention and Visitors Bureau,** at 211 E. Huron St., #6 (995-7281), offers free guides to area attractions, cultural activities, accommodations, and the university. (Open Mon.-Fri. 8:30am-5pm.) **University of Michigan Information** is reached at 763-4636 (call Mon.-Thurs. 7am-1pm, Fri.-Sat. 7am-2pm, Sun. 9am-1pm for listings of campus events). **Amtrak** runs out of 325 Depot St. (994-4906 or 800-872-7245). Trains go to Chicago ($24) and Detroit ($7.50; open daily 7am-11:30pm). **Greyhound,** 116 W. Huron St. at Ashley St. (662-5212), downtown, 1 block off Main St., offers frequent service to Detroit ($6.75) and Chicago ($43; open daily 7:30am-7pm). The **Ann Arbor Transportation Authority** (973-6500 or 996-0400) runs 25 routes serving Ann Arbor and a few nearby towns. Most buses operate 6:45am-9:45pm. (Fare 60¢, seniors and students 30¢. Open Mon.-Fri. 8am-5pm.)

Ann Arbor's **time zone** is Eastern. The **post office** is at 2075 W. Stadium Blvd. (665-1100; open Mon.-Thurs. 8:30am-5pm, Fri. 8:30am-6pm). The **ZIP code** is 48106. The **area code** is 313.

Lake Michigan Shore

The 350-mile eastern shore of Lake Michigan stretches from the Mackinaw Bridge in the north to the Indiana border in the south. Tourists flock here to enjoy high dunes of sugar sand, superb fishing, abundant fruit harvests through October, and deep snow in winter. Many of the region's attractions center around forked **Grand Traverse Bay** and **Traverse City,** the "cherry capital of the world," at the southern tip of the bay. Fishing is best in the **Au Sable** and **Manistee Rivers.** The rich fudge sold in numerous specialty shops seems to have the biggest pull on tourists, however, whom locals dub "fudgies." The **West Michigan Tourist Association,** 136 Fulton E., Grand Rapids 49503 (616-456-8557), offers copious free literature on this area. (Open Mon.-Fri. 9am-4:30pm.) **Greyhound** and the infrequent **North Star Bus Lines** (616-946-5180), in Traverse City, serve the coast.

Traverse City and Environs

In summer, vacationers head to Traverse City for its sandy beaches and annual **Cherry Festival,** held the first full week in July. Traverse City produces 50% of the world's sweet and tart cherries. The locals are friendly and the city is full of intimate cafés and overpriced knick-knack shops. The surrounding landscape of sparkling blue water, cool forests, and magnificent sand dunes makes this region a Great Lakes paradise, albeit a crowded and expensive paradise. **Grand Traverse Bay** is the focal point for swimming, boating, and scuba diving. Free beaches and public access sites dot its shores. Look for the large flock of white swans.

According to local legend, the mammoth sand dunes 30 miles northwest of Traverse City are a sleeping mother bear, waiting for her cubs—the **Manitou Islands**—to finish a swim across the lake. According to Western theory, ice-age glaciers left behind the islands which now comprise the **Sleeping Bear Dunes National Lakeshore.** Nature constantly resculpts the dunes, and some rise precipitously 400 feet above the shore of Lake Michigan. A ferry (256-9061 or 271-4217) runs out of Leland to South Manitou Island in summer. (Ferries leave daily at 9:30pm, return at 5pm. Round-trip $14, $16 if you are camping, under $12 get $2 discount.). The park and centers rent canoes, and are open for cross-country skiing in winter.

The renowned **Interlochen Center for the Arts** (276-9221) rests between two lakes just south of Traverse City on Rte. 137. Performances of the high-powered **National Music Camp,** held almost every day in summer, usually cost $1-2, and many are free. (Open Tues.-Sun. 8:30am-9pm.) The 1200-acre wooded grounds are open year-round, and free tours leave the information center at 10am and 2pm. The **Interlochen Arts Academy** offers performances almost every weekend in winter as well. Across the road, the huge **Interlochen State Park** (276-9511) has camping (primitive campsites $4, with hookup $8). The park store rents row boats and kayaks ($2.50 per hr., $12 per day; $5 deposit) and cross-country skis.

Traverse City has a multitude of fast food restaurants along E. Front St., but there are also many smaller, cheaper, and more appetizing restaurants throughout town. **Stone Soup,** 115 E. Front St. (941-1190), downtown, serves splendid salads for $2-5.35 and "sandriginals" for $5.25. (Open Mon.-Sat. 7am-4pm, Sun. 9am-3pm.) The **Omelette Shop and Bakery,** 124 Cass St. (946-0912), has great omelettes ($3.15-4.89)—try the ratatouille *frittata.* (Open daily 7am-3pm.) **D.J. Kelly's,** 120 Park St. (941-4550), has enough bowties and green upholstery to remind you of the clubhouse after the 18th hole. (Fondues $5-5.50; open Mon.-Sat. 11am-3pm, daily 5-11pm.)

Sleep in the woods at the **Brookwood Home Hostel (AYH),** 538 Thomas Rd., Frankfort (352-4296), near the Sleeping Bear Dunes, almost 50 miles south of Traverse City on Hwy. 31. The large cottage has 12 beds. ($6. Open mid-June to Labor Day.) Another option is the **Honey House Home Hostel,** 613 S. Bayshore (264-9768), in Elk Rapids, 18 miles north of Traverse City. There are 15 beds but no showers. ($5, nonmembers $6. Open May-Oct.) The **Victoriana Bed and Breakfast,** 622 Washington St. (929-1009), near downtown, has three comfortable, almost grand, rooms decorated with family heirlooms. (Singles and doubles $45. Suite $65. Big breakfast and afternoon tea included.) The **Northwestern Michigan Community College,** East Hall, 1701 E. Front St. (922-1406), is over a mile from the bus station. (Dorms with shared bath. Doubles $25, suite with private bath $40. Reservations recommended. Open in summer only.) **D. Orr Haus Motor Lodge,** 894 Munson Ave. (974-9330), has clean, no-frills motel rooms. Right across the street is a nice state beach. (Singles $26.50-31.80. Doubles $34-40. Weekends $5 more.)

There are hundreds of **campgrounds** around Traverse City—in state parks and forests, the Manistee and Huron National Forests, and various parks run by local townships and counties. The West Michigan Tourist Association's *Carefree Days* gives a comprehensive list of public and private sites. State parks usually charge

$7-9. As usual, national forests (723-2211 or 723-3161) are probably the best deal ($4-7). Sleeping Bear Dunes National Lakeshore has two campgrounds: **DH Day** (334-4634) in Glen Arbor and **Platte River** (325-5881) in Honor. Both cost $6 per vehicle and fill up on mid-summer weekends.

The **Greyhound** station is at 717 Woodmere (946-5180), about 2½ miles from downtown. Serves Detroit ($38). (Open Mon.-Fri. 6am-8:30pm, Sat.-Sun. 6am-noon and 5:30pm-8:30pm.) **Bay Area Transportation Authority** (941-2324) buses run once per hour ($1). They also provide personal transportation. (One-way fare $1 up to 15 miles, $1.50 over 15 miles. Call 30 min. in advance. Open Mon.-Fri. 6am-6pm, Sat. 9am-5pm.)

For visitor information, contact the **Grand Traverse Chamber of Commerce,** 202 E. Grandview Pkwy. (947-5075; open Mon.-Sat. 9am-5pm), or the **Grand Traverse Convention and Visitors Bureau,** 900 E. Front St., #100 (947-1120 or 800-872-8377; open Mon.-Fri. 9am-5pm). Ask for the *Traverse City Guide* and *Carefree Days.* Call the **Michigan Department of Natural Resources** for information on state parks (947-7193) or state forest campgrounds (946-4920; open Mon.-Fri. 8am-5pm). For a listing of local events and entertainment, pick up the weekly *Traverse City Record-Eagle Summer Magazine,* free at the visitors bureau and in many stores.

The area's **time zone** is Eastern. The **post office** is at 202 S. Union St. (946-9616. Open Mon.-Fri. 8:30am-5pm, Sat. 6:30am-noon.) Traverse City's **ZIP code** is 49685; the **area code** is 616.

North of Traverse City: Charlevoix and Mackinaw City

Hemingway set some of his Nick Adams stories on the stretch of coast near **Charlevoix** (pronounced "SHAR-le-voy"), north of Traverse City on U.S. 31. The town, which lies on a ½-mile-wide ribbon of land between Lake Michigan and Lake Charlevoix, has become considerably more touristy since Hemingway's time, as upscale downstaters triple Charlevoix's population in summer. It's an artsy and artistically beautiful town, and, whether or not you're a Hemingway fan, it's worth the trip.

Fort Michilimackinac (436-5563) guards the straits between Lakes Michigan and Superior, just as it did in the 18th century, though **Mackinaw City,** the town that grew around the fort, is something of a tourist trap. (Tours of the fort daily 9am-7pm. Admission $5.50, ages 6-12 $2.75.) **Mackinac Island** (on which cars are not allowed) has another fort, **Fort Mackinac** (847-3328), many Victorian homes, and the **Grand Hotel** (906-847-3331), an elegant, gracious summer resort that boasts the world's longest porch. Horse-drawn carriages drag guests all over the island (906-847-3323; $2.50-5 per person; open 24 hours). This island is also where tourist fudge shops began. (Ferries Memorial Day-Labor Day every hr.; May and Sept.-Nov. every other hr.; round-trip $9, ages 6-12 $5.75.) **Greyhound** has a flag stop at the Standard gas station in downtown Mackinaw City. (See Upper Peninsula below for ferry service to Mackinac Island and St. Ignace.)

The small **Durance Home Hostel (AYH),** 541 N. Mercer (547-2937), is run by a delightful woman who feeds you plenty of stories and raspberries ($3.25). Rough it if you prefer at **Fisherman's Island State Park,** 3 miles southwest of Charlevoix. The **Petoskey Regional Chamber of Commerce,** 401 E. Mitchell (347-4150), has information on the area's attractions. Fall is most beautiful here, with fiery foliage reflected in clear, cold water. The Mackinaw **travel information center** (436-5566), off I-75, is loaded with tourist brochures.

Upper Peninsula

A multimillion-acre forestland bordered by three of the world's largest lakes, Michigan's Upper Peninsula (U.P.) is one of the most scenic and unspoiled stretches of land in the Great Lakes region.

Greyhound is the major carrier on the U.P., though its routes may be reduced in upcoming service cuts. Lower Peninsula schedules connect at St. Ignace to Sault

Ste. Marie and U.S. 2 across to Escanoba. In Escanoba and in Ironwood, routes from Wisconsin, Duluth, and Chicago link with service to Marquette and the Keweenaw Peninsula. If you are traveling by bus in the U.P., prepare to wait for connections for approximately one day and half of a night, since buses travel only at night. While this may help save on accommodations costs, it'll soon make you a weary traveler. Try to get some sleep on the beautiful beaches; life is very safe in the U.P.

Eastern Upper Peninsula

The low, eastern reaches of the U.P. contain vast quiet lakes and forests, deserted lake shore dunes, and lonely, mosquito-infested marshes—havens for hikers, cross-country skiers, anglers, canoeists, and compulsive scratchers. Contact the **Upper Peninsula Travel and Recreational Association,** P.O. Box 400, Iron Mountain 49801, for general information. The **U.S. Forestry Service,** Hiawatha National Forest, 2727 N. Lincoln Rd., Escanoba 49829, has guides and maps to help you plan a trip into the wilderness. The towns of Manistique on the Lake Michigan shore and Grand Marais (see Superior North Shore above) on the Superior coast offer supplies, information, food, and accommodations. Contact the Grand Marais Chamber of Commerce, P.O. Box 303, Grand Marais 49839 (494-2766).

Les Cheneaux Islands, due south of the Soo Canal on Lake Huron, are a labyrinth of 35 forest-covered islets and pure, delicious water. Hill's Marina in **Hessel** on MI Rte. 134 (484-2640) rents 14-foot aluminum motor boats (17½ horsepower, $35 per day). **Government Island** is maintained as an uninhabited area by Hiawatha National Forest. You can dock your boat and camp here.

U.S. 2 from the north end of the bridge in St. Ignace west to Naubingway follows some lovely, unspoiled, and practically deserted lakeshore. The white sand dunes of enormous Lake Michigan resemble ocean beaches. Numerous inexpensive motels line U.S. 2. Sleep in or near **Manistique,** where the locals are among the friendliest, and you can find a whole range of accommodations. The **Marina Guest House,** 230 Arbutas (341-5147), is a clean, well-kept B&B. (Singles $30. Doubles and suites $45-50. Reservations recommended.) Most motels are priced from $32 to $36; for slightly more, the **Beachcomber Motel** (341-2567) offers clean rooms. At night, guests are lulled to sleep by the waves of Lake Michigan and the semis on U.S. 2. (Singles $40. Doubles $44.) You can eat next door at **Sunny Shores Restaurant** (341-5582; big sandwiches $3.19-3.69, fisherman's platter $7.65). For supplementary information, contact the **Manistique Chamber of Commerce,** on U.S. 2 (341-5010; open Mon.-Fri. 8am-6pm, Sat.-Sun. 10am-4pm).

The swimming is excellent around Manistique. An especially beautiful, sandy beach lies 2 miles west of the city limits, just off Rte. 2. Pretty, clean **Indian Lake State Park** (341-2355) lies 5 miles west. (300 sites; $8. Tents or tepees $4 per night.) **Camper's Market** (341-5614) rents canoes. ($10 per day, $7 per half-day. $20 deposit required.) Downtown, you may unknowingly cross the **Siphon Bridge,** the nation's only "floating bridge." Twelve miles west of Manistique, visit the amazing **Big Spring,** a 45-foot deep, 45° pond of crystal clear water and brown trout—early natives called it the "mirror of heaven."

Northwest of Seney, between Munising and Grand Marais, is the **Pictured Rocks National Lakeshore** (387-2607). Here, the rain, wind, and ice of Lake Superior have carved the sandstone cliffs into multicolored arches and columns, with caves dotting the steep walls about the lake. The lakeshore offers beaches and primitive camping and inland lakes for fishing and swimming. For a better perspective on the stone formations, the **Pictured Rocks Boat Cruises** (494-2611) will take you along the shoreline, with frequent departures in summer and early fall. (Tickets $10, ages 6-12 $5, under 5 free.) A section of the scenic **North Country Hiking Trail** traverses the park, with free campsites en route. This trail crosses the entire U.P. and winds south through the Lower Peninsula into Ohio.

The **area code** for the U.P. is 906.

Isle Royale National Park

No cars are allowed in America's most unspoiled national park, a 45-by-9-mile island. The ponds, lakes, and forest wilderness cover the rock foundation of Isle Royale and create a natural sanctuary where humans are only guests. One hundred and twenty miles of hiking trails lace the island, threading past beaches and lookout points, through thick hardwood forests to ancient Indian copper mining pits. The **Greenstone Ridge Trail** follows the backbone of the island from Rock Harbor Lodge. **Ojibway Lookout,** on Mt. Franklin, affords a good view of the Canadian shore 15 miles away. **Monument Rock,** 70 feet tall, challenges even experienced climbers. **Lookout Louise,** also on the trail, offers one of the most beautiful views in the park. For a superlative time, go to **Ray's Island,** the largest island in the largest lake on the largest island in the largest freshwater lake in the world. The park is open for **camping** between mid-June and Labor Day, but beware of fog and mosquitoes in June and early July. Nights are always cold, so bring warm clothes. Plan to bring your own tent rather than relying on shelters. There are 31 campsites along the shores and on inland lakes. Permits, free and available at any ranger station, are required for backcountry camping. Be sure to boil your water for at least two minutes or use a 25-micron filter—the water is infested with a nasty tapeworm, and iodine tablets and charcoal purification are not sufficient. Campers can buy supplies and groceries at Rock Harbor and limited amounts at Windigo. **Ferries** run from **Houghton** (906-482-0984; $35 one way) and **Copper Harbor** (906-289-4437; $28 one-way) in Michigan, or **Grand Portage,** MN (218-728-1237; $25-35 one-way depending on Isle Royale destination. Full-day cruise 9:30am-6pm $30). Reservations recommended.

Minnesota

Minnesota's nickname, "Land of 10,000 Lakes" epitomizes the state's modest character. Although the total number of lakes actually tallies closer to 15,000, Minnesotans prefer to round it off to the nearest power of 10. Inclement weather ("Cold enough for you?") and sparsely populated land have imbued Minnesotans with an energetic, cooperative spirit. State residents are almost always ready to help a neighbor or a stranger, whether aid comes as a push out of a snowdrift or as social welfare policies championed by natives such as Hubert Humphrey and Walter Mondale.

The Midwestern prairie meets the North Woods in this state. Neatly laid out family farms give way to wild tracts of lake-spangled forest toward the Canadian border. Minnesota's Boundary Waters is one of the most beautiful canoeing areas in the country, weaving through wilderness that has never felt the rubber tread of the dreaded Winnebago. This landscape felt like the old country to 19th-century immigrant farmers from Germany and Scandinavia, whose descendants still populate much of the state. Even in the cosmopolitan Twin Cities of Minneapolis and St. Paul, natives pronounce "Minn-eh-soh-ta" with a Nordic sweetness, stretching their "ohs" nice and long.

Practical Information

Capital: St. Paul.

Tourist Information: Minnesota Travel Information Center, 375 Jackson St., 250 Skyway Level, St. Paul 55101 (296-5029 or 800-657-3700). Open Mon.-Fri. 8am-5pm.

Time Zone: Central (1 hr. behind Eastern). **Postal Abbreviation:** MN.

Minneapolis and St. Paul

The Twin Cities are hardly twins. First-class museums and theater, trendy shops and restaurants, and shining lakes scattered throughout the city give Minneapolis the edge on tourists. The music scene in Minneapolis has made its mark in the last decade, uncovering hard-driving bands like Hüsker Dü, the Replacements, and, lately, Prince and Trip Shakespeare.

Legend has it that while Minneapolis was born of water power harnessed at the Mississippi's St. Anthony Falls, St. Paul was born of whiskey. Originally dubbed Pig's Eye, after one-eyed whiskey seller "Pig's Eye" Parrant, St. Paul has since undergone tremendous transformation. It has kept a distinctive style, more gritty than cosmopolitan, that many prefer to Minneapolis's urban charms. Take some time to cross the Mississippi and take in the state capital's constellation of small, grassy college campuses, Victorian houses, historic landmarks, and nationally recognized performing arts.

Practical Information

Emergency: 911.

Visitor Information: Minneapolis Convention and Visitors Association, 1219 Marquette Ave. (348-4313 or 800-445-7412). Open Mon.-Fri. 9am-5pm, Sat. 10am-4pm. **St. Paul Convention and Visitors Bureau,** 600 NCL Tower, 445 Minnesota St. (297-6985 or 800-627-6101). Open Mon.-Fri. 9am-5pm. **Greater Minneapolis Chamber of Commerce,** 15 S. 5th St. (370-9132). Open Mon.-Fri. 8am-5pm. **St. Paul Chamber of Commerce,** #701, North Central Life Tower, 445 Minnesota St. (222-5561). Open Mon.-Fri. 8am-4:30pm. **Arts Events,** 870-3131.

Travelers Aid: 404 S. 8th St. (335-5000), Minneapolis. Open Mon.-Fri. 8:15am-4:30pm. Also at the airport (726-9435), across from Braniff. Emergency shelter help. Open Mon.-Sat. 8am-8pm, Sun. 11am-8pm.

Twin Cities International Airport: 7 miles south of the cities, on I-494 in Bloomington. **Northwest Airlines** has its headquarters here. Limousines (726-6400) run to downtown and suburban hotels, leaving from the lower level near baggage claim. (6am-midnight; $7.50.) Take bus #35 to Minneapolis (fare 85¢; 6-8am and 3-4:45pm). Otherwise, take bus #7 to Washington Ave. In Minneapolis, or transfer at Fort Snelling for bus #9 to downtown St. Paul. Ask for a transfer. Taxis are about $15-20 to Minneapolis and $15 to St. Paul.

Amtrak: 730 Transfer Rd. (339-2382 or 800-872-7245), on the east bank off University Ave. SE, between the Twin Cities. A nice station, but inconvenient. Trains to Chicago (10 hr., $66).

Greyhound: In **Minneapolis,** 29 9th St. and 1st Ave. N. (371-3311), 1 block northwest of Hennepin Ave. Very convenient. 24-hour security. To: Chicago ($52), New York ($125), and Seattle ($139). Open daily 5:45am-2:15am. In **St. Paul,** 7th and St. Peter (222-0509), 3 blocks east of Civic Center, downtown. A little deserted, even in the daytime. Open 5:30am-9pm.

Local Transit: Metropolitan Transit Commission, 560 6th Ave. N. (827-7733). Schedules and route maps available at the tourism information center, Coffman Student Union, 300 Washington Ave. SE, University of Minnesota; and in the booth in the Crystal Court on the 1st floor of the IDS Tower, 7th and Nicollet, downtown Minneapolis. Bus service for both cities. Call for information and directions Mon.-Fri. 6am-11pm, Sat.-Sun. 7am-11pm. Some buses operate 5am-1:30am, others shut down earlier. Fare 75¢ peak, 50¢ off-peak, under 18 20¢. **University of Minnesota Bus,** 625-9000. Buses run 7am-9pm. Free to campus locations and even into St. Paul, if you look like a student. Off-campus routes 50¢, 75¢ peak.

Car Rental: Ugly Duckling Rent-A-Car, 6405 Cedar Ave. S. (861-7545), Minneapolis, near the airport. From $17 per day with 100 free miles. Weekly from $100. Open Mon.-Fri. 8:30am-6pm, Sat. noon-3pm, or by appointment. Must be 21 with major credit card or a $200 deposit.

Taxi: Yellow Taxi, 824-4444, in Minneapolis. **Yellow Cab,** 222-4433, in St. Paul. Base rate $1.25, $1.20 per mile.

Help Lines: Gay-Lesbian Helpline, 822-0127.

Post Office: In **Minneapolis,** 1st St. and Marquette Ave. (349-4935), next to the Mississippi River. General Delivery open Mon.-Fri. 8:30am-5pm, Sat. 9am-noon. **ZIP code:** 55401. In **St. Paul,** 180 E. Kellogg Blvd. (293-3021). Open same hours. **ZIP code:** 55101.

Area Code: 612.

Minneapolis and St. Paul lie 405 miles northwest of Chicago on I-94 and 252 miles north of Des Moines, IA, on I-35. The two cities are on either side of the curving **Mississippi River;** Minneapolis is 8 miles northwest of St. Paul on I-94. Minneapolis's layout is straightforward—streets run east-west and avenues run north-south. **Hennepin Avenue** crosses the Mississippi and goes through downtown, curving south towards uptown. Outside of downtown, most avenues are in alphabetical order as you travel west. St. Paul streets are more confusing to navigate. **Grand Avenue** (east-west) and **Snelling Avenue** (north-south) are major thoroughfares. **University Avenue** connects the two cities.

Accommodations and Camping

Budget lodgings are hard to find in the Twin Cities. While cheap airport hotels abound, their cleanliness and safety are often inadequate. The convention and visitors bureaus have useful lists of **Bed and Breakfasts.** The **University of Minnesota** housing office (624-2994), in Comstock Hall, has a list of rooms that rent on a daily ($5-15) or weekly basis. The **Oakmere Home Hostel** (944-1210), Bloomington, has singles for $10. Its fairly remote suburban location makes it a difficult option for those without a car.

College of St. Catherine, Caecilian Hall, 2004 Randolph Ave. (690-6604), St. Paul. Take bus #14 or call for directions. 103 pleasant, quiet dorm rooms. Shared bath, kitchenette. Singles $12. Doubles $20. Open June to mid-Aug.

Evelo's Bed and Breakfast, 2301 Bryant Ave. (374-9656), in S. Minneapolis. A 15-min. walk from uptown or take bus #17 from downtown. Three quaint, comfortable rooms in a beautiful house filled with Victorian artifacts. Friendly owners. Singles $35. Doubles $45. Reservations required.

Town and Country Campground, 12630 Boone Ave. S. (445-1756), 15 miles south of downtown Minneapolis—the closest sites to the Twin Cities. From I-35W, go west on Rte. 13 to Rte. 101 for ½ mile, then left onto Boone Ave. 68 sites. Plenty of shade, friendly, and family-run, but you can hear the freeway. Sites $10, with electricity $13, with sewer $15. Each additional person $1.

Minneapolis Northwest I-94 KOA, (420-2255), on Rte. 101, west of I-94's exit 213, 15 miles north of Minneapolis. Noisy kids and all the KOA amenities: pool, sauna, and showers. Sites $13-16.50, each additional adult $2.

Food

The Twin Cities specialize in casual dining, and a gourmet sandwich or salad and a steaming cup of coffee is the favored fare. Changing demographics and tastes mean the Scandinavian smorgasbords you might have spotted a decade ago are giving way to dozens of Vietnamese and natural food restaurants. **Uptown** and the **Warehouse District** in Minneapolis and St. Paul's **Victoria Crossing** are trendy spots, while **Dinkytown** and the **West Bank** cater to student needs. For cheaper food and ethnic specialties, try **Northeast Minneapolis** or explore St. Paul.

Minneapolis

It's Greek to Me, 626 Lake St. (825-9922), at Lyndale Ave. Take bus #52C. Great Greek food, complemented by traditional costumes hanging on the walls. Gyros with fries and salad $3.85. Dinners $6-10. Open daily 11am-11pm.

Matin, 416 1st Ave. N. (340-0150), downtown. Elegant Vietnamese food with French flair. Lunch buffet $5.25, entrees $3.25-5.75. Open Mon.-Fri. 11am-2:30pm, Mon.-Thurs. 5-10pm, Fri.-Sat. 5-11pm.

Vescio's, 406 14th Ave. SE (378-1747), in Dinkytown. Solid Mom-and-Pop Italian fare. Pesto spaghetti with bread $6.25. Open Tues.-Thurs. 11am-11pm, Fri.-Sat. 11am-12:30am, Sun. 3-10pm.

Annie's Parlor, 315 14th Ave. SE (379-0744), in Dinkytown, and 406 Cedar Ave. (339-6204), West Bank. Malts that are a meal in themselves ($2.75-3) and great hamburgers ($2.75-3.85). Open Mon.-Thurs. 11am-11pm, Fri.-Sat. 11am-midnight, Sun. noon-11pm.

The New Riverside Cafe, 329 Cedar Ave. (333-4814), West Bank. Take bus #73. The self-proclaimed "Biomagnetic Center of the Universe." Full vegetarian meals served cafeteria-style amidst unframed works by local artists and nightly live jazz and bluegrass. Sandwiches and Mexican dishes $2-4. Open daily Mon.-Thurs. 7am-11pm, Fri. 7am-midnight, Sat. 8am-midnight, Sun. 9am-1:30pm. Performances Tues.-Sat. 7pm, Fri. 9pm, Sat. 5pm. No cover.

My Lam's Café, 2827½ Hennepin Ave. (870-0220), uptown. Narrow diner barely fits its proudest possession, a 50s Schwinn just like Pee Wee Herman's. Vietnamese entrees $3.55-5.75. Open Mon.-Thurs. 6am-9pm, Fri. 6am-10pm, Sun. 8am-8pm.

Two Pesos, 1320 W. Lake St. (825-8264), uptown. Reminders of fast food joints are quickly forgotten on the outdoor patio, which is cool in even the most sweltering weather. Two soft tacos $3.39. Bottled Mexican beer $1.90, Margaritas $1-1.40. Open Mon.-Sat. 10:30am-2am, Sun. 10:30am-midnight.

The Malt Shop, 50th St. and Bryant Ave. (824-1352), S. Minneapolis or Bandana Square (645-4643), St. Paul. An old-time soda fountain; try a phenomenal fresh fruit malt or shake ($2.60).

St. Paul

Sawatdee, 289 E. 5th St. (222-5859), downtown, 2 streets from the Greyhound station. Take bus #50. Nationally acclaimed Thai food enhanced by great ambience—antique street lamps light the tables. Stir-fried shrimp with peppers $8, other entrees $6-18. Open Mon.-Thurs. 11am-10pm, Fri.-Sat. 11am-11pm.

Café Latté, 850 Grand Ave. (224-5687), across the street from Victoria Crossing. Cafeteria-style, but elegant, with bilevel seating and neon accents. Try the *café Jé* (coffee with chocolate milk). Delicious soups, salads ($2.95-4.25), and pastries. Long lines at lunch. Open Mon.-Thurs. 10am-11pm, Sat. 10am-midnight, Sun. 9am-10pm.

Mickey's Dining Car, 36 W. 9th St. (222-5633), across from Greyhound. Small, cheap, and convenient, a great spot for wee-hour munchies runs. Steak and eggs from $3.85, lunch and dinner from $3. Open 24 hours.

St. Paul Farmers Market, 5th and Wall Market (227-6856), downtown. Fresh produce and baked goods. Get there before 10am on Sat. Call to verify location and hours. Open Sat. 6am-1pm, Sun. 9am-1pm.

Sights

Minneapolis

One look at the beautiful lakes right in the middle of the city explains Minneapolitans' pride in their city. **Lake of Isles,** off Franklin Ave., about 1½ miles from downtown, is ringed by stately mansions. It's hard to believe you're in the middle of the city when you walk among throngs of Canadian geese and breathe the countrified air. **Lake Calhoun,** on the west end of Lake St., a hectic social and recreational hotspot, is constantly ringed by bikers, skaters, and joggers. Rent skates and roller blades at **Rolling Soles,** 1700 W. Lake St. (823-5711; skates $3 per hr., $7.50 per day; blades $5 per hr., $10 per day. Open daily 10am-9pm.) The **Minneapolis Park and Recreation Board** (348-5406) rents canoes at several locations ($4.50 per hr.) Situated in a more residential neighborhood, **Lake Harriet** has a tiny steamboat and an endless stream of joggers. The city presents 28 miles of trails along these lakes for cycling, roller skating, roller blading, jogging, or strolling on a sunny afternoon. The circumference of each lake is about 3 miles and paths are well maintained.

One of the top modern art museums in the country, the **Walker Art Center,** 725 Vineland Place (375-7600), a few blocks from downtown, draws thousands with daring exhibits and an impressive permanent collection, including works by Roy

Lichenstein and Andy Warhol. Inside is an excellent, not-too-expensive café, and adjacent to the museum is the Guthrie Theater (see Entertainment). (Open Tues.-Sat. 10am-8pm, Sun. 11am-5pm. Admission $3, ages 12-18 $2, seniors free.) Next to the Walker, the **Minneapolis Sculpture Garden** displays dozens of sculptures and a fountain in a "room" of exquisitely landscaped trees and flowers. The **Minneapolis Institute of Arts,** 2400 3rd Ave. S. (870-3131), holds Egyptian, Chinese, American, and European art, including yet another casting of Rodin's *Gates of Hell* in the lobby. (Open Tues.-Sat. 10am-5pm, Thurs. 10am-9pm, Sun. noon-5pm. Admission $2, students and under 18 $1, seniors and under 12 free; free to all Thurs. 5-9pm.) **Loring Park,** near the Walker Art Center, is the focal point of Minneapolis's large and politically powerful gay community. On Monday evenings in the summer, the park hosts free concerts by local bands, followed by vintage films, on the hill toward the north edge. (Take bus #1, 4, 6, or 28 going south to the park and the Walker Art Museum-Guthrie Theater complex.)

St. Anthony Falls and Upper Locks, 1 Portland Ave. (333-5336), has a free observation deck that overlooks the Mississippi River. (Open April-Nov. daily 8am-10pm.) Several miles downstream, Minnehaha Park provides a breathtaking view of **Minnehaha Falls,** immortalized in Longfellow's *Song of Hiawatha.* (Take bus #7 from Hennepin Ave., downtown.)

St. Paul

The state capital is fairly sedate and frankly sterile on weekends. Battle the school field trip crowds to see the golden horses atop the ornate **state capitol** (296-3962), on Cedar St. (Open Mon.-Fri. 9am-5pm, Sat. 10am-4pm, Sun. 1-4pm.) Nearby, the **Minnesota Historical Society,** 690 Cedar St. (296-6126), records the early history of St. Paul's Scandinavian settlers in its extensive libraries. (Open Mon.-Sat. 8:30am-5pm, exhibits only on Sun. 1-4pm. Free.) The **Landmark Center,** 75 W. 5th St. (292-3272), hovers over the Greyhound station. This grandly restored 1902 federal court building, with its towers and turrets, houses a collection of pianos and keyboard instruments, art exhibits, a concert hall, and four restored courtrooms. (Call to arrange a tour. Open Mon.-Wed. and Fri. 10am-5pm, Thurs. 10am-8pm, Sat. 10am-5pm, Sun. 1-5pm. Free.) **St. Paul's Cathedral,** 239 Selby Ave. (228-1766), is a scaled-down version of St. Peter's in Rome, minus the Vatican. (Open daily 7:30am-6pm.)

Summit Avenue, west of downtown, displays the nation's longest stretch of Victorian homes, including the Governor's Mansion and the former homes of F. Scott Fitzgerald and railroad magnate James J. Hill. Known as the "Grand Old Ladies of Summit Avenue," these homes were built mainly with railroad fortunes in the 19th century.

St. Paulites are justifiably proud of their space-age **Science Museum,** 30 E. 10th St. (221-9400 or 221-9451), across from the cathedral, near the intersection of Exchange and Wabasha St. Outside, a giant iguana sculpture stands guard, while inside the **McKnight-3M Omnitheater** presents a literally dizzying array of films. (Open Mon.-Sat. 9:30am-9pm, Sun. 11am-9pm. Tickets for exhibits $3.50, for theater $4.50, combination $5.50; seniors and under 12 get $1 discounts.)

When you tire of touring, come inside and have a brew at **Stroh Brewing Company,** 707 E. Minnehaha (778-3100), with free tours and samples. (Open Mon.-Fri. 1-4pm.)

Entertainment

With more theaters per capita than any U.S. city outside of New York, the Twin Cities' vibrant drama scene has something for everyone.

The shining star of the Twin Cities' thriving theater community is the **Guthrie Theater,** 725 Vineland Place (377-2224), just off Hennepin in Minneapolis, adjacent to the Walker Art Center. The Guthrie repertory company performs from June to March. (Box office open Mon.-Fri. 9am-9pm, Sat. 9am-9pm, Sun. 11am-9pm. Tickets $6-32, rush tickets 15 min. before the show $5.)

The **Children's Theater Company,** 3rd Ave. and 24th S. (874-0400), adjacent to the Minneapolis Institute of Art, puts on classic favorites and innovative productions for all ages from September to June. (Box office open Mon.-Fri. 9am-5pm, Sat.-Sun. noon-4pm except summer. Tickets $11-18, seniors, students, and children $8-14. Student rush tickets, available 15 min. before any performance, $6.)

In the summer, **Orchestra Hall,** 1111 Nicollet Mall (371-5600 or 371-5656), downtown Minneapolis, hosts **Summerfest,** a month-long celebration of Viennese music. (Box office open Mon.-Sat. 10am-6pm, Sun. noon-8pm. Tickets $8-19.50. Student rush 15 min. before show $4.) Don't miss the free coffee concerts at 11am or the free dance lessons at night at nearby **Peavey Plaza,** with its spectacular fountain (no wading allowed).

For information on the local music scene and other events, pick up the free *City Pages* or **Twin Cities Reader,** available throughout the cities. Free outdoor blues, jazz, and rock concerts are held along the riverfront near St. Anthony Falls. (Call 724-8437 for information.) For swinging singles fun, go to **St. Anthony's Wharf** (378-7058), in St. Anthony Main, a restored mattress warehouse next to Riverplace.

St. Paul's glass-and-brick, accordion-fronted **Ordway Music Theater,** 345 Washington St. (224-4222), is one of the most beautiful public spaces for music in the country. It opened its doors in January, 1985 to the **St. Paul Chamber Orchestra,** then under the direction of Pinchas Zukerman. The **Minnesota Orchestra, Schubert Club,** and the **Minnesota Opera Company** perform here. (Box office open Mon.-Sat. 10am-5:30pm. Tickets $5-10.)

The many comedy and improvisational clubs make the Twin Cities a downright hilarious place to visit. Dudley Riggs' **Brave New Workshop,** 2605 Hennepin Ave. (332-6620), has consistently good musical comedy shows in an intimate club. (Box office open Tues.-Sat. 4-10pm. Performances Tues.-Sat. 8pm, Fri.-Sat. 10:30pm. Tickets $10 weekdays, $12 weekends.) The **Ha Ha** lives up to its name at the corner of Hennepin and W. 28th St., in S. Minneapolis. (872-0305; shows Fri.-Sat. at 8pm and 10:30pm, Sun. at 7:30pm. Cover $6.) A sizzling downtown club (and Prince's old haunt) is **First Avenue and 7th St. Entry,** (338-8388), with reggae, rock 'n' roll, funk, house music, thrash, and heavy metal. Live bands every night. (Open Mon.-Sat. 9pm-1am, Sun. 9pm-midnight. Cover for concerts $4-18, otherwise $3-5.) The "Homerdome," also know as the **Hubert H. Humphrey Metrodome,** 501 Chicago Ave. S. (375-1366), downtown Minneapolis, is home to most of the Twin Cities' professional sports teams.

Some of Minneapolis's most popular forms of entertainment take place outside. In January, the 10-day **St. Paul Winter Carnival,** near the state capitol is the ideal antidote for cabin fever. Both cities get into the swing of things in July—St. Paul celebrates **Taste of Minnesota,** on the Capitol Mall during the fourth, then **Riverfront Days,** with big name bands, food stands, and rides for a week. Finally, the 9-day **Minneapolis Aquatennial** begins, with concerts, parades, art exhibits, and kids dripping sno-cones on their strollers (call 922-9000 for information). During late August and early September, spend a day at the **Minnesota State Fair,** at Snelling and Como, the second-largest in the nation. If the human zoo has become too much, talk to the animals at the **Minnesota Zoo,** Hwy. 32 (432-9000). Walk around or ride the all-weather monorail. (Open daily 10am-6pm, off-season 10am-4pm. Admission $4, seniors $2, ages 6-16 $1.50. Parking $1.50.)

Northern Minnesota

Chippewa National Forest Area

The Norway pine forests, interspersed with lovely strands of birch, thicken as you move north into **Chippewa National Forest,** source of the mighty Mississippi River. Camping is a popular activity, and there are hundreds of lakes to canoe on. Leech, Cass, and Winnibigoshish (or simply "Winnie") are the largest, but also the most crowded with speedboats. The national forest shares territory with the **Leech Lake Indian Reservation,** home of the remaining members of the Chippewa tribe.

Use the town of Walker on Leech Lake as a gateway to the Chippewa National Forest. Travelers can find information on the tourist facilities at the **Leech Lake Area Chamber of Commerce** (547-1313; open daily 9am-5pm.) Information on abundant, cheap camping, hiking, fishing, and other activities is available one block west at the **forest office** (335-2226; open daily 7:30am-5pm). Both offices are on Rte. 371 in the east end of town. **Greyhound** runs from Minneapolis to Walker (2 per day, 4 hr., $21), stopping at the Standard gas station, 4th Ave. and Minnesota St., across from the chamber of commerce.

The **Headwaters of the Mississippi** are not very mighty as they trickle out of **Lake Itasca,** 30 miles west of Walker on Rte. 200. Here is the only place where mere mortals can easily wade across the Mississippi. Campsites in the park are usually not crowded. (Sites $8, with electricity $10. 2-day vehicle permit $3.25.) The **Itasca State Park Office** (266-3654) has more information. (Open daily 8am-10pm.) You can also get there via Bemidji and Park Rapids, both of which have **Greyhound** and **Triangle** stops (Duluth-Bemidji $14.45, Minneapolis-Park Rapids $25).

The **area code** is 218.

The Superior North Shore

The North Shore begins with the majestic Sawtooth Mountains just north of Duluth and extends 150 wild and wooded miles to Canada. This stretch, defined by Highway 61 (North Shore Drive), is home to virtually all of Minnesota's Superior lakeshore—and multitudes of bears, moose, and the only remaining wolf population in the contiguous 48 states. In summer thousands flock to the towns dotting the coastline to fish, camp, hike, and canoe, attracted by the cool and breezy weather.

During the warmer months, it's fun to drive or bike your way up the 150-mile-long coast along Hwy. 61, beginning in Duluth. Bring warm clothes, since even in summer temperatures can drop into the low 40s at night. And bring your money bags unless you plan to camp. Over 200 years ago, locals trapped beaver, but now they prey on tourists.

Developers are at work on a new trail that will take hikers from Duluth to Canada, and completion is scheduled for 1990. Paths between **Temperance River** and **Cascade State Park** (35 miles) and near **Split Rock Lighthouse** (10 miles) are already well trod. For tenderfoot daytrippers, the trail provides easy access to accommodations, transportation, and food along the way. For more information on where to hook up with the trail, write to the **Superior Trail Hiking Association,** P.O. Box 2157, Tofte 55615. Caramel-colored water splashes over the jagged rocks at **Gooseberry Falls,** a popular swimming hole 40 miles up the coast from Duluth. Sleep within earshot of the falls at the **Gooseberry Falls Campground** (834-3787; sites $11.73, including state park sticker. Make reservations for July and Aug.) Just north of the falls, **Split Rock Lighthouse** looks out over one of the most treacherous stretches of water around. The rocks below, endowed with strange magnetic qualities, made compasses useless and lured unwary sailors into their Scylla-and-Charybdis-like arms. The **History Center** (226-4372), atop a 120-foot cliff, offers exhibits on famous shipwrecks and a film on the old days of Split Rock. (Open daily May 15-Oct. 15 9am-5pm, off-season Fri.-Sun. noon-4pm. Admission is a state park sticker, $3.25.) Camp next door, at **Split Rock Lighthouse State Park** (226-3065; sites $11.73, including state park sticker.) Make reservations two weeks in advance.

Grand Marais is a good base for excursions into nearby portions of the **Boundary Waters Canoe Area.** The 60-mile-long **Gunflint Trail,** now widened into an auto road, begins in Grand Marais and continues northwest into the BWCA. Reward yourself at the end of the trail at the simple but pleasant **"Spirit of the Lake" Island AYH Hostel** (388-2241), in Seagull Lake. ($10. $2 boat transport. Meals $3-5. Closed Nov.-Dec. and April.) The **Tip of the Arrowhead Tourist Information Center,** Broadway and 1st Ave. (387-2524), houses both a chamber of commerce and a forest service desk. The National Forest Ranger station at the base of the trail,

¼ mile south of town, offers even more information, and issues BWCA permits for individual ports of entry into BWCA. (Open in summer daily 7am-5pm; rest of the year Mon.-Fri. 7:30am-4pm.) **Wilderness Waters Outfitters** (387-2525), 2 miles south of Grand Marais on Rte. 61, rents canoes for $12 per day (less for longer trips; $10 deposit, reservations required). Paddles, life jackets, and a car rack are included. (Open May-Oct. daily 7am-8pm.)

Motels cost at least $25 for a single, but campground space is easy to find. The **Grand Marais Recreation Area** (387-1712), off Rte. 61 in town, offers a great view of Lake Superior. Pitch your tent by the small inlet and eat breakfast with the ducks. (Office open daily 6am-10pm. Sites $9.50, with water and electricity $11, with full hookup $12. Open May to mid-Oct.)

Grand Marais's **area code** is 218.

Duluth

This once-booming railroad hub is still an active port (the largest on the Great Lakes), but today Duluth also counts on the thousands of tourists who come to see the city's historic mansions, beautiful parks, and spectacular views of Lake Superior. Minnesota's "refrigerated city" is also a great place to gear up for a fishing, camping, or driving excursion in northwestern Minnesota.

The best thing about Duluth is the view. Take a tour of the harbor on **Duluth Superior Excursions,** 5th Ave. W. and Waterfront (722-1728), behind the Duluth Arena and Auditorium. (Boats depart May-late Oct. 9:30am-5:30pm every hr. and at 7:30pm, but hours fluctuate. Admission $7, ages 3-11 $3.25.) Reach new heights in the summer by climbing to the top of **Enger Tower,** 18th Ave. W. on Skyline Parkway. You can see all of Duluth-Superior Harbor, and as far as 30 miles away on a clear day. **Hawk Ridge** is a birdwatcher's paradise. A tremendous number and variety of hawks cruise by between late August and early November on their way south.

For indoor entertainment, visit **The Depot,** 506 W. Michigan St. (727-8025), in the old Amtrak depot, with its museum delineating Duluth's railroad and logging heritage. (Open daily 10am-5pm; Labor Day-Memorial Day Mon.-Sat. 10am-5pm, Sun. 1-5pm. Admission $4, seniors $3, ages 6-17 $2, families $11.) Directly adjacent to the depot is the **Performing Arts Center.** (722-0349; box office open Mon.-Fri. 9am-4pm, until 8pm on nights of performances. Tickets $5-6, seniors and students $4-5.) Mansion-lovers should head to **Glensheen,** 3300 London Rd. (724-8863). This 39-room neo-Jacobean spectacle with beautiful Edwardian furnishings and landscaped grounds overlooks the lakes. (Open Jan. Sat.-Sun. 1-3pm; Feb.-Dec. Thurs.-Tues. 9am-5pm; more tours in summer and on weekends. Admission $5.50, seniors and ages 13-17 $4.25, under 12 $2.50; less in winter. Make reservations in summer.)

After a day of sight-seeing, head to one of the city parks. Free outdoor concerts are held at **Chester Bowl** or **Zoo-Fairmont Park** (724-9832). **Bayfront Park** hosts the **International Folk Festival** (727-8025 or 722-7425) on the first Saturday in August.

Two downtown shopping centers, the restored **Fitger's** brewery and the more modern **Holiday Center,** have a number of pleasant restaurants ranging from fast-food joints to elegant dining spots. **Grandma's Saloon and Deli,** 522 Lake Ave. S. (727-4192), packs people into a room that combines old-time atmosphere and lots of cool signs. Those under under 21 can't go in unless accompanied by an adult. (Sandwiches $2-6, spaghetti $4. Open daily 11am-1am.) **Sir Benedict's Tavern on the Lake,** 805 E. Superior St. (728-1192), is much more laid-back. Pick up a made-to-order sandwich ($3.40-4.20) and choose from the many imported beers ($2.25). Outside tables overlook the lake. (Live bluegrass Wed., jazz Thurs. Open Sun.-Tues. and Thurs. 11am-11pm, Wed. 11am-midnight, Fri.-Sat. 11am-12:30am.) Afterwards, head to the **Portland Malte Shoppe,** 714 E. Superior, for a malt ($2.80; open daily 11am-11pm).

The **youth hostel (AYH)** at the **YWCA**, 202 W. 2nd St. (722-7425), is an exception to Duluth's inflated bedroom prices, but for a reason. Dorms are small and cots are available for free in the closet on the second floor. The mattresses, linen, and bathrooms are all of a questionable nature. ($9, nonmembers $22 per night or $55 per week.) The **College of St. Scholastica**, 1200 Kenwood Ave. (723-6483), often has room in summer at its secluded campus. There is no occupant limit for their spacious, pleasant rooms. (Doubles with shared bath $25. Make reservations.) **Jay Cooke State Park** (384-4610), southwest of Duluth on I-35, has 80 campsites. (Open 8am-10pm. Sites $8.48. Vehicle permit $3.25.) **Spirit Mountain**, 9500 Spirit Mountain Pl. (628-2891), near the ski resort of the same name, is 10 miles south on I-35, on the top of the hill. (Sites with electricity $11, with electricity and water $13.)

Greyhound, 2212 W. Superior (722-5591), 2 miles west of downtown, serves Michigan's Upper Peninsula, Hancock, and Calumet ($66). **Turner Bus Lines** sends one bus per day up the Superior Drive (North Shore) to Grand Portage ($23.55) and Thunder Bay ($31.50). The express to the Twin Cities costs $19. (Open daily 6:45am-10pm, last tickets sold at 5pm.) The **Duluth Transit Authority (DTA)** serves the downtown and outlying areas. Consult maps in bus shelters or call 722-7283. (Fare 60¢, seniors 50¢.)

The **Convention and Visitors Bureau**, at Endion Station, 100 Lake Place Dr. (722-4011), north side of town (open Mon.-Fri. 8:30am-5pm), and the summer **visitors center** on the waterfront on Harbor Dr. (722-6024; open daily 9am-7:30pm), have an ample supply of brochures and Duluth maps. The **Fun Line** (724-0872) provides 24-hour entertainment information. Duluth is 154 miles northeast of the Twin Cities on I-35.

The Duluth **post office** is at 2800 W. Michigan (723-2561), near the bus station. (Open Mon.-Fri. 7:30am-5pm, Sat. 9am-noon.) **ZIP code:** 55806.

Duluth's **area code** is 218.

Ohio

Ohio just doesn't quit. Undaunted by the rustbelt depression of the late 1970s, the Ohio Seven—a constellation of cities representing nearly four fifths of the nation's leading industries—pushes ahead with plans for the future. At opposite ends of the state, Cleveland and Cincinnati have revamped their downtowns, cleaned up pollution, and fostered a resurgence in the arts, all the while retaining their own distinct flavor. In the center of the state, Columbus is now recognized as one of the best places to live in the country (according to a 1989 *Newsweek* article). And for two centuries, farmers in central and northeastern Ohio have raised plentiful crops and tended unblemished dairylands.

On the eastern edge of the Midwest, Ohio lays claim to several major waterways and some of the nation's most fertile pastures. The geography that fosters industry and agriculture also features numerous attractions for lovers of the outdoors. With vacation spots like the Lake Erie Shore and the lush southern forests, it's no surprise that the state's name comes from an Iroquois word meaning "beautiful."

Practical Information

Capital: Columbus.

Tourist Information: State Office of Travel and Tourism, 77 S. High St., Box 1001, Columbus 43215 (466-8844). **Greater Columbus Convention and Visitors Bureau**, 1 Columbus Bldg., 10 W. Broad St., #1300, Columbus 43215 (221-6623 or 800-821-5784). Open Mon.-Fri. 8am-5pm.

Time Zone: Eastern. **Postal Abbreviation:** OH.

REE Items In Red

Feel Confident, You'll Have The Basics.

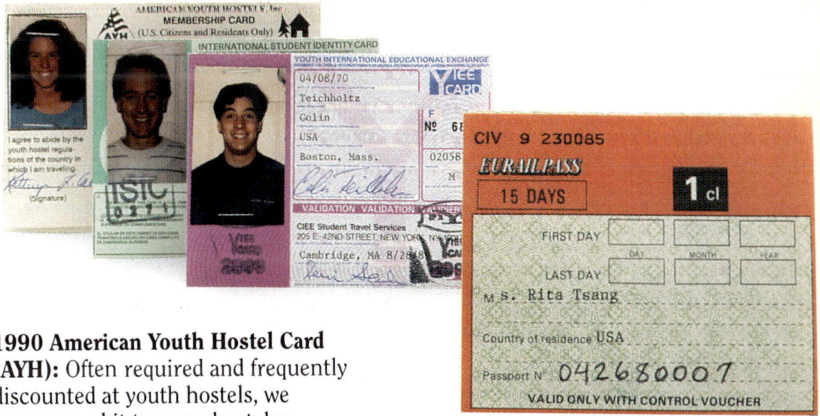

1990 American Youth Hostel Card (AYH): Often required and frequently discounted at youth hostels, we recommend it to every hosteler.
10022 AYH Card $25.00 ($.75)
10023 Plastic Case $.75
FREE directory of hostels in the USA.

1990 International Student Identification Cards (ISIC): Available to currently enrolled full-time students, provides accident/medical insurance, discount air fares, countless discounts on cultural events, accomodations, and more.
10020 ISIC $10.00 ($.75)
FREE "International Student Travel Guide"

1990 Youth International Educational Exchange Card (YIEE): All the same benefits of ISIC (above), for non students under 26 years of age.
10021 YIEE $10.00 ($.75)
FREE "Discounts for Youth Travel," a 200 page guide to discounts all around the world.

1990 International Teacher Identification Card (ITIC): Same benefits as the ISIC. Applicants must be full time teachers at a school or university.
10024 ITIC $10.00 ($.75)

Eurail Pass: (Please include an additional $4.00 for Certified Mail)

First Class		
10025	15 Day	**$340**
10026	21 Day	**$440**
10027	1 Month	**$550**
10028	2 Months	**$750**
10029	3 Months	**$930**

Flexipass		
10030	5 Days within 15	**$198**
10031	9 Days within 21	**$360**
10032	14 Days in 1 month	**$458**

Eurail Youth Pass (Under 26)		
10033	1 Month	**$380**
10034	2 Months	**$500**

All Eurail Pass orders include FREE: Eurail Map, Pocket Timetable, and Traveler's Guide.

LET'S GO Travel

THE travel authority for 30 years

Postage prices are within parentheses.

Cleveland

The glitz of Gilded Age magnates like Rockefeller and Hanna no longer shimmers over Cleveland, but MBAs, attachés, and resumés still reflect the capitalist heritage. Planners have sunk billions into downtown construction, waterfront development, and historic renovation as the city tries to move beyond its sooty, gritty industrial image to a more slick corporate one. The City on the Lake now basks in a national spotlight, in part because of its thriving arts community. Cleveland has not entirely shaken its seedy past, however. Travelers are advised to exercise extra caution here.

Practical Information

Emergency: 911.

Visitor Information: Cleveland Convention and Visitors Bureau, 3100 Tower City Ctr. (621-4110 or 800-321-1001), in Terminal Tower at Public Square. Free maps and helpful staff. **Cleveland Fun Phone,** 621-8860. 24-hour entertainment hotline. **Language Bank** and **Nationalities Service Center,** 781-4560, 24 hours.

Cleveland Hopkins International Airport: in Brookpark, some distance west of downtown, but accessible on the RTA airport rapid line, which goes to the Terminal Tower on bus #66X ("Red Line") for $1.

Amtrak: 200 Cleveland Memorial Shoreway, NE (861-0105 or 800-872-7245), east of City Hall. Open Mon.-Sat. 4am-1pm, 2-5:30pm, midnight-3am; Sun. 4-8:45am and midnight-3am. To New York ($88) and Chicago ($69).

Greyhound: 1465 Chester Ave. (781-0520; schedules and fares 781-1400), at E. 14th St., near Regional Transit Authority (RTA) bus lines and about 7 blocks east of Terminal Tower. Frequent and convenient service to Chicago and New York City. Good coverage of Ohio. To: Pittsburgh ($19), Cincinnati ($36), and Indianapolis ($39).

Regional Transit Authority (RTA): 2019 Ontario Ave. (566-5074), across the street from Terminal Tower. Schedules for city buses and rapid transit lines. Open Mon.-Fri. 7:30am-5:30pm. Information by telephone Mon.-Sat. 6am-6pm (621-9500). Daily service 4:30am-12:30am. Bus lines, connecting with the Rapid stops, provide public transport to most of the metropolitan area. Fare $1 (free transfers to buses), buses 85¢.

Taxi: Yellow Cab, 623-1500. 24 hours.

Time/Weather Line: 931-1212. 24 hours.

Help Line: Rape Crisis Line, 391-3912. 24 hours.

Post Office: 2400 Orange St. (443-4199). Open Mon.-Fri. 8am-7pm. **ZIP code:** 44101.

Area Code: 216

Cleveland spreads out south of Lake Erie and extends to crowded suburbs, including Cleveland Heights and Shaker Heights to the east, Garfield Heights to the southeast, and Parma to the southwest. **Terminal Tower** in **Public Square** divides the city into east and west. To reach Public Square from I-90 or I-71, follow the Ontario Ave./Broadway exit. From I-77, take the 9th St. exit to Euclid Ave., which runs into the Square. From the Amtrak station, follow Lakeside Ave. and turn onto Ontario, which leads to the tower. Cleveland is getting safer, but it is still not advisable to walk alone.

Accommodations

Safe, cheap lodgings are simply not available in downtown Cleveland. Travelers are better off staying in the suburbs. Hotel taxes are hefty; add approximately $5 to all of these prices.

If you know your plans well in advance, it's worth calling **Cleveland Private Lodgings** (321-3213), which places people in homes around the city for as low as

$25. All arrangements are made through the office. Leave enough time for a letter of confirmation. (Open Mon.-Tues. and Thurs.-Fri. 9am-noon and 3-5pm.)

Stanford House Hostel (AYH), 6093 Stanford Rd., Peninsula (467-8711), 22 miles south of Cleveland. Exit 12 off I-80. Take bus #77F to Snowville Rd. Beautifully restored Greek Revival farmhouse is on National Register of Historic Places. Excellent facilities, friendly houseparent. Expect a small chore, but it's worth it. Check-in 5-9pm, flexible curfew 11pm. $8, sleep sack $2. Reservations only.

Gateway Motel, 29865 Euclid Ave. (943-6777), 10 miles east of Public Sq. in Wickliffe. Take Euclid Ave. exit off I-90 or bus #28X. Renovated in the past year, it now has A/C and color TV. Singles $22. Doubles $30.

Lakewood Manor Motel, 12019 Lake Ave., Lakewood (226-4800). Take bus #55CX. Neat, severe. Vinyl furniture, TV, central A/C. Complimentary coffee and doughnuts. Singles $30. Doubles $40.

Red Roof Inn, I-90 and Crocker Rd., exit 156, Westlake (892-7920). Singles $31. Doubles $40.

Forty minutes east of downtown, off I-480, in Streetsboro, are two campgrounds: **Woodside Lake Park,** 2256 Frost Rd. (626-4251; tent sites for 2 $15, with electricity $19. Each additional guest $2, ages 3-17 75¢); and **Valley View Lake Resort,** 8326 Ferguson (626-2041; tent sites $17, water and hookup available).

Food

You'll find Cleveland's culinary treats in the tiny neighborhoods that surround the downtown area. If you lust for hot corned beef, just step into one of the dozens of delis in the city center.

Corky & Lenny's, 13937 Cedar Rd., S. Euclid (321-3310), 12 miles from downtown. Pleasant deli-restaurant has good sandwiches for $2.50-4. Harried service. Open daily 7am-midnight.

Mama Santa's, 12305 Mayfield Rd. (231-9567), in Little Italy, just east of University Circle. Friendly owner, subdued lighting. Medium pizza $3.25, spaghetti $4.25. Open Mon.-Thurs. 11am-midnight, Fri.-Sat. 11am-1am.

Tommy's, 1820 Coventry (321-7757), on Coventry Rd., just up the hill from University Circle. Take bus #9X east to Mayfield and Coventry Rd. Although fire damage temporarily cramps its style, enjoy great sandwiches ($2.40-5.25) and bright-eyed service. Try the Brownie Monster. Open Mon.-Sat. 7:30am-10pm, Sun. 9am-5pm.

Downtown Coffee Shoppe, 1150 Huron Rd. (771-1055), 8 blocks from Public Sq. This Mom and Pop diner is situated on a calm street behind Euclid Ave. Sandwiches and burgers $1.75-3. Open Mon.-Fri. 6am-5pm.

West Side Market, W. 25th and Lorain Ave. (664-3386). Fresh produce, meats, and baked goods from 185 vendors. Tasty ethnic food. Open Mon. and Wed. 7am-4pm, Fri.-Sat. 7am-6pm.

Sights and Entertainment

Cleveland claims a wide variety of historic sights and cultural events. Overlooking the Flats to the east, the **Warehouse District** is a nice place for an afternoon walk. The city's former downtown features a cluster of newly restored 19th-century buildings, shops, and restaurants. Located five miles east of the city, **University Circle** is a cluster of 75 cultural institutions. Check with the helpful visitors bureau for details on museums, live music, and drama. The world-class **Cleveland Museum of Art,** 11150 East Blvd. (421-7340), in University Circle, contains a fine collection of 19th-century French and American impressionist paintings, as well as a version of Rodin's "The Thinker." The beautiful plaza and pond that face it are great places to stroll. (Open Tues. and Thurs.-Fri. 10am-6pm, Wed. 10am-10pm, Sat. 9am-5pm, Sun. 1-6pm. Free.) Nearby is the **Cleveland Museum of Natural History,** Wade Oval (231-4600), where you can see the only skull of the fearsome Pygmy Tyrant *(Nanatyrannus).* (Open Mon.-Sat. 10am-5pm, Sun. 1-5pm. Admission $3.50, seniors and children $1.75, students $1.50. Free Tues. and Thurs.) Also in University

Circle, the renowned **Cleveland Orchestra,** one of the nation's best, performs in Severance Hall, 11001 Euclid Ave. (231-1111. Prices vary.)

Since downtown Cleveland got its multi-million dollar face-lift in 1988, the **Flats,** a restored warehouse district, has become the heart of the city's rock scene and the favorite haunt of thousands of swinging singles. On weekend nights, you can expect huge crowds and lots of traffic jams. Watch the sunset from the outdoor "Beach Bar" at **Fagan's,** 996 Old River Rd. (241-6116), although remodeling has made it an expensive, jet-set experience. (Open daily 11:30am-2am, no cover except for selected bands.) **Peabody's Down Under,** 1059 Old River Rd. (241-0792 or 241-2451), has a younger crowd and plays harder rock. (Open daily 8pm-2:30am. $4-18 cover depending on the band.) Cleveland's much-anticipated Rock & Roll Hall of Fame, designed by I.M. Pei, won't start rockin' until 1992. Until then, you'll have to satisfy yourself with "Hang On, Snoopy" (the official state song), and the city's innovative rock radio stations.

If the crowd you see pouring into downtown doesn't seem to go with Flats nightlife, it's probably coming from **Cleveland Stadium,** home of the Indians baseball team (861-1200) and the Browns football team (696-5555).

In contrast to Cleveland's metropolitan hustle and bustle lie the Amish communities of rural **Holmes County.** Originally Swiss Mennonites, the Amish broke with the main body to create their own sect. Following Jacob Amman, they came to America in 1728 to practice their more austere lifestyle undisturbed. In Ohio, they settled south of Cleveland in rural Holmes, Wayne, and Tuscavaras counties. Outsiders can visit the **Amish Farm** (893-2951) in Berlin. The farm offers a film presentation, demonstrations of non-electrical appliances, and a tour of the grounds. (Open April 1-Nov. 1 Mon.-Sat. 10am-5pm. Tour $2, children $1. Buggy ride $2.50.) Unserved by public transportation, Berlin lies 70 miles south of Cleveland on Rte. 39, 17 pastoral miles west of I-77.

Lake Erie Islands

If you long for the sea, visit the Lake Erie Islands, but make sure you take a car because the ferries cannot be reached by public transportation. "Ohio's scenic playground" is the place to take the kids, the dog, and the mobile home, but not your honeymoon sweetheart. The scenery of the islands takes backstage to the schlocky fun of the amusement park.

Sandusky, on the mainland, is the regional center. The city lies on Rte. 2, 55 miles west of Cleveland and 45 miles southeast of Toledo. Sandusky was once the last stop in the U.S. for escaped slaves fleeing to Canada via the underground railroad. To escape the hum-drum of daily life, visit **Cedar Point** amusement park (627-2350). Take the Ohio Turnpike (I-80) to exit 7 and follow signs north on U.S. 250. (Open daily mid-May to mid-September, usually 9am-10pm; call for daily information. Admission $18.50, seniors $12.75, under 48 inches $10, under 3 free. After 5pm the lines go down, and starlight admission is only $10.50).

Sandusky and the Erie Islands lost their monopoly on U.S. wine production after Prohibition and the Great Depression, but today the area still bubbles and ferments. Each fall, from mid-September through October, the **Erie County Vineyard Days,** an orgy of libations, do Dionysus proud. For more information, contact the **Visitors and Convention Bureau,** 231 W. Washington Row (625-2984; open Mon.-Fri. 7:30am-5pm, Sat. 10am-4pm), or the **Tourist Information Center,** 5510 Milan Rd. (626-5721; open daily Memorial Day-Labor Day 8am-6pm).

Greyhound, 6513 Milan Rd. (625-6907) offers service from Lake Erie Islands to Cleveland ($13.25), Detroit ($24), and Chicago ($48). The **Greyhound Shuttle** runs to downtown Sandusky and Cedar Point ($4).

Cheap accommodations are difficult to find in Ohio's vacationland, especially during summer weekends. Rates are extremely flexible and tend to soar upwards during the peak tourist season, so try to schedule an off-season visit. In Sandusky, try one of the motels east of downtown along Cleveland Rd. The **Tudor Inn Motel,**

2214 Cleveland Rd. (626-0775), sometimes has a cabin for $25. A hundred yards away, **Bayshore Estates RV Park and Campsite,** 2311 Cleveland Rd. (625-7906), has tent sites for $11, with hookup $13. On the northeast side of Marblehead, **Lakeside,** on North Shore Blvd., is one of the last of the Chautauqua villages. This 19th-century Methodist retreat has economy rooms in its **Hotel Lakeside** (798-4461). (Take Rte. 2 to Rte. 163, heading toward the tip of Marblehead. Singles $20-22. Doubles $22-32.50. Grounds admission fee $6.50, children $4.50. Overnight auto pass $1.50, includes free entertainment at the compound's Hoover Auditorium.) **Poor Richard's Inn,** 317 Maple St. (798-5405), is 2 blocks up the street from the Hotel Lakeside. (Singles $18. Doubles $23.) Camping is available here at **Lakeside** (tent sites $7, with hookup $11), or at the **Crystal Rock Campground,** 710 Crystal Rock Rd. (684-7177), on Rte. 250 south of Rte. 2, which offers extensive facilities, including a pool ($15.50, with hookup $19). A couple of miles from the Catawba ferry dock, try the **East Harbor State Park** (734-4424), on Rte 269 off I-65. (Open 24 hours. Tent sites $8.)

Although **Kelleys Island** is the largest American island in Lake Erie, a leisurely bike ride around it takes only about two and a half hours. Near the town on the island's southern shore you can see **Inscription Rock,** a slab of limestone covered with Erie Indian pictographs over four centuries old. On the north shore, somewhat older at 30,000 years, **glacial grooves** gouge the limestone, an impressive 15 feet deep, 35 feet wide, and 400 feet long.

To tour the island, you can rent bicycles from **Kim's** (746-2292) or golf carts from **Popeye's** (746-2551) near the ferry dock on the southwest shore. (Bikes $1.50 per hr., $6 per day; golf carts $8-10 per hr., $25 per half-day.) **Kelleys State Park** (746-2546), on the north shore near the glacial grooves, has tent sites for $6. **Newman Boat Line,** 101 E. Shoreline Dr., Sandusky (626-5557), serves Kelleys Island by ferry. Ferries run more frequently between Kelleys Island and **Marblehead** (798-5800), on the tip of the peninsula just northwest of Sandusky. (April 5-Sept. 2, every hr. dawn to dusk, more frequently depending on the season. Taking your vehicle across can add hours to your wait. One way $3.50, children 6-11 $2, car $6.50, bike $1.)

The **Bass Island chain** extends far into Lake Erie to the west of Kelleys Island. **South Bass,** shaped like an irregular hourglass, is the largest of the three Bass Islands. On South Bass Island, you can camp and swim at **South Bass Island State Park** (285-2112; open 8am-5pm, tent sites $7). **Perry's Victory and International Peace Memorial** is stuck to the hourglass's waist at the town of Put-In-Bay. The world's tallest doric column (352 feet), it was erected to commemorate Commodore Oliver Hazard Perry's monumental victory over the British in the War of 1812. (Open mid-June to Labor Day daily 9am-6pm; late April to mid-June and Labor Day-late Oct. 9am-5pm. Elevator 50¢.) Also located in Put-In-Bay, the **Heineman Winery,** Catawba Ave. (285-2811), gives intimate tours of its grounds, including a look at **Crystal Cave,** one of the world's largest geodes. (Open late May to mid-Sept. Mon.-Sat. 11am-5pm, Sun. noon-5pm. Admission $2.50, children $1.) The **Miller Boat Line** (285-2421) serves Put-In-Bay from Catawba Dock on the mainland. (Ferries mid-May to early Sept. 7am to 7pm on the hr.; more frequently during summer. One-way $3.50, children $1, cars $6.50.)

Miller Boat Line also serves **Middle Bass Island,** just north of South Bass Island. Once there, visit the fortress-like **Lonz Winery** (285-5411) and sample their vintage wines. (Open May 13-Sept. 30; call for more information.)

The **area code** for the islands is 419.

Southern and Central Ohio

The pun about Ohio being round on both ends and high in the middle is hardly accurate. In the southeastern end of the state, Pleistocene glaciers plowed into the land narrow valleys, steep hills, and ragged rock formations currently swathed in dense green forests. **U.S. 50,** running east from Cincinnati to Parkersburg, roughly follows the southern route of the Buckeye Trail.

Along U.S. 50 lie the spectacular Native American burial grounds constructed by the "Moundbuilders," the Adena, Hopewell, and Fort Ancient tribes. Among the most interesting is the **Mound City Group National Monument** (774-1125), on Rte. 104, 3 miles north of Chillicothe. Within a 13-acre area hunch 24 still-mysterious Hopewell burial mounds. The adjoining museum elucidates theories about Hopewell society based on the mounds' configuration. (Monument open daily dawn-dusk. Museum open daily 8am-8pm. Admission $1 or max. $3 per vehicle. Seniors and under 17 free.) Check with park officials for information on other nearby mounds. **Chillicothe** itself merits a visit for the Greek Revival mansions of the northwest territory's first capital.

Ten miles south of Chillicothe off U.S. 23, you can camp at **Scioto Trail State Park** (663-2125; open Mon.-Fri. 8am-11pm. Sites $4, $8 for electricity). Four miles from the bus station is the **Chillicothe Home Hostel** (775-3632 or 773-3989). $4, members only. Reservations are required.

Greyhound, 302 E. Main St. (775-2013), serves Chillicothe from both Cincinnati (via Portsmouth, not U.S. 50; $27.25) and Columbus ($11.25).

About 30 miles east of Chillicothe, U.S. 50 passes near **Hocking Hills State Park,** accessible by Rte. 93 north or 56 west. Rugged terrain filled with waterfalls, gorges, cliffs, and caves make this area the most beautiful in the state. **Ash Cave,** east of South Bloomingville on Rte. 56, gouges 80 acres out of a horseshoe-shaped rock. A trickling stream falls over the edge of this cliff to a pool at the cave entrance. **Cantwell Caves,** southwest of Rockbridge on Rte. 374, is another horseshoe-shaped precipice. Also visit the deep gorge **Cedar Falls, Conkles Hollow,** and **Rock House,** a stone structure stuck perilously in a perpendicular cliff. All of these sights are preserved and run by the state park system. Camp at **Old Man's Cave** (385-6165; sites $7, $10 for electricity; swimming pool available).

The **area code** for this area is 614.

Columbus

In the heart of the state lies **Columbus,** Ohio's capital and most populous city. The downtown area sprawls around the architecturally stellar **state capitol** and **Capitol Square** at Broad and High St. (466-2125; open Mon.-Fri. 8am-4pm, Sat.-Sun. 9am-4:30pm). Downtown is also home to Columbus' two excellent museums. The **Columbus Museum of Art,** 480 E. Broad St. (221-6801), has a fine collection of European masterpieces. (Open Tues.-Fri. 11am-5pm, Sat. 10am-5pm, Sun. 11am-5pm. Admission $3.50, seniors, students, and ages 6-17 $1. Fri. free.) Ohio's **Center of Science and Industry (COSI),** 280 E. Broad St. (228-2674), has hands-on mechanized exhibits. (Open Mon.-Sat. 10am-5pm, Sun. 1-5:30pm. Admission $5, seniors, students, and children $3, families $15.)

If you're hungry, head to **Bernie's Bagels and Deli,** 1896 N. High St. (291-3448), for warm sandwiches ($3.25-4.25). The place resembles a fall-out shelter, but the live gigs make it cozy instead of claustrophobic. For a more airy dining experience, choose from 7000 bottles of wine to accompany the moderately priced Mediterranean cuisine at **A La Carte,** 2333 N. High St. (294-6783). The outdoor tables are particularly popular. (Open Mon.-Thurs. 11:30am-9:30pm, Fri.-Sat. 11:30am-11pm.) Just south of Capitol Square is the **German Village,** first settled in 1843 and now the largest privately funded restored historical area in the U.S. Visitors can tour the stately brick homes and patronize old-style beer halls and restaurants. At **Schmidt's Sausage House,** 240 E. Kossuth St. (444-6808), tap your feet to the nightly live music and order brats and German potato salad. (Open daily 11am-1am.) For information, call the helpful German Village Society, 634 S. 3rd St. (221-8888). (Open Mon.-Fri. 9am-4pm, Sat.-Sun. 11am-3pm.)

Two miles north of downtown Columbus is gargantuan **Ohio State University (OSU),** whose 59,000-plus students support a lively nightlife. Bars and clubs rocks late into the night on **North High Street,** the focus of activity. **Papa Joe's,** 1573

N. High St. (421-7272), is a popular pick-up spot for rowdy underclass students. On Wednesdays, buckets of beer are only $4. (Open daily 11am-2:30am, admission 50¢ Wed.-Sat.) Underage hipsters groove to hard-core rock at **Newport's,** 1722 N. High St. (291-8829), where bands big and small energize a sweaty, dancing crowd (call for cover and admission information).

The beautiful **Heart of Ohio Hostel (AYH),** 95 E. 12th Ave. (294-7157), 1 block from OSU, has outstanding facilities for $6 in the summer, $7 in the winter. Check-in 5-9pm. Rooms in apartment houses near campus are cheap, abundant, and well advertised during the summer, when OSU students leave them vacant. Contact **De Santis Properties** (291-7368; 451-8715 evenings). Downtown accommodations are much more expensive.

Visitors to the city can contact the **Greater Columbus Convention and Visitors Bureau,** 10 W. Broad St., #1300 (221-6623 or 800-821-5784). Open Mon.-Fri. 8am-5pm. **Greyhound,** 111 E. Town St. (221-5311), offers the most frequent and complete service from downtown Columbus to Cincinnati ($21), Cleveland ($22), and Chicago ($56). Public transportation in the city is run by the **Central Ohio Transit Authority (COTA),** 177 S. High St. (228-1776). (Open Mon.-Fri. 8:30am-5:30pm. Fare 75¢, express $1, transfers 10¢.)

The **Area code** for Columbus is 614. The **ZIP code** is 43016.

Cincinnati

Longfellow called it the "Queen City of the West." In the 1850s, less romantic folk nicknamed it "Porkopolis," a tribute to its position as the world's largest pork-packing center. As a legacy of this era, winged pigs guard the entrance of the city's **Sawyer Point Park** downtown. Though swine no longer snort through the streets and the West has since expanded to the Pacific, Cincinnati still combines cosmopolitan charm with pig-in-a-poke comfort.

Mark Twain purportedly claimed that if the world suddenly stopped dead, it would take Cincinnati 20 years to figure it out. Snuggled in a valley surrounded by seven rolling hills and the Ohio River, downtown Cincinnati is much more reminiscent of an old-fashioned town square than of an urban center—but this is mostly because the streets are so clean and the people so friendly. 1988 witnessed the opening of spanking new buildings, parks, and plazas during the city's year-long bicentennial birthday party.

Practical Information

Emergency: 0.

Visitor Information: Cincinnati Convention and Visitors Bureau, 300 W. 6th St. (621-2142). Pick up an *Official Visitors Guide*. Open Mon.-Fri. 9am-5pm. **Info Line,** 421-4636. Lists plays, opera, cruises, and symphonies.

Airport: Greater Cincinnati International Airport, in Covington, KY, directly across the river. The **Jetport Express** (283-3702) shuttles passengers to downtown (about $8).

Amtrak: 1901 River Rd. (579-8506, 921-4172, or 800-872-7245). To Indianapolis ($28) and Chicago ($56).

Greyhound: 1005 Gilbert Ave. (352-6000), just past the intersection of E. Court and Broadway. To: Indianapolis ($23), Louisville, KY ($19), and Cleveland ($36). Open 24 hours.

Queen City Metro: 6 E. 4th St. (621-4455). Downtown office has bus schedules and information. Telephone information Mon.-Fri. 6:30am-7pm, Sat.-Sun. 8am-5pm. Most buses run out of Government Sq. at 5th and Main St., to outlying communities. Peak fare 65¢, other times 50¢, weekends 35¢.

Taxi: Yellow Cab, 241-2100. Base fare $1.50, about $1.20 per mile.

Weather Line: 241-1010.

Post Office: 122 W. 5th St. (684-5664), between Walnut and Vine St. Open Mon.-Fri. 8:30am-5pm, Sat. 8am-noon. **ZIP code:** 45202.

Area Code: 513.

Cincinnati is in southwestern Ohio, 78 miles due north of Lexington, KY and 100 miles southeast of Indianapolis.

Fountain Square, E. 5th at Vine St., is the focal point of the downtown business community. Cross streets are numbered and designated East or West, with Vine Street as the divider. The **Riverfront Stadium,** the **Serpentine Wall,** and the **Riverwalk** are down by the river. The University of Cincinnati spreads out from Clifton, north of the city. Overlooking downtown from the east, **Mt. Adams,** adjoining Eden Park, harbors some of Cincinnati's active nightlife.

Accommodations and Camping

Cincinnati has many motels, but most of the cheap places are outside the heart of the city. Cars and reservations are recommended, especially on nights of Reds baseball games and on weekends. Campgrounds are also a long way out of town.

Cincinnati Youth Hostel, 2200 Maplewood Ave. (651-5537). Singles around $8.

College of Mount St. Joseph, 5701 Delhi Pike (244-4327), about 8 miles west of downtown off Rte. 50. Immaculate rooms in a quiet, though remote location. Excellent facilities. Singles $15. Doubles $20. Cafeteria lunch $3, dinner $4.

Evandale Motel, 10165 Reading Rd. (563-1570), ½ hr. from downtown. Small, dark, but clean rooms. Singles and doubles $23.

Red Roof Inn, 5300 Kennedy Ave. (531-6589), off I-71 at Ridge Rd. Run-of-the-mill basics from the national chain. Singles $34. Doubles $42.

Ohio Valley Bed and Breakfast, 6876 Taylor Mills Rd., Independence, KY (606-356-7865). Singles and doubles in a variety of area homes $30-55. Call well in advance for reservations.

Camp Shore Campgrounds, Rte. 56, Aurora, IN (812-438-2135), 30 miles west of Cincinnati on the Ohio River. Tent sites with hookup $11.

Rose Gardens Resort-KOA Campgrounds, I-75 exit 166 (606-428-2000), 30 miles south of Cincinnati. Award-winning landscaping. Tent sites $15. Cabins $22, including water and electricity. Make reservations.

Food

The city that gave us the first soap opera and the first baseball franchise presents as its great culinary contribution **Cincinnati chili.** To the usual meat and beans, locals add your choice of spaghetti, onions, and cheese, often with a hot dog to boot, all for about $2.50. With few exceptions, natives swear by the abundant fast-food chains **Gold Star Chili, Skyline,** and **Empress.**

Camp Washington Chili, Hopple and Colerain Ave. (541-0061), 1 block west of I-95 at Hopple. A legendary greasy spoon. CBS called it the best chili in the country. Open Mon.-Sat. 24 hours, Sun. 10am-6pm.

Izzy's, 819 Elm St. (721-4241), also at 9th St. downtown and 610 Main St. (241-6246). A Cincinnati institution founded in 1901. Izzy has passed away, but his tradition of good-natured insults endures. Overstuffed kosher sandwiches with potato pancake $2.85-4. Izzy's famous reuben $4.45. Open Mon.-Fri. 7am-5pm, Sat. 7am-4pm.

Montgomery Inn, 9440 Montgomery Rd. (791-3482), east off I-71, exit 12. Few customers would contest their boast of the world's best ribs. Friendly family atmosphere. Ribs $10-13. Open Mon.-Thurs. 11am-11pm, Fri. 11am-midnight, Sat. 4pm-midnight, Sun. 4-9:30pm.

Graeter's, 41 E. 4th St. (381-0653), downtown and 11 other locations. Since 1870, Graeter's has dished out fresh ice cream with giant chocolate chips. Medium cone $1.45. Open Mon.-Sat. 7:30am-6pm.

Findlay Market, 18th at Elm St. (352-3282), downtown. Produce and picnic items $3-5. Open Wed. 7am-1:30pm, Fri. 7am-6pm, Sat. 6am-6pm.

Sights and Events

Downtown Cincinnati is focused around the **Tyler Davidson Fountain,** the ideal spot to people-watch while you feign admiration of the gorgeous architecture. If you squint your eyes, you can almost see Les Nesman rushing to WKRP to deliver the daily hog report. Check out the expansive gardens and daring design at **Procter and Gamble Plaza,** just east of Fountain Square, or walk along **Fountain Square South,** a shopping and business complex connected by a series of second-floor skywalks. If the visual stimuli exhaust you, perk up your ears for a free concert in front of the fountain. The **Downtown Council,** 120 W. 5th St. (241-9000) has more information. (Open Mon.-Fri. 8:30am-5pm.)

Close to Fountain Square, the controversial **Contemporary Arts Center,** 115 E. 5th St., 2nd floor (721-0390), by Walnut, changes its exhibits frequently and offers evening films, music, and multi-media performances. (Open Mon.-Sat. 10am-6pm. Admission $2, seniors and students $1; Mon. free.)

The **Cincinnati Zoo,** 3400 Vine St. and Forest Ave. (281-4700) can be reached by car (take Dana Ave. or exit 6 off I-75, Dana Ave. off I-71), or by bus (#78 or 49 from Vine and 5th St.) *Newsweek* called it one of the world's "sexiest zoos." The lush greenery and cageless habitats evidently encourage the zoo's gorillas and famous white Bengal tigers to reproduce enthusiastically. (Open in summer daily 9am-8pm, entrance closes at 6pm; rest of the year daily 9am-6pm, entrance closes at 5pm. Admission $5.25, seniors and children under 12 $2.)

On a cliff overlooking downtown from the east, the Mt. Adams/Eden Park area gives Cincinnati a bit of bohemian charm. Shaded by the trees of Eden Park, the **Cincinnati Art Museum** (721-5204) features a permanent art collection spanning 5000 years, as well as exceptional exhibits of musical instruments and Middle Eastern artifacts. (Open Tues.-Sat. 10am-5pm, Sun. 1-5pm. Admission $2, seniors $1, students $1.50; Sat. free. Take bus #49 to Eden Park Dr. By car, follow Gilbert Ave. northeast from downtown.) Step into a tropical rain forest in the **Krohn Conservatory** (352-4086), one of the largest public greenhouses in the world. (Open daily 10am-5pm. Suggested donation $1.50, seniors and children under 15 $1.) The **Taft Museum,** 316 Pike St. (241-0343), downtown, has a beautiful collection of painted enamels, as well as pieces by Rembrandt and Whistler. (Open Mon.-Sat. 10am-5pm, Sun. 2-5pm. Suggested donation $2, seniors and students $1.)

On the west side of town, the **Union Terminal,** 1031 Western Ave. (241-7257), near the Ezzard Charles Dr. exit off I-75 (take bus #1), is a fine example of art deco architecture. It also has the world's highest unsupported dome. Renovations have closed the terminal museum until 1991.

Procter and Gamble offers good, clean fun on its tours of its home plant, **Ivorydale,** 5201 Spring Grove Ave. (721-8230), accessible from 75N exit left on Mitchell Ave. Watch the world's largest soap manufacturer at work, learn a little about the history of American industry, and pick up a free gift pack. (Tours Tues.-Thurs. Reservations required.)

Cincinnati is fanatical about sports. The **Reds** baseball team (421-7337) and the **Bengals** football team (621-3550) both play in **Riverfront Stadium.** The **Riverfront Coliseum** (241-1818), a Cincinnati landmark, hosts other sports events and major concerts year-round. During the second week of July **Summerfair** (800-582-5804), a large annual art festival, is held at **Coney Island** (232-8230).

Outdoor roller skating is the craze at the **Riverwalk** by the **Serpentine Wall,** and free summer concerts are held at the **Pavilion.** The area was totally revamped for the bicentennial. At the new **Bicentennial Commons,** a timeline of Ohio history and exquisite recreational facilities span about a mile. Even those who have graduated from jungle gym days should go for a bounce on the rubber floor. If you are in town for Labor Day, get early seats for **Riverfest,** one of the nation's largest fireworks displays.

Entertainment and Nightlife

The cliff-hanging communities that line the steep streets of Mt. Adams also support a vivacious arts and entertainment industry. Perched on its own wooded hill is the **Playhouse in the Park,** 962 Mt. Adams Circle (421-3888), a theater-in-the-round remarkably adaptable to many styles of drama. The regular season runs October to June, with cabaret in the summer. Accessible to the vision and hearing impaired. (Tickets $10-25.50, student rush tickets $8.50.)

For a drink and a voyage back to the 19th century, try **Arnold's,** 210 E. 8th St. (421-6234), Cincinnati's oldest tavern, between Main St. and Sycamore, downtown. After 9pm, traditional jazz, ragtime, and swing are served along with sandwiches ($4-5) and dinners ($6-10). (Open Mon.-Fri. 11am-10pm, Sat. 5-10pm.) Peruse the antique toys inside or listen to jazz and blues in the courtyard at **Blind Lemon,** 936 Hatch St., Mt. Adams (241-3885), at St. Gregory St. Draft beer $1.90. (Open Mon.-Fri. 4pm-2:30am, Sat. 6:30pm-2:30am, Sun. 3pm-2:30am. Music at 9:30pm.) The **City View Tavern,** 403 Oregon St., Mt. Adams (241-8439), is a self-proclaimed dive. A notice in the bar reads, "No California Coolers, no Perrier, no cute drinks." The deck in back overlooks the panorama of glittering downtown towers. Local draft beer 90¢. (Open Mon.-Fri. 11:30am-1am, Sat. 1pm-1am, Sun. 2-11pm.)

The University of Cincinnati's **Conservatory of Music** (556-9430) often gives free classical and experimental concerts. Slightly more upscale, the **Music Hall,** 1241 Elm St. (721-8222), by Ezzard Charles Dr., has wonderful acoustics. The **Cincinnati Symphony Orchestra** (621-1919) performs here September to May. (Tickets $7-32. Discounted rush tickets 10 min. before the performance.) Other companies performing at the Music Hall are the **Cincinnati Opera** (241-2742; limited summer productions; tickets $7-32) and the **Cincinnati Ballet Company** (621-5219; Sept.-May; tickets $6-42). For updates, call **Dial the Arts** (751-2787).

Near Cincinnati

If you can't get to California's Napa or Sonoma Valleys, the next best thing may be **Meiers Wine Cellars,** 6955 Plainfield Pike (891-2900). I-71 to exit 12 or I-75 to Galbraith Rd. Free tours of Ohio's oldest and largest winery allow you to observe the entire wine-making operation and taste its goods. (Free tours Memorial Day-Oct. 31 Mon.-Sat.; Nov.-May 10am-3pm by appointment only.)

In Mason, 24 miles north of Cincinnati off I-71 at exit #24, the amusement park **Kings Island** (241-5600) ranks just behind the Disney parks in size, and is home of The Beast, reputedly the world's fastest and highest roller coaster. Admission entitles you to unlimited rides and attractions, but emphatically not the food. Pack a picnic or a very thick wallet. Lines diminish after dark. (Open Memorial Day-Labor Day Sun.-Fri. 9am-10pm, Sat. 9am-11pm. Admission $19.)

Wisconsin

The state that calls itself "America's Dairyland" is also one of the nation's most popular playlands, with forests, rivers, and lakes to suit the tenacious and the tenderfoot alike. Wisconsin residents take up the fun where the wilderness leaves off. Here you can enjoy such diverse pleasures as a Madeline Island fishboil, one of Milwaukee's ethnic festivals, or, in the state capital, the annual march to legalize marijuana.

Practical Information

Capital: Madison.

Tourist Information: Division of Tourism, P.O. Box 7606, Madison 53707 (266-2161, 266-6797, or 800-372-2737).

Time Zone: Central (1 hr. behind Eastern). **Postal Abbreviation:** WI.

Milwaukee

One of Milwaukee's original trademarks was *gemutlichkeit*—hospitality. Though the Teutonic culture has long been diffused by an international array of immigrants, including Italians, Irish, Poles, and Hispanics, the city now welcomes more travelers than ever to its beautiful lakefront. For the visitor, the best part of Milwaukee may be its vital ethnic communities—during the summer, one of them throws a city-wide party every weekend. The self-proclaimed "City of Fabulous Festivals" has whatever you're looking for—whether it's beer 'n' brats, baklava, or bagpipes.

Practical Information

Emergency: Police, 749 W. State St. (765-2323).

Visitor Information: Greater Milwaukee Convention and Visitors Bureau, 756 N. Milwaukee St. (273-3950), downtown. Open Mon.-Fri. 8:30am-5pm. Also at the airport (open daily 7am-7pm) and Grand Avenue Mall (open Mon.-Fri. 10am-8pm, Sat.-Sun. 10am-4pm). Pick up a copy of *The Greater Milwaukee Dining and Visitors Guide.* **Fun Line** (799-1177) and **Rockline** (276-7625) give local entertainment information. Both 24 hours.

Travelers Aid: 3517 W. Burleigh and the airport (873-1521). Open Mon.-Thurs. 9am-5pm, Fri. 9am-4pm.

Amtrak: 433 W. St. Paul Ave. (933-3081 or 800-872-7245), at 5th St., 3 blocks from the bus terminal. To Chicago ($14.50). Open Mon.-Fri. 6am-9pm, Sat.-Sun. 6am-9pm.

Buses: Greyhound, 606 N. 7th St. (272-8900), off W. Michigan St. downtown. Open 24 hours. To: Chicago ($13) and Madison ($5.85). **Wisconsin Coach,** Greyhound terminal (542-8861). To outlying areas of Wisconsin. Open 6am-9pm. **Badger Bus,** 608-255-6773, across the street. Runs to Madison (6 per day, $6).

Milwaukee County Transit System, 1942 N. 17th St. (344-6711). Efficient service in metro area. Most lines run 5:30am to the wee hours. Fare $1, seniors 50¢.

Car Rental: Suburban Car Rental, 4939 S. Howell (482-0300), across from Mitchell airport. $23 per day. 150 free miles, 15¢ each additional mile. $10 collision insurance. Open Mon.-Fri. 7:30am-6pm, Sat. 9am-5pm, Sun. noon-9pm. Must be 21 with liability insurance and major credit card.

Auto Transport Company: Auto Driveaway Co., 9039 W. National Ave. (962-0008), W. Alice. Open Mon.-Fri. 9am-5pm, Sat. 9am-noon. Must be 21 with a good driving record.

Help Lines: Crisis Intervention Center, 257-7222. 24 hours. **Rape Crisis Line,** 278-4617. **Gay People's Union Hotline,** 562-7010.

Post Office: 345 W. St. Paul Ave. (287-2530), south along 4th Ave. from downtown, next to the Amtrak station. **ZIP code:** 53201.

Area Code: 414.

Wisconsin's largest city occupies about 15 miles of the shore of **Lake Michigan** in the southeastern corner of the state. It lies 90 miles north of Chicago, 80 miles east of Madison on I-94, and 340 miles east of Minneapolis on I-90/94. The downtown area is a few miles back from the lakeshore. The city's grid pattern is broken by the **Milwaukee River,** flowing north-south just east of downtown and dividing streets east-west.

Accommodations and Camping

Sleeping is rarely cheap in downtown Milwaukee. There are, however, three hostels nearby, including the small **Halter Home Hostel (AYH),** 2956 N. 77th St. (258-7692; members only, $5; take bus #57 to 76th and Center St.) and two larger, attractive hostels.

Tyme Out II Hostel (AYH), 3680 S. Kinnickinnic (769-2680 or 483-5706), in South Milwaukee. Take bus #15 5 miles south to Crawford and Kinnickinnic. Run by a friendly group of nuns on the beautiful grounds of a Catholic seminary, convent, and retreat center along Lake Michigan. $8. Great breakfast $2. Reservations required. Open June-Aug.

Red Barn Youth Hostel (AYH), 6750 W. Loomis Rd. (529-3299), 13 miles southwest of downtown Milwaukee via Rte. 894, exit Loomis. Take bus #10 or 30 westbound on Wisconsin Ave., then get off at 35th St. to take the #35 southbound to the Loomis and Ramsey intersection; cross over to Pick and Save store and walk ¾ mile. Rustic, slightly dark rooms. Friendly houseparents. $5, nonmembers $8. Open May-Oct.

University of Wisconsin at Milwaukee (UWM): Sandburg Halls, 3400 N. Maryland Ave. (229-4065). Take bus #30 north to Hartford St. Look for tall stone building. Private rooms are part of suites. Laundry, cafeteria available. Singles with shared bath $20. Doubles $25-35. Open May 31-Aug. 15.

Hotel Wisconsin, 720 N. 3rd St. (271-4900), across from the Grand Avenue Mall. 250 pleasant, if shabby, rooms. Very clean bathrooms. Convenient downtown location. Singles $42. Doubles $48. Key deposit $3. Phone deposit $2.

Motel 6, 5037 S. Howell Ave. (482-4414), near the airport. Take bus #80 southbound at the corner of 6th and Wisconsin; get off at Edgerton and Howell. Outdoor pool. Singles $29. Doubles $30. Fills quickly.

State Fairgrounds (257-8800), Madison exit off I-94 west, then 84th St. to the fairgrounds. No tents, only RVs. Often noisy. Sites $12. Gets very full for the State Fair (early Aug.).

Country View Campgrounds, S. Craig Rd., 4 miles west of Big Bend (662-3654), a 40-min. drive southwest. Take Rte. 15, exit at Hwy. F, turn left to reach Big Bend, turn right on Rte. 24, drive 4 miles, and then turn right onto Craig. Tent sites for 2 $14, full hookup $16. Each additional adult $7, each additional family member $3.

Food

Milwaukee is not for dainty eaters—prices here are small, and portions are big. The bohemian **Brady Street** area to the north has many Italian restaurants, and the **South Side** is heavily Polish. Many students and young professionals have lunch at the **Grand Avenue Mall's** third floor, which is a huge **Speisegarten** ("meal garden") of reasonable ethnic and fast food places. **East Side** eateries are a little more cosmopolitan, often serving cappuccino in place of *kielbasa.* The UWM cafeteria, on the main floor of the student union, offers good, cheap food.

Kalt's, 2856 N. Oakland (332-6323), at Locust, on the East Side. German beer mugs hang everywhere. Lunch $2.50-5.50, dinner $7.25-12.25. Live comedy Thurs.-Sun. at 7:30pm, additional show Fri.-Sat. at 10pm. Admission $7. Call Comedy Sportz (962-8888) for reservations. Free hors d'oeuvres Mon.-Fri. 3-6pm. Open Mon. 4pm-midnight, Tues.-Thurs. 11am-1am, Fri.-Sat. 11am-2am, Sun. 3pm-midnight.

Webster's Bookstore and Cafe, 2559 Downer St. (332-1719), at Webster Place on the East Side. French-American café hangout for would-be poets. Try the *croque monsieur* (ham 'n' cheese croissant; $4.50), or the soufflé pizza ($3.85). Outdoor seating, great bookstore, and friendly staff. Open Mon.-Sat. 7am-midnight, Sun. 8am-5pm.

Abu's Jerusalem of the Gold, 1978 N. Farwell (277-0485), at Lafayette on the East Side. A poem dedicated to Abu on the wall, exotic tapestries, and plenty of kitsch adorn this tiny, corner restaurant. Try the rosewater lemonade. Plenty of veggie entrees, including felafel sandwich ($2.25) and kebab dinner ($6.50). Open Mon.-Thurs. 11:30am-9pm, Fri. 11:30am-2am, Sat. 11:30am-4am, Sun. 1:30-9pm.

Albanese's, 701 E. Keefe Ave. (964-7270), on the East Side, 3 blocks west of Humboldt. Generous portions of homemade Italian food (pasta dishes $5-5.75). Open Mon.-Thurs. 11:30am-1:30pm and 5:30-10:30pm, Fri. 11:30am-1:30pm and 5:30-11:30pm, Sat. 5:30-11:30pm, Sun. 5-9:30pm.

Sights

Historic Milwaukee, Inc., P.O. Box 2132 (277-7795), offers tours focusing on ethnic heritage, original settlements, and architecture ($2-3). Ask about Milwaukee's many beautiful churches, including **St. Josaphat's Basilica,** 2336 S. 6th St.

(645-5623), a turn-of-the-century landmark with a dome larger than the Taj Mahal's.

Riverwest is an integrated neighborhood where activists and workers rub shoulders. The **Woodland Pattern Book Center,** 720 E. Locust (263-5001), has a large selection of small press publications. The center also sponsors poetry readings, lectures, and gallery shows that attract local and national artists.

If the center doesn't satisfy your craving for art, turn to one of Milwaukee's excellent museums. The **Milwaukee Public Museum,** 800 W. Wells St. (278-2700), at the corner of N. 8th St., has incredibly realistic exhibits of the streets of Old Milwaukee, a European village, Native American settlements, and world wildlife. (Open daily 9am-5pm. Admission $3, under 17 $1.50.) The **Milwaukee Art Museum,** in the War Memorial Building, 750 N. Lincoln Memorial Dr. (271-9508), on the lakefront, houses a diverse collection of Haitian art, 19th-century German art, and American sculpture and paintings. (Open Tues.-Wed. and Fri.-Sat. 10am-5pm, Thurs. noon-9pm, Sun. noon-5pm. Admission $3, seniors, students, and the disabled $1.50.) Visit the **Villa Terrace,** 2220 N. Terrace Ave. (271-3656), an Italian-style villa, now a decorative arts museum on the East Side. (Open Wed.-Sun. 1-5pm. Free.) Also try the large and picturesque **Bradley Sculpture Garden,** 2145 Brown Deer Rd. (271-9509; 276-6840 to schedule a tour; tours Mon.-Wed. and Fri. 9am-1pm, Thurs. 1-5pm; admission with scheduled tour group $2.50, students $1.50, seniors and children $1; personal guide $1 extra.) The **Charles Allis Art Museum,** 1801 N. Prospect Ave. (278-8295), is an English Tudor mansion with a fine collection of Chinese, Japanese, Korean, Persian, Greek, and Roman artifacts, American and European period furniture, Barbazon paintings, and Renaissance bronzes. (Open Thurs.-Sun. 1-5pm, Wed. 1-5pm and 7-9pm. Free. Take bus #30.) The **Mitchell Park Conservatory,** 524 S. Layton Blvd. (649-9800), at 27th St., better known as "The Domes," is a series of three seven-story conical glass domes containing a desert, a rain forest, and seasonal displays. (Open daily 9am-5pm. Admission $2.50, seniors $1.25, under 18 and the disabled $1. Take bus #27.) Nearby, you'll find the **Milwaukee County Zoo,** 10001 W. Bluemound Rd. (771-3040), where zebras and cheetahs roam together in the only prey-predator exhibit in U.S. Also look for the black rhinos and the trumpeter swans (*not* together in the same exhibit). (Open Mon.-Sat. 9am-5pm, Sun. 9am-6pm; shorter hours in winter. Admission $4.50, under 12 $2.50. Parking $3. Take bus #10.)

Beer made Milwaukee famous, so be cultured and tour a brewery. The **Miller Brewery,** 4521 W. State St. (931-2467), offers free one-hour tours with free samples. (3 tours per hour 10am-3:30pm. Must be 21.)

Events and Entertainment

During almost any weekend in summer, there is a city-wide party or ethnic festival on the lakefront in Milwaukee. One of the best is the lakefront **Summerfest,** held over 11 days in late June and early July, a potpourri of musical performances, culinary specialties from 30 restaurants, and an arts and crafts marketplace. There's also a circus watershow and a children's theater. (Admission $6 in advance.) For more information on Summerfest and dozens of other festivals, call 273-3378. The **Rainbow Summer** is a series of free, lunchtime concerts throughout the summer, featuring jazz, bluegrass and country music. Concerts are held weekdays at 1:15pm in the Peck Pavilion (see below). Milwaukeeans line the streets for **The Great Circus Parade** (273-7877), an authentic recreation of turn-of-the-century processions, with performing animals, daredevils, costumed performers, and 75 original wagons. (Call their office for information on special weekend packages at local hotels and motels during the parade.) In early August the **Wisconsin State Fair** (257-8800) rolls into town and totes big-name entertainment, 12 stages, exhibits, contests, rides, fireworks, and, of course, a pie-baking contest. (Admission $4, under 11 free.)

If you're looking for entertainment on a strict budget, Milwaukee's colleges and universities can satisfy you with films, concerts, lectures, theater, and exhibits. Call the **Marquette University Information Center** (288-7250; open Mon.-Fri. 9am-9pm and Sat. noon-8pm; 224-7115 24 hours) or the **University of Wisconsin-Milwaukee Union** (229-4825).

The modern white stone **Performing Arts Center (PAC),** 929 N. Water St., across the river from Père Marquette Park (800-472-4458), hosts the Milwaukee Symphony Orchestra, First Stage Milwaukee, Ballet Company, and the Florentine Opera Company. (Tickets $10-30.) The stone and ivy building across the river from the PAC is the **Milwaukee County Historical Center,** 910 N. 3rd St. (273-8288; open Mon.-Fri. 9:30am-5pm, Sat. 10am-5pm, Sun. 1-5pm; free). **Skylight Comic Opera,** 813 N. Jefferson, at E. Wells St. (271-8815) specializes in contemporary and classic opera. (Box-office open Mon.-Fri. noon-6pm and ½ hr. before shows. Tickets $5, seniors and students $4.)

Nightlife

If you've got the time, Milwaukee has the bars. By some estimates, there are over 6000 of them here—about one for every 100 Milwaukeans. Downtown bars are more accessible to tourists, but more expensive. For lower prices and less hype, head east to the campus area. (Downtown pitchers $4-4.50, mixed drinks $1.75-2; campus area, pitchers $2-4.50, mixed drinks $1.35.)

If you're downtown, come in from the cold to **Safehouse,** 779 N. Front St. (271-2007). Enter through a bookcase passage and leave through a telephone booth. A brass plate labeled "International Exports, Ltd." marks the entrance. Draft beer $1.25, simple dinners $4-5. (Open Mon.-Thurs. 11:30am-1:30am, Sat. 11:30am-3am, Sun. 5pm-1:30am. Cover $1-2 on weekends.) For British drinking fun, dip inside **John Hawk's Pub,** 607 N. Broadway (562-2137; open daily 11am-2am, live jazz Fri.-Sat. at 9:30pm).

The college crowd dances at **Bermudas,** 500 N. Water (765-0891), at Clybourn, 1 block from Broadway, downtown. (Open Tues.-Thurs. 8pm-2am, Fri.-Sat. 8pm-2:30am. Cover Thurs.-Sat. $1-2.) Nearby is the **Stackner Cabaret,** 108 E. Wells (272-1994), in Milwaukee Center. Here the Milwaukee Repertory Theater puts on shows for dinner crowds from September through May. (Entrees $9.50-12.50, tickets $7-9.50.) For live, no-frills entertainment, go to the **Odd Rock Cafe,** 2010 S. Kinnickinnic (483-7625). Chain link fence replaces walls in this energized music den. (Open Sun.-Thurs. 8pm-2am, Fri.-Sat. 8pm-2:30am. Cover up to $2.)

On the East Side, North Avenue has a string of campus bars. **Von Trier's,** 2235 N. Farwell (272-1775), at North, is the nicest. Don't miss the ceiling mural of the town of Trier. No pitchers—strictly bottled imports in a lavish German interior or on the large outdoor patio. Bottles average $2.75. **Hooligan's,** at 2017 North Ave. (273-5230), a block or so south, is smaller, louder, and rowdier. (Live music on Mon. starts at 9:30pm. Cover $2-4.) **RC's,** 1530 E. North (273-1100), next to McDonald's a few blocks down, is younger, preppier, and slightly more expensive. (Pitchers $4.) **Judge's Irish Pub,** 1431 E. North (224-0605), across the street, has a better mix of people, a tented beer garden (pitchers $3.75-6), and Friday fish fry (11am-8pm, $4.50).

Madison

In the predominantly conservative Midwest, Madison is famous for the liberal attitudes that flourish in Wisconsin's intellectual and political center. Despite the city's drift away from hippiedom, the mixture of punkers, frat boys, socialists, and Bible-thumping fundamentalists spices up life on the isthmus encompassing the downtown/university area. Four sparkling lakes, wide, bike-safe streets, a huge University Arboretum, and over 150 city parks take the edge off urban life in this capital city.

Practical Information

Emergency: Police, 211 S. Carroll St. (266-7422).

Visitor Information: Greater Madison Convention and Visitors Bureau, 425 W. Washington Ave. (255-0701). Open Mon.-Fri. 8am-5pm. **State of Wisconsin Tourist Information Center,** 123 W. Washington St. (266-6797 or 800-372-2737), a few blocks from the visitors bureau and 1 block from the capitol. Open Mon.-Fri. 7:45am-4:30pm. **Campus assistance,** 420 N. Lake St. (263-2400), near State St. Open Mon.-Fri. 8am-8pm, Sat. 10am-2pm. (Longer weekend hours during the school year.) **Gay-Lesbian Center,** 257-7575. 24-hour recording. **Madison Telefun Line,** 256-6222. 24 hours. **Coliseum Concerts,** 271-7625. 24 hours.

Dane County Airport: 4000 International Lane (246-3380), in the northeast corner of town, about a 20-min. drive from campus. Badger Cab to campus $5-6. The "Burr Oaks" bus is only 75¢, but with suitcases it's a long walk to the Packer Ave. bus stop.

Buses: Greyhound, 931 E. Main St. (257-9511), off E. Washington, 10 blocks from the capitol. Open daily 7am-6pm, sporadically late at night, but always 15 min. before buses leave or arrive. To: Milwaukee ($5.85), Green Bay ($19), and Minneapolis ($34). **Badger Bus,** 2 S. Bedford (255-6771), at W. Washington Ave. Open 7am-10pm. Regular runs to Milwaukee only (6 per day, 1½ hr., $6). Usually faster than Greyhound. **Jen Calder Bus,** 217 S. Hamilton (255-0525). Main office a few blocks southeast of the capitol, but call to find convenient on-campus ticket stops. $14 trips "directly to your airline" at Chicago's O'Hare Airport. Buses leave 5am-6pm 9 times per day; buses at 8:30pm available on Fri. and Sun.

Local transit: Madison Metropolitan Bus Transit (MMTA), (266-4466). Excellent system, efficient service to all parts of the city. All buses eventually converge on Capitol Sq., at the top of State St. Buses operate daily 6am-11pm. Fare 75¢, students 45¢. **Women's Transit Authority,** 263-1700. Offers free, safe rides for women. Sept.-April 7pm-2am; May-Aug. 8pm-2am. Service prompt in an emergency; otherwise, expect a 1- to 2-hr. wait.

Taxi: Badger Cab, 256-5566. Ride-share system with $1.50 base fare, additional 50¢ per zone. Greyhound to the UW campus about $2. **Union Cab,** 256-4400. From Greyhound to UW campus $3-4, airport to campus $8-9.

Car Rental: Ajax Car Rental, 1601 W. Beltline Hwy. (271-5008). $26 per day with 100 free miles, 15¢ each additional mile; $55 weekend rate with 200 free miles. Must be 21.

Bike Rental: Budget Bicycle Center, 1202 Regent St. at Charter St. (251-8413). $6 per day, $11 per weekend, $18 per week. Free tour maps. Open Mon.-Fri. 10am-8pm, Sat. 10am-7pm, Sun. 1-5pm.

Help Lines: Rape Crisis, 251-7273. 24 hours. **Gay Crisis Line,** 255-4297. 9am-6pm.

Post Office: 3902 Milwaukee St. (246-1287). 15-min. bus ride from downtown on the "Buckeye" bus. Open Mon. 8:30am-7pm, Tues.-Fri. 8:30am-5pm, Sat. 9:30am-1pm. 24-hour pickup in the lobby. **ZIP code:** 53714.

Area Code: 608.

U.S. 12 surrounds Madison to the south and west; I-90/94 comes around on the north and east. U.S. 151 intersects both and runs into Washington St., which goes downtown. Madison overflows from a narrow isthmus between large **Lake Mendota** on the northwest and small **Lake Monona** on the southeast. Most sights are on the isthmus. **State Street** is a tree-lined pedestrian concourse that runs from the capitol towards the student union, the cultural center of the city. Madison is a cyclist-oriented city, complete with bike traffic lights and bike cops.

Accommodations and Camping

There are several reasonably priced accommodations in Madison, but rooms are often booked, even on weeknights; try to make advance reservations. Inexpensive motels are located almost exclusively off U.S. 12 near its intersection with I-90/94.

University of Wisconsin dorms: Six hotel rooms in the **Memorial Union,** 800 Langdon (262-1583), overlooking Lake Mendota. 14 rooms at **Union South,** 255 N. Randall St. (263-2600), near the football stadium. Nice, comfortable, convenient. Singles $41. Doubles $45. **Lowell Hall** (262-4395 or 256-2621) and **Friedrick Center,** 1950 Willow Dr. (231-1341), have convention-style rooms for $31-36. **Short Course,** 1450 Linden Dr. (262-1234), has standard dorm rooms. Singles $15. Doubles $22. Dorms available mid-March to Sept. for those who have a legitimate reason to visit campus. (Visiting friends at UW qualifies.) Reserve by phone.

University YMCA (AYH), 306 N. Brooks St. (257-2534), right beside the UW campus. From the Greyhound station, turn left on Main St. and walk 2 blocks to bus stop; all local buses here go to University Ave. Get off at N. Brooks St. and walk left. Room for 4 men and 4 women in run-down, dingy dorms. Houseparent won't answer AYH questions until check-in, 7pm-6am. $8, will accept nonmembers (same price) if there is room.

YWCA, 101 E. Mifflin (257-1436), at Capitol Sq. and Rickney, 11 blocks from Greyhound Station; turn left onto Main St. and walk 2 blocks to the bus stop. Take any bus to Capitol Sq. Women only. Clean, pleasant rooms. No male visitors except relatives. Singles $16, with bath $19.

Lake Kegonsa State Park (873-9695), about 15 miles southeast of Madison off U.S. 51. Attractive tent sites $12.75 for non-WI residents (park admission $6, camping fee $6.75). Open April-Nov.

Babcock County Park (246-3896), just 5-10 min. out to Kegonsa in the town of MacFarland, by Lake Waubesa. Not as big or beautiful as Kegonsa, but has showers, flush toilets, and a nearby laundromat. $10, electricity included. Open May-Nov.

Madison KOA (846-4528), 11 miles north off I-94 (exit 126). More of an RV park, with no shade and lots of gravel. Tent sites $13 for 2, trailer $15.50; each with full hookup. Each additional person $1. Open April 15-Nov. 1.

Food and Entertainment

At lunchtime, carts selling fresh cherries, ethnic specialties such as felafel, and blended fruit smoothies fill the square at the end of State St. Buy inexpensive fresh fruits, vegetables, breads, cakes, and cheeses at the open-air Farmers Market, Capitol Sq. concourse (Sat. 6:30am-2pm).

Ella's Kosher Deli and Ice Cream Parlor, 425 State St. (257-8611), halfway between the capitol, and also Lake St. location at 2902 E. Washington (241-5291). Voted Madison's best deli. Hot-fudge fantasies $2.35-2.85. Sandwiches $2.10-4.45. Open Mon.-Wed. 8am-11pm, Thurs.-Sat. 8am-midnight, Sun. 9am-11pm.

Sunprint Cafe, 638 State St. (255-1555), on the 2nd floor. A light, vegetarian alternative. Delicious salads and sandwiches $3.50-5. Open Mon.-Thurs. 7am-10pm, Fri.-Sat. 7am-11pm, Sun. 9am-3pm.

El Charro, 600 Williamson St. (255-1828), in the Gateway. If you don't mind plastic plates and cutlery, this place is authentic, tasty, and inexpensive. Breakfast $2.75, 4 chicken tamales $3. Open Mon.-Sat. 8am-9pm, in off-season Mon.-Sat. 8am-9pm and Sun. noon-8pm.

Steep and Brew, 544 State St. (256-2902). One of the best of Madison's many new tea houses. Doubles as a small gallery. Open Mon.-Wed. 8am-9pm, Thurs.-Fri. 8am-11pm, Sat. 9am-6pm, Sun. 11am-6pm.

Madison's bars are smaller, less glittery, and less gimmicky than those in Milwaukee. However, while Milwaukee's brewing industry shrinks, Madison now bottles the local Capital Garten Brau. For jocks and cheap drink specials, patronize **Joe Hart's,** 704 University Ave., at Lake St. (Open daily 11am-12:45pm.) **T.C. Katz's,** 303 N. Henry (251-2700), covers the top of the charts for underage dancers. (Open 9pm-12:45am). For more variety, walk from the capitol down King St. to Wilson, turn left, and 2 blocks down is the **Cardinal Bar,** 418 E. Wilson (251-0080). Dance Tuesday and Wednesday (progressive music), Thursday (latino, reggae, African), Friday (funk), and Saturday (free-for-all—hardcore to disco) from 9pm to 2am. (Fri.-Sat. open until 2:30am. Cover $2.)

For a low-key, smoky, intellectual atmosphere go to the **602 Club,** at 602 University Ave. (256-5204). (Mixed drinks $1.30-1.75. Draft pints 95¢. Open Mon.-Wed. 11:30am-1am, Thurs. 11:30am-2am, Fri.-Sat. 11:30am-2:30am.) For good live music, go to the **Club de Wash Tavern,** 636 W. Washington at Francis St. (256-3302), in the Hotel Washington Building. Artists belt out blues, rock, and reggae nightly. (Open Sun.-Thurs. 10:30am-2am, Fri.-Sat. 10:30am-2:30am.) **Essenhaus,** 514 E. Wilson (255-4674), at Blair St., claims an authentic German bar experience, complete with live polka Tuesday through Saturday. Servers in lederhosen and dirndels bring Boots o' Beer (about 2 liters each) for $8.40. (Open Tues.-Wed. and Sat.-Sun. 3pm-1am, Thurs. 11:30am-2am, Fri. 11:30am-1am.) The nightspot that combines all these different types is the **Memorial Union.** Indoors is the **Rathskeller,** strewn with tables and beer mugs; outdoors is the **Union Terrace** whose multicolored tables overlook beautiful Lake Mendota. You'll find everything from chess to raucous live bands here—check *Forecast,* the free union magazine, for events. With any college ID you can get a cheap pitcher ($2.75). The union is open until 11pm on weeknights, 1am on weekends. All events at the union are free.

Sights and Activities

Madison is a city of lakes and parks where hiking, picnicking, biking, swimming, and sailing are the order of the day. Many Madisonians turn out to feed the ducks at the free **Vilas Park Zoo,** at Drake and Grant St. (266-4732; open daily 9:30am-8pm; take the "Burr Oaks" bus.) **Vilas Beach** is full of windsurfers and blaring radios. **Wingra Park** (233-5332), off Monroe St., a 15-minute walk from the Vilas area on Knickerbocker Rd., has a more sedate, family atmosphere. Rent windsurfing equipment for under $10 per hour.

The Memorial Union is a pleasant place in the daytime, where local musicians occasionally accompany those swimming off the dock. If people-watching is your game, there are few better arenas on the planet. Leave yourself time for some **Babcock Hall Ice Cream** (262-5959), made by UW's dairy service students (80¢). Work it off with a run out to **Picnic Point** from Memorial Union. The Union boathouse (262-7351) rents canoes for $3 per hour, $10 per day. (Open daily 11am-sunset.)

Free guided tours of the **state capitol** (266-0382) are available daily on the hour between 9am and 5pm, except at noon. The ascending triangles of the **Unitarian Church,** 900 University Bay Dr., south of downtown, are yet more examples of Frank Lloyd Wright's work. (Take the L line or G line bus.)

The University of Wisconsin is a magnet for cultural activities. Its **Elvehjem Museum of Art,** 800 University Ave. (263-2246), has art, graphics, furniture, and decorative arts from ancient and modern times. (Open Mon.-Sat. 9am-4:45pm, Sun. 11am-4:45pm. Free.) Over a dozen campus theater, music, and dance groups perform regularly. Check kiosks for campus events, as well as notices for Madison's professional theater groups and movie houses.

The **Madison Art Center,** 211 State St. (257-0158), features changing exhibits and workshops and sometimes has performances in the lobby. The collection of 19th-century Japanese prints is particularly fine, as is its contemporary collection. (Open Tues.-Thurs. 11am-5pm, Fri. 11am-9pm, Sat. 10am-5pm, Sun. 1-5pm. Free.) In the same building, the **Civic Center** (266-9055) is the home of Madison's own repertory company and hosts concerts by national and local musicians. (Box office open Mon.-Fri. 11am-5:30pm, Sat. 10am-2pm. Take the "Mendota" or "A West" bus.) At the **Coliseum,** 1881 Exposition Center Mall E. (257-5686), more renowned rock groups perform. (Box office open Mon.-Fri. 9am-5pm, Sat. 9am-noon.) During the school year, the **University Theater,** Vilas Hall, 821 University Ave. (262-1500), offers classical music events. Tickets for all three average $8-12. For live improvisational comedy, go to the **Ark Improvisational Theatre,** 220 N. Bassett (256-6624; admission $4.50-6; call ahead during the summer; shows are sometimes held in local restaurants and public spaces.)

Door County

Door County, a 40-mile long peninsula stretching north into Lake Michigan, includes five state parks, 250 miles of shoreline, and eight inland lakes. The area sees more tourists every year. The peninsula (technically an island cut off from the rest of Wisconsin by the Sturgeon Bay Canal), often has no street addresses; business hours are also indefinite, set by personal or climatic idiosyncrasies.

Practical Information

Emergency: Southern Door County (743-2244); northern Door County (868-3237). The dividing line is at Egg Harbor Village.

Visitor Information: Door County Chamber of Commerce, 6443 Green Bay Rd. (743-4456), on Hwy. 42/57 entering Sturgeon Bay. Friendly staff with free brochures from every village on the peninsula and a county map ($1). Mailing address is P.O. Box 346, Station A. **Triphone:** 24-hour free service outside the chamber of commerce allows you to call every hotel on the peninsula, as well as restaurant, police, weather, and fishing hotlines. Each village has its own visitors center.

Wisconsin-Michigan/Greyhound Bus Depot: 222 S. Madison Ave. (743-7709), at Earl's Qwik-Stop in Sturgeon Bay. Wisconsin-Michigan and Greyhound in Green Bay, bring people to Door County. Daily bus from Madison (at noon, $26), Chicago's O'Hare airport (several buses daily 9am-6pm, $26) and Green Bay ($8). Student and senior discount of 15%.

Phil Young Car Rental: 120 N. 14th Ave. (743-9228). $19.95 per day, 10¢ per mile. Must be 21 with $40 deposit plus estimated cost in advance. Call a week ahead in summer. Open Mon.-Fri. 7am-5pm, Sat. 8am-noon.

Other Rentals: Nor Door Sport and Cyclery, Fish Creek (868-2275), at the entrance to Peninsula State Park. Mountain bikes $7 per hr., $20 per day; 5- and 10-speeds $5 per hr., $15 per day, $30 for 3 days. Open mid-May to Oct. **The Boat House,** Fish Creek (868-3745). Mopeds $10 for the 1st hr., $8 each additional hr. Rent includes $5 admission fee to nearby Peninsula State Park. **Nan and Jerry's,** Fish Creek, across from the information center. Canoes $6 per hr.; rowboats $7 for 2 hr. Open April 15 to Nov. 7am-6pm. **Kurtz Corral,** 3 miles east of Carlsville on C.R. "I" (743-6742). Horseback riding on 300 acres. $17 per hr., 14 and under $14; instruction included. Open May-Oct. daily 9am-3pm.

Police: 123 S. 5th Ave.

Post Office: 359 Louisiana (793-2681), at 4th St., Sturgeon Bay. Open 9am-5pm.

Area Code: 414.

The county line is south of **Sturgeon Bay,** but the real Door County begins north of this city. Highway 42 and 57 converge and flow through Sturgeon Bay and then split again—57 running up the eastern coast of the peninsula, 42 on the western side. The peninsula is 200 miles northwest of Madison (take 151 and then 57 north) and 150 miles north of Milwaukee (take Hwy. 43, then 42, north), and has no land access except Sturgeon Bay. Summer is high season in Door's 12 villages, the biggest of which are Fish Creek (rhymes with fish stick), Sister Bay, and Ephraim. There is no public transportation on the peninsula.

Accommodations and Camping

Motels are uniformly expensive. There are few exceptions to the $50-70 range, but if you arrive on a slow night you might be able to bargain down to $40 or below; otherwise, camping brings you closer to the peninsula's beauty.

If you must stay in a motel, try **Liberty Park Lodge** (864-2025), in Sister Bay. (Lodge rooms $38-46.) **Chal-A Motel,** 3910 Hwy. 42-57 (743-6788), in Sturgeon Bay, has rooms for $25-40. The outgoing manager will offer you advice on your trip; she runs a museum on the grounds with over 1,000 dolls, antique cars, and Christmas window mechanicals.

Camping is the way to go in Door County, and the **state parks** (all except Rock Island; open 6am-11pm) are the places to camp (nonresident park admission sticker good for 1 year $30). The five parks in the county are all worth visiting. Daily admission costs $5. Camping is an additional $10 (electricity $1.75 extra) at each park. **Peninsula,** P.O. Box 218, Fish Creek 54212 (868-3258), by Fish Creek village, is the largest, with 467 sites. Reserved sites (with showers and flush toilets) are hard to get in high season, but 125 sites are kept open for walk-ins—try to come early in the morning. Peninsula has 20 miles of shoreline, a spectacular view from Eagle Lighthouse, and 17 miles of hiking. **Potawatomi State Park,** 3740 Park Dr., Sturgeon Bay 54235 (743-5123), just outside Sturgeon Bay off Hwy. 42/57, has 125 campsites (no showers or flush toilets), half of which are open to walk-ins. Write for reservations. **Newport,** at the tip of the peninsula, 6 or 7 miles from Ellison Bay off Hwy. 42, has only 16 sites and does not allow motorized vehicles. To get to **Rock Island,** take the ferry from Gill's Rock to Washington Island ($4 for people, $11 for cars) and another ferry to Rock Island. (40 sites. Open May-Dec.)

The best private campground is **Path of Pines** (868-3332), in Fish Creek, which has scenic sites and a truly hospitable staff. It's a mile east of perennially packed Peninsula, on County "F" off Hwy. 42. ($13.50 includes water and electricity, each additional adult $2.25.)

Food and Drink

Many people come to Door County just for the **fish boils,** a Scandinavian tradition dating back to nineteenth-century lumbermen. The boil is as much a ceremony as it is a meal and the billowing heat of the elaborately manipulated fire and cauldron meet with the cool twilight air off Lake Michigan. The best fish boils (all $8-9) are at: **White Gull Inn,** in Fish Creek (868-3517; May-Oct. Wed. and Fri.-Sun.; Nov.-April Wed. and Sat. 5:45-8:15pm; reservations recommended); the **Edgewater Restaurant,** in Ephraim (854-4034; June to mid-Oct. Mon.-Sat. 5-8pm; reservations recommended); and **The Viking,** at Ellison Bay (854-2998; July-Aug. Tues.-Sun.; June and Sept. to mid-Oct. Tues. and Fri.-Sat. 4:30-8pm). Cherries are another county tradition, and each fish boil ends with a big slice of cherry pie. Cherries are also used extensively at the **Door Peninsula Winery** (423-7431), 9 miles south of Sister Bay on Hwy. 42., which also makes pear, apple, and plum wine. The winery in Carlsville gives tours daily from 9am and 5pm, complete with wine tasting and cheese ($1).

In Door County, you're better off stocking up at grocery stores and farm markets than sitting down at a restaurant. **Piggly Wiggly,** Country Walk Rd. (854-2391), in Sister Bay, is probably the best place to get groceries. Another is located at Cherry Point Mall in Sturgeon Bay. (Open Mon.-Thurs. and Sat. 8am-8pm, Fri. 8am-9pm, Sun. 8am-4pm.) **Hy-Line Orchards,** on Hwy. 42 between Juddville and Egg Harbor, is a huge barn full of produce and a few old Model T's. (Open 8am-8pm.) Door County wines and fresh produce are sold at **Ray's Cherry Hut,** ½ mile south of Fish Creek on Hwy. 42. (Open mid-May. to Nov. daily 7:30am-8pm.)

Al Johnson's Swedish Restaurant, Sister Bay (854-2626), on Hwy. 42, down the hill past the information center, 2 blocks away. Excellent, authentic Swedish food popular with locals as well as visitors. Goats keep the grass trimmed on the sod roof. Swedish pancakes and meatballs $4.95). Open mid-April to Oct. 6am-9pm; Nov. 1 to mid-April 6am-8pm.

Bayside Tavern, Fish Creek (868-3441), on Hwy. 42. Serves serious burgers ($2-4) and a delicious Friday perch fry ($6.95). Also a hip bar. Open daily 10am-1am.

The Fish Creek General Store, Fish Creek (868-3351). The best deal on prepared food on the peninsula. Thick deli sandwiches with potato chips $2-4. Carry-out only. Open May-Nov.; early season 8am-6pm; summer hours 8am "until nightfall or thereabouts."

Kirkegaard's Yum-Yum Tree (839-2993), in Bailey's Harbor. Floats $1.75, sundaes $1.75-2.45, cones 81¢, beer brats $1.50, and deli sandwiches $2-4. Open mid-May to Nov. daily 10am-10pm.

Sights and Activities

Door County is best seen by bike. You miss much of Door's beauty by driving. **Cave Point County Park,** the most photographed spot in Wisconsin, offers the most stunning views of the peninsula. The park is on Cave Point Rd. off Hwy. 57, just south of Jacksonport. (Open daily 6am-10pm. Free.) Next door is **Whitefish Dunes State Park,** with 10 miles of hiking through a well-kept wildlife preserve. (Open daily 6am-11pm. Admission $5.) There are small public beaches all along Door's 250-mile shoreline; one of the nicest is at **Jacksonport.** The beach is wide and sandy, backed by a shady park and playground. (Open daily 6am-10pm. Free.) You can go windsurfing off the public beach at Ephraim, in front of the Edgewater Restaurant and Motel. **Windsurf Door County** (854-4324), across from the information booth, at South Shore Pier, rents boards ($8 per hr., $49 per day; $25 deposit). **Peninsula State Park,** a few miles south of Ephraim in Fish Creek, has 3763 acres of forested land. Ride a moped or bicycle along the 20 miles of shoreline road, or mix, mingle, and sunbathe at **Nicolet Beach.** From the immense observation tower, 110 steps up, you can see clear across the lake to Michigan. (Open daily 6am-11pm. Admission $5 for cars, $1 for bikes, under 18 free.) **Kangaroo Lake,** the largest of the eight inland lakes on this thin peninsula, offers warmer swimming and a less intimidating stretch of water. The **Kangaroo Resort,** south of Bailey's Harbor off Hwy. 57, offers public swimming and canoeing access; follow the county roads around the lake to find your own secluded swimming spot. The **Ridges Sanctuary,** north of Bailey's Harbor off Hwy. "Q," has an appealing nature trail that leads to an abandoned lighthouse. (Open daily 10am-6pm. Free.) Newport State Park, 6 miles east of Ellison Bay on Newport Dr. off Hwy. 42, provides more satisfying hiking than Peninsula (vehicles not allowed). Newport has an expansive 3000-foot swimming beach and 13 miles of shoreline on Lake Michigan and on inland Europe Lake.

For more scenic seclusion, seek out **Washington Island,** off the tip of the Door Peninsula; ferries leave Gills Rock and Northport Pier several times daily. (Washington Island Ferry Line 847-2546, Island Clipper 854-2972. Both $5 round-trip, children $2.50. Washington Island offers bike transport for $1, autos from Northport $12.)

Apostle Islands

Glaciers in the past million years have sculpted the Great Lakes with the scenic archipelago known as the Apostle Islands. Today 20 of the 22 islands are protected as a National Lakeshore. Thousands of summer tourists visit the wind- and wave-whipped caves and camp on the unspoiled sandstone bluffs.

Legend has it that the islands were named in the 18th century when a band of pirates called the Twelve Apostles hid out on Oak Island. Today you don't have to hide to stay there, as long as you get a free camper's permit, available at the **National Lakeshore Headquarters Visitors Center,** 410 Washington Ave. (779-3397). The permit allows you to camp on 21 of the 22 islands. Madeline Island has two campgrounds. **Big Bay Town Park** is 6½ miles from the island's only town, La Pointe, right next to the beautiful Big Bay Lagoon. (Primitive sites $6.50.) Across the lagoon, **Big Bay State Park** has sites for $10.75, including state park sticker.

All Apostle Islands excursions begin in the sleepy mainland town of **Bayfield.** If you're hungry here, you can find filling burgers and fresh fish sandwiches in the few restaurants that line Main St. At **Beach House** (747-3955), enjoy the relaxed atmosphere and a view overlooking the lake. (Svelte chicken or pasta salad with shrimp $5. Open daily 10:30am-3:30pm and 5:30-9:30pm, in summer only.) Join the bronzed and beautiful post-windsurfing crowd at **The Pub** (747-6315). Sandwiches are a bit pricey ($4-7), but the seafood or steak dinners ($10-13) are tasty. (Open April-Nov. daily 7:30am-10pm. Hours fluctuate each month.) For live music and good cheer, head for the **Bates Bar,** 14 S. Broad St. (779-5356), Bayfield, where grinning gargoyles are imprisoned in wood around the bar. (Open in summer daily 1pm-2am. Blues or rock 'n' roll Fri.-Sat. Cover $2.)

The "high season" summer months make accommodations scarce, so reserve in advance. The **Frostman Home,** 24 N. 3rd St. (779-3239), Bayfield, has three comfortable rooms for $20. Down the street and around the corner, **Greunke's Inn,** 17 Rittenhouse Ave. (779-5480), has pleasant, old-fashioned rooms from $30. Madeline Island has several motels. The **Madeline Island Motel** (747-3000), on Colonel Woods Blvd., has clean rooms. (Singles $37-41, off-season $28. Doubles $4 more.) Across the street, you can be surrounded by four walls of knotty pine at **La Pointe Lodgings Motel** (747-5205 or 779-5596. Singles $55, off-season $35.) Make reservations in summer. Camping is available on the mainland at **Apostle Islands View**

Campground, Hwy. 13 (779-5524; 742-3303 in winter), ½ mile south of Bayfield. (Sites $9-14, depending on season.)

Madeline Island is the most accessible of the Apostles, since it allows car traffic and has frequent ferry service (4 per hr.) from the mainland center of Bayfield. Of the non-natural sights, the **Madeline Island Historical Museum** (747-2415), right off the dock, is a great place to learn about the Chippewa, trading, and logging history of the islands. (Open late May-early Oct. daily 9am-5pm. Admission $1.50, seniors $1.20, ages 5-17 50¢.) **Indian Burial Ground** has meandering dirt paths that lead to the graves of early settlers and Christianized Chippewa, including Chief Great Buffalo. Towards the end of the day, head to **Sunset Bay** on the north side of the island. **Madeline Island Tours** (747-2051) offers 1¼-hour tours of the island. (3-4 buses daily. Admission $6.75, ages 5-11 $4.50.)

The other islands have charms, albeit more hidden, of their own. The sandstone quarries of Basswood and Hermit Island, as well as the abandoned logging and fishing camps on some of the others, are mute remainders of a more vigorous and animated era. Some of the sea caves on Devils Island are large enough to maneuver a small boat inside. Museums in their own right, the restored lighthouses on Sand, Raspberry, Michigan, Outer, and Devils Island offer spectacular panoramas of the surrounding country. A good way to visit all of these sights is on one of three narrated cruises provided by the Apostle Islands Cruise Service. (Tickets $17, children $9.)

The Apostle Islands are off the northern tip of Wisconsin and are easily accessible from Bayfield, off Hwy. 13. They are 90 miles from Duluth, 220 miles from the Twin Cities, and 465 miles from Chicago. Transportation to some of the islands is provided by the **Apostle Islands Cruise Service** (779-3925; $17). The rest of the islands can be reached by the **Water Taxi** (779-5153) for a considerably higher price. Ferry service to and from Bayfield and La Pointe to the islands is also provided by **Madeline Island Ferry Line** (747-2051). (Summer ferries run Sat.-Thurs. every 15 min. 7am-10:30pm, Fri. 7am-12:30am. Tickets $2.25, ages 6-11 $1.50. Cars $5.) A nearby **Greyhound** station is in **Ashland, WI,** 101 2nd St. (682-4010), 22 miles southeast of Bayfield. (Ashland to Duluth $15.25.) The **Bay Area Rural Transit (BART) offers a shuttle. (Last one at 4:20pm to Bayfield. 4 per day. Fare $1.80, seniors $1.10, students $1.50.) Rent mopeds at Motion to Go** in the La Pointe Lodgings Motel. ($7-10 per hr., $45 per day. Open in summer daily 9am-9pm. Driver's license as deposit.) Rent fat-tired bicycles at **Island Bike Rental** (747-5442), ½ block north of the town dock in La Pointe. ($2 per hr., $14 per day. Tandem or bike and bugger $5 per hr. Open Memorial Day-early Oct. daily 10am-5:30pm.)

The **Bayfield Chamber of Commerce,** 42 S. Broad St. (779-3335) and the **Madeline Island Chamber of Commerce,** Main St. (747-2801), are helpful for information and accommodations. (Both open in summer daily 9am-5pm.) The **Apostle Islands National Lakeshore Headquarters Visitors Center,** 410 Washington Ave. (779-3397) can answer more questions. (Open in daily 8am-6pm, off-season Mon.-Fri. 8am-4:30pm.)

The La Pointe **post office** (747-3712) is right off the dock on Madeline Island. (Open Mon.-Fri. 9am-4:30pm, Sat. 9:30am-1pm.) **ZIP code:** 54850.

The **area code** for the Apostle Islands is 715.

GREAT PLAINS

The Great Plains are to be explored as they are lived—slowly and to the fullest. Over 200 years ago, a newborn nation stretched westward onto this land. In U.S. culture, this is the territory of Laura Ingalls Wilder and Wild Bill Hickok, the farmer and the pioneer. Less well-remembered are the land's original inhabitants, although their names grace numerous towns, rivers, streets, and monuments. However, there are more monuments to the "conquest" of the prairie than to the prairie's original dwellers. Native Americans retain ownership rights to only a small fraction of their homeland, and the socio-economic consequences of such displacement are quite evident. Relegated to reservations and natural history museums, the people at times still referred to as the "Indian problem" remain an obvious and unresolved issue, although movements have begun to return the land—at least some of it—to its first settlers.

Before the Homestead Act of 1862, Anglo-Americans saw the plains simply as a huge, flat barrier to be traversed on the way to the fertile valleys of the West Coast. The new law, and the new transcontinental railroad, began an economic boom that essentially lasted until the Great Depression of the 30s, when the fertile "bread basket" became an impoverished Dust Bowl. Since then, thanks to modern farming techniques, the region has become the nation's largest grain and livestock producer. Cities thrive with industry and the trading of farm commodities.

The land itself, in its natural state, without skyscrapers, thoroughfares, or other obvious monuments to civilization, continues to rule the Great Plains. Miners still search for gold in the Black Hills of South Dakota and farmers still cultivate the expansive fields of the south. The wind never stops blowing across the prairies. The burning sun of summer and winter's cold take their toll in turn. The tides of nature dominate the plains.

Travel

More than a few corn fields separate the towns of the Great Plains—the cross-country driver can expect to pass many hours watching fence posts go by. Those with the time and the inclination can enjoy the rural life and landscape as they experience it at a leisurely pace. The plains are far more than a sparsely populated, two-dimensional void that sits in the center of the country.

Greyhound/Trailways follows the major interstates. In Iowa, Greyhound connects with other local lines that honor the Ameripass, including South Dakota's **Jack Rabbit** and Arkansas' **Iowa Lines. Jefferson Lines,** another Greyhound affiliate, breaks the east-west pattern by running a few lines from central Minnesota through Iowa, Kansas, and Missouri to Arkansas and Oklahoma. **Amtrak** crosses the plains states on three routes from Chicago. Since the trains usually run at night, Amtrak is a relaxing option for getting across the region, but not for exploring it.

Car travel is the best way to explore the Plains. Rentals are cheap, but beware of extreme heat in the summer and biting cold in the winter. **Hitchhiking** along local routes is all right, but the corn might grow five inches before you catch a ride. Ask in town for rides; more likely than not, someone with a pick-up truck will give you a lift. Don't hitch along the dangerous interstates.

If you're **bicycling,** try to plan your route west to east. In the summer, a strong wind blows across the unbroken horizon out of the Rockies. Those traveling from east to west might consider taking their bikes onto a bus for portions of the trip.

The Great Plains have a notably low density of hostels—seven hostels in seven states—but there are numerous cheap motels. Local motels are usually the least expensive, at times as low as $15 per night. The best deals often line the interstates outside of towns. Campsites are plentiful, and car travelers can sleep all over the region in state park campsites.

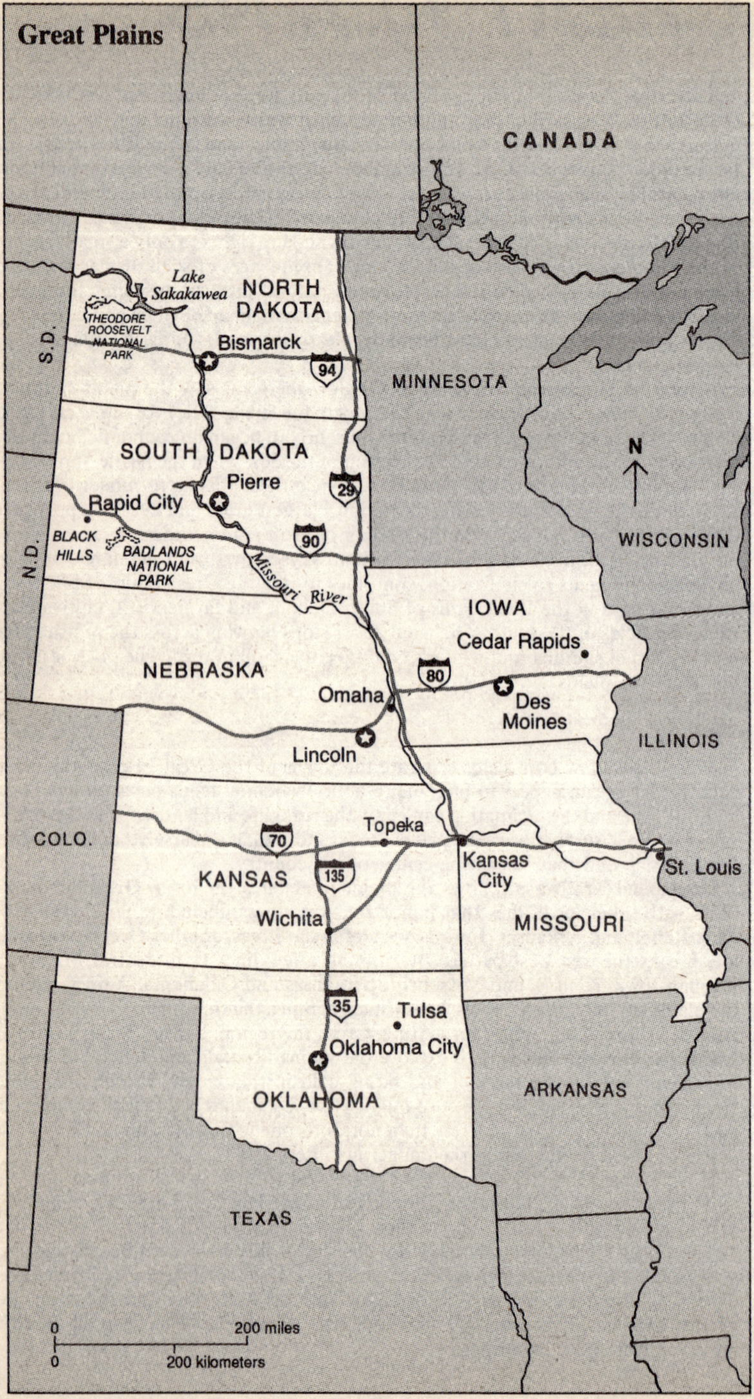
Great Plains
CANADA
Lake Sakakawea
NORTH DAKOTA
THEODORE ROOSEVELT NATIONAL PARK
Bismarck
94
MINNESOTA
S.D.
SOUTH DAKOTA
Pierre
29
Rapid City
BLACK HILLS
BADLANDS NATIONAL PARK
90
Missouri River
N.D.
N
WISCONSIN
IOWA
Cedar Rapids
80
NEBRASKA
Omaha
Des Moines
Lincoln
ILLINOIS
COLO.
70
Topeka
Kansas City
St. Louis
135
KANSAS
Wichita
MISSOURI
35
Tulsa
Oklahoma City
OKLAHOMA
ARKANSAS
TEXAS
0
200 miles
0
200 kilometers

Outdoors

The "amber waves of grain" originally sprouted out of the Great Plains, and still form a veritable ocean of corn and wheat. Early travelers actually experienced seasickness riding through the waves of wild grass. Three vacation areas bait tourists and break the undulating rhythm of the plains: the **Badlands** and **Black Hills** of South Dakota, and the picturesque **Ozarks** of Missouri. All have extensive state and/or national park services and recreational facilities.

Many travelers in the plains are on constant lookout for an Uncle Henry look-alike screaming, "It's a twister, it's a twister!" Tornadoes actually occur quite infrequently, and most collapse back into the clouds from which they came without touching the ground.

Many animals make this harsh land their home. Several species of deer lope through the hills, while rabbits and prairie dogs burrow in the sod and geese and pheasant fly overhead. You can see wild bison in some isolated areas such as the Badlands. Most of the wild prairie has been put to the plow, but occasional patches are protected by state and national parks. For information on the national park properties in the Great Plains, contact the National Parks Midwest Regional Office, 1709 Jackson St., Omaha, NB 68102 (402-221-3471).

Iowa

Native Americans named this area Iowa, "the beautiful country," but they didn't see the state from the freeways. Cruise control was probably born here—Iowa's freeways streak as straight as lead pipe through the flattest parts of a flat state.

To see the real "beautiful country," you have to turn off the freeway and onto the old roads that wind and plunge through fairy-tale meadows, hills, and thickets. Here, off the beaten concrete trail, you can cast your line into one of more than 19,000 miles of fishing streams, bike the 52-mile Cedar Valley Nature Trail from Cedar Rapids to Cedar Falls, or travel through time to one of the many traditional communities established in Iowa.

Practical Information

Capital: Des Moines.

Tourist Information: Iowa Development Commission, 600 E. Court Ave., Suite A, Des Moines 50309 (281-3100). **Conservation Commission,** Wallace Bldg., Des Moines 50319.

Time Zone: Central (1 hr. behind Eastern). **Postal Abbreviation:** IA.

Des Moines

If you're expecting downtown Des Moines, the capital of Iowa, to be a friendly, safe, quiet place where the tallest building is the two-story chamber of commerce, forget it. Friendly and safe, yes. Quiet, no—at least not during business hours. Des Moines's workforce bustles in and out of downtown's cluster of mini-skyscrapers. Headquarters to over 50 insurance companies, and home to a world class art museum and musical events, Des Moines exhibits a growing array of big-city pleasures. However, the capital never loses sight of the state it represents. Every year, Des Moines hosts the **Iowa State Fair,** bringing cows, pigs, and corn to the nine-to-five city.

Practical Information

Emergency: 911.

Visitor Information: Des Moines Convention and Visitors Bureau, in the Skywalk Kaleidoscope Building at 6th and Walnut St. (244-2444), at the Hub. Open Mon.-Sat. 10am-5:30pm. The office at **Des Moines International Airport** (287-4396) has similar information for airborne travelers. Open Mon.-Fri. 10am-10pm, Sun. 2-10pm. **Events Hotline,** 283-2220.

Des Moines International Airport: Fleur Dr. at Army Post Rd. (285-5857), about 5 miles southwest of downtown.

Greyhound: 1107 Keosauqua Way (243-5283), at 12th St., just northwest of downtown. To: Kansas City (4 per day, 4 hr., $38.50); St. Louis (6 per day, 9½ hr., $59); and Chicago (9 per day, 8-9 hr., $59). Open 24 hours.

Metropolitan Transit Authority (MTA): 1100 MTA Lane (283-8100), just south of the 9th St. viaduct. Open Mon.-Fri. 6am-6pm, Sat. 7am-5pm. Pick up maps at the MTA office or any Dahl's market. Routes converge at 6th and Walnut St. Buses operate Mon.-Sat. 6am-7pm. Fare 60¢, transfers 5¢.

Taxi: Capitol Cab, 282-8111. **Yellow Cab,** 243-1111. $2.50 first mile, $1.20 each additional mile. Airport to downtown $9-10.

Car Rental: Budget, 287-2612, at the airport. $37 per day, 100 free miles. Open daily 6am-10pm. Must be 25 with major credit card.

Help Lines: Crisis Intervention, 244-1000. **Gay/Lesbian Support,** 246-5600, ext. 1930.

Post Office: 1165 2nd Ave. (283-7500), just north of I-235, downtown. Open Mon.-Fri. 8:30am-5:30pm. **ZIP code:** 50314.

Area Code: 515.

Des Moines lies near the center of Iowa at the intersection of I-35 and I-80. Numbered streets run north-south, named streets east-west. Numbering begins at the **Des Moines River** and increases east or west, or at **South Union** when the river twists east. **Grand Avenue** divides addresses north-south along the numbered streets. Other east-west thoroughfares are **Locust Street, Park Avenue, Douglas Avenue,** and **Hickman Road.**

Accommodations and Camping

Finding cheap accommodations in Des Moines is usually no problem, though you should make reservations for visits in March, when high school sports tournaments are held, and in August, when the state fair comes to town. Several cheap motels are clustered around I-80 and Merle Hay Rd., 5 miles northwest of downtown. Take bus #4 ("Urbandale") or #6 ("West 9th") from downtown.

YMCA, 101 Locust St. (288-0131), at 1st St. downtown, on the west bank of the river. Men only. Singles $19.50. Key deposit $5.

YWCA, 717 Grand Ave. (244-8961), across from the Marriott Hotel, downtown. Fairly safe area. Women only. Clean dorm-style rooms with access to lounge, kitchen, and laundry. Beds $8. Key deposit $1.

Econo Lodge, 5626 Douglas Ave. (278-1601), across from Merle Hay Mall. Nice neighborhood. Bus stop in front. Large, newly furnished rooms with cable TV and complimentary coffee, doughnuts, and newspaper. Spa and sauna. Singles $30. Doubles $33.25.

Royal Motel, 3718 Douglas Ave. (274-0459), northwest of downtown, 1 mile from Merle Hay Mall. Take bus #6. Cottage-like motel with clean, comfortable rooms. Singles $27. Doubles $35.

Iowa State Fairgrounds Campgrounds, E. 30th St. and Grand Ave. (262-3111). Take bus #1 or 2. 2000 campsites on a grassy, wooded hill. Very nice when not crowded at fair time. Water spigots at all sites, but no fires allowed. Open Mon.-Fri. 8am-4:30pm, fee collected in the morning. $7 per vehicle.

Walnut Woods State Park, SW 52 Ave. (285-4502), 4 miles south of the city on Rte. 5. Floods out about once a year; if the front gate is locked, it's for a good reason. Primitive sites $4, with electricity $6.

Food and Entertainment

Des Moines's cheap, clean fast-food places are located on the lower level of the **Locust Mall,** downtown on 8th and Locust St. (Mall closes at 5:30pm.) **Court Avenue,** 2 blocks south of Locust, around 3rd St., has a few reasonable Mexican and Italian restaurants in a renovated warehouse. A popular **farmers market** (286-4987) is held at 4th and Court Ave. every Saturday from 7am to 1pm.

Spaghetti Works, 310 Court Ave. (243-2195). Old-fashioned interior with a 50-foot fresco of a sea-serpent. Spaghetti dinners with salad and garlic bread $3.70-6, lunch versions $3-4. Large portions. Open Mon.-Thurs. 11:30am-2pm and 5-10pm, Fri.-Sat. 11:30am-2pm and 5-11pm, Sun. 11:30am-2pm and 4-9:30pm.

Babe's, 417 6th St. (244-5857), across from the Locust Mall. This 50-year-old restaurant has attracted such luminaries as Diane Sawyer and Bob Barker. Veal scallopini $4.50, chicken breast $4.

Juke Box Saturday Night, 206 3rd St. (243-0707). Hot spot for fun and drink. Main decorative motif is the '57 Chevy. Aid your digestion by participating in the frequent hula-hoop, twist, and jitterbug contests. Drinks average $2.50, happy hour Mon.-Fri. 4-7pm. Open Mon.-Fri. 11am-2am, Sat. 5pm-2am, Sun. 5pm-midnight.

Sights

From downtown you can see the green and gold domes of the **state capitol,** E. 9th St. (281-5591), across the river and up Grand Ave., rising majestically from atop a barren hill. (Tours Mon.-Fri. 10am-3pm on the hour; reservations 281-5591. Legislative observation Mon.-Fri. 8am-4:30pm, Sat.-Sun. and holidays 8am-4pm. Take bus #5 "E. 6th and 9th St.," #1 "Fairgrounds," #2, 4, or 7.) Three blocks away, the **Iowa State Historical Museum and Archives,** E. 12th at Grand Ave. (281-5111), features a monolithic neon outdoor sculpture called the *Plains Aurora* and exhibits on Iowa's history. (Museum open Tues.-Sat. 9am-4:30pm, Sun. 1-5pm. Free. Take bus #7.)

Most cultural sights cluster west of downtown. The **Des Moines Art Center,** 4700 Grand Ave. (277-4405), is acclaimed for its wing of stark white porcelain tile designed by I.M. Pei. Modern art predominates, but the museum also has Native American, impressionist, and optics exhibits. (Open Tues.-Sat. 11am-5pm, Sun. noon-5pm. Free. Take bus #1 "West Des Moines.") Down the street across Greenwood Park, the **Science Center of Iowa,** 4500 Grand Ave. (274-4138), is full of entertaining permanent exhibits and also hosts traveling exhibits. (Open Mon.-Sat. 10am-5pm, Sun. 1-5pm. Admission $3.50, under 12 $1.50.) Flapper-era cosmetic manufacturer Carl Weeks's fantasy of owning a home just like the King of Britain's was realized after he had salvaged enough ceilings, staircases, and artifacts from English Tudor mansions to complete **Salisbury House,** 4025 Tonawanda Dr. (279-9711; open Mon.-Fri. 8am-4:30pm. Admission $2. Take bus #1 to 42nd and Grand Ave. and go 5 blocks south.) Two miles away stands the grandiose Victorian mansion **Terrace Hill,** 2300 Grand Ave. (281-3604), built in 1866 and currently the governor's mansion. (Open March-Dec. Mon.-Thurs. 10am-1:30pm.)

The **Iowa State Fair,** one of the largest in the nation, captivates Des Moines for 10 days during the middle of August. Traditional events include agricultural displays, tractor pulls, chuckwagon races, and demolition derbies, but many open contests have been added to the fair over the years: tobacco-spitting, rolling-pin-throwing, and hog-calling. For information contact the Administration Building, Iowa State Fair Grounds, Des Moines 50306 (262-3111).

Iowa City

Iowa City, once seat of Iowa's territorial and state government, lost its capital status in 1857 to the more centrally located Des Moines. Today, the city is dominated by the University of Iowa, with students comprising one half of the town's winter population. Not only is Iowa City remote, but it is also one of the state's few remotely hip towns.

After it was vacated by the legislature, the **Old Capitol** (335-0548) became the first building owned by the University of Iowa. Recently renovated for the second time, the gold dome is now the centerpiece of both the university and the town. Stop by the **Old Capitol National Monument** for a tour. (Call ahead for larger groups. Open Mon.-Sat. 10am-3pm, Sun. noon-4pm.) MacBride Hall, next door, houses the **Museum of Natural History** (335-0480), on Clinton St. at Jefferson. (Open Mon.-Sat. 9:30am-4:30pm, Sun. 12:30-4:30pm.) Five blocks west of the Old Capitol, the eclectic **Museum of Art** (335-1727), on N. Riverside Dr., houses painting and sculpture, antique silver, traveling exhibits, and U of I student and faculty work. (Open Tues.-Sat. 10am-5pm, Sun. noon-5pm. Free.) While at the university, you may want to stop by the **Iowa Memorial Union,** at Madison and Jefferson, ½-block from the Old Capitol. (Open Mon.-Sat. 8am-9pm, Sun. noon-4pm.) Students and ducks frequent the outdoor patios and gardens. Pitchers of beer are $2 ($1 deposit) at the river-level **Wheelroom.**

At **The Kitchen,** local "cooking artists" concoct dishes in a small open kitchen, spreading a smorgasbord of spicy aromas through the café. All dishes are $5-7. (Open Mon.-Sat. 11am-2:30pm and 5-9:30pm.) For dessert, no place beats the **Great Midwestern Icecream Co.,** 126 Washington (337-7243), at the head of the pedestrian concourse. Generous cones $1.11. (Open Mon.-Thurs. 7am-11pm, Fri. 7am-midnight, Sat. 8am-midnight, Sun. 10am-11pm.) On Wednesday nights (5:30-7pm) and Saturday mornings (7:30-11:30am), a **farmers market** (356-5000) is held at Van Buren and Washington next to City Hall.

The **Wesley Youth Hostel (AYH),** 120 N. Dubuque St. (338-1179), 6 blocks from the Greyhound station, has cots in clean rooms with access to showers and a kitchen. Take your valuables with you. Free medical clinic operates downstairs. (Check-in 7-9pm. 10pm curfew. Members and students $8, others $16.) The cheapest motel rooms around are in Coralville, 2 miles west of Iowa City, off I-80 exit 242. Take the "First Ave. Coralville" bus from the University of Iowa Pentacrest. The **Motel 6,** 810 1st Ave., Coralville (354-0030), has an outdoor pool and HBO. (Singles $25. Doubles $31.) Nearby, the **Sunset Motel,** 28 1st Ave. (354-4009), has simple rooms with cable TV and free coffee. (Singles $20. Doubles $24.)

Iowa City is 110 miles east of Des Moines, just south of I-80. The Greek Revival buildings of the Old Capitol area are known as the **Pentacrest.** To the east is a pedestrian concourse filled with trees, benches, and fountains, and lined with restaurants and shops. **Greyhound, Burlington Trailways,** and **Jefferson Bus Lines,** 404 E. College Ave. (337-2127), at Gilbert St., connect Iowa City to Minneapolis, St. Louis, Des Moines, and Omaha. (Open Mon.-Fri. 6:30am-9pm, Sat. 6:30am-8pm, Sun. 6:30am-8pm and 10pm-8am.) **Iowa City Transit, Cambus,** and **Coralville Transit** service the entire area for 50¢. For visitor information, stop by the **chamber of commerce,** 323 E. Washington St. (337-9637), or the **Campus Information Center** (335-3055), on the first floor of the Iowa Memorial Union. (Open Mon.-Sat. 8am-9pm, Sun. noon-4pm.)

The **post office** is at 400 S. Clinton (354-1560); the **ZIP code** is 52240. Iowa City's **area code** is 319.

The Amana Colonies

In 1714, the religious movement known as the Community of True Inspiration was founded in Germany. Migrating to America in 1842, the followers headed west to Iowa in 1855, where they settled in the seven villages known as the Amana Colonies. Initially, the inhabitants' lifestyle was close to pure communism. The experiment fell through during the Depression, and today it is primarily the church that gives the colonies a sense of cultural and spiritual unity. Although affiliated with neither the Amish nor the Mennonites, the Amana colonists adhere to a similarly spartan existence.

In keeping with the old world village feel, there are no addresses in the colonies, only place names. Anything that isn't on the road leading into town is easily found by following the profusion of signs that point to attractions off the main thoroughfare.

Start your visit with a history lesson at the **Museum of Amana History,** on the "central artery" (622-3567). The museum runs an overly sentimental and patriotic, but informative, slide show every half-hour. (Open Mon.-Sat. 10am-5pm, Sun. noon-5pm; off-season by appointment. Admission $2, children $1.) The **Woolen Mill Machine Shop Museum,** Rte. 220 (622-3432), gives noisy tours and is the best and cheapest place to buy Amana blankets, sweaters, and clothes. (Tours Mon.-Fri. every ½ hour 8am-4pm. Open Mon.-Sat. 8am-5pm, Sun. noon-5pm.) Across the street, watch artisans plane, carve, and sand wooden creations in an open workshop at the **Amana Furniture and Clock Shop** (622-3291; open Mon.-Sat. 9am-5pm, Sun. noon-5pm). In Middle Amana, the **Communal Kitchen Museum** (622-3567), displays the colonies' only functional open-hearth oven as you tour the former site of all local food preparation. (Open May-Oct. daily 9am-4pm. Admission $1.) Its scrumptious products are sold at **Hahn's Hearth Oven Bakery** (622-3439), next door. (Open April-Oct. Mon.-Sat. 7:30am to sell-out; Nov.-Dec. Wed. and Sat. only.)

Amana is probably best known for its delicious, wholesome food. The **Amana Society Bread and Pastry Shop** (622-3600), across from the Amana Museum, near the center of the colonies, sells fragrant, fresh breads and pastries. A 6-inch honey loaf costs only 50¢, while an opa (5-inch cinnamon pastry) is yours for 80¢. (Open mid-April to mid-Nov. Mon.-Sat. 8:30am-5pm.) Once you've had your loaf of bread, go on a free wine-tasting spree at one of the several wineries in Amana. Wines range from the standard grape to brews fermented from rhubarb and dandelions. When you're ready for heartier fare, try the **Colony Inn** (622-3471), which serves hefty portions of delicious German and American food, such as ham, fried chicken, or delicious bratwurst and sauerkraut ($9-12). Breakfast ($6) is an orgy of fruit salad, huge pancakes, fried eggs, thick sausage patties, bacon, and a bowl piled with hashbrowns. (Open Mon.-Sat. 7:30am-10:30pm, Sun. 11am-8pm.)

Most lodging options consist of pricey but personal B&Bs such as Lucille's Bett und Breakfast (668-1185), **Snoozies Bed and Breakfast** (364-2134), and **Joy's Bed and Breakfast** (642-7787). The **Rettig House Bed and Breakfast** (622-3386), in Middle Amana, has been in the family for four generations. It does not allow smoking, drinking, or children under 12. (Singles and doubles $38.50.) The only camping is at the **Amana Community Park** (622-3732). (Sites $3.50 per vehicle, $4.50 with electricity.)

The Amana Colonies lie 10 miles north of I-80, clustered around the intersection of U.S. 6. Rte. 220, and Rte. 149. From Iowa City, take Rte. 6 west to Rte. 149; from Des Moines, take exit 220 off I-80 east to Rte. 6 and Rte. 149. Stop by the **Amana Colonies Visitor Center,** Hwy. 151 and 220 (622-6262; open Mon.-Sat. 9am-5pm, Sun. 10am-5pm.)

Amana's **ZIP code** is 52203; the **area code** is 319.

Cedar Rapids

Although Cedar Rapids is the principal industrial city of eastern Iowa, the pace of life in this "City of Five Seasons" (the fifth being the time to relax and enjoy oneself) remains slow and easygoing. Named after the surging rapids of the Cedar River running through its center, Cedar Rapids is home to citizens who meander rather than march and who are never too pressed for time to strike up a conversation.

The **Science Station,** 427 1st St. SE (366-0968), across the street from the Ground Transportation Center, features hands-on scientific fun. (Open daily 9am-5pm. Admission $2.) Due to open in late 1989 is the **Cedar Rapids Museum of Art,** 324 3rd St. SE (366-7503), whose permanent collection features the works of Marvin Cone,

Grant Wood, and Mauricio Jasansky, plus a children's gallery. (Open Tues.-Wed. and Fri.-Sat. 10am-5pm, Thurs. 10am-8pm, Sun. 2-5pm. Free.) From 1870 to 1910, thousands of Czechoslovakian immigrants settled in Cedar Rapids. Take bus #7 to 16th Ave. and C St. to visit the Czech Village, on 16th Ave. between 1st St. and C St. SW, where you can stroll along the historic streets and visit traditional Czech watering holes and bakeries. At the end of the block is find the **Czech Museum and Library,** 10 16th Ave. SW (362-8500), which houses the largest collection of traditional costumes outside Czechoslovakia. (Open April 15-Nov. 15 Tues.-Fri. 10am-4pm; Jan.-Dec. Sat. 9:30am-4pm. Admission $2.)

Downtown Cedar Rapids is filled with moderately priced restaurants and delis. At the **4th St. Diner,** 214 4th St. SE (362-7472), be-bop nostalgics share booths and counter space with regulars addicted to the diner's pies, sandwiches ($1.50-2.80), and soups ($1). (Open Mon.-Sat. 7am-2:30pm.) For free chips with your dinner, stop by **Gringo's Mexican Restaurant,** 207 1st Ave. SE (363-1000), downtown. Try the beef enchiladas with rice and beans ($3.50). (Open Mon.-Thurs. 11am-10:30pm, Fri.-Sat. 11am-11pm, Sun. 4:30-9pm.) In the Czech Village sample *knedliky* (Czech dumplings) or *kolace* (fruit-filled sweet rolls) at family-owned **Sykora's Bakery,** 73 16th Ave. SW (364-5271; open daily 6am-5pm). Try more substantial Czech cuisine at the **Lion's Pride,** 95 16th Ave. (362-1216). Dinners are a tad pricey ($7-10), but you can sample pork and dumplings, *jaternice* (sausage and potatoes), or goulash for $4-5. (Open daily 11am-2pm and 5-9pm.)

There are plenty of budget motels on 16th Ave. SW. The **Shady Acres Motel,** 1791 16th Ave. (362-3111), is a row of cottage-like, primitive, but spotlessly clean rooms atop acres of rolling hills and huge oaks. Rooms have A/C, showers, and TV, but no phone. (Singles $18. Doubles $22. Take bus #10 to the K-Mart 5 blocks away.) **The Village Inn Motel,** 100 F Ave. NW (366-5323), across the river from the Quaker Oats factory, is 4 blocks from downtown and 8 blocks from the Greyhound station. The motel has large, quiet rooms with cable TV. (Singles $30. Doubles $34-38.) **Exel Inn,** 616 33rd Ave. SW (366-2475), 5 miles from downtown, has clean rooms, comfortable beds, free coffee, and HBO. (Singles $26. Doubles $33.)

Cedar Rapids is 150 miles east of Des Moines at the junction of I-380 and Rte. 30 and 151. The Amana Colonies are 19 miles to the southwest. The **Greyhound/Trailways** station, 145 Transit Way SE (364-4167), has buses to: Des Moines (3 per day, 3 hr., $16.50); Chicago (4 per day, 6½ hr., $41); and Kansas City (3 per day, 7-11 hr., $56). Get around town in **Easyride** buses. (Run daily 6am-6pm; fare 50¢, seniors 35¢, transfers 10¢, reduced fare with receipts from many local restaurants.) All routes stop at the **Ground Transportation Center,** 200 4th Ave. SE (398-5335), across the street from the Greyhound station. For taxis, try **Yellow Cab** (365-1444).

For information on sights, accommodations, and attractions, contact the **Cedar Rapids Area Convention and Visitors Bureau,** 119 1st Ave. SE (398-5009; open Mon.-Fri. 8am-5pm.) Or call the **Visitor Info Line** (398-9660).

The **post office** is at 616 6th Ave. SE (399-2911; window open Mon.-Fri. 8:30am-5pm, Sat. 9am-noon; lobby open daily 5am-12:30am. Cedar Rapids' **ZIP code** is 52401; the **area code** is 319.

Kansas

Disappointed settlers leaving Kansas in the 1800s did not share Dorothy's enthusiasm for the state when they wrote: "In God we trusted, in Kansas we busted." From the early frontier days to the present, the people of Kansas have faced a succession of calamities: border wars in the 1850s, guerilla raids in the Civil War, locusts, dust storms, droughts, falling wheat prices, and endless taunts from the rest of the country. Yet the product of these adversities is a special breed driven by a will to succeed and an overwhelming affection for the state. Kansas produces more wheat than any other state (every Kansas farmer feeds you and 75 others), and more than most nations in the world. Industry plays a strong role in Kansas as well, with Wichita known as the "air capital of the world" because of its concentration of aircraft manufacturers.

Kansans do not proceed at cyclone speed, but work and welcome visitors at a friendly, thoughtful pace. The state fair, held in Hutchinson during the second and third weeks of September, is more delightful than dizzying—sure, it has ferris wheels and roller coaster rides, but the fair also features delicious country baked goods, quilting contests, and hog auctions. Unbeknownst to most, Kansas is also the home of the Garden of Eden (at the corner of 2nd and Kansas, in Lucas, just off I-70 on Hwy. 181 in the virtual center of the U.S.). This meticulous re-creation was first planted in 1907. (Open in summer daily 9am-6pm; in winter daily 10am-4pm.)

Practical Information

Capital: Topeka.

Tourist Information: Department of Economic Development, 400 W. 8th, 5th floor, Topeka 66603 (296-2009). **Kansas Park and Resources Authority,** 503 Kansas Ave., 6th floor, Topeka 66603 (296-2281).

Time Zone: Central (1 hr. behind Eastern). **Postal Abbreviation:** KS.

Wichita

When Coronado, the first European to explore the Great Plains, came to the present-day site of Wichita, he was so disappointed that he had his guide strangled for misleading him. But by the 1870s, settlers had taken a permanent liking to the place and stubbornly called their woolly home town such colorful names as the "Peerless Princess of the Plains," and the "Wonderfully Worthy Wombat." Today, the Plains Princess is starved for tourists to appreciate her beauty, and offers a huge number of festivals and attractions to lure them in.

The **Old Cowtown Historic Village Museum,** 1871 Sim Park Dr. (264-6398), takes you back to boisterous cowboy days as you walk through the 44 buildings that comprised the town during the Reconstruction. (Open daily 10am-5pm; Jan.-Feb. Mon.-Fri. 10am-5pm. Admission $2.50, ages 6-12 $1.50, under 6 free.) Equally worthwhile is the **Wichita-Sedgwick County Historical Museum,** 204 S. Main (295-9314). Posh antique furniture and heirlooms sit beside such historical oddities as the hatchet used by crusading prohibitionist Carrie Nation when she demolished the bar of the Carey Hotel. (Open Tues.-Fri. 11am-4pm, Sat.-Sun. 1-5pm. Admission $1, ages 6-16 50¢.) Two blocks away is the **Wichita Children's Museum,** 124 S. Broadway (267-3844), with a short-wave radio that links kids up with visitors in children's museums in Germany, England, Holland, and Puerto Rico. (Open Tues.-Fri. 9am-4pm, Sat. 9am-5pm, Sun. 1-5pm. Admission $2.) Further from the center of town is the **Mid-American All-Indian Center and Museum,** 650 N. Seneca (262-5221), which showcases traditional and modern works by Native American artists. The late Blackbear Bosin's monolithic sculpture, *Keeper of the Plains,* always stands guard over the grounds. (Open Mon.-Sat. 10am-5pm; off-season Tues.-Sat. 10am-5pm, Sun. 1-5pm. Admission $1.75.)

Wichita State University's campus, at N. Hillside and 17th St., contains an outdoor sculpture collection comprised of 42 works, including pieces by Rodin, Moore, and Hepworth. Free sculpture maps are available at the **Edwin A. Ulrich Museum of Art** (689-3664), also on campus. You can't miss this building—one whole side is a gigantic glass mosaic mural by Joan Miró. (Open Wed. 9:30am-8pm, Thurs.-Fri. 9:30am-5pm, Sat.-Sun. 1-5pm. Free. Take "East 17th" or "East 13th" bus from Century II.)

Meat is the main event when Wichita serves up a meal. If you have only one meal in Wichita, go to **Doc's Steakhouse,** 1515 N. Broadway (264-4735). The most expensive entree is the 18-oz. T-bone at $7.75. (Open Mon.-Thurs. 11:30am-9:30pm, Fri. 11:30am-11pm, Sat. 4-11pm.) The **Old Mill Tasty Shop,** 604 E. Douglas, recalls a long-lost Wichita with its old time soda fountain and spitoons. Sandwiches and ice cream treats are 50¢-$2. (Open Mon.-Fri. 11am-3pm, Sat. 8am-5pm.) **Le Monde,** 217 E. Douglas (262-3383), offers healthful meals with many meatless options. (Breakfast $1-2, sandwich with chips or salad $2-3; open Mon.-Sat. 7am-3pm.) **Dyne Quik,** 1202 N. Broadway (267-5821), is homey, albeit grotesquely misspelled and cramped. It serves catfish with potatoes, bread, and coffee for $3.50 or a 21-piece shrimp dinner for $5. (Open Mon.-Sat. 5:15am-3pm.)

Wichita is a haven of cheap hotels. Try South Broadway, though watch the neighborhood. The **Mark 8 Inn,** 1130 N. Broadway (265-4679), is hard to beat, with clean rooms, huge pillows, in-room movies, and refrigerators. (Singles $23. Doubles $25.) Closer to downtown and the bus station is the **Royal Lodge,** 320 E. Kellogg (263-8877), with a dated but clean interior and cable TV. (Singles $25. Doubles $34.) Several other cheap but palatable motels line East Kellogg 5 to 8 miles from downtown. The **Wichita KOA Kampground,** 15520 Maple Ave. (722-1154), has private showers, a laundromat, game room, pool, and convenience store. (Office open daily 8:30am-6pm. Tent sites $11.25 for 2, with hookup $16; each additional person $1.50. 5 miles west of I-235 on U.S. 54; no bus service.)

Wichita sits on I-35, 170 miles north of Oklahoma City and about 200 miles southwest of Kansas City. **Main Street,** the major north-south thoroughfare, divides the town east-west. **Douglas Avenue** lies between numbered east-west streets to the north and named east-west streets to the south. The **Convention and Visitors Bureau,** on 100 S. Main St. (265-2800), has a "Quarterly Calendar" of local events (open Mon.-Fri. 8am-5pm). You can also try the message on the **Wichita Fun Phone** (262-7474), which lists current festivals, activities, sports, and entertainment.

The closest **Amtrak** station is in Newton, 25 miles north of Wichita, at 5th and Main St. (283-7533). Tickets are sold Mon.-Fri. 9am-1pm and 1:30-5:30pm. Trailways provides bus service to the Newton Amtrak station for $6; schedules vary. The **Trailways** station is located at 312 S. Broadway (265-7711), 2 blocks east of Main St. and 2 blocks south of Douglas Ave. Buses serve: Kansas City (4 per day, 4 hr., $36); Denver (3 per day, 10½ hr., $86); and Dallas (4 per day, 9 hr., $63). The station is open daily 3:30am-10pm. Get around town with **Metropolitan Transit,** 1825 McLean Blvd. (265-7221). Most buses pass the Century II Convention Center at 225 W. Douglas, in the heart of downtown. Schedules are posted there, at the City Library, Wichita State University, and City Hall. (Service Mon.-Fri. 6am-6:30pm, Sat. 7am-7pm. Buses run every 20-30 min. Fare 75¢, seniors 35¢, students and ages 6-18 50¢, transfers 25¢.) **Steven's Discount Car Rental,** 1925 E. Douglas (262-3590), rents cars for $18 per day plus 18¢ per mile. (Open Mon.-Fri. 8am-5pm, Sat. 8am-noon. Must be 21 with major credit card.) Or, if you prefer getting around on two wheels, head for the **Riverside Bike and Skate Shop,** 1908 W. 13th St. (264-2782). Five- and 10-speed bikes are $5 per hr., $15 per day. (Open Mon.-Wed. 1-8pm, Thurs.-Sun. 10am-8:30pm. Deposit driver's license or credit card. Take "Riverside" bus to 13th and Coolidge.) The **Post Office** is at 7117 W. Harry (946-4511), at Airport Rd. (Open Mon.-Fri. 8am-4:30pm, Sat. 11am-1pm.) Wichita's **ZIP code** is 67276; the **area code** is 316.

Dodge City

Legends haunt Dodge City, the quintessential cowtown. At the turn of the century, wranglers, gunfighters, prostitutes, and other lawless types used the town as a stopover along the Santa Fe trail. Chaos ensued. At one time **Front Street,** the main drag, had one saloon for every 50 citizens. So many people died "with their boots on" in drunken brawls and heated gunfights that the makeshift cemetery where they were laid to rest became known as Boot Hill. Today, longhorn cattle parade through town only during Dodge City Days at the end of July, when the city recalls its past with a rodeo and a huge festival.

For a taste of life as it was during Dodge City's wild heyday, saunter on down to the **Boot Hill Village Museum,** a block-long complex replicating the Boot Hill cemetery and Front Street as they looked in the 1870s. Among the buildings is the **Boot Hill Museum,** which displays a 1903 Santa Fe Locomotive and the restored and furnished **Hardesty House,** a rancher's home in the Gothic Revival style. On summer evenings the **Long Branch Saloon** holds a variety show at 7:30pm ($3.75; open daily 8am-7:30pm; Sept.-May Mon.-Sat. 9am-5pm, Sun. 1-5pm. Admission to museum $4.25, seniors and children $3.75, families $13; off-season $3, $1, and $13, respectively.)

Dodge City is a fast-food lover's fantasy, but if your taste is more refined, the pickings are slim. Near the Boot Hill Museum is the **Golden Corral,** 700 Wyatt Earp Blvd. (227-7455), a steak house that also offers a delicious and complete buffet for $5. (Dinners $5-7, all-you-can-eat shrimp $8.) Inside the Boot Hill Museum you can get all the barbecued beef and fixings that you can eat at the **Chuckwagon Barbecue.** ($6, ages 6-12 $4; open June-Aug. daily 5:30-7:30pm.) At the center of town, **Pam's Place,** 614 2nd Ave. (227-3886), offers sandwiches ($1.20-1.75) and soup ($1; open Mon.-Sat. 9am-5pm).

A warning to the carless: except for the Western Inn Motel across from the bus station ($30-40), most motels are 4 miles west along Wyatt Earp Boulevard, a very busy highway. (Wyatt Earp Blvd. becomes U.S. 50 outside of town.) The **Holiday Motel,** 2100 W. Wyatt Earp (227-2169), boasts cheap, clean, big rooms with HBO. (Singles $19. Doubles $25. Seniors get a 10% discount. Breakfast included.) The **Econo Lodge,** 1610 W. Wyatt Earp (225-0231), has resort-style facilities at bargain rates. The hotel has large, clean rooms with free HBO, indoor pool, jacuzzi, sauna, gameroom, dry cleaning service, laundry facilities, and shuttle service. (Singles $25. Doubles $30.) There are two adequate campgrounds close to town, the highly developed **Gunsmoke Campground,** W. Hwy. 50 (227-8247), 3 miles west of Front St. (tent sites $9 for 2, RV sites with hookup $12; each additional person $1.50) and the **Water Sports Campground Recreation,** 500 Cherry St. (225-9003), on a small lake 10 blocks south from Front St. on 2nd Ave. (Sites $9; swimming $1.50.)

Dodge City is 150 miles west of Wichita on Rte. 54, north of the Oklahoma panhandle. **Trailways,** 910 E. Wyatt Earp Blvd. (225-1617), serves the town from Wichita once in the morning and once in the evening for $23. (Open Mon.-Sat. 8am-5pm.) Stop in at the **chamber of commerce,** at 4th and W. Spruce St. (227-3119), 1 block north of Front St., for visitor information. The center of town and hub of all business activity is the railway. **Amtrak** (800-872-7245) runs out of the **Santa Fe Station,** a century-old national historic landmark at Central and Wyatt Earp Blvd. Contact a travel agent, since no tickets are sold at the station. **Greyhound,** 910 E. Wyatt Earp St. (225-1617), has very limited service in Dodge City. Buses run to Wichita daily at 6:15am and 9:15pm. There is no public transportation in town. The **post office** is at 700 Central (227-8616; open Mon.-Fri. 8:15am-4:30pm, Sat. 11am-1pm). Dodge City's **ZIP code** is 67801; the **area code** is 316.

Lawrence

With its wide tree-lined avenues and gracious Victorian houses, Lawrence's placidity hides a stormier side. In the mid-19th century it stood in the crossfire of antebellum disputes over slavery and was repeatedly burned, sacked, and raided before and during the Civil War. The town was founded by the abolitionist New England Emigrant Aid Company, who considered naming the town "New Boston." While radicals and rebels no longer dominate the town, Lawrence, home to the University of Kansas, doesn't fit the stereotype of the conservative Kansas town.

The small but stately **Elizabeth Watkins Community Museum,** 1047 Massachusetts St. (841-4109), displays the relics of Lawrence's tumultuous past, with emphasis on the Civil War era. The bottom floor is devoted to the Kansas **Sports Hall**

of Fame, with bios, photos, and mementos of all its members. (Open Tues.-Sat. 10am-4pm, Sun. 1:30-4pm. Donation.) On the **University of Kansas** campus you can see **Comanche,** a currently dead horse, who, when alive, was the only survivor of Custer's Last Stand. He, along with other stuffed animals, is in the **Museum of Natural History,** in Dyche Hall at 14th and Jayhawk Blvd. (864-4540; 864-4450 on weekends). (Open Mon.-Sat. 8am-5pm, Sun. 1-5pm. Donation.) Aesthetes should stop by the **Helen Foresman Spencer Museum of Art,** 1301 Mississippi St. (864-4710), to appreciate a fine collection of Renaissance and baroque painting and sculpture. (Open Tues.-Sat. 8:30am-5pm, Sun. noon-5pm. Free.)

The large student population in Lawrence supports several tasty, reasonably priced restaurants. The **Paradise Café,** 728 Massachusetts St. (842-5199) will toss you a veggie-burger made of lentils, oats, walnuts for $3. (Open Mon.-Tues. 8am-2:30pm, Wed.-Sat. 6:30am-2:30pm and 5-10pm, Sun. 8am-2:30pm.) The **Drake Snack Shop,** 907 Massachusetts St. (843-0561), serves bargains such as an unpredictable "oops omelette" ($3.50) or a meatloaf dinner ($4; open Mon.-Sat. 6:30am-3:30pm, Sun. 8:30am-3pm). The crowded **Tin Pan Alley,** 1105 Mass. St. (749-9756), has great Mexican and American food. (Open Mon.-Sat. 11am-10pm, Sun. 11am-9pm.) For great live jazz, go to the **Jazzhaus,** 926½ Massachusetts St. (749-3320; open daily 4pm-2am).

If you feel like spending the night, try the **College Motel,** 1703 W. 6th (843-0131), a short walk up the hill from the bus station. Rooms are clean, with A/C and a pool. (Singles $22-28. Doubles $28-32.) The small **Jayhawk Motel,** 1004 N. 3rd (843-4131), farther from the center of town, has fairly clean rooms. (Singles $20. Doubles $24.) Another option is the **G.S. Pearson Dormitory,** 500 W. 11th St. (864-4884), at the end of Louisiana St. The dorm rooms are standard, with shared bathrooms and no phone, but spotlessly clean and ultra-secure. Not primarily intended for tourists, but mention *Let's Go* and see if they take you. (Singles $15. Doubles $20.)

Lawrence lurks 25 miles east of Topeka. The main drag is **Massachusetts Street,** between 7th and 11th Avenue. The **Amtrak** station is at 413 E. 7th St. (843-7172 or 800-872-7245), a few blocks east of downtown. Trains run once per day to: Kansas City (1 hr., $11.50); St. Louis (8 hr., $52); and Chicago (10 hr., $94). No tickets are sold at the station, so try a travel agency, such as the one at 704 Massachusetts St. (842-4000; open Mon.-Fri. 9am-5pm, Thurs. 9am-8pm, Sat. 9am-12:30pm). **Greyhound/Trailways** and **Jefferson Lines** share a depot at 1401 W. 6th St. (843-5622), at Michigan, 7 blocks from Massachusetts St. (Open Mon.-Fri. 7am-10:30pm, Sat. 7am-4:30pm and 7-10:30pm, Sun. 7-9am, noon-4:30pm, and 7-10:30pm). Buses go to: Kansas City (10 per day, 1 hr., $12); Wichita (4 per day, 4 hr., $24.25); and Des Moines (3 per day, 6½ hr.). The **Lawrence Bus Co.,** 841 Pennsylvania (842-0544 or 864-3506) runs full service September through May. Over the summer, buses run only between the campus and downtown. (Buses daily 7am-6pm. Fare 75¢.) For a cab, call **A-1 City Cab** (842-2432; bus station to K.U. $3.50).

The **chamber of commerce,** 823 Vermont (843-4411), has listings of historic buildings and a map of town. (Open Mon.-Fri. 8:30am-5pm.) For information on goings-on in town, call the **University of Kansas Information Hotline** (864-3506).

Lawrence's **ZIP code** is 66044; the **area code** is 913.

Missouri

Two types predominate in Missouri: the progressive city slickers from St. Louis and Kansas City who live in "Missouree," and the farmers and small townspeople who inhabit an earthier "Missourah." Politicians jump from one pronunciation to the other with admirable readiness to demonstrate their earnestness. Harry Truman, master of the eloquent expletive, epitomizes the Missourian blend of caution and warmth.

Defined by the nation's two greatest rivers, the Missouri landscape rolls from plains in the east and north into the low Ozark Mountain Range in the south. The state is home to a fascinating hill culture that is rich in handmade crafts and traditional music. T.S. Eliot and Tennessee Williams began their lives, if not careers, in St. Louis, and composer Scott Joplin perfected and popularized the indigenous ragtime rhythm. Samuel Clemens (Mark Twain) of Hannibal wrote *Tom Sawyer* and *Huckleberry Finn,* the novels that immortalized the state's frontier years. Twain's broadside irony and his refusal to knuckle under to "civilization," lends meaning to Missouri's stubborn state motto: Show Me.

Practical Information

Capital: Jefferson City.

Tourist Information: Missouri Division of Tourism, 301 W. High St., P.O. Box 1055, Jefferson City 65102 (751-4133). **Missouri Department of Natural Resources,** 1915 Southridge P.O. Box 176, Jefferson City 65102 (751-3443 or 800-334-6946).

Time Zone: Central (1 hr. behind Eastern). **Postal Abbreviation:** MO.

St. Louis

When Pierre Laclede founded this trading post over two centuries ago, he envisioned it becoming one of the great cities of the New World. Steamboat trade on the Mississippi and the birth of powerful brewing and distilling industries helped realize Laclede's ambition. Today, the city is a vibrant and diverse cultural center.

St. Louis is a pleasure to tour, thanks in great part to the city government's renewed interest in preserving historic housing and in developing and beautifying neighborhoods. When it opened in 1894, **St. Louis Union Station** was an important transportation center. Now it marks a National Historic Landmark, as well as a fun and festive shopping center in the downtown district. Flowers and trees grace the **Soulard Historic District** in South St. Louis, only recently rescued from urban neglect. Further west is the charming **Central West End** and the many attractions in **Forest Park,** the largest urban park in the country. At the **Riverfront** and **Laclede's Landing,** riverboats rest along the banks of the muddy and mighty Mississippi.

Practical Information

Emergency: 911.

Visitor Information: Convention and Visitors Bureau, 10 S. Broadway, #300 (421-1023 or 800-247-9791). Open daily 8:30am-5pm. Stop by the **St. Louis Visitors Center,** 445 N. Memorial Dr. (241-1764), at Mansion House, for the *St. Louis Visitors Guide,* maps, brochures, and friendly advice. Open daily 9:30am-4:30pm. Other tourist information centers are located at the airport and at Kiener Plaza. **Fun Phone,** 421-2100, lists special events. **Entertainment Hotline,** 725-2582.

Travelers Aid: 809 N. Broadway (241-5820). Open Mon.-Fri. 8:30am-5pm, Sat. 10am-2pm.

Lambert St. Louis International Airport: (426-8000), 12 miles northwest of the city on I-70. Served by Bi-State (bus #104 "Natural Bridge"; runs 5:50am-5:45pm, once per hour from 9th and Locust St.) and Greyhound.

Amtrak: 550 S. 16th St. (241-8806 or 800-872-7245), at Market St., downtown. To: Chicago, Dallas, New Orleans, Denver, and Kansas City, MO. Prices vary. Open daily 7am-12:30am. Additional passenger station in Kirkwood at Argonne Dr. and Kirkwood Rd. (966-6475).

Greyhound: 809 N. Broadway (231-7800 or 800-528-0447), north of the business district. A major hub for the midwest. To: Kansas City, MO (4-5 per day, $36); Chicago ($35); Indianapolis ($29); Oklahoma City ($88); Memphis ($49). Airport service. Open 24 hours. Additional station in Kirkwood, 11001 Manchester (965-4444); open Mon.-Fri. 8am-9pm, Sat. 8am-noon and 4:30-9pm.

Bi-State: 231-2345 in St. Louis, 618-875-4144 in E. St. Louis. Extensive service, but buses come infrequently during off-peak hours. Buses operate daily, with reduced service on weekends and holidays. Pick up maps and schedules at the Bi-State Development Agency, 707 N. 1st St., on Laclede's Landing, or at the reference desk of the public library's main branch, 13th and Olive St. Fare 85¢, transfers 15¢; seniors and disabled 40¢, transfers free. Free in the downtown area (bordered by I-40, Broadway, Jefferson, and Cole). The **Levee Line** also offers free service to points of interest between Union Station and the Riverfront.

Taxi: Yellow Cab, 991-1200. First 1/9 mile $1, each additional 1/9 mile 10¢, each additional person 50¢.

Car Rental: Cut-Rate Car Rental, 10232 Natural Bridge (426-2323) $25 per day; 100 free miles, 18¢ each additional mile. Open Mon.-Fri. 7am-10pm, Sat.-Sun. 9am-10pm. Must be 21 with major credit card. **Freewheelin' Bike Rental,** 5854 Delmar Blvd. (361-5854), near Washington University. $10 per day, $25 per weekend, $35 per week. Tandems available. Major credit card for deposit.

Weather Line: 321-2222.

Help Lines: Rape Crisis, 531-2005. 24 hours. **Gay and Lesbian Hotline,** 367-0084.

24-Hour Pharmacy: 351-2100.

Post Office: 1720 Market St. (436-5255). Open Mon.-Fri. 7am-5pm. **ZIP code:** 63166.

Area Code: 314.

The **Mississippi River** divides St. Louis from its unsafe Illinois neighbor, East St. Louis. The city of St. Louis is a small crescent hugging the river; the suburbs (the "county") fan out in all directions. I-44, I-55, I-64, and I-70 meet in St. Louis. **Route 40/64** is the main drag running east-west through the entire metropolitan area. Downtown, **Market Street** divides the city north-south. Numbered streets begin at and run parallel to the river, with **1st Street** closest to the river.

Accommodations

The motels and universities that offer budget accommodations are generally several miles from downtown. Buses do serve the major suburban arteries, but it takes a while to get back to the city.

Huckleberry Finn Youth Hostel (AYH), 1904-1906 S. 12th St. (241-0076), 2 blocks north of Russel St., in S. St. Louis. From downtown, take bus #73 ("Carondelet"), but don't walk, since it is just past an unsafe neighborhood. If you don't mind the shabby alleyway entrance and the flies, the small rooms are neat. Open doors, so guard your belongings. $9, nonmembers $13.

Washington University: Shepley and Eliot Halls at corner of Big Bend Blvd. and Forsyth. Clean rooms offer bare essentials. A/C. Singles $14. Doubles $24. Call 889-5050 or 727-6337 to make reservations. Open May 25-Aug. 20.

Motel 6, 4576 Woodson Rd. (427-1313), in N. St. Louis County. Inconvenient, but dependable. Singles $28. Doubles $34.

Food

Although noted for its German and French heritage, St. Louis' best culinary efforts emerge from kitchens in the Italian and American traditions. The young and affluent gravitate to two areas: **Laclede's Landing** and the **Central West End.** Downtown on the riverfront, Laclede's Landing has experienced an amazing transformation from an industrial wasteland to a popular nightspot. The bars and dance clubs in this area are in restored 19th-century buildings. (Most places have no cover charge.) You can reach the landing by walking north along the river from the Gateway Arch. Less touristy and more established, the Central West End caters to a slightly older crowd. Just north of Lindell Blvd., for 5 blocks along Euclid Ave., a slew of restaurants has won the urban professional seal of approval. Take bus #93 ("Lindell") from Broadway and Locust downtown.

Further west, **Clayton** offers a pleasant setting for window shopping and dining. Historic **South St. Louis,** the "Italian Hill," and the University City Loop (Delmar Blvd. west of Skinker) offer dozens of restaurants.

Amighetti Bakery, 101 N. Broadway (241-3700), downtown, and 5141 Wilson Ave. (776-2855) in S. St. Louis, near I-44. Take bus #95 to Wilson Ave. Order one of Amighetti's locally renowned sandwiches ($4-5) from the express window or join the white-collar lunch crowd inside. Open Mon.-Fri. 10am-3pm, Sat. 10:30am-2pm; express window Mon.-Fri. 11am-6:30pm.

Blueberry Hill, 6504 Delmar (727-0880), near Washington University. The jukebox is rumored to have a library of 30,000 records. Live entertainment in the Elvis Room every Fri.-Sat. Sandwiches and specialties $3-5. Open Mon.-Wed. 11am-9pm, Thurs.-Sat. 11am-1am.

Rossino's, 204 N. Sarah (371-7774), 1 block south of Lindell, just outside the eastern edge of the Central West End. Take bus #93 from Washington and Broadway. A slightly upscale, though downstairs establishment serving Italian food. Lunch Mon.-Fri. 11am-2pm; dinner Mon. 6-11pm, Tues.-Thurs. 5pm-midnight, Fri.-Sat. 5pm-1am, Sun. 5-10pm.

Uncle Sam's Plankhouse, 710 N. 2nd St. (421-0000), at Laclede's Landing. Serves $3-4 chicken and burger specials from various states of the Union. The Hawaii special, broiled in teriyaki and crowned with a ring of pineapple, is $4 with fries. Live entertainment and no cover on weekend nights. Open Mon.-Thurs. 11am-midnight, Fri.-Sat. 11am-3am, Sun. noon-11pm.

Posh Nosh, 8115 Maryland (862-1890), in Clayton. Under the yellow awning you'll find containers of complimentary dill pickles to appease your appetite while you wait for $3 deli sandwiches. Open Mon.-Fri. 10am-8pm, Sat. 10am-7pm, Sun. 11am-3pm.

Ted Drewe's Frozen Custard, 6726 Chippewa (481-2652), and 4224 S. Grand (352-7376). In summertime, it's the place for the true St. Louisian to go. Stand in line, order your chocolate-chip banana concrete, and join the crowd across the street on the grassy banks of the river. Open March-Dec. Sun.-Thurs. 11am-midnight, Fri.-Sat. 11am-1am.

Sights

On Memorial Dr. by the Mississippi, the **Gateway Arch** (425-4465) is visible from 10 miles away. At 630 feet, it stands as the nation's tallest monument. The stainless steel arch is an inverted catenary curve (the shape assumed by a chain hanging freely between two points). Designed by the Finnish architect Eero Saarinen, the arch celebrates St. Louis's former role as a pioneer gateway. On a cloudless day you can see 30 miles of city stretching lazily on one side as the "monstrous big" Mississippi flows by on the other. A train rides up the monument daily in summer 8am to 9:15pm; in winter 9am to 6pm. (Tickets $2.50, children 50¢.) You can spend your one- to two-hour wait at the **Museum of Westward Expansion,** under the arch. Don't miss the *Monument to the Dream,* a half-hour documentary chronicling the sculpture's construction ($1; shown in summer 17 times per day. Museum open same hours as arch.)

Facing the arch two blocks to the west, the **Old Courthouse,** site of the Dred Scott decision, is a wonderful place to view downtown St. Louis. (Open daily 8am-4:30pm. Free.) From the courthouse, walk up Market St. for about a mile to the magnificent old **Union Station.** Currently an indoor shopping mall, the station nostalgically recalls the demise of the St. Louis railroad in the 1950s.

Walk south of downtown (down Tucker Blvd., preferably during daylight hours) or take bus #73 ("Carondelet") to **South St. Louis.** Proclaimed a historic district by the city in the early 70s, this area was home to German and East European immigrants, great numbers of whom worked in the breweries. Young couples and families are now revitalizing South St. Louis, but have not yet displaced an older generation of immigrants.

Walk to the end of 12th St. in the historic district to the **Anheuser-Busch Brewery,** 1127 Pestalozzi St. (577-2626 or 577-2153), at 13th and Lynch. Take bus #40 ("Broadway") or #73 from downtown. Watch the beer-making process from barley to bottles and meet the famous Clydesdale horses. The 70-minute tour stops in the hospitality room, where guests can sample each beer Anheuser-Busch produces. Don't get too excited about the free beer, however—they kick you out after only 15 minutes. (Tours in summer Mon.-Sat. 10am-5pm; rest of the year 9:30am-4pm. Free, but you must pick up a ticket at the office first. Make reservations for groups of 20 or more.)

Also in South St. Louis, built on grounds left by botanist Henry Shaw, are the internationally acclaimed **Missouri Botanical Gardens,** 4344 Shaw (577-5100), north of Tower Grove Park. From downtown, take bus #99 ("Lafayette") from 4th and Locust St. going west. Get off at Shaw and Tower Grove. The gardens display plants and flowers from all over the world. (Open Memorial Day-Labor Day daily 9am-8pm; in winter 9am-5pm. Admission $2, seniors $1, under 12 free. Free Wed. and Sat. mornings.)

To the north and west of downtown you will find **Forest Park,** site of the 1904 World's Fair and St. Louis Exposition. Take bus #93 ("Lindell") from downtown. The park contains two museums, a zoo, a planetarium, a 12,000-seat amphitheater, a grand canal, and countless picnic areas, pathways, and flying golf balls. Of special note is the **Missouri Historical Society** (361-1424), at the corner of Lindell and DeBaliviere, on the north side of the park. It is filled with American memorabilia, and has an exhibit devoted to Charles Lindbergh's flight across the Atlantic in the "Spirit of St. Louis." (Open Tues.-Sun. 9:30am-4:45pm. Free.) Just to the southwest, high atop Art Hill, stands an equestrian statue of France's Louis IX, the city's namesake. The king beckons with his raised sword toward the **St. Louis Art Museum,** which contains masterpieces of Asian, Renaissance, and impressionist art. (721-0067; open Tues. 1:30-8:30pm, Wed.-Sun. 10am-5pm. Free.) Near the southern edge of the park lies the **St. Louis Zoo** (781-0900). Marlin Perkins, rugged former host of the TV show *Wild Kingdom,* turned the zoo into a world-class institution. At the Living World exhibit, you can see computer-generated images of future evolutionary stages of humans. (Open daily 9am-5pm. Free.) The **St. Louis Science Center-Forest Park** (289-4400) offers hands-on exhibits and a planetarium projector. (Admission to planetarium $3, children $2. Admission to Discovery Room 50¢.)

The **Cathedral of St. Louis,** 4431 Lindell Ave. (533-2824), just north of Forest Park at Newstead, is a bizarre but successful combination of Romanesque, Byzantine, Gothic, and baroque styles. Gold-flecked mosaics depict episodes from 19th-century church history in Missouri. (Free tour Sun. 1pm. Open daily 8am-8pm. Take bus #93 ("Lindell") from downtown.)

The **Magic House,** 516 S. Kirkwood Rd. (822-8900) can be a hair-raising good time—place your hand on the van de Graff generator to find out how. (Open Memorial Day-Labor Day Tues.-Thurs. 10am-6pm, Fri. 10am-9pm, Sat. 10am-6pm, Sun. noon-6pm; in winter Tues.-Thurs. 3-6pm, Fri. 3-9pm, Sat. 10am-6pm, Sun. noon-6pm. Adults $2.50, under 12 $2.)

The Crafts Alliance Gallery, 6640 Delmar Blvd. (725-1151), north of Washington University, shows ceramic, enamel, glass, metal, and textile works by American craftspeople. (Open Tues.-Fri. noon-5pm, Sat. 10am-5pm. Free. From downtown, take bus #91 ("Delmar-Forsyth") on Washington St.)

Laumeier Sculpture Park, 12580 Rott Rd. (821-1209), is the second largest in the U.S., with over 50 sculptures on 96 acres. The park also hosts free outdoor jazz concerts on Sunday evenings during the summer. (Open daily 8am-½ hr. past sunset. Gallery hours Wed.-Sat. 10am-5pm, Sun. noon-5pm. Free.)

See the only 1936 vintage bowling pin car at the **National Bowling Hall of Fame and Museum,** 111 Stadium Plaza (231-6340). Even if bowling isn't your favorite sport, the museum can provide an afternoon's entertainment. (Open Memorial Day-Labor Day Mon.-Sat. 9am-7pm, Sun. noon-7pm; in winter Mon.-Sat. 9am-5pm, Sun. noon-5pm. Adults $3, seniors $2, children $1.50.)

Sightseers can also view St. Louis from the water on a **river cruise** (621-4040). Departures in summer every 45 minutes begin at 10:15 daily; in spring and fall every 1½ hr., beginning at 11am. (Cruise $6.50, children $3.50.)

Entertainment

St. Louis's heart belongs to ragtime and brassy Dixieland jazz. In the early 1900s, showboats carrying Dixieland and rag regularly traveled to and from Chicago and New Orleans. St. Louis, a natural stopover, fell head over heels in love with the music and, happily, has never recovered. If you, too, are enamored of the style, try the **Goldenrod Showboat,** 700 Lenore K. Sullivan Blvd (621-3311), along the river. (Jazz and dixieland bands Tues.-Wed. at 9:30pm, Thurs.-Sat. at 8:30pm. Balcony seats $14.90-17.90. Buffet dinner before every show.) For purists, the annual **National Ragtime Festival** is held on the riverboat in mid-June. If your wallet is thin (tickets are $19.50), you could probably sit by the boat and hear the music from the pavement. Float down the Mississippi while listening to jazz on the *President* (241-5500), a five-story paddleboat. (2½-hr. cruise Tues. 10:30am, Wed.-Sun. 10:30am and 7pm. Adults $9, children $4.25. Rates higher at night. Open June-Oct.)

Laclede's Landing, just north of the arch, is St. Louis's evening hotspot. Bars and restaurants featuring jazz, blues, and reggae fill "the landing." Try **Muddy Waters,** 724 North 1st St. (421-5335), for live music on weekends. (Open Mon.-Sat. 11am-3am, Sun. noon-3am.) The **Funnybone Comedy Club,** 940 W. Port Plaza (469-6692), offers national headliners for a modest price and a two-drink minimum. (Sun. and Wed.-Thurs. $5, Fri. $7, Sat. $8.)

Founded in 1880, the **St. Louis Symphony Orchestra** is one of the finest in the country. **Powell Hall,** 718 N. Grand (534-1700), which houses the 101-member orchestra, is acoustically and visually magnificent. (Performances Sept.-May Thurs. at 8pm, Fri.-Sat. at 8:30pm, Sun. at 3 and 7:30pm. Box office open Mon.-Sat. 9am-5pm and before performances. Tickets $9-40. take bus #97 to Grand Ave.)

St. Louis offers the theater-goer many choices. The **Municipal Opera** (361-1900) performs hit musicals in Forest Park during the summer. Tickets cost up to $28.50, but the rear 1200 seats, quite far from the stage, are free. Arrive around 6:15pm for 8:15pm shows and bring a picnic (no bottles). Hot dogs and beer are sold at moderate prices. **The Opera Theatre of St. Louis,** 130 Edgar Rd., Webster Groves (961-0171) features new and classic operas in English. (Performances Tues.-Sun. Tickets $7.50-45.) Tour the **Fabulous Fox Theatre** (534-1678) for $2.50, under 12 $1.50 (Sat. at 10:30am. Call for reservations), or pay a little more for Las Vegas, country, and rock stars, Broadway shows, or classic films. Renovated and reopened in 1982, the Fox Theatre was originally a 1930s movie palace.

St. Louis Cardinals baseball games (421-3060; April-Oct. Tickets $5-8) are held at Busch Stadium, downtown. **Blues** hockey games (781-5300) take place at the **Arena.** (Sept.-May; tickets $10-21.)

Kansas City

A haven for 1920s gamblers, prostitutes, stray cowpokes, and the jazz musicians who entertained them, Kansas City underwent a thorough clean-up by reformers disgusted with what they deemed a corrupt and amoral town. By the 50s, jazz musicians were sparse indeed, but have since made a remarkable comeback. In contrast, gone forever are the formerly bustling stockyards, now inert vestiges of the city's once-vibrant agriculture and beef production. Rather than moving out, however, Kansas City residents have returned downtown, where recent construction and renovation have produced a slew of shopping malls, moderately priced restaurants, nightclubs, and cultural festivals.

All listings are for Kansas City, MO unless otherwise stated.

Practical Information

Emergency: 911.

Visitor Information: Visitors Center, 1100 Main St., #2550 (221-5242 or 800-767-7700), in the City Center Square bldg. downtown. Pick up *A Visitor's Guide to Kansas City.* Open Mon.-Fri. 8:30am-4:30pm. Also at 4010 Blue Ridge Cutoff (861-8800), just off I-70, next to the stadium. **Daily Visitors Information** (474-9600) is a recorded listing of theater in the downtown area. **Jazz Hotline,** 936-2888. **Concert Line,** 931-0077. **Fine Arts Line,** 756-0123.

Kansas City International Airport: 243-5237, 18 miles northwest of Kansas City, off I-29. The **KCI Express Bus** (243-5950) departs from airport gate #63 at 6:30am, then every ½ hr. 8am-9pm, and at 11:30pm; it goes to the Greyhound station, Crown Center, and Country Club Plaza (Fare $11). Bus #29 goes to the airport for 85¢ but takes much longer and leaves only in the early morning and late afternoon.

Amtrak: 2200 Main St. (421-3622 or 800-872-7245), directly across from Crown Center. Take bus #28, 31, 40, 51, 53, 54, 56, or 57. To: St. Louis (2 per day, 5½ hr., $40-60) and Chicago (2 per day, 9 hr., $74). Open 24 hours.

Greyhound/Trailways: 1101 N. Troost (698-0080 or 221-2835), To: St. Louis (8 per day, 4-5 hr., $36); Chicago (5 per day, 11 hr., $49); and Des Moines (4 per day, 5 hr., $39). Open daily 4:30am-12:30am.

Kansas City Area Transportation Authority (Metro): 1350 E. 17th St. (221-0660; Mon.-Fri. 6am-6pm), at Brooklyn. Excellent downtown coverage. Fare 75¢, plus 10¢ for crossing zones. Free transfers; free return receipt available downtown. Pick up maps and schedules at headquarters, airport gate #62, or on buses.

Taxi: Economy Cabs, 621-3436. **Yellow Cab,** 471-5000. About $22 from airport downtown; determine fare before trip.

Car Rental: Thrifty Car Rental, 2001 Baltimore (842-8550 or 800-367-2277), 1 block west of 20th and Main St. Compact $28 per day Mon.-Thurs., $18 Fri.-Sun. 150 free miles, 25¢ each additional mile. Must be 21 with major credit card.

Post Office: 315 W. Pershing Rd. (374-9275), near the train station. Open Mon.-Fri. 8am-6:30pm, Sat. 8am-12:30pm. General Delivery Mon.-Fri. only. **ZIP code:** 64108.

Area Codes: 913 in Kansas, 816 in Missouri.

Kansas City is actually two cities rolled into one—the west side sits in Kansas and the east in Missouri. Each has its own police department, government, area code, and alcohol laws. The metropolitan area of Kansas City is huge and spread out, so traveling may take a while. Almost every sight worth visiting lies south of the Missouri River, on the Missouri side of town, which is organized like a grid: numbered streets run east-west and named streets run north-south. **Main Street,** the central artery, divides the city east-west and cuts north-south close to the farmers market and the central business district, Crown Center, Westport, and the Country Club Plaza.

Accommodations

Kansas City is a big convention center and can usually accommodate everyone looking for a room. The least expensive lodgings are near the interstates. The highways leading from Kansas City to Independence, MO are lined with lodging bargains. Downtown, most hotels are either expensive or uninhabitable, with a few exceptions.

Travelodge, 921 Cherry St. (471-1266) at 9th St. The best downtown motel deal. Large, clean, secure rooms. Bus schedules in lobby. Singles $30. Doubles $40.

Traveler's Inn, 606 E. 31st (861-4100), off I-435 at I-70 and U.S. 40. Take bus #28. Pleasant rooms, indoor pool, spa, gameroom, laundry, free cable TV. Singles $25-30. Doubles $27-32. Key deposit $2.

Motor-Inn Hotel, 2018 Main St. (471-7872). Most buses traveling south from downtown, such as #40 along Main, pass nearby. A few blocks from Crown Center, but a potentially unsafe neighborhood. Rooms are cramped and dingy; a last resort for the carless. No visitors after 11pm, and you must leave your room key at desk when you leave the building. Singles $16.50, with bath $19.10. Doubles $19.

Food

Kansas City boasts a herd of meaty, juicy barbecue restaurants. Equally notable are K.C.'s unusually tangy ribs. For fresh produce, visit the **farmers market** in the morning, especially on Saturday. It's in the River Quay area, at 5th and Walnut St.

Arthur Bryant's, 1727 Brooklyn St. (231-1123), about 1 mile east of downtown at 17th. Take bus #71 ("Prospect"). A local legend. The meat and sauce are superb and the servings are more than generous. Barbecued beef sandwiches ($5.25) are enough to stuff any living human. Open Mon.-Thurs. 10am-9:30pm, Fri.-Sat. 10am-10pm, Sun. 11am-8pm.

The Golden Ox, 1600 Genesee (842-2866). Take bus #12 to the stockyards. Lunch $4-6, dinner $10-17. Open Mon.-Fri. 11:20am-10pm, Sat. 5-10:30pm, Sun. 4-9pm. The restaurant runs a more reasonably priced **cafeteria** next door—enter through the Stockyards Building. Dine with livestock locals on hearty entrees for about $3. Open 6am-1:30pm.

Stanford and Sons, 504 Westport Rd. (756-1450). A lively place in the middle of Westport, and a favorite singles haunt. Sandwiches $5-6, entrees $7-15. Open Mon.-Thurs. 11:30am-11pm, Fri.-Sat. 11:30am-1am, Sun. 10am-11pm.

The Pumpernickel Deli, 319 E. 11th St. (421-5766), 4 blocks from downtown. Friendly, busy place with rustic decor. Often sells cheap, fresh veggies outside. Sandwiches $1-2.50, with the jumbo hoagie topping the menu at $2.60. Open Mon.-Fri. 7:30am-6:30pm, Sat. 9am-3pm.

Stephenson's Old Apple Farm Restaurant, 16401 E. U.S. 40 (373-5400). Several miles from downtown, but the hickory-smoked specialties are worth the trip. The dishes that accompany all entrees (fruit salad, apple fritters, and corn relish) are almost as notable as the specialties. Open Mon.-Fri. 11:30am-10pm, Sat. 11:30am-11pm, Sun. 10am-9pm.

Lamar's Do-Nuts, 240 E. Linwood (931-5166). Amazingly fresh, sweet, scrumptious doughnuts. Open Mon.-Sat. 6am-6pm, Sun. 6:30am-4pm.

Sights

Built in 1922, the **Country Club Plaza** (known as "the plaza") is the oldest and perhaps most picturesque American shopping center, located 2½ miles south of Crown Center. Modeled after Seville, Spain, the plaza seems to sprout fountains, scuptures, hand-painted tiles, and reliefs of grinning gargoyles on every corner.

A few blocks to the northeast, the **Nelson-Atkins Museum of Fine Art,** 45th Terrace and Rockhill (931-4278), is renowned for its East Asian collection. Check out the fluorescent statue of Picasso scratching himself. (Open Tues.-Sat. 10am-5pm, Sun. 1-5pm. Admission $3, students $1. Free admission Sun. to permanent exhibits. Take bus #40, 56 or 57 from Main downtown, or from Crown Center at Grand and Pershing.)

Two miles north of the plaza is **Crown Center,** 2450 Grand Ave. (274-8444), at Pershing. The headquarters of Hallmark Cards, it houses a maze of restaurants and shops and a hotel with a five-story indoor waterfall. Inside, the **Hallmark Visitors Center** (274-5672) fetchingly illustrates the company's history and the process of greeting card production. (Visitors center open Mon.-Fri. 9am-5pm, Sat. 9:30am-4:30pm. Free.) Also in the Crown Center are the **Coterie Children's Theatre** (474-6552) and the **Ice Terrace** (274-8411), K.C.'s only public ice skating rink (take bus #40, 56, or 57 or take any trolley from downtown for $3). The Crown Center has free **Concerts in the Park** every Friday evening at 8pm during the summer. Last summer's performances included Diana Ross, The Who, and the Grateful Dead. Run through a huge fountain designed for this purpose; you can't have more fun on a hot summer night with your clothes on. Just to the west stands the **Liberty Memorial,** 100 W. 26th St. (221-1918), a tribute to those who died in World War I. Ride the elevator to the top for a fantastic view. The Memorial also includes a museum. (Open Tues.-Sun 9:30am-4:30pm. Free. Elevators $2, students 50¢, under 11 25¢.)

Entertainment

Most of K.C.'s bars and nightclubs are in the Missouri half of the city; those on the Kansas side are all "private" (over 21 only) and require a membership fee of $10-25. Formerly the crossroads of the Santa Fe, Oregon, and California Trails, and an outfitting post for travelers to the west, the restored **Westport** area (931-3586), near Broadway and Westport Rd., about ½ a mile north of the plaza, is packed with nightspots. **Blayney's,** 415 Westport Rd. (561-3747), is in a small basement and hosts live bands six nights per week, playing reggae, rock, or jazz. Monday is "Blues Night." (Open Mon.-Sat. 7pm-3am. Cover $2 or less.) Old-fashioned **Kelly's Westport Inn,** 500 Westport Rd. (753-9193), gets rowdy around sundown. (Open Mon.-Sat. 6am-1am.) Next door, Stanford & Sons offers one of the only live comedy shows in K.C. (Showtimes Mon.-Thurs. 9pm, Fri. at 8 and 11pm, Sat. at 6, 8:30 and 11pm. Cover: Mon.-Thurs. $2-4, Fri.-Sat. $5-7.)

There is no shortage of jazz in K.C. In the 20s, it was part of the famous triangle that included Chicago and New Orleans. Count Basie and his "Kansas City Sound" reigned at the River City bars, while Charlie "Yardbird" Parker, whose fame was made in New York, thrived in the open environment. Stop by the **Grand Emporium Hotel and Saloon,** 3832 Main St. (531-1504), to hear jazz bands play on Friday and Saturday. (Weekdays feature rock, blues, and reggae bands; open Mon.-Sat. 9pm-3am.) The wild times have passed, but they are fondly remembered in **Milton's Tap Room,** 3241 Main St. (753-9384). The late Miltie once sponsored Basie, Parker, and other jazz greats. (Live music Fri.-Sat. 8pm-1am.) **City Lights,** 7425 Broadway (444-6969) may not be as nostalgic, but it is dependable and fun. Live bands Tues.-Sat. 9pm-1am; house jazz band. (Open Mon.-Sat. 5pm-1:30am. Cover $2.)

Sports fans will be bowled over by the massive **Harry S. Truman Sports Complex.** Even Howard Cosell did not have enough inscrutable superlatives to describe **Arrowhead Stadium,** 1 Arrowhead Dr. (924-3333), home of the Chiefs football team (924-9400) or **Royals Stadium,** 1 Royal Way (921-8000), home of the Royals baseball team. The stadium express bus runs from downtown on game days.

Nebraska

The Platte River gave Nebraska its name, which comes from an Omaha word meaning "river in the flatness." Many of Nebraska's place names recall the people who populated the harsh territory prior to European settlement, such as Tecumseh, Weeping Water, Ogallala, and Otoe. But very little else has been left to the plains tribes. For almost two decades after the Homestead Act of 1862, Nebraska was often a battlefield, as settlers fought with Crazy Horse, Red Cloud, and Dull Knife.

Agriculture dominates Nebraska, which produces much of the food consumed by the other 49 states. Thomas Jefferson once said that "cultivators of the earth are the most virtuous citizens"—and Nebraskans heartily agree.

Practical Information

Capital: Lincoln.

Tourist Information: Nebraska Department of Economic Development, P.O. Box 94666, Lincoln 68509 (471-3796). **Nebraska Game and Parks Commission,** 2200 N. 33rd St., Lincoln 68503 (464-0641). Permits for campgrounds and park areas. Open Mon.-Fri. 8am-5pm.

Time Zone: Central (1 hr. behind Eastern) and Mountain (2 hr. behind Eastern). **Postal Abbreviation:** NE.

Omaha

Omaha was at the center of many of the great migrations westward in the 19th century. The Mormons spent the winter here in 1846 before continuing on to Utah and, in 1863, the city was the center point for the first Transcontinental Railroad. Always a stop-over point for transients, Omaha today offers travelers a little culture and a great selection of ethnic food.

Practical Information

Emergency: 911.

Visitor Information: Nebraska/Omaha Tourist Information Center, 1212 Deer Park Blvd. (554-3990), at I-80 and 13th St. (Rte. 73/75). Take bus #6 from downtown. Open April-Oct. daily 9am-5pm. **Douglas County Tourism and Convention Bureau,** 1819 Farnam St., #1200 (444-4660), in the Omaha-Douglas Civic Center. City bus schedules in the basement, behind the cafeteria area. **Events Hotline,** 444-6800.

Amtrak: 1003 S. 9th St. (342-1501 or 800-872-7245). One train once per day to: Chicago (9 hr., $91); Denver (9 hr., $96) and Salt Lake City (24 hr., $161). Open Mon.-Fri. 7am-3:30pm and 9:45pm-7am, Sat.-Sun. 9:45pm-7am.

Greyhound: 1601 Jackson (341-1906). To: Kansas City (4 per day, 4 hr., $38.50); Chicago (9 per day, 9-12 hr., $69) and Denver (5 per day, 10-13 hr., $59). Open 24 hours.

Metro Area Transit (MAT): 2615 Cuming St. (341-0800). Maps available at the Park Fair Mall, 16th and Douglas, near the Greyhound station. Open daily 9:30am-5:30pm. Buses run Mon.-Fri. 5am-10pm, Sat. 7am-10pm. Fare 75¢, transfers 5¢. Bus #28 ("Airport") from 10th St. serves the airport twice early in the morning and twice late in the afternoon.

Taxi: Happy Cab, 339-0110. $1.20 first mile, $1 each additional mile. To airport $7.

Car Rental: Rent-a-Wreck, 501 N. 17th St. (344-2001), at Cass St. $18 per day; 50 free miles, 10¢ each additional mile. Open Mon.-Sat. 7:30am-6pm. Must be 21 with major credit card or $100 deposit.

Help Lines: Crisis Line, Inc., 341-9111 or 341-9112. **Mayor's Commission on the Handicapped,** 444-5021. Information on transportation, access, and services. Open Mon.-Fri. 8am-4:30pm.

Time Zone: Central (1 hr. behind Eastern).

Post Office: 1124 Pacific St. (348-2861). Open Mon.-Fri. 7:30am-5pm, Sat. 8:30am-noon. **ZIP code:** 68108.

Area Code: 402.

Omaha sits along the **Missouri River,** halfway up Nebraska's eastern border, a little over 125 miles west of Des Moines on I-80. I-80 cuts horizontally through southern greater Omaha, then dips down to the southwest for a 50-mile trek to Lincoln. I-480 runs south along the western edge of downtown to join I-80. I-29 runs north-south on the western side of the Missouri River. Numbered north-south streets begin at the river; named roads run east-west. **Dodge Street** divides the city north-south. When night falls, avoid 24th Street, and stay close to Creighton University. The area from 10 to 19th Street between Dodge and Jackson is considered safe.

Accommodations and Camping

Many motels are off the L or 72nd St. exits from I-80, 5½ miles southwest of downtown. Buses #11, #21, and #55 service the area.

Motel 6, 10708 M St. (331-3161), near 108th and L St. Bus #55 will get you only as close as 108th and Q. Safe area. Clean rooms with HBO and pool. Near a mall and restaurants. Singles $26. Doubles $32.

Motel 89, 4303 S. 89th St. (331-0646), at H St. Take bus #55 to 84th and H St. from 24th and Farnham. Small, dark rooms with cable TV. Singles $19. Doubles $21.

Super 8, 7111 Spring St. (390-0700), near 72nd and Grover St. Take bus #11 or #21. Non-smoking rooms, cable TV. Restaurants nearby. Singles $31. Doubles $37. Also at 108 and L St. (339-2250). Singles $28. Doubles $34.

Bellevue Campground, at Haworth Park (291-3379), on Rte. 370 near the Bellevue Bridge. Take the infrequent bus #50 ("Bellevue") from 17th and Dodge, get off at Mission and Franklin, and walk down Mission. Bus #60X, the Offutt Air Force Base line, travels south once in the morning, and north once in the afternoon. Showers, toilets, and shelters. On the Missouri River. Tent sites $4, with hookup $7. Water 75¢ extra. Open daily 7am-10pm, but stragglers can come after hours.

Food and Entertainment

The **Old Market,** 10th and Howard St., in the southeastern corner of downtown, was once a warehouse district, but is now filled with shops, bars, and restaurants. South Omaha includes an old Slavic neighborhood (Bohemians, Poles, and Slovaks). Farnam, near Creighton University, a few blocks past I-480, is fast-food row. **Bohemian Café,** 1406 S. 13th St. (342-9838), will stuff you with liver dumplings, duckling, kraut, rye bread, and Czech specialties for under $6. (Open daily 11am-10pm.) **Joe Tess' Place,** 5424 S. 24th St. (731-7278), at U St. in South Omaha (take bus #6 from Farnam and 16th) is renowned for its fresh, fried carp and catfish, served with thin-sliced potatoes and rye bread. (Entrees $3-7. Open Mon.-Thurs. 10:30am-11pm, Fri.-Sat. 10:30am-midnight, Sun. 11am-11pm.) **Chicago,** 3259 Farnam St. (346-7300; take bus #1, 2, 3, or 28), a popular hangout for Creighton and University of Nebraska students, serves delicious hamburgers with fried mushrooms and potatoes and sandwiches ($2-4; open Mon.-Sat. 11am-11pm, Sun. noon-11pm). **The Choice,** 10803 John Galt Blvd. (592-5110), is a pleasant family restaurant featuring a huge smorgasbord (lunch $4.40, dinner $5.40; open Mon.-Sat. 11am-8pm, Sun. 8am-8pm).

For nightlife in the Old Market area, head to the **Howard St. Tavern,** 1112 Howard St. (341-0433). The local crowds and good music create a pleasant atmosphere. Cover usually $2-3.50. (Open Mon.-Sat. 2pm-1am, Sun. 6pm-1am). **Omaha's Magic Theater,** 1417 Farnam St. (346-1227; call Mon.-Fri. 9am-5:30pm), specializes in satirical musical comedy. (Performances Fri.-Mon. evenings. Tickets $5, seniors and students $2.)

Sights

Omaha's **Joslyn Art Museum,** 2200 Dodge St. (342-3300), is a three-story art deco landmark with a fantastic courtyard and an excellent display of local artifacts. In the summer, they host "Jazz on the Green," Thursdays from 7-9pm. (Open Tues.-Sat. 10am-5pm, Sun. 1-5pm. Admission $2, seniors and under 12 $1.)

The **Omaha History Museum,** 801 S. 10th St. (444-5071), has a historic schoolroom and soda fountain among its exhibits, but its main feature is the architecture. Built in the old Union Pacific Railroad Station in 1929, the museum glitters with kitsch. (Open Tues.-Sat. 10am-5pm, Sun. 1-5pm. Admission $2, under 12 $1.) For a non-traditional view of how the West was won, visit the **Great Plains Black Museum,** 2213 Lake St. (345-2212), an exhibit on black pioneer history. (Open Mon.-Fri. 8am-5pm. Admission $1. Take bus #8 from 19th and Farnam or #9 from Dodge.) The **Omaha Children's Museum,** 551 S. 18th St. (342-6163), features hands-on science and art exhibits. (Open Tues.-Sat. 10am-5pm, Sat. 1-5pm; Sept.-May Tues.-Fri. 1-5pm, Sat. 10am-5pm, Sun. 1-5pm.) The **Henry Doorly Zoo,** 3701 S. 10th St. (733-8400), at Deer Park Blvd., has Siberian tigers and a good aviary. (Open April-Oct. Mon.-Sat. 9:30am-5pm, Sun. 9:30am-6pm. Admission $5, children $2.50.)

Lincoln

From nearly 20 miles away you can see the Nebraska State Capitol soaring far above the city and farmlands below. The "Tower on the Plains," remarkable for its streamlined exterior and detailed interior, is an appropriate centerpiece for Lincoln, an oasis of learning, government, and culture on the prairie.

In 1867, the settlement of Lancaster was renamed Lincoln, in honor of the recently deceased president, and became the state's capital. This hospitable pioneer town is now the seat of Nebraska's unique one-house legislature, and home of the big red Cornhuskers, Nebraska's beloved football team.

Practical Information

Emergency: 911.

Visitor Information: Tourist Offices, #606, 1221 N St. (477-6300). Open Mon.-Fri. 8am-4:45pm. Downtown branch, 105 S. 9th St. (477-6300), at O St. Open late May-Sept. daily 9am-5pm.

Amtrak: 201 N. 7th St. (476-1295 or 800-872-7245). One train east, one west daily. To: Omaha (1 hr., $13) and Denver (7½ hr., $94). Open Mon.-Wed. 6am-3pm and 11pm-7am, Thurs.-Sun. 11pm-7am.

Greyhound: 940 P St. (474-1071), close to downtown and campus. To: Omaha (6 per day, 1 hr., $10) and Chicago (6 per day, 10-12 hr., $90.50). Buses run east-west. Open Mon.-Fri. 7am-9:30pm, Sat. 8am-9:30pm, Sun. 9am-9:30pm.

Lincoln Transportation System: 710 J St. (476-1234). Open Mon.-Fri. 7am-4:30pm. All buses stop at 11th and O St. "Star shuttle" buses serve downtown Mon.-Fri. 9:30am-4:50pm (10¢). Service Mon.-Sat. 6am-7pm. Fare 65¢.

Taxi: Yellow Cab, 477-4111. $2.50 first mile, $1 each additional mile.

Car Rental: Economy Rent-a-Car, 2912 N. 38th St. (466-3344), 1 block south of Adams. $10 per day with 50 free miles, 12¢ each additional mile. Cars cannot cross state line. Open Mon.-Fri. 7:30am-5:30pm, Sat. 8am-1pm. Must be 21 with major credit card or $2.50 cash deposit.

League of Human Dignity: 1423 O St. (471-7871). Advice and aid, including local transportation for disabled persons. Open Mon.-Fri. 8am-5pm.

Help Lines: Rape Crisis, 471-7273. 24 hours. **Gay/Lesbian Support Line,** 475-4967. **Lodging Hotline,** 476-2192.

Post Office: 700 R St. (473-1695). Open Mon.-Fri. 8am-5pm, Sat. 8am-noon. **ZIP code:** 68508.

Area Code: 402.

Lincoln is in southeastern Nebraska, 55 miles southwest of Omaha on I-80. **O Street** is the main east-west drag and splits the town north-south. Alphabetized streets increase northwards. **First Street,** running north-south, sits along **Salt Creek,** west of downtown. Numbers increase to the east. The **University of Nebraska** (472-7211) is on the northern border of downtown. Check the **student union** on 14th at R St. for ride boards (south at main entrance) and cheap food. Most places of interest are within walking of distance downtown, except for the university's **East Campus.** Take the university shuttle from Lyman Hall or bus #4 ("University Place").

Accommodations and Camping

There are several budget motels on West O St. (about a $5 cab ride from downtown), including the **Senate Inn,** 2801 West O. St. (475-4921), with clean rooms, pool, cable TV, and café. (Singles $24. Doubles $30-32. Take bus #12.) You may want to avoid cab fares and pay to stay downtown at the gorgeous, family-run **Town House Mini-Suite Motel,** 18th and M St. (475-3000). Each room is a one-bedroom apartment with a kitchen, cable TV, great beds, and access to a microwave. (Singles

$33. Doubles $38.) If you're flying to Lincoln, try the **Motel 6,** 3001 NW 12th (475-3211), near the airport and I-80, for standard motel rooms with cable TV. (Singles $24. Doubles $30.)

The best place to camp is at **Branched Oak Lake** (464-0641, ext. 245), north on Rte. 34, 12 miles out of town, where facilities include showers and restrooms. (Sites $6, $8 with electricity.) Campers need a Nebraska park entry permit ($2), available at lake headquarters or at the Nebraska Game and Parks Commission in Lincoln (see Nebraska Practical Information).

Food and Nightlife

Lincoln abounds with fast-food places, most of them on the southern edge of the campus. Students and locals alike flock to **Valentino's,** 3457 Holdrege (467-3611), near the East Campus, for great pizza, pasta, antipasto, and buffets. Medium pizzas cost about $9. (Open Sun.-Thurs. 11am-11pm, Fri. 11am-12:30am, Sat. 11am-1am. Take the shuttle from Lyman Hall or bus #4 "University Place" from downtown.) A second Valentino's is at 232 N. 13th St. (475-1501), near the city campus. **Kerrey's,** 201 Sun Valley Blvd. (475-3677), just west of Salt Creek, has hearty and delicious fare. Quiche, soup, and vegetable are $5.50. Seniors get a 10% discount. (Open Mon.-Thurs. 11am-2pm and 5-10pm, Fri. 11am-2pm and 5-11pm, Sat. 11am-11pm.)

Local bar patrons' favor rests with **P.O. Pears,** 322 S. 9th St. (476-8551), a lively place with fascinating mechanized decor. Draft beer is 69¢, bottles $1.09, burger and fries $3. (Open Mon.-Sat. 11:30am-1am, Sun. 1-11pm.) The best live music in town can be heard at the **Zoo Bar,** 136 N. 14th (435-8754; open Mon.-Sat. noon-1am, Sun. 6-11pm. Cover $2-8.) **Speakeasy's,** 13th and Arapahoe St. (423-9883), at Indian Village, has a renowned house band that plays rock, oldies, blues, and country in a nostalgic, memorablilia-laden bar. (Open Mon.-Sat. 11am-1am. One-drink minimum.)

Sights

The **capitol building,** 14th at K St. (471-0448), maintains all the pomp and majesty of an art deco museum. A statue of a sower stands on top of the tower, spreading his seed over the state to insure fertility. (Tours Mon.-Fri. on most hours and half-hours; Sept.-May on the hour; year-round hourly Sat. 10am-4pm, Sun. 1-4pm. Open daily 9am-5pm. Free.)

The **Sheldon Memorial Art Gallery,** 12th and R St. (472-2461), on the University of Nebraska city campus, is not to be missed. The cool, white building designed by Philip Johnson is as great a work of art as its collection of rural paintings by Cole, Davies, and Innes. (Open Tues.-Sat. 10am-5pm, Sun. 2-5pm.)

An unusually large mammoth named "Archie," short for its genus name, *Archidiscodon,* poses with several other fossil relatives in the **University of Nebraska State Museum,** Elephant Hall, in Morrill Hall, 14th and U St. (472-2642; open Tues.-Sat. 8am-5pm. Donation.)

North Platte

Close to Fort McPherson, an important stop on the Oregon Trail, North Platte is famed as the home of William Cody, otherwise known as "Buffalo Bill." Every year during the third week in June, the town holds **Nebraskaland Days** in memory of the legendary showman. Highlights include a road run, contests (featuring hog calling and cake baking), parades, and a rodeo.

Buffalo Bill used **Scouts Rest Ranch,** Buffalo Bill Ave. (532-4795), as his home during the heyday of his Wild West Shows. Follow Jeffers north over the railroad tracks, turn west on Rodeo Rd. (Rte. 30), then north on Buffalo Bill Ave. Mementos of Cody's career as an Indian fighter, army scout, buffalo hunter, and showman are displayed in the Gothic mansion and brightly-colored barn. (Open Memorial

Day-Labor Day daily 10am-8pm; rest of the year by appointment only.) A Nebraska Park entry permit is required for entrance ($2), available at the ranch or at the Nebraska Game and Parks Commission in Lincoln (see Nebraska Practical Information). From the beginning of July through mid-August, the Ranch holds a Buffalo Stew cook-out and cowboy sing-along. (Wed.-Fri. 6pm. Admission $3.)

Down the road from Scouts Rest, the **Lincoln County Historical Museum,** 2403 Buffalo Bill Ave. (534-5640), displays possessions of the other illustrious settlers of the area. (Open daily 9am-8pm. Free.) For some western excitement, head out to the **Rough Riders Rodeo,** in the arena across the street from the Historical Museum. (Rodeos late June-late Aug. nightly 8:30pm. Admission $4, children $2.)

The **Greyhound** station is at 4th and Chestnut St. (532-2324; open Mon.-Fri. 7:30am-6pm, Sat. 10am-6pm, Sun. 11:30am-6pm). The **Lincoln County Tourist Bureau,** 509 E. 4th St. (532-4966), is 1 block from the bus depot. (Open Mon.-Fri. 9am-5pm.) A **Nebraska Tourist Information Center** is located at the intersection of I-80 and Rte. 83. (386-4806; open May-Sept. daily 8am-4pm.)

North Dakota

Though North Dakota was proclaimed the 39th state in 1889, most of its windswept lands still remain a mystery to travelers in the U.S. Those that do visit often pass as quickly as they can through the eastern prairie to the more sensational "badlands," the infertile, pock-marked buttes that dominate the western half of the state. Sojourners searching for solitude, however, would be well advised to savor the tranquil expanses of farmlands before moving on to the tourist-filled western towns.

No matter where you go in North Dakota, you will find the locals eager to make you feel at home. People here are about as sparse as snow in June (there are fewer than 10 per square mile), but they are twice as amenable. Whether you are in search of a ride down the interstate or a bed for the night, you have only to ask. North Dakotans are the epitome of the Midwestern adage: cold hands, warm heart. In the words of one long-time resident, "If you want clean air, good food, and people who give a damn, come to North Dakota."

Practical Information

Capital: Bismarck.

Tourist Information: Tourism Promotion Division, Liberty Memorial Bldg., Capitol Grounds, Bismarck 58505 (800-437-2077, 224-2525, or 800-472-2100 in ND). **Parks and Recreation Department,** 1424 W. Century Ave., #202, Bismarck 58502 (224-4887).

Time Zone: Central (1 hr. behind Eastern) and Mountain (2 hr. behind Eastern). **Postal Abbreviation:** ND.

Area Code: 701.

Bismarck

As a port on the east bank of the Missouri River, this pleasant frontier town grew more rapidly than any of its neighbors. When the first rails were laid across the slopes of the Rockies, it became the terminus for the Northern Pacific Railway and was renamed in honor of the current Chancellor of Germany in hopes of attracting German investment in the budding railroad company.

Practical Information

Emergency: Police, 700 S. Ninth St. (223-1212).

Bismarck-Mandan Convention and Visitors Bureau: 523 N. 4th St. (222-4308). Open Mon.-Fri. 8am-5pm.

Bismarck Municipal Airport: 2½ miles south of Bismarck, near the intersection of University Dr. (Rte. 1804) and Airport Rd.

Greyhound: 1237 W. Divide (223-6576), 3 inconvenient miles west of downtown, off I-94 exit 35. To: Minneapolis (10 hr., $47) and Seattle (1½ days, $145). Open Mon.-Fri. 3:30-5am, 8am-1pm, and 4-9pm, Sat.-Sun. 3:30-5am, 9am-12:30pm, and 6-9pm.

Taxi 9000: 223-9000. $1.25 per mile.

Time Zone: Central (1 hr. behind Eastern), except for Fort Lincoln, which is Mountain (2 hr. behind Eastern).

Post Office: 220 E. Rosser Ave. (221-6517). Open Mon.-Fri. 8am-5pm, Sat. 10-noon. **ZIP code:** 58501.

Area Code: 701.

Most of **Bismarck** is contained within an oval formed by I-94 and its corollary Business 94, otherwise known as **Main Street.** Bismarck's small downtown shopping district is located in the southwest curve of this oval, bounded by Washington St. and 9th St. on the west and east, and Rosser Ave. and Business 94 on the north and south.

Accommodations, Camping, and Food

The **Highway Motel,** 6319 E. Main St. (223-0506), 2 miles east on Rte. 10, rents rooms to local workers by the month, but they often have space for those staying only a night or two. (Singles $19.90. Doubles $23—couples should use the same last name.) **Motel 6,** 2433 State St. (255-6878), right off I-94, offers clean, small rooms and a pool. (Singles $25. Doubles $31. Under 18 free). Your best bet closer to town is the **Bismarck Motor Hotel,** 2301 E. Main Ave. (223-2474). (Singles $17.90. Doubles $34.)

The **Hillcrest Campground** (255-4334), 1½ miles out of town on E. Main St., provides showers and scenery from April-Sept. (Sites $5). **General Sibley Park** (222-1844), 4 miles south of Bismarck on S. Washington St., is a Garden of Eden worthy of a visit even if you don't stay the night. If you do decide to stay, call ahead for reservations, and then set up camp in a glen of huge, shady trees on the banks of the Missouri River. The park has showers. (Sites $5, with full hookup $9.) **Fort Lincoln State Park** (663-9571), 5 miles south of Mandan on Rte. 1806, has a quiet campground on the east bank of the Missouri. (Sites $8, with water and electricity $10. Daily pass to park and showers included.)

There are several local diners that serve tasty, inexpensive meals. The **Little Cottage Cafe,** 2513 E. Main St. (223-4949), brings in droves of workers at the lunch whistle and families at dinnertime. (Fantastic muffins 90¢, 8-oz. sirloin steak $5.25. Open daily 6am-10pm.) The **Drumstick Cafe,** 307 N. 3rd St. (223-8449), serves breakfast all day. The home-baked desserts (fresh strawberry pie 95¢) and fresh-ground coffee are superb. Sandwiches are $2-3.50. (Open Mon.-Sat. 24 hours.) For an intimate family dinner complete with classical music, try **Caspar's East 40,** 1401 E. Interchange Ave. (258-7222). The service is fast and friendly, the food delicious. (Chicken teriyaki dinner $5.25.) Reservations preferred.

Sights and Entertainment

Bismarck takes every opportunity to tout its 20-story art deco **State Capitol,** 900 East Blvd. (224-2480). However, a walk through the main lobby and a ride to the observation platform will show you everything noteworthy.

Walk across the wide green lawn in front of the capitol to reach the **North Dakota Heritage Center** (224-2666). The exhibits inside on the Plains tribes, the buffalo, and the history of white settlement are extensive and sophisticated. (Open Mon.-Thurs. 8am-5pm, Fri. 8am-8pm, Sat. 9am-5pm, Sun. 11am-5pm. Free.)

The less showy but equally informative **Camp Hancock Historic Site,** at the intersection of 1st Ave. and Main St. (224-2666), was originally constructed to house the workers on the Northern Pacific Railroad. (Open Wed.-Sun. 1-5pm.) Below Mandan, on the opposite bank of the Missouri, lies **Fort Lincoln,** a campsite built for the same purpose. Today it is known as the starting point of General Custer's march towards his fatal meeting with Sitting Bull at Little Bighorn. The fort is part of the **Fort Lincoln State Park** (663-9571), which also features a reconstructed Mandan village on its original site, renovated army blockhouses, and a small collection of artifacts and memorabilia from native peoples and early settlers. It is worth an afternoon trip and is never crowded. (Park open daily 8am-sunset; Sept.-May Mon.-Fri. 9am-sunset. Museum open daily 9am-9pm; Sept.-May Mon.-Fri. 9am-5pm.)

To find out about local entertainment, drop by the new **Bismarck Civic Center,** at the terminus of Sweet Ave. E.(222-6491), for a schedule of events.

If you're in town at the end of July, join the lifetime fans of the **Annual North Dakota Prison Rodeo,** held at the penitentiary east of Bismarck. In the first week of August, watch for the **Art Fair,** held on the Capitol Mall lawn. And in early September, call 701-255-3285 for information on the **United Tribes Pow Wow,** one of the largest gatherings of Native Americans in the nation. Enjoy the dancing, singing, foods and crafts of many tribes, but be sure to call ahead.

Theodore Roosevelt National Memorial Park and Medora

It's called "rough-rider country" in honor of President Theodore Roosevelt, who recognized the beauty of the badlands' red and brown-hued lunar formations. After Roosevelt's mother and wife died on the same day, he came here in search of "physical and spiritual renewal;" today's visitor can find the same peace among the park's quiet canyons and dramatic rocky outcroppings.

The park is divided into a south unit and a north unit. The entrance to the better-developed **south unit,** (Time Zone: Mountain) is just north of I-94 in the historic frontier town of **Medora.** Restored with the tourist in mind, Medora is a place to hold tightly to your purse strings. Limit your shopping to **Joe Ferris' General Store** (623-4447), spotless and still inexpensive. (Open daily 8am-8pm.) If you're in need of immediate nourishment, stop by the **Badlands Bake Shoppe,** four doors to the left of Ferris, for a midday snack. Large muffins 85¢, loaf of Dakota bread—perfect hiking food—$2.19. (Open daily May-Sept. 8am-5pm.) Budget motels are even harder to find than budget food, but the **Dietz Motel,** 401 Broadway (623-4455), offers clean spacious basement rooms for the lowest rates in town. (Singles $18-$20. Doubles $22-$26.) Reserve a month in advance. Medora's only sight is the **Badlands Wax Museum,** on Main St. (623-4451), which tells you all there is to know about the town. (Open Tues.-Sat. 10am-9pm, Sun.-Mon. 10am-7pm. Admission $2, children $1).

Start your exploration of the park at the **visitors center** (623-4466) on the western edge of town. The center serves as a mini-museum, displaying a few of Teddy's guns, spurs, and old letters, and showing a beautiful film of winter badlands scenes. (Open daily 7am-7pm; Sept.-May 8am-4:30pm. Inquire at desk for the showtimes of the film.) Here you pay the park entrance fee ($3 for vehicles, $1 for pedestrians.) Then either walk or drive along the 36-mile scenic loop through the park, or drive to one of the unpaved trails that start from the loop and foot it deep into the wilderness. Don't miss the world's third-largest **petrified forest,** 14 miles into the park. **Painted Canyon Overlook,** 7 miles east of Medora, has a **visitors center** (575-4020; open daily 8am-5pm), picnic tables, and a breathtaking view of the badlands.

The **north unit** of the park is 75 miles from the south unit on Rte. 85. (Time zone: Central.) Most of the land is wilderness; very few people visit, and fewer still stay overnight. Backcountry hiking possibilities are endless. Check in at the ranger station (623-4466 or 842-2333) for information and a free overnight camping permit. (Open daily 8am-4:30pm.) The park maintains **Squaw Creek Campground,** 5 miles west of the north unit entrance. (Sites $6.)

Greyhound serves Medora from the Dietz Motel, with two buses daily to Bismarck ($20) and Billings, MT ($53).

For more information on the park, write to Theodore Roosevelt National Memorial Park, Medora 58645.

Oklahoma

The foothills of the Ozarks roll into the Oklahoma plain, creating a dry, bumpy land that the pioneers called the Great American Desert. President Andrew Jackson populated this desert with Native American nations displaced from the Southeast. Although Jackson assured Congress that this "Trail of Tears" was the last time the tribes would be forced to move, 60 years later they were again forcibly relocated to permit a dramatic land rush that brought droves of white settlers to the territory. Oklahoma still calls itself the Sooner state in honor of the homesteaders who got to the territory before it was officially opened.

In recent years, Oklahoma has been plagued with economic uncertainty. Parts of the state dried up and blew away during the Great Depression, forcing many farmers, similar to the Joad family in John Steinbeck's *Grapes of Wrath,* to migrate west. Oil and new conservation methods helped the state to recover, but in the last decade both oil prices and crops have shriveled. The Oklahomans' friendly, smiling faces belie their past struggles and future uncertainty.

Practical Information

Capital: Oklahoma City.

Tourist Information: Oklahoma Tourism and Recreation Department, 215 NE 28th St., Oklahoma City 73105 (521-2409), 2 blocks west of Lincoln Blvd.

Time Zone: Central (1 hr. behind Eastern). **Postal Abbreviation:** OK.

Alcohol: Many areas outside the major cities are "dry."

Tulsa

Back in the 20s, oil was found in the Oklahoma dirt and Tulsa earned the nickname "Terra Cotta City" as ambitious new millionaires built a cavalcade of art deco skyscrapers. Falling oil prices have recently created plenty of cheap office space, and downtown rattles like a ghost town. Tulsa now promotes itself as an "Indian" town, claiming the highest percentage Native American population of any U.S. metropolitan region.

Practical Information

Emergency: 911.

Visitor Information: Convention and Visitors Division, Metropolitan Tulsa Chamber of Commerce, 616 S. Boston 74119 (585-1201 or 800-558-3311). **Information Center,** in the kiosk on the east side of the Civic Center, Denver and 5th St., 5 blocks west of the bus depot. Open Mon.-Thurs. 7am-5pm, Fri. 7-11am. **Events Line,** 585-2787. 24-hour recording.

Greyhound/Trailways: 317 S. Detroit (584-4427). To: Oklahoma City (11 per day, 2 hr., $12); St. Louis (11 per day, 7½-9½ hr., $58); Kansas City (9 per day, 6-8 hr., $47); and Dallas (8 per day, 7 hr., $50). Lockers $1. Open 24 hours.

Local Transit: Metropolitan Tulsa Transit Authority, 510 S. Rockford (582-2100). Buses run every 30-60 min. until about 6pm. Fare 60¢, transfers 5¢, seniors and disabled 30¢, ages 5-18 50¢. Free trolley around downtown 11:30am-1:30pm and 4:30-6:30pm. Maps and schedules available at the main office (open Mon.-Sat. 7am-5:30pm), the chamber of commerce, the kiosk in front of the Tulsa Central Library at 5th and Denver, and most other libraries.

Taxi: Yellow Cab, 582-6161.

Bike Rentals: River Trail Sports Center, 3949 Riverside Dr. (743-5898), at 41st St. 5-speeds $4 per hr., $12 per day. Open Mon.-Sat. 10am-7pm, Sun. 11am-6pm. Must have driver's license or cash deposit.

Help Lines: 583-4357. 24-hour information, referral, and crisis intervention. **Gay Information Line,** 743-4297; daily 8-10pm.

Post Office: 333 W. 4th St. (581-7555). Open Mon.-Fri. 8:30am-5pm. **ZIP code:** 74101.

Area Code: 918.

Tulsa sits on I-44, 100 miles from Oklahoma City in the northeastern corner of the state. All "South" addresses are along the numbered east-west streets, which begin downtown. Named streets lie in alphabetical order, with the alphabet beginning at north-south avenues on both sides of **Main Street,** and at east-west streets 1 block north of **First Street.** Streets named after the western cities are on the west side of town, eastern on the east side.

Accommodations and Camping

Most cheap accommodations in Tulsa are outside the city center. An exception is the **YMCA,** 515 S. Denver (583-6201), open to men only. Ask for a room on the third floor—they're cleaner. Guests have access to pool and gym and the office is open 24 hours. (Singles only, $10.) The cheapest downtown motel is the **Darby Lane Inn,** 416 W. 6th St. (584-4461). Clean, recently remodeled rooms have cable TV. (Singles $28. Doubles $36. Reserve ahead.) Outside downtown, budget motels abound along I-244 and bordering streets. The **Gateway Motor Inn** is at 5600 W. Skelly Dr. (446-6611), off I-44, 8 miles outside of downtown. Take bus #17 and get off at Reasor's Grocery. Rooms are clean with enormous beds, cable TV, and HBO. (Singles from $19. Doubles $27.) Across I-44 (but inaccessible by bus), **Days Inn,** 1016 N. Garnett Rd. (438-5050), about 7 miles east of town off I-244, has clean rooms with HBO. (Singles $18. Doubles $23.) The **KOA,** 193 East Ave. (266-4227), ½ mile west of the Will Rogers Turnpike Gate off I-44, has a pool, laundry room, and game room. (Sites $14.50, with hookup $15.50.) Three **state parks** (865-4991) with campgrounds grace the shores of Keystone Reservoir, 20 miles west of Tulsa on the Cimarron Turnpike (U.S. 64). Four-person cabins are also available ($40; call 800-522-8565 for reservations).

Food

The menu changes every day at **Nelson's** popular cafeteria, 514 S. Boston (584-9969). Generous breakfast specials ($2-3) are served from 8:30 to 10:30am; lunches cost $3-4. (Open daily 6am-3pm.) In the eastern section of Tulsa, **Mark's Super Subs and Health Food,** 3208 E. 11th St. (583-4397), has a stunning array of subs ($2-4; open Mon.-Sat. 10:30am-9pm.) Two blocks away is one of Tulsa's finest eating establishments, the 50s-style **Metro Diner,** 3001 E. 11th St. (592-2616), at College. The colorful interior has checkerboard Winthropian floors, a ton of 50s memorabilia, and a soda fountain. They specialize in sinfully rich fountain treats and homemade pies ($1.75). Dinners are $4-6 and burgers are $2-4.50. Seniors get a 10% discount. (Open Sun.-Thurs. 7am-1am, Fri.-Sat. 7am-2am.) Keep in mind that most downtown restaurants close at 3pm on weekdays and 1pm on Saturdays.

Sights and Entertainment

The **Thomas Gilcrease Museum**, 1400 Gilcrease Museum Rd. (582-3122), at Newton St. and 25th Ave., 2 miles northwest of downtown, specializes in American art and history. It houses a large collection of Remington sculptures and Russell paintings. It also has Native American jewelry, masks, and weapons. (Open Mon.-Sat. 9am-5pm, Sun. 1-5pm. Donation. Take bus #7 "Gilcrease" from downtown; walk north from 25th West Ave. and Independence Pl.)

The **Philbrook Art Center,** 2727 S. Rockford Rd. (749-7941), in the former Renaissance villa of an oil baron, now houses a collection of Native American pottery and artifacts and Renaissance paintings and sculpture. Half the building will be closed for renovation until 1990. Picnic by the lovely pond on the grounds. (Open Tues.-Sat. 10am-5pm, Sun. 1-5pm. Admission $3, seniors and college students $1.50, high school students and children free. Take bus #16 "S. Peoria" from downtown.)

You won't find any student bars around **Oral Roberts University (ORU),** 7777 S. Lewis (495-6161): no smoking, drinking, or dancing is allowed on this emphatically Christian campus. Many local residents call it the "University of Mars" because of its futuristic, gold-mirrored, angled architecture—like an alien imitation of art deco. Inside the "Prayer Tower" (a.k.a. "Prayer Rocket;" 495-6807), visitors can walk through an exhibition idolizing the university's founder. Choirs sing in the background, spotlights illuminate mementos from Roberts's childhood, and, like the gates of heaven, the doors open and close automatically. A 700-foot Jesus appeared to Oral Roberts and instructed him to build the **O.R. City of Faith Hospital** (493-8065 to schedule tours). At the entrance stands an imposing pair of 80-foot-high praying hands. The **ORU Healing Outreach** (496-7700) hosts a "Journey Through the Bible" tour, where old testament scenes are re-created in life-like, three-dimensional exhibits. (Tours every 15-20 min. Mon.-Sat. 10:30am-4:30pm, Sun. 1-5pm. Free.) The university is about 6 miles south of downtown Tulsa between Lewis and Harvard Ave. (Prayer Tower and visitors center open Mon.-Sat. 9am-4:30pm, Sunday 1-4:30pm. Take bus #9 "S. Lewis").

Fans of art deco architecture will want to visit the **Boston Avenue United Methodist Church,** 1301 S. Boston (583-5181). Built in 1929, it is faintly suggestive of the witch's palace in *The Wizard of Oz.* Climb the 14-story tower for a skyline view of downtown Tulsa. Free tours are given after the 11am services on Sunday or for specially scheduled groups.

Rodgers and Hammerstein's *Oklahoma!* is performed at the **Discoveryland Amphitheater** (245-0242), 10 miles west of Tulsa on 41st St. The play gives a *somewhat* romanticized introduction to Oklahoma's history. Just the same, a night under the stars is a treat. Be sure to arrive early for the pre-show barbecue, starting at 5:30pm. (Shows June-Aug. Mon.-Sat. at 8pm. Admission $11, under 11 $7. Pre-show starts at 7:30. Barbecue $6.50, children $4.50.) For tickets call 245-6552 or write 2502 E. 71st St., Tulsa 74136.

At night, get out of downtown and try the bars along 15th St. east of Peoria, or in the 30s along S. Peoria. The **Sunset Grill,** 3410 S. Peoria (744-5550), never charges for its rowdy rock bands. There is a free buffet at midnight and live music every night. (Drinks $2-3; free popcorn. Open daily 8pm-2am.) To keep up-to-date on Tulsa's nightlife, pick up a free copy of *Uptown News* at a newsstand or bookstore.

Oklahoma City

Oklahoma City began on April 22, 1889 with a gunshot that sent settlers swarming by foot, horseback, covered wagon, and bike into the newly opened Oklahoma territory. Soon the Sooners found oil, and during the early 1930s Oklahoma City was liberally sprayed with "oil from the sky," spewing out of the city's wells. Today, a working well is still right on the grounds of the capitol building, but that's about all the activity you'll find in downtown OKC. Stand outside Santa Fe Plaza in the heart of downtown at 9am and you'll see only a scarce handful of people trickle by. More than a third of OKC's offices are empty and people are still moving out. Not surprisingly, tourists are also in short supply.

Those who do visit be forewarned: neighborhoods change quickly from decent to dangerous, and the bus system is lousy. Buses run only once an hour even on weekdays, and stops are few and far between. Those without cars should plan their sight-seeing carefully. Try not to travel alone and avoid being stranded in an unsavory area.

Practical Information

Emergency: Police, 231-2121.

Visitor Information: Chamber of Commerce Tourist Information, 4 Santa Fe Plaza (278-8912), at the east end of Park Ave. Open Mon.-Fri. 8am-4:30pm.

Travelers Aid: Located in the Greyhound station. Open Mon.-Fri. 9am-4pm.

Will Rogers Memorial Airport: (681-5311), southwest of downtown. **Airport Limousine, Inc.,** 1800 S. Meridian (685-2638), has van service to downtown ($9).

Greyhound/Trailways: 427 W. Sheridan Ave. (235-6425) at Walker. The station is in a seedy part of town, but near a stop for city buses #5, 6, 11, and 12. To: Tulsa (11 per day, 2 hr., $11); Dallas (4 per day, 5 hr., $36); and Kansas City (5 per day, 10 hr., $49). Open 24 hours.

Local Transit: Masstrans, 300 E. California Blvd. (235-7433). Bus service Mon.-Sat. 6am-5:40pm. All routes radiate from the station at Reno and Gaylord, where maps are available. Route numbers vary depending on the direction that buses travel. Fare 75¢

Taxi: Yellow Cab, 232-6161. $2 1st mile, $1 each additional mile. Airport to downtown $12.

Car Rental: Rent-a-Wreck, 2930 NW 39th St. (956-9288). Used cars $25 per day with 150 free miles, 20¢ each additional mile. Open Mon.-Fri. 8am-5:30pm, Sat. 8:30am-noon. Must be 21 or over.

Bike Rental: Miller's Bicycle Distribution, 739 Asp Ave. (321-8296). 10-speeds $2 per day. Open Mon.-Fri. 9am-5:30pm, Sat. 9am-3pm. Must have major credit card or a $75 deposit.

Help Lines: Crisis Hotline, 848-2273. **Rape Crisis,** 524-7273. Both 24 hours.

Post Office: 320 SW 5th St. (278-6246). Open Mon.-Fri. 8:30am-5:30pm, Sat. 9am-noon. **ZIP code:** 73125.

Area Code: 405.

Oklahoma City lies virtually at the center of the state. I-35 and I-40 intersect at right angles in the city. Dallas is about 200 miles to the south. Streets are organized more or less on a grid. **Main Street** divides the town east-west.

Accommodations, Camping, and Food

If you can stand it, the **YMCA,** 125 NW 5th St. (232-6061), will put you up for only $10.50. (Men only. Shared baths.) The **Myriad Motor Inn,** 1305 Classen (235-2384), at NW 13th and N. Shartel, is one of the best deals in the city. It is in a pleasant neighborhood close to downtown, with indoor pool, color TV, and adjacent restaurant. Large country breakfast is included. (Singles $23. Doubles $28.) The **Brass Lantern Inn,** 700 NW 9th St. (232-0505), across from St. Anthony's Hospital, has clean, quiet, comfortable rooms. (Singles $25. Doubles $30.) I-35 near Oklahoma City is lined with inexpensive hotels with singles for under $25.

Oklahoma City has two readily accessible **campgrounds. RCA,** 12115 NE Expressway (478-0278), next to Frontier City Amusement Park, 10 miles north on I-35, has a pool, laundry room, and showers. (Tent sites $11 for 2, RV sites with hookup $14. Each additional person $2.) **Briscoe's RV,** 6002 South I-35 (632-1901) at 59th, has parched sites for $8. The nearest state park with camping lies on Lake Thunderbird about 30 miles south at **Little River State Park** (360-3572 or 364-7634;

tent sites $3; showers included). Take I-40 East to the Choctaw Rd. exit, then south until the road ends. (Office open 8am-5pm.)

Since Oklahoma City has the largest feeder cattle market in the U.S., beef tops most menus. Downtown, the concourse under **Skirvin Plaza** is filled with lunch spots. Enter from the Skirvin or Sheridan Century hotels. (Open 11am-3pm.) The **Cattlemen's Café,** 1309 S. Agnew (236-0416), near the stockyards, serves its namesake well. (Prime rib dinner $5, navy bean soup with cornbread $1, sandwiches $2-3.50. Open 24 hours.) Try "Oklahoma crepes" (chicken, cream cheese, and jack cheese enchiladas topped with sour cream) at **Pump's Bar and Grill,** 5700 N. Western (840-4369). (Burgers, sandwiches, and specialties $3.50-7. Open Sun.-Thurs. 11am-10:30pm, Fri.-Sat. 11am-midnight.)

Sights and Entertainment

The **Oklahoma City Stockyards,** 2500 Exchange Ave. (235-8675; take bus #11 from Hudson downtown to S. Agnew Ave.) are the busiest in the world. Cattle auctions, held here Monday through Thursday, begin at 7 or 8am and sometimes last into the night. Monday and Tuesday are the busiest days, and mornings are the best time to visit. The auctioneer fires bids in a rapid-fire monotone as cowhands chase the cattle through a maze of gates and passages into the auction building. Visitors can reach this building via a catwalk over the pens, leading from the parking lot east of the auction house.

The plight of Native Americans along the "Trail of Tears" is commemorated by James Earle Fraser's *The End of the Trail.* His sculpture of a man slumped over an exhausted pony is on display at the **National Cowboy Hall of Fame and Western Heritage Center,** 1700 N.E. 63rd St. (478-2250). Along with Frederic Remington sculptures and cowboy memorabilia, you'll find John Wayne's collection of Pueblo kachina dolls. Every summer, the museum showcases 150 works of the National Academy of Western Art. (Open daily 8:30am-6pm; Labor Day-Memorial Day 8:30am-5pm. Admission $4, seniors $3, ages 6-12 $1.50. Take bus #22 from downtown.)

Gas lamps and spacious mansions are the hallmarks of **Heritage Hill,** a grand neighborhood of restored turn-of-the-century houses. The **Overholser Mansion,** 405 NW 15th St. (528-8485), built in 1903, is a good example of Victorian architecture and is filled with elaborate Limoges china services, Venetian crystal, and Meissen vases. For many years, this mansion was the social center of Oklahoma City. (Free tours every hr. Tues.-Fri. 10am-4pm, Sat.-Sun. 2-4pm.) Another area of gorgeous homes is **Nichols Hills,** a community just north of Oklahoma City. Take bus #5 (from Walker and Main) past 63rd and wander west.

The **Kirkpatrick Center Museum Complex,** 2100 NE 52nd St. (427-4561), a sort of educational amusement park, looks like a mall but is actually divided (in an undecipherable pattern) into eight separate museums, each of which is colorful and entertaining. Highlights are the **Air and Space Museum** and the **International Photography Hall of Fame.** (Admission to all 8 museums $5, seniors and ages 5-12 $3. Open Mon.-Sat. 9am-6pm, Sun. noon-6pm; Labor Day-Memorial Day Mon.-Fri. 9am-5pm, Sat. 9am-6pm, Sun. noon-6pm. Take bus #22.)

For a night of country dancing and music, try **Doc Severinson's,** 201 N. Meridian (946-2300). When Doc's own band doesn't play, other groups do. (Open Wed.-Sat. from 4:30pm. Ticket office open 10am-10pm. Prices vary with performers; no charge for the house band.) The **Oklahoma Opry,** 404 W. Commerce (632-8322), is home to many country music stars. (Regular performances Sat. 8pm.) The **Black Liberated Arts Center,** 1901 N. Ellison (528-4666), provides plays and musical events at the Classen Theater from October to May.

South Dakota

You may be surprised by all that this state has to offer. In the east, the wind blows over the expansive grasslands where buffalo once roamed. Farther west, the Missouri River never veers from its southeastern course towards the mighty Mississippi Along the Wyoming border, the Black Hills rise in a magnificent jumble of rocky spires, forested slopes and convoluted caverns, and the sandstone vistas of the Badlands continue to fall prey to the winds and rain. Tourism is the second-largest industry in South Dakota—make the most of local hospitality.

Practical Information

Capital: Pierre.

Tourist Information: Division of Tourism, 221 S. Central, in Capitol Lake Plaza, P.O. Box 1000, Pierre 57051 (773-3301 or 800-952-2217; 800-843-1930 outside SD). Open Mon.-Fri. 8am-5pm. **U.S. Forest Service,** Custer 57730 (673-2551). Camping stamps for National Forest, Golden Eagle passes for ages over 62, and Black Hills National Forest maps ($1). Open Mon.-Fri. 8am-5pm. **Division of Parks and Recreation,** Capitol Bldg., Pierre 57501 (773-3391). Information on state parks and campgrounds. Open Mon.-Fri. 8am-5pm.

Time Zones: Central (1 hr. behind Eastern) and Mountain (2 hr. behind Eastern). **Postal Abbreviation:** SD.

Rapid City

Rapid City's location, approximately 40 miles east of the Wyoming border, makes it an ideal base from which to explore both the Black Hills and the Badlands. Every summer the area is visited by about 2.2 million tourists, over 40 times the city's permanent population.

Practical Information

Emergency: 911.

Visitor Information: Rapid City Chamber of Commerce, Visitors Bureau, 444 Mt. Rushmore Rd. N. (343-1744), in the Civic Center. Visitors bureau open Memorial Day-Labor Day daily 7am-6pm; chamber of commerce (343-1744) open year-round Mon.-Fri. 8am-5pm.

Buses: Milo Barber Transportation Center, 333 6th St. (348-3300), downtown. **Jack Rabbit Lines** runs east of Rapid City. To: Pierre (1 per day, 3 hr. $33) and Sioux Falls (2 per day, 8 hr., Mon.-Thurs. $49). **Powder River Lines** service Wyoming and Montana. To: Cheyenne (2 per day, 8½ hr., $53.50) and Billings (2 per day, 9 hr., $65). **Arrow Stage Lines** run to Nebraska and Iowa. To: Omaha (3 per day, 13 hr., $49). All 3 honor the Greyhound Ameripass. Station open Mon.-Fri. 6am-11pm, Sat. 6am-5:30pm and 9:30-11pm, Sun. 6am-1pm, 4-5:30pm, and 9:30-11pm.

Local Transit: Milo Barber Transportation Center, 348-7433. City bus transportation available by reservation. Call 24 hours in advance. One way trip $1, seniors 50¢. Office open Mon.-Fri. 6am-5:30pm.

Taxi: Rapid Taxi, 348-8080. Base fare $2, $1 per mile.

Car Rental: Black Hills Car Rental, 301 Campbell (342-6696). $15 per day plus 15¢ per mile. $89 per week plus 12¢ per mile and $250 deposit. Budget cars $13 per day plus 12¢ per mile, subject to availability. Open Mon.-Fri. 8am-6pm, Sat. 8am-3pm. Must be 21 with a major credit card or at least $100 deposit.

Time Zone: Mountain (2 hr. behind Eastern).

Post Office: 500 East Blvd. (394-8600), several blocks east of downtown. Open Mon.-Fri. 8am-5pm, Sat. 9:30am-12:30pm. **ZIP code:** 57701.

Area Code: 605.

Orienting yourself may be difficult at first, since Rapid City sprawls across 27 flat square miles, and few of the buildings in town stand taller than four stories. The center of the downtown area is bordered on the east and west by 6th and 9th Street, and on the north and south by Omaha and Kansas City Street.

Accommodations, Camping, and Food

The **AYH hostel** is in the **YMCA,** 815 Kansas City St. (342-8538), downtown. It consists of 12 cots, with no separation between men and women. Access to kitchen and YMCA facilities is available, but no bedding is provided. A cot for the night costs $4 for AYH members or any young foreigner.

Rapid City accommodations are considerably more expensive during the summer. Make reservations, since budget motels often fill up weeks in advance. The **Tip Top Motor Hotel,** 405 St. Joseph St. (343-3901), downtown, has an outdoor pool and cable TV. It's a little musty, but clean. (Singles $39.50. Doubles $52.50. In off-season, $24.50 and $27.50, respectively.) **Motel 6** is less conveniently located northeast of town, off I-90 exit 59, about a $4 cab trip from downtown. Some rooms have disabled access. (Pool. Singles $30. Doubles $36.) A last resort is the **Golden Hills Motel,** 206 Main St. (342-6232), 5 blocks from the bus station. It's a bit dingy but clean and cheap, with access to a kitchenette. (Singles $29. Doubles $36.) **The Berry Patch Campground,** 1860 E. North St. (341-5588), 1 mile east of I-90 off exit 60, has 14 grass campsites, gameroom, playground, showers, and swimming. (Tent sites $12.50 for 2, with hookup (April 12-Oct. 1 only) $16. Each additional person $1.50.)

When your thoughts turn to food, check out **Aunt Jane's,** 807 Columbus (341-4529), on the first floor of a Victorian house and stuffed with antiques. Aunt Jane prepares her own recipes, such as Rocky Mountain salad sandwich (ham, swiss cheese, and peaches; $3.25). (Open Mon.-Fri. 8am-4:30pm, Sat. 9am-2pm.) **Tally's,** 530 6th St. (342-7621), downtown, under the orange awning, serves family-style country meals such as chicken and dumplings ($3.65. Open daily 7am-8pm; Labor Day-Memorial Day 7am-7pm.) Don't miss the 5¢ cookies at **Ray's Retail Bakery,** 729 Main (343-4720; open Mon.-Sat. 5am-5pm). The **Flying T** (342-1905), 6 miles south on U.S. 16, next to the Reptile Gardens, serves a chuck wagon meal on a tin plate for $9, singing cowboys included. Dinner (7:30pm) and a show (8:15pm) are offered every night. (Open 24 hours, but only in the summer.)

Sights and Entertainment

Tourism rears its flashing neon head in Rapid City. Those who wish to explore the town should try the self-guided **Circle Tour,** which begins at the Rushmore Plaza Civic Center, 444 Mt. Rushmore Rd. The **Sioux Indian Museum** and the **Pioneer Museum** (both 348-0557), 515 West Blvd., between Main and St. Joseph St. in Halley Park, present interesting but limited exhibits. (Open Mon.-Sat. 9am-5pm, Sun. 1-5pm; Oct.-May Tues.-Sat. 10am-5pm, Sun. 1-5pm.) **The Museum of Geology,** 501 E. St. Joseph St. (394-2467), in the administration building of the School of Mines and Technology, just east of Main St., exhibits the beautiful minerals and textbook fossils of the Badlands. (Open Mon.-Sat. 8am-6pm, Sun. noon-6pm; off-season Mon.-Fri. 8am-5pm, Sat. 9am-2pm, Sun. 1-4pm. Free.) The **Dahl Fine Arts Center,** 7th and Quincy St., houses rotating exhibits of local and Native American art. It also has the enormous "Cyclorama of American History"—a 200-foot, circular mural. (Open Mon.-Thurs. 9am-8pm, Fri.-Sat. 9am-5pm, Sun. 1-5pm.) For more information, ask at the civic center.

For nightlife, try Main Street between 9th and Mt. Rushmore St. **Filly's Food, Fun, and Firewater** (348-8300), in the **Hilton,** is a fantastic spot for a quiet drink or a comedy show. (Shows Fri.-Sat. at 9 and 11pm. Open Mon.-Sat. 11am-2am, Sun. noon-midnight. Cover $5-6.) For boot-stompin' country-western music and dancing, head to **Boot Hill,** 826 Main St. (343-1931), where live bands perform nightly. (Open Mon.-Sat. 3pm-2am, Sun. 5-11:30pm. Cover Tues.-Sat. $2.)

Black Hills

The Black Hills, so named for the dark sheen that distance lends to the green pines covering the hills, have long been considered sacred by the Sioux Indians living to the north. The treaty of 1868 gave the Black Hills and the rest of South Dakota west of the Missouri River to the Sioux, but the treaty was broken in the gold rush of 1877-79. Since then, Anglo-Americans have dominated the forested hills, white granite spires, and expansive underground caves with logging, mining, and tourism. Recently, the Sioux took their claims to federal courts and, in 1980, the Supreme Court awarded them a "just compensation" of $200 million. The Sioux, however, refused to accept the money, wanting only the return of their land. Legislative efforts to address this conflict have, to date, met with slow death by Congressional inertia.

I-90 skirts the northern border of the Black Hills through Spearfish in the west and Rapid City in the east; the interconnecting road system through the hills is difficult to navigate without a good map. Pick up a free South Dakota tourism map at the Rapid City Chamber of Commerce.

Powder River Lines serves only Deadwood, Lead, and Hot Springs (see Rapid City Practical Information). If you have the time and the money, rent a car to explore the area thoroughly. Hitching a ride with vacationers can be tough, but the locals are helpful. Alternatively, take advantage of the excellent and informative **Gray Line** tours (342-4461). Tickets are available at Rapid City motels, hotels, and campgrounds. Make reservations, or call one hour before departure. They will pick you up at your motel. Tour #1 is the most complete Black Hills tour: Mt. Rushmore, Black Hills National Forest, Custer State Park, Needles Highway, and the Crazy Horse Monument (mid-May to mid-Oct. daily, 8 hr., $24). Tour #2 goes north through the Black Hills to the historic western towns of Lead and Deadwood, Mt. Moriah Cemetery (see Lead and Deadwood below), and the Black Hills mining museum. (June-Aug. daily 8 hr., $26.) Tour #4 heads to Spearfish for the Black Hills Passion Play (June-Aug. Sun., Tues., and Thurs., 5 hr., $18). Tour #5 provides nighttime transportation to Mt. Rushmore, which is illuminated for viewing. (June 1-Labor Day, daily, 3½ hr., $8.)

Hiking in the hills is a joy—there is little underbrush beneath the conifer canopy, and there are many abandoned mines and strange rock outcroppings to explore. Rainy, cool weather is common in May and June, so dress accordingly.

Black Hills National Forest

The national forest that encompasses most of the hills is open for business and pleasure. Tourists hike, fish, and boat; loggers log; ranchers herd cattle; and mining companies dig for gold. Then they pose for the cover of a Richard Scarry book.

The most convenient information centers are the **Pactola Ranger District,** 803 Soo San Dr., Rapid City (343-1567; open Mon.-Fri. 8am-5pm), and the **Spearfish Ranger District,** 226 Colorado Blvd., Spearfish (642-4622; open Mon.-Fri. 8am-5pm). The main information office and visitors center at **Pactola Reservoir,** 17 miles west of Rapid City on U.S. 385, has forestry exhibits in the summer in addition to the usual tourist literature. You can buy supplies before you head off to the hinterland at small grocery stores in Keystone and Custer, or at the KOA campground 5 miles west of Mt. Rushmore on Rte. 244.

Camping in the national forest is virtually unrestricted. To save money the adventurous way, you can disappear down one of the many dirt roads (make sure it isn't someone's driveway) and set up camp. It's safe, free, legal, and fun, but watch for poison ivy and afternoon thunder showers. The most popular established campgrounds include **Bear Gulch** and **Pactola** (343-4283), on the Pactola Reservoir just south of the junction of Rte. 44 and U.S. 385. ($9, $11 for sites near the lake.) **Willow Creek Horse Camp,** in the North Cave Gap Area ($10 reservation fee, $15 charge for 1-10 people) and **Sheridan Lake Campground** (574-2873 or 800-283-2267), east of Hill City on U.S. 385 ($9, $11 for lakefront sites) are also favorites. They provide campsites with picnic tables, pit toilets, and water hydrants. These campgrounds often fill up in the summer, but you can reserve a spot by calling or writing ahead to send your money one day in advance. For more information, contact the Pactola or Spearfish Ranger District (see above). As a last resort, try the **Hill City-Mt. Rushmore KOA** (574-2525), 5 miles west of Mt. Rushmore on Rte. 244. The KOA cabins come with facilities including showers, a stove, a heated pool, laundry facilities, and free shuttle service to Mt. Rushmore. (Office open daily 7am-11pm; Oct.-April 8am-10pm. Sites $15 for 2, $18 with water and electricity, $20 with full hookup.)

Mt. Rushmore National Monument

Originally conceived as a memorial for local Western heroes such as Kit Carson, this "shrine of democracy," completed in 1941, portrays the 60-foot-tall faces of George Washington, Thomas Jefferson, Abraham Lincoln, and Theodore Roosevelt. Millions of Americans have stood in awe before the four granite patriarchs. Some, however, find it odd and distasteful that white Americans are enshrined in sacred Sioux hills.

From Rapid City, take U.S. 16 to Keystone and Rte. 244 up to the mountain. The **visitors center** (574-2523) has the usual multi-media exhibitions and also braille brochures and wheelchairs. Programs for the disabled are held daily at 9pm. (Visitors center open 8am-10pm; Sept. 18-May 14 8am-5pm.) Nearby, **Borglum's Sculptor's Studio** holds the plaster model of the sculptor's mountain carving, as well as his tools and plans. (Ranger talks are held in summer every hr. 9:30am-6pm; the studio is open daily 9am-8pm.) Between the visitors center and the studio is the **Mt. Rushmore Memorial Ampitheater,** the locale of the evening sculpture-lighting programs. (May 14-Sept. 4 program 9pm, sculpture lit 9:30-10:30pm; Sept. 5-16 program 8pm, sculpture lit 8:30-9:30pm.)

Custer State Park

Peter Norbeck, governor of South Dakota during the 1970s, loved to hike among the thin, towering rock formations that haunt the area south of Sylvan Lake and Mt. Rushmore. Norbeck created Custer State Park to preserve the area's treasures, as well as spectacular **Needles Highway,** which follows his favorite hiking route. He purposely kept the highway narrow and winding so that newcomers could experience the pleasures of discovery. Watch for mountain goats and bighorn sheep among the rocky spires. For information, contact HCR 83, P.O. Box 70, Custer 57730 (255-4515); open Mon.-Fri. 7:30am-5pm. There is a $3 daily entrance fee (under 11 free), or $6 per car load. At the entrance, ask for a copy of *Tatanka,* the informative Custer State Park newspaper. The **Peter Norbeck Welcome Center** (255-4464), on 16A, 1 mile west of the State Game Lodge, is the park's central information center. (Open June-Aug. daily 8am-8pm.) All eight **state park campgrounds** charge $7-8 per night and have showers and restrooms. Restaurants and concessions are available at any of the four park lodges—State Game, Blue Bell, Sylvan Lake, and Legion Lake—but you can save money at the local general stores in Custer, Hermosa, or Keystone.

Sylvan Lake, Needles Hwy. (Rte. 87), is lovely, with hiking trails, fishing, horse concessions, paddle boats, and canoes. Horse rides are available at Blue Bell Lodge ($12 per hr., under 12 $10; $20 for 2 hr., under 12 $17). Boat rentals are available at Legion Lake Lodge ($2.50 per person for 30 min.). Fishing is permitted in all lakes and streams, with a $6 daily license available at the four area lodges. Five-day nonresident licenses are $14, or $16 per group. There is a limit of eight trout per day, six times per summer. The best fishing is in the summer, especially around the first of the month when officials stock the waters.

Ranger programs offer lectures, stargazes, and films. The **Night Barn Dance** is particularly fun. **South Dakota Junior Ranger Program,** geared for children 7 to

12, is a one-hour, interactive program revolving around environmental preservation and protection. (Open Mon.-Fri. 10am-5pm, Sat. 1-4pm.)

Caves

In the cavern-riddled Black Hills, the scenery underground often rivals that above. Private concessionaires will attempt to lure you into the holes in their backyards, but the government owns the area's prime real estate. **Wind Cave National Park,** adjacent to Custer State Park on Rte. 87, and **Jewel Cave National Monument,** 14 miles west of Custer on U.S. 16A, are in the southern hills. There is no public transportation to the caves.

In the summer, both Wind and Jewel cave visitors centers offer daily tours, including short candlelight tours and more strenuous but exhilarating spelunking tours, during which tourists crawl on the floor of the cave just like real explorers. Guides provide knee pads, helmets with lanterns, and instruction. Wear well-soled shoes, preferably ankle-high lace boots, and expendable clothing. Bring a sweater on all tours—Jewel Cave remains a constant 47°, Wind Cave 53°.

Wind Cave was discovered in 1881, although most of it was explored in 1890 by 17-year-old Alvin McDonald, whose name can still be seen burned on the walls of some of the deeper chambers. The cave lies 12 miles north of Hot Springs on U.S. 385. Besides several short walks, Wind Cave Park offers three tours. The **Garden of Eden Tour,** the easiest one, gives a quick overview of the cave's interior. (6 tours per day, 1 per hr. 10:40am-3:40pm. Admission $1.) The one-hour **Natural Entrance Tour** leaves on the hour and covers ½ mile of the cave. (Admission $3, ages 6-15 $1.) The more strenuous, hour-and-a-half **Fairgrounds Tour** winds ½ mile through two levels of the cave. (Admission $4, ages 6-15 $1.) The four-hour spelunking tour, limited to 10 people, leaves at 1pm (4 hr., ages 14 and over only, $5; reservations required). To make reservations for the spelunking tours, contact **Wind Cave National Park,** Hot Springs 57747 (745-4600; open daily 8am-7pm; Aug. 24-June 4 8am-5pm).

Jewel Cave sprawls underground in one of the largest unexplored labyrinths in the world. It is formed of the same limestone as Wind Cave, but the similarity ends there. Grayish calcite crystal walls are the highlight of the tours. Guides sponsor three tours during the summer. The ½-mile scenic tour takes you over 700 stairs (every 20 min., 1¼ hr., admission $3, ages 6-15 $1). Make reservations for the spelunking tour, limited to 10 people, and be sure to wear sturdy foot gear (ages 16 and over only, $5). Contact **Jewel Cave National Monmument,** Custer 57730 (673-2288; open June 12-Aug. 27 8am-4:30pm).

The **Wind Cave Campground** offers primitive sites with flush toilets for $7. There are no overnight accommodations at the Jewel Cave Monument, but you can camp at the national forest's facility 6 miles east on Rte. 16A.

Lead and Deadwood

The Black Hills are dusted with many interesting small towns, but Lead and Deadwood are true standouts. During the 1877 gold rush, the towns became legendary for their idiosyncratic prospectors and boom-town exploits.

In **Lead** (pronounced "LEED"), as in Deadwood, almost everybody works for Homestake, the locally prominent gold-mining corporation. Here, after the hills had been "panned out" in 1878, hardrock or lode mining began in earnest. Homestake still owns much of the northern Black Hills and continues to operate the largest gold mine in the Western Hemisphere. The **Open Cut,** a yawning chasm where a mountain once stood, is a monument to Homestake's handiwork. You'll see huge vats of tailings, conveyor belts loaded with ore, and contraptions that lower the miners down almost a mile into the earth. Operations there have ceased for quite some time—long enough for a Piggly-Wiggly store and many miners to make their homes in its path. The **Lead Civic Association** (584-3110) gives surface tours of the mine. (Tours June-Aug. Mon.-Fri. 8am-5pm, every ¼ hr.; May and Sept.-Oct. Mon.-Fri.

8am-4pm, every ½ hr. Admission $2, high school students $1.75, elementary school students $1.25.)

Gunslinging hero-outlaws Wild Bill Hickok and Calamity Jane sauntered into **Deadwood** at the height of the Gold Rush. Bill stayed just long enough—two months—to spend eternity there. He was shot while playing poker, so the legend goes, and since he fell while holding eights and aces, a full house was henceforth known as "the dead man's hand." Visit **Mt. Moriah Cemetery,** where Bill and Jane are buried beside each other on a hillside overlooking the city.

The **Nugget Café,** 815 W. Main St. (584-3337), in Lead, is almost a museum in its own right, decorated with photos documenting the town's history. Try the spaghetti dinner ($4) or the tasty omelettes ($2.50-3.50; open Mon.-Sat. 6am-7pm). Jack McCall, Wild Bill's assassin, was captured at **Goldberg Grocery and Soda Fountain,** 672 Main St. (578-1515), Deadwood, where you can down an old-fashioned phosphate for 50¢ or a huge "Goldburger" for $1.50-3.50. (Open June-Labor Day Mon.-Sat. 6:30am-6pm.) The **#10 Saloon,** 657 Main St. (578-3346), claims to own Wild Bill's "death chair." (Open Mon.-Sat. 10am-2am, Sun. noon-8pm.)

The best place to stay is the sleepy old **Fairmont Hotel,** 628 Main St. (578-2205), in the heart of Deadwood, next door to the bus station. Upcoming change in ownership and renovations may boost prices. (Singles $10. Doubles $15.) Since the Fairmont often fills in the summer, try the **Franklin Hotel,** 700 Main St. (578-2241), a beautiful historic monument completed in 1903. (Singles $35. Doubles $39. Off-season $27 and $35, respectively.)

The most scenic route to Lead and Deadwood is from Spearfish south via Rte. 14A, which traverses **Spearfish Canyon,** a densely-wooded canyon of steep limestone cliffs and tumultuous waterfalls. **Powder River Lines,** 10 Water St. (578-2604), serves both towns from Rapid City twice per day (1 hr., $9).

Check in at the **chamber of commerce,** 735 Main St., Deadwood (578-1876; open Mon.-Fri. 8:30am-5pm). In the summer, they run a booth on Pine Street. The towns are in the Mountain time zone (2 hr. behind Eastern). The **post office** in Lead is at 329 W. Main St. (584-2110; open Mon.-Fri. 8:15am-4:15pm, Sat. 10am-noon); the **ZIP code** is 57754. The Deadwood **post office** is at the Deadwood Federal Building (578-1505); the **ZIP code** is 57732.

The **area code** for Lead and Deadwood is 605.

Badlands National Park

Some 60 million years ago, when much of the Great Plains was under water, the earth's plates shifted, heaving up the Rockies and the Black Hills. Silt carried from these highlands by mountain streams was deposited in what is now known as the Badlands, preserving in layer after pink layer the remains of the wildlife that once wandered the flood plains. Erosion has created spires and steep gullies, a landscape that contrasts sharply with the plains of eastern South Dakota. The Sioux called these arid and treacherous formations "Mako Sica," or "bad land;" Gen. Alfred Sully, the opposition, called them "hell with the fires out."

The Badlands are about 50 miles east of Rapid City on I-90. Highway 240 winds through the wilderness in a 32-mile detour off I-90 (take exit 131 or 110). There is almost no way to visit the park by highway without being assaulted by employees from **Wall Drug,** 510 Main St. (279-2175), in Wall. An overgrown monument to entrepreneurial skill, Wall Drug gives out free ice water and 5¢ coffee, the only bargains in the store. (Open daily 6am-10pm; Sept.-Nov. and May 7am-5pm; Dec.-April Mon.-Sat. 7am-5pm.) All of the other cafés and shops on Main Street are just as ridiculously overpriced, and there is no reason to stay the night in Wall.

From Wall, take Rte. 240, the road that loops through the park and returns to I-90 30 miles east of Wall in Cactus Flats. From Rapid City, take Rte. 44 and turn northeast at Scenic, where it leads to Sage Creek and Rte. 240. There are ranger stations at both entrances off I-90, although the western portion of the park is much less developed. **Jack Rabbit Buses** (348-3300) make two stops daily at Wall from Rapid City ($13). You can probably hitch a ride into the park from Wall.

The **Cedar Pass Visitors Center** (433-5361), 5 miles inside the park's eastern entrance, is more convenient than the **White River Visitors Center** (455-2878), 55 miles southwest, off Rte. 27 in the park's less-visited southern section. Both centers distribute a free paper detailing park programs and trail guides for sale. (Cedar Pass open daily 7am-8pm; Labor Day-May 8am-4:30pm; White River open June-Aug. 9am-5pm.) Stock up on gasoline, water, food, and insect repellent before entering the park. The Badlands suffer extreme temperatures in midsummer and winter, but late spring and fall offer pleasant weather and few insects. Always watch (and listen) for rattlesnakes.

Accommodations, Camping, and Food

There are two campgrounds in the park. **Cedar Pass Campground,** near the visitors center, has covered picnic tables and a bathroom with running water, but no showers. (Sites $7). The **Sage Creek Campground,** 11 miles from the Pinnacles entrance south of Wall, is just an open field with pit toilets and no water. But it's free.

Try backcountry camping for a more intimate introduction to this desert-like landscape. Bring plenty of water and set up camp at least half a mile from a road. It's great fun to share the stars with local wildlife, but don't cozy up to the bison, especially in the spring when overprotective mothers may become nervous.

For tenderfoot tourists, the **Cedar Pass Lodge** (433-5460), P.O. Box 5, Interior 57750, next to the visitors center, has air-conditioned cabins. (Singles $28. Doubles $32. Each additional person $3. Open May to mid-Oct. Try to make reservations; leave a 50% deposit). There's a mid-priced restaurant at the lodge (open June-Aug. approximately 7am-9pm).

Sights and Activities

The park protects large tracts of native prairie along with the stark rock formations. The Cedar Pass visitors center has an audio-visual program on the Badlands, and the park rangers of both centers lead free tours, all of which leave from the Cedar Pass amphitheater. The nature hikes (1½ hr., 8am and 6pm) are an easy way to appreciate the Badlands, and you may find Oligocene fossils right at your feet. The evening amphitheater slide program narrates Badlands history, but the mosquitoes can be ravenous, so cover up. A one-hour night-prowl or sky-trek follows the program.

You can also hike through the Badlands on your own. Try the short but steep **Saddle Pass Trail** or the scenic hike following a 5¼-mile loop that runs between the **Fossil Exhibit** and the **Windows,** both sights along the Loop Road. Other highlights of the Loop Road are **Robert's Prairie Dog Town** and the **Yellow Mounds Overlook,** where brilliant red and yellow formations relieve the bleached rose. Keep your eyes peeled along the Sage Creek Rd. for the park's herd of about 400 bison. Respect the intense mid-day sun, and at all times be wary of crumbly footholds, cacti, and occasional rattlesnakes. It's easy to lose your bearings in this confusing territory, so talk to a ranger or bring a map.

Pierre

Pierre (pronounced "peer") is South Dakota's capital, and lies smack in the center of the state, on the Missouri River. This commercial center for farmers and ranchers was once a bustling cow town. Western garb is still a common sight, even in the copper-topped **capitol building** (773-3765; free 40-min. tours Mon.-Fri. 9am-4pm every ½ hr., Sat. 10am-3pm every hr., Sun. 11am-2pm every hr. Building open Mon.-Fri. 8am-10pm, Sat.-Sun. 8am-9pm.) Behind the capitol, the unusual flaming fountain spouts natural gas deposits. Across the street, in the **Cultural Heritage Center,** 900 Governor's Dr. (773-3458), is the **Robinson State Museum,** with excellent displays on the Sioux and South Dakota. (Open Mon.-Fri. 9am-4:30pm, Sat.-Sun. 1-4:30pm; off-season Mon.-Fri. 9am-4:30pm.)

Eat at the cozy little **D & E Cafe,** 115 W. Dakota Ave. (224-7200), where an entree with soup, potato, toast, beans, and a bowl of ice cream costs $4-5 (open 24 hours). Grab a kup of koffee at the **Kozy Korner Restaurant,** 217 E. Dakota Ave. (224-9547), a family place with generous dinners for $5-6 (open daily 5am-10pm). **Zesto,** 213 W. Capitol Ave. (224-4681), serves generous heaps of great ice cream (cones 15-80¢, sundaes 60¢-$1.40; open Mon.-Sat. 11:30am-10:30pm, Sun. noon-10:30pm).

Sleep cheap at the **Waverly Hotel,** 442 S. Pierre St. (224-7358), 1½ blocks from Sioux Avenue. The old, dusty rooms are lovingly maintained, but have neither phones nor A/C. (Singles with bath $15.) Conveniently located across the street from the bus station, the **Days Inn,** 520 W. Sioux Ave. (224-0411), serves free doughnuts, coffee, and milk every morning. (Singles $25. Doubles $36). The popular **Farm Island State Park** (224-5605), 3 miles east on Rte. 34, has campsites for $7, $9 with hookup.

To reach Pierre from I-90, go 30 miles north on U.S. 83. **Greyhound/Jack Rabbit** buses stop in the Phillips 66 station at 621 W. Sioux Ave. (224-7657). To: Omaha ($69), Rapid City ($33), and Minneapolis ($73). Visit the **chamber of commerce,** 108 E. Missouri St. (224-7361; open Mon.-Fri. 8am-5pm). Pierre is in the Central time zone (1 hr. behind Eastern). The **post office** is at 225 S. Pierre St. (224-4140; open Mon.-Fri. 8am-5:30pm, Sat. 8am-noon); the **ZIP code** is 57501.

Pierre's **area code** is 605.

TEXAS

Texas is both bilingual and bicultural. One culture celebrates Texas's past as an independent republic and touts its image of rugged masculinity typified by the cattle rancher with the mile-long Cadillac and the avaricious oil-baron J.R. Ewing. This culture's creed, "the bigger, the better," pervades urban centers such as Houston and Dallas with their conglomerations of shiny new skyscrapers. Alongside this longhorn tradition, a vibrant Mexican-American culture has developed. Its most palpable and visible contributions to Texas are the state's addictively spicy cuisine and its distinctive architecture.

Practical Information

Capital: Austin.

Tourist Information: Texas Division of Tourism, Dept. AAA, P.O. Box 12008, Austin 78711 (512-463-8586). **U.S. Forest Service,** P.O. Box 130, Lufkin 75901 (409-831-2246). **State Parks and Recreation Areas,** Austin Headquarters Complex, 4200 Smith School Rd., Austin 78744 (512-463-4630).

Time Zones: Central (1 hr. behind Eastern) and Mountain (2 hr. behind Eastern). **Postal Abbreviation:** TX.

Travel

Car travelers have the run of most of this huge state, but public transportation serves areas frequented by tourists. The constellation of major cities in eastern Texas form a triangle with **Dallas/Ft. Worth, San Antonio,** and **Houston/Galveston** at the corners, and **Austin** part way along the San Antonio-Dallas leg. Each leg is 200-300 miles long. Interstate highways, frequent bus schedules, and Amtrak routes connect the corners. **Kerrville Bus Lines,** a Greyhound affiliate, covers the entire region, while Greyhound/Trailways zooms along the edges.

Outside this triangle, the two areas of greatest interest to visitors are **western Texas** and the **Gulf Coast/Mexican Border** area, accessible by interstates and bus routes. Greyhound has frequent service on I-10 and I-20 into western Texas and convenient service to Corpus Christi and the southern border towns. Greyhound's affiliate, **TNM&O Coaches,** gives thorough regional coverage in northwestern Texas and southern New Mexico. El Paso/Ciudad Juárez, a major urban area straddling the Mexican border, is a convenient base for exploring western Texas and southern New Mexico. (See Desert Survival in the Southwest section.)

San Antonio, El Paso, Austin, Dallas, and Houston each have a hostel, and the state's very own bed and breakfast organization arranges stays in private homes in many Texas cities and towns. The "budget" class charges $25-40 for singles, $30-50 for doubles.

Regional cuisine, like most of Texan culture, is enriched by the state's Mexican heritage. "Tex-Mex" is a variation of the dishes served across the border. Chefs throw jalapeño peppers into chili as casually as you might shake salt on french fries. Mexican pastries and genuine longhorn beef are a must. Have your steak "chicken-fried" and pour on cream sauce, or try a big ol' Texas-style T-bone.

Outdoors

Some folks say Texas has only two seasons: summer and January. It's hot in summer. Really hot. The heat is more bearable in the west, where the air is dry, but the humidity in the coastal area is stifling. Winter varies across the state, from warm and mild in the south to potentially severe and blizzardy in the northern panhandle.

Take advantage of the state's wide open space by camping. Bring a tent and tons of repellent to deter the plagues of mosquitoes. The state park system has excellent

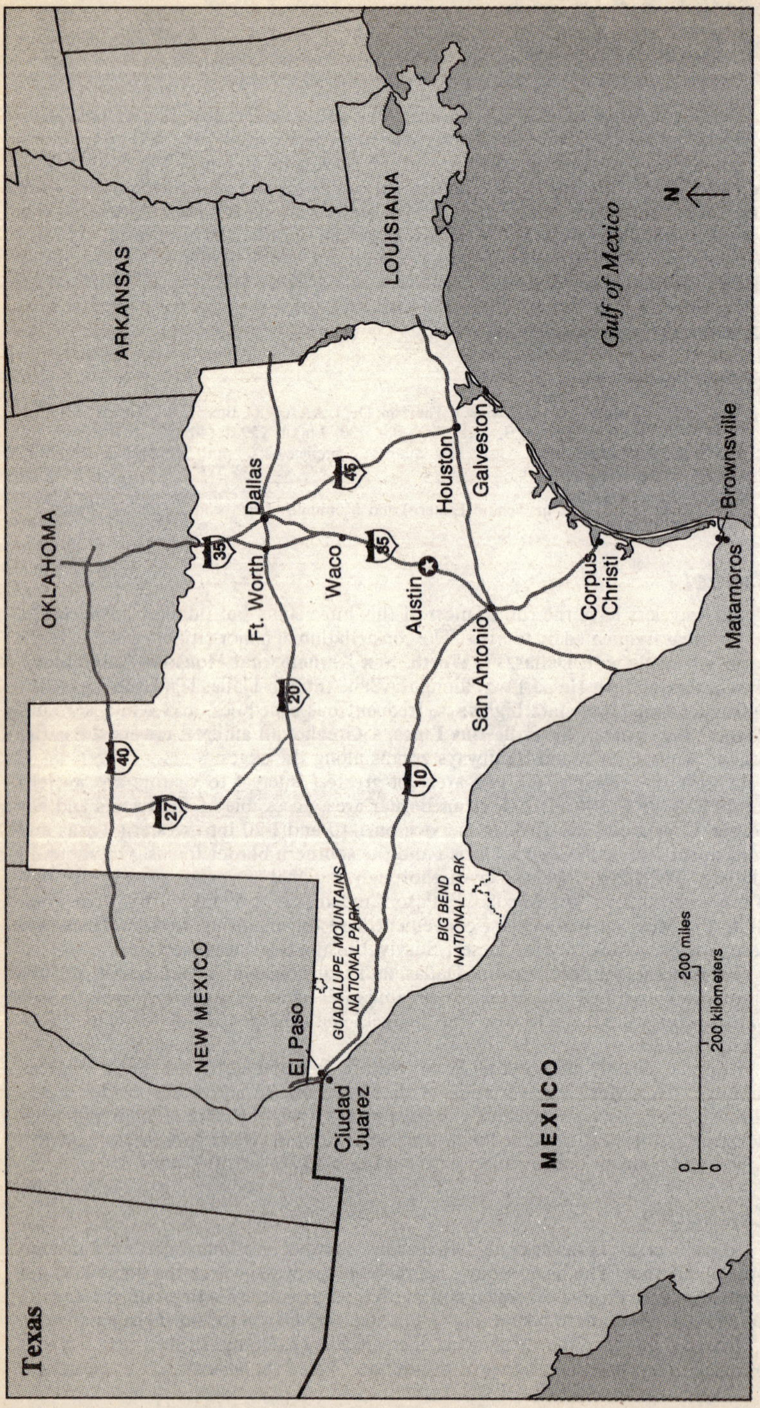
OKLAHOMA
ARKANSAS
LOUISIANA
NEW MEXICO
MEXICO
Gulf of Mexico
N
Dallas
Ft. Worth
Waco
Austin
Houston
Galveston
San Antonio
Corpus Christi
Brownsville
Matamoros
El Paso
Ciudad Juarez
GUADALUPE MOUNTAINS NATIONAL PARK
BIG BEND NATIONAL PARK
35
45
20
40
27
10
200 miles
200 kilometers
0
0

Texas

camping at over 60 parks, recreation areas, and historic sites. Some parks charge an admission fee of $2 per car, 50¢ per pedestrian or bicyclist. Sites usually cost $4. In the open ranching countryside of western Texas or in the Hill Country, finding sites should present few problems. For a broader overview of the region, see the Southwest Introduction.

Dallas

Local institutions such as Neiman-Marcus stores, the colorful nocturnal skyline, and the Dallas Cowboys typify the city's preoccupation with commerce and hype. Business is a primary interest in the "silicon prairie," where affluence is emphasized, not downplayed. Yet Dallas also has an unmistakable Bible-belt flavor, evident in its moral tone and numerous conservative churches.

Practical Information

Emergency: 911

Visitor Information: Dallas Convention and Visitors Bureau, 1201 Elm St., #200 (746-6702). Open Mon.-Fri. 8:30am-5pm. **Union Station Visitor Center,** 400 S. Houston Ave. (954-1111), in a booth in the lobby. Open daily 9am-5pm. **Dallas Artsline,** 385-1155.

Dallas-Ft. Worth International Airport: (212-574-6701), 17 miles northwest of downtown. **Love Field** (670-7275; take bus #39) has mostly intra-Texas flights. To get downtown from either airport, take the **Super Shuttle,** 729 E. Dallas Rd. (817-329-2001; in terminal, dial 02 on phone at ground transport services.) 24-hr. service. DFW airport to downtown $12, Love Field to downtown $8.

Amtrak: 400 S. Houston (653-1101 or 800-872-7245), in Union Station, next to Reunion Tower. To: Houston (3 per week, 6 hr., $39) and St. Louis (3 per week, 14 hr., $120).

Greyhound/Trailways: Commerce and Lamar St. (655-7000), 3 blocks east and 1 block north of Union Station. To: Houston (9 per day, 6 hr., $32); San Antonio (13 per day, 6 hr., $34); El Paso (8 per day, 12½ hr., $75); New Orleans (6 per day, 12½ hr., $65). Open 24 hours.

Dallas Area Rapid Transit (DART): 601 Pacific Ave. (979-1111 or 934-3278). Serves most suburbs; routes radiate from downtown. Service 5am-midnight, to suburbs 5am-6pm. Base fare 75¢, more with zone changes. Information desk open Mon.-Fri. 8:30am-4:45pm. Maps available at Main and Akard St. Mon.-Fri. 8am-5pm, or at Elm and Ervay St. Mon.-Fri. 7am-6pm. **Hop-a-Bus** (979-1111) is DART's downtown Dallas service, with a park-and-ride system. Three routes (blue, red, and green) run about every 10 min. Fare 35¢, transers free. Look for buses with a blue bunny, a red kangaroo, or a green frog.

Taxi: Yellow Cab Co., 426-6262. $2.30 first mile, $1 each additional mile. Dallas-Ft. Worth Airport to downtown $20.

Car Rental: All-State Rent-a-Car, 3206 Live Oak (741-3118). $23 per day with 100 free miles. Open Mon.-Sat. 7:30am-5pm.

Bike Rental: Bicycle Exchange, 11716 Ferguson Rd. (270-9269). Rates from $45 per week. Open Mon.-Fri. 9am-7pm, Sat. 9am-5pm.

Help Lines: Gay Hotline, 368-6283. Open daily 7:30pm-midnight. Community Center, 3920 Cedar Springs (528-4233). **Senior Citizen Call Action Center,** 744-3600. Information on reduced fares, recreational activites, and health care.

Time Zone: Central (1 hr. behind Eastern).

Post Office: 400 N. Ervay St. (760-7200), on Thanksgiving Sq., downtown. Open Mon.-Fri. 8am-5pm, Sat. 8am-12:30pm. **ZIP code:** 75201.

Area Code: 214.

Dallas is in the northeast corner of Texas, near the border of Oklahoma and Arkansas. Houston is 240 miles to the south and El Paso is 620 miles to the west. Downtown Dallas will confuse pedestrians and drivers alike. Streets are laid out

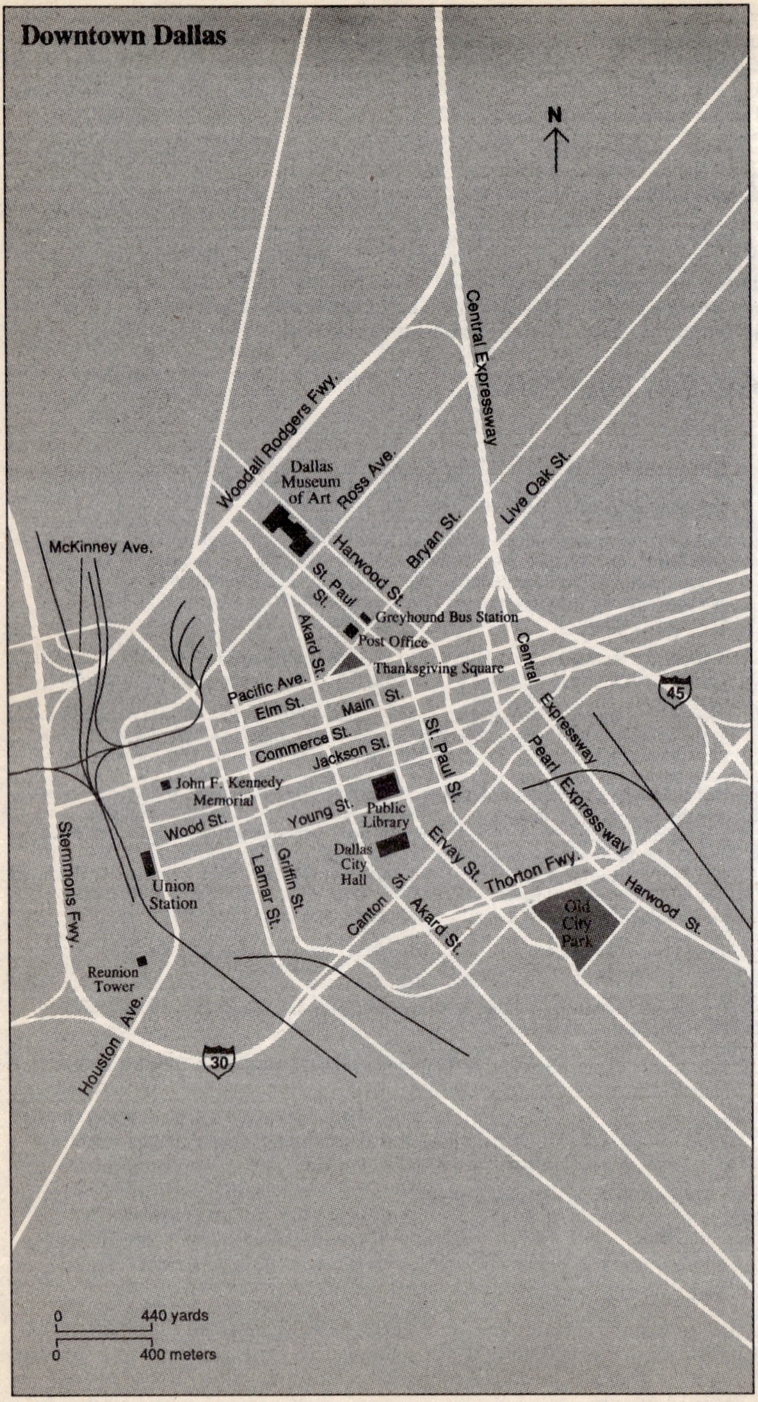
Downtown Dallas
N
Woodall Rodgers Fwy.
Central Expressway
Dallas Museum of Art
Ross Ave.
Live Oak St.
Bryan St.
Harwood St.
McKinney Ave.
St. Paul St.
Greyhound Bus Station
Akard St.
Post Office
Thanksgiving Square
Central Expressway
Pacific Ave.
Elm St.
Main St.
45
Commerce St.
Jackson St.
St. Paul St.
Pearl Expressway
John F. Kennedy Memorial
Public Library
Young St.
Wood St.
Dallas City Hall
Ervay St.
Thorton Fwy.
Stemmons Fwy.
Union Station
Lamar St.
Griffin St.
Canton St.
Akard St.
Old City Park
Harwood St.
Reunion Tower
Houston Ave.
30
0 440 yards
0 400 meters

along two separate grids that meet at a 45° angle. Pedestrians beware: jaywalking is illegal and subject to a $25 fine.

Accommodations and Camping

Conventions are big business in Dallas, and their demand for rooms boosts rates, as do big events such as the Texas State Fair (mid-Oct.) and the Cotton Bowl (Jan. 1). Most restaurants and nightlife are well outside of downtown, so it's not always worthwhile to stay there. The suburbs of Irving and Arlington are full of inexpensive motels. **Motel 6** (505-891-6161) has 11 locations in the greater Dallas area. Also consider **Exel Inns** (800-356-8013) and **Red Roof Inns** (800-843-7663).

Dallas International Hostel (AYH), 1451 E. Northgate (438-6061), Irving, at the University of Dallas Conference Center off Carpenter Fwy. From downtown, take bus #202 to N. Station Transit Center and transfer to #306. Get off at University of Dallas. Although infrequent buses limit its accessibility, the large, clean rooms, A/C, and peaceful environment compensate. Check-in 7-9am and 5-11pm. $9, nonmembers $12. Linen $1. Breakfast $1.50.

Bed and Breakfast Texas Style, 4224 W. Red Bird Lane, Dallas 75237 (298-5433 or 298-8586). Hosts are friendly Dallas families who'll meet you at a hotel or the bus station. Singles $25-29. Doubles $30-40. Reservations strongly recommended.

Grande Lodge Motel, 1401 N. Zang Blvd. (942-8335), at the Colorado exit. Take bus #22 or 62 to Zang Blvd. and walk 3 blocks toward downtown. Central location. Spacious, clean rooms in a resort-like setting. Pool, spa, sauna, restaurant, and lounge. Singles $30. Doubles $35.

Dallas Budget Inn, 4001 Live Oak (826-7110), take bus #1 or 20 from downtown. The neighborhood is seedy and rooms are damp and musty, but it's close to downtown. Singles $25. Doubles $28.

If you have a car and camping gear, head up I-35 to **Lewisville Lake Park,** 5 Lake Park Rd. (221-5754), at Lake Park and Kingfisher, 1 mile east of I-35. There is a golf course and a pretty lake with sailing and fishing. (Tent sites $5 for 2, $7 with electricity. $1 each additional person.) South of town, try the **Hi-Ho Campground,** 200 W. Bear Creek Rd. (223-8574). Take I-35 14½ miles to exit 412, turn right, and go 2 more miles. (Tent sites $10 for 2, $14.50 with hookup. $1 each additional person.) Sleeping in Dallas parks is illegal and unsafe.

Food

Greenville Avenue in North Dallas has miles of restaurants. (Take bus #1 down Greenville.) **McKinney Avenue** also offers an econorama of cheap eats. For more ideas, pick up a copy of the Friday weekend guide of the *Dallas Morning News.* The touristy **West End Historic District** supplies ample food, beverage, and entertainment in the heart of downtown. For fast Tex-Mex food and a variety of small shops, explore the **West End Marketplace,** 603 Munger St. (954-4350). The **Farmers Produce Market,** 1010 S. Pearl Expressway (748-2082), between Pearl and Central Expressway near I-30, has good buys. (Open sunrise to sunset.)

Guadalajara, 4405 Ross (823-9340). Piñata-packed interior, while exterior boasts a patio view of Dallas. Combination dinners $5, steak and seafood specialties $7-10. Open Mon.-Fri. 11am-3am, Sat.-Sun. 8am-3am.

Farmer's Grill, 807 Park Ave. (741-9361), at corner of Cadiz and Canton. Excellent cobbler, prepared with market fruit each morning. Complete Texas country dinners $4. Open Mon.-Fri. 6am-3pm, Sat. 7am-3pm. Bar open until 8:30pm.

Herrera's Cafe, 4101 Maple Ave. (528-9644). Take bus #29. You can often judge a Mexican restaurant by its appearance; the dumpier it looks, the more authentic the Tex-Mex food and the better the value. Herrera's is such a place. Filling meals $4-6. Bring your own beer, and expect to wait on weekends. Open Mon. and Wed.-Thurs. 10am-9pm, Fri.-Sat. 9am-10pm, Sun. 9am-9pm.

Old Spaghetti Warehouse, 1815 N. Market (651-8475), in the heart of the West End. Italian food in a colorful interior. Spaghetti plates $3-5, specialties $6-9. Crowded at lunchtime. Open Mon.-Thurs. 11am-11pm, Fri. 11am-1am, Sat. noon-1am, Sun. 11am-10pm.

White Rock Yacht Club, 7324 Gaston Ave. (328-3866), near the junction of Gaston and Garland. A quirky, unpretentious place with pool tables and peanut-shell-littered floors. Yacht club tacos $4.50. No entree over $6, but portions are small. Free peanuts. Open Mon.-Sat. 11am-2am, Sun. noon-2am.

Colter's, 11827 Abrams (680-1990). Over 10 locations in the Dallas area. Generous portions of hickory-smoked barbecue in a rustic country interior. Great onion rings. Bring a church bulletin on Sun. to get 15% off your bill. Sandwiches $2.80, dinners $5-7. Open Sun.-Thurs. 11am-9:30pm, Fri.-Sat. 11am-10pm.

Sights

Dallas has no easily discernible history. Originally an inland port in the mid-19th century, it eventually became a railroad town and then an oil town. Take in the panorama from the top of **Reunion Tower** (741-3663; open daily 10am-midnight; admission $1.88). On your way out of the tower, explore the adjoining **Union Station,** 400 S. Houston, one of Dallas's few grand old buildings.

Walking north along Houston you'll come upon the **Texas School Book Depository,** from where, on Nov. 22, 1963, Lee Harvey Oswald shot President John F. Kennedy. The site is now **The Sixth Floor,** 411 Elm St. (653-6666), an unabashedly worshipful museum commemorating Kennedy's life and detailing his assassination. (Admission $4, seniors $3, students $2. Audio tours $2. Open Mon.-Thurs. 9:30am-6pm, Fri.-Sun. 9:30am-7pm.) The **John F. Kennedy Memorial,** designed by Philip Johnson, stands at Market and Main St.

Continue north along Houston to reach the heart of the **West End Historic District** (747-7470), which perhaps should be renamed the West End Dining and Drinking District. The red-brick, converted warehouse neighborhood culminates in the **West End Marketplace,** crowded with fast-food eateries, bars, and shops.

Walking east along Ross Avenue from the historic district leads you to the new **Arts District,** the centerpiece of which is the **Dallas Museum of Art,** 1717 N. Harwood St. (922-1200). The museum offers an excellent collection of Indonesian, impressionist, modern, and American decorative art. There is also an outdoor sculpture garden and a drop-in art room for children. (Museum open Tues.-Wed. and Fri.-Sat. 10am-5pm, Thurs. 10am-9pm, Sun. and holidays noon-5pm. Children's room open Wed.-Thurs. and Sat. noon-5pm. Admission to both free.)

Walking south from the museum on St. Paul, toward the downtown area, turn right on Bryan St. and walk 1 block to **Thanksgiving Square,** (969-1977), a tiny park beneath massive towers. Built below street-level, with gardens and quiet waterfalls, the square is both an example of successful urban design and a haven from the city's busy streets. (Open Mon.-Fri. 9am-5pm, Sat.-Sun and holidays 1-5pm.) Continue south from Thanksgiving Square along Ervay St. to the imposing, $32 million **Dallas City Hall** (670-5680), designed by I.M. Pei.

South of City Hall on Ervay St. is the **Old City Park,** Gano and Ervay St. (421-5141). The park is indeed the oldest in the city and is also one of the most popular recreation areas and lunch spots. Open spaces and picnic facilities are scattered among restored buildings which include a railroad depot and a church. (Open dawn to dusk. Exhibit buildings open Tues.-Fri. 10am-4pm, Sat.-Sun. 1:30-4:30pm. Tours $4.)

State Fair Park (565-9931), southeast of downtown on 2nd Ave., is home to numerous exhibits. A standout is the **Museum of Natural History** (421-2169), which has a small permanent display on prehistoric life. (Admission free for permanent exhibits, prices vary for temporary exhibits.) Other exhibits include the **Aquarium** (670-8466; open daily 9am-5pm); the **Age of Steam Museum** (421-8754; open Sat.-Sun. 11am-5pm. Admission $2, under 16 $1); the **Science Place** (428-8351); and the **Dallas Garden Center,** at 2nd and Forest Ave. (428-7476; open Mon.-Sat. 10am-5pm, Sun. 12:30-5pm).

The **Dallas Arboretum and Botanical Garden** (327-3990), off Garland Rd. in northeast Dallas, is 66 acres of country just outside the city. (Open March-Oct. Tues.-Sun. 10am-6pm; Nov.-Feb. Tues.-Sun. 10am-5pm. Admission $3, seniors $2, under 12 $1.)

Entertainment

Dallas offers a mix of the serious and the frivolous. Check the *Dallas Observer* or weekend sections of local papers for complete entertainment listings. Enjoy free summer theater at the **Shakespeare in the Park** festival (954-0199) during July and August, in the Fair Park Bandshell. Two plays are performed each year, and they alternate nights Tuesday through Sunday. The **Music Hall** (565-1116), in State Fair Park, houses the Dallas Symphony Orchestra (692-0203) in September and from January through May (tickets $6.50-18); the **Dallas Civic Opera** (827-3320) in November and December (tickets $6-45, 50% student discount in certain sections); the **Dallas Ballet** performing the *Nutcracker* in late December; and the **Dallas Summer Musicals** (787-2000) from June through August, with performances nightly (tickets $5-35, cash only). **KVIL** (369-8500) sells half-price tickets on performance days. (Tickets on sale noon-6pm, 9am-noon for matinees.)

Greenville Avenue is home to a variety of bars and nightclubs such as **Aw Shucks,** 3601 Greenville Ave. (821-9449), an outdoor seafood bar just south of Mockingbird Lane. Sit outside on a warm Texas evening, enjoying a cool beer and raw oysters ($3-7). (Open Mon.-Thurs. 11am-11pm, Fri.-Sat. 11am-11:45pm, Sun. 11:30am-10pm.) **McKinney Avenue,** parallel to and a few blocks west of Central Expressway, is another center of nightlife, with the **Hard Rock Cafe,** 2601 McKinney (855-0007), at its hub. Enjoy live music and dancing every night. (Open daily 11am-2am. No cover Tues.) The **Historic West End** also has a thriving nightlife. Pay one cover charge ($5-8) for all eight of the packed clubs on **Dallas Alley.** Look for the colorful neon cylinders at the tip of the West End. Nearby is the **Outback Pub,** 1701 N. Market (761-9355), a thoroughly Aussie lounge/restaurant with a large selection of beers to wash down your vegemite sandwich. The pub has live rock nightly. (Open daily 11am-2am. No cover.) One of the most popular clubs is **Dick's Last Resort,** Ross Ave. at Record St. (747-0001), which plays "loud and obnoxious Dixieland" and prides itself on its insolent employees. But heck, it's free.

Although Dallasites like to think of themselves as a refined and reserved group, sometimes the rowdy Texan spirit and those afflicted head to country-western dance halls. **Belle Star,** 7724 N. Central Expressway at Southwestern (750-4787), takes its name from a tough outlaw of the 19th century. Like Belle herself, some of the patrons here get rambunctious. The large dance floor has made this place a popular hangout, but the action doesn't begin until late. (Open daily 7pm-2am. Cover $2. Free dance lessons Sun. 4-8pm.)

Six Flags Over Texas (640-8900), 15 miles from downtown off I-30 in Arlington, is the original link of the nationwide amusement park chain. The name alludes to the six governments that have ruled over the state. This is a thrill-lover's paradise, replete with rides, restaurants, shops, and entertainment theaters. The admission charge ($20, over 55 years or under 4 feet $14) will drain your dollars, but it includes unlimited access to all rides and attractions. (Open June-Aug. Sun.-Thurs. 10am-10pm, Fri.-Sat. 10am-midnight; March-May and Sept.-Oct. Sat.-Sun. 10am-8pm. Parking $3.)

Austin

Austin has a reputation as a sanctuary for panhandlers and a destination for intellectuals, music lovers, the young, and the restless. If it weren't for the magnificent capitol building and the omnipresent longhorns of the state university, you'd never guess that Austin is in Texas. Unlike Houston and Dallas, downtown Austin has not sprouted towering glass boxes, and the 50,000-plus student body of the University of Texas (UT) generates unpredictability and a dose of radicalism. Amidst the rapid urban growth, which has tapered in recent years, Austin is still dominated by state politics and university students. If you've had your fill of Lone Stars, explore the Hill Country of Texas, with Austin as your base.

Practical Information

Emergency: 911.

Visitor Information: Austin Tourist Center, 412 E. 6th St. (478-0098). Open Mon.-Fri. 8:30am-5pm, Sat.-Sun. 1-5pm. **Tourist Information Center,** 11th and Congress, in the state capitol. Open 8am-5pm. **Highland Lakes Tourist Association,** 499-9383. Open Mon.-Fri. 8:30am-5pm. **Texas Parks and Wildlife,** 479-4991 or 800-792-1112 in TX. Open Mon.-Fri. 8am-5pm. Information on camping outside Austin. Contact Texas Parks and Wildlife Dept., 4200 Smith School Rd., Austin 78744.

Amtrak: 250 N. Lamar Blvd. (476-5684 or 800-872-7245). To: Dallas (3 per week, 7 hr., $36); San Antonio (3 per week, 2½ hr., $13); El Paso (3 per week, 7 hr., $115). No service to Houston.

Greyhound/Trailways: 916 E. Koenig (458-5267), several miles north of downtown, off I-35. Pick up buses to downtown at the Highland Mall across the street. To: San Antonio (11 per day, 2-3 hr., $11); Houston (11 per day, 3-4 hr., $16); Dallas (10 per day, 4 hr., $27); El Paso via San Antonio (5 per day, 14 hr., $75). Open 24 hours.

Austin Transit System: Capitol Metro, 504 Congress (474-1200; line open Mon.-Sat. 6am-midnight, Sun. 6am-7pm). Maps and schedules available here Mon.-Fri. 7am-6pm, Sat. 9am-1pm or at the Austin Chamber of Commerce, across from the visitors center. Fare 50¢, seniors, children, and disabled 25¢. Downtown, the **Armadillo Express** (look for old-fashioned green trolley cars) connects major downtown points and runs every 10-15 min. Mon.-Thurs. 6:30am-7pm, Fri. 6:20am-midnight, Sat. noon-midnight. Fare 25¢.

University of Texas Shuttle Bus: Service in the campus area. Map and schedule at the UT Information Center (472-3434) or any library, including the Main Library, 9th and Lavaca St.

Taxi: Yellow Cab, 472-1111. $1 per mile. Airport to downtown $6.

Car Rental: Rent-A-Wreck, 6820 Guadalupe (454-8621). $20-22 per day plus 12¢ per mile. Open Mon.-Fri. 8am-6pm, Sat. 8am-2pm, Sun. 10am-1pm. Must be 21 with major credit card.

Bike Rental: University Schwinn, 2901 N. Lamar Blvd. (474-6696). $20 per day, $300 deposit. Open Mon.-Fri. 10am-7pm, Sat. 10am-6pm.

Help Lines: Crisis Intervention Hotline, 472-4357. **Austin Rape Crisis Center,** 472-7273.

Time Zone: Central (1 hr. behind Eastern).

Post Office: 300 E. 9th St. (482-5414). Open Mon.-Fri. 7:30am-6pm, Sat. 8am-noon. **ZIP code:** 78767.

Area Code: 512.

Austin lies 78 miles from San Antonio and 192 miles from Dallas on I-35, and 164 miles from Houston on U.S. 290. Highway signs lead you to the **capitol area** on Congress Ave. and 11th St., in the center of the city. **Congress Avenue** runs from the **Colorado River** in the south 12 blocks to the capitol and then 7 more blocks to the **University of Texas (UT)** in the north. It splits numbered streets into east and west and includes most tourist spots in this stretch. Austin is a biker's paradise, with roller-coaster hills and clearly marked bikeways.

Accommodations and Camping

Cheap accommodations are plentiful in Austin. Half the reason to visit Austin is the **AYH Hostel,** 707 W. 21st St. (467-8209), where you can get a bed and three meals for only $10 or simply a bed for $7. Rooms are large and comfortable; facilities include TV room, laundry, recreation room, and piano; and the staff is unbeatable. (To get from the bus station to the hostel, take bus #15 to 7th and Congress

St., walk down 7th 1 block to Colorado, and take #3 to 21st and Nueces St.) Just a few blocks away is their sister hostel in **Taos Hall (AYH),** 2612 Guadalupe (474-6905), with the same attractions at the same price. As if that's not enough, a couple blocks away is the **Goodall Wooten Dorm,** 2112 Guadalupe (472-1343). Private rooms with a small refrigerator, plus access to a TV room and basketball courts. ($15. Call ahead.)

I-35, running north and south of Austin, is home to a string of inexpensive hotels, but they are pretty far from downtown. **Motel 6** has two locations along I-35, both of which have clean rooms, a pool, and color TV with HBO. **North,** 9420 N. I-35 at the Rundberg exit (339-6161), is 12 miles north of the capitol off N. Lamar and E. Rundberg Lane. Take a bus to Fawnridge and walk 4 blocks. (Singles $20. Doubles $26.) **South,** 2707 I-35 (444-4842), near the Woodward exit, is 7 miles south of the capitol, near St. Edward's University. (Singles $22. Doubles $28.) Camping is no problem if you don't mind a 15- to 45-minute drive. The **Austin Capitol KOA** (444-6322), on I-35, 6 miles south of the city, offers a pool, game room, laundry, grocery, and playground. Some cabins are available. (Sites $14 for 2.) The **Emma Long Metropolitan Park,** 2000 Barton Spring (346-1831), a large preserve in the bend of the Colorado River, 6½ miles off Rte. 2222, has year-round hookups, tent sites, and a boat ramp. Contact the visitors center and the Highland Lakes Tourist Association for more information (see Practical Information above).

Food

Two main districts in town compete for Austin's restaurant trade. Along the west side of the UT campus, **Guadalupe Street** has scores of fast-food joints and convenience stores, including the **Party Barn,** with drive-through beer. Those who disdain the $3 all-you-can-eat pizza buffets and sub shops that line the drag can eat for $2 to $5 in the UT Union. The second district clusters around **Sixth Street,** south of the capitol. Here the battle for happy-hour business is waged with special intensity (to the delight of many) and three-for-one drink specials and free hors d'oeuvres are common.

Sam's Bar-B-Que, 2000 E. 12th St. (478-0378), take bus #12 or 6 eastbound. In a rough neighborhood. Some of the best barbecue in the Southwest. Tiny, dive-like interior gets cramped on weekends. Barbecue plates (with beans and potato salad) $3.50. Open Mon.-Thurs. 10am-3:30am, Fri.-Sat. 10am-5am, Sun. 10am-3am.

Trudy's Texas Star, 409 W. 30th St. (477-0646). Fine Tex-Mex dinner entrees $7-9, with a fantastic array of margaritas. Famous for their *migas,* a corn tortilla soufflé ($4). Open Mon.-Thurs. 7am-midnight, Fri.-Sat. 7am-4am, Sun. 8am-midnight.

Beans, 311 W. 6th (477-8999). Great little spot with menu printed on a bean can. Burgers, fries, chili, chicken, and beans. Huge meals $4-8. Happy hour Mon.-Fri. 2-7pm. Open Mon.-Sat. 11am-midnight, Sun. 11am-3pm.

Sholz Garden, 1607 San Jacinto (477-4171), near the capitol. An Austin landmark recognized by the legislature as "epitomizing the finest traditions of the German heritage of our state." Great chicken-fried steaks and Tex-Mex. Meals under $8. Live country-rock music and excellent jazz. German only in name. Open Mon.-Thurs. 11am-midnight, Fri.-Sat. 11am-2am.

Texas Chili Parlor, 1409 Lavaca (472-2828). Hot chili and Tex-Mex ($5-7) in a bar atmosphere as spicy as its food. Happy hour daily 3-7pm. Open daily 11am-1am.

Old Bakery and Emporium, 1006 N. Congress, near the capitol. Cheap sweets and light lunches in an old stone home. Sandwiches $1.75-$2. Open Mon.-Fri. 9am-4pm.

Sights

Not to be outdone by Washington, in 1882 Texans built their **state capitol,** Congress Ave. (475-3070), seven feet higher than the national capitol. The capitol is colossal, with colorful inlaid marble floors and "Texas" inscribed on everything from door hinges to hallway benches. (Free tours Mon.-Sat. 8:15am-4:30pm. Tourist information center open daily 8am-5pm. Open 24 hours when the legislature is in session; 6am-11pm when it's not.) Across the street from the capitol, at 11th and Colorado St., is the **Governor's Mansion** (463-5516), built in 1856. The bottom level stores the furniture of the past 10 Texas governors. (Tours Mon.-Fri. 10am-11:40am every 20 min. Free.)

The **University of Texas at Austin,** with an enrollment of over 50,000, is the largest university in the state and the wealthiest public university in the country. The **visitors centers** (471-1421) are in Sid Richardson Hall, adjacent to the LBJ Library, and at the corner of Martin Luther King and Red River Rd. The **Harry Ransom Center,** Guadalupe and 21st St. (471-1833), displays a Gutenburg Bible and medieval, 20th-century American, and Latin American art. (Open Mon.-Sat. 9am-5pm, Sun. 1-5pm. Free.)

The **Laguna Gloria Art Museum,** 3809 W. 35th St. (458-8191), 8 miles from the capitol (take bus #21 or 24.), in a Mediterranean villa-lookalike, displays the city's best exhibits on a rotating basis and features 20th-century artwork. With rolling, spacious grounds that overlook **Lake Austin,** the Laguna often hosts evening concerts, plays, and seasonal festivals. (Tickets $4.) (Docent tours Sun. 2pm. Open Tues.-Sat. 10am-5pm, Thurs. 10am-9pm, Sun. 1-5pm. Admission $2, seniors and students $1, under 16 free.)

Near the capitol is **St. Mary's Cathedral,** E. 10th St. and Brazos, an ornate sanctuary with the closest Austin comes to Gothic architecture. Riverside **Zilker Park,** 2201 Barton Springs Rd., just south of the Colorado River, is the place to head on hot afternoons. **Barton Springs Pool,** in Zilker Park (476-9044), is a popular swimming hole. The unchlorinated, spring-fed pool is 1000 feet long and 200 feet wide. Walnut and pecan trees line the banks. Beware: the pool's temperature rarely rises above the 60s. If you don't want to pay and need to get away from the crowds, walk upstream (take an inner tube) and swim at any spot that looks nice. (Admission $1.50, ages 12-18 25¢, under 12 free. Nov.-Jan. swimming is free and at your own risk.) Also in Zilker Park are a botanical garden (477-8672), canoes for rent (478-3852), playgrounds, playing fields, and picnic grounds. Parking inside the grounds is $2, but it's free on the roads near the entrance.

Entertainment

Austin is one of the country's few music magnets and has boosted many bands to fame. Others come from all over the country to play. Pick up a free copy of the **Austin Chronicle,** available at book and record stores. For honky-tonks and two-steppin' action visit the **Broken Spoke,** 3201 S. Lamar Blvd. (442-6189), Austin's liveliest dance hall. (Open Mon.-Tues. 9am-midnight, Wed. and Fri. 9am-1am, Thurs. 9am-12:30am, Sat. 10am-2am. Dancing Wed.-Sat. Cover $3-6.) The **Continental Club,** 1315 S. Congress (441-2444), is popular with students for everything from punk-a-billy and new wave to folk music. (Cover $4.) Wander along 6th Street, especially on weeknights when there are no crowds and no cover charges, to sample the bands from the sidewalk. For solid Texan music, try **Raven's Garage** (482-9272), on Red River just north of 6th St., where you actually sit in an old garage. Within the university, the **Cactus Cafe,** 24th and Guadalupe (471-8228), hosts different bands almost every night. (Hours vary, but usually open 8am-1am. Cover $2-12.) Next door, the **Texas Tavern** (471-9231) favors country music and serves fast food. (Hours vary, but usually open 11:30am-1:45am. Cover $2-5.) Those journeying out to Lake Travis can take advantage of **Oasis Cantina De Lago,** 6550 Comanche Trail (266-2441), a restaurant and bar with a gorgeous sunset view. (Open Sun.-Thurs. 11am-9pm, Fri.-Sat. 11am-10pm. No cover.)

From early May through late August, the **Zilker Park Hillside Theater,** 2000 Barton Springs Rd., Rte. 2244 (499-2000), produces free variety shows and concerts under the stars. Shows usually start between 7 and 9pm. The **Austin Symphony Orchestra** sponsors concerts of all kinds in the amphitheater at 1101 Red River Rd. (476-6064), downtown, while UT's **Performing Arts Center,** 23rd and E. Campus Dr. (471-2787), houses major touring theater companies, operas, and the like.

Film fans can try the **Varsity Repertory Theater,** 2402 Guadalupe (474-4351), which hosts new and unusual movies and foreign films. The historic **Paramount Theater,** 713 Congress (472-5411), has a daily double-feature oldies film festival ($4, seniors, students, and under 12 $2.50).

San Antonio

The Alamo lurks in the town center as the spiritual sub-conscious of San Antonio. However, the historical markers around town deferentially refer to Santa Anna's legions as the "brave" enemy, and today the Mexican-American influence is still powerful in the culture, politics, and economy of San Antonio. Spanish architecture, south-of-the-border food, and an ethnically diverse population give the city its distinctive appeal.

Practical Information

Emergency: 911.

Visitor Information Center: 321 Alamo Plaza (299-8155), downtown, across from the Alamo. Open daily 9am-5:30pm.

San Antonio International Airport, due north of town. Served by I-410 and Hwy. 281. Cabs to downtown $11.25.

Amtrak: 1174 E. Commerce St. (223-3226 or 800-872-7245), off the I-37 Montana St. exit. To: Dallas (3 per week, 8 hr., $42); Houston (3 per week, 9 hr., $41); El Paso (3 per week, 10 hr., $104).

Greyhound: 500 N. St. Mary's St. (227-8351, in Spanish 227-8387), or 2321 Vance Jackson (732-7441), 1 mile south of I-10. To: Houston (10 per day, 4 hr., $27); Dallas (13 per day, 6 hr., $34); El Paso (4 per day, 11 hr., $72). Open 24 hours.

VIA Metropolitan Transit: 112 Soledad (227-2020), between Commerce and Houston. Buses operate 5am-11:30pm, but many routes stop at 5pm. Service to outlying areas is inconvenient. Fare 40¢, express 75¢. Downtown, cheap (10¢) and frequent **streetcars** operate Mon.-Fri. 7am-8pm, Sat. 9am-8pm. Open Mon.-Fri. 7am-8pm, Sat. 9am-6pm.

Taxi: Yellow Cab, 226-4242. **Checker Cab,** 222-2151. Both $2.45 for 1st mile, $1 each additional mile.

Car Rental: Chuck's Rent-A-Clunker, 3249 SW Military Dr. (922-9464). $13-25 per day with 100 free miles. Must be 19.

Help Lines: Rape Crisis Center, 349-7273. 24 hours. In Alamo area, 674-4900. **Presa Community Service Center,** 532-5295. Referrals and transport for elderly and disabled.

Time Zone: Central (1 hr. behind Eastern).

Post Office: 615 E. Houston (227-3399), 1 block from the Alamo. Open Mon.-Fri. 8:30am-5:30pm. **ZIP code:** 78205.

Area Code: 512.

San Antonio is about 100 miles south of Austin and about 150 miles north of the Mexican border at Nuevo Laredo. I-35 and I-10 meet just south of town and I-37 shoots southeast to Corpus Christi. The **Riverwalk** forms a rough circle in the center of town. The **Alamo** (northeast), **Hemisfair Plaza** (southeast) and **La Villita** (south) lie just outside the circle. **Commerce Street** connects downtown to **Market Square** and **El Mercado,** about 10 blocks west.

Accommodations and Camping

San Antonio is a popular city, and downtown hotel managers have no reason to keep prices low. Further, San Antonio's dearth of rivers and lakes means that there are few good campsites. The best value in public camping is about 60 miles north of town at Canyon Lake in **Guadalupe River State Park** (512-438-2656; sites $4).

Bullis House Inn San Antonio International Hostel (AYH), 621 Pierce St. (223-9426), 2 miles northeast of the Alamo, across the street from Fort Sam Houston. From downtown take bus #11 to Grayson St. and get off at the stop after the 7-11 store. Friendly hostel in a quiet neighborhood. Cramped but clean rooms. Pool, kitchen. Open 7:30-11am and 5-11pm. Curfew 11pm, but night key available ($5 deposit). $10, nonmembers $12. Private singles from $17, nonmembers from $19. Doubles from $24, nonmembers from $26. Linen $2. Fills in summer.

Elmira Motor Inn, 1126 East Elmira (222-9463), off N. St. Mary's, a little over 1 mile north of downtown. Large, clean rooms. Singles $24. Doubles $26.

The Traveler's Inn, 220 N. Broadway (226-4381), about 5 blocks northwest of the Alamo. Comfortable, clean rooms, eccentric residents. Large singles for 1 or 2 $15. Doubles $35.

Motel 6, 138 North W. White Rd. (333-1850), 8 miles west of the Alamo, near I-10. Take bus #24 from downtown. Clean, though sparsely furnished. TV and pool. Singles $24. Doubles $30. Reservations a must.

El Tejas Motel, 2727 Roosevelt Ave. (533-7123), Rte. 281 S., at corner of Roosevelt and E. Southcross, 3 miles south of downtown. Take bus #42. Some waterbeds, color TV, pool, but rooms are a bit musty and the linens are ancient. Singles $22. Doubles $28. $2 extra on weekends.

San Antonio KOA, 602 Gembler Rd. (224-9296), 6 miles from downtown. Take bus #24 ("Industrial Park") from the corner of Houston and Alamo downtown. Showers, laundry, pool, playground, movies, fishing pond. Sites $12.50 for 2, each additional person $2.

Yogi Bear's Jellystone Park, 2617 Roosevelt Ave. (532-8310), 3 miles south of downtown. Showers, laundry, pool, spa, playground. Next to golf course and restaurants. Careful of your picnic lunch. Open daily 8am-5:30pm. Tent sites $12 for 2. RV sites $16 for 2. Each additional person $2.

Food

Downtown San Antonio's Mexican food is disappointingly bland and uninspiring. Explore the area east of S. Alamo and S. St. Mary's for better Mexican food and barbecue pits. The Riverwalk abounds with waterfront cafés. **Pig Stand** diners offer decent, cheap food all over this part of Texas; the one at 801 S. Presa, off S. Alamo, is open 24 hours. North of town, many East Asian restaurants line Broadway across from Breckenridge.

Casa Río, 430 E. Commerce (225-6718). Brightly decorated tables along the river, serenading mariachis, tasty Mexican cuisine, and a bargain to boot. Entrees $4-7. Open Mon.-Sat. 11:30am-9:30pm, Sun. noon-9:30pm. Usually crowded—large parties should make reservations.

Big Bend, 511 Riverwalk (225-4098), near the Hyatt. Best *fajitas* on the river. A bit expensive, but large portions and good atmosphere. Margaritas $1.25 during happy hour (Mon.-Fri. 4-7pm). Open Sun.-Thurs. 9am-midnight, Fri.-Sat. 9am-3am.

Hung Fong Chinese and American Restaurant, 3624 Broadway (822-9211), 2 miles north of downtown, take bus #14. The oldest Chinese restaurant in San Antonio. Consistently good and crowded, big portions. Try the egg rolls and lemon chicken. Meals $3-8. Open daily 11am-midnight.

Josephine Street Cafe, 400 East Josephine (224-6169), just northeast of downtown. Poor neighborhood. A semi-anonymous hangout for longtime locals, immortalized as the sultry neon diner on tourist posters. Steaks, chicken, fish, and Cajun dishes $4-9. Open Mon.-Thurs. 11am-10pm, Fri. 11am-11pm, Sat. 5:30-11pm.

Sights

The Missions

The four missions established along the San Antonio River formed the basis of the city and their remains are preserved by the **San Antonio Missions National His-**

torical Park. To reach the missions by car or bike, follow the blue-and-white "Mission Trail" signs beginning on S. St. Mary's St. downtown. If you lack a car, **San Antonio City Tours** (680-8724), in front of the Alamo, provides a two-hour tour of all the missions and the Alamo for $10, while **Tours for Kids,** 15411 Aviole Way (496-6030), offers tours just for children (9am-3pm). Bus #42 gets you within walking distance of Mission Concepción, and stops right in front of Mission San José. All of the missions are open 9am-6pm daily. For information on the missions, call 229-6000.

Mission Concepción, 807 Mission Rd., 4 miles south of the Alamo off E. Mitchell St. Traces of the once-colorful frescoes are still visible. This is the oldest unrestored church in North America (1731). Mass Sunday at 10am.

Mission San José (1720), 6529 San Jose Blvd. (921-4770). The "queen of the missions" has its own irrigation system, a church with a gorgeous sculpted rose window, and numerous restored buildings. The largest of San Antonio's missions, it provides the best sense of these self-contained Spanish institutions. Catholic services, including a "Mariachi Mass," are held five times on Sunday.

Mission Espada, 10040 Espada Rd. (627-2021). The main features here are the tiny chapel and a functioning mile-long aqueduct, built between 1731 and 1745. **Mission San Juan Capistrano** (229-5734) and **Mission San Francisco de la Espada** (627-2021), both off Roosevelt Ave., 10 miles south of downtown, are smaller and simpler than the other missions, but they best evoke the sense of isolation these imperial outposts once knew. (Open daily 9am-6pm; Sept.-May 8am-5pm.)

Downtown Tourist District

"Be silent, friend, here heroes died to blaze a trail for other men." Disobeying orders to retreat with their cannons, the defenders of the Alamo, outnumbered 20 to 1, held off the Mexican army for 12 days. Then, on the morning of the 13th day, Mexican buglers blew the infamous *deguello*—"No Quarter, No Prisoners." The rest is history. Now only tourists attack the **Alamo** (255-1391), at the center of Alamo Plaza, by the junction of Houston and Alamo St., and sno-cone vendors are the only defenders. A single chapel and a barracks preserved by the state are all that remain of the former Spanish mission. (Open Mon.-Sat. 9am-5:30pm, Sun. 10am-5:30pm. Free.) The **Long Barracks Museum and Library,** 315 Alamo Plaza (224-1836), houses Alamo memorabilia. (Open daily 9am-5:30pm.)

Heading southwest from the Alamo you'll soon see the black signs indicating access points to the **Paseo del Río (Riverwalk),** the shaded stone pathways following a winding canal built in the 30s by WPA workers. Lined with picturesque gardens, shops, and cafés, it is especially beautiful at night and is well patrolled and safe. The Riverwalk connects most of the major downtown sights. Ride the entire length of the Riverwalk by taking a boat ($1.75) from in front of the Hilton Hotel. The **Alamo Imax Theater** (225-4629), in River Center, shows a docudrama Alamo film on its six-story screen. Nearby is **La Villita** (299-8614), which has been transformed into a haven for crafts shops and art studios. (Open daily 10am-6pm.)

Hemisfair Plaza, on S. Alamo (229-8570), the site of the 1968 World's Fair, is another top tourist spot. The plaza, surrounded by restaurants, museums, and historic houses, is often used for special events in the city. The **Tower of the Americas,** 200 S. Alamo (299-8615), rises 750 feet above the dusty plains and dominates the meager skyline. Among the free museums to stroll through within the plaza is the **Institute of Texan Cultures,** (226-7651; open Tues.-Sun. 9am-5pm; free; parking $1) and the **Mexican Cultural Institute** (227-0123), filled entirely with modern Mexican art. (Open Tues.-Fri. 10am-7pm, Sat.-Sun. noon-6pm. Free.) Near Hemisfair on Commerce St., across from the San Antonio Convention Center, is **St. Joseph's Church,** erected in 1868 by German-Americans. This beautiful old church stubbornly refused to move, so a local department store chain built their establishment around it.

A few blocks west, between Commerce and Dolorosa St. at Laredo, is the Main Plaza and city hall. Directly behind the city hall is the **Spanish Governor's Palace,** 105 Plaza de Armas (224-0601). Built in 1772, the house is in the Colonial Spanish style with carved doors and an enclosed, shaded patio and garden. (Open Mon.-Sat. 9am-5pm, Sun. 10am-5pm. Admission 50¢.)

Market Square, 514 W. Commerce (229-8600), is a center for the sale of both schlocky souvenirs and handmade local crafts. The walkway **El Mercado** continues the block-long retail stretch. Nearby is the **Farmers Market,** where you can buy produce, Mexican chilis, pastries, candy, and spices. Come later in the day, when prices are lower and vendors are willing to haggle. (Open daily June-Aug. 10am-8pm; Sept.-May 10am-6pm.)

San Antonio North and South

Head to **Brackenridge Park,** main entrance 3900 N. Broadway (735-8641), 5 miles north of the Alamo, for a day of unusual sight-seeing. The 343-acre showplace includes an aerial tramway (rides $1.75), sunken gardens, stone bridges, and a miniature railway. At the **Witte Museum,** 3801 Broadway (226-5544), new shows are always being mounted, while permanent exhibits focus on Texas folklore. (Open Tues. 10am-9pm, Wed.-Sat. 10am-5pm, Sun. noon-5pm. Admission $3, seniors and students $1.50, ages 6-12 $1; Thurs. free 3-9pm.) The nearby **San Antonio Zoo,** 3903 N. St. Mary's St. (734-7183), also in the park, has over 3500 animals from 800 species in natural settings, and an extensive African mammal exhibit. (Open daily 9:30am-6:30pm; Nov.-March 9:30am-5pm. Admission $5, seniors $3.50, ages 3-11 $1.) The 38-acre **Botanical Center** (821-511), a mile east of Brackenridge Park, includes the largest conservatory in the Southwest. (Open Wed.-Sun. 9am-6pm. Admission $2.50.)

The **San Antonio Museum of Art,** 200 W. Jones Ave., just north of the city center, is in a restored Lone Star Brewery building. Towers, turrets, and spacious rooms decorated with ornate columns house pre-Columbian, Native American, Spanish Colonial, and Mexican folk art, Texan furniture, and decorative arts. (Open Tues.-Sat. 10am-5pm, Sun. noon-5pm. Admission $3, seniors and students $1.50, ages 6-12 $1; free Thurs. 3-9pm.) The former estate of Marion Koogler McNay, the **McNay Art Institute,** 6000 N. New Braunfels (824-5368), displays a collection of mostly post-impressionist European art. It also has a charming inner courtyard with sculpture fountains and meticulous landscaping. (Open Tues.-Sat. 9am-5pm, Sun. 2-5pm. Free.)

The **Lone Star Brewing Company,** 600 Lone Star Blvd. (226-8301), is about 2 miles south of the city. Gun-happy Albert Friedrich had managed to accumulate a collection of 3500 animal heads, horns and antlers when he opened the Buckhorn in 1887. What better place to put them than in his bar? Tours leave every 30 minutes, and include samples of beer and root beer. (Open daily 9:30am-5pm. Admission $2.50, seniors $2, ages 6-11 $1.)

Entertainment

For spur-of-the-moment fun after dark, stroll down the Riverwalk. Otherwise, peruse the Friday *Express* or the weekly *Current* for a guide to concerts and entertainment. The romping, stomping **Farmer's Daughter,** 542 North W. White Rd. (333-7391), lures crowds and features local entertainers. (Open Wed.-Thurs. 5pm-midnight, Fri.-Sat. 5pm-1am, Sun. 2-11pm. Cover Tues. and Thurs. $2, Wed. and Sun. $1, Fri. $4, Sat. $4.50.) **Floores Country Store,** on Helotes (695-8827), out Bandera St. toward the northwestern outskirts, is an old hangout of country star Willie Nelson. Dancing takes place outside on a large cement platform. (Cover varies.) **Mendiola's Ballroom,** 16490 U.S. Rte. 81 south (622-9204), is the city's best Mexican dance hall. On Saturdays, the doors are thrown open and dancers of all ages crowd the gigantic dance floor. (Take I-35 south from downtown. Admission $5.) Some of the best jazz in the city plays at **Jim Cullen's Landing,** 123 Losoya at the Hyatt (222-1234), also downtown. The music inside starts at 9pm and goes until around 2am. A jazz quartet performs on Sunday nights. The riverside café outside opens at 11:30am. (Cover $3.) **Fiesta San Antonio** rocks the city in mid-April.

Corpus Christi

Located smack dab on the Gulf of Mexico shoreline, Corpus Christi combines longhorn pride with the attractions of a coastal town. The local eagerness for tourists, fueled by the downswing of the petroleum industry, adds to the town's drawing power, particularly for the budget traveler. The part of Corpus Christi discovered by Spanish explorer Alonzo de Pineda in 1515 now serves as a base for the two major industries of petroleum and agriculture and remains the hub of city life. The city looks toward the water, as downtown hotels reach to the gulf, and area restaurants reflect the city's unique blend of Tex-Mex and seafood tastes. Corpus Christi is essentially an outdoor city, so come prepared to swim, sail, waterski, golf (there are numerous facilities), or otherwise enjoy the pier. What Corpus Christi lacks in high culture, it makes up for in sunshine.

Practical Information

Emergency: 911

Visitor Information: Convention and Visitors Bureau, 1201 N. Shoreline (882-5603), where I-37 meets the water. Lots of pamphlets, bus schedules, and local maps. Open Mon.-Fri. 8:30am-5pm. **Phone-a-Fact** (993-7414) provides information on weather, senior citizen and local activities, sports, entertainment, and horoscopes.

Greyhound: 702 N. Chaparral (882-2516), at the corner of Chaparral and Starr, downtown. To: Dallas (5 per day, 8 hr., $51); Houston (12 per day, 5 hr., $28); Austin (6 per day, 5 hr., $29). Open 24 hours.

Regional Transit Authority (The "B"): 882-1722. Pick up routes and schedules at the main station on the corner of Water and Schatzel St. or at the visitors bureau. Central transfer point is City Hall, downtown. Service ends around 8pm; no service Sun. or holidays. Fare 50¢, seniors, disabled, and children 25¢.

Taxi: Island Shuttle Cab Company, 949-8850. Airport to downtown $10 (per van, not per person). Major credit cards accepted. Call 800-543-6467 for reservations.

Help Lines: 24 Hour Crisis Hotline, 993-7410. **Crisis Services,** 993-7411. **Women's Shelter,** 881-8888. 24 hours.

Post Office: 809 Nueces Bay Blvd. (886-2200). Open Mon.-Fri. 7:30am-5:30pm, Sat. 8am-noon. **ZIP code:** 78469.

Area Code: 512.

Corpus Christi's tourist district follows **Shoreline Drive,** which borders the gulf coast. The downtown business district lies one mile north.

Accommodations and Food

Sandwiched between the Corpus Christi Visitors Center and the ultra-plush Wyndham Hotel is the **Sand and Sea Budget Inn,** 1013 N. Shoreline (882-6518), where I-37 meets the water. Rooms are clean and comfortable, and you can't beat the location; ask for a room with a bay view. (Singles $25. Doubles $27. Key deposit $5.) While the northwest section of Corpus Christi lacks the convenience of downtown lodging (public transportation is sparse outside downtown), the best motel bargains can be found there. Sleep cheap at the **Ecomotel,** 6033 Leopard St. (289-1116), exit I-37 at Corn Products and turn left at light. By bus, take #27 from downtown right to the motel—be sure to check a schedule, since the bus runs infrequently. Clean, comfortable, dimly lit rooms. (Singles $20. Doubles $27.) Campers should head to **Padre Island** or **Mustang Island State Park** (See Padre Island National Seashore below.) **Nueces River City Park** (241-1464), north on I-37, has free 3-day RV permits.

The downtown area is home to many inexpensive, tasty eating establishments. **Bahia,** 224 Chaparral (884-6555), serves simple but rib-sticking Mexican breakfasts and lunches. The authentic food compensates for the tacky decor. Try *nopalitos* (cactus and egg on a tortilla; $1.10) or a taco and 2 enchiladas with rice beans, tea, and dessert ($3.75). Live entertainment Fri. 7-9pm. (Open Mon.-Thurs. 7am-3pm, Fri. 7am-9pm, Sat. 8am-3pm.) Just down the street is the **Sea Gulf Villa Cafe,** 412 N. Chaparral (888-9238), where you can build your own breakfast *tacquito* (any 4 items $1.25) or try three-bean, cheese, and veggie *chalupas* for $3.15. Large portions and quick service. The **Cajun Reef,** 1002 N. Chaparral (883-5123) offers a large, all-you-can-eat lunch buffet for $4.80. Run-down exterior but inviting interior. Dinner entrees $8-10.

Corpus Christi is the home of **Whataburger,** a chain of superior fast-food joints. With 30 locations in the city, there is ample chance to sample their made-to-order burgers ($1.79) or malts ($1.05). Most locations open 24 hours.

There are few restaurants within walking distance of the Ecomotel and other northwest area motels except for the **Little Venice Restaurant** (289-1116), inside the Ecomotel, which offers an Italian all-you-can-eat buffet for $3.75, as well as a filling and inexpensive breakfast of pancakes, eggs, and ham or sausage for $2. (Open Mon.-Fri. 6am-10pm, Sun. 6am-4pm.)

Sights

Corpus Christi's shoreline seems ready-made for tourists; wide sidewalks with distance markers (for joggers) and graduated steps leading up from the water (for more sedentary sea-gazers) border almost two miles of Corpus Christi Bay. Docks and piers are also more suited to tourism than industry; restaurant showboats and sightseeing ferries abound.

Sights are concentrated along the gulf shore. On the north end of Shoreline Dr., the Convention Center houses the **Art Museum of South Texas,** 1902 N. Shoreline (884-3844), whose small but impressive collection includes works by Monet, Matisse, Picasso, Rembrandt, Goya, and Ansel Adams. Disabled access. (Open Tues.-Fri. 10am-5pm, Sat. 10am-6pm, Sun. 1-6pm. Free.) **The Harbor Playhouse,** less than 100 yards away, presents two plays a week. Showtimes and ticket prices vary. Across the street is the quirky **Corpus Christi Museum,** 1900 N. Chaparral (883-2862), with hands-on exhibits for kids. (Open Tues-Fri. 10am-5pm, Sat.-Sun. noon-5pm. Free.) Two blocks to the southwest is **Heritage Park,** a neighborhood with the old homes of nine of the city's patriarchs, all open to visitors. Tours are quick and fun. (Generally open Mon.-Fri. 10am-4pm, but hours vary in each house. Call 883-0639 to arrange group tours. Free.)

Corpus Christi also works to attract shoppers in an effort to pump money into its weary economy. Take the **trolley** from the north shoreline to the **Sunrise** or **Padre Island Mall.** The trolley travels along the posh and scenic Ocean Dr. Fashioned after an old-time model, the trolleys run every hour from the motels on Shoreline Dr. to the malls. (Fare Mon.-Fri. 50¢, Sat. 25¢.)

Padre Island National Seashore

One of only eight national seashores, Padre Island National Seashore (PINS) boasts unadulterated seascapes, clean sand dunes, perfectly preserved wildlife refuges, and an ideal environment for jet skiing and surf sailing. Condos and tacky souvenir shops are beginning to spring up around the junction of the Padre Isles and the John F. Kennedy Causeway (the only access route). The majority of the 80.5 miles of seashore, however, remain in their natural state.

Driving and hiking along the beach are two of the most popular activities at PINS. Because of the loose sand, four-wheel drive vehicles are needed to traverse the length of the beach. Cars must stop 30 miles shy of the end of the national seashore at the Mansfield Cut, since there is no bridge across the channel. There are no hiking trails on the seashore, but the **Malaquite** (pronounced MAL-a-kee) **Ranger Station,** 3.4 miles south of the park entrance, conducts hikes and programs throughout the year. (Call 949-8060 for information on group programs.)

The headquarters for PINS lie, ironically, outside the island in nearby Corpus Christi. The **PINS Visitors Center,** 9405 S. Padre Island Dr. (512-937-2621) provides information on camping, tide, and weather conditions, safety precautions, and sightseeing opportunities in nearby **Mustang State Park** and **Port Aransas.** (Open Mon.-Sat. 8:30am-4:30pm.) Within the national seashore, the **Malaquite visitors center** (512-949-8068), about 14 miles south of the JFK Causeway turn-off, supplies the above information and also offers exhibits and the sale of bird and wildlife guidebooks. (Open June-Aug. 9am-6pm, Sept-May 9am-4pm.) The Malaquite Ranger Station (949-8173) provides first-aid and emergency assistance. Entry into PINS costs $3.

While **Padre Island** (nearby, but not part of the national seashore) resorts and hotels are overpriced, camping sites are plentiful, scenic, and inexpensive. The **PINS Campground** (949-8173) consists of an asphalt area for RVs, with restrooms and cold-rinse showers (sites $4). Five miles of beach are devoted to primitive camping, and free camping is also allowed wherever vehicle driving is allowed. Near the national seashore is the **Balli County Park** (949-8121), on Park Rd. 22, 3½ miles from the JFK Causeway. Running water, electricity, and hot showers are available. (3-day max. stay. Sites $4, $8.50 with hookup.) If you value creature comforts, a few miles farther north is the **Mustang State Park Campground** (749-5246), on Park Rd. 53, 6 miles from the J.F.K. Causeway, with electricity, running water, dump stations, restrooms, hot showers, shelters, trailer sites, and picnic tables. (Entry fee $2. Camping fee $9.)

Motorists enter the PINS via the JFK Causeway, which runs through the Flour Bluff area of Corpus Christi. PINS is difficult to reach by public transportation. Corpus Christi bus #10 (which makes only 2 trips per day Mon.-Fri.) takes you to the tip of the Padre Isles (get off at Padre Isles Park-n-Ride). To reach the national seashore, call the **Island Shuttle Service** (949-8850; fare $1 per mile. Note that round-trip distance from bus stop to Malaquite Visitors Center is over 30 miles.) There is no post office on the PINS; mail should be sent general delivery to Flour Bluff sub-station, Corpus Christi. ZIP code: 78418.

Houston

The oil-bust hit Houston hard and many of the skyscrapers downtown are half-empty. But the Houston skyline remains one of the most magnificent, with the vibrant colors and exquisite modern architecture reflecting the pride of this great city. Watching the sun set over these luminious structures on a late summer evening is particularly memorable.

Built in the lush pine forests of East Texas, Houston epitomizes the sprawling urban giant. In all, the city covers almost 500 square miles. The absence of zoning laws, combined with a recklessly swift building boom in the 70s and early 80s, have resulted in a peculiar architectural mix. A museum, a historic home, a 7-Eleven, and a mini-mall may share the same city block.

Practical Information

Emergency: 911.

Greater Houston Convention and Visitors Bureau: 3300 Main St. (523-5050), at Stuart, outside of the downtown area, 10 blocks south of I-45. Take any bus serving the southern portion of Main St. (#7, 8, 14, 25, 65, 70, or 78). Open Mon.-Fri. 8:30am-5pm. Information booth in parking lot is open Sat. 9am-3pm.

Travelers Aid: 1600 Louisiana St. (223-8946) at the YMCA. Open daily 6am-midnight. 24-hour help line: 668-0911. Offices also at 2630 Westridge St., off Main St. near the Astrodome, and at Greyhound Station and Houston Intercontinental Airport.

Airport: Houston Intercontinental Airport (230-3000), 25 miles north of downtown. Get to the city center via the **Airport Express** (523-8888). Buses depart between 5am and 11:30pm every 20 minutes ($8.50, children $4.25). **Hobby Airport** is 9 miles south of downtown, just west of I-45. Take bus #50 downtown. **Hobby Airport Limousine Service** leaves Hobby for downtown every ½ hr. Tickets $4. **Southwest Airlines** (237-1221) has commuter flights to most major Texas cities. Flights from Hobby to San Antonio, Dallas, and Austin as low as $19 one way with 21-day advance purchase. Standard one way fare to San Antonio $39, to Austin and Dallas $44.

Amtrak: 902 Washington Ave. (224-1577 or 800-872-7245). Rough neighborhood. During the day, catch a bus by walking west on Washington (away from downtown) to the intersection with Houston Ave. At night, call a cab. To: San Antonio (3 per week, 4 hr., $41); New Orleans (3 per week, 9 hr., $67); and El Paso (3 per week, 16 hr., $130).

Greyhound/Trailways: 2121 S. Main St. (222-1161), on or near several local bus routes. Walk west toward downtown on Texas to the intersection of Main St. for local buses. Unsafe area. To: San Antonio (6 per day, 4 hr., $27); New Orleans (8 per day, 9 hr., $40); Dallas (5 per day, 5 hr., $24-$32); El Paso (4 per day, 16 hr., $90); Corpus Christi (5 per day, 5 hr., $28); and Galveston (5 per day, 1½ hr., $9). Open 24 hours.

Metro Bus System: Route and schedule information: 635-4000, Mon.-Fri. 6am-8pm, Sat.-Sun. 8am-5pm. An all-encompassing system that can take you from NASA (15 miles southeast of town) to Katy (25 miles west of town). Get system maps at the Customer Services Center, 912 Dallas St. (658-0854; open Mon.-Fri. 10am-6pm). Individual route maps can also be obtained at Metro headquarters, 901 Jefferson at Smith, 12th floor; the Houston Public Library, 500 McKinney at Bagby (224-5441); or at the Metro Ride store at Fannin and Capitol. Buses operate 6am-midnight. Fare 70¢, zone changes 10¢.

Taxi: Yellow Cab, 236-1111. Base rate $2.45, $1.05 per mile.

Car Rental: Rent-A-Heap Cheap, 5722 Southwest Freeway (977-7771). Cars from $22 a day with 100 free miles, 20¢ each additional mile. Open Mon.-Fri. 9am-6pm, Sat.-Sun. 9am-5pm. Must be 21 with major credit card.

Help Lines: Crisis Center Hotline, 228-1505. 24 hours. **Rape Crisis,** 528-7273. 24 hours.**Gay Switchboard of Houston,** 529-3211. Counseling, medical and legal referrals, and entertainment information. Daily 3pm-midnight.

Time Zone: Central (1 hr. behind Eastern).

Post Office: 401 Franklin St. (227-1474). Open Mon.-Fri. 9am-5pm, Sat. 9am-1pm. **ZIP code:** 77052.

Area Code: 713.

Houston lies 35 miles inland from the Gulf of Mexico. New Orleans is 350 miles east on the same coastline, which is paralleled by I-10; Dallas is a 240-mile drive north on I-45; San Antonio is 200 miles nearly due west on I-10. The flat Texas terrain supports several mini-downtowns. True "downtown" Houston, a squarish grid of interlocking one-way streets, borders the Buffalo Bayou at the intersection of I-10 and I-45. The city's notorious traffic jams will slow drivers during rush hour, but a car in Houston is almost a must—distances are vast and bus service is infrequent. Houstonians orient themselves by **"The Loop"**—I-610 lassoes the city center at a radius of 6 miles. Anything inside the Loop is easily accessible by car or by bus. Find rooms on the southern side of the city, near Montrose Avenue, the museums, Hermann Park, Rice University, and Perry House for easy access to points of interest and several bus lines.

Accommodations and Camping

Houston is an important convention center offering hundreds of motels. Those downtown are the most expensive. The cheaper motels are concentrated in the southeast by the Astrodome and **South Main Street** and along the **Katy Freeway** (I-10 east) on the other side of the city. Singles are as low as $18, doubles as low as $20. The rooms may be decent once you get inside, but this part of town is quite dangerous at night. (Buses #8 and 9 go down S. Main, and #19, 31, and 39 go out along the Katy Freeway.)

Houston is sadly lacking in safe rooms in the $25-35 range. But many of the best hotels in the city offer rooms for 1-4 people at under $50 on the weekends.

Perry House, Houston International Hostel (AYH), 5302 Crawford (523-1009), at Oakdale. From the Greyhound station, take bus #8 or 9 south to the Oakdale stop and then walk east 6 blocks on Oakdale to Crawford. Clean and friendly, in a quiet neighborhood near museums and restaurants. Closed between 10am and 5pm. Under $10. Linens $1.50.

Houston Youth Hostel, 5530 Hillman, #2 (926-3444). Take bus #36 to Lawndale at Dismuke. Only six beds, but rarely full. A less hectic atmosphere than most AYH-affiliates, but also less roomy. Coed dorm room. No curfew. $7. Linen $1.

YMCA, 1600 Louisiana Ave. (659-8501), between Pease and Leeland St. Women allowed. Good downtown location and a short ride from the Westheimer nightlife. Clean but minimalist rooms. No private baths. Rooms $15. $2 key deposit. The Y at 7903 South Loop E. (643-4396) is farther from downtown but has cheaper rooms. Take bus #40 ("Telephone"). Men only. $11.30. $5 key deposit.

Grant Motor Inn, 8200 Main St. (668-8000). Near the Astrodome. Clean and safe. Cable TV and pool. Singles $27. Doubles $35.

The Roadrunner, 8500 S. Main (666-4991) near the Astrodome. Mediocre rooms with significant variance in tidiness. Ask to see a few before you unpack. Singles $20. Doubles $24.

Comfort Inn, 9041 Westheimer (785-1400). Far from downtown, but close to the Galleria. Pool and cable TV. (Singles $29. Doubles $33.)

There are only two campgrounds in the Houston area. Both the **KOA Houston North,** 1620 Peachleaf (442-3700), off north Loop 610, and the **Houston Campground,** 710 State Hwy. 6 S. (493-2391), are out in the boondocks, inaccessible by Metro bus, and crowded on weekends. Make reservations at either location. KOA charges $14.50 per site for two, $3 each additional adult, $1.50 each additional child. Houston Campground charges $11 per site for two, $2.50 each additional adult, $1 each additional child.

Food

As a port town, Houston has been blessed with many immigrants (today its Indochinese population is the second largest in the nation), and its restaurant selection reflects this. Houston cuisine includes Mexican and Vietnamese food, and the state specialty, barbecue. Look for reasonably priced restaurants among the shops and boutiques along **Westheimer Street,** especially near the intersection with **Montrose.** This area, referred to as "Montrose," is Houston's answer to Greenwich Village. This area is also popular with gay men. Bus #82 follows Westheimer from downtown to well past the Loop. For great Vietnamese cuisine, go to **Milam Street,** where it intersects **Elgin,** just south of downtown.

Good Company Barbecue, 5109 Kirby Dr. (522-2530). A Texas tradition, complete with picnic tables and loud country music. Sliced pork and rib barbecue, as well as chicken and sandwiches ($3-7). Open Mon.-Sat. 11am-10pm, Sun. noon-10pm.

Hobbit Hole, 1715 S. Sheperd Dr. (528-3418), a few blocks off Westheimer. Take bus #35. For the hard-core Tolkien buff or the dedicated vegetarian. Try the "Gandalf," a vegetarian treat with mushrooms, avocado, and melted cheese ($5.25). Entrees $4-8. Open Mon.-Thurs. 11am-11pm, Fri.-Sat. 11am-midnight, Sun. 11:30am-10pm.

Pappasitos Cantina, 6445 Richmond (784-5253). Great Mexican food (entrees $5-14), including award-winning, *fajitas,* served to the vibrant strains of *mariachi* music. Open Sun.-Thurs. 11am-11pm, Fri.-Sat. 11am-midnight.

Luther's Barbeque, 8777 S. Main St. Good Texas barbecue entrees ($3-6) and free refills on soft drinks. Open Sun.-Thurs. 11am-10pm, Fri.-Sat. 11am-11pm.

Van Loc, 3010 Milam St. (528-6441). Vietnamese and Chinese food at reasonable prices (entrees $5-8). A great all-you-can-eat luncheon buffet, including iced tea ($3.65). Open Mon.-Thurs. 9:30am-11:45pm, Fri.-Sat. 9:30am-2:45am.

The Marble Slab, 3939 Montrose (523-3035). The latest "in" ice cream spot—special flavors and mix-ins prepared on its namesake tabletop. Homemade ice cream in a cone with one mix-in $2. Open Mon.-Thurs. 11:30am-11pm, Fri. 11:30am-midnight, Sat. noon-midnight, Sun. 1-11pm.

Cadillac Bar, 1802 N. Shepherd Dr. (862-2020), at the Katy Freeway (I-10), northwest of downtown. Take bus #75, change to #26 at Shepherd Dr. and Allen Pkwy. Wild fun and authentic Mexican food. Try a "Mexican Flag," a flaming shot of liquor. Tacos and enchiladas $5-7; heartier entrees more expensive. Open Mon.-Thurs. 11am-10:30pm, Fri. 11am-midnight, Sat. noon-midnight. Sun. noon-10pm.

Sights

Houston's gigantic urban sprawl has seen the creation of several clusters of skycrapers: Galleria and the Medical Center by themselves would dwarf the skyline of some comparable cities. But start your journey in the true downtown, the focal point of virtually all of the city's bus routes.

In the southwest corner of the downtown area is **Sam Houston Park,** just west of Bagby St. between Lamar and McKinney St. **St. John's Lutheran Church,** built in 1891 by German farmers, contains the original pulpit and pews. Catch a one-hour tour of four buildings in the park. (Tours Mon.-Sat. 10am-4pm on the hr., Sun. 1-5pm. Tickets $4, students $2).

Central downtown is a shopper's paradise, with a twist. Hundreds of shops and restaurants line the underground **Houston Tunnel System.** The system connects all the major buildings in downtown Houston, extending from the Civic Center to the Tenneco Building and the Hyatt Regency. On hot days, everyone ducks into the air-conditioned passageways to escape the heat and humidity. To navigate the tunnels, pick up a map at the Houston Public Library, the Pennzoil Place, or the Texas Commerce Bank.

Head westward along Westheimer to the **Galleria,** an extravagant, Texas-size shopping mall with an ice-skating rink surrounded by pricey stores. Next door is the **Transco Tower,** 2800 Post Oak Blvd. (439-2000), Houston's latest monument—the view from the top is impressive. Just walk in and take an elevator to the 51st floor. Don't miss the **Wall of Water Fountain,** in front of the Transco—it's on the scale of a waterfall.

Back toward downtown, just east of Montrose, are two of the city's smaller but most highly acclaimed museums.The **Menil Collection,** 1515 Sul Ross (525-9400), displays both ancient and 20th-century art. One block away, the **Rothko Chapel,** 1409 Sul Ross (524-9839), houses some of the artist's works. (The Menil open Wed.-Sun. 11am-7pm; the Rothko open daily 10am-6pm.)

Antique lovers will want to see **Bayou Bend,** in **Memorial Park,** the palatial mansion of millionaire Ima Hogg (yes, that's her *real* name), daughter of turn-of-the-century Texan governor Jim Hogg. Admire the collection of 17th- to 19th-century decorative art. The **museum,** 1 Wescott St. (529-8773), is 3 miles from downtown, just off Memorial Dr., and quite at home in posh River Oaks. Take bus #16, 17 or 84. (Tours Tues.-Sat. Call ahead. Closed Aug. Disabled access.)

On Main Street, 3½ miles south of downtown, lies the beautifully-landscaped **Hermann Park,** near all of Houston's major museums. The **Houston Museum of Natural Science** (639-4600) offers a splendid display of gems and minerals, permanent exhibits on petroleum, a hands-on gallery geared toward children, and a planetarium and IMAX theater to boot. (Open Sun.-Mon. noon-5pm. Tues.-Sat. 9am-5pm. Admission $2, children $1.) The **Houston Zoological Gardens** (523-5888) features small mammals, hippopotami, and alligators. (Open Tues.-Sun. 10am-6pm. Free.) Adjacent to Hermann Park on the north side is the **Museum of Fine Arts,** 1001 Bissonet (526-1361). Designed by Mies van der Rohe, it is noted for its collection of impressionist and post-impressionist works, as well as for its Remingtons. (Open Tues.-Wed. and Fri.-Sat. 10am-5pm, Thurs. 10am-9pm, Sun. 12:15-6pm. Admission $2, seniors and college students $1, under 18 free, free Thurs.) Across the street, the **Contemporary Arts Museum,** 5216 Montrose St. (526-3129), has multi-media exhibits. (Open Tues.-Sat. 10am-5pm, Sun. noon-6pm. Free.) Also located on the park grounds are sports facilities, a zoo, a kiddie train, and the Miller Outdoor Theater (see entertainment below). The University of Houston, Texas Southern University, and Rice University are in this part of town.

The **Astrodome,** Loop 610 and Kirby Dr. (799-9555), a mammoth indoor arena and baseball stadium, is the home of the Oilers football team and the Astros baseball team. (Tours daily 11am, 1pm, 3pm, and 5pm; off-season 11am, 1pm, and 3pm. Admission $2.75 under 7 free. Parking $3). At these prices, you're better off paying admission to a game. Football tickets are hard to get, but seats for the Astros are usually available and cost only $3.

Wander down Space Age memory lane at NASA's **Lyndon B. Johnson Space Center** (483-4321), where models of Gemini, Apollo, Skylab, and the space shuttle are displayed in a free walk-through museum. This NASA is the home of Mission Control: when astronauts ask, "Do you read me, Houston?" the folks here answer. (Control center open daily 9am-3:30pm. Free. By car, go 21 miles south of downtown on I-45. The car-less should take the Park and Ride Shuttle #246 from downtown.)

Free one-and-a-half-hour guided harbor tours are offered on the inspection boat *Sam Houston.* Terminus of the gruesomely polluted Houston Ship Channel, the **Port of Houston** leads the nation in foreign trade. (Tours Tues.-Wed. and Fri.-Sat. at 10am and 2:30pm, Thurs. and Sun. at 2:30pm.) Reservations for these deservedly popular tours must be requested four to six weeks in advance, but you can join one if the boat doesn't reach its 90-person capacity. Call to make last-minute reservations. Drive 5 miles west from downtown on Clinton Dr., or take bus #48 to the Port Authority gate. For more information or reservations, write or call Port of Houston Authority, P.O. Box 2562, Houston 77252 (225-4044; open Mon.-Fri. 8am-5pm).

Entertainment

Whether you're in the mood for a few cool beers in an urban-professional hangout or some serious country "kicker" dancing, Houston has the bar for you. The Westheimer strip offers the largest variety of places. Rub elbows with venture capitalists and mod New Wavers alike at **The Ale House,** 2425 W. Alabama at Kirby (521-2333). The downstairs bar and beer garden offers over 100 brands of beer served with a British accent. Upstairs you'll find mostly New Wave music and dancing. (Open daily 11am-2am.) A similar mix can be encountered at the more exclusive **Cody's Restaurant and Club,** penthouse of 3400 Montrose (522-9747), which offers a view of the skyline. Sit inside or out on the balcony, and listen to live jazz. (Open Tues.-Fri. 4pm-2am, Sat. 6pm-2am. Informal dress.) **Sam's Place,** 5710 Richmond Ave. (781-1605) is a real Texan hangout, especially on Sunday afternoons, when a band plays outside (4-10pm), and they set up various booths with different beers. Proper dress required. (Happy hour 4-7pm and 11pm-closing. Open Mon.-Sat. 11am-2pm, Sun. noon-2am.) **The Red Lion,** 7315 Main St. (795-5000), features cheap beer and nightly entertainment that ranges from bluegrass to heavy metal. (Open Mon.-Fri. 11am-2am, Sat. 4pm-2am, Sun. 4-10pm.)

Houston offers ballet, opera, and symphony at **Jones Hall,** 615 Louisiana Blvd. Tickets for the **Houston Symphony Orchestra** (224-4240) cost $5-23. During July, the symphony gives free concerts on Tuesday, Thursday, and Saturday at noon in the Tenneco Building Plaza. The season runs from September to May. The **Houston Grand Opera** (546-0200) produces seven operas per season, with performances from October through May. (Tickets $5-25; 50% student discount ½ hr. before performance.) Call 227-2787 for information on the ballet, opera, or symphony. If you're visiting Houston in the summer, take advantage of the **Miller Outdoor Theater** in Hermann Park (520-3291). The symphony, opera, and ballet companies stage free concerts here in the evenings from May to August, and an annual **Shakespeare Festival** in the last week of July and first week in August. The **Alley Theater,** (228-8421) downtown, stages Broadway-caliber productions at moderate prices. (Tickets $14-28. Student rush seats available 15 min before curtain $5.) Comedy lovers should visit the **Comedy Workshop,** 2105 San Felipe (524-7333; nightly shows $2-4). For last minute, half-price tickets to many of Houston's sports, musical and theatrical events, and nightclubs, take advantage of **Showtix** discount ticket center, located at 400 Rusk at Smith, Tranquility Park (227-9292; open Tues.-Sat. 11am-5:30pm); and 11140 Westheimer St. at Wilcrest (open Mon.-Fri. 11am-5pm, Sat. 10am-noon).

Near Houston: Galveston Island

Fifty miles southeast of Houston on I-45, the narrow, sandy island of **Galveston** offers not only a beach resort's requisite tacky t-shirt shops, ice cream stands, and video arcades, but also beautiful historic homes, shady, oak-lined streets, and even a few quiet, deserted beaches.

It's hard to believe, but prior to the devastating hurricane of 1900, this was the largest and wealthiest city in Texas. With the city almost fully decimated, the survivors of that storm swore that Galveston would be rebuilt better and stronger than ever. Although the city never regained its prominence, the ten-mile concrete **"seawall"** that gives the main thoroughfare its name is testament to the "stronger than ever" Galveston.An unfortunate result is that your "beachside" motel may not be precisely that. The island's natural beaches are located at the extreme islands; below the seawall the shoreline is rocky and the waves are treacherous.

A warning to visitors: Galveston's streets are set up in a grid that appears elementary. Lettered streets (A to U½) run north to south, numbered streets run east-west, with Seawall following the southern coastline. But it's incredibly simple to get completely lost because most streets have two names. For example, Avenue J and Broadway are the same, as are 25th Street and Rosenberg.

You can surround yourself with families and high-spirited volleyball games at **Stewart Beach,** near 4th and Seawall. If you prefer a student crowd and a quieter beach, try **Pirates Beach,** near 95th and Seawall. There are two **Beach Pocket Parks** on the west end of the island, with bathrooms, showers, playgrounds, and a concession stand. (Parking $3.)

After a day at the beach, visit the **Strand,** on Strand St., between 20th and 24th St., a national historic landmark which today consists of restaurants, gift shops, and clothing stores. Cool off with a delectable root-beer malt at **LaKing's Confectionery,** 2323 Strand (762-6100), a large, old-fashioned ice-cream parlor and candy factory. (Open Sun.-Thurs. 10am-9pm, Fri.-Sat. 10am-10pm.) One of the island's two **visitors centers** is located 2 blocks over at 2016 Strand (765-7834). The center functions as the depot for the **Galveston Island Trolley** running between the Strand and the Seawall and to most major attractions and hotels. (Tickets $2, seniors and children $1. Trains leave hourly Oct.-Apr. and every ½-hour May-Sept.) Galveston's other visitors information center is the **Convention and Visitors Bureau,** at 21st St. and Seawall (763-4311 or 800-351-4236; open Mon.-Fri. 8:30am-5pm, Sat.-Sun. 9am-5pm.)

Seafood is abundant in Galveston, along with traditional Texas barbecue. Plenty of eateries line Seawall and the Strand. For seafood, go to **Benno's on the Beach,** 1200 Seawall (762-4621). Try a big bowl of the shrimp gumbo ($3.50) or one of their crab variations.

Prices for accommodations in Galveston usually fluctuate with the season. The least expensive option is to make Galveston a daytrip from Houston. There are a few cheap motels along Seawall, but most are notoriously shabby and singles range from $25-60. Probably the best of the bunch is the **Treasure Isle Motor Hotel,** 1002 Seawall (763-0582). Rooms are decent, and the owners are making some attractive renovations for the 1990 season. (Summer weekdays: Singles $29. Doubles $35.) The familiar **Motel 6,** 7404 Broadway (740-3794), is about 1½ miles from the beach, with decent rooms and a pool. (Singles $22. Doubles $26.) You can camp at **Galveston Island State Park,** on 13 Mile Rd. (737-1222), about 10 miles southwest of the visitors center. (Sites $12.) The **Bayou Haven Travel Park,** 6310 Heards Lane (744-2837), on Offatts Bayou, is much more convenient to downtown and has laundry facilities and clean showers. (Full hookup $12 for 4, waterfront sites $15. Each additional person $2. From the bus station, go left off 61st St., then ½mile to Heards.)

Texas Bus Lines, a **Greyhound** affiliate, operates out of its station at 4913 Broadway (765-7731). To Houston (6 per day, 1½ hr., $9). Galveston's **time zone:** Central

(1hr. behind Eastern). Its main **post office** is at 601 25th St. (763-1527; open Mon.-Fri. 8:30am-1pm and 2-5pm, Sat. 9am-12:30pm.) Galveston's **ZIP code** is 77550; the **area code** is 409.

East Texas

What is generally known as East Texas—the vast area north and east of Houston and east of Dallas—defies the conventional Texas stereotype of flat, treeless ranch country. A swath of thick, hilly woods and lake country, it offers a shady alternative to the often sweltering city-scapes of Dallas and Houston.

The major cities of this region are Beaumont in the south and Lufkin in the north. In the area are four national forests. **Sam Houston National Forest** about 50 miles north of Houston, borders Lake Livingston in the northeast and Lake Conroe in the southwest. The **Lone Star Hiking Trail** and the **Big Creek Scenic Area** run through here. Ranger offices are located in Cleveland (713-592-6462) off U.S. 59 and in New Waverly (409-344-6205) off I-45. On the outskirts of the Forest, the **Sam Houston Memorial Museum Complex,** 1836 Sam Houston Ave. (409-295-7824) in Huntsville, off U.S. 75, includes the general's two homes and his law office as well as a commemorative mini-model of the Eiffel tower and Taj Mahal rolled into one.

Davy Crockett National Forest and **Angelina National Forest** lie 10 miles west and east of Lufkin, respectively. The Davy Crockett incorporates the scenic **Four C National Recreation Trail,** a 20-mile pass from the Neches Overlook to Ratcliff Lake. Ranger stations are located in Crockett (409-544-2046) and Apple Springs (409-831-2246). The Angelina is split in two by the pristine *Sam Rayburn Reservoir,* in which catfish and bass are plentiful. The ranger station is located at 1907 Atkinson Dr. (409-634-7709) in Lufkin. For more information, contact the Forest Supervisor, 701 N. First St., Lufkin 75901.

The **Sabine National Forest** lies at the Louisiana border, 60 miles south of Shreveport and just due east of the Angelina National Forest, on the other side of U.S. 96. The Sabine overlooks the *Toledo Bend Reservoir,* which teems with bluegill. Rangers can be reached in Hemphill (409-787-2791) and in San Augustine (409-275-2632). Camping in designated areas of the national forests is usually free unless amenities (RV hookups, showers, etc.) are provided. There are also many private camping facilities in the area. Stop by the Park Service office in Lufkin for maps and permits.

Established to protect the rich biological diversity of the region, the **Big Thicket National Preserve** (just north of Beaumont) offers nature trails, canoeing, and undeveloped camping in designated areas. Stop by the **Big Thicket Visitors Center** on Rte. 420 off U.S. 287, 10 miles north of Kountze and 35 miles north of Beaumont. For more information, write or call the Superintendent, Big Thicket National Preserve, 8185 Eastex Freeway, Beaumont 77708 (409-839-2689). Permits are required for fishing and camping, and you should check in with the forest ranger at the visitor information center before venturing out.

West Texas

On the far side of the Rio Pecos lies a region whose stereotypically Texan character is so extreme that it borders on self-parody. This land was colonized in the days of the Texan Republic, during an era when "Law West of the Pecos" meant a rough mix of vigilante violence, frontier gunslinger machismo, and lip service to the niceties of U.S. jurisprudence. This desolate region does not lack attractions. Here are the mountain ranges (such as they are) of Texas and the border city of El Paso and its Chihuahuan neighbor, Ciudad Juárez.

Guadalupe Mountains National Park

The Guadalupe Mountains are Texas's highest and carry a legacy of unexplored grandeur. Early westbound pioneers avoided the area, fearful of the arid climate and the Mescalaro Apaches who controlled the region. Even by the early 20th century, the only inhabitants of this rugged area were a few homesteaders and guano miners. Today the mountains maintain their primitive state and ensure challenging hikes in a mostly desert environment for those willing to journey to this remote part of the state. The passing tourist who hopes to catch only the most established sights will stop to see **El Capitan,** a 2000-foot limestone cliff, and **Guadalupe Peak,** 8549 feet tall, the highest point in Texas. More leisurely travelers can hike to **McKittrick Canyon,** with its spring-fed stream and oak and maple forest, and **The Bowl,** a high forest of Douglas fir and ponderosa pine. Both are day hikes from the **Frijole Information Center** (915-828-3251), right off US 62/180, where you can pick up topographical maps, hiking guides, backcountry permits, and information. (Open daily June-Aug. 7am-6pm; Sept.-May 8am-4:30pm.)

Guadalupe National Park's undevelopment may be a bonus for backpackers, but it makes just getting by tough. All water in the backcountry is reserved for wildlife and no food is available nearby. Bring water for even the shortest, most casual hike. The **Pine Springs Cafe** (915-828-3338), directly across from the campground, sells only ready-made sandwiches, sodas, and beer. You can get ice cream and hamburgers at **Nickel Creek Cafe** (915-828-3348), 5 miles east, or a pancake and coffee breakfast for $3-6; fill up here before visiting McKittrick Canyon, which is 3 miles farther east.

Guadalupe Mountains Park Service conducts half- and full-day hikes June to August, as well as evening programs. Information is available at the Frijoles Visitor Center or on radio station 1610 AM. An additional visitor contact station is staffed during the fall and sporadically throughout the year at McKittrick Canyon. Visit the park in the fall to marvel at the trees, while avoiding the hot summers and windy springs.

The **Pine Springs Campgrounds** (915-828-3251), 1½ miles west of the Frijole station, right on the highway, has water and restrooms. No fires are allowed. (Sites $5; Golden Age and Golden Access Passport holders receive a 50% discount.) **Dog Canyon Campground** (505-981-2418), at the north end of the park, just south of the state line, can be reached only by a 70-mile drive from Carlsbad, NM, on Rte. 137. A primitive campground, Dog Canyon has no hookups or running water, but you can camp in the backcountry for free with a permit from the visitors center.

The park is less than 40 miles west of Carlsbad Caverns in New Mexico (see Southern New Mexico), 110 miles east of El Paso, and a 90-mile drive from Kent. **TNM&O Coaches,** an affiliate of Greyhound, runs along U.S. 62/180 between Carlsbad, NM, and El Paso, passing Carlsbad Caverns National Park and Guadalupe National Park en route. This schedule (#734) makes flag stops at the park three times per day in each direction ($5.70 round-trip if you buy a special ticket from Greyhound in El Paso). Guadalupe Mountains National Park is in the Mountain time zone (two hours behind Eastern).

For further information, contact the Superintendent, Guadalupe Mountains National Park, 3325 National Parks Hwy., Carlsbad, NM 88220 (505-785-2233).

Big Bend National Park

Roadrunners, coyotes, wild pigs, mountain lions, and 350 species of birds make their home at Big Bend National Park, a huge, 700,000-acre tract that lies within the great curve of the Rio Grande. The spectacular canyons of the Rio Grande, the vast Chihuahuan Desert, and the cool **Chisos Mountains** have all witnessed the 100 million years it took to mold the park's natural attractions. Although the Chihuahuan Desert covers most of the park, colorful wildflowers and plants abound.

You must get a free **wilderness permit** at the visitors center if you want to take an overnight hike. The park rangers will suggest places to visit and hikes to take according to your time constraints and energy levels. It is possible to see much of the park by car (fortunately, most roads are well paved), but many of the most scenic places are only accessible by foot. The **Lost Mine Peaks Trail,** an easy three-hour hike up a peak in the Chisos, leads to an amazing summit view of the desert and the Sierra de Carmen in Mexico. Another easy walk leads up the **Santa Elena Canyon** along the Rio Grande. The canyon walls rise up as much as 1000 feet over the banks of the river. Three companies offer river trips down the 133-mile stretch of the Rio Grande owned by the park. Information on rafting and canoeing is available at the visitors center. The **park headquarters** (915-477-2251) are at Panther Junction. (Open daily 8am-7pm; 1-week vehicle pass $5) For information, write National Park Concessions, Inc., Big Bend National Park 79834. The other **ranger stations** are at Rio Grande Village and Castolon.

There are **grocery stores** in the Chisos Basin at Castolon, Panther Junction, and Rio Grande Village. Get damp at the park's only public shower for 75¢ per 5 minutes at the Rio Grande Village store.

The only motel-style lodging is the **Chisos Mountain Lodge** (915-477-2291) in the Chisos Basin. This lodge offers four types of service: a new hotel (singles $53, doubles $58), an older motel (singles $42.50, doubles $50), lodge units located ¼ mile away from the lodge complex (singles $45, doubles $53), and stone cottages housing up to three people ($60). Reservations are a must, since the lodge is often booked six months to a year in advance. The lodge also runs a restaurant/coffee shop, where entrees cost $5-12. (Open 7am-8pm, off-season 7am-7:30pm.) The entire complex is located in the **Chisos Basin,** 10 miles from the park's visitor center. Designated **campsites** within the park are given out on a first come, first serve basis. **Chisos Basin** and **Rio Grande Village** have sites with running water ($5); Cottonwood has toilets but no running water ($3); there are free primitive sites along the hiking trails. Due to the relatively high temperatures at the river, you won't have to worry about getting a site at Rio Grande Village, but you may have to negotiate with the resident flock of buzzards. The best (and coolest) campsites by far are those in Chisos Basin. Try to get a campsite near the perimeter. Get here early, as the basin sites fill up fast.

Big Bend may be the most isolated spot you'll ever visit. El Paso is 300 miles to the northwest and San Antonio is a 450 miles away. The park is only accessible by car via I-118 or I-385. Rental cars are available in the Davis Mountain towns of Fort Davis and Alpine, approximately 100 miles north of the park. Amtrak serves Alpine three times per week. Hitching is not a good idea; the roads to Big Bend are not well traveled, and you may wind up stranded.

El Paso

Over 400 years ago, Spanish refugees fleeing the Pueblo Revolt forded the Rio Grande River to explore what is now New Mexico. That passage, dubbed El Paso del Norte (passage of the north) gave this city its name and also its character of impermanence. Across the river from the Mexican city of Ciudad Juárez, El Paso forms half of a binational metropolis. Neither passport nor special ID is required for entrance, and cities on both sides of the border are home to a population of transients. The aura of flux has persisted since the first Spanish settlers arrived here.

Although 33 million legal crossings are made each year, El Paso is embroiled in a long-running controversy over U.S. immigration control, a political issue that affects tourists (especially those of Hispanic origin) who cross the Mexican border or encounter a random INS checkpoint on the open road. The "open border" concept is still opposed on *both* sides of the fence. Historically, immigrants have been used in this region to bust unions and keep wages low on the U.S. side of the line.

Practical Information

Emergency: 911. **Juárez Police,** 2-48-35.

Visitor Information: Convention and Visitors Center, 5 Civic Center Plaza (534-0686), on the western edge of downtown, within 1 block of both Greyhound and Trailways. Booth open Mon.-Fri. 8:30am-4:30pm, Sat.-Sun. 9am-noon and 1-5pm.

El Paso International Airport: in northeast El Paso (722-4271). Bus #50 stops about ½ mile south of the terminal building, at the corner of Montana and Airway Blvd. **Sprint Airport Shuttle System** (833-8282) departs from curb outside the Continental Airlines desk every 10 min. Door-to-door service offered. Advance reservations required for trips to the airport. Airport to downtown Plaza $10.

Amtrak: 700 San Francisco (545-2247; reservations 800-872-7245), on the western side of the Civic Center, near Greyhound. Office open daily 11am-7pm. To San Antonio (3 per week, $103, continues to Dallas) and Tucson (3 per week, $68, continues to Phoenix and Los Angeles). Reservations required.

Greyhound: 111 San Francisco (544-7200; current rates and schedules 533-3837), at Santa Fe, across from the Civic Center. Office open 24 hours. To: Albuquerque (4 per day, $39); Dallas (8 per day, $75); San Antonio (4 per day, $72); Tucson (9 per day, $42, continues to Los Angeles); and the Mexican city of Chihuahua.

Sun City Area Transit (SCAT): 533-3333. Extensive service. All routes begin downtown at San Jacinto Plaza (Main at Mesa). Fewer routes in the northwest. Connects with Juárez system. Maps and schedules posted in the Civic Center Park and available at 700-A San Francisco Ave. Mon.-Fri. 8am-noon and 1-5pm. The visitors bureau puts out a pamphlet on sightseeing by bus. Most buses stop around 5pm; limited services on Sundays. Fare 75¢, seniors and students with ID 35¢. **Handy-SCAT** is a curb-to-curb transportation service for the disabled. Call 544-2514 Mon.-Fri. 7am-9pm, Sat.-Sun. 8am-4pm.

Car Rental: Rent-a-Heap, P.O. Box 2184 (532-2170). $15 per day, unlimited free mileage; 3-day min. rental. Cars must be kept within a 50-mile radius of El Paso. Must be 18 with a cash deposit. Will deliver.

Help Lines: Crisis Hotline, 779-1800, 24 hours. **U.S. Customs Service,** 534-6837, 24 hours.

Post Office: 5300 E. Paisano (775-7519), at Alameda, about 5 miles from downtown. Open 24 hours. **ZIP code:** 79910.

Area Codes: El Paso, 915. International direct dialing to Ciudad Juárez is 011 + 52 (country code) + 161 (city code) + local number.

El Paso is at the westernmost tip of Texas on I-10, 40 miles south of Las Cruces, New Mexico, and 570 miles west of San Antonio. The geographical intrusion of the Rio Grande and the Franklin Mountains complicates the city's road planning. Split by the Franklins, the city is roughly shaped like the letter "Y," angling northwest to southeast along the river.

Accommodations, Camping, and Food

The cheapest hotel rooms are across the border, but downtown El Paso has several good budget hotels within easy walking distance of San Jacinto Plaza. The **Gardner Hostel (AYH)**, 311 E. Franklin (532-3661), at Stanton, is 1 block northeast of the plaza. Bank robber John Dillinger stayed at this historic landmark just before the feds nabbed him in Tucson. Affordability comes before luxury; some of the furnishings (including the bedsheets) may also be pretty historic. Simple but sunny hostel rooms have four beds and a semi-private bath. ($10.50, nonmembers $12.80. Singles with private bath $16. Doubles $21.) Quality budget motels are concentrated along **N. Mesa Drive,** including **Warren Inn,** 4548 N. Mesa Dr. (544-4494), 5 miles north of downtown. Large clean rooms with kitchenette and cable TV. Continental breakfast included. (Singles $24. Doubles $28.) Farther to the north (about 8 miles from downtown) is **Motel 6,** 7840 N. Mesa (584-2125), off I-10. While far from downtown, it has clean rooms with free movies. (Singles $22. Doubles $32.)

There is no public transportation to campgrounds outside of town. **Hueco Tanks State Park** (857-1135) is 32 miles east of El Paso on U.S. 62/180. (Sites with utilities and showers $6-9.) **Desert Oasis Park** is at 12705 Montana (855-3366). (Sites $11 for 2, each additional person $1. $2 park entrance fee.)

Forti's Mexican Restaurant, 321 Chelsea (772-0066), offers fantastic fajitas at a convenient location a few blocks south of I-10. (Entrees $5-7. Take-out available. Open Sun.-Thurs. 11am-10pm, Fri.-Sat. 11am-11pm. Take bus #22.) **Chico's Tacos,** 4230 Alameda (533-0975), offers cheap and filling burritos, burgers, and tacos. Beef stew burrito 85¢, 3 rolled beef tacos 84¢. Three other locations: 5305 Montana (772-7777), 3401 Dyer (565-5555), and 1235 McRae (592-8484). Open daily 9am-1:30am. Near the hostel, the **Brown Bag Deli,** 500 Stanton, offers 31 different sandwiches for $3-5. Serves breakfast too. (Open Mon.-Fri. 7am-7pm, Sat. 8am-6pm.)

Sights

Murchison Park, northeast of downtown on Rim Rd. (which becomes Scenic Dr.), at the base of the mountains, offers a fine view of El Paso, Juárez, and the Sierra Madre. The city center is a couple of miles to the south; the University of Texas at El Paso and the Sun Bowl are off to the west; Fort Bliss and the airport sprawl several miles to the east.

El Paso has a number of interesting museums that focus on local culture and history. The **El Paso Museum of Art,** 1211 Montana (541-4040), contains samples from the French, Venetian, and Sienese schools, a hodge-podge of silverware, crucifixes, and candelabras, as well as a plethora of Spanish religious paintings. (Decent tours Sun. 1:30pm. Open Tues.-Sat. 10am-5pm, Sun. 1-5pm. Free.) The **Fort Bliss Replica Museum,** 5051 Pleasanton Rd. (568-4518), 7 miles from downtown, recreates the 1854 fort built to fight the Apache and includes a cactus garden. (Open daily 9am-4:30pm. Free.) The small but ambitious **Americana Museum,** Civic Center Plaza (542-0394), downtown, is dedicated to the display and study of U.S., pre-Columbian, and historical art of the Americas. Exhibits include models of cliff houses, local and regional photography, and artifacts from the Hohoka and Anasazi cultures. (Open Tues.-Sat. 10am-5pm. Free.) El Paso's most controversial organization is the subject of the **Border Patrol Museum of the Immigration and Naturalization Service,** 310 N. Mesa (533-1816), in the Merrill Lynch building. Focus is on the colorful history and artifacts of the Border Patrol's three branches—Canadian, Mexican, and coastal. When the service was established in 1924, Border Patrol officers were given a badge, pistol, and rifle, but had to supply their own horse; today they receive 17 weeks of classes in Spanish and immigration law. The museum doesn't skimp on nostalgia; at its hub is a commemorative statue, "The Silent Sentinel." (Open Mon.-Fri. 10am-4pm, Sat. 9am-noon. Free.)

For a more thorough exploration of El Paso, try one of the visitors bureau's three tours. The **walking tour** directs you to the colorful relics of El Paso's "wild west" phase, most of which are in or near downtown. The **bus tour** trasports you to most of the cultural highlights from the El Paso Museum of Art to the **Museo de Arte y Historia,** across the river in Juárez. The **car tour** covers the most territory, including a short drive up Alabama Rd. and McKelligon Rd. into **McKelligon Canyon,** high in the Franklins, northeast of downtown.

ROCKY MOUNTAINS

The thousands of towering peaks that have brought the Rocky Mountains their fame shelter secluded spots of unbelievable beauty. Stretching from the Canadian border to central Utah, the mountains are full of colorful alpine meadows, fordbidding rocky gorges, and clear, relatively unpolluted streams gushing down either side of the Continental Divide. Certain vistas, certain moments of profound silence defy description: don't be surprised if you have trouble squeezing the essence of these "purple mountains' majesty" onto a postcard.

The surrounding states are properly and grandly spacious. The whole Rocky Mountain area supports less than five percent of the population of the U.S., and much of the land belongs to the public, preserved in national parks, forests, and wilderness areas. The stunning Waterton-Glacier International Peace Park lies at Montana's border with Alberta, Canada; Idaho encompasses two impressive back-country regions, as well as acres of state and national forests; Wyoming and Colorado are the proud landlords of Yellowstone and Rocky Mountain National Parks.

Not surprisingly, most residents of the mountain states live close to the land; even in Colorado, agriculture is still bigger business than tourism. The people of Denver, the only major metropolis in the region, combine big-city sophistication with an abiding appreciation for the area's rich natural endowment. Most other cities are oil towns, ski villages, university seats, or mining towns—commercial centers are in short supply in the mountains. Although acid rain threatens alpine lakes and streams, and new proposals for damming the Colorado and Columbia Rivers are made every year, the simple truth is that few sections of the high-and-dry Wild West can support big cities. The Rockies are likely to remain thankfully empty and relatively unspoiled.

Travel

This place is big. Really, really big. It is possible to drive for hours through these states without seeing another car, and long-time residents think nothing of spending four or five hours behind the wheel in order to do the Sunday shopping. The roads are mountainous and full of switchbacks, so that a 50-mile trip can take up to three hours to accomplish. The rugged terrain and remoteness of the most interesting parts of the region discourage public transportation. Outside the cities and the well-served Yellowstone-Teton axis (which everyone and their battleship-sized Winnebagos visit), hitching or driving are the best options. Buses generally get you close enough so that one friendly ride or local car rental can finish the last leg of the trip.

The interstate highway system makes some gorgeous, remote areas of the Rockies accessible as easy side trips from a cross-country bus or car tour. **I-90** skirts Devil's Tower and the Bighorns in Wyoming, the mountain valleys near Bozeman, and the ghost towns and ranges of western Montana and northern Idaho. The Medicine Bow Range of Wyoming is just south of **I-80,** as are the impressive Uintas of northeastern Utah. Colorado's **I-70** burns past some of the best scenery in central Colorado, including Rocky Mountain National Park to the north, and the ranges around Aspen to the south. **Powder River Transportation,** in Wyoming, **Intermountain Transportation,** in Montana, and **Rocky Mountain Stages,** in Colorado, accept Greyhound/Trailways passes and tickets.

Amtrak (800-872-7245) has two excellent routes though the Rockies. The amazing **"California Zephyr"** opens up a prime slice of the Colorado Rockies for exploration between Denver and Salt Lake City (1 per day, $98); the **"Empire Builder"** serves Glacier National Park directly and conveniently from Chicago (1 per day,

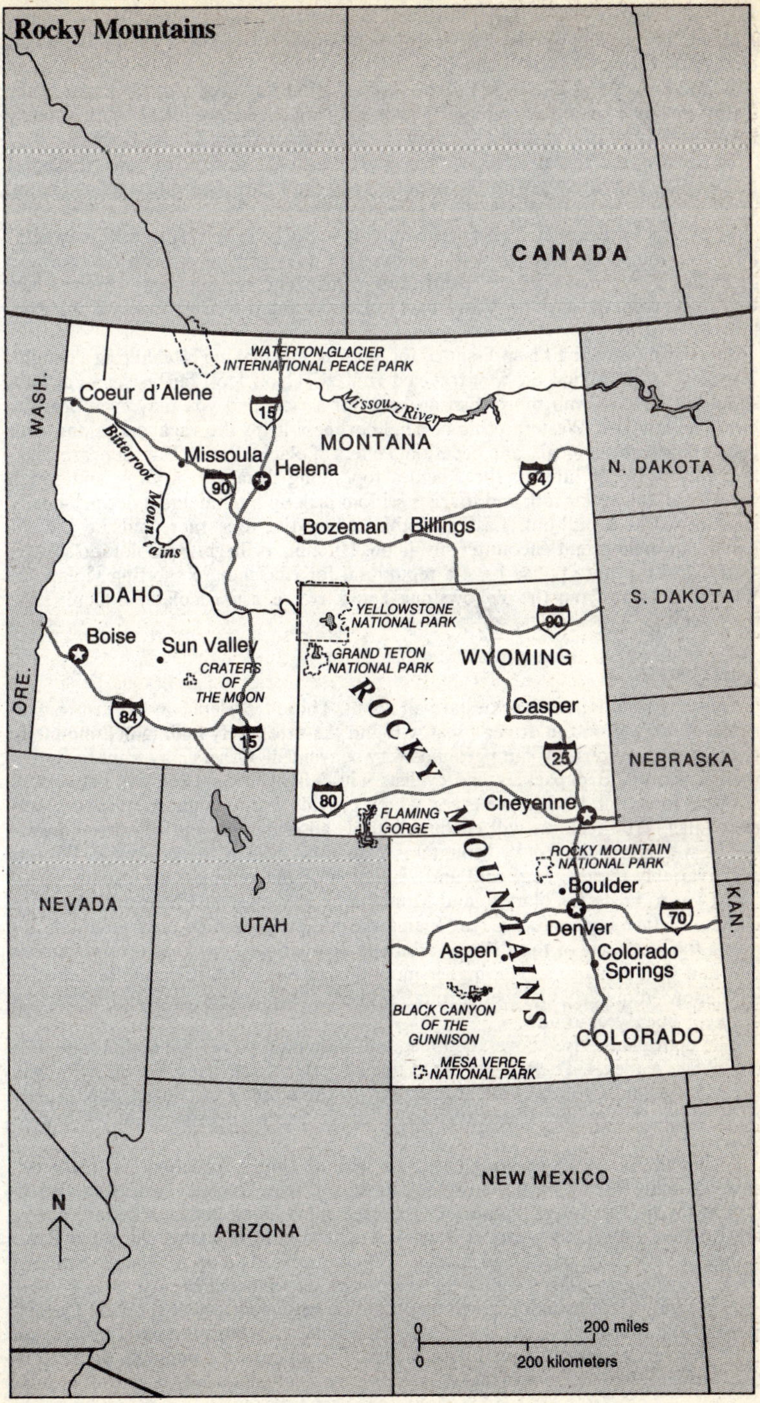
Rocky Mountains
CANADA
WATERTON-GLACIER
INTERNATIONAL PEACE PARK
WASH.
Coeur d'Alene
15
Missouri River
Bitterroot Mountains
MONTANA
Missoula
Helena
90
94
N. DAKOTA
Bozeman
Billings
IDAHO
S. DAKOTA
YELLOWSTONE
NATIONAL PARK
90
Boise
Sun Valley
GRAND TETON
NATIONAL PARK
WYOMING
CRATERS
OF
THE MOON
ORE.
ROCKY MOUNTAINS
84
Casper
15
25
NEBRASKA
80
Cheyenne
FLAMING
GORGE
ROCKY MOUNTAIN
NATIONAL PARK
Boulder
KAN.
NEVADA
UTAH
70
Denver
Aspen
Colorado
Springs
BLACK CANYON
OF THE
GUNNISON
COLORADO
MESA VERDE
NATIONAL PARK
NEW MEXICO
N
ARIZONA
0
200 miles
0
200 kilometers

$240) and Seattle (1 per day, $114). But besides these two transmountain routes, Amtrak has nothing to offer. **Air travel** on a budget is possible if you're flying into base cities Denver or Salt Lake City.

Sound brakes and a reliable radiator are essential for successful **car travel.** Take it slow (trapped behind a creeping RV, you may not have any choice). With a sturdy two-wheel-drive car, you can see almost every famous spot in the Rockies.

In general, **car rental** prices vary inversely with the size of the town (cheapest in Denver), and directly with the popularity of the sights. Cut-rate used car rental agencies are banned in Wyoming. These companies might not offer the best deals, anyway, since mileage charges add up quickly in the wide open spaces. It may actually save you rental costs to waste a couple of days driving in from Los Angeles or Dallas if you plan a longer rental. **Auto transport** companies may offer the best way to get from the East or West Coast to Denver and the larger towns in the Rockies.

The dry mountain air is well-suited for outdoor life, making **hitchhiking** a delight. It's easy to get a ride on well-traveled routes. If you look fairly clean-cut, you shouldn't have to wait more than an hour for a ride, and you may even beat the bus. The low-key, Western ethic of neighborliness helps the vagabond along with good conversation, meals, and occasional offers of places to stay. But there are negative factors to hitching in the Rockies too. Long distances, aridity, and rough weather all take their toll; and tourists seldom pick up hitchhikers if not personally approached at a pull-out. Lastly, in this conservtive area those outside the all-American mold might encounter suspicion. Hitching is illegal on Colorado's interstates, and the state police have a reputation for efficiency in spotting violations. Wyoming, away from the Yellowstone-Teton axis, is a particularly difficult state for hitching.

Outdoors

Outdoors is what the Rockies are all about. Those travelers content just to gaze at the scenery from the driver's seat will find the excellently maintained mountain roads and numerous RV campgrounds very convenient. Others may want to stretch their legs a bit. Backpackers and cyclists will delight in the extensive network of national forests and other preserves, which provide a quiet night in unspoiled surroundings. True recluses will encounter trails absolutely devoid of other hikers.

The weather in the Rocky Mountains is about as even as the landscape. Winters are invariably tough—very cold and very snowy—but summers are usually pleasantly warm. Eastern Colorado and Montana lie in the Great Plains and share the climate of that region (see Great Plains introduction). Where cold mountain air meets the warm air of the Plains, turbulent weather systems whip up tremendous hail and thunderstorms. The higher mountain passes (9000 ft.) are often clogged with snow from early October through mid-May. Major highways and interstates are kept open year-round.

The high plains rise above 5000 feet, and mountain passes are commonly 8000 feet above sea level. The thinner air at this altitude means that heavy exertion will tire you out until you become accustomed to the scarcity of oxygen; this usually takes about two weeks. Less oxygen also means more direct sunlight, so beware of severe sunburns.

Although America's growing obsession with all things outdoorsy has made circuses of many Rocky Mountain sights, most of the backcountry is seldom visited. Ask at the nearest ranger station for deserted spots. Even better, hike into one of the Rockies' little-known ranges, such as the Sawtooths of Idaho, the Wind River Range of Wyoming, or the San Juans of Colorado. Head on up to Glacier National Park and the Canadian Rockies for even more unpopulated beauty.

Any sight worth examining will be on public land, courtesy of the U.S. Department of the Interior. Access is generally excellent, since both the park service and the forest service maintain well-paved roads throughout their domains. In general, the **National Park Service** manages most areas of truly outstanding natural beauty.

The parks now charge hefty entrance fees (generally $5 per car). If you plan to visit several, get a **Golden Eagle Passport** (see the General Introduction). The lower-profile **National Forest Service** offers many more campgrounds in areas spared the throngs of tourists. Camping in undeveloped national forest spots off major roads is the cheapest way to enjoy the Rockies.

Almost every good-sized town within 50 miles of the mountains has its own forest service or Bureau of Land Management office, where you can pick up information on backpacking, hiking, and climbing. Most **ranger districts** (sub-units of national forests) publish suggested hikes and sights within their territory. Armed with an NFS map and the more detailed U.S. Geological Survey topographical maps (available at better sporting-goods stores), you're ready for the woods.

Inquire about the national properties through Rocky Mountain regional offices. The National Park Service is at 655 Parfet St., P.O. Box 25287, Denver 80225 (303-234-3095). The National Forest Service office for Colorado and eastern Wyoming is at 11177 W. 8th Ave., P.O. Box 25127, Lakewood, CO 80225; for Montana and northern Idaho, the Northern Regional Office, Federal Bldg., P.O. Box 7669, Missoula, MT 59807; for western Wyoming or central and southern Idaho, contact the Intermountain Regional Office, Federal Bldg., 324 25th St., Ogden, UT 84401.

Colorado

For many travelers, mention of the "Silver State" brings one image to mind—the world-class ski slopes of America's staggeringly beautiful Rocky Mountains. But the Spanish explorers who christened this region between the plains and the desert intended the apellation "Colorado" (meaning colored or colorful) to describe the diversity of the area's terrain. It speaks equally of snowy peaks and checkerboard farmland, of glacier-gouged canyons and silent mesas. Colorado's inhabitants are as diverse as her countryside. Such die-hard conservatives as the Coors family and James Watt reside only a few miles from the New Age Center that is Boulder. The state's many natural wonders fuel an active tourist industry, an industry so well developed that even budget travelers can enjoy a journey through Colorado's varied attractions.

Bus transportation is readily available throughout the Denver-Boulder area and most of the north, but to see the more remote south you might consider renting a car. Hitching is relatively easy along the east-west expanse of I-70 and the north-south thoroughfare of U.S. 550, but becomes difficult near Denver and Colorado Springs. Luckily, finding accommodations is easier than getting around; Colorado possesses 21 of the Rockies' 24 youth hostels, and offers camping in 13 national forests and eight national parks. Contact the Rocky Mountain Council of AYH, 1058 13th St., P.O. Box 2370, Boulder 80306 (442-1166; open Tues.-Thurs. 10am-4pm). Colorado also has the majority of **bed and breakfasts** in the Rockies. The budget category starts around $25 for singles and $30 for doubles. For information, write Bed and Breakfast of Colorado, Ltd., P.O. Box 12206, Boulder, CO 80303. (Send $5 for a list of hosts. Rates start at $23; no reservation fee.) To reserve a campsite in any state park or recreation area, call 800-365-2267.

Practical Information

Capital: Denver.

Tourist Information: Colorado Board of Tourism, 1625 Broadway, #1700, Denver 80202 (592-5410 or 800-433-2656). Open Mon.-Fri. 8am-5pm. **U.S. Forest Service,** Rocky Mountain Region, 11177 W. 8th Ave., Lakewood 80225 (236-9431). Tour maps free or forest maps $2. Open Mon.-Fri. 7:30am-4:30pm. **Ski Country USA,** 1540 Broadway, #1300, Denver 80203 (837-0793; recorded message 831-7669; open Mon.-Fri. 8am-5:30pm). **National Park Service,** P.O. Box 25287, Denver 80255-0287 (236-4648). Handles some reservations for Rocky Mountain National Park. Open Mon.-Fri. 9am-4pm. **Colorado State Parks and Recre-**

ation, 1313 Sherman St., #618, Denver 80203 (866-3437). Guide to state parks and Metro-area trail guide. Open Mon.-Fri. 8am-5pm.

Road Conditions: 639-1234 (I-25 and East), 639-1111 (Denver and West).

Time Zone: Mountain (2 hr. behind Eastern). **Postal Abbreviation:** CO.

Denver

Gold! In 1858 the word went out from the South Platte River Valley—there was money for the taking at the confluence of the South Platte and its smaller neighbor, Cherry Creek. Within weeks the rumor of riches drew thousands of miners to Northern colorado, and Denver, complete with Colorado's first saloon, was born. Though the mines have since gone out of business, and sporting goods stores now contribute more to Denver's economy than saloons ever did, Colorado's capital city is still the Rockies' fastest growing metropolis. Centrally located between Colorado's eastern plains and western ski resorts, Denver today serves as the industrial, commercial, and cultural center of the Silver State.

Denver is home to a curious mix of burnt-out New York yuppies, rednecked cowboys, and starry-eyed New Age enthusiasts eagerly awaiting the appearance of a kinder, gentler world. But if betting and meditation at various locals' hangouts don't intrigue you, explore fine museums, numerous parks, and the nation's first symphony in the round, all the while enjoying the glorious mountain view.

Practical Information and Orientation

Emergency: 911 (Denver), 759-1511 (Glendale), 279-2557 (Golden), 340-2200 (Aurora), 987-7111 (Lakewood), 287-2844 (Commerce City).

Visitor Information: Denver and Colorado Convention and Visitors Bureau, 225 West Colfax Ave. (892-1112), near Civic Center Park, just south of the Capitol. Open Mon.-Fri. 8am-5pm. Pick up a free copy of the comprehensive *Denver and Colorado Official Visitors Guide.* **Big John's Information Center,** 1055 19th St., at the Greyhound/Trailways Bus Station. Big John is a great guy who offers enthusiastic information on hosteling in Colorado. Open Mon.-Sat. 6:15am-noon. **Stapleton Airport Information Center,** between C and D concourses. Open Mon.-Fri. 8am-5pm, brochures available 24 hours. **16th St. Ticket Bus:** Double-decker bus on the 16th St. Mall at Curtis St. Visitor information, half-price tickets to local theater performances, and RTD bus information. Open Mon.-Fri. 10am-6pm, Sat. 11am-3pm.

Stapleton International Airport (398-3844), in northeast Denver. Easily accessible to downtown. RTD bus lines #32 and 38 serve the airport. A cab will cost you $8-9. This is the 6th busiest airport in the world; delays are common.

Amtrak: Union Station, 17th St. (534-2812), at Wynkoop, in northwest corner of downtown. To: Salt Lake City (1 per day, 14 hr., $98); Omaha, NE (1 per day, 9 hr., $96); and Chicago, IL (1 per day, 18 hr., $142).

Buses: Greyhound/Trailways, 1055 19th St. (292-6111; 800-531-5332 for Spanish-speaking visitors), downtown. To: Cheyenne (4 per day, 3 hr., $23); Albuquerque (4 per day, 12 hr., $55); Kansas City (4 per day, 15 hr., $100); and Salt Lake City (4 per day, 12 hr., $90); also comprehensive service within CO. **Estes Park Bus Company** (447-0770), in the Greyhound/Trailways office. Serves Boulder and Rocky Mountain National Park. Also leaves from Stapleton Airport lower level, near gate 6, and the bus terminal.

Regional Transportation District (RTD): 626 E. 16th St. (778-6000). Service within Denver and to Longmont, Evergreen, Conifer, Golden, and the suburbs. Many routes shut down by 9pm or earlier. Fare Mon.-Fri. 6-9am and 3-6pm 75¢, all other times 50¢. Free 16th St. Mall Shuttle covers 14 blocks downtown. Over 20 buses per day to Boulder (45 min., $2). Call Mon.-Fri. 5am-10pm, Sat.-Sun. 7am-10pm. Bus maps $1.

Gray Line Tours: at the bus station (289-2841). 2½ hr. tours of Denver in summer twice daily, once during the rest of the year. $12, under 12 $7. The 3½-hr. Denver Mountain Parks tour includes many of the sights outside of Denver, including a stop at the Coors Brewery ($15, under 12 $9).

Taxi: Zone Cab, 861-2323. **Yellow Cab,** 777-7777. Both $1.25 base fare, $1 per mile.

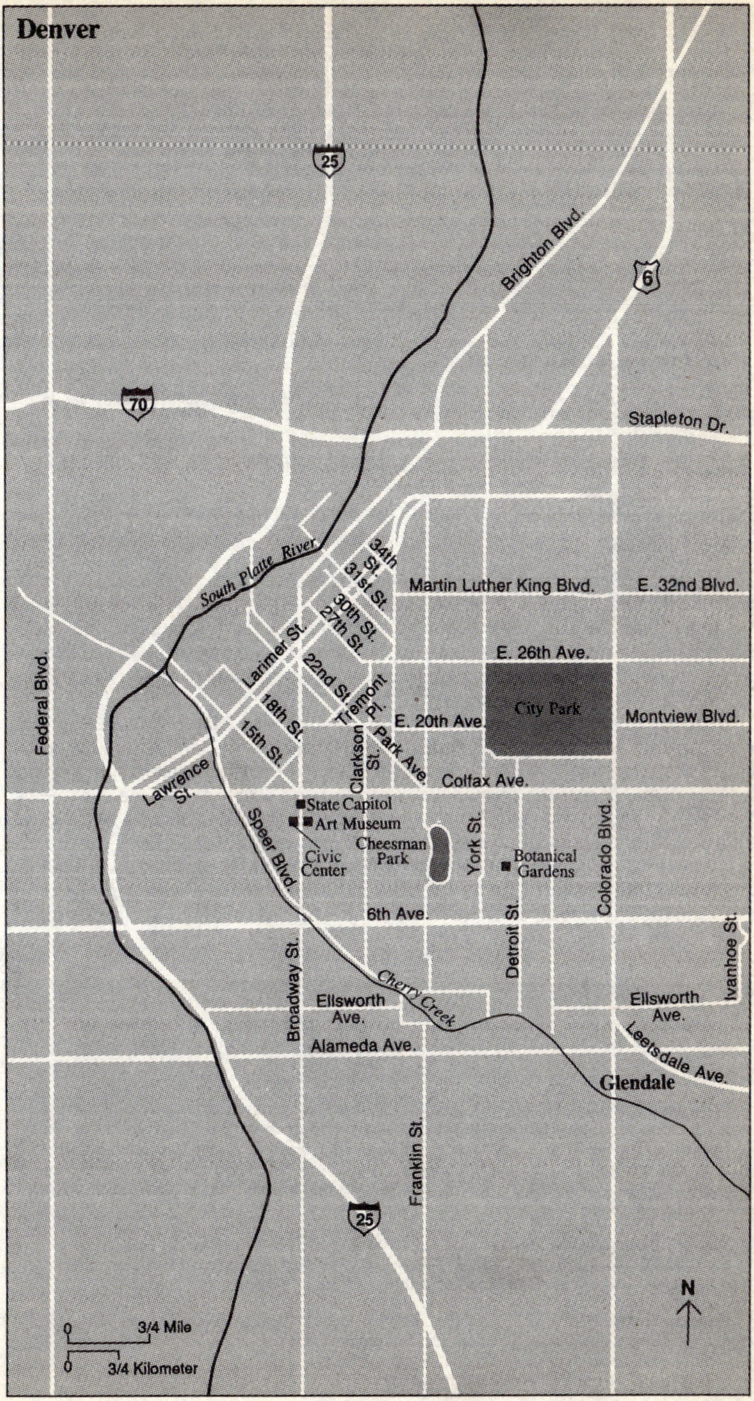
Denver
25
70
6
Brighton Blvd.
Stapleton Dr.
South Platte River
34th St.
31st St.
30th St.
27th St.
Larimer St.
22nd St.
Tremont Pl.
18th St.
15th St.
Lawrence St.
Martin Luther King Blvd.
E. 32nd Blvd.
E. 26th Ave.
City Park
Montview Blvd.
E. 20th Ave.
Park Ave.
Clarkson St.
Colfax Ave.
Federal Blvd.
State Capitol
Art Museum
Civic Center
Cheesman Park
York St.
Botanical Gardens
Colorado Blvd.
Speer Blvd.
6th Ave.
Broadway St.
Detroit St.
Ivanhoe St.
Cherry Creek
Ellsworth Ave.
Ellsworth Ave.
Alameda Ave.
Leetsdale Ave.
Glendale
Franklin St.
25
N
0 3/4 Mile
0 3/4 Kilometer

Car Rental: For all three establishments you must be at least 21 years old and you may not drive out of CO. If you will be driving in the mountains, be wary of renting heaps. **Rent-a-Heap,** 2397 W. Dartmouth Ave. (781-1816); take I-25 south to the Santa Fe exit, or call and they might pick you up. $15 per day ($18 to go into the mountains), unlimited free mileage. $110 per week. Must have your own insurance and a $50 deposit. Open Mon.-Fri. 9am-6pm, Sat. 9am-3pm. **Cheap Heaps Rent-a-Car,** 4839 Colifax Ave. (393-0028), 8 blocks east of Colorado Blvd. $15 per day with 30 free miles per day, 12¢ each additional mile. $13 if you're heading for the mountains, and $21 for unlimited free mileage. $100 deposit required. Open Mon.-Fri. 8am-6pm, Sat. 8am-2pm. **People's Rent-a-Car,** 2222 S. Colorado Blvd. (758-5159). Call them and they'll pick you up. $20 per day with 100 free miles per day, 16¢ each additional mile. Open Mon.-Thurs. 7:30am-5:30pm, Fri. 8am-6pm, Sat. 8:30-noon. Must have a credit card.

Auto Transport Company: Auto Driveaway, 5777 E. Evans Ave. (757-1211); take bus #21 to Hollis and Evans. Open Mon.-Fri. 8:30am-4:30pm. Must have a $150 cash deposit, be at least 21, and have three local references (this last requirement is waived for foreigners).

Bike Rental: J & E Sports, 4365 Santa Fe Dr. (781-4415). $10 per day, $5 each additional day, $100 deposit. Open Mon.-Sat. 10am-6pm.

Help Lines: Contact Lifeline, 458-7777. 24-hour. **Rape Crisis,** 430-5656 or 329-9922. 24 hours.

Gay and Lesbian Community Center: 1245 E. Colfax Ave. (837-1598). Open daily 10am-10pm.

Post Office: 1823 Stout (297-6016). Open Mon.-Fri. 8am-5pm. **ZIP code:** 80201.

Area Code: 303.

I-25 bisects Denver north-south, connecting Denver with Cheyenne, WY (100 miles north) and Sante Fe, NM (360 miles south). I-70 links Denver with Grand Junction (250 miles west) and Kansas City (600 miles east). Route 285 cuts south through the central Rockies, opening up the Saguache and Sangre de Cristo Ranges to easy exploration. Hitchhiking along the lesser routes is easy once you've left Denver, as is getting a ride into the city.

Broadway divides east Denver from west Denver, and **Ellsworth Avenue** forms the north-south dividing line. Streets west of Broadway are in alphabetical order, while the streets north of Ellsworth are numbered. Streets downtown run diagonal to those in the rest of the metropolis. Keep in mind that many of the avenues on the eastern side of the city become numbered streets downtown. Most even-numbered thoroughfares downtown run only east-west.

The hub of downtown is the **16th Street Mall.** There is little crime to worry about in this area, but the east side of town beyond the capitol, the west end of Colfax Ave., and the upper reaches of the *barrio* (25th-34th St.) should be avoided at night, especially by women traveling alone.

Accommodations

Denver is a hosteler's heaven, with more than its fair share of excellent and inexpensive places to stay, many within easy reach of downtown. Campgrounds are plentiful.

Melbourne Hotel and Hostel, 607 22nd St. (292-6386), downtown, at the corner of Welton St., 6 blocks from the 16th St. Mall. Large singles and doubles with refrigerator. Kitchen and free coffee. Gentlemanly proprietor "Professor K" leads an all-day tour around downtown Denver, Boulder, and the mountains. (Tours Mon.-Sat. The Professor also picks up guests at the Denver hostel. $11 fee includes lunch at the University of Colorado, and a short hike.) $8 per person. Call ahead.

Denver International Youth Hostel, 630 E. 16th Ave. (832-9996), 10 blocks east of bus station, and 4 blocks north of downtown. Take bus #15 to Washington St., 1 block away. Dorm-style rooms with kitchen and laundry facilities. Check-in 8-9:30am and 5-10pm. $6.

Franklin House, 1620 Franklin St. (331-9106), a block off Colfax Ave.; take bus #15. 15-min. walk from downtown. The comfortable rooms in this converted Victorian will remind you of home. Bathrooms down the hall. Singles from $16, with bath from $20. Doubles from $24, with bath from $28. Breakfast included.

The Standish, 1530 California St. (534-3231), downtown by 15th St. Neat and clean. Many rooms have TV, or you can rent one for $1 per day. Giant bathtubs in many rooms, showers in others. Singles from $12, with bath $22. Doubles from $14, with bath $26.

YMCA, 25 E. 16th St. (861-8300). In 3 parts: old section (men only), new section, and family section. You can use the Olympic-size pool, and other sports facilities ($4). Old section: Singles $14, with bath $16. Doubles $25 with bath. New section: Singles $17, with bath $18. Doubles $28, with bath $29. Family section: 3-person room $34, 4-person room $40.

Motel 6, 4 locations in the greater Denver area, all with A/C and pool. North: 6 W. 83rd Place (429-1550), Northwest: 10300 S. I-70 Frontage Rd. (467-3172), East: 12020 E. 39th Ave. (371-1980), West: 480 Wadsworth Blvd. (232-4924). Singles $24. Doubles from $30.

Cherry Creek Lake Recreation Area (699-3860, for reservations 671-4500). Take I-25 to exit 200, then west on Rte. 225 for about 3 miles and south on Parker Rd.—follow the signs. 102 sites that fill only on summer weekends. Sites $7, entrance fee additional $6.

Chatfield Reservoir (791-7275); take Rte. 75 or 85 4 miles past the center of Littleton. 153 well-developed sites. Open mid-May to late Sept. ($7, with electricity $10.) Make reservations for weekends.

Chief Hosa Campground (526-0364), in Genesee Park off I-70 exit 253. 200 sites complete with heated pool, athletic field, laundry, grocery store, showers, and restrooms. (Sites $12, with electricity and water $15.) No reservations accepted.

Golden Gate Canyon State Park (592-1502), 20 miles west of Golden on Rte. 6 past Black Hawk. **Reverend's Ridge Campground.** 156 sites. Developed sites $7. Open late May-late Sept. **Aspen Meadows Campground,** 19 miles south of Nederland. Sites $6, $3 entrance fee. Contact the Metro-Regional office of **Colorado Division of Parks and Recreation** (791-1957; open Mon.-Fri. 8am-5pm) for more information on campgrounds.

National Forest Campgrounds are plentiful in the mountains 25 miles west of Denver near **Idaho Springs,** Rte. 103 and 40 (893-1474), and in the region around **Deckers,** which is 30 miles southwest of downtown on Rte. 67. Sites are marked, but may be difficult to find. Open May-Sept. Sites $5-8. Call ahead or pick up maps at the **National Forest's Rocky Mountain Regional Headquarters,** 11177 W. 8th Ave., Lakewood (236-9431). Open Mon.-Fri. 8am-5pm.

Food

The *barrio,* north of the mall between 20th and 30th St., is home to many inexpensive—if slightly downtrodden—bars and Mexican restaurants, while **Sakura Square,** at 19th St. and Larimer, offers several Japanese restaurants surrounding a pleasant rock garden. A young crowd haunts Sheridan, Wadsworth, and Federal Avenues in the west, and Colfax Avenue in the east. If you're over 21, you'll find the cheapest food at the Glendale nightclubs.

The Goodmorning House, 1530 Blake St. (620-0077). A friendly diner where you can get a juicy burger for $2.75 or a large bowl of chili and a piece of cornbread for $2.50. (Open Mon.-Fri. 6:30am-2pm, Sat. 7am-2pm.)

City Spirit Café and Bookstore, 1434 Blake St. (575-0022), a few blocks from the north end of the 16th St. Mall. After your meal in the funky restaurant, browse among the architecture books. Specialties $4, tasty sandwiches $5. Live entertainment most evenings. Open Mon.-Thurs. 11am-midnight, Fri.-Sat. 11am-1am.

The Old Spaghetti Factory, 18th and Lawrence (295-1864), 1 block from Larimer St. Part of a national chain. Located in a gorgeously renovated old tramway building. Large, delicious spaghetti dinner only $5. Open Mon.-Thurs. 11:30am-2pm and 5-10pm, Fri. 11:30am-2pm and 4-11pm, Sat. 4-11pm, Sun. 4-10pm. No credit cards accepted.

The Eggshell, 1520 Blake St. (623-7555). A local yuppie favorite. Huge breakfast specials daily $2. Sandwiches $4-5. Open Mon.-Fri. 6:30am-2pm, Sat.-Sun. 7am-2pm.

Casa de Manuel, 2010 Larimer (295-1752), at 20th St. in the *barrio.* Huge portions of authentic Mexican dishes. *Menudo,* an excellent, thick soup made with tripe and hominy, *barbacoa* (barbecue) taco, and other specialties $5-6. Open Tues.-Thurs. 11:30am-8:30pm, Fri.-Sat. 11:30am-10:30pm.

It's Greek to Me, 2680 E. Colfax (321-7051), bus #15. The gyros ($4.59) are good, and the baklava ($1.39) scrumptious. Open Mon.-Sat. 6am-11pm, Sun. 7am-10pm.

Daddy Bruce's Bar-B-Q, 1629 E. 34th St. (295-9115), at Gilpin; take bus #38. The sign on the back of the owner's truck says: "God loves you. So does Daddy Bruce." If that's not enough of a welcome, wait until you get inside and taste the best barbecue in Denver. If you're lucky, you'll meet the 86-year-old Daddy himself. Ribs $5.15, honey-fried chicken $2.40. Open Tues.-Thurs. 9am-10:30pm, Fri. and Sat. 11am-midnight.

Sights

With over 205 spotless picnic and relaxation areas, Denver claims the prize for the American city with the most open-air parks. Of these, **City Park,** a green-and-blue rectangle between 17th and 23rd Ave. from York St. to Colorado Blvd., is the largest; take bus #20 or #23 to Colorado Ave. **Cheesman Park,** 4 blocks to the south, is known for its gay socializing and good views of the snowy mountains rising above the Denver skyline. (Take bus #6 or 10.) These parks are terrific for bicycling and strolling, but are not safe after dark. The **Denver Municipal Band** performs summer concerts at 7:30pm at the various parks. Pick up a schedule at the visitors bureau (see Practical Information above). For a wilder park experience, from June-September, take I-70 from Golden to Idaho Springs, and then pick up Rte. 103 south over the summit of **Mt. Evans,** a mere 14,260 feet in elevation. Or, journey to **Red Rocks** (see below) or other parts of Denver's 25,000 acre park system. Check with **Denver Parks and Recreation,** 1805 Bryant Ave. (459-4000) about current road conditions in fall and winter. (Open Mon.-Fri. 8am-5pm.)

The **16th St. Mall,** a 14-block pedestrian area in the heart of downtown, is Denver's biggest tourist attraction. The shuttle buses which patrol this strip from 6am-8pm are the only free convenience you'll find here. **Larimer Square,** between 14th and 15th St., has been restored to Victorian elegance, and now houses pricey souvenir shops, galleries, and restaurants. Larimer's wild Octoberfest also draws large crowds.

A gold-leaf dome tops the gray Colorado granite of the **Capitol** on Colfax and Broadway between Grant and 14th St. (866-2604). For a great view of the Rocky Mountains, climb the steps to the gallery around the dome. (Free tours from the foyer every hour on the ½ hr. from 9am-3:30pm. Open Mon.-Fri. 7am-5:30pm, Sat. 9:30am-3:30pm.)

The **U.S. Mint,** 320 W. Colfax (844-3332), issues the U.S. coins with a small "D" printed under the date. Free 20-minute tours, every 20 minutes in summer and every 30 minutes in winter, will lead you past a million-dollar pile of gold bars and expose you to the deafening roar of money-making machines that churn out a total of twenty million shiny coins a day. Unfortunately, no free samples are given. Come early in summer. (Open Mon., Tues, Thurs., and Fri. 8:15am-3:30pm, Wed. 9:15am-3:30pm.)

Denver's museums cover every subject from pioneer history to space-age technology. The **Natural History Museum** (370-6357) in City Park presents amazingly lifelike wildlife sculptures and dioramas. (Open Sat.-Tues. 9am-5pm, Wed.-Fri. 9am-10pm.) The Natural History Museum complex includes the **Gates Planetarium** (with its popular "Laserdrive" show) and an **IMAX theater** (370-3600). Combination tickets to the museum, planetarium, and IMAX cost $6.50, seniors and ages 4-12 $4.50. Across the park from the museum complex lies the **Denver Zoo** (331-4110), where you can view the live versions of the museum specimens. (Open daily 10am-6pm. Admission $4, seniors and ages 6-15 $2.)

Just a few blocks from the U.S. Mint, and right behind Civic Center Park, stands the **Denver Art Museum,** 100 W. 14th Ave. (575-2793). Architect Gio Ponti designed this "vertical" museum in order to accommodate totem poles and period architecture. The museum's collection of Native American art is one of the finest in the world (575-5928; museum open Tues.-Sat. 10am-5pm, Sun. noon-5pm; admission $3, seniors and students $1.50.) Downtown's second most popular museum, the **Colorado History Museum,** 13th and Broadway (866-3682), chronicles the state's colorful history through artifacts, dioramas, and original documents. (Open Mon.-Sat. 10am-4:30pm, Sun. noon-4:30pm. Admission $3, seniors and ages 6-16 $1.50.) The **Museum of Western Art,** 1727 Tremont Place (296-1880), features numerous stellar Russell and O'Keeffe paintings. (Open Tues.-Sat. 10am-4:30pm. Admission $3, seniors and students $1.50.) **The Black American West Museum and Heritage Center,** 608 26th St. (295-1026) will show you a side of western history not propounded by John Wayne fans or white ranchers. Come here to learn why 1/3 of all cowboys were black, and other details often left out of textbooks. (Open Wed.-Fri. 10am-2pm, Sat. noon-5pm, Sun. 2-5pm. Admission $2, seniors $1.50, ages 12-16 75¢, under 12 50¢.) Finally, the **Brown Palace** (297-3111) is an historic, grand hotel that once hosted presidents, generals, and movie stars. (Free tours Wed. at 2pm.) The museum is housed in the Navarre Building, which used to be the brothel for the Brown Palace.

The dramatic **Red Rocks Amphitheater and Park** (575-2637), 12 miles west of Denver and south of U.S. 6 on I-70, is carved into red sandstone. As the sun sets over the city, even the most well-known of performers must compete with the natural spectacle behind them. (For tickets call 623-8497 Mon.-Fri. 8am-5pm. Park admission free. Shows $9-16.)

Entertainment and Nightlife

Denver is a "young" city—a lot of singles in search of a good time are turned loose every evening. Clubs downtown tend to come and go, but some have gained a lasting reputation. One tried and true favorite is **Basin's Up,** 1427 Larimer St. (623-1204), where you can wallow in live rock music all evening. (Open Mon.-Sat. 8pm-2am. Cover Fri. and Sat. $4. Must be 21 or over.) Another popular spot is the jazz club **El Chapultepec,** 20th and Market St. (295-9126; open daily 7am-2am; no cover.) The magazine *Westwood* has more details on the downtown club scene. To find the happening places in the 'burbs, head for Glendale, where the night-time bar-hoppers can show you the best places to have a quiet intimate evening, or go slam dancing. At **Bangles,** 4501 E. Virginia (377-2702), live bands rock the floor in the evening, and the afternoon volleyball matches often become jubilant free-for-alls after a few pitchers of beer ($4.50). (Open Mon.-Sat. 8pm-2am. Volleyball games at 4pm. Cover $3 Wed.-Mon. night.) **Meo,** 350 S. Birch (320-0118), is a hot top-40 dance club which grants admission at the manager's discretion. Thurs. night all beer $1 a glass. (Open Tues.-Thurs. 8pm-2am, Fri. and Sat. 8pm-4am.)

For those who prefer to shun the booze in favor of arts and academics, Denver now boasts some cafés where the thickness of the espresso is only rivalled by that of the cigarette smoke. **Muddy's Java Café,** 2200 Champa St. (298-1631), has leopard skin seat coverings and African reed music for your listening pleasure. Try the coffee and steamed with almond milk ($1.50; open daily 7pm-4am.) **Paris on the Platte,** 1553 Platte St. (455-2451), is the local impoverished artists' favorite night spot. (Open Mon.-Fri. 11am-3am, Sat. and Sun. 7pm-3am.)

The Denver Center Theater Company performs at the **Denver Arts Center,** 12th and 14th St. (893-4100), between Stout and Arapahoe St. and the Denver Center Theater. Performances run from September to May; tickets cost $9-21, but students and seniors can get half-price tickets 30 minutes before the show. (Box office open Mon.-Sat. 9am-5pm.)

Denver's two most popular festivals are the **Greek festival** and **A Taste of Colorado.** The Greek festival takes place in June, downtown, and features good Greek food, music, and dancing. A Taste of Colorado is an outdoor fête that spans a couple of weekends in August, during which food vendors line the streets near the capitol and there are good open-air concerts.

Near Denver

68 miles northwest of Denver on U.S. 40, surrounded by 600 miles of skiing, hiking, and biking trails, the incredibly beautiful town of **Winter Park** nestles amonst the mountain pines. On the town's southern boundary, the **Winter Park Hostel (AYH)** (726-5356), sits next to sporting goods stores and restaurants. One block from the Greyhound stop and two miles from Amtrak (free shuttle), the hostel fea-

tures bunks in spotless, cheery trailers and a kitchen. (Nov. 1-April 20 $9, nonmembers $11. June 20-Oct. $6, nonmembers $8. Call for reservations in winter. Closed April 20-June 20.) Next door **Le Ski Lab** (726-9841) offers 10% discounts on bike and ski rentals for hostelers (Mt. bikes $5 per hr., $14 per day; skis $9 per day. Open daily in winter 8am-8pm, in summer 9am-6pm. With a note from hostel manager Polly no deposit required.) The **Winter Park-Fraser Valley Chamber of Commerce,** 50 Vasquez Rd. (726-4118; from Denver 800-422-0666), can give you information about skiing at the Winter Park Mary Jane Ski Area. (Open daily in winter 9am-8pm, in summer 10am-5pm.) It also serves as the Greyhound/Trailways depot. (From Denver 2 buses per day, 2 hr., $12. Polly will meet either bus if you call ahead.)

If you're strong of heart and lung, head out to **Frisco,** (55 miles west of Denver on I-90) for some hiking in the Rockies. Along with Breckenridge, Dillon, Copper Mountain, Keystone, and Silverthorne, Frisco hosts numerous sporting events throughout the year. All six towns fall under the jurisdiction of the **Summit County Chamber of Commerce,** P.O. Box 214, Frisco, CO 80443, 110 Summit Blvd. (668-5800), which can easily provide information on current area events. (Open Mon.-Fri. 9am-5pm. Weekends 9am-6pm. Hours subject to change.) The only reasonable accommodations in the county are at the **Alpen Hütte,** 471 Rainbow Dr. in Silverthorne (468-6336). A bed in the sparsely decorated, gleaming bunk rooms is $18 during Christmas and March, Nov. 18-May $15, and May-Nov. 17 $12. (Guest rooms closed 9:30am-3:30pm. Curfew. Reservations recommended.)

115 miles beyond Frisco and 170 miles west of Denver on I-70 you will find the semi-resort town of **Glenwood Springs.** Not nearly as touristy or over-priced as Aspen (40 miles further west), this village relies upon the nearby natural hot springs for most of its income. The **Glenwood Hot Springs,** 401 N. River Rd. (945-6571) are open daily from 7:30am to 10pm. (All day pass $5.25, children $3.)

Within walking distance from the springs you'll find the **Glenwood Springs Hostel (AYH),** 1021 Grand Ave. (945-8545), a former Victorian home with spacious dorm and communal areas and a full kitchen. ($9.50, nonmembers $11.50, linen $2. Closed 10am-4pm.)

Greyhound serves Glenwood Springs from a terminal at 118 W. 6th Ave. (945-8501). 4 buses daily to Denver (4 hr., $14.90) and Grand Junction (2 hr., $7.50). Open Mon.-Fri. 5:45am-6pm, Sat. 9am-1pm and 4-5pm, Sun. 3-5pm. For further information on Glenwood Springs, contact the **Glenwood Springs Chamber Resort Association,** 1102 Grand Ave. (945-6589). (Open Mon.-Fri. 8am-5pm, Sat.-Sun. 10am-2pm.)

Boulder

Boulder residents have put a new kink in conspicuous consumption. Rather than indulge in Cadillacs and chinchilla coats, the leisure class in Boulder splurges on spiritual retreats and yoga classes, where hip adults—many of whom are recent transplants from the East—pay big bucks to get in touch with the Tao and learn how to move with a crane's grace. Every self-respecting Boulderite owns tennis shoes, biking shoes, and rock shoes (for climbing), loafers (for work), sandals (for kicking around), running shoes (for the Bolder Boulder), and flip-flops (for aprés-hot tub), and hiking- and ski-boots. Add to this their sizeable tofu and yogurt bills, and casual living puts a serious strain on the Boulderite budget.

But travelers can live fairly cheaply in Boulder. With the Flatiron Mountains—baby peaks on the fringe of the Rockies—towering over the town, and mimes, break dancers, and itinerant fire-eaters plying their trades on the Pearl St. pedestrian mall, Boulder makes a colorful gateway to Rocky Mountain National Park.

Practical Information

Emergency: 911.

Visitor Information: Boulder Chamber of Commerce/Visitors Service, 2440 Pearl St. (442-1044 or 800-444-0447), at Folsom, about 10 blocks from downtown. Take bus #200. Well-equipped. Pick up the comprehensive seasonal guides and the *Boulder Surprise.* Open Mon. 9am-5pm, Tues.-Fri. 8:30am-5pm. **University of Colorado Information** (492-6161), 2nd floor of UMC Student Union. Campus maps and information. Open Mon.-Thurs. 7am-11pm, Fri.-Sat. 7am-1am, Sun. 11am-11pm. **U.C. Ride Board,** UMC, Broadway at 16th. Lots of rides, lots of riders—even in the summer.

Local Transit: Boulder Transit Center, 14th and Walnut St. (778-6000). Routes to Denver and Longmont as well as intracity routes. Buses operate Mon.-Fri. 5am-10pm, Sat.-Sun. 7am-10pm. Fare 50¢, 75¢ Mon.-Fri. 6-9am and 3-6pm. Long-distance $1.50 to: Nederland ("N" bus) and Lyons ("Y" bus); $2 to Golden ("G" bus) and Boulder Foothills and Denver ("H" bus). Several other lines link up with the Denver system (see Denver Practical Information). You can get a bus map for $1 at the RTD terminal. **Estes Park Bus Company,** 205 Park Lane (586-8108), in Estes Park. 2 buses per day between Estes Park and Boulder in the summer (after June 16), 1 per day otherwise. (2 hr., $6.50 one way, $12 round-trip). Station open daily 7am-4:30pm.

Taxi: Boulder Yellow Cab, 442-2277. $1 first ½ mile, $1 each additional mile.

Car Rental: Dollar Rent-a-Car, 2100 30th St. (442-1687). $27 per day, $139 per week. Open Mon.-Fri. 8am-8pm, Sat. 8am-6pm. Must be 21 with a major credit card.

Bike Rental: University Bicycles, 839 Pearl St. (444-4196), downtown. 10-speed bikes $9 per ½-day, $12 per day. Mountain bikes $10 per day, $55 per week. Open Mon.-Fri. 8:30am-7:30pm, Sat. 9am-6pm, Sun. 10am-5pm.

Help Lines: Rape Crisis, 443-7300. 24 hours. **Crisis Line,** 447-1665. 24 hours. **Gays, Lesbians and Friends of Boulder,** 492-8567.

Post Office: 1905 15th St. (938-1100), at Walnut, across the road from the RTD terminal. Open Mon.-Fri. 8:45am-5:15pm, Sat. 9am-noon. General Delivery 7am-5pm. **ZIP code:** 80302.

Area Code: 303.

Boulder is a small, manageable city, 26 miles northwest of Denver on U.S. 36, which becomes 28th St. in the center of town. Rte. 119 intersects with Rte. 36 and becomes **Canyon Boulevard** on the city's west side. **Hitchhiking** from Boulder to Denver is easy, especially if you catch a ride from S. Broadway to Golden first, or go from 28th St. in Boulder down Rte. 36 directly to Denver. Thumbing into Boulder from Denver is more difficult, but hitching up Boulder Canyon should be a cinch.

The most developed part of Boulder lies between **Broadway** (Rte. 93) and **28th Street** (Rte. 36), two busy streets that run parallel to each other north-south through the city. The main part of the **University of Colorado** campus is bounded by **Baseline Road,** which connects the Flatirons with the eastern plains, and Canyon Boulevard (Rte. 7), which follows the scenic Boulder Canyon up into the mountains. UC and its surroundings are known locally as the **"Hill."** The pedestrian-only **Pearl Street Mall,** between 11th and 15th St. is at the heart of the hip life in Boulder. Most east-west roads have names, while north-south streets have numbers (Broadway is a conspicuous exception).

Accommodations and Camping

Even though Boulder's a college town, you won't find many student-rate places to bunk for the night. In summer, you can rely on the **Boulder International Youth Hostel (AAIH),** 1107 12th St. (942-0522), on the Hill, 2 blocks west of the UC campus and 15 minutes south of the RTD station. Reasonably clean. Bring your own sheets, towel, and pillow, or rent them. (Towel 50¢. Linen $2. Open 7:30-10am and 5pm-midnight. $10 per person. Private rooms: Singles $20. Doubles $25. Closed Aug.-May.) The **Chautauqua Association,** 9th St. and Baseline Rd. 80302 (442-

3282), has quaint, highly popular cottages available May-Sept. (Singles $24. Doubles $28. Reservations recommended. Take bus #203.) Guests at this cultural institution can take in movies and other productions, including the Colorado Music Festival (see Sights and Activities below). **The Boulder Mountain Lodge,** 91 Four Mile Canyon Rd. (444-0882), is a 2-mile drive west on Hwy. 119. Clean, reasonably large accommodations range from bunks ($12.50) to motel rooms (from $38) to campsites ($14 check-in by 8pm).

You'll have an easier time finding camping spots. Information on campsites in **Roosevelt National Forest** is available from the Forest Service Station at 2995 Baseline Rd., #16, 80303 (444-6001; open Mon.-Fri. 8am-5pm). Excellent maps of the forest are available ($2). A site at **Kelly Dahl,** 3 miles south of Nederland on Rte. 119, costs $7. **Rainbow Lakes,** 6 miles north of Nederland on Rte. 72, then 5 miles west on Arapahoe Glacier Rd., is free, but no water is available. (Campgrounds open from Memorial Day to mid-September.) **Peaceful Valley** and **Camp Dick** (north on Rte. 72, $7 per site) have cross-country skiing in the winter.

Food and Entertainment

The streets on the "Hill" and those along the Pearl St. Mall bristle with good eateries, natural foods markets, burger-joints and colorful bars. Many more restaurants and bars line **Baseline Road.** Throughout Boulder, the restaurants and night spots are high quality, and therefore expensive.

New Age Foods, 1122 Pearl St. Mall (443-0755), at the back of the health food store. The cheapest meals in town, featuring healthful and veggie food. Cafeteria-style restaurant offers soup, large salad, sandwiches, and specials such as lasagna and black-bean burritos. Choose 1 for $2.50, 2 for $3.50. Open Mon.-Fri. 11:30am-3pm.

The L.A. Diner (for "Last American"), 1955 28th St. (447-1997). Waitresses and waiters on roller skates serve green chili in a silver space-ship of a restaurant. 10.-oz. sirloin steak, potato, vegetables, soup or salad $6. Open Mon.-Thurs. 6:30am-midnight, Fri. 6:30am-3am, Sat. 8am-3am, Sun. 8am-midnight.

Harvest Restaurant and Bakery, 1738 Pearl St. (449-6223), at 18th St., inside a little mall. A fine example of mellow, "back-to-nature" Boulder. Very popular among UC students. Try the turkey-cashew salad on toasted whole-wheat bread ($4.35). Open Sun.-Thurs. 7am-10pm, Fri.-Sat. 7am-11pm.

1st Wok, 1718 Broadway (444-8886), on the way up the hill from downtown. The students' favorite for its $5 lunch buffet. Full course dinners $6.50-12. Open Sun.-Thurs. 11:30am-10pm, Fri.-Sat. 11:30am-11pm.

UC Student Cafeteria, 16th and Broadway (492-6578), downstairs in the Student Union (UMC). The large **Alfred Packer Grill** (named after the West's celebrated cannibal) serves burgers ($1.65) and sizeable burritos ($3). Open Mon.-Fri. 7am-7pm, Sat. 10am-4pm, Sun. 11am-4pm.

Eddie's Mexican Cafe, 2865 Baseline Dr. (442-7512). The local up-and-coming business folk make a habit of munching nachos at this place. Enchiladas from $2.35. Combination dinners from $5.75. Open daily 11am-11pm.

The Walrus Café, 1911 11th St. (443-9902). A universally popular night spot. All-you-can-eat spaghetti and garlic bread $4. Pints of beer from $1. Open Mon.-Sat. 4pm-whenever.

Sights and Activities

Intellectuals at the **University of Colorado,** numerous yuppies, and back-to-nature fanatics constantly collaborate to find innovative things to do. Check out the perennially outrageous street scene on the Mall and the Hill and watch the kiosks for the scoop on downtown happenings.

The university's **Cultural Events Board** (492-8409) has the latest word on all UC-sponsored activities. The most massive of these undertakings is the annual **Arts Fest,** which takes place in the middle of July. Phone for tickets or stop by the ticket office in the UMC. (Open Mon.-Fri. 10am-4pm, Sat.-Sun. noon-4pm.) Concurrently with Arts Fest, the **Chautauqua Institute** (442-3282; see Accommodations above) hosts the **Colorado Music Festival** (449-1397; 8am-5pm, on concert days 8am-6pm; performances June 23-Aug. 5; tickets $10-22). The **Parks and Recreation Department** (441-3400; open Mon.-Fri. 8am-5pm) sponsors free performances in local parks from May-August; dance, classical and modern music, and children's theater are traditional. The **Boulder Center for the Visual Arts,** 1750 13th St. (443-2122), focuses on the finest in contemporary regional art and has national exhibits as well. (Open Tues.-Sat. 11am-5pm, Sun. 1-5pm. Free.)

The intimate and impressive **Leanin' Tree Museum,** 6055 Longbow Dr. (530-1442) presents a beautifully arranged panorama of western art and sculpture. (Open Mon.-Fri. 8am-4:30pm. Free.) View similar scenes in 3-D at the **University of Colorado Museum,** Henderson Building between 15th and 16th streets. (692-6892 or 492-6165; open Mon.-Fri. 9am-5pm, Sat. 9am-4pm, Sun. 10am-4pm. Free.)

The Flatiron Mountains, acting as a backdrop to this bright and vibrant town, offer the visitor plenty of chances to go walking, hiking, and biking. Take a walk or bike ride along Boulder Creek Path, a beautiful strip of park that lines the creek for 15 miles. Farther back in the mountains lie treacherous rocky outcroppings for the more adventurous. Trails weave through the 6000-acre **Boulder Mountain Park,** beginning from several sites on the western side of town. **Flagstaff Road** winds its way to the top of the mountains from the far western end of Baseline Rd. The **Boulder Creek Canyon,** accessible from Rte. 119, is well known for its splendid rocky scenery. Some of the best rock climbing in the world is found in nearby **Eldorado Canyon,** as well as on the Flatirons themselves.

Running and biking competitions far outnumber any other sports events in the Boulder area, and draw large crowds. The biggest foot race by far is the 10km Memorial Day challenge known as the **"Bolder Boulder."** This event brings in 25,000 international athletes and the winner takes home $4000. For information on any running event, call the Boulder Roadrunners (443-9615; open daily 9am-8pm).

The **Boulder Brewing Company,** 7880 Wilderness Place (444-8448), offers tours for those who prefer dietary pleasures to exercise. Yes, there's free beer at the end (25-min. tours Mon.-Sat. at 11am and 1pm; open Mon.-Fri. 8am-5pm, Sat. 11am-3pm).

Rocky Mountain National Park

In Rocky Mountain National Park, you can lounge on the cool rocks next to a bright blue alpine lake and dangle your feet in the icy water. All around, snow-streaked crags pierce a clear summer sky, while nearby elk gambol below a waterfall, and hawks glide overhead. Is this nirvana? It all depends on how far you had to hike to get away from the crowds below and how sore those feet are.

Although purists disparage Rocky Mountain National Park for its overpopularity, this remarkable sanctuary makes even the slickest of city dwellers don flannel shirts and take in some of the best scenery in the Rockies. The mountain wilds are made accessible by the two tourist towns on the park's borders: **Estes Park** on the east and **Grand Lake** on the west. These two are connected by Trail Ridge Rd., which crosses the park from east to west, peaking at 12,183 feet. Since hiking at such elevations is not for amateurs, the way to see Rocky Mountain National Park is by car. You can rent one in Boulder or just stick out your thumb—within minutes you'll have a ride.

Practical Information and Orientation

Emergency: 911. Estes Park police 586-4465; Grand Lake police 627-3322.

Visitor Information: Estes Park Chamber of Commerce, P.O. Box 3050, Estes Park 80517, at 500 Big Thompson Hwy. (586-4431 in Estes, or 800-443-7837), on Rte. 34, slightly east of downtown. Open June-Aug. Mon.-Sat. 8am-8pm, Sun. 8am-6pm; Sept.-May Mon.-Fri. 8am-5pm, Sat.-Sun. 10am-4pm. **Grand Lake Area Chamber of Commerce,** 14700 Hwy. 74, just outside of the Park's west entrance. Open daily 9am-5pm, off-season Mon.-Fri. 10am-5pm.

Park Entrance Fees: $5 per vehicle, $2 per biker or pedestrian. Under 16 free. Good for 7 days.

Park Visitor and Ranger Stations: Park Headquarters and Visitors Center, 2 miles west of Estes Park, on Rte. 36 (586-2371), at the Beaver Meadows entrance to the park. Call for park information, or to make sure the Trail Ridge Rd. is open. Headquarters open Mon.-Fri. 8am-5pm. Visitors center open daily 8am-9pm, off-season Mon.-Fri. 8am-5pm. **Kawuneeche Visitors Center** (627-3471), just outside of the park's western entrance. Open daily 7am-7pm, off-season 8am-5pm. **Moraine Park Visitors Center and Museum,** (586-3777) on the Bear Lake Rd. Open 9am-5pm in summer only. **Alpine Visitors Center,** at the crest of Trail Ridge Rd. (586-4927). Open daily June to mid-July 10am-4pm, mid-July to mid-Aug. 9am-5pm.

Local Transit: Estes Park Bus Company, 205 Park Lane (586-8108). Driver will drop you off at the Chamber of Commerce or the YMCA. To Boulder $6.50 one way, $12 round-trip. Also offers full-day tours to Grand Lake ($25, under 12 $17) and 4-hour trips up Trail Ridge Rd. ($15, under 12 $10.) **Estes Park Trolley** (586-8866). Red trolleys operate in summer only daily 10am-9pm. Frequent service connects everything you could want to see in Estes Park; guided tour included. $1 for each trip, $3 for a full day.

Horse Rental: Sombrero Ranch, 1895 Big Thompson Rd. (586-4577), in Estes Park 2 miles from downtown on Hwy. 34 E, and on Grand Ave. in Grand Lake (627-3514). $10 for 1 hour, $18 for 2. The 7am breakfast ride includes a 2 hr. ride and a huge breakfast ($18). Call ahead. Both open daily 7am-7pm. Hostelers get 10% discount.

Help Lines: Roads and Weather, 586-2385. **Hearing Impaired Visitors,** 586-8506.

Post Office: In Estes Park, 215 W. Riverside (586-8177). Open Mon.-Fri. 9am-5pm, Sat. 10am-12:30pm. In **Grand Lake:** 520 Center Dr. (627-3340). Open Mon.-Fri. 8:30am-5pm. **ZIP code:** 80517.

Area Code: 303.

The national park is most easily reached from Boulder via Rte. 36 or from Loveland up the **Big Thompson Canyon** via Rte. 34. Both routes lead to Estes Park, are busy during the summer, and are easy hitching or biking trails. From Denver, it's best to take the RTD bus to its last stop in Boulder, transfer (free) to bus #202 or 204, and hitchhike from U.S. 36 W. In Boulder you can find the entrance to U.S. 36 at 28th and Baseline. Estes Park is 65 miles from Denver, 39 miles from Boulder, and 31 miles from Loveland. Hitching along these well-traveled routes is unbelievably easy. Hitching within the park is prohibited, but many people do it.

The western side of the park is reached from Granby (50 miles from I-70) via Rte. 40. Route 7, which approaches the park from the southeast out of Lyons or Nederland, is one of the most scenic entrances, and gives access to the **Wild Basin Trailhead,** the starting point for some of the most glorious hikes. If Trail Ridge Rd. is closed, you can drive from one side of the park to the other through Walden and Fort Collins, via Rte. 125 out of Granby and then Rte. 14 to Fort Collins. Or take the more traveled Rte. 40 over spectacular **Berthoud Pass** to I-70, then Rte. 119 and 72 north to the park. Either way, if the Trail Ridge Rd. is closed, the drive jumps from 48 to 140 miles.

Accommodations

Although Estes Park and Grand Lake have an overabundance of expensive lodges and motels, there are a few good deals for indoor sleeping near the national park, especially in winter, when the hostels close down.

H Bar G Ranch Hostel (AYH), P.O. Box 1260, Estes Park 80517 (586-3688). Hillside cabins, international patrons, tennis courts, kitchen, and a spectacular view. Proprietor Lou drives you out to the park entrance or into town every morning at 7:30am, and picks you up again at the chamber of commerce. He will also pick up anyone arriving on Estes buses at 5pm. $7.50, members only. Rent a car for $23 per day. Open May-Sept. Call ahead.

YMCA of the Rockies, 2515 Tunnel Rd., Estes Park Center 80511 (586-3341), 2 miles south of the park headquarters on Rte. 66 and 5 miles from the chamber of commerce. Caters largely to family reunions and conventions. Extensive facilities on the 1400-acre complex, as well as daily hikes and other events. Four people can get an individual cabin for $35 and up; kitchen and bath included. Guest membership $3. For $30 you can get a lodge with bunk beds that sleeps up to 5. Disabled access.

The Colorado Mountain School, 351 Moraine Ave., Estes Park (586-5758 or 800-444-0730). The dorm-style accommodations are opened to travelers unless already booked by mountain-climbing students. Wood bunks with comfortable mattresses $16. Call for reservations.

The American Wilderness Lodge, 481 W. Elkhorn, Estes Park (586-4402). Luxurious rooms with queen-sized beds. Singles from $30. Doubles from $40.

Shadowcliff Youth Hostel (AYH), P.O. Box 658, Grand Lake 80447 (627-9966), near the western entrance to the park. Entering Grand Lake, take the left fork after the visitors center on West Protal Rd.; their sign is 2/3 mile down the road on the left. Beautiful, rustic lodge on a cliff; offers easy access to the trails on the western side of the park and to the lakes of Arapahoe National Recreation Area. $6, nonmembers $8. Private rooms $18-24. Open June-Sept.

Sunset Motel, 505 Grand Ave., Grand Lake (627-3318). Gorgeous singles with rates in the $30 range.

Camping

National Park Campgrounds: Moraine Park and **Glacier Basin** ($8) require reservations in the summer; **Aspenglen, Longs Peak** (tents only), and **Timber Creek** are first come-first serve ($6). A three-day limit is enforced at Longs Peak, a one-week limit elsewhere. Timber Creek is the only campground in the western portion of the park. One campground, usually near park headquarters near Estes Park, is kept open year-round; the rest close when the snow falls. Reservations can be made at select Ticketrons. In winter there is no water but also no charge.

Handicamp: The Park's backcountry campsite for the disabled (586-2371). Open in summer 7am-7pm. Free.

Backcountry camping: Backcountry offices at Park Headquarters (586-2371) and Kawuneeche Visitors Center (627-3741). Open 8am-5pm. Get reservations and permits at these offices or write the Superintendent, Rocky Mountain National Park, Estes Park 80517 (586-4454). There are no charges for backcountry camping, but many areas are in no-fire zones, so you may want to bring along a campstove.

Olive Ridge Campground, 15 miles south on Rte. 7, in Roosevelt National Forest. First come-first serve sites $6. Contact the **Roosevelt-Arapahoe National Forest Service Headquarters,** 161 2nd St., Estes Park (586-3440). Open daily 8am-noon and 1-5pm; Aug.-May Mon.-Fri. 9am-noon and 1-4pm.

Indian Peaks Wilderness, just south of the park, jointly administered by Roosevelt-Arapahoe National Forests. Permit is required for backcountry camping during the summer. If you're on the east slope, contact the Boulder Ranger District, 2915 Baseline Rd. (444-6003; open Mon.-Fri. 8am-5pm). If you're on the west slope, contact the Hot Sulphur Ranger District, 100 U.S. 34 in Granby (887-3331; open Memorial Day-Labor Day daily 8am-5pm).

Sights and Activities

For those with wheels, the star trail of this park is the **Trail Ridge Road.** At its highest point, this 50-mile-long road is 12,183 feet above sea level. The round-trip drive takes three hours by car, 12 hours by bicycle. Much of the road is above timberline. For a closer look at the fragile tundra environment, walk from roadside to the **Forest Canyon Overlook,** or take the half-hour round-trip **Tundra Trail. Fall River Road,** a one-way dirt road merging with Trail Ridge Rd. at the alpine center, offers even more impressive scenery, but also sharp cliffs and tight cutbacks along the road.

Rangers can help plan a hike to suit your interests and abilities. Since the trailheads in the park are already so high, just a few hours of hiking will take you into unbeatable alpine scenery along the Continental Divide. Be warned that it takes time to adjust to the high altitudes. Some easy trails are the 3.6-mile road trip from

Wild Basin Ranger Station to **Calypso Cascades** and the 2.8-mile round-trip from the **Long Peaks Ranger Station** to **Eugenia Mine.** From the nearby **Glacier Gorge Junction** trailhead, take a short hike to **Mills Lake** or up to the **Loch.**

Some moderately taxing trails are not too touristed and might be fun once your body's acclamated to the thinner air. From the **Twin Owls** or **Gem Lakes Trailheads,** pace yourself along the 3.6-mile steep climb to Gem Lake. If you still haven't escaped the crowds, head for the less popular western slope of the park. From the town of Grand Lake, a trek into the scenic and remote **North** or **East Inlets** will leave the camera-toting tourists behind. Both of these wooded valleys offer excellent trout fishing. The park's gem is prominent **Long's Peak** (14,255 ft.), which dominates the eastern slope. The Peak's monumental East Face, a 2000-foot vertical wall known simply as the **Diamond,** is the most challenging rock climbing spot in Colorado.

Traversing the park on a **mountain bike** is a fun and challenging alternative to hiking. **Colorado Bicycling Adventures,** 184 E. Elkhorn (586-4241), rents bikes ($9 for 2 hr., $14 per ½-day, $19 per day; discounts for hostelers). Guided mountain bike tours are also offered ($12.50 for 2 hr., $25 for 4 hr.; open daily 9am-8pm; off-season 10am-5pm). Of the three bike routes in the park, Horseshoe Park/Estes Park Loop is the least traveled, because its tight turns and sheer drops require expertise. In the winter, **cross-country skiing** is popular in the high snows around Bear Lake and Wild Basin. The **Ski Estes Park** ski resort (586-8173) is within the park's boundaries, just off Trail Ridge Rd., 10 miles west of Estes Park. Cross country, snowshoeing, and snowboarding are also available. (Lift tickets $16, lessons $15. Skis, boots, and poles can be rented for about $13 per day. Open in winter only.)

For those seeking to learn more about the park's ecology, the three major campgrounds have good nightly amphitheater programs. The visitors centers have information on these and on many enjoyable ranger-led interpretive activities, including nature walks, birding expeditions, and artists' forays.

You probably won't be spending every day in the National Park, and both entry towns have their attractive points, including good food. In **Estes Park,** try:

Johnson's Cafe, (586-6624, 2 buildings to the right of Safeway, across from the chamber of commerce. Everything is made from scratch and the Johnsons are friendly. Great waffles $2.10, sandwiches $3.25, luscious pies $1.75. Open Tues.-Fri. 7am-4pm, Sat.-Mon., 8am-2pm.

O'Shea's, 225 Riverside (586-2815), next to the post office. Great homemade soups $1, full meal daily specials $3.45. Open Mon.-Fri. 7am-3pm.

Polly's Pizza, 181 W. Riverside (586-6081). Free delivery of spicy fresh pizza. 13-inch pizza $5.50. Open Sun.-Thurs. 11am-midnight, Fri.-Sat. 11am-1am.

Ed's Cantina, 362 E. Elkhorn (586-2919). The best Mexican in the park area. A combination plate of cheese enchilada, bean burrito, and bean tostada $5. Open daily 7am-10pm.

Grand Lake, Estes's western cousin, is less touristed in the summer, but inaccessible without a car in the winter. It offers unbeatable snowmobile and cross-country routes. Ask at the visitors center about seasonal events. Camp on the shores of adjacent **Shadow Mountain Lake** and **Lake Granby.**

Colorado Springs

The idle elegance of this long-time resort is reflected in the large, Victorian houses and wide streets of the city's older sections. Today's visitors come for the same reasons that 19th-century travelers did: clean, dry air, and easy access to the mountains, especially Pikes Peak, which springs up from the Great Plains to 14,110 feet. Some sections of town, especially Manitou Springs to the west, are overrun with tourists and tourist-oriented establishments, and there may be more nearby **ghost towns** than there ever were cowboys. Last year's tourists poured $399 million into the Colorado Springs economy. The U.S. government pours in even more: North American Air Defense Command Headquarters (NORAD) lurks beneath nearby

Cheyenne Mountain. Still, the city is worthwhile as a daytrip from Denver or as a point of departure for mountain pilgrimages.

Practical Information and Orientation

Emergency: 911.

Visitor Information: Colorado Springs Convention and Visitors Bureau, 104 S. Cascade, #104 80903 (635-1632 or 800-888-4748), at Colorado Ave. Check out the *Colorado Springs Pikes Peak Park Region Offical Visitors Guide* and the city bus map. Open daily 8am-5pm; Nov.-March Mon.-Fri. 8:30am-5pm. **Manitou Springs Chamber of Commerce,** 354 Manitou Ave., Manitou Springs 80829 (685-5089 or 800-642-2567). Near the trailhead for climbing Pikes Peak. Open in summer Mon.-Fri. 8:30am-5pm, Sat.-Sun. 8am-4pm. **Funfone,** (635-1723). Information on local events.

Colorado Springs Airport: 596-0188. Directly to the east of the downtown area, off Nevada Ave. at the end of Fountain Blvd.

Greyhound/Trailways: 327 S. Weber St. (635-1505). To: Denver (9 per day, 1½ hr., $7); Pueblo (9 per day, 50 min., $4); and Albuquerque, NM (4 per day, 7-9 hr., $52). Tickets available Mon.-Sat. 5am-midnight, Sun. 8am-midnight. Open 24 hours.

Colorado Springs City Bus Service: 125 E. Kiowa at Nevada (475-9733), 2 blocks from Greyhound/Trailways. Serves the city and Widefield, Manitou Springs, Fort Carson, Garden of the Gods, and Peterson Air Force Base. Service Mon.-Fri. 6am-6pm, Sat. variable hours. Fare 60¢, seniors and children 25¢, students 40¢; long trips 15¢ extra.

Tours: Gray Line Tours, 322 N. Nevada Ave. (633-1747 or 800-423-9515 outside CO), downtown. Trips to Cripple Creek and back, as well as tours of Pikes Peak, Garden of the Gods, and the U.S. Air Force Academy. Tours (½-day $20, children $10; full day $35, children $17.50) are not offered daily, so call for reservations. Office open Mon.-Fri. 7am-6pm, Sat. 8am-5pm, Sun. 9am-5pm. **Pikes Peak Region Tours:** 3704 W. Colorado Ave. (633-1181), at the Garden of the Gods Campground. Offers 4-hr. tours to Pikes Peak, the U.S. Air Force Academy, and Children of the Gods ($20, children $10), and a night tour of Cave of the Winds and Seven Falls. Open Mon.-Fri. 7am-5pm.

Taxi: Yellow Cab, 634-5000. $2.60 first mile, $1.10 each additional mile.

Car Rental: Ugly Duckling, 2128 E. Bijou (634-1914). $15.88 per day, $97 per week. Must stay in CO. Open Mon.-Sat, 9am-5pm. Must be 21 with major credit card or $150 deposit. **Payless Auto Rental:** 316 N. Nevada (578-1133). $22 per day, $119 per week. 100 free miles per day, 20¢ each additional mile. Open Mon.-Fri. 7am-6pm, Sat. 8am-5pm, Sun. 9am-5pm. Must be 21 with major credit card.

Help Lines: Crisis Emergency Services, 471-8300. 24 hours. **Gay Community Center of Colorado Springs,** 512 W. Colorado Ave. (471-4429). Phones answered Mon.-Fri. 6-9pm, Sat. 3-5pm.

Post Office: 201 Pikes Peak Ave. (570-5336), at Nevada Ave. Open Mon.-Fri. 7:30am-5pm. **ZIP code:** 80903.

Area Code: 719.

Colorado Springs is composed of well-groomed, wide thoroughfares laid out in a fairly consistent grid. **Nevada Avenue** is the main north-south strip, known for its bars, restaurants, and high crime rate. **Pikes Peak Avenue** serves as the east-west axis, and runs parallel to **Colorado Avenue,** which connects with U.S. 24 on the city's west side. U.S. 25 from Denver (70 miles north of The Springs) plows through the downtown area. Downtown itself is comprised of the square bounded on the north by Fillmore St., on the south by Colorado Ave., on the west by U.S. 25, and on the east by Nevada Ave. A word of warning—the city's attractions are spread out over a wide area, and are serviced by an inefficient bus system.

Accommodations and Camping

Avoid the shabby motels along Nevada Ave. If the youth hostel fails you, head for the establishments along W. Pikes Peak Ave. or a nearby campground. For information on B&Bs, contact Bed and Breakfast of Colorado (see Colorado Practical Information).

Garden of the Gods Youth Hostel (AYH), 3704 W. Colorado Ave. (475-9450). Clean, sparsely furnished 4-bunk cabins. Swimming pool, jacuzzi, laundry and showers. $7, nonmembers traveling with members $9.50. Open April-Oct.

Apache Court Motel, 3401 W. Pikes Peak Ave. (471-9440); take bus #1 west down Colorado Ave to 34th St., walk 1 block north. In a quiet residential area. A/C and TV. Singles $25. Doubles $28-30.

Amarillo Motel, 2801 W. Colorado Ave. (635-8539); take bus #1 west to 34th St. Slightly worn, but reasonably clean. Nice management. TV and laundry facilities. Singles $20. Doubles $35. Off-season $18 and $20, respectively.

Motel 6, 3228 N. Chestnut St. (520-5400), at Fillmore St., just west of I-25 exit 145; take bus #8 west. TV, pool, A/C. Some rooms with unobstructed view of Pikes Peak. Singles $24. Doubles $30.

Right in the city is the **Garden of the Gods Campground,** 3704 W. Colorado Ave. (475-9450). Sites in this gorgeous grove are $15, with electricity and water $17, full hookup $19. There are several popular **Pike National Forest** campgrounds in the mountains flanking Pikes Peak, generally open May through September. Some clutter around Rte. 67, 5 to 10 miles north of **Woodland Park,** which is 18 miles northwest of the Springs on U.S. 24. Others fringe U.S. 24 near the town of Lake George. (Sites $8; they fill only on summer weekends.) If they are full, you may camp off the road on national forest property for free. The **Forest Service Office,** 601 S. Weber (636-1602), has maps ($2) of the campgrounds and wilderness areas. (Open Mon.-Fri. 7:30am-4:30pm.) Farther afield, you can camp in the **Eleven Mile State Recreation Area** (748-3401), off a spur road from U.S. 24 near Lake George. (Sites $6, $3 admission fee. Reserve on weekends. Call 800-365-2267.) Last resorts include the **Woodland Park KOA** (687-3535), ¼ mile north of U.S. 24 on Rte. 67, 3 blocks west on Bowman Ave. (sites $14, with water and electricity $17, full hookup $18); and the **Monument Lake Resort and Campground,** 19750 Mitchell Ave. (481-2223), in nearby Monument (sites $9, with water and electricity $14, full hookup $15).

Food

Cheap, straightforward fare is available downtown, while some moderately priced foreign cuisine is served on 8th St. north of town.

Kennedy's 26th St. Café, 2601 W. Colorado Ave. (634-1007). One of the cheapest places in Colorado Springs. The enormous Ranchman's breakfast (2 eggs, ham, and all the pancakes you can eat) goes for $4. Cheeseburger with large fries $2-3. Open Mon. 6:30am-4pm, Tues.-Sat. 6:30am-8pm, Sun. 8am-2pm.

Catalona's Deli and Subs, 219 E. Platte Ave. (389-0243), downtown and 3 blocks north of Colorado Ave. A plain little place with everything from macaroni to milkshakes; try the 6-inch subs ($1.50). Ravioli dinner $3. They deliver. Open Mon.-Fri. 10am-6pm, Sat. 10am-4pm.

Kings Table, a regional chain with 2 local locations: 3015 N. Nevada Ave. (473-8471) and 3020 E. Platte Ave. (634-5182). The place to go if you're famished, with all-you-can-eat, cafeteria-style food (roast beef and ham on weekdays). Discounts for seniors. Lunch with amazing corn bread $4.50; dinner $6. Open Mon.-Thurs. 11am-8:30pm, Fri.-Sat. 11am-9pm, Sun. 8am-8pm.

Dale St. Café, 115 Dale St. (578-9898). Where locals go for gourmet pizza. Try the mediterranean ($4.75), and wash it down with some draft Sam Adams beer ($1.75). Open Mon.-Thurs. 11:30am-9pm. Fri.-Sat. 11:30am-9:30pm.

Henri's, 2427 W. Colorado Ave. (634-9031). Genuine, excellent Mexican food. This locally popular restaurant has been around for 40 years, and the margaritas are fantastic. Two cheese enchiladas $4.75. Open Tues.-Sat. 11:30am-10pm.

Giuseppe's Old Depot Restaurant, 10 S. Sierra Madre St. (635-3711). The best Italian food in the city served in a renovated train station. The daily special is $3.25, and a large plate of delectable spaghetti with garlic bread costs $5.50. Open daily 11am-10pm.

Sights

The town's major attraction looms large on its western horizon; you can see **Pikes Peak** from the town as well as from the quieter expanses of the **Pike National Forest.** If you're up to it, climb the peak via the 13-mile **Barr Burro Trail.** (The trailhead is in Manitou Springs by the "Manitou Incline" sign. Catch bus #1 to Ruxton.) Otherwise, pay the fee to drive up the **Pikes Peak Highway,** which is administered by the Colorado Department of Public Works. (684-9383. Open daily May-June 10 9am-3pm, June 11-Labor Day 7am-6:30pm. Admission $4, under 13 $1.) Expect to find snow and ice on the roadway even in summer. You can also reserve a seat on the **Pikes Peak Cog Railway,** 515 Ruxton Ave. (685-5401; open May-Oct. 8 daily; round-trip $17, ages 5-11 $8). Expect cold weather. At the summit, you'll see Kansas, the Sangre de Cristo Mountains, and the ranges along the Continental Divide.

Pikes Peak is not Colorado Springs' only outdoor attraction. The **Garden of the Gods City Park,** 1401 Recreation Way (578-6939), is composed of red rock monuments, once part of a Native American holy land, which now ring a pleasantly secluded picnic and hiking area. (Free. Visitors center open 9am-5pm, off-season 10am-4pm.) Be sure not to miss the "kissing camels," just a few minutes walk from the park's south entrance. For more strenuous hiking, head for the **Cave of the Winds** (685-5444), 6 miles west of exit 141 off I-25. Guided tours of the fantastically contorted caverns are given every 15 minutes daily 9am-9pm, off-season 10am-5pm. Just above Manitou Springs on Rte. 24 lies the **Manitou Cliff Dwellings Museum** (685-5242), U.S. 24 bypass, where you can wander through a pueblo of ancient Anasazi buildings. (Open June-Aug. 9am-6pm; May-Oct. 10am-5pm. Admission $2.75, under 11 $1.25.)

Buried in a hollowed-out cave 1800 feet below Cheyenne Mountain, the **North American Air Defense Command Headquarters (NORAD)** (554-7321) lies in wait. This telecommunications complex is one of the key elements in America's nuclear strategy. Headquarters for the controversial "Star Wars" space defense system are being erected nearby. The **Peterson Air Force Base,** on the far east side of the city, offers a visitors center and the **Edward J. Peterson Space Command Museum** (554-7321; open Tues.-Fri. 9am-5pm, Sat. 10am-5pm; off-season Mon.-Sat. 9am-5pm; free). Take bus #2.

The **United States Air Force Academy,** a college for future officers, is 12 miles north of town on I-25. It has some of the most distinctive architecture in Colorado. On weekdays during the school year, uniformed cadets gather at 11:55am near the chapel for the cadet lunch formation—it seems like a big production just to chow down. The **visitors center** (472-2000) has self-guided tour maps, information on the many special events, and guided tours every 30 minutes during the summer. (Open daily 9am-5pm.)

The **Pioneers' Museum,** 215 S. Tejon St. (578-6650), downtown, covers the settling of Colorado Springs, including a display on the techniques and instruments of a pioneer doctor. (Open Mon.-Sat. 10am-5pm, Sun. 1-5pm.) Everything you ever wanted to know about mining is on display at the **Western Museum of Mining and Industry,** 1025 N. Gate Rd. (598-8850; open daily 9am-4pm; admission $3, ages 5-17 $1). Take exit 156-A off I-25. And all your questions about those famous Olympians will be answered at the **U.S. Olympic Complex,** 1750 E. Boulder St. (578-4618 or 578-4644), which offers informative 1½-hour tours that include a film. (Open Mon.-Sat. 9am-4pm and Sun. noon-4pm.) Take bus #1 east to Farragut.

For information about the arts in Colorado Springs, drop in at the **Colorado Springs Fine Arts Center,** 30 W. Dale (634-5583; open Tues.-Fri. 9am-5pm, Sat. 10am-5pm, Sun. 1-5pm). Or call **Colorado College** (473-2233, ext. 2655), which provides the city with theater, dance and art exhibits. (Open Mon.-Fri. 8am-5pm.)

Near Colorado Springs: Cripple Creek

The area about Colorado Springs is peppered with forgotten mining towns, crumbling reminders of the state's glory days. **Cripple Creek,** 2 hours from Colorado Springs via Rte. 67 off U.S. 24, features the **Mollie Kathleen Gold Mine** (689-2465), 1 mile north of town on Hwy. 67. Every 15-20 minutes during the day, miners lead tours down a 1000-foot-deep shaft. (Open May-Oct. daily 9am-5pm. Tours $6, under 12 $5.) For information about other activities, try the **Cripple Creek Chamber of Commerce,** P.O. Box 650, Cripple Creek 80813 (689-2169 or 689-2307).

If your car is in good shape (check the suspension), the most exciting way to get to Cripple Creek is via the **Phantom Creek Road.** This route takes off from U.S. 50, some 30 miles southwest of Colorado Springs, and meanders up an ever-narrowing canyon, in which the vertical walls get closer and closer to the road. Finally, near the touristy mining town of Victor, the road reaches a 9000-foot highland. Cripple Creek is 6 miles ahead. On the return trip, the most scenic route is over the dirt **Gold Camp Road** (open only in summer), and once described by Teddy Roosevelt as the "trip that bankrupts the English language."

Aspen

Aspen: luxurious ski resort, world-renowned hermitage of dedicated musicians, and every budget traveler's worst nightmare.

Like countless other Colorado tourist traps, Aspen was once a prosperous mining town. When its streams of silver began to dry up in the 1940s, the shanty settlement went into a 20-year decline. But the Aspen of the 90s exhibits no signs of its past economic difficulties; condos with 6 digit retail values line the outskirts of the nation's best-known resort community. Some have been so audacious as to suggest that this community has become too exclusive, but these objections have done little to reverse Aspen's popularity with the upper class, and it is more than likely that low-budget living will remain as much a thing of the past in this town as the forsaken mining industry.

Practical Information

Emergency: 911.

Visitor Information: Visitors Center, at the **Wheeler Opera House,** 320 E. Hyman Ave. (925-1940). Pick up free *What to Do in Aspen and Snowmass.* Open daily 8am-7pm, in winter 10am-5pm. **Aspen Resort Association,** 303 E. Main St. (925-1940). Open Mon.-Fri. 8am-5pm. **Aspen District of the White River National Forest Ranger Station,** 806 W. Hallam at N. 7th St. (925-3445). Information for hikers and a map of the whole forest ($2). Open in summer Mon.-Sat. 8am-5pm. **24-Hour Forest Information,** 920-1664 (recording).

Pitkin County Airport: 4 miles west of town on Hwy. 82. General information 920-5380. **Continental** (925-4350) and **United** (925-3400) each offer 2 daily flights from Denver ($84). Roaring Fork buses shuttle visitors into town from the Airport Business Center (50¢).

Roaring Fork Transit Agency: 450 Durant Ave. (925-8484), 1 block from the mall. Service in winter daily 7am-1am; in summer 7am-midnight. Buses to Snowmass, Woody Creek, and other points down valley as far as El Jebel daily 6:15am-12:15am, in winter 6:15am-1am. One bus per day round-trip to Maroon Bells. ($3 each.) Free shuttles around town. Out-of-town service 50¢-$2.50.

Taxi: High Mountain, 925-8294. $2.85 base fare, $1.80 per mile. Fare to airport $10. In winter, call **Aspen Carriage Co.** (925-4289) for a horse-drawn sleigh ride.

Car Rental: 800-227-7368, at the airport. Economy cars $29 per day, $116 per wk. Unlimited mileage. Must be 25 with a major credit card.

Bike Rental: The Hub, 315 E. Hyman St. (925-9434). Mountain bikes $6 per hr., $20 per day. Open daily 9am-8pm. Credit card or $500 deposit required.

Help Lines: Crisis Line, 800-332-6804. 24 hour. **Gay Community of Aspen,** 925-9249.

Weather Line: 831-7669.

Post Office: 235 Puppy Smith Rd. (925-7523). Open Mon.-Fri. 9am-5pm, Sat. 9am-noon. **ZIP code:** 81611.

Area Code: 303.

Aspen lies 195 miles southwest of Denver in the summer, but in the winter you must take I-70 west to Glenwood Springs before you can pick up CO Rte. 82 south to Aspen, thus adding about 70 miles to the trip.

Once you reach Aspen, you will have no trouble getting around. CO Rte. 82 forms **Main Street,** to the south of which lies the downtown shopping district, and to the north of which lie the opulent homes of the permanent residents. Virtually everything in Aspen shuts down between the closing of the lifts in late April and the beginning of the summer season in June.

Accommodations and Camping

Pickings are pretty slim for budget accommodations in Aspen. Luckily, though, surrounding national forests offer inexpensive summer camping, and some skiers' dorms are reasonably priced, doubling as guest houses in summer. The most crowded and expensive times are Christmas and February to March.

Little Red Ski Haus, 118 E. Cooper (925-3333), 2 blocks west of downtown. Clean, bright, wood-paneled rooms. In winter, singles and dorm bunks from $25, off-season from $20. Doubles from $40, $48 respectively. Breakfast included.

Aspen International Hostel at the St. Moritz Lodge (AAIH), 334 W. Hyman Ave. (925-3220). Dorms, shared baths. Pool, jacuzzi, sauna. Slightly dingy. Look at your room before you hand over any money. In winter $29, off-season $19.

Unless the ground is covered with 6 feet of snow, try camping in the mountains nearby. Hike well into the forest and camp for free, or use one of the nine **national forest campgrounds** within 15 miles of Aspen. **Maroon Creek** offers beautiful forest service campgrounds: Maroon Lake, Silver Bar, Silver Bell, and Silver Queen are on Maroon Creek Rd. just west of Aspen. (Open July-Labor Day. 3-day max. stay. No reservations; sites fill well before noon.) Southeast of Aspen on Rte. 82 toward Independence Pass there are six campgrounds: **Difficult, Lincoln Gulch, Dispersed Sites, Weller, Lost Man, and Portal.** Difficult is the only one with water. (14-day max. stay. Sites $6.) The others are free and have a 5-day max. stay.

Food

The In and Out House, 233 E. Main St. (925-6647). A miniscule hole-in-the-wall doling out huge sandwiches on fresh-baked bread ($1.80-3.25) to long lines of music students at lunch. Come around 11:30am to beat the crowd. Open Mon.-Fri. 9am-9pm, Sat.-Sun. 9am-4pm.

Pizza-n-Stuff, 303 Aspen Airport Business Center (925-8239). This local favorite serves the cheapest and tastiest pizza in town (12-inch cheese $6.15) as well as lots of other Italian "stuff." Large plate of spaghetti $4. Open Mon.-Thurs. 10am-2pm and 4-10pm, Fri.-Sat. 4pm-midnight, Sun. 4-10pm.

Pour la France, 411 E. Main (920-1151). The local coffeehouse. Croissants in the morning, pastries and coffees in the evening. Continental breakfast $3.25. A good place for late-night conversation.

The Red Onion, 420 E. Cooper St. (925-9043). Almost 100 years old and still on the original site with lots of antique woodwork. Burgers and sandwiches $4-5, good *fajitas* $7.75. Look for coupon in visitors center. Open daily 11:30am-10pm.

Entertainment and Nightlife

Not surprisingly for a popular resort, Aspen has an active nightlife. Students frequent the **Cooper Street Pier,** 500 E. Cooper St. (925-7758), where a chili dog and fries ($3) and a glass of draft beer (75¢) are the combo to order. (Open 11am-2am, restaurant 11am-11pm.) At **The Tippler,** 535 E. Dean Ave. (925-4977), you'll find a more seasoned crowd, also sipping 75¢ drafts. (Open Tues.-Sat. 9am-2am.) **Little Annie's,** 517 E. Hyman St. (925-1098), has been known to host the jet set, but usually has a wide range of patrons. Beer from $1.50. (Restaurant open daily 11:30am-11:30pm. Bar open 11am-2am.) **André's** is another spot where the scene changes every time you turn around; business talk, student antics, and gay socializing make this one of the liveliest places in town. Intellectual discussions, esoteric jokes, and mouth-watering scents fill the air at the **Explore Booksellers and Coffee Shop.** Here you can read as many of the shop's books as you'd like for free. (Pot of tea $1.50, succulent apricot pie $4.25. Open Sun.-Thurs. 10am-10pm, Fri.-Sat. 10am-midnight.)

In addition to a parcel of annual artistic happenings, Aspen hosts many seasonal and even nightly cultural events. For tickets and the scoop on local dance, theater, and film in the entire Aspen area, call the **Wheeler Opera House Box Office,** 320 E. Hyman Ave. (925-7250; open Mon.-Sat. 10am-5pm.)

Activities and Sights

The hills surrounding town contain four ski areas: **Aspen Mountain, Buttermilk Mountain,** and **Snowmass Ski Area** (925-1221) sell interchangeable lift tickets. ($33-35, seniors with ID $20, under 12 $17. Daily hours: Aspen Mountain 9am-3:30pm, Buttermilk Mountain 9am-4pm, Snowmass 8:30am-3:30pm.) **Aspen Highlands** (925-5300) does not provide interchangeable tickets. ($33, seniors with ID and children $17. Open daily 9am-4pm.)

Needless to say, you can enjoy the mountains without shelling out money to ski. The ghost towns of **Ashcroft** and **Independence** are open to visitors in the summer, and hiking in the **Maroon Bells** and **Elk Mountains** is permitted at any time the snow isn't too deep. **Maroon** and **Crater Lakes** are popular destinations in this relatively unspoiled area. The shuttles run twice every hour and have been instituted to spare the Maroon Creek Valley from automobile emissions and noise. (Fare $2.50, seniors and children $1.) Free shuttle buses to Highlands leave from Aspen's Rubey Park 15 and 45 minutes after the hour. Biking up to Maroon Lake is popular and fairly strenuous. From the trailhead, hike the 1.6-mile turnpike through aspen groves to Crater Lake, and continue through high passes to more distant destinations in the **Maroon Bells-Snowmass Wilderness.** Be sure to pick up a topographical map in Aspen before beginning your ascent. The **Ute Mountaineer,** 308 S. Mill St. (925-2849; open daily 9am-8pm), and **Carl's Pharmacy,** 306 E. Main St. (925-3273; open daily 8am-10pm), both sell maps for $2.50.

Undoubtedly Aspen's most famous event, the **Aspen Music Festival** (925-9042) holds sway over the town every June-August. Free bus transportation is provided from Rubey Park downtown to "the Tent," south of town, before and after all concerts. Picnic outside the tent and listen for free; afternoon rehearsals are also free. (Student and Festival Orchestra concerts June-late Aug. Tickets $8-20. Sun. rehearsals $2.) Aspen's only museum, the **Wheeler-Stallard House,** 620 W. Bleecker St. (925-3721), is also home to the **Aspen Historical Society.** The society offers tours of the house daily from 1-4pm during peak tourist season. The talk includes many fascinating details about the mining history of Aspen. (Admission $3, children 50¢.)

Great Sand Dunes National Monument

If Colorado's splendid mountains are all beginning to look the same, make a path for these unique mountains of sand. At the northwest edge of the **San Luis Valley,** 700-foot sand dunes lap the base of the **Sangre de Christo Range.** For thousands of years, wind-blown sand has accumulated in dunes at passes in the range, its progress checked by the shallow but persistent **Medano Creek.** Visitors can wade across the creek from April to mid-July. For a short hike, head out on Mosca Trail, a ½-mile jaunt into the desert sands. Avoid the intense afternoon heat.

Rangers preside over daily naturalist activities, hikes, and other programs. Full schedules are available at the **visitors center** (378-2312), ½ mile past the entrance gate, where you can also view a 15-minute film on the dunes, shown every 15 minutes. (Open daily 8am-8pm; Labor Day-Memorial Day 8am-5pm. Entrance fee for vehicles $3, pedestrians and bikers $1.) For more information contact the Superintendent, Great Sand Dunes NM, Mosca 81146 (378-2312).

If you'd care to see more than just the first wave of dunes, the **Oasis** complex (378-2222) on the southern boundary also provides four-wheel-drive tours of the backcountry. The tour takes the rugged Medano Pass Primitive Road into the nether regions of the Monument. (4 tours daily, 3 hr., $14, under 12 $8. Discounts for seniors.)

Pinyon Flats, the monument's campground, fills quickly in summer. Camping here among the prickly pear cacti is first come-first serve. Bring mosquito repellent in June. (Sites $6.) If the park's sites are full, you can camp at Oasis. (Sites for 2 $8, with hookup $11.50. Each additional person $2.50. Showers included.) **Backcountry camping** requires a free permit. For information on nearby National Forest Campgrounds, contact the Rio Grande National Forest Service Office, 1803 W. Hwy. 160, Monte Vista, CO 81144 (852-5941). All developed sites $5-7.

Great Sand Dunes National Monument is 32 miles northeast of Alamosa and 112 miles west of Pueblo, on Rte. 150, off U.S. 160. **Greyhound/Trailways** sends one bus per day out of Denver to Alamosa (5 hr., $35). The Alamosa depot is at 511 4th St. (589-4948) and is open Mon.-Fri. 9am-1pm and 4-6pm, Sat. 11am-12:30pm and 5-6pm. Hitching to the Monument is a simple maneuver, especially from Rte. 150. Avoid the poorly maintained country road from Mosca on Rte. 17. For emergencies within the park, call the **Colorado State Patrol** (589-5807).

Mesa Verde National Park

Six long centuries ago, nameless tribes settled and cultivated the desert mesas of southwestern Colorado. In 1200 C.E., they began to construct the cliff dwellings, but in 1376, they mysteriously abandoned their shelters. When Navajo bands arrived in the area in 1450, they named the previous inhabitants the Anasazi or the "ancient ones."Today only four of the 1000 archeological sites are open to constant touring, because the fragile sandstone wears quickly under human feet. This caution causes some congestion within the park, so get there early.

Entrance fees to the park are $3 per car, $2 per pedestrian or cyclist. The southern portion of the park is divided into the **Chapin Mesa** and the **Wetherill Mesa.** A stop at the **Chapin Mesa Museum and Visitors Center** (529-4461), near the cliffs at the southern end of the park, offers information and 3-hour guided tours. (2 tours each morning. $8, under 12 $4. Open daily 8am-7pm; off-season Mon.-Fri. 8am-5pm.) On Wetherhill Mesa tours run only from June-Sept. and leave from Far View Lodge (6 hr.; $10, under 12 $4). You may take self-guided tours up ladders and through passageways of the apartments of these stone age people. Spruce Tree House is one of the better-preserved ruins. To get an overview of the Anasazi lifestyle, visit the **Spruce Tree Museum,** (529-4475) at the Chapin Visitors Center. (Open daily 8am-5pm.)

The **Far View Visitors Center** (529-4543), close to the north rim on the way to the Morfield campground (see below), can also be of assistance. (Open in summer daily 8am-5pm.) The **Morfield Ranger Station** in the park's northwest corner (529-4548), offers a 6-hour excursion departing from the Morfield campground. ($10, under 12 $4. Station open in summer daily 8am-5pm.)

Mesa Verde's only motel, **Far View Motor Lodge** (529-4421), is extremely expensive, but a few motels can put you up for under $30. Try the **Ute Mountain Motel,** 531 S. Broadway (565-8507). (Singles from $24. Most doubles from $32.) It's best to stay at the nearby **Durango Hostel** (see Durango). The only camping in Mesa

Verde is at **Morfield Campground,** (529-4474; off-season 529-4421) 4 miles inside the park, with some beautiful and secluded sites. (Sites $7, with full hookup $14.50. Showers 85¢ for 10 min.) Outside the park, ¼ mile east on Hwy. 160, is the **Double A Campground and R.V. Park** (565-3517; sites $11, full hookup $14).

The park's main entrance is off U.S. 160, 36 miles from Durango and 10 miles from Cortez. **Greyhound/Trailways** will drop you off in either town on its daily Durango-Cortez run, but only in the wee hours of the morning. Stations are at Frontier Plaza (565-7379) in Cortez, and 225 8th Ave. (247-1581) in Durango. From Cortez, you can ride the park employee shuttle, which leaves from 317 E. Main St. between May 15 and October 15 at 6:45am, and returns from the park at 5:30pm ($3.60 one way). **Durango Transportation** (259-4818) will take you on a nine-hour tour of the park ($27, children $13.50). Bring your own lunch. Hitching to and around Mesa Verde is fairly easy, especially in the morning. Once you're in the park, you'll need to hitch, as the sights are rather far apart (up to 40 miles).

Mesa Verde's **ZIP code** is 81330; nearby Mancos is 81328. The **area code** is 303.

San Juan Mountains

Ask Coloradans about their favorite mountain retreats and they'll most likely name a peak, lake, stream, or town in the San Juan Range of southwestern Colorado. Four national forests—the Uncompahgre (pronounced un-cum-PAH-gray), the Gunnison, the San Juan, and the Rio Grande—encompass this sprawling range.

Durango is an ideal base camp for forages into these mountains. In particular, the **Weminuche Wilderness,** northeast of Durango, tempts the hardy backpacker with a particularly large expanse of alpine territory. You can hike for miles without seeing a tree, and sweeping vistas of wild terrain are the rule. Get maps and information on hiking in the San Juans from **Pine Needle Mountaineering,** Main Mall, Durango 81301 (247-8728; open Mon.-Sat. 9am-9pm, Sun. 11am-4pm; maps $2.50).

The San Juan area is readily accessible. Each summer, hundreds of thousands of tourists travel U.S. 550, the main road in the region. **Greyhound/Trailways** and **Rocky Mountain Stage** service the area, but very poorly. **Hitchhiking** is an only slightly better alternative.

On a happier note, the San Juans are full of AYH hostels and campgrounds, making them one of the most economical places to visit in Colorado.

Durango

As Will Rogers once put it, Durango is "out of the way, and glad of it." Despite its increasing popularity as a tourist destination, Durango still retains its small-town feeling, and exudes an almost insidiously relaxed atmosphere. Come to see nearby Mesa Verde and to raft down the Animas River, but don't be surprised if you end up staying longer than you expected. Winter is Durango's busiest season, when nearby **Purgatory Resort** (800-358-3400), 20 miles north on U.S. 550, hosts skiers of all levels. (Lift tickets $30, children $14.)

Durango is best known for the **Narrow Gauge Railroad,** 479 Main St. (247-2733), which runs along the Animas River Valley to the touristy town of Silverton. Old-fashioned locomotives pull a string of sight-seeing cars through the mountains on a regular schedule. The ride is worth even the $32.30 round-trip (children $16.25). They have four trips per day but you must make reservations at least a day in advance. If you want to backpack into scenic **Chicago** and **New York Basins,** buy a round-trip ticket to Needleton ($30). The train (3 per day) will drop you off here on its trip to Silverton. When you decide to leave the high country, return to Needleton and flag the train, but you must have exactly $16 to board. For more information on the train and its services for backpackers, contact the Durango and Silverton Narrow Gauge Railroad, 479 Main St., Durango 81301. Offices open May-Aug. 6am-9pm, Aug.-Oct. 7am-7pm, Oct.-May 8am-5pm.

If you want to try river rafting, **Rivers West,** 865 Main St. (259-5077), has the best rates. ($10 per hr., $19 for 2 hr. plus lunch, $22 for an hr. plus a steak dinner. Open daily 9am-9pm.) **Durango Rivertrips,** 720 Main St. (259-0289), organize two-hour rides in two-person rafts ($15). Open daily 9am-9pm. If you feel like biking about town, pick up gear from **Hassle Free Sports,** 2615 Main St. (259-3874. Bikes $5 per hr., $15 per day. Open Mon.-Sat. 8.30am-6pm.)

Food in Durango is mostly overpriced. Buy provisions at **City Market,** on Hwy. 550 1 block down 9th St., and at 3130 Main St. (open 24 hours), or breakfast with the locals at **Carver's Bakery,** 1022 Main Ave. (259-2545), which has good bread and breakfast specials ($2-4. Open Mon.-Sat. 6:30am-10pm, Sun. 6:30am-2pm.) The **Durango Diner,** 957 Main St. (247-9889) serves ample cheeseburgers ($2.25) and boasts a singing cook. (Open Mon.-Sat. 5:30am-2pm, Sun. 5:30am-1pm.) **Clancy's Bar,** 128 E. 6th St. (247-2626), serves good sandwiches ($4.50) and has live entertainment on weekends. (Open daily 4:30pm-midnight. Bar open 4:30pm-1am.)

The simplest way to ensure a pleasant stay in Durango is to rest up at the **Durango Youth Hostel,** 543 E. 2nd Ave. (247-9905 or 247-5477), a quaint old building 1 block from downtown. David, the friendly host, will give you sightseeing tips as well as fresh vegetables from his garden. (Check-out 7-10am, check-in 5-10pm. $7, nonmembers $9. Make reservations in winter.) The **Central Hotel and Hostel,** 975 Main St. (247-0330), has a TV in each of the clean and pleasant rooms. (Singles $20. Doubles $25.) 1/3 mile west of town, the **Cottonwood Camper Park,** on U.S. 160 (247-1977), has tent sites for $12, with electricity and water $12.50, full hookup $14.

Durango is at the intersection of U.S. 160 (east to Alamosa, 150 miles) and U.S. 550 (south to Farmington, NM, 45 miles), and can easily be reached by hitching. Streets run perpendicular to avenues, but everyone calls Main Avenue "Main Street." **Greyhound/Trailways,** 275 E. 8th Ave. (259-2755), serves Grand Junction ($28), Denver ($47), and Albuquerque ($33). Open Mon.-Fri. 7am-5:30pm, Sat. 7am-noon and 4:30-5:30pm, Sun. 7-10am and 4:30-5:30pm.

Durango's **ZIP code** is 81301; the **area code** is 303.

Ouray

Once upon a time Ouray (pronounced yer-RAY) was—yes, you guessed it—a gold and silver mining town. This ½ by ¼ mile hamlet in the Uncompahgre National Forest is dwarfed by the 5000-foot peaks that rise on all sides. The town is well prepared for hikers and climbers, and its numerous sports shops can equip you and keep track of you through their hiker registration service. After a hike or a ski tour, soak in the **Onvis Hot Springs,** right off the "Million Dollar Highway" (U.S. 550) on the northern outskirts. (Open Mon.-Sat. 9am-10pm, Sun. 9am-7pm; off-season Wed.-Mon. noon-9pm. Admission $4, seniors and children $2.75, ages 13-17 $3.50.) The Million Dollar Highway was that immigrant's dream come true—it was originally paved with gold and silver ore valued at over a million dollars.

Experience the heritage of Ouray on a tour of the **Bachelor-Syracuse Mine,** Country Road 14, P.O. Drawer 380 W. (325-4500), just off Hwy. 550. Sit in an ore cart and be driven 3350 feet along a real mine shaft right into the heart of the mountain. If you've ever wanted to know why gold is so expensive, don't miss this. (Open late May-late Sept. 9am-5pm. Admission $6.75.) Once you resurface, head to the southwest end of town to see the **Box Canyon Falls,** a 285-foot waterfall. (Open mid-May to mid-Oct. 9am-10pm. Admission $1.25, seniors 65¢, under 13 75¢.)

Rent a jeep in Ouray and four-wheel over the Imogene Pass to Telluride (see Telluride). The prices are steep but you'll never forget the stupendously beautiful trip past waterfalls, mountain peaks, alpine flowers, ice fields, yellow-bellied marmots, and old mining towns. Reserve a jeep as far in advance as possible. **San Juan Scenic Jeep Tours,** 480 Main St. (325-4444 or 325-4154), rents jeeps for $50 per ½ day, $75 per day. (Open daily 7am-6pm. $50 deposit required.) If you'd prefer to pedal in the mountains, rent a bike from the **Basic Training Gym and Massage** behind the Hot Springs (325-4367). $12 per ½ day, $18.75 per day. (Open Mon.-Fri. 7am-7pm, Sat.-Sun. 10am-4pm.)

A national forest **campground** perches above Ouray, a mile or so south on U.S. 550. (Sites $5. Open May-Sept.) The **Ouray KOA** (325-4736) has some streamside sites, and comfortable grassy spots for primitive camping. (Sites $14, with electricity and water $16, full hookup $17.) For indoor accommodations, journey the 10 miles down valley to **Ridgway,** at the intersection of U.S. 550 and Rte. 62. The most pleasant, most affordable place to stay in the area is Ridgway's **Adobe Inn,** Lidell Dr. (626-5939), where friendly management and comfortable beds welcome you. Bunks $12, singles $37, and doubles $45.

Ouray's **ZIP code** is 81427; its **area code** is 303.

Telluride

Skiing is the sport that put Telluride on the map. Every winter ski pros zoom down the state's most gut-wrenching trails, known as "Jaws" and "The Telluride Plunge." For more information, contact the **Telluride Company,** P.O. Box 307, 81435 (728-3856).

Neither rockslide nor snowmelt signal the end of the tourist season in Telluride. The quality and number of summer arts festivals is staggering when you consider that only 1000 people call Telluride home. Just about every weekend in summer and fall some get-together occurs, but the most renowned include the **Bluegrass and Country Music Festival** (mid-June), the **Jazz Festival** (mid-Aug.), and the **Chamber Music Festival** (early Aug.). You can often hear the music festivals all over town, all day, and far into the night when you are trying to sleep. Above all, there's the **Telluride International Film Festival** in early September, now in its 13th year, and the fall **Colorfest** (late Sept.-Oct.) of dances, concerts and hiking trips. Contact the **Telluride Chamber Resort Association,** upstairs at Rose's (728-3041), at the entrance to town, for more information. (Open Mon.-Fri. 9am-7pm, Sat.-Sun. 10am-7pm.) For 24-hour recorded information call the **Festival Hotline** (728-6079).

The visitors center is located next to the **Coonskin Chairlift,** which will haul you up 10,000 feet for an excellent view of Pikes Peak and the La Sal Mountains. (Open Thurs.-Mon. 11am-3pm. Fare $5, seniors and children $3.) The biking, hiking and backpacking opportunities around Telluride are endless; the wild terrain is filled with ghost towns and lakes tucked behind stern mountain crags. For a fun day hike, trek up the San Miguel River Canyon to **Bridal Veil Falls.** Drive to the end of Rte. 145 and hike a steep, misty dirt road to a spectacular waterfall. **Paragon Ski and Sport,** 213 W. Colorado Ave. (728-4525), is the place to go for camping supplies, bikes and skis. (Open in winter daily 8am-9pm, in summer Mon.-Thurs. 9am-7pm, Fri.-Sun. 9am-8pm.) Stop at the local sportshop or **Between the Covers** bookstore, 224 W. Colorado Ave., for trail guides and maps.

The **Oak Street Inn (AYH),** 134 N. Oak St. (728-3383), has two-level loft dorms complete with saunas. ($14.50, in summer $12.50. Nonmembers $22. Showers $3.) If they're out of beds, head for the **New Sheridan Hotel,** 231 W. Colorado (728-4351), where a 3-bunk room for 1-3 people goes for $26. You can **camp** in the east end of town in a town-operated facility with water, restrooms, and showers. (2-week max. stay. Sites $5. Open mid-May.) **Sunshine,** 4 miles southwest on Rte. 145 toward Cortez, and **Matterhorn,** 10 miles farther on Rte. 145, are well-developed national forest campgrounds, and the latter can accommodate trailers with hookup. (2-week max. stay. Sites $5.) There are several free primitive campgrounds nearby, accessible by jeep roads. During festival times, you can crash just about anywhere in town.

Fun food in Telluride can be found at the **Park Bench Barbeque,** 136 E. Colorado (728-5134). Try the incredible pumpkin yogurt pancakes ($3) or the vegetable pita with fries ($4.25). For delicious Italian fare, head for **Eddie's Café,** 300 W. Colorado (728-5335). 8-inch pizzas $4.25, dinner specials $7-11. At **Froggies's Popcorn Wagon,** on the corner of Fir and Colorado Ave. (728-6105), grab a vegetarian crêpe

($1.85) and sit on the shaded outdoor deck admiring the mountains. (Open daily 11am-closing.)

You can only get to Telluride by car, on Rte. 550 or Rte. 145. Telluride's **post office** is located at 101 E. Colorado Ave. (728-3900; open Mon.-Fri. 9am-5pm, Sat. 10am-noon). The **ZIP code** is 81435; the **area code** is 303.

Black Canyon of the Gunnison National Monument

According to the geologist who first mapped this area, "no other canyon in North America combines the depth, narrowness, sheerness, and somber countenance of the Black Canyon." Sculpted by the Gunnison River, this canyon drops 2,500 feet into the earth's crust. Sunlight strikes the canyon floor once a day at high noon.

The **North Rim** of the canyon is more remote, accessible only via a 12-mile dirt road which leaves CO Rte. 92 near the Crawford Reservoir. Seven overlooks are positioned along the rim, and a self-guiding nature trail starts from the campground. The better developed, more populated **South Rim** is most easily reached from U.S. 50 via CO Rte. 347 just outside of Montrose. Along this rim, there is an 8-mile scenic drive boasting spectacular **Chasm View,** where you can peer down a sheer vertical drop of 2,000 feet. The most inspired hikes go down to the bottom of the canyon. The least difficult drops 1800 feet over a distance of 1 mile, and even this is more like a controlled slide. At certain points you'll need to hoist yourself on a chain in order to gain ground—this hike is not to be undertaken lightly. Registration and advice from a ranger are required before any descent. For more information, write the Superintendent, Gunnison National Monument, P.O. Box 1648, Montrose 81401, or call the **visitors center** (249-1915). (Guided nature walks hourly 10am-2pm. Open Memorial Day-Labor Day 8am-8pm.) A short walk down from the visitors center affords a view so startling in its steepness that the chest-high rails are positioned to protect the dizzy from falling.

Camp in either rim's beautiful desert **campground.** Each has pit toilets and charcoal grills; the southern one has an amphitheater with evening programs in summer. Water is available, but use it sparingly. (Sites $6.) Collecting wood is difficult, but a store sells it at the turn-off from U.S. 50. Backcountry camping in the canyon bottom is permitted; beware of the abundant poison ivy. Only fires using driftwood are permitted.

The closest town to the monument is **Montrose,** where the administrative offices for the monument are located at 2233 E. Main St. (249-7036. Open Mon.-Fri. 8am-4:30pm.) For rooms, look to the **Mesa Hotel** at the junction of Rte. 550 and 50 (249-3773), which has quaint, clean, and cheap rooms. (Singles $12. Doubles $21.) The town's best food is at the **Cameo Buffet,** 613 E. Main St. (249-0633), where an all-you-can-eat dinner is $8. (Open Mon.-Sat. 6am-9pm, Sun. 6am-8pm.)

Greyhound serves Montrose and Gunnison, which are about 55 miles upriver on U.S. 50. (Montrose 249-6673; Gunnison, 303 E. Tomichi St., 641-0663.) The bus will drop you off at the junction of Rte. 50 and 347, 6 miles from the canyon. Hitching is not difficult, though, and often more convenient. **Western Express Taxi** (249-8880) will drive you in from Montrose (about $14). Entrance to the monument is $3 for vehicles, $1 for pedestrians and bikers.

Monrose's **ZIP code** is 81401; the **area code** for the region is 303.

Grand Junction

Grand Junction gets its hyperbolic name from the confluence of the **Colorado** and **Gunnison River.** As western Colorado's trade and agricultural center, this quiet city serves as a fantastic base for explorations of the Gunnison Valley and the western San Juans.

Grand Junction is home to some excellent restaurants. **Dos Hombres Restaurant,** 421 Branch Dr. (242-8861), just south of Broadway (Rte. 340), on the southern bank of the Colorado River serves great Mexican food in a casual, family-style setting. A second Dos Hombres is in the Coronado Plaza in Clifton. (Combination dinners $3.75-5.25. Open daily 11am-10pm.) **A Touch of Greece,** 1059 N. Ave. (242-4457) serves scrumptious *souvlaki* for $3.75. (Open Mon.-Sat. 6am-10pm, Sun. 6am-8pm.)

Affordable lodging isn't all that easy to come by in Grand Junction. The **Melrose Hotel (AYH),** 337 Colorado (242-9636), between 3rd and 4th St., is an immaculate, well-maintained old hotel with lots of old-fashioned charm. ($10, nonmembers $14, with bath $15. Doubles $18, with bath $20.) **La Court Motor Lodge,** 120 S. 1st St. (242-3310), offers A/C, huge tubs, beautiful wood furniture, and general luxury. (Singles $25. Doubles $29.) And there's always **Motel 6,** 776 Horizon Dr. (243-2628. Singles $24. Doubles $30.) Camping in **Highline State Park** (858-7208), 22 miles from town and 7 miles north of exit 15 on I-70, or **Island Acres State Park** (464-0548), 15 miles east, on the banks of the Colorado River, costs $6 plus a $3 day-use pass. There is also a **KOA** at 3238 F Rd. (434-6644), in Clifton, just east of Grand Junction, off I-70. (Sites $13.75, with electricity and water $15.75, full hookup $17.75.)

For literature on the area, visit the **Tourist Information Center,** 759 Horizon Dr. Suite F (243-1001; open Mon.-Sat. 9am-8pm, Sun. 9am-5pm; off-season Mon.-Sat. 9am-5pm, Sun. 9:30am-1pm). Write to the **Chamber of Commerce** at P.O. Box 1330, Grand Junction 81052.

Grand Junction lies at the juncture of U.S. 50 and U.S. 24 in northwestern Colorado. U.S. 6 connects these two highways in town. Denver is 228 miles to the east, Salt Lake City 240 miles to the west. The **bus station,** 230 S. 5th S. (242-6012) serves Durango ($28), Salt Lake City ($50), and Denver ($40). Open 24 hours.

Grand Junction's **ZIP code** 81501; the **area code** is 303.

Grand Mesa

Fifty miles east of Grand Junction lies Grand Mesa, the world's largest flat-top mountain. Some 600 million years ago, a 300-foot-thick flow of lava covered the area where the mesa now stands. Since then, erosion has worn down the surrounding land by over 5000 feet, but the mesa's lava cap has preserved its original height. Take I-70 eastbound to Plateau Creek, where Route 65 cuts off into the long climb through the spruce trees to the top of the mesa. Near the top is the Land's End turnoff leading to the very edge of Grand Mesa, some 12 miles down an improved dirt road. On a clear day, you can see halfway across Utah from here. The National Forest Service maintains a dozen **campsites** on the Mesa (free, with water $7). The district **forest service,** 764 Horizon Dr., Grand Junction (242-8211), has more information. (Open Mon.-Fri. 8am-5pm.) You can buy a map of the mesa's trails, campsites, and trout ponds ($2.15) here, or at **Surplus City,** 200 W. Grand Ave. (242-2818; $4). Surplus City is a good place to get cheap backcountry equipment. (Open Mon.-Fri. 8am-8pm, Sat. 8am-7pm, Sun. 8am-6pm.) **Vega State Park** (487-3407), 12 miles east of Colbrain off Rte. 330, is another possibility for camping in the high country.

Besides camping, the Monument offers fine backcountry hiking. Rock climbers covet the soft-rock climbs here, including the Monument Spire. A good auto tour also runs all around the rim of the canyon. Stop by the ranger stations on Hwy. 65 and on Land's End Road for details on rock climbing and registration. (Both open June-Sept. daily 9am-6pm.)

Colorado National Monument

The red, fearsome canyons and dry striated sandstone of the Colorado National Monument were once scorned by settlers as arid and unusable land. Were it not for trapper and hunter John Otto, who in 1911 declared the land a national monument, it would have been left to succumb to a slow process of desertification.

If you only have time for a quick look, the monument's **Rim-Rock Drive** (a 35-mile round-trip from Grand Junction) offers unforgettable photo opportunities. To more fully appreciate the stark, powerful beauty of the desert, leave the pavement and delve into the canyons. Many trails off the Rim-Rock Drive offer spectacular views of monoliths as they meander down the 1000-foot canyon. Campsites in the monument at **Saddlehorn Campground** are offered on a first come-first serve basis and have picnic tables, grills, and restrooms. (Sites $6. Free in winter.) The **Bureau of Land Management** (243-6552; open Mon.-Fri. 9am-5pm) maintains three less-developed "campgrounds" near Glade Park. Bring your own water. (Free.) **Little Dolores Fall,** 10½ miles west of Glade Park, has fishing and swimming. The monument charges an additional admission fee of $3 for vehicles and $1 for cyclists and hikers. The monument headquarters and visitors center, near the campground on the Fruita side of the monument, issue backcountry permits (Open daily 8am-8pm, off-season Mon.-Fri. 8am-4:30pm).

Idaho

When Abraham Lincoln declared Idaho a territory in 1863, he could not find an easterner willing to govern the area's 82,413 square miles of wilderness. Only after the first two appointees accepted the post, took the money, and failed to arrive in Boise did Lincoln finally locate a man committed to the job.

Today's visitor will soon come to appreciate the reasons for the pioneers' hesitation. Termed Ee-da-ho ("Gem of the Mountains") by Native Americans, Idaho contains some of the most primitive wilderness in the United States. Acres of ponderosa pine forest dominate the northern panhandle, while the **Selway-Bitteroot Wilderness** and **Idaho Primitive Area** occupy the central portion of the state. The western border is marked by the **Snake River,** whose turbulent waters have carved out **Hell's Canyon,** the deepest gorge in North America. Only in the southernmost regions do the mountains and forests yield to the agricultural plains, where those "famous potatoes" are grown.

Practical Information

Capital: Boise.

Tourist Information: Idaho State Tourism, 800-635-7820. **Tourism Department,** Capitol Bldg., 700 W. 8th St., Boise 83720 (334-2470). Open Mon.-Fri. 8am-5pm. **Parks and Recreation Department,** 2177 Warm Springs Ave., Boise 83720 (334-2154). Open Mon.-Fri. 8am-5pm.

Idaho Outfitters and Guide Association: P.O. Box 95, Boise, ID 83701 (342-1438). Information on companies leading whitewater, packhorse, and backpacking expeditions in the state. Free vacation directories.

Time Zones: Mountain (2 hr. behind Eastern) and Pacific (3 hr. behind Eastern). **Postal Abbreviation:** ID.

Area Code: 208.

Boise

According to noted Boisean N.J. Hayashi, Idaho's capital city is "a great place to grow up." Hundreds of shady trees and numerous grassy parks make this pleasantly small city a residential oasis at the edge of the state's dry southern plateau—a relaxing way station on a cross-country jaunt, but not exactly a tourist haven. Most of Boise's sights (or lack thereof) lie between the capitol and I-80, a few miles south. You can manage pretty well on foot, and the **Boise Urban Stages** (336-1010) run several routes through downtown; route maps are available from any bus driver.

(Buses operate Mon.-Fri. 6:45am-6:15pm, Sat. 8:30am-6:30pm. Fare 50¢, seniors 25¢.)

The **Boise Tour Train** (342-4796) It will show you everything you ever wanted to know about Boise, and oh-so-much more. 1¼-hr. tours leave from either the State Historical Museum, 610 Julia Davis Dr. (334-2120) in Julia Davis Park, or at the 8th St. Marketplace. Mon.-Sat. 10am-3pm, Sun. noon-5pm. (Fare $4.25, seniors $3.25, ages 3-12 $2.25.) Or, if you prefer to learn about Idaho at your own pace, walk through the **Historical Museum** itself. (Open Mon.-Sat. 9am-5pm, Sun. 1-5pm. Free.) Also in the Julia Davis Park, the **Boise Art Museum,** 670 Julia Davis Dr. (345-8330), displays international and local art. (Open Tues.-Fri. 10am-5pm, Sat.-Sun. noon-5pm. Admission $2, under 18 free.) Beyond these two buildings lies the tiny and crowded **Boise Zoo** (384-4260). (Open Mon.-Wed. and Fri.-Sun. 10am-5pm, Thurs. 10am-9pm. Admission $2, seniors and ages 3-12 $1, under 3 free. Thurs. ½-price.) If the zoo doesn't sate your appetite for wildlife, pay a visit to the rare raptors at the fantastic **World Center for Birds of Prey,** 6 miles south of I-84 on Cole Rd. (Call 362-3716 to set up an appointment.)

Perched on the northern edge of the Great Basin, Boise makes a perfect starting point for forays into the **Basque Country** of eastern Oregon, Nevada, and southwestern Idaho. Local ranchers have been employing hardy, skilled shepherds from the mountainous Basque region of France and Spain for generations, and the Basque community is now well established in the Great Basin and the Western Rockies. Fiercely proud of their heritage, the Basques maintain the **Basque Museum and Cultural Center,** 6th and Grove St. (343-2671), in downtown Boise. This one-time boarding house for Basque immigrants is now a public museum with informative exhibits. (Call for hours.) If you have no luck there, you could either buy a Basque *chorrizo* from a hot-dog stand downtown, or make a day trip to **Jordan Valley, OR** for a taste of authentic Basque food. The pride of this little village, **Old Basque Inn** (586-2298), prepares Basque specialties for $6-10. (Open daily 6am-10:30pm.)

In terms of food, Boise has it all: the heavy pasta of southern Italy, the spicy specialties of northern Spain, and a good measure of down-home American burgers and fries. For huge, delectable servings of the latter, try The **Red Robin Burger and Spirits Emporium,** 211 Parkcenter Blvd. (344-7470), on the west side of town. (Salads $1.35-5, burgers $2.90-4.25. Open Mon.-Sat. 11am-midnight, Sun. 11am-10pm.) For slightly lighter fare, stop by the unusual **Moon's Kitchen,** 815 W. Bannock St. (342-5251), at the back of Moon's Gun and Tackle. Enjoy one of the best milkshakes in town ($1.80) while you contemplate the murals of the rugged Rocky Mountains. (Open Mon.-Fri. 7am-3pm, Sat. 10am-2pm.) For night-time entertainment, head for Old Boise, the area between S. 1st and S. 6th St., where the town's bars will vie for your patronage.

The lodging situation in Boise is pretty dismal; neither the YMCA nor the YWCA provide rooms, and even the cheap hotels don't charge less than $20 per night. The more reasonable ones tend to fill quickly, so make reservations. One of the most spacious motels is the **Capri Motel,** 2600 Fairview Ave. (344-8617), where well air-conditioned rooms come with coffee and queen-sized beds. (Singles $21. Doubles $26.) Farther out of town, the **Boisean,** 1300 S. Capitol Ave. (343-3645), has smaller rooms but a more personable staff. (Singles $23. Doubles $33.) Three miles north of town lies the unimproved **Forest Service Campground.** Contact **Boise National Forest,** 1715 Front St. (334-1516), for a map. (Open Mon.-Fri. 7:30am-4:30pm.) The nearest campground with hookups is **Fiesta Park,** 11101 Fairview Ave. (375-8207). (Sites $14, with electricity and water $17, full hookup (sewer included) $17.70.)

Amtrak (800-872-7245) serves Boise from the beautiful Spanish-mission style **Union Pacific Depot,** 1701 Eastover Terrace (336-5992), easily visible from Capitol Blvd. One train goes east daily to Salt Lake City (7 hr. 40 min., $55) and beyond; one also goes west to Portland (11hr., $75) and Seattle (15½ hr., $101). **Greyhound/Trailways** serves the capital on their I-84 schedules from a terminal at 1212 W. Bannock (343-7531), a few blocks west of the main downtown area. Two buses per day head for Portland (8-10 hr., $49), and three for Seattle (11 hr., $80).

Boise's main **post office** is on 770 S. 13th St. (383-4211; open Mon.-Fri. 7:30am-5:30pm, Sat. 9am-3pm. The **ZIP code** is 83701 and the **area code** is 208.

Sawtooth National Recreation Area (SNRA)

This recreation area's 756,000 acres of wilderness are filled with jagged peaks whose pinnacles serrate the clouds. Home to the **Sawtooth** and **White Cloud Mountains** in the north, and the **Smokey** and **Boulder** ranges in the south, the **SNRA** is surrounded by four national forests, and encompasses the headwaters of five of Idaho's major rivers. Whether you're looking for a pleasant place to camp beneath the pines, or a strenuous climb up a sheer granite face, you're sure to find it here.

Getting to the heart of the SNRA is easy, as long as you have a car. Don't miss the chance to pause at the **Galena Summit** (just after Ketchum on Idaho 75). The 8,701 foot peak provides an excellent introductory view of the range. If you don't have a car, take the bus to Missoula (250 miles north on U.S. 75) or Twin Falls (60 miles south on the same road). From there, hitchhike (extremely easy from most points), rent a car with at least 6 cylinders, or plan for a long beautiful hike.

Information centers in the SNRA are almost as plentiful as the peaks themselves. The **Stanley Chamber of Commerce** (774-3411), is on Hwy. 21 about three-quarters of the way through town. (Open daily 9am-noon and 12:30-5:30pm.) Three miles south of Stanley on U.S. 75 lies the **Stanley Ranger Station** (774-3681; open daily June 16-Sept. 6 8am-5pm; off-season Mon.-Fri. 8am-5pm); and the **Redfish Visitors Center** (774-3376) is 8 miles south and 2 miles west of Stanley at the **Redfish Lake Lodge.** (Open June 19-Labor Day daily 8am-5pm.) Whatever you can't find at these three places will be available at **SNRA Headquarters** (726-8291), 53 miles south of Stanley, off U.S. 75. (Open daily 8am-5:30pm, off-season Mon.-Fri. 8am-4:30pm.) All three ranger stations provide maps of the Sawtooths ($4) and free auto tape tours of the impressive Ketchum-Stanley trip on U.S. 75.

Hiking, boating and fishing opportunities in all four of the SNRA's little-known ranges are unbeatable. Two miles northwest of Stanley on Rte. 21 lies the 3-mile dirt road which leads to the trailhead of the **Sawtooth Lake Hike.** This 5½ mile trail is steep but well worn, and not overly difficult if you stop to rest. Bolder hikers who want to survey the White Cloud Range from above should head woutheast of Stanley to the **Casino Lakes** trailhead. This trek terminates at **Lookout Mountain,** 3000 feet higher than the far-away town of Stanley. (Make sure you have a camping permit, and plan to stay overnight.) The long but gentle loop around **Yellow Belly, Toxaway,** and **Petit Lakes** is recommended for beginning hikers, or any tourists desiring a leisurely overnight trip.

In the heat of summer, the cold rivers are ideal for fishing, canoeing or white water rafting. **McCoy's Tackle Shop** (774-3377), on Ace of Diamonds St. in Stanley, rents gear and sells most types of outdoor equipment. (Open daily 8am-8pm.) The **Redfish Lake Lodge Marina** (774-3536), rents paddleboats ($3 per ½ hr.), canoes ($5 per hr., $15 for 4 hr., $25 per day), and more powerful boats for higher prices. (Open daily in summer 9am-7pm.) **The River Company** based in Ketchum (726-8890) but with an office in Stanley (774-2250) arranges white water rafting and float trips. (Ketchum office open daily 8am-6pm. Stanley office open in summer daily 8am-6pm, unless a trip is in progress.)

The most inexpensive way to enjoy the SNRA waters is to visit the hot springs just east of Stanley. Watch for the rising steam on the roadside. The best of these is the **Sunbeam Hot Springs,** 13 miles from town; there is a stone bathhouse here. Be sure to bring a bucket or cooler, as you'll need to add about 20 gallons of cold Salmon River water before you can get into these *hot* pools (free). For evening entertainment, try to get in on the regionally famous **Stanley Stomp,** when fiddlers in the local bars play non-stop from 8am-midnight or beyond, and the dancers' foot-stomping is heard for miles around.

The **Sawtooth Hotel and Cafe,** Diamond St., Stanley (774-9947) is the perfect place to stay after a wilderness sojourn. (Singles $15, with private bath $22. Doubles $19.50, with private bath $26.) Or try one of the cabins at the **McGowan Resort** on Hwy. 75 in Lower Stanley (774-2290; cabins for 1-3 $45, Sept.-early June $27.) Campgrounds line U.S. 75. The biggest concentrations are at **Redfish Lake,** at the base of the Sawtooths, and **Alturas Lake,** in the Smokies. At Redfish, the pick of the spots is the small campground at the Point, which has its own beach. The two campgrounds on nearby Little Redfish Lake are the best spots for trailers. All sites in the SNRA cost $4-6; primitive camping is free.

The SNRA's **time zone** is Mountain (3 hr. behind Eastern). The **Post Office** is located on Diamond St. (774-2230; open Mon.-Fri. 8am-5pm. ZIP code: 83278.)

Craters of the Moon National Monument

Sixty miles south of Sun Valley on U.S. 20/26/93, the black lava plateau of **Craters of the Moon National Monument** rises from the surrounding fertile plains. Windswept and remarkably quiet, the stark, twisted lava formations are spotted with sparse, low vegetation. Volcanic eruptions occurred here as recently as 2000 years ago. The eerie, dark landscape is considered a natural work of art by many and as interesting as a torn-up parking lot by others.

The **visitors center** (527-3257) just off Rte. 20/26/93 has displays and videotapes on the process of lava formation, and printed guides for hikes to all points of interest within the park. (Open daily 8am-6pm; off-season 8am-4:30pm.) Campfire programs are held in summer daily at 9:30pm (Aug.-Sept. at 9pm) in the amphitheater, ¼ mile from the visitors center, near the park entrance on U.S. 93. Twice daily, free **guided walks** from the Cave Area parking lot (5 miles past the visitors center) carry you over the frozen lava beds and through the cave-like lava tubes, which can spread as much as 30 feet in diameter and extend several hundred feet long. The **Indian Tunnel,** a furrow that shoots straight down for a ½-mile, is one of the most spectacular.

Park admission is $3 per car, and the bizarre black campsites cost $5. Wood fires are prohibited, so you might want to camp in the adjacent Bureau of Land Management properties. (Free.) The park's sites often fill by 9 or 10pm on summer nights. Unmarked sites in the monument are free, but even with the $4 topographical map from the visitors center it may be hard to find a comfortable spot. The first explorers couldn't sleep in the lava fields for lack of bearable places to lie down. The more tender-backed tourist should head 18 miles east of the monument to **Arco,** where the **Lost River Motel,** on Hwy. 26 (527-3600), will put you up with A/C and coffee. (Singles $22.50. Doubles $32.) The **Lazy-A** motel, 318 W. Grand Ave. (527-8263) charges the same amount for smaller rooms with fewer amenities. From MacBride's Grocery Store, **Salmon River Stages** (527-3144) can transport you between Arco and Blackfoot (1½ hr., $5.15), or Pocatello (2hr., $6.25) on Tuesdays or Fridays only. From those points you can connect with Greyhound. However, there is no public transportation to the national monument.

Coeur d'Alene

Droves of tourists can do little to mar this isolated spot's rustic beauty. No matter how many people clutter its beaches, Lake Coeur d'Alene's serene expanse commands the viewer's attention and belies the surrounding bustle of human activity. **Sandpoint,** to the north, is less touristy and equally spectacular.

Practical Information

Emergency: 911.

Visitor Information: Chamber of Commerce, Front Ave. and 2nd St. (664-3194; 800-232-4968 outside ID). Open Mon.-Fri. 8am-5pm. Also a branch in the parking lot at U.S. 95 and Appleway. Open in summer daily 9am-4pm.

Bus Station: 1923½ N. 4th St. (664-3343), 1 mile north of the lake. **Greyhound** serves Spokane, WA (1 hr., $4) and Missoula, MT (5 hr., $29.95). **Empire Lines** connects Coeur d'Alene to Sandpoint at 5th and Cedar St. (1 per day, $3.45.) A **Roadrunner** bus connects with Lewiston (1 per day, $16.90). Open Mon.-Fri. 8:30am-noon and 1-8pm, Sat. 8:30-10am and 4-8pm.

Car Rental: Auto Mart Used Car Rental, 120 Anton Ave. (667-4905), 3 blocks north of the bus station. $25 per day, $160 per week. With 150 free miles per day, 18¢ each additional mile. Open Mon.-Sat. 8:30am-6pm, but phone line is open 24 hours. If you have your own insurance you can rent a car at age 18. Must have a credit card or a $50 cash deposit.

Help Lines: Crisis Services, 664-1443. 24 hours.

Time Zone: Pacific (3 hr. behind Eastern).

Post Office: 111 N. 7th St. (664-8126), 5 blocks east of the chamber of commerce. Open Mon.-Fri. 8:30am-5pm, Sat. 9am-noon. **ZIP code:** 83814.

Area Code: 208.

Accommodations, Camping, and Food

Cheap lodging are scarce in this booming resort town; you'll have better luck in the eastern outskirts of the city. The **Blackstone Motel,** 2009 E. Sherman Ave. (664-5410) has tiny singles for $19, doubles for $29. The property is being sold to another owner, so call ahead to check the rates. **El Rancho Motel,** 1915 E. Sherman Ave. (664-8791), has singles for $23 and doubles for $37. A mile from downtown, **Motel 6,** 416 Appleway (664-6600), offers singles for $22, doubles for $28. Ages 18 and younger not allowed without a parent or guardian. If you head up to Sandpoint, by all means stay at the elegant **Whitaker House,** 410 Railroad Ave. (263-0816), right on the lake. **AYH** members get the bargain of a lifetime for $10, $2 more for a hefty breakfast. (Nonmembers $27.)

There are four **public campgrounds** within 20 miles of Coeur d'Alene. The closest is **Beauty Creek,** a forest service site 10 miles south along the lake. Camp alongside a lovely stream against the side of the mountain. Drinking water and pit toilets are provided. (Free. Open May 5-Oct. 15.) **Honeysuckle Campground,** about 25 miles to the northeast, has nine sites with drinking water and toilets. (Sites $5. Open May 15-Oct. 15.) **Bell Bay,** on the shores of Lake Coeur d'Alene, off U.S. 95 south, then 14 miles to Forest Service Rd. 545, has 40 sites, a boat launch, and good fishing. (Sites $5. Open May 5-Oct. 15.) **Farragut State Park** (683-2425), 20 miles north on Rte. 95, is an extremely popular park with 4000 acres dotted with hiking trails and beaches along Lake Pend Oreille (pronounced "pon-do-RAY"). (Memorial Day-Labor Day, sites $7, with hookup $9. $2 day-use fee for each motor vehicle not camping in the park.) Call the Fernan Ranger District Office, 2502 E. Sherman Ave. (765-7381), for information on these and other campgrounds. (Open Mon.-Fri. 7:30am-4:30pm.)

A spirited resort community, Coeur d'Alene entertains with several unusual eateries and nightspots. Adventurous diners should look for a place to eat "Rocky Mountain oysters," a delicacy created from bull testicles. Or step into the exotic **Third Street Cantina,** 201 N. 3rd St. (664-0581), for a filling and delicious "Dos Combinaciones" selection ($6). (Open Mon.-Sat. 11:30am-whenever, Sun. 1pm-whenever.) Offerings at the **Coeur d'Alene Natural Foods & Restaurant,** 301 Lakeside Ave. (664-5916), are guaranteed to satisfy the health nut in you and please your taste buds as well. Garden burgers $3.75, pasta salad $4.50. (Open Mon.-Fri. 11am-3pm.) For a sandwich, pop into **Mr. J's Stuff-n-Such,** 206 N. 4th St. (664-8522).

The "pocket" (cream cheese, avocado, and tomatoes on pita bread) is a delightful eccentricity ($3.40). (Open Mon.-Fri. 8am-5pm, Sat. 10am-4:30pm.)

Sights and Activities

The lake is Coeur d'Alene's major attraction. Hike up **Tubbs Hill** to a scenic vantage point, or head for the **Coeur d'Alene Resort** and walk along the world's longest floating boardwalk (3,300 ft.). You can tour the lake on a **Lake Coeur d'Alene Cruise** (765-4000), which departs from the downtown dock every afternoon between June and Sept. (Cruises at 1:30pm and 4pm, return at 3pm and 5:30pm respectively. Fare $6.50, seniors $5.50, under 11 $4.50.) Rent a canoe from **Coeur d'Alene Canoe Rentals** (664-1175) at the city dock and explore the lake yourself ($5 per hour, $15 per half-day, $25 per day, $40 per weekend).

To absorb some of the region's history, explore the **Museum of Northern Idaho,** 115 Northwest Blvd. (664-3448). Exhibits primarily deal with white settlement and provincial development. (Open April-Oct. Tues.-Sat. 11am-5pm. Donation required.) Or drive up to **Silverwood,** 15 minutes north of Coeur d'Alene off I-90 (772-0513), a theme park where you can "step into yesteryear"—see old movies, ride horse-drawn carriages and a steam locomotive—all for $9 (seniors $8, under 12 $4.) Twenty miles east of town on I-90 is the **Old Mission at Cataldo** (682-3814), now contained in a day-use state park. Built in 1853 by Native Americans, the mission is the oldest-known building in Idaho. (Free tours daily. Open June 1-Aug. 1 daily 8am-6pm; Aug. 2-May 31 daily 9am-7pm. $2 vehicle entry fee.) Near Sandpoint, about 50 miles north of Coeur d'Alene, the **Roosevelt Grove of Ancient Cedars** nurtures trees up to 12 feet across.

Continue another 35 miles east on I-90 through mining country to the town of **Wallace.** Here you will find retail shops shaped like mining helmets. Learn about the **Wallace Mining Museum,** 509 Bank St. (753-7151), which features turn-of-the-century mining hardware and equipment. (Open Mon.-Sat. 8:30am-6pm, Sun. 9am-5pm; off-season Mon.-Fri. 9am-noon and 1-5pm. Admission $1, seniors and children 50¢.) Next door, take the **Sierra Silver Mine Tour** (1 hr., leaves from museum) through a recently closed mine. (Tours June-Sept. daily 9am-4pm every 20 min. Admission $4.50, seniors and under 12 $3.50.)

Montana

The license plate is appropriately labeled "Big Sky Country." Everything in this sparsely populated area feels spacious, from the alpine meadows of Glacier National Park to the empty lanes of the interstates. Rolling prairies rising gently from the Great Plains grasslands occupy the eastern two-thirds of Montana; the Rocky Mountains, which gave the state its original Spanish name of *montanã,* punctuate the western third, complete with three million acres of wilderness, national parks, national forests, glaciers, and grizzlies.

Tourists will find that another of this state's assets is its people, who like to quote local painter Charles Russell in assuring visitors that, in Montana, "the robe of welcome will always be spread, and the peace pipe will be forever lit."

Practical Information

Capital: Helena.

Tourist Information: Montana Promotion Division, Dept. of Commerce, Helena 59620 (444-2654 or 800-541-1447). Write for a free *Montana Travel Planner.* **National Forest Information,** Northern Region, Federal Bldg., 5115 Hwy. 93, Missoula 59801 (329-3511). **Gay and Lesbian tourists** can write to the **Lambda Alliance,** P.O. Box 7611, Missoula, MT 59807, for information on gay community activities in Montana.

Time Zone: Mountain (2 hr. behind Eastern). **Postal Abbreviation:** MT.

Area Code: 406.

Billings

Big city life still receives only a hesitant welcome in Billings, Montana's fastest growing city (population still well under 100,000). Throughout the city, seasoned Western gentility holds sway. Although you may not want to linger long, the town makes a good base from which to explore the nearby Custer Battlefield National Monument or Beartooth Highway.

The **Custer Battlefield National Monument** is located, ironically, on the Crow Indian Reservation, 60 miles southeast of Billings, off I-90. On June 26th, 1876, Lt. Col. George Armstrong Custer and five companies from the Seventh Cavalry were wiped out here by Sioux and Cheyenne warriors fighting to protect land ceded to them by the Laramie Treaty of 1868. A 5-mile self-guided car tour takes you past the area where Custer made his "last stand." You can also see the park on a 45-minute bus tour ($2) or pay $5 for a semi-private, hour-long van tour. The **visitors center** (638-2622) has a small museum that includes hundred-year-old drawings by an eyewitness, depicting the Native American warriors' account of the battle. (Museum and visitors center open daily 8am-7:45pm; off-season daily 8am-4:30pm. Free. Battlefield open daily 8am-sunset. Entrance fee $3.)

A mere 60 miles southwest of Billings on U.S. 212 lies Red Lodge, a scenic, mining-turned-tourism town that is best known as the entrance to the scenic **Beartooth Highway.** (Open in summer only; ask at the chamber of commerce for exact dates.) This gorgeous section of U.S. 212 leaves Red Lodge, climbs to **Beartooth Pass** at 11,000 feet and descends to the northeast entrance to Yellowstone National Park. The highway is only 62 miles long, but allow plenty of time. Even the most jaded travelers stop for the spectacular roadside views. If you're lucky, you'll hit the pass on the undisclosed date in July when the **Red Lodge Chamber of Commerce** (446-1718; open Mon.-Fri. 9am-5pm; Oct.-April 9am-4pm) hosts a bar at the summit.

If you decide to shack up in Billings, try the **Red Gables Motel,** 1511 1st Ave N. (252-9319), with clean rooms, phone, cable TV, and A/C. (Singles $21. Doubles $28. $2 less in off-season. Reservations required.) The **Lazy KT Motel,** 1403 1st Ave. N. (252-6606), at 14th St., has rooms with phone and color TV. The neighborhood is not the best. (Singles $22. Doubles $28.) **Motel 6,** far removed from town at 5400 Midland Rd. (252-0093), has spacious singles and slightly smaller doubles, A/C and an outdoor pool. (Singles $22. Doubles $30.) Campers should press on to the Rocky Mountains or look for a state park in the far eastern stretches of Montana; Billings has little to offer.

Hungry travelers should head for the **Lobby Cafe,** 2408 1st Ave. N., 1 block east of the bus station. The metal tables and fake leather seats may not be the Ritz, but $4.25 buys you entree, soup, salad, and potato. (Open Mon.-Thurs. 7am-5:30pm, Fri. 7am-5pm, Sat. 7am-2pm.) The best burgers in town are at the venerable, if somewhat seedy, **Hamburger Shop,** 17 N. 29th St., where 30¢ buys a small burger, and $2 pays for the substantial chili special. (Open daily 10am-7pm.) Grab a hearty burrito at **El Burrito Cafe,** 301 N. 29th St. (256-5234), where the combination of Mexican and modern decorations will keep your eyes entertained for the duration of the meal. For more traditional suroundings, have dinner at **The Stirrup Cafe,** 415 N. 29th St. (259-5561), right next to the Dude Rancher Motel. (Spaghetti, soup, salad $4.25. Open Mon.-Sat. 6am-9pm, Sun. 6am-6pm.)

Billings rests on the lonely high plains of eastern Montana, not far from the mountains. Bozeman lies 140 miles to the west on I-90; the North Dakotan border is 250 miles east. Billings's Logan International Airport serves cities in Montana, as well as Salt Lake City, Denver, Minneapolis, and Chicago. **Greyhound** (245-5116), **Powder River Transportation, RimRock Stages,** and **Cody Bus Lines** all serve Billings from a terminal at 2502 1st Ave. Greyhound runs to: Bozeman (3 per day, 3 hr., $14.50); Great Falls (1 per day, 5 hr., $25); and Helena (2 per day,

10 hr., $25.90). Powder River runs south through Wyoming, while Cody and Rim-Rock cover Montana. **Billings Metropolitan Transit** (657-8218) serves downtown (fare 50¢, seniors and disabled free 9:45am-3:15pm). Across the street, **Rent-a-Wreck** (252-0219) has the cheapest cars in town. ($16-18 per day, $2 less in winter. $120-130 per week. 300 free miles, 12¢ each additional mile. Open Mon.-Fri. 9am-5pm, Sat. 9am-2pm. Sun. by appointment. Must be 21 with a credit card and have liability insurance.) Call 252-2806 for **local road information** (24-hour recording) and 800-332-6171 for statewide highway reports.

The **visitors center** is at 1239 S. 27th St. (252-4016), exit 450 from I-90. (Open Memorial Day-Labor Day Mon.-Fri. 8:30am-5pm.) Information is also available at the **chamber of commerce,** 200 N. 34th St. (245-4111; open Mon.-Fri. 8:30am-5pm.)

The main **post office** is at 841 S. 26th St. (657-5745; open Mon.-Fri. 8am-6pm). The **ZIP code** for Billings is 59101; the **area code** is 406.

Bozeman

Bounded by the **Bridger and Madison Mountains,** Bozeman is a growing metropolis in Montana's broad Gallatin River Valley. The valley was originally settled by farmers who sold food to Northern Pacific Railroad employees living in the neighboring town of Elliston. Today, the fertile farmlands stretch from the city limits to the timberline and supply foodstuffs to a large portion of southern Montana. Bozeman's rapid expansion has lent it a cosmopolitan air, but visitors are still sure to find plenty of down-home, Western hospitality in both the city bars and the farmhouse kitchens.

The **Gallatin County Pioneer Museum,** 317 W. Main St., features exhibits concerning the political and judicial history of the county. A quick visit will tell you all you ever wanted to know about the development of Montana's plains. (Call 282-7220 to check hours.) The more spectacular **Museum of the Rockies,** on S. 6th St. and Kasy Blvd. (994-2251), has extensive displays on wildlife and Native American tribes of the northern Rockies. Particularly entertaining for families traveling with children. (Open daily 9am-9pm; Labor Day-Memorial Day Tues.-Sat. 9am-5pm, Sun. 1-5pm. Admission $3, ages 5-8 $2, under 5 free.)

Winter in Bozeman is synonymous with snow sports. **Bridger Bowl,** 15795 Bridger Canyon Rd. (586-2787), 15 miles northeast of town, offers 800 acres of alpine skiing. (Lift tickets $18, under 12 $7. Call 586-2389 for the ski and weather report.)

A good spot for nightlife is the **Cat's Paw,** 721 N. 7th Ave. (586-3542), where you'll find MSU students around the bar. (You must be 21 to enter. Open Mon. and Wed.-Sat. 10am-2pm, Tues. 9am-2pm, Sun. noon-2am.) The annual **Sweet Pea Festival** (587-8848), held from late July to the first weekend in August, brings Bozemanians to Lindley Park for folk music and all the ethnic food they can put away.

Eat cheaply and well at the **Western Cafe,** 443 E. Main St. (587-0436), known for its sweet rolls and burgers. The Hamburger Deluxe here ($2.45) is a local favorite. (Open Mon.-Fri. 5am-7:30pm, Sat. 5am-2pm.) In the **Baxter Hotel,** 105 W. Main St., the **Rocky Mountain Pasta Company** serves an Italian spaghetti dinner with bread and salad for $4.25. In the same building, the **Bacchus Pub** provides cocktails and ample soup and salad plates to Bozeman's intellectual and yuppie crowd ($3.50). (Phone for both: 586-1314. Both open daily 7am-10pm. Reservations highly recommended.) For impromptu picnics, the **Town and Country Warehouse,** 220 N. 20th St. (587-5541), provides supplies (open daily from 9am-6pm).

Summer travelers support a number of budget motels in Bozeman. The **Alpine Lodge,** 1017 E. Main St. (586-0356), takes the honors with fairly clean but rather small rooms for extraordinary prices. (Singles $10.35. Doubles $12.43.) The **Ranch House Motel,** 1201 E. Main St. (587-4278), has larger rooms with free cable TV and A/C. (Singles $21. Doubles $24.) The **Bobcat Lodge,** 2307 W. Main St. (587-5241), is more expensive (singles $25; doubles $32), but the spacious suites include a full kitchen (use of stove $4), TV and lounge area, and access to the indoor heated pool.

Bozeman lies in the southeastern quarter of Montana. It is bounded on the north and east by I-90. The town itself is laid out on a grid and is easily navigable. **Downtown** lies by the intersection of 7th Ave. and Main St. **Greyhound, RimRock Stages,** and **TW Services** all serve Bozeman from 625 N. 7th St. (587-3110). Greyhound runs to: Butte (3 per day, $10.45) and Billings (3 per day, $14.15). RimRock runs two buses per day to Helena ($11.75) and Missoula ($23). TW runs one bus per day to West Yellowstone ($10), Mammoth Hot Springs ($13.35), and Old Faithful ($14.90). **Rent-a-Wreck,** 112 N. Tracey St. (587-4551), rents cars for $24.50-26.50 per day, with 100 free miles, 14¢ each additional mile. (Open Mon.-Sat. 8am-6pm, Sun. by appointment.) You must be 21 with a major credit card. The **Bozeman Area Chamber of Commerce,** 1205 E. Main St. (586-5421), has ample information concerning geography and local events. (Open Mon.-Fri. 8am-5pm.)

The **post office** is at 32 S. Tracey St. (586-1508; open Mon.-Fri. 9am-5pm). Bozeman's **ZIP code**is 59715; the **area code** is 406.

Near Bozeman

Seventeen miles south of Bozeman on MT Rte. 85 (U.S. 191) lie the **Bozeman Hot Springs,** at 133 Lower Rainbow Rd. (586-6492). The three successive pools here increase both in size and temperature in order to allow customers to accustom themselves to the thermal heat. (Open Sun.-Thurs. 8am-10:45pm, Fri. 8am-8:30pm, Sat. 9:30am-11:45pm. Admission $2.50, seniors and ages 5-11 $2, under 5 free.) Adjacent to the bathing pools is the **Bozeman Hot Springs KOA Campground.** (Sites $12 per couple with water and electricity $13. Each additional adult $1.)

Virginia City, famous for its violent frontier town history, is 17 miles south on U.S. 287 and 15 miles west on MT Rte. 287. The territorial capital for ten years before Helena took over, and the site of the world's richest placer gold discovery, Virginia City once clanged with the prospecting pans of over 10,000 latter-day Midases. Once the gold source was exhausted, however, the population quickly thinned out, down to today's 100 or so. **Main Street** offers two museums, the **Watkins Memorial** and **Virginia City Museum.** The latter considers its pride and joy the foot of outlaw Clubfoot George, who was hanged in Virginia City one winter day in 1863. Main St. also possesses a restored print shop, blacksmith shop, stores, and a fully renovated hotel. At the stately **Fairweather Inn** (843-5377), cozy, well-kept rooms go for $26, with bath $28-34. The **Virginia City Campground** (843-5493) offers showers and toilets. (Sites $9, with electricity and water $10.50, full hookup $11.25.)

Even more intriguing than Virginia City is **Nevada City,** 1½ miles west on MT Rte. 287. All the buildings on the single street have been restored to their turn-of-the-century appearance. At the **music hall,** dozens of player pianos, organs, and horn machines play old-time tunes for a quarter. Don't miss the Famous and Obnoxious Horn Machine, the building's most ear-catching device. Call ahead to find out the hours of Nevada's showcase buildings; American Playhouse is filming a movie there and has temporarily interrupted all tourism. For more information, call or write the **Chamber of Commerce,** Box 145, Virginia City, MT 59755 (406-843-5341).

Helena

In 1864, four penniless prospectors decided to make their last go of mining at a site they dubbed **Last Chance Gulch.** Soon enough, four very happy men had discovered deposits bearing over 20 million dollars worth of gold. Though the ore was mined out long ago, Last Chance Gulch, now Helena's Main Street pedestrian mall (south of 6th St.), still manages to attract prospectors who chisel money from the wallets of unsuspecting tourists. The developed gulch is a pleasant fountain- and sculpture-lined place for window-shopping. More impressive are the mansions built by luckier last chance prospectors on streets in the northwest corner of the city.

As the "Queen City of the Rockies," Helena in 1890 felt obliged to build a capitol worthy of its status. The massive, granite, Greek revival **capitol building** that stands between 6th and Lookey Ave. is a testament to the youthful city's pride and enthusiasm. Inside, murals depict early mining activity, Old West culture, and white/Native American conflicts, including local artist Charles Russell's largest painting (12 × 25 ft.), **Lewis and Clark meet the Flatheads.** Godzilla watch out. (Open daily 9am-5pm. Free.) Across from the capitol at the **State Historical Museum,** 225 N. Roberts St. (444-2694), you'll find more Russell paintings as well as interpretive exhibits on early railroad history, cattle-drives, and mining activities. (Open Mon.-Fri. 8am-6pm, Sat.-Sun. 9am-5pm; Labor Day-Memorial Day Mon.-Sat. 8am-6pm. Free.) One-hour tours of historic Helena leave from the State Historical Museum on 6th and Roberts St. (every hr. on the ½ hr. daily 8:30am-4:30pm; admission $3, under 12 $2). Also of interest are the surprisingly good **Holter Museum of Art,** 12 E. Lawrence St. (442-6400), and the historic **Old Governor's Mansion.** (Museum open Tues.-Sat. 10am-5pm, Sun. noon-5pm. Mansion open Tues.-Sun. noon-5pm, tours every hour on the hour. Both free.)

Helena has plenty of unpretentious restaurants that won't strain your budget. **4 B's,** 900 N. Last Chance Gulch (442-5275), is right across from the bus station, and provides a scrumptious chicken pot pie for $4. (Open 24 hours.) The **Country Kitchen,** 2000 Prospect Ave. (443-7457), is 4B's biggest competitor and serves a superior breakfast (Eggs, toast, hash-browns, and coffee $3. Open 24 hours.) **Big Al's Sandwich Shop,** 11 W. 6th Ave. (443-7422), charges $2.75-$5.25 for a hefty sandwich made to order. (Open Mon.-Fri. 6:30am-4pm, Sat. 8am-2:30pm.)

Like restaurants, lodgings in Helena are extremely reasonable. The **Iron Front Hotel,** 415 Last Chance Gulch (443-2400), offers some of the cheapest and cleanest beds in town. (Singles $10-12. Doubles $14-16. Key deposit $5. No private baths.) Across the road, the **Park Hotel,** 432 N. Last Chance Gulch (442-0960), has older, less spacious rooms. Singles $13, with bath $15. Doubles $20, with bath $22. There are many public **campgrounds** within 25 miles of Helena, but none has showers or flush toilets. Try the **Porcupine Campground** (free) in the Helena National Forest, 13 miles west on U.S. 12, or **Cromwell Dixon,** a few more miles west on Rte. 12. (Sites $4.) Call the Fish, Wildlife, and Parks Department (444-2535) for information, or contact the **Helena National Forest Office,** 301 S. Park St. (449-5201). The chamber of commerce also has complete listings of campgrounds in their free *Montana Travel Planner.*

Helena lies in the Missouri River Valley, about halfway between Yellowstone and Glacier National Parks. Major highways connect Helena to Missoula (112 miles west on U.S. 12 and I-90), Bozeman (100 miles southwest on U.S. 12/287 and I-90), and Great Falls (90 miles north on I-15). **Intermountain** and **Rimrock Stage Lines** (442-5860) serve Helena from 5 W. 15th St. Service to: Butte ($9.50), Great Falls ($13.10), Bozeman ($11.75), Billings ($20.70), Kalispell ($49), and Missoula ($13.25). (Open Mon.-Fri. 8am-7:15pm.) For short trips around Helena, you might look into **Rent-a-Dent,** 1485 Cedar (443-7436). Cars are $15 per day (100 free miles, 15¢ each additional mile), $95 per week (700 free miles). (Open Mon.-Fri. 8am-6pm, Sat. 8am-4pm.) You must be 21 with a major credit card or a $250 deposit.

Helena's **post office,** 2300 N. Harris (443-3304), is in the north end, by I-15. (Open Mon.-Fri. 8:30am-5pm.) The **ZIP code** is 59601; the **area code** is 406.

Missoula

Missoula is one of the few cities in the U.S. that you visit in order to enjoy the great outdoors. So many of the locals are nature-enthusiasts that you'll be hard pressed to resist the flow and catch the city's cultural sights. If you do take the time to seek out some indoor recreation, however, you'll be well rewarded. Thanks to the presence of the University of Montana, the city has a pleasantly intellectual atmosphere and several sights to match.

Cycling enthusiasts have put the town on the map, instituting the rigorous **Bikecentennial Route.** The **Bikecentennial Organization Headquarters,** 113 W. Main St. (721-1776), has information on the route, while the **Missoula Bicycle Club,** P.O. Box 8903, Missoula 59807, furnishes enthusiasts with other bicycling news through the mail. To rent a bike and participate in Missoula's most popular sport, visit the **Braxton Bike Shop,** 2100 South Ave. W. (549-2513) and procure a bike for a day ($12), overnight ($15), or a week ($75). (Open Mon.-Sat. 10am-6pm.) You must have a credit card or leave a blank check as deposit.

Ski trips, raft trips, backpacking and day hikes are other popular Missoula diversions. The **University of Montana Outdoor Program Office,** University Center #164 (243-5172), posts sign-up sheets for all these activities and is a good source of information on guided hikes. (Open Mon.-Fri. noon-5pm, Sat. 11am-2pm.) The **Department of Recreation** (243-2802) organizes some day hikes and overnight trips for varying fees. (Open Mon.-Fri. 9am-5pm.) A great day of hiking can be spent in the **Rattlesnake Wilderness National Recreation Area,** a few miles northwest of town off the Van Buren St. exit from I-90. Wilderness maps are available from the **U.S. Forest Service Information Office,** 340 N. Pattee St. (329-3511; open Mon.-Fri. 7:30am-4pm. Maps $2.) The Clark Fork, Blackfoot, and Bitterroot Rivers provide great opportunities for float trips. For river maps ($1), visit the **Montana Department of Fish and Game,** 3201 Spurgin Rd. (542-5500; open Mon.-Fri. 8am-5pm).

The **Museum of the Arts,** 335 N. Pattee St. (728-0447), has classical art displays for those hankering for more metropolitan diversion. (Open Mon.-Sat noon-5pm.)The hottest sight in town, however, is the **Aerial Fire Depot Visitors Center** (329-4900), 7 miles west of town on Broadway (U.S. 10). Here you'll learn to appreciate the danger aerial firefighters encounter when jumping into flaming, roadless forests. (Open daily 8:30am-5:30pm; Oct.-Apr. by appointment. Hourly tours in the summer, except noon-1pm.) If firefighters don't spark your interest, take a drive to the south end of town to see **Fort Missoula** and the **Historical Museum,** both spruced up for Montana's centennial year. The museum's wordy displays are worth only a quick glance. (Open Tues.-Sat. 10am-5pm, Sun. noon-5pm; Labor Day-Memorial Day Tues.-Sun. noon-5pm. Free.)

Missoula's **Old Town Cafe,** 127 W. Alder St. (728-9742), provides budget fare with little grease and friendly service. Fill up with the hot veggie browns ($2.50). (Open daily 6am-8pm.) **Torrey's,** 1916 Brooks St. (721-2510), serves hearty health food at absurdly low prices (8-oz. sirloin steak $4.25). **Zorba's,** 420 S. Orange St. (728-9259), offers an escape from Americana. A large Greek salad is $3.50, and entrees run $5-7. (Open Mon.-Thurs. 11am-9:30pm, Fri.-Sat. 11am-10pm.)

Spend the night in Missoula at the **Birchwood Hostel (AYH),** 600 S. Orange St. (728-9799), 13 blocks east of the bus station on Broadway, then 8 blocks south on Orange. Most of the guests are cyclists. The spacious, immaculate dormitory room sleeps 22. There are admirably clean laundry, kitchen, and bike storage facilities. ($5, off-season $6. Open daily 5-10pm. Closed 2 weeks at Christmas.) The **Broadway Motel,** 1021 E. Broadway (549-4091), has clean, unremarkable singles for $19 and doubles for $26.50. A "sleeper" (no A/C or heater) goes for only $16.50. Right next door, the **Canyon Motel,** 1015 E. Broadway (543-4069 or 543-7251), has newly renovated rooms for the same price. (Single $18-20. Doubles $20-25.) Closer to the bus station, the **Sleepy Inn,** 1427 W. Broadway (549-6484), has singles for $22 and doubles for $26.

The **Greyhound terminal** is at 1660 W. Russel St. (549-2339). Catch a bus to Bozeman (5 per day, $23) or Spokane (3 per day, $30). **Intermountain Transportation** serves Kalispell (2 per day, $16) from the same terminal. This bus station sends **RimRock Stages** to Helena (2 per day, $13). **Rent-a-Wreck,** 2401 W. Broadway (728-3838), offers humble autos for $19.95 per day, $119 per week; 100 free miles, 26¢ each additional mile. You must be 21 with a credit card or a $100 cash deposit.

The **Missoula Chamber of Commerce,** 825 E. Front St. (543-6623), provides bus schedules. Traveling within Missoula is easy; the city **buses** (721-3333) operate Mon.-Fri. 6:15am-6:15pm, Sat. 9am-5:30pm. The fare is 40¢.

The **post office** is at 1100 W. Kent (329-2200), near the intersection of Brooks, Russell, and South St. (Open Mon.-Fri. 8:30am-5pm, Sat. 9am-1pm.) The **ZIP code** is 59801; the **area code** is 406.

Wyoming

Whoopee ti yi oh, git along little dogies
For you know Wyoming will be your new home.

Life on the ranch is still a reality for many Wyoming inhabitants. Here, the Wild West lives on, and not just through a macho image. The same state which still breeds American cowboys—complete with silver belt buckle, cowboy hat, boots, bolo tie, and other curios—is also the "equality state," the first to grant women suffrage (1869). This pioneering spirit is reflected in Wyoming's other firsts: the nation's first national park (Yellowstone), the first national monument (Devil's Tower), and the first national forest (the Shoshone). Today, Wyoming offers 30 of the nation's best-preserved parks and recreation areas for travelers eager to explore the Wild West on their own.

Practical Information

Capital: Cheyenne.

Tourist Information: Wyoming Travel Commission, I-25 and College Dr. at Etcheparc Circle, Cheyenne 82002 (777-7777). If you plan to camp, write for their free *Wyoming Vacation Guide.* **Wyoming Recreation Commission,** Cheyenne 82002 (777-7695). Information on facilities in Wyoming's 10 state parks. Open Mon.-Fri. 8am-5pm. **Game and Fish Department,** 5400 Bishop Blvd., Cheyenne 82002 (777-7735). Open Mon.-Fri. 8am-5pm.

Highway Patrol: 800-442-9090 (in Wyoming), or 777-7301.

Time Zone: Mountain (2 hr. behind Eastern). **Postal Abbreviation:** WY.

Cheyenne

Wyoming's capital was given its official name to honor the Native Americans who once owned its land, but within Wyoming it is also known as the "Magic City of the Plains." This grandiose nickname owes its origins to the Union Pacific Railroad; when the tracks were laid through the territory the city seemed to grow up overnight, or by magic, if you like. The magic seems to have waned over the years; Cheyenne today is struggling to balance the city and state economies in the wake of the oil crisis.

Perhaps because the economy has not continued to boom as it did back when the first ties were banged in on the UP line, Cheyenne has remained a pleasantly small city, and serves as an excellent gateway for all of northwestern Wyoming.

Practical Information

Emergency: 911.

Visitor Information: Cheyenne Visitors Center, 301 16th St. (778-1401; 800-426-5009 outside WY), just west of Capitol Ave. Extensive accommodations and restaurant listings. Open Mon.-Fri. 8am-5pm. **Howdy Wagon,** next door, open Sat.-Sun. 10am-3pm in summer only.

Cheyenne Street Railway: (778-1401). 2-hr. trolley tours of Cheyenne leaving in summer only Mon.-Sat. 10am and 1pm, and Sun. at 1pm. Tickets $5, seniors $4.50, children $2.50 (can be purchased from the chamber of commerce). Tours depart from 16th and Capitol Ave.

Buses: Greyhound, 1503 Capitol Ave. (634-7744), at 15th St. 3 buses daily to: Salt Lake City ($78), Chicago ($104), Laramie ($8) and Rock Springs ($31). 4 buses daily to Denver ($19). Open 24 hours. **Powder River Transporation:** in the Greyhound terminal (634-2128). South to Rapid City twice daily ($56); north to Casper ($29) and Billings ($83) 3 times daily. Greyhound passes honored.

Taxi: Ace Cab, 637-4747. $1.20 per mile.

Help Lines: Rape Crisis, 637-7233. 24 hours.

Post Office: 2120 Capitol Ave. (772-6580), 6 blocks north of the bus station. Open Mon.-Fri. 8:30am-5pm, Sat. 8:30-10:30am. **ZIP code:** 82001.

Area Code: 307.

Cheyenne's downtown area is small and manageable. Central, Capitol and Carey Avenues form a grid with 16th-19th Streets, which encompasses most of the downtown sights and accommodations. 16th St. is part of I-80; it intersects I-25/84 on the western edge of town. Denver lies just 90 minutes south on I-25.

Accommodations, Camping, and Food

It's not hard to land a cheap room here, unless your visit coincides with Frontier Days (see Sights and Entertainment), when rates almost double. Many budget motels line **Lincolnway** (U.S. 30, 1 mile east down 16th St.). The cheapest hotel in Cheyenne is the creaky old **Pioneer Hotel,** 208 W. 17th St. (634-3010), 2 blocks north of the bus station. The 80 rooms are in decent to good shape and feature elaborate Western decor. (Singles $15, with private bath $19. Doubles $22-30. Communal kitchen.) Right up the street, the **Plains Hotel** has beautifully renovated singles for $20, and doubles for $40. On the south side of town you'll find the **Lariat Motel,** 600 Central Ave. (635-8439). The rooms are quite presentable and the owner works hard to please. (Singles $22. Doubles $30.)

For campers, spots are plentiful (excepting the week of Frontier Days) at the **Restway Travel Park,** 4212 Whitney Rd. (634-3811), 1½ miles east of town. (Sites $12.50, electricity and water $13.50, full hookup $14.50. Prices go up by $1 in July. Each pet $1 per night. You might also try **Curt Gowdy State Park,** 23 miles west of Cheyenne on Rte. 210 (632-7946). Shade, scenery, and friendly management. (Sites $4, grill provided.)

Cheyenne is basically a meat 'n' potatoes town, but there are a few cheap, good ethnic eateries sprinkled around downtown. Here, the price difference between the humble café and posh restaurant can be a mere $4-6. If you want cow and tuber type American cuisine, try the **Driftwood Café,** 200 E. 18th St. (634-5304), where a Cheyenne burger costs $2.75. (Open Mon.-Fri. 7am-4pm.) **Jose O'Toole's,** 507 E. 16th St. (635-6403), won't charge you a pot 'o gold for their Irish and Mexican cuisine. Chili $4, Bucking Ham Palace sandwich $4. (Open daily 6am-10pm.) Even more authentic Mexican food is served at **Los Amigos,** 620 Central Ave. (638-8591), where burritos are $1.75-3.90 and humongous dinners start at $7. You might want to go with a ½ order (60% of the price), or come for the $4 lunch specials. (Open Mon.-Sat. 11am-8:30pm.) Lunch specials are also available in the **Twin Dragon Chinese Restaurant,** 1809 Carey Ave. (637-6622) on Fridays and Saturdays. ($4. Regular dinners from $5.50. Open Mon.-Sat. 11am-10pm, Sun. noon-9pm.)

When the urge to guzzle comes upon you, the aptly named **D.T.'s Liquor and Lounge,** 2121 Lincolnway, 1 mile east down 16th St., will quench your thirst. Look for a pink elephant above the sign; if you are already seeing two, move on. (Open daily 6am-11pm.) The **Cheyenne Club,** 1617 Capitol Ave. (635-7777), is a spacious good-time country nightspot, offering free, oily hors d'oeuvres from 5 to 7pm and live bands nightly from 8pm to 1:30am. You must be 19 to enter and 21 to drink. (Open Mon.-Sat. 4pm-2am. $1 cover after 8pm.)

Sights and Entertainment

If you're within 500 miles of Cheyenne between July 21 and 30, make every possible effort to attend the **Cheyenne Frontier Days,** nine days of non-stop Western hoopla. The town doubles in size as anyone worth a grain of Western salt comes to see the world's oldest and largest rodeo competition, and partake of the free pancake breakfasts (every other day in the parking lot across from the chamber of commerce), parades, and square dances. Most remain inebriated for the better part of the whole crazy week. Reserve accommodations in advance or camp nearby. For information, contact Cheyenne Frontier Days, P.O. Box 2666, Cheyenne 82003. (800-543-2339; 800-227-6336 outside WY. Open Mon.-Fri. 8am-5pm.)

If you miss Frontier Days, don't despair; Old West events are the major source of entertainment for Cheyenne's history-oriented public. Throughout June and July the **Cheyenne Gunslingers** perform the mock **Old Cheyenne Gunfight** to prove that justice reigns in Wyoming territory. (West 16th and Carey St. Mon.-Fri. 6pm, Sat. noon. Free.) The **Cheyenne Frontier Days Old West Museum** (778-7290), in **Frontier Park** at 8th and Carey St., is a half-hour walk north down Carey St. The museum chronicles the rodeo's history from 1897 to the present and houses an extensive collection of Oglala Sioux clothing and artifacts and an "Old West" saloon. (Open Mon.-Sat. 8am-7pm, Sun. 10am-6pm; off-season daily 11:30am-4:30pm.)

The **Wyoming State Museum,** 2301 Central Ave. (777-7024), describes the history of "boys who packed a long rope" (cattle rustlers) and of the women's suffrage movement, and traces the development of the Plains tribes. (Open Mon.-Fri. 8:30am-5pm, Sat. 9am-5pm, Sun. 1-5pm; in off-season closed on Sun. Free.) Around the corner you'll find the beautiful **capitol building,** on the north end of Capitol Ave. (Open Mon.-Fri. 8am-5pm. Guided tours every 15 min. in summer.)

This oversized cowtown rolls up the streets at night; except for a few bars, the downtown goes to sleep at 5pm. One delightful exception is the **Old Fashioned Melodrama,** which plays at the **Old Atlas Theater** (638-6543 mornings, 635-0199 aft. and eve.), an old vaudeville house at 211 W. 16th St., between Capitol and Carey Ave. (Shows July to mid-Aug. Wed.-Sat. 7-9pm; mid-late July Mon.-Sat. 7-9pm. Tickets $4, under 12 $2.50.) To find out about other theatrical events contact the **Cheyenne Civic Center,** 2101 O'Neile St. (637-6363). Box office open Mon.-Fri. 11am-5:30pm.

Casper and Environs

Built primarily as the stop for the Union Pacific Railroad, Casper's history is not much different from that of the hundreds of other similar railroad towns. Nonetheless, Casperites are proud of their city's one claim to fame—nine of the pioneer trails leading west, including the Oregon and Bozeman trails, met and intersected at a point not far from what is today the city's southern limit. Hence Casper's nicknames, "the Hub" and "the Heart of Big Wyoming." Disparage them within earshot of local residents at your own risk.

Casper's pride and joy, **Fort Casper,** 4205 W. 13th St., is a reconstruction of an old army fort on the western side of town. There is an informative museum on the site. (Open Mon.-Fri. 9am-6pm, Sat. 9am-5pm, Sun. noon-5pm; off-season Mon.-Fri. 9am-5pm, Sun. 2-5pm. Free.) From here you can hike to Muddy Mountain or Lookout Point to survey the terrain that hosted some of the last bloody conflicts between the Native Americans and the white pioneers.

Forty-five miles northwest of Casper on U.S. 20/26, you can see **Devil's Kitchen** (also called **Hell's Half Acre**), a 320-acre bowl serving up hundreds of crazy colorful spires and caves. Fifty-five miles out on WY Rte. 220, **Independence Rock** still welcomes travelers to the entrance of a hellish stretch of the voyage across Wyoming. In 1840, Father Peter DeSmet nicknamed it the "Great Registry of the Desert," honoring the godless renegades and Mormon pioneers who etched their name into the rock. Explore the abandoned prospecting town on **Casper Mountain** or follow the **Lee McCune Braille Trail** through Casper Mountain's **Skunk Hollow.** If you're here at the end of August, check out the week-long **Central Wyoming Fair and Rodeo,** 1700 Fairgrounds Rd. (266-4228), which keeps the town in an extended state of Western hoopla with parades, demolition derbies, livestock shows, and, of course, rodeos.

Eleven miles south of Casper, Casper Mountain hosts the **Hogadon Ski Area** (266-1600), with 60 acres of trails and runs rising 8000 feet above sea level. For ski rental, stop in at **Mountain Sports,** 543 S. Center St. (266-1136), where downhill and cross-country skis go for $15 per day, $70 per week. Open in winter Mon.-Sat. 9am-6pm, and Sun. noon-5pm; in summer Mon.-Sat. 9am-6pm.) Credit card or cost of equipment in cash required. For information on ski conditions, contact **Community Recreation, Inc.** (235-8383; open Mon.-Fri. 8am-5pm.)

Due to the recent failure of the oil economy, prices are conveniently low in Casper. In the nourishment department, **Signe's,** 429 E. A St. (265-8911), is currently the rage. Get the filling soup, bread, potato, and pie special ($5) and eat it at a wooden table. Country pictures line the walls. (Open daily 6am-9pm.) At the **Cheese Barrel,** 544 S. Center St. (235-5202), cheese is incorporated into nearly every concoction except the beverages. Try the pita vegehead ($3.35), and be sure to have at least one order of cheese bread ($1 for 2 gooey slices; open Mon.-Sat. 7am-3pm.) **Anthony's,** 241 S. Center St. (234-3071), serves huge portions of Italian food by candlelight (spaghetti $4.75; open Mon.-Sat. 11:30am-2pm and 5-10pm, Sun. 9am-2pm and 5-10pm).

If you're looking to stay overnight in Casper, check out the **Travelier Motel,** 500 E. 1st St. (237-9343), which offers spotless rooms near the center of town. (Singles $16.50. Doubles $18.) The **Virginian Motel,** 830 E. A St. (266-9731), has been renovated in Victorian style but has not been repriced. (Singles $18. Doubles $24.) The **Topper Motel,** 728 East A St. (237-8407), 6 blocks east of the bus depot, is a spacious and clean double decker. (Singles $18.50. Doubles $23-40.)

Campers can bunk down at the **Ft. Caspar Campground,** 4205 W. 13th St. (234-3260). (Tents $10. Full hookup $13.) **Casper Mountain Park,** 12 miles south of Casper on Rte. 251, near Ponderosa Park, has $4 sites. **Alcova Lake Campground,** 32 miles southwest of Casper on County Rd. 407 off Hwy. 220, is a popular recreation area with beaches, boats, and private cabins. (Sites $4.) The **Hell's Half Acre Campground** (472-0018), 45 miles west on U.S. 20-26, has showers and hookups (full hookup $10.40 for 2). The **Natona County Parks Office,** 182 Casper Mt. Park, provides information about camping in the greater Casper area. (Open Mon.-Fri. 9am-5pm.)

The informative **Casper Chamber of Commerce** is at 500 N. Center St. (234-5311; open Mon.-Fri. 8am-7pm, Sat.-Sun. 10am-7pm; off-season Mon.-Fri. 8am-5pm.) The **Powder River Transportation Services,** 315 N. Wolcott (266-1904; 800-433-2093 outside WY), sends three buses per day to: Buffalo ($20), Sheridan ($25), Cheyenne ($29), and Billings ($56); two per day to Rapid City ($46). **Casper Affordable Used Car Rental,** 131 E. 5th St. (237-1733), rents cars for $22 per day; 100 free miles, 15¢ each additional mile. $150 per week; 100 free miles, 15¢ each additional mile. (Open Mon.-Fri. 8am-5:30pm. Must be 22 with a major credit card or $200 deposit.)

Casper's main **post office** is on 150 East B St. (266-4000; open Mon.-Fri. 7:30am-5:30pm). The **ZIP code** is 82601; the **area code** is 307.

Bighorn Mountains

The Bighorns erupt from the hilly pastureland of Northern Wyoming, a dramatic backdrop to the grazing cattle and sprawling ranch houses at their feet. In the 1860s the area was the site of violent clashes between the Sioux Indians, who had their traditional hunting grounds here, and incoming settlers. Cavalry posts such as **Fort Phil Kearny,** on U.S. 87 between **Buffalo** and **Sheridan,** could do little to protect the settlers. The war reached a climax at the **Fetterman Massacre,** in which several hundred Sioux warriors wiped out Lt. Col. Fetterman's patrol. As a result, settlers and soldiers left the Bighorns to the Sioux. However, although the Native Americans won the battle, they lost the war. Within 20 years, the Bighorns became permanent cattle country.

For sheer solitude, you can't beat the Bighorns' **Cloud Peak Wilderness.** To get to **Cloud Peak,** the 13,175-foot summit of the range, most hikers enter at **Painted Rock Creek,** accessible from the town of Tensleep, 70 miles west of Buffalo on the western slope. The most convenient access to the wilderness area, though, is from the trailheads near U.S. 16, 25 miles west of Buffalo. From the **Hunter Corrals** trailhead, move to beautiful **Mistymoon Lake,** an ideal base for strikes at the high peaks beyond. You can also enter the wilderness area from U.S. 14 out of Sheridan in the north.

The forest is filled with campgrounds, and all sites cost $6 per night. Near the Buffalo entrance **Lost Cabin Middle Fork** and **Crazy Woman** are recommended for their scenery, as are **Cabin Creek** and **Porcupine** campgrounds near Sheridan. If you choose not to venture into the mountains, you can spend the night free just off Coffeen St. in Sheridan's grassy **Washington Park.**

Most travelers will want to use either Buffalo or Sheridan as a base town from which to explore the mountains. The **Mountain View Motel** is by far the most appealing of Buffalo's cheap lodgings. Pine cabins with TV, A/C and/or heating are complemented by the owners' assiduous service. (Singles $18-$20. Doubles $28-32. $2 less in the off-season.) Stock up on sandwiches at the **Breadboard,** 57 S. Main St. (684-2318), where a large "Freight Train" (roast beef and turkey with all the toppings) costs $3.20. (Open Mon.-Sat. 11am-8pm.)

If you get tired of the outdoors, you might want to visit the **Museum of the West,** 10 Fort St. (684-9331), or the museum and outdoor exhibits at the former site of Fort Phil Kearny (on U.S. 97 between Buffalo and Sheridan; open daily 8am-6pm, Oct. 16-May 14 Sat.-Sun. 1-5pm). Both testify to the tangled relations between local Native Americans and the encroaching pioneers.

The **Buffalo Chamber of Commerce** is at 55 N. Main St. (684-5544), 8 blocks south of the bus station. (Open Mon.-Fri. 9am-5pm.) In the summer, you can also visit the Buffalo summer information center, 2 miles east on Hwy. 16. (Open July-Aug. 10am-7pm; Sept.-June 11am-6pm.) The **U.S. Forest Service Offices,** at 300 Spruce St. (684-7981), will answer your questions about the Buffalo District in the Bighorns, and sell you a road and trail map of the area ($2). (Open Mon.-Fri. 8am-4:30pm.) At **Alabam's,** 421 Fort St. (684-7452), you can buy topographical maps for $2.50 and hunting, fishing, or camping supplies. (Open daily 6am-9:30pm; off-season 6am-8pm.)

The town of Sheridan, 30 miles to the north of Buffalo, escaped most of the military activity of the 1860s. But Sheridan has its own claim to fame; Buffalo Bill Cody used to sit on the porch of the luxurious **Sheridan Inn,** at 5th and Broadway, as he interviewed hopeful cowboys for his *Wild West Show.* Travelers counting their pennies will find the **Triangle Motel,** 540 Coffeen St. (674-8031), a better bargain than Cody's fabled inn. It boasts comfortable beds in rooms with A/C and is near the central business district. (Singles $15.60. Doubles or kitchenettes $24.) The **Parkway Motel,** 2112 Coffeen Ave. (674-7259), provides larger, more cheerfully decorated rooms for slightly more. (Singles $18. Doubles $24.)

The **U.S. Forest Service Office** in Sheridan, 1969 S. Sheridan Ave. (672-0751), offers $2 maps of the Bighorns, along with numerous pamphlets on how to navigate them safely. The **Sheridan Chamber of Commerce,** 5th St. and I-90 (672-2485), can also provide information on the National Forest, as well as other useful tips for lodging and activities in Sheridan. (Open daily 8am-8pm.)

Nestled at the junction of I-90 (east to the Black Hills area and north to Billings, MT) and I-25 (south to Casper, Cheyenne, and Denver), Buffalo is easy to reach. **Powder River Transportation** serves Buffalo from a terminal at the **Frontier Inn,** 800 N. Main St. (684-7453), where you can catch a bus north to Sheridan ($8) and Billings ($33), or south to Cheyenne ($33) (buses twice daily in each direction). Buffalo, as the crossroads of north-central Wyoming, is a good place for hitchhikers to catch rides to the southern cities of Casper and Cheyenne. Getting a lift on the freeway in Sheridan is more difficult. But never fear—**Powder River buses** run from the depot at the **Rancher Motel,** 1552 Coffeen Ave. (672-8147), to Billings ($27.25, 2 per day), Buffalo ($8, 2 per day), and Cheyenne ($44, 2 per day). The bus station is open Mon.-Fri. 8am-5am; Sat. 9am-noon, 4-5:30pm, 9:30-11pm, and 2:30-5:30am; Sun. 10am-noon, 4-5:30pm, 9:30-11pm, and 2:30 5:30am.

The **Time Zone** for both Sheridan and Buffalo is Mountain (2 hr. behind Eastern.) The **ZIP code** for Buffalo is 82834, and for Sheridan 82801. The **area code** for the Bighorns is 307.

Eastern Wyoming

Medicine Bow Range, Laramie, and Saratoga

As you travel west from Cheyenne into the **Pole Mountain** division of **Medicine Bow National Forest,** the gentle prairie gives way to hilly forests and parks that have yet to lure tourists in any great numbers. **Happy Jack Road** (Rte. 210) parallels I-80 for a scenic 38 miles from Cheyenne to Laramie, home of the University of Wyoming. **Curt Gowdy State Park,** mid-way between the two cities, is a prime hiking area with beautiful lakes and great fishing, and is popular with university students (see Cheyenne accommodations). The **Vedauwoo** (pronounced vee-dah-voo) **National Park,** 20 miles west of Cheyenne off I-80, offers some of the finest rock climbing in the world (entrance fee $2). Nearby, just south of I-80, is **Sherman Ghost Town.**

Greyhound can get you from Cheyenne to the **Laramie Terminal,** 1358 N. 2nd St. (742-0896; 2 per day, $8.32; terminal open Mon.-Fri. 8:30am-5:30pm, Sat. 9am-1pm). Laramie does make a rather interesting rest stop if you arrive during June, when the UW campus hosts a **Western Arts Music Festival,** or during July when the town parties Western style with **Jubilee Days.** The **Laramie Chamber of Commerce,** 3rd and Park St. (745-7339), has information on all events. (Open daily 9am-6pm; off-season 8am-5pm.) The **UW Department of Theater and Dance,** P.O. Box 3951 University Station, Laramie 82071-3951, can provide information on campus and cultural occasions. The box office, in the lobby of the Fine Arts building (766-3212), is open each week before a production from noon-4pm.

Stop in for a quick bite in Laramie at the **Downtown Café,** 215 Grand Ave., for a $3 cheeseburger, order of fries, coke and dessert. (Open Mon.-Sat. 6am-2pm.) Stay in Laramie at the **Thunderbird Motel,** 1369 N. 3rd St. (745-4871), 2 blocks south of the bus station. Clean, spacious rooms with A/C and cable TV. (Singles $19.50. Doubles $22.50.)

The **North Platte River Valley** and its central town, Saratoga, are even better-kept secrets than **Medicine Bow.** Rte. 130 from Laramie west to Saratoga is a stunning, summer-only route directly up and over the 11,000-foot **Snowy Range Pass** (742-8981; 800-442-8321 in southeastern WY). This route over the mountains will save you 40 miles. Just before the summit, you'll pass through **Centennial,** a tiny ski resort town legendary for its lost gold mine. Not far from Centennial, you'll come upon **Saratoga,** still unsullied by massive tourist invasions. 100 miles from Laramie and only 20 miles south of I-80 (exit 235), Saratoga draws locals to bask in delightful **Hobo Hot Springs,** a natural 110°F mineral water source that is directed into a large sand-bottomed pool. When you get too hot, simply climb over the low wall into the rejuvenating North Platte River.

Wyoming has designated the 70 miles of the **North Platte River** that connect Saratoga to Colorado's norther border a "blue ribbon" trout stream. Contact the **Game and Fish Department,** Medicine Bow (379-2337), or inquire at the well-equipped **Saratoga-Platte Valley Chamber of Commerce,** 102 W. Bridge (326-8855). The chamber of commerce has a list of tour companies that operate 1½-hour to 3-day float trips on the North Platte, and a list of local accommodations. (Open June-Sept. Mon.-Fri. 9am-6pm, Sept.-June Mon.-Fri. 9am-5pm.)

If you return without a creel full of brook trout, try **Wally's Pizza,** 110 E. Bridge St. (326-8472), the only budget alternative in town and a culinary rarity in this part of Wyoming. It serves the "vegetarian special" (cheeses, avocado, mushroom, cucumber, and sprouts) and huge sandwiches on fresh-baked bread ($4.50) in a cozy setting. (Open Mon.-Sat. 11am-10pm, Sun. noon-9pm.)

The best place to stay in Saratoga is the **Wolf Hotel** (326-5525), at the town's only main corner on WY Rte. 130 (1st and Bridge St.). This charming, renovated old building is a registered national historic landmark. The only thing the rooms lack are telephones. (Singles $12, $17 with bath. Doubles $23.) The saloon and dining rooms downstairs evoke the 1890s. Reservations are needed for busy summer weekends. The **Silver Moon Motel,** 412 E. Bridge St. (326-5974), is near the river. Clean rooms come with TV. (Singles $18. Doubles $24; off-season singles $6 and doubles $20.)

Medicine Bow National Forest is a camper's paradise. Of the over 30 campgrounds, about half are free, and all have toilets and drinking water. The closest ones to Saratoga are: **Jack Creek Campground,** 20 miles west on Rte. 500, then 8 miles south on a forest service road (open mid-June to Oct., free); **Lincoln Park Campground,** 21 miles southeast on Rte. 130, then 4 miles north on a forest service road (open mid-May to Sept., $3); and **South Brush Creek,** 2 miles beyond Lincoln Park (open mid-May to Sept., $4). Other sites cluster around Centennial and Laramie. Call the ranger station (326-5258) for more information.

Some of the best camping and hiking in the national forest is in the **Sierra Madre Range,** on the western slope of the North Platte Watershed. The town of **Encampment,** just 40 miles south of I-80 on Rte. 230, is a good base for forays into these mountains. A 16-mile long aerial tramway—the longest in the world—used to supply the hungry copper smelters of Encampment with a steady supply of ore. The town now claims an excellent **museum** of mining days, with several complete buildings from the town's turn-of-the-century boom period. (327-5310 or 327-5744; open daily 1-5pm, Labor Day-Memorial Day weekends 1-5pm. Free guided tours by appointment.)

For maps and information on hiking, camping, cross-country skiing, and other kinds of recreation in this area, contact the Medicine Bow National Forest, 605 Skyline Dr. Laramie 82070. (745-8971; open Mon.-Fri. 7:30am-5pm, weekends 7:30am-4pm; off-season Mon.-Fri. 7:30am-5pm. Maps $2.) There is also a **ranger station** in Saratoga, 212 S. 1st St. (326-5258; open Mon.-Fri. 7:30am-5pm), and a chamber of commerce, P.O. Box 456, Medicine Bow 82329 (379-2255; open Mon.-Wed. 8am-2pm). The **post office** in Laramie is on 105 W. Main St. (326-5611; open Mon. and Fri. 8:30am-5pm, Tues.-Thurs. 8am-5pm, Sat. 8:30-9:30am). The **ZIP code** is 82331; the **area code** is 307.

Yellowstone National Park

Had legendary mountain man John Colter been versed in the classics of world literature, he probably would have compared his 1807 trek into the Yellowstone area with a descent into Dante's Inferno. As it was, his graphic descriptions of boiling, sulfuric pits, spouting geysers, and smelly mudpots inspired a half-century of popular stories about "Colter's Hell." In 1870 the first official survey party, the Washburn Expedition, reached the area. As they came over a mountain ridge, the explorers were shocked by a fountain of boiling water and steam jetting 130 feet into the air. Members of the expedition watched it erupt nine times and named it "Old Faithful" before leaving the Upper Geyser Basin. One year later, President Grant declared Yellowstone a national park, the world's first ever.

Visitors in Grant's time might have encountered 50 other tourists in Yellowstone's 3,472 square miles. Today's tourist will find the park cluttered with the cars and RV's of 50,000 people or more. The park's main attractions are huge, tranquil Yellowstone Lake, the 2100-foot deep Yellowstone River Canyon, and the world's largest collection of reeking, sputtering geysers, mudspots, hot springs and fumaroles. In the back country, you'll get the chance to observe the park's abundant bear, elk, moose, bison and bighorn sheep, and will escpape the hordes of tourists in the bargain.

One note: in 1988 Yellowstone was ravaged by a blaze that charred almost half the park. In an extraordinary example of disaster tourism, crowds in Yellowstone doubled in 1989 as people poured in to see "what really happened." Lodgings in 1990 will be scarce, as more of the curious seek out the park. Make reservations early unless you don't mind sleeping under the stars.

Practical Information

Emergency: 911.

Park Information and Headquarters: Superintendent, Mammoth Hot Springs, Yellowstone National Park 82190 (344-7381). The switchboard serves all visitors centers and park service phones. General information, campground availability, and emergencies. Headquarters open in off-season Mon.-Fri. 8am-5pm. **Park admission:** (good for one week) $10 for non-commercial vehicles, $4 for pedestrians and bikers.

Visitors Centers and Ranger Stations: Most regions in the vast park have their own center/ranger station. The district rangers have a good deal of autonomy in making regulations for hiking and camping, so be sure to check in at each area. All visitors centers give backcountry permits, or have a partner ranger station that does, and have guides for the disabled. Each visitors center's displays concentrate on a theme. **Mammoth Hot Springs** (344-2357): natural and human history. Open Sept.-May 8:30am-5pm; June-Aug. 8am-7pm. **Grant Village** (344-6602): wilderness. Open in summer only, 8am-6pm. **Old Faithful/Madison** (344-6001): geysers. Open 8am-6pm; Dec.-Mar. 8am-4:30pm. **Fishing Bridge** (344-6150): wildlife and Yellowstone Lake. Open daily 8am-6pm; off-season 9am-5pm. **Canyon** (344-6205): natural history and history of canyon area. Open July-Aug. 8am-6pm; Sept.-June 9am-5pm. **Norris** (344-7733): park museum. Open daily 8am-6pm. **Tower/Roosevelt Ranger Station** (344-7746): special temporary exhibits. Open daily 8am-5pm. *Discover Yellowstone,* the park's activities guide, has a thorough listing of tours and programs at each center.

Radio Information: Tune to 1606AM for service information and interpretive discourse within the park.

Foreign Visitors Aid: 800-225-3050. Park has a multilingual staff of rangers. Brochures available in French, German, Spanish, and Japanese.

West Yellowstone Chamber of Commerce: P.O. Box 458, West Yellowstone, MT 59758 (406-646-7701). Located at the intersection of Canyon and Yellowstone St., 2 blocks west of the park entrance. Open daily 9am-6pm; off-season Mon.-Fri. 9am-6pm.

Greyhound: 127 Yellowstone Ave., W. Yellowstone, MT (406-646-7666). Two daily buses northeast to Bozeman (2 hr., $10), and 1 per day south to Salt Lake City (7½ hr., $59). Open in summer only, daily 8am-8pm.

TW Services, Inc.: 344-7311. Monopolizes concessions within the Park. 9-hr. bus tours of the lower portion of the Park leave daily from all lodges ($22, under 12 $18). Similar tours of the northern region leave Gardiner, MT, and the lodges at Mammoth Lake and Fishing Bridge ($14-21, depending on where you start and end). Individual legs of this extensive network of tour loops can get you as far as the Grand Tetons or Jackson, but the system is inefficient, and costs much more money than it's worth. Fares add up quickly. (West Yellowstone to Old Faithful 3 per day $6.40, chidren $3.20. Does not include park entrance fee.)

Gray Line Tours: 211 W. Yellowstone Ave, West Yellowstone, MT (406-646-9374). Offers full-day tours from West Yellowstone around the lower loop ($24.50, under 12 $9), upper loop ($22.50, under 12 $8), and Grand Tetons ($32.50, under 12 $12). Open daily 8am-5pm.

Car Rental: Payless Auto Rental, 225 W. Yellowstone Ave., West Yellowstone, MT. (406-646-9561), inside the Traveler's Lodge. $35 per day with 100 free miles, 25¢ each additional mile. Open daily 8am-7pm.Must be 21 with a credit card, $100 deposit, or passport.

Bike Rental: Yellowstone Bicycles, 132 Madison Ave., West Yellowstone, MT (406-646-7815). $12.50 per day. Open daily 8am-9pm.

Horse Rental: Mammoth Hot Springs Hotel, end of May to mid-Sept. **Roosevelt Lodge,** mid-June to Labor Day. **Canyon Lodge,** June 4 to Labor Day. $10.30 per hr. $19.50 for 2 hr. Call TW Services for information (394-7901).

Medical Facilities: Lake Clinic, Pharmacy, and **Hospital** at Lake Hotel (242-7241). (Clinic open daily May-Sept. 8:30am-5pm. Hospital Emergency Room open May-Sept. 24 hours.) **Old Faithful Clinic,** at Old Faithful Inn (545-7325; open May-Oct. daily 8:30am-5pm). **Mammoth Clinic,** at Mammoth Hot Springs (342-7965; open Mon.-Fri. 8:30am-5pm).

Post Office: 17 Madison Ave., West Yellowstone, MT. Open Mon.-Fri. 8:30-5pm. ZIP code: 59758. Also office at Old Faithful Station, in the park, behind the visitors center. Open Mon.-Fri. 8:30am-4pm. The **ZIP code** for the whole park is 82190; address mail to Old Faithful Station.

Area Code: 307 (in the park), 406 (in West Yellowstone and Gardiner). Unless otherwise indicated phone numbers have a 307 area code.

Yellowstone National Park lies in the northwest corner of Wyoming and spills into Montana and Idaho. **West Yellowstone** and **Gardiner, MT,** are the most built-up towns along the edge of the park and are quite pricey. The south entry to the park is through Grand Teton National Park. **Hitchhiking** into Yellowstone from nearby towns is easy. Hitching within the park is illegal, but is done.

Yellowstone's extensive system of roads circulates its millions of visitors. Side roads branch off at most of the corners to the park entrances and some of the lesser-known sights. It's unwise to bike or walk around the deserted roads at night since you may risk startling large wild animals. Approaching any wild animal at any time is illegal and extremely unsafe, and those who don't remain at least 100 feet from bison, bear, or moose risk being mauled or gored to death.

Food and Accommodations

Be very choosy when buying food in the park. If possible, stick to the **general stores** at each lodging location (open daily 7:30am-10pm) and try to stock up on price-regulated items.

Lodging in the Park

TW Services (344-7311) controls all of the accomodations within the park, and uses a special set of classifications for budget cabins. All cabins or rooms should be reserved well in advance of the June-September tourist season.

Old Faithful Inn and Lodge. Near the west Yellowstone entrance. Offers pleasant Roughrider cabins ($17) and Frontier cabins ($30). Inn provides well-appointed hotel rooms starting at $32, $47 with private bath.

Roosevelt Lodge, in the northwest corner. So named because it was a favorite campsite for Teddy Roosevelt. Provides the cheapest and most scenic indoor accommodations in the area. Rustic shelters $16, each with a wood-burning stove (bring your own bedding and towel). Also Roughrider cabins $17 (bring you own towel) and more spacious "family" cabins with toilet ($33).

Mammoth Hot Springs, 18 miles west of Roosevelt area, near the north entrance. Unremarkable budget cabins $19. Frontier cabins with private baths start at $46.

Lake Yellowstone Hotel and Cabins, near the south entrance. Overpriced, but with a nice view of the lake. Frontier cabins identical to Old Faithful's frontier accommodations ($39) and Western Cabins with a little more space ($59).

Canyon Village: Frontier Cabins $46, Western cabins $59. Less authentic and more expensive than Roosevelt's cabins, but slightly closer to the popular Old Faithful area.

Lodging in West Yellowstone

West Yellowstone International Hostel at The Madison Hotel and Motel, 139 Yellowstone Ave. (406-646-7745), in West Yellowstone. The cheapest respectable rooms in town and a friendly manager. Singles $20, with bath $24. Doubles with bath $28. Rooms $2 cheaper in the spring. Hostelers stay in more crowded rooms for $10, nonmembers $15. Open Memorial Day to mid-Oct.

Ho-Hum Motel, 126 Canyon Rd. (646-7746). Small, dark, but clean. Singles $24. Doubles $26.

Traveler's Lodge, 225 W. Yellowstone Ave. (406-646-9561). Comfortable, large singles $27. Doubles $35. $5 off if you rent a car from them (see Practical Information: Car Rental above).

Alpine Motel, 120 Madison (406-646-7544). Nondescript singles with bath, and cable TV $27. Doubles $30.

Lodging in Gardiner, MT.

Hillcrest Cottages (848-7353), on U.S. 89 near where it crosses the Yellowstone River. Small but clean singles $21. Doubles $26. 7 nights for the price of 6.

The Town Motel, across from the park's northern entrance (848-7322). Wood paneling, A/C, and color TV $24. Doubles $28.

Wilson's Yellowstone River Motel, ½ block east of U.S. 89 (406-848-7303). Large, well-decorated rooms. Singles $30. Doubles $34. $3 each additional person.

Camping

All developed campsites are available on a first come- first serve basis; during summer months, most fill by 2pm. All regular sites cost $5-9. Arrive very early, especially on weekends and holidays. If all sights are full, try campgrounds outside the park in the surrounding national forest land or off the main roads (free). Bring a stove or plan to hike a bit in search of firewood. Except for **Mammoth Campground,** all camping areas close for the winter.

Two of the most beautiful and restful areas are **Slough Creek Campground,** 10 miles northeast of Tower Junction (open May-Oct.), and **Pebble Creek Campground,** 15 miles farther down the same road (open June-Sept.). Both have good fishing and are relatively uncrowded. **Canyon Village** and **Fishing Bridge** campgrounds are for hard-sided campers only ($17 for RV hookup. Open June-Sept.). The popular (and scenic) campgrounds at **Norris** (open May-Sept.) and **Madison** (open May-Oct.) fill early (11am-1pm), while others, such as Fishing Bridge, Canyon, and Pebble Creek, sometimes have sites until 6pm. **Bridge Bay** (open May-Sept.), **Indian Creek** (open June-Sept.), and **Mammoth** (open year-round) campgrounds are treeless and less scenic. You'd be better off camping in the **Gallatin National Forest** to the north and west. Good sites line Hwy. 20, 287, 191, and 89. Call the Park headquarters (344-7381) for information on any of Yellowstone's Campgrounds. Madison, Norris, Bridge Bay, Grant, and Lewis Lake campgrounds all have special hiker/biker areas in several campgrounds, and charge only $1 to set up a tent.

More than two million acres, 95% of Yellowstone, is backcountry.

To venture overnight into the wilds of Yellowstone, you must obtain a free **wilderness permit** from a ranger station or visitors center. Be sure you understand the most recent instructions regarding closing of campgrounds and trails due to bears and other wildlife. The more popular areas fill up in high season, but you can reserve a site up to 48 hours in advance.

The campgrounds at Grant, Village Lake, Fishing Bridge, and Canyon all have coin-operated laundries and pay showers ($1 plus 25¢ for towel or soap). The lodges at Mammoth and Old Faithful will let you use their showers for $1.50, but they have no laundry facilities.

To discourage bears, all campers should keep clean camps and store food in a locked car or suspended 10 feet above ground and 5 feet horizontally from a post or tree trunk.

Sights and Activities

TW Services, for unbelievable amounts of money, will send you on tours, horseback rides, and chuckwagon dinners to your heart's content. But given enough time, your eyes and feet will do an even better job than TW's tours, without placing you in danger of bankruptcy. Hiking to the main attractions is a lot easier if you make reservations in the cabins closest to the sights you most want to see.

The geysers that made Yellowstone famous are clustered on the eastern side of the park, near the West Yellowstone entrance. **Old Faithful** (neither the largest, the highest, nor the most regular geyser, but certainly the most popular) is located in the **Upper Geyser Basin,** 16 miles south of **Madison Junction** where the entry road splits north-south. Since it was discovered in 1870, it has consistently erupted with a whoosh of spray and steam (5000-8000 gallons worth) every 45 to 70 minutes. There's almost no way to avoid crowds here in summer unless you come for the blasts at dusk or in the wee hours of the morning. Enjoy other geysers and elk in the surrounding **Firehole Valley.** Swimming in any hot springs or geysers is prohibited, but you can swim in the **Firehole River,** ¾ of the way up **Firehole Canyon Drive** (turn south just after Madison Jct.), or in the **Boiling River,** 2½ miles north of Mammoth. Do not swim alone, and beware of strong currents. From Old Faithful, take the easy 1½-mile walk to **Morning Glory Pool,** a park favorite, or head 8 miles north to the **Lower Geyser Basin,** where examples of all four types of geothermic activity (geysers, mudpots, hot springs, and fumaroles) steam, bubble, and spray together.

The regular star here is **Echinus,** which erupts about every hour from a large basin of water. If you are lucky enough to witness it, the biggest show of all is put on by **Steamboat,** the largest geyser in the world. Eruptions can last 20 minutes and top 400 feet. The last such enormous eruption occured on May 5, 1989, after almost a decade of inactivity. Don't hold your breath for another one soon. If that's any indication of increasing activity, you might get lucky. But whether you're waiting for geysers to erupt or watching them shoot skyward, don't go too close: the crust of earth around a geyser is only two feet deep, and falling into one of these boiling sulfuric pits could be detrimental to your health. Pets are not allowed in the basin.

Pause at the sparkling **Obsidian Cliff,** about 9 miles north of the Norris Geyser Basin. Legend has it that mountain man Jim Bridger once attempted to shoot an elk that was standing on this mountain, not realizing he was actually only seeing its reflection. Every tour guide tells a different version of this story, but the "mountain of glass" is worth a glance no matter how much credence you give to the tale.

Mammoth Hot Springs boast the famous **hot springs terraces,** built of multicolored limestone deposits—6 inches are added every year. **Wildlife** is quite abundant in the northern part of the park, both on the road from Mammoth to Roosevelt and also past Roosevelt in the Lamar Valley. If you can hitch from Mammoth to Roosevelt, you might want to try the short, scenic hike south to **Tower Falls** (about 4 miles).

The pride of the Western area of the park is the **Grand Canyon of the Yellowstone,** carved through glacial deposits and amber, volcanic bedrock. For the best views, hike or drive to the 308-foot Lower Falls at Artist Point, on the southern rim, or head for Lookout Point on the northern rim. All along the canyon's 19 mile rim, keep an eye out for the rare bighorn sheep, and at dawn or dusk the bear-viewing management area (at the intersection of the northern rim and Tower roads) should be filled with opportunities to use your binoculars.

Yellowstone Lake at the southeastern corner of the park, is 16 miles south of the Canyon's rim. With a free Yellowstone fishing permit, you can catch your own trout here, and have the chef prepare it for you in the **Yellowstone Hotel Dining Room.** Most other lakes and streams are catch-and-release fishing only. The walks around the main body of the lake, as well as those that take you around one of the lake's three fingers, are scenic but serene rather than strenuous. Nearby **Mud Volcano,** near Yellowstone Lake, features boiling sulfuric earth and the **Dragon's Mouth,** a vociferous steaming hole that early explorers reportedly heard all the way from the lake. You'll smell it from nearly as far away.

Although most of the spectacular sights in the park are accessible by car, a hiking trip through the backcountry will get you away from crowds. The multilayered petrified forest of **Specimen Ridge** and the geyser basins at **Shoshone** and **Heart Lakes** are only accessible by well-kept trails. **Cascade Corner,** in the southwest, is a lovely area accessible by trails from Belcher. Over 1000 miles of trails crisscross the park, but many are poorly marked. If you plan to hike, pick up a topographical trail map ($2.50) at any visitors center and ask a ranger to describe all forks in the trail and the wording of trail markings. Even then, allow yourself extra time (at least 1 hr. per day) in case you lose the trail.

Winter

Yellowstone can be as rewarding blanketed with snow during winter as blanketed with tourists during summer. The native animals can still be seen clustered around the sparse vegetation, and the traveling humans convert the park into snowboarding city. Cross-country skiing, ranger-sponsored snowshoe tours, and evening programs with hot chocolate and noisy snowmobile excursions are all available at off-season rates. Contact Park Headquarters (344-7381), **Snowmobile Touring** (545-7249), or the **visitors center** at Mammoth Hot Springs, Old Faithful (mid-Dec. to mid-March), or in West Yellowstone (mid-Dec. to mid-March). In winter, the Mammoth Hotel converts two rooms into a youth hostel, each of which holds 6 people ($6 per person).

Roads are plowed and bus service is available to West Yellowstone and Flagg Ranch on the west and south borders, and the Mammoth-Tower-Cooke City park road is kept open and accessible from Bozeman via Gardiner. All other roads are used by snowmobilers and the snowcoach only. The **snowcoach,** a tank-like vehicle, heated, enclosed, and run by TW Services, provides transportation from the south gate at Flagg Ranch, the west gate at West Yellowstone, and the north gate at Mammoth to bring travelers to the Old Faithful Lodge. With a permit (free from any visitors center), you may use the undeveloped backcountry sites, but exercise caution. People do get snowed in. You can find heated restrooms at Madison and Mammoth campgrounds. Food is available at Old Faithful and the **Canyon Snack Shop,** snowmobile fuel at Old Faithful, Mammoth, and Canyon. The **Three Bears Hotel,** 217 W. Yellowstone Ave. (646-7353), rents snowmobiles ($68 per day, $72 for 2 people).

Grand Teton National Park

When French fur trappers first peered into Wyoming's wilderness from the eastern border of Idaho, they were somewhat discouraged to find themselves face to face with three craggy peaks all topping 12,000 feet. In an attempt to make the imposing landscape seem more trapper-friendly, they christened the mountains "Les Trois Tetons," French for "the three breasts." When they found the three Tetons had numerous smaller companions, the Frenchmen named the entire range "Les Grand Tetons."

Though the discovery of the Teton Mountains utterly failed to please the tired 19th-century trappers, the snowy heights of Grand Teton National Park delight modern hikers and cyclists with their miles of strenuous trails. The less adventurous appreciate the Tetons's rugged appearance; the craggy pinnacles and shining glaciers possess an extraordinary beauty.

Practical Information

Emergency: 911.

Park Headquarters: Superintendent, Grand Teton National Park, P.O. Drawer 170, Moose 83012 (733-2820). Office at the Moose Visitors Center. Open Mon.-Fri. 8am-4:30pm.

Park Entrance Fees: $10 per car, $4 per pedestrian or bicycle, $5 per family (non-motorized). Good for 7 days for both the Tetons and Yellowstone. Under 16 (non-motorized) free.

Visitors Center: Moose, Rockefeller Pkwy. at the southern tip of the park (733-2880). Open daily 8am-7pm; Labor Day-May 8am-4:30pm. **Jenny Lake,** next to the Jenny Lake Campground. Open daily 8am-7pm; Labor Day-Memorial Day 8am-5pm. **Colter Bay,** on Jackson Lake in the northern part of the park (543-2467). Open daily early June-early Sept. 8am-7pm,

May and late Sept. 8am-5pm. **Signal Mountain,** between Colter Bay and Moose (543-2516). Open daily May 13-June 30 8am-5pm. Park information brochures available in Braille, French, German, Japanese, and Spanish. Topographical maps ($3). Pick up the free *Teewinot* newspaper for a list of park activities, lodgings, and facilities services.

Park Information and Road and Weather Conditions: 733-2220; 24-hour recording.

Bike Rental: Colter Bay General Store. 1-speed bikes $1.75 per hr., $8 per day. Open daily 7:30am-10pm. $20 deposit and 2 IDs required. Call the **Grand Teton Lodge Co.** (733-2811 or 543-2855) for more information. **Mountain Bike Outfitters, Inc.** (733-3314), at Dorman's in Moose. Quality mountain bikes $4.50 per hr., $14 per ½-day, $20 per day. Open in summer daily 9am-6pm. Credit card or deposit required.

Bike Tours: Off the Deep End Travels (733-8707; 800-223-6833 outside WY). $15 for a 3-hr. twilight tour of the Jackson Hole area, including wine and cheese. $50 for morning bike trip and afternoon whitewater trip, including breakfast and lunch. Call in advance and they'll pick you up at your hotel. Open Mon.-Fri. 9am-5pm.

Grand Teton Medical Clinic: Jackson Lake Lodge (543-2514), near the Chevron station. Open June to mid-Sept. daily 10am-6pm. After hours, call 733-8002. In a dire emergency, contact **St. Johns's Hospital,** (733-3636) in Jackson.

Post Office: in Colter Bay General Store. Open Mon.-Fri. 8am-noon and 1-5pm, Sat. 9am-1pm; closed in the off-season. **ZIP codes:** Colter Bay 83001, Moose 83021, Moran 83013, Kelly 83011.

Area Code: 307.

The national park occupies most of the space between Jackson to the south and Yellowstone to the north. **Rockefeller Parkway** connects the two parks and is open year-round. The park is directly accessible from all directions except the west. Hitching from Jackson is easy; hitching from Yellowstone may be more time-consuming.

Food

As in Yellowstone, the best way to eat in the Tetons is to bring your own food. If this isn't possible, stick to what non-perishables you can pick up at the **Flagg Ranch Grocery Store** (open daily 7am-10pm, reduced hours in winter), or **Dornan's Grocery** in Moose (open daily 8am-9pm, reduced hours in winter).

Accommodations

If you want to stay indoors, grit your teeth and open up your wallet. **The Grand Teton Lodge Co.** controls nearly all the lodging within the park. Make reservations for any Grand Teton Lodge establishments by writing the Reservations Manager, Grand Teton Lodge Co., P.O. Box 240, Moran 83013 (543-2855 or 733-2811). Accommodations are available late May through early October, and are most expensive from late June to early August. See Jackson (below) for accommodations outside the park.

Colter Bay Tent Cabins: The cheapest accommodations in the park, but not the place to stay if it's extremely cold. Canvas shelters with wood-burning stoves, table, and bunks for 4. Sleeping bags, wood, cooking utensils, and ice chests available for rent. (Call Maintenance, 543-1081). $17 for 2, each additional person $2. Restrooms and showers ($1.50) nearby.

Colter Bay Log Cabins: Quaint and clean 1-room cabins $25 with semi-private bath, $44-62 with private bath. 2-room cabins $62 and up.

Flagg Ranch Village: P.O. Box 187, Moran 83013 (543-2861 or 800-443-2311), on the Snake River. Simple, clean cabins with semi-private bath $26. Slightly larger rustic cabins $36, with private bath $38. Reservations recommended.

Camping

Camping is the way to see the Tetons without emptying your savings account. The park service maintains six campgrounds all on a first come-first serve basis (sites

$7). In addition, there are two trailer parks and acres of backcountry open to visitors whenever the snow's not too deep. RVs are welcome in all but Jenny Lake but no hookups are available. Information is available at any visitors center.

Park Campgrounds: All campgrounds have rest rooms, cold water, fire rings, grocery store, and picnic tables. Jenny Lake: 49 highly coveted sites; arrive early. No RVs. **Signal Mountain:** A few miles south of Colter Bay. 86 spots, usually full by noon. **Colter Bay:** 310 sites, shower and laundromat. Usually fills by 2pm. **Snake River and Lizard Creek:** Northern campgrounds, with 60 sites, convenient to Yellowstone. Fills in late afternoon. **Gros Ventre:** On the park's southern border. 360 sites. A good bet if you arrive late. Max. stay in Jenny Lake 7 days, all others 14 days. Reservations required for large groups.

Colter Bay Trailer Park: 112 sites, electrical hookups. Reserved through Grand Teton Lodge Co. (733-2811 or 543-2855). Grocery store and eateries. (Sites June-Aug. $17, May-June and Aug.-Sept. $15. Showers $1.50, towel rental $1.25.)

Flagg Ranch Village Camping: Operated by Flagg Ranch Village (543-800-443-2311). Grocery and eateries on the grounds. $9.50 for 2, $13.50 for hookups. Make reservations.

Backcountry Camping: Reserve a spot in a camping zone in a mountain canyon or on the shores of a lake by submitting an itinerary Jan. 1-June 1 to the permit office at **Moose Ranger Station** (733-2880). Pick up the permit the morning of the first day of your hike. Two-thirds of all spots left open on a first come-first serve basis; you can get a permit up to 24 hours before you set out at the Moose or Jenny Lake Ranger Stations. Open daily 8am-7pm. There are also off-trail backcountry areas where camping is unrestricted (though you must have a permit). Wood fires are not permitted above 7000 ft.

Sights and Activities

As the youngest mountain range in North America, the Tetons provide hikers, bikers, climbers, rafters and sightseers with challenges and vistas not found in more eroded ranges. **Cascade Canyon Trail,** one of the least arduous (and therefore more popular) hikes, originates at Jenny Lake. To start, take a boat trip (operated by Teton Lodge Co.) across Jenny Lake (fare $3 round-trip, $2.25 one way; children $1.50 round-trip, $1.25 one way), or hike the 2-mile trail around the lake. Trail guides (25¢) are available at the trailhead. A half-mile from the trail entrance lies the **Hidden Falls Waterfall;** the hardy can trek 6 miles further to **Lake Solitude.** Another pleasant day hike, popular for its views of wildlife, is the 4-mile walk from Colter Bay to **Hermitage Point.** The **Amphitheater Lake Trail,** which begins just south of Jenny Lake at the Lupine Meadows parking lot, will take you 9 breathtaking miles up to one of the park's many glacial lakes. Those who were bighorn sheep in past lives can take the challenge of **Static Peak Divide,** a 15-mile trail that climbs 4020 feet and offers some of the best lookouts in the park. All information centers provide pamphlets about the day hikes and sell the *Teton Trails* guide ($1.85).

Those who prefer floating to walking can rent boats at the **Colter Bay Marina** for a leisurely afternoon on Jackson Lake. (Rowboats $4.50 per hr., canoes $5 per hr. $30 deposit required. Motorboats $9 per hr., 2 hr. minimum. $50 deposit required. Open daily 7am-6pm.) Call Grand Teton Lodge Co. for more information (733-2811 or 543-2811). **Signal Mountain Marina** (543-2831) rents a greater variety of boats, but charges more. (Rowboats and canoes $5 per hr., motorboats $12.50 per hr., waterski boats and pontoons $25 per hr. Open daily 7am-6pm.) For a small fee, **Triangle X Float Trips** (733-5500) in Moose will do the work for you. (10-mile, 2- to 3-hr. trip $20, under 17 $12.50. 20-mile lunch float $40, under 17 $30.) Reservations by phone are easiest, but you can also visit the ticket office at Sirk Shirts, 245 Cache (733-8269), in Jackson. (Open daily 9am-10pm.) **Fishing** in any of the park's waters is unparalleled. A permit costs $5 for one day, $15 for five days.

The **American Indian Art Museum** (543-2467), in the Colter Bay Visitors Center, offers an extensive private collection of Native American artwork and artifacts, movies and workshops. (Open daily June-Sept. 8am-7pm, May and late Sept. 8am-5pm. Free.) During July and August you can see Cheyenne, Cherokee, Apache, and Sioux dances at Jackson Lake Lodge (Fri. at 8:30pm).

In the winter, all hiking trails and the unplowed section of Teton Park Road are open to cross-country skiers. The trail map "Winter in the Tetons" is available at the Moose Visitors Center. From January through March, naturalists lead snowshoe hikes from Moose Visitors Center (snowshoes distributed free). Make reservations at the visitors center (733-2880). Snowmobiling along the Park's well-powdered trails and up into Yellowstone is a noisy but popular winter activity. Pick up a map and guide at the Jackson Chamber of Commerce, 10 miles south at Moose. For a steep fee you can rent snowmobiles at Signal Mt. Lodge, Flagg Ranch Village, or down in Jackson (there's a $5 registration fee for all snowmobile use in the park). All campgrounds close during the winter. The Colter Bay parking lot is available for RVs and cars, and backcountry snow camping is allowed with a free permit from Moose—only for those who know what they're doing. Check with a ranger station for current weather conditions and avalanche danger. Many early trappers froze to death in the 10-foot drifts.

Jackson

Jackson overflows with camera-snapping tourists who make comical efforts to look like "real Westerners." But Jackson was the cowboy's domain long before the Tetons became a recreational destination, and plenty of Marlboro men still call this uninhibitedly Western city home. These native gentlemen are the genuine articles—their hats are Stetsons, their ragged bandanas are for more than show, and the stuff on their boots—don't ask, it's genuine.

Practical Information

Emergency: 911.

Jackson Hole Area Chamber of Commerce: 532 N. Cache St. (733-3316), in the modern wooden split-level with grass on the roof. A crucial information stop. Open daily 8am-8pm; Sept. 16-June 14 8:30am-5pm.

Bridger-Teton National Forest Headquarters: 340 N. Cache St. (733-2752), 2 blocks south of the chamber of commerce. Maps $2-8. Open daily 7:45am-5:30pm, off-season daily 7:45am-4:30pm.

Bus Lines: Jackson-Rock Springs Stages: 72 S. Glenwood St. (733-3135). Daily bus to Pinedale ($9.75) and Rock Springs ($17.78). Greyhound passes not honored. Open Mon.-Fri. 10-11:30am, Sat. and Sun. 10:30-11:30am. Connections with **Greyhound** at the Rock Springs terminal, 1005 Dewar Ave. (362-2931). Open Mon.-Fri. 8am-5pm, Sat. 8am-noon. **Powder River Transportation,** 565 N. Cache St. (733-4152), will send you east to Casper (1 per day, $34) where you can connect to Cheyenne (3 per day, $29). Also operates in conjunction with TW tours. (See Bus Tours below.) Terminal open daily 7:30am-5:30pm; off-season Mon.-Fri. 7:30am-5:30pm. **Grand Teton Lodge Co.** (733-2811) runs a shuttle twice daily in summer to Jackson Lake Lodge ($5.25, park entrance fee not included). Reserve your place at the Powder River office.

Bus Tours: Powder River Tours, 565 N. Cache St. (733-2136). Full-day tour of the Tetons with boat ride on Jenny Lake $34. **Grayline Tours,** 330 N. Glenwood St. (733-4325) in front of Dirty Jack's Theatre. Full-day tours of Grand Teton National Park and Yellowstone National Park lower loop $36. Call for reservations. **Wild West Jeep Tours** (733-9036), P.O. Box 7506. In summer only, half-day tours of the Grand Tetons and other areas. $27, seniors $24.30, under 12 $14. Make reservations.

Car Rental: Rent-A-Wreck, 1650 W. Martin Lane (733-5014). $20 per day, $109 per week; 135 free miles, 25¢ each additional mile. Open Mon.-Fri. 8:30am-5:30pm. Must be 21 with credit card or a $300 cash deposit. Must stay within 200 miles of Jackson.

Ski and Bike Rental: Hoback Sports, 40 S. Millward (733-5335). 10-speeds $12 per day, mountain bikes $17 per day; rates are lower the longer you rent the bike. Ski rental $13 per day. Open daily 9am-7pm. Must have credit card or enough cash to cover the cost of the equipment. **Skinny Skis,** 65 W. Delovey St. (733-6094). Skis $9 per day, $17 for mountaineering. Open daily 9am-9pm. Major credit card or deposit for value of equipment.

Bike Tours: Off the Deep End Travels, 733-8707; 800-223-6833 outside WY. See Grand Tetons Practical Information for prices.

Help Lines: Rape Crisis Line, 733-5162. **Weather Line,** 733-1731. 24 hour recording. **Road Information,** 733-9966; 800-442-7850 outside WY.

Post Office: 220 W. Pearl St. (733-3650), 2 blocks east of Cache St. Open Mon.-Fri. 8:30am-5pm. **ZIP code:** 83001.

Area Code: 307.

Although most services in Jackson are terribly expensive, the town makes an ideal base for trips into the Tetons, 10 miles north, or the Wind River Range, 70 miles southeast. U.S. 191 ties Jackson to I-80 at Rock Springs (180 miles south), and is the usual southern entry into town. This road continues north into Grand Teton Park and eventually reaches Yellowstone, 70 miles to the north. The streets of Jackson itself are centered around **Town Square,** a small park on Broadway and Cache St.

Accommodations, Camping, and Food

Jackson's constant influx of tourists ensures that rooms all over will be small and expensive at best, and non-existent at worst if you don't book ahead. Fortunately you can sleep affordably in one of the two local hostels. The **Bunkhouse,** in the basement of the Anvil Motel, 215 N. Cache St. (733-3668), has a lounge, kitchenette, laundromat, ski storage, and one large but quiet sleeping room with comfortable bunks. ($15; off-season $10. Linens $2.) **The Hostel (AYH),** P.O. Box 546, Teton Village 83025 (733-3415), 12 miles northwest of Jackson, is a budgetary haven among the condos and lodges of Teton Village, and a favorite of skiers because it's near the slopes. Game room, TV room, ski waxing room, and movies nightly. The rooms range from dorm-style ($13.50 per bunk, $15 for nonmembers) to private suites ($31 for 2, $42 for 3 or 4). All are clean and well maintained. If you prefer to stay in a Jackson motel, the **Lazy X Motel,** 325 N. Cache St. (733-3673), offers moderately priced attractive rooms during the summer. (Singles $28. Doubles $34.) You can always fall back on **Motel 6,** 1370 W. Broadway (733-1620), even though their rates go up steadily as the peak season approaches. (Singles from $31. Doubles from $37.)

Jackson has an RV/tent campground, the **Wagon Wheel Village,** which, though it doesn't offer amazing scenery, does not charge an arm and a leg. Call 733-4588 to reserve one of their 8 sites. (From $12.) You can also camp in the **Bridger-Teton National Forest** surrounding Jackson. Hike up Cache Creek to the south of town, or drive toward Alpine Junction on U.S. 26/89 to find spots. Check the map at the chamber of commerce for a complete list of campgrounds. (Sites $4-10.)

The Bunnery, 130 N. Cache St. (773-5474), in the "Hole-in-the-Wall" mall, has the most delicious food in town. (2 eggs, peaches, cottage cheese, toast $3.50. Sandwiches $3.50-4. Open daily 7am-9pm.) Great burgers are flipped at **Billy's Burgers,** N. Cache St. (733-3297), across from the Town Square. Get a ½-lb. cheeseburger and fries for $3.75. (Open Mon.-Sat. 11:30am-10:30pm, Sun. 11:30am-10pm.) On weekdays, a mixture of Western BBQ and Mexican delicacies is set out at **Pedro's,** 139 N. Cache St. (733-9015). $3 all-you-can-eat buffet. (Open in summer only daily 11am-8:30pm.) Just down the street, **Alexander's Lone Star Cafe,** 335 N. Cache St. (733-2850), specializes in great barbecue. (Sandwiches $3-3.75, giant dinners $6-8. Open daily 7am-9:30pm.) Bring the family to the **Wagon Wheel,** 435 N. Cache St. (733-2492), where you can wolf down all-you-can-eat rib dinners for $9, salad bar included. (Open daily 7am-10pm.)

Nightlife and Activities

Western saddles serve as bar stools at the **Million Dollar Cowboy Bar,** 25 N. Cash Dr. (733-2207), Town Square. This Jackson institution attracts a mixed group of cowpokes, high society types, and even some gay cowboys—you can't feel out of place here. (Live music Mon.-Sat. 9pm-2am, Open Mon.-Sat. 10am-2am, Sun. 11am-2am. $3-6 cover after 8:30pm.)

Cultural activities in Jackson fall into two camps—the rambunctious foot-stomping Western celebrations and the more formal, sedate presentations of music and art. Every summer evening except Sunday, the Town Square hosts an episode of the **Longest-Running Shoot-Out in the World.** For $2.50 on Friday evenings at 8pm, you can join in at the **Teton Twirlers Square Dance,** in the fair building on the rodeo grounds (733-5269 or 543-2825). In June, the town will celebrate the opening of the 47th consecutive **Jackson Hole Rodeo** (733-2805; open June-Aug. Wed. and Sat. 8pm. Tickets $5-8.) And on Memorial Day, the town bulges at the seams as tourists, natives, and local Native American tribes pour in for the dances and parades of **Old West Days.**

The Wildlife Museum (733-4909), in Grand Teton Plaza on Broadway exhibits the trophies of local hunters in extremely realistic settings. (Open May-Oct. daily 9am-6pm. Admission $2, ages 6-12 $1, under 6 free. Families $5.) The prestigious **Grand Teton Music Festival** (733-1128) holds court in Teton Village from mid-July through August. (Performances nightly at 8:30pm. Student tickets $3-5. Fri. and Sat. symphony at 8:30pm. Student tickets $9. Reserve in advance.) Throughout September, the **Jackson Hole Fall Arts Festival** attracts painters, dancers, actors, and musicians to Jackson's four main theaters.

Between May 15 and Labor Day over 100,000 city slickers and backwoods folk go white-water rafting out of Jackson. **Mad River Boat Trips,** 1060 S. Hwy. 89 (733-6203), offers the cheapest white-water and scenic raft trips (from $20), though the **Barker-Ewing Co.,** 45 W. Broadway (733-1000), is stiff competition. (Trips from $25.) Cheaper thrills include a lift 10,452 feet up Rendez-Vous Mountain on the **Jackson Hole Aerial Tram** (733-2292; fare $10, seniors $8, teens $6, ages 6-12 $2). In winter, the **Jackson Hole Ski Resort** (733-2292) offers spectacular slopes. (Lift tickets $32, under 13 $16.)

Wind River Range

The Arapahoe named the range for the turbulent rivers that tumble down to the sloping, windswept farmlands on the Wind River Range's eastern border. This simple appellation captures the beauty of the winds better than volumes of prose ever could. With its seven enormous glaciers, acres of virgin forests, and miles of primitive wilderness, the Winds are the most spectacular of Wyoming's mountains, and yet relatively undiscovered by tourists.

There are no roads into the range. It lies smack in the middle of a tremendous oval formed by U.S. 191, which runs along the western side, and U.S. 26/28/287, which follows along the range's eastern edge. From the western side, the trails are accessible from **Pinedale;** if you're coming from the east, the closest you'll get is **Lander.** Since most of the range's finest scenery lies in the **Budger Wilderness Area** on the western slope, Pinedale is a better starting point for hiking expeditions than Lander. Stop at **Pinedale Ranger District Office,** 210 W. Pine St., P.O. Box 220 (367-4326), before you venture into the range. (Open Mon.-Sat. 7:45am-4:30pm; off-season Mon.-Fri. 7:45am-4:30pm.) Fishing permits and information are available at sporting goods stores and at the **Wyoming Game and Fish Department,** 117 S. Sublette (367-4352; open Mon.-Fri. 8am-5pm; permits $5 per day, $15 per week, $40 per month). **Faler's Hardware,** 341 E. Pine (367-2324), provides excellent topographic maps ($4). (Open Mon.-Sat. 7am-7pm, Sun. 8am-5pm.)

The two most popular trailheads are at the end of the 16-mile access road that heads east out of Pinedale. The trails begin at **Elkhart Park** above giant Fremont Lake, where you will find yet another information center. (Open daily 8am-8pm.) From there, head 9 miles up the trail to the beautiful **Seneca Lakes;** hardy mountaineers will want to continue 18 miles through **Indian Pass** to the glaciers beyond. You can climb **Fremont Peak** (13,745 ft.) from here. The other trailhead at Elkhart will take you into the empty **Pine Creek** drainage, nirvana for those who love fishing. Beyond the canyon, the trail continues up to **Crows Nest Lookout** and **Glimpse Lake** which provide a beautiful bird's eye view of the icy surroundings.

Other popular destinations from Pinedale include **Gannett Peak** (at 13,800 ft., the highest mountain in the state), 10 miles east, and **Big Sandy,** 50 miles southeast on U.S. 191. Rock climbers from all over the world gather at the Big Sandy trailhead for the 8-mile jaunt into **Cirque of the Towers,** where hikers are hemmed in by sheer cliffs. At the northwestern end of the wilderness sits its most famous peak, **Squaretop.** Begin at **Green River Lake,** northwest of Pinedale on Rte. 352 off U.S. 191, for a good two-day loop around this appropriately named peak. This area and the trail leading to the Cirque are the only crowded ones in the Winds.

Access to the Winds from the other side is more time-consuming because of the longer, gentler eastern slope. One of the showpieces of this area is the broad **Shoshone Lake,** which lies at the crest of the **Shoshone Trail.** A few miles beyond the lake, the Shoshone Trail joins the **Fork Trail,** which leads into the tangled heart of the **Popo Agie** (pronounced "po-PO-zhuh") **Wilderness.** Approach this unspoiled area from Lander via the Sinks Canyon Rd. west through impressive **Sinks Canyon State Park** on Rte. 131. There are two small campgrounds here (sites $4; arrive by 3pm).

The **Lander Ranger District Offices** (332-5460), on U.S. 287, can give you information on the Popo Agie Wilderness. (Open Mon.-Fri. 8am-noon and 1-5pm.) For information on hiking in **Fitzpatrick Wilderness** in the northwestern Winds, you can write to the forest service offices at P.O. Box 186, Dubois 82513. For information on the eastern side of the Winds, write the Shoshone National Forest, P.O. Box 961, Cody 82414. To find out about the **Wind River Indian Reservation,** contact the Joint Council of Shoshone and Arapahoe Tribes, Box 217, Fort Washakie 82514.

In Pinedale, everyone's favorite place to eat is **The Wrangler Cafe,** 310 E. Pine St. (367-4233), where burgers with all the fixin's go for $3.25 and fantastic homemade pie is dished out for $1.85. (Open Mon.-Fri. 6am-10pm, Sat.-Sun. 6am-8pm.) South of town on U.S. 191, you'll find **King Cone,** home of the much vaunted Roadkill Burger ($2), as well as to a variety of shakes and sweets. To eat in Lander, try **The Breadboard,** 125 E. Main St. (332-6090), where a hardy sub costs $3. (Open Mon.-Fri. 11am-8pm. Sat. 11am-4pm.) A local favorite is **The Commons,** 170 E. Main St. (332-5149). Wrap yourself around the $2.60 waffles and bacon breakfast. (Open daily 6am-11pm.)

To stay in Pinedale, first stop in at the the **Pinedale Chamber of Commerce,** 32 E. Pine (367-2242), which has a list of accommodations and area sights. (Open in summer only, daily 8:30am-5:30pm.) Clean, comfortable rooms with A/C are available at both the **Teton Court Motel,** 123 E. Magnolia (367-4317), and the **Pine Creek Motel,** 650 W. Pine St. (367-2191). Singles at Teton from $21, at Pine Creek from $23. Doubles at both from $28. Nearby **Trail's End** campground is free, and **Fremont Lake** sites go for $6 (367-4326).

If you decide to shack up in Lander stop at the **Lander Chamber of Commerce,** 160 N. 1st St. (332-3892), for information on lodgings and current activities. (Open Mon.-Fri. 9am-5pm.) For bikers and hikers, the cheapest place to stay in Lander is **Ma's Boarding House,** Mortimer Lane (332-3123, ask for Pat Focht), at the southern end of Lander. (Overnight bunk with shower $5. Camping $1. Don't miss the breakfast-and-a-hug for $3.) Your next best bet is the **Teton Motel,** 886 Main St. (332-3582), where decent singles go for $23, and doubles for $27.

Jackson-Rock Springs Stages serves Pinedale once a day from the terminal at 1005 Dewar Ave. (362-2931), in Rock Springs ($8.32), and from the stop at 72 S. Glenwood St. (733-3135) in Jackson ($9.75). The flag stop in Pinedale is at the northern Phillips 66 station (367-4311). Greyhound passes are not honored. **Powder River Transportation** can connect you with Lander from Jackson or Casper; Greyhound passes are honored.

Pinedale's **ZIP code** is 82941; Lander's is 82520. The **area code** in the Winds is 307.

Near the Winds

The great plains stretch southwest from Lander as far as the eye can see and the lonely expanses of sagebrush are broken only by the glaring blacktop of U.S. 28. Thirty miles from Lander down this empty highway lie the remains of **South Pass City** and **Atlantic City,** two erstwhile mining towns whose crumbling wooden buildings stand as monuments to both the stamina and avarice of Wyoming's first pioneers.

Recent restoration efforts have helped to refurbish both communities, and the interesting historical displays in the **South Pass Visitors Center** are worth the drive down the 5-mile dirt detour from the highway. (Open Mon.-Fri. 9am-5pm. Ask a local for directions.) This rough-and-ready frontier community also played an important role in the women's suffrage movement. William Bright, a representative from South Pass City, wrote and introduced the bill which, when passed in 1869, made Wyoming the first territory to allow women the right to vote and hold office. The National Forest Service maintains a splendid forested **campground** just out of town near Atlantic City. (Sites $4.) 85 miles northeast of Lander on U.S. 20, the city of Thermopolis maintains the world's largest single mineral hot springs at **Hot Springs State Park** (864-3771). In 1896, the U.S. purchased the springs from the Shoshone and Arapahoe tribes for $60,000 worth of cattle and food supplies. Once a year (usually in Aug.), Thermopolis celebrates with the **Gift of Waters Pageant. Bighorn Hot Springs** gush over 18 million gallons of 135°F water daily, constantly replenishing the soothing steam at the **State Bath House,** at the northeast edge of town on U.S. 20 and Rte. 789. The bath house maintains the thermal brew at 100-105°F in a clean and well-kept indoor and outdoor soaking pool. (Open Mon.-Fri. 8am-6pm, Sat.-Sun. noon-6pm. Towel and bathing suit rental 30¢.)

The **chamber of commerce,** 220 Park St. (864-2636), in the State Park Building, provides adequate assistance and a schedule of special events in Thermopolis. (Open Mon.-Fri. 8am-5pm.) You can stay at the simple **Plaza Hotel** (864-2251), on the park ground. (Singles $15. Doubles $22.) **Pumpernicks,** 512 Broadway (864-5151), serves delicious sandwiches ($2.50-5), salads, and steaks, and has Old West memorabilia strung up all over the walls. (Open Mon.-Sat. 7am-9pm, Sat.-Sun. 9am-10pm.) **The Sideboard Cafe,** 109 S. 6th St., serves ample hamburgers for $2.75 and dinners for $4.59-7. Simple but good. (Open daily 6am-10pm.)

SOUTHWEST

The Southwestern states lure visitors with warm weather and a relaxed lifestyle, but the four states also have much more to offer. Some of the world's most awe-inspiring scenery, including the Grand Canyon and Carlsbad Caverns, can be found in the region, as well as a rich history of cultural interaction unmatched in the rest of the U.S.

The Anasazi of the 10th and 11th centuries were the first to discover that the arid lands of the Southwest, with proper management, could support an advanced agricultural civilization. The Navajo, Apache, and Pueblo nations migrated into the region later, sharing the land with the Hopi descendants of the Anasazi. Spanish conquest came early in the 17th century, bringing European and *mestizo* colonists to modern-day Texas and New Mexico. Mexican independence in 1821 was followed by Anglo-American conquest of the region: the Texan War of Independence in 1836, which began as a revolt by Mexican and U.S. settlers against Santa Anna's dictatorship, led to the Mexican-American War. Santa Fe, Nuevo Mexico, became the first foreign capital ever to fall to the U.S., and, in 1853, Mexico's beaten government agreed to sell a tract of land south of the Gila River that today forms a large part of Arizona and New Mexico.

The legacy of this history is still seen throughout the Southwest, in the large Hispanic and Native American populations, in the Spanish and tribal place names, and in the numerous historical sites. But much of the land retains the tranquility of nature undisturbed by human forces. The grand, lonely beauty of the desert stretches for miles, and the water- and wind-scored landscape—the cliffs of the Guadalupe Mountains, the gorges of the Colorado and Rio Grande, the redstone arches and twisted spires of southern Utah and northern Arizona—stands as testament to past and present battles waged by erosion.

Travel

Travel in the Southwest introduces extremes of temperature and distance unknown in other regions. **Amtrak** serves cross-country routes; lines from Dallas and Houston converge in San Antonio and continue through El Paso, Tucson, and Phoenix on the way to Los Angeles, while another line passes through Santa Fe, Albuquerque, and Flagstaff en route to Los Angeles. (Call 800-872-7245 for details.) **Greyhound** serves the major cities and towns along the interstates; service in rural northern New Mexico is provided by **Texas, New Mexico, & Oklahoma (TNM&O) Coaches,** a Greyhound affiliate.

Nothing can substitute for a car when touring the Southwest. Public transportation serves a few of the cities, but cities are not the reason for traveling to the Southwest. **Hitching** is usually safe but unreliable, especially in the more remote regions, and is unadvisable in larger cities such as Phoenix. **Flying** to the Southwest is relatively inexpensive. Phoenix is the hub of **America West Airlines,** which serves Los Angeles, Denver, and Chicago.

Balmy winter weather in the lower elevations of the Southwest attracts many travelers, so make reservations for accommodations if you travel from December to April. Crowds understandably diminish in summer, when temperatures regularly top 100°. **Youth hostels** are becoming more plentiful; call ahead or mail in reservations to stay in the more popular ones at the Grand Canyon, Phoenix, Taos, Salt Lake City, and Las Vegas.

Outdoors

While predominantly arid, the landscapes of every Southwestern state include everything from hot, desolate flatlands to breezy mountain ridges. In one season, you can camp out under a desert sky, ski down powdered slopes, and hike through

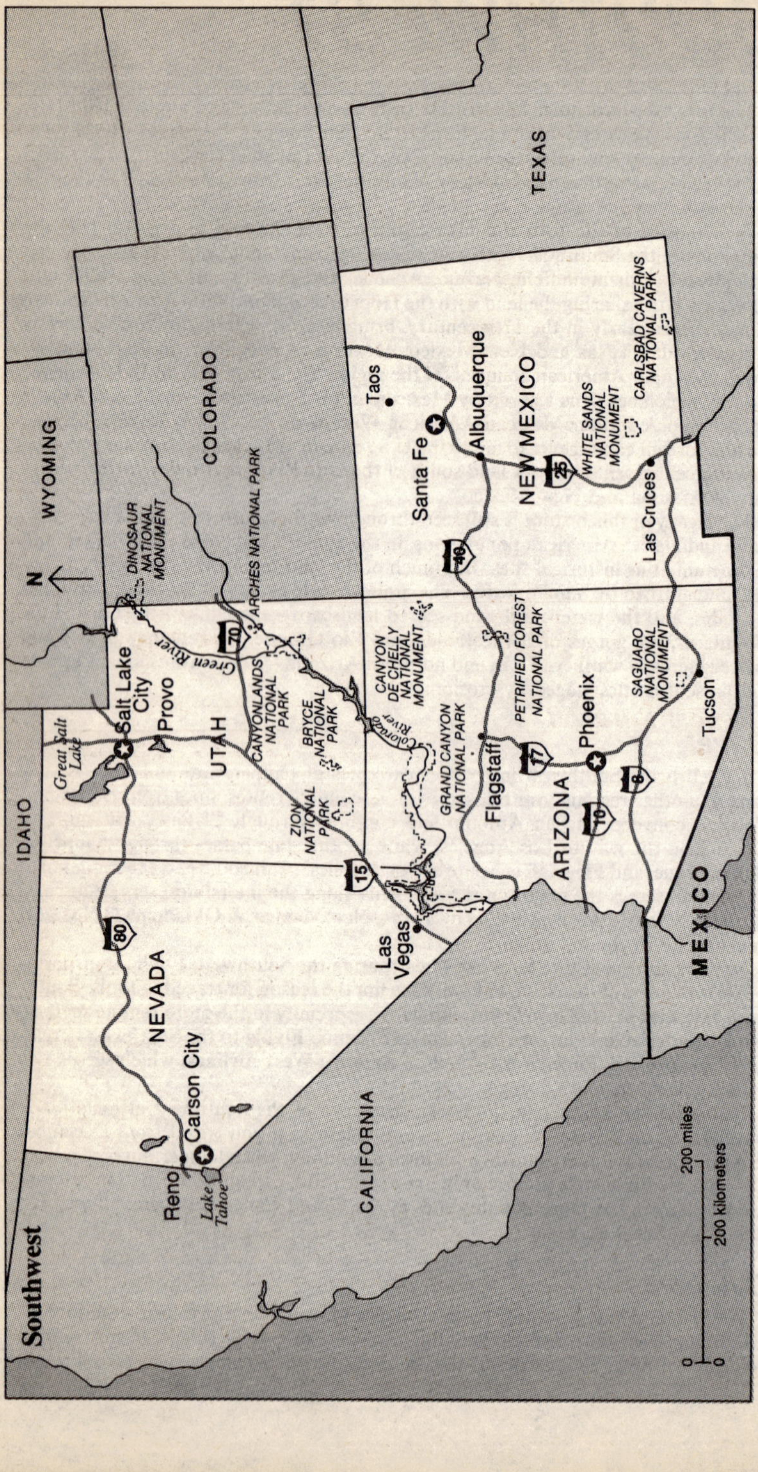
Southwest
N
IDAHO
WYOMING
COLORADO
TEXAS
NEVADA
UTAH
ARIZONA
NEW MEXICO
CALIFORNIA
MEXICO
Reno
Lake Tahoe
Carson City
Salt Lake City
Great Salt Lake
Provo
Las Vegas
Flagstaff
Phoenix
Tucson
Santa Fe
Taos
Albuquerque
Las Cruces
DINOSAUR NATIONAL MONUMENT
ARCHES NATIONAL PARK
CANYONLANDS NATIONAL PARK
BRYCE NATIONAL PARK
ZION NATIONAL PARK
GRAND CANYON NATIONAL PARK
CANYON DE CHELLY NATIONAL MONUMENT
PETRIFIED FOREST NATIONAL PARK
SAGUARO NATIONAL MONUMENT
WHITE SANDS NATIONAL MONUMENT
CARLSBAD CAVERNS NATIONAL PARK
Green River
Colorado River
80
15
70
40
17
10
8
25
200 miles
200 kilometers
0
0

piñon forests. In southern Arizona, you'll find the barren sandy flats and saguaro cacti of the Sonoran Desert, home of Wile E. Coyote and speedy roadrunners. Southern New Mexico shares the Chihuahuan Desert's tenacious, brilliant flowers and pine-covered mountains with West Texas and Northern Mexico. To the north, in southern Utah and northern Arizona, lies the slickrock country of the Painted Desert, where running water has gouged the sandstone bedrock into fantastic shapes and dramatic canyons. The southern Rockies tumble out of Colorado into the Sangre de Cristo, San Juan, Sandia, Manzano, Jicarilla, and Sacramento ranges of New Mexico. The Guadalupe range straddles the Texas-New Mexico border between El Paso and Carlsbad; farther south the Davis Mountains complete the picture. The desolate Llano Estacado plain covers eastern New Mexico and western Texas.

Much of this incredible scenery is yours: The federal government owns a hefty portion of the region, and access is, for the most part, cheap and easy. Well-maintained park service campgrounds dot the region. By all means see the tourist magnets such as the Grand Canyon, but also take advantage of the less publicized, less crowded, and more plentiful forest service and Bureau of Land Management (BLM) holdings. The forest service or BLM offices in most major towns are great places to ask about outdoor activities. Best of all, you can pretty much wander and camp at will throughout their property without cost. Get a free campfire permit at the nearest ranger station before starting out.

The **National Park Service** has two regional offices in the Southwest region: the **Southwest Regional Office,** with jurisdiction over New Mexico, Utah, and eastern Arizona (P.O. Box 728, Santa Fe, NM 87504-0728; 505-988-6375); and the **Western Regional Office,** which covers Nevada and most of Arizona (450 Golden Gate Ave., P.O. Box 36063, San Francisco, CA 94102; 415-556-4122). The appropriate **National Forest Regional Offices** are the **Southwestern Office,** Federal Bldg., Albuquerque, NM 87102, and the **Intermountain Office,** Federal Bldg., 324 25th St., Ogden, UT 84401.

Desert Survival

The body loses a gallon or more of liquid per day when it is hot, and water must be replaced. Whether you are driving or hiking, tote two gallons of water per person per day; less is adequate at higher altitudes and during winter months. Drink regularly, even when you're not thirsty. You can't merely drink huge quantities of water after you've become dehydrated—indeed, it may be dangerous to do so. If you're drinking sweet beverages, dilute them with water to avoid a reaction to high sugar content. Even juices should be diluted by at least 50%. Alcohol and caffeine cause dehydration; if you indulge, compensate with more liquid. Avoid salt tablets, which shock your system and can be dangerous.

Travelers should allow a couple of days to adjust to the climate, especially if planning a hike or other strenuous activity. This warning applies to activity at high altitudes as well as in low-lying deserts. The desert is not the place to sunbathe. A hat, long-sleeved loose-fitting shirts of a light fabric, and long trousers actually keep you cooler and protect you from exposure to the sun.

In winter, nighttime temperatures can drop below freezing at high elevations, even though afternoon temperatures may be in the 60s or 70s. The desert is infamous for its flash floods, mostly during spring and fall. A dry gulch can turn into a violent river with astonishing speed; if you're camping, try to locate a site that is uphill or at least flat.

Hitching in the desert is safest heat-wise between October and April, but is possible year-round. Carry a lot of water and count on delays.

Those **driving** in the desert should carry water for the radiator. A two- to five-gallon container should be adequate. Drivers should purchase a desert water bag (about $5-10) at a hardware or automotive store; this large canvas bag is strapped onto the front of the car and filled with water. If you see the temperature gauge climbing, turn off the air-conditioning. If an overheating warning light comes on, stop immediately and wait about a half-hour before trying again. Don't shut off the engine; the fan will help cool things down under the hood. Turning your car's heater on full force will help cool the engine. Never open the radiator until it has cooled, because internal pressure will cause scalding steam to erupt out of it. And never pour water on the engine to cool it off: the temperature change may crack the engine block.

For any trips off major roads, a board and shovel are useful in case your car gets stuck in sand; the board can be shoved under a tire to gain traction and the shovel can take care of minor quagmires. Letting some air out of your tires can also help you drive free.

Reservations

Visiting Native American reservations can either be an enlightening cultural experience or the cheapest sort of imperialistic voyeurism. Avoid the latter by learning about the beliefs, customs, and politics of the various tribes before you blunder through their territories—which are considered sovereign areas by the U.S. government. The museums of Flagstaff, the **Pueblo Indian Cultural Center** in Albuquerque, the **University of New Mexico Museum of Anthropology,** Phoenix's **Heard Museum,** and the **Native American Folk Art Center** in Santa Fe each offer a general background of Southwest Native American life.

Books and museums, however, say little about contemporary tribal life. The overall picture is not pretty; unemployment on the reservations is well above 50%. Although federal law prohibits alcohol on the reservations, wet towns such as Gallup exist just outside their borders and fuel the rampant alcoholism among Native Americans. This disease combines with wandering livestock to make nighttime driving in these areas very dangerous. Realize as well that reservations are not strictly preservations: most Native Americans live in modern houses, drive trucks, and wear clothes that accord with our conception of a Southwestern cowboy's.

For all this, the reservations are still fascinating places to visit. Talk to rangers at national parks and monuments near reservations, who are often informal experts on local customs and sights. General stores and gas stations in tribal capitals such as Window Rock are often the best places to find Native Americans who don't mind talking to outsiders. While you may wear shorts on the reservation, avoid tight-fitting or "provocative" clothing. Don't photograph anyone without permission—some residents believe that one's fate is tied with the artificially-produced likeness. Abide by laws intended to protect customs and rights of privacy; you may be arrested or fined by tribal police if you violate a village ordinance prohibiting non-native travel on local trails. Visitors may be deliberately ignored in stores and roads, particularly by the elderly.

Facilities for tourists on most reservations are minimal and overpriced. Camp and picnic if you can; primitive sites are usually free. Many back roads, usually unpaved, are passable only by four-wheel drive. Bus service is scarce, but Gray Line Tours runs to many reservations.

Arizona

Arizona has some of the world's most awe-inspiring natural scenery. Within the Cactus State lie the Grand Canyon's immense labyrinths, the four-story cliff-dwellings tucked into the striated walls of Canyon de Chelly, Monument Valley's fantastic sandstone formations, the streaked and arid landscape of the Painted Desert, and the *saguaro* cacti and old mining towns dotting the Sonoran Desert. Compared with these wonders, the state's cities often appear as little more than massive, horizontal air-conditioners, but the towns aren't just rest stops. In the cities and towns live Arizon's multicultural people, from retirees in search of sun to Native American tribes trying to preserve their heritage.

Practical Information

Capital: Phoenix.

Tourist Information: Arizona Office of Tourism, 3507 N. Central Ave., #506, Phoenix 85012 (255-3618). **Arizona State Parks,** 1688 W. Adams St., Phoenix 85007.

Time Zone: Mountain (2 hr. behind Eastern). Arizona (with the exception of the reservations) does not follow Daylight Saving Time, so in summer it is 1 hr. behind the rest of the Mountain Time Zone. **Postal Abbreviation:** AZ.

Official Neckwear: The bolo tie, with big rhinestones.

Grand Canyon

All human works and words fade to insignificance when confronted with the Grand Canyon. Next to the canyon's vastness, 277 miles long, 13 miles wide, and over a mile deep, our greatest structures are like models built of matchsticks. And most epic words to describe its shimmering rose and violet buttes are like whispers in the canyon's immense stillness. Big? Hoo boy, you bet!

Until six million years ago, the Grand Canyon was just another hill. Then, for reasons still disputed, the Colorado Rim began to flow right through it. Against the rushing might of the Colorado, the canyon's soft limestone, sandstone, and shale yielded quickly. Look at the incredibly intricate pattern the river cut, though, and you might find equally plausible the legend of the Grand Canyon as a sort of Native American Garden of Eden.

Grand Canyon National Park consists of three areas: the South Rim, which includes Grand Canyon Village, the North Rim, and the canyon gorge itself. Because it is more accessible, the slightly lower South Rim draws 10 times more visitors than the higher, more heavily forested North Rim.

The 13-mile distance that traverses the canyon is a two-day adventure for sturdy hikers, while the 214 miles of road are a good 5-hour drive for those who would rather explore from above. Remember that, despite commercial exploitation, the Grand Canyon is still untamed; every year several careless hikers also take what locals morbidly refer to as "the 12-second tour."

South Rim

In summer, everything on two legs or four wheels for miles around converges on this side of the Grand Canyon. If you plan to visit during the summer, make reservations for everything, and be prepared for crowds. During the winter there are fewer tourists; however, many of the canyon's hotels and facilities are closed.

Practical Information

Emergency: 911 or 638-2477.

Visitor Information: Park Headquarters, 638-7888; open 8am-5pm. **Main Switchboard,** 638-2631. 24 hours. **Lodging reservations,** Reservations Dept., Grand Canyon National Park Lodges, Grand Canyon 86023 (638-2401). South Rim hotel information, 638-2631. **Visitors Center,** Grand Canyon Village. Open 8am-8pm; off-season 8am-5pm. **Transportation Information Desk,** in Bright Angel Lodge (638-2631). Reservations for mule rides, bus tours, Phantom Ranch, and taxi. Open daily 6am-6pm. **Visitor Activities Line,** 638-9304. 24-hour recording. **Weather and road conditions,** 638-2245. 24-hour recording. **Backcountry Information Line,** 638-2474. Current trail and weather conditions. Open 11am-5pm. At the South Rim, grab a copy of the informative *The Guide,* available in the village.

Nava-Hopi Bus Lines: 774-5003. Leaves Flagstaff Greyhound station daily at 7:25am, 9:05am, and 2:50pm. Leaves Bright Angel Lodge at Grand Canyon for Flagstaff daily at 9:45am and 5pm. Round-trip $22.30, with Greyhound Ameripass $10.70.

Post Office: 638-2512, across the street from the visitors center. Open Mon.-Fri. 8:30am-5pm, Sat. 10am-2pm; in winter Mon.-Fri. 8:30am-5pm. Lobby open 24 hours. **ZIP code:** 86023.

Area Code: 602.

From Flagstaff, the fastest and most scenic route to the South Rim is Hwy. 93 south to I-40 east; Rte. 64 north then takes you to the Desert View entrance in the eastern part of the park. From Flagstaff Rte. 64 can also be reached by driving west on I-40, but Rte. 180 north is the quickest way to the South Rim (83 miles). Admission to the Grand Canyon is $5 per car, $2 for travelers using other modes of transportation—even bus passengers must pay.

The National Park Service operates two free **shuttle buses.** The **West Rim Loop** runs between West Rim Junction and Hermit's Rest, with stops at all the scenic vistas along the way (operates Memorial Day-Labor Day every 15 min. 7:30am-6:45pm). The **Village Loop** covers Bright Angel Lodge, West Rim Junction, the visitors center, Grand Canyon Village, and Yavapai Point (operates year-round, every 15 min. 5:45am-11pm).

Thanks to the efforts of the park service, the South Rim is quite accessible by wheelchair; pick up the free pamphlet "Access for Visitors" at the visitors center.

Accommodations and Camping

Most accommodations on the South Rim except those listed below are outrageously expensive. The campsites listed are usually full by 10am in summer. Campground overflow usually winds up in the **Kaibab National Forest,** adjacent to the park along the southern border, where you can pull off a dirt road and camp for free. Greyhound stops at Bright Angel Lodge and you can check your luggage at the lodge for 50¢ per day.

Grand Canyon International Hostel (AYH), 76 Tonto St., P.O. Box 270, Grand Canyon Village 86023 (638-9018). Take the Village Loop shuttle bus to the rangers headquarters; the hostel is ¼ mile away on a clearly marked route. Show up at 4pm to move into unreserved beds. You'll be awakened at 7am to do designated chores. Open 7-9am and 4-11pm. Curfew 11pm. $8; extra $1 for sleepsack, 50¢ if you have a sleeping bag. Try to reserve at least 2 days in advance.

Bright Angel Lodge (638-2401), Grand Canyon Village. Scout-style rustic cabins with plumbing but no heat. Very convenient. Singles $40. A few rooms with no plumbing $27. Each additional person $6. Reserve rooms at least 6 months in advance for summer, 6 weeks in advance for winter.

Maswik Lodge, Grand Canyon Village (638-2401). Small, clean cabins $34 (singles or doubles). Each additional person $8. Reservations required.

Mather Campground, Grand Canyon Village, ½ mile from the visitors center. Shady, relatively isolated sites $6. Make reservations through Ticketron outlets or request information from Mather Campground, National Park Service, Grand Canyon 86023.

Trailer Village, next to Mather Campground. This campground was clearly designed with the RV in mind. Campsites resemble driveways and aren't secluded. Sites $10 with hookup. For reservations, contact Grand Canyon National Park Lodges.

Desert View Campsite, 25 miles east of Grand Canyon Village. 50 sites; $6 each. No reservations accepted, so get there early. Open May 15-Oct. 30.

Ten-X Campground (638-2443), in the Kaibab National Forest, 10 miles south of Grand Canyon Village on Hwy. 64. Chemical toilets, water. 70 sites; $6 each. No reservations. Open April-Nov.

Phantom Ranch, on the canyon floor, a 4-hr. hike down the Kaibab Trail. Dorm beds $18. Cabin for 1 or 2 people $50, each additional person $10. Reservations required 6 months in advance for the April-Oct. season, but check at the Bright Angel Transportation Desk (see above) for last-minute cancellations.

To camp overnight on the canyon floor (free), you must make reservations at the **Backcountry Reservations Office,** South Rim, Grand Canyon National Park, Grand Canyon 86023 (638-2474; open daily 7am-5pm). They start taking reservations for the following year on Oct. 1; reserve a site as early as possible. Some people resort to sleeping in their cars.

Food

Haute cuisine is not the local specialty. There are crowds everywhere and restaurant owners pull every trick to inflate prices. Buy groceries (and anything else you need) at **Babbit's General Store** (638-2262), across from the visitors center. (Open daily 8am-8pm.) You may find the best deals in the rowdy employees' canteen on Center Rd., near the hostel.

Yavapai Lodge Cafeteria, Grand Canyon Village (638-7509), has reasonable prices. Sandwiches cost $2-3, small salads about $1. (Open Mon.-Sat. 6-11am and 11:30am-9pm.) **Bright Angel Restaurant,** in Bright Angel Lodge (638-6389), serves edible fare at practically palatable prices in synthetic Western surroundings. The best deal is the three-egg omelette with fries, vegetable, and roll for $3.45. (Open daily 6:30am-10pm.) After a hot hike around the canyon, the soda fountain at Bright Angel Lodge beckons seductively. (Open daily 11am-9pm.)

Activities

Give yourself two days to see the Grand Canyon. Few experiences are as frustrating as climbing on the 5pm bus to Flagstaff just as the shadows begin to lengthen and the hazy pinks and blues of midday give way to the more dramatic sunset shades. If you have the time, the best way to see the canyon is to hike down into it. The park service maintains two trails: **Bright Angel Trail,** which begins below the Bright Angel Lodge, and **South Kaibab Trail,** which begins at Yaki Point. The Bright Angel trail is less strenuous than the Kaibab and has rest houses (with water during summer) 1½ miles and 3 miles from the rim and water, shade, picnic tables, and toilets at **Indian Gardens,** 4½ miles out. The Kaibab trail has better vistas, but it is much steeper, and no water is provided. For detailed descriptions of these trails, pick up copies of "Hiking the Bright Angel and Kaibab Trails" and "South Rim Day Hikes and Walks" at the visitors center. One local rule: If you meet a mule train, stand quietly by the side of the trail and obey all the wrangler's instructions so as not to spook the animals.

If you have made arrangements to spend the night on the canyon floor, the best route is to hike down the Kaibab trail (3-4 hr., depending on conditions) and back up the Bright Angel (7-8 hr.) the following day. The hikes down Bright Angel trail to Indian Gardens and Plateau Point, where you can look down 1360 feet to the river, make excellent daytrips. A free **Hiker's Special Bus** departs daily from the Backcountry Reservation office for the south Kaibab Trailhead at 7:30 and 10:30am, and returns at 8:30 and 11:30am.

If you don't feel like descending into the depths of the canyon, follow the **Rim Trail** east to Grandeur Point and the **Yavapai Museum,** or west to **Hermit's Rest,** using the shuttles as desired. There are no fences or railings between you and oblivion. The Eastern Rim trail is packed at dusk with sunset-watchers and the Yavapai Museum at the end of the trail has a sweeping view of the canyon during the day from a glassed-in observation deck. (Museum open daily 8am-6pm. Free.) The Western Rim trail leads to some incredible vistas, notably **Hopi Point,** a favorite for sunsets, and the **Abyss,** where the canyon wall drops almost vertically to the Tonto plateau 3000 feet below.

A funny thing often happens in the Grand Canyon. Otherwise reasonable people, who would no sooner walk 8 miles on flat ground than they would attempt to swim the Atlantic, suddenly think they can hike that distance straight up a cliff in 100° heat. Though some hikers can travel to the canyon floor and fight their way back in a single day, rangers advise strongly against it. The heat and the height will take their toll. You don't have to be superhuman to hike the canyon, but if you're not in reasonably good shape, don't go farther than a mile or two down the trail. Pick up a copy of the pamphlet "Hiking Safely at Grand Canyon" at the visitors center before you leave, and bring lots of water.

The park service rangers present a variety of free informative talks and hikes. Listings of each day's events are available at the visitors center or in the *Grand Canyon Guide* (10¢), available everywhere in the village. Every evening at 8:30pm, a free presentation highlights some aspect of the Grand Canyon in Mather Amphitheater, behind the visitors center. The park also offers a variety of activities for younger visitors. Pick up a copy of *Grand Canyon's Young Adventurer,* available at the visitors center, with entertaining stories, scavenger hunts, and puzzles.

In addition to the freebies offered by the National Park Service, a variety of commercial tours cover the South Rim. Tours by helicopter, airplane, inflatable raft, and mule are beyond the reach of most budget travelers. Of the three bus tours, the Sunset and West Rim tours cover mostly places accessible by free shuttle buses. You may decide to take the tour to West Desert View (3 hr. 45 min., 2 per day in summer, 1 per day in winter; tickets $16, children $8). Unless you have a car, this tour is the only way to reach Desert View, 26 miles east of the village, with an even more commanding panorama of the canyon to the north and west, as well as the Painted Desert to the east. Contact the Bright Angel Transportation Desk (638-6576) for information on all commercial tours.

North Rim

Those who are coming from Utah or Nevada, or want a more rugged, less crowded Grand Canyon experience, should consider the North Rim. Here things are a bit less tamed, a bit cooler, and much more serene. The view from the North Rim is at least as spectacular as the view from the South Rim.

Unfortunately, getting to the North Rim without a car is difficult, since there is virtually no public transportation. Canyon visitors seem wary of those on foot, so hitching is not an option.

The North Rim is a 200-mile-plus, stunningly scenic drive from the South Rim. Take Rte. 64 east to 89 north; 64 south then hits Rte. 67, the road leading into the canyon. Between the first snows at the end of October and May 15, Rte. 67 is closed to traffic. Only a snowmobile can get you to the North Rim.

There is no visitors center on this side of the park, but you can direct questions to rangers at the entrance station and the information desk in **Grand Canyon Lodge** (638-2611; open daily 8am-8pm). The lodge is at the very end of Rte. 67. The front desk is open 24 hours. The North Rim **emergency** phone (638-7805) is monitored 24 hours a day.

Accommodations, Camping and Food

As camping within the confines of the Grand Canyon National Park is limited to designated campgrounds, only a lucky minority of North Rim visitors get to spend the night "right there." If you can't get in-park lodgings, the **Kaibab National Forest** runs from north of Jacob Lake to the park entrance. Camp in an established site, or pull off the main road onto any forest road and camp for free. Another option is **Canyonlands International Youth Hostel** (801-644-5554), Kanab, UT 84741. It is 1½ hours north of the Grand Canyon, up Rte. 89, an equal distance south of Bryce Canyon in Utah. The hostel sleeps 40 in newly restored cabins. There is also a large kitchen and free beverages. (Office open daily 8-10am and 5-10pm. Non-AYH, but all hostel cards honored; $8, nonmembers $10. Reservations recommended.)

Grand Canyon Lodge, on the edge of the rim. Rooms start at $43 for 2. Write or call TW Recreational Services, P.O. Box 400, Cedar City, UT 84720 (801-586-7686).

Kaibab Lodge, on Rte. 67 (638-2389), 5 miles north of the Park entrance station. A quiet, secluded lodge with a restaurant. Singles $41. Doubles $54. For reservations, contact Kaibab Lodge, North Rim, Rural Rte., Fredonia 85719. Open May 28-Oct. 1.

North Rim Campground, on Rte. 67, near the rim. You can't really see into the canyon from the pine-covered site, but you know it's there. Near food store, recreation room, and showers. Sites $6. Reserve by writing to North Rim Campground, Grand Canyon National Park, Grand Canyon 86023.

Kaibab National Forest Sites: DeMotte Park Campground, 18 miles north of the North Rim Entrance Station. 20 pleasant, shaded, and remote sites. Water and restrooms. **Jacob Lake**

Campground, 32 miles north of the park entrance, at the junction of U.S. 89A and Rte. 67 (643-7395). 48 sites. Both charge $6 and operate on a first come-first serve basis.

Activities

A ½-mile paved trail takes you from the Grand Canyon Lodge to **Bright Angel Point,** which commands a fantastic view of the Canyon. **Point Imperial** overlooks Marble Canyon and the lesser known **Grand Canyon East Gorge** where thickets of whitebark aspen turn yellow in the autumn. Jutting out of the canyon in the east, the **Walhalla Plateau** obscures a full view of the canyon's sweep. **Point Sublime,** to the west, is accessible by Sublime Road, recommended for rugged trucks and four-wheel drive vehicles only.

The North Rim offers nature walks and evening programs, both at the North Rim Campground and at Grand Canyon Lodge. Check at the information desk or campground bulletin boards for schedules. Half-day mule trips ($25) descend into the canyon from Grand Canyon Lodge (638-2292, in winter 801-679-8665; open daily 7:30am-9pm). Trips depart daily at 7:30am and 12:30pm. Ask at the desk in the lobby about the much more scenic full-day trips ($52).

On warm evenings, the Grand Canyon Lodge fills with an eclectic group of international travelers, American families, and rugged adventurers. Some frequent the **Lodge Saloon** for drinks, jukebox disco, and the enthusiasm of a young crowd. Others look to the warm air rising from the canyon, a full moon, and the occasional shooting stars for their intoxication at the day's end.

Northeastern Arizona

Navajo and Hopi Reservations

Window Rock, near the edge of a reservation stretching from Lake Powell, Utah, to south of Crownpoint, New Mexico, is the capital of the Navajo Nation. This is the largest reservation in the U.S., only the beginning of what may be a strange and foreign journey through a desert that is part America and part Third World. The Navajo and their neighbors, the Hopi, whose reservation is enclosed by the Navajo Reservation, have lived in this region for centuries and, despite U.S. citizenship, don't really consider themselves part of a national "melting pot." They, and not the U.S. government, have sovereignty over this large but agriculturally unproductive land. Over the years they have been treated brutally by Spanish, Mexican, and U.S. governments; don't expect too much hospitality.

A visit to these two reservations gives a unique glance at a land that most U.S. residents never see. Reservation politics are lively but obscure, written up only in the *Navajo Times* or in regional sections of Denver, Albuquerque, or Phoenix newspapers. Recently an activist from outside the reservation used a headlock to attempt an unsuccessful citizen's arrest of the local Bureau of Indian Affairs director, and scandals regularly erupt over tribal leadership and misappropriated federal funds.

There are no central visitors centers for the reservations. For information on the Hopis, visit their cultural center (see below). The Navajo Nation is more spread out; several tribal parks have their own small information booths. Pick up their excellent *Visitors Guide to the Navajo Nation* ($3), which includes a detailed map. (Both open in summer 7am-8pm; in winter 8am-5pm.)

The "border towns" of Gallup, NM, and Flagstaff, AZ, are good entry points to the reservations; rent cars in one of these towns. Both are served by frequent **Greyhound** schedules along I-40. No public transportation goes into or within the reservations, with the notable exception of the **Navajo Transit Authority** (729-5457) in Fort Defiance, 6 miles north of Window Rock. One bus per day leaves Tuba City, AZ, at 6am and travels along Rte. 264 through the Hopi mesa towns (flag stops) to Window Rock, arriving at 9:50am. (Leaves Window Rock heading west at 3pm, $14.) The only reasonable way to see this part of the country is to rent a sturdy car and spend a few days. One good route is a loop along Rte. 264 from Tuba City east through Hopi land to Ganado, then north along U.S. 160 to Monument Valley and Navajo National Monument. A great detour is the drive northwest along Rte. 98 to Lake Powell, near Page, AZ, on the Utah border (see Utah). Plan to camp at the national monuments or Navajo campgrounds, and expect to pay dearly for the privilege.

In addition to the town and tribal government, Window Rock features the geological formation that gives the town its name. The tribal park is an ideal (and free) picnic spot.

On the Hopi Reservation, the **Hopi Cultural Center** (734-2401), on Rte. 264 in the community of **Second Mesa,** delineates the world of the tribe whose ancestors, the Anasazi, lived here centuries before the Navajo and their cousins the Apache arrived. The center consists of a museum of pottery, photography, and handicrafts, along with four gift shops, a motel, and a restaurant. The motel (734-2401) is expensive but decent and requires reservations two weeks to a month in advance. (Singles $50. Doubles $55.) The restaurant is surprisingly reasonable. Sandwiches cost $3.50-4.50, Native American dishes $3-5. (Open daily 6:30am-9pm. Museum open Mon.-Fri. 9am-5pm. Admission $2, students $1.50, children 75¢.)

Inquire at the cultural center or at the Flagstaff Chamber of Commerce for the dates and sites of the **Hopi village dances.** These religious ceremonies are announced only a few days in advance and last from sunrise to sundown. The dances are highly formal occasions; tourists may come to watch, but should not wear shorts, tank tops, or other casual wear. Picture-taking is strictly forbidden.

Monument Valley and Navajo National Monument

You will probably recognize the red rock towers of **Monument Valley Navajo Tribal Park** from the numerous western movies filmed here. The 1000-foot monoliths helped boost John Wayne to great heights of heroism. The best and cheapest way to see the valley is via the Park's 17-mile looping **Valley Drive.** This dirt road winds in and out of the most dramatic monuments, including the famous paired **Mittens** and the slender **Totem Pole.** The gaping ditches, large rocks, and mudholes on this road will do horrible things to your car. Drive at your own risk, and hold your breath. Much of the valley can be reached only in sturdy four-wheel-drive vehicles or by a long hike. In winter, the rocky towers are laced with snow, and almost all the tourists are gone. (Inquire about snow and road conditions at the Flagstaff Chamber of Commerce.)

The valley drive begins at the **visitors center** (672-2366), 4 miles off U.S. 163. The park entrance is 24 miles north on U.S. 163 from the town of Kayenta and the intersection with U.S. 160. (Park open May-Sept. 7:45am-6pm; off-season 8am-5pm. Free.)

Twenty miles past Kayenta on U.S. 160, Rte. 564 takes you to **Navajo National Monument.** This stunning site consists of three Anasazi cliff-dwellings, including **Keet Seel,** the best-preserved site in the Southwest. Inscription House has been closed, and entrance into Keet Seel and **Betatakin,** a 135-room complex, is limited to 25 people per day in ranger-led groups. (Tours daily at 9am, noon, and 2pm; try to make reservations at least two months in advance. Write Navajo National Monument, Tanalea 86044.) For $50, Navajo guides will put you on a horse, lead you down the 8-mile trail, and leave you with a ranger to explore the 400-year-old ruins left by the Anasazi. Allow a full day for the ride and the strenuous hike. Rangers also lead 5-mile hikes. You can hike on your own, but you need a permit. The **visitors center** (672-2366) has a craft shop and pottery and artifacts displays. (Open 8am-6pm; off-season 8am-5pm.)

The Navajo maintain a small campground with water next to the Monument Valley Tribal Park Visitors Center. (Sites $7.) The one at the National Monument has no showers or hookups, but it's free and has the added advantage of nightly ranger talks. If you need hookups, there is a **KOA** (801-727-3280), in Monument Valley, UT, 4 miles west of Monument Valley Park off U.S. 163 (sites $11 for 2, each additional person $2.)

Petrified Forest National Park

On a trip from Flagstaff to New Mexico, **Petrified Forest National Park,** 107 miles east on I-40, makes an alluring detour off the Navajo/Hopi reservation circuit. The park includes some of the most scenic areas of the **Painted Desert,** so named for the magnificent multicolored bands of rock that cut across its hills. Petrified logs of agate inlaid with quartz and amethyst crystals are scattered across the desert floor, creating a stunning kaleidoscope of color.

Entrances are off I-40 to the north and U.S. 180 to the south (entrance fee $3 per vehicle). The **Painted Desert Visitors Center,** near the north entrance, shows a film explaining petrification. A 28-mile park road through desert landscapes connects the two entrances, winding past piles of petrified logs and Indian ruins. Stop to look at **Newspaper Rock,** covered with Indian petroglyphs. At **Blue Mesa,** a hiking trail winds through the desert. **Long Logs Crystal** and **Jasper Forest** contain some of the most exquisite fragments of petrified wood. It is illegal and traditionally unlucky to pick up fragments of petrified wood in the park. If you must take one home, buy it at the stores along I-40. You can camp overnight if you make arrangements at the visitors center in the **Rainbow Forest Museum,** at the park's southern entrance (542-6228; open in summer daily 6am-7pm; in spring and fall 7am-6pm; in winter 8am-5pm). The Petrified Forest is inaccessible by public transportation; several bus lines stop in Holbrook, on I-40, 27 miles away.

Canyon de Chelly National Monument

A narrow canyon traced by park roads rises eastward out of Beautiful Valley, and the sandstone walls rise 30 to 1000 feet above the flat, sandy wash. The hollowed arcs of 12th-century adobe ruins, the remnants of Anasazi civilization, hide in the canyon walls. The caves and crevices created by seepage and erosion afforded the 19th-century Navajo protection until frontiersman Kit Carson starved the tribe out. The Navajo have since returned to the lush valley as farmers, inhabiting modern-day hogans on the canyon floor.

The land constituting Canyon de Chelly National Monument is owned by the Navajo Nation and administered by the National Park Service. All but one of the park trails are closed to public travel unless hikers are escorted by Navajo. Although the park service offers free short tours into the canyon (check with the visitors center), the only way to get far into the canyon or close to the Anasazi ruins is to hire a Navajo guide. Guides usually arrive at the visitors center at about 9am, and charge $7 per hour to walk or drive into the canyon. If you wish to drive into the canyon with a guide, you must provide your own four-wheel-drive vehicle. Horseback tours can be arranged through **Justin's Horse Rental** (674-5678), on the South Rim. Drive at the mouth of the canyon. (Open approximately 8am-6pm. Horses $7 per hr.; mandatory guide $7 per hr.) The **visitors center** (674-3436), 2 miles east of Chinle on Navajo Rte. 64, off U.S. 191, houses a small museum. The staff can arrange for guides and tours at any time of day. Advance reservations are helpful, but you can try dropping in. (Open daily 8am-6pm; off-season 8am-5pm.)

Seven miles from the visitors center, the 1-mile trail to **White House Ruin,** off South Canyon Rd., winds down a 400-foot face, past a Navajo farm and traditional hogan, through an orchard, and across the stream wash. This is the only trail you can walk without a guide, but it's well worth the trip, especially in the spring when you can hike miles in the canyon heat with the cool stream swirling about your ankles. Make sure you take one of the paved **Rim Drives** (North Rim 44 miles, South Rim 36 miles), which skirt the edge of the 300- to 700-foot cliffs. The South Rim is the more dramatic. Try to make it all the way to the **Spider Rock Overlook,** 20 miles from the visitors center, a narrow sandstone monolith that towers hundreds of feet above the canyon floor. Native lore has it that the whitish rock at the top of Spider Rock is actually composed of bleached bones of victims of the kachina spirit, Spider Woman. A written guide to the White House Ruins and the North or South Rim Drives costs 50¢ (available at the visitors center).

Camp for free in the park's **Cottonwood Campground,** ½ mile from the visitors center. It's a giant campground in a pretty cottonwood grove, but at night you'll probably feel as though you're camped with a noisy army. Stray dogs tend to wander around. Don't expect to find any budget accommodations in nearby Chinle.

It's impossible to take an ugly approach to the park. The most common route is from Chambers, at the intersection of I-40 and U.S. 191. The park is 75 miles north of Chambers and 40 miles north of Ganado on U.S. 191. The other approach is from the north, where U.S. 191 leaves U.S. 160 in Colorado near Four Corners, 50 miles from the monument. There is no public transportation. Please remember to respect the privacy of the Navajo.

Flagstaff

Flagstaff is a mountain town with a split personality. Most of the year it is a gracious host to a handful of skiers and the students of **Northern Arizona University.** Come May, however, the townspeople turn to the business of plundering tourists who use the town as a jumping-off point for journeys to the Grand Canyon and other local attractions. Flagstaff itself is a good place to relax for a few days between photography binges. While the mountain elevation cools Flagstaff down during the day, local bands heat the town up at night.

Practical Information

Emergency: 911. **Police/Medical Assistance,** 774-1414.

Visitor Information: Flagstaff Chamber of Commerce, 101 W. Santa Fe Ave. (800-842-7293), across from the Trailways and Amtrak stations. Free city map, national forest map $2. Open Mon.-Sat. 8am-9pm, Sun. 8am-5pm. **Special Events Hotline,** 779-3733. 24-hour recorded message.

Amtrak: 1 E. Sante Fe Ave. (774-8679 or 800-872-7245). One train per day to Los Angeles ($79) and Albuquerque ($61). Open daily 5:15am-10:15pm.

Buses: Greyhound, 399 S. Malpais Lane (774-4573), across from NAU campus, 5 blocks southwest of the train station on U.S. 89A. To: Phoenix (5 per day, $21); Albuquerque (6 per day, $45); Los Angeles (5 per day, $75); and Las Vegas via Kingman, AZ (3 per day, $51). Terminal open 24 hours. **Gray Line/Nava-Hopi,** 774-5003; 800-892-8687 outside AZ. Shuttle buses to the Grand Canyon (3 per day, $22.30 round-trip, $10.70 with Greyhound's Ameripass).

Pine Country Transit: 113 W. Butler Ave. (779-6624 or 779-6635). Three routes covering most of town. Fare 75¢. In summer a free trolley runs to the mall Mon.-Sat.

Tours: Grey Line/Nava-Hopi, 774-5003; 800-892-8687 outside AZ. One-day sight-seeing tours to: the Grand Canyon ($30, under 12 $16); Monument Valley and the Navajo Reservation and Monument ($70, under 12 $35); the Hopi Reservation and Painted Desert ($62, under 12 $31); and the Museum of N. Arizona, Sunset Crater, Wupatki, and Walnut Canyon (May-Oct.; $28, under 12 $14). Reservations required for all but the Grand Canyon bus. Purchase tickets at the Amtrak and Greyhound stations.

Camping Equipment Rental: Peace Surplus, 14 W. Santa Fe Ave. (779-4521), 1 block from the hostel. Three-day rental of dome tents ($15), packs ($12), stoves ($9), plus a good stock of cheap outdoor gear. Open Mon.-Fri. 9am-9pm, Sat. 9am-7pm, Sun. 9am-6pm.

Bike Rental: Inner Basin, 111 S. San Francisco St. (779-0259), downtown. Mountain bikes $18 per day, "commuter" bikes $8 per day. Open Mon.-Fri. 9:30am-5:30pm, Sat. 9am-5:30pm.

Taxi: Fleet Taxi, 774-9102 or 774-9103. $3 one-way in Flagstaff, $5 from airport to anywhere in Flagstaff.

Car Rental: Allstar Rent-A-Car, 602 Mikes Pike (774-7394 or 800-367-2277). $20 per day with 100 free miles, 20¢ each additional mile. Open Mon.-Sat. 7am-7pm, Sun. 9am-4pm. Must be 21 with major credit card.

Post Office: 104 N. Agassiz. Open Mon.-Fri. 9am-3pm. **ZIP code:** 86001.

Area Code: 602.

The center of Flagstaff is the intersection of **Beaver Street** and **Santa Fe Avenue** (U.S. 89A), where the train station is located. Within a ½-mile of this spot are both bus stations, both youth hostels, the Peace Surplus, the chamber of commerce, and several inexpensive restaurants. Other commercial establishments lie on **South Sitgreaves Street** (U.S. 89A), near the NAU campus.

Flagstaff is a mountain town, so it's cooler than much of the rest of the state, and gets frequent afternoon thundershowers. You can walk around most of downtown, but to get to anything worth seeing, rent a car, take a tour bus, or hitch.

Accommodations and Camping

Three competing hostels downtown, as well as other cheap motels on East Santa Fe Avenue, make sleeping in Flagstaff easily affordable. Don't expect to find budget lodgings in the vicinity of the the Greyhound station or around the NAU campus. Camping in **Cocino National Forest** is a pleasant and inexpensive option.

The Weatherford Hotel (AYH), 23 N. Leroux (774-2731). Friendly management and convenient location. Dorm rooms, hall baths, kitchen, and a cozy common area; ride board in the lobby. Open daily 7am-3pm and 5-11pm; off-season 7am-1pm and 5-10pm. Check-out 9:30am. Curfew 1am. $9, nonmembers $12, required sleepsheet $1. Private singles $22. Doubles $24. Guests receive ½-off cover at **Charly's,** downstairs.

Hotel Du Beau (non-AYH), 19 W. Phoenix (774-6731), just behind the train station. This registered National Landmark hotel, built in 1929, once hosted Los Angeles film stars and Chicago gangsters. Kitchen, library, nightly videos, gift and necessities shop. No charge to borrow bikes. 4 campsites. Check-out 11am. $11. International travelers only. Breakfast included.

Downtowner Independent Youth Hostel, 19 S. San Francisco (774-8461). Flexible management will send a Mercedes to shuttle between hostel and bus station. Very clean, well-maintained rooms. Kitchen, hall baths. Open approximately 7am-9:30pm. Private rooms $10, more crowded $8. Linens included. Open mid-May to mid-Aug.

KOA, 5803 N. Hwy. 89 (526-9926), 6 miles northeast of Flagstaff. Municipal bus routes stop nearby. Sites $16 for 1 or 2, with hookup $17. Each additional person $2.50.

Though hitching is possible, you'll probably need a car to reach the public campgrounds that ring the city. Campgrounds at higher elevations close during the winter; many are small and fill up quickly during the summer, particularly on weekends when Phoenicians flock to these cool mountains. If you stake out your site by 3 to 4pm, you shouldn't encounter problems. National forest sites are usually $2 to 3 a night. Pick up a **Coconino National Forest** map ($2) in Flagstaff at the chamber of commerce. **Lake View,** 13 miles southeast on Forest Hwy. 3 (U.S. 89A), has 30 sites ($5). **Bonito,** 2 miles east on Forest Rd. 545, off U.S. 89, has 44 sites at Sunset Crater ($5). All have running water and flush toilets. If you can live without the amenities, you can camp for free on any national forest land outside the designated campsites, unless there are signs to the contrary. For more information, call the Coconino Forest Service (527-7400; Mon.-Fri. 7:30am-4:30pm; 24-hour emergency 526-0600).

Food

As befits a college town, Flagstaff is liberally sprinkled with cafés and coffee shops. Naturally, because the town is in a state abutting Mexico, there are many affordable Chinese restaurants.

Alpine Pizza, 7 Leroux St. (779-4109) and 2400 E. Santa Fe Ave. (779-4138). Excellent, huge *calzones* ($4.75) and *strombolis* ($5.29). At night, pizzas sail through the air and beer flows freely. Open Mon.-Thurs. 11am-11pm, Fri.-Sat. 11am-midnight, Sun. noon-11pm.

Kathy's, 7 N. San Francisco (774-1951), 1 block east of Leroux St. Great omelettes ($3-4), sandwiches ($2.50-4), and full dinners ($6 includes entree and salad). Open Mon.-Fri. 6:30am-8pm, Sat.-Sun. 9:30am-3pm.

Choi's Chinese and American Diner, 7 E. Aspen (774-3492). Blandness matched only by cheapness. Full omelette breakfast $2, enormous but excellent pastries $1, such as jelly doughnuts with hyperactive pituitary glands.

Bun Huggers, 901 S. Milton Rd. (779-3743), just off Sitgreaves near NAU; and 3012 E. Santa Fe Ave. (526-0542). Genuine charbroiled hamburgers, lots of beef, excellent onion rings, and do-it-yourself toppings (from $2.25). Open daily 10:30am-10pm.

Macy's, 14 S. Beaver St. (774-2243). One of many Flagstaffian coffee cafés, but conveniently next to a laundromat. Espresso machine put to bewildering uses—they even steam eggs with it. Way to go! Open daily 7am-8pm.

Near Flagstaff

Most of Flagstaff's legions of tourists are Grand Canyon-bound, but Flagstaff sits in the middle of six other "natural wonders," most of which are not nearly as crowded.

Seventeen miles north on U.S. 89 lies **Sunset Crater National Monument** (527-7042). This volcanic crater erupted in 1065, forming cinder cones and lava beds; oxidized iron in the cinder gives the pre-nuclear crater its dramatic color. Stop in at the **visitors center.** (Open daily 7am-6pm; off-season 8am-5pm; in winter may close due to snow. Admission $3 per car or $1 per person.) Guided bus trips take off to **O'Leary Peak** three times per day (fare $2; make reservations at the visitors center). From the top you can look down the mouth of Sunset Crater (its treacherous terrain is closed to hiking). A ½-mile self-guided tour wanders through the plain's surreal lava formations, 1½ miles east of the visitors center. All interpretive materials along the trail are also available in Spanish, Dutch, French, and German. Guided tours of the lava tubes begin daily at noon and 3pm; if you're an aspiring spelunker, rent a hard hat and light from the visitors center, don a coat, and explore as far as you dare.

Eighteen miles north and several hundred feet down from Sunset Crater on a scenic loop road is **Wupatki National Monument.** The ancestors of the Hopi moved here around 900 C.E. when they discovered the black-and-red soil was ideal for agriculture. However, by 1215, droughts and overfarming precipitated the abandonment of their pueblos. Today Wupatki boasts some of the Southwest's most scenic ruins, perched on the sides of arroyos in view of Monument Valley and the San Francisco Peaks. Four major abandoned pueblos stretch along a 14-mile park road from U.S. 89 to the visitors center. The largest and most accessible, **Wupatki Ruin,** rises three stories high. Below the ruin, you can see one of Arizona's two stone ball-courts, the sites of ancient games employing a rubber ball and a stone hoop in a circular court. Get information at the **Wupatki Ruin Visitors Center** (774-7000; open daily 7am-7pm; off-season 8am-5pm). When visiting Wupatki or Sunset Crater you can camp at the park's **Bonito Campground** just across from the Sunset Crater Visitors Center. (Running water, no hookups. Sites $5. Overflow campers can pitch their tents for free in the national forest.)

Walnut Canyon National Monument lies 8 miles east of Flagstaff off I-40. In the 13th century, the Sinagua people built more than 300 rooms under hanging ledges in the walls of this 400-foot-deep canyon. From a glassed-in observation deck in the visitors center you can survey the whole canyon, out of whose striated gray walls sprout a stunning variety of plants. A trail snakes down from the visitors center past 25 cliff dwellings; markers along the trail describe aspects of Sinagua life, and identify the plants they used for food, dyes, medicine, and hunting.

Rangers now lead hikes down a rugged trail to the original Ranger Cabin and many remote cliff dwellings. These strenuous two-and-a-half-hour hikes leave daily from the visitors center at 10am. Hiking boots and long pants are required. A walk along the main trail takes about 45 minutes. (Open daily 7am-6pm; Labor Day-Memorial Day 8am-5pm. Admission $3 per car, $1 for motorcycles, bikes, or hikers.)

The **San Francisco Peaks** are the huge, snow-capped mountains you can see to the north of Flagstaff. **Humphrey's Peak** is the highest point in Arizona at 12,670 feet; it is sacred to the Hopi, who believe that the Kachina spirits live there. Nearby **Mount Agassiz** has the area's best skiing. The **Fairfield Snow Bowl** operates four lifts from mid-December through mid-April; its 35 trails receive an average of 8 to 9 feet of powder each winter. Lift tickets cost $18 on weekdays, $24 on weekends. Call the **Fairfield Resort** switchboard (800-352-3524; 24 hours) for information on ski conditions, transportation, and accommodations.

During the summer, the peaks are perfect for **hiking.** When the air is clear, you can see the North Rim of the Grand Canyon, the Painted Desert, and countless square miles of Arizona and Utah from the top of Humphrey's Peak. If you're not up to the hike, take the chairlift up the mountain (runs Memorial Day-Labor Day; $7, seniors $5, ages 6-12 $3.50). The vista from the top of the lift is almost as stunning. Picnic facilities and a cafeteria are open from May to October. Since the mountains are national forest land, **camping** is free, although there are no organized campsites. To reach the peaks, take U.S. 180 about 7 miles north to the Fairfield Snow Bowl turnoff. **Gray Line/Nava-Hopi** offers a tour of the Museum of Northern Arizona, Walnut Canyon, Sunset Crater, and Wupatki National Monument (see Flagstaff Practical Information). There is no other public transportation to these sights, nor, during the summer, to the San Francisco Peaks.

From Flagstaff to Phoenix

The quickest way to make the 142-mile trip from Flagstaff to Phoenix is to head straight down I-17. However, the drive down 89A is worth the extra time. A few miles south of Flagstaff, U.S. 89A descends into **Oak Creek Canyon,** a trout-stocked creek bordered by trees and reddish canyon cliffs. You can pull over to swim or fish at several points along the route; look for **Slide Rock,** an algae-covered natural water chute. National forest campsites are scattered along 12 miles of Oak Creek Canyon on the highway. Get there early—they fill up quickly. Most of the **campgrounds** are open from April to October. Call the forest service (282-4119) for information. **Manzanita** has a three-day limit, and **Cave Spring** and **Pine Flat** have seven-day limits. All have running water and toilets. (Sites $8.)

Twenty-seven miles south of Flagstaff, the walls of Oak Creek Canyon open up to reveal the striking red rock formations surrounding **Sedona,** the setting for many western movies. The town itself, an incongruous blend of wealthy retirees and organic trend-followers, boasts a wide variety of restaurants and resort hotels.

Twenty miles southwest of Sedona (take U.S. 89A to Rte. 279 and continue through the town of Cottonwood) lies **Tuzigoot National Monument,** which consists of a dramatic Sinaguan ruin overlooking the Verde Valley. (Open daily 8am-7pm. Access $3 per vehicle.)

From Sedona, Rte. 179 leads south to I-17. An amazing five-story cliff dwelling is 10 miles south back on I-17. **Montezuma Castle National Monument** (567-3322) is a 20-room adobe abode. Say it five times fast. The dwellings were constructed around 1100 C.E., when overpopulation in the Flagstaff area forced the Sinagua south into the Verde Valley along Beaver Creek. Visitors can view the "castle" from a path below. (Path open daily 7am-7pm, visitors center open daily 8am-6pm. Admission $3 per car.) Eleven miles away is the little-known **Montezuma Well National Monument.** (Open daily 7am-7pm. Free.)

From Montezuma Castle, follow I-17. From the turnoff at Cordes Junction, 28 miles south, a 3-mile dirt road leads to **Arcosanti.** When completed around the turn of the century, Arcosanti will be a self-sufficient community embodying Italian architect Paolo Soleri's concept of **arcology,** somewhat mysteriously defined as "architecture and ecology working together as one integral process." Budgetarians will appreciate the architect's vision of a city where personal cars are obsolete. The complete city, with its subterranean parks, will surprise even the most imaginative Legoland architect. (Tours every hour 10am-4pm. Open to the public daily 9am-5pm. Donation. For more information, contact Arcosanti, HC 74, Box 4136, Mayer 86333 (632-7135).) **Arizona Central** buses (see Phoenix Practical Information) can drop you off in Cordez Junction, 1½ miles away from Arcosanti.

Gray Line/Nava-Hopi runs a tour from Flagstaff to Oak Creek Canyon, Sedona, Montezuma Castle, and **Jerome,** a picturesque ghost town south of Sedona on U.S. 89A. (Tickets $28, under 12 $14. See Flagstaff Practical Information.)

Phoenix

Arizona's capital rose from the ruins of a Hohokam city of the 1100s to become the cultural and commercial center of the Southwest region. In practical terms, this means northerners peregrinate to Phoenix for winter golf and major league baseball's spring training. Balmy in the winter, Phoenix is *hot* in the summer (the hottest major city outside the Islamic world), so avoid the "Valley of the Sun" after May unless you have a swimming pool reserved and ready. Avoid Phoenix year-round if you lack a car. The city sprawls 60 miles from the Mormon-dominated mesa to the retirement community of Sun City and continues, cancer-like, to multiply past these boundaries. The constituent unit of this growth has not been the neighborhood or community, but the shopping mall.

Practical Information

Emergency: 911.

Visitor Information: Phoenix and Valley of the Sun Convention and Visitors Center, 505 N. 2nd St. (254-6500). Open Mon.-Fri. 8am-5pm. Convenient branch offices downtown on 2nd St. at Adams (open Mon.-Fri. 8am-4:30pm), and in Terminals 2 and 3 at Sky Harbor Airport (open Mon.-Fri. 9am-9pm, Sat.-Sun. 9am-5pm). **Weekly Events Hotline,** 252-5588. 24-hour recorded information.

Amtrak: 401 W. Harrison (253-0121 or 800-872-7245), 2 blocks south of Jefferson St. at 4th Ave. Dangerous at night. Three per week to: Los Angeles ($79) and El Paso ($79). Station open Sun.-Mon. and Thurs. 5:15am-12:45pm and 5:15-10:45pm, Tues.-Wed. 5:15-10:45pm, Fri.-Sat. 5:15am-12:45pm.

Greyhound: 5th and Washington St. (248-4040). To: Flagstaff (5 per day, $21); Tucson (14 per day, $14.90 local, $18.45 nonstop); and Los Angeles (10 per day, $25). Open 24 hours.

Local Transit: Phoenix Transit, 253-5000. Most lines run to and from the **City Bus Terminal,** Central and Washington. Buses operate Mon.-Fri. 6am-7pm, reduced service on Sat. Some routes run as late as 9:30pm. Even major lines run only once every ½hr., so expect long, hot waits. Fares 75¢, disabled and seniors 35¢. To Mesa 85¢. 10-ride pass $7.25, all-day $2.50, disabled and seniors half-price. Pick up free time tables, maps of the bus system (75¢, good for free ride), and bus passes at the terminal. City bus #13 runs between the **Sky Harbor International Airport** and the city (every ½ hr. Mon.-Fri. 5:30am-9:30pm, Sat. 7:30am-7pm, Sun. 7am-7pm; call Dial-A-Ride). Cab fare to downtown Phoenix costs about $6. **Dial-A-Ride,** 271-4545. Takes passengers anywhere in Phoenix only on Sun. and holidays 7am-7pm. Fare $1.50 plus 60¢ for each additional zone. Call 258-9977 for weekday service in specified areas only.

Car Rental: Rent-a-Wreck, 2422 E. Washington St. (254-1000). $20 with unlimited mileage, local driving only. Open Mon.-Fri. 7am-6:30pm, Sat.-Sun. 9am-4:30pm. Must be 21 with credit card or a cash deposit. **Associated Rent-a-Car,** 14 S. 22nd St. (275-6992). $22 per day with 100 free miles, 20¢ each additional mile. Open Mon.-Thurs. 7am-6pm, Fri. 7am-7pm, Sat. 8am-5pm, Sun. 9am-4pm. Must be 21 with credit card or a cash deposit and Arizona driver's license.

Auto Transport Company: Auto Driveaway, 3530 E. Indian School Rd. (952-0339). First tank of gas free. Open Mon.-Fri. 9am-5pm. Must be 21 with a $200 refundable deposit.

Taxi: Ace Taxi, 254-1999. **Yellow Cab,** 252-5252.

Help Line: Center Against Sexual Assault, 257-8095. 24 hours.

Post Office: General Delivery: 1543 E. Buckeye. Not downtown. Open Mon.-Fri. 8:30am-5:30pm. **ZIP code:** 85026.

Area Code: 602.

The **city bus terminal** at Central Avenue and Washington Street is in the heart of downtown Phoenix. **Central Avenue** runs north-south; "avenues" are numbered west from Central and "streets" are numbered east. **Washington Street** divides streets north-south.

Phoenix's sights are scattered throughout the valley. Getting around with a car can be pleasant with air conditioning and a tape deck, but the summer heat and the city's dismal joke for bus service can turn an afternoon's recreation into an infernal ordeal.

Accommodations and Camping

Expect motel rates during the peak winter season to be 30 to 50% higher than summer prices. If you don't have reservations, which are usually required in winter, cruise the 25-mile row of motels on occasionally decrepit, slightly dangerous East and West **Van Buren Street** or on **Main Street** (Apache Trail) in Tempe and Mesa. The city's notorious anti-vagabond ordinances make crashing in Phoenix parklands a bad idea. **Bed and Breakfast in Arizona,** P.O. Box 8628, Scottsdale 85252 (995-2831), can help visitors find accommodations in homes in Phoenix and throughout Arizona. (Preferred 2-night min. stay. Singles from $25. Doubles $35. Reservations recommended.) During the hot summer months, you can sleep in Phoenix in style by taking advantage of special packages offered by sun-battered resorts. Check for additional discounts for seniors and children.

Valley of the Sun International Hostel (AYH), 1026 N. 9th St. (262-9439), a few blocks northeast of downtown. From the city bus terminal, take bus #7 to 7th and Roosevelt St., then walk 2 blocks east to 9th St. and turn left—the hostel is a ½ block north. Far from the action. Dorm-style rooms and common showers. Kitchen, porch and common room, coin-op laundry. Office open 8am-10pm. Check-in 7-9:30am and 5-11pm. $8, nonmembers $11. Linens $1. Bike rental $3 per day.

YMCA, 350 N. 1st Ave. (253-6181), downtown. From the city bus terminal, take bus #6 or walk 1 block west and 3½ blocks north. Mediocre rooms, hall bathroom. Men and women segregated by floor. Mostly retired people; rooms usually filled in winter. Singles $17, $60 per week. Key deposit $10.

Motel 6, 2323 E. Van Buren St. (267-7511), near the airport. Other locations north, east, and west of downtown, but this is the most central and, of course, they're all the same. Clean, comfortable rooms. A/C, pool, and TV with free movies. Singles $20. Doubles $27.

Budget Lodge Motels, 402 W. Van Buren St. (254-7247), near downtown. Attractive rooms. Pool, A/C, and TV. Singles $22. Doubles $25. Check for summer specials.

KOA, at 2550 W. Louise (869-8189), 3 miles north of Bell Rd. on I-17 at Black Canyon City. Sites $12.50 for 1 or 2, each additional person over 18 $2.

Food

Nowhere in Phoenix is there a concentration of good, bad, or indifferent restaurants—least of all downtown. Foraging for food means mall-hopping.

Golden Phoenix Restaurant, 6048 N. 16th St. (263-8049). A local favorite. Lunch is the best deal (4-course meal $4.50). Dinners are also excellent (from $6). Open Sun.-Fri. 11:30am-10pm, Sat. 4-10pm.

La Pasadita, 1731 E. Van Buren St. (253-7237). Choose from a variety of *burritos, chimichangas,* and *crispitos* (from $2). Open Mon.-Wed. 7am-4pm, Thurs.-Fri. 7am-6pm, Sat. 7am-3pm.

Tacos de Juárez, 1017 N. 7th St. at Roosevelt (258-1744), near the hostel. Standard Mexican fare at rock-bottom prices. *A la carte* items all under $2.50. Open Thurs.-Mon. 11am-9pm, Wed. 11am-3pm.

The Spaghetti Company, 1418 N. Central Ave. (257-0380). Dinners include salad, bread, beverage, and dessert ($5-7.50). The personal luncheon pizza ($5) is the best deal. Open Mon.-Thurs. 11am-10:30pm, Fri.-Sat. 11am-11:30am, Sun. 11:30am-10pm.

The Purple Cow, 200 N. Central (253-0861), in the San Carlos Hotel; also in the Park Central Mall. Kosher-style deli, but no lox here in the Southwest unless you give advance warning. Great for lunch or fro-yo. Open Mon.-Fri. 7am-4pm.

It's Ginzey's Again, 618 N. Central (254-1990). Another deli-type place, but with executive clientele and a healthy attitude. Known for peanut-butter-banana sandwiches (like Elvis used to eat), fruit juices, and yogurt shakes. Drink in the "South Pacific" (berry yogurt and strawberry coconut juice, $2.25). Open Mon.-Fri. 7am-3pm.

Sights

The **Heard Museum,** 22 E. Monte Vista (252-8848), 1 block east of Central Ave., has outstanding collections of Navajo blankets, jewelry, pottery, and kachina dolls. The museum also promotes the work of contemporary Native American artists and craftspeople, many of whom give free demonstrations. Educate and prepare yourself for the journey into the Southwest's omnipresent Native American artifacts vending. (Guided tours daily. Open Mon.-Sat. 10am-5pm, Sun. 1-5pm. Admission $3, seniors $2.50, students and children $1.) The **Phoenix Art Museum,** 1625 N. Central Ave. (257-1222), 3 blocks south, has excellent exhibits of European, modern, and American folk art. (Open Tues. and Thurs.-Sat. 10am-5pm, Wed. 10am-9pm, Sun. 1-5pm. Admission $3, seniors $2.50, students $1.50. Free Wed.)

The **Desert Botanical Gardens,** 1201 E. Galvin Way (941-1225), in Papago Park, 5 miles east of the downtown area, grow a beautiful and colorful collection of cacti and other desert plants. Visit in the morning or late afternoon to avoid the midday heat. (Open 7am-sunset. Admission $3.50, seniors $3, children $1. Take bus #3 east to Papago Park.)

Just south of Phoenix across the dry Salt River lies Tempe's **Arizona State University (ASU),** where you'll find the **Gammage Memorial Auditorium** (965-3434), one of the last major buildings designed by Frank Lloyd Wright. The pink-and-beige edifice draws both exclamations of amazement and snickers of derision from visitors. (20-minute guided tours every afternoon. At Mill Ave. and Apache Trail, take bus #60 on weekdays, #22 on weekends.) The poolside atmosphere and nearby mountains distract students and entice visitors.

Entertainment

Phoenix is the progressive rock and country capital of the Southwest, with an active (though awfully fashion-conscious) nightclub scene. New Music bands with names like Feedhog and Dead Hot Workshop blister the paint on the dark walls of the **Sun Club,** 1001 E. 8th St. (968-5802), in Tempe. (Music nightly at 8 or 9pm. Cover $3 and up.) **Char's Has the Blues,** 4631 N. 7th Ave. (230-0205), is self-explanatory. Dozens of junior John Lee Hookers rip it up nightly. (Music nightly 9pm. Cover $4 and up.) Headbangers find their black leather, big guitar Eldorado in the bottom of the **Mäson Jar,** 2303 E. Indian School (956-6271). (*Heavy* jams nightly 9 or 10pm. Cover $2 and up.) The free *New Times Weekly,* on local magazine racks, lists club schedules. Pick up a copy of the **Cultural Calendar of Events,** a concise guide covering three months of area entertainment activities.

Near Phoenix

The drive along the **Apache Trail** to Tonto National Monument makes a great daytrip from Phoenix. Take Rte. 60-89 to Apache Junction, about 30 miles east of Phoenix, then turn right onto Rte. 88, which follows the Apache Trail through the Superstition Mountains. Three miles after Canyon Lake, the first of three artificial lakes along the trail, is the good-humored town of Tortilla Flat, a way station for hot and dusty travelers. Five miles east of Tortilla Flat begins a spectacular stretch of scenery. A well-maintained dirt road winds its way through 22 miles of mountains and canyons to **Roosevelt Dam,** an enormous arc of masonry set between two huge red cliffs. Four miles beyond the dam is the turn-off for **Tonto National Monument** (467-2241), where preserved dwellings of the Saledo tribe are tucked into sheltered caves in the cliffs. A one-hour self-guided hike up the mountainside, through the apartments and back, gives you a lovely view of Roosevelt Lake. (Monument open daily 8am-5pm. Admission $3 per car or $1 per person.)

Tucson

Once the capital of Arizona, Tucson lost its title to the overgrown city of Phoenix, but gained the University of Arizona. A city of 700,000 with burgeoning high-tech industry, Tucson nevertheless retains a sense of neighborhood and a certain funkiness. The Mexican *barrios* are intact, and the downtown along North 6th Street and the end of East Congress is attempting a revival based, quixotically, on art. Display windows at vacant downtown shops, for example, have been converted into "phantom galleries" to display local works until businesses move in. The renewal is new enough that the avante-garde still outweighs the investment aesthetic.

Practical Information

Emergency: 911.

Visitor Information: Metropolitan Tucson Convention and Visitors Bureau, 130 S. Scott Ave. (624-1889). Ask for a city bus map and the Arizona campground directory. Open Mon.-Fri. 8:30am-5pm, Sat.-Sun. 10am-3pm.

Tucson International Airport: on Valencia Rd., south of downtown. Take bus #8 to the central city.

Amtrak: 400 E. Toole at 5th Ave. (623-4442 or 800-872-7245), across from Greyhound. Three trains per week to: Phoenix ($25), Los Angeles ($95), and El Paso, TX ($68).

Greyhound: 2 S. 4th Ave. (792-0972), downtown, between Congress St. and Broadway. To: Phoenix (14 per day, $16-$18.45); Los Angeles (11 per day, $44); Nogales (10 per day, $6); El Paso (8 per day, $42). Open 24 hours.

Sun-Tran: 792-9222. Buses operate 5:30am-10pm. Fare 60¢.

Car Rental: Ugly Duckling (747-3825). $16 per day with 200 free miles, 15¢ each additional mile. Local driving only. Open Mon.-Sat. 8am-5:30pm. Must be 21 with major credit card.

Help Lines: Crisis Counseling/Suicide Prevention, 323-9373. 24 hours.

Post Office: 1501 S. Cherry Bell (620-5157). Open Mon.-Fri. 8:30am-5pm. **ZIP code:** 85726.

Area Code: 602.

Tucson catches the sun from the western flanks of the **Santa Catalina Mountains,** 65 miles north of Nogales and the Mexican border on I-19 and 120 miles southeast of Phoenix on I-10. The downtown area is just east of I-10, around the intersection of Broadway (running east-west) and Stone Avenue, and includes the train and bus terminals. The **University of Arizona** is 1 mile northeast of downtown at the intersection of Park and Speedway Boulevard.

Accommodations and Camping

The historic **Congress Hotel,** 311 E. Congress (622-8848), is conveniently located across from both Greyhound and Amtrak stations. The hotel also serves as a hostel, with three beds to a small room. Clean, airy rooms with private baths are also available. (Hostel bed $12, nonmembers $15. Singles $28. Doubles $32.) Tucson's motel row is along **South Freeway,** the frontage road along I-10 just north of the junction with I-19, where you'll find **Motel 6,** 960 S. Freeway (628-1339). The usual amenities include clean rooms with A/C, phones, TV with free movies, and a pool. (Singles $22. Doubles $28.) **Old Pueblo Homestays Bed and Breakfast,** P.O. Box 13603, Tucson 85732 (790-2399 daily 8am-8pm), arranges overnight stays in private homes. (Singles from $25. Doubles $35-40. More expensive in winter. Reservations usually required.)

The best place to camp is the **Mount Lemmon Recreation Area** in the **Coronado National Forest.** Campgrounds and picnic areas are two minutes to two hours outside Tucson via the Catalina Hwy. The best unofficial camping in the forest is in Sabino Canyon, on the northeastern outskirts of Tucson. **Rose Canyon,** at 7000 feet, is heavily wooded, comfortably cool, and has a small lake. Sites at higher elevations fill quickly on weekends. (Sites $5 at Rose and Spencer Canyons; General Hitchcock Campground free, but no water available.) For more information, contact the **National Forest Service,** Ochoa St. and Scott Ave. (629-6483), 7 blocks west of Greyhound. (Open Mon.-Fri. 7:45am-4:30pm.) Among the commercial campgrounds near Tucson, try **Cactus Country RV Park** (574-3000), 19 miles southeast of Tucson on I-10 off the Houghton Rd. exit. (Sites $10.50 for 1 or 2 people, with full hookup $14.50. Each additional person $2.)

Food

Sánchez Burrito Co., 2530 N. 1st Ave. (622-2092), with 6 locations at all points of the compass. Might be the Southwest's best Mexican diner. Try the red chile tamales, fajitas, or legendary giant burritos. Most items under $4. Hours vary among locations, but all are open for lunch and dinner.

El Minuto, 354 S. Main Ave. (351-4145), next to the south barrio. Voted Tucson's best in 1988. Like Sánchez Burrito, largely local clientele. Three cheese enchiladas $4.25, *chimichangas* $4-5.50. Open daily 11am-1am.

El Charro, 311 N. Court Ave. (622-5465), 4 blocks north of the Civic Center. Their specialty is sun-dried *carne seca* ($4 for a side order). Entrees of enchiladas and *flauta* (long, rolled tortillas stuffed with beef and topped with avocados) are $6. Open Sun.-Thurs. 11am-9pm, Fri.-Sat. 11am-10pm.

Café Magritte, 254 E. Congress (884-8004), downtown. A taste of Southwest surrealism, this gourmet homage to the 20th-century artist serves up an original blend of healthful salads and mildly spicy food for under $6. Beware of green apples falling from the ceiling. Open Tues.-Thurs. 11am-11, Fri. 11am-1am, Sat. 5pm-1am, Sun. 5-11pm.

Entertainment

Tucsonites rock and roll near U of A on Speedway Boulevard, and several country music lounges hunker down on North Oracle. Ask at the visitors center for the "Nightlife Locator."

Terry & Zeke's, 4376 E. Speedway Blvd. (325-3555). A great and longstanding institution of live Texas blues and R&B. This hole-in-the wall has a great beer selection. Open daily noon-1am.

Berkey's, 5769 E. Speedway (722-0103). A slightly grungy, smoke-filled blues and rock club. Open Mon.-Sat. 11am-1am, Sun. noon-1am. Live music Wed.-Sat. 9pm. Cover Fri.-Sat. $2.

Hotel Congress Historic Tap Room, 311 E. Congress (622-8848). Frozen in its 1938 incarnation. Eclectic, perhaps even weird, crowd, but very friendly. Open daily 11am-1am.

The **Tucson Parks and Recreation Department** (791-4079) sponsors free concerts every Sunday evening in May, June, and September. Concerts begin at 7:30pm at the **De Meester Outdoor Performance Center.** Check the Thursday evening *Citizen* or call the office for information on other productions. The annual **Tucson Summer Arts Festival** runs from June through August, featuring dance, theater, music, and the visual arts. Pick up a schedule of events at the visitors center.

Sights

Several free museums cluster near the east side of the beautiful University of Arizona campus. (Take bus #1 or #4 from downtown.) The **Arizona State Museum's** (621-6302) archeological displays are little more than a nice break from the heat. (Open Mon.-Sat. 9am-5pm, Sun. 2-5pm. Free.) The **University of Arizona Museum of Art** (621-7567) displays lesser-known works ranging from 16th-century bronze sculpture to photographic prints. (Open in summer Mon.-Fri. 10am-3:30pm, Sun.

noon-4pm; during the school year Mon.-Fri. 9am-5pm, Sun. noon-4pm. Free.) From Incan mummy masks to Southwestern modernism, the **Tucson Museum of Art,** 140 N. Main Ave. (624-2333), sticks to regional themes for an enticing and impressively coherent exhibit. (Open Tues.-Sat. 10am-4pm, Sun. noon-4pm. Admission $2, seniors and students $1. Free Tues.)

A vibrant local event is the **mariachi mass** at **St. Augustine,** 192 S. Stone Ave., downtown. The singing and dancing, which are not intended as tourist attractions, take place in Tucson's old white Spanish cathedral. (Sun. 8am mass in Spanish.)

Near Tucson

Pima's **Titan II Missile Museum,** La Canada Dr. (791-2929), in Green Valley, 25 miles south of Tucson, is a chilling monument built around a deactivated missile silo. (Open Wed.-Sun. 9am-5pm; Nov.-April daily 9am-5pm. Admission $4, seniors $3, ages 10-17 $2.) The Southwest is the desert graveyard for many an outmoded aircraft; low humidity and sparse rainfall preserve the relics. Over 20,000 warplanes, from World War II fighters to Vietnam War jets, are parked in ominous, silent rows on the **Davis-Monthan Air Force Base** (750-4570), 15 miles southeast of Tucson. Take the Houghton exit off I-10, then travel west on Irvington to Wilmont. You can view the 2-mile long graveyard through the airfield fence.

A forest of giant cacti grows in **Saguaro National Monument** (296-8576). The tall, forked *saguaro* cactus often lives 200 years and grows over 40 feet tall. The monument is divided into two areas. The **Tucson Mountain Unit,** on N. Kinney Rd. at Rte. 9 (883-6366), has limited hiking trails for day use only and an auto loop. (Visitors center open daily 8am-5pm. Free.) The **Rincon Mountain Unit** (296-8576), on the Old Spanish Trail east of Tucson, offers the same services and has overnight hikes as well. (Visitors center open daily 8am-5pm. Admission $3 per vehicle.)

Old Tucson, a preserved movie set, purports to convey the feel of the old cowboy-and-rustler Southwest, but the real thing exists in nearby **Tombstone.** An old silver mining town, Tombstone was the scene of the famous shootout at the O.K. Corral and the home of such legendary Western figures as Wyatt Earp, Bat Masterson, and Doc Holiday. The **O.K. Corral,** on Allen St. (457-3456), next to City Park, is open to visitors, and doubles as a general tourist information center. (Open daily 8:30am-5pm. Admission $1. Tickets $2.75; includes a movie screening, a copy of the *Epitaph,* and a cold *sasparilla.*) Tombstone's sheriffs and outlaws, very few of whom died of natural causes, were laid to rot in the **Boothill Cemetery.** Try to catch the mock gunfights staged every Sunday at 2pm alternately between the O.K. Corral and the town streets. Come prepared to open your wallet; "the town too tough to die" touts an almost irresistible assortment of kitschy curios in several shops. For more information on Tombstone's sights, contact the O.K. Corral or the **Tombstone Tourism Association,** 9 S. 5th St. (457-2211; open Mon.-Fri. 9am-5pm, Sat.-Sun. 10am-5pm).

Nevada

Nevada once walked the straight and narrow path. Explored by Spanish missionaries and settled by Mormons, the Nevada Territory's searing, arid climate seemed a perfect place for ascetics to strive for moral uplift. But the discovery of gold in 1850 and silver in 1859 won the state over permanently to the worship of filthy lucre. When the boom-bust roller coaster finally stalled at the bottom during the Great Depression, Nevadans responded by shaking off even the last vestiges of traditional virtue. Unique in America, they made gambling and marriage-licensing the state industries. Logically, Nevada is also home of the drive-through divorce. In a final break with the rest of the country, Silver Staters legalized prostitution (though not in Reno and Las Vegas), and began paying Wayne Newton enormous amounts of cash for his concerts.

But there is a Nevada outside the gambling towns. The forested slopes of Lake Tahoe, shared with California, offer serenity in little resorts away from the casinos of the south shore. Much of the rest of Nevada is expansive, arid, "basin-and-range" countryside, where the true West lingers in its barren glory.

Practical Information

Capital: Carson City.

Tourist Information: Nevada Commission on Tourism, #2075 Valley Bank Building, U.S. 50, Carson City 89710 (885-4322). Open Mon.-Fri. 8am-5pm. **Nevada Division of State Parks,** Nye Building, 201 S. Fall, Carson City 89701 (885-4384). Open Mon.-Fri. 8am-5pm.

Time Zone: Pacific (3 hr. behind Eastern). **Postal Abbreviation:** NV.

Area Code: 702.

Las Vegas

Forget Hollywood images of Las Vegas glamor. The city at base is nothing but an adult Disneyland in the desert. As an arena for mild, middle-aged debauchery, Vegas simply trades in Mickey and Minnie for overbright neon marquees, monolithic hotel/casinos, besequinned Ziegfieldesque entertainers, and rococo wedding chapels.

And yet, amazingly, the city takes itself very seriously—employees literally wear poker faces, and fail to see anything amusing about a nightmarishly overdecorated casino lobby or a chorus of cocktail waitresses forced to wear outfits combining the worst of ancient Athens with contemporary Victoria's Secret. Mostly what Vegas is serious about is making money. The city rakes in a substantial share of the annual $126 billion spent at American gambling tables and the $37 billion dropped into American slot machines. Serious money. The visiting voyeur will find, however, that the best show in town is not an opulent "stage spectacular" but simply the bizarre spectacle of decadent Las Vegas itself.

Practical Information and Orientation

Emergency: 911

Visitor Information: Las Vegas Convention and Visitors Authority, 3150 Paradise Rd. (733-2323, ext. 2471), at the Convention Center, 4 blocks from the Strip, by the Hilton. Pick up a free copy of the *Official Visitors Guide.* Open Mon.-Fri. 8am-5pm.

McCarran International Airport: 798-5410, at the southeast end of the Strip. The main terminal is on Paradise Rd. The University of Nevada campus and the southern casinos are within walking distance, and buses and taxis run downtown.

Amtrak: 1 N. Main St. (386-6896, for fares and schedules 800-872-7245), in the Union Plaza Hotel. To: L.A. ($61), San Francisco ($110), and Salt Lake City ($80). Open daily 6am-9pm.

Buses: Greyhound, 200 Main St. (382-2640), at Carson Ave. downtown. To: L.A. ($34), Reno ($37.60), Salt Lake City ($45), and Denver ($86). **Las Vegas-Tonopah-Reno Lines** provides service to Phoenix ($30). Open 24 hours.

Las Vegas Transit: (384-3540). Common transfer point at 200 Casino Center downtown. Trolley shuttle runs along Vegas Blvd. to here ($1, non-transferable). Most buses operate 5:45am-8:45pm. Strip buses (#6) 6:30am-1:30am every 15 min., 1:30-6:30am every ½ hr. Fare $1, ages 6-18 40¢, 6 tokens $4.80, transfers 15¢.

Tours: Gray Line Tours, 1550 S. Industrial Rd. (384-1234). Bus tours to Hoover Dam/Lake Mead (5 hr., $21, departs Mon.-Sat. 9 and 11am, Sun. 9am); the Grand Canyon (2 days, $88 double occupancy, departs Mon. and Wed. 7:30am; Oct.-April Mon., Wed., and Fri. 7:30am); Old Nevada (7 hr., $26.50, departs daily 10am). **Ray and Ross Tours,** 300 W. Owens St. (646-4661). Bus tours to Hoover Dam (6 hr., $17, departs daily at 10am) and Hoover Dam/Lake Mead (7 hr., $24, departs daily at 10am). **Allstate Tours,** 798-5002. To Hoover

Dam ($21), Laughlin/Bullhead City ($15), and Colorado River rafting (1 day, $60, departs daily at 9am). Ticket booths in hotels list departure times.

Taxi: Checker Cab, 873-2227. $1.70 first 1/7 mile, $1.40 each additional mile.

Car Rental: Brooks Rent-a-Car, 3039 Las Vegas Blvd. S. (735-3344). $26 per day with unlimited mileage. Free pickup from airport. Open daily 6am-1am. Must leave credit card number or return airline ticket. **Thrifty,** 5168 Paradise Rd. (736-4706), by the airport. Sub-compacts $25 with 150 free miles, 20¢ each additional mile. Open daily 5am-midnight.

Help Lines: Crisis Line, 382-4357. **Rape Crisis,** 366-1640. **Gambler's Anonymous,** 385-7732. All 24 hours.

Post Office: 1001 Circus Circus Dr. (388-6229), behind Circus Circus. Take the Circus Circus Skyway shuttle (free) from the Strip to Circus Circus Manor. Open Mon.-Fri. 8am-5pm, Sat. 9am-1pm. General delivery window open Mon.-Fri. 10am-5pm, Sat. 9am-1pm. **ZIP code:** 89114.

Area Code: 702.

Las Vegas lurks in the southwest corner of Nevada, about 240 miles northeast of Los Angeles and 425 miles southeast of San Francisco. From L.A., the drive takes five to six hours, going east on I-10 and turning north on I-15 in San Bernardino. **Gambler's specials** are among the cheapest and most popular ways to reach Las Vegas. These bus tours leave early in the morning and return at night or on the next day; ask in L.A., San Francisco, or San Diego tourist offices. You can also call casinos for information. Prices include everything except food and gambling.

There are two major casino areas. The **downtown** area, around Fremont and 2nd Street, is very amenable to walkers. Casinos cluster close together, their big doors open and all-too-welcoming; some of the sidewalks are even carpeted. The other main area, known as the **Strip,** is a collection of mammoth casinos on both sides of intimidatingly busy Las Vegas Boulevard South. Except for the neighborhoods just north and west of downtown, Vegas is generally, and especially on the Strip, a safe place for late-night strolling. Security guards and lights are plentiful, and there is almost always pedestrian traffic.

Accommodations and Camping

Las Vegas is one of the easiest cities in which to find cheap food and lodging, thanks to casino owners who make their money on gambling. Watch the travel and entertainment sections of local newspapers for specials. Also, small motels along **Las Vegas Boulevard North** are often willing to bargain.

Las Vegas Independent Hostel, 1208 Las Vegas Blvd. S. (385-9955). Not AYH-affiliated, but gives members discounts. Very friendly, well-run hostel. Free coffee, tea, and lemonade. Ride board in the kitchen. Tours every Mon. to North Rim of the Grand Canyon. Office open daily 7-10am and 3-11pm. Check-out 10am. Students and AYH members $8, others $10. Key deposit $2.

Las Vegas International AYH Hostel, 1236 Las Vegas Blvd. S. (382-8119). Small kitchen. Rooms for 3 and 4. Not especially friendly, but there is a pool table and a patch of grass. Office open daily 7-10am and 5-11pm. $8, nonmembers $11. Key deposit $5.

Jackie Gaughan's Nevada Hotel and Casino, 235 S. Main St. (385-7311; 800-637-5777 for reservations). TV and phone in large, clean rooms. Singles and doubles $18.

El Cortez, 600 E. Fremont (385-5200; 800-634-6703 for reservations). TV, phone, and A/C. Singles and doubles $20.

Stardust, 3000 Las Vegas Blvd. S. (732-6441), on the Strip. TV, phone, and A/C. Pool and one of Vegas's largest casinos. Singles and doubles Sun.-Thurs. $25, Fri.-Sat. $38.

Motel 6, 195 E. Tropicana Ave. (798-0728), near the airport, 3 blocks from the Strip. Pool and jacuzzi. Even with 577 rooms, it fills up quickly, so make reservations in summer and during holidays. Singles $28. Doubles $34.

Crest Motel, 207 N. 6th St. (382-5642), at Ogden St. Very eager, friendly management. TV, phone, and refrigerators in room. Singles Sun.-Thurs. $30, Fri.-Sat. $32. Doubles Sun.-Thurs.

$40, Fri.-Sat. $42. Breakfast with jumbo danish included. Key deposit $3. Be sure to ask about discounts for *Let's Go* readers.

For all the luxuries of a hotel except room service, park your RV next door to the **Hacienda,** 3950 Las Vegas Blvd. S. (739-8214), for $9.58; the **Stardust,** 3000 Las Vegas Blvd. S. (732-6564; 800-824-3000 for reservations), for $8.56; or **Circus Circus,** 500 Circus Circus Dr. (734-0410; 800-634-3450 for reservations), $7.54 Mon.-Thurs., $9.58 Fri.-Sat., with free shuttle service to the Strip. Tent campers have to settle for the **KOA Campground,** 4315 Boulder Hwy. (451-5527), east of the Desert Inn. Sites start at $16 for two, each additional adult $4, each additional child $2.50. Pool, spa, recreation hall, and free shuttle to the Strip are included.

You'll need a car to reach any of the noncommercial campsites around Vegas. Twenty miles west of the city on Rte. 159 is **Red Rock Canyon** (363-1921), where you can see an earthquake fault-line and other geological marvels. Camp here for free, but only in **Oak Creek Park.** Twenty-five miles east, **Lake Mead National Park** (293-4041) has several campgrounds. Fifty-five miles northeast via I-15 and Rte. 169, **Valley of Fire State Park** also has campsites.

Food

Prime rib dinners, all-you-can-eat buffets, and champagne brunches at astonishingly cheap prices beckon high- and low-rollers alike into the casinos. In most cafeterias, buffet food is served nonstop from 11am to 10pm. Expect the quality that comes from leaving food on a warming table for three hours. Cruise the Strip or roam around downtown at any time of day watching for advertisements for specials. The Visitors Authority (see Practical Information) keeps a reasonably up-to-date list of buffets. **El Rancho,** 2755 Las Vegas Blvd. S. (796-2222), serves a brunch buffet on weekends and is not as crowded as the bigger casinos ($3.25; Sat.-Sun. 8am-4pm). The **Hacienda,** 3950 Las Vegas Blvd. S. (739-8911), is a cut above comparably priced buffets, with champagne at breakfast and 12 entrees at lunch (either meal $4; Mon.-Fri. 7am-3pm). **Caesar's Palace,** 3570 Las Vegas Blvd. S. (731-7110), is considerably more expensive than most; yet its comfortable chairs, friendly service, and especially appetizing display of desserts, sliced meats, fresh salads, fruits, and cheeses make it *the* place to go for a gastronomic orgy. Go for breakfast to get the most for your money ($5; Mon.-Fri. 8:30-10:30am. Other meals cost upwards of $10.) Downtown's **Golden Nugget,** 129 E. Fremont (385-7111), serves a similarly high-class morning meal ($4.75; Mon.-Fri. 8-11am).

Like inexpensive food, liquid meals are easy to come by and operate on the same principle: Casino operators figure that a tourist drawn in by cheap drinks will stay to spend tons more playing the slots or losing at cards. Drinks in most casinos cost 75¢-$1, or are free to those who look like they're playing. Look for 50¢ shrimp cocktail specials and offers of free champagne at entrances to casinos.

"Lay" restaurants—those not owned by casinos—cannot match the prices of the buffets, but are a nice respite for those suffering the effects of too many helpings of chipped beef and fish croquettes. Downtown is home to a number of Thai, Chinese, and Italian restaurants. Sahara Boulevard and Flamingo Road both cut across the Strip and are studded with such places. One of the best is the **Silver Dragon Restaurant,** 1510 E. Flamingo Rd. (737-1234), 1 block east of Maryland Pkwy., which serves Cantonese and Szechuan meals. Their "graveyard menu" caters to those on the 24-hour schedule. (Open daily 11:30am-5am.) Those who desire more typical Southwestern fare should visit **Mi Casa,** 2710 E. Desert Inn Rd. (369-5440), which offers enchiladas, strawberry *sopapillas,* and live Latin music every night. (Open daily 11am-3am.)

Casino-Hopping and Nightlife

Casinos and their restaurants, nightclubs, and even wedding chapels are all open 24 hours. You'll almost never see clocks or windows in a casino—the owners are afraid that players might realize it's past midnight, turn into pumpkins, and neglect to lose a nickel more. You'll quickly discern which games are suited for novices and which require more expertise, from **penny slots** in laundromats to **baccarat,** in which the stakes can be as high as tens of thousands of dollars. The hotels and most casinos give first-timers "funbooks," with gambling coupons that can stretch your puny $5 into $50 worth of wagering. But remember that casinos function on the basis of most tourists leaving considerably closer to the poverty line than when they arrived; don't bring more than you're prepared to lose cheerfully. Keep your wallet in your front pocket, and beware of the thieves who prowl casinos to nab big winnings from unwary jubilants. You can get an escort from the casino security, or leave your winnings with the cashier, to be picked up later. Seniors are favorite targets and should be especially careful.

Visit several casinos if you can (entrance is always free) to survey the atmosphere, decor, and clientele. **Caesar's Palace,** 3570 Las Vegas Blvd. (731-7110), is the most elegant casino on the Strip. Along the moving sidewalk to the door, you'll pass a full-sized, if inexact, replica of Michelangelo's *David,* be whisked over a miniature Thai temple, and listen to a live band surrounded by silky water on Cleopatra's Barge. Across the street is the brighter **Holiday Casino,** 3475 Las Vegas Blvd. S. (369-5000), where some folks actually seem to be having a good time amid the wild western hoopla. Downtown, the **Golden Nugget,** 129 E. Fremont (385-7111), is definitely the most enjoyable casino in Las Vegas. Eschewing traditional tackiness for polished marble and brass, the Golden Nugget is the place to sip a drink and relax in relative splendor. **Circus Circus,** 2880 Las Vegas Blvd. S. (734-0410), cultivates a family atmosphere, embodied by the huge clown on its marquee. While parents run to the card tables and slot machines downstairs, their children can spend 50¢ tokens upstairs on the souped-up carnival midway. Two stories above the casino floor, tightrope-walkers, fire-eaters, and acrobats perform from 11am to midnight.

Aside from gambling, every major casino has nightly shows. Some, like the **Union Plaza,** 1 Main St. (386-2110), feature free performances by live bands. Extra bucks will buy you a seat at a made-in-America phenomenon: the Vegas spectacular. The overdone but stunning twice-nightly productions feature marvels such as waterfalls, explosions, fireworks, and huge casts. The "Lido de Paris" at the **Stardust,** 3000 Las Vegas Blvd. S. (732-6325), costs $27.50 and includes two drinks, tax, and tip. (Wed.-Mon. at 7 and 11pm.) "Les Folies Bergère," a similar francophile musical farce at the **Tropicana,** 3801 Las Vegas Blvd. S. (739-2222), also offers an all-inclusive dinner for $27.50 (Fri.-Wed. at 6:15, 8, and 11pm). The **Holiday Casino** (369-5222) brings back "The Roaring Twenties" six nights per week for only $16, which includes the usual two drinks, tax, and tip (Mon.-Sat. at 8 and 10:30pm). Later shows often cost less.

You can also see Broadway plays and musicals, ice revues, and individual entertainers in concert. Musical stars in Las Vegas tend to be such libido-driven performers as Wayne Newton and Frank Sinatra, whose shows cost far more than you'll ever be willing to pay. The lowest price for a cocktail show is $5. Dinner shows (steak is the norm) start at $10. To see someone such as Diana Ross or Mel Tillis, people fork over $35 or more. Far more reasonable are the many "revues" featuring imitations of (generally deceased) performers. In Vegas you can't turn around without bumping into an aspiring Elvis clone . . . or perhaps the *real* Elvis in disguise.

Pick up a copy of *Las Vegas Today,* which has plenty of discount coupons, show information, and up-to-date special events listings, or *What's On,* distributed by the Visitors Authority (see Practical Information). Also good are *Entertainment Today, Vegas Visitor,* and *Fun and Gaming. The Games People Play,* distributed by the Golden Nugget Hotel, explains how each casino game is played. Many casinos also offer gambling classes for novices.

Nightlife in Vegas gets rolling around midnight, and keeps going until everyone drops. The casino lounge at the **Las Vegas Hilton,** 3000 Paradise Rd. (732-5111), has a disco every night (no cover, 1-drink min.). **Gipsy,** 4605 Paradise Rd. (731-1919), southeast of the Strip, is a popular disco. At 11pm the place is deserted, but by 1am the medium-sized dance floor is packed. The crowd is mixed. **Carrow's,**

1290 E. Flamingo Rd. (796-1314), has three outdoor patios, plus plenty of people and plants. During the 4-7pm Happy Hour, filling hors d'oeuvres are free.

Reno

Gambling is what lures most tourists to Reno, and some gamblers are so desperate that there is even a bank of slot-machines in the local supermarket (**J.J.'s Food Co. Market,** Virginia and 5th St.). Only casinos outnumber the pawn-shops, and their neon lights spread onto the sidewalk flower beds. The **Reno Arch** (on Virginia at Commercial), originally launched across the road with its "Biggest little city in the world" slogan in 1926, was remodeled with 1600 bulbs a few years ago. Each casino claims fame and uniqueness for its "loosest slots" or accountant-certified "highest paybacks." The **Cal Neva,** 38 E. 2nd St. (323-1046), currently holds the world jackpot record ($6.8 million, made in February 1988). Most venues have live music in the evenings, while at **Bally's,** 2500 E. 2nd St (634-3450) the enormous stage hosts stars like Sinatra and Liza Minnelli. Check details in the weekly freebie *Showtime.* A free shuttle leaves the Cal Neva for Bally's every 40 minutes from 10am till 2am. **Circus Circus,** 500 N. Sierra (634-3450), has free "big-top" performances every night. **The Ponderosa,** 515 S. Virginia (786-6820), recently opened as Reno's first 100% non-smoking casino. The owners even fine their hotel guests $250 for puffing in their rooms. Before you "stack 'em or rack 'em" (your chips, that is), you might try the "Behind the Scenes" gaming tour, which takes you to the other side of the one-way mirrors, and teaches you the rudiments of the games—the only time you'll be given chips for nothing (well, almost nothing: tours at 12:30pm and 2pm daily, $5; leave from Ticker Station, 135 N. Sierra, 348-7788 or 348-7403).

Eating in Reno is amazingly cheap. The casino buffets make McDonalds seem expensive. To entice gamblers in, or to prevent them wandering out in search of food, there are a range of all-you-can-eat places. **Circus Circus,** 500 N. Sierra, offers enormous quantities on plastic plates. "Eat all you want, but eat all you take," they ask. Breakfast (6-11:30am, $2.29), brunch (11:30am-4pm, $2.69), dinner (4:30-11pm, $3.89). Friday seafood (4:30-11pm, $5.99). Drinks are also cheap downstairs where the gaming is (beer for 75¢), either at the bar or on trays from sadly stereotypical bunny-girls. But be warned: a recent Supreme Court judgement making Atlantic City casino owners responsible for the debts of gamblers they are deemed to have gotten drunk does not apply to Nevada (after all, what's the point of cheap liquor otherwise?)

For an alternative to casino fare, drop by the **Bamboo House,** 231 W. 2nd St. (323-6333), across from the Comstock. Largely undiscovered, this spot dishes out spicy Thai and Chinese lunches for about $4 in a jungle-green setting (served Mon.-Fri. 11:30am-2:30pm). Dinners about $7. Open daily 11am-10pm.

Nevada has a large Basque population, and they've brought their fiery cooking with them. **Louis' Basque Corner,** 301 E. 4th St. (323-7203), is a local institution. A hefty $10.50 will buy you a full-course meal, including wine, soup, and salad; $6 will get you an a la carte entree. (Open Mon.-Fri. 9am-11pm, Sat. 10am-11pm, Sun. 4-11pm.) The **Santa Fe Hotel,** 235 Lake St. (323-1891), offers Basque dinners for $11. (Open for lunch at 12:30pm and for dinner 6:30-9pm.)

Downtown Reno is compact, and its wide streets and 24-hour activity make most areas seem safe. The cheapest places are in the southern part of town. **Windsor Hotel,** 214 West St. (323-6171), 2 blocks from Greyhound toward Virginia, is definitely worth trying. The hall showers and rooms are wonderfully clean. Large fans wave lazily overhead to compensate for the lack of A/C. Laundry facilities, friendly staff. (Singles $16, with bath $20; Fri.-Sat. $16, with bath $24. Doubles $22; Fri.-Sat. $26.) **El Cortez,** 239 W. 2nd St. (322-9161), 1 block east of Greyhound, features pleasant management and great bargains. TV. Ask for a private bath. The cheapest singles don't have A/C. (Singles and doubles $19-22, triples $24; in winter singles and doubles $14-17, triples $19. Add $3 on weekends and holidays.) **Motel 6** has 3 locations in Reno, all about 1½ miles from the downtown casinos: 866 N. Wells

(786-9852), north of I-80 off Well Ave. exit; 1901 S. Virginia (827-0255), 1½ miles down Virginia to Plumb Lane, near Virginia Lake; 1400 Stardust St. (747-7390), north of I-80 off Keystone Ave. exit, then west on Stardust. Singles $27, each additional adult $7.

You can park your RV overnight at **Bally's,** 2500 E. 2nd St. (789-2000), for $15. But the **Toiyabe National Forest** begins only a few miles southwest of Reno, and you can try the woodland sites of **Davis Creek Park** (849-0684), 17 miles south on U.S. 395, then ½ mile west (follow the signs), with full service, including showers, but no hookups. (Sites $6.) The nearest Forest Service campground sits high atop **Mount Rose** (784-5030), 20 miles southwest of Reno on Rte. 431. (No showers or hookups; sites $6.)

Only 14 miles from the California border, 443 miles north of Las Vegas, Reno glitters at the intersection of I-80 and U.S. 395, which runs along the eastern slope of the Sierra Mountains. Scan West Coast big-city newspapers for **gambler's specials** on bus and plane fare excursion tickets. Some include rebates and casino credits.

Although the city sprawls for miles, most of the major casinos are clustered downtown along **Virginia** and **Sierra Streets,** between 2nd and 4th St. The adjacent city of **Sparks** also has several casinos along I-80. The bus station and all the hotels listed are downtown or within five to 10 minutes' walking distance.

The **Chamber of Commerce,** 135 N. Sierra (329-3558), offers a friendly staff and the usual deluge of maps and brochures. The *Reno/Tahoe Travel Planner* is an excellent guide to the city. The weekly *Showtime* lists current events and performers. (Open Mon.-Fri. 9am-5pm, Sat. noon-5pm.) Adjacent booth to the chamber, **Ticketron,** sells tickets for shows (348-7788). **Cannon International Airport** is on East Plumb Lane and Terminal Way (785-2575), on I-580 3 miles southeast of downtown. To get there, take bus #24 on Lake Ave. near 2nd St., or the shuttle from the Reno Hilton ($2), which leaves every hour on the hour 9am-4pm. For more information, call 322-6343 or 348-2281. The **Amtrak** station, on E. Commercial Row and Lake St. (329-8638 or 800-872-7245), offers 1 per day to San Francisco ($62), to Salt Lake City ($101), and Chicago ($192). **Greyhound** is on 155 Stevenson St. (322-2970), ½ block from W. 2nd St., in a nice, modern depot. To San Francisco (15 per day, $49.50 each), Salt Lake City (3 per day, $70), and L.A. (10 per day, $54.95). (Open daily 6am-11pm.) **Las Vegas-Tonopah-Reno Lines,** 1155 Glendale (358-9666), in Sparks, offers service from the Greyhound terminal and the Reno airport. To Carson City (6 per day, $5), South Lake Tahoe (5 per day, $13.50), and Las Vegas (4 per day, $54.95). **Gray Line Tours,** 2570 Tacchino St. (329-1147; outside NV 800-822-6009), offers bus tours to Virginia City (4 hr., Tues., Thurs., Sat. at 11am, $15) and Lake Tahoe/Virginia City (8½ hr., daily at 9am, $30). Local transit is provided by **Reno Citifare** at Plaza and Center St. (348-7433). Routes operate 24 hours. (Fare 60¢, seniors and disabled 25¢, students 35¢.)

The **post office** is on 50 S. Virginia St. (786-5523; open Mon.-Fri. 7am-5pm.) General Delivery ZIP Code: 89501. The General Delivery office is open Mon.-Fri. 10am-3pm. The **area code** is 702.

New Mexico

Vast, quiet spaces tell New Mexico's story, from the mysterious ruins whose cliff-dwelling residents left 1000 years ago, to the menacing silence of the world's first atomic testing ground. The first arrivals to New Mexico ambled there during the Stone Age, setting up house in the area's many caves. Twenty thousand years later, the Anasazi made cliff-dwelling an art, constructing masterful apartment buildings in the caves and valleys of this semi-arid landscape. They were followed by other Native American nations, Spanish conquistadors, and Mexicans, who lost control of the area following the Mexican-American War of 1848.

After 140 years of U.S. domination, New Mexico is still a heterogeneous ethnic stew. On the reservations, Navajo and Pueblo tribes try, with varying degrees of success, to preserve parts of their heritage in the face of poverty and dependence upon Anglo tourism and government. In the cities, descendants of the Anglo-American conquerors and the vanquished Spanish- and Mexican-Americans have attempted to live peacefully, incorporating elements of Native American culture into their own. Along with new immigrants from Latin America and Asia has come a sustained invasion of North American New Age devotees, seeking heightened spirituality in the ancient native religions and the awe-inspiring beauty of New Mexico.

Practical Information

Capital: Santa Fe.

Tourist Information: Dept. of Economic Development, 1100 St. Francis Dr., Santa Fe 87503 (827-6291 or 800-545-2040). **Park and Recreation Division,** Villagra Bldg., P.O. Box 1147, Santa Fe 87504-1147 (827-7465). **U.S. Forest Service,** 517 Gold Ave. SW, Albuquerque 87102 (842-3292).

Time Zone: Mountain (2 hr. behind Eastern). **Postal Abbreviation:** NM.

Taos

Taos, a small town at the foot of the Sangre de Cristo range, has been a cultural mosaic since the Spanish arrived in 1615. Like the U.S. conquerors who descended in the 19th century, the Spanish found it impossible to wipe out the Taos Pueblo culture. Today, Taos provides the clearest example of the tricultural legacy of northern New Mexico: Anglo-Americans, Hispanics, and Native Americans maintain their own identities even as they share the natural beauty they have inherited.

Practical Information

Emergency: Police, 758-2216. Ambulance, 758-1911.

Visitor Information: Chamber of Commerce, Paseo del Pueblo Sur (Rte. 68) (758-3873 or 800-732-8267), just south of McDonald's. Open Mon.-Fri. 9am-6pm, Sat.-Sun. 9am-5pm. **Information booth** (no phone) in the center of the plaza open Mon.-Sat. 9am-4pm. Pick up maps and tourist literature from either.

Greyhound: S. Santa Fe Rd. (Rte. 68) (758-1144), about 1 mile south of Taos. To Albuquerque (4 per day, $21).

Pride of Taos Trolley: 758-8340. Serves several hotels and motels as well as the town plaza and Taos Pueblo. Schedules available in the plaza, the chamber of commerce, and most lodgings. Runs Mon.-Sat. 9:15am-5:30pm, Sun. 10am-5pm. Fare $1.

Bike Rental: Bicicletas Corp.: 758-3522, next to Greyhound. Magnificent cycles $14 per day, including equipment. $2 discounts for hostel guests and Greyhound passengers. Open Mon.-Fri. 9am-6pm. Deposit passport or major credit card.

Rape Crisis: 758-2910. 24 hours.

Post Office: N. Pueblo Rd. (Rte. 68) (758-2081), ¼ mile north of the plaza. Open Mon.-Fri. 8:30am-5pm. **ZIP code:** 87571.

Area Code: 505.

Taos is 70 miles north of Santa Fe. Drivers should park on **Placitas Road,** 1 block west of the Plaza, or at the Park-and-Ride lots along Rte. 68 at Safeway and Fox Photo.

Accommodations and Camping

The **Plum Tree Hostel (AYH),** Rte. 68 (758-4696 or 800-678-7586), in Pilar 15 miles south of Taos, is a gorgeous little hostel right next to the Rio Grande. They're angling more for the B&B crowd (hot-tub and massage $45), but the manager still organizes river rafting on the Rio Grande in summer and leads free hikes into the surrounding mountains every Monday if enough guests are interested. The hostel is a flag stop on the bus route between Santa Fe and Taos, so getting in and out of town isn't a problem. (Office open 7:30am-10pm. $9.50, nonmembers $11.50. Breakfast included. Linen $2.) The **Abominable Snowmansion Hostel (AYH)** (776-8298), so named for its proximity to the Taos Ski Valley, is in Arroyo Seco, a tiny town 10 miles northeast of Taos on Rte. 150 via Rte. 3. (Office open 8-10am and 4-11pm. Flexible 11pm curfew. $8.50, nonmembers $10.50; in winter $18.50 and $28, respectively, and breakfast included.) The only hostel in Taos is the independent **Gateway Hostel and San Francisco Hotel,** Hwy. 3 (758-5537). Currently undergoing renovation and changing management, it is a bit of an unknown quantity. The hostel is within walking distance of galleries and shops, and is a short drive from the hot springs and ski areas. (Office open daily 4:30pm-midnight. Check-out 10:30am. Dorm rooms $9, nonmembers $10. Semi-private rooms $12.) Hotel rooms are expensive in Taos. The cheapest are at the **Taos 6,** Rte. 68 (758-2524), 3 miles south of the Plaza. (Singles $28.75. Doubles $32.)

Camping around Taos is easy if you have a car. Up in the mountains on wooded Rte. 64, 20 miles east of Taos, the **Kit Carson National Forest** operates three campgrounds. Two are free but have no hookups or running water; look for campers and tents and pull off the road only at a designated site. **La Sombra,** also on this road, has running water (sites $5). The other six campgrounds are located on the road to Taos Ski Valley and are free. No permit is required for backcountry camping in the national forest. For more information, including maps of area campgrounds, contact the forest service office (758-6200; open Mon.-Fri. 8am-5pm, Sat. 8am-4:30pm). On Rte. 64 west of town, next to the awesome **Rio Grande Gorge Bridge** (758-8851), is a campground operated by the Bureau of Land Management. (46 sites with water and porta-potty. $6. Visitors center open daily 8am-5pm.)

Food

The **Apple Tree Restaurant,** 111 Bent St. (758-1900), 2 blocks north of the plaza, serves up some of the best New Mexican food in the state. Dinner ($7-13) includes a huge entree (swimming in melted cheese and liberally garnished with chiles), homemade bread, and soup or salad. (Open daily 8am-9:30pm.) **Michael's Kitchen,** N. Pueblo Rd. (758-4178), makes mainstream American munchies such as doughnuts, sandwiches ($4), and great apple pie (95¢). (Open daily 7am-8:30pm.) The **El Pueblo Cafe,** N. Pueblo, near the Gateway hostel, is *the* spot for local sheriff's deputies and late night munchers—their peak serving hour is often 2am. In the rear of **Amigo's Natural Foods,** S. Sante Fe Rd. (758-8493), across from Jack Donner's, sits a small but holistic deli serving such politically and nutritionally correct dishes as a not-so spicy tofu on many-grained bread ($2.75). (Open daily 11am-5pm.) For other cheap eats, check out the pizza and fast food places on the strip south of the plaza.

Sights and Activities

Artists have been inspired by the spectacle of the Taos area since the days when the Pueblo exclusively inhabited this land. Many "early" Taos paintings can be found at the **Harwood Foundation's Museum,** 25 Ledoux St. (758-3063) off Placitas Rd. (Open Mon.-Fri. noon-5pm, Sat. 10am-4pm. Free.) Other galleries featuring works by notable locals such as R.C. Gorman can be found in the plaza, along **Kit Carson Road** and **Ledoux Street,** and along **Route 3** in El Prado, a village just north of Taos. Taos's galleries range from high-quality operations of international reputation to upscale curio shops. In early October, the **Taos Arts Festival** celebrates local art.

The **Mission of St. Francis of Assisi,** patron saint of New Mexico, is a favorite of Taos painters. It also holds a "miraculous" painting that changes into a shadowy figure of Christ with a cross when the lights go out. Open Mon.-Sat. 10am-noon and 1-4pm.) Exhibits of Native American art, including a collection of beautiful black-on-black pottery, are displayed at the **Millicent Rogers Museum** (758-2462), north of El Prado St., 4 miles north of Taos on Rte. 3. (Open daily 9am-5pm; Nov.-April Tues.-Sun. 10am-4pm. Admission $3, seniors and children $1, families $6.)

Remarkable for its five-story adobes, pink and white mission church, and striking silhouette, **Taos Pueblo** is a vibrant community that unfortunately charges visitors dearly to look around. Much of the pueblo is off-limits to visitors. If this is the only pueblo you will see, make the trip; otherwise, skip it. (Open daily 9am-5pm. Admission $5 per car, $2 per pedestrian. Camera permit $5, sketch permit $10, painting permit $15.) Beautiful tribal dances are held on Feast Days, including during San Gerónimo's Feast Day (Sept. 29-30), which features a fair and races. Contact the tribal office (758-8626) for schedules of dances and other information.

The less-visited **Picuris Pueblo** is 20 miles south of Taos on Rte. 75, near Peñasco. Smaller and somewhat friendlier to the occasional visitor, Picuris is known best for its sparkling pottery, molded from mica and clay.

Taos Ski Valley, about 5 miles north of town on Rte. 150, is the state's premier ski resort, with powder conditions rivaling those of Colorado, as well as bowl sections and "short but steep" downhill runs. Reserve a room well in advance if you plan to come during the winter holiday season. (Lift tickets $32, equipment $17. For information and ski conditions, call the Taos Valley Resort Association at 776-2233 or 800-992-7669.) In summer, the ski valley area offers some great hikes.

After a day of strenuous sight-seeing, soak in one of the natural hot springs near Taos. To reach one of the most accessible, drive 9 miles north on Rte. 3 to **Arroyo Hondo,** and turn left onto a dirt road immediately after you cross the river. Follow the dirt road for about 3 miles; when it forks just after crossing the Rio Grande, turn left—the hot spring is just off the road at the first switchback. Because the spring is so near the road, it isn't very private, but its dramatic location part way up the Rio Grande Gorge more than compensates. The U.S. 64 bridge over the Rio Grande Gorge is the nation's second-highest span. Located 17 miles west of Taos, it affords a spectacular view of the canyon and is also a good spot to take in a New Mexico sunset.

Santa Fe

Santa Fe has always been aware of its historic role in the Southwest. Capital of the region after the Spanish conquest in the early 17th century, the town continued as a state capital in the Mexican Republic. After earning the dubious distinction of first foreign capital to fall to the U.S. Army during the Mexican-American War, Santa Fe lent its name to the Santa Fe Trail, one of the most important trade routes of the Old West.

City leaders have clung to this history, freezing the past in adobe. By law all buildings near the downtown plaza—restaurants, rug shops, even parking ramps—must be 17th-century-style adobe, painted in one of 23 approved shades of brown. Such earth-toned beauty, as well as the mountains that fringe the city, has attracted a large community of artists to Santa Fe. Hard on their heels have come yelping packs of well-to-do tourists. For all that, the town is a wonderful place to visit—manageably small, relaxed, and a nationwide center of chili-fueled New Mexican cuisine.

Practical Information

Emergency: 911.

Visitor Information: Chamber of Commerce, 333 Montezuma at Guadalupe (983-7317 or 800-528-5369). Open Mon.-Fri. 8am-5pm, Sat. 9am-3pm, Sun. 10am-3pm; off-season Mon.-Fri. 8am-5pm. **Information booth** in the First National Bank building on the west side of the Plaza. Open June-Aug. Another booth inside the lobby of the **Santa Fe Convention Cen-**

ter, 200 W. Marcy. Open Mon.-Fri. 8am-5pm. **National Park Service Southwest Regional Office,** 1900 Old Santa Fe Trail (988-6340). Information on camping and sights in the region. Open Mon.-Fri. 8am-4:30pm.

Greyhound/Trailways: 858 St. Michaels Dr. (471-0008). To: Denver (via Raton, NM, 4 per day, $55); Taos (4 per day, 1½ hr., $12.50); and Albuquerque (7 per day, 1½ hr., $10.40).

Local Transit: Santa Fe Trolley, St. Francis Dr. (989-8595), also known as the Chile Line. Two lines operate daily 9am-6pm, also with some evening runs. The Red Line goes along Cerrillos Rd.; the Green Line is the historic tour and museum route. Fare $1, seniors and children 50¢. **Shuttlejack** (982-4311) provides transportation from the Albuquerque and Santa Fe airports. Also runs shuttle to the opera.

Gray Line Tour: 471-9200 or 983-9491. Free pickup from downtown hotels. Tours Mon.-Sat. to: Taos and Taos Pueblo (at 9am, $38.50); Bandelier, Los Alamos, and San Ildefonso (at 1pm, $28.50); and around Santa Fe (at 9:30am and 1pm, 3 hr., $12.75). Also operates the Roadrunner, a sight-seeing trolley around Old Santa Fe leaving from the plaza at Lincoln and Palace (5 per day, 1½ hr., $6, under 12 $3.)

Taxi, 982-9990. Not exactly punctual, so leave yourself extra time. Coupons for a substantial discount on taxi fare available free from the public library, behind the Palace of the Governors.

New Age Referral Service: 984-0878. Information clearinghouse for holistic healing services and alternative modes of thought.

Post Office: (988-6351), in the Montoya Office Building, S. Federal Place, next to the Federal Courthouse. Open Mon.-Fri. 8am-5:30pm, Sat. 9:30am-12:30pm. **ZIP code:** 87501.

Area Code: 505.

Except for a cluster of museums southeast of the city center, the major sights and most restaurants are within a few blocks of the plaza and inside the loop formed by the circular **Paseo de Peralta.** The narrow streets make driving troublesome, so park your car and hit the pavement. You'll find brown adobe parking lots behind Santa Fe Village, near Sena Plaza, and 1 block east of the Federal Courthouse near the plaza. Parking is available at two-hour meters on some streets.

Accommodations and Camping

Hotels are swamped with requests as early as May for the week of the **Fiesta de Santa Fe** in early September, so make reservations or plan on sleeping in the streets. At other times, look around the Cerrillos Road area for the best prices. At many of the less expensive adobe motels, bargaining is acceptable. The **Santa Fe Hostel (AAIH),** 1412 Cerrillos Rd. (988-1153), 1 mile from the bus station, and 2 miles from the plaza, is a beautiful adobe with kitchen, library, and very large dorm-style beds. ($8, nonmembers $10. Linen $2. $1 kitchen fee includes lots of free food. Also bed & breakfast rooms $24-35. Chile Line flag stop.)

If you plan to camp around Santa Fe, you'll need a car or a lucky thumb. Several miles out of town, **Santa Fe National Forest** (988-6940) has numerous campsites as well as free backcountry camping in the beautiful Sangre de Cristo Mountains. **New Mexico Parks and Recreation** (827-7465) operates the following free campgrounds on Rte. 475 northeast of Santa Fe from May through October (sites with hookup $4-6): **Black Canyon** (8 miles away); **Big Tesuque** (12 miles); and **Aspen Basin** (15 miles).

Food and Nightlife

In Santa Fe you have no reason to eat anything but spicy Mexican food on blue corn tortillas. The better restaurants near the plaza dish up their chilis to a mixture of government employees, well-heeled tourists, and local artistic types. Many serve only breakfast and lunch, so you should also look for inexpensive meals along **Cerrillos Road** and **St. Michael's Drive** south of downtown. One little-known fact: because it has served the local Native American vendors for decades, the **Woolworth's** on the plaza actually serves a mean bowl of chili.

Tomasita's Santa Fe Station, 500 S. Guadalupe (983-5721), near downtown. Locals and tourists line up for their blue corn tortillas and fiery green chili dishes ($4.50-5). Indoor and outdoor seating. Open Mon.-Sat. 11am-10pm.

Josie's, 225 E. Marcy St. (983-5311), in a converted house. Lunch only. Family-run for 23 years. Josie's incredible Mexican-style dishes are worth the 20-minute wait, as are the multifarious mouthwatering desserts. Open Mon.-Fri. 11am-4pm.

Tortilla Flats, 3139 Cerrillos Rd. (471-8685). Frightenly bland family atmosphere belies the ineffably edible Mexican masterpieces ($6-8). Open daily 7am-10pm.

Upper Crust Pizza, 329 E. Old Santa Fe Trail (983-4140). Practically the only downtown restaurant open in the evening. Thick, chewy ten-incher with whole-wheat crust $7. Open Mon.-Sat. 11am-10pm, Sun. noon-10pm.

Sights

Since 1609, religious ceremonies, military gatherings, markets, cockfights, and public punishments have been held on the **Plaza de Santa Fe.** The city was also a stop on two important trails: the **Santa Fe Trail** from Independence, MO, and *El Camino Real* from Mexico City. The plaza is a good starting point for exploring the city's museums, sanctuaries, and galleries. Take the tour on the Chile Line ($1) for a corny but informative introduction to Santa Fe's sights and history.

The following four museums are commonly owned, so their hours are identical and a two-day pass bought at one of them admits you to the other three. (Open March-Dec. daily 10am-5pm; Jan.-Feb. Tues.-Sun. 10am-5pm. Admission $3.50, under 16 free. Two-day passes $6, children $2.50.) The **Palace of the Governors** (827-6483), the oldest public building in the U.S., on the north side of the plaza, was the seat of seven successive governments after its construction in 1610. The *hacienda*-style palace is now a museum with changing and permanent exhibits on Native American, Southwestern, and New Mexican history. If you want to buy Native American crafts or jewelry, check out the displays spread out in front of the Governor's Palace each day by artists from the surrounding pueblos. Their wares are often cheaper and of better quality than those found in the "Indian Crafts" stores around town.

Across Lincoln St., on the northwest corner of the plaza, the **Museum of Fine Arts** (827-4455) is a large, undulating "adobe" building with thick, cool walls illuminated by sudden shafts of sunlight. Its exhibits include works by major Southwestern artists, including Georgia O'Keeffe and Edward Weston, and an amazing collection of 20th-century Native American art.

The other two museums also merit visits. Find them southeast of town on **Camiro Lejo,** just off Old Santa Fe Trail. The **Museum of International Folk Art,** 705 Camiro Lejo (827-8350), 2 miles south of the plaza, houses the Girard Collection of over 100,000 works of folk art from around the world. Amazingly vibrant but jumbled, the collection is incomprehensible without the gallery guide handout. Nearby in the **Museum of American Indian Arts and Culture,** photographs and artifacts unveil the essence of the Native American tradition.

The galleries of Santa Fe may not match those of Taos in fame or number, but trading art, local or imported, is big business here. **Shidoni Sculpture Gallery** (988-8001), in Tesuque, mounts huge summer collections of obelisks and wind harps, abstracts, and golden pigs in its "gallery-in-the-fields" outside Santa Fe. The pieces are impressive, despite the junkyard atmosphere. (Gallery open daily 9am-6pm; off-season 9am-5pm. Field is always accessible. Free. Take Washington Ave. north from the plaza and continue 5 miles north on Bishop's Lodge Rd.—Shidoni will be on your left.)

Santa Fe Detours (983-6565) offers two-and-a-half-hour walking tours of the city daily at 9:30am and 1:30pm ($10). Tours leave from the La Fonda Hotel, on the corner of the Plaza.

Entertainment

With numerous musical and theatrical productions, arts and crafts shows, and Native American ceremonies, Santa Fe offers rich entertainment year-round. Fairs, rodeos, and tennis tournaments are also common. World-famous musicians often play in Santa Fe's clubs, and the theater scene is quite active. For information, check *Pasatiempo* magazine, a supplement to the Friday issue of the *Santa Fe New Mexican.*

Don Diego De Vargas's peaceful reconquest of New Mexico in 1692 marked the end of the 12-year Pueblo Rebellion and the beginning of the traditional three-day **Fiesta de Santa Fe** (988-7575). Held in early September, the celebration reaches its height with the burning of the 40-foot *papier-mâché* **Zozobra** (Old Man Gloom). Festivities include street dancing, processions, and political satires. Most events are free. The *New Mexican* publishes a guide and schedule for the fiesta's events.

The **Santa Fe Chamber Music Festival** (983-2075) celebrates the works of great baroque, classical, and 20th-century composers. (Performances July to mid-Aug. Sun.-Mon. and Thurs.-Fri. in the St. Francis Auditorium of the Museum of Fine Arts. Tickets from $5 Sun. matinee to $25 some evenings. Not easily available.) The **Santa Fe Opera,** P.O. Box 2048 (982-3855), 7 miles north of Santa Fe on Rte. 84, performs out in the open, so bring a blanket. (Performances July-Aug. All shows begin at 9pm. Downtown box office at Galisteo News and Ticket Center, 201 Galisteo St. (984-1316); open Mon.-Sat. 10am-4pm.) Standing-room only tickets can be purchased for as little as $5. **Shuttlejack** (982-4311) runs a bus from downtown Santa Fe to the opera before each performance.

In August, the nation's largest and most impressive **Indian Market** is held in the plaza. Tribes from all over the U.S. are represented; activities include dancing as well as over 500 exhibits of fine arts and crafts. The **Southwestern Association on Indian Affairs** (983-5220) has more information.

Near Santa Fe

Pecos National Monument, located in the hill country east of Santa Fe, 25 miles southeast of town on I-25 and Rte. 63, features ruins of a pueblo and Spanish mission church. The small monument includes an easy 1-mile hike through various archeological sites. Especially notable are Pecos's renovated kivas. These underground ceremonial chambers used in Pueblo rituals were built after the Rebellion of 1680 drove the Spanish from the area. Off-limits at other ruins, these kivas are open to the public. (Open daily sunrise-sunset. Admission $1) The monument's **visitors center** has a small but informative museum and a 10-minute introductory film, shown every half-hour. (Open daily 8am-6pm; Labor Day-Memorial Day 8am-5pm. Free.) Greyhound sends early-morning and late-evening buses daily from Santa Fe to the town of Pecos, 2 miles north of the monument. There are campsites, as well as free backcountry camping, in the **Santa Fe National Forest,** 6 miles north on Rte. 63 (see Santa Fe Accommodations above).

The Pecos hostel, **Wilderness Inn (AYH),** P.O. Box 1040 (757-6351), is 2 miles from the monument and accessible by **Greyhound** as a flag stop, by the **Lamy Shuttle** (982-8829). Llama hikes and other outdoor activities abound. ($8, linen $1.75.)

Bandelier National Monument, 40 miles northwest of Santa Fe (take U.S. 285 to Rte. 4), features some of the most amazing pueblo and cliff dwellings in the state (accessible by 50 miles of hiking trails), as well as 50 square miles of dramatic mesas and tumbling canyons. The most accessible of these is **Frijoles Canyon,** site of the **visitors center** (672-3861; open daily 8am-7pm; off-season 8am-5pm). A 5-mile hike from the parking lot to the Rio Grande descends 600 feet to the mouth of the canyon, past two waterfalls and fascinating mountain scenery. The **Stone Lions Shrine** (12 miles, 8-hr. round trip from the visitors center), sacred to the Anasazi, features two stone statues of crouching mountain lions. The trail also leads past the unexcavated **Yapashi Pueblo.** A two-day, 20-mile hike leads from the visitors center past the stone lions to **Painted Cave,** decorated with over 50 Anasazi pictographs, and to the Rio Grande. Both hikes are quite strenuous. Free permits are required for backcountry hiking and camping; pick up a topographical map ($6) of the monument lands at the visitors center. A less taxing self-guided one-hour tour takes you through a pueblo and past some cliff dwellings near the visitors center. You can camp at **Juniper Campground,** ¼ mile off Rte. 4 at the entrance to the monument. (Sites $6.) Evening campfire programs are conducted by park rangers at 8:45pm. (Park entrance fee $5 per vehicle.)

Los Alamos, 10 miles north of Bandelier on NM Loop 4, stands in stark contrast to nearby towns such as Santa Fe, Taos, or Española. A small mountain village at the outset of World War II, Los Alamos was selected as the site for the U.S. top-secret nuclear weapons development program; today, nuclear research continues at the **Los Alamos Scientific Laboratory.** The facility perches eerily atop several mesas connected by highway bridges over deep gorges, and supports a community with more PhD.s per capita than any other city in the U.S. The public may visit the **Bradbury Museum of Science,** Diamond Dr., for exhibits on the Manhattan Project, the strategic nuclear balance, and the technical processes of nuclear weapons testing and verification. (Open Tues.-Fri. 9am-5pm, Sat.-Mon. 1-5pm. Free.) The **Los Alamos County Historical Museum,** Central Ave. (662-6272), details what life was like in the 1940s, when Los Alamos was a government-created "secret city." (Open in summer Mon.-Fri. 9am-6pm, Sat. 10am-4pm, Sun. 1-4pm.)

Albuquerque

I knew I shoulda toined left at Albuquerque.
Bugs Bunny

Approximately one third of New Mexico's population thrives amidst the youthful energy of New Mexico's only "real" city. Against the dramatic backdrop of the Sandía Mountains, Albuquerque spreads across a desert plateau. The town's Spanish past gave rise to touristy Old Town, but the cheesy roadside architecture lining Route 66 (I get my kicks) and the city's high-tech industry underlie Albuquerque's modern image. Despite their understandable difficulty with spelling the city's name, Albuquerque's youthful residents (average age 29) view their home as a new and growing great American city.

Practical Information

Emergency: 911.

Albuquerque Convention and Visitors Bureau: 625 Silver SW (243-3696). Willing to part with a free map and the useful *Official Albuquerque Travel Guide.* Open Mon.-Fri. 8am-5pm. After hours, the visitors bureau phone has recorded events information. **Old Town Visitors Center,** Romero St. and N. Plaza. (243-3215). Open Mon.-Sat. 10am-5pm, Sun. 11am-5pm.

Albuquerque International Airport: Gibson St. (842-4366), south of downtown. Take bus #50 from Yale and Central downtown Mon.-Sat. 7:20am-6:20pm. Cab fare to downtown $7.25.

Amtrak, 314 1st St. SW (242-7816 or 800-872-7245). Open daily 10am-6:30pm. To: Los Angeles ($89) and Kansas City ($159).

Bus Station: 300 2nd St. SW, 3 blocks south of Central Ave. **Greyhound/Trailways** (243-4435) and **TNM&O Coaches** serve: Oklahoma City (7 per day, $76); Denver (4 per day, $55); Phoenix (6 per day, $45); and Los Angeles (3 per day, $65).

Sun-Tran Transit, 601 Yale Blvd. SE (843-9200 for schedule information Mon.-Fri. 7am-5pm, Sat. 8am-4:30pm). Most buses run Mon.-Sat. 6am-6pm. Pick up system maps at transit office or at the main library. Fare 60¢, ages 5-18 35¢.

Albuquerque Trolley: 242-1407. Provides transportation with tour commentary. Stops at most major hotels. Operates Tues.-Thurs. and Sat. 10am-5:30pm, Fri. 10am-6:30pm, Sun. 11am-6:30pm. Fare $1, seniors and children 50¢.

Taxi: Albuquerque Cab Co., 883-4888. Fare $1.10 for the first mile, $1.20 each additional mile.

Car Rental: Rent-a-Wreck, 500 Yale Blvd. SE (256-9693). Cars with A/C from $20 per day. 100 free miles, 10¢ each additional mile. Open Mon.-Fri. 8am-6pm, Sat. 8am-4pm, Sun. 8:30am-3:30pm. Must be 21 with credit card.

Bike Rental: The Wilderness Center, 4900 Lomas Blvd. NE (268-6767). Mountain bikes $15 per day, $25 per weekend, $50 per week. Open Mon.-Sat. 10am-6pm.

Help Lines: Rape Crisis Center, 247-0707. 24 hours.

Post Office: 1135 Broadway NE (848-3880). Open Mon.-Fri. 8am-6pm. **ZIP code:** 87101.

Area Code: 505.

Albuquerque lies between the **Sandía Mountains** to the east and the **Rio Grande** to the west. **Central Avenue** and the **Santa Fe railroad tracks** create four quadrants used in city addresses: Northeast Heights (NE), Southeast Heights (SE), North Valley (NW), and South Valley (SW). The all-adobe campus of the **University of New Mexico (UNM)** stretches scenically along Central Ave. NE from University Ave. to Carlisle St.

Accommodations and Camping

Central Avenue, the old U.S. 66, is the site of the international hostel and dozens of cheap motels. The **Albuquerque International Hostel (IYHF),** 1012 W. Central (243-6101), at 10th St., is a large adobe house with comfortable rooms and perhaps the only non-sagging mattresses in an American hostel. (Office open Mon.-Fri. 7am-noon and 5-11pm, Sat.-Sun. 7am-noon and 4-11pm. Check-out noon. $8, nonmembers $10. Linen $2. $1 kitchen fee includes plenty of free food.) If you'd prefer to try your luck at one of the motels along Central Ave., the **De Anza Motor Lodge,** 4301 Central Ave. NE (255-1654), has clean, secure, and well-kept rooms. (Singles $18. Doubles $26.) The **Gaslight Inn,** 601 Central Ave. NE (247-0416), is a slightly faded vision in pink and blue, with pool and TV. (Singles $16.50. Doubles $21.)

Named for the Spanish adventurer who burned some 250 natives shortly after his arrival in 1540, the **Coronado State Park Campground** (867-5589), 1 mile west of Bernalillo on Rte. 44, about 20 miles north of Albuquerque on I-25, offers unique camping. Adobe shelters on the sites provide respite from the heat. The view of the Sandía Mountains is haunting, especially in a full moon. Sites are equipped with toilets, showers, and drinking water. (2-week max. stay. Open daily 7am-10pm. Sites $5, with hookup $8. No reservations.) Albuquerque's nearby **KOA,** 5739 Ouray Rd. NW (831-1911), has a swimming pool. (Sites $10.50 for 2. Each additional person $2. Take I-40 west from downtown to the Coors Blvd. N. exit, or bus #15 from downtown.) Camping equipment can be rented from the friendly folks at **Mountains & Rivers,** 2320 Central Ave. SE (268-4876), across from the university. (For 1 weekend: tents $15, backpacks $8-10. Deposit required; reservations recommended.) Canoes are also available. (Open Mon.-Fri. 10am-6pm, Sat. 9am-6pm.)

Food and Nightlife

Downtown Albuquerque has great Mexican food. If you have one Mexican meal to eat before heading into the desert, it should be the *carne adovada burrito* ($3.50) at **M and J Sanitary Tortilla Factory,** 403 2nd St. SW (242-4890), at Lead St. in the hot pink and blue building. The M and J tends to be crowded at lunchtime. (Open Mon.-Sat. 10am-3:30pm.)

The area for tasty, inexpensive food borders the **University of New Mexico,** which stretches along Central Ave. NE. **Nunzio's Pizza,** 107 Cornell Dr. SE (262-1555), claims, somewhat erroneously to some, the best pizza west of New York, at $1 for a huge slice. (Open Sun.-Thurs. 11am-10pm, Fri.-Sat. 11am-11pm.) "Feed your Body with Love, Light, and high VIBRATIONAL Food," advises **Twenty Canots,** 2110 Central Ave. SE (242-1320). Wheatgrass smoothies ($2.25) and bulk organic food are, apparently, sufficiently vibratory. (Open and accepting Mon.-Sat. 10am-8pm, Sun. noon-6pm.) Similarly laid back is **E.J.'s Coffee and Tea Co.,** 2201 Silver SE (268-2233), at the corner of Yale, with baked goods and a bewildering number of variations on the cup of coffee. (Open Mon.-Fri. 7am-11pm, Sat. 8am-midnight, Sun. 8am-2pm.) At the nearby **Purple Hippo,** 120 Harvard Dr. SE (266-1997), a regular scoop of rich, homemade ice cream is only 75¢ and pastry is just as inexpensive. (Open Mon.-Thurs. 7:30am-10:30pm, Fri.-Sat. 7:30am-11:30pm, Sun. 10am-9pm.)

Rub elbows with **Cowboys',** 3301 Juan Tabo Blvd. NE (296-1959), in this country-western bar and nightclub at the eastern end of town. Ranchers hang out here when they come to town. You can also kick up your spurs at **Caravan East,** 7605 Central Ave. NE (265-7877), but watch your step for tobacco-juice puddles. (Continuous live music every night 5pm-1:30am. Thurs. tight jeans contest. Cover $2-3.) Less rurally-inclined music lovers can hear rock and blues bands at the **El Ray,** 622 Central Ave. SW (242-9300), a spacious old theater renovated into a bar and nightclub. (Music usually Wed.-Sat. at 8:30pm. Cover $2-20.)

Sights

Old Town, on the western end of downtown, is Albuquerque's obligatory Spanish plaza surrounded by restaurants and galleries. Located at the northeast corner of the intersection of Central Ave. and Rio Grande Blvd., 1 mile south of I-40, Old Town is the best place to hang out and watch tourists.

The **National Atomic Museum,** 20358 Wyoming Blvd., Kirkland Air Force Base (844-8443), tells the story of the development of the atomic bombs "Little Boy" and "Fat Man," and of the obliteration of Hiroshima and Nagasaki and its aftermath. *Ten Seconds that Shook the World,* an hour-long documentary on the development of the atomic bomb, is shown four times daily at 10:30am, 12:30pm, 2pm, and 3:30pm. (Open daily 9am-5pm. Free. The Air Force base is several miles southeast of downtown, just east of I-25. Access is controlled; ask at the Visitor Control Gate on Wyoming Blvd. for a pass to visit the museum.)

The **Indian Pueblo Cultural Center,** 2401 12th St. NW (843-7270), just north of I-40, provides a sensitive introduction to the nearby Pueblo reservations. The cafeteria serves authentic Pueblo food (fry-bread $1.50). Colorful Pueblo dances are performed on weekends during the semester at 11pm and 2pm. (Open mid-May to Oct. Mon.-Sat. 7:30am-5:30pm, Sun. 9am-5:30pm; off-season Mon.-Sat. 7:30am-5:30pm. Admission $2.50, seniors $1.50, students $1. Take bus #36 from downtown.) The **New Mexico Museum of Natural History,** 1801 Mountain Rd. NW (841-8837), houses fascinating exhibits on biology, geology, and paleontology in a futuristic building. Take the "evolator" 70 million years into the past. (Open daily 9am-5pm. Admission $3, seniors $2, under 11 $1.)

Near Albuquerque

Located at the edge of suburbia on Albuquerque's west side, **Indian Petroglyphs State Park** (897-7201) includes a trail leading through lava rocks written on by the area's earliest residents. Take the Coors exit on I-40 north to Atrisco Rd. to reach this free attraction, or take bus #15 to Coors and transfer to bus #93. (Open daily 8am-6pm; off-season 8am-5pm. $1 parking fee.)

On the east side of the city, the **Sandía Peaks** rise 10,000 feet, providing a pleasant escape from Albuquerque's heat and noise. Sandía means "watermelon" in Spanish, and the mountains were so named for the color they turn at sunset. These mountains are convenient to Albuquerque by car. Take Tramway Rd. from either I-25 or I-40 to the **Sandía Peak Aerial Tramway** (298-8518) for a thrilling ride to the top of Sandía Crest. You ascend the west face of Sandía Peak and gaze out over Albuquerque, the Rio Grande Valley, and western New Mexico. Try to make the ascent at sunset. (Operates daily 9am-10pm; Labor Day-Memorial Day Sun.-Tues. and Thurs. 9am-9pm, Fri.-Sat. 9am-10pm. Fare $9.50, seniors and students $7. 9-11am rates are $8 and $6, respectively.)

North of Albuquerque, on the scenic "Turquoise Trail," sits (in lotus position) the hippie town of **Madrid** (pronounced "MA-drid"). Like a wildlife preserve for certain species of humans, Madrid maintains natural habitats such as communes and psychedelic bars. For information on its many music festivals see the posters in Albuquerque.

A trip in the **Sandía Ski Area** makes a beautiful 58-mile, day-long driving loop. Take I-40 east up Tijeras Canyon 17 miles and turn north onto Rte. 44., which winds through lovely piñon pine, oak, ponderosa pine, and spruce forests. Route 44 then descends 18 miles to Bernalillo, through a gorgeous canyon. A 7-mile trail toll-road (Rte. 536) leads to the summit of **Sandía Crest,** and a dazzling ridge hike covers the 1½ miles and 300 feet separating the crest and **Sandía Peak.** Rangers offer guided hikes on Saturdays in both summer and winter. Reservations are recommended for the challenging winter snowshoe hikes (281-3304).

Western New Mexico

West of Albuquerque lies a vast land of forests, lava beds, and desert mesas populated by Native Americans and boomtown coal and uranium miners. It is a difficult region to explore without a car, but can be very rewarding for the dedicated adventurer.

Chaco Culture National Historical Park

Sun-scorched and water-poor, Chaco Canyon seems like an improbable setting for the first great flowering of the Anasazi. At a time when most farmers were relying on risky dry farming, Chacoans created an oasis of irrigated fields. They constructed sturdy five-story rock apartment buildings at a time when most Europeans were living in squalid wooden hovels. By the 11th century, the canyon residents had set up a major trade network, with dozens of small satellite towns in the surrounding desert. Around 1150 C.E., the whole system gave out. With no food and little water, the Chacoans simply abandoned the canyon for greener pastures.

Only the ruins remain, but these are the best-preserved sites in the Southwest. **Pueblo Bonito,** the canyon's largest town, demonstrates the skill of Chacoan masons. Among many other structures, one four-story wall still stands. Nearby **Chetro Ketl** houses one of the canyon's largest great kivas, used in the Chacoans' religious rituals. Bring water, since even the visitors center occasionally runs dry.

The **visitors center** (988-6727 or 988-6716; 24 hours), at the eastern end of the canyon, houses an excellent museum that includes exhibits on Anasazi art and architecture, as well as a description of the sophisticated economic network by which the Chacoan Anasazi traded with lesser tribes of modern Colorado and northern Mexico. (Open daily 8am-6pm; Labor Day-Memorial Day 8am-5pm. Entrance fee $1 per person or $3 per carload.) **Camping** in Chaco is free, but space is limited (46 sites), so arrive by 3pm.

Chaco Canyon is a 160-mile, three-and-a-half-hour drive northwest from Albuquerque; it lies 90 miles south of Durango, CO. When the first official Washington archeologist left for the canyon at the turn of the century, it took him almost a year to get here. Today's visitor faces unpaved Rte. 57, which reaches the park from paved Rte. 44 (turn off at the tiny town of Nageezi) on the north (29 miles), and from I-40 on the south (about 60 miles, 20 miles of it unpaved). **Greyhound's** I-40 run from Albuquerque to Gallup serves Thoreau, at the intersection of Rte. 57, five times per day. It is very difficult to hitchhike from Nageezi or Thoreau to the park.

El Morro National Monument and Gallup

Located just west of the Continental Divide on Rte. 53, 4 miles southeast of the Navajo town of **Ramah,** this is the site of **Inscription Rock,** where Native Americans, Spanish conquistadors, and Anglo-American pioneers made their mark while traveling through the scenic valley. Today, self-guided trails allow access to the rock as well as to ruins further into the park. (Open 8am-6:30pm.) The visitors center (open 8am-8pm) includes a small museum as well as several dire warnings against emulating the graffiti artists of old by marking the rocks. For those unable to resist the inscription urge, an alternate boulder is provided.

Southern New Mexico

Carlsbad Caverns National Park

East of the Sacramento Mountains lies the dusty plain named Llano Estacado. The lonely towns of southeastern New Mexico—Roswell, Artesia, and Carlsbad—would attract few visitors were it not for the spectacular underground scenery. Dangling on the edge of nowhere, Carlsbad Caverns attract hordes of visitors from all over the world to their fantastic, often spectacular formations. Another draw is the massive bat flight sunset, in which the entire bat population of the caverns (currently 250,000) fly out of the cave's entrance in a long, twisting line on their way to feeding grounds. The caverns' bats gave explorers in this desolate region the first clue that another world lay underground here. Indeed, before becoming a national park, Carlsbad Caverns supported the profitable mining of guano (bat dung, used as fertilizer), found in 100-foot deep deposits in some of the caves.

The **visitors center** (785-2232) has a restaurant, an outrageously expensive gift shop, an information desk, a 24-hour information recording, and lockers (50¢). For another 50¢ you can rent a small radio which transmits a guided tour. (Open Memorial Day-Labor Day daily 8:30am-7pm; Labor Day-Memorial Day 8:30am-5:30pm.) There are two ways to see the caverns. Those with strong knees and solid shoes can take the "blue tour," traveling by foot down a steep (but paved) 3-mile descent. This tour will give you the best sense of the depth and extent of the caverns. The "red tour," an easier, shorter route, descends from the visitors center by elevator. Most of the trail is wheelchair-accessible, and both tours are self-guided. Almost all visitors return to the surface by elevator, the last of which leaves a half-hour before the visitors center closes. After that it's just you and the bats. (Tours June-Aug. 8:30am-5pm, Sept.-May 8:30am-3pm. $4, ages 6-15 $3, over 62 $2.50).

Tours of the undeveloped **New Cave** (785-2232) are offered Memorial Day to Labor Day daily at 9am and 12:30pm; in off-season weekends only. Two-hour, 1¼-mile flashlight tours traverse difficult and slippery terrain; there are no paved trails or handrails. Just getting to the cave takes some energy—the parking lot is 23 miles on a dirt road from the Carlsbad Caverns Visitors Center (there is no transportation from the visitors center or from White's City) and the cave entrance is a steep, strenuous half mile from the lot. Reservations (and a flashlight) are necessary for the cave tour, as the park limits the number of persons allowed to visit each day. (Tours $5, children 6-15 $3. Children under 6 not admitted; Golden Eagle passes not valid.)

The nightly flight of the caverns' bats is also open to public viewing; the **Bat Flight Program** takes place in the amphitheater of the natural entrance to the cave just before sundown every night from May to October. Free guano samples.

No camping is permitted in Carlsbad Caverns National Park. The **Carlsbad Caverns International Hostel** (785-2291) is easily accesssible by bus (3 times per day from El Paso and Carlsbad). Spacious six-bed rooms include bathroom, access to kitchen, TV, pool and spa, and a nightly display of six-legged, non-paying guests. Check in at the RV park 7am-10pm or at the Texaco station after 10pm. ($10. Linens $2.) The privately-run (and usually overrun) **Park Entrance Campground** (785-2291; ask to be connected), in White's City, is just outside the park entrance. (Sites for up to 6 people $13.50) Pay at the office adjacent to the laundromat. The **Lake Carlsbad Campground** (885-4435), off U.S. 62/180, is about 2 miles east of the Carlsbad bus depot. ($1 per tent.) Both campgrounds provide water, showers, restrooms, and free swimming. Find cheap beds at the **Motel 6,** 3824 National Parks Hwy. (885-0011). Make reservations, especially if you plan to arrive in the late afternoon or evening. (Singles $23. Doubles $29.) Additional campsites are available at nearby Guadalupe Mountains National Park (see Texas).

The tiny, rather tacky town of **White's City,** on U.S. 62/80, is the access point to the caverns. White's City is 20 miles southeast of the town of Carlsbad, and the caverns are 7 miles away, up a steep, winding mountain road. (Flash floods occasionally close the road, so call ahead before making the trek.) From Las Cruces on I-25, take U.S. 82 east to Alamogordo, crossing the Sacramento Mountains, and then take U.S. 285 south to Carlsbad, a trip of 213 miles total. From El Paso, TX, also on I-25, take U.S. 62/180 east 150 miles, passing Guadalupe Mountains National Park, which is 40 miles southwest of White's City. Greyhound, in cooperation with **TNM&O Coaches** (887-1108), runs three buses per day from El Paso or Carlsbad to White's City. Two of these routes have White's City only as a flag stop. ($5.70 round-trip). From White's City, you can take **Carlsbad Cavern Coaches** to the visitors center ($14 round-trip for 1-4 people; buy tickets in the White's City Gift Shop where Greyhound drops you off), but linking up with another party or hitching the 7 miles to the caverns from the White's City parking lot should be simple.

Utah

Utah's varied terrain, once home to dinosaurs, now beckons smaller travelers. Human visitors come to witness the rugged landscape, including a vast lake of salt water and a multitude of bizarre rock formations. Southern Utah is a weird wonderland of redstone canyons, deep river gorges, and fantastic, naturally carved arches, spires, and columns. Northeastern and central Utah feature mountains (the Uinta range) and national forests, dotted with lakes and covered with aspens and ponderosa pine.

The native Mormons (Church of the Latter-Day Saints), with their unusual religious beliefs and patriotic, family-oriented conservatism, complete Utah's strange picture; over 80% of the state belongs to the faith of Joseph Smith and Brigham Young. It is essential to acclimate yourself to the evangelical Mormons, but don't let this effort distract you from the state's overwhelming natural beauty.

Practical Information

Capital: Salt Lake City.

Tourist Information: Utah Travel Council, Council Hall/Capitol Hill, 300 N. State St., Salt Lake City 84114 (530-1030), across the street from the Capitol building. Information on national and state parks, campgrounds, and accommodations. Open in summer only, Mon.-Fri. 8am-5pm. Pick up a free copy of the *Utah Travel Guide,* with a complete listing of motels, national parks, and campgrounds. **Utah Parks and Recreation,** 1636 W. North Temple, Salt Lake 86116 (538-7220). Open Mon.-Fri. 8am-5pm.

Time Zone: Mountain (2 hr. behind Eastern). **Postal Abbreviation:** UT.

Area Code: 801.

Salt Lake City

When Brigham Young led the Mormon pioneers across the Rocky Mountains in 1847, he looked out at the vast valley surrounded by mountains and a great lake in the distance and declared, "This is the place." Today, Salt Lake City is still the place, both the spiritual and secular center of Utah. The gargantuan Mormon Temple is the leading church of the Mormon faith, while the University of Utah, the art museums, and the symphony are the state's major cultural institutions.

Practical Information

Emergency: 911.

Salt Lake Valley Convention and Visitors Bureau: 180 S. West Temple (521-2868 or 800-831-4332), 2 blocks south of Temple Sq. Open Mon.-Fri. 8am-7pm, Sat. 9am-4pm, Sun. 10am-4pm; off-season Mon.-Fri. 8am-5:30pm, Sat. 9am-6pm, Sun. 10am-4pm. Other visitors centers at: the Crossroads Mall, 50 S. Main St.; the ZCMI Mall, 36 S. State St. (321-8745; open Mon.-Fri. 7:30am-9pm, Sat. 8am-6pm); and terminal 2 at the airport. The *Salt Lake Visitors Guide* (free) details a good self-guided tour.

Salt Lake City International Airport: 776 N. Terminal Dr. (539-2205), 4 miles due west of Temple Sq. UTA buses are the best way to get to and from the airport. Bus #50 serves the terminal directly. Delta/Western Airlines flies here from Los Angeles and San Francisco, and several airlines will take you to Denver for about $50.

Amtrak: 325 S. Rio Grande (364-8562 or 800-872-7245). Trains once daily to: Denver (13½ hr., $98); Las Vegas (8 hr., $80); Los Angeles (15 hr., $127); and San Francisco (17 hr., $130). Ticket office open Mon.-Sat. 5-9am, 10:30am-2pm, 4:15-7pm, 8pm-midnight; Sun. 4:15pm-1:20am.

Greyhound/Trailways: 160 W. South Temple (355-4684), 1 block west of Temple Sq. To: Cheyenne (3 per day, 9 hr., $60); Las Vegas (2 per day, 10 hr., $42); San Francisco (3 per day, 15 hr., $76); Boise (3 per day, 7 hr., $40); West Yellowstone (1 per day, 9 hr., $66); and Denver (3 per day, 12 hr., $55). Ticket counter open daily 1:45am-10pm; off-season 7am-10pm. Terminal open 24 hours.

Utah Transit Authority: 287-4636 (until 7pm). Frequent service to University of Utah; buses to Ogden, suburbs, airport, and east to the mountain canyons. Buses ½ hr. or more apart 6:30am-11pm; to Provo 5:30am-10pm. Fare 50¢, seniors 25¢, under 5 free. To Provo, $1.25. Maps available from libraries or the visitors bureau.

Tours: Old Salty Tours, run by Lewis Brothers Stages, 549 W. 500 South (359-8677). 1½-hr. guided tour of Salt Lake City in an open-air train. Tours leave (6 per day) from the North Side of Temple Sq. and Trolley Sq. Water Tower. Fare $5, seniors $4, under 12 $3. Purchase tickets at the **Sport Stalker,** in Trolley Sq. (533-9999; open Mon.-Sat. 10am-5pm, Sun. noon-5pm), or call the Old Salty phone any day between 8am and 9pm. **Gray Line,** 553 W. 100 South (521-7060). Open Mon.-Fri. 7am-5pm, Sat. and Sun. 7am-3pm. 2½-hr. tours of the city focusing on Mormon historical sites. Departures in summer daily 9am and 2pm. Fare $12, children $6.

Taxi: City Cab, 363-5014; **Ute Cab,** 359-7788; or **Yellow Cab,** 521-2100. 95¢ base fare, plus $1.30 per mile. $9-10 from the airport to Temple Sq.

Car Rentals: Payless Car Rental, 1974 W. North Temple (596-2596). $21.50 per day with 200 free miles, or $109 per week with 1200 free miles, 14¢ each additional mile. Open Mon.-Fri. 7am-10pm, Sat. and Sun. 8am-6pm. **Low Cost Car Rental,** 935 W. Temple (596-1155). $17 per day with 100 free miles, or $99 per week with 700 free miles, 15¢ each additional mile, $5 mandatory insurance. You must be 21 with a major credit card and may only drive in Utah.

Bike Rental: Wasatch Touring, 702 E. 100 South St. (359-9361). 15-speed mountain bikes $15 per day. Open Mon.-Sat. 9am-7pm.

Post Office: 250 W. 200 South St. (530-5902), 1 block west of the visitors bureau. Open Mon.-Fri. 8am-5:30pm, Sat. 9am-2pm. **ZIP code:** 84101.

Area Code: 801.

Salt Lake is 750 miles inland from San Francisco, 420 miles northeast of Las Vegas, and 500 mountainous miles west of Denver. I-80 and I-15 meet in the city. **Hitchhiking** out of Salt Lake City is easier going east-west than north-south. The city's sprawl has been checked by the **Wasatch Mountains** to the north and east, and by the **Great Salt Lake,** 17 miles from downtown to the west. Most of the built-up suburbs lie in the **Salt Lake Valley,** toward the south.

Salt Lake's grid system makes navigation quite simple. Brigham Young, the city's founder, designated **Temple Square,** in the heart of today's downtown, as the center. Street names define how many blocks east, west, north, or south they lie from Temple Square. **Main Street,** running north-south, and **Temple Street,** running east-west, are the "0" points. Smaller streets and streets that do not fit the grid pattern often have non numerical names. Occasionally, a numbered street reaches a dead end, only to resume a few blocks farther on.

The city's main points of interest lie within the relatively small area bounded by the railroad tracks around 400 W., the **University of Utah** at 1300 E., the **State Capitol** at 300 N., and **Liberty Park** at 900 S. The downtown is equipped with audible traffic lights for the convenience of blind pedestrians. A "cuckoo" a green light for east-west travel while "chirps" indicate a green light for north-south travel.

Accommodations

Avenues Youth Hostel (AYH), 107 F St. (363-8137), 5 blocks east of Temple Sq. Good rooms. Kitchen and laundry available. No check-ins after 10pm. Dorm rooms $9.75, nonmembers $13. Private singles $19, doubles $30.

Austin Hall at the **University of Utah** (581-6331), 15 blocks east of downtown, off Wasatch Dr. Take bus #14 or 3. Minute but clean dorm rooms for rent mid-June to Aug.; off-season go next door to Baliff Hall for the same rooms and rates. Singles $17. Doubles $22. Reservations recommended.

Colonial Village Motel, 1530 Main St. (486-8171). Friendly management keeps cheap rooms in good shape. (Singles $18. Doubles $21.)

Kendell Motel, 667 N. 300 West (355-0293). Clean rooms with refrigerators (some ovens), cable TV, and A/C $25.

Carlton Hotel, 140 E. South Temple (355-3418), 2 blocks from the temple. The top of the budget line. Singles $20, with continental breakfast and bath $29, with full breakfast and shower $39. Doubles $29, with bath and continental breakfast $34, with full breakfast and bath $49.

Motel 6, 3 locations: 176 W. 600 South (531-1252); 1990 W. North Temple (364-1053), 2½ miles from the airport (take bus #50); and 496 N. Catalpa (561-0058), just off I-15. Singles $23. Doubles $29. Catalpa and downtown locations $2 more. All fill quickly.

The **Wasatch National Forest** (524-5030) skirts Salt Lake on the east, with many established sites. The terrain by the city is so steep, though, that the best camping is on the far side of the mountains. Three of the closest campgrounds lie near I-215, which runs along the mountain fronts off I-80. Between mile 11 and 18 out of Salt Lake on I-80, there are four campgrounds with more than 100 sites altogether (no hookups). It's first come-first serve—go early on weekends. (Sites $5.) The **Utah Travel Council** (538-1030) has detailed information on all campsites in the area, including the three near the ski areas off Rte. 152 and 210 to the south of Salt Lake. The **state parks** around Salt Lake also offer camping, though none on the lake itself. **East Canyon State Park,** 30 miles from Pioneer State Park in Salt Lake, near the junction of Rte. 65 and 66, has sites by East Canyon Reservoir—a good place to go boating and fishing. (Open April-late Nov.) State parks normally charge $2 for day use and $6-9 for sites. For more information, contact **Utah Parks and Recreation** (see Utah Practical Information above). If you need a hookup, then the **KOA,** 1400 W. North Temple (355-1192; sites $13.75, with water and electricity $15, full hookup $18), and other private campgrounds are your only alternatives.

Food

Affordable food is bountiful in Salt Lake City, but don't expect to find too many cheap eats downtown. Fill up on **scones** (a Utah specialty via England), a popular fast food staple throughout the area. Otherwise stick to ethnic food downtown and the cheap, slightly greasy eateries on the outer fringe.

Bill and Nada's Cafe, 479 S. 6th St. (359-6984). One of Salt Lake's oldest, most revered cafés. Two eggs, hash browns, toast $2.75. Roast leg of lamb, salad, soup, vegetable and potatoes $5. Open 24 hrs.

Rio Grande Cafe, 270 Rio Grande (364-3302), in the Rio Grande Railroad depot, 4 blocks west of the temple. Take bus #16 or 17. Stylish, fun Mexican restaurant with neon and glass decor. Two tacos with rice and beans $4.50. Open Mon.-Thurs. 11:30am-2:30pm and 5-10pm, Fri.-Sat. 11:30am-2:30pm and 5-10:30pm, Sun. 4-9pm.

Union Cafeteria, at the university (581-7256). Serves the cheapest grub in town. Chat with students while you eat a $1-2 breakfast or a $2-3 lunch or dinner. Open Mon.-Fri. 7am-9pm, Sat. 8am-7:30pm, Sun. 11am-7:30pm.

Bistro to Go, 271 S. Main St. (363-5300). Great food, friendly service, intellectual conversation and the aroma of capuccino typify this college hang-out. Try the Scandinavian spinach torte ($3.75) and top it off with one of their exotic coffees ($1.25-2.50; open Mon.-Sat. 9am-3pm).

Salt Lake Roasting Company, 249 E. 400 South (363-7572). Classical or jazz music amid big burlap bags of coffee beans. Coffees and pastries; quiche complete with soup and French bread $3. Open Mon.-Thurs. 7am-midnight, Fri.-Sat. 8am-midnight.

The Sconecutter, 2040 S. State St. (485-9981). The king of sconemakers. Your favorite flavor of fluffy but stuffing scone only 85¢. Open 24 hours.

Mormon Sights

Salt Lake City is the world headquarters of the **Church of Jesus Christ of Latter-day Saints.** The faithful are called Mormons, from the **Book of Mormon,** which contains the revelations received by their first prophet, Joseph Smith. The Bible, as well as the Book of Mormon, is held to be the word of God. The triumvirate First Presidency is the highest authority in the Mormon church, and makes its headquarters in Salt Lake City. The largest and most important Mormon temple, built by the earliest Anglo-American Utah community, is also here.

Temple Square (240-2534) is the symbolic center of the Mormon religion. Feel free to wander around the flowery and pleasant 10-acre square, but non-Mormons may not enter the sacred temple itself. Sitting atop the highest of the building's three towers, a golden statue of the angel Moroni watches over the city. The square has two **visitors centers** (north and south), each of which is liberally stocked with information and armies of smiling guides. If you only have a little time join in on the 30-minute **Pioneer Tour;** for more history and sightseeing try the 45-minute **Historical Tour.** (From the flagpole, the Pioneer Tour leaves every 15 minutes, the Historical Tour every 30 minutes.) Visitors center open daily 8am-9pm; off-season 9am-8pm. The pamphlet "Truth Restored" (75¢) is available at both centers and provides further explanation of the Mormon religious creed.

Visitors on any tour in Temple Square will visit the **Mormon Tabernacle,** the flying-saucer-like building that houses the Mormon Tabernacle Choir. One-and-a-half-hour rehearsals on Thursday evenings (8pm) and Sunday morning broadcasts from the tabernacle (be there by 9am) are open to the public. Impressive as it may be, the choir can't match the size and sound of the 10,814-pipe organ that accompanies the singers. (Recitals Mon.-Fri. at noon, weekends at 4pm.) There are also various concerts at **Assembly Hall,** next door, almost every evening in summer.

Around the perimeter of Temple Square are several other buildings commemorating the history of the Mormons in Utah. The **Genealogical Library,** 35 N. West Temple (240-2231) provides the resources for Mormons to research their lineage, in accordance with their belief that they must baptize their ancestors by proxy in order to seal them into an eternal family. If you've ever wanted to research your own family heritage, this is the place to do it; the library houses the largest collection of geneological documents in the world. (Tours every 15-20 minutes. Open Mon. 7:30am-6pm, Tues.-Fri. 7:30am-10pm, Sat. 7:30am-5pm).

The **Museum of Church History and Art,** 45 N. West Temple. (240-3310) houses Mormon memorabilia from 1820 to the present. (Open Mon.-Fri. 9am-9pm, Sat.-Sun. and holidays 10am-7pm; off-season Tues. and Thurs.-Sun. 10am-7pm, Mon.

and Wed. 10am-9pm. Free.) The **Beehive House,** N. Temple and State St. (240-2671), 2 blocks east of Temple Sq. was the official residence of Brigham Young while he served as governer of the territory and president of the church. ½-hr. guided tours every 10 min. Open Mon.-Sat. 9:30am-6:30pm, Sun. 9:30am-2pm; off-season Mon.-Sat. 9:30am-4:30pm, Sun. 9:30am-2pm. Free.)

The city of Salt Lake encompasses the **Pioneer Trail State Park,** (533-5881) in Emigration Canyon on the eastern end of town. Follow 8th South St. until it becomes Sunnyside Ave., then take Monument Rd. (Bus #4.) The **"This is the Place" Monument,** 2601 Sunnyside Ave. (533-5920), commemorates Brigham Young's decision to settle down at last, and a visitors center will tell you all about the Mormons' toilsome immigration from the Midwest. Tour **Brigham Young's forest farmhouse,** where the dynamic leader held court with his numerous wives. (Park grounds open in summer 8am-8pm, but visit 9am-7:30pm for the best welcome. $1 entrance fee.)

Secular Sights and Activities

The **capitol**'s grey dome lies behind the spires of Temple Square. Tours (521-2822) are offered daily from 9:30am-3:30pm. For more information, contact the **Council Hall Visitors Center** (538-1030), across from the main entrance. (Open daily 9am-6pm; Labor-Memorial Day Mon.-Fri. 8am-5pm.) While you're in the capitol area hike up City Creek Canyon to **Memory Grove,** and savor the shade as you gaze out over the city. Or, better yet, stroll down to the **Church of Jesus Christ of Latter-Day Saints Office Building,** 50 East N. Temple St., and take the elevator to the 26th floor observation desk. (Open Oct.-April Mon.-Fri. 9am-5pm; April-Oct. Mon.-Sat. 9am-5pm.) Also on capitol hill is the **Hansen Planetarium,** 15 S. State St. (535-7007 or 538-2048). Even if you don't wish to pay for a show, the free exhibits are fabulous. (Open daily 10am-8pm.) Head for the **Children's Museum,** 840 N. 300 West (328-3383), if you've always wanted to pilot a 727 jet or implant a Jarvik artificial heart in a life-size "patient." (Open Tues.-Sat. 9:30am-5pm. Admission $2. Take bus #61.) Or stroll through the U. of Utah campus to the **Utah Museum of Natural History,** where you can marvel at the variety of life that has lived on the Salt Lake plain. (Open Mon.-Sat. 9:30am-5:30pm, Sun. noon-5pm. Admission $2, under 12 $1.) Right next door is the **Utah Museum of Fine Arts's,** eclectic collection. (Open Mon.-Fri. 10am-5pm, Sat.-Sun. 2-5pm.)

For information on university happenings contact the Information Desk in the U. of Utah Park Administration Building (581-6515; open Mon.-Fri. 8am-8pm), or the **Olpin Student Center,** (581-5888; open Mon.-Sat. 8am-9pm, Sun. 10:30am-9pm).

The **Utah Symphony Orchestra** (533-6407) performs in **Symphony Hall,** one of the most spectacular auditoriums in the country, in Salt Palace Center, 100 S. West Temple. (Free tours Mon.-Fri. at 1, 1:30, 2, and 2:30pm; off-season Tues. and Thurs. only. Concert tickets $10-15, student rush $5.) Dance and opera performances occur at the neighboring **Salt Lake Art Center.** (Open Mon.-Sat. 10am-5pm. Donation.)

Alcohol and Nightlife

A number of restrictions have arisen from the Mormon Church's prohibitions against alcohol consumption among its members. Utah law requires that all liquor sales be made through state-licensed stores, so don't be surprised if you can't get more than a beer at most restaurants or bars. The drinking age is well-enforced. (State liquor stores open Mon.-Sat. 11am-7pm. There are 6 within 3 miles of downtown Salt Lake.) A number of hotels and restaurants are licensed to sell mini-bottles and splits of wine, but consumers must make the drinks themselves. Public bars serve only beer but you can bring your own liquor (and pay 75¢-$2.50 for a set-up). Private clubs requiring membership fees are allowed to serve mixed drinks. Some clubs have two-week trial memberships for $5. Others will give you a free, temporary membership if you will only be in town for a night or two.

The 18-21 yr. old crowd tends to party at **The Bay,** 1130 E. 200 South (466-3733), and even though smoking and drinking are prohibited, this Top-40 club is boppin'. (Open Tues.-Wed. 9pm-1am, Fri.-Sat. 9pm-2am, Wed. 25 plus only. Cover $3-5.) **Xenon,** 909 E. 2100 South (486-4261), is a slightly less popular but still frequented 18-and-over bar with modern and Top-40 hits. (Open Thurs.-Sat. 9pm-2am. Cover $5.) **The Zephyr,** 79 W. 300 South (355-2582), has live rock bands and dancing nightly. (Open daily 7pm-2am; off-season 7pm-1am. Cover $3-10.) For rock and good old country and western music, mosey on down to the **Barb Wire,** 348 W. 500 South (363-2870). (Dance floor open Thurs.-Sat. 8pm-2am, bar open Mon.-Sat. 11am-2am. Cover $5-10.) If you're in the mood for a small, friendly bar, head for the remote **Cotton Bottom Inn,** 2829 E. 6200 South (273-9830). Their garlic burgers are famous ($3.50) and they play all types of music from country to new wave. (Open Mon.-Thurs. 11am-1am, Fri. and Sat. 11am-2am, Sun. 11am-8pm.)

Near Salt Lake City

The **Great Salt Lake,** a remnant of primordial Lake Bonneville, is a bowl of salt water where only blue-green algae and brine shrimp can live. The salt content varies between 5 and 15%, and provides such buoyancy that it is almost impossible for the human body to sink. Unfortunately, flooding sometimes closes the state parks and beaches on the lakeshore, but if you are desperate to swim you can try Saltair Beach 17 miles to the west, or head north 40 minutes to fresh-water **Willard Bay.** Contact the visitors center or the state parks (538-7220) for up-to-date information on access to Salt Lake.

In the summer, escape the heat with a drive or hike to the cool breezes and icy streams of Salt Lake City's beautiful mountains. One of the prettiest roads over the **Wasatch Range** is **Route 210.** Heading east from Sandy, 12 miles southeast of the city, this road goes up **Little Cottonwood Canyon** to the Alta ski resort. The **Lone Peak Wilderness Area** stretches away southward from the road, around which the range's highest peaks (over 11,000 ft.) tower. **City Creek, Millcreek,** and **Big Cottonwood** are also good spots to picnic or hike.

There are seven ski resorts within 40 minutes of downtown Salt Lake. **Snowbird** (521-6040; lift tickets $32) and **Park City** (649-8111; lift tickets $30) are two of the best, but also the most expensive. For a more affordable alternative, try the nearby **Alta** (742-3333; lift tickets $19). UTA runs buses from SLC to the resorts in winter, with pick-ups at downtown motels. You can rent equipment from **Breeze Ski Rentals** (800-525-0314), at Snowbird and Park City ($13-14, 10% discount if reserved over 2 weeks in advance, lower rates for rentals over 3 days). Call or write the Utah Travel Council (see Utah Practical Information above). Pick up the free *Ski Utah* for listings of ski packages and lodgings. The **Utah Handicapped Skiers Association,** P.O. Box 108, Roy 84067, provides information, specialized equipment, and instruction for disabled skiers.

Some resorts offer summer attractions as well. Snowbird's aerial tram climbs to 11,000 feet and offers a spectacular view of the Wasatch Mountains and the Salt Lake Valley below. (Fare $6, seniors and under 16 $3.50. Open daily 11am-8pm.) Park City offers a gondola ride (Fri.-Mon. noon-6pm $5, under 12 $4) during the summer along with an alpine slide, the fastest way down the mountain. (Fare $3.75, seniors and children $2.75. Open daily 10am-10pm. Take I-80 east 30 miles from Salt Lake.)

Three Corners Area

Monstrous bones in Dinosaur National Monument memorialize the giant lizards that once lived in long-vanished marshes, and the broad spine of the snow-capped Uinta Range rises from the desert plateau like a sleeping dragon. The terrain here changes with impossible abruptness from desert to pine forest to alpine meadow to boulder-strewn canyon. The Green River defies nature by flowing from flatlands into the mountains, creating an enormous expanse of water in a parched land.

In this little-known region where Utah, Colorado, and Wyoming meet, you'll find the entire history and landscape of the west encapsulated. Luckily, no fewer than five perfectly respectable roads (U.S. 40, Rte. 150, Rte. 414, Rte. 530, and U.S. 191) break away from mind-numbing I-80, greatly facilitating exploration. **Greyhound** sends its beasts of burden down I-80 six times per day and lumbers past the Uintas and Dinosaur Monument on the south, along U.S. 40. Even the farthest corners of the area are within a half-day's drive of Salt Lake City.

Vernal

Vernal is central to Flaming Gorge and the Uinta Mountains and 16 miles west of the Dinosaur National Monument on U.S. 40. The town is a perfect base for exploring the Three Corners Area; you'll find information about the whole region, including a list of 66 public campgrounds. Visit the Utah Travel Council's desk at the Natural History Museum (789-4002; see below) for many brochures on one-day drives in the area. (Open daily 8am-8pm, off-season shorter hours.) Or contact the **chamber of commerce,** 50 E. Main St., Vernal 84078 (789-1352; open Mon.-Fri. 8am-5pm). The **Ashley National Forest Service,** 355 N. Vernal Ave. (789-1811), has jurisdiction over much of this area and most public campgrounds.

Stop in at the **Utah Fieldhouse of Natural History and Dinosaur Garden,** 235 Main St. (789-3799). The full-scale dinosaur models strutting among garden plants somehow come off as less than grandiose. The well-run museum has excellent displays on the natural and human history of the area, with special attention to the Ute Indians and the region's geology. Check out the fluorescent minerals: your shoelaces will glow in the dark. (Open daily 8am-9pm; Labor Day-Memorial Day 8am-4pm. Admission $1, children 50¢.)

Sleeping cheaply in Vernal is easy. The **Ute Motel,** 236 E. Main St. (789-0687), has pleasant rooms and friendly management. (Singles $20. Doubles $25, $1 more after June.) Just up the street is the simple **Sage Motel,** 54 W. Main St. (789-1442). (Singles $22. Doubles $26.) The closest campground is **Campground Dina RV Park,** 930 N. Vernal Ave. (789-2148), about 1 mile north of Main St. on Hwy. 46 and 191. (2-person sites $10, with electricity and water $13, full hookup $14).

Dinosaur National Monument

Dinosaur National Monument is more than just a pile of bones. The Green and Yampa Rivers have created vast, colorful gorges and canyons here, and the harsh terrain still evokes eerie visions of the massive reptiles that roamed about the continent 140 million years ago.

The park entrance fee is $5 per car, $2 for bikers, pedestrians, and those in tour buses. The more interesting western side lies along Rte. 149 off U.S. 40 out of Jensen. Seven miles from the intersection with U.S. 40 is the **Dinosaur Quarry Visitors Center,** P.O. Box 128, Jensen 84035 (789-2115), accessible from the road by free shuttle bus or a fairly strenuous ½-mile walk (cars prohibited in summer). Inside the center is a hill that has been partially excavated to reveal the gargantuan remains of dinosaurs. You can see paleontologists chipping away at the rock, hear a brief lecture, and tour the excellent exhibits. (Open daily 8am-7pm; off-season 8am-4:30pm. You can drive your car in after closing.) It's lonely and cold up here in winter; there is no shuttle service and the tour is self-guided. A few miles farther along Rte. 149 you'll find the **Split Mountain Gorge Campground,** which is scenic but hot, and the **Green River Campground,** with shady, green sites. Both have flush toilets, drinking water, and tent and RV sites. (Open late spring-early fall. Sites $5 per night. There are also several free primitive campsites in and around the park; call the visitors center for information.) Split Mountain Gorge Campground has evening programs in its own amphitheater. Past the campgrounds on Rte. 149, just beyond the end of the road, you can see one of the best examples of the monument's many ancient Native American petroglyphs.

The eastern side of the park is accessible only from U.S. 40, outside **Dinosaur,** CO. The 25-mile-long road (closed in winter) to majestic **Harper's Corner,** where the Green and Yampa River gorges meet, begins 2 miles east of Dinosaur. From the road's terminus, a 2-mile round-trip nature hike leaves for the corner itself. It's worth the sweat—from here you can view the river canyons of the Green and Yampa Rivers, thousands of feet below. The **Dinosaur National Monument Headquarters,** on U.S. 40 in Dinosaur (303-374-2216), at the intersection with the park road, provides orientation to the canyonlands of the park and information on river rafting. (River office 374-2468. Open Mon.-Fri. 8am-7pm; Sept.-May 8am-4:30pm. Call 8am-4:30pm.) For more information on this side of the park, write to the Monument Superintendent, P.O. Box 210, Dinosaur, CO 81610.

In Dinosaur, the **Terrace Motel,** 301 Brontosaurus Blvd. (374-2241), has clean, beautiful rooms in mobile home units. (Singles $21. Doubles $26.) The **Park Motel,** 105 E. Brontosaurus Blvd. (374-2270), offers kitchenettes with A/C. (Singles $18. Doubles $22).

Dinosaur's **post office** is at 198 Stegasaurus Dr. (374-2353; open Mon.-Fri. 8:30am-12:30pm and 1-5pm).

Greyhound/Trailways makes a daily run both east and west along U.S. 40 (July-Aug. 2 per day), stopping in Vernal and Dinosaur en route from Denver and Salt Lake City. Jensen is a flag stop, as is the monument headquarters, 2 miles west of Dinosaur (disembark only). The Vernal depot is at 45 E. Main St. (789-0404). The Dinosaur depot is at 103 W. Brontosaurus Dr. (374-2711; open daily 8am-10pm). From Salt Lake City to Vernal is $29; to Dinosaur $37.

Flaming Gorge and Brown's Hole

Curiously, Flaming Gorge never suffered a firestorm and Brown's Hole is not a hole. It is the bright red canyons of northeastern Utah that give the Flaming Gorge Recreation Area its name, and "Brown's Hole" simply refers to the valley (in 1870 trapper-speak). This peaceful retreat offers ample opportunities for hiking and water sports. **Flaming Gorge National Recreation Area** is part of the **Ashley National Forest,** which spans southwestern Wyoming and northeastern Utah. A towering army dam built in the 60s on the Green River created the 91-mile Flaming Gorge Reservoir.

From Wyoming, the most scenic route to the gorge is the amazing U.S. 191 south from I-80 (exit between Rock Springs and Green River). Route 530 closely parallels the reservoir's western shore, but the only scenery you'll see will be an occasional pronghorn antelope. Take this route only if you want to camp on the flat beaches of the lake's Wyoming portion. Hitching on either of these roads is difficult because of limited traffic. To reach Flaming Gorge from the south, take U.S. 191 north from Vernal, over the gorgeous flanks of the **Uinta Mountains** (see below), to **Dutch John,** UT. Wyoming has much of the recreation area, but the most scenic and best-developed area of the park is in Utah, at the base of the Uinta Range.

The Flaming Gorge Dam Visitors Center (885-3135) is off U.S. 191 just outside the government building complex of Dutch John. Guided tours of the dam area are offered every hour and ½ hour, and maps of the area are $2. (Open daily 9:30am-4:30pm; off-season 8am-4pm). The **Red Canyon Visitors Center** (889-3713), a few miles off U.S. 191 on Hwy. 44 to Manila, perches a breathtaking 1360 feet above Red Canyon and Flaming Gorge Lake. (Open daily 9:30am-4:30pm. Closed winter.)

The diversity of activities in the recreation area parallels the startling variation in terrain. Watch the locals shooting carp with bows and arrows in the high desert of the Wyoming lakeshores, or try your own hand at fishing along the steep, forested slopes of the Green River gorge below the dam. The gorge has superb trout fishing (in 1987 the 3rd largest trout in the world was caught here), but you must have a license from Wyoming and a stamp of approval from Utah, or vice versa. Call the Utah Department of Wildlife Resources, 152 E. 100 North (789-3103). You can rent fishing rods and boats at **Cedar Springs Marina** (869-3795), 3 miles before the dam in Dutch John, and also at **Lucerne Valley Marina** in Manila (784-3483; boats $6-12 per hr., with 8-hr. and all-day rates. Rod rentals a few dollars per day. Open April-Aug. 7am-8pm.) **Hatch River Expeditions** (789-4316 or 800-342-8243; 789-4715 after hours) offers a wide variety of summer float trips, including a one-day trip for $36, under 12 $25.

Inexpensive, albeit primitive, campgrounds are plentiful in the Flaming Gorge Area. You can camp right next to the **Red Canyon Visitors Center** in the Red Canyon Campground ($5), or in one of the numerous national forest campgrounds along Rte. 191 and 44 in the Utah portion of the park. (2-week max. stay. Sites $5.) **Buckboard Crossing** (307-875-6344) and **Lucerne Valley** (801-784-3293), located farther north, tend to be drier and unshaded, but are close to marinas on the reservoir (flush toilets, swimming; sites $6-7). Either visitors center provides information on campgrounds. If you'd rather sleep indoors, try the **Flaming Gorge Lodge** (801-889-3773) near the dam in Dutch John. The immaculate rooms have A/C and cable TV, but prices you may not appreciate. (Singles $39. Doubles $45.)

For a hideout from tourists, visit **Brown's Park,** a large valley 23 only-partially-paved miles east of Flaming Gorge. Hitching is not good on this lonely road. The valley's incredible isolation attracted western outlaws, most notably local boy **Butch Cassidy** and his gang, the **Wild Bunch.** The outlaws also made creative use of the proximity of three state lines—great for getting out of a state posse's jurisdiction. There are primitive **campsites** ¼ mile from the camp in either direction. Just up the Green River lies **Indian Crossing,** while **Indian Hollow** is just downstream (no water; free). Chances are you'll see more people than the outlaws ever did, but the Green River's shore is a beautiful place to camp or land your raft after a brisk ride downstream. To get to Brown's Park, head north from Dutch John about 10 miles on U.S. 191 until you reach Minnie's Gap; from here follow the signs east to Clay Basin (13 miles) and to the park (23 miles).

For further information, contact the **Flaming Gorge National Recreation Area,** Dutch John 84023 (801-885-3315; open Mon.-Fri. 8am-4:30pm) or, if you're coming from Wyoming, stop by the **Green River Chamber of Commerce,** 1450 Uinta Dr., on Rte. 530, Green River 82936 (307-875-5711; open Mon.-Fri. 9am-4:30pm). **Rock Springs,** WY, has a well-marked **visitors center,** 1897 Dewar Dr. (307-362-3771; open Mon.-Fri. 8am-5pm), a few blocks south of I-80. This is the most convenient brochure stockpile for those planning to go south on U.S. 191.

Finally, you can write or call the Ashley Natl. Forest Service in Vernal (see Vernal) or Manila. (Manila address: P.O. Box 278, Manila, UT 84046; 784-3445).

Uinta Mountains

The first white people in the Three Corners area were trappers, drawn by the high wooded valleys populated by beaver. During the 1820s and 1830s, the Uintas were inundated with mountaineers like Jim Bridger and Jedediah Smith, who clashed with the Ute. The trappers managed to hold on until the beaver ran out, and even held some of their wild annual rendezvous in the area. Today, the Uintas' inscrutable peaks and silent valleys attract more hikers and sight-seers than mountain folk.

The **Ashley** and **Wasatch National Forests** encompass most of the mountains; Utah's tallest peaks lie within the **High Uintas Wilderness Area,** a subsidiary of these two government territories. Here, even the most harassed city-dweller can find peace amid the tundra-covered meadows of the Uintas high country. The only major east-west range in the U.S., the Uintas have different environments on the shaded northern and exposed southern slopes. The mountains parallel U.S. 40, the main road connecting Vernal, UT, with Salt Lake City. Although the southern slope is the more developed and accessible of the two, hiking connoisseurs claim that the northern slope is prettiest. This slope is most accessible to I-80 via Rte. 414 or 530, or U.S. 191 out of southwestern Wyoming. Most trailheads on the northern side can be reached from **Manila, Utah,** on Rte. 44. **Browne Lake** and **Deep Creek campgrounds** are accessible from Hwy. 44 (pit toilets, water (which should be boiled before drinking); free). From here, the well-equipped backpacker can plunge into the wilder regions to the south and west. For more information, contact Ashley National Forest's Flaming Gorge ranger district in Manila, at the intersection of Rte. 43 and 44 (801-784-3445; open Memorial Day-Labor Day daily 8am-4:30pm). Several campgrounds line U.S. 191 as it winds through the aspen glens from Flaming Gorge south into Vernal and the arid Ashley Valley. Neither as remote nor as scenic as those near Manila, they are bigger and much more convenient. **Lodgepole,** 30 miles north of Vernal on Hwy. 91, is the best of the bunch. (Sites $5. Open June-Sept.)

Some easy trails out of Vernal include the East Park and Oak Park Trails, but hardier backpackers will want to head straight for the wilderness area, where 13,000-foot peaks tower over an unsullied wilderness (no vehicles allowed). The best launch sites are from the southern slope, 12 miles off U.S. 40. **Moon Lake** and **Yellow Pine** campgrounds (Sat.-Sun. only) in the **Rock Creek Canyon** are each just outside the primitive area boundary. Both are a few miles north of the tiny hamlet of **Mountain Home,** 20 miles north of U.S. 40 on Rte. 87. The High Uintas can also be approached from the west, through Wasatch National Forest off Rte. 150. The road provides the quickest access to the range from Salt Lake City. For information on southern access to the primitive area, contact the **Duchesne Ranger District,** P.O. Box 1, Duchesne, UT 84021 (801-738-2482), or stop by their office in Duchesne, on U.S. 40. (Open Mon.-Fri. 8am-6pm, Sat. 8am-4:30pm.) For western access, contact the **Wasatch National Forest,** 125 S. State St., Salt Lake City 84138 (801-524-5030).

Southern Utah

All five of Utah's national parks and three of her six national monuments grace the southern half of the state with their narrow canyons and broad swaths of desert. Although **Arches, Bryce,** and **Zion** have a tendency to become overcrowded during the summer months, **Capitol Reef, Natural Bridges** and **Cedar Breaks** offer a refreshing reprieve from the tourist crush. Traveling without a car here is difficult, and renting one in Salt Lake City or Provo might be well worth the cost. Cars can be used as campers in the extensive Dixie and Mani-La-Sal National Forests, or on the shores of Lake Powell and the Green and Colorado Rivers.

Bryce Canyon National Park

The fragile, slender spires of pink and red limestone that rise gracefully out of Bryce's canyons often seem part of an impressionist painting rather than the result of whimsical wind and water currents. But beautiful as they are, these barren canyons made life extremely difficult both for the native Paiute and for the first white settlers who attempted to settle here. Ebenezer Bryce, the first white man to view the canyon, called it "one hell of a place to lose a cow." It's also the perfect place to lose your big-city blues.

The park's **visitors center** (801-834-5322) is the place to begin a tour. Pick up a copy of the free Bryce Canyon *HooDoo,* which lists all park services, events, suggested hikes, and sight-seeing drives. (Open daily 8am-8pm; off-season 8am-4:30pm).

There are 23 **hikes** that let you explore Bryce. The best scenery is concentrated within 2 miles of the visitors center. Three spectacular lookouts—**Sunrise Point, Sunset Point,** and **Inspiration Point**—will refresh even the weariest traveler. Sunrises are especially rewarding sights. The section between Sunrise and Sunset Points is suitable for wheelchairs. The 3-mile loop of the **Navajo** and **Queen's Garden** trails takes you into the canyon itself. A strenuous way to escape the crowds is to conquer the **Trail to the Hat Shop,** 3.8 miles down an extremely steep descent. From the bottom, several pinnacles with gravel stones perched on their peaks are visible. The strenuous part, of course, is climbing back.

If you don't want to hike, you can drive the 15 miles from the visitors center to **Rainbow Point** and stop at the various lookouts along the way. Or take a **TW Services** bus tour. ($16, under 12 $3, departs from Bryce Lodge). Two-hour horseback rides to the canyon bottom are available at the corral across from the lodge ($15).

Bryce has two campgrounds planted among the tall ponderosa pines: **North Campground** and **Sunset Campground.** (Sites at both $6.) Public showers and a small grocery store are located at Sunrise Point, west of both campgrounds. (834-5361. Open 8am-8pm. Showers, $1.25 for 10 minutes available 8am-10pm). **Backcountry camping** at designated sites is a lovely way to become intimate with the canyon's changing moods and its wildlife. A free permit is required, available at the visitors center. There are six **Dixie National Forest** campgrounds, most about an hour away, just off Rte. 14. The best are **TE-AH Campground, Spruce Campground,** and the **Navajo Lake Campground.** (All $6 per night; no showers; running water and toilets.) The nearest Forest Service Office is in Panguitch, 225 E. Center St. (676-8815; open Mon.-Fri. 8am-4:30pm).

Bryce Canyon is in southwestern Utah, five hours south of Salt Lake City. From U.S. 89 at Bryce Junction (7 miles south of Panguitch), turn east on Rte. 12 and drive 17 miles to the park entrance (entrance fee $5 per car, $2 per pedestrian). There is no public transportation within the park. The **Cowboy Jubilee,** featuring singing, dancing, and rodeo rowdiness is a Bryce summer institution at Ruby's Inn (834-5341). Another popular annual event is the **Fiddler's Association Contest** in early July. Bryce has a **post office** at Ruby's Inn (open Mon.-Fri. 8am-5:15pm). The park's **ZIP code** is 84764.

Near Bryce

The recent paving of Hwy. 12 has now opened up some of the wilderness surrounding Bryce, including the beautiful towns of **Escalante** and **Boulder,** a reconstructed Anasazi village dating from about 1100 C.E. If you don't mind dodging cows and driving on dirt roads, head out 3 miles to **Lower Bowns Reservoir Lake** (425-3702; no drinking water, pit toilets; free). Near Escalante, try **Escalante State Park** (826-4466) where you may even find some petrified wood (showers, trailer space; sites $8). To hike into the unsullied desert environment of the **Phipps Death Hollow Outstanding Natural Area,** just north of Escalante, contact the Bureau of Land Management (826-4221), on Hwy. 12, about a mile west of town (Escalante Ranger District, Escalante, UT 84726). (Open Mon.-Fri. 7am-4:30pm, Sat. 8am-4:30pm, off-season Mon.-Fri. 8am-4:30pm.)

Wandering out of Bryce in the opposite direction, on Rte. 14 to Cedar City, you'll come across **Cedar Breaks National Monument** (admission $3 per car). The rim of the giant amphitheater is a lofty 10,350 feet above sea level; 2000 feet of flowered slopes separate the rim from the chiseled depths (disabled access). At **Point Supreme** you'll find a 30-site **campground** (sites $5) and the **visitors center.** (Open in summer only Mon.-Thurs. 8am-6pm, Fri. and Sat. 8am-7pm.) For more information, contact the **Superintendent,** Cedar Breaks National Monument, P.O. Box 749, Cedar City 84720.

Cedar City's **Iron Mission State Park,** 585 N. Main St. (586-9290) has an amazing horse-drawn vehicle collection and merits a visit. (Open daily 9am-7pm, off-season 9am-5pm. $1, under 6 free.) The cheapest place to stay is the **American Siesta Motel,** 427 S. Main St. (586-2700). Unfortunately, the grungy, tiny rooms are hardly comfortable or inviting. (Singles $21. Doubles $27.) For more information, contact the **Cedar City Visitor's Center,** 100 E. Center St. (586-4484; open Mon.-Fri. 8am-5pm).

Zion National Park

In contrast to Bryce's delicate beauty, the allure of Zion lies in its massiveness, in the feeling that no matter how deeply you penetrate into the wilderness, there will always be another breathtaking sight around the next bend. The landscape here inspired early Mormon and Methodist visitors with visions of paradise—hence the name of the park and of sights such as East Temple, Angel's Landing, and Cathedral Mountain. The waters of the **Virgin River,** which sculpted the canyon, offer a cool retreat from the summer heat. On the way to **Zion Canyon,** stop off at the **main visitors center** (722-3256), ½ mile past the entrance. The **ride board** in the visitors center can help you find a lift to more remote parts of the park. (Open daily 8am-9pm; off-season 8am-5pm.) Buses also travel to more remote regions ($4.50, seniors and children $2.25). The **Kolob Canyons Visitors Center** (586-9548) welcomes folks to the park's less-known region, in the northwest quadrant off I-15 (open daily 8am-8pm; off-season 8am-5pm; park entrance fee $5 per car, $2 per pedestrian). Make sure that you carry water wherever you go in the park. If you need emergency assistance, call 772-3256 or 800-624-9447.

Even if you plan to visit the Kolob Canyon's backcountry (a great idea), be sure to make the pilgrimage to **Zion Canyon.** Drive along the 7-mile dead-end road that follows the floor of the canyon, take the bus-tram (in summer only; $4.50, children $2.25), or catch a ride at the visitors center. You'll be going right between such giant formations as the **Sentinel, Mountain of the Sun,** and the overwhelming symbol of Zion, the **Great White Throne.** Short hikes to the base of the cliffs may be made on foot, as well as by wheelchair. A challenging trail takes you to **Observation Point,** where steep switchbacks let you explore an impossibly gouged canyon. Another difficult trail ascends to **Angel's Landing,** a lonely monolith that offers a heart-stopping path along the ridge and an amazing view of the canyon (5 miles). A great short hike runs to the Upper Emerald Pool (2 miles), passing the less spectacular lower and middle pools on the way. For fun without sweat, rent an inner tube ($5) from the shop across from the Canyon supermarket and float down the Virgin River near the campgrounds at the southern entrance.

The park maintains two campgrounds at the south gate, **South Campground** and **Watchman Campground** (772-3402). Bathrooms and drinking water available, but no showers. (Sites $6, 2-week max. stay. Open daily 9am-10pm.) Showers are $2 at Zion Canyon Campground 8am-8pm. There is a grocery store just outside the south entrance, about a 10-minute walk from the campgrounds. The visitors' center rangers present campfire programs nightly at 9pm at these two locations. The park's only other campground is a primitive area at Lava Point, accessible from a hiking trail in the midsection of the park or from the gravel road that turns off Rte. 9 in **Virgin.** You must obtain a free permit from the visitors center for **backcountry camping.** You cannot camp within Zion Canyon itself; hike up to the mesa top above. Observation Point is one of the only spots on the canyon rim where you can pitch a tent. Many backpackers spend a few nights on the 27-mile **West Rim Trail** (too long for a day's hike) or in the **Kolob Canyons,** where there's never a crowd. Zion Campground doesn't take reservations and often fills on holiday and summer weekends; if you don't get in, try one of the six campgrounds in Dixie National Forest (see Bryce Canyon).

The best place to stay outside the park is in **Kanab,** in the **Canyonlands International Youth Hostel.** The hostel offers roomy bunks and a fun-loving management. ($8, nonmembers $10.)

Zion National Park is most easily reached from I-15 between St. George and Cedar City. Zion Canyon, 30 miles from the interstate, is reached from exit 16 via Rte. 9 or from exit 27 on Rte. 17, then Rte. 9 to the park entrance. The park's Kolob Canyons region is directly accessible from I-15, exit 40, just south of New Harmony. From southernmost Kanab and points east, take U.S. 89 to Rte. 9, and enter through the eastern entrance by Checkerboard Mesa and several tunnels.

Greyhound serves the towns along I-15; ask if you can be let off at one of the exits if there is no scheduled stop. In St. George, Greyhound stops on St. George

Blvd., about 20 blocks from the turnpike. One bus arrives daily at each terminal from Salt Lake City (6 hr., $48.88) and Los Angeles (15 hr., $87) on schedules serving I-15, including Las Vegas and Provo. Hitching into the park is relatively easy, especially if you hold up a "Zion" sign. (Again, make sure you carry water.)

Capitol Reef National Park

Spiny and forbidding, like the backbone of an immense prehistoric sea creature, Capitol Reef's **Waterpocket Fold** dominates the terrain of south central Utah. This 100-mile-long line of sheer cliffs cuts the state's southern region in half. To the west lie Zion and Bryce Canyon; to the east lie Arches and Canyonlands. Major bus lines don't serve the park itself.

You'll want to make at least a brief stop at the park's **visitors center** (801-425-3791), on Rte. 24, for information on the Capitol Reef and daily activities. (Open 8am-7pm; off-season 8am-4:30pm.) Maps here are $6, guides to specific trails 10¢. The 25-mile round-trip **scenic drive** is the best way to see the park by car. This 90-minute jaunt takes you out along the "reef" itself. Nearby **Capitol Dome,** which resembles the U.S. Capitol, explains the other half of the park's unusual name. If you have a few days to spare, explore the park's desert backcountry. Foot trails and four-wheel-drive roads crisscross the region, giving access to the area's most inspiring, remote scenery. Keep in mind that summer temperatures average 95°F and most water found in seep springs and rain-holding waterpockets is contaminated.

For **backcountry camping,** you must obtain a free permit from the visitors center. Sites at the pleasant, grassy main campground cost $5 and are available on a first come-first serve basis. Located just a mile from the visitors center, the campground lies in the heart of the old orchard town of **Fruita.** When the Park Service bought the land for Capitol Reef back in the 60s, they suddenly found themselves with the town's extensive fruit orchards on their hands, with no one to pick the fruit. Summer tourists can now harvest fruit from late June (cherries) to mid-October (apples). In between are bountiful harvests of apricots, peaches, and pears, all for ridiculously low prices.

For accommodations and restaurants in this region, try: **Torrey,** 11 miles west of the visitors center on U.S. 24; **Boulder,** 50 miles south of the visitors center on U.S. 12; or **Hanksville,** 37 miles from the visitors center on U.S. 24. The **Redrock Restaurant and Campground** (542-3235), in Hanksville, are the main tourist services here. Meals at the restaurant are $4-$7 (Open daily 7am-10pm). Tent suites at the campground $6, with electricity and water $7, full hookup $10.

If you've ever wanted to see real *wild* buffalo, not the mangy kind they pen up at tourist traps, head for Hanksville and the **Henry Mountains,** 30 miles east of the visitors center near the intersection of Rte. 24 and 95. The largest free-roaming buffalo herd in the continental U.S. lives here. From an original group of 18 transplanted here in 1941, the herd has grown to its present size of about 100. In winter, the sturdy bison graze in the mountains' lower meadows. The warmth of summer makes them more elusive; look for them in high alpine valleys.

Arches National Park

In Arches National Park, nature has been experimenting with avant-garde sculpture for millions of years. One hundred million years ago, the constant movement of a primordial sea deposited an uneven, unstable salt bed on the Colorado Plateau. The sea evaporated, but periodic washes, along with the tireless winds, deposited layer after layer of debris upon the new salt crust. Unable to bear the weight of the debris, which became compacted into extremely heavy rock, the salt twisted, buckled, and crumbled. It left some of the most fantastic natural shapes in the world: towering spires, pinnacles, and, of course, arches. Arches National Park has the highest density of arches in the world (more than 200), and these are often so perfectly formed that early explorers thought the huge arches were, like Stonehenge in England, works of some lost culture. Don't miss this spot, especially since you can stay for $5 at the **Lazy Lizard Hostel** in nearby Moab.

The park **visitors center**, 27 miles south of I-70, 3½ miles north of Moab on U.S. 191, provices 35¢ auto tour guides. (Open daily 8am-6pm; off-season 8am-4:30pm.) For additional information, contact Superintendent, Arches National Park, P.O. Box 907, Moab 84532 (259-8161). $5 per car will get you an entrance pass good for seven days at both Arches and nearby Canyonlands. Pedestrians and bikers pay only $1.

You will find plenty of scenic wonders along the 25-mile road between the visitors center and Devil's Garden. No matter how short your stay, be sure to see the **Windows Section** at **Panorama Point**, about ½ way along the road. Cyclists will also enjoy this ride in spring or fall, but the steep inclines make the trip unbearable in the summer heat. **Rim Cyclery**, 94 W. 100 N. (259-5333), offers bikes for $20 per day, including helmet and water bottle. (Open Mon.-Sat. 9am-9pm, Sun. 9am-6pm; off-season daily 9am-6pm.) At the end of the paved road by the campground, **Devil's Garden** has an astounding 64 arches. The climax of your visit should be **Delicate Arch**, the symbol of the monument. Take the Delicate Arch turn-off from the main road 2 miles down a graded unpaved road (impassible after rainstorms). Once you get to Wolfe Ranch, go down a 1½-mile foot trail to Delicate Arch. The free-standing arch spans 33 feet and rises 45 feet. Beyond it you can get a glimpse of the Colorado River gorge and the La Sal Mountains. If you're lucky, you may come across petroglyphs—writings on the stone walls left by the Anasazi and Ute who roamed the area from 1000 to 100 years ago. Please don't touch—preserve them for future wanderers.

Of course, arches aren't the only natural wonders here. Two of the most popular trails, the 1-mile **Park Avenue** stroll and the moderately strenuous 2-mile **Fiery Furnace Trail** lead downward into the canyon bottoms, providing views of the cliffs and monoliths above. Unless you are an experienced hiker don't attempt the **Fiery Furnace** trail alone; there are no guide markers and the ranger on duty will be more than happy to guide you safely through the labyrinth.

The park's only **campground**, Devil's Garden, has 53 sites; get there early since all the sites are often snatched up by 1pm. The campground is 18 miles from the visitors center and has running water. (2-week max. stay. Sites $5. Open April-Oct.) **Dead Horse Point State Park**, perched on the rim of the Colorado Gorge south of Arches and 14 miles south of U.S. 191, is accessible from Rte. 313. The campground has modern rest rooms, water, hookups, and covered picnic tables. (Sites $6-8. Open April-Oct.) Winter camping is allowed on Dead Horse Point itself. For more information, contact the Park Superintendent, Dead Horse Point State Park, P.O. Box 609, Moab 84532 (259-6511). **Backcountry camping** in Arches National Park is a free adventure. Register at the visitors center first, and pick up a **USGS map** to avoid getting lost. Bring plenty of water and avoid hiking on summer afternoons. Better than either the campground at Arches or Dead Horse Point in the summer, however, is the **Manti-la-Sal National Forest**, where you can escape the heat, the crowds, and the biting gnats. These campgrounds are about 4000 feet higher up, and about 20 to 25 miles southeast of Moab off U.S. 191. All are free, except **Warner**, which charges $4. Three miles down a dirt road is **Oowah Lake**, a rainbow trout heaven (fishing permit $5 per day). Camping is free (no water, pit toilets). For more information on the forest, contact the Manti-la-Sal National Forest Service office in Moab, 125 W. 200 S. (259-7155. Open Mon.-Fri. 8am-4:30pm.)

Moab (pop. 5500) and the surrounding area is also speckled with private campgrounds. The **Holiday Haven Mobile Home and RV Park**, 400 West (259-5834) charges $10 per site, with water $11, with electricity and water $12, full hookup $13. The **Canyonland Campark**, 555 S. Main St. (259-6848) asks $10 per site, with electricity and water $14, full hookup $16. The **Moab KOA**, 4 miles south on U.S. 191 (259-6682) charges $12 for a tent site, with electricity and water $13, full hookup $14-16. The town of Moab, just below the park, is the ideal place to find food and indoor lodging during a visit to Arches. The **Lazy Lizard Hostel**, 1213 S. Hwy. 191 (259-6057) has clean bunk rooms and extremely friendly management

($6 per night. Private singles $10, doubles $15). The **Prospector Motel,** 186 N. 100 W. has fantastic A/C and assiduous service. (Singles $20. Doubles $25).

Moab is also a popular departure point for river raft, kayak, and canoe trips. **Descent River Expeditions** (801-259-7252), 321 N. Main St., Moab, UT 84532, and **Tex's River Expeditions** (801-259-5101) N. Hwy. 191, Moab, UT 84532, offer trips for $25-35 per day. Whitewater raft tours run daily.

The entrance to the park is on the paved road that winds for 25 miles into its interior. This road is accessible from U.S. 191 at the junction 5 miles north of Moab. Arches is 230 miles from Salt Lake City. Buses will stop along I-70, in Crescent Junction, where you can hitch south along 191. (Note: There is no place to stay in Crescent Junction.) If you're driving in from I-70, take Rte. 128 from Cisco; it follows the Colorado River Gorge all the way to 191. **Hitching** is tough only because of the heat—bring lots of water on summer afternoons.

The **Moab Visitor's Center,** 191 Main St. (259-8825) can provide information on lodging and dining in Moab. (Open Mon.-Sat. 8am-7pm. Sun. 8am-6pm; Labor Day-Memorial Day Mon.-Sat. 8am-6pm, Sun. 8am-5pm). The **Moab Post Office,** 39 S. Main St. (644-2760) is open Mon.-Fri. 8:30am-4pm, Sat. 9am-noon. Moab's **ZIP code** is 84741.

Canyonlands National Park

The scenery at the confluence of the Green and Colorado Rivers in **Canyonlands National Park** proves conclusively that when these two mighty waterways joined they refused to be satisfied with an uneventful meeting. The merging rivers gouged out rifts and gorges that sink into the desert's crust with a dizzying starkness. At those points in the park which the rivers bypassed, the harsh desert prevails. The entire park, with its scenic but arid terrain, has remained remote and wild. Roads here are unpaved, trails primitive, and the vistas some of the most breathtaking in the southwest.

Outside the park, there are two information centers. In **Monticello's National Park Service Office,** 32 S. 1st E. (587-2737) sells maps for $2.50-6. In **Moab,** the **Park Service** resides at 125 W. 200 S. (259-7164) and has the same business hours. Both can provide information for French, German, and Spanish visitors.

The park has three distinct areas. The most easily reached region is **Needles** (ranger station 259-6568), in the park's southeast corner. (Open daily 8am-5pm.) To get there, take Rte. 211 west from U.S. 163, about 40 miles south of Moab. This well-maintained paved road begins 34 miles from the park entrance, so be sure to have plenty of gas and water, and register with the park ranger before entering this area. Farther north, deep within the "Y" formed by the two rivers, sits the **Island in the Sky** (ranger station 259-6568; open Sun.-Wed. 8am-5pm, Thurs.-Sat. 8am-6pm). Access to this dramatic mesa is a little more difficult; take Rte. 313 west from U.S. 163 about 10 miles north of Moab. The road becomes dirt before it enters the park, but it's kept in good condition. The most remote district of the park is the rugged **Maze** area (ranger station 259-6513; open daily 8am-4:30pm), to the west of the canyons, accessible only by four-wheel drive. Once you've entered a section of the park, you're committed. Transferring from one area to another involves retracing your steps and re-entering the park, a tedious trip lasting from several hours to a full day.

Each ranger station has a booklet of possible hikes (including photos), so you can pick your own. Hiking options from the Needles area are probably the best. Cyclists should check at the visitor's centers for lists of trails.

If hiking in desert heat doesn't appeal to you, you can rent jeeps and mountain bikes at the **Needles Outpost,** or take an airplane ride ($25 for a 25-min. flight). **Lin Ottinger Tours,** 137 N. Main St., Moab (259-7312), leads all-day jeep and backpacking tours ($25-35) that teach you how to survive on local flora.

Each region has its own official **campground.** In the Needles district, **Squaw Flat** is situated in a sandy plain surrounded by giant sandstone towers. Avoid this area in June, when flying insects swarm. Water is usually available from April through

September. A $5 fee is also charged during these months. **Willow Flat Campground,** in the Island in the Sky unit, sits high atop the mesa. You must bring your own water, but sites are free. Willow Flat and Squaw Flat both have picnic tables, grills, and pit toilets, and both operate on a first come-first serve basis. The campground at the **Maze Overlook** has no amenities at all. Dead Horse Point State Park (adjacent to Island in the Sky) and Manti-la-Sal National Forest (adjacent to the Needles) provide alternative campsites. (See Arches National Park.) Before **backcountry camping** be sure to get a free permit from the ranger's office in the proper district, and to take along plenty of water (at least one gallon per person per day). Summer temperatures regularly climb to over 100°F.

There are no food services in the park. Just outside the boundary in the Needles district, however, the **Needles Outpost** houses a limited, expensive grocery store and gas pumps. Hauling groceries in from Moab or Green River (for the Maze) is the best budget alternative.

CALIFORNIA

California is often singled out as the apex of modern American life. Hot tubs, roller skates, and suntans are necessities in California, not merely privileges. And nowhere in America has the automobile been held in greater reverence. Some would further claim that people here adopt a different language filled with affected pauses and vacuous phrases, as if the Good Life defies description, or, in the end, simply doesn't require description. The claims are true—to a point. Fads seem to sweep the state with seasonal regularity, and every esoteric cause has its California champion. Natives of the state show a loyalty to their lifestyle they feel no compunction to explain.

Among its superlatives, California can count the highest and lowest points in the continental U.S., most populous state in America, and more performances of Disneyland's Horseshoe Revue than any other show in the nation. Disneyland itself is the country's most famous tourist spot: The Emperor of Japan wore a Mickey Mouse watch for years after his visit, and Krushchev was livid when he couldn't get in.

For more comprehensive coverage of California than we can provide here, consult *Let's Go: California & Hawaii.*

Practical Information

Capital: Sacramento.

Visitor Information: California Office of Tourism, 1121 L St., #103, Sacramento 95814 (916-322-1396). **National Park Information,** 213-888-3770. **Weather in California National Parks,** 415-556-6030.

Time Zone: Pacific (3 hr. behind Eastern). **Postal Abbreviation:** CA.

San Diego

San Diego's clean air, miles of beaches, perfect weather, and crescent bay have moved San Diegans to name their town "America's Finest City." Underlying these natural advantages is the prosperity that comes from being a center of the defense industry during the Reagan era. As a result the city has recently exploded in size and population and is currently California's second-largest city and the U.S.'s sixth-largest. No one wants San Diego to turn into another L.A. jungle, but natives who want to preserve a small-town feel fight a hard battle against the forces of expansion.

San Diego offers ample tourist attractions. Your most enjoyable destination, however, might simply be a patch of sand at one of the superb beaches. It's also a great city for frittering days away just relishing the climate and the diffuse amiability. When exploring, don't neglect residential communities such as Hillcrest, La Jolla, and Ocean Beach. If you need relief from city noise, and the beach isn't enough, get away to the nearby mountains and deserts or head for Mexico.

Practical Information

Emergency: 911.

Visitor Information Center: 11 Horton Plaza (236-1212), downtown at 1st Ave. and F St. Open daily 8:30am-5:30pm. **Old Town and State Park Information,** 4002 Wallace Ave. (237-6770), in Old Town Square next to Burguesa. Take the Taylor St. exit off I-8 or bus #5. Historical brochures on Old Town $2. Open 10am-5pm. **Arts/Entertainment Hotline,** 234-2787.

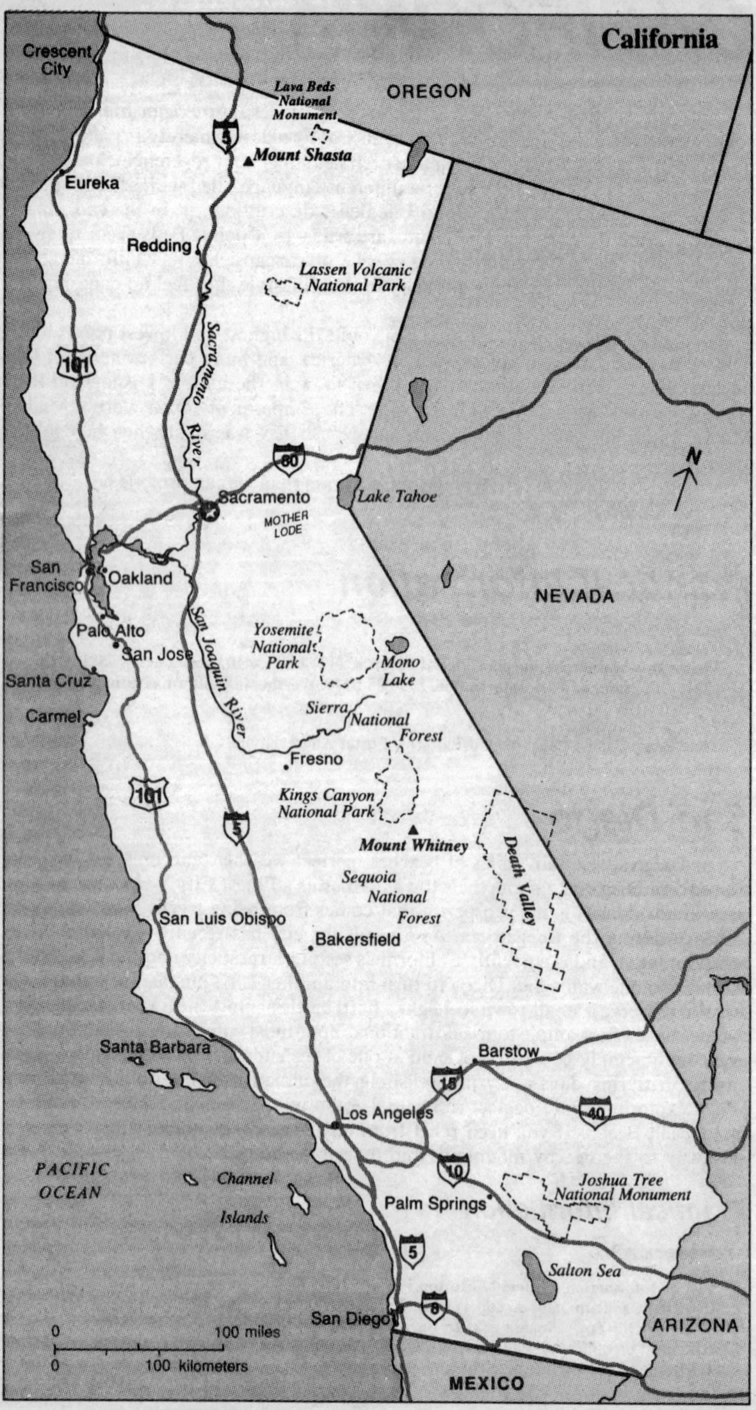
California
Crescent City
OREGON
Lava Beds National Monument
Mount Shasta
Eureka
Redding
Lassen Volcanic National Park
101
Sacramento River
80
Sacramento
Lake Tahoe
MOTHER LODE
N
San Francisco
Oakland
NEVADA
Palo Alto
San Jose
San Joaquin River
Yosemite National Park
Mono Lake
Santa Cruz
Carmel
Sierra National Forest
Fresno
101
Kings Canyon National Park
Mount Whitney
Death Valley
Sequoia National Forest
San Luis Obispo
Bakersfield
Santa Barbara
Barstow
15
40
Los Angeles
10
PACIFIC OCEAN
Channel Islands
Joshua Tree National Monument
Palm Springs
5
Salton Sea
8
San Diego
ARIZONA
0 100 miles
0 100 kilometers
MEXICO

San Diego Council American Youth Hostels: 1031 India St., 92101 (239-2644), between Broadway and C St. Student travel information, bike accessories, travel gear, and guides. Sponsors domestic and European trips. Open Mon.-Fri. 9:30am-5:30pm, Sat. 9:30am-4:30pm. After hours, you'll get a recorded listing of hostels in San Diego.

Travelers Aid: Airport (231-7361), with 1 station in each terminal. Open daily 9am-10pm. **Downtown,** 1122 4th Ave., #201 (232-7991). Open Mon.-Fri. 8:30am-5pm.

San Diego International Airport (Lindbergh Field): at the northwestern edge of downtown, across from Harbor Island. San Diego Transit bus #2 ("30th and Adams") goes downtown ($1). Buses depart every 20-30 min. 5:50am-11:30pm. Cab fare downtown around $7.

Amtrak: Santa Fe Depot, 1050 Kettner Blvd. (239-9021 or 800-872-7245), at Broadway. Reasonably safe area. To L.A. (8 per day, $23, round-trip Mon.-Thurs. $30, Fri.-Sun. $46). Information on bus, trolley, car and boat transportation available at the station. Ticket office open daily 5:10am-9pm.

Greyhound: 120 W. Broadway (239-9171), at 1st Ave. Reasonably safe area. To L.A. (12 per day, $15).

Local Transit: see Getting Around below.

Car Rental: Rent a Car Cheep, 1747 Pacific Hwy. (238-1012). $18 per day with unlimited mileage. Open daily 7am-11pm. Must be 18 with major credit card. **Rent-a-Wreck,** 3309 Midway Dr. (224-8235). $22 per day. 100 free miles, 20¢ each additional mile. $99 per week includes 700 miles. Open Mon.-Fri. 8am-5pm, Sat. 8am-3pm, Sun. 10am-3pm. Must be 21 with major credit card. **Aztec Rent-a-Car,** 2401 Pacific Hwy. (232-6117). $25 per day. 150 free miles, 25¢ each additional mile. $135 per week includes 1000 miles. Open Mon.-Fri. 7am-10pm, Sat.-Sun. 8am-5pm. Must be 21 with major credit card. Cars may go south of the border, but only if you purchase Mexican insurance.

Bike Rental: Hamel's Bike and Skate Rentals, 704 Ventura Place, Mission Beach (488-5050). Bicycles, roller skates, rollerblades, or surfboards $4 per hr., $15 per day. Boogie boards $3 per hr., $10 per day. Tandem bikes $8 per hr., $30 per day. Open Mon.-Fri. 10am-7pm, Sat.-Sun. 9am-7pm; off-season daily 10am-6pm. Must have driver's license. **Alexander's,** 4315 Ocean Blvd. (273-0171), Mission Beach. Bikes and skates $2 per hr., $8 for 6 hr. Boogie boards $3 per hr., $9 per 6 hr. Open daily 9am-9pm.

Taxi: Yellow Cab, 234-6161.

Help Lines: Crime Victims Help Line, 236-0101. 24 hours. **Rape Crisis,** 233-3088. 24 hours. **Women's Center,** 2467 E St. (233-8984). Open Mon.-Fri. 8:30am-4:30pm.

Lesbian and Gay Men's Center: 3780 5th Ave. (692-2077). For counseling hotline call 692-4297 Mon.-Sat. 6-10pm. Young people can contact the **Gay Youth Alliance,** 4190 Front St., Hillcrest (233-9309), a support and social group for gay men and lesbians under 24. For a listing of all gay events and establishments check the *Update* (225-0282), available at virtually all gay businesses, bookstores and bars.

Senior Citizen's Services: 202 C St. (236-5765), in the City Hall building. Provides ID cards so that seniors can take advantage of discounts. Plans daytrips and serves meals at 8 "nutrition sites." Open Mon.-Fri. 8am-5pm.

Community Service Center for the Disabled: 2864 University Ave., Hillcrest (293-3500). Attendant referral, wheelchair repair and sales, emergency housing, motel/hotel accessibility referral, and **TDD Line** services for the hearing impaired (293-7757). Open Mon.-Fri. 9am-5pm.

Post Office: 2535 Midway Dr. (547-0477). Open Mon.-Fri. 7am-5pm, Sat. 8am-4pm. **ZIP code:** 92138.

Area Code: 619.

Orientation

San Diego rests in the extreme southwestern corner of California, 127 miles south of L.A. and 15 miles north of the Mexican border. **I-5** runs south from Los Angeles and skirts the eastern edge of downtown San Diego. Suburbanites north of downtown spend a sizable fraction of their lives on this six-lane strip. **I-8** runs east-west along downtown's northern boundary, connecting the desert in the east with Ocean

Beach in the west. The major downtown thoroughfare, **Broadway,** also runs east-west.

A cluster of skyscrapers in the block surrounding **Horton Plaza,** 4th Ave. and Broadway, makes up downtown San Diego. The downtown street scheme is frustrating because it tries to make sense, but fails. Streets running parallel to the bay on the western end of downtown are simply given names until they hit Horton Plaza in the east and streets farther east are numbered consecutively. Cutting east-west across these north-south avenues are the lettered streets, with A St. farthest north and L St. farthest south. In between, Broadway replaces D St. and runs directly east from the bay. Easterners who are accustomed to muscling their way across a street against the light will either be impressed or amused by the San Diegan habit of waiting obediently for the walk signal, no matter how clear the coast. Jaywalking is taboo and tickets are issued freely.

On the northeastern corner of downtown, **Balboa Park,** larger than the city center, is bounded by 6th Ave. on the west, I-5 and Russ St. on the south, 28th St. on the east, and Myrtle Way and Upas St. on the north. To the north and east of Balboa Park are the main residential areas. **Hillcrest,** San Diego's most cosmopolitan district and a center of the gay community, is located at the park's northwestern corner, centered on 5th and University Ave. (also a major bus transfer point). **University Heights** and **North Park** sit along the major east-west thoroughfares of University Ave., El Cajon Blvd., and Adams Ave.

West of downtown is the bay, 17 miles long and formed by the Coronado Peninsula (jutting northward from Imperial Beach), and Point Loma (dangling down from Ocean Beach). North of Ocean Beach are Mission Beach (with neighboring Mission Bay), Pacific Beach, and La Jolla.

Getting Around

A car is extremely helpful in San Diego, but it is possible to reach most areas of the city by bus. The regional transit systems (San Diego Transit, North County Transit, DART, FAST, and Dial-A-Ride) cover the area from Oceanside in the north to Tijuana, Mexico and inland to Escondido, Julian, and other towns.

Public Transportation Information answers questions daily 5:30am to 8:25pm (233-3004). Bus service is scanty after 9pm. Most urban routes originate or pass through downtown. Another principal transfer point is in Hillcrest at 5th and University Ave. A good resource is the **Transit Store,** 449 Broadway (234-1060), at 5th Ave. (Open Mon.-Sat. 8:30am-5:30pm, Sun. noon-5:30pm.) Ask for the *Regional Transit Guide,* a well-designed route map and compendium of facts. Fares vary: North County Transit routes 75¢, local routes $1, express routes $1.25, and commuter routes about $2.25. Transfers within San Diego are free, other transfers cost 25¢ and more on premium-fare routes. Exact change is required. Most city buses accept dollar bills. At least one wheelchair-accessible bus travels per hour. Those over 62 receive discounts. Buses on some routes, especially those to the beaches, are equipped with bike racks. Those in San Diego for an extended stay may purchase **Ready Passes** ($45), good on all rides except commuter express routes.

The **San Diego Trolley** runs on two lines from a starting point near the Santa Fe depot (on C St. at Kettner). One heads east to **La Mesa.** The other, popularly known as the Tijuana Trolley, crosses 16 barren miles south to **San Ysidro** at the Mexican border daily every 15 to 20 minutes 5:30am to 9pm. From the border, cabs to the Tijuana Cultural Center or shopping district are less than $5. The trolley also provides access to local buses in National City, Chula Vista, and Imperial Beach. The trolley is wheelchair-accessible. (Fare $1.50, ages 63 and over and disabled passengers 50¢, rides confined to C St. and 12th Ave. downtown 25¢. Transfers free.) You're on the honor system; purchase a ticket from machines at stations and board the trolley. There are no turnstiles or ticket takers, but occasionally an inspector will check for tickets. The **Molly Trolley** (233-9177), primarily for sightseers, also provides transportation to points of interest such as Balboa Park and Seaport Village. It also picks up tourists at Hotel Circle. All-day passes can be purchased for $6 whenever you climb aboard. Trolleys run once per hour daily 9am-7pm during spring and summer and 9am-7pm during fall and winter.

Accommodations

Although San Diego attracts visitors throughout the year, both lodging rates and the number of tourists skyrocket in summer, particularly on weekends. However, residential hotels offering inexpensive weekly rates are numerous, especially downtown, and usually safe, although those who desire Holiday Inn sterility should probably find a motel. If you have a car, consider camping outside San Diego (see Camping).

Downtown

Most hotels listed are in a safe area to the north and south of the bus and train stations.

Armed Services YMCA Hostel (AYH), 500 W. Broadway (232-1133), has 2 types of accommodations. The first, which requires AYH membership, is stark rooms with frame beds and old mattresses (linen not included). Check-out 9:30am. Beds $8. The second is newly remodeled rooms with communal baths. Check-out noon. Singles $20. Doubles $30. Key deposit $2.

YWCA Women's Hostel, 1012 C St. (239-0355), at 10th Ave. Women only. Quite friendly. Dorm rooms for ages 18-34. Hall bathrooms. 12 beds. No upper age limit for AYH members. Check-out 11am. $8.25; nonmembers over 34, singles $17, doubles $26. Linen $5. Key deposit $5. Often full.

Siesta Motor Inn, 1449 9th Ave. (239-9113), at Beech St. Close to Balboa Park. Comfortable, attractive rooms. A/C and pool. Check-out 11am. Singles $37. Doubles $41. Key deposit $2.

Clarke's Flamingo Lodge, 1765 Union St. (234-6787), 7 blocks north of Broadway, with a stunning pink and blue color scheme. Color TV, pool, A/C, telephone, coffee maker. Check-out 1pm. Singles $33. Doubles $43. Reservations often necessary.

The Maryland Hotel, 630 F St. (239-9243). The raspberry and white lobby is fancier than the clean but spare rooms. Mostly houses older residents. Housekeeping, laundry, and telephone service available. Beauty shop and pharmacy on the premises. Singles $17, with bath $22. Doubles with bath $30.

Mission Hills, Hillcrest, Mission Valley

E-Z 8 Motels, 4 locations: 2484 Hotel Circle Pl., Mission Valley (291-8252); 4747 Pacific Hwy., Old Town (294-2512); 3325 Midway Dr. (224-3166), between Point Loma and Old Town; 3333 Channel Way (223-9500), near the Sports Arena. All have TV, pool, A/C. Check-out 11am. Singles $31.88. Doubles $34.88. Triples and quads $37.88.

Eaglecrest Motel, 3942 8th Ave. (298-0350), between University and Washington. Take bus #16 or 25. Pleasant, yellow stucco building in good neighborhood. Check-out 11am. Simple sleeping rooms with no frills and no bath $20, with TV and phone $30-34, with bath $35.

South and East of Downtown

Imperial Beach Hostel (AYH), 170 Palm Ave. (423-8039). Take bus #901 from the train station or take the trolley on C St. to Palm St. Station (35 min.). Transfer to bus #33 westbound every hour on the half-hour. In a converted firehouse 2 blocks from the beach. 5 miles from Mexico. Quiet, with well-equipped kitchen and large common area with a TV. 37 bunkbeds. Open 7:30-9:30am and 4:30-11pm, registration 4:30-10pm. $8, nonmembers $11. Key deposit $2. Reserve by phone or send 1st night's lodging.

Point Loma Hostel (AYH), 3790 Udall St. (223-4778). Take bus #35 from downtown, get off at the Alpha Beta shopping center at Voltaire and Worden St., and walk 1 block south to Udall St. An airy 2-story building 20 min. from Ocean Beach, also convenient to downtown and the airport. 78 bunk beds, common room, kitchen. Open 7:30-9:30am and 4:30-11pm. Check-out 9:15am. $8, nonmembers $11. Reserve by sending first night's lodging.

Camping

All state campgrounds charge bikers $2 per night and state law requires that no cyclist be turned away due to overcrowding. The only campground within city limits is Campland on the Bay. For information on state park camping, call the helpful people at San Elijo Beach (753-5091). Camping reservations are handled by MISTIX (800-444-7275). Most parks are completely full in summer and it's common to make reservations eight weeks in advance.

Campland on the Bay, 2211 Pacific Beach Dr. (274-6260). Take I-5 to Grand Ave. exit and follow the signs, or take bus #30 and get off on Grand at the sign on the left. Expensive and crowded because it's the only central place to pitch a tent or plug in an RV. The cheapest sites are in a "dirt area" with nothing to block the wind coming off the water. Sites $33-43; Labor Day-Memorial Day $24-29.

San Elijo Beach State Park, Rte. 21 south of Cardiff-by-the-Sea (753-5091). 171 sites set on cliffs over the sea. Good landscaping makes it seem less crowded than it is. Hiker/biker campsites. Sites $12. Reserve in summer.

San Diego Metropolitan KOA, 111 N. 2nd Ave. (427-3601), in Chula Vista, south of the city. Check-out noon. For 2 people: tent sites $22, RV sites $27, each additional adult $3, each additional child $2. Reserve a week ahead in summer.

Food

If speedy burritos set your heart ablaze, the best Mexican fast food spot is probably **Roberto's,** 3202 Mission Blvd. and other locations. Pick up cheap, high-quality fruits and vegetables at the **Farmer's Bazaar,** 205 7th Ave. (233-0281), at L St. (open Tues.-Sat. 9am-5:30pm, Sun. 9am-5pm) or at one of Ocean Beach's several organic grocery stores. Pick up a copy of the *San Diego Metropolitan* for a full listing of downtown emporia.

Kansas City Barbeque, 610 W. Market St. (231-9680), south of Broadway near the bay. Chicken, pork, or beef dinners (under $7) include two of the following: slaw, beans, fries, or rings. Open daily 11am-10pm.

Kiyo's, 531 F St. (238-1726). Proudly claims to be the oldest sushi bar in the San Diego area. Try one of their specials (from $4). Open Mon.-Fri. 11:30am-2:30pm and 5-10pm, Sat. 5-10pm.

Chuey's Café, 1894 Main St. (234-6937), in Barrio Logan. Get off at the Barrio Logan trolley stop and walk 1 block toward stoplight. A stretch out of downtown, but people go out of their way for this combination restaurant/cocktail bar/pool hall. Excellent Mexican entrees ($4-6), huge combination plates, and gringo food. Open Mon.-Fri. 11am-7:30pm, Sat. 11am-3:30pm.

Veva's Mexican Café, 739 E St. (234-7795). Open the screen door to a justifiably busy lunch counter. Two enchiladas with rice $3. Open Mon.-Fri. 7am-3pm.

San Diego Chicken Pie Shop, 3801 5th Ave. (295-0156), at Robinson. Owner George Whitehead has been selling great food at low prices for 51 years. An average of 3000 pies sold daily. The namesake dish comes with whipped potatoes, vegetable, roll, and dessert ($3.20). Open daily 10am-8pm.

Hong Kong Restaurant, 3871 4th Ave. (291-9449). Good, cheap Cantonese, Mandarin, and Szechuan dishes served with soup, rice, and eggroll $3-4. Kung pao chicken $6, pork chop suey $5. Open Mon.-Fri. 11am-2:30pm and 4:30pm-11pm, Sat. and Sun. 4:30pm-11pm.

The India St. Colony, 3700 block of India St., off Washington. An informal collection of inexpensive restaurants serving Japanese, Greek, Mexican, and American food. Highlights include **El Indio,** 3695 India St. (299-0333), where the line stretches down the block. Extremely busy, but they have speedy service, high quality, and large portions. The beef burrito ($3.06) is great. Open daily 10am-9pm. **Fish Pier VII,** 3701 India St. (574-7758), has huge portions of grilled fish with rice and vegetables ($5-7) and a large salad bar ($5). Open Mon.-Fri. 11am-10pm, Sat. noon-10pm.

Point Loma Seafoods, 2805 Emerson (223-1109 or 223-6553), off Rosecrans by the bay. Take bus #29 from downtown. They claim to be "The Freshest Thing in Town" and sell fish directly from the boat. Good, gooey crab sandwich $4.50. Always crowded at lunch. Open Mon.-Sat. 9am-8pm, Sun. noon-8pm.

Margarita's, 4955 Newport Ave., Ocean Beach (224-7454). Everyone, from local Kiwanis to O.B. surf bums, eventually eats here. Good for any meal, but the best deal is breakfast (2 fried eggs, toast, and hash browns $2.25). If Margarita's doesn't appeal to you, check out the boulevard for plenty of other restaurants engaged in the breakfast price war. Open Sun.-Fri. 8am-9pm and Sat. 8am-9:30pm; in winter open 8am-9pm.

Nicolosi's Pizza, 4009 El Cajon Blvd. (282-9919). This family-owned establishment prides itself on its homemade baked lasagna (with soup or salad and oven-fresh bread $6.50). Open Mon.-Sat. 11am-11pm, Sun. noon-10pm.

Julio's, 4502 University Ave. (282-6837). Another one of San Diego's dimly lit Mexican restaurants with good food, set apart only by its late hours. Try big burritos with dressings ($3.25; $2.75 at lunch) or 2 enchiladas ($4.70). Open Mon.-Thurs. 11am-11pm, Fri.-Sat. 11am-3am, Sun. 9am-11pm.

Don Jose's, 4551 El Cajon Blvd. (284-9519), take bus #15. Natives swear by this little-known place whose specialty is sour cream enchiladas ($4.60). Also famous for its avocado soft tacos. Open daily 11am-11pm.

Quel Fromage, 523 University Ave. (295-1600). Popular café with an East Coast atmosphere. Pep up with potent espresso ($1), or sedate yourself with cheesecake ($2.25). Energy Adjustment Hour 5-7pm (double espresso for the price of single). Open Sun.-Thurs. 7:30am-11pm, Fri-Sat. 7:30am-midnight.

Sights

In contrast to the rest of southern California, where the pre-fab houses and mobile homes make the cities appear like newborn, low-rent infants, San Diego's buildings are a tangible record of the city's long history. The oldest buildings are the early 19th-century adobes of **Old Town.** Just up Juan St. from Old Town, **Heritage Park** displays old Victorian homes, carefully trimmed and painted like gingerbread houses. Extending from Broadway south to the railroad tracks and bounded by 4th and 6th Ave. on the west and east, the **Gaslamp Quarter** is home to a concentration of pre-1910 commercial buildings now undergoing gentrification with a retail flair. Lastly, fine houses and apartment buildings from 1910 to 1950, in dozens of styles from Mission Revival to zig-zag Moderne, are found on almost every block. The **Gaslamp Quarter Foundation** 410 Island Ave. (233-5227), in the William Heath Davis House, offers free two-hour walking tours of the city, departing from the foundation office on Sat. at 10am and 1pm.

For less structured fun, kick back at the beaches, where surfers catch totally tubular waves, sun-worshippers catch basal cell carcinoma, and eventually everybody is caught up in beach-induced lassitude.

Downtown

The centerpiece of San Diego's redevelopment is **Horton Plaza,** at Broadway and 4th Ave. This pastel-colored confection of glass and steel is an open-air, multi-level shopping center encompassing seven city blocks. Only M.C. Escher could navigate the inner staircases. (Free 3-hr. parking in garage.) Along with its neighbor, the million-dollar-per-unit condominium project known as **Meridian,** Horton Plaza signals San Diego's renewed interest in downtown. Another notable example of local architecture, just 3 blccks west of Horton Plaza, is the **Santa Fe Depot,** Kettner Blvd., a Mission Revival building whose grand arches welcomed visitors to the 1915 exposition. The building is currently the San Diego Amtrak depot.

South of downtown the **Coronado Bridge** stretches westward from Banio Logan to the Coronado Peninsula. A breathtaking sight (for squat San Diego), the sleek, sky-blue arc rests upon spindly piers but executes a near-90° turn over the waters of San Diego Bay before touching down in Coronado. Although its eastern end cuts a swath through San Diego's largest Chicano community, residents have prevented it from dividing their neighborhood by taking legal possession of the land beneath the bridge, creating **Chicano Park.** They have also taken spiritual possession of the bridge itself by painting splendid murals on the piers. The murals, visible from I-5 but fully appreciated only by walking around the park, are heroic in scale and theme, drawing on Hispanic-American, Spanish, Mayan, and Aztec imagery. (Take bus #13 or the San Ysidro trolley to Banio Logan Station.)

The **Embarcadero,** a fancy Spanish name for dock, sits at the foot of Broadway on the west side of downtown. Along with North Island's seaplanes, Point Loma's submarine base, and South Bay's mothball fleet, the vessels on the Embarcadero are reminders of San Diego's number-one industry and its role throughout the years as a major West Coast naval installation. **San Diego Harbor Excursions** (234-4111) has offered trips around the bay since 1885. (2-hr. cruises mid-Sept. to mid-June daily at 2pm; mid-June to mid-Sept. daily at 10am, 12:30pm, and 2pm. Fare $11.50, ages 3-11 and over 55 $5. 1-hr. cruises mid-Sept. to mid-June at 10am, 11:15am, 12:45pm, and 4:15pm; mid-June to mid-Sept. at 11:15am, 12:45pm, 2:45pm, and 4:15pm. Fare $8, ages 3-11 and over 55 $3.50.) Harbor Excursion also sells tickets for the ferry departing for Coronado (every hour 10am-10pm, returning on the half-hour; fare $1.50). The ferry docks at the Olde Ferry Landing in Coronado on 1st and Orange St., a 10-block walk or trolley ride from the Hotel del Coronado (see Near San Diego). **Invader Cruises** (234-8687) next door offers the same kind of cruise as Harbor Excursion, but also uses a sailing vessel for many of its tours. (2-hr. cruises $10, 1-hr. cruises $7, over 55 and ages 4-12 ½ price, under 3 free.)

Balboa Park

Balboa Park was established in 1868, when San Diego's population was 2301. Now millions are entertained each year at the 1000-acre park, which features outdoor concerts and theater, street entertainers, Spanish architecture, rich vegetation, and a zoo. It has hosted the Panama-Pacific International Exposition and the 1935 California-Pacific Exposition. Most of the present buildings are renovations of the structures erected for these fairs. The park has the greatest concentration of museums in the U.S. outside of the Mall in Washington, DC. All museums are free on the first Tuesday of each month. Purchase a *Passport to Balboa Park* if you'll be spending more than an afternoon here.

The **San Diego Zoo** (231-1515) earns its reputation as one of the best in the country. One hundred acres of exquisitely designed natural habitats re-create such environments as a Southeast Asian rain forest and an African savannah. Animal shows (over 6 per day) are held in the Wedgeforth Bowl, near the entrance, and kids can ride elephants and camels near the elephant mesa. The latest addition is **Tiger River,** a simulated rain forest that exhibits the natural wonders of the tropics while illustrating and explaining the world's impending ecological doom. The **Children's Zoo** (ages 3 and over 50¢) is a barnyard delight.

You can see about 80 acres of the zoo, a lot more than you can cover on foot, on the double-decker bus tour ($2.50, ages 3-15 $2). The "skyfari" aerial tramway ($1.50, ages 3-17 $1) belongs more in an amusement park than in the zoo, and the bird's-eye tour lacks the thrill of the bus trip. The main zoo entrance is open July-Labor Day 8am-5:30pm, must exit by 7:30pm; Labor Day-Oct. 4 9am-4pm, exit by 6pm. Admission is $8.50, children $2.50. Group rates are available. Free on Oct. 1.

The focus of Balboa Park is the **Plaza de Panama,** on El Prado (a street running west to east through the plaza), where the Panama-Pacific International Exposition took place in 1915 and 1916. Designed by Bertram Goodhue in Spanish colonial style, many of the buildings were built as temporary structures, but their elaborate ornament and colorfully tiled roofs were thought too beautiful to demolish. The star of the plaza's western axis is Goodhue's California State Building, now the **Museum of Man** (239-2001), whose castle-like tower and dome are covered with shiny tiles in a Spanish design. Inside, millions of years of human evolution are traced in exhibits on primates, early humans, the Maya, Hopi and other Native American cultures. It is one of those rare museums not designed for fifth graders. (Open daily 10am-4:30pm. Admission $3, ages 13-18 $1, ages 6-12 25¢, under 6 free.)

Behind the Museum of Man is the **Old Globe Theater** (239-2255), California's oldest professional theater. Shakespearean and other plays are performed nightly (Tues.-Sun.), with weekend matinees. (Tickets $22, but prices begin at $14 for seniors and students at weekend matinees.) The **Spreckels Organ Pavilion** at the south end of the Plaza de Panama, opposite the Museum of Art, resounds with concerts on a very large outdoor organ. (Sun. at 2pm. Free. Closed Feb.)

Across the Plaza de Panama is the **San Diego Museum of Art** (232-7931) with a comprehensive collection ranging from ancient Asian to contemporary Californian. In between are works by Renaissance, 16th-century Dutch, American Western, and German expressionists. Excellent temporary exhibits of less canonic works punctuate the galleries. (Open Tues.-Sun. 10am-4:30pm. Admission $5, over 65 $4, college students with ID and ages 6-18 $2, under 6 free.) Nearby is the outdoor **Sculpture Court and Garden** (236-1725), with a typically rounded and sensuous Henry Moore presiding over other large abstract chunks of inspiration. (Sculpture garden open until 4:30pm.)

Next door the **Casa de Balboa,** a recent reconstruction of the 1915 Electricity Building, contains four museums: the **Museum of Photographic Arts** (239-5262; admission $2.50), the **San Diego Hall of Champions** (234-2544), the **Research Archives,** and the **Museum of San Diego History** (both 232-6203). Admission to the last three museums is $2. To complete your tour of the Casa de Balboa, climb aboard the **San Diego Model Railroad Museum** (696-0199), which features a genuine semaphore in operation. (Open Wed.-Fri. 11am-4pm, Sat.-Sun. 11am-5pm. Admission $1, children free.)

From the end of El Prado St. (closed to cars), a left onto Village Place St. will take you to **Spanish Village,** a crafts center that offers free demonstrations and exhibits in 39 different studios. At the other end of Village Place is the **Natural History Museum** (232-3821), which features state-of-the-art taxidermic specimens. Visit the Sefton Hall of Shore Ecology and you'll be able to impress friends later at the beach. The museum also sponsors whale-watching trips in winter (reserve in the autumn). (Open daily 10am-4:30pm. Admission $4, ages 6-18 $1, under 6 free.)

South of the Natural History Museum is the **Reuben H. Fleet Space Theater and Science Center** (238-1168), where two Omnimax projectors, 153 speakers, and a hemispheric planetarium whisk viewers inside the human body, up with the space shuttle, or 20,000 leagues under the sea. The world's largest motion pictures play here about eight times per day. (Admission $5, over 59 $3.50, ages 5-15 $3, under 5 free.) At night lasers whirl to music on the ceiling of the **Laserium.** (Admission $5.50, seniors $4, children $3.50.) Tickets to the space theater are also good for the science center, where visitors can play with the cloud chamber, the telegraph, a light-mixing booth, and other gadgets. (Open 9:45am until the last show of the day, usually around 9:30pm. Science center admission alone $2, ages 5-15 $1.)

Old Town, Mission Valley, and Mission Hills

Old Town is the site of the original settlement of San Diego. Take bus #4 or 5 from downtown. Before becoming a museum, Old Town was the site of the county courthouse, the town gallows, and a busy commercial district. Now the partially enclosed pedestrian mall is a tourist trap. Tuning out hundreds of camera-clicking shutterbugs is the key to enjoying the free walking tours, offered by the state park (daily at 2pm) and originating at the Casa de Machado y Silvas (237-6770). In **Presidio Park,** next to and north of Old Town, the less-than-scintillating **Serra Museum** (297-3258) is a 1929 replica of the original San Diego mission on the same site. (Open Tues.-Sat. 10am-4:30pm, Sun. noon-4:30pm. Admission $2.)

Entertainment

San Diego is not renowned for its nightlife, but a certain amount of spelunking could turn up some action. To find out what's happening in San Diego, consult the Thursday *Reader,* a free weekly newspaper that lists places, dates, and prices. *Varieties,* a guide to UCSD events, is available on campus. 5th St., south of Broadway, has a lot of live music on weekends. **Arts Tix,** 121 Broadway (238-3810), at 1st Ave., offers half-price tickets to shows on the day of performance.

No. 1 Fifth Avenue, 3845 5th Ave., Hillcrest (299-1911). Comfortable piano bar, frequented by gay people. Open daily noon-2am. No cover.

Confetti's, 5373 Mission Center Rd. (291-8635). A singles hot spot. Lots of confetti and lots of scoping. Drinks $1.75-3.75. Happy hour 5-8pm includes free buffet. Serves pizza 8:30pm-1am. Open Mon.-Fri. 5pm-2am, Sat. 7pm-2am, Sun. 9pm-2am. Cover Mon.-Wed. $2, Thurs. and Sun. $3, Fri.-Sat. $5. No cover before 8pm.

Diego's Club and Cantina, 860 Garnet Ave. (272-1241), Pacific Beach. Dance to top-40 and surfing music. The place keeps the crowd entertained with close-ups of dancers on big video screens. Large portions of respectable food. Open nightly until 2am. Cover Sun.-Thurs. $2, Fri.-Sat. $5. No cover before 9:30pm.

The Comedy Store, 916 Pearl St. (454-9176), La Jolla. Drinks $3. Potluck night Mon.-Tues. 8pm, when uninhibited local comics climb on stage. (Call after 3pm to sign up.) Well-known comedians featured other evenings. Shows Wed.-Thurs. 8pm ($6), Fri. 8pm and 10:30pm ($8), Sat. 8pm and 10:30pm ($10). Wed.-Thurs. 2-for-1 admission with any college ID. 2-drink minimum.

Gorgeous weather and a strong community spirit breed a variety of local festivals, many of which are long-standing traditions. The visitors bureau (see Practical Information) publishes an events brochure and runs a 24-hour **Events Hot Line** (696-8700). Notable seasonal events include **Penguin Day Ski Fest** (276-0830), New Year's Day, De Anza Cove on Mission Bay; **Ocean Beach Kite Festival** (223-1175), mid-March, 4741 Santa Monica Ave. at Ocean Beach Elementary School; **Pacific Beach Spring Art Festival** (488-0273), April; and **Surf, Sand, and Sandcastle Days** (424-3151), mid-July, Imperial Beach, by the pier at 9am, in conjunction with the 8th annual **U.S. Open Sandcastle Competition.**

Near San Diego: The Coast

There are 70 miles of beaches in this city, each with a pronounced personality. Loyal canine companions have a place at Dog Beach, while the disposable and the wasted can visit Garbage Beach. The coast, from Imperial Beach (a town that feels a little like Oklahoma) in the south to La Jolla in the north, is choked with sun-worshippers, and it may take a little ingenuity to find room to bask. Chic places like Mission Beach and La Jolla are likely to be as packed as funky Ocean Beach (see below) come prime sunning time on summer weekends. Coastal communities do have more to offer than waves and white sand, so wander inland a few blocks and explore.

The **Hotel del Coronado,** Orange Ave. (435-6611), on the Coronado Peninsula, is one of the world's great hotels. (Take the Coronado Bridge from I-5 (toll $1), bus #901 from downtown, or ferry from San Diego Harbor Excursions ($1.50); see Downtown Sights). The "Hotel Del" is a monumental, shingled structure with long, white verandas and red, circular towers. Wander onto the white, seaweed-free beach, one of the prettiest in S.D. It's seldom crowded, even on weekends.

Point Loma walks a fine line between residential community and naval outpost, but the Navy is contained near the base of the point. The people of Point Loma range from Ocean Beach hippies to more sedate and moneyed residents up the hill in the "wooded area." **Cabrillo National Monument** (557-5450), is known for its views of San Diego and for the migrating whales that pass the offshore kelp beds December to February. From downtown, take I-5 to Rosecrans Blvd. and follow the signs, or take bus #2 to 30th and Redwood and transfer to bus #6. The 2-mile **Bayside Trail** winds through the brush along the coast on the harbor side. Exhibits describe the life of the Native Americans who lived here before João Rodríguez Cabrillo's arrival in 1542. At the highest point of the peninsula sits **Old Point Loma Lighthouse,** which operated from 1855 to 1891 and is now a museum. (Park and visitors center open daily 9am-sunset, off-season 9am-5:15pm. Lighthouse closes 15 min. earlier. Parking $3 per car or $1 per passenger, whichever is less.)

Ocean Beach, a former drug mecca, has been cleaned up. What remains of its depraved subculture simply adds piquancy to the community. Although scorned by hot-dog surfers, the waves here are perfect for beginners. O.B. also hosts some spirited afternoon volleyball games.

Mission Beach and **Pacific Beach** have more rugged waves than O.B. **Ocean Front Walk** is packed with joggers, walkers, and bicyclists. The 3 blocks between the sea and Mission Blvd. are quintessentially suburban. Low cottages inhabited by those who are rich or lucky line alleys bearing the names of the world's famous resort cities.

La Jolla's beaches are superb. Grassy knolls run right down to the sea at **La Jolla Cove,** and surfers are especially fond of the waves at **Tourmaline Beach** and **Windansea Beach,** some of the best in the San Diego area. At **Black's Beach,** people run, sun, and play volleyball in the nude. Take I-5 to Genesee Ave., go west and turn left on N. Torrey Pines Rd. until you reach the **Torrey Pines Glider Port** (where hang gliders leap off the cliffs).

The University of California at San Diego (UCSD) (452-2230) rests above La Jolla, surrounded on three sides by Torrey Pines Rd., La Jolla Village Dr., and I-5. To get to UCSD cheaply and quickly from downtown San Diego, take bus #3 to the UCSD Hospital in Hillcrest. The university's CIEE office operates a free shuttle bus between the hospital and the campus bookstore. (In summer every 15 min. 6am-6:30pm; during school year every 15 min. 7am-7:30pm.) Drivers will honor only UCSD identification—or any facsimile thereof. Eucalyptus trees surround the four colleges (each in a different architectural style) that make up the campus.

Los Angeles

Los Angeles is diverse in all respects, partly the result of its immensity. The geography ranges from the flat and open spaces of the central city areas, to the rugged cliffs of Pacific Palisades, to the wide beaches of Santa Monica. The population of 3.4 million consists of all nationalities; indeed, by the year 2010, 60% of the inhabitants will be minorities, the bulk being Black, Hispanic, and Asian. The images of Los Angeles that pervade the national consciousness are of infinite variety—from the glamorous Hollywood and opulent Beverly Hills to the smog-choked freeways and inner-city neighborhoods torn by gang-wars. But all told, there is a common though indefinable sensibility, apparent in the love of being outdoors or the leisurely everyday attitudes, that identifies one as an Angeleno, a label worn with immense pride.

The city was founded as part of the Spanish empire in 1781, the same year Cornwallis surrendered to Washington at Yorktown to end the American struggle for independence. Governor Felipé de Neve christened the city *El Pueblo de Nuestra Señora la Reina de los Angelenos de Porciúncula,* the Porciúncula being the creek on whose banks the original settlement was built. The city joined the U.S. in 1847, and the completion of the railroad in 1869 turned the stream of settlers into a flood. Sometime along the way, the Porciúncula dried up, and today, natural water is practically non-existent. Most of the supply comes from the Colorado River or from Northern California, placing a collective chip on the shoulders of L.A.'s upstate neighbors. The dearth of water did nothing to stop Los Angeles' uncontrollable expansion into the San Fernando Valley and elsewhere.

Traffic, tremors, and toxic smog aside, Los Angeles offers a limitless string of possibilities for those of all interests. As the United States cultivates its relations with the peoples on the other side of the other ocean, the City of the Angels has become the gateway to the East (or further West) and to the future. This is a young city still growing strong. The innumerable portraits of the city each represent only a slice of its sweeping and indescribable grandeur. Though it may not be heaven as its name suggests, there is a special attraction that implores curious visitors to return and loyal residents to remain.

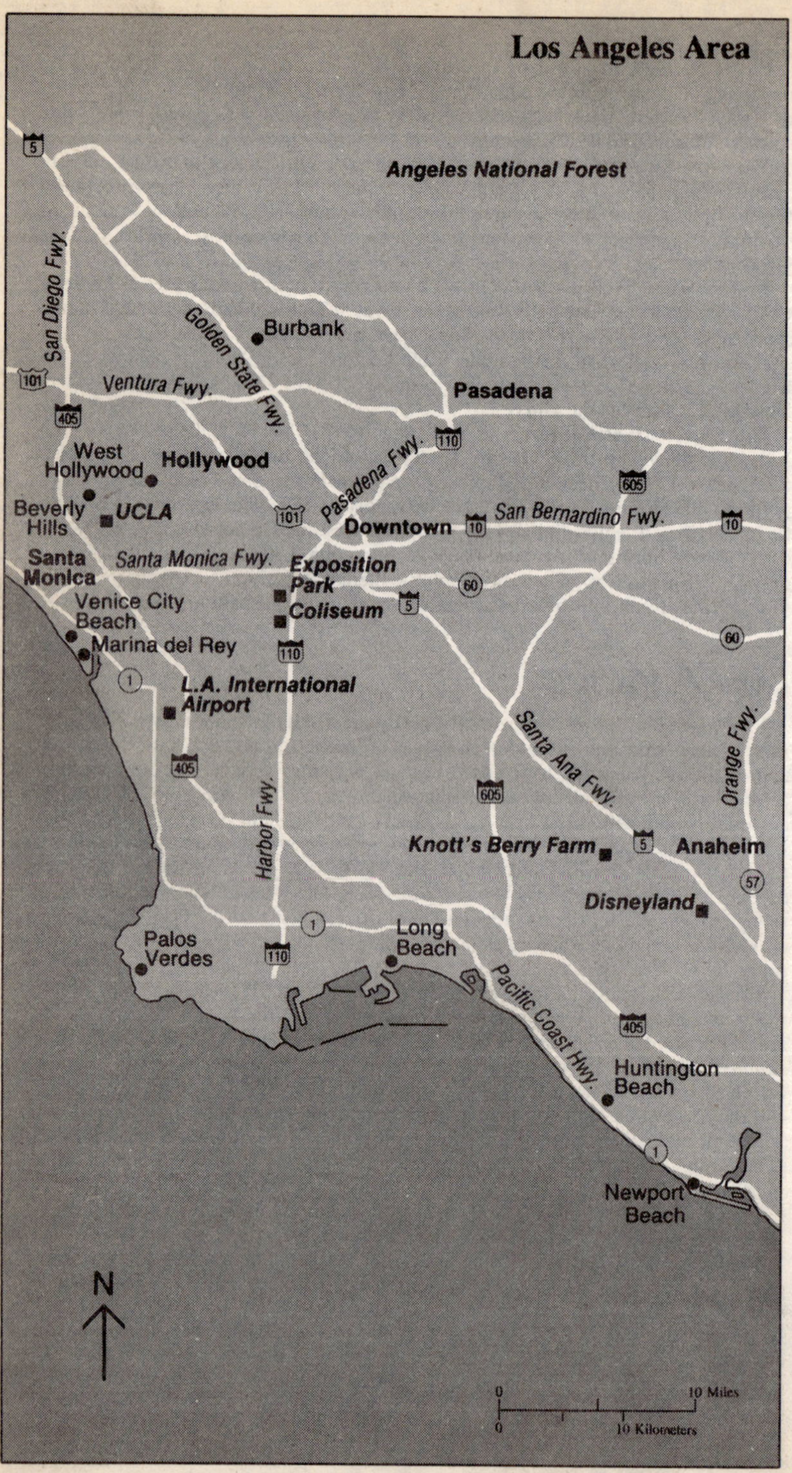
Los Angeles Area
Angeles National Forest
5
San Diego Fwy.
Golden State Fwy.
Burbank
101
Ventura Fwy.
Pasadena
405
110
Pasadena Fwy.
West Hollywood
Hollywood
605
Beverly Hills
UCLA
101
Downtown
10
San Bernardino Fwy.
10
Santa Monica
Santa Monica Fwy.
Exposition Park
60
Venice City Beach
Coliseum
5
Marina del Rey
60
110
1
L.A. International Airport
Santa Ana Fwy.
Orange Fwy.
405
605
Harbor Fwy.
Knott's Berry Farm
5
Anaheim
57
Disneyland
1
Palos Verdes
Long Beach
110
Pacific Coast Hwy.
405
Huntington Beach
1
Newport Beach
N
0
10 Miles
0
10 Kilometers

Practical Information

Emergency: 911

Visitor Information: Greater Los Angeles Visitors and Convention Bureau, 695 S. Figueroa St. 90015 (689-8822), downtown between Wilshire and 7th St. Helpful staff speaks French, German, Hungarian, Italian, Japanese, Portuguese, and Spanish. Discount coupons and free tickets to TV shows sometimes available. Good maps for downtown streets, sights, and buses. Publishes *Datelines,* a rundown of special events, 4 times per year. Their information-packed guide to L.A. is free and available by mail (allow 3 weeks for delivery). Open Mon.-Sat. 8am-5pm.

National Park Service, 22900 Ventura Blvd. (818-888-3770), Woodland Hills, in the San Fernando Valley. Information on the Santa Monica Mountains and other parks. Open Mon.-Sat. 8am-5pm. Call their "Parkcast" (710-9488) for park weather. **Los Angeles County Parks and Recreation,** 433 S. Vermont (738-2961). Open Mon.-Fri. 8am-5pm.

Council Travel: 1093 Broxton Ave. (208-3551), Westwood Village. Cheap flights, IYHF/AYH passes, ISICs. Open Mon.-Fri. 9:30am-5pm; April-June also Sat 10am-2pm.

Los Angeles Council AYH: 335 W. 7th St. (831-8846), San Pedro. Information and supplies for travelers. Guidebooks, low-cost flights, rail passes, and ISICs. Open Tues.-Sat. 10am-5pm.

Consulates: Britain, 3701 Wilshire Blvd. (385-7381). Open 9am-5pm for calls, hours vary by department for visits. **Japan,** 250 E. 1st St. (624-8305). Open Mon.-Fri. 9:30-11:30am and 1-5pm for calls, until 4pm for visits.

Los Angeles International Airport: See Getting There, By Air below.

Amtrak and **Greyhound/Trailways:** See Getting There, By Train and Bus; and Getting Out below.

Rapid Transit District Bus: See Orientation, Public Transportation, below.

Car Rental: Rent-a-Car Cheep, 4760 W. Century Blvd. (678-9146), Inglewood, just east of LAX. $18 per day, $126 per week. Unlimited mileage, but insurance is $9 per day. Open Mon.-Sat. 7am-11pm, Sun. 8am-9pm. Must be 18. Cash or credit card deposit required. **Penny Rent-a-Car,** 12425 Victory Blvd. (818-786-1733), N. Hollywood. $9 per day plus 15¢ per mile or $15 per day with 75 free miles. $98 per week with 500 free miles. Insurance $5 per day. Open Mon.-Fri. 8am-6pm, Sat. 9am-4pm, Sun. 9am-2pm. Must be 21 with major credit card. **Avon Rent-a-Car,** 8459 Sunset Blvd. (654-5533). Also at LAX (322-4033) and Sherman Oaks (818-906-2277). $20 per day with unlimited mileage, $119 per week. Insurance $12 per day. Open Mon.-Fri. 7:30am-9pm, Sat.-Sun. 8am-8pm. Must be 18 with major credit card, but drivers 18-22 face a $15 per day surcharge, $5 per day for those 22-25.

Auto Transport Companies: Dependable Car Travel Service, Inc., 8730 Wilshire Blvd., #414 (659-2922), Beverly Hills. References from L.A. or destination. Most cars to the northeast, especially New York, but also to Florida and Chicago. $75 refundable deposit. Call 1-2 days ahead to reserve. Open Mon.-Fri. 9am-5pm, Sat. 9am-noon. Must be 18. **Auto Driveaway,** 3407 W. 6th St. (666-6100). Cars go nationwide. Application requires a photo. Call not more than 1 week before you want to leave. Open Mon.-Fri. 9am-5pm. Must be 21 and have references in both L.A. and your destination city. $200 deposit required.

Gay and Lesbian Community Services Center: 1213 N. Highland Ave. (464-7400), Hollywood, near Santa Monica Blvd. Youth, employment, housing, seniors, education, counseling, and medical services. Open Mon.-Sat. 8:30am-10pm, but most offices close around 5pm.

Help Lines: Rape Crisis, 392-8381. 24 hours. Response service, 855-3506. **Suicide Prevention,** 381-5111. 24 hours. **Committee for the Rights of the Disabled,** 2942 W. Pico Blvd. (731-8591). Open Mon.-Fri. 8:30am-5pm. Call for appointment. **Area Agency on Aging,** 1102 S. Crenshaw Blvd. (857-6411). Open Mon.-Fri. 8am-5pm.

Beach Information: 457-9701, recording for Malibu, Santa Monica, and South Bay. Most FM radio stations have a surf report at noon.

Post Office: main office at Florence Station, 7001 S. Central Ave. (586-1723; rates and schedules 586-1467). General Delivery at 901 S. Broadway (617-4413), at 9th St. Open Mon.-Fri. 8:30am-3pm. General Delivery ZIP code: 90055.

Area Codes: southern half of Los Angeles County (Downtown, Beverly Hills, Westside, Malibu, Santa Monica, Venice, South Bay, Long Beach) 213, northern half (including San

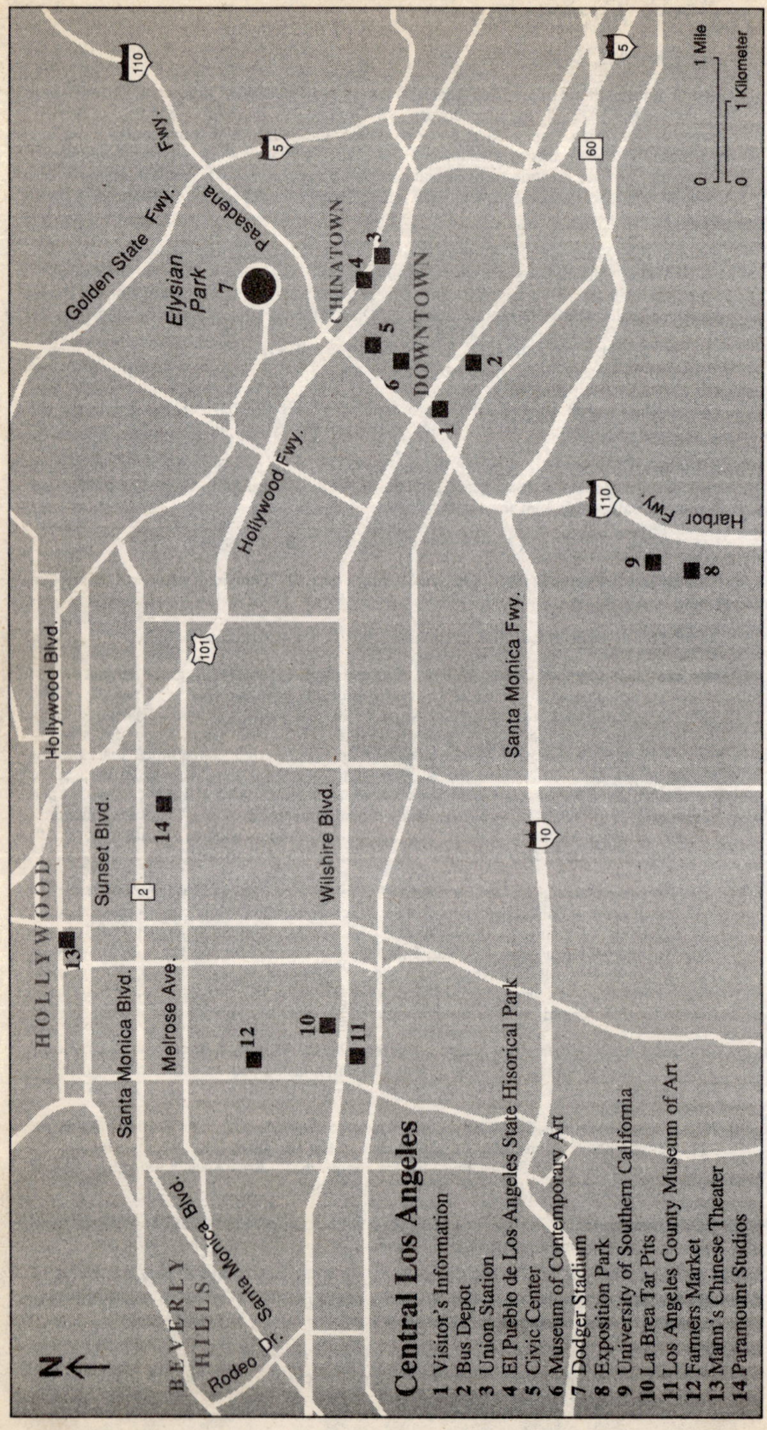
Central Los Angeles
1 Visitor's Information
2 Bus Depot
3 Union Station
4 El Pueblo de Los Angeles State Hisorical Park
5 Civic Center
6 Museum of Contemporary Art
7 Dodger Stadium
8 Exposition Park
9 University of Southern California
10 La Brea Tar Pits
11 Los Angeles County Museum of Art
12 Farmers Market
13 Mann's Chinese Theater
14 Paramount Studios
N
BEVERLY HILLS
HOLLYWOOD
CHINATOWN
DOWNTOWN
Elysian Park
Hollywood Blvd.
Sunset Blvd.
Santa Monica Blvd.
Melrose Ave.
Wilshire Blvd.
Santa Monica Blvd.
Rodeo Dr.
Santa Monica Fwy.
Hollywood Fwy.
Golden State Fwy.
Pasadena Fwy.
Harbor Fwy.
110
5
60
101
2
10
0
1 Mile
1 Kilometer

Fernando Valley and Pasadena) 818, Orange County 714, San Diego County 619, Ventura County 805.

Check out the Monday *Daily News* "L.A. Life" section under "Helplines" for almost a hundred different hotlines. Also useful are the *Los Angeles Times,* the *Los Angeles Herald-Examiner,* the *LA Weekly,* and *The Outlook,* a small Westside daily.

Hollywood

Visitor Information: The Janes House, 6541 Hollywood Blvd. (461-4213), in Janes House Sq. Provides L.A. visitor guide. Open Mon.-Sat. 9am-5pm. **Hollywood Chamber of Commerce,** 6255 W. Sunset Blvd., #911 (469-8311).

RTD Customer Service Center: 6249 Hollywood Blvd. (972-6000). Free information, maps, timetables, and passes. Open Mon.-Fri. 10am-6pm. **Important buses:** #1 along Hollywood Blvd., #2 and 3 along Sunset Blvd., #4 along Santa Monica Blvd., #10 along Melrose. Buses also serve the major north-south streets; see Wilshire District Sights below for a list.

Greyhound: 1409 N. Vine St. (466-6381), 1 block south of Sunset. Blvd. Open daily 7:15am-11:15pm. To Santa Barbara (6 per day, $12.90), San Diego (bus change in downtown L.A., 14 per day, $15.10), and San Francisco (9 per day, $42).

Area Code: 213.

Santa Monica

Visitor Information: 1400 Ocean Ave. (393-7593), in Palisades Park. Local maps, brochures, and information on attractions and events. Open daily 10am-5pm; off-season 10am-4pm.

Santa Monica Municipal (Big Blue) Bus Lines: 1660 7th St. (451-5445), at Olympic. Open Mon.-Fri. 8am-5pm. Bus #10 provides express service between downtown L.A. and downtown Santa Monica for 80¢ (faster than RTD—but so is walking). Catch it along Flower St. between 3rd and 6th St., or on Grand Ave. down to the Santa Monica Fwy. (the I-10). Buses #1 and 2 run between Santa Monica and Venice and are free with a transfer from the #10; otherwise fare 50¢.

Greyhound: 1433 5th St. (395-1708), between Broadway and Santa Monica Blvd. Open Mon.-Fri. 7:15am-5:30pm, Sat.-Sun. 7:15am-1pm. To Santa Barbara (6 per day, 2½, $13), San Diego (some require bus change in downtown L.A., 8 per day, 3½-5-hr., $15.50), and San Francisco (8 per day, most require bus change in downtown L.A., 10-12-hr., $46).

Surfboard Rental: Natural Progression Surfboards, 22935½ W. Pacific Hwy. (456-6302), Malibu. Boards $15 per day, plus $5 insurance. Wetsuits $5. Windsurfers $35 per day, plus $5 insurance. Lessons available. Open daily 9am-6pm.

Post Office: 5th and Arizona (393-0716). Open Mon.-Fri. 9am-2pm, 3-5:30pm, Sat. 9am-12:30pm.

Area Code: 213.

Pasadena

Visitor Information: Convention and Visitors Bureau, 171 S. Los Robles Ave. (795-9311), across from the Hilton Hotel. Open Mon.-Fri. 9am-5pm, Sat. 10am-4pm.

Greyhound: 645 E. Walnut (792-5116). Open Mon.-Fri. 6:30am-4:45pm, Sat. 6:30am-1:15pm. To San Francisco (4 per day, 11 hr., $44.25) and San Diego (3 per day, 4 hr., $13.30).

Post Office: 600 N. Lincoln (304-7122), at Orange. Open Mon., Wed., Fri. 8am-6pm; Tues., Thurs. 8am-5pm; Sat. 9am-2pm.

Area Code: 818.

Getting There

Los Angeles sprawls away from the coast of Southern California, 127 miles north of San Diego and 403 miles south of San Francisco. You can still be "in" L.A. if you're 50 miles from downtown. Originally a Spanish mission on the banks of the Los Angeles River, "Greater L.A." now encompasses the urbanized areas of Orange, Riverside, San Bernadino, and Ventura counties.

By Car

General approaches to Greater L.A. are I-5 from the south, I-1 or I-5 from the north, and I-10 or I-15 from the east. The city itself is crisscrossed by over a dozen freeways. Driving into L.A. can be trying if you've never before run a gauntlet of ramps, exits, and four-story directional signs.

By Train and Bus

Amtrak pulls into Union Station, 800 N. Alameda (624-0171), at the northwestern edge of the heart of downtown Los Angeles. Bus #1 travels west into Hollywood and can be caught at the corner of Broadway and Arcadia to the west of the station.

Visitors arriving by **Greyhound** bus will disembark at 208 E. 6th St. (620-1200), at Los Angeles St. downtown, in a rough neighborhood near skid row. Greyhound also stops in Hollywood, Santa Monica, Anaheim, and other parts of the metropolitan area. RTD buses #22-322 stop on 7th and Main St., 2 blocks southwest of the downtown station, and carry passengers westward along Wilshire Blvd. Bus #1 stops at 6th and Broadway, 4 blocks to the west, and travels westward along Hollywood Blvd.

By Air

Once a nightmare of disorganization and delay, **Los Angeles International Airport (LAX)** has been transformed by $700 million worth of renovations into an efficient regulator of the third largest passenger volume handled by any airport in the world. The airport complex is located in Westchester, about 15 miles southwest of downtown, 10 miles southeast of Santa Monica, and 1 mile east of the coast.

Many car rental agencies service the airport directly via shuttle buses (see Cars). All **Rapid Transit District (RTD)** service to and from the airport stops at the **transfer terminal** at Vicksburg Ave. and 96th St. To get downtown, take bus #439 (Mon.-Fri. rush hours only) or #42 from the transfer terminal. Bus #42 operates from LAX daily from 5:30am to 11:15pm, from downtown daily from 5:45am to 12:10am. To get to UCLA, take express #560; to Long Beach, #232; to West Hollywood and Beverly Hills, #220. From West Hollywood to Hollywood, take bus #1, 4, or 304 along Santa Monica Blvd. For further information, pick up one of the Rapid Transit District information courtesy phones, in most terminals. **Metered cabs** are costly: about $1.90 for the first mile and $1.50 each additional mile.

A final option—more expensive than an RTD bus but cheaper than a cab—is to use the shuttle buses, which stop outside the baggage claim area of each terminal. The **Funbus** (800-962-1976 or 714-776-9210) runs continually to hotels in downtown ($6.50), Long Beach, Pasadena ($8.50), Disneyland ($9.75), and elsewhere. Buy tickets at the ground transportation kiosks outside baggage claim areas or from the driver. The **Super Shuttle** (838-1111; must reserve 24 hours in advance) offers door-to-door service to Beverly Hills ($16) and Pasadena ($18). The **Coast Shuttle** (417-3988) provides door-to-door service to Marina del Ray ($8), Venice ($10), and Santa Monica ($12).

For specific information regarding RTD buses, cabs, and shuttles, ask at the information kiosks located on the sidewalks directly in front of the terminals. **Travelers Aid** (686-0950) offices are located in all terminals. (Open Mon.-Fri. 8:30am-5pm; all stations have extensive printed information round-the-clock, and a recording when stations are closed.)

Getting Out

To reach Los Angeles International Airport (LAX) by car from downtown take I-10 west to I-405 south and get off at Century Blvd. heading west. Traffic tends to be bumper-to-bumper during rush hour. There is no shortage of parking at the airport. Lots are metered (25¢ for 15 min.). On busier days, some of the hassle can be eliminated by parking in the aptly named "remote" lots at the airport's eastern edge and taking the free tram to the terminals. Lots C and D sit at Sepulveda and

96th St., lot VSP at La Cienaga and 11th St. Your first two hours at these lots are free. Disabled travelers needing assistance should park in Lot C and call 646-8021 for a van to pick them up.

LAX can be reached by bus from downtown on the #42, from UCLA express #560, from Long Beach #232, and from West Hollywood and Beverly Hills #220. At the airport, the tram marked "A" makes frequent free trips among terminals. Terminal two serves international carriers. For information on shuttles to LAX, see Getting There. Special flight bargains to San Francisco are offered by many airlines.

Amtrak: Union Station, 800 N. Alameda (624-0171), downtown. To San Diego (7 per day, 3 hr., $23) with stops in San Juan Capistrano, San Clemente, Oceanside, and Del Mar. To San Francisco $69.

Buses: Greyhound, 208 E. 6th St. (620-1200 for fare and schedule information). To: San Diego (16 per day, 2½ hr., $15); Tijuana (12 per day, 3½ hr., $18); Santa Barbara (15 per day, 2-3½ hr., $13); and San Francisco (10 per day, 8 or 13 hr., $46). **Green Tortoise,** 392-1990, San Francisco headquarters 415-285-2441. Their north-bound mobiles depart only on Sun. from Venice at 2321 Lincoln Blvd., at 8pm; from downtown, 536 E. 8th, at 9pm; and from Hollywood at Sunset and Vine, near the McDonalds, at 9:30pm. To San Francisco ($30), Eugene ($59), Portland ($69), Seattle ($69). Call for reservations. They also sponsor 11-day cross-country "adventures" (see Getting There in the General Introduction).

Getting Around

Orientation

With its 40,000 intersections and 6500 miles of streets, the centerless sprawl of Los Angeles transcends all human understanding. A legitimate **downtown** Los Angeles does exist, but this small district merely acts as a reference point to explain where all the "suburbs in search of a city" lie. Immediately east of downtown are the thriving Latino districts of Boyle Heights, Montebello, and El Monte; to the south is the University of Southern California (USC), Exposition Park, and Watts; and farther along Rte. 11 is Long Beach.

Los Angeles is a city of boulevards; its shopping areas and business centers are distributed evenly along these broad arteries, each with a distinctive character. Streets throughout L.A. are designated east, west, north, and south from First and Main St.

The area west of downtown is known as the **Wilshire District** after its main boulevard. Wilshire is built up in a continuous wall of tall buildings (called the "Miracle Mile") with bungalows and duplexes huddled on either side of it.

North of the Wilshire District is **Hollywood.** *Grande dame* Sunset Boulevard, the main artery, runs from the ocean to downtown. It presents a cross section of virtually everything L.A. has to offer: beach communities, the lavish wealth of Beverly Hills, L.A.'s best and most famous nightclubs along "the strip," the old elegance of Silver Lake, and Chicano murals. North of Sunset is Hollywood Boulevard, running just beneath Hollywood Hills, where many of the split-level buildings perched precariously on hillsides are home to Hollywood's screenwriters, actors, and producers.

Beverly Hills, an independent city geographically swallowed by L.A., lies west of the Wilshire District and east of **Westwood** (home of UCLA). Still farther west, **Santa Monica** stretches its wide and crowded beaches along the ocean. Just south is the beach community of **Venice.**

On the other side of the hills is the **San Fernando Valley** (like, you know, the *Valley*). One-and-a-quarter million people totally inhabit this far out basin bounded on the north and west by the Santa Susanna Mountains and the Simi Freeway, on the south by the Hollywood Hills and the Ventura Freeway, and on the east by the Golden State Freeway.

Eighty miles of beach line L.A.'s coast. **Zuma** is northernmost, followed by **Malibu,** 15 miles up the coast from Santa Monica. The beach towns south of Santa Monica and Venice, comprising the area called the **South Bay,** are Marina del Rey,

El Segundo (with the airport just inland there), Manhattan, Hermosa, and Redondo Beaches. The coast bulges south of Redondo Beach to form the **Palos Verdes Peninsula** (which is indeed mostly green hills). Beyond the peninsula the coast once again turns east. **San Pedro,** L.A.'s port, is both the terminus of the Harbor Freeway and the point of departure for **Catalina Island.** East of San Pedro is **Long Beach,** a city of a half-million people. Finally, farthest south are the **Orange County** beach cities: Seal Beach, Sunset Beach, Huntington Beach, Newport Beach, and Laguna.

The moral? Buy a good map, and sleep with it under your pillow. The best investment you can make is the *Thomas Guide Los Angeles County Street Guide and Directory.* It's definitely worth the $13 for stays longer than a day or two.

Once the sun sets, those on foot should exercise caution outside West L.A. and off well-lit main drags. Women alone should not stroll *anywhere* after dark. Hollywood and the downtown area, east of Western Ave., are notably crime-ridden at night. Women should exercise caution also in parking structures, even if in such "safe" areas as UCLA.

Public Transportation

Nowhere in America is the great god Automobile held in greater reverence than in L.A. Although most Angelenos will insist that it's impossible to live in or visit Los Angeles without a car, the **Southern California Rapid Transit District (RTD)** does work. Slowly. Write for a **Tourist Kit,** RTD, Los Angeles 90001 (this address is sufficient), or stop by one of the 10 **customer service centers** once you've arrived. There's one across the hall from the visitors and convention bureau in ARCO Plaza (open Mon.-Fri. 7:30am-3:30pm). Two other downtown locations are 419 S. Main St. (open Mon.-Fri. 8am-4:30pm) and 1016 S. Main St. (open Mon.-Fri. 10am-7pm, Sat. 10am-6pm). Ask for the free **Bus System Map,** which contains a diagram of major bus routes for the greater L.A. area and a directory of customer service centers, RTD information numbers, and points of interest. The brochure *RTD Self Guided Tours* describes how to reach most sights from downtown. The visitors and convention bureau offers a map for Hollywood-based visitors.

Bus service is best downtown and along the major thoroughfares west of downtown. (There is 24-hour service, for instance, on Santa Monica and Wilshire Blvd.) The downtown **DASH shuttle** is only 25¢ and serves most points of interest, including Chinatown, Union Station (you can use the DASH to get from Union Station to downtown), Olvera Street, City Hall, Little Tokyo, the Music Center, and ARCO Plaza. (DASH operates Mon.-Fri. 7am-6pm and Sat. 9am-4pm.) Bus service is dismal in the outer reaches of the city, and two-hour journeys are not unusual. The buses themselves are speedy, but transferring from one to another often involves interminable waits.

For **transit information,** call 626-4455 (lines open daily 6am-midnight). If you tell the operator your point of origin and destination, you will be told the proper bus route. To avoid staying on hold forever, call late (after 11pm), or use a phone at a customer service center, where the call will go directly to the operators. Spanish-speaking operators are available.

RTD's **basic fare** is $1.10, disabled passengers 55¢. Additional charges for express buses, buses taking the freeway, special services for sports events, etc., sometimes raise total fare to $1.50-3.00. Exact change is required. Transfers are 25¢, whether you're changing from one RTD line to another or from RTD to another transit authority, such as the Santa Monica Municipal Bus Lines, Culver City Municipal Bus Lines, Long Beach Transit, or Orange County Transit District. For information on other transit systems, see the appropriate city below. All route numbers given are RTD unless otherwise designated. If you plan to use the buses extensively, buy a **bus pass.** Unlimited use for a month costs $42, $10 for the disabled, $25 for college students, $18 for students under 18.

Over 150 of RTD's lines offer **wheelchair-accessible buses.** Get their brochure *The New Mobility.* All bus stops with accessible service are marked with the international symbol of access.

If you don't want to spend hours on an RTD bus to travel from one end of the L.A. basin to the other, consider paying a bit more to take Greyhound or Trailways to such places as Long Beach, Huntington Beach, and Anaheim.

The answer to rapid transit blues is patience. A subway from downtown to the Valley, the Metro Rail, should be completed by 1998, and a bullet train between L.A. and San Diego might be operational by 2010. No promises.

Freeways

The *real* concrete jungle is not composed of the skyscrapers of New York, but the massive stretches of the Los Angeles freeways. Having acquired an almost mythological status in the American imagination, the elephantine concrete haunches of these thoroughfares loom over the cityscape like grand aisles in an automotive cathedral. Riding the freeways is a phantasmagoria of speed, chrome, and concrete as well as a whirl of queer place names (Azusa, Cucamonga, Tarzana, Panorama City). The highway is without question one of the most curious, albeit unnerving, shows this city has to offer.

In a city the size of Los Angeles, freeways are a must for efficient travel. Traffic means, however, that the same freeways can also be a most *inefficient* way to get anywhere (or, perhaps more accurately, nowhere). For those who know the local streets (many residents don't), the major thoroughfares are often faster than freeways. It is best to avoid the freeways between 6 and 10am and between 3 and 7pm. In L.A., the decentered city, there is nothing so forthright as an "inbound" jam in the morning and an "outbound" one in the afternoon. Traffic is snarled in all directions, in many places, and at all hours. Tie-ups are not limited to rush hours and can begin from something so simple as Caltrans (the Transportation Department) deciding to sweep the inside lane on a Sunday morning.

Perhaps to help them "get in touch with their freeway," Californians refer to the highways by names rather than by numbers. These names are little more tahn hints of a freeway's route and at best harmless, at worst misleading.

The most comprehensive **rideboard** is at UCLA's Ackerman Union, Floor B. Ackerman is in the center of campus, 2 blocks north of the Westwood Blvd. terminus. Also check the classified section of papers such as *The Chronicle.*

Bicycles

The most popular bike route is the **South Bay Bicycle Path.** It runs from Santa Monica to Torrance (19 miles), winding over the sandy beaches of the South Bay past sunbathers, boardwalks, and roller skaters. (Even the police ride bicycles here.) Other bike paths include the **California Aqueduct Bikeway,** 107.2 miles disengaged from traffic, along the aqueduct; **San Gabriel River Trail,** 36.6 miles along the river with views of the San Gabriel Valley; **Upper Rio Hondo** and **Lario Trails,** 9.1 and 22.1 miles, both free from traffic; **Kenneth Newell Bikeway,** 10 miles through residential Pasadena; **Sepulveda Basin Bikeway,** 7.3 miles around the Sepulveda Dam Recreation Area, a large loop of some major San Fernando Valley streets; **Griffith Park Bikeway,** 4.5 miles past the L.A. Zoo and Travel Town train park; **Bolsa Chica Bike Path,** 10 miles along Huntington Beach; **Santa Ana River Bike Trail,** 22 miles along—you guessed it—the Santa Ana River; and the **Santa Ana Canyon Bikeway,** 7.3 miles split between street and canyon.

For maps and advice, write to any **AAA office.** L.A. headquarters is at 2601 S. Figueroa (741-3111), near Adams. It's worth calling just to talk to helpful and friendly Norty Stewart, "the Source" for bicycling information in Southern California.

Walking and Hitchhiking

L.A. pedestrians are a lonely breed. The largely deserted streets of even commercial centers will seem eerie to the first-time visitor, and the long distances between sights may be frustrating. However, traveling on foot allows you the chance to see L.A. architecture up close, and if you're not too ambitious about "doing" all the tourist spots in the area, a stroll through such colorful areas as Chinatown, Hollywood, or Westwood Village can be rewarding. Venice Beach is perhaps the most enjoyable place to walk in L.A. You'll be in the company of the thousands of Venetian beach-goers, and Venice's sights and shopping areas are all relatively close to one another. You may also wish to call **Walking Tours of Los Angeles** for tours of El Pueblo de Los Angeles State Historic Park (628-1274), City Hall (485-4423), or the Music Center (972-7483). Tours of historic theaters, and a variety of other artistic sights, are given by the **Los Angeles Conservancy** (623-CITY, that's 623-2489).

Do not hitchhike, especially if you are a woman traveling alone. It is simply not safe. It is also illegal on freeways, and illegal on streets unless you are on a sidewalk and not disturbing traffic.

Accommodations

Many inexpensive lodgings in Los Angeles bear a frightening resemblance to the House of Usher. Dozens of flophouses around the Greyhound station charge between $10 and $20 per night, but those unnerved by skid-row street life should look elsewhere. Tolerable lodgings fall roughly into four categories: hostels and Ys, run-down but safe hotels, residential hotels offering weekly rates (these can save you a bundle), and budget motels located well off the beaten track but reasonably close by car. Reservations are a good idea year-round, though only summer is high tourist season. It never hurts to ask for off-season or student discounts, and occasionally managers will lower prices to snare a prospective but hesitating customer. The comprehensive *L.A. Lodging Guide* is available at the Los Angeles Visitors Center. **Youth hostel passes** may be obtained from UCLA's Ackerman Union, #A-213 (825-0611, see also Practical Information).

Los Angeles has no **campgrounds** convenient to public transport. Even motorists face at least a 40-minute commute from campsites to downtown. The only place to camp in L.A. County that's vaguely nearby is **Leo Carrillo State Beach,** on PCH (Rte. 1), 28 miles northwest of Santa Monica at the Ventura County line (818-706-1310), which lays out 134 developed sites at $12 per night. In summer, make reservations through MISTIX (800-444-7275).

Downtown

All of these hotels are in areas that are tolerable by day, dangerous by night. Women may feel uncomfortable walking the deserted streets alone even during the daytime; both men and women should travel in groups at night.

Clark Hotel, 426 S. Hill St. (624-4121), 1 block north of Pershing Sq. on the east side. From the Harbor Fwy. take the 4th St. off-ramp to Hill St. The rooms have been renovated, but the neighborhood hasn't been. Cocktail lounge, TV, room service, A/C, 24-hour security. Basic rooms $25.20. Singles and doubles with bath $35

Park Plaza Hotel, 607 S. Park View St. (384-5281), on the west corner of 6th St. across from MacArthur Park. This eerily grandiose Art Deco monument, built in 1927, comes with a 3-story marble-floored lobby and monumental staircase (both of which seem incongruous in the dimly-lit entryway). Caters largely to young students from the Otis Art Institute next door. A/C in the clean but small rooms; pool in the adjacent YMCA. Singles $25. Doubles $30. Twin beds $35. Weekly: singles $125. Doubles $150.

Mary Andrews Clarke Home YWCA, 306 Loma Dr. (483-5780). This arresting Moroccan-style mansion was unfortunately damaged by the October '87 earthquake and is closed as *Let's Go* goes to press. Nevertheless, women travelers (the residence does not admit men) should call to see if it has reopened because it's their safest option. About $30, nonmembers $35. Breakfast and dinner included.

Budget Inn Motel, 1710 W. 7th St. (483-3470). Color TV with free HBO and waterbed for the ultimate budget hotel night. Singles $30. Doubles $40.

City Center Motel, 1135 W. 7th St. (628-7141). Within walking distance of the downtown area. A/C, 24-hour security. Singles $31. Doubles $35.

Hollywood

Hollywood is an ideal base for tourists, although it gets creepy after dark. Side streets can be dangerous, vigilance and caution should preempt most problems.

Hollywood Hostel (AYH), 1553 Hudson Ave. (467-4161), 1½ blocks south off Hollywood Blvd. From Union Station, walk west along Macy St./Sunset Blvd. to Spring St., take bus #33 to Sunset and Grand, then take bus #1. From LAX take Airport Service bus to Roosevelt Hotel in Hollywood and walk 6 blocks east. The facility maintains a hotel and a hostel. The hostel recently underwent renovation, and features a kitchen, laundry, lounge, and dorm-style cots. 5-day max. stay. Curfew midnight. Hostel rates: $9, nonmembers $11. Hotel rates: singles $29, doubles $39. Arrive early to secure a room.

Howard's Weekly Apartments, Cine Lodge, 1738 N. Whitley Ave. (466-6943), ½ block north of Hollywood Blvd. between Highland Ave. and Cahuenga Blvd. In a busy, slightly seedy neighborhood, but security is tight. Small, pleasant studio apartments with refrigerators, snack bars, private baths, and A/C. Some have furnished kitchenettes. Weekly housekeeping service. Many international guests. 3-night min. stay. 3-night rates: singles $80; doubles $95, with kitchenette $105; suite (3 people) $120. Weekly: singles $133; doubles $145, with kitchenette $165; suite $175. Security deposit $50-75. Garage $20 per week. Rollaway $35 per week. TV $15 per week. Reservations recommended.

Hastings Hotel, 6162 Hollywood Blvd. (464-4136). Youth-oriented hotel in the thick of Hollywood, near RTD bus lines. 85 rooms. Singles $20-25. Doubles $25-35.

Beverly Hills, Wilshire District, West Los Angeles

The Westside is an attractive and much safer part of town, but for the most part, room rates are out of sight. Call the **UCLA Off-Campus Housing Office** (825-4491), 100 Sproul Hall, and see if they can put you in touch with students who have a spare room with their "roommate share board."

UCLA: Mira Hershey Hall, 801 Hilgard (825-3691). From LAX take bus #560; from Union Station take bus #68, 70, or 71 to Wilshire Blvd., then catch #21. Share a 2-bed room in this large Italian villa-style dormitory. Single-sex shared bath and laundry on each floor. Singles $32 during summer break (mid-June to mid-Sept.). Breakfast included. Doubles $16 per person. Make reservations at least one month in advance.

Deseret Motel, 10572 Santa Monica (474-2035), in West L.A. on the south side of the divided highway at Westholme Ave. Prime location between Westwood and Century City. From LAX take bus #560 to Santa Monica Blvd., then #4 or 304. From downtown and Hollywood, take bus #4 or 304. Small, simple rooms with A/C and cable TV. Singles $33.50. Doubles $36.50. Weekly: singles $185. Doubles $195.

Santa Monica and Venice Beach

One lovely way to experience L.A. if you only have a few days is to spend your visit staying at one of the cheap hostels in Venice. You may miss the Sunset Strip (and L.A. traffic), but you'll find dazzling white beaches, kooky architecture, and a mellow and unpretentious community devoted to worshipping the sun and cultivating its own eccentricities.

Venice Beach Hotel Cotel, 25 Windward Ave., Venice (399-7649), on the boardwalk between Zephyr Ct. and 17th Ave. Shuttle from LAX. You must show your passport to stay here. A friendly, lively hostel full of young international travelers. Located close to beaches. 3-6 people share each of the clean, functional rooms. No food allowed. 5-day max. stay. No curfew. $12, with bath $15. Private rooms with ocean view $25-45 $35 (no passport required for these).

Marina Hostel, 2915 Yale Ave., Marina Del Rey (301-3983), 3 blocks from Lincoln Blvd. Just outside of Venice in a quiet residential neighborhood. A privately owned, friendly household with lockers, linens, laundry, and a microwave-equipped kitchen. Some bunks, some floor mattresses. Living room with cable TV. $11.

Interclub Hostel, 2221 Lincoln Blvd., Venice (305-0250), near Venice Blvd. Shuttle from LAX. Passport required. Festive after-hours common-room atmosphere as many nationalities bump elbows. Rooms sleep 6, or you can sleep in the 30-bed dorm. Grubby kitchen with stove and fridge. Linen. Laundry room. Mixed-sex accommodations. 5-day max. stay. Lockout 11am-4pm. Curfew 4am. $12. Deposit $5.

Share-Tel International Hostel, 20 Brooks Ave. (392-0325), Venice. Airport shuttle. Outstanding location ½ block off the boardwalk. Student ID or passport required. Family-style atmosphere; clean, pleasant rooms with kitchen facilities and bathroom sleep 4-12 each. Linen service. No curfew. $15.

Stardust Motor Hotel of Santa Monica, 3202 Wilshire Blvd. (828-4584), Santa Monica. The red, white, and blue structure a few miles from the beach. Pool, kitchen units, parking. Singles $35-40. Doubles $45-50. Cottages for up to 4 people $60 per day or $350-375 per week.

Food

Angelenos count eating among their favorite pastimes, and the range of cuisine is astounding. Jewish and Eastern European, especially in the Fairfax area; Mexican, especially in East L.A. but nearly everywhere as well; Japanese, Chinese, Vietnamese, and Thai around Little Tokyo and Chinatown; excellent seafood along the coastal area; Hawaiian, Indian, Ethiopian, and much more. The places themselves cover the spectrum from simple, family-run nooks to glitzy, neon yuppie magnets. Familiarity with foreign foods is an easy way to feel cultured, and so ethnic cuisine is often trendy and vice versa.

Fresh produce is plentiful but of surprisingly uneven quality, considering the proximity to the San Joaquin Valley, the state's major agricultural region. California farmers ship much of their harvest elsewhere; thus everything is picked half-ripe. Find a health-food store or cooperative market that sells organic and small-farm produce.

Visit one of the big public markets to appreciate the variety and sheer volume of foodstuffs. **Farmer's Market,** 6222 W. 3rd St. (933-9211), at Fairfax in the Wilshire District, has over 160 produce stalls, meat vendors, sidewalk cafés, and small restaurants. (Open Mon.-Sat. 9am-6pm, Sun. 10am-6pm.) A less touristed, less expensive source of produce is the **Grand Central Public Market,** 317 S. Broadway (624-2378), a large baby-blue building downtown. The main market in the Hispanic shopping district, Grand Central has more than 50 stands selling not only produce, but also clothing, housewares, costume jewelry, vitamins, and fast food. (Open Mon.-Sat. 9am-6pm.)

If you don't want to leave your restaurant selection to chance, consult *Daily News* food critic Larry Lipson's guide to cheap L.A. dining, the monthly features in *Los Angeles* magazine, or the *L.A. Times.*

Downtown

Gorky's, 536 E. 8th St. (627-4060), at San Julian St. Free parking in the lot across 8th. Russian cuisine served in a casual, avant garde cafeteria setting. Charles Bukowski might have eaten here, or so the customers hope. *Piroshki* $1.75. Live music every night from 8:30pm, brewery on the premises. Open 24 hours.

Philippe's, The Original, 1001 N. Alameda (628-3781), 2 blocks north of Union Station. The Olvera St. location isn't as good. An L.A. institution, opened in 1908, Philippe's claims to have invented the French dip sandwich. It's the centerpiece of the menu, and rightly so. Order your choice of beef, pork, ham ($2.80) or lamb ($3.10). Take your sandwich, potato salad or coleslaw (50¢), and lemonade (45¢) or coffee (still 10¢) to one of the long tables where you'll rub elbows with CEOs and construction workers. Breakfast $2-3. Open daily 6am-10pm.

Home Cafe, 859 N. Broadway (624-6956), in Chinatown. From downtown take bus #45 or 46 on Broadway or the DASH shuttle. A tiny soup and noodles joint that receives high marks from local publications. Fill up on *jook* (rice porridge with scallions and egg, $2.25) or a meat and rice plate for $3-3.25. Open Sun.-Fri. 8am-4pm, Sat. 8am-5pm.

Miriwa, 750 A N. Hill St. (687-3088), in Chinatown. This huge restaurant is among the most popular—and the best—*dim sum* places anywhere in the city. Weekend lunch hours are always crowded. Choose your dishes from the carts pushed by your table; a full lunch is about $10 per person. Open daily 9am-3pm and 5-9:30pm.

Hollywood and West Hollywood

Some of L.A.'s best restaurants are here, with an especially strong showing of ethnic places on and around Hollywood Blvd. Most of the celebrity hangouts (such as the **Brown Derby,** 1628 Vine St.) are high-priced so that tourist riff-raff will stay away. But others do fish for visitors, who come peering in through the darkness for invariably elusive stars.

The Old Spaghetti Factory, 5939 W. Sunset Blvd. (469-7149). Part of a national chain. Decorated in pure Hollywood kitsch, from the purple velveteen wallpaper to the authentic trolley in the middle of the dining room. Full dinner (bread, salad, spaghetti, and spumoni) $4-5. Open Mon.-Thurs. 11:30am-2pm and 5-11pm, Sat. 5-11pm, Sun. 4-10pm.

Johnny Rocket's, 7507 Melrose Ave. (651-3361). Very popular and in a hip location. The 30s Moderne architecture puts you right back into a lost, pre-golden-arches era of American diners. Patsy Cline on the jukebox. Always packed. Great burgers from $2.70. Sandwiches ($2.25-4.25), and *real* cherry Cokes ($1.20). Open Sun.-Thurs. 11am-midnight, Fri.-Sat. 10am-2am.

Center's Fairfax Restaurant, Delicatessen, and Bakery, 419 N. Fairfax Ave. (651-2287). Impeccably ordered shelves with matzoh and gefilte fish. The sandwiches are expensive ($7), but plenty big enough to share. Open 24 hours.

Duke's, 8909 Sunset Blvd. (652-3100), at San Vicente. In a neighborhood of trendy boutiques and rock clubs. Walls are a kaleidoscope of posters and autographed album covers. Great for brunch, but bring a newspaper to pass the time while you wait to share a table with some of Hollywood's uppercrust. Entrees $5-7. Open Mon.-Fri. 7am-9pm, Sat.-Sun. 8am-4pm.

Tail O' The Pup, 311 N. La Cienega Blvd., across from the Beverly Center shopping mall in West Hollywood. A classic of Southern California roadside architecture: a hot dog stand in the shape of a hot dog—oozing with yellow mustard. Completely redefines the notion of form following function. Dogs from $2.50. Open daily 11am-6pm.

Beverly Hills, Westside, Wilshire District

John O'Groat's, 10516 W. Pico Blvd. (204-0692). They lay the Scottish theme a wee bit thick, but John O'Groat is the genuine article. He's usually standing out front soothing the lassies and laddies hungry for his mouthwatering biscuits, pancakes, and omelettes. Breakfast and lunch $3-6. Open daily 7am-3pm.

El Nopal, 10426 National Blvd. (559-4732), in West L.A., between Motor and Overland, just south of the Santa Monica Fwy. Known as the "home of the pregnant burrito." The famed burrito *embarrasado* ($4.50), made with chicken and avocado, lives up to its name. Smaller models $2-3. Take-out available. Open Mon.-Thurs. 11am-9pm, Fri.-Sat. 10am-10pm, Sun. 3-10pm.

Sak's Teriyaki, 1121 Glendon Ave. (208-2002), in Westwood. Excellent, cheap Japanese plates including chicken and beef teriyaki ($3.50-4.75). Popular with students. Happy hour special ($2.50) 3-6pm. Open Mon.-Thurs. 11am-10pm, Fri.-Sat. 11am-11pm, Sun. 11am-9pm.

Santa Monica and Venice

Cafe 50s, 838 Lincoln Blvd. (399-1955), Venice. Diner-style interior with 50s memorabilia plastering the wall and a jukebox to match. All-American fare at low prices. Hamburger $2.75. Open Sun.-Thurs. 7am-11pm, Fri.-Sat. 7am-1am.

The Oar House, corner Marine and Main St., Venice. Cheap pub, turns into a popular bar after 7pm. Funky, eclectic decor: a stuffed coyote holding a beer stein grins broadly from a wall. Experience "Burger Madness" Tues., Thurs., Sun. 11:30am-10pm, when you can get their burger and a heaping portion of fries for $2. Happy Hour 7:30-9pm.

The Rose, on Rose at Pacific Blvd. (399-0711), in Venice. A chic young crowd frequents this pricey but pretty café. The desserts are delightful just to ogle, let along eat. A variety of pasta salads with fresh produce ($5). Ultra-*nouvelle* dinners from $8. Open Mon.-Fri. 8am-11pm, Sat. 9am-11pm, Sun. 9am-5pm.

Jody Maroni's Sausages, on the boardwalk by Venice Blvd., Venice Beach. Free samples of these delectable sausages. Try his Yucatan chicken and duck ($3.75) if you have always equated sausages with greasy red meat.

Pasadena

Fair Oaks Ave. and Colorado Blvd., in the Old Town section of Pasadena, are punctuated with cafés and Mexican restaurants.

Acapulco Mexican Restaurant, 2060 E. Foothill Blvd. (818-449-7273). A white-bread version of the rougher Hispanic cafés in the Old Town, but the food is tasty and plentiful. Excellent combination dishes around $5.75. Kids eat free on Tues. Open Mon.-Thurs. 11am-10pm, Fri.-Sat. 11am-11pm, Sun. 10am-10pm.

Rose City Diner, 45 S. Fair Oaks Ave. (818-793-8282), just south of Colorado Blvd. Another restaurant that recalls the 50s. Hardly authentic, but so peppy that you can't fault it. Generous portions of vintage food $3-7. Bazooka gum presented with your check. Open daily 6:30am-2am.

The Espresso Bar, 34 S. Raymond (818-356-9095), in an alley *behind* the Raymond St. façade. Just when you thought there were no hip cafes in Pasadena, this bare, ratty little place rides to the rescue. Bagel with brie $2.75, steamed milk $1.25. And—inevitably—espresso ($1). Open Mon.-Thurs. noon-1am, Fri.-Sat. noon-2am, Sun. noon-midnight.

Sights

Downtown

The Los Angeles downtown is an odd mixture of neighborhoods. The skyscrapers of the financial district soar in the center of downtown (in an area bounded roughly by 3rd and 6th St. and Figueroa St. and Grand Ave). L.A.'s top-quality jewelry is sold on Hill St. only a block away from the tawdry five-and-dime stores of Broadway; Chinatown's spice shops crowd each other a short distance from the Civic Center, site of one of the largest concentrations of office buildings outside of Washington, DC.

The city was founded on the banks of the Los Angeles River 200 years ago, in the area where the downtown now stands. Today 90% of L.A.'s water is imported, and three-fourths of the year the river is an arid ditch. In the place where the original city center once stood, **El Pueblo de Los Angeles State Historic Park** (680-2525) preserves a number of historically important buildings from the Spanish and Mexican eras. Start out at the **docent center,** 130 Paseo de la Plaza (628-1274). They offer free walking tours (Tues.-Sun. 10am-1pm on the hour) and a free bus tour of L.A., for which you must make reservations (1st and 3rd Wed. of each month. Open Mon.-Fri. 10am-3pm.) The **Old Plaza,** with its century-old Moreton Bay fig trees and airy bandstand, sprawls at the center of the pueblo. Tours start here and wind their way past the **Avila Adobe,** 10 E. Olvera St., the oldest house in the city (it's actually made of concrete now, thanks to the 1971 earthquake), followed by **Pico House,** 500 N. Main St., once L.A.'s most luxurious hotel. Founded in 1818, the **Plaza Church,** 535 N. Main St., almost melts away from the street with its soft, rose adobe facade. Most tours also include the catacombs where Chinese immigrants ran gambling and opium dens. The **visitors center** is located in the **Sepulveda House** (1887), 622 N. Main St. (628-1274; open Mon.-Sat. 10am-3pm).

One of the original pueblo's roads, **Olvera Street,** has been turned into Tijuana North: one tawdry stand after another sells low-quality Mexican handicrafts. On **Cinco de Mayo,** huge celebrations mark Mexican Independence Day. L.A.'s population today is about thirty-percent Hispanic, and Chicanos form the majority downtown. Everyone joins the festivities for this holiday.

The **Civic Center,** a solid wall of bureaucratic architecture bounded by the Hollywood Fwy. (U.S. 101), Grand, 1st, and San Pedro St., ends at **City Hall,** 200 N. Spring St. There's an observation deck on the 27th floor (free elevator), but don't waste your time unless the air is clear. Right.

Bustling **Chinatown** lies north of this area, roughly bordered by Yale, Spring, Ord, and Bernard St. (From downtown, take the DASH shuttle. See Getting Around, Public Transportation.) Excellent Chinese food can be eaten in this once vice-ridden neighborhood where Jake Giddis learned what a tough, unforgiving world this is.

Little Tokyo is centered at 2nd and San Pedro St. on the eastern edge of downtown. Due to the increased commerce among Pacific Rim nations, the Japanese have invested heavily in Los Angeles. The **Japanese Village Plaza,** in the 300 block of E. 2nd St., offers a weird symbiosis of U.S. shopping mall and Japanese design. Don't miss the Japanese-style Shakey's Pizza Parlor. The **Japanese American Cultural and Community Center,** 244 S. San Pedro St. (628-2725), was designed by Buckminster Fuller and Isamu Noguchi. Noguchi created a monumental sculpture for the courtyard. (Open Mon.-Fri. 8:30am-6pm.)

Neon (both old and new essays in the art form), electric, and kinetic art are enshrined at the **Museum of Neon Art,** 704 Traction Ave. (617-1580), on the eastern edge of Little Tokyo, in an area with several other small art galleries. Traction is the continuation of 2nd St. east of Alameda St. (Open Tues.-Sat. 11am-5pm. Admission $2.50, students and seniors $1, under 17 free.)

Across from City Hall East, between the Santa Ana Fwy. and Temple in the L.A. Mall, is the **L.A. Children's Museum,** 310 N. Main St. (697-8800), where everything can be handled. (Open Mon.-Fri. 11:30am-5pm, Sat.-Sun.10am-5pm; off-season Wed.-Thurs. 2-4, Sat.-Sun. 10am-5pm. Admission $4.)

Undoubtedly the most striking and chic museum in the area is the **Museum of Contemporary Art (MOCA),** showcasing art from 1940 to the present. The main museum is at California Plaza, 250 S. Grand Ave. (626-6222), and is a sleek and geometric marvel of architecture. Its collection focuses on abstract expression, and includes works by Pollack, Calder, Miró, and Giacometti. The second MOCA facility is at the **Temporary Contemporary,** 152 N. Central Ave. in Little Tokyo. Unlike the main museum, the TC focuses on today's avant-garde. Admission covers both places; the DASH shuttle goes between them. (Open Tues.-Wed. and Sat.-Sun. 11am-6pm, Thurs.-Fri. 11am-8pm. Admission $4, seniors and students with ID $2. Under 12 free, everyone free Thurs. 5-8pm. Disabled access.)

The arts are also alive at the **Music Center,** 135 N. Grand Ave. (972-7211), showcasing the **Dorothy Chandler Pavillion,** the **Mark Taper Forum,** and the **Ahmanson Theatre.** The center is home to the Los Angeles Philharmonic Orchestra and the Joffrey Balley.

Los Angeles, always a melting pot, is becoming increasingly Hispanic. It is somewhat ironic that this originally Spanish settlement has taken so long to regain the flavor of its roots. **Broadway** south of 1st St. is one of the predominantly Mexican sections of the city. All billboards and store signs are in Spanish, and the **Grand Central Public Market** (see Food) takes a center seat. One of many Spanish-language cinemas housed in old movie palaces is the **Million Dollar Theater,** 307 S. Broadway (624-6272). Get a look at the baroque auditorium, and inspect the stars in the sidewalk out front, each bearing the name of a Chicano celebrity—a *rambla de fama* to complement Hollywood's Walk of Fame.

Among the most notable downtown sights is **Exposition Park.** The park is southwest of downtown, just off the Harbor Fwy., and is bounded by Exposition Blvd., Figueroa St., Vermont Ave., and Santa Barbara Ave. From downtown, take bus #40 (from Broadway) or 42 (from Olive) to the park's southern edge. From Hollywood, take #204 down Vermont. From Santa Monica, take bus #20, 22, 320, or 322 on Wilshire, and transfer to #204. The park is dominated by several large museums, including the **California Museum of Science and Industry,** 700 State Dr. (744-7400). Enter at the corner of Figueroa and Exposition: You can't miss the United DC-8 parked out front. Many of the exhibits are either corporate or governmental propaganda; those left to the MSI's own devices are rather amateurish. The museum also houses the **Kinsey Hall of Health,** which features a transparent woman named Clearissa and a machine that answers questions about substance abuse. The **Hall of Economics and Finance** does its best to enliven what even its practitioners call "the dismal science"; and the **Aerospace Building,** as big as a hangar, exhibits $8 million worth of aircraft, including the Gemini 11 space capsule. (Open daily 10am-5pm. Free. Parking 50¢.)

The **Los Angeles County Natural History Museum,** 900 Exposition Blvd. (744-3430; 744-3466 for a recorded message), houses an astounding range of exhibits, including the E. Hadley Stuart, Jr. Hall of Gems and Minerals, where displays of gold nuggets and precious gems will light up even the least materialistic eyes. (Open Tues.-Sun. 10am-5pm. Admission $3, seniors and students $1.50, ages 5-12 75¢, under 5 free.)

The **University of Southern California (USC)** campus is opposite Exposition Park on Exposition Blvd. The campus is beautiful, but the neighborhood is dangerous after dark. The **Fisher Gallery,** 823 Exposition Blvd. (743-2799), includes the Armand Hammer collection of 18th- and 19th-century baking soda boxes, or rather, Dutch paintings. (Open early Sept.-early May Tues.-Sat. noon-5pm. Free.)

Three concentric, concrete-coated towers, the tallest standing 104 feet, rise from the district of Watts. Major riots erupted here during the 60s, frustrating hopes for peaceful racial progress. The **Watts Towers,** 1765 E. 107th St. (569-8181), were built single-handedly by Simon Rodia, an immigrant tinsetter. For 33 years until 1954 (when he deeded the monument to a neighbor and disappeared), Rodia fashioned fountains and labyrinths from steel, wire mesh, shells, bottle tops, broken glass, and concrete embedded with broken tiles. For a tour of the towers, visit the **Watts Tower Arts Center,** 1727 E. 107th. (Open Tues.-Sat. 9am-5pm.) Watts is quieter than it once was, but go only in the company of street-wise friends.

Wilshire District and Hancock Park

Wilshire Boulevard, especially the "Miracle Mile" between Highland and Fairfax Ave., played a starring role in Los Angeles' westward suburban expansion. On what was then the end of the boulevard, the Bullocks Corporation gambled on attracting shoppers from downtown and opened what remains one of L.A.'s classiest buildings, the massive bronze-colored **Bullocks Wilshire** at 3050 Wilshire Blvd., near Vermont Ave. Many stores and businesses followed, but, unfortunately, Wilshire Blvd. now supports a dozen boring, glass-and-steel monoliths for every art-deco skyscraper. The neighborhood houses a nine-to-five high-rise warren of office workers, but the residential areas are worth exploring, particularly if you're interested in 1920s domestic architecture (the streets south of Wilshire opposite Hancock Park are lined with Spanish-style bungalows and the occasional modernist house). The streets of Hancock Park (a residential area bounded by Melrose, Wilton, Wilshire, and Highland) and St. Elmo Drive offer some of the finest architecure in Los Angeles.

The **La Brea Tar Pits** in Hancock Park is one of the most popular hangouts in the world for fossilized early mammals. Most of the one million bones recovered from the pits between 1913 and 1915 are now housed in the excellent **George C. Page Museum of La Brea Discoveries,** 5801 Wilshire Blvd. at Curson, Wilshire (857-6311; 936-2230 for a recorded message). Wilshire buses stop right in front. The museum includes not only reconstructed Ice Age animals, but also two movies, a laboratory where paleontologists work behind plate-glass windows, and a display where you can feel what it's like to stick around in the tar. (Open Tues.-Sun. 10am-5pm. Admission $3, students and seniors $1.50, children 75¢. Free 2nd Tues. of each month. Call ahead to see if tours are being run. Combined admission to Page and L.A. County Museum of Art $4.50, students and seniors $2.25.)

The Los Angeles County Museum of Art (LACMA), 5905 Wilshire Blvd. (857-6000), at the west end of Hancock Park, has a distinguished, comprehensive collection that should be required viewing for Easterners who think L.A. culture is yogurt. Opened in 1965, LACMA is the largest museum in the West and still growing. A pavilion for Japanese art has recently been completed. LACMA's four huge floors represent all major periods, with extensive collections in the arts of Asia, the classical world, and Renaissance and impressionist-era Europe. The **Robert O. Anderson Building,** a 1986 addition to the museum framed in salmon-colored sandstone and glass blocks, is home to provocative 20th-century painting and sculpture. There are numerous free talks and tours almost daily. Check with the information desk at the museum entrance or contact the Docent Council at 857-6109. (Open Tues.-Fri. 10am-5pm, Sat.-Sun. 10am-6pm. Admission $3, seniors and students and seniors $1.50.)

Similar to Jerusalem's famous Yad VaShem is **Martyrs Memorial and Museum of the Holocaust** (852-1234, ext. 3200), located in the Jewish Community Building, 6505 Wilshire Blvd., just east of Beverly Hills. Horrifying photographs and prisoners' personal items are on display next to paintings and drawings done by people in the ghettos and death camps. The museum is on the twelfth floor; sign in at the security desk. (Open Mon.-Thurs. 9am-5pm, Fri. 9am-3pm, Sun. 1-5pm. Free.)

More positive aspects of human nature are celebrated at **St. Elmo Village,** 4830 St. Elmo Dr. (936-3595), 2½ blocks east of La Brea Ave. between Venice and Washington Blvd. Most Angelenos have never heard of St. Elmo, yet this little clutch of 10 bungalows has admirers and supporters worldwide. A community of artists that has evolved over the past 24 years under the guidance of Rozzell and Roderick Sykes, St. Elmo is vivid testimony to its inhabitants' belief that harmony in the community is only possible if its members are allowed to express their creativity. Everything—window screens, walls, sidewalks, driveways—explodes in an astonishing array of colors. There are free workshops in the garage every week (Tues. and Thurs. at 8pm, children Sat. at 1pm); participants are encouraged to act on their own creative impulses, and "non-artists" are especially welcome.

Hollywood

For decades, this small section of a massive city defined the glamour of the West Coast. Hollywood today has lost much of its sparkle. The major studios have moved over the mountains into the San Fernando Valley, where they have more room to weave ever more elaborate fantasies, and Hollywood is left with mere relics of filmdom's heyday. Hollywood Boulevard and other thoroughfares, once sparkling and glamorous, are now sleazily evocative of Times Square. At night, prostitutes outnumber other streetwalkers; women work Hollywood and Sunset Boulevards, while boys ply their trade on Santa Monica Boulevard (also known as S&M Blvd.). Hollywood is still a fascinating place, but far from the Emerald City it was once thought to be.

The **Hollywood sign**—those 50-foot-high, slightly erratic letters perched on Mt. Cahuenga north of Hollywood—stands with New York's Statue of Liberty and Paris' Eiffel Tower as a universally recognized symbol of its city. The original 1923 sign, which read HOLLYWOODLAND, was an advertisement for a new subdivision in the Hollywood Hills (a caretaker lived behind one of the "L"s). Over the years, people came to think of it as a civic monument, and the city, which by 1978 had acquired the sign, reconstructed the crumbling letters, leaving off the last syllable. For a closer look at this legendary site, follow Beachwood Dr. up into the hills (bus #208; off Franklin Ave. between Vine St. and Western Ave.). Drive along the narrow twisting streets of the Hollywood Hills for glimpses of some bizarre homes of the rich and famous.

Hollywood Boulevard, lined with souvenir shops, prono houses, clubs, and theatres, is a bustling center of activity both day and night. The facade of **Mann's Chinese Theater** (formerly Grauman's), 6925 Hollywood Blvd. (464-8111), between Highland and La Brea, is Hollywood kitsch at its finest, with an odd mix of Chinese and Polynesian. There's always a crowd of tourists in the courtyard, staring with stooped backs at cement impressions of the stars' anatomy and trademark possessions. Al Jolson's knees, Trigger's hooves, R2D2's wheels, and George Burns's cigar join everyone else's hands and feet in concrete perpetuity. If you want to stroll among stars, have a look at the **Walk of Fame** along Hollywood Blvd. and Vine St. More than 2500 bronze-inlaid stars are embedded in the sidewalk—some 1800 of them have been inscribed with names and feats so far.

Two blocks east of Mann's is the **Hollywood Wax Museum,** 6767 Hollywood Blvd. (462-8860), where you'll meet over 200 figures from Jesus to Linda Blair. (Open Sun.-Thurs. 10am-midnight, Fri.-Sat. 10am-2am. Admission $6, children $4, senoir discount.) For a guide to nondescript places made famous by the fact that stars courted, married, fooled around, were discovered, made movies, or committed suicide there, stop at **Larry Edmund's Cinema and Theatre Bookshop,** 6658 Hollywood Blvd. Call **Hollywood Fantasy Tours,** 1721 N. Highland Ave. (call FAN-

TASY, that's 469-8184), for the most creative and least patronizing tours available. Ride a double-decker bus for two hours with hammy guides who try to take seriously questions they've heard a million times. (Beverly Hills tour $19, ages 5-12 $8. Hollywood tour $12.)

The **Hollywood Studio Museum,** 2100 N. Highland Ave. (874-2276), across from the Hollywood Bowl, provides a refreshing look at the history of early Hollywood film-making, without the glitz of Mann's. Back in 1913, when it was a barn, famed director Cecil B. DeMille rented this building as a studio and shot Hollywood's first feature film, **The Squaw Man.** Antique cameras, costumes, props, and other memorabilia clutter the museum along with vintage film clips. (Open Tues.-Sun. 10am-4pm. Admission $2, students and seniors $1.50, children $1. Ample free parking.)

Although dozens of film and TV crews take to L.A.'s streets to shoot scenes on location daily, it's unlikely that you'll stumble across one. If you're determined to see stars, stop by **Hollywood on Location,** 8644 Wilshire Blvd. (659-9165), 3 blocks west of La Cienega. Each weekday morning at 9:30am they publish a list of shooting locations with detailed maps, directions, stars, titles, subjects, shooting times, and types of shot. To get your money's worth ($29), rent a car, start early, and keep star-chasing until late.

Barnsdall Park, 4800 Hollywood Blvd., relatively small and discreet, contains the **Municipal Art Gallery,** 4804 Hollywood Blvd. (485-4581), a modern building showcasing the works of Southern California artists. (Open Tues.-Sun. 12:30-5pm. Admission 50¢, under 13 free.) Near the museum, on top of the hill, Frank Lloyd Wright's **Hollyhock House,** 4808 Hollywood Blvd. (662-7272), commands a 360° view of Los Angeles and the mountains. (Tours Tues.-Thurs. at 10am, 11am, noon, 1pm; Sat. and all but last Sun. each month at noon, 1pm, 2pm, 3pm. Admission $1.50, seniors $1, ages 12 and under free.) Buy tickets at the Municipal Art Gallery, and call to arrange tours of Hollyhock House in foreign languages.

Griffith Park sprawls over a mammoth 4108 acres of hilly terrain; this formidable recreational region stretches from the hills above Hollywood north to the intersection of the Ventura and Golden State Freeways. Pick up a map at any of the entrance points (small entrance fee for motorists). The park contains a zoo, a Greek theatre, and a planetarium complete with laser shows. For information, stop by the **visitors center and ranger headquarters,** 4730 Crystal Spring Dr. (665-5188; open daily 5am-10pm).

The 113-acre **L.A. Zoo,** at the park's northern end (666-4650), is home to 2000 animals. (Open daily summer 10am-6pm; winter 10am-5pm. Admission $4.50, seniors $3.50, ages 2-12 $2; under 2 free. Ticket office closes 1 hr. before the zoo.)

Located within Griffith Park but separate from the City of Los Angeles facilities is the **Gene Autry Western Heritage Museum,** 4700 Zoo Dr. (667-2000), at the junction of Golden State and Ventura Fwy. The museum's collection covers both the fact and fiction of the Old West, with exhibits on pioneer life and on the history of western films. (Open Tues.-Sun. 10am-5pm. Admission $4.75, seniors $3.50, children $2.)

West Hollywood

Though West Hollywood once was considered the dissolute neighbor of Beverly Hills and Hollywood, it is now a proud California city. West Hollywood has the distinction of being the first city to be largely governed by avowed gays and lesbians. Three of the five members of its first city council, including its first mayor, are publicly acknowledged homosexuals.

In the years before incorporation in 1985, lax zoning and other liberal laws gave rise to decadent **Sunset Strip.** Long the nightlife center of L.A., the Strip was originally lined with posh nightclubs frequented by stars and is now the home of several rock clubs (see Music).

Melrose Avenue, south of West Hollywood, is lined with unique restaurants, ultra-trendy boutiques, punk clothing pits, and art galleries. The choicest stretch is between La Brea and Fairfax, but the *Repo Man*-like spectre of apocalyptic apathy haunts the whole 3-mile distance between Highland and Dohemy. At Beverly and La Cienaga sits the massive **Beverly Center,** an extraordinary, opulent shopping complex. At the corner of Beverly and La Cienaga is the Los Angeles **Hard Rock Cafe** (276-7605). A 57 pistachio-green Chevy juts out of the roof, and the place is even groovier within. Indiana Jones's leather jacket, one of Pete Townshend's guitars, a 6-foot-tall martini glass, license plates, and school banners from every college in the country all adorn the interior. Be prepared for a wait every night of the week—over an hour on weekends. The line to buy T-shirts is formidable as well. (Open Sun.-Thurs. 11:30am-midnight, Fri.-Sat. 11:30am-1am.)

Beverly Hills

Early residents of Beverly Hills must have believed that urban blight could simply be gerrymandered out of existence. To protect themselves from creeping poverty, they incorporated their city decades ago. Its artificial boundaries might as well be the padlocked gates to the Emerald City, so successful has Beverly Hills been in keeping out "undesirables." The world of *Hollywood Wives* is alive and spending in the **Golden Triangle,** a wedge formed by Wilshire and Santa Monica Blvd., with **Rodeo Drive** at its beating heart of gold. There are simply too many pricey, flaky clothing boutiques to list by name. Rodeo Drive is one of the few places where you can feel underdressed even if you're simply window-shopping.

To see the most luxurious homes, drive up Benedict, Coldwater, or Laurel Canyon, north of Beverly Hills. Property values, as elsewhere in L.A., rise with elevation from the smoggy basin floor. Contractors today commonly purchase and then tear down $1 million homes to build $2 million ones which they then turn around and sell for $3 million. The "star maps" advertised by little signs on street corners aren't for astronomers—they're for tourists looking for addresses of their favorite actors and actresses.

The **Los Angeles Institute of Contemporary Art,** 2020 S. Robertson Blvd. (306-7388), is not actually in Beverly Hills, but it's close. There are changing exhibits, as well as information on happenings at the smaller galleries. (Open Wed.-Sat. noon-6pm. Reach Beverly Hills or West Hollywood by an east-west bus, then take #220 south along Robertson.)

Also close to Beverly Hills is the **Simon Wiesenthal Center,** 9760 W. Pico Blvd. (553-9036), near Roxbury Dr., one of the largest U.S. institutions for Holocaust studies. Located in the **California Yeshiva University,** the Wiesenthal Center was founded to promote tolerance as well as the cessation of various human rights abuses around the world. Named after the survivor of Mauthausen who has brought over a thousand Nazis to justice since the end of World War II, the institute comprises both a museum and a library; the opening of **Beit Hashoah, The Museum of Tolerance,** next door is projected for 1991. (Museum open Mon-Fri. 9:30am-5pm, in winter Fri. 9:30-2pm. Library open Mon.-Thurs. 9am-5pm and 7-10pm, Fri. 9am-2pm, Sun. 1:30-4pm. Both free.)

Westwood and UCLA

Appropriately huge, the University of California at Los Angeles (UCLA) sprawls over 411 beautiful, well-maintained acres in the foothills of the Santa Monica Mountains, bounded by Sunset, Hilgard, Le Conte, and Gayley. The school is so big that most of its 33,000 deep-tanned students use cars or mopeds to get around. Some joke that the most exciting thing about being an Alumni/ae Scholar is the guaranteed parking—everyone else pays $3 per day to park. Free campus maps are available at information kiosks near entrances. For general information 206-5333.

Campus highlights include the **Dickson Art Center** (825-1462), which houses the University Galleries (open Sept.-June Tues. 11am-8pm, Wed.-Fri. 11am-5pm, Sat.-Sun. 1-5pm; free); the **Museum of Cultural History** in Haines Hall (825-4361), offering changing exhibits (open year-round Wed.-Sun. noon-5pm); and the **Botanical Gardens** (825-1260), encompassing a subtropical canyon where redwoods and venerable palms mingle brook-side (open year-round Mon.-Fri. 8am-5pm, Sat.-Sun. 8am-4pm).

Ackerman Union, 308 Westwood Plaza (825-0611), is the campus information hub. A calendar lists the month's line-up of movies (first-runs often free), lectures, and campus activities. On level B is the Expo Center, with travel information and a complete **rideboard.** (Open Mon.-Fri. 8:30am-6pm, Sat. 10am-5pm, Sun. noon-5pm.)

To reach UCLA, take bus #20, 21 (best), 22, 320, or 322 along Wilshire Blvd. to Westwood. Use the free UCLA shuttle from Lot 32 on Weyburn Ave. (1 block west of Gayley Ave.) to get to the center of campus. RTD runs a **Westwood shuttle** (10¢; Fri. 6:30pm-1:30am, Sat. 11am-1:30am). Pick up a map in Westwood or at an RTD customer service center. There is free parking behind the Federal Building at Veteran and Ashton, just south of Wilshire Blvd. (An evening shuttle runs the 3 blocks to Westwood Village.) Or you can stop at any campus entrance, pay $3, and park all day in the student garages.

Westwood Village is perhaps the least collegiate of college towns—bookstores and stationers give way to movie theaters, fashionable clothing boutiques, frozen yogurt shops, restaurants, and bars. Crowded and happening on weekends, the area has experienced gang activity, but there are enought police around to keep things in control. There are also hundreds of tourists, high school students, street performers, and actual UCLA collegians roaming the village.

Santa Monica

It's hard to believe that Santa Monica, once a distant beach resort, is now comprised of condominiums, shopping malls, and high-rise office complexes. A Sunday on the beach to a resident of turn-of the-century L.A. meant a long trek over poor roads. Today, the trip takes well under an hour on Big Blue express bus #10 or on the Santa Monica Freeway (I-10) from downtown. No longer far away, SaMo is still far out, with an avowedly socialist city council and the soon-to-be-divorced Mr. Jane Fonda (Tom Hayden, one of the Chicago Seven) as one of its assemblymen. The beach is the closest one to L.A. proper, and thus is crowded and dirty. However, Santa Monica demands a look for its seaside spectacle of luxury condominiums and art deco hotels. The **Santa Monica Pier** is colorful and popular, if a bit dilapidated. The gem of the pier is the magnificent turn-of-the-century **carousel** that starred opposite Robert Redford in *The Sting* and was restored in 1984.

Venice

Although once-seedy Venice is becoming increasingly gentrified, it's still the place where L.A.'s eccentrics go to be their earthy, colorful, artsy selves. Abbot Kinney, a midwestern tobacco magnate, did his best to bring Venezia to the Pacific Coast, but the oil in the canals doomed the gondoliers, and the city's personalities have stolen center stage.

Ocean Front Walk in Venice is a drastic demographic departure from Santa Monica's Promenade. Street people converge on shaded clusters of benches, blatantly healthy folk play paddle tennis (a cross between tennis and ping pong), and bodybuilders of both sexes in skimpy outfits pump iron at the original **Muscle Beach** (1800 Ocean Front Walk, closest to 18th and Pacific Ave.). This is where the roller-skating craze began, and this is probably where it will breathe its last. Even the police wear Jams, cheerily handing out $55 fines to nude sunbathers. New Wave types, cyclists, joggers, gay people, groovy elders (such as the "skateboard grandma"), and bards in Birkenstocks make up the balance of this funky playground population. The **Sidewalk Cafe,** 1407 Ocean Front Walk (399-5547) offers delicious pizza and is nearly always packed, Fri.-Sat. 8am-1am. (Open Sun.-Thurs. 8am-midnight, and offers free live music most evenings.)

Venice's **street murals** are another free show. Don't miss the brilliant, grafitti-disfigured homage to Botticelli's *Birth of Venus* on the beach pavilion at the end of Windward Ave.: an angelically beautiful woman, wearing shorts and a Band-aid top, disco-skates out of her seashell while pedestrians walk by on either side, unfazed.

To get to Venice from downtown L.A., take bus #33, 333 (or 436 during rush hour). From downtown Santa Monica, take Santa Monica bus #1 or 2.

Malibu

Malibu is a tiny collection of multi-million-dollar homes. The beach lies along the 23200 block of the Pacific Coast Highway (PCH); you might want to walk out onto the sand by the **Zonker Harris access way,** named after the quintessential Californian from *Doonesbury,* at 22700 PCH.

East of Malibu Beach, on a cliff high above the ocean, what looks like a Roman villa is the **J. Paul Getty Museum,** 17985 PCH (458-2003). Multi-zillionaire Getty built this mansion as a re-creation of the Villa dei Papiri in Herculaneum. Appropriately, the collection of Greek and Roman sculpture is given center stage—it includes a bronze athlete that is the only surviving work of Lysippos, a sculptor contemporaneous with Alexander the Great. Although Getty himself collected 13th- to early 20th-century European paintings (with an emphasis on Renaissance and Baroque art), there is an incredible variety of artwork housed in the museum. Access to the museum is more difficult than it should be. Because the parking lot is small, reservations are needed, a day in advance most of the time, weeks in advance in summer. You are *not* permitted to park outside the museum, unless you do so at the county lot. Bicyclists and motorcyclists are admitted without reservations. (Open year-round Tues.-Sun. 10am-5pm. Free. Take RTD #434 from either Sunset and PCH in Malibu or Ocean and Colorado in Santa Monica; be sure to ask the driver for a free **museum pass.**) If the Getty won't admit you, try the **Malibu Lagoon Museum,** 23200 PCH (456-8432), 300m west of the Malibu pier, for a complete history of Malibu. (Tours Wed.-Sat. 10am-2pm.)

Pasadena

At the western end of Pasadena, near the intersection of the foothill and Ventura Fwy., lies the **Norton Simon Museum of Art,** 411 W. Colorado Blvd. (449-3730), at Orange Grove Blvd. The collection is superb; there are numerous Rodin and Brancusi bronzes, and the paintings include masterpieces by Rembrandt, Raphael, and Picasso. (Open Thurs.-Sun. noon-6pm. Admission $3, seniors and students $1.50, under 13 free. From downtown L.A. take bus #483 from Olive St., anywhere between Venice Blvd. and 1st St., to Colorado Blvd. and Fair Oaks Ave. in Pasadena. The museum is 4 blocks west.)

The museum is about a ½-mile from a quiet, shady neighborhood that contains several examples of gorgeous Pasadena architecture. The most renowned of these is the **Gamble House,** 4 Westmoreland Pl. (793-3334). Designed in 1908 by brothers Charles and Henry Greene for the heirs to the Procter and Gamble fortune, this bunalow-style masterpiece has become part of USC's School of Architecture. (1-hr. tours Thurs.-Sun. noon-3pm. Admission $4, seniors $3, college students $2, high school students and children free. From the Norton Simon, walk north along Orange Grove Blvd., over the Ventura Fwy. Turn left after you see Walnut St. on the right, then right onto Westmoreland.) A self-guided tour of this area is available in the **Gamble House bookstore** for 50¢.

The **Pacific Asia Museum,** 46 N. Los Robles Ave. (449-2742), between Colorado Ave. and Union St., has an extensive and impressive collection. (Open Wed.-Sun. noon-5pm. Admission $1.50, under 12 free.)

The **California Institute of Technology,** 1201 E. California Blvd. (356-6328), lies near the intersection of Mill Ave. and California Blvd. The fantastic proliferation of plants on this campus manages to distract visitors from the war between the architectural styles of the various buildings; the campus is a jumble of Spanish, Italian Renaissance, and modern architecture. Appearances aside, **CalTech,** founded in 1891 as Throop University, boasts a faculty which includes many Nobel prizewinners and a student body which demonstrates its high I.Q. through ingenious practical jokes, occasionally as outrageous as making the Hollywood sign read "CalTech."

One half-mile to the south of CalTech lies the **Huntington Library, Art Gallery, and Botanical Gardens,** 1151 Oxford Rd., San Marino 91108 (213-792-6141, 818-405-2100, ticket information 818-405-2273). Despite the ban on picnics and sunbathing, families and tourists still flock here on Sundays to stroll around the lush grounds and visit the library and galleries. The astounding botanical gardens nurture 207 acres of plants, many of them rare. The library houses one of the world's most important collections of rare books and English and American manuscripts, including a Gutenberg Bible and Benjamin Franklin's handwritten autobiography. The art gallery is best known for its 18th- and 19th-century British paintings; American art is on view in the recently added Virginia Steele Scott Gallery. (Open Tues.-Sun. 1-4:30pm, ticket information from 12:30pm. Free. Parking donation. To visit on Sunday, write for advance tickets. Include a self-addressed, stamped envelope (visitors from out of state don't need reservations). The museum sits between Huntington Dr. and California Blvd. in San Marino, just south of Pasadena. From downtown L.A. catch bus #79 along Olive St. The bus travels along Huntington Dr. Get off at San Marino Ave., and walk north to Stratford Rd. Turn left. From the Huntington, take bus #79 or 379 along Huntington Dr., transfer to #485 at Oak Knoll, and then again to the #177 at California.)

The grandaddy of the bowl games is played New Year's Day at the **Rose Bowl,** 991 Rosemont Blvd. (818-793-7193). The classic West-meets-Midwest showdown follows the **Tournament of Roses Parade,** where thousands line Pasadena's streets to get a look.

Entertainment

"Vast wasteland" mythology to the contrary, L.A.'s cultural scene is in fact active and diverse. The *L.A. Weekly* routinely runs 120 pages, trying to keep up with the city's film, music, art, theater, radio, television, and other entertainment events. The *L.A. Times Calendar* section is a super source of accurate and up-to-date information on what's going on where. The *L.A. Life* section of Friday's *Los Angeles Daily News* is tremendously useful in planning a weekend.

Film and Television Studios

All of the major TV studios offer free tickets to show tapings. Some are available on a first come-first serve basis from the **visitors information center** of the Greater L.A. Visitor and Convention Bureau, or by mail. Networks won't send tickets to out-of-state addresses, but they will send a guest card or letter that can be redeemed for tickets. Be sure to enclose a self-addressed, stamped envelope. Write ABC-TV, 4151 Prospect, Hollywood 90027 (557-7777); CBS-TV, 7800 Beverly Blvd., Hollywood 90036 (852-2624); or NBC-TV, 3000 W. Alameda Ave., Burbank 91523 (840-3537). Tickets don't guarantee admittance, so arrive early. The following studios offer tours:

KCET Public Television, 4401 Sunset Blvd. (667-9242), near Santa Monica Blvd. Served by buses #2 and 3. Free 1½-hr. tours, an opportunity to be treated like an adult while getting a glimpse of how the entertainment industry works. Tours Tues. and Thurs. mornings. Call to arrange a time.

Universal Studios, Universal City (508-5444). Hollywood Fwy. to Lankershim. Take bus #424 to Lankershim Blvd. On the trolley tour, visit sets, be attacked by Jaws, get caught in an earthquake, and witness many special effects and other demonstrations of movie-making magic. After the tour, wander the amusement park and visit the special effect and stunt shows. You can even be videotaped aboard the U.S.S. *Enterprise.* Reservations for the tour are not accepted; it's best to arrive early to secure a ticket. Open daily 9am-5pm; Sept.-June Mon.-Fri. 10am-3:30pm, Sat.-Sun. 9:30am-3:30pm. Tours in Spanish on Sat. and Sun. Allow 2½ hr. for the tour. Admission (includes both tour and amusement park shows) $20; ages 3-11 $14.50. Parking $3.

NBC Television Studios Tour, 3000 W. Alameda Ave. (840-3537), is in Burbank, at Olive, 2 miles from Universal. Hollywood Fwy. north, exit east on Barham Blvd., which becomes Olive Ave. Take bus #420 from Hill St. downtown. A cheaper, smaller, and in many ways better tour than Universal's. A good chance to see shows being taped and to bump into a wandering star. Arrive early to avoid crowds and improve your chances of receiving free tickets to a live show taping. Tickets for shows (including *The Tonight Show*) available by mail or at the box office (off California) Mon.-Fri. 8am-5pm, Sat. 9:30am-4pm. Studios open Mon.-Fri. 8:30am-4pm, tours every ½ hr.; Sat.-Sun. 10am-2pm, tours every hr. Tours $6.50, ages 5-14 $4.50.

Burbank Studios VIP Tour, 4000 Warner Blvd., Burbank (954-1744). Personalized, unstaged tours (maximum 12 people) through the home of Warner Bros. and Columbia Pictures. These technical, 2-hr. tours get to the guts of the movie-making industry. No children under 10. Tours 4 times per day, $20 per person. Make reservations.

Cinema

Just about every major block of every major street in L.A. owns a movie theater. A handful are worth mentioning as opportunities to see a film the way it was meant to be seen: in a big auditorium, on a big screen, in a big city, in a big way.

Cineplex Odeon Universal City Cinemas, atop the hill at Universal Studios (818-508-0588). Take the Universal Center Dr. exit off the Hollywood Fwy. (U.S. 101). Opened in 1987 as the world's largest cinema complex. The 18 wide-screen theaters, 2 *Parisienne*-style cafés, and opulent decoration puts all others to shame. Hooray for Hollywood.

Pacific Cinerama Dome, 6360 Sunset Blvd. (466-3401), near Vine. The screen stretches nearly 180° around the theater. You can't miss the geodesic-like dome illuminated at night.

Mann's Chinese (formerly Grauman's), 6925 Hollywood Blvd. (464-8111). Opulent, moviegoer's fantasy. For more details, see Hollywood Sights.

Devotees of second-run, foreign language, and just plain weird films are also rewarded. Check the midnight show at a first-run theater. The following show **classic and cult films** all the time:

New Beverly Cinema, 7165 Beverly Blvd. (938-4038), in L.A. Classics, old and new.

Nuart Theatre, 11272 Santa Monica Blvd. (478-6379), in L.A., at the San Diego Fwy. Perhaps the best known. The playbill changes nightly, so drop by for a copy of the monthly guide. Classics and documentaries.

Rialto Theater, 1023 Fair Oaks Ave. (799-9567), in South Pasadena, at Oxley. *Rocky Horror* Sat. at midnight.

UCLA's Melnitz Theater, on the northeastern corner of campus near Sunset and Hilgard. An eclectic range of film festivals.

Foreign films can be found consistently at the four **Laemmle Theaters** in Beverly Hills, West L.A., and Hollywood.

Comedy

L.A. is a great place to catch the newest and wackiest stand-up comedians, or to watch the pros hone new material. This is where HBO scouts and shoots. Some clubs are open only a few nights per week. Call ahead to check age restrictions.

Comedy Store, 8433 Sunset Blvd. (656-6225), in West Hollywood. Take bus #2 or 3. Big names often try out their new routines here. 3 different rooms, depending on the type of comedy you want. Cover $8 and up, plus 2-drink minimum.

The Improvisation, 8162 Melrose Ave. (651-2583), in L.A. Bus #10. Consistently hilarious. Bar, restaurant cafe. Cover $6.50-10, 2-drink minimum.

The Laugh Factory, 8001 W. Sunset Blvd. (656-8860), in West Hollywood. Cover $5-8 plus 2-drink minimum. Must be 18 or over.

Theater and Classical Music

Los Angeles has the most active theater circuit on the West Coast. One hundred and fifteen Equity Waiver theaters (under 100 seats) offer a dizzying choice for theater-goers, who can also enjoy small productions in museums, art galleries, universities, parks, and garages. During the summer hiatus, TV stars frequently return to their acting roots. Mainstream theater is often worth the high prices to see shows that are either Broadway-bound or beginning their national tour after a New York run. Most of the following double as sites for musical performances as well as drama.

Hollywood Bowl, 2301 N. Highland Ave. (850-2000), in Hollywood. Perfect for a summer evening. Although sitting in the back of this outdoor, 18,000-seat amphitheater makes even the L.A. Philharmonic sound like AM radio, the bargain tickets ($1-3) and the sweeping views of L.A. from the bowl's south rim make it worthwhile. You're free to bring your own food, and buckets of Kentucky Fried Chicken are at least as numerous as classy gourmet baskets. Going to the bowl can mean a major production by car; parking is complicated and expensive. It's easier and more relaxing to use RTD's Park 'n' Ride service (get a brochure listing parking lots from where shuttle service is available). If you're willing to do a little hiking, park away from the bowl and walk up Highland. Bus #150 takes you to the Bowl from the Valley, and bus #420 runs from downtown.

Music Center, 135 N. Grand Ave., downtown (972-7475), at the corner of 1st in the heart of the city. Includes the **Mark Taper Forum** (972-7353) and the **Dorothy Chandler Pavilion,** (972-7200) where the Academy Awards are often held.

Schubert, 2020 Ave. of the Stars, Century City (800-223-3123). Big Broadway shows, such as *A Chorus Line.*

Pantages, 6233 Hollywood Blvd. (410-1062). L.A.'s other place for big Broadway spectacles.

Nightclubs

Music in L.A. falls into two major categories: clubs and concerts. Clubs are crowded and intimate; concerts are crowded and impersonal. Clubs tend to be experimental, uneven in quality, and ephemeral. To find a club to suit your taste, scan the *L.A. Weekly News.*

Club Lingerie, 6507 Sunset Blvd., Hollywood (466-8557), 21 and over. Rock/reggae/ska/funk from 9pm on. Two full bars.

Palomino, 6907 Lankershim Blvd. (818-764-4010), in North Hollywood. Popular country and folk club. Cover $4-8. All ages.

Anti-Club, 4658 Melrose Ave. (661-3913). Avant-garde, smoky, and dim, this famous lair has been supporting innovative bands like Elizabeth's Children for years. Acts range from traditional to underground rock sounds. Full bar, cover varies.

Gazzarrio's, 9039 Sunset Blvd. (273-6606). An enormously popular heavy metal club on the Sunset Strip. Don't go if you're disturbed by the thought of long-haired crazies sharing your space. Cover $6-10. Must be 18.

Roxy, 9009 Sunset Blvd. (276-2222). This is the *biggest* club on the strip. Cover varies, no age limit.

Whiskey a Go-Go, 8901 Sunset Blvd. (652-4202). Like the Roxy, a part of L.A.'s music history. Hosted many progressive bands in the late 70s and early 80s, and took part in the punk explosion. Mostly metal nowadays. Full bar, cover varies. No age limit.

Dance Clubs

Excellent listings describe both trendy and tried-and-true dance spots in the *L.A. Weekly News.* For more extensive listings of women's and men's bars contact the Gay and Lesbian Community Services Center (see Practical Information).

Baxter's Underground, 1050 Gayley Ave., Westwood (208-3716). Hot spot with the UCLA crowd. Must be 21. Grill until 10 pm.

Coconut Teaszer, 8117 Sunset Blvd., W. Hollywood (654-4773). Big, popular club with DJs and live entertainment. Must be 21; over 18 during weekend after-hours.

Code Blue L.A., call for location and info. (281-9903). Flashy, upscale club for lesbians.

Florentine Gardens, 5951 Hollywood Blvd. (464-0706). College kids jam this huge dance space every Thurs.-Sun. Must be 18.

The Palace, 1735 N. Vine St. (462-3000). In the heart of Hollywood, this stylish art deco club features live acts and dancing nightly until 4am. Dazzling lights and lasers, restaurant, 3 bars. Cover varies. Must be 18.

Rage, 8911 Santa Monica Blvd. (652-7055), W. Hollywood. Dance and R&B sounds for a mostly gay and male crowd. Must be 21.

Disneyland

The recent growth of Mike Eisert's Disney empire, with its cable-TV channel, movies, and new studio park in Florida, has breathed new life into the most famous, and still perhaps the best, amusement park in the world. Opened in 1955, "The Happiest Place on Earth" has delighted even the most hardened cynics, including resident Donald Duck. Grown adults walk through the park sporting ridiculous-looking hats, but this silliness is all part of the fun. The attractions are inspired testaments to the charm of child-like creativity, and they are executed with technological sophistication.

Admission to the spotless, gleaming fantasy world is gained through the **Unlimited Use Passport** ($23.50, ages 3-11 $18.50). The park is open daily in summer from 8am-1am. Off-season hours vary; call 714-999-4000 for more information.

Disneyland is divided into four main areas that branch out from the end of Main Street, USA: **Adventureland, Frontierland, Fantasyland,** and **Tomorrowland.** There are also two areas not directly connected to Main St.: **New Orleans Square** and **Bear Country. Main Street, USA** does not feature rides but serves as a place of orientation. Shops, banking services, entertainment information, and first aid are all located here.

Once inside, you'll face a barrage of attractions. The newest addition to the park is **Splash Mountain,** a "Song of the South"-themed log ride. The other thrill rides, **Space Mountain, Thunder Mountain,** and the Matterhorn are always crowded. Other notable rides are the **Jungle Cruise,** the **Submarine Voyage,** the **Haunted Mansion,** and the **Pirates of the Caribbean.** The recently added **Star Tours** and teen dance club **Videopolis** are also among the big draws.

Food services in the park range from sit-down establishments to fast-food eateries such as the Lunch Pad. Food is decent, but you can save much time and money by packing a picnic lunch and eating a big breakfast before you leave home. If you're looking for a martini, you'll be left high and dr: no alcohol is served in the park.

No matter when you go, you'll probably feel as if every Huey, Dewey, and Louie has picked the same day to visit. Fall months and weekdays are frequently less crowded than summer days and weekends. To avoid long waits, arrive early. Lines for the most popular attractions are shorter just after opening and late at night; try mid-day and you'll see why some call it "Disneyline."

The Unofficial Guide to Disneyland ($7.95) is available from Simon and Schuster, Attn.: Mail Order Dept., 200 Old Tappan Rd., Old Tappan, NJ 07675 (201-767-5937). The authors have earned their mouska-ears by cramming the book with time-saving hints. The guide evaluates every attraction in the park, and the researchers suggest several specific itineraries for visitors, including adults with young children, senior citizens, and those pressed for time.

Disneyland is located at 1313 Harbor Blvd., in Anaheim and is bounded by Katella Ave., Harbor Blvd., Ball Rd., and West St. Take **bus #460** from 6th and Flower St. downtown, about one-and-a-half hours to the Disneyland Hotel. (Service to the Disneyland Hotel from 4:53am, back to L.A. until 1:20am.) From the hotel take the free shuttle to Disneyland's portals. Also served by Airport Service, OCTD, Long Beach Transit, and Gray Line (see Public Transportation for prices). If you're **driving,** take the Santa Ana Fwy. to the Katella Ave. exit. Be forewarned, however: while parking in the morning should be painless, leaving in the evening often will not be. In addition, when the park closes early, Disneygoers must contend with L.A. rush hour traffic, one of the slowest-moving attractions.

Other Amusement Parks

Six Flags Magic Mountain, 26101 Magic Mountain Pkwy. (818-367-2271), in Valencia, 30 miles north of downtown L.A. just off the Golden State Fwy. (I-5). From L.A. take Gray Line. A combination amusement park, petting zoo, and country fair. For the thrill-seeker, the rides are among the best in Southern California. Colossus is the largest wooden roller coaster in the world, the Revolution features a vertical 360° loop. Free Fall has been known to cause even those with ice water in their veins to prostrate themselves and kiss the ground as they step off. The fair, in a pioneer village, includes glass-blowers, candlestick-makers, and blacksmiths. Bugs Bunny World offers children's rides. Open Memorial Day to mid-Sept. and Christmas and Easter weeks Mon.-Fri. 10am-6pm, Sat. 10am-midnight, Sun. 10am-10pm; otherwise weekends only. Admission $20, seniors and those shorter than 48" $10.

Knott's Berry Farm, 8039 Beach Blvd., Buena Park (714-220-5200 for a recording), 30 miles south of L.A. at La Palma, just 5 miles northeast of Disneyland. Take the Santa Ana Fwy. south, exit west on La Palma Ave. Bus #460 stops here on its way to Disneyland. An actual berry farm in its early days, Knott's now cultivates a country fair atmosphere with a re-created ghost town, Fiesta Village, Roaring Twenties Park, rides, and a replica of Independence Hall. Open Mon.-Thurs. 10am-10pm, Fri. and Sun. 10am-midnight, Sat. 10am-1am; off-season usually Sun.-Thurs. 10am-6pm, Fri.-Sat. 10am-9pm. Admission $20, seniors and ages 3-11 $16, teenagers $10 after 6pm.

Raging Waters Park, 111 Raging Waters Dr. (714-592-6453 for recorded message, for directions 714-599-1251), in San Dimas. Near the intersection of the San Bernardino and Foothill Fwy. (I-10 and I-210). 44 acres and 5 million gallons of slides, pools, whitewater rafts, innertubes, fake waves, and a fake island offer a cool alternative to the beach. Hurl yourself over the 7-story water-slide "Drop Out" if you dare. Open Mon.-Thurs. 10am-6pm., Fri.-Sat. 10am-8pm, Sun. 10am-7pm. Admission $14.50, under 5 $8.50, under 2 free.

The Desert

Mystics, misanthropes, and hallucinogenophiles have long shared a fascination with the desert and its vast spaces, austere scenery, and sometimes brutal heat. California's desert region has worked its spell on generations of passersby, from the Native Americans and pioneering fortune hunters of yesterday to today's city slickers disenchanted with smoggy L.A. The fascination stems partly from the desert's cyclical metamorphosis from a pleasantly warm refuge in winter to a technicolored floral landscape in spring, and then to a blistering wasteland in summer. Despite a climate that allows only six inches of rain to trickle onto the parched sand each year, the desert supports an astonishing array of plant and animal life.

Southern California's desert is the fringe of the North American Desert, a 500,000-square-mile territory stretching east into Arizona and New Mexico, northeast into Nevada and Utah, and south into Mexico. The California portion claims desert parks, shabby towns around Death Valley, unlikely resorts such as Palm Springs, and dozens of ordinary highway settlements serving as pit stops for those speeding to points beyond.

Orientation

The desert divides roughly into two major regions with different climatic zones. The **Sonoran,** or **Low Desert,** occupies southeastern California from the Mexican border north to Needles and west to the Borrego Desert; the **Mojave,** or **High Desert** spans the southcentral part of the state, bounded by the Sonoran Desert to the south, San Bernardino and the San Joaquin Valley to the west, the Sierra Nevada to the north, and Death Valley to the east.

The differences between the Low and High Desert stem essentially from the elevation and are reflected in the climate. The Low Desert is flat, dry, and barren. The sparse vegetation makes shade-providing plants a necessary but scarce commodity, one that relies on an even rarer one, water. Human and animal life alike exists in the oases in this area, the largest supporting the super-resort of Palm Springs. Despite the arid climate, much of this region has become agriculturally important. Water from the Colorado River irrigates Blythe, the Imperial Valley, and the Coachella Valley. Anza-Borrego Desert State Park and the Salton Sea are other points of interest here.

By contrast, the High Desert consists of foothills and plains nestled within mountain ranges approaching 5000 feet. Consequently, it is cooler (by about 10°F in summer) and wetter. Though few resorts have developed, Joshua Tree National Monument remains a popular destination for campers. Barstow is the central city of the High Desert as well as a rest station on the way to Las Vegas or the Sierras.

Death Valley serves as the eastern boundary for the Mojave but might best be considered a region unto itself, since it has both high and low desert areas. Major highways cross the desert east-west: I-8 hugs the California-Mexico border, I-10 goes through Blythe and Indio on its way to Los Angeles, and I-40 crosses Needles to Barstow, where it joins I-15, which runs from Las Vegas and other points east to L.A.

Desert Survival

For special health and safety precautions in the desert, see Desert Survival in the Southwest regional introduction.

Palm Springs

Leave your telescope at home; you won't need it to see the stars come out in Palm Springs. One of the most visible, of course, is Mayor Sonny Bono, who joined the ranks of California's celebrities-turned-politicians in 1988. Cher's former husband/sidekick is perhaps the only star of a John Waters movie to govern a major American resort town, yet Bono's "popularity" has nonetheless sparked everything from "Sonny Palm Springs" logos on t-shirts to the Bonoburger, the latest in Palm Springs cuisine.

And then, of course, there are the tourists. Today the swimming pool reigns as the supreme, if slightly chlorinated, emblem of Eden for the thousands who make their pilgrimage each year in unabashed worship of the sun. Spring vacation now brings Palm Springs thousands of college and high school students, transforming it into the Ft. Lauderdale of the West. Things turned ugly a few years ago, however, when wild spring break partying turned led to mayhem and destruction of property. "Cruising the strip" is now prohibited during Spring Break, when dozens of police monitor the streets.

The San Jacinto Mountains come grinding to a halt only blocks from **Palm Canyon Drive,** the city's one-way main drag. The elevation changes over 5000 feet from the base station to the terminal on Mt. San Jacinto at the **Palm Springs Aerial Tramway,** Tramway Dr., which intersects Rte. 111 just north of Palm Springs. Within 14 minutes the gondolas glide from the arid foothills through five climate zones to snow and pine trees at 8516 feet, with a temperature change of as much as 50°. Stairs from the deck lead up to a 360° viewing platform, but they are covered with snow drifts except in high summer. The tramway station is also the gateway to **Mt. San Jacinto State Park.** At the bottom of a lengthy concrete ramp is the Long Valley Ranger Station (327-0222), which can provide information on the park. Two short trails (under 1½ miles) start here and introduce you to the sub-alpine ecology, with walks guided by volunteer naturalists. Take the *Desert View Trail* for the most panoramic glimpses of the Valley.

Palm Springs's wealth has endowed the city with **The Desert Museum,** 101 Museum Dr. (325-7186), between Tahquitz-McCallum Way and Andreas Rd., behind the Desert Fashion Plaza on Palm Canyon Dr. The museum is housed in a gorgeous, expensive building; it showcases a very strong collection of southwestern art, including Native American and contemporary artists. The museum also sponsors curator-led field trips ($3) to observe wildflowers or explore the canyons. They leave the museum every Friday at 9am. Some of these involve as many as 9 miles of hiking. (Open late Sept.-early June Tues.-Fri. 10am-4pm, Sat.-Sun. 10am-5pm. Admission $4, ages under 17 $2, accompanied children free. Free for all the first Tuesday of every month.)

The **Living Desert Reserve** in Palm Desert is at 47900 Portola Ave. (346-5694), south of Rte. 111. Take bus #19 to Portola, and walk south 1 mile. This wild animal park and botanical garden contains tracts recreating various desert environments, from Saharan to Sonoran, a small aviary, and desert wildlife. It is also home to slender-horned gazelles and bighorn sheep, both endangered species. The 6 miles of nature trails are open from September to mid-June daily from 9am to 5pm. (Admission $3.50, ages 3-15 $1, senior citizens $2.50 on Tues. Disabled access.)

But most visitors to Palm Springs have no intention of studying the desert or taking in high culture. Palm Springs means sunning and swimming, with no activity more demanding than drinking a gallon or so of iced tea each day to keep from dehydrating. When lazing about becomes tiring, however, there are enough attractions here to keep you otherwise occupied.

Those not blessed with a pool in their backyard will probably want to use the **Olympic-sized pool** at the Palm Springs Leisure Center, Sunrise Way at Ramon Rd. (323-8278). (Open daily 11am-5pm also 7:30-9:30pm Tues. and Thurs. in summer. Admission $2, ages 3-13 $1.) For complete information about other recreactional facilities (including tennis and golf), call the Leisure Department at 323-8272. (How many places do you know with a Leisure Department?)

The most delightful sport, however, is sitting around in the naturally hot **mineral pools** of Desert Hot Springs, which are said to have curative properties. The **Desert Hot Springs Spa,** 10805 Palm Dr. (329-6495), has pools of different temperatures, a bar, saunas, and house masseurs. Unfortunately, on crowded days the deck becomes littered with cups and cigarette butts, and the pools are awash in uninviting slicks of suntan oil. (Open daily 8am-10pm. Admission Mon.-Fri. $5, after 3pm $4; Sat.-Sun. $7, after 3pm $5; holidays $8. Refundable $3 lock deposit, $3 towel deposit, plus 50¢ rental.) **The Hacienda Riviera Spa,** 67375 Hacienda (329-7010), attracts younger bathers. (Open Sept.-June daily 9am-5pm; July Wed.-Mon. 9am-5pm. Admission $4, children $1.)

Residents who want to hear good music invest in a stereo system or go to Los Angeles for the evening. Do what the locals do and see a movie on Monday or Tuesday night, when all the cinemas lower their ticket prices. The behemoth disco (with the ambience of a glitzy airplane hanger) is **Zelda's,** 169 N. Indian Ave. (325-2375), Palm Springs' best S&M (that is, Stand and Model) bar. (Open daily 8pm-2am.) For a more elegant evening, **Pernina's,** 340 N. Palm Canyon Dr. (325-6544), offers lyrical piano music in a more intimate setting.

Palm Springs's accommodations and food establishments cater to visitors (and residents) with fat wallets. The cheapest lodgings are at nearby state parks and national forest campgrounds. The sign in front of the **Motel 6,** 595 E. Palm Canyon Dr. (325-6129; take bus #20) says "Hotel 6" because of an ordinance banning the word "motel" from public view in Palm Springs. A/C. Usually booked up—sometimes 6 months in advance for winter, 3 months for summer. And no wonder; this is by far the best deal for your budget dollar. Reservations accepted up to one year in advance. Some on-the-spot rooms are available around 9am, and no-shows are frequent; so keep trying. (Singles $23. Doubles $29.) The **Mira Loma Hotel,** 1420 N. Indian Ave. (320-1178), has 12 smartly-decorated rooms in a one-story complex; all have refrigerators and color TV, and open onto the poolside. (Singles Dec.-Sept. $33-48; up to $63 in winter. Children in summer only.) The **Monte Vista Hotel,** 414 N. Palm Canyon Dr. (325-5641), is conveniently located downtown. All 34 cheery rooms have color TV and A/C. (Sept.-May $39.50-45; June-Aug. $32.50-37.50. Suites with kitchens $60-65. Children in summer only.)

If you're stocking up for a foray into the desert, there are plenty of large, chain supermarkets in Palm Springs. **Ralph's,** 1555 S. Palm Canyon (323-8446), and **Vons,** in the Palm Springs Mall on Tahquitz-McCallum (322-2192), are reliably low-priced. **Palm Springs Leisure Center,** on Sunrise at Ramon, and the **Ruth Hardy Park,** on Tamarisk, 4 blocks east of Indian Ave., are good places to picnic. For sit-down food, try the **El Gallito Cafe,** 68820 Grove St. (328-7794), Cathedral City, within sight of Rte. 111, 2 blocks west of Date Palm Dr.; look for the Mag Gas station on Rte. 111. Take bus #20. Juan and Petra Cantu serve up the best *comida mexicana* in Palm Springs. The *combinaciones* (2 entrees, beans, rice, and tortillas) are fit for a glutton ($6.25). Try a burrito ($3) with compimentary chips and salsa and one of several Mexican beers ($1.75). Always loud and busy. (Open Sun.-Fri. 11am-9:30pm, Sat. 10am-9:30pm.) **Nate's Delicatessen,** 100 S. Indian Ave. (325-3506), is the oldest (est. 1948) and best known of Palm Springs's delis. Full sandwiches are $4.50-7, but a half sandwich ($3.75, with soup $5) should suffice. Huge hunks of fresh avocado adorn a vegetarian sandwich. (Open daily 7am-8:30pm.) **The Sizzler,** 725 S. Palm Canyon Dr. (325-1851), offers an all-you-can-eat *tostada* with fixings. (Open Sun.-Thurs. 11am-9:30pm, Fri.-Sat. 11am-10:30pm.) The **Hamburger Hamlet,** 105 N. Palm Canyon Dr. (325-3231), has burgers galore for under $5.

Palm Springs lies off I-10, 120 miles east of L.A., just beyond a low pass that marks the edge of the Colorado Desert. The **chamber of commerce** is at 190 W. Amado (325-1577). Ask for a map ($1) and a free copy of *The Desert Guide.* (Open Mon.-Fri. 8am-5pm, Sat. 10am-2pm.) **Amtrak,** Jackson St. and the railroad tracks in Indio, 25 miles southeast of Palm Springs (connect to Greyhound in Indio) sends 3 trains per week to and from L.A. ($28). **Greyhound,** 311 N. Indian Ave. (325-2053) is much more convenient. Nine buses per day to and from L.A. ($15.25). **Desert Stage Lines** (367-3581) serves Twenty-nine Palms and Joshua Tree National Monument (3 buses per day, $8.45); Friday service to L.A. ($16.05) and San Diego ($20). **Sun Bus** (343-3451) is the local bus system, serving all Coachella Valley cities daily 6am-6pm (50¢, plus 25¢ per zone and 25¢ per transfer). Rent a car at **Rent-a-Wreck,** 67501 Rte. 111 (324-1766) for $14-50 per day or $121 per week, with 700 free miles, 10¢ each additional mile. (Must be 21 with major credit card.)

The Palm Springs **post office** is at 333 E. Amado Rd. (325-9631). (Open Mon.-Fri. 8:30am-5pm.) Palm Springs's **ZIP code** is 92262; the **area code** is 619.

Joshua Tree National Monument

The low, scorching Sonoran Desert and the higher, cooler Mojave Desert meet here, resulting in an area of over a half-million acres with an extraordinary variety of scenery. The star of the monument is the Joshua tree, a member of the lily family whose erratic limbs sometimes reach 50 feet in height. The Mormons who came through here in the 19th century thought the crooked branches were like the arms of Joshua leading them to the promised land. Spare forests of gangly Joshuas extend for miles in the high central and eastern portions of the Monument, punctuated by great piles of quartz monzonite boulders, some over 100 feet high. Tremendous movements of the earth left the rock exposed to the elements, and the two forces together have created fantastic textures and shapes. Beside the natural environment are vestiges of human existence: ancient rock pictographs, dams built in the 19th century in order to catch the meager rainfall for livestock, and the ruins of gold mines that operated as late as the 1940s.

The monument's main **visitors center** is at 74485 National Monument Dr., Twentynine Palms 92277 (367-7511), ¼ mile off Rte. 62. The center offers displays, lectures, and maps. (Open daily 8am-5pm.) Other visitors centers are located at the southern gateway, approximately 7 miles north of I-10 (exit 4 miles west of the town of Chiriaco Summit), and at the west entrance on Park Blvd., several miles southeast of the town of Joshua Tree.

Over 80% of the monument is designated wilderness area; for those experienced in **backcountry desert hiking and camping,** Joshua Tree is a fantastic opportunity to explore truly remote territory. Hikers should go to one of the visitor's centers for the rules and recommendations on use of isolated areas of the monument, and for a topographic map ($2.50). There is no water in the wilderness except when a flash flood comes roaring down a wash, and even this evaporates quickly. Carry at least a gallon of water per person per day. You must register at roadside boxes before setting out (see maps), so that the monument staff knows where you are, and so that your car is not towed from a roadside parking lot.

Less hardy desert rats should not be put off. Joshua Tree can be enjoyed for a day or a weekend in relative comfort. The most popular time, as with other desert parks, is **wildflower season** (mid-March to mid-May), when thousands come to see the floor of the desert exploding in yucca, verbena, cottonwood, mesquite, and dozens of other wildflowers. Summer is the hottest and slowest season. Bear in mind that no off-road driving is permitted.

A drive along the winding road from Twentynine Palms to the town of Joshua Tree (34 miles) passes by the **Wonderland of Rocks,** a most spectacular concentration of rock formations. The longer drive between Twentynine Palms and I-10 through the monument offers a sampling of both desert landscapes. Along the way on both of these tours, explore as many of the side roads as time allows—some are paved, some are dirt, and some are suitable only for four-wheel-drive vehicles. All roads indicate which vehicles are safe. One site that must not be missed is **Key's View,** off the park road just west of Ryan Campground, a spectacular scenic point. You can see as far as Palm Springs and the Salton Sea on a clear day. The **palm oases** (Twenty-nine Palms, Forty-nine Palms, Cottonwood Spring, Lost Palms) are also worth seeing, as is the **Cholla Cactus Garden,** off Pinto Basin Rd.

A number of hiking trails lead to the most interesting features of Joshua Tree: five oases, mine ruins, and fine vantage points. Short trails run near picnic areas and campsites. Visitor center brochures describe these trails, which range from a mere 200 yards (the Cholla Cactus Garden) to 35 miles (a section of the California Riding and Hiking Trail). The degree of difficulty varies almost as widely; the staff at the visitors center can help you choose a trail. Plan on at least one hour per mile on even relatively short trails.

Campgrounds in the monument accept no reservations, except for group sites at **Cottonwood, Sheep Pass,** and **Indian Cove,** where Ticketron handles reservations (mandatory at these 3 sites). Sites are also available at **White Tank** (closed in summer), **Belle, Black Rock Canyon, Hidden Valley, Ryan,** and **Jumbo Rocks.** All campsites have tables, fireplaces, and pit toilets; all are free except Cottonwood ($6) and Black Rock Canyon ($8). Water is available only at Black Rock Canyon and Cottonwood, you must bring your own firewood. To secure a fee waiver for group sites, write to the monument on your best official stationery and explain your "bona fide educational/study group" purposes. There is unlimited backcountry camping. Your tent must be more than 500 feet from a trail, 1 mile from a road. Your camping stay is limited to 14 days Oct.-May, and to 30 days in the summer. The entrance fee to the monument is $2 per individual or $5 per vehicle which is good for a 1-week stay at any California state park. In the summer, only a few primitive sites are open, and all are entirely free.

Joshua Tree National Monument occupies a vast area northeast of Palm Springs, about 160 miles (3-3½ hr. by car) from west L.A. It is ringed by three highways: I-10 to the south, Rte. 62 (Twentynine Palms Hwy.) to the west and north, and Rte. 177 to the east. From I-10, the best approaches are via Rte. 62 from the west, leading to the towns of Joshua Tree and **Twentynine Palms** on the northern side of the monument, and via an unnumbered road that exits the interstate about 25 miles east of Indio. **Desert Stage Lines** (367-3581), based in Palm Springs, stops in Twentynine Palms.

Barstow

Barstow is a fine place to prepare for forays into the desert. Once a booming mining town, this desert oasis (pop. 20,000) now thrives on business from local military bases, tourists, and truckers. Stop in at the California Desert Information Center, 831 Barstow Rd. (256-3591), which has superb exhibits on the forest and a large topographical model of the Mojave, as well as free maps and information on hiking, camping, and exploring.

What Barstow lacks in charm (and boy does it lack) is made up for by its abundant supply of inexpensive motels and eateries. The **El Rancho Motel,** 112 E. Main St. (256-2401), is convenient to Greyhound and Amtrak stations. Clean and newly decorated rooms come complete with TV, A/C, pool. (Singles and doubles $23-$27.) The **Economy Motel,** 1590 Coolwater Lane (256-1737), has singles for $20, and doubles for $27.50. The **Calico KOA,** I-15 and Ghost Town Rd. (254-2311), is uncomfortably crowded with Ghost Town devotees, but what did you expect? (Tents $13, electric hookup $15, full hookup $16. All fees for 2 people per night per site. Each additional person $2.50.)

In Barstow, of fast-food rules. To prevent a SoCal Big Mac attack, head for the **Barstow Station McDonald's,** on E. Main St. Made from old locomotive cars, this Mickey D's is the busiest in the U.S. If Filet-O-Fish does not agree with you, you may wish to try **Vons** on E. Main St., where you may purchase a variety of supermarket specialties.

Barstow is midway between Los Angeles and Las Vegas on I-15; it is the western terminus of I-40. At the **Amtrak** station, N. 1st St. (800-872-7245), you can get on or off a train—that's all. Two trains per day to L.A. ($30.60); San Diego ($46); and Las Vegas ($41). **Greyhound,** 120 S. 1st St. (256-8757), at W. Main St., sees 3 buses per day to L.A. ($15) and 9 to Vegas ($25). Open daily 8am-6pm.

Death Valley

Though Milton and Dante needed no further inspiration for their visions of Hell, they could have received it by visiting Death Valley. Nowhere in England or Italy even begins to approach the searing temperatures that are everyday here, especially in the summer.

The *average* high temperature in July is 116°, with a nighttime low of 88°. Ground temperatures hover near an egg-frying 200°.

Much of the lanscape resembles the Viking photographs of the surface of Mars, with its reddish crags and canyons, immobile and stark. The strangeness of the landscape lends it a certain beauty. The earth-hues of the sands and rocks change hourly in the variable sunlight. The elevation ranges from 11,049 ft. Telescope Peak down to Badwater, the lowest point in the hemisphere at 282 ft. below sea level. There are pure white salt flats on the valley floor, impassable mountain slopes, and huge, shifting sand dunes. It appears that nature focuses all of its extremes and varieties here at a single location.

The region sustains a surprisingly intricate web of life. Casual tourists and naturalists alike may observe a tremendous variety of desert dwellers, such as the great horned owl, roadrunner, coyote, and kit fox, gecko, chuckwalla, and raven.

Practical Information

Emergency: 911.

Visitor Information: Furnace Creek Visitors Center (786-2331), on Rte. 190 in the east-central section of the valley. For information by mail, write the Superintendent, Death Valley National Monument, Death Valley 92328. Simple and informative **museum.** Slide show every ½-hour and nightly lecture. Office open daily 8am-5pm. Center open daily 8am-5pm; Nov.-Easter 8am-8pm.

Entrance Fee: $5 per car. Good for 7 days.

Ranger Stations: Grapevine, junction of Rte. 190 and 267 near Scotty's Castle; **Emigrant,** 8 miles west of Stove Pipe Wells on Rte. 190; **Wildrose,** Rte. 178, 20 miles south of Emigrant via Emigrant Canyon Dr.; and **Shoshone,** outside southeast border of the valley at junction of Rte. 178 and 127. Weather report, weekly naturalist program, and park information posted at each station. Also provides emergency help. All are open year-round.

Gasoline: Tank up outside Death Valley at Olancha, Shoshone, or Beatty, NV. Otherwise, you'll pay about 20¢ per gallon more at the stations across from the Furnace Creek visitors center, in Stove Pipe Wells Village, and at Scotty's Castle (all Chevron). Don't play chicken with the fuel gauge: Death Valley takes no prisoners. **Propane gas** available at the Furnace Creek Chevron, **white gas** at the Furnace Creek Ranch and Stove Pipe Wells Village stores, **diesel fuel** pumped in Las Vegas, Pahrump, and Beatty, NV, and in Lone Pine, Olancha, Ridgecrest, and Trona, CA.

Groceries and Supplies: Furnace Creek Ranch Store, expensive and well-stocked. Open daily 7am-9pm. **Stove Pipe Wells Village store,** same price range. Both sell charcoal and firewood. Ice is available at the Furnace Creek Chevron and the Stove Pipe Wells Village Store. Open daily 7am-8pm. Both sell charcoal and firewood.

Post Office: Furnace Creek Ranch (786-2223). Open Mon.-Fri. 7am-7pm. **ZIP code:** 92328.

Area Code: 619.

Death Valley spans over 2 million acres (1½ times the size of Delaware), and is quite isolated. However, visitors from the south will find it only a small detour on the road to Sierra Nevada's Eastern slope, and those from the north will find it reasonably convenient to Las Vegas. The monument lies about 300 miles from Los Angeles, 500 miles from San Francisco, and 140 miles from Las Vegas.

There is no regularly scheduled public transportation into Death Valley. The only way to get there by bus is to hook up with a charter. **Las Vegas-Tonopah-Reno Stage Lines** (702-384-1230) sends an occasional charter between Las Vegas and Furnace Creek.

Bus tours within Death Valley are monopolized by **Fred Harvey's Death Valley Tours,** the same organization that runs Grand Canyon tours. They begin at Furnace Creek Ranch, which also handles reservations (786-2345, ext. 61; $15-25).

The best way to get into and around Death Valley is by **car.** With two or more Death Valley pilgrims to share gas expenses, renting a car will prove far cheaper and more flexible than any unreliable bus tour. The nearest agencies are in Las Vegas, Barstow, and Bishop. Be sure to rent a reliable car. This is emphatically *not* the place to cut corners.

Of the 13 monument entrances, most visitors choose Rte. 190 from the east. The road is well-maintained, the pass is much less steep, and you arrive more quickly at the visitors center, located at the approximate midpoint of the 130-mile north-south route through the valley. But since most of the major sights adjoin not Rte. 190 but the north/south road, the daytripping visitor with a trusty vehicle will be able to see more of the monument by entering from the southeast (Rte. 178 west from Rte. 127 at Shoshone) or the north (direct to Scotty's Castle via NV Rte. 267 from U.S. 95). Unskilled mountain drivers should probably not attempt to enter via the smaller roads Titus Canyon or Emigrant Canyon Drive, since no guard rails prevent cars from sailing over the canyon's precipitous cliffs.

Eighteen-wheelers have replaced 18-mule teams, but transportation around Death Valley still takes stubborn determination. Radiator water (*not* for drinking) is avaliable at critical points on Rte. 178 and 190 and NV Rte. 374, but not on any unpaved roads. Trust the signs that say "four-wheel-drive only." Those who do bound along the backcountry trails by four-wheel-drive should carry extra tires, gas, oil, water (both to drink and for the radiator), and spare parts, and leave an itinerary with the visitors center. Be sure to check which roads are closed—especially in summer.

Hitching is suicidal.

Death Valley has **hiking** trails to challenge the mountain lover, the desert daredevil, the backcountry camper, and the fair-weather dayhiker. Ask a ranger for advice, and see Sights below. Backpackers and dayhikers alike should inform the visitors center of their trip, and take appropriate topographic maps. During the summer the National Park Service recommends that valley floor hikers spend several days prior to the hike acclimating to the heat and low humidity, plan a route along roads where assistance is readily available, and outfit a hiking party of at least two people with another person following in a vehicle to monitor the hikers' progress. Carrying salve to treat feet parched by the nearly 200° earth is also a good idea.

Check the weather forecasts before setting out—all roads and trails can disappear during a winter rainstorm. The dryness of the area, plus the lack of any root and soil system to retain moisture, transforms canyon and valley floors into deadly torrents during heavy rains. For other important tips, see Desert Survival in the introduction to the Southwest.

Accommodations

Fred Harvey's Amfac Consortium retains its vise-like grip on the trendy, resort-style, incredibly overpriced concessions in Death Valley. Look for cheaper accommodations in the towns near Death Valley: **Olancha** (west), **Shoshone** (southwest), **Tecopa** (south), and **Beatty, NV** (northwest).

The National Park Service maintains nine **campgrounds,** none of which accepts reservations. Call the visitors center to check availability and be prepared to do battle if you come during peak periods (see When to Visit). Park Service campgrounds include **Mesquite Springs** ($5), **Stove Pipe Wells** ($4), **Emigrant** (free), **Furnace Creek** ($5), **Sunset** (tent sites $8, RV sites $4), **Texas Springs** ($5), **Wildrose** (free). (Camping fees are not pursued with vigor in the summer.) All campsites have toilets; all except Thorndike and Mahogany Flat have water; all except Sunset and Stove Pipe Wells have tables. Open fires are prohibited at Stove Pipe Wells and Sunset; bring a stove and fuel or eat raw meat. Fires are permitted at Thorndike and Mahogany Flat, though there are no fireplaces and collecting wood, be it alive or dead, is *verboten* anywhere in the monument. **Backcountry camping** is free and legal, as long as you check in at the visitors center and pitch tents at least 1 mile from main roads and 5 miles from any established campsite.

Sights

If you're doing Death Valley in one day, you should adopt a north-south or south-north route, rather than head directly to the Furnace Creek visitors center via Rte. 190, which connects east with west.

The **Visitors Center and Museum** (see Practical Information) offers information on tours, hikes, and special programs. Visit the nearby museums as well. If you're interested in astronomy, speak to one of the rangers; some set up telescopes at Zabriskie Point and offer freelance shows. In **wildflower season** (Feb.-April 11), there are tours to some of the best places for viewing the display. **Hells Gate** and **Jubilee Pass** are especially beautiful, **Hidden Valley** even more so, though it is accessible only by a difficult, 7-mile four-wheel-drive route from Teakettle Junction (itself 25 miles south of Ubehebe Crater).

Artist's Drive is a one-way loop off Rte. 178, beginning 10 miles south of the visitors center. The road twists and winds through rock and dirt canyons on the way to **Artist's Palette,** a rainbow of green, yellow, and red mineral deposits in the hillside. Be aware that the dizzying 9 miles turn back upon themselves again and again, ending up on the main road only 4 miles north of the drive's entrance. About 5 miles south of this exit, you'll reach **Devil's Golf Course,** a huge plane of spiny salt crust, the precipitate left from the evaporation of ancient Lake Manly. Walk around on this gigantic sponge; the salt underfoot sounds like crunching snow.

Immortalized by Antonioni's film of the same name, **Zabriskie Point** is a marvelous place (particularly at sunrise) from which to view Death Valley's corrugated badlands. The trip up to **Dante's View,** 15 miles by paved road south off Rte. 190 (take the turn-off beyond Twenty Mule Team Canyon exit) will reward you with views of Badwater, Furnace Creek Ranch, the Panamint Range, and, on a clear day, the Sierra Nevadas. Faintly visible are the tracks of the 20-mule-team wagons across Devil's Golf Course, itself intricately patterned. It can be snowy up here in mid-winter and cold anytime but mid-summer.

Late November through February are the coolest months (40-70° in the valley, freezing temperatures and snow in the mountains) and also the wettest, with infrequent but violent rainstorms which can flood the canyons. Desert wildflowers bloom in March and April, accompanied by moderate temperatures and tempestuous winds that can whip sand and dust into an obscuring mess for hours or even days. Over 50,000 people vie for Death Valley's facilities and sights during the **49ers Encampment** festival, held the last week of October and the first two weeks of November. Other times that bring traffic jams, congested trails and campsites, hour-long lines for gasoline, and four-hour waits at Scotty's Castle include three-day winter holiday weekends, Thanksgiving, Christmas through New Year's Day, and Easter.

Central Coast

San Franciscans and Los Angelenos rarely agree. However, both Northerners and Southerners beam proudly at the mention of the Central Coast, proclaiming it the most dramatic coastline in California—if not the world. This coast combines the best of Southern and Northern California. There are wide beaches on swimmable waters without the pollution and frenetic autoculture of the southland. The coast also has lush, breathtaking scenery—from rocky cliffs to glorious parks—and cozy bars and restaurants without northern pretensions to urbanity.

Big Sur

The untamed coastal region known as Big Sur simultaneously welcomes and ignores visitors. Its dramatic beaches, mountains, and redwood forest are entirely accessible, thanks to the government's protection of large wilderness areas for public use. At the same time, however, the human inhabitants of Big Sur do little to make strangers feel at home. There is no "village" or "town" *per se;* no banks, no theaters, no mini-golf. While perfectly willing to sell tourists sandwiches and postcards, residents often hide their houses in the woods and religiously remove signs giving directions to their loveliest beach. Such seclusion is in keeping with Big Sur's history as a hideaway for artists and hippie-types seeking both solitude and transcendence in its vast expanses.

Places to camp are abundant, beautiful, and cheap. The **Fernwood Motel,** Hwy. 1 (667-2422), 2 miles north of the post office, offers friendly management, 65 campsites, and cabins for the tent-less. (Registration 8am-midnight. Check-out 11am. Sites $14, with hookup $16. Cabin doubles $47.) The **Pfeiffer Big Sur State Park** (667-2315), just south of Fernwood, 26 miles south of Carmel, is a popular inland park; sometimes all 217 developed campsites (no hookups) are full. (Hot showers. Sites $10. Reservations 800-444-7275.) **Limekiln,** south of Big Sur (667-2403), is a privately run campground with grocery, showers, and beach access. (60 sites. $9 per vehicle, $4 per person. $3 reservation fee.) **Los Padres National Forest** includes two U.S. Forest Service Campgrounds: **Plaskett Creek** (927-4211), south of Limekiln, near Jade Cove, and **Kirk Creek,** about 5 miles north of Jade Cove. (Toilets and cold running water. Check-out 2pm. Sites $8, hikers $2.)

The Fernwood Hotel includes the **Fernwood Burger Bar,** Rte. 1 (667-2422). Fish and chips or chicken are $5.50-6.50, hamburgers start at $3. There's also a bar, a grocery store, and cheap gas here. (Open daily 11:30am-midnight.) The **Center Deli,** right beside the Big Sur post office (667-2225), serves the cheapest sandwiches ($2.50-4.95) in the area. (Open daily 8am-9pm.) At the Monterey-Salinas Transit bus stop, **Café Amphora** (667-2660), in **Nepenthe Restaurant** serves coffee and liquor on an outdoor patio spectacularly situated on the edge of a Big Sur cliff. (Open daily 10am-5pm.)

The Big Sur area state parks and wilderness areas are exquisite natural settings for dozens of outdoor activities, including especially beautiful hiking. The northern end of **Los Padres National Forest** has been designated the **Ventana Wilderness** and contains the popular 12-mile **Pine Ridge Trail.** Pick up a map and a required permit at the USFS **ranger station** (667-2423; ¼ mile south of Pfeiffer Big Sur State Park, down the hill from the post office). Within **Pfeiffer Big Sur State Park** are six trails of varying lengths; pick up a 25¢ map at the park entrance. Try the **Valley View Trail,** a short, steep path; at its apex you'll find a remarkable view of miles of redwood country. Big Sur's most jealously guarded treasure is USFS-operated **Pfeiffer Beach,** reached by an unmarked narrow road 100 yards or so south of the ranger station. Take the road 2 miles to the parking area, then follow the footpath to the beach. The small cove, partially protected from the Pacific by a huge offshore rock formation, is safe for wading, but riptides make swimming risky. For the uninhibited, there's a nude beach just to the north of the cove. **Big Sur Mountain Bike,** Rte. 1 (667-2468), in the Village Shops, rents mountain bikes.

The **Old Coast Road** offers a more inclusive, uncrowded vista than Hwy. 1 but shows less of the coastline. The 10-mile gravel road can be entered from the south through Andrew Molera State Park or from the north from Bixby Bridge (don't try if it's rained recently). It winds down through groves of redwood and up over barren hills. At one point, the road affords a breathtaking view of one of the old, concrete cantilever bridges of Rte. 1 silhouetted against the sea. Both roads are stunning to drive, but perhaps the most leisurely way to see northern Big Sur is out the windows of Monterey-Salinas bus #22.

Big Sur stretches between Salmon Cove in the south (San Simeon's Hearst Castle is 17 miles below) and Carmel in the north. It lies two hours by car south of the cultivated Monterey Peninsula. For a guide to the area, send a stamped, self-addressed envelope to the **Chamber of Commerce,** P.O. Box 87, Big Sur 93920 (667-2100). The **post office** is on Hwy. 1 (667-2305), next to the Center Deli. Big Sur's **ZIP code** is 93290; the **area code** is 408.

Near Big Sur: Hearst Castle

In San Simeon did William Hearst a stately pleasure dome decree. Popularly known as Hearst Castle (927-2020), the Hearst San Simeon Historic Monument perches high on a hill 5 miles east of Rte. 1 near San Simeon. Satirized as Charles Foster Kane's "Xanadu" in Orson Welles' *Citizen Kane,* the castle lives up to every adjective ever applied to the state of California itself: opulent, plastic, beautiful, fake, dazzling, and intent on instant gratification. William Randolph Hearst, tycoon of yellow journalism, began building this Hispano-Moorish indulgence in 1919, and abandoned the project during the Depression. The three houses and two pools are undeniably grand and yet simultaneously unsettling. Once a weekend getaway for Hearst's celebrity friends, today the castle has an air of blighted bloom. On one side of the hill the remains of Hearst's miniature zoo rot peacefully, long abandoned.

Visitors have a choice of four **tours,** each an hour and 45 minutes long. It's possible to take all four in one day, but each costs $10, ages 6-12 $5, under 6 free (if well-behaved—otherwise they are escorted off the premises). Groups are taken up the hill in old school buses and shepherded around, then taken back down. Tours are given at least once an hour October through March from 8am until 3:30pm (except tour #4, which runs April-Sept. only), more frequently and later according to demand in summer. If you really want to see the Castle in summer, it's a good idea to make reservations (800-444-7275) since tours sell out quickly. The gates to the visitors center open at 6am in summer, 7am in winter, and tickets go on sale at 7:45am, in winter at 8:45am.

Carmel

Upper-class Californians take refuge in Carmel to live out fantasies of life before the City. Well-preserved, although a bit precious, the town possesses one of Northern California's most beautiful beaches, a gloriously restored Spanish mission, and a set-piece main street lined with stores that sell jewelry, silk dresses, and fine art. The town works hard to maintain its image. Local ordinances forbid parking meters, normal-sized street signs, billboards, home mail delivery, and numbers on houses—all undesirable symbols of urbanization. All of the houses have names instead of numbers, and franchise stores are forbidden in the city proper. Because development early this century caused flooding when steep hills were denuded, the town passed a law in 1916 decreeing it a felony to cut down any tree. As a result, pines and cypresses grow everywhere—in the middle of streets, sidewalks, and houses. Carmel beckons visitors with the tastefulness of a town that makes its living from tourism but pretends otherwise.

Spend some time strolling around Carmel's quaint downtown area, and then head for the nature. **Carmel City Beach,** at the end of Ocean Ave., is where the northern Big Sur coast actually begins. There are no signs proclaiming the event, but it's unmistakable. A crescent of white sand frames a cove of clear aquamarine water, but the beach ends abruptly at the bases of distant dark red cliffs. Surrounding the whole area are cyprus-covered hills wreathed in clouds. Access to the beach and its barbecue pits is free. Beautiful though it may be, the city beach and its tourists are shunned by locals who prefer the more remote **Carmel River State Beach,** around the southern point at the end of city oeach. This beach, windier and colder than the city beach but blessed with bigger surf, can be reached by walking about 1 mile along Scenic Rd. or by driving to the end of Carmelo St. off Santa Lucía Ave.

One and a half miles south of Carmel on Rte. 1 is the **Point Lobos Reserve** (624-4909), a state-run, 1276-acre wildlife sanctuary, popular with skindivers, dayhikers, and wildlife-watchers. Bring a windbreaker and field glasses out to the ledge; Point Lobos offers tide pools and good vantage points for the winter whale migration. (Open daily 9am-7pm; in winter 9am-5pm. On weekends there is frequently a line of cars waiting to get in by 8am. Admission $3 per car plus 50¢ for a map. No dogs allowed. Park outside the tollbooth and walk or bike in for free.) To reach Point Lobos, take MST bus #22 ("Big Sur") from Monterey.

Mission Basilica San Carlos Borromeo del Rio Carmelo, 3080 Rio Rd. (624-1271), off Rte. 1, is crowned by a Mudéjar tower supporting four bells and a number of swallows' nests. The three **museums** at Carmel Mission display the original silver altar furnishings, handsome vestments, a library, and other souvenirs from the days when missionaries swore allegiance to the sovereign with one hand on the gospels, the other on the sword. (Self-guided tours Mon.-Sat. 9:30am-4:30pm, Sun. 10:30am-4pm. Donation.)

You can eat very well in Carmel. You can eat relatively inexpensively in Carmel. But it is almost impossible to do both simultaneously unless you are willing to buy food at the local supermarket and cook it yourself. **Nelson Brothers' Grocery** (624-6441), on the corner of San Carlos and 7th, stocks the usual groceries, deli products, liquors, and, of course, rare wines. **Em Le's,** on Dolores between 5th and 6th St. (625-6780), offers various breakfast specials (huge blueberry waffles $4.35). (Open daily 6am-3pm.) **Dilli Deli,** at Ocean and Monte Verde (624-1277), serves 35 different sandwiches, plus hot dogs, bagels, beer, and wine. (Entrees $4-5. Open daily 10am-6pm.)

Carmel makes it difficult for budget travelers to get a foothold in town. This side of paradise is private property. The streets swarm with police alert for ragtag travelers or wandering indigents, and there are few inexpensive places to eat or sleep. Few motel rooms in Carmel are under $60 (double-occupancy). A 15-minute bus ride north to Monterey will bring better hunting. Camping is illegal within the city limits. If you have a car or van and like it well enough to sleep with it, you may wish to join the few travelers who park along Rte. 1 about 2 miles south of town for a cramped night. Some travelers also crash on the river beach, where thick bushes provide cover from patrolling police. The wind at this beach can be fierce, however—make sure you have warm clothing. The **Carmel River Inn,** Rte. 1 (624-1575), by Carmel River Bridge, is the cheapest of an expensive bunch. (Cottages with private baths and TVs $36-75; 2-month advance reservations recommended.) The cheapest camping in Carmel Valley is 4½ miles east of the city at **Saddle Mountain Ranch** (624-1617), a private resort on Schulte Rd. (50 sites. Showers. $14, with full hookup and sanitary dump $16.50.)

Carmel lies at the southern base of the Monterey Peninsula, off Rte. 1. The downtown is contained within a large square bounded by Rte. 1 (east), the beach (west), 5th Ave. (north), and Rio Rd. and Santa Lucia Ave. (south). Ocean Ave. is a wide boulevard cutting east to west through the town's center. Pick up a free map of the town at any motel or at the **Carmel-by-the-Sea Business Association,** San Carlos St. and 7th Ave. (624-2522). The **post office** is at 5th St. between San Carlos and Dolores St. (624-1525). Carmel's **ZIP code** is 93921; the **area code** is 408.

Santa Cruz

Santa Cruz sports an uncalculated hipness that other coastal towns can only envy. The town is often seen as the epitome of California cool, and its beaches and bookstores even lure visitors from San Francisco, 75 miles to the north. Santa Cruz's location is crucial to its identity. Without a beach, it would be Berkeley; with a better one, it would be Coney Island. The downtown area, centered on the tree-lined **Pacific Grove Mall,** is exceptionally pleasant. Lined with cafes and bookstores, it has the mellow feel that is quintessential Californian. Stroll down the sidewalks as street musicians growl Bob Marley tunes and vendors patiently display hand-woven bracelets.

The **Boardwalk,** a 3-block arcade of ice cream, caramel apples, games, rides, and taco restaurants, dominates the Santa Cruz beach area. Video games, pinball, shooting galleries, and Bing-o-Reno complement miniature golf and amusement-park rides. The 1929 **Giant Dipper** roller coaster far outdoes the other rides; one of the largest remaining wooden coasters in the country, it's well-worth the $2 charge. (Boardwalk open Memorial Day-Labor Day daily; weekends the rest of the year. Call 432-5590 for current hours.)

The **Santa Cruz beach** itself is broad and sandy, and generally packed with high school students from San Jose during summer weekends. If you're looking for solitude, try the banks of the San Lorenzo River immediately east of the boardwalk. Nude sunbathers should head for the **Red White and Blue Beach.** Take Rte. 1 north to just before Davenport and look for the line of cars to your right; women should not go alone. ($5 per car.) If you don't feel like paying for the privilege of an all-over tan, try the **Bonny Doon Beach,** at Bonny Doon Rd. off Hwy. 1, 11 miles north of Santa Cruz. This surfer hangout is free but somewhat untamed.

A pleasant 10-minute walk along the beach to the southwest will take you to two wacky Santa Cruz museums. The first is the **Shroud of Turin Museum,** 544 Cliff Dr. (423-7658), at St. Joseph's shrine. Earnest curators shepherd you through the museum's many exhibits, including one of only two replicas of the now-discredited shroud. It is often unintentionally amusing. (Open Sat.-Sun. noon-5pm. Call ahead to visit during the week.) Just south of this museum lies Lighthouse Point, home to the **Santa Cruz Surfing Museum** (429-3429). Opened in 1986, the museum is the first of its kind in the world. Its cheerful, one-room exhibit featuring vintage boards and surfing videos shows no sign of the tragedy that inspired its creation. The lighthouse and gallery are actually a gift in memory of a local boy who drowned in a surfing accident. (Open Wed.-Mon. noon-4pm. Donation.) You can still watch people challenge the sea right below the museum's cliff. The stretch of Pacific along the eastern side of the point is famous **Steamer Lane,** a hotspot for local surfers for over fifty years. A recent rash of drownings has inspired a sign there asking "lame tourists" not to surf; novices should stick to the city beach.

The 2000-acre **University of California at Santa Cruz (UCSC)** hangs out, in its entirety, five miles northwest of downtown. Take bus #1 or ride your bike along a scenic path to the campus. Then-governor Ronald Reagan's attempt to make it a "riot-proof campus" without a central point where radicals could inflame a crowd resulted in beautiful, sprawling grounds. University buildings appear intermittently, like startled wildlife, amid spectacular rolling hills and redwood groves. The school itself remains more Berkeley than Berkeley; extracurricular leftist politics supplement a curriculum offering such unique programs as the "History of Consciousness." Guided tours start from the **visitors center** at the base of campus. If you drive on weekdays make sure you have a parking permit. (Parking permits and maps available at the police station, 429-2231.)

Directly south of UCSC, the inaccurately named **Natural Bridges State Beach** (423-4609), at the end of W. Cliff Drive, offers a nice beach, tidepools, and tours twice per day during Monarch butterfly season from October to February. October 9th is "Welcome Back Monarch Day," but the best time to go may actually be from November to December, when thousands of the little buggers swarm along the beach. (Open daily 8am-sunset. Parking $3 per day.)

Santa Cruz innkeepers double or triple rates for the "in" season, rendering $20 winter singles $60-100 summer retreats. If you're really desperate, you can sleep in your car near the campgrounds, or take your chances hiding from the wind and police in the tall grass near the Surfing Museum. The **Santa Cruz Youth Hostel,** 511 Broadway (423-8304), offers 16 beds. Reservations are recommended; send one half of the $10 fee to Box 1241, Santa Cruz, 95601 (AYH/IYHF members only). The enormous **St. George Hotel,** 1520 Pacific Garden Mall (423-8181), houses a combination of permanent older residents and aging hippies energetically arguing the *Bhagavad Gita* all night. (Singles $16, with bath $20. Doubles $18, with bath $22. Call for reservations.) The **American Country Inn,** 645 7th (476-6424), 5 blocks from the beach just north of Eaton St., is a small, pleasant hotel off the main drag.

One bed per room; bathrooms are clean and spacious. (Weekdays $20, with bath $30; weekends $40, with bath $50. Weekly $150, with bath $170. The small RV camp in back has full hookup. Sites $18; $95 per week. Reservations with deposit recommended.)

Reservations for state campgrounds can be made by calling 800-444-7275. The **New Brighton State Beach,** 4 miles south of Santa Cruz off Rte. 1 near Capitola (688-3241), offers 115 lovely campsites on a high bluff overlooking the beach. (One-week max. stay. No hookups. Check-out 2pm. Weekdays $12, weekends $14. Reservations highly recommended. Take SCMDT bus #58 ("Park Avenue").) The **Henry Cowell Redwoods State Park,** off Rte. 9 (335-9145), is 3 miles south of Felton. (Take Graham Hill Rd., or SCMDT bus #34, 35, or 36.) 113 campsites in summer, 35 in winter, hot showers, and restaurants. (One-week max. stay. Sites $10.) **Big Basin Redwoods State Park,** north of Boulder Creek (338-6132), is worth the 45-minute trip from downtown. (Take Rte. 9 north to Rte. 236 north, or the infrequent SCMDT bus #37.) Big Basin offers the best camping south of Point Reyes and north of Big Sur, so reservations are recommended. Rent mountain bikes and horses nearby. (188 sites. Showers. 15-day max. stay. Sites $10. Backpackers $1 at special backcountry campsites. Security parking $3 per night.)

Santa Cruz cultivates two distinct types of eateries. On the one hand, you have corn dogs, burgers, and tacos in gastronomically threatening fast-food stands. On the other hand, there are places that serve lovingly hand-rolled pita bread, sprouts, tofu, and cauliflower sandwiches with grated carrots sprinkled meticulously on top. Try the first variety on the Boardwalk, the second at places such as the Pacific Garden Mall. **Positively Front St.,** 44 Front St. (426-1944), is friendly and hip, with over 40 beers and a lit model train that runs around the ceiling. Good burgers and sandwich dinners are about $4. (Open daily 11:30am-10pm.) **Zachary's,** 819 Pacific Ave. (427-0646), is perhaps the mall's only spark of life early in the morning, as locals crowd in for Breakfast Number 1: 2 eggs, great cottage fries, and toast ($2.49). (Open Tues.-Sun. 7am-2:30pm. Come before 9am to avoid long waits.) The **Saturn Cafe,** 1230 Mission St. (429-8505), cooks up vegetarian meals at their Santa Cruz best (generally for under $4). Cracked wheat is positively right-wing around here. (Open Mon.-Fri. 11:30am-12:30am, Sat.-Sun. noon-12:30am.) **Zoccoli's Delicatessen,** 1534 Pacific Garden Mall (423-1711), has great food at great prices. The lunch special of lasagna, salad, garlic bread, salami and cheese slices, and an Italian cookie goes for $4. (Open Mon.-Sat. 9am-5:30pm.)

Santa Cruz thinks of itself as a high-class operation, and most bars frown on backpacks and sleeping bags. Carding at local bars is stringent. The restored ballroom at the Boardwalk makes a lovely spot for a drink in the evening, and the Boardwalk bandstand also offers free Friday night concerts. The **Kuumbwa Jazz Center,** 320-322 E. Cedar St. (427-2227), has regionally renowned jazz, and music lovers under 21 are welcome. The big names play here, and it's rarely sold out. (Tickets $5-11.50. Most shows at 8pm.) The **Blue Lagoon,** 923 Pacific Ave. (423-7117), is a relaxed gay bar with a giant aquarium in the back of the room. Taped music, videos, dancing. (No cover. Drinks about $1.50. Open daily 4pm-2am.) **The Poet and the Patriot,** 320 E. Cedar St. (426-8620), is a left-wing Irish pub with great music and a wide selection of tap beer ($1-2.50). (Happy hour Mon.-Fri. 5-7pm. Open Mon.-Fri. and Sun. noon-midnight, Sat. noon-2am.) The **Front Street Pub,** just off the mall, is also a relaxed watering hole popular with UCSC students.

Call the **Live Theatre Hotline** (476-2166) for the latest shows. The **Barn Theatre,** Bay and High St. (429-2159), on the UCSC campus, is home to student theatrical productions in winter. In summer, local repertory companies perform. (Tickets Thurs. and Sun. $7, Fri.-Sat. $8; $2 off for the self-described "low income.") **Shakespeare Santa Cruz,** Performing Arts Building Complex, UCSC campus (429-2121), features outdoor and indoor modern interpretations of Shakespeare (July-Aug.). (Tickets for regular performances in the Performing Arts Theatre $10-15.) Watch for occasional, free outdoor performances.

Santa Cruz is about one hour south of San Francisco on the northern lip of Monterey Bay. Hitching to or from the city is fairly easy. **Greyhound/Peerless Stages** is at 425 Front St. (423-1800). Buses to San Francisco (4 per day, $11.35) and L.A. via Salinas (2 per day, $39.95) or via San Jose (2 per day, $50). (Open daily 7:30am-8pm.) **Santa Cruz Metropolitan District Transit (SCMDT),** 920 Pacific Ave. (425-8600 or 688-8993), serves the city and environs. Pick up a copy of *Headways* here for route information. (Open Mon.-Fri. 7am-6pm, Sat.-Sun. 9am-1pm and 2-5:30pm.) The **Chamber of Commerce** is at 105 Cooper St., 95060 (423-1111; open Mon.-Fri. 9am-5pm), but is more easily reached at 811A Front St.; the **post office** is at 850 Front St. (426-5200; open Mon.-Fri. 9am-5pm). Santa Cruz's **ZIP code** is 95060; the **area code** is 408.

Sierra Nevada

The Sierra Nevada is the highest, steepest, and most physically stunning mountain range in the contiguous United States. The heart-stopping sheerness of Yosemite's rock walls, the craggy alpine scenery of Kings Canyon and Sequoia National Parks, and the abrupt drop from the eastern slope into Owens Valley are like nothing else in the country. At 14,494 ft., Mt. Whitney is the highest point in the U.S. outside Alaska.

The **Sequoia National Forest** encompasses the southern tip of the Sierras as they march from Kings Canyon and Sequoia down to the low ranges of the Mojave Desert. The forest includes both popular recreational areas and isolated wilderness areas. **Forest headquarters** is located in Porterville, 900 W. Grand Ave. (209-784-1500), 15 miles east of Rte. 99 between Fresno and Bakersfield. The **Sierra National Forest** fills the area between Yosemite, Sequoia, and Kings Canyon. Although not on the Winnebago warpath, the forest is not exactly the "undiscovered" Sierras; droves of Californians jam the busier spots at lower elevations, and even the wilderness areas are popular in the summer. The main **information office** is at the Federal Building, 1130 O St., #3017, Fresno (209-487-5155; 209-487-5456 for 24-hour recorded information). Pick up an excellent map of the forests here or in Porterville ($1) or order one ($2) from the Three Forest Interpretive Association (3FIA), 13098 E. Wire Grass Lane, Clovis 93612.

Yosemite

Three million tourists pour into Yosemite every year for a glimpse of its stunning waterfalls, rushing rivers, alpine meadows, and granite cliffs. The resulting congestion poses a knotty question to the overtaxed park service: Whose park is it anyway? Purists bemoan Yosemite's accessibility and the amenities that pamper the droves of tourists: snack shops, delis, photo galleries, and grocery stores. Casual visitors counter that the valley's unique splendors belong to everyone, not just to backpackers. Fortunately, the embattled valley occupies only a handful of the nearly 1200 square miles encompassed by this national park. Yosemite graciously manages to accommodate all its suitors.

Yosemite National Park is divided into several areas, **Yosemite Valley** being the most spectacular and consequently the most heavily trafficked. Bus tours operate throughout the valley, as well as up to **Glacier Point** and the giant sequoias in the **Mariposa Grove.** In addition to the bus crowd, there are the day-hikers who venture up the falls' trails and into **Little Yosemite Valley.** If you're interested in a moderate hike with varying landscapes, lots of water (big rivers, lakes, falls), and an optional ridge or two, head toward **Lake Merced** from Glacier Point and then down toward the **Clark Range.** Hiking during the week almost guarantees privacy. The two main backcountry trailhead areas, **Tuolumne Meadows** and **Happy Isles Nature Center,** are accessible from Yosemite Valley by hitching along Tioga Rd. or by bus (372-1240) after July 1; ask to be let off at the trailhead. Buy both a topographical and a trail route map from a visitors center. The best cheap one is *Guide to Yosemite High Sierra Trails* ($2.50). A map of valley trails is also available (50¢).

Practical Information

Visitor Information: General Park Information, 372-0265; 372-0264 for 24-hour recorded information. Advice about accommodations, activities, and weather conditions. TTY users call 372-4726. Open Mon.-Fri. 8am-5pm. **Yosemite Valley Visitors Center,** Yosemite Village (372-4461, ext. 333). Open daily 8am-8pm. **Tuolumne Meadows Visitors Center,** Tioga Rd. (372-0263), 55 miles from Yosemite Village. The headquarters of high-country activity, with trail information, maps, and special programs. Open in summer daily 8am-7:30pm. **Big Oak Flat Information Station,** Rte. 120 W. (379-2445), in the Crane Flat/Tuolumne Sequoia Grove Area. Open in summer daily 7am-6pm. **Wawona Ranger Station,** Rte. 141 (375-6391), at the southern entrance near the Mariposa Grove. Open daily 8am-5pm, in winter Mon.-Fri. 8am-5pm. **Backcountry Office,** P.O. Box 577, Yosemite National Park 95389 (372-0308; 372-0307 for 24-hour recorded information), next to Yosemite Valley Visitors Center. Backcountry and trail information. Open Sun.-Fri. 7:30am-7:30pm, Sat. 6:30am-7:30pm. With a map of the park and a copy of the informative *Yosemite Guide,* both available for free at visitors centers, you should be equipped to explore the park. Information folders and maps are available also in French, German, Japanese, and Spanish. Wilderness permits are available at all visitors centers.

Yosemite Park and Curry Co. Room Reservations, 5410 E. Home, Fresno 93727 (252-4848, TTY users 255-8345). Except for the campgrounds, Y.P.&C. has a monopoly on all the facilities of what has become a full-fledged resort within the park. Contact them for information and reservations.

Tour Information: Yosemite Lodge Tour Desk (372-1240), in Yosemite Lodge lobby. Open daily 7:30am-8pm, or contact any other lodge in the park.

Bus Tours: McCoy's Charter Service, 1819 E. Olive, Fresno 93701 (268-2237). Connects the park with Fresno on weekdays. Buses stop at Greyhound, the train station, and the airport. Call ahead to be picked up anywhere along the Fresno-Yosemite route. $14, including a $2 park entry fee. **Yosemite Via,** 300 Grogan Ave., Merced 95340 (384-1315 or 722-0366). 2 trips per day from the Merced Greyhound station to Yosemite ($15; discount for seniors). **California Yosemite Tours,** P.O. Box 2472, Merced 95344 (383-1563 or 383-1570). Meets the morning train arriving in Merced from San Francisco and takes passengers to Yosemite. Returns to Merced in time to catch return train to San Francisco ($13). The **Yosemite Transportation System** (372-1240) connects the park with Greyhound in Lee Vining ($32.50). Reservations required; runs July-Labor Day.

Green Tortoise, based in San Francisco. Two- or 3-day trip. Buses leave San Francisco at 9pm. "Sleep-aboard" bus arrives at popular sites before they get crowded. 2-day trip $49, 3-day trip $59, food $6 per day. Reservations required. See General Introduction for more information.

Equipment Rental: Yosemite Mountaineering School, Rte. 120 at Tuolumne Meadows (372-1335; Sept.-May 372-1244). Sleeping bags $4 per day, backpacks $3.50 per day, snow shoes $5 per day. Driver's license or credit card required.

Post Offices: Yosemite Village, next to the visitors center. Open Mon.-Fri. 8:30am-5pm; Sept.-May Mon.-Fri. 8:30am-12:30pm and 1:30-5pm. **Curry Village,** near Registration Office. Stamps available from machines year-round. Open June-Sept. Mon.-Fri. 8am-4:30pm. **Yosemite Lodge,** open Mon.-Fri. 9am-4pm. General Delivery **ZIP code:** 95389.

Area Code: 209.

Yosemite crowns the central Sierra Nevada, 180 miles due east of San Francisco and 320 miles north of Los Angeles. It can be reached by taking Rte. 140 from Merced, Rte. 41 north from Fresno, and Rte. 120 east from Sonoma and west from Lee Vining. Park admission is $2 if you're entering on foot, $5 for a 7-day vehicle pass.

Drivers intending to visit the high-country in spring or fall should have snow tires; they are sometimes required in early and late summer. Of the five major approaches to the park, Rte. 120 to the Big Oak Flat entrance is particularly brutal. The easiest route from the west is Rte. 140 into Yosemite Valley. The eastern entrance, Tioga Pass, is closed during snow season. The road to Mirror Lake and Happy Isles is forbidden to private auto traffic, but is served by free shuttle buses during the summer. In winter, snow closes the road to Glacier Point and sections of Tioga Road.

Accommodations

Those who prefer some kind of roof over their heads can shell out for a small, clean, sparsely furnished cabin at Yosemite Lodge. (Singles $21.65-38.75. Doubles $34.35-51.25.) Southeast of Yosemite Village, Curry Village offers noisy but clean cabins close to pizza and ice cream spots. (Cabins $21.65-38.75, with bath $34.35-51.25. Canvas-sided cabins $19.40-25.90.) Reservations are necessary for all hotels, lodges, and cabin tents in the park; send one night's rent to Yosemite Park & Curry Co. Reservations. (See Practical Information.) **Housekeeping Camp** has canvas and concrete units that accommodate up to six people. Bring your own utensils, warm clothes, and industrial-strength insect repellent. (1-4 people $30.50, each additional person $4.) **Tuolumne Meadows,** on Tioga Rd. in the northeast corner of the park, has canvas-sided tent cabins. (2 people $29, each additional person $5.) **White Wolf,** west of Tuolumne Meadows on Tioga Rd., has similar cabins ($29) and cabins with bath ($48.75).

For the be-one-with-nature set, Yosemite provides many options. Most of the park's campgrounds are crowded, many with trailers and RVs. In Yosemite Valley's drive-in campgrounds, reservations are required from April to November and can be made through Ticketron up to eight weeks ahead. Sleeping in cars is emphatically prohibited. With the exception of major holidays, you should be able to camp in one of the first come-first serve campgrounds if you arrive at a reasonable hour. In summer, there is a 14-day limit for campers outside Yosemite Valley and a seven-day limit for those in the valley, except at **Backpacker's Camp** (2-day limit in the valley, 1-day for the sites at Tuolumne). This camp is for backpackers with wilderness permits and without vehicles; "walk-in" camps do not require reservations.

Backcountry camping (for general information 372-0307) is prohibited in the valley (you'll get slapped with a stiff fine if caught), but it's unrestricted along the high-country trails with a free wilderness permit. Reserve specific sites by mail February through May (write Backcountry Office, Box 577, Yosemite National Park 95389), or take your chances with the remaining 50% quota held on 24 hour notice at the Yosemite Valley Visitors Center, the Wawona Ranger Station, or Big Oak Flat Station. Popular trails like **Little Yosemite Valley** and **Clouds Rest** fill up regularly. To receive a permit, you must show a planned itinerary, although you needn't follow it exactly. Most hikers stay at the undeveloped mountain campgrounds in the high country for the company and for the **bear lockers,** used for storing food (not bears). These campgrounds often have chemical toilets.

Kings Canyon and Sequoia National Parks

If your impression of national parks has been formed by the touristy Grand Canyon and Yosemite, you'll be surprised by the lack of sightseers in most of Sequoia and Kings Canyon, two separate and enormous parks administered jointly by the National Park Service. Glacier-covered Kings Canyon displays a beautiful array of imposing cliffs and sparkling waterfalls. Home to the deepest canyon walls in the country, turnouts along the roads offer vistas breathtakingly like aerial photography. In Sequoia, the Sierra Crest lifts itself to its greatest heights. Several 14,000-foot peaks scrape the clouds along the park's eastern border, including Mt. Whitney, the tallest mountain in the contiguous U.S. at 14,495 feet. Both parks contain impressive groves of massive sequoia trees in addition to a large and troublesome bear population, and both are worth visiting for an opportunity to view natural beauty free from transistor radios and tourist traps. Visitors like to cluster around the largest sequoias, which are near the entrances to the parks; vast stretches of backcountry are relatively empty.

The "summer season" usually runs from Memorial Day through Labor Day; "snow season" runs November through March.

Kings Canyon's **Grant Grove Visitors Center,** 2 miles east of the Big Stump Entrance by Rte. 180 (335-2315) has books, maps, and exhibits. (Open daily 8am-5pm.) Sequoia's **Ash Mountain Visitors Center,** Three Rivers 93271 (565-3456), on Rte. 198 out of Visalia, has information on both parks; the **Lodgepole Visitors**

Center (565-3341, ext. 631), is in the heart of sequoia, near the big trees and all of the tourists.

The two parks are accessible to vehicles from the west only. Trailheads into the John Muir Wilderness and Inyo National Forest on the eastern side are accessible from spur roads off U.S. 395, but no roads traverse the Sierras here. From Fresno follow Rte. 180 through the foothills; it's about 60 miles to the entrance of the **Grant Grove** section of Kings Canyon. Rte. 180 ends 28 miles later in the **Cedar Grove,** an island of park land enveloped within Sequoia National Forest. The road into this region is closed in snow season. From **Visalia,** take Rte. 198 to Sequoia National Park. This road, which passes Lake Kaweah and runs alongside the Kaweah River, offers an overwhelming number of scenic views and turnouts. Both roads are maintained by snow plows in winter. **Generals Highway** (Rte. 198) connects the Ash Mountain entrance to Sequoia with the **Giant Forest,** and continues to Grant Grove in Kings Canyon.

In summer (June-Nov.), the treacherous road to **Mineral King** opens up the southern parts of Sequoia. From Visalia, take Rte. 198; the turnoff to Mineral King is 3 miles past Three Rivers, and the **Lookout Point Ranger Station** lies about 10 miles along the Mineral King Rd. Take a break from driving here: Atwell Springs Campground and the nearby town of Silver City are 10 miles (but 45 min.) farther. Cold Springs Campground, Mineral King Ranger Station, and several trailheads lie near the end of Mineral King Rd. in a valley framed by 12,000-foot peaks on the north and east. The route to Mineral King includes stunning scenery that you will enjoy if you can tear your eyes away from the tortuous road while making 698 turns between Rte. 198 and the Mineral King complex. Allow two hours for the trip from Three Rivers.

The northern two-thirds of Kings Canyon and the eastern two-thirds of Sequoia are untouched by roads; here the backpacker and packhorse have free rein. Check at a ranger station or visitors center for more detailed information.

Sequoia Guest Services, Inc., P.O. Box 789, Three Rivers 93271 (561-3314), has a monopoly on indoor accommodations and food in and near the parks. Their rustic **cabins** cluster in a little village in Sequoia's Giant Forest; there are some at Grant Grove, too. (Cabins available May-Oct., $25-30 per person, $3.50 per each additional person up to 8.) Most park service **campgrounds** are open from mid-May to October (two-week limit year-round). For information about campgrounds, contact a ranger station or call 565-3351 for 24-hour recorded information. Kings Canyon offers sites for $6 at **Sunset, Azalea,** and **Crystal Springs,** all within spitting distance of Grant Grove Village, and at **Sheep Creek, Sentinel, Canyon View,** and **Moraine,** at the Kings River near Cedar Grove. Sequoia has sites without hookups at **Lodgepole** (565-3338), 4 miles northeast of Giant Forest Village in the heart of Sequoia National Park. (Sites $6-8; free in winter; reserve up to 8 weeks in advance through Ticketron mid-May to mid-Sept.) Other options are **Atwell Mill** and **Cold Springs,** about 20 miles along the Mineral King Rd., in the Mineral King area ($4).

Lake Tahoe

2.5 million years ago, an area of land between two geological faults sank as the Sierra mountains rose by uplift on either side. Lava flows sealed the depression, which filled with water and formed the third deepest lake in North America—Tahoe. Today the clear blue lake, surrounded by evergreens and mountains, forms an Alpine-like oasis which draws millions of tourists. For decades, wealthy families from San Francisco came to Lake Tahoe on vacation and built houses on its shores. An increasing number and range of people visit each year, heading for the beaches in summer and the ski slopes in winter. Adjacent Stateline is a modest extension of the town into Nevada, to accomodate a few casinos. But most use the area simply as a base for the many activities going on all around the face.

The stylish way to see the lake itself is by boat—the glass bottom *Tahoe Queen* (541-3364) provids lunch on board, and the **M.S. Dixie** sails across while serving a champagne brunch on Sundays.

In the summer, **Windsurf Tahoe** will rent you a windsurfer for $12 per hour. You may want to hire a wet-suit, too, since the base temperature of the lake remains a chilling 39°F. Several marinas rent out fishing boats, although you can get paddle boats for under $10 per hour. It might be worth sharing the costs with several people, and renting a motorboat and waterskis for $49 per hour, or a jet-ski for $45 per hour at **Zephyr Cove** on U.S. 50 (702-588-3833), 4 miles north of the casino. You're more likely, incidentally, to bump into the friendly green monster "Tahoe Tessie" in gift shops than in the water.

Incline Village, just into Nevada north of Tahoe, is named after an incline-railway which supplied local mines in the late-19th century. The village is home to the famed *Bonanza* **Ponderosa Ranch** (702-831-0691) on Tahoe Blvd. (Open daily 10am-5pm; admission $5.50, ages 5-11 $4.50, under 5 free.) Both the **Forest Service Fire Lookout** and the **Mount Rose Scenic Overlook** (Rte. 431 from Incline to Reno) give good vantage points on the lake. The **Heavenly Mountain** ski resort chairlift ride (541-7544) will lift you up 2000 feet for a different birds-eye view (open Mon.-Sat. 10am-10pm, Sun. 9am-10pm).

For those who prefer to earn their views with boot leather, the U.S. Forest Service (573-2674) produces a series of leaflets and can advise on many different trails. On the western side of Tahoe, there is the **Tahoe State Recreation Area** (583-3074), **Sugar Pine Point Park** (525-7982), and the **D.L. Bliss** and **Emerald Bay State Parks** (both 525-7277). The ultimate hike is the 150-mile **Tahoe Rim Trail,** which loops around the entire lake and takes about 15 days (call 576-0676 for information).

In winter, there are 16 Alpine ski resorts, 9 cross-country skiing areas, and a number of snowmobile routes to choose among.

The strip off U.S. 50 on the California side of the state line supports the bulk of Tahoe's 200 motels. Others reside on Park Avenue, which is less noisy. Be wary of hotels. That $15 dump on Tuesday may become a regal $80 chamber on Friday. Most hotels sell out on weekends. Try to book ahead and get written confirmation of the price. Scout around for discount coupons (as much as $10 off weekday rates). The cheapest deals are clustered near Stateline on U.S. 50 and tend to display their prices. The **Motel 6,** at 2375 Lake Tahoe Blvd., 95731 (542-1400), is standard issue but very popular, especially on weekends. Pool. (Singles $28, each additional adult $6. Make reservations in advance or forget it.) **Jack Pot Inn,** 3908 U.S. 50 (541-5587), about 1 mile south of the casinos, is a bit tatty but fine. Some rooms have kitchenettes. (Singles $16. Doubles $20. Fri.-Sat. rooms from $30.) **Four Seasons Lodge,** on U.S. 50 at Ski Run Ave. (544-2751), offers rooms with TV and A/C. (Singles $20. Doubles $28. Fri.-Sat. rooms from $32.)

The forest service at the visitors bureau provides up-to-date information on the abundance of good camping around Lake Tahoe. There are over 30 sites around the lake. You can make reservations at state park campgrounds by calling 800-444-7275. Call the Forest Service (see Practical Information) for more details. Free campsites include **Bayview** (573-2600, max. stay 1 night, open June-Sept.) and **Granite Flat** (587-3558; open April-Oct.).

The **Visitors Bureau and Chamber of Commerce,** 3066 U.S. 50 (541-5255 or 800-822-5922), at San Francisco Ave., has tons of helpful brochures and maps. Pick up a free copy of *101 Things to Do in Lake Tahoe.* Disabled visitors should pick up the *Handbook for Handicapped,* an extensive directory of facilities and information. Open Mon.-Fri. 8:30am-5pm, Sat.-Sun. 9am-4pm.The **U.S. Forest Service,** Emerald Bay Rd., S. Lake Tahoe (541-0209), publishes the free, informative *Lake of the Sky Journal* and supervises campgrounds. Open daily 8am-6pm, in fall Sat.-Sun. 10am-4pm. **Greyhound,** 1099 Park Ave. (544-2351), on the state line, has service to San Francisco (10 per day, $27), Las Vegas (2 per day, $28), Reno (6 per day, $5), and Los Angeles (8 per day, $62). Open daily 7:45am-6:15pm. **Tahoe Regional Transport (TART),** (581-6365), connects to the western and northern shores from Tahoma to Incline Village. Buses run daily 6:30am-6:30pm every hour. (Fare

$1, unlimited travel day pass $2.50.) **South Tahoe Area Ground Express (STAGE),** (573-2080) offers 24-hour bus service around town, and 7-hour daily service to the beach (1 per hr.). (Fare $1, ages under 8 free. 12-ride pass $10.) If you're traveling without luggage, the major hotels all offer free shuttle service along U.S. 50 to and from their casinos. **Harvey's** runs theirs daily from 8am-2am (588-2487). Rent bikes at **Anderson's Bicycle Rental,** 645 Emerald Bay Rd. (541-0500), convenient to the well-maintained west shore bike trail. (Full day $14, half-day $10. Open daily 8:30am-6pm. Leave driver's license as deposit.) **Sierra Cycleworks,** 3430 U.S. 50 (541-7505), has lightweight mountain bikes from $3 per hour, or $15 per day. (Open daily 9am-6pm.)

The **post office** is at 1085 Park Ave. (544-6162), next to Greyhound. (Open Mon.-Fri. 8:30am-5pm.) Lake Tahoe's **ZIP Code** is 95729; the **area code** is 916 in California, 702 in Nevada.

San Francisco

While other West Coast natives glory on sunkissed beaches, San Franciscans must endure a mild climate that brings fog in summer, rain in winter, and rarely produces the beach party atmosphere for which California is famous. But they're not complaining; in fact, natives take a singular pride in their city's unique character in the land of sun. The hills and cable cars, the Marin Headlands visible just across the Golden Gate Bridge, and the striking skyline dominated by the distinctive pyramid of the Transamerica Building combine to produce a panorama equal to that of any of the world's other great cities.

In 1776, the Spanish occupied the area in the name of the King of Spain. They founded a mission and dedicated it to St. Francis—*San Francisco.* However, they failed to protect the area against their eastern neighbors. The U.S. occupied the Presidio in 1846. During the 1848 Gold Rush, San Francisco became one of the busiest ports in the country overnight. The next topsy-turvy 50 years produced one of San Francisco's most beloved cult figures, Emperor Norton I. Many saw the 1906 earthquake and the resultant three-day fire, which burned down half of San Francisco, as a judgment by God on the city's sinful nature. The stunned metropolis set about the business of rebuilding. World War II gave the city a new importance as the staging ground for all Pacific operations and guaranteed a new prosperity. A receptiveness to cultural trends allowed North Beach to serve as home to the Beat Generation in the 1950s; the 60s saw Haight-Ashbury become the hippie capital of the world; and in the 70s, the gay population emerged as one of the most powerful and visible groups in the city. In recent years, San Francisco's gay population has been decimated by the onslaught of the AIDS epidemic. Yet the community has rallied heroically to this tragedy, limiting the spread of the disease through safe-sex education and providing aid and comfort to the afflicted.

San Francisco remains very much a confederation of neighborhoods; the average San Franciscan thinks in terms of the Mission District, Chinatown, and Nob Hill rather than the city as a whole. Subdivisions follow no discernible logic: A few blocks will take you from ritzy Pacific Heights to the impoverished Western Addition; the crime-ridden Tenderloin abuts the steel-and-glass wonders in the Financial District. Quaint small-scale streets, superb restaurants, and extensive parks afford a European air, and turreted houses line the avenues. The people are friendly, the food unbeatable, and the atmosphere tolerant. Everyone leaves inhibitions behind in San Francisco; you'll have to fight against the odds not to leave your heart.

Practical Information

Emergency: 911.

Visitor Information: Visitor Information Center, Hallidie Plaza (391-2000), at Market and Powell St., beneath street level. Open Mon.-Fri. 9am-5:30pm, Sat. 9am-3pm, Sun. 10am-2pm. 24-hour event and information recordings in English (391-2001), French (391-2003), German

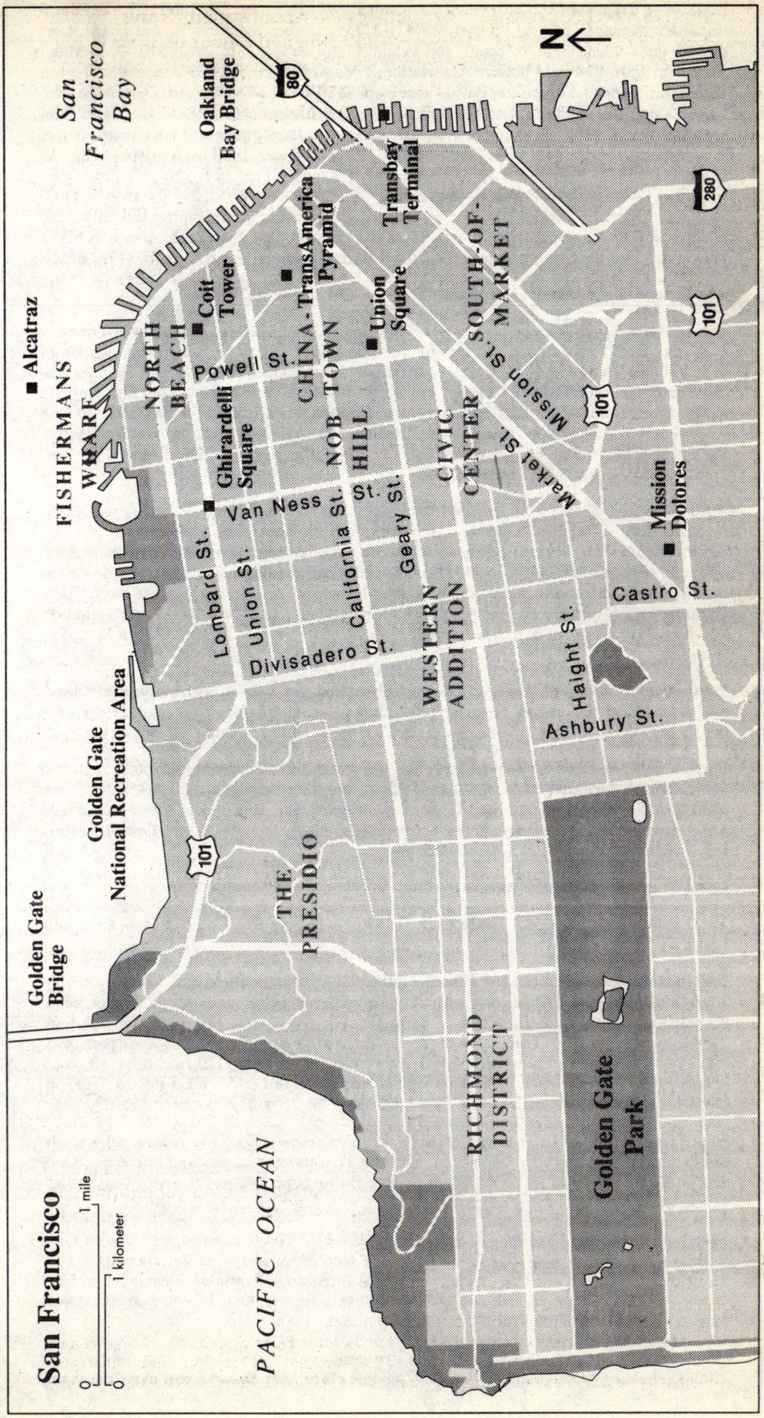
San Francisco
1 mile
1 kilometer
PACIFIC OCEAN
San Francisco Bay
Oakland Bay Bridge
80
280
101
Alcatraz
Golden Gate Bridge
Golden Gate National Recreation Area
THE PRESIDIO
FISHERMANS WHARF
NORTH BEACH
Coit Tower
Ghirardelli Square
Powell St.
CHINA-TOWN
TransAmerica Pyramid
Transbay Terminal
Union Square
NOB HILL
SOUTH-OF-MARKET
Mission St.
Market St.
CIVIC CENTER
Van Ness
California St.
Geary St.
Lombard St.
Union St.
Divisadero St.
WESTERN ADDITION
Haight St.
Ashbury St.
Castro St.
Mission Dolores
RICHMOND DISTRICT
Golden Gate Park

(391-2004), Japanese (391-2101), and Spanish (391-2122). **Center for International Educational Exchange (CIEE),** 312 Sutter St. (421-3473), between Stockton St. and Grant Ave., downtown. Student-flight, discount, and lodgings information. ISIC cards $10. Open Mon.-Fri. 10am-5pm. **Redwood Empire Association,** 1 Market Plaza (543-8334), Spear St. Tower, 10th floor. Maps and brochures on the area from San Francisco to Oregon. Open Mon.-Fri. 9am-4:30pm. **Sierra Club Store,** 730 Polk St. (923-5600), just north of the Civic Center. Tremendous resource for those planning wilderness trips. They prefer and encourage visitors to join the club. Open Mon.-Fri. 10am-5:30pm. **Wine Institute,** 165 Post St. (986-0878), 1½ blocks east of Union Square. Free newsletter about planning a trip to the Napa Valley. Open Mon.-Fri. 9am-5pm. **San Francisco Ticket Box Office Service (STBS),** 251 Stockton St. (433-7827), near Post St. Tickets to concerts, clubs, and sports events. Half-price tickets on day of show. Cash only. Open Tues.-Thurs. noon-7:30pm, Fri.-Sat. noon-8pm. Also sells BASS tickets to sports events, concerts, and clubs. **Concert Information,** KMEL-FM, 397-5635.

San Francisco International Airport (SFO): See Getting There, below.

Trains: Amtrak, 425 Mission St. (for ticket information 800-872-7245), 1st floor of Transbay Terminal. Really just a boarding area for the free shuttle bus to the actual train station in Oakland on 16th St. (982-8512). Shuttle trip takes 30 min. Open daily 6:30am-10pm. **Southern Pacific Transportation Company,** 4th St. (495-4546), between Townsend and Key St., nearly 1 mile south of Market St. Regional train service between San Francisco and San Jose 4:50am-10pm. Fare $4. **CalTrain,** 4th and Townsend St. (557-8661), 6 blocks south of Market St. Trains between San Francisco and San Jose along the peninsula. Open Mon.-Fri. 7am-7pm, Sat. 8am-5pm, Sun. 8am-3pm.

Buses: Greyhound, 50 7th St. (558-6616), between Mission and Market St. downtown. Coin-operated storage lockers ($1 per day) frequently full. Baggage check $1.50 per day per bag. Security lounge for ticketed passengers. Unsafe neighborhood at night. Open daily 5am-midnight. **Green Tortoise,** 285-2441. Runs friendly and regular bus trips up and down the coast to L.A. ($30) and to Seattle ($59). Also to New York and Boston (both 14 days, $279). Organized tours of Yosemite ($69-89) and other national parks. Must make reservations in advance. Bus pick up at 1st and Natoma St., behind the Transbay Terminal. Open Mon.-Fri. 8am-8pm.

Tours: Gray Line Tours, 896-1515. Reasonably priced, short tours of the city. Audio tapes available in French, German, Spanish, Italian, Japanese, and English. Tour conducted 6 times per day, leaving from the Transbay Terminal or from Union Square (3½ hr., $21.50).

Ferries: San Francisco-Larkspur Ferry, San Francisco Ferry Terminal (332-6600), east end of Market St. Operates Mon.-Fri. 6am-8:25pm, Sat.-Sun. and holidays 10:45am-6:45pm. Mon.-Fri. one way $2.20, Sat.-Sun. $3; seniors half-price; Sat.-Sun. under 12 with parent free. **San Francisco-Sausalito Ferry,** Ferry Terminal (332-6600). One way $3.50. Operates Mon.-Fri. 7:50am-8pm; Sat.-Sun. 11:30am-6:55pm.

Local Transit: See Getting Around, below.

Taxi: Yellow Cab, 626-2345; **Luxor Cabs,** 282-4141; **DeSoto Cab Co.,** 673-1414. First mile $1.40, $1.50 each additional mile.

Car Rental: Rent-A-Wreck, 555 Ellis St. (776-8700), between Hyde and Leavenworth St. Used, mid-sized cars $22 per day with 150 free miles, $119 per week with 700 free miles; 20¢ each additional mile. Under 25 $3 extra per day. Open Mon.-Fri. 8am-7pm, Sat.-Sun. 9am-4pm. Must be 21 with major credit card. **Bob Leech's Auto Rental,** 435 S. Airport Blvd. (583-3844), South San Francisco. New Toyotas $20 per day with 150 free miles, 10¢ each additional mile. Travelers coming into SFO should ask Bob Leech's for a ride to the shop. Open Mon.-Fri. 8am-9pm, Sat.-Sun 8am-6pm. Must be 25 with major credit card.

Auto Transport: Auto Driveaway Company, 330 Townsend (777-3740). A large selection of destinations. Open Mon.-Fri. 9am-5pm. Must be 21 with valid license and references. Cash deposit $250. **A-1 Auto,** 1300 Old Bayshore Rd., Burlingame (342-9611). Call 10 days in advance. Open Mon.-Fri. 8am-5:30pm. Must be 21 with major credit card. Cash deposit $150.

Bike Rental: Lincoln Cyclery, 772 Stanyan St. (221-2415), on the east edge of Golden Gate Park. 3-speeds $2 per hr., 10-speeds $3 per hr. Open Mon. and Wed.-Sat. 9am-5pm, Sun. 11:30am-5pm. Driver's license or major credit card required. **Presidion Bicycle Shop,** 5335 Geary (752-2453), between 17th and 18th Ave. 10-speed or mountain bike $25 per day. Open Mon. and Sat. 10am-6pm, Tues.-Fri. 10am-7pm, Sun. 11am-4pm.

Help Lines: Drug Line, 752-3400. **Suicide Prevention,** 221-1423. **Rape Crisis Center,** 647-7273. Operated by San Francisco Women Against Rape. **Gay Switchboard and Counseling**

Services: 841-6224. Information on gay community events, local clubs, etc., as well as counseling. Open Mon.-Fri. 10am-10pm, Sat.-Sun. noon-4pm.

Post Office: 7th and Mission St. (621-6838), opposite Greyhound. Open Mon.-Fri. 9am-5:30pm, Sat. 9am-1pm. **ZIP code:** 94101. **Rincon Annex,** 99 Mission St. Open Mon.-Fri. 8am-10pm, Sat. 9am-5pm. Other branches open at least Mon.-Fri. 9am-5:30pm.

Area Code: 415.

Getting There

San Francisco, the cultural capital of Northern California and third largest city in the state (pop. 750,000), is 548 miles north of San Diego, 403 miles north of Los Angeles, and about 390 miles south of the Oregon border. The city proper lies at the northern tip of a peninsula separating San Francisco Bay from the Pacific Ocean.

San Francisco International Airport (SFO) is located on a small nub of land in San Francisco Bay about 15 miles south of the city center on U.S. 101. There are two ways to commute from SFO to the city by public transportation. First, **San Mateo County Transit (samTrans)** (761-7000), runs two buses from SFO to downtown San Francisco. The express (#7F) takes 30 minutes, but you can only bring carry-on luggage (every ½ hr. 6am-1am; $1.25, seniors and under 17 75¢). Bus #7B takes a little longer (45 min.), but you can carry all the luggage you want (every ½ hr. 5:40am-1:30am; seniors and under 17 75¢). An **Airporter** bus runs a shuttle route between all three terminals and a downtown terminal at 301 Ellis St. (every 15 min. 5:30am-9:15pm, after 9:15pm every 30-40 min., $6).

Taxi rides to downtown San Francisco from SFO cost about $20.

Lorrie's Travel and Tour (334-9000), on the upper level at the west end of all three terminals provides convenient door-to-door van service to and from the airport. Reserve at least six hours in advance for service to the airport. No reservations are needed for travel from the airport. (Vans run 4:25am-10:25pm. One way $8, ages 2-12 $5, under 2 free.) **Franciscus Adventures** (821-0903) runs a small bus between San Francisco and SFO ($7, $5 per person for groups of five or more). Call ahead to arrange a time.

The San Francisco airport is more out of the way than you would expect. Give yourself plenty of time as traffic can get very bad, especially during the evening commute.

If you're a driver who needs a passenger or a passenger who needs a driver, call the **Berkeley Ride Board** (527-0352) for free, 24-hour listings. The San Francisco International Hostel and San Francisco State University (469-1842, located in the student union; open Mon.-Fri. 7am-10pm, Sat. 10am-4pm), also have ride boards. KALX radio (642-5259), on the Berkeley campus, broadcasts a ride list Monday through Saturday at 10am and 10pm. Call them to put your name and number on the air for free. KSAN radio (986-2825) provides a similar service.

Getting Around

The hilly city of San Francisco, surrounded by water on three sides, is an amalgam of distinct neighborhoods organized along a few central arteries. Each neighborhood is compact enough to explore comfortably on foot.

San Francisco radiated outward from its docks, on the northeast edge of the peninsula just inside the lip of the bay. Most visitors' attention still gravitates to this area, although the city now extends south and west from this point. Here, within a wedge formed by Van Ness Ave. running north-south, Market St. running northeast-southwest, and the Embarcadero (waterfront road) curving along the coast are concentrated many of San Francisco's attractions. Taking the diagonal course, Market Street disrupts the regular grid of streets and accounts for an exceptionally confusing street-numbering system. The streets radiating north from Market and west from Market and the Embarcadero are numbered beginning at those thoroughfares, although you should keep in mind that parallel streets do not bear the same block numbers.

At the top of this wedge lies **Fisherman's Wharf** and **North Beach,** a district shared by Italian-Americans, artists, and professionals. The focal point of North Beach is Telegraph Hill, topped by Coit Tower and fringed counterclockwise from the northwest to the southeast by Columbus Avenue. Across Columbus begin the **Nob Hill** and **Russian Hill** areas, resting places of the city's old money. This fan-shaped area is confined by Columbus along its northeast side, Van Ness along the west, and (roughly) Geary and Bush Streets on the south. Below Nob Hill and North Beach, and still north of Market, **Chinatown** covers around 24 square blocks between Broadway in the north, Bush Street in the south, Powell Street in the west, and Kearny Street in the east. The heavily-developed **Financial District** lies between Washington St. in the north and Market in the south, east of Chinatown and south of North Beach. Going down Market from the Financial District, heading toward the bottom of the wedge, you pass through the core downtown area centered on **Union Square** and then, beyond Jones Street, the **Civic Center,** an impressive collection of municipal buildings including City Hall, the Opera House, and Symphony Hall. The Civic Center occupies the base of the wedge and spills out over Van Ness to Gough Street, 2 blocks west.

Also within this wedge is the **Tenderloin,** which still qualifies as a somewhat seedy region to avoid at night, despite the sprouting high-rises. The Tenderloin is roughly bounded by Larkin Street to the west and to the east by Taylor Street extending from Market Street north to Geary. Some of the area's seediness, however, seeps across Market to the area near the Greyhound station (6th and 7th St.).

Below Market St. lies the aptly-named **South-of-Market-Area (SOMA),** home to much of the city's nightlife. The South-of-Market extends inland from the bay to 10th Street, at which point the Hispanic **Mission District** begins and spreads south. The **Castro** area, center of the gay community, abuts the Mission District at 17th and also extends south, centered upon Castro Street.

West of Van Ness Avenue, the city distends all the way to the ocean side of the peninsula. At the top of Van Ness, the commercially developed **Marina** area embraces a yacht harbor, Fort Mason, and the Youth Hostel. Fisherman's Wharf lies immediately to its east. Above the marina rise the wealthy hills of **Pacific Heights.** South of Pacific Heights, across Van Ness from the Civic Center, is the somewhat seedy **Western Addition,** extending west to Masonic Avenue. **Japantown,** is located within the Western Addition. Farther west is the rectangular **Golden Gate Park,** extending to the Pacific and bounded by Fulton Street in the north and Lincoln Street in the south. At its eastern end juts a skinny Panhandle bordered by the **Haight-Ashbury** district. North of **Golden State Park** nods San Francisco's token suburb within the city, the **Richmond District.**

Although San Franciscans love to complain about it, their city's mass transportation is superb. Buses run frequently and punctually and are generally clean. Even better, despite its location in a state of automobile worshipers, San Francisco has not neglected rail transportation. Connections to neighboring cities are well-coordinated and speedy. See San Francisco Bay Area for information on transportation beyond San Francisco.

San Francisco Municipal Railway (MUNI) (673-6864) operates buses, streetcars, cable cars, and a subway. Except on cable cars, fare is 85¢, ages 5-17 25¢, disabled passengers and seniors 15¢. Exact change is required. A Fast Pass ($25) allows unlimited travel on MUNI for one month. Ask for a free transfer, valid in any direction for several hours, when boarding. The MUNI subway runs along Market St. in part, and should not be confused with BART (see below). The subway and bus lines along a few major streets (Market, Geary, Union, and Mission) run all night. Most buses, however, run daily 7am-1am. Smoking is prohibited on all MUNI vehicles. The excellent *San Francisco Street & Transit Map,* available at most bookstores ($1.50), contains a special map of public transportation after midnight and enough information for all but the most devoted bus-riders.

San Francisco's **cable cars** were named a national historic landmark in 1964. Overhauled in 1983 and '84, they are back on the streets, still the most novel (albeit crowded) way to see parts of the city. There are three lines, serving parts of Hyde,

Jackson, Washington, Taylor, California, Mason, and Powell St. Hyde is the most dramatic stretch of track. The fare is $2, ages 5-17 75¢, seniors 15¢, under 5 free. Unlimited transfers allowed within a given three-hour period. Cars run daily 7am-1am.

Bay Area Rapid Transit (BART) (778-2278) does not (alas) really serve the entire Bay Area. It does operate modern, fully carpeted trains connecting San Francisco with the East Bay, including Oakland, Berkeley, Concord, and Fremont. It is not a local transportation system within the city of San Francisco; use MUNI for that. One way fares range from 80¢ to $3. A special excursion deal for $2.60 is designed for tours of the system. You must begin and end at the same station, and your trip must not take more than three hours. BART trains run Monday through Saturday from 6am to midnight, Sunday from 9am to midnight. Maps and schedules are available at the visitor information center and all BART stations. Bring fresh dollar bills, as the automatic ticket printers are infamously picky.

Other, more local lines serve the greater Bay Area as well as parts of San Francisco. **AC Transit** (839-2882) offers primarily East Bay service, but lines F,N, and T run between the East Bay and San Francisco. **Golden Gate Transit** (332-6600) serves Marin and Sonoma Counties. **San Mateo County Transit (samTrans)** (761-7000) runs between San Francisco and San Mateo County and from Transbay Terminal to SFO.

A car is not the necessity it is everywhere else in California. Furthermore, parking spots are scarce and very expensive. A car is, however, definitely the best way to explore the outer reaches of the Bay Area. In the city, contending with the hills is the first task; if you've arrived in a standard-shift car, you'll need to develop a fast clutch foot, since all the hills have stop signs at the crests. If you're renting, get an automatic. And remember, in San Francisco, cable cars have the right of way.

The street signs admonishing you to "PREVENT RUNAWAYS" refer not to wayward youths but rather to cars improperly parked on hills. When parking on an incline, cramp the wheels against the curb and always set the parking brake.

Accommodations

Unlike most cities, San Francisco has a wide selection of conveniently located, relatively satisfying budget accommodations. Don't expect miracles for these prices. Note that a rather hefty 11% bed tax is not included in the prices given below. Most hotels listed here are in areas such as the Tenderloin, the Mission District, Union Square, and downtown, where caution is advised both on the streets and within the buildings, particularly at night. Women, especially, should go elsewhere and pay more if suspicious about a particular neighborhood or establishment.

The International Network Globe Hostel, 10 Hallam Place (431-0540), near Greyhound, just off Folsom St. in the South of Market district. Clean and very convenient. Four beds to a hotel room with chairs and tables. No kitchen. This friendly, lively hostel serves a continental breakfast and has its own sauna and jacuzzi. Over 100 beds, many filled by international student travelers. Community lounge and laundry room are good places to meet people. $12, off-season $10. Key deposit $5.

San Francisco International Hostel (AYH), Bldg. 240, Fort Mason (771-7277). Entrance at Bay and Franklin St., 1 block west of Van Ness Ave., at the northern end of the peninsula. From Greyhound, walk to 9th and Market St., then take MUNI bus #19 ("Polk") to Polk and Bay St. Turn left, and walk 2 blocks to Franklin St.; follow signs to hostel. One of the largest AYH-affiliated hostel in the nation. The General Motors of hosteling: clean, well-run, and efficient. Chore-a-day rule enforced. Extensive lounges, large kitchen, spic-and-span food-storage areas, and pay lockers for valuables. Good ride board. Frequented by students, families, and seniors. Crowded in summer. 3-day max. stay in summer, 5-day in winter. Registration 7am-2pm and 4:30pm-midnight. Dorms closed 10am-4:30pm. Check-out 10am. Curfew midnight. Members and nonmembers $10. Get here very early or send a night's fee 3 weeks ahead of time to reserve a place.

International Guest House, 2976 23rd St. (641-1411), at Harrison St. in the Mission District. More of a home than a hostel. The owner adheres strictly to a foreign-travelers-only rule.

2 fully equipped kitchens for 28 guests. Common room, TV, and stereo. 5-day min. stay. No curfew. Bunks $10 in 2- or 4-person rooms. Rooms for couples $20. No singles. No reservations.

European Guest House, 761 Minna St. (861-6634), near 8th St., 2 blocks south of Greyhound and west on Minna in a quiet but run-down neighborhood. Free-wheeling, relaxed, improvised, friendly. People sleep on sofas, mats, cushions. Even if you aren't foreign, chances of getting in are good if you're from out of town. Mixed-sex rooms. TV room, laundry facilities, kitchen, small information board. Register any time. No curfew. $9 per night.

Youth Hostel Centrale, 116 Turk St. (346-7835), just north of Market. From Greyhound, walk northeast along Market to Turk, then turn left. Aging building in the Tenderloin. Porno theaters lurk on all sides, but the hostel's locked gate inspires confidence. TVs monitor the front door. Clean but uninviting. TV lounge. Primarily international, but traveling Americans usually accepted. Check-in 7:30am-noon. Curfew 2am. Male only bunks $10. Singles $18. Doubles $25. Key deposit $5.

Hancourt Residence Club, 1105 Larkin (673-7720). One of the city's most popular residence clubs offers rooms by the week or by the month. Price includes maid service, color TV, and 2 meals a day except Sundays. Filled by a younger set of traveling students and local residents. Regular cocktail parties and dances are organized by Harcourt. Single rooms for 1 or 2 people from $125 per week, with bath $150.

YMCA, 166 Embarcadero (392-2191), between Mission and Howard St., in Financial District. Men and women. 269 rooms. Best of the city's YMCAs: conveniently located, attractive lobby, friendly people. Unfortunately, its future is uncertain, so call before rushing over. Use of pool, sauna, and gym. Register at any time. Check-out 11am. No curfew. No membership required. Singles $24. Bunk beds $33. Doubles $35, with TV $37.

YMCA Hotel, 220 Golden Gate Ave. (885-0460), at Leavenworth St., 2 blocks north of Market St. Men and women. One of the largest hotels in the city. Impressive post-modern facade, although the inside rooms are spartan. Has the only indoor track in the city, which is just as well given the uninviting surroundings. Double locks on all doors. Pool and gym. Register any time. No curfew. Singles $26. Doubles $35. Triples with toilet and shower, $53.

YMCA Chinatown, 855 Sacramento St. (982-4412), between Stockton St. and Grant Ave. Good location for those wanting to be near the center of the city. Men over 18 only. Friendly young staff, pool, and gym. Registration Mon.-Fri. 6:30am-10pm, Sat. 9am-5pm, Sun. 9am-1pm. Check-out 1pm. No curfew. Singles $22.45-24.25, with bath $28.85. Doubles $28.85. Weekly: singles $116-140, with bath $158.70; doubles $158.70.

San Francisco State University, 800 Font Blvd. (338-2721), a trip from downtown. Take BART to Daly City and bus #70 to Font (Mon.-Fri.), or bus #17 to Font and Holloway. A short walk from the intersection. Dorm rooms for traveling students only. 3-day max. stay. Registration and check-out at any time. Singles $35. Doubles as low as $20. Rooms available early June to mid-Aug.

Sheehan Hotel, 620 Sutter St. (775-6500), near Mason St. Excellent location with nearby access to calbe cars, buses, and BART. Across the street from trendy art galleries. The elegant lobby is busy and something of a scene on warm summer evenings. Many international students take advantage of the clean, comfortable rooms. Singles $35, with bath $50. Doubles $45, with bath $60.

The Red Victorian Bed and Breakfast Inn, 1665 Haight St. (864-1978), 3 blocks west of Masonic Ave., 2 blocks east of Golden Gate Park in Haight-Ashbury. For the Haight experience, this Vicorian hotel offers 14 rooms uniquely decorated to recall the Summer of Love and the beauty of Golden Gate Park. Swedish and shiatsu therapeutic massage ($40 per hr.), meditation rooms, and a peace gallery. A non-smoking, angst-free environment that you won't want to miss if your wallet is up for the experience. Summer rates $65-125 depending on room size and karma; in winter $55-120. For $10 they will put an extra futon in your room. Breakfast and coffee and tea in the evenings included. Make reservations well in advance for the summer months.

Olympic Hotel, 140 Mason St. (982-5010) at Ellis St., a few blocks from Union. Caters mostly to Japanese students and Europeans. Clean comfortable kitschy design. Helpful, friendly management. Tends to fill up during the summer months. Olympic Deli next door has cappuccino ($1.20) and sandwiches ($2.80). Singles $28, with bath $35. Doubles with bath $42.

Pacific Bay Inn, 520 Jones St. (673-0234), 3 blocks west of Union Sq. Entirely renovated after fire. Singles and doubles $55-65; only $45 if you bring your copy of *Let's Go.* Continental breakfast included.

The Ansonia, 711 Post St. (673-2670), 3 blocks west of Union Sq. This busy, attractive hotel offers the weary traveler comfortable accommodations, a good location, and a wlecoming environment. The more expensive rooms have large claw-foot bathtubs. Singles $35-50. Doubles $45-60. Hearty American-style breakfast included. Dinner served for $5; free if you stay for six nights. Call in summer for reservations.

The Amsterdam, 749 Taylor St. (673-3277 or 800-637-3444), between Bush and Sutter St., 2 blocks from Nob Hill. This "European-style" hotel peddles attractive rooms with queen-sized beds. It usually fills up in summer with foreign student travelers and the occasional business person. Singles $38, with bath $52. Doubles $42, with bath $56. Continental breakfast included.

Golden Gate Hotel, 775 Bush St. (392-3702), between Powell and Mason St., 2 blocks north (uphill) of Union Sq. A warm, charming, and well-located turn-of-the-century hotel with antique furnishings. Spotless hall toilets and bath. Color TV. Multi-lingual host. Check-out noon, but late-fliers can store their luggage. Singles and doubles $45-50, with shower $48-53. Continental breakfast included. Garage parking available. One-week advance reservations recommended June-Sept.

All Season's Hotel, 417 Stockton St. (986-8737 or 989-9355), between Sutter and Bush St., 1 block north of Union Sq. Excellent location. Clean but somewhat weary and worn. The noise from the parking garage across the street penetrates the thin walls. TV. Check-out 11am. Singles $42, with bath $50. Doubles $47, with bath $65. Continental breakfast included. Reservations usually needed for the weekend.

Obrero Hotel and Basque Restaurant, 1208 Stockton (989-3960), between Pacific Ave. and Broadway in Chinatown. Warm and enthusiastic proprietor, comfortable rooms, great location, and a huge breakfast (including ham, eggs, cheese, sourdough bread, hot chocolate, and coffee). European atmosphere in the center of Chinatown. No private baths. Registration 8am-noon and 5-10pm. Check-out 11am. Singles $35. Doubles $42.

Gum Moon Women's Residence, 940 Washington (421-8827), at Stockton in Chinatown's center. Women only. Kitchen and laundry facilities. All rooms with shared bath. Primarily a boarding house, so call ahead to make sure there are rooms available. Registration 9am-6pm. Check-out noon. Singles $23. Doubles $38. Weekly: singles $88; doubles $146.

Food

Even when the mouths of late 20th-century Americans are dust, it will be remembered that San Francisco in the 1980s and 90s was a culinary paradise. The city feasts on Chinatown's tantalizing *dim sum,* the *cleantro*-spiced burritos of the Mission, and the freshest seafood. The pizzas that emerge from the wood ovens of the Bay Area range from North Beach Neapolitan to the trendy but tasty goat cheese and *pancetta.* The sourdough is a city landmark and San Franciscans are as serious about their coffee as they are about the wines of Napa valley.

The ethnic diversity of San Francisco makes the city a perfect place to explore the world's exotic cuisines. The urban professionals of San Francisco may have sold their souls for the earthly pleasures of great food, but money need not be a limiting factor for gourmet dining. Ethnic food will consistently get you the very best value and can often be better than the most expensive meals. Head out to the Mission for excellent and inexpensive cuisine. Chinatown offers wonderful food for paltry sums. The Haight has a fabulous selection of bakeries and Columbus Avenue in North Beach lures visitors to café after café.

North Beach

Cafe Sport, 574 Green St. (981-1251), near Columbus Ave. Terrific food served in an oddly decorated, claustrophobic dining room. Go for lunch and order the garlicky *pesto* over pasta ($8), worth every penny. Dinner can cost over $15. Tues.-Sat. noon-2pm; dinner sittings at 6:30, 8:30, and 10:30pm. Reservations essential.

Bohemian Cigar Store, 566 Columbus Ave. (362-0536), corner of Union Sq. Excellent espresso ($1) and agreeable Italian food. Try their Italian sandwiches ($4-5). Open Mon.-Sat. 11am-midnight.

Unites States Restaurant, 431 Columbus Ave. (362-6251), at Stockton St. Popular with young San Franciscans (a patriotic lot). Long wait at dinner. Large, tasty portions. Garlicky pot roast $7.50. *Calamari* ($7.50) is their most popular dish. Most dishes under $10. Open daily 6:30am-9pm.

Caffe Trieste, 609 Vallejo St. (392-6739), at Grant. Only a few beatniks now, but sip coffee and remember the exciting Eisenhower years when Ginsberg and Ferlinghetti hung out here. Loud live music Sat. noon-4pm. Otherwise settle for a tune from the opera jukebox. Coffees $1-2. Open Mon.-Thurs. 7am-11:30pm, Fri.-Sat. 7am-12:30am, Sun. 7am-10:30pm.

Tommaso's, 1042 Kearny St. (398-9696), just below Van Ness Ave. For a break from *nouvelle pizza* try some of the very best traditional Italian pizza anywhere. The super deluxe, piled high with mushrooms, peppers, ham, and Italian sausage sates two ($12). Francis Ford Coppola is known to toss some pizza dough every once in a while in front of Tommaso's huge wood burning ovens. The wait is sometimes long but always worth it. Open Tues.-Sat. 5-10:45pm.

Specs' Twelve Adler Museum Cafe, 19 Adler Place (421-4112), off Columbus Ave. This bar is another last resting place for Bay Area beatniks. Although not regularly scheduled, you can often hear excellent local jazz musicians jam until all hours of the morning. Drinks $2-4. Open Mon.-Fri. 4:30pm-2am, Sat.-Sun. 5pm-2am.

Chinatown

Hunan, 924 Sansome St. (956-7727). Has been called the best Chinese restaurant in the U.S. Everything is delicious and moderately priced. The pot-stickers ("Peking Ravioli" on the East coast) are meaty and good ($3.50). The Harry special, a generous assortment of fresh shrimp, scallops, and prawns, is a favorite among seafood lovers around the Bay ($9.50).

Tung Fong, 808 Pacific Ave. (363-7115), just off Stockton St. Excellent *dim sum* in this relaxed, comfortable restaurant. The foil-wrapped chicken ($1.50) is highly recommended. *Dim sum* dishes $1.50-2.50. Open Tues.-Thurs. 9am-3pm. Reservations accepted.

Yuet Lee, 1300 Stockton St. (982-6020), at Broadway. A favorite among knowing locals, this ugly lime-green restaurant with evil fluorescent lighting is your best choice for Chinese seafood. Celebrity gourmets flock here to sample the exciting menu. Most dishes under $10. Open Wed.-Mon. 11am-3am.

King of China, 939 Clement St. (668-2618). A huge 2nd-floor dining room seats at least 300. *Dim sum* is their specialty ($1.50 a dish). Excellent roast duck is dispensed by the plate, Hong Kong style. You can eat lavishly for about $10 with many interesting dishes to choose from. The friendly service is something of a rarity in Chinatown. Considered among the city's finest. Open daily 9am-10pm.

Mission District and Castro Street

La Cumbre, 515 Valencia St. (863-8205). Excellent food often attracts long lines in early afternoon. Great barbecued beef burrito ($2.29). Pleasant dining hall is covered with bright folk murals and has hand-carved wooden picnic tables. Open Mon.-Sat. 11am-10pm.

Taqueria San Jose, 3 locations: 2830 Mission St. (282-0203), 2282 Mission St. (558-8549), 3274 24th St. (282-7018). These popular *taquerias* comprise what has been called the best-tasting fast food chain in America. Generous portions of chopped *cilantro* add an interesting flavor to simple food made with the freshest ingredients. Tacos with split-roasted pork $1.55. Caution is advised at night in the Mission. #1 open Mon.-Thurs. 8am-1am, Fri.-Sat. 8am-4am. #2 open daily 8:30am-2:30am. #3 open daily 8am-midnight.

Manora, 3226 Mission (550-0856). This attractive Thai restaurant serves delicious cuisine at reasonable prices. Manora is especially light with its sauces so the food isn't smothered in peanut butter as it can be at lesser Thai places. The red beef curry gets good reviews ($5.25). Most dishes under $8. Open daily 5-10pm.

La Victoria, 2937 24thSt. (550-9292). You have to walk through the bakery to get to the dining room. Fill yourself for about $5. The menu is in Spanish but the staff can translate. Enchanting *tamales.* Open daily 10:30am-10pm.

Marina and Pacific Heights

Coffee Cantata, 2030 Union St. (931-0770). the window opening onto the street makes this Union St. establishment a great place to watch people. The Cantata sampler for lunch offers *dolmas,* ratatouille, and chicken curry with rice pilaf for $6. Spinach and feta strudel $6.25. Full bar. Open Mon.-Fri. 10am-12:30am, Sat.-Sun. 11:30am-2am.

Jackson Fillmore, 2506 Fillmore St. (346-5288). Where the staff from Chez Panisse goes on their day off. There is almost always a wait at this popular and hip *trattoria.* Great southern Italian cuisine and a lively atmosphere. The portions are large and you might sneak out for less than $10 per person. Open Tues.-Thurs. 5:30-10:30pm, Fri.-Sat. 5:30-11pm, Sun. 5-10pm.

Mai's Vietnamese, 1838 Union St. (921-2861). Sidewalk dining. The crab claws get good marks ($6.25) as does the vegetarian imperial role ($4.75). A romantic spot on warm summer nights. Open Mon.-Fri. 11am-10pm, Sat.-Sun. noon-10pm.

Haight-Ashbury

Cha Cha Cha, 1805 Haight St. (386-5758). Love children fighting against the stream of late capitalist society join hands with the yuppies who urge it on in order for a chance to eat at this trendy Latin restaurant. Thought to be the best in the Haight. Try the topaz. Entrees $5-8. Open Mon.-Thurs. 5-11pm, Fri.-Sat. 5:30-11:30pm.

Crescent City Cafe, 1418 Haight St. (863-1374). Tasty Cajun and Creole food served in what looks to be a neighborhood diner in the middle of the Haight. Terrific BBQ sandwiches ($5). Open Wed.-Fri. 10am-4pm and 5-10pm, Sat. 8am-10pm, Sun. 8am-3pm, Tues. 5-10pm.

Dish, 1398 Haight St. (431-3534), at Masonic. Remarkable range of food—everything from corned beef to waffles to *quesadillas* ($3.25-6.75). Clean, classic decor. Open Mon.-Fri. 8am-2pm and 6-10pm, Sat.-Sun. 8am-10pm.

Tassajara Bread Bakery, 1000 Cole St. (664-8947), at Parnassus, 5 blocks south of Haight St. One of the best bakeries in the city. Famous for its outstanding poppy seed cake ($7, 85¢ per piece). There's a branch at Fort Mason (771-6331), but the purist will want to make the pilgrimage to Haight-Ashbury for the original. Open Mon.-Thurs. 7am-7pm, Fri. 7am-10pm, Sat. 8am-10pm, Sun. 8am-2pm.

Sights

While San Francisco has many recognizable districts and well-known sights, the conventional landmarks fail to communicate the city's elusive identity. Leave enough time for leisurely strolls through the city's diverse but compact neighborhoods. Off-beat bookstores, Japanese folk festivals, Chinese *dim sum,* cosmopolitan Union Street, Pacific Heights nightlife, reminders of the 60s in Haight-Ashbury, Strawberry Hill in Golden Gate Park, the Club Fugazi on North Beach—these define San Francisco.

North Beach

North of Broadway and west of Columbus lies North Beach. Its two nicknames, "The Latin Quarter" and "Little Italy," reflect the split within the district between the bohemian Beats who made it their home—Jack Kerouac, Allen Ginsberg, Lawrence Ferlinghetti—and the residents of a traditional Italian neighborhood. North Beach bohemianism flourished in the 1950s when the artists and brawlers nicknamed the Beats (short for "beatitude" according to Kerouac) first moved in. Drawn to the area by low rents and cheap bars, the group came to national attention when Ferlinghetti's **City Lights Bookstore** (see Entertainment) published Allen Ginsberg's anguished and ecstatic dream poem *Howl.* More than one poet still tinkers with the language of Blake and Whitman, but the Beats are gone. Through the middle of North Beach runs Broadway, the neon netherworld of pornography purveyors. Above it all stands the pleasant old residential district of Telegraph Hill, topped by Coit Tower. North Beach is most fun to visit at night as the after-dinner, after-show crowd flocks to the area's numerous cafés for a relaxing cappuccino.

At its northern limit, North Beach curls along the Embarcadero to embrace **Fisherman's Wharf,** a lively tourist trap for camera-toting dollar droppers. Ferries for Alcatraz Island leave from the wharf. If you're willing to wake up at 4am, put on a heavy sweater, and go down to the piers, you can see the real Fisherman's Wharf: the loading and outfitting of small ships, the animated conversation, and the blanket of morning mist. Arrive later, and steel yourself against the most rapacious tourist scene in the city.

Chocolate lovers have been known to come to San Francisco just to see **Ghirardelli Square** (GEAR-a-deli), 900 N. Point St. (Information booth, 775-5500; open daily 10am-9pm.) The only remains of Ghirardelli's chocolate factory now lie in the back of the **Chocolate Factory,** a soda fountain (open daily 11am-midnight). Drool over the huge vats of melted chocolate before purchasing one of the "factory's" magnificent desserts. Pricey boutiques now fill the rest of the old factory's red brick buildings, and local musicians and magicians entertain the masses. Take MUNI bus #19 ("Polk"), #30 ("Stockton"), or #42 ("Downtown Loop").

American shopping mall mania hit North Beach with a vengeance. **The Cannery,** 2807 Leavenworth St. (771-3112) near Beach St., and Pier 39, about ½ mile east of the Cannery along the Wharf, compete with Ghirardelli Square for the tourists' crisp greenbacks. Housing a fruit warehouse and silver smelter in its early days, The Cannery now packs enough stores and people within its walls to justify it claustrophobic name. Nonetheless, **Pier 39** remains the most unabashedly fabricated and gratuitous of the three complexes.

To escape from this morass, take one of the **tour boats** or ferries from the wharf. Cruises usually pass by Alcatraz, Angel Island, the Golden Gate Bridge, the residential hills of San Francisco, and the Financial District before returning. Boats of the **Blue and Gold Fleet** (781-7877) leave from Pier 39 for a 75-minute trip around the harbor. (Departures daily 10am-7pm. Fare $12, seniors and ages 5-18 $6, under 5 free.) The **Red and White Fleet** (546-2896) runs a 45-minute cruise under the Golden Gate Bridge and around Alcatraz. (Departures from Pier 43½ daily 10:45am-3:45pm, every 30-45 min. Fare $12, seniors and ages 12-18 $8, ages 5-11 $5, under 5 free.) Red and White also operates regularly scheduled ferry service to Angel Island and Sausalito (see Getting Around). For a really pleasant escape, try one of the **sailboat charters** that line the wharf. Run by an experienced sailor, the *Rondo* (421-8353) sails two to six people on one- to three-hour voyages ($10 per person per hr., March-Nov. Mon.-Fri. 1-5pm, Sat.-Sun. noon-6pm). Depending on tides and winds, voyages head for Angel Island, Sausalito, and the Golden Gate Bridge. The *Ruby* (861-2165) sails at lunchtime (with sandwiches) daily from May to October. The sloop departs from the China Basin building at 12:30pm and returns by 2pm, but call as the schedule often changes (tickets $25, under 10 $12.50). The *Ruby* also takes a turn in the bay on Friday and Saturday at 6pm. Reservations are required for sailboat charters. Be sure to bring a heavy sweater in summer and a jacket in winter.

No prisoner who's tried to escape from **Alcatraz Island** has ever been heard of again. A former federal prison, the island looms over the San Francisco Bay, 1½ miles from Fisherman's Wharf. The island was named in 1775 for the *alcatraces* (pelicans) that flocked to it. During the Civil War "the Rock," then little more than barren stone, was fortified with a massive cannon and a garrison of several hundred Union soldiers to protect San Francisco from a possible Confederate attack. After the war the army decided to take advantage of the island's isolation and resident police force to incarcerate troublemakers from across the country. In 1934, Alcatraz became a maximun-security prison, only to be closed 20 years later due to high maintenance costs. Alcatraz is currently a part of the Golden Gate National Recreation Area, administered by the National Park Service. The Red and White Fleet (546-2805) runs boats to Alcatraz from Pier 41. (Departures every 1½ hr. from Pier 43½. The first boat leaves daily at 8:15am; the last boat back leaves daily at 6:15pm. Fare $7.50, ages 5-11 $4, under 5 free. Reserve tickets in advance through Ticketron for $1 extra or suffer long lines and risk not getting a ride.) Once on Alcatraz, you can take a free audiotape-guided, two-hour tour, or wander around by yourself, trail map in hand.

Those who aren't sure of their sea legs can inspect docked vessels along the wharf. **The Golden Gate National Recreation Area,** at Jefferson and Hyde St., harbors five boats, two of which are open to the public. The nearby museum displays related memorabilia and is worth popping into just to stand on the terrace overlooking the bay. (Boats and museum open daily 10am-6pm; off-season 10am-5pm. Free.) At the Haight Street Pier floats the famous windjammer the *Balclutha* (929-0202), a swift trading vessel that plied the Cape Horn route in the 1880s and 90s and was featured in the first Hollywood version of *Mutiny on the Bounty.* (Open Wed.-Sun.

10am-5pm. Admission $2, under 16 free.) At Pier 45 you can board a World War II submarine—the *U.S.S. Pampanito.* (Open daily 9am-9pm; off-season Sun.-Thurs. 9am-6pm, Fri.-Sat. 9am-9pm. Admission $3, seniors and ages 6-12 $1, ages 13-18 $2, under 6 free.)

Southeast of Pier 39 are Columbus Ave. and Telegraph Hill. Next to pleasant **Washington Square Park,** at the foot of Telegraph Hill between Stockton and Powell, stands the **Church of St. Peter and St. Paul,** beckoning tired sightseers to an island of quiet in its dark, wooden nave. Farther up Columbus Ave. lie numerous bookstores, restaurants, cafés, and small shops.

High above the North Beach streets atop Telegraph Hill stands one of the city's more conspicuous landmarks, **Coit Tower.** The tower is the legacy of Lillie Hitchcock Coit, an eccentric heiress known for her interest in firemen. It is often said that the tower was built to resemble a fire nozzle. At any rate, Coit Tower's spectacular 360° view makes it one of the most romantic spots in the city. An elevator will take you to the top. (Open daily 10am-6pm. Elevator fare $3, seniors $2, ages 6-12 $1, under 6 free.) The murals inside depicting scenes of manual labor, were sponsored by the WPA in the 30s. There is very limited parking, so leave your car on Washington St. and walk up the **Filbert Steps** which rise from the Embarcadero to the eastern base of the tower. The walk is short, allows excellent views, and passes by many gorgeous Art Deco buildings.

Nob Hill and Russian Hill

Until the earthquake and fire of 1906, Nob Hill was home to the mansions of the great robber barons. Even today, Nob Hill remains one of the nation's most prestigious addresses. The streets are lined with many fine buildings, and the overall feeling is that of settled wealth. Sitting atop a hill and peering down upon the masses can be a pleasant afternoon diversion. Nearby Russian Hill is named after Russian sailors who died during an expedition in the early 1800s and were buried on the southaest crest.

Grace Cathedral, 1051 Taylor St. (776-6611), crowns Nob Hill. The castings for its portals are such exact imitations of Ghiberti's on the Baptistry in Florence that they were used to restore the originals. Inside, modern murals mix San Franciscan and national historic events with biblical scenes. The view from **Huntington Park,** opposite Grace Cathedral, is superb.

The notorious **Lombard Street Curves,** on Lombard between Hyde and Leavenworth St. at the top of the hill, afford a fantastic view of the city and harbor—that is, if you can keep your eyes open down this terrifying plunge. The curves were installed in the 1920s to allow horse-drawn carriages to negotiate the extremely steep hill. Devising transportation on the city's steep streets also inspired the vehicles celebrated at the **Cable Car Museum,** at the corner of Washington and Mason St. (474-1887). The building is the cable-winding terminus for the picturesque cars, the working center of the cable-car system. (Open daily 10am-6pm; Dec.-March 10am-5pm. Free.)

Chinatown

The largest Chinese community outside of Asia, Chinatown is also the most densely populated of San Francisco's neighborhoods. Chinatown was founded in the 1880s when, the gold dug and the tracks laid, bigotry fueled by unemployment engendered a racist outbreak against what was then termed the "Yellow Peril." Chinese banded together to protect themselves in a small section of the downtown area. As the city grew, speculators tried to take over the increasingly valuable land, especially after the area was leveled by the 1906 earthquake, but the Chinese were not to be moved, and Chinatown, which has gradually grown beyond its original borders, remains almost exclusively Chinese. The Grant Ave. bazaars aside, Chinatown is not a Fisherman's Wharf tourist fabrication. The overly ornate **Chinatown Gate,** flanked by stone lions, misrepresents a very real and vibrant community.

Get onto the less famous streets; Jackson and Stockton give you a much better feel for the neighborhood. Live quail are sold out of a truck at Stockton and Washington St., and buckets of tender baby corn lie next to the day's catch of black eels in the markets. Although most visitors to Chinatown do little other than eat, there are other activities. Watch fortune cookies being shaped by hand in the **Golden Gate Cookie Company,** 56 Ross Alley (781-3956), between Washington and Jackson St. just west of Grant Ave. Nearby **Portsmouth Square,** at Kearny and Washington St., made history in 1848 when Sam Brennan brought the news of the gold strike at Sutter's Mill. The **Chinese Historical Society Museum,** 17 Adler Place (391-1188), off Grant Ave. near Broadway, houses a small but interesting collection of artifacts, photos, and descriptions of Chinatown's formative years. (Open Wed.-Sun. noon-4pm. Free.)

For two-hour guided tours of Chinatown and general information, stop at the **Chinese Culture Center,** 750 Kearny St., 3rd floor (986-1822).

The largest celebration of the year occurs at **Chinese New Year** (in 1990, Jan. 27-30), incorporating massive fireworks displays, parades, and feasting.

Financial District

North of Market and east of Kearny, snug against the bay, beats the West's financial heart, or at least one of its ventricles. Montgomery Street, the Wall Street of the West, is only of passing interest to the visitor and is best seen before the workday ends. After 7:30pm, the heart stops, to be resuscitated the next morning.

Parking is next to impossible during business hours. If you must drive, park your car South-of-Market and walk from there. To reach the Financial District by public transportation take MUNI Metro line J, K, L, M, or N to the Transbay Terminal, MUNI bus #2, 7, 8, 9, 11, 12, 14, or 21 to the terminal, samTrans bus #7A to Beale St., or BART to Embarcadero Station.

Commemorative plaques nailed to skyscraper flanks tell two stories: the explicit one, about intriguing events that transpired in the once raucous city center, and the implicit one, about a part of the city rendered homogeneous and hyper-efficient by development, smothering the Barbary Coast out of existence. Modern architecture enthusiasts may have a field day in this glass-box wonderland, but for the casual observer, a glimpse from afar will suffice.

San Francisco's most distinctive structure, totally out-of-scale with the surrounding buildings, is the 853-foot **Transamerica Pyramid,** at Montgomery St. between Clay and Washington St. The building's pyramidal shape and subterranean concrete "anchor" base (it was completed in 1972) make it one of the city's most stable, earthquake-resistant buildings. There is an observation deck on the 27th floor. (Open daily 9am-4pm. Free.)

Diagonally across from the pyramid is the **Old Transamerica Building,** 701 Montgomery St., at Washington St., the opulent showpiece of the corporation and a gem of older commercial architecture. The elaborate entryway is fenced with wrought iron and finished in gilt.

To see the Financial District at work, stop for a quick look at the **Pacific Stock Exchange,** 301 Pine St., at Sansome St. The statues to the side of the main entrance are impressive art nouveau. (Active Mon.-Fri. 9am-5pm. Closed to visitors at all times.)

The **Wells Fargo History Museum** 420 Montgomery St. (396-3174), is on the ground floor of the Wells Fargo Bank Building, near the intersection with Californai St. One of the zillion exhibits is an authentic Old West stagecoach. Information sheets are printed in seven languages. (Open Mon.-Fri. 9am-5pm. Free.) Those intent on breaking the tenth commandment can visit the **Museum of Money of the American West,** 400 California St. (863-8800), at Sansome St., on the lower level of the Bank of California Building. It displays gold and silver nuggets and coins as well as other historical tidbits. The privately minted coins are the most interesting attraction. (Open Mon.-Fri. 9am-4:30pm. Free.)

Downtown

Union Square is the center of San Francisco. Now an established shopping area, the square has a rich and somewhat checkered history. During the Civil War, a large public meeting was held here to decide whether San Francisco should secede. The square became the rallying ground of the Unionists, who bore placards reading "The Union, the whole Union, and nothing but the Union." At the **Sheraton Palace Hotel,** a few blocks away on Market St. at New Montgomery St., Warren Harding died in 1923, presumably of food poisoning. And on the square itself, by a side entrance of the **St. Francis Hotel,** Sara Jane Moore's attempt to assassinate President Gerald Ford was foiled on September 23, 1975.

The best free ride in town is on the outside elevators of the St. Francis Hotel. As you glide up the building, the entire Bay Area stretches out before you. The "elevator tours" offer an unparalleled view of Coit Tower and the Golden Gate Bridge. The newly renovated Powell St. cable cars also grant an excellent view of the square.

Even when the Barbary Coast (now the Financial District) was down and dirty, Union Square was cheaper. **Morton Alley,** in particular, offered off-brand alternatives to the high-priced prostitutes and stiff drinks of the coast; the prices were low, but the action was just as sizzling. At the turn of the century, murders averaged one per week on Morton Alley, and prostitutes with shirts unbuttoned waved to their favorite customers from second-story windows. After the 1906 earthquake and fire destroyed most of the flophouses, a group of proper merchants moved in and renamed the area **Maiden Lane** in hopes of changing the street's image. The switch worked. Today Maiden Lane, extending 2 blocks from Union Square's eastern side, is home to smart shops and classy boutiques. Traces of the old street live on, however, in words like "hoodlum," "shanghaied," and "Mickey Finn," all added to the American vocabulary by the people who frequented the area.

Civic Center

There are two ways to see the **Civic Center:** by day, for the architecture and museums, and by night, when the city's principal mainstream music groups perform. Although the **San Francisco Museum of Modern Art,** Van Ness Ave. (863-8800), at McAllister St. in the Veterans Building, is planning a move to a larger home, the current site displays an impressive collection of Abstract Impressionist painting, including a large collection of Clifford Still's jagged canvases. (Open Tues.-Wed. and Fri. 10am-5pm, Thurs. 10am-9pm, Sat.-Sun. 11am-5pm. Admission $3.50, seniors and under 16 $1.50. Tues. 10am-5pm free. Thurs. 5-9pm $2.)

By night **Louise M. Davies Symphony Hall,** 201 Van Ness Ave. (431-5400), at Grove St., rings with the sounds of the San Francisco Symphony. Next door, the **War Memorial Opera House,** 301 Van Ness Ave. (864-3330), at Grove St., hosts the well-regarded San Francisco Opera Company and the San Francisco Ballet. The Civic Center has two other theaters: the **Orpheum,** 1192 Market St. (474-3800), tends to draw flashy overblown shows, while the smaller **Herbst Auditorium,** 401 Van Ness Ave. (552-3656), at McAllister St., hosts string quartets, solo singers, and ensembles. Tours of the symphany hall, opera house, and Herbst Auditorium leave on the hour and half-hour from the Grove St. entrance of the Davies Hall. (½ hr., Mon. 10am-2:30pm. Admission $3, seniors and students $2. For more information, call 552-8338).

Mission District and Castro Street

Castro Street and the Mission District are far enough south that both areas may still be enjoying sunshine when fog blankets Nob Hill. The area is home to two thriving cultures: the gay community around Castro Street and the Hispanic community to the east. Although the scene has mellowed considerably from the wild days of the 70s as AIDS has taken its toll, Castro Street still remains a proud and assertive emblem of gay liberation. In the Hispanic Mission District, the colorful murals along 24th Street reflect the rich cultural influences here of Latin America.

The best way to see Castro Street is to wander, peering into shops or stepping into bars. Two popular hangouts are **Cafe Flor,** 2298 Market St. (621-8579), and **Cafe San Marco,** 2367 Market St. (861-3846).

At 16th and Dolores St. lies the old heart of San Francisco, **Mission Dolores,** said to be the oldest building in the city. The Mission was founded in 1776 by Father Junípero Serra and, like San Francisco itself, was named in honor of St. Francis of Assisi. However, the Mission sat close to a marsh known as *Lagoon de Nuestra Señora de los Dolores* (Laguna of Our Lady of Sorrows) and, despite Serra's wishes, it gradually became known as *Misión de los Dolores.* The artists constructing the chapel really let loose on the ceiling, painting it with vegetable colors—yellow, white, and deep red—that remain bright today. Exotic bougainvillaea, poppies, and birds of paradise bloom in the cemetery, which was featured in Alfred Hitchcock's *Vertigo.*

Western Addition and Japantown (Nihonmachi)

Nihonmachi, or Japantown, is a popular, modern complex of shops and light manufacturing located near the corner of Webster and Geary St. Built in 1968, the center was intended to be a gathering place for San Francisco's large Japanese-American population. Instead, it now exists mainly for tourists; few Japanese hang out here. The **Peace Pagoda,** a memorial to the victims of Hiroshima and Nagasaki, stands in the center of **Peace Plaza.** Japanese folk festivals animate the plaza in April (Cherry Blossom Festival), early July (Star Festival), September (Fall Festival), and December (*Mochi,* or rice loaf, Pounding Festival). There is free outdoor entertainment on Saturdays during the summer.

Marina and Pacific Heights

The Marina, Pacific Heights, and the adjoining Presidio Heights are the most sought-after residential addresses in San Francisco. Centered about Union and Sacramento St., Pacific Heights boasts the greates number of Victorian buildings in the city. The 1906 earthquake and fire destroyed most of the northeast part of San Francisco, but left the Heights area west of Van Ness Ave. unscathed. Victorian restoration has become a full-fledged enterprise; consultants try to determine the original form of fretwork, friezes, fans, columns, corbels, cartouches, pediments, stained glass, rosettes, rococo plaster, and so on. The **Octagon House,** 2645 Gough St. (885-9796), and **Haas-Lilienthal House,** 2007 Franklin St. (441-3004) allow the public a look inside a Victorian building. Rather sedate tours of the impeccably preserved octagon house are given for free on the first Sunday and second and fourth Thursdays of each month between 1 and 4pm. The Haas-Lilienthal House, 2007 Franklin St., is open Wed. noon-3:15pm, Sun. 11am-4pm. (Admission $4, seniors and under 18 $2.)

If you prefer shopping to Victoriana, however, **Union Street** is the place to be. Between Scott and Webster St., Union Street is chock-full of upscale shops, bars, restaurants, and bakeries. Try to catch the Union Street Spring Festival, one weekend in late May or early June.

Down from Pacific Heights toward the bay, is the **Marina** district. **Marina Green** by the water seethes with joggers and walkers and is well-known for spectacularly flown kites. To the west lies the **Palace of Fine Arts,** on Baker St. between Jefferson and Bay St. The strange, domed structure and two curving colonnades are reconstructed remnants of the 1915 Panama Pacific Exposition, which commemorated the opening of the Panama Canal and symbolized San Francisco's completed recovery from the great earthquake. In 1959, a wealthy citizen, dismayed by the erosion, paid to have it rebuilt in stone. On summer days performances of Shakespeare are sometimes given in the colonnade section.

The domed building houses the **Exploratorium** (561-0360). Hundreds of interactive exhibits may teach even poets a thing or two about the sciences. (Open Wed. 11am-9:30pm, Thurs.-Fri. 11am-5pm, Sat.-Sun. 10am-5pm. Admission $5, seniors $2, under 18 $1. Tickets valid 6 months.) Within the Exploratorium sits the **Tactile Dome** (561-0362), a pitch-dark maze of tunnels, slides, nooks, and crannies designed to help refine your sense of touch; as you might guess, this museum is a wonderful place to bring children. (Admission $5. Reservations required two weeks in advance.)

Haight-Ashbury

The 60s live on in Haight-Ashbury, though more self-consciously than 20 years ago. The Haight willfully preserves an era that many seek to forget. Originally a quiet lower-middle-class neighborhood, the Haight's large Victorian houses—perfect for communal living—and the district's proximity to the University of San Francisco drew a large hippie population in the mid- and late-1960s. LSD, possession of which was not a felony at the time, flooded the neighborhood. The hippie scene reached its apogee in 1966-67 when Janis Joplin, the Grateful Dead, and the Jefferson Airplane all lived or played in the neighborhood. During 1967's "Summer of Love," young people from across the country converged on the grassy Panhandle of Golden Gate Park for the celebrated "be-ins." Despite recent gentrification, Haight-Ashbury remains cheap and exciting. Many of the bars and restaurants are remnants of a past era, with faded auras, games in the back rooms, and live-in regulars.

Walk down Haight St. and stick your head in as many stores as you like. **Aardvark's Odd Ark,** 1501 Haight St. (621-3141), at Ashbury, has an immense selection of used new wave jackets, good music in the background, and prices that will take you back in time. (Open Sat.-Thurs. 11am-7pm and Fri. 11am-8pm.) **St. Vincent's De Paul Thrift Shop,** 1519 Haight St. (863-3315), beneath the surplus 7-Up sign near Haight and Ashbury, is the real thing: no music, no lighting, no service, and rock-bottom prices. (Open Mon.-Sat. 9:30am-4:45pm.) **Great Expectations Bookstore,** 1512 Haight St. (863-5515), would make Abbie Hoffman and Herbert Marcuse proud. Each of its hundreds of T-shirts is emblazoned with a different political or social critique. (Open Mon.-Thurs. 9:30am-11pm, Fri.-Sat. 9:30am-midnight, Sun. 10am-10pm.) **Reckless Records,** 1401 Haight St. (431-3434), is the place to find those long-lost Fairfield Parlour and John's Children discs. (Open Mon.-Sat. 10am-11pm, Sun. 10am-8pm.)

The Holo Gallery, 1792 Haight St. (668-4656), is an off-beat museum whose amazing collection of holograms is the closest today's USF students come to the visions of the 60s LSD users. (Open Mon.-Sat. 11am-6pm, Sun. noon-6pm. Free.)

Resembling a dense green mountain in the middle of the Haight, **Buena Vista Park** has a predictably bad reputation. Enter at your own risk, and once inside, be prepared for those doing their own thing.

Golden Gate Park

No visit to San Francisco is complete without a picnic in Golden Gate Park. Frederick Law Olmsted, designer of New York's Central Park, said it couldn't be done when San Francisco's 19th-century leaders asked him to build a park to rival Paris's Bois de Boulogne on their city's western side. But the engineer William Hammond Hall and the Scottish gardener John McLaren proved him wrong. Hall designed the 1000-acre park—gardens and all—when the land was still shifting sand dunes, and then constructed a mammoth breakwater along the oceanfront to protect the seedling trees and bushes from the sea's burning spray.

Most of the park is bounded by Fulton Street to the north, Stanyan Street to the east, Lincoln Way to the south, and the Pacific Ocean to the west. The major north-south route through the park is named Park Presidio By-Pass Drive in the north and Cross Over Drive in the south. The **Panhandle,** a thin strip of land bordered by Fell and Oak Street on the north and south respectively, is the oldest part of the park. Originally the "carriage entrance," it contains the oldest trees in the park, surrounded by the intriguing Haight-Ashbury. **Park headquarters,** where you can obtian information and maps, is at Fell and Stanyan St. (558-3706), in McLaren Lodge on the eastern edge of the park. (Open Mon.-Fri. 8am-5pm.)

There are three museums in the park, all in one large complex on the eastern side between South and John F. Kennedy Dr., where 9th Ave. meets the park. The **California Academy of Sciences** (221-5100; 750-7145 for a recording; 750-7138 for Laserium), the West Coast's oldest institution of its kind, contains several smaller museums. The **Steinhart Aquarium** is more lively than the natural history exhibits.

The alligator and crocodile pool is engaging but pales in comparison with the unique Fish Roundabout, a large tank shaped like a doughnut where the fish swim around you. (Seals and dolphins fed Fri.-Wed. 10:30am-4:30pm every 2 hr.; penguins fed daily at 11:30am and 4pm.) The academy also includes the **Morrison Planetarium** with its shows about white dwarves and black holes. (Additional charge of $2.50, seniors and students $1.25. The schedule of shows changes, so call 750-7141.) The Laserium orients its argon laser show to such robust themes as the Summer of Love and the legend of Jim Morrison. Call for the current schedule. The synesthetic spectacle may be too intense for children under six. (Ticket office open daily 10am-7pm; Sept. 2-July 3 10am-5pm. Admission $4-6, seniors and ages 12-17 $2, ages 6-11 $1, under 6 free. Free first Wed. of every month until 8:45pm.)

The **M. H. de Young Museum** (750-3600) contains a wonderful collection of art from Europe and Africa, as well as Nelson Rockefeller's collection of over 150 works by American artists. Next to the de Young is the **Asian Art Museum** (668-8921), located in the west wing of the building. (Both museums open Wed.-Sun. 10am-4:45pm. Admission $4, ages 12-17 $2, under 12 free. Free first Sat. of every month 10am-noon and the first Wed. of every month all day.)

Despite its sandy past, the soil of Golden Gate Park appears rich enough today to rival the black earth of the Midwest. Flowers blossom everywhere, particularly in spring and summer. The **Conservatory of Flowers** (386-3150) is the oldest building in the park, allegedly constructed in Ireland and shipped from Dublin via Cape Horn. The delicate and luminescent structure is modeled after Palm House in London's Kew Gardens and houses brilliant displays of tropical plants. (Open daily 9am-6pm. Admission $1.50, seniors and ages 6-12 $1, under 6 free.) The **Strybing Arboretum,** on Lincoln Way at 9th Ave. (661-1316), southwest of the academy, shows 3000 varieties of plants. Walk through the **Garden of Fragrance** for the vision-impaired, where the labels are in braille and the plants are chosen especially for their texture and scent. (Tours daily at 1:30pm. Open Mon.-Fri. 8am-4:30pm, Sat.-Sun. 10am-5pm. Free.) Near the Music Concourse on a path off South Dr., the **Shakespeare Garden** contains almost every flower and plant ever mentioned by the herbalist of Avon. Plaques with the relevant quotations are hung on the back wall, and there's a map to help you find your favorite hyacinths, cowslips, and gillyvors. (Open daily 9am-dusk; in winter Tues.-Sun. 9am-dusk. Free.)

A relic of the 1894 California Midwinter Exposition, the **Japanese Tea Garden** is a serene, if overpriced, collection of dark wooden buildings, small pools, graceful footbridges, carefully pruned trees and plants, and tons of tourists. Buy some tea and cookies for $1 and watch the giant goldfish swim placidly in the central pond. (Open daily 8:30am-5:30pm. Admission $2, seniors and ages 6-12 $1, under 6 free. Free 8:30-9am, 5-5:30pm, and all national holidays.)

At the extreme northwestern corner, the **Dutch Windmill** turns and turns again. Rounding out the days of old is the **Carousel** (c. 1912), which is accompanied by a $50,000 Gebruder band organ. (Open daily 10am-5pm; Oct.-May Wed.-Sun. 10am-5pm. Tickets $1, ages 6-12 25¢, under 6 free.)

The multinational collection of gardens and museums in Golden Gate Park would not be complete without something expressly American: its own herd of buffalo. A dozen of the shaggy beasts roam a spacious paddock at the western end of John F. Kennedy Dr., near 39th Ave.

To get to the park, hop on bus #5 or 21. On Sundays traffic is banned from park roads, and bicycles and roller skates come out in full force. Bike rental shops are plentiful. Skates, although harder to come by, are also available. Numerous MUNI buses cover the streets that surround Golden Gate Park and the north-south Park Presidio By-Pass/Cross Over Dr.

The Richmond District

The **Golden Gate Bridge,** the rust-colored symbol of the West's bounding confidence, sways above the entrance to San Francisco Bay. Built in 1937 under the directions of chief engineer Joseph Strauss, the bridge is almost indescribably beautiful from any angle on or around it.

Lincoln Park, at the northwest extreme of the city, is the Richmond district's biggest attraction. To get there, follow Clement St. west to 34th Ave., or Geary Blvd. to Point Lobos Ave. The park's California Palace of the Legion of Honor (750-3659) houses one of the best Rodin collections in the U.S. as well as excellent Monets and Manets. (Open Wed.-Sun. 10am-5pm. Admission $4, seniors and ages 12-17 $2, under 12 free. Free first Wed. and Sat. of each month 10am-noon.) Take the **Land's End Path,** running northwest of the cliff edge, for a romantic view of the Golden Gate Bridge.

Entertainment

San Francisco abounds with free publications listing the events in the Bay Area. The two that natives rely on most are the *San Francisco Bay Guardian* (824-7660) and the *East Bay Express.* The *Guardian* lives by Wilbur Storey's statement that "It is a newspaper's duty to print the new and raise hell." It is filled with reviews, some news, and a detailed weekly calendar. For a more detailed listing of Berkeley theater and the Oakland jazz scene, try the *Express* (652-4610). For listings of the visual and performing arts, try the monthly *CenterVoice* (398-1854), the downtown neighborhood newspaper.

Two newspapers worth buying are the daily *San Francisco Chronicle* (25¢), particularly the Sunday edition ($1) with its ample, pink-paged entertainment listings, and the weekly *Advocate,* whose own pink pages are another thing entirely. This national newsmagazine for gay people offers a large amount of information on San Francisco's gay community.

Publications are distributed in record stores (try Tower Records in North Beach—see below), bookshops, and street corner distribution boxes. If you can't find a magazine, call the publication itself for the nearest distribution point. Or call the **Entertainment Hotline,** 391-2001 or 391-2002.

Clubs

Firehouse, 3160 16th St. (621-1617). This hip Mission District habitat delivers excellent rap and underground music. Live bands on Sun. Open Mon.-Sat. 9pm-until the crowd tires. Cover Fri.-Sat. $5.

Southside, 1190 Folsom St. (431-3332). A popular danceria that can accommodate upwards of 2000 upwardly mobile singles. Food served. Open daily 5pm-4am. Cover $5.

Channel's, #1 Embarcadero Center (956-8768). This Financial District watering hole is a bustling reservoir of eligible young men and women. Open daily 4pm-2am.

Kimballs', 300 Grove St. (861-5555), at Franklin St. Great jazz musicians scare off the New Age/fusion frauds at this popular club/restaurant. Shows Wed.-Thurs. 9pm, Sat.-Sun. 11pm. Cover usually $8-12.

The I-Beam, 1748 Haight St. (668-6086), Haight-Ashbury. Specializes in post-Branca bands and DJs playing high-tech rock. Decor includes shooting light beams and 2 screens featuring clips from cartoons, golden oldies, and Japanese monster flicks. Often free student night Wed. or Thurs. Used to be a gay scene, and some nights still is. Carding fairly stringent. Open 9pm daily. Cover $5-10. Must be age 21.

The Fillmore, 1805 Geary St. (567-2060, 474-2995 for recording), opposite Japantown. Big name bands for the younger set. All ages welcome. You pay dearly to recall the times when everyone from Janis Joplin to Herbert Marcuse entertained here. Box office open day of show only, generally around 7pm. Advance tickets available from BASS. Call for show times.

Wolfgang's, 901 Columbus Ave. (441-4334, 474-2995 for recording), at Lombard St. Rock, video, vinyl, acoustic—you name it, they'll have it. Bands or DJ every night after 9pm. Cover $15 plus 2-drink minimum ($5).

Gay and Lesbian Clubs

While gay nightlife in San Francisco has become less visible in recent years, it still flourishes. Most of the popular bars can be found in the city's two traditionally gay areas—the Castro (around the intersection of Castro St. and Market St.) and

Polk St. (for several blocks north of Geary St.). In the Castro, stop for a drink at the **Metro Bar and Restaurant,** 3600 16th St. (431-1655), near Market St. or at **Castro Station,** 456 Castro (626-7220). **The Stallion,** 749 Polk (775-2213), provides a convenient, central starting point for a survey of Polk folk. For something more elegant, try **Imo's,** 1351 Polk (885-4535). Although the gay stronghold on the South-of-Market has given way to the invasion of straight clubs, one landmark remains: **Trocadero Transfer,** 520 4th St. (495-0185) is reputed to be the largest gay disco in the union. **Amelia's,** 647 Valencia St. (552-7788), is a popular lesbian bar and dance club.

San Francisco Bay Area

Berkeley

A quarter-century ago Mario Salvo climbed on top of a police car and launched Berkeley's free speech movement. Today, Berkeley is still a national symbol of political activism and social iconoclasm. In the 1980 presidential election Ronald Reagan finished fourth. Even as today's students prefer climbing corporate ladders to digging ditches in underdeveloped coutnries, the Berkeley City Council eagerly considers an initiative to curb "excess profits" in real estate. Berkeley's rent control law, now in its ninth year, has served as a model to the rest of hte country.

The site of one of the country's most radical universities, Berkeley is as renowned for its academics and chefs as for its political cadres and streetpeople. Chez Panisse is regarded as having originated California Cuisine, now imitated in almost every major city. Northwest of campus, the shopping area around Chez Panisse has been termed the "Gourmet Ghetto." Stylish clothing boutiques and gourmet specialty stores blanket the city. Miraculously, Berkeley revels in these bourgeois accoutrements while maintaining its idealistic rhetoric. By purchasing free-range chickens and avoiding styrofoam, citizens contentedly strike their blows against mechanized farming and the destruction of the environment. In Berkeley when you consume, you "shop for peace."

Practical Information

Visitor Information: Chamber of Commerce, 1834 University Ave. (549-7000). Open Mon.-Fri. 9am-5pm. **Council on International Educational Exchange (CIEE) Travel Center,** 2511 Channing Way (848-8604), at Telegraph Ave. Open Mon.-Fri. 10am-5pm. **Recorded Event Calendar,** 835-3849. **U.C. Berkeley Switchboard,** 1901 8th St. (642-6000). Information on community events. Irregular hours.

Local Transit: Bay Area Rapid Transit (BART): 465-2278. The free university **Humphrey-Go-BART shuttle** (642-5149) connects the BART station with the central and eastern portions of campus. During the school year, the shuttle leaves the station every five to ten minutes from 7am to 5:45pm, and every 15 minutes after that until 7pm, Monday through Friday—not on university holidays. **Alameda County Transit (AC Transit),** 839-2882. Buses leave from Transbay Terminal for Berkeley every 15 minutes from 6am-11pm, less frequently at other times. City buses operated by AC Transit run frequently. Fare 75¢, seniors 15¢, under 18 50¢.

Ride Boards: Berkeley Ride Board, ASUC building near the bookstore, on the 1st floor. Or call KALX-FM at 642-1111.

Transportation Information: Berkeley TRIP, 644-7665). Information on public transport, biking, and carpooling. Mostly local transportation, but not confined to daily commuting.

Help Lines: Rape Hotline, 845-7273. 24 hours. **Suicide Prevention,** 849-2212. 24 hours.

Post Office: 2000 Allston Way (845-1100). Open Mon.-Fri. 8:30am-5pm, Sat. 10am-2pm. **ZIP code:** 94704.

Area Code: 415.

Berkeley lies across the bay northeast of San Francisco, just north of Oakland. There are two efficient ways to reach the city: by car (I-80 or Rte. 24) or by public transportation from downtown San Francisco. Crossing the bay by **BART** ($1.85) is quick and easy, and both the university and Telegraph Ave. are a short, 5-minute walk from the station.

Lined with bookstores and cafés, **Telegraph Avenue** is the spiritual center of the town. The north side of campus has a few places to grab a snack but is mostly residential. The **downtown** area contains what few businesses Berkeley will allow. The public library and central post office can be found there. The **Gourmet Ghetto** encompasses the area along Shattuck Ave. and Walnut St. between Virginia and Rose St. West of campus and by the bay lies the **Fourth St. Center,** home to great eating and window shopping. To the northwest of campus, **Solano Avenue** offers countless ethnic restaurants (the best Chinese food in the city is found here), book stores, and movie theaters as well as more shopping.

Accommodations

It is surprisingly difficult to sleep cheaply in Berkeley. There are no good hostels, and clean, cheap motels seem disconcertingly lacking. Most of the city's hotels are flophouses; open spaces suitable for safe crashing are few. You might try renting a **fraternity room** for the night. Check the classified ads in the *Daily Californian* for possibilities.

YMCA, 2001 Allston Way (848-6800), at Milvia St. Men over 17 only. No membership required. 14-day max. stay. Registration daily 8am-10pm. Check-out 11:30am. Small rooms $18. Medium rooms $19. Key deposit $2.

The Berkeley Motel, 2001 Bancroft Way (843-4043), at Milvia St. Typical small motel with glitter on the ceiling and plastic showers. Clean rooms with TV. Fills up fast, so arrive early. Doubles $34, with 2 beds $45.

University of California Housing Office, 2700 Hearst Ave. (642-5925), in Stern Hall, at the northern end of campus. Rents rooms in summer to anyone who claims connection with the school (e.g. thinking of transferring). Call ahead. Open daily 8am-11pm. Singles $30. Doubles $38.

California Motel, 1461 University Ave. (848-3840), 2 blocks from the North Berkeley BART station. A clean but truly uninspiring motel. TV. Singles $39. Doubles $50.

Food

Eating takes on an existential significance in Berkeley. Choosing between radicchio or endive for a lunchtime salad is an anxiety-filled act of self-creation. **Telegraph Avenue** has more than its share of places to munch pizza, sip coffee, and lick frozen yogurt. The espresso is excellent but the food, with the exception of La Fiesta, is generally mediocre. For reasonably priced and tasty food, head downtown (Shattuck Ave.) or to Solano Ave.

Plearn Thai Cuisine, 2050 University Ave. (841-2148), between Shattuck and Milvia. Elegant decor. One of the best Thai places in the Bay Area. Long lines at peak hours. Entrees $5-8.50. Open Mon.-Sat. 11:30am-3pm and 5-10pm, Sun. 5-10pm.

Mario's La Fiesta, 2444 Telegraph Ave. (848-2588), at Haste St. Great Mexican food and a friendly atmosphere. Long lines. Huge entrees $3.50-6. Extremely filling lunch specials under $5. Open Mon.-Sat. 10:30am-10:30pm, Sun. 10:30am-10pm.

Yogurt Park, 2433 Durant Ave. (549-0570), 1 block west of Telegraph. 31 rotating flavors of fro yo. The best deal is the 2-flavor 65¢ minicup. Open daily 10am-midnight.

Manuel's, 2521 Durant (849-1529), near Telegraph Ave. A frat-jammed student hang-out with low prices and a juke box. Regular burrito fare ($3-4) with $3-4 pitchers of beer and $3 pitchers of margaritas when its liquor license is not suspended. Happy hour daily 3:30-5pm. Open Mon.-Thurs. 11am-midnight, Fri. 11am-2am, Sun. noon-midnight.

Flint's Barbecue, 6609 Shattuck Ave. (653-0593), in Oakland. Just over the city line, and worth the trip. Considered the best BBQ around. Service can be rude. Ribs $6.25. Open Mon.-Fri. 11am-2am, Sat.-Sun. 11am-4am.

The Blue Nile, 2525 Telegraph Ave. (540-6777). East African cuisine. Make sure you sit upstairs amid the leaves and windows so you can overlook the action on Telegraph. Food is served communally on a large platter, and you scoop up dollops with scraps of Ethiopian *injera* bread. Vegetarian entrees $5.25, others $5-6. Lunch specials $3.50-4 (served 11:30am-4pm). Open Mon.-Sat. 11am-10pm, Sun. 5-10pm.

Fat Apple's, 1346 Martin Luther King Dr. (526-2260), northwest of campus. Natural foods and hamburgers piled high with cheese and fixings ($5.50) make this a popular restaurant. Don't miss the fresh apple pie ($2), baked here daily, or the cream puffs. Open Mon.-Fri. 6am-11pm, Sat.-Sun. 7am-11pm.

Berkeley Fish, 1504 Shattuck (845-7166). Fresh take-out *sushi* in packages of 5 ($3.25) or 10 ($6.50). Open Mon.-Sat. 9am-6:30pm.

Café Fanny, 1603 San Pueblo (524-5447). This excellent stand-up café is owned and run by Alice Walters of Chez Panisse fame. Although the portions are small and prices somewhat high ($5-7), the food is wonderful. The open-faced sandwiches (about $5) are always interesting. Open Mon.-Sat. 7:30-5pm. Sunday brunch 9:30am-2:30pm.

Panini, 2115 Allston Way (849-0405), in the Trumpet Vine court. The best gourmet bargain around. Exotic sandwiches change daily. Some are hot, and all are delicous ($3.75-5). Tasty homemade soup $1.50. Open Mon.-Fri. 7:30am-5pm, Sat. 9am-4pm (food served 11am-2:30pm).

Caffe Mediterraneum, 2475 Telegraph Ave. (841-5630). Many great things have been thought here, few done. Also known as "Café Depresso". About a dollar for tea or cappuccino and an afternoon's lodgings. Try the hot almond milk (85¢). Daily food specials ($5) and soups ($1.50). Open Mon.-Fri. 7am-midnight, Sat.-Sun. 7:30am-midnight.

Espresso Strada, 2300 College Ave. (548-2384), at Bancroft. Philosophy and art grad students throng this glittering jewel of a culinary—intellectual complex. Get your cappucino cold when the sun's hot, and enjoy the beautiful outdoor terrace. Coffee 85¢-$1.25. Open Mon.-Fri. 7:30am-11pm, Sat.-Sun. 8:30am-11pm.

Sights

Pass through **Sather Gate** into **Sproul Plaza** and enter the university's world of gracious buildings, grass-covered hills, and sparkling streams that give the impression of an intellectual Arcadia. The **visitors information center,** in the Student Union Building (642-5215; open Mon.-Fri. 9am-5pm), sponsors walking tours of the campus weekdays at 1pm, or you can follow the self-guided tour (by pamphlet). The Berkeley campus swallows 160 acres, bounded on the south by Bancroft Way, on the west by Oxford St., by Hearst Ave. to the north, and by extensive parkland to the east. Founded in 1868 and moved to Berkeley in 1873, the school has an enrollment of over 30,000 and more than 1000 full professors. Imposing **Bancroft Library,** with nearly six million volumes, is among the nation's largest.

The most dramatic attraction is **Sather Tower,** the 1914 monument to Berkeley benefactor Jane K. Sather. For 50¢, you can ride to the top of the tower, known affectionately as the *Campanile* because it's modeled after the clock tower in Venice's St. Mark's Square. (open daily 10am-4:15pm). The tower's 61 bells are played manually most weekdays at 8am, noon, and 6pm.

The **University Art Museum,** 2626 Bancroft Way (642-1124; 24-hour events hotline 642-0808), holds a diverse and interesting permanent collection. Innovative directors have put together a number of memorable shows over the years on everything from cubism to the interaction of American painting and popular culture in the 50s. (Museum open Wed.-Sun. 11am-5pm. Admission $3; seniors, students and under 19 $1.)

The **Lawrence Hall of Science** (642-5132), standing above the northeast corner of the campus in a concrete building, shares honors with San Francisco's Exploratorium for finest science museum in the Bay Area. Take the free express shuttle from the BART station weekdays during museum hours. Exhibits stress learning science through hands-on use of everyday objects. (Open Fri.-Wed. 10am-4:30pm, Thurs. 10am-9pm. Admission $3.50; seniors, students, and ages 7-18 $2.50; ages under 7 free.)

Back in the campus center, the excellent **Lowie Museum of Anthropology** (642-3681) displays selections from its 500,000 catalogued items in Kroeber Hall. (Open Mon.-Tues. and Thurs.-Fri. 10am-4:30pm, Sat.-Sun. noon-4:30pm. Admission $1, seniors and under 16 35¢.) Also in Kroeber Hall is the **Worth Ryder Art Gallery** (642-2582) in Room 116. The gallery displays contemporary works of wildly varying quality by students and local artists. (Open Tues.-Thurs. 11am-4pm. Free.)

The Earth Sciences Building houses the **Museum of Paleontology,** the **Museum of Geology** and the **Berkeley Seismographic Station.** The paleontology division displays hundreds of fossils and dozens of skeletons, including an extremely-detailed exhibit on the evolution of the horse. The geology museum devotes its galleries to maps exploring the sedimentary structure of California and nearby states. The seismographic station is quiet unless there happens to be an earthquake. (Earth Sciences Building open Mon.-Fri. 8am-5pm, Sat.-Sun. 1-5pm. Free.)

Bancroft Library in the center of campus contains exhibits ranging from California arcana to folio editions of Shakespeare's plays. You can see the tattered bronze plaque left by Sir Francis Drake in the 16th century, vainly claiming California for England. A gold nugget purported to be the first one plucked from Sutter's Mill, the catalyst for the Gold Rush, is also displayed. Open to the public. (Open Mon.-Fri. 9am-5pm, Sat. 1-5pm. Free.)

The **Botanical Gardens** (642-3343) spread over 30 acres in Strawberry Canyon, contain over 10,000 species of plant life. (Open daily 9am-5pm. Free.) The **Berkeley Rose Garden** is on Euclid Ave. at Eunice St., north of the campus. Built by the WPA during the Depression, the garden spills from one terrace to another in a vast semi-circular amphitheater. You can see Marin County and the Golden Gate Bridge from the far end. While in bloom, from May through September, the gardens are always open.

The city itself is not devoid of its own museums and noteworthy architecture. The **Judah Magnes Museum,** 2911 Russell St. (849-2710), displays one of the West Coast's leading collection of Judaica. (Open Sun.-Fri. 10am-4pm.) The **Julia Morgan Theater,** 2640 College Ave. (548-7234), is housed in a beautiful former church designed by its namesake and constructed of dark redwood and Douglas fir.

People's Park on Haste St., 1 block off Telegraph Ave., is an unofficial museum of sorts, featuring a mural that depicts the 60s struggle between the city and local activists over whether to leave the meager block a park or to develop it commercially. During that struggle, then-governor Ronald Reagan sent in state police to break a blockade, resulting in the death of one student. In 1989, a rally was held to protest the university's renewed threats to convert the park. The demonstrators quickly forgot their noble purpose and began turning over cars, looting stores, and setting fires. The future of the area is still in question, and presently, crack dealers and the homeless have claimed this dismal site. Avoid it at night.

An off-beat experience can be had at the **Takara Sake Tasting Room,** 708 Addison St. (540-8250), at 4th St. You can request a sample of several varieties, all made with California rice. A narrated slide presentation on *sake* brewing is shown on request. (Open daily noon-6pm.)

Entertainment

Hang out with procrastinating students in front of or inside the **student union** (642-5215). The ticket office, arcade, bowling alleys, and pool tables are all run from a central desk. (Open Mon.-Fri. 8am-6pm, Sat. 10am-6pm; off-season Mon.-Fri. 8am-10pm, Sat. 10am-6pm.) The **Bear's Lair,** a student pub, is next door (486-0143). A pitcher of Bud goes for $3.50. (Open Mon.-Thurs. noon-midnight, Fri. 11am-8pm.) **CAL Performance,** 101 Zellerbach Hall (642-7477), is a university-wide concert and lecture organizer. Information on all the rock, classical, and jazz concerts, lectures, and movies on campus is available here. Big concerts are usually held in the Greek Theatre or Zellerbach Hall. (Open Mon.-Fri. 10am-5:30pm, Sat. noon-4pm.)

Berkeley is awash with **free publications** that explain where to go and what to do. Most reliable and interesting is *The Berkeley Monthly* (848-7900), a magazine with comprehensive listings. It's delivered free to local residents, but costs $1 on the stands (you may have to look around a bit). For more up-to-date news, the **Daily Californian** (548-8300), published by Berkeley students, prints information on university happenings. It's available in Sproul Plaza daily during the term, on Tuesday and Thursday in summer. The *Express* (642-4610) has a vast listings section and is widely available at book and record stores.

Ashkenaz, 1317 San Pablo Ave. (525-5054), between Gilman St. and Camelia. A folk-dance co-op that often swings with reggae bands. Children welcome. Cover depends on performer; usually $4-7. Open some afternoons and most evenings from 9:30pm-1am.

The Griffin, Virginia St. at Shattuck Ave. Lively jazz club popular with students. Top-line acts. Cover $3-5.

Brennan's, 4th St. and University Ave. (841-0960), down by the waterfront in nonstudent Berkeley. Cheap liquor and large crowds from every part of the city combine for the perfect Bacchanalian budget-obliteration. Steam tables at one end offer cheap food for the fearless. Great Irish coffee $2.25. Open Tues.-Sat. 11am-1am, Sun.-Mon. 11am-midnight. Food served until 9pm.

Starry Plough, 3101 Shattuck Ave. (841-2082). A pub with Irish bands and Anchor Steam on tap. Posters espouse the pro-Irish, anti-nuclear, and U.S.-out-of-Nicaragua points of view. Open daily 4pm-2am.

Larry Blake's Downstairs, 2367 Telegraph (848-0886), at Durant Ave., through the college's upstairs dining room and down a flight. An excellent drinking and meeting spot. Sawdust on the floor and live jazz. Drinks from $2. Cover $3-6. Bar open until 1am. Food served until midnight.

Bertola's, Telegraph Ave. and 41st St. (547-9301), in Oakland. The student's place to get smashed. Well drinks $1.50, double bourbons $1.75, triples $2. Open daily 4-10pm.

Triple Rock Brewery, 1920 Shattuck Ave. (843-2739). This micro-brewery produces 3 regular beers (2 pale ales and 1 porter) and occasional specialties. All are delicious, and a bargain at $2.25 per pint. Old beer logos grace the walls, and there's a roof garden. After 7pm, standing is all you can do in the crowded barroom, but in the afternoon, come to meet friendly noncollegiates who really enjoy their beer. Open daily 11:30am-1:30am.

Spats, Shattuck Ave. (841-7225), in the Gourmet Ghetto. Looks like your aunt's attic except for the taxidermy victims standing here and there. Have a drink on a ramshackle sofa amid parasols, and a sign reading "Bachelor Officers Quarters." Hors d'oeuvres served 2-7pm. 8-page drink menu (drinks from $1.75). Open Mon.-Sat. 11:30am-1am, Sun. 4pm-1am.

Marin County

The wealthiest county in the United States, Marin (pronounced ma-RIN) is also by some reports the most vapid. An unmistakably Californian conflation of hedonism and mysticism has produced a sort of New Age opulence; residents confer in hot tubs, worship crystals, consume macrobiotic food, and accumulate obscene heaps of wealth.

The undeveloped hills just to the west of the Golden Gate Bridge comprise the **Marin Headlands,** part of the Golden Gate National Recreation Area which sprawls across the Bay Area. The view from the Headlands back over the bridge to San Francisco is arguably the most spectacular vista in the Bay Area. The Headlands (and the viewpoints) are easily accessible by car; simply take the Alexander Ave. exit off US 101 and take your first left. You'll go through an underpass and up a hill on your right. You should consider hiking the ¾-mile trail which leads from the parking area down to the sheltered (and usually deserted) beach at **Kirby Cove.**

About 5 miles west along the Panoramic Hwy. off U.S. 101 is **Muir Woods National Monument,** a stand of primeval coastal redwoods. A loop road takes you through the most outstanding area. (Open daily 8am-sunset.) The visitors center (388-2595) is near the entrance and keeps the same hours as the monument. West of Muir Woods lies Muir Beach, which offers a tremendous view of San Francisco from its surrounding hills.

North of Muir Woods is the isolated, largely undiscovered, and utterly beautiful **Mount Tamalpais State Park.** The heavily forested park has a number of challenging trails that lead to the top of the peak, to a natural stone amphitheater, and to **Stinson Beach,** a local favorite for sunbathing. Park headquarters is at 810 Panoramic Hwy. (388-2070). The park opens a half-hour before sunrise and closes a half-hour before sunset.

Encompassing 100 miles of coastline along most of the western side of Marin, the **Point Reyes National Seashore** juts audaciously into the Pacific from the eastern end of the submerged Pacific Plate. Here is where the infamous San Andreas Fault comes to an end. The remote position of the point brings heavy fog and strong winds in winter, a special flora and fauna, and crowds of tourist to gawk at it all.

Limantour Beach, at the end of Limantour Rd., west of the seashore headquarters, and **McClures Beach,** at the extreme north of the seashore near the end of Pierce Point Rd., are two of the nicest beaches. Both have high, grassy dunes and long stretches of sandy beach. In summer a free shuttle bus runs to Limantour Beach from seashore headquarters. Strong ocean currents along the point make swimming suicidal. To reach the dramatic **Point Reyes Lighthouse** at the very tip of the point, follow Sir Francis Drake Blvd. to its end and then head right along the long stairway to Sea Lion overlook. From December to February, gray whales can occasionally be spotted off the coast from the overlook.

Marvelous Marin, to its credit, has managed to avoid the cheap motel plague that can ruin lovely areas overnight. The **Golden Gate Youth Hostel (AYH)** (331-2777), a few miles south of Sausalito, sits close to a waterbird sanctuary and houses 60 beds in an old, spacious building that is part of deserted Fort Barry. (Check-in 4:30-10pm. Curfew 11pm. $7 per person. Linen 50¢. Reservations recommended in summer. By car from San Francisco, take the Alexander Ave. exit off U.S. 101; take the second Sausalito exit if going toward San Francisco. Follow the signs into the Golden Gate National Recreation Area, then follow the hostel signs through the park about 3 miles to the hostel. Golden Gate Transit buses #2, 10, and 20 stop at Alexander Ave. From there, you'll have to hitch. A taxi from San Francisco costs $11-12.)

Farther north, the spectacularly situated **Point Reyes Hostel (AYH),** Limantour Rd. (663-881), is open nightly for groups and individuals. You're more likely to get a late-notice room here than in the Golden Gate Hostel, although reservations are advised on weekends. Hiking, wildlife, birdwatching, and Limantour Beach are all within walking distance. You need foresight to use the well-equipped kitchen; the nearest market is 8 miles away. (Registration 4:30-9pm. $7 per person. By car take the Seashore exit west from Rte. 1, then follow Bear Valley Rd. to Limantour, 6 miles from the hostel. For public transportation information, contact Golden Gate Transit (332-6600) or call the hostel.)

Campsites on Pt. Reyes are more plentiful than in more populated areas. The campground closest to Sausalito is in **Samuel Taylor State Park** (488-9897), on Sir Francis Drake Blvd. 15 miles west of San Rafael (itself 10 miles north of Sausalito on U.S. 101). The park has 65 sites ($10) with hot showers and is open year-round. Make reservations from April to September (800-444-7275, 1 week in advance). There are four campgrounds (accessible only by foot) on the national seashore in the south, inner cape portion of Pt. Reyes. All are fairly primitive, with pit toilets, firepits, and tap water; all require permits from the **Point Reyes National Seashore Headquarters,** Bear Valley Rd. (663-1092; open Mon.-Fri. 9am-5pm, Sat.-Sun. 8am-5pm). All camps command exquisite views of the ocean and surrounding hills.

The **Sausalito Chamber of Commerce** can be reached at 332-0505. **Point Reyes National Seashore Headquarters,** on Bear Valley Rd. (663-1092), ½ mile west of Olema, offers wilderness permits, maps, and campsite reservations. (Open Mon.-Fri. 9am-5pm, Sat.-Sun. 8am-5pm.) There is little public transportation in Marin. **Golden Gate Transit** (453-2100; 332-6600 in San Francisco) provides daily bus service between San Francisco and Marin County via the Golden Gate Bridge, as well as local service within the county. Buses #10, 20, 30 and 50 run from the Transbay Terminal at 1st and Mission St. in San Francisco (one way $1.85). The **Golden Gate**

Ferry (453-2100) serves Sausalito, departing from Pier 43½ for a 25-minute crossing (Mon.-Fri. 11:20am-4:50pm, Sat.-Sun. 10:55am-6:10pm; in winter the last ferry leaves at 4:50pm). Boats return from Sausalito roughly one hour later than departures. One way fare $5, off-season $3.

The **area code** is 415.

Northern California

Napa Valley

Napa Valley has long been the center of the American wine industry. Transplanted Europeans recognized the Dionysian virtues of this area (75 miles northeast of San Francisco) when California was still a part of Mexico. Prohibition, however, turned the vineyards into fig plantations, and only in the last 20 years have vintners recovered lost ground. Today, the wine-tasting carnival lasts from sunup to sundown, dominating the life of the valley's small towns.

Napa Valley is home to wine country's heavyweights; vineyards include national names such as Inglenook, Christian Brothers, and Mondavi. The large vineyards are good for neophytes since tours are well organized, and there's no pressure to spout obscure adjectives at the tastings. Once you've got a feel for things, head to the smaller wineries of Sonoma Valley (Kenwood and Château St. Jean are especially good) or Oregon to discuss vintages with the growers themselves.

There are more than 100 wineries in Napa County, and nearly two-thirds are in Napa Valley. Almost all give free tours and tastings. The vineyards listed below are some of the valley's larger operations. To reach the smaller places, pick up a list of vineyards from the chamber of commerce in Napa or look for signs along the roadside.

Robert Mondavi Winery, 7801 St. Helena Hwy. (963-9611), in Oakville. Spirited tour takes visitors through marvelous catacombs and past towering stacks of oaken barrels with mellowing wine. The best free tour and tasting for the completely unknowledgeable, and the wine itself is fairly decent. Open daily 9am-5pm; Nov.-April 10am-4:30pm. Reservations required—and they book up fast in summer.

Domaine Chandon, California Dr. (944-2280), next to the Veteran's Home in Yountville. One of the finest tours in the valley, which can be given in several languages by prior arrangement. Owned by Moët Chandon of France (makers of Dom Perignon), this company is best able to share the secrets of champagne making. Champagne tastings $1 per glass at the restaurant attached to the winery. Open daily 11am-6pm; Nov.-April Wed.-Sun. 11am-6pm.

RMS Vineyards, 1250 Cuttings Wharf Rd. (253-9055). For yet another different type of Napa alcohol, try this new and unique brandy distillery. Tours Mon.-Fri. at 10:30am and 2:30pm. Sales room open until 4pm.

Hanns Kornell Champagne Cellars, 1091 Larkmead Lane (963-2334), 4 miles north of St. Helena. A 1-room testing area with excellent dry champagne (try the Sehr Trocken). Entertaining, informative tours until 3:45pm. Open daily 10am-4pm.

Beaulieu Vineyard, 1960 St. Helena Hwy. (963-2411), in Rutherford. Tour includes a brief, imaginative audio-visual presentation. First tour at 11am, last tour at 3pm. Tasting daily 10am-4pm.

Clos Du Val Wine Company Ltd., 5330 Silverado Trail (252-6711), in Napa. An outdoor picnic area with whimsical drawings by Ronald Searle. Tours by appointment at 10am and 2pm. Tasting room open all day. Open daily 10am-4pm.

Budget motels are scarce and inaccessible to those without cars. Everpresent **Motel 6,** 3380 Solano Ave. (257-6111), in Napa at Redwood Rd., off Rte. 29, has rooms with TV and A/C; small pool. (Registration after 1pm, usually full by 6pm in summer. Check-out noon. Singles $31. Doubles $37.) The best deal in the valley may be the all-wood cabins at the **Triple S Ranch,** 4600 Mountain Home Ranch Rd. (942-6730), in Calistoga (take Rte. 29 north to Calistoga, turn left on Petrified Forest Rd., and then right on Mountain Home Ranch Rd. Registration 9am-6pm.

Singles $27. Doubles $35. Open April-Oct.) Campers can try the **Bothe-Napa Valley State Park,** 3601 St. Helena Hwy. (942-4575; 800-444-7275 for reservations), north of St. Helena on Rte. 29. (Open 8am-10:30pm; Oct.-April 9am-5pm. Sites with hot showers $10. Reservations recommended.)

Sit-down meals are often expensive here, but Napa and its neighboring communities support numerous delis where you can buy inexpensive picnic supplies. **The Diner,** 6476 Washington St. (944-2626), in Yountville, is a white-bread Mexican restaurant that serves huge, delicious dinners. It's off the beaten tourist track and cherished by locals. (*Chile relleno* with rice, beans, and salad $7. (Open Tues.-Sun. 8am-3pm and 5:30pm-closing.) Enormous portions are also the norm at **Barney's Rib House,** 2766 Old Sonoma Rd. (224-3465), with everything made on the premises. (Open daily 6am-2am.)

Route 29 runs through the middle of the valley with the main town of **Napa** at its southern end and **St. Helena** to the north. The best way to see the area is by bicycle since the valley is dead level and no more than 30 miles long. The **tourist information office,** 4076 Byway E. (257-1112), in Napa, recommends that bicyclists use the Silverado Trail rather than jammed Rte. 29, which it parallels. Rent a bike at **Napa Valley Cyclery,** 4080 Byway E. (255-3377), in Napa. ($4 per hr., $15 per day. Open Mon.-Sat. 9am-6pm, Sun. 10am-5pm. Major credit card required.) **Greyhound** stops in Napa, Yountville, St. Helena, and Calistoga. (Yountville office California Dr., 944-8377; open Mon.-Fri. 7am-5pm, Sat.-Sun. 7-11am and 1-5pm. Napa office 1620 Main St., 226-1856; open Mon.-Fri. 7:45am-noon and 1:15-6pm, Sat. 9:15-10:15am.)

The Napa **post office** is at 1625 Trancas St. (255-1621). (Open Mon.-Fri. 8:30am-5pm.) Napa's **ZIP code** is 94558; the **area code** in the valley is 707.

Redwood National Park

Redwood National Park flaunts an astonishing variety of flora and fauna. The park begins just south of the Oregon border and extends down the coast for almost 40 miles, encompassing three state parks. While the abundance of redwoods is spectacular, the park's attractions include far more than these 500-year-old mammoths with more rings than Liberace. The region is famous for its fishing, and the variegated terrain is ideal for hikers and backpackers. The lack of public transportation within the park, however, demands of the carless both perseverance and well-honed hitchhiking skills. Beaches line the coastal trail which marches most of the length of the park. Day use of state parks costs $3 per car.

Campsites are numerous and range from the well equipped (flush toilets and free hot showers; sites $10, hikers $1) to the primitive (outhouses at best; free). Peak season begins in the third week of June and concludes in early September. The ideal time to visit is mid-April to mid-June or September to mid-October, when the park is less crowded and is free of summer fog. Call MISTIX (800-444-7275) for reservations ($3.75; highly recommended in the peak season).

The most pleasant roost in this neck of the woods is the **Redwood Youth Hostel (AYH),** 14480 U.S. 101, Klamath 95548 (482-8265). This hostel, housed in the historic DeMartin House, features modern facilities and rugged coastal outlooks. Kitchen, dining room, and laundry facilities. Disabled access. (Family rooms available by reservation. $7, under 18 with parent $3.50. Linen $1.)

Practical Information

Visitor Information: Redwood Information Center (488-3461), 2 miles south of Orick on U.S. 101. **Orick Chamber of Commerce,** at the same station. Open June 21-Labor Day daily 8am-6pm; off-season 9am-5pm. **Prairie Creek Ranger Station,** on U.S. 101 (488-2171), in Prairie Creek State Park. Open daily 8am-5pm; mid-Sept. to mid-June hours subject to change. **Hiouchi Ranger Station,** on U.S. 199 (458-3134), in **Jedediah Smith Redwoods State Park.** Open daily 8am-7pm; Sept. 2-June 20 8am-5pm. **Redwood National Park Headquarters and Information Center,** 1111 2nd St., Crescent City 95531 (464-6101). Open daily 8am-7pm; Sept. 2-June 20 8am-5pm. **Crescent City Chamber of Commerce,** 1001 Front St. (464-3174), at J St. Open Mon.-Fri. 9am-5pm.

Park Activity Information: 464-6101. 24 hours.

Greyhound: 1125 Northcrest Dr. (464-2807), in Crescent City. Buses can supposedly be flagged down at 3 places within the park: Shoreline Deli (488-5761), 1 mile south of Orick on U.S. 101; Paul's Cannery in Klamath on U.S. 101; and the Redwood Hostel. Capricious bus drivers may decide to ignore you. Call the Greyhound station directly preceding your stop, and ask the attendant to alert the driver of your presence.

Local Transit: Del Norte Senior Center (464-3069) offers a very limited service connecting Klamath and Crescent City.

Post Office: 751 2nd St. (464-2151), in Crescent City. Open Mon.-Fri. 8:30am-5pm. **ZIP code:** 95531.

Area Code: 707.

The park divides naturally into five segments (Orick, Prairie Creek, Klamath, Crescent City, and Hiouchi) stacked from south to north along Rte. 101, each with its own ranger station. The scenery is extremely variegated, but always present are the imposing *Sequoia sempervirens.* The Orick region includes the southernmost section of the park. Its new **ranger station** lies about 2 miles south of Orick on U.S. 101 and 1 mile south of the Shoreline Deli (the Greyhound stop). The staff provides up-to-date information about the area. The main attraction is the **tall trees grove,** an 8-mile hike from the ranger station. In peak season, a shuttle bus (fare $3, seniors $1.50, children $1) runs three to five times per day from the station to the tall trees trail. From there, it's a rather strenuous 3-mile hike to the tallest known tree in the world (367.8 feet—bring a tape measure if you're skeptical). The same trail is accessible to backpackers, who may camp anywhere along the way after obtaining a permit at the ranger station.

Orick itself (population 400) is sleepy and uninteresting, overrun with souvenir stores selling "burl" (tacky, expensive wood carvings). Nevertheless, the town provides some amenities. Along U.S. 101 are a laundromat, a post office, the reasonably priced **Orick Market** (488-3225), and some motels. The market delivers groceries to Prairie Creek Campground daily at 7:30pm. Call in your order in before 6pm (minimum order $10; delivery free). Two miles north of Orick on U.S. 101 (Fern Canyon exit) lies the area's only gourmet restaurant, the **Prairie Creek Park Cafe** (488-3841; open Jan. to mid-Dec. daily 8am-8:30pm). The adventurous traveler may select dishes ranging from elk steak to wild boar roast, but prices are rather steep, with dinner entrees about $10.

The **Prairie Creek** Area, equipped with a ranger station and state park campgrounds, is perfect for hikers. The 10-mile **James Irvine Trail** winds through magnificent redwoods, around clear and cold creeks, through **Fern Canyon** (famed for its 50-foot fern walls and mossy bottom), and by a stretch of the Pacific Ocean. The trail starts at the Prairie Creek Visitors Center (see Practical Information). To the north, the **Klamath** Area comprises a thin stretch of park land connecting Prairie Creek with Del Norte State Park. The main attraction here besides the rugged coastline is the Klamath River, renowned for its salmon. (Fishing permit required.) There is no ranger station in this area. Check out the home cooking at the **Klamath Café** (482-7245), south of town.

Crescent City is worth a visit for refueling—but not much else. Seven miles south of the city lies the **Del Norte Coast Redwoods State Park,** an extension of the Redwood Forest. The park's magnificent ocean views—along with picnic areas, hiking trails, and nearby fishing—lure enough campers to keep the sites full during peak season. (RV and tent sites $6, day-use $2.) Crescent City itself, technically not part of the park, was largely destroyed by a 1964 *tsunami.* The town struck back, rebounding uglier than ever. South of the city, across the highway from the beach picnic area, the **Elk Captain Motel,** 100 Elk Valley Rd. (464-5313), provides the park's cheapest motel lodging. (Singles $18. Doubles $22.) The **Mexican Cafe** at 607 U.S. 101 N. (464-1422), serves Mexican dinners for about $7. (Open Mon.-Sat. 11am-8pm.)

The **Hiouchi** region sits in the northern part of the park inland along Rte. 199 and offers several excellent trails. The **Stout Grove Trail,** an easy ½-mile walk, boasts the park's widest redwood, 16 feet in diameter. The path is also accessible to the disabled; call 458-3310 for arrangements. **Kayak** trips on the Smith River leave from the ranger station.

Sacramento

Sacramento is so unexceptional, some say, that it is often used by market researchers to test new brands of soap. But the city turns a deaf ear to its maligners, confident that its several excellent museums and interesting historical sights, all nestled among leafy, quiet streets, will continue to attract a steady stream of visitors.

From a hobo-hangout in the 1960s, **Old Sacramento** has been restored as a tourist attraction with many up-market shops filling the original building shells. There's a pleasant atmosphere, and a number of historically interesting structures, including the **B.F. Hastings** building at the corner of 2nd and J. St. Dating from 1852, the building houses Wells Fargo's offices, a museum, and the reconstructed chambers of the California Supreme Court. Pick up a walking tour guide at the Old Sacramento Visitors Center, or join a tour beginning at the Center (322-3676) on weekends at 11:30am and 1:30pm.

Once you've had your fill of souvenir stores and cutesy-pie potpourri gift shops, try one or two of the excellent historical museums in Old Sacramento's northern end. The **California State Railroad Museum,** 111 I St. (448-4466), at 2nd St., open daily 10am-5pm, will delight even those who don't know the difference between a cowcatcher and a caboose. The museum houses a fascinating collection of historical locomotives in its over 100,000 square feet of exhibition space. The same ticket admits you to the **Central Pacific Depot and Passenger Station,** at 1st and J St., a reconstruction of a station that once stood here. (Open daily 10am-5pm. Admission $3, ages 6-17 $1.)

The **Sacramento History Center,** 101 I St. (449-2057), at Front St., does a fair job with lively, informative exhibits on California history set in a two-story glass-and-chrome extravaganza. Dazzle yourself with their collection of specimens from the '49 Gold Rush. (Open daily 10am-5pm. Guided tours at 11am and 2pm. Adults $2.50, ages over 64 $1.50, ages 6-17 $1.)

Especially good for inquisitive children of all ages, is the **Sacramento Science Center,** 3615 Auburn Blvd. (449-8255). The center has a good selection of "exploratory" exhibits, as well as a planetarium and an aviary. (Open Mon.-Fri. 9:30am-5pm, Sat.-Sun. noon-5pm. Admission $2.50, seniors $1.50, children $1.)

Art connoisseurs will enjoy popping into the small but elegant **Crocker Art Museum,** 216 O St. (449-5423), at 3rd St. The museum shows mainly 19th century European and American oil paintings, with one large gallery devoted to photography and another showcasing contemporary works by California artists. (Open Tues. 1-9pm, Wed.-Sun. 10am-5pm. Admission $2, seniors and ages 7-18 $1.)

The **state capitol,** at 10th St. and Capitol Mall (324-0333), in Capitol Park, was very nearly replaced by two twin modern towers in the 1970s, when the old and abused structure began to crumble. Fortunately, the generous Californian taxpayer forked out $68 million, and the building was finally restored in 1982 to its glorious 1906 finery: glorious pink and green decor, oak staircases, gilt, and all-too-flattering oil paintings of forgotten governors. The "Restoration" tour covers the chambers; the "Historic" delves into the re-created office spaces, decorated as they were decades ago. Both are free, last one hour, and are given daily 9am-4pm on the hour. Another tour explores the gardens, including the elaborate Vietnam Memorial (daily at 10am). For information and an excellent 10-minute free film, go to Room B-27 in the basement (324-0333). Self-guided walking tour brochures are also available there.

Before the arrival of a certain Ronald Reagan, who demanded more spacious surroundings, the **Old Governor's Mansion,** 16th and H St. (323-3047) fit the bill. This

15-room Victorian masterpiece (c. 1877) was home to 13 of California's governors. The building practically bursts with gables and attics, displaying the architectural subtlety of a three-tiered wedding cake. (Open daily 10am-5pm, ½-hr. tours on the hour. Last tour 4pm. Admission $1, ages under 18 50¢.)

Across town at 27th and L St., **Sutter's Fort** (445-4422) is a reconstruction of the 1839 military settlement that launched Sacramento. All supplies had to be dragged overland from the river to build the settlement, which now contains the **State Indian Museum** (349-0971). The Maiden Legend puppet show is given daily at 11:30am. Rangers fire the fort's cannon at 11am and 2pm. (Both open daily 10am-5pm. Admission to each $1, ages under 18 50¢.)

Those brave few who still resist the compact disc invasion will be rewarded by a trip to the original **Tower Records,** at the corner of Landpark Dr. and Broadway (444-3000). Tower started out with a small shelf of records in the back of his dad's drugstore in the '40s, and now owns a national chain of stores. The store's overwhelmingly large selection and late hours are replicated in the adjacent Tower Books, Drugs, Theater, Tobacco, *ad nauseum.* Prices have moved into the 90s, however. (Record store open 9am-midnight.)

The kid in you (or with you) will enjoy the **Sacramento Zoo,** 3930 W. Land Park Dr. (449-5885). If mere animals aren't enough, get off your tuffet and head for the zoo's **Fairytale Town,** a 6-acre theme park with puppet shows throughout the day. (Admission $2.50, seniors and ages 3-12 $1. Take bus #5 or 6 to William Land Park, 3 miles south of the capitol. Open daily 9am-5pm.)

Downtown Sacramento supports numerous breakfast and lunch spots; unfortunately, many close by 3 or 4pm. Once the government yuppies go home for the day, so do the restaurateurs. Old Sacramento is the place to go for ice cream, light snacks, and classier wining and dining. **Zelda's Original Gourmet Pizza,** 1415 21st St. (447-1400), has the best deep-dish pizza in Sacramento—ask any passerby. This dark, cool retreat from Sacramento's heat is some distance from the center of town. Medium cheese pizza $6. (Open Mon.-Thurs. 11:30am-2pm and 5-10pm, Fri. 11:30am-2pm and 5-11:30pm, Sat. 5-11:30pm, Sun. 5-9pm.) **Orpheum Cafe and Bar,** 1015 14th St. (448-3263), is veritably boffo. (Sandwiches and beer $5-6. Open Mon.-Fri. 11:30am-2pm.) In Old Sacramento, **Annabelle's,** 200 J St. (448-6239), next to the parking lot, has Italian food (and decor) that is about rendered worthwhile by the all-you-can-eat lunch buffet ($3.25), which includes pasta, lasagna, pizza, and salad bar. (Buffet served daily 11am-4pm.)

Sacramento has an extraordinary supply of motel rooms. However, if a large convention is taking place (and they are frequently), you'll find all but the sleaziest dives are fully booked by midweek; it's best to make advance reservations. The cheapest places lie near the Greyhound station across from Capitol Park. Several motels east of Capitol Park, along 15th and 16th St., also average $30 for singles. For even cheaper rates go to West Sacramento, a 10- to 30-minute walk along W. Capitol Ave. from Old Sacramento. Call the West Sacramento Motel & Hotel Association (372-5378 or 800-962-9800) or the West Sacramento Chamber of Commerce (372-5378; open 8am-5pm). Yolo buses #40, 41, or 42 go to West Sacramento from the L St. terminal.

The **Central Motel,** 818 16th St. (446-6006), next to the Governor's Mansion, has A/C and TV in the clean rooms. (Singles $25. Doubles $28.) **Capitol Park Hotel,** 1125 9th St. (441-5361), at L St., 2 blocks from Greyhound. Classy, cheap digs with large windows keeping them comfortably cool. (Singles $28. Doubles $35.) The **Americana Lodge,** 818 15th St. (444-3980), is the nicest in the range, featuring a small pool, A/C, TV. (Singles from $30. Doubles $37. Confirm reservations with advance payment.) **Gold Rush Home Hostel (AYH),** 1421 Tiverton Ave. (421-5954), on the outskirts of town, has a few beds.

Sacramento not coincidentally commands the center of the Sacramento Valley. No fewer than seven major highways converge on the city from all points of the compass. As in many other cities, each block represents one hundred numbers. These numbers also correspond to the lettered cross-streets, so 200 3rd St. intersects B St., 1700 C St. is on 17th St., 300 3rd St. intersects C, and so on. The capitol and endless state government buildings occupy the rectilinear **downtown** area. The **Broadway** area, home of the original Tower Records, lies beyond Z St. The 40 avenues north of Broadway, known as the "fabulous forty," contain the mansions of Sacramento's industrial barons. One was home to Ronald Reagan during his term as governor. **West Sacramento** lies, strangely enough, west of downtown, on the other side of the river.

The **Sacramento Convention and Visitors' Bureau,** 1421 K St. (442-5542), between 14th and 15th St. is small and congenial, with a tidy stand of brochures discreetly displayed on the corner table. The only accommodations guide is in the free "Sacramento" produced by the city. (Open 8am-5pm.) The **Old Sacramento Visitors Center,** 1104 Front St. (442-7544), also has a modest handful of brochures. The **Discover Sacramento Hotline** (449-5566) offers 24-hour recorded information on arts, sports, and special events.

Amtrak, at 4th and I St. (444-9131), has a huge terminal open daily 5:15am-11pm. Daily connections to Reno ($48.50), Chicago ($273), L.A. ($73), Seattle ($113), and San Francisco ($14.50). The **Greyhound** station is at 715 L St. (444-6800), between 7th and 8th St. It is relatively safe, though not in the most pleasant of neighborhoods. Buses to Reno (gambler's special round-trip weekdays $18, weekends $19; one-way $28.75), L.A. ($47), and San Francisco ($10). Open 24 hours. **Sacramento Regional Bus Transportation** (321-2877) offers bus service in downtown Sacramento Mon.-Fri. 6am-6pm; some lines run 6am-9pm. Saturday buses run later. (Fare 85¢. Express buses ($1) run Mon.-Fri. 6:30-9am and 3:30-6pm.) A trolley connects downtown with Old Sacramento via the I-5 underpass on K St. Mon.-Fri. 11am-4pm. The cheap fare (25¢) makes it worth hopping on, but don't wait around for it—the distance is walkable. An 18.3-mile **light rail** transit line connects the central business district with the eastern regions of the city. (Trains run every 15 min. from 6am-8:30pm. Fare 85¢.) The **Yolo Bus Commuter Lines** (371-2877) connect downtown with Old Sacramento, West Sacramento, Davis, and Woodland. (Fare 60¢, rush hour 75¢; 50¢ surcharge from Davis or Woodland into Sacramento or West Sacramento.)

The **post office** is at 2000 Royal Oak Dr. (921-0280; open Mon.-Fri. 8:30am-5pm. On weekends, holidays, and after 5pm, call 921-4564.) **General Delivery** mail can be picked up at Metro Station, 801 I St. (442-0764), at 8th. (Open Mon.-Fri. 8am-5pm.) The General Delivery ZIP Code is 95814. The **area code** is 916.

Whiskeytown-Shasta-Trinity National Recreation Area

Not quite park and not quite playground, the Whiskeytown-Shasta-Trinity National Recreation Area encompasses a huge expanse of forest and lakes. On weekend afternoons, Shasta Lake and Whiskeytown Lake are dotted with sailboats and crisscrossed by water-skiers. Trinity Lake to the north takes its natural heritage more seriously. It's set in unspoiled wilderness and ringed with dozens of hike-in campsites for nature enthusiasts, and there's a paucity of RV parks and superettes. The best place to go for information on the area is the **Shasta-Cascade Wonderland Association,** 1250 Parkview Ave. (243-2643), in Redding. (Open Mon.-Fri. 8am-noon and 1-5pm.) The **U.S. Forest Service** area headquarters are in Redding, at 2400 Washington St. (246-5222; open Mon.-Fri. 7:30am-4:30pm.)

Further north lies magnificent **Mount Shasta,** a mecca for mountain walkers and huggers alike. The snow-capped 14,162-foot dormant volcano can be seen from over 100 miles away. Climbers should seek advice from the **Shasta-Trinity National Forest Service Office,** 204 W. Alma St. (926-3781), or **5th Season,** 426 N. Shasta Blvd. (926-3606). Nearby **Black Butte** is a shorter but strenuous hike. The best place to stay is **Das Alpenhaus Motel,** 504 S. Mt. Shasta Blvd. (926-4617; singles from $19).

THE PACIFIC NORTHWEST

The drive of "manifest destiny" brought 19th-century pioneers to the Pacific Northwest, some of the most beautiful and awe-inspiring territory in the United States. Lush rainforests, snow-covered mountains, and the deepest lake on the continent all reside in this corner of the country. Oregon's Dunes, Washington's Cascades, miles and miles of the Pacific Crest Trail, and a long, stormy coast inhabited by giant redwoods and sequoias draw the mountaintop-born outdoorsperson and the adventurous city-slicker alike.

Settled amidst the wildlands of the Pacific Northwest are cities with all the urban flair of their northeastern counterparts. But unlike New York, Washington, DC, or Boston, the cosmopolitan cities of Seattle and Portland have mountain ranges at their back doors. The northwestern traveler can hike the Cascade Range by day and club-hop by night, ride Seattle's monorail or raft down wild river rapids.

For more comprehensive coverage of the Pacific Northwest than we can provide here, please consult *Let's Go: Pacific Northwest, Western Canada, & Alaska.*

Travel

The best strategy for getting to the Pacific Northwest by air is probably to fly by budget airline to San Francisco, and then travel by land. **Amtrak** can also take you from the East Coast or Midwest to Seattle. The "Pioneer" and the "Empire Builder" trains run from Chicago to Seattle along two different routes. The "Coast Starlight" train runs along the seashore, making stops at Seattle, Los Angeles, and numerous points in between.

Hitchhiking in the Pacific Northwest is generally safe and easy. The only place hitchers should avoid is Seattle. Hitching the coastal routes is made difficult only by summertime competition.

The accommodations in this region are terrific. **Hostels** throng Oregon's coast, Willamette Valley, Washington's Puget Sound, and most are well established and seldom full. Inexpensive **bed & breakfasts** are multiplying in the area.

Outdoors

In the Northwest, the coastal region remains cool and misty year-round. The densely populated central valleys enjoy a mild climate, with warm summers and rainy winters. The Cascade Range keeps moisture and cool air from reaching eastern Washington and Oregon, where the arid climate resembles that of the Rocky Mountain states.

In addition to camping and hiking, a variety of unusual activities invite you to explore the Coast. Whitewater rafting is a huge business in the Pacific Northwest, offering the adventurous a chance to view areas otherwise inaccessible. Canoeing and kayaking are two other perenially popular water sports. Mountain schools at Mt. Rainier and elsewhere offer instruction in rock-climbing and mountaineering. The Pacific Crest Trail stretches from the Mexico/California border all the way into Canada. This rugged, challenging trail is particularly attractive for one- or two-week hiking trips.

For information on national parks, contact the **Pacific Northwest Regional Office,** National Park Service, 2001 6th Ave., Seattle, WA 98121 (206-442-0170). The national forest system manages huge expanses of land, including the West Coast's least spoiled natural landscapes, the designated wilderness areas. Reach the **Pacific Northwest Region** at U.S. Forest Service, P.O. Box 3723, Portland, OR 97212. State parks are rarely booked up even on popular summer weekends. Sites are about $8. All along the West Coast, state parks and forests, especially those by the ocean, offer hiker/biker campsites, where those on two feet or two wheels can camp for 50¢.

Oregon

Although their shoreline, inland forests, and parks share all the lush drama of those in California, Oregon residents for years disdained the gaggles of tourists that overran their southern neighbor. They could afford to be protective of their solitude. The 1980s brought hard times for Oregonians, however, and with them a reconsideration of this once-widespread disdain. Bumper stickers that read "Don't Californicate Oregon" and "SNOBS" (Society of Native Oregonian Born) have disappeared, replaced by giant "welcome" signs in every backwater town. Cities that once thrived on Oregon's now dwindling mining and foresting industries are resurrecting themselves as tourist towns.

But tourism is by no means new to the state. Lewis and Clark slipped quietly down the Columbia River when their transcontinental trek brought them to Oregon; later, waves of settlers surged along the Oregon Trail. Today the best-worn corridor of travel is the coastal route along U.S. 101, a narrow strip of roadway clinging to the shore. You will, however, have to venture off the highway to reach many of Oregon's natural glories.

Practical Information

Capital: Salem.

Time Zone: Pacific (3 hr. behind Eastern) and Mountain (2 hr. behind Eastern). **Postal Abbreviation:** OR.

Tourist Information: State Tourist Office, 595 Cottage St. NE, Salem 97310 (800-547-7842). **Oregon State Parks,** 525 Trade St. SE, Salem 97310 (378-6305). **Department of Fish and Wildlife,** 506 SW Mill St., Portland 97208 (229-5403). **Oregon Council American Youth Hostels,** 99 W. 10th St., #205, Eugene 97402 (683-3685).

Portland

Nature keeps a watchful eye over Portland, as if the city's presence were only uneasily tolerated in Oregon's glorious wilderness. Mammoth Mt. Hood guards the eastern reaches of the city. The Willamette and Columbia Rivers encircle it and every so often an army of thunder clouds rumbles into town, just to keep everyone honest.

The people of Portland make full use of their natural surroundings. Fanatic runners, hikers, and windsurfers, Portlanders are as concerned about their personal health as they are about the health of the environment. They are proud of their casual, almost neo-hippie lifestyle: birkenstocks and bran are in, beluga and BMWs are out. Portlanders are also renowned for their sense of humor. Current Mayor Bud Clark posed for the notorious "Expose yourself to Art" poster, depicting a man in a trenchcoat flashing a public sculpture.

Practical Information

Emergency: 911.

Visitor Information: Portland/Oregon Visitors Association, 26 SW Salmon St. (275-9750), at Front St. Their free *Portland Book* contains maps, general information, and historical trivia. Open Mon.-Fri. 8:30am-5pm, Sat. 10am-3pm.

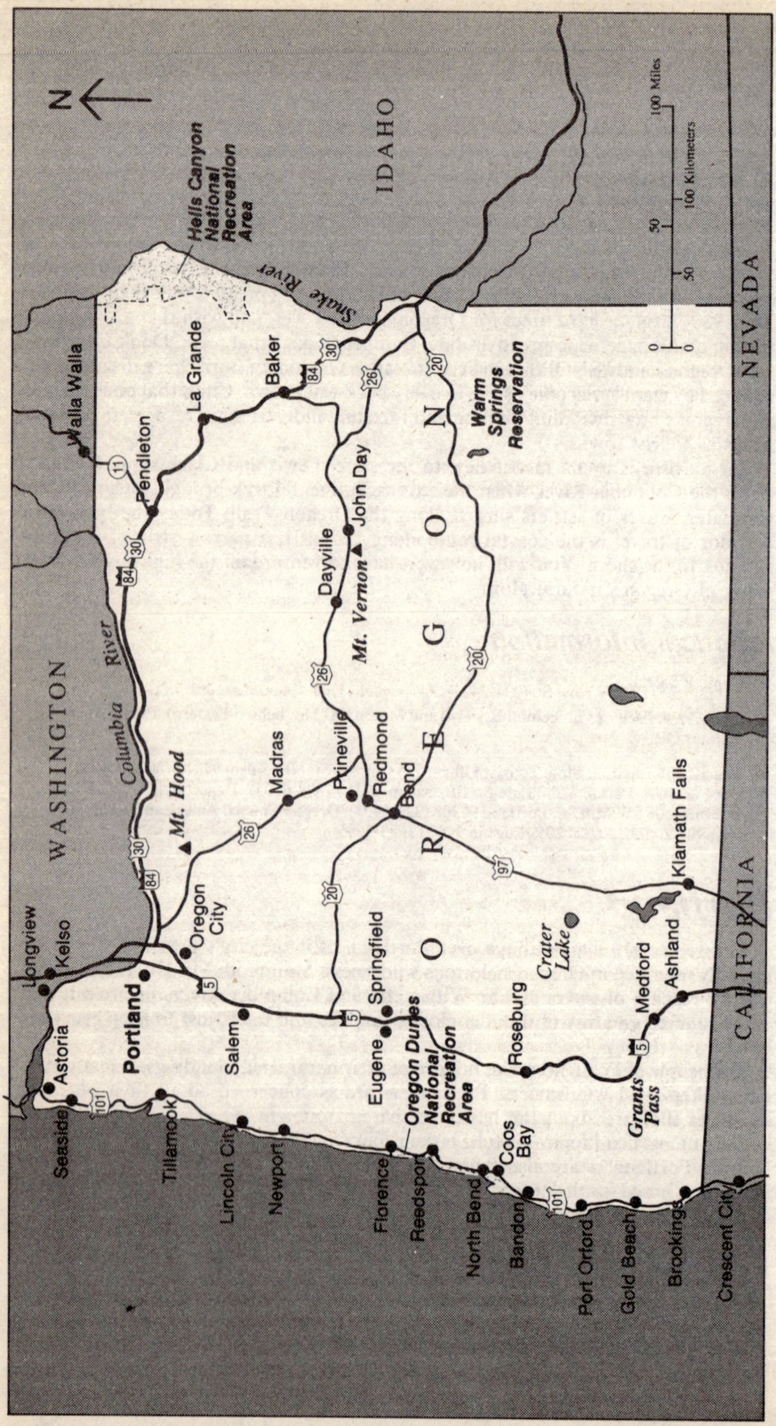
N
WASHINGTON
IDAHO
NEVADA
CALIFORNIA
OREGON
Columbia River
Snake River
Hells Canyon National Recreation Area
Warm Springs Reservation
Oregon Dunes National Recreation Area
Mt. Hood
Mt. Vernon
Crater Lake
Longview
Kelso
Astoria
Seaside
Portland
Tillamook
Lincoln City
Newport
Salem
Oregon City
Florence
Reedsport
Eugene
Springfield
North Bend
Coos Bay
Bandon
Port Orford
Gold Beach
Brookings
Crescent City
Roseburg
Grants Pass
Medford
Ashland
Klamath Falls
Bend
Redmond
Prineville
Madras
Dayville
John Day
Baker
La Grande
Pendleton
Walla Walla
101
5
84
30
26
20
97
11
0 50 100 Miles
0 50 100 Kilometers

Airport: Portland International Airport, north of the city on the banks of the Columbia. Served by Hwy. 205. To get downtown, take Tri-Met bus #12, which will arrive on SW 5th Ave. (fare 85¢). **Rad Tranz** (recorded information 246-4676) provides an airport shuttle that leaves every 20 min. and takes 35 min. to reach major downtown hotels and the Greyhound station. (Fare $5, under 12 $1.)

Amtrak: 800 NW 6th Ave. (241-4290), at Hoyt St. Open daily 7:30am-5:30pm.

Greyhound/Trailways: 550 NW 6th St. (243-2323; recorded information 243-2313). Buses almost every hr. to Seattle ($24). Ticket window open daily 5:30am-12:30am.

Green Tortoise (225-0310). To: Seattle (Tues., Sat. at 4pm, $15) and San Francisco (Sun., Thurs. at 12:30pm, $49).

City Buses: Tri-Met, Customer Service Center, #1 Pioneer Courthouse Sq., 701 SW 6th Ave. (24-hr. recorded information; 233-3511). Bus routes are grouped into seven regional service areas, each with its own color totem. A few buses with black and white totems cross color-coded boundaries. The crux of the bus system is the **mall,** with covered bus stops and information centers. Fare 85¢-$1.15. All rides are free within *fareless square,* bounded by the Willamette River, NW Hoyt St., and I-405. Center open Mon.-Fri. 9am-5pm. Service generally 7am-midnight, reduced Sat.-Sun. **MAX** is Tri-Met's light rail system. It only serves one line (running between downtown and the city of Gresham), but uses the same fare system as the buses.

Taxi: Broadway Cab (227-1234). **New Rose City Cab Co.** (282-7707). Both charge $1.30 for the first mile, $1.40 each additional mile.

Car Rental: Rent-A-Wreck, 2838 NE Sandy St. (231-1640). $14 per day. 50 free miles, 15¢ each additional mile. Must be 25. **Budget,** 2033 SW 4th St. (222-9123), and at the airport (249-4550). $46 per day, unlimited mileage. Must be 21.

Help Lines: Crisis Line, 223-6161. **Rape Hotline,** 235-5333. Both 24 hours. **Senior Citizens Crisis Line,** 223-6161. **Gay and Lesbian Services,** 223-8299.

Time Zone: Pacific (3 hr. behind Eastern).

Post Office: 715 NW Hoyt St. (294-2424). **ZIP Code:** 97208. Open Mon.-Fri. 7:30am-6:30pm, Sat. 8:30am-5pm.

Area Code: 503.

Portland sits just south of the Columbia River about 75 miles inland from the Oregon coast. The city is 637 miles north of San Francisco and 172 miles south of Seattle. The primary east-west highway, I-84 (U.S. 30), follows the route of the Oregon Trail through the Columbia River Gorge. West of Portland, U.S. 30 follows the Columbia downstream to Astoria. I-405 curves around the west side of the business district to link I-5 with U.S. 30.

Portland can be divided into five districts. **Burnside Street** divides the city into north and south, while east and west are separated by the Willamette River. **Williams Avenue** slices off a corner of the northeast sector, which is called simply "North." The **Southwest district** is the city's hub, encompassing the downtown area, historical Old Town in the northern end, and a slice of ritzy West Hills. The very core of the hub is the downtown mall area between SW 5th and 6th Avenues. Car traffic is prohibited here; this is the transit system's turf. The **Northwest district** contains the southern end of Old Town, warehouses to the north, and a residential area, culminating in the posh Northwestern hills area to the west. Most students enrolled in Portland's several colleges and universities live in the Northwest. The **Southeast district** is a poorer neighborhood. Anomalous amidst its poorer surroundings, **Laurelhurst Park** is a collection of posh houses around E. Burnside Street and SE 39th Street. The **North** and **Northeast** districts are chiefly residential, punctuated by a few quiet, small parks, but are becoming increasingly commercial.

Accommodations and Camping

With Portland's increasing gentrification, finding cheap lodgings is becoming more and more challenging. **Northwest Bed and Breakfast,** 610 SW Broadway, Portland 97205 (243-7616), has an extensive listing of member homes in the Portland area and throughout the Northwest. You must become a member for $25 per year to use their lists and reservation services. They promise singles from $25-40 and doubles from $30-60.

The few remaining cheap hotels downtown are somewhat dingy and primitive, but are generally good deals nonetheless. Parts of Oldtown can be fairly sleazy and occasionally dangerous at night. Southwest of the city, several motels offer a few more conveniences for a few more dollars; you can also opt for the selection on N. Interstate Ave., where the respectable motels placidly cohabitate with pay-by-the hour establishments.

Campers can call the **Oregon State Parks Campsite Info Line** at 238-7488.

Portland International AYH Hostel (AYH), 3031 SE Hawthorne Blvd. (236-3380), at 31st Ave. Take bus #5. Cheerful, clean, and crowded. Sleep inside or on the porch. Kitchen facilities; laundromat across the street. Open 8-9:30am and 5-11pm. $8.75, nonmembers $11.75. Reserve in summer.

Youth Hostel Portland International, 1024 SW 3rd St. (241-2513). Not as inviting, but more vacancies. Laundromat. Open 24 hours. $8.75, nonmembers $13-18; with private bath $18. Key deposit $5.

YWCA, 1111 SW 10th St. (223-6281). Women only. Close to major sights, clean, and safe. Small rooms. Shared double $8.72, single $17.44, with bath $20.71.

The Unicorn Inn Motel, 3040 SE 82nd (774-1176), off I-205 at exit 19. A clean and beautiful (albeit obscure) hotel with cable, A/C, and pool. Rooms from $25. Senior citizen discount.

Bel D'air Motel, 8355 N. Interstate Ave. (289-4800), just off I-5. Take bus #5 from SW 6th Ave. Its name is a bit pretentious, but its decor is certainly not. Very small, so call a week in advance. Singles $25. Doubles $31.

Aladdin Motor Inn, 8905 SW 30th at Barbur Blvd. (246-8241), about 10 min. from downtown by bus #12 from SW 5th Ave. Clean and comfortable. A/C and kitchens available. Singles $32.70. Doubles $35.

Mel's Motor Inn, 5205 N. Interstate Ave. (285-2556). Take bus #5 from 6th Ave. No aspirations to elegance, but clean and comfortable with A/C and cable TV. Singles $26. Doubles $30.50.

Ainsworth State Park, 37 miles east of Portland on I-84, up the Columbia River Gorge. Hot showers, flush toilets, and hiking trails along the gorge. Sites $8, with electicity $9, with full hook up $10.

Milo McIver State Park, 25 miles southwest of Portland, off Oregon Rte. 211, 5 miles west of the town of Estacada. Fish, boat, and bicycle along the nearby Clackamas River. Hot showers and flush toilets. Sites $8, with electricity $9, with full hookup $10.

Jack London Hotel, 415 SW Alder St. (228-4303) downtown. Ask the management to discuss *Call of the Wild* and they'll look at you as if you were insane. Not particularly clean, and few female tenants. Singles $14.17, $19.62 with bath. Doubles $17, $21.80 with bath. Key deposit $5.

Food

Some of the best fresh produce in town is available at the **Corno Foods,** 711 SE Union St., under the Morrison Bridge (232-3157), a labyrinthine market whose offerings consist mainly of fruits and veggies.

The Original Pancake House, 8600 SW Barbur Blvd. (246-9007). Take green bus #12, 41, or 43. Great place for breakfast ($3.50-5). Hour-long lines on Sat. and Sun. morning. Open Wed.-Sun. 7am-3pm.

Escape from New York Pizza, 913 SW Alder St. (226-4129). The best pizza in town. Tiny and crowded. Cheese slices $1. Medium cheese pie $5.80 plus $1 per additional topping. Large from $7.75. Open Mon.-Thurs. 11:30am-9pm, Fri.-Sat. 11:30am-11pm. Also at 622 NW 23rd St. (227-5423).

Chang's Mongolian Grill, 1 SW 3rd St. (243-1991) at Burnside. Also at 2700 NW 185th (645-7718) and 1600 NE 122nd (253-3535). All-you-can-eat lunches ($5.50) and dinners ($7.50). You select your meal from a buffet (fresh vegetables, meats, and fish), mix your own sauce to taste, and then watch your chef make a wild show of cooking it on a grill the size of a Volkswagen. Rice and hot-and-sour soup included. Open daily 11:30am-2:30pm and 5-10pm.

Foothill Broiler, 33 NW 23rd Place, in Uptown Shopping Center (223-0287), take bus #20 up Burnside. Fantastic homemade food served by energetic, pseudo-hippie staff. The utter lack of macrame has to be seen to be appreciated. Best burgers in the Northwest from $2. Come off-hours or be prepared to wait. Open Mon.-Fri. 7:30am-7pm, Sat. 7:30am-4pm.

Macheesmo Mouse, 715 SW Salmon St. (228-3491). Fast, authentic Mexican food for the health-conscious, in a setting that is part Hard Rock Café, part Pompidou Center. The $2.65 veggie burrito stands out. Open Mon.-Sat. 11am-10pm, Sun. noon-9pm. Locations also at 811 NW 23rd St. (274-0500), 3553 SE Hawthorne Blvd. (232-6588; 5 blocks from the AYH hostel), and 1200 NE Broadway (249-0002).

Hamburger Mary's, 840 SW Park St. (223-0900) at SW Taylor St. Good food near the museums and theaters, with a relaxed atmosphere and eclectic decor: floor lamps hang upside down from the ceiling. As popular with straights as it is with gays (its original and most faithful clientele). Burgers with everything and fries $4.80. Plenty of vegetarian fare. Open daily 7am-midnight.

Rose's Deli, 315 NW 23rd Ave. (227-5181), at Everett St. Take bus #53. Rose has her own cookbook now, but the fame hasn't corrupted her cooking. She still serves up the city's best bagels in a noisy and crowded atmosphere. Great matzoh-ball soup ($2), cheese blintzes, and a pastry case that is fattening by osmosis. Lunches $5-6.50. Open Mon.-Thurs. 7am-11pm, Fri. 7am-midnight, Sat. 8am-midnight, Sun. 8am-11pm.

Jarra's Ethiopian Restaurant, 617 SE Morrison St. (230-8990). Take bus #15. Authentic and hot cuisine served by a friendly staff. Eat with your fingers here, using spongy pancakes served on side plates to scoop up mouthfuls. *Doro wat* (chicken in a hot sauce) $6.50. Open Mon.-Tues. 5-10pm, Wed. 11:30am-2pm and 5-10pm, Thurs.-Fri. 5-10pm, Sat. 4-10pm.

Sights

Portland can be exciting any time of year, but try to avoid the rains of fall, winter, and spring. Visit instead during the summer, when you can take advantage of the temperate weather and many free cultural events. This is also the best season in which to appreciate Portland's fountains, all of which seem to have long, intricate histories. Those with the best known biographies include the 20 bronze drinking fountains located on strategic street corners throughout Portland. These were donated to the city by Simon Benson, a wealthy Prohibition-era Portlander, ostensibly to ease the thirst of native loggers. **Benson Memorial Fountains** can be recognized by their four-spigoted heads and pump cold "Bull Run" spring water, one of Portland's greatest natural assets. Other objets d'art dot the downtown area, the product of a city law requiring that one percent of the costs of all construction and renovation work be devoted to public art projects.

Almost all the major sights are grouped **downtown** in the southwest district. Portland's downtown area is centered on the **mall,** running north-south between 5th and 6th Ave. and closed to all traffic except city buses. The **Pioneer Courthouse** sits at 5th Ave. and Morrison St., the tribal elder of downtown landmarks. The monument now houses the U.S. Ninth Circuit Court of Appeals and is the centerpiece of **Pioneer Courthouse Square,** 701 SW 6th Ave. (223-1613), opened in 1983. Forty-eight thousand citizens supported its construction by sponsoring personalized bricks, and it seems as though all 48,000 make a daily pilgrimage to visit their gift to the city. Live jazz, folk and ethnic music draws the rest of Portland to the square for the **PB and Jam Sessions,** held every Tues. and Thurs. from noon-1pm.

Certainly the most controversial building in the downtown area is Michael Graves's postmodern **Portland Building,** which is also on the mall. This amazing confection of pastel tile and concrete has been both praised to the stars and condemned as an overgrown jukebox. Make sure to visit the interior as well, which looks like something out of *Blade Runner.* The **Standard Insurance Center,** 900 SW 5th Ave., nearby, has also engendered controversy for the white marble sculpture out front, "The Quest," in which the quest is done *au naturel.* The sculpture is more commonly known to locals as "three groins in the fountain."

West of the mall are the **South Park Blocks,** a series of shady, rose-laden enclosures running down the middle of Park Ave. Facing the parks, the **Portland Art Museum,** 1219 SW Park Ave. (226-2811), at Jefferson St., has an especially fine exhibit of Pacific Northwest Native American art, including masks, textiles, and sacred objects. International exhibits and local artists' works are interspersed. (Open Tues.-Fri. 11am-7pm, Sat.-Sun. noon-5pm. Admission $3, seniors and students $1.50, Thurs. 5-9:30pm free.) The **Northwest Film and Video Center** (221-1156), in the same building, screens classics and off-beat flicks.

Old Town, to the north of the mall, was filled a century ago with rowdy sailors who docked in the ports from which the city takes its name. The district has been revived with large-scale refurbishment of store fronts, and the opening of a bevy of shops and restaurants. A popular people-watching vantage point, the **Skidmore Fountain,** at SW 1st Ave. and SW Ankeny St., marks the entrance to the quarter. Had the city accepted resident draftsman Henry Weinhard's offer to run draft beer through the fountain, it would have been a truly cordial watering hole indeed. Old Town marks the start of **Waterfront Park,** an enormous expanse of grass and flowers that offers little shade but provides great views of the Willamette River.

From March until Christmas, the area under the Burnside Bridge is given over to the **Saturday Market** (222-6072), 108 W. Burnside St. Saturdays from 10am to 5pm and Sundays from 11am to 4:30pm, the area is filled with street musicians, artists, craftspeople, chefs, and produce sellers.

Portland's finest galleries are centered downtown. The **Image Gallery,** 1026 SW Morrison St. (224-9629), presents an international potpourri of Canadian Eskimo sculpture and Mexican and Japanese folk art. (Open Mon.-Fri. 10:30am-6pm, Sat. 11am-5pm.)

Less than 2 miles west of downtown, in the posh **West Hills, Washington Park** is crisscrossed with looping trails for day hiking, running, and picnic-laden expeditions. Obtain trail maps at the information stand near the parking lot of the arboretum, or refer to the maps posted on the windows. **Hoyt Arboretum,** 4000 SW Fairview Blvd. (228-8732), at the crest of the hill above the other gardens, features a large collection of conifers and 10 miles of trails. (Free nature walks Apr.-Oct. on Sat. and Sun. at 2pm, and June-Aug. on Tues. at 9:30am.) The five-acre **Japanese Garden** (223-1321) is a formal arrangement of idyllic ponds and bridges; ask to see the "Sand and Stone Garden." Cherry blossoms ornament the park in summer, thanks to sibling city Sapporo, Japan. (Open daily 10am-6pm; Sept. 16-April 14 daily 10am-4pm. Admission $3.50, over 62 and under 12 $2.) Roses galore and spectacular views of the city await a few steps away at the **International Rose Test Garden,** 400 SW Kingston St. (248-4302).

Below the Hoyt Arboretum lies Portland's favorite tourist-attracting triad: the **Washington Park Zoo,** 4001 SW Canyon Rd. (226-1561; recorded message 226-7627; open daily 9:30am-7pm; call for winter hours; admission $3, seniors and children $1.50, Tues. after 3pm free); the **World Forestry Center,** 4033 SW Canyon Rd. (228-1367; open daily 10am-5pm; admission $3, seniors and children $2); and the **Oregon Museum of Science and Industry,** (better known as **OMSI**), 4015 SW Canyon Rd. (228-6674; open Sun.-Thurs. 9am-7pm, Fri. 9am-8pm; admission $5, seniors and under 17 $3.50). The #63 "zoo" bus connects the park with Morrison St. in the downtown mall, and a miniature railway also connects the Washington Park gardens with the zoo (fare $1.75). Beginning in late June, the zoo sponsors **Your Zoo and All That Jazz,** a nine-week series of open-air jazz concerts (Wed. 6:30-8:30pm), free with regular zoo admission. Bring a picnic dinner. **Zoograss Concerts** features a 10-week series of bluegrass concerts (Thurs. 6:30-8:30pm). The World Forestry Center specializes in exhibits of Northwestern forestry and logging, but is now trying to broaden its scope. OMSI will keep children and adults occupied with a plethora of do-it-yourself science, computer, and medical exhibits. The **Kendall Planeterium** (228-7827) within gives daily shows (50¢) and also puts on laser rock shows most evenings (schedule of shows 242-0723; admission $4.50). **Terra One,** an experimental solar-heated residence operated by OMSI, teaches principles of energy conservation. (Open Mon.-Fri. 9am-5pm, Sat.-Sun. noon-5pm. Free.) The new and tastefully done **Vietnam Memorial** is a few steps up the hill. From Washington Park, you have easy access to sprawling **Forest Park,** filled with hiking trails and picnic areas with spectacular views of Portland.

Southeast Portland, largely a residential district, nourishes an enclave of progressive politics at **Reed College,** SE 28th and Woodstock, a small liberal arts school founded in 1909. Reed sponsors numerous cultural events and in 1968 became the first undergraduate college to open a nuclear reactor. Tours of the campus leave Eliot Hall twice per day during the school year. (Call 771-7511 for hours.)

Farther southeast is **Mt. Tabor Park,** the only city park in the world on the site of an extinct volcano. More of a molehill than a mountain, the volcano is easily eclipsed by Mt. Tabor itself. Take bus #15 from downtown, or drive down Hawthorne to SE 60th Ave.

Entertainment

Portland is no longer the hard-drinking, carousing port town it once was. A newer, more sophisticated brand of entertainment now exist. The best sources of current listings are the Friday edition of the 35¢ *Daily Oregonian* and a number of free handouts: *Willamette Week, Multnomah Monthly,* the *Main Event, Clinton St. Quarterly,* and the *Downtowner.* The first of these caters to students, the last to the upwardly mobile. Each is available in restaurants downtown and in boxes on street corners.

The **Oregon Symphony Orchestra** plays in Arlene Schnitzer Concert Hall at the Portland Center for the Performing Arts, on the corner of SW Broadway and SW Main St. (228-1353). (Tickets $9-28. "Symphony Sunday" afternoon concerts $5-8. Performances Sept.-April.) **Chamber Music Northwest** performs summer concerts at Reed College Commons, 3203 SE Woodstock Ave. (223-3202). (Classical music Mon., Thurs., and Sat. at 8pm. Admission $13, under 15 $9.)

Portland's many fine theaters produce everything from off-Broadway shows to experimental drama. At

Portland Civic Theatre, 1530 SW Yamhill St. (226-3048), the mainstage often presents musical comedy, while the smaller theatre-in-the-round puts on less traditional shows. Tickets around $10. **Oregon Shakespeare Festival/ Portland,** at the Intermediate Theatre of PCPA, corner of SW Broadway and SW Main St. (248-6309), has a five-play season running Nov.-Feb. **New Rose Theatre,** 904 SW Main St. in the Park Blocks (222-2487), offers an even mix of classical and contemporary shows (tickets $9-14).

The best clubs in Portland are not the easiest ones to find. Neighborhood taverns and pubs often can be tucked away on backroads. Flyers advertising upcoming shows are always plastered on telephone poles around town. Those with happy feet should bop down the length of 6th Ave. to find most of the dancing clubs. The under-21 crowd ought to head for the **Confetti Club,** 126 SW 2nd St.(274-0627), for new wave music, or the **Warehouse,** 320 SE 2nd St. (232-9645), for top-40 tunes. At the **Produce Row Cafe,** 204 SE Oak St. (232-8355), they have 21 beers on tap ($1), 72 bottled domestic and imported beers (ranging in origin from China to Belgium), and a lovely outdoor beer garden. (Open Mon.-Fri. 11am-1am, Sat. noon-1am, Sun. 2pm-midnight.) The **Mission Theater and Pub,** 1624 NW Glisan St. (223-4031), serves excellent home-brewed ales as well as delicious and unusual sandwiches. Relax in the balcony of this old moviehouse with a pitcher of Ruby, a fragrant raspberry ale ($1.25 glass, $6.50 pitcher). (Open daily 5pm-1am.) **Key Largo,** 31 NW 1st Ave. (223-9919), has an airy, tropical atmosphere. Dance to rock, R & B, or jazz on the patio when it's not raining. (Cover $2-8. Open Mon.-Fri. 11am-2:30am, Sat.-Sun. noon-2:30am.) **The Goose Hollow Inn,** 1927 SW Jefferson (228-7010; bus #57 or 59), always a popular neighborhood tavern, is currently wall-to-wall with aspiring progressive politicos. (Sandwiches $3-6.50. Open daily 11:30am-1am.) **Brasserie Montmartre,** 626 SW Park (224-5552), is a high-class joint with live jazz every night. (Lunch $7, dinner $10. Open Mon.-Fri. 11:30am-2:30pm, Sat. 5:30-10pm.)

During the **Rose Festival** (first 3 weeks of June), the city bedecks itself in all its finery. Waterfront concerts, art festivals, parades, lots of Navy ships, and Native American pow-wows take center stage. (Call 248-7923 for general information, 227-2681 for the offices.)

Oregon Coast

The so-called "Pacific" hurls itself at the Oregon Coast with abandon, amidst impressive explosions of spray. Only the most daring swim in this ice-cold surf; others are more than satisfied by the matchless views and huge stretches of unspoiled beach.

Possessively hugging the shore, **U.S. 101,** the renowned coastal highway, is edged by a series of high-perched viewpoints. From northernmost Astoria to Brookings in the south, it laces together the resorts and historic fishing villages clustered around the mouths of rivers feeding into the Pacific. It is most beautiful between the coastal towns, where hundreds of miles of state and national park allow direct access to the beach. Whenever the highway leaves the coast, look for a beach loop road. These are the quieter ways, the "roads less traveled," which afford some of the finest scenery on the western seaboard.

Drive or bike for the best encounter with the coast. The major flow of traffic is south. Portlanders, like spawning salmon, head down-road to vacation. While biking is good, the long days are also wet. The *Oregon Coast Bike Route Map* (available free from the Oregon Dept. of Transportation, Salem 97310 or at virtually any visitors center or chamber of commerce on the coast) provides invaluable information on campsites, hostels, bike repair facilities, temperatures, wind speed, etc. For those without a car or bike, transportation becomes a bit tricky.

Greyhound's coastal routes from Portland run only twice per day, with half of the routes running in the middle of the night. Local public transportation goes from Tillamook to Astoria, but no public transportation links Tillamook and Lincoln City.

Gasoline and grocery prices en route to the coast are about 20% higher than in inland cities. Motorists may want to stock up and fill up before reaching the coast-bound highways.

Reedsport and the Dunes

For 42 miles between Florence and Coos Bay, the beach widens considerably to form the **Oregon Dunes National Recreation Area.** Shifting hills of sand rise to 300 feet and extend inland up to 3 miles (often to the brink of U.S. 101), clogging mountain streams and forming numerous small lakes. The dunes were created by glaciation 15,000 years ago. Reaching their maximum development 9000 years later, the dunes are maintained by a unidirectional, seasonally regular wind. Hiking trails wind around the lakes, through the coastal forests, and up to the dunes themselves. In many places, no grasses or shrubs grow, and you can see only bare sand and sky. In other places, however, you might feel more like you're in the Gator Bowl parking lot rather than in the Gobi. Campgrounds fill up early and loudly with dunebuggy and motorcycle enthusiasts, especially on summer weekends. The blaring radios, thrumming engines, and swarms of drunk people might drive you, like Lawrence of Arabia, into the sands seeking eternal truth—or at least a quiet place to crash.

Visit the **Oregon Dunes National Recreation Area Information Center,** 855 U.S. 101, Reedsport (271-3611), just south of the Umpqua River Bridge, to pick up their free guide with details on camping, hiking, fishing, boating, wildlife observation, environmental exploration, and dune-buggy access for each side the NRA maintains. (Open Mon.-Fri. 8am-4:30pm, Sat.-Sun. 9am-5pm; Labor Day-Memorial Day Mon.-Fri. 8am-4:30pm.) The **Reedsport Chamber of Commerce,** U.S. 101 and Rte. 38 (271-3495), is across the street from the NRA office. (Open Mon.-Fri. 9am-5pm.)

Sand Dunes Frontier, 83960 U.S. 101 S. (997-3544), 4 miles south of Florence, gives 25-minute **dune buggy rides** ($5, under 11 $2.50, under 5 free). But if you really want to experience the dunes, shell out $25 for an hour ($15 each additional hour) on your own dune buggy; **Dunes Odyssey,** on U.S. 101 in Winchester Bay (271-4011), and **Spinreel Park,** Wildwood Dr., 8 miles south on U.S. 101 (759-3313; open daily 8am-6pm), both offer rentals. The best access to the dunes is at **Eel Creek Campground,** 11 miles south of Reedsport. Leave your car in the parking lot of the day-use area and hike a short and easy distance through scrubby pines and grasses; suddenly, the dune piles will tower above you. It's easy to get lost wandering from one identical, stark rise to the next. The ocean is another 2 miles to the west.

Inside **Umpqua Lighthouse State Park,** 6 miles south of Reedsport, the Douglas County Park Department operates the **coastal visitor center** (440-4500), in the old Coast Guard administration building. The center has small exhibits on the shipping and timber industries of the turn-of-the-century era. (Open May-Sept. Wed.-Sat. 10am-5pm, Sun. 1-5pm. Free.)

Restaurateurs of Winchester Bay (3 miles south of Reedsport) pride themselves on their seafood, especially salmon. The **Seven Seas Cafe,** Dock A, Winchester Bay (271-4381), at the end of Broadway at 4th St., is a small diner crowded with marine memorabilia and navigational charts. The local fishing crowd gathers here to trade big fish stories. The café is, in fact, the self-proclaimed "haunt of the liars." (Fish and chips $4, deep-fried prawns $5.75, coffee 35¢. Open Fri.-Tues. 8am-2pm.) The **Seafood Grotto and Restaurant,** 8th St. and Broadway, Winchester Bay (271-4250), is a peaceful restaurant with excellent seafood and a large Victorian doll house. *Cioppino* with rich tomato sauce goes for $11; a large salmon steak will cost you $10. (Open Sun.-Thurs. 8am-9pm.) The **Pepper Pot Deli,** 1061 U.S. 101, Reedsport (271-5114), a few blocks south of the information centers, is too antiseptic to qualify as a true deli, but the sandwiches are fine nonetheless. (Reuben or pastrami, $3.25. Open Mon.-Sat. 10:30am-6pm. Winter hours may be shorter.)

Whether you prefer motels or campsites, head to peaceful Winchester Bay. The **Harbor View Motel,** on Beach Blvd. (271-3352), across from the waterfront, is a little shabby, but fairly clean with color TV and some kitchenettes. (Singles $21. Doubles $26. Mid-Sept.-April: singles $18.50; doubles $23.) The **Winchester Bay Motel,** at the end of Broadway (271-4871), at 4th St. past dock A, is a good place to blow dough after weeks of camping out and feeling grungy. Color TV and free coffee. (Singles $28. Doubles $35. Labor Day-Memorial Day: singles $25; doubles $30.) The rooms in the **Fir Grove Motel,** 2178 Winchester Ave., Reedsport (271-4848), are rather small, but come with color TV, free coffee, and a pool. (Singles $34. Doubles $38. In winter: singles $25; doubles $28.)

The National Forest Service's pamphlet *Campgrounds in the Siuslaw National Forest* covers campgrounds in the dunes. The sites closest to Reedsport are in Winchester Bay. The campgrounds that allow dune-buggy access—South Jetty, Lagoon, Waxmyrtle, Driftwood II, Horsfall, and Bluebill—are generally loud and rowdy. The **Surfwood Campground,** ½ mile north of Winchester Bay on U.S. 101 (271-4020), has all the luxuries of home—including a laundromat, heated pool, grocery store, sauna, tennis court, and hot showers. (Sites $6, full hookup $9.50. Call at least a week in advance in the summer.) The **Windy Cove Campground** (271-5634), adjacent to Salmon Harbor in Winchester Bay, is a county park with rather steep rates for tent camping. (75 sites with drinking water, hot showers, flush toilets, and beach access. Sites $7.35.)

Reedsport's **post office** is at 301 Fir St. (271-2521; open Mon.-Fri. 9am-5pm). General Delivery ZIP code is 97467. The **area code** is 503.

Klamath Falls and Crater Lake National Park

Iceless in winter and flawlessly circular, Crater Lake (at an elevation of over 6000 ft.) plunges to a depth of an astonishing, mirror-blue 2000 feet, making it the nation's deepest lake. **Route 62** through Crater Lake National Park circumnavigates the lake and then heads west to Medford or east to Klamath Falls. To get to the park from Portland, take I-5 to Eugene, then Rte. 58 east to U.S. 97 south. Call ahead for road conditions during winter (1-238-8400). Admission to the park (charged only in summer) is $5 for cars, $3 for hikers and bikers. The tiny **visitors center** (594-2211) on the lake shore at **Rim Village,** distributes books and maps on hiking and camping. (Open daily 8am-7pm.) Rangers conduct nightly talks in the **Rim Center** across the street starting at 8pm.

The **Rim Drive,** open only in summer, is a 33-mile route high above the lake. Points along the drive offer views and trailheads for hiking. Among the most spectacular are **Discovery Point Trail** (from which the first pioneer saw the lake in 1853), **Garfield Peak Trail,** and **Watchman Lookout.**

The hike up **Scott Peak,** the park's highest (9000 ft.), begins from the drive near the lake's eastern edge. Although steep, the 7½-mile trail to the top gives the persevering hiker a unique overhead view of the lake which repays the sweat spent getting there. Steep **Cleetwood Trail,** a 1-mile switchback, is the only trail that leads down to the water's edge. From here a boat tours the lake (fare $8.50, under 13 $5; check with the lodge for times). Both **Wizard Island,** a cinder cone 760 feet above lake level, and **Phantom Ship Rock** are fragile and tiny specks when viewed from above, yet prove surprisingly large from the surface of the water. Picnics and fishing are allowed, as is swimming, if you can stand the frigid 50° temperature. Park rangers lead free walking tours daily in the summer and periodically in winter (on snowshoes). Call the ranger station for exact times.

If you're pressed for time, walk the easy 100 yards from the visitors center down to the **Sinnott Memorial Overlook.** The view is the area's best and most accessible. For a short lecture on the area's history, attend a ranger talk at Rim Village.

Eating inexpensively in Crater Lake is difficult. Crater Lake Lodge has a small dining room, and Rim Village has several groceries that charge high prices for a skimpy selection of foodstuffs. As in most national parks, the best plan is to buy supplies at nearby towns and cook your own meals once inside. If you're coming from the south, **Fort Klamath** is the final food frontier before the park. Stock up here at the **Old Fort Store** (381-2345; open daily 8am-8pm). In **Klamath Falls,** try **McPherson's Old Town Pizza,** 722 Main St. (884-8858), for some of the tastiest and cheapest food in the area. (Small pizzas from $2.55. Open daily 11am-11pm.)

The only hotel in the park is **Crater Lake Lodge,** Rim Village (594-2511), open from June to September. Call far in advance for reservations; renovations due to safety hazards have closed parts of the lodge for extended periods of time. Staying here will put a crater in your wallet; cottages cost $36, and rooms with views of the lakes start at $47.

Nearby Klamath Falls, however, features several affordable hotels; you may be wise to sack out in the town and base your visits to Crater Lake from there. The **Pony Pass Motel,** 75 Main St. (884-7735) in Klamath Falls, offers clean, comfortable rooms at the edge of town with A/C and TV. (Singles $32. Doubles $34.) The **Maverick Motel,** 1220 Main St. (882-6688), down the street from Greyhound in the center of Klamath Falls. (TV, A/C, and a handkerchief-sized pool. Singles $24.60. Doubles $27.50.) **Molatore's Motel,** 100 Main St. (882-4666), across the street from the Pony Pass, caters mostly to business travelers. 104 immense rooms all have A/C. (Singles from $30.75. Doubles $33.90.)

Mazama Campground (594-2211), is a monster facility, usually usurped by equally mammoth RVs in summer. This is camping with the ambiance of a parking lot. (Sites $7.) **Lost Creek Campground** (594-2211), is hidden at the southwest corner of the park. (12 sites. Arrive by morning to secure a spot.)

Washington

Washington has two personalities, clearly split by the Cascade Range. The western ridge of the range blocks Pacific moisture heading east and hurls it back toward the ocean, bathing the Olympic Peninsula with an average annual rainfall of 135 inches (compared to 15 inches inland). It is on this side, around Puget Sound, that most of the inhabitants cluster. And though raindrops keep falling on its head, this portion of Washington not only sings in the rain, but takes fitting pride in its seafood.

But pity not the residents of eastern Washington, blessed with seafood thanks only to the miracle of modern refrigeration. Time that might otherwise be devoted to cracking crab shells can be spent savoring fresh fruit in Yakima. This is Washington's less congested side. Residents and tourists can both enjoy its rolling countryside without jostling for space.

Washington runs the gamut of terrain; desserts, volcanoes, untouched Pacific Ocean beaches, and the world's only non-tropical rain forest await exploration. There's rafting on the Skagit, Suiattle, Sauk, Yakima, and Wenatchee Rivers; sea kayaking in the San Juan Islands; and sand castle building on the Strait of Juan de Fuca (beware of razor clams). Beach bums can sleep on the banks of the Columbia or the shores of the Pacific. Mount Rainier has fantastic hiking, while the Cascades boast perfect conditions for nearly any winter activity. Seattle and Spokane drape themselves over equally beautiful green landscapes, showing that botany and bottom line can still intersect. Best of all, Washington is a compact state by Western standards—everything is less than a daytrip away.

Practical Information

Visitor Information: State Tourist Office, Tourism Development Division, 101 General Administration Building, Olympia 98504 (206-753-5600). **Washington State Parks and Recreation Commission,** 7150 Clearwater Lane, Olympia 98504 (206-753-2027; summers within WA 800-562-0990). **Forest Service/National Park Service Outdoor Recreation Information Office,** 1018 1st. Ave., Seattle 98104 (206-442-0170).

Capital: Olympia.

Time Zone: Pacific (3 hr. behind Eastern). **Postal Abbreviation:** WA.

Seattle

A city in the shadow of a mountain, Seattle is both physically and spiritually an odd fusion of alpine candor and urban illusion. Here octogenarian architects tote backpacks, thirtysomething accountants wear clogs, and everyone else paws through the fresh greens and sea creatures at the Pike Place Market.

Seattle spends nearly three quarters of the year blanketed by clouds. Prompted by a hometown organization called Lesser Seattle, many inhabitants ballyhoo their city's reputation as the rain capital of the U.S. in an effort to keep the city to themselves. (In reality, Seattle catches less precipitation each year than quite a few other major cities.) Undaunted by precipitation, residents spend as much time as possible in the great outdoors.

Practical Information

Visitor Information: Seattle-King County Visitors Bureau, 666 Stewart St. (461-5890), in the Vance Hotel near Greyhound. Open Mon.-Fri. 8:30am-5pm, Sat. 10am-4pm. From 5-

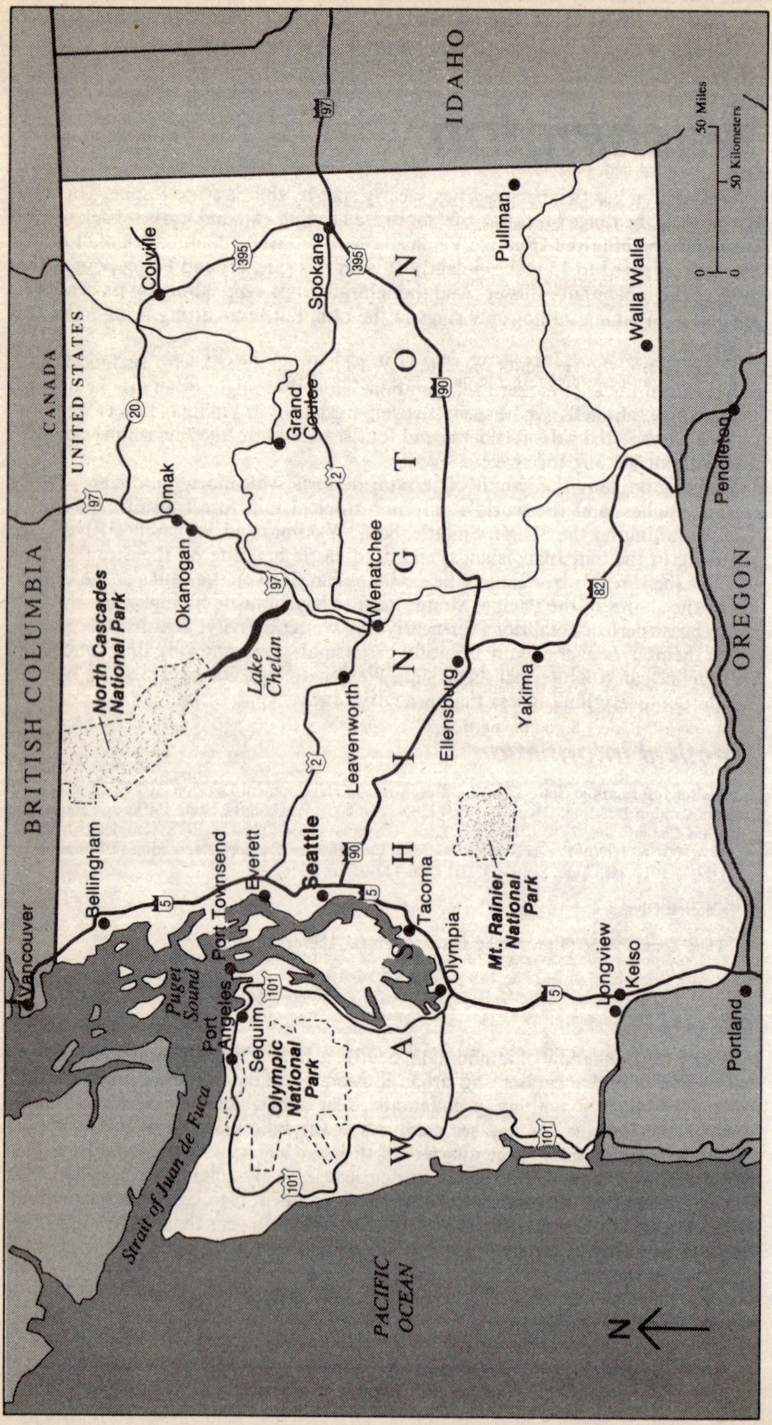
BRITISH COLUMBIA
CANADA
UNITED STATES
IDAHO
OREGON
WASHINGTON
PACIFIC OCEAN
Strait of Juan de Fuca
Puget Sound
Lake Chelan
North Cascades National Park
Olympic National Park
Mt. Rainier National Park
Vancouver
Bellingham
Port Townsend
Everett
Seattle
Tacoma
Olympia
Port Angeles
Sequim
Longview
Kelso
Portland
Leavenworth
Ellensburg
Yakima
Wenatchee
Okanogan
Omak
Grand Coulee
Colville
Spokane
Pullman
Walla Walla
Pendleton
5
90
2
97
20
395
82
101
50 Miles
50 Kilometers
0
0
N

7:30pm, call the airport branch at 433-5218. **Tourism B.C.,** 720 Olive Way, Seattle 98101 (623-5937, 9am-4pm). Information on travel to British Columbia. Open Mon.-Fri. 8:30am-1pm and 2-4:30pm. **Ticket Agency: Ticket Master,** 201 S. King St. #38, Seattle 98104 (628-0888). Open Mon.-Sat. 10am-10pm, Sun. 10am-6pm. **Jazz Hotline,** 102 S. Jackson (624-5277). Recorded information on area happenings. **Arts Hotline,** 447-2787.

Seattle Parks and Recreation Department, 5201 Green Lake Way N., Seattle 98103 (684-4075). Open Mon.-Fri. 8am-6pm. **National Park Service, Pacific Northwest Region,** 83 S King St., 3rd floor (442-4830).

Travelers Aid: 909 4th Ave., #630 (461-3888), at Marion, in the YMCA. Free services to stranded travelers with lost wallets, lost relatives, or lost heads. Open Mon.-Fri. 8:30am-9pm, Sat.-Sun. and holidays 1-5pm.

Seattle-Tacoma International Airport (Sea-Tac), on Federal Way, south of Seattle proper. General information (433-5217). **Sea-Tac Visitors Information Center** (433-5218), in the central baggage claim area across from carousel 10. Open daily 9:30am-7:30pm. **Gray Line** coaches and limousines operate between airport and downtown. $5 one way, $9 round-trip. Metro buses #174 and 194 run daily every half-hour from 6am-1am. Fare $1.25 during peak hours, 85¢ off-peak; under 18 75¢ during peak, 55¢ off-peak.

Amtrak: King Street Station, 3rd and Jackson St. (464-1930 or 800-872-7245). Trains to Portland (3 per day, $27), Tacoma ($9), Vancouver ($27), and San Francisco ($139). Station open daily 6am-10pm; ticket office daily 6am-5:30pm.

Buses: Greyhound, 8th Ave. and Stewart St. (624-3456). To Sea-Tac Airport (5 per day, $2.50); Vancouver (2 per day, $23); and Portland (2 per day, $23). Open daily 5:45am-7:45pm, 10-10:30pm, and 11:45pm-1:20am. **Green Tortoise Alternative Travel,** 324-7433 or 800-227-4766. Buses leave from NE Campus Parkway and 15th Ave. NE in the University District and then swing by the downtown Greyhound station. Trips leave Thurs. and Sun. at 8am for Portland (5 hr., $15); Berkeley, CA (26 hr., $49); and San Francisco (27 hr., $59). Reservations required.

Metro Transit: Customer Assistance Office, 821 2nd Ave., in the Exchange Building downtown. Open Mon. 8am-5:30pm, Tues.-Fri. 8am-5pm. 24-hour information (447-4800; TTY service 447-4826). Buses run 6am-1am. Fare 55¢, during weekday peak hours 75¢. One-day pass ($2.50). Ride free in the area bordered by Jackson St. on the south, 6th Ave. and I-5 on the east, Battery St. on the north, and the waterfront on the west. Transfers valid for 1 hr. and for Waterfront Streetcars as well.

Ferries: Washington State Ferries, Colman Dock, Pier 52 (464-6400; in WA 800-542-0810 or 800-542-7052). Service to Bremerton on Kitsap Peninsula and Winslow on Bainbridge Island. Ferries leave frequently daily 6am-midnight. Fares from $1.65, car and driver $6.65. **B.C. Steamship Company,** Pier 69, 2700 Alaskan Way (624-6663). Daily cruises on the *Princess Marguerite* and the *Vancouver Island Princess* to Victoria, BC, early May-late Sept. Round-trip $32; seniors $28; ages 5-11 round-trip $16. Bikes $3, motorcycles $11. Car and driver $40.

Car Rental: Five & Ten, 14120 Pacific Hwy. S. (246-4434). $18 per day with 100 free miles, each additional mile 5¢. Airport pickup. Mon.-Sat. 8am-6pm, Sun. 12:30pm-6pm. Must be 21 with credit card or $120 deposit. **A-19.95-Rent-A-Car,** (364-6300). $20 per day with 100 free miles plus 15¢ each additional mile. Free delivery. Qualified drivers under 21 welcome; call ahead for appointment.

Bike Rental: Gregg's, 7007 Woodlawn Ave. NE (523-1822). 10-speeds and mountain bikes $25 per day; other bikes $3.50 per hr. Open Mon.-Fri. 9:30am-9pm, Sat.-Sun. 9:30am-6pm. Credit card or $20 deposit. **Alki Bikes,** 2722 Alki Ave. SW (938-3322). Mountain bikes $7 per hr., $17 per day; 10-speeds $4 per hr., $13 per day. Open Mon.-Thurs. 10am-7pm, Fri. 10am-8pm, Sat. 10am-6pm, Sun. 10am-5pm; Oct.-April daily 10am-6pm. Credit card or license required as deposit.

Help Lines: Crisis Clinic, 461-3222. **Senior Citizen Information and Referral,** 100 W. Roy (285-3110). Open Mon.-Fri. 9am-5pm. **Gay Counseling: Dorian Group,** 340 15th Ave. E. (322-1501). Support and referral for gay men and women. Open Mon.-Fri. 9am-midnight.

Post Office: Union St. and 3rd Ave. (442-6255), downtown. Open Mon.-Fri. 8am-5:30pm. **ZIP code:** 98101.

Area Code: 206.

Seattle is a long, skinny city stretched out north to south between long, skinny **Puget Sound** on the west and long, skinny **Lake Washington** on the east. The head

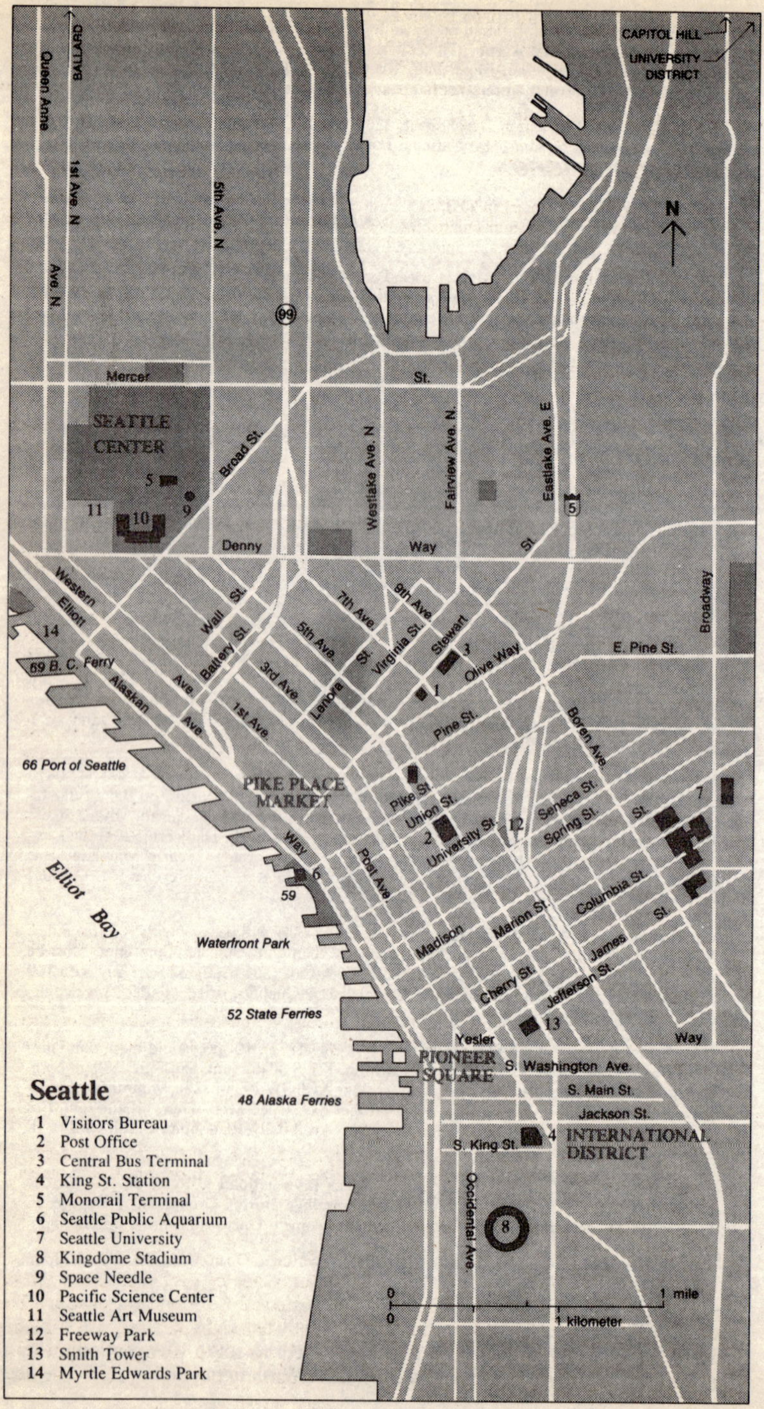
CAPITOL HILL
UNIVERSITY DISTRICT
BALLARD
Queen Anne Ave. N
1st Ave. N
5th Ave. N
N
99
Mercer St.
SEATTLE CENTER
Broad St.
Westlake Ave. N
Fairview Ave. N
Eastlake Ave. E
5
Denny Way
Western
Elliott
Wall St.
Battery St.
7th Ave
9th Ave
5th Ave.
Virginia St.
Stewart
3rd Ave.
Lenora St.
Olive Way
E. Pine St.
Broadway
59 B. C. Ferry
Alaskan
Ave.
Ave.
1st Ave.
Pine St.
Boren Ave.
66 Port of Seattle
PIKE PLACE MARKET
Pike St.
Union St.
Seneca St.
University St.
Spring St.
St.
Way
Post Ave.
Elliot Bay
59
Columbia St.
Madison
Marion St.
St.
Waterfront Park
James
Cherry St.
Jefferson St.
52 State Ferries
Yesler
Way
PIONEER SQUARE
S. Washington Ave.
S. Main St.
Jackson St.
48 Alaska Ferries
S. King St.
INTERNATIONAL DISTRICT
Occidental Ave.
0
1 mile
0
1 kilometer
Seattle
1 Visitors Bureau
2 Post Office
3 Central Bus Terminal
4 King St. Station
5 Monorail Terminal
6 Seattle Public Aquarium
7 Seattle University
8 Kingdome Stadium
9 Space Needle
10 Pacific Science Center
11 Seattle Art Museum
12 Freeway Park
13 Smith Tower
14 Myrtle Edwards Park

of the city is cut from its torso by Lake Union and a string of locks, canals, and bays. In the downtown area, avenues run northwest to southeast and streets southwest to northeast. Outside the downtown area everything is vastly simplified: avenues run north to south and streets east to west, with only a few exceptions. The city is split into quadrants: 1000 1st Ave. NW is a far cry from 1000 1st Ave. S.

Accommodations

Seattle International Hostel (AYH), 84 Union St. (622-5443), at Western Ave. downtown. 125 beds in sterile rooms, immaculate facilities, and plenty of modern amenities. Sleep sacks required. Open daily 7-10am and 5pm-midnight. Extended curfew on weekend nights (until 2am; $1 fee). $11, nonmembers $14.

YMCA, 909 4th Ave. (382-5000), near the Madison St. intersection. Men and women welcome; must be 17. Luxury lodgings for the budget traveler. Good downtown location. TV lounge on each floor, laundry facilities, and use of swimming pool and fitness facilities. Well-run, clean, and friendly. Singles from $22. Doubles from $26. Weekly: from $78 and $96 respectively. AYH members pay $12 for a dorm bunk, or 10% off the regular price.

YWCA, 1118 5th Ave. (461-4888), near the YMCA. Take any 4th Ave. bus to Seneca St. Women only, ages under 18 require advance arrangement. Great security and location, but an older facility than the YMCA with smaller rooms. Housing desk open 24 hours. Singles $22, with bath $27. Doubles $33, with bath $38. Weekly: singles $124, with bath $150. Additional charge for health center use. Key deposit $2.

Commodore Hotel, 2013 2nd Ave. (448-8868), at Virginia. Downtown. Where the hostel sends its overflow. Those with AYH card and sleep sack can get a dorm bed for $9. Tight security and fairly clean. Private room for 2 $31.50.

Pacific Hotel, 317 Marion St. (622-3985), between 3rd and 4th Ave., across from the YMCA. Quiet and safe location. The small rooms are very small but the large singles can hold 2 people. No visitors after 10pm. Small singles $24; large singles $25, with bath $30. Doubles $27, with bath $32. Key deposit $2.

St. Regis Hotel, 116 Stewart St. (448-6366), conveniently located 2 blocks from the Pike Place Market. The rooms are dark and your lamp may not work, but the place is clean and the management pleasant. The neighborhood, however, is unsafe after dark. Laundromat on the first floor. Singles $22, with bath $28. Doubles $27, with bath $34.

Hillside Motel, 2451 Aurora N. (285-7860). Take bus #6 or 16. One of a number of relatively inexpensive motels along noisy Aurora. 11 units with hot plates. Singles $23, doubles $27.

Park Plaza Hotel, 4401 Aurora Ave. N. (632-2101). Another option along this endless strip of car dealerships and fast-food joints. Clean rooms, in-room coffee, cable TV. Singles $25. Doubles $27.

Nites Inn, 11746 Aurora Ave. N. (365-3216). Large rooms. Movie channel. Singles $30. Doubles $32.

Bush Hotel, 621 S. Jackson (623-8079). Take bus #1, 7, or 14. In the heart of the International District. Newly remodeled, but still not particularly presidential or safe. Singles from $17. Doubles from $20. Key deposit $5.

Motel 6, 18900 47th Ave. S. (241-1648), just off I-5 at exit 152. Take bus #170 during peak hours; otherwise take #174 to Sea-Tac. Noisy but clean. Pool and TV. Singles $25. Doubles $32.

The College Inn, 4000 University Way NE (633-4441). European-style B&B in the University District. Breakfast served in a lovely refinished attic. Antiques and individual wash basins in every room. Service not always reliable. Singles from $44. Doubles from $52.

Food

By a Sound full of fish and in a state tacked in place by orchards, Seattle rivals San Francisco in culinary excitement and eclecticism. Seafood and produce here are always fresh in season. If you want to eat in, buy fish right off the boats at **Fisherman's Wharf,** at NW 54th St. and 30th Ave. NW in Ballard, along bus route #43. The wharf is usually open from 8am to 3 or 4 pm.

Pike Place Market

Farmers have been selling their produce here since 1907, when angry Seattle citizens demanded an alternative to the middle merchant. Crazy fishmongers and produce sellers yell at customers and at each other, while street performers do their thing and tourists wonder what they've walked into. Seattlites accept the whole affair with equanimity and sail through at day's end in search of something special for dinner. (Market open Mon.-Sat. 9am-6pm; many stands also open Sun.)

El Puerco Llorón, 1501 Western Ave. (624-0541), at the 2nd level of the Hillclimb overlooking the waterfront. Some of the best Mexican food in Seattle—no nachos here. The entire place has been transported from Tijuana. Unfortunately, portions fall short of hearty. *Tacos de carne asada* (charcoal-broiled flank steak in soft tortillas) $4. Open Mon.-Sat. 11:30am-9pm, Sun. noon-8pm.

World Class Chili, 1411 1st Ave. (623-3678), in the South Arcade. Order up a Texas-sized portion of Seattle's best chili here ($3.19) and quickly grab a stool at the crowded bar. Four different kinds to choose from; California-style contains chicken instead of beef. Open Mon.-Sat. 11am-6pm.

The Pink Door, 1919 Post Alley (682-3241), in the alley. Unmarked; look for the pink door. A tastefully decorated Italian restaurant, worth the price. Dinners cost up to $12, but you can eat lunch for $6. Outdoor dining. Open Tues.-Sat. 11:30am-10pm.

Ying Hei Restaurant, 664 S. King St. (622-4229). A spacious place decorated with paper lanterns and a fish tank. Excellent barbecue and soy sauce chicken. Try the individual portion soups or shrimp with black bean sauce ($5.75). Good seafood selection. Open Mon.-Wed. and Fri.-Sun. 11:30am-8:30pm, Thurs. 11:30am-4pm.

Phnom Penh Noodle Soup House, 414 Maynard Ave. S. (682-5690). Excellent Cambodian cuisine. Head to the upstairs dining room for a good view of the park and a spicy, steaming bowl of *battambany* noodles ($3.75). Open Mon.-Fri. 8:30am-7pm, Sat.-Sun. 9am-7pm.

Ivar's Fish Bar, Pier 54 (624-6852), on the waterfront. One of a string of seafood restaurants owned by and named for Seattle celebrity Ivar Haglund. This locals' favorite charges $2.89 for fish and chips. Dine with the gulls and pigeons in outdoor, covered booths. Open daily 11am-2am.

Fran-Glor's Creole Cafe, 547 1st Ave. (682-1578). Genuine gumbo with crabmeat, sausage, and who knows what else. The bric-a-brac and the jazz are classic New Orleans. Lunches from $4.50. Open Mon.-Sat. noon-9:30pm.

Kokeb Restaurant, 926 12th Ave. (322-0485). Behind Seattle University at the far south end of Capitol Hill, near the First Hill neighborhood. An intriguing Ethiopian restaurant offering hot and spicy meat stews served on *injera,* a soft bread. Colorful decor. Lunch $3.50-5, dinner $5-6.50. Open Mon.-Thurs. 11:30am-9pm, Fri.-Sat. 4-10pm, Sun. 11:30am-3pm and 6-9pm.

The Cause Célèbre, 524 E. 15th Ave. (323-1888), at Mercer St., at the other end of Capitol Hill. The special province of Seattle's well-fed left. Stay away if you don't like feminist music or discussions on the struggle for Chinese succession. The ice cream and baked goods are sublime. Free evening entertainment. Lunch $3-6. Open Mon.-Thurs. 7:30am-9:30pm, Fri. 7:30am-midnight, Sat. 8am-midnight, Sun. 8am-9:30pm.

Lox, Stock and Bagel, 4552 University Way NE (634-3144). In spite of a somewhat pricey menu—bagels go for 75¢ each—Huskies flock to the Stock nightly. $1 drinks and $2.75 pitchers between 4-7pm contribute to their zeal. High ceilings and low hanging lamps add to the cool, relaxed atmosphere. Open Mon.-Sat. 9am-2am.

Espresso Roma Cafe, 4201 University Way NE (633-2534). Rather like an undecorated basement. Students and professors study, chat, or watch the crowds walk by from outdoor streetside tables. Croissants 95¢. Open Mon.-Fri. 7am-midnight, Sat.-Sun. 8am-midnight.

Sights and Activities

If you only have a day to spare in Seattle, despair not. In one day of dedicated sightseeing you can cover a good deal of the city. If you've got a little more time, head out to Seward Park for a late afternoon dip in Lake Washington, or cycle along the lake's western bank.

The **Pike Place Market,** at the bottom of Pike St. between 1st and Western Ave. somehow crowds produce stands, fish vendors, bakeries, craft sellers, restaurants, and boutiques into a 3-block indoor/outdoor area. An information table at the corner of Pike St. and Pike Place (in front of the bakery) provides information about market history and shop (and rest room) locations. **Freeway Park,** on Seneca St. at 7th Ave., is a smashing place for picnicking. Its waterfall and playground are built right on top of I-5, in the midst of Seattle's high-rises. At the south end of the market begins the **Pike Place Hillclimb,** a set of staircases leading down past more chic shops and ethnic restaurants to Alaskan Way and the **waterfront.** (An elevator is also available.)

The waterfront docks once played Ellis Island to shiploads of gold coming in from the 1897 Klondike gold rush. Today, on a pier full of shops and restaurants, the credit card is firmly established as standard currency. On Pier 59 at the base of the hillclimb, the **Seattle Aquarium** (625-4357) explains the history of marine life in Puget Sound and the effects of tidal action. (Open daily 10am-7pm; Labor Day-Memorial Day daily 10am-5pm. Admission $3.25, seniors and ages 13-18 $1.50, ages 6-12 75¢.)

Four blocks inland from Pier 70 you'll find **Seattle Center.** The 74-acre, pedestrians-only park was originally constructed for the 1962 World's Fair and still attracts thousands of sightseers daily. Take the monorail from Pine St. and 5th Ave. downtown. (Fare 60¢, seniors and children 25¢.) The **Pacific Science Center** (443-2001), within the park, houses a laserium and IMAX theater. (Science Center open daily 10am-6pm; Labor Day-June Mon.-Fri. 10am-5pm, Sat.-Sun. 10am-6pm. Admission $4.50, seniors and students $3.50, ages 2-5 $1.50. Laser shows $5, $2.50 on Tues. evenings.) The **Space Needle** (443-2100), sometimes known as "the world's tackiest monument," has an observation tower and restaurant. On clear days, the view from atop is without peer. (Admission $4.25, ages 5-12 $2.) After working up an appetite in the Center's amusement park, head next door to the **Center House,** home to dozens of shops and restaurants serving everything from Mongolian to Mexican. (Open in summer daily 11am-9pm; in spring 11am-7pm; in fall and winter Sun.-Thurs. 11am-6pm, Fri.-Sat. 11am-9pm.) The Center has an **information desk** (625-4234) on the court level in the Center House. (Open daily 11am-7pm.)

Pier 57 is also home to Seattle's new maritime museum, **The Water Link** (624-4975). Wallow in Seattle's waterfront history or probe the geological mysteries of the ocean floor. (Open May 17-Sept. 30 Tues.-Sun. noon-6pm. Admission $1.) From Pier 56, **Harbor Tours** (623-1445) leaves for a one-hour cruise south to the Coast Guard outposts around Harbor Island (June-Sept. 5 per day; May and Oct. 3 per day. Fare $6.50, seniors $6, children $3.)

From the waterfront, it's just 2 blocks to historic **Pioneer Square,** where 19th-century warehouses and office buildings were restored in a spasm of prosperity during the 70s. The *Compleat Browser's Guide to Pioneer Square,* available in area bookstores, provides a short history and walking tour.

When Seattle nearly burned to the ground in 1889, an ordinance was passed to raise the city 35 feet. At first, shops below the elevated streets remained open for business and were moored to the upper city by an elaborate network of stairs. In 1907 the city moved upstairs permanently, and the underground city was sealed off. Tours of the vast underworld are now given by **Bill Speidel's Underground Tours** (682-4646). Speidel spearheaded the movement to save Pioneer Square from the apocalypse of renewal. The tours are informative and irreverent glimpses at Seattle's beginnings; just ignore the rats that infest the tunnels. Tours (1½ hr.) leave from Doc Maynard's Pub at 610 1st Ave. (March-Sept. 6 per day 10am-6pm. Reservations strongly recommended. Admission $4, seniors $2.75, students $3.25, ages 6-12 $2.)

Once back above ground, learn about the next major event in the city's history at the **Klondike Gold Rush National Historic Park,** 117 S. Main St. (442-7220). The center depicts the lives and fortunes of the miners. Saturday and Sunday at 3pm, the park screens Charlie Chaplin's 1925 classic, *The Gold Rush.* (Open daily 9am-5pm. Free.)

Three blocks east of Pioneer Square, up Jackson on King St., is Seattle's **International District.** Though sometimes still called Chinatown by Seattlites, this area is home to peoples from all over Asia. The 45-minute slideshow *Seattle's Other History,* presented at the Nippon Kan Theater, 628 Washington St. (624-8801), reveals the years of treatment as noncitizens that Asians in Seattle experienced and the strength with which they met hardship. (Presentation given whenever large enough groups accumulate; call ahead. Admission $2.) Whether or not you see the show, be sure to pick up the brochure *Chinatown Tour: Seattle's Other History,* which is available free at the **Nippon Kan Theater,** itself a good place to start your tour of the district. The theater was built in 1909 to house weddings and cultural events. The Nippon Kan fell into disrepair during World War II and was only restored and reopened in 1981.

Capitol Hill inspires extreme reactions from both its residents and neighbors. The former wouldn't live anywhere else, while the latter never go near the place. The district's leftist and gay communities set the tone for its nightspots (see Entertainment), while the retail outlets include a large number of collectives and radical bookstores. Saunter down Broadway or its cross streets to window-shop, or walk a few blocks east and north for a stroll down the hill's lovely residential streets, lined with beautifully maintained Victorian homes. Bus #10 runs along 15th St. and #7 along Broadway.

Volunteer Park, between 11th and 17th Ave. at E. Ward St., north of the main Broadway activity, beckons tourists to travel east of the city center. Named for the "brave volunteers who gave their lives to liberate the oppressed people of Cuba and the Philippines," the park boasts lovely lawns and an outdoor running track. Climb the water tower at the 14th Ave. entrance for stunning 360° views of the city and the Olympic Range, rivalling the views from the Space Needle. The **Seattle Art Museum,** 14th St. E. and Prospect (625-8901), houses an excellent permanent collection of Asian art. Pick up a program listing or call 443-4670 for information about special exhibits. (Open Tues.-Wed. and Fri.-Sat. 10am-5pm, Thurs. 10am-9pm, Sun. noon-5pm. Admission $2, seniors, students, and under 12 $1; free Thurs.)

The **University of Washington Arboretum** (325-4510), 10 blocks east of Volunteer Park, has great cycling and running trails. The tranquil **Japanese Garden** (625-2635) is in the southern end of the arboretum at East Helen St. Take bus #43 from downtown. The nine acres of sculpted gardens include fruit trees, a reflecting pool, and a traditional tea house. (Open March-Nov. daily 10am-5pm. Admission $1.50, seniors, under 18, and disabled 75¢. Arboretum open daily dawn to dusk; greenhouse open Mon.-Fri. 10am-4pm.)

With 35,000 students, the **University of Washington** is the state's cultural and educational center of gravity. The "U district" swarms with bookstores, shops, taverns, and restaurants. Stop by the friendly and helpful **visitors information center,** 4014 University Way NE (543-9198), to pick up a map of the campus and to obtain information on the university. (Open Mon.-Fri. 8am-5pm.)

On the campus, visit the **Thomas Burke Memorial Washington State Museum,** NE 45th St. and 17th Ave. NE (543-5590), in the northwest corner of the campus. The museum houses artifacts of the Pacific Northwest Native American tribes. Especially good are the scrimshaw display. (Open Mon.-Wed. and Fri.-Sat. 10am-5pm, Thurs. 10am-8pm.) The **Henry Art Gallery,** 15th Ave. NE and NE 41st St. (543-2256), houses a collection of 18th- to 20th-century European and American art. (Open Tues.-Wed. and Fri. 10am-5pm, Thurs. 10am-7pm, Sat.-Sun. 11-5pm. Admission $2, students and seniors $1.) The **UW Arts Ticket Office,** 4001 University Way NE, has information and tickets for all events. (Open Mon.-Fri. 10:30am-4:30pm.) To reach the U-district, take buses #71-74 from downtown, #7 or 43 from Capitol Hill.

Waterways and Parks

A string of attractions stud the waterways linking Lake Washington and Puget Sound. House and sailboats fill **Lake Union.** Here, the **Center for Wooden Boats,** 1010 Valley St. (382-2628), maintains a moored flotilla of new and restored small craft for rental. (Sailboats $7.50-8.50 per hr., 15-min. check of your sailing skills $2.50. Open Mon.-Fri. noon-8pm, Sat.-Sun. 10am-8pm. Must be 16; no deposit required.) **Kelly's Landing,** 1401 NE Boat St. (547-9909), below the UW campus, rents canoes for outings on Lake Union. ($4.50 per hr., $15 per 5 hr.; $100, a credit card, or car keys required for deposit.) Tour the houseboat moorings along Lake Union's shores or go through the Montlake Cut to Lake Washington.

Watch trout and salmon as they struggle up 21 concrete steps at the **Fish Ladder** (783-7059) on the south side of the locks. Take bus #43 from the U District or #17 from downtown. Further north, on the northwestern shore of the city, lies the **Golden Gardens Park** in the Loyal Heights neighborhood, between NW 80th and NW 95th. The frigid beach is for the brave. Several expensive restaurants are located on the piers to the south, and the unobstructed views of the Olympics almost make their uniformly excellent seafood worth the price. (See Food.)

Directly north of Lake Union, the beautiful people run, roller skate, and skateboard around **Green Lake.** Take bus #16 from downtown Seattle to Green Lake. The lake is also popular with windsurfers, but woe those who lose their balance. Whoever named Green Lake wasn't kidding; even a quick dunk results in gobs of green algae clinging to your body and hair. Next door is Woodland Park and the **Woodland Park Zoo,** 5500 Phinney Ave. N. (789-7919), best reached from Rte. 99 or N. 50th St. Take bus #5 from downtown. The park itself is shaggy, but this makes the animals' habitats seem all the more realistic. (Open daily 8:30am-6pm; off-season daily 8:30am-4pm. Admission $2.50, ages 13-17 $1, seniors, disabled and ages 6-12 50¢.)

Entertainment

Obtain a copy of *The Weekly* (75¢) at newsstands and in boxes on the street, for a complete calendar of music, theater, exhibits, and special events. The free *Rocket,* available in music stores throughout the city, is a monthly off-beat guide to the popular music scene around the Puget Sound area, and *Seattle Gay News* (25¢) lists events and musical happenings relevant to the gay community. The *Area 206* Friday insert of the *Seattle Post-Intelligencer* has a "Hot Tix" column of free performances and discount tickets.

During summertime lunch hours downtown, city-sponsored free entertainment of the **"Out to Lunch"** series (623-0340) brings everything from reggae to folk dancing to the parks and squares of Seattle.

One of the joys of living in Seattle is the abundance of community taverns dedicated not to inebriating or scooping, but rather to providing a relaxed environment for dancing and spending time with friends. In Washington a tavern serves only beer and wine; a fully licensed bar or cocktail lounge must adjoin a restaurant. You must be 21 to enter bars and taverns. The Northwest produces a variety of local beers (none bottled): **Grant's, Imperial Russian Stout, India Pale Ale, Red Hook, Ballard Bitter,** and **Black Hook.**

For $4 or so, catch an evening of live stand-up comedy in one of Seattle's comedy clubs, such as Pioneer Square's **Swannie's Comedy Underground,** 222 S. Main St. (628-0303; acts Wed.-Sun. 9:30pm and 11pm.

The University Bistro, 4315 University Way NE (547-8010). Live music (everything from blues to reggae) nightly. Happy Hour (4-7pm) finds schooners of Bud for 75¢, well drinks $1.25. Cover Tues. $2, Wed.-Sat. $3-5. Open Tues.-Sat. 10am-2am; off-season daily 10am-2am.

Murphy's Pub, 2110 N. 45th St. (634-2110), in Wallingford, west of the U district. Take bus #43. A classic Irish pub with a mile-long beer list. Popular with the folksy crowd, Murphy's has live Irish and folk music nightly with no cover charge. Open daily 2pm-2am.

Squid Row Tavern, 518 E. Pine (322-2031). Bizarre paintings, black booths, a bar, and earfuls of delightful punk rock. Cover $4. Open Mon.-Fri. noon-2am, Sat. 4pm-2am.

The Borderline, 608 1st Ave. (624-3316), in the heart of Pioneer Sq. Under-25 crowd dances to a mix of music from Motown to new-wave. Occasional live bands. Happy hour (8-10pm) features 50¢ pints of Bud and free snacks. Fri.-Sat. cover $2 for men, $1 for women. Open Thurs.-Sat. 8pm-2am.

The Double Header, 407 2nd Ave. in Pioneer Sq. (464-9918). Claims to be the oldest gay bar in the country. An oom-pah band plays nightly to a mostly middle-aged crowd of gay men and women. A Seattle institution. Open daily 10am-2pm. No cover.

San Juan Islands

The San Juan Islands are an uncorrupted treasure. Bald eagles circle above ragged hillsides dotted with family farms, pods of killer whales spout offshore, and the sun shines perpetually. To travelers approaching from summer resorts infested with vacationers, the islands will seem blissfully quiet. Even in mid-summer, it is possible to drive the back roads and pass another car just once per hour. For this reason, islanders don't begrudge admission to their towns and campsites. Although tension is starting to build between the locals and the Seattle vacationers who are buying up huge chunks of the islands, quiet well-behaved tourists and their dollars are still very welcome on the San Juans.

An excellent guide to the area is *The San Juan Islands Afoot and Afloat* by Marge Mueller ($10), available at book and outfitting stores on the islands and in Seattle. *The San Juans Beckon* is published annually by the *Islands Sounder,* the local paper, to provide up-to-date information on island recreation. You can pick it up free on the ferries and in island stores. The *San Juanderer* is another freebie geared toward tourists, available on the ferries and at visitors centers.

Washington State Ferries serve the islands daily from **Anacortes** on the mainland. To reach Anacortes, take I-5 north from Seattle to Mt. Vernon. From there, Rte. 20 heads west; the way to the ferry is well marked. **Evergreen Trailways** buses to Anacortes depart Seattle from the **Greyhound depot** at 8th Ave. and Stewart St. twice per day. Call Evergreen Trailways (728-5955) for exact times.

In Anacortes, you can purchase a ticket to Lopez, Shaw, Orcas, or San Juan Island. You pay only on westbound trips to or between the islands; no charge is levied on eastbound traffic. (In effect, any ticket to the islands bought in Anacortes is a round-trip ticket.) You can thus save money by traveling directly to the westernmost island on your itinerary, and then making your way back, island by island. The ferry unloads first at Lopez Island, followed by Shaw, Orcas, and finally San Juan. It is also possible to purchase one-way tickets to Sidney, B.C., or from Sidney to the islands. Foot passengers travel in either direction between the islands free of charge. Fares from Anacortes to San Juan Island are $4.65 for pedestrians ($2.35 for seniors and ages 5-11), $6.25 for bikes, and $9.50 for motorcycles; cars cost $19 in the summer. Fares to the other islands en route are generally a few dollars cheaper. Inter-island fares average $2.25 for bikes and motorcycles, $7.75 for cars. The one-way fare to Sidney, B.C. costs $6.05 for pedestrians, $8.55 for bikes, $13.15 for motorcycles, and $31.25 for cars in summer, $26.05 in winter. Some car spaces are available from the islands to Sidney, but reservations are recommended. Call Washington State Ferries (206-464-6400; in WA 800-542-0810) before noon on the day before your trip to ensure a space. They're also the people to call for specific departure times and rates. The ferry authorities only accept cash or in-state checks as payment. You may park your vehicle for free in Anacortes at the parking lot on the corner of 30th and T St. A free, reliable shuttle then whisks you 4 miles to the terminal.

San Juan Island

Although San Juan is the last stop on the ferry's route, it is the most frequently visited island and is home to the largest town in the group, **Friday Harbor.** Since the ferry docks right in town, the island is the easiest to explore.

The **National Park Service Information Center** and **Chamber of Commerce Information Center,** 1st and Spring (378-2240), will answer questions about the British and American camps (see below). (Open Mon.-Fri. 8am-4:30pm, Sat.-Sun. 10:30am-3:30pm.) For those without private transportation, **San Juan Tours and Transit Co.,** 470 Hillcrest Dr. (378-5545), runs two sight-seeing tours of the island every afternoon (June-Sept.). The two-hour tours circle the island, stopping at Roche Harbor, English and American Camps, and Limekiln Lighthouse ($8, ages 5-11 $5). The company also runs hourly shuttle buses from the ferry to Lakedale campground ($3) and Roche Harbor ($4).

To begin a loop of the island, head south out of Friday Harbor on Argyle Rd., which merges into Cattle Point Rd. on the way to **American Camp** (378-2240), a total of 5 miles south of Friday Harbor. The camp dates to the infamous Pig War of 1859, when the U.S. and England were at loggerheads over possession of the islands. An interpretive shelter near the entrance to the park explains the history of the war; there is also a self-guided interpretive trail from the shelter through the buildings and past the site of the English sheep farm.

Returning north on Cattle Point Rd., consider taking the gravel False Bay Rd. to the west. The road leads to **False Bay,** home to a large number of nesting bald eagles. The bay is a University of Washington biology preserve, and student projects are all indicated by markers. Farther north on False Bay Rd., you'll run into **Bailer Hill Road,** which turns into West Side Rd. when it reaches Haro Straight. (You can also reach Bailer Hill Rd. by taking Cattle Point Rd. to Little Rd.) Along the road, sloping hills blanketed with wildflowers rise to one side, and rocky shores fall to the other. **San Juan County Park** on Smallpox Bay provides a convenient opportunity to park your bike or car and examine this scenery more closely.

English Camp, the second half of San Juan National Historical Park, is on West Valley Rd. amid the forest surrounding Garrison Bay. From West Side Rd., take Mitchell Bay Rd. east to West Valley Rd. Here, four original buildings have been preserved, including the barracks, now used as an interpretive center. The center explains the history of the "war" and sells guides to the island. (Park open year-round; buildings open Memorial Day-Labor Day daily 9am-6pm. Free.)

Friday Harbor is less than charming when the tourists are out in full force, but quite appealing in the winter. Take the time to poke around the galleries, craft shops, and bookstores. The **Whale Museum,** 62 1st St. (378-4710), will teach you everything you ever wanted to know about cetaceans (but were afraid to ask), with skeletons, sculptures, and information on new research. The museum even has a **whale hotline** (800-562-8832) for you to report sightings and strandings. (Open daily 10am-5pm, in winter daily 11am-4pm. Admission $2.50, seniors and students $2, children under 12 $1.)

Walking south a block will take you to the **Friday Harbor Youth Hostel (AYH),** 35 1st St. (378-5555) in the Elite Hotel. It earns low marks for cleanliness, elegance, and security, but its location can't be beat. ($9, nonmembers $14.) An alternative is **San Juan County Park,** 380 Westside Rd. (378-2992), 10 miles west of Friday Harbor on Smallpox and Andrews Bays. (Cold water and flush toilets. Bikers and hikers $3; cars, campers, and trailers $10.) The parks and shoreline drives beg you to pack a picnic lunch and leave Friday Harbor behind. Stock up on bread and cheese at **King's Market,** 160 Spring St. (Open daily 8am-10pm.)

The **post office** is at Blair and Reed St. (378-4511; open Mon.-Fri. 8:30am-4:30pm; **ZIP code:** 98250). San Juan Island's **area code** is 206.

Whidbey Island

This 50-mile-long, crescent-shaped island sits in the rain shadow of the Olympic Mountains. Clouds are wrung dry by the time they pass over Whidbey, so the island receives a mere 25 inches of rain per year and a luxurious ration of sunshine. This leaves visitors free to enjoy rocky beaches bounded by bluffs blooming with wild roses and crawling with blackberry brambles.

Whoever named **Useless Bay** certainly did not do so based on aesthetic criteria. On the west side of the bay, uninterrupted beach stretches from Bayview Beach along **Double Bluff Park** to the tip of the peninsula of Double Bluff. Comb the 1½-

mile beach, explore the bluffs, or just gaze across the water at Seattle and Mt. Rainier. Another ideal spot for the wanderer is **South Whidbey State Park,** 4128 S. Smuggler's Cove Rd. (321-4559), about 7 miles north of Freeland. The park wraps around the west coast of the island, covering 87 acres of virgin forest. Park by the tiny outdoor amphitheater and walk down the bluff to the beach (10 min.). Wander along the pebbly beach approximately 1½ miles in either direction—to Lagoon Point in the north or to a lighthouse on Bush Point in the south.

Around the bend to the north, **Fort Casey State Park,** 1280 S. Fort Casey Rd. (678-4519), is right next to the Keystone ferry terminal, 3 miles south of Coupeville. The park is situated on the site of a late 1890s fort designed to defend against a long-anticipated attack from the west. (Interpretive center open in winter only for large groups by appointment. The rest of the park is open year-round.) **Fort Ebey State Park,** 395 N. Fort Ebey Rd. (678-4636), is accessible from Libbey Rd. off Rte. 20 north of Coupeville, by Valley Drive's park entrance. The park is also the driest spot on the island; prickly pear cacti grow right up next to the beach.

Both parks and the town of **Coupeville** are contained within **Ebey's Landing National Historical Reserve,** federally established for the "preservation and protection of a rural community." Many of Coupeville's homes and commercial establishments date from the 19th century, and the city also maintains the **Island County Historical Museum** at Alexander and Coveland St. (Open May-Sept. daily noon-4pm, April Sat.-Sun. noon-4pm only. Free.) The town extends along E. Front St. between two blockhouses. Constructed in 1855, the four blockhouses were meant to withstand an anticipated Skagit tribe uprising that never occurred. Two of the zealously fortified buildings that remain standing are the **John Alexander Blockhouse,** at the west end of town, and the **Davis Blockhouse,** at the edge of the town's cemetery. A few miles north of Oak Harbor on Rte. 20, fruit fiends and aviation afficionados peacefully coexist at the **U-pick Strawberry Farms,** where the roar from low-flying Navy "Prowler" jets virtually rattles the fruit from the plants.

When the Skagit tribe lived and fished around Deception Pass, it was often raided by the Haida tribe from the north. A bear totem of the Haidas now stands on the north end of West Beach in **Deception Pass State Park,** 5175 N. Rte. 20 (675-2417). This is the most heavily used of Whidbey's state parks, and its views will take your breath away. Eight and a half miles of trails, camping facilities, a saltwater boat launch, and a freshwater lake for swimming, fishing, and boating, allow for a closer look at the tidal pools, beaches, and natural life of the area. (A fishing license, available at most hardware stores, is required for fishing in the lake; the season runs from mid-April to Oct. Park open year-round.)

Smoked salmon is the dish of choice on Whidbey; every town (and every milepost along the highway) has its share of salmon shacks. In Clinton, **Hong Kong Gardens,** 4643 S. Hwy. 525 (221-2828), across from Tara Properties, up a steep hill to the right as you leave town, overlooks the sound and the mainland to the east. Go up for a drink ($1.25-2) even if you skip the Cantonese food. Try the *chow sai foon,* a mix of shrimp, pork, mushrooms, and tiny noodles ($5.75). (Open Sun.-Thurs. 11:30am-11:30pm, Fri.-Sat. 11:30am-2am.) In Langley, **Mike's Place,** 215 1st St. (321-6575) serves the best clam chowder on the island ($2.25). The all-you-can-eat nightly specials are also highly recommended. (Breakfast $5, lunch $4-6, dinner under $10. (Open Mon.-Fri. 7am-10pm, Sat.-Sun. 8am-10pm.) **Knead and Feed** in Coupeville serves small but good sandwiches on homemade bread ($4.15). (Open Mon. and Wed.-Fri. 10:30am-3pm, Sat.-Sun. 10am-4pm.) In Oak Harbor, locals swear by the mushroom burger ($4.50) at **Jason's,** 5355 Hwy. 20 (679-3535), at Goldie Rd. (Breakfast under $5, lunch $3-4, dinner $5-8. Open 24 hours.)

Inexpensive motels are few and far between on Whidbey, while those that do exist are frequently a little run-down. A number of bed and breakfasts offer elegant rooms for a few more dollars. Contact **Whidbey Island Bed and Breakfast Association,** P.O. Box 259, Langley 98260 (321-6272) for a full listing; reservations are necessary. The **Tyee Motel and Cafe,** 405 S. Main St., Coupeville (678-6616), offers clean, straightforward rooms. The setting is bleak but it's within walking distance of Coupeville center and the water. (Cafe open daily 6:30am-9pm. Singles $24, each additional person $2.) The **Acorn Motor Inn,** 8066 Rte. 20 (675-6646), in Oak Harbor, across the street from Safeway, is a beautifully maintained motel run by friendly management. (Singles $36. Doubles $39. Continental breakfast included.) On the northern edge of Oak Harbor is the **Crossroads Motel,** 5622 Hwy. 20 (675-3145). The cinderblock construction is discouraging, but the rooms are immaculately kept. Fully equipped kitchens available. Singles $28. Doubles $39, with kitchens $43.

There are four state parks on the island. **South Whidbey State Park,** 4128 S. Smuggler's Cove Rd. (321-4559), 7 miles northwest of Freeland via Bush Point Rd. and Smuggler's Cove Rd, is on a cliff in a virgin stand of Douglas-firs. A steep ¼-mile trail leads down to a rocky beach. (Open year-round. Sites $7.) **Fort Casey State Park,** 1280 S. Fort Casey Rd. (678-4519), right next to the Keystone ferry terminal, has 35 sites interspersed with turn-of-the-century military memorabilia. It fills early in the summer because it's near the ferry. (Sites $7.) **Fort Ebey State Park** (678-4636) is on N. Fort Ebey Rd., north of Fort Casey and just west of Coupeville. Miles of hiking trails and easy access to a pebbly beach make this, the island's newest campground, also the island's best. (50 sites for cars and RVs $7, 3 sites for hikers and bikers $3.) **Deception Pass State Park,** 5175 N. Hwy. 525 (675-2417), 8 miles north of Oak Harbor, has 8½ miles of hiking trails and Cranberry Lake, for good freshwater fishing and swimming. (Sites $7. 4 rustic sites for hikers and bikers $3.)

Unfortunately, **Island Transit** (678-7771 or 321-6688) only runs one intra-island bus line—the automobile still reigns. There is, however, only one main road: "Rte. 525" on the southern half of the island and "Rte. 20" at Coupeville and beyond. **Hitchhiking** is therefore fairly good, but not recommended for women traveling alone, especially in the northern part of the island.

The southern tip of Whidbey Island is 40 miles directly north of Seattle. The 20-minute **ferry** to Clinton leaves from Mukilteo (pronounced mu-kul-TEE-o), a small community just south of Everett. Take I-5 north from Seattle and follow the large signs to the ferry. (Ferries leave Mukilteo every ½-hr. 6am-11pm, and return ferries leave Clinton every ½-hr. 5:30am-11:30pm. Exact schedule changes with the seasons, so call Washington State Ferries (800-542-7052) for times. Car and passenger $3.75, bicycle and rider $3, walk-on $1.65, each additional passenger $1; over 65, ages 5-12, and disabled travelers 50¢, under 5 free. Small surcharges are added in the summer.) Avoid commuter traffic eastbound in the morning and westbound at night.

Whidbey Island can also be reached from Port Townsend on the Olympic Peninsula. Ferries leave the terminal in downtown Port Townsend for Keystone, on the west side of the island, 8 times per day between 7am and 5:45pm. Ferries return from Keystone to Port Townsend 8 times per day between 7am and 6:30pm. More ferries are scheduled for weekends; extra daily ferries are added in August. (35 min. Car and passenger $5.55. Bicycle riders $3.50. Walk-on $1.65, 65 and over, ages 5-12 and disabled travelers 80¢. Under 5 free. For more information, call 800-542-7052.)

To reach Whidbey from the north, take exit 189 off I-5 and head west toward Anacortes. Be sure to stay on Rte. 20 when it heads south through the stunning Deception Pass State Park (signs will direct you); otherwise you will fly on to Anacortes. **Evergreen Trailways** runs a bus to Whidbey from Seattle.

The **post office** in Langley is at 115 2nd St. (321-4113), **ZIP code** 98260; in Coupeville at 201 NW Coveland (678-5353), **ZIP code** 98239; in Oak Harbor at 7035 70th NW (675-6621), **ZIP code** 98277. The **area code** for Whidbey is 206.

The Olympic Peninsula

In the fishing villages and logging towns of the Olympic Peninsula, locals joke about having webbed feet and using Rustoleum instead of suntan oil. The area's heavy rainfall (up to 200" per year on Mt. Olympus) is wrenched out of the moist Pacific air by the Olympic Mountains. While this torrent supports bona fide rain forests in the western peninsula's river valleys, towns such as Sequim in the range's rain shadow are the driest in all of Washington, with as little as 17 inches of rain in a typical year.

The peninsula's extremes of climate are matched in its geography. The beaches along the Pacific strip are a hiker's paradise—isolated, windy, and beautiful. The glaciated peaks of the Olympic range sport spectacular alpine scenery; the network of trails covers an area the size of Rhode Island. These wild, woody mountains resisted exploration well into the 20th century.

Because it compresses such variety into a relatively small area, the Olympic Peninsula is one of Washington's best destinations for those seeking accessible wilderness and outdoor recreation. U.S. 101 loops around the peninsula, stringing together scattered towns and attractions around the nape of the mountains. The numerous secondary roads departing from 101 were specially designed with exploration in mind, although some are gravel-covered, making bicycling into the heart of the park difficult. Heart o' the Hills Road to Hurricane Ridge makes a particularly good detour, offering an unbeatable panorama of the mountains. Route 112 follows the Strait of Juan de Fuca out to Neah Bay, the driftwood-laden coastal town near Cape Flattery. Greyhound provides service only as far as Port Angeles to the north and Aberdeen/Hoquiam to the south. Although local transit systems extend public transportation a little farther, the western portion of the peninsula and the southern portion of Hood Canal are not on any regular routes.

Hitchhiking is illegal on U.S. 101 southwest of Olympia. Where it is legal, hitching can often be slow, and you may be stranded in the rain for hours. Bicycling is dangerous in some spots, particularly along Crescent Lake just west of Port Angeles, as the shoulders are narrow or nonexistent, the curves are sharp, and the roads serve as race tracks for any number of speeding logging trucks. Motoring suits the peninsula best, although some of the beaches and mountain wilds can be reached only on foot. Extended backpacking trips are particularly rewarding.

Camping

Although many towns on the peninsula cater to tourists with motels and resorts, the beautiful outdoors make camping the more attractive option. **Olympic National Park** maintains a number of campgrounds. (Sites $5.) The numerous **state parks** along Hood Canal and the eastern rim charge $4 per night, with an occasional site for tenters at only $1-3 per night. The **national forest** and the park services welcome backcountry camping (free everywhere), but a permit, available at any ranger station, is required within the park. Camping on the **beaches** is especially easy, although you should be sure to pack a supply of water. The beaches in the westernmost corner of Neah Bay and from the town of Queets to Moclips farther south fall within Native American reserve land. Reservation land is private property: Travelers are welcome, but local regulations prohibiting alcohol, fishing without a tribal permit, and beachcombing should be respected. The Quinault Indian Reservation gained fame 20 years ago by forcibly ousting vandals trespassing on their beaches.

Washington's **Department of Natural Resources (DNR)** manages huge tracts of land on the Kitsap Peninsula and along the Hoh and Clearwater Rivers near the western shore, as well as smaller, individual campsites sprinkled around the peninsula. In DNR areas, camping is free and uncrowded; no reservations are required. DNR areas, however, can be hard to find. For maps, write the Department of Natural Resources, Olympic Area, Rte. 1, Box 1375, Forks, WA 98331, or call 206-374-6131.

Hood Canal and the Kitsap Peninsula

The long ribbon of the Hood Canal reaches down from Puget Sound, nearly separating the Kitsap Peninsula from its parent Olympic Peninsula. The Canal's structure invites comparison with Scandinavia's famous fjords—the same narrow, steeply banked waterway, the same jagged peaks for backdrops, the same little towns tucked in the crevices of the coastline. U.S. 101 adheres to the western shore of the canal from Potlatch State Park on its southern tip to Quilcene in the north.

Here, the **Olympic National Forest** rims the eastern edge of the national park. Much of the forest is more developed and more accessible than the park and gives those with little time or small appetites for the outdoors a taste of the peninsula's wildlife. Stop by one of the forest's **ranger stations** along the canal to pick up information on camping and trails in the forest. The two stations are in **Hoodsport,** P.O. Box 68 (877-5254; open Memorial Day-Labor Day daily 8am-4:30pm, business office open year-round Mon.-Fri. 7am-4:30pm) and **Quilcene,** U.S. 101 S. (765-3368; open Mon.-Fri. 7:30am-5pm, Sat.-Sun. 8:30am-5pm). Both are clearly marked with signs on the highway. Adjacent to the Hoodsport Ranger Station is a **post office** (877-5552; open Mon.-Fri. 8am-12:30pm and 1:30-5pm, Sat. 8:30-11:30am; **ZIP Code:** 98548.). Many of the forest service **campgrounds** cost only $4, including **Hamma Hamma,** on Forest Service Rd. 25, 7 miles northwest of Eldon; **Lena Creek,** 2 miles beyond Hamma Hamma; **Elkhorn,** on Forest Service Rd. 2610, 11 miles northwest of Brinnon; and **Collins,** on Forest Service Rd. 2515, 8 miles west of Brinnon. All are marked on U.S. 101 and have drinking water, as well as good fishing, hiking, and gorgeous scenery. Unfortunately, many of these are accessible only by gravel roads, which are difficult to navigate by bicycle.

Lake Cushman State Park (877-5491), 7 miles west of Hoodsport on Lake Cushman Rd., stretches by a beautiful lake with good swimming beaches. The park is popular as a base camp for extended backpacking trips into the national forest and park. Lake Cushman has 80 sites ($6, $8.50 with full hookup) with flush toilets and pay showers. Clinging to a quiet cove is **Mike's Beach Resort and Hostel,** N. 38470 U.S. 101 (877-5324), just north of Eldon. The hostel lacks a kitchen, and too many bunks crowd its tiny rooms, but it does have a small grocery store. ($5, nonmembers $7.50. Open May 15-Oct. 1.) The **Hungry Bear Cafe,** in Eldon (877-5527), serves the Hood Canal specialty: geoduck (GOO-ey-duck) steak ($8). The geoduck, a giant mollusk which lives 2½ to 7 feet below the surface of Hood Canal's beaches, has a taste somewhere between that of a razor clam and a scallop and is especially delectable here, served with mounds of great french fries and some of the best homemade tartar sauce anywhere. Those feeling less daring might want to stick with the burgers ($1.50-5). (Open Mon.-Thurs. 9am-7pm, Fri. 9am-8pm, Sat. 8am-8pm, Sun. 8am-7pm.)

Topologically, the amorphous **Kitsap Peninsula** resembles a half-completed landfill project jutting into Puget Sound. The new bridge over the northern end of Hood Canal links the Kitsap Peninsula with the towns along the Strait of Juan de Fuca; no pedestrian traffic is allowed, but hitchhiking across is easy. Kitsap can also be reached by ferry: from Seattle to Bremerton or Winslow on connected Bainbridge Island, or from Edmonds, north of Seattle, to Kingston on the northern end of the peninsula.

In **Bremerton** you'll swear that you have stepped into the setting of a Tom Clancy novel; every third person has a Navy security pass swinging officially from their neck. The city is basically an overgrown repair shop for U.S. Naval ships. There are plenty of chain hotels along Kitsap Way in Bremerton, but you might prefer **Scenic Beach State Park,** near the village of Seabeck, featuring 50 campsites with water and bathrooms. (Sites $7, walk-in sites $3.) From Silverdale, take Anderson Hill Rd. or Newberry Hill Rd. west to Seabeck Hwy., then follow the highway 7 miles south to the Scenic Beach turn-off. Cyclists should beware of the staggering hills along this route. The Department of Natural Resources' **Tahuya Multiple Use Area** encompasses eight free campgrounds, each with drinking water, and many with good swimming beaches and boat launches. These are hard to find, however, and must be reached via some difficult gravel roads.

The Kitsap's most appealing attraction is the **Suquamish Museum** (598-3311), 6 miles north of Winslow, just over the Agate Pass Bridge on Rte. 305. Run by the Port Madison Indian Reservation, this small but well-presented museum is devoted entirely to the history and culture of the Puget Sound Salish Native Americans. (Open daily 10am-5pm. Admission $2, seniors $1.50, under 12 $1.)

Olympic National Park

Lodged among the august Olympic mountains, Olympic National Park covers 900,000 acres of velvet rainforest, jagged snowcovered peaks, and dense evergreen forest. This enormous region at the center of the peninsula affords limited access to four-wheeled traffic. No scenic loops or roads cross the park, and only a handful of secondary roads make insignificant attempts to penetrate the interior. The roads that do exist serve mainly as trailheads for over 600 miles of hiking trails. Come prepared for rain; a parka, good boots, and a waterproof tent are essential in this area.

Stop at the **Park Service Visitors Center,** 3002 Mt. Angeles Rd., Port Angeles (452-4501, ext. 230), for backcountry camping permits and map of the locations of other park ranger stations. (Open daily 8am-6pm; in off-season call for hours.) The park service runs **interpretive programs** such as guided forest walks, tidal pool walks, and campfire programs from its various ranger stations (all free). For a full schedule of events everywhere in the park, obtain a copy of the park newspaper, available at ranger stations and the visitors center. A $3 entrance fee per car is charged at the more popular entrances, such as the Hoh, Heart O' the Hills, and Elwaha. The fee buys an entrance permit good for 7 days. A similar pass for hiker/bikers costs $1.

July, August, and September are the best months for visiting Olympic National Park, since much of the backcountry often remains snowed-in until late June, and only the summer has a good number of rainless days. **Backcountry camping** requires a free wilderness permit, available at ranger stations and trailheads. The park service's shelters are for emergencies only; large concentrations of people attract bears.

Never drink untreated water in the park. *Giardia,* a very nasty microscopic parasite, lives in all these waters and causes severe diarrhea, gas, and abdominal cramps. Symptoms often don't appear for weeks after ingestion. Bring your own water supply, or boil local water for five minutes before drinking it. Dogs are not allowed in the backcountry, and must be restrained at all times within the park.

Berry picking ranks high on the list of summer activities on the peninsula. Newly cleared regions and roadside areas yield the best crops; raspberries, strawberries, blueberries, and huckleberries are all prevalent. (Bears are also fond of this fruit; if one stumbles onto your favorite berry patch, don't argue.) **Fishing** within park boundaries is allowed without a permit, but you must obtain a state game department punch card for salmon and steelhead trout at outfitting and hardware stores locally, or at the game department in Olympia.

The **Eastern Rim** of the park is accessible through the Olympic National Forest from U.S. 101 along Hood Canal. For information on camping in the forest see Hood Canal and the Kitsap Peninsula above. The car-accessible campgrounds are popular with hikers who use them as trailheads to the interior of the park. **Staircase Campground** (877-5569), 19 miles northwest of Hoodsport at the head of Lake Cushman, has a ranger station with interpretive programs on weekends. (Open year-round. Sites $5.) **Dosewallips,** on a road that leaves U.S. 101 3 miles north of Brinnon (27 miles north of Hoodsport) is free, but less developed, and only open June-Sept.

On the park's **Northern Rim, Heart o' the Hills** (452-2713) and **Elwha Valley** (452-9191) campgrounds both have interpretive programs and ranger stations, as does **Fairholm Campground** (928-3380), 30 miles west of Port Angeles at the western tip of Lake Crescent. (Open year-round. Sites $5.) The **Lake Crescent** station (928-3380) has an extensive interpretive program but no camping. The **information booth** here is open Memorial Day to Labor Day daily from 11:30am to 4:30pm. **Soleduck Hotsprings Campground** (327-3534), to the southeast of Lake Crescent, 13 miles off U.S. 101, is adjacent to the hot springs resort. (Sites $5.)

The main attraction of the northern area, especially for those not planning backcountry trips, is **Hurricane Ridge,** which affords magnificent views of Mt. Olympus, the Bailey Range, and on clear days, even Canada.

At the top of the Hoh River Rd. is the park service's **Hoh Rain Forest Campground and Visitors Center** (374-6925). The center is wheelchair-accessible, as are trails leading from the center into the only temperate (as opposed to tropical) rain forest in the world. Camping costs $5. (Visitors center open daily 9am-5pm; off-season call for hours.) Farther south, after U.S. 101 rejoins the coast, the park's boundaries extend southwest to edge the banks of the **Queets River.** The road here is unpaved and the campground at the top is free. (Open June-Sept.) The park and forest services share the land surrounding **Quinault Lake** and **Quinault River.** The park service land is accessible only by foot. The forest service operates a day-use beach and an information center in the **Quinault Ranger Station,** South Shore Rd. (288-2525; open in summer daily 7:30am-5pm; in winter Mon.-Fri. 7:30am-5pm).

Mora (374-5460) and **Kalaloch** (962-2283), have campgrounds (sites $7) and ranger stations. The Kalaloch (kuh-LAY-lok) Center, including lodge, general store, and gas station, is the more scenic with 195 sites near the ocean. The **South Beach Campground** is south of the Kalaloch campground. It's free, but really is little more than a parking lot by the shore, packed solid with RVs. Escape the hubbub by hiking up the bluffs at South Beach.

Cascade Range

Formed by centuries of volcanic activity, the relatively young Cascade Range is still evolving—as the 1980 eruption of Mt. St. Helens attests. While a handful of white-domed beauties attract the most interest, the bulk of the range consists of smaller systems that together form a natural barrier from the Columbia Gorge to Canada. The mountain wall intercepts moist Pacific air, and is responsible both for Seattle's cloudy weather and the 300 rainless days per year in the plains of eastern Washington.

Although much of the heavily forested range is accessible only to hikers, horseback riders, and the Sasquatch, four major roads cut through the mountains along river valleys, each offering good trailheads and impressive scenery. **Route 12** through White Pass goes nearest Mt. Rainier National Park; **Interstate 90** sends four lanes past the major ski resorts of Snoqualmie Pass; scenic **Route 2** leaves Everett for Stevens Pass and descends along the Wenatchee River, a favorite of whitewater rafters; and **Route 20,** the **North Cascades Highway,** provides access to North Cascades National Park from April to November, weather permitting. These last two roads are often traveled in sequence as the **Cascade Loop.**

Greyhound travels the routes over Stevens and Snoqualmie Passes to and from Seattle, while **Amtrak** cuts between Ellensburg and Puget Sound. Rainstorms and evening traffic can slow **hitchhiking** down; locals warn against thumbing across Rte. 20, where a few hapless hitchers have apparently "vanished" over the last decade. The mountains are most accessible in the clear months of July, August, and September; many high mountain passes are snowed in the rest of the year. The best source of general information on the Cascades is the **National Park/National Forest Information Service,** 915 2nd Ave., Seattle 98174 (442-0181 or 442-0170).

North Cascades

The North Cascades, an aggregation of dramatic peaks north of Stevens Pass on Rte. 2, is administered by a number of different agencies. Pasayten and Glacier Peak are designated wilderness areas, each attracting large numbers of hardy backpackers and mountain climbers. Ross Lake Recreation Area surrounds the Rte. 20 corridor, and **North Cascades National Park,** 2105 Hwy. 20 Sedro Wooley, WA 98284 (206-856-5700; open Sun.-Thurs. 8am-4:30pm, Fri.-Sat. 8am-6pm), extends north and south of Rte. 20. The **Mt. Baker/Snoqualmie National Forest,** 1018 1st Ave., Seattle 98104 (206-442-0170), borders the park on the west; the **Okanogan National Forest,** 1240 2nd Ave. S., P.O. Box 950, Okanogan 98840 (509-422-2704) to the east; and **Wenatchee National Forest,** 301 Yakima St., P.O. Box 811, Wenatchee

98801 (509-662-4335) to the south. Route 20, the North Cascades Highway, provides the major access to the area, as well as astounding views past each new curve in the road.

Route 20 from Burlington (exit 230 on I-5) across the mountains gives the best first impression of the North Cascades. A feat of modern engineering, Rte. 20 follows the Skagit River to the Skagit Dams and lakes, whose hydroelectric energy powers Seattle, then crosses the Cascade Crest at Rainy Pass (4860 ft.) and Washington Pass (5477 ft.), finally descending to the Methow River and the dry Okanogan rangeland of eastern Washington.

Route 9 leads north from the rich farmland of **Skagit Valley** through inspiring forested countryside, with roundabout access to **Mount Baker** via the forks at the Nooksack River and Rte. 542. Mt. Baker (10,778 ft.) has been belching since 1975, and in winter, jets of steam often rise from its dome. You would only have to sneeze four times in succession to miss the town of **Concrete** and its three neighbors—and perhaps you may want to do so. If you drive through at lunchtime, stop at the **Mount Baker Café,** 119 E. Main St. (853-8200; open Mon.-Sat. 6am-4pm). The road from Concrete to Mt. Baker runs past the lakes created by the Upper and Lower Baker Dams. Solid facts are available from the **Concrete Chamber of Commerce** (853-8400), in the old depot, tucked between Main St. and Hwy. 20—follow the railroad tracks upon entering town. (Open Sat.-Sun. 9am-4pm.)

Neighboring **Rockport** borders **Rockport State Park,** which features magnificent Douglas-firs, a trail that accommodates wheelchairs, and 50 campsites that are among the nicest in the state ($7). The surrounding **Mount Baker National Forest** permits free camping closer to the high peaks. From Rockport, Hwy. 530 stems south to **Darrington,** oddly enough home to a large population of displaced North Carolinians, and therefore host to a rapidly-growing **Bluegrass Festival** on the third weekend of July. Darrington's **ranger station** (436-1155) is on Hwy. 530 at the north end of town. (Open Mon.-Fri. 6:45am-4:30pm, Sat.-Sun. 8am-5pm., in off-season weekends only.)

Pitch your tent at the free sites at the **Cascade Islands Campground,** on the south side of the Cascade River. Ask for careful directions in town, and bring heavy-duty repellent to ward off the swarms of mosquitoes.

From Marblemount, drive up the Old Cascade Rd. for a short hike over **Cascade Pass,** and catch the park service's **shuttle** from Cottonwood or High Bridge to Stehekin on the eastern slope. (Shuttles: 3 per day, 2 hr., $4. Runs mid-June to mid-Sept.) Always check at the **Marblemount Ranger Station,** 1 mile north up a marked raod at the west end of town (873-4590), to see if the shuttle is running. (Open daily 8am-4:30pm.)

Newhalem, a buffer zone between Rte. 20 and North Cascade National Park, is the first town in the **Ross Lake National Recreation Area.** A small grocery store and hiking trails to the dams and lakes nearby are the town's largest attractions. Information is available at the **visitors center,** on Rte. 20. (Open late June-early Sept. Thurs.-Mon. 8am-4pm.) At other times, stop at the general store. (Open daily 8am-8pm.)

The artificial expanse of **Ross Lake** extends back into the mountains as far as the Canadian border, and is plugged up by Ross Dam. It is ringed by 15 campgrounds, some accessible only by boat, others by trail. The trail along Big Beaver Creek, a few miles north of Rte. 20, leads from Ross Lake into the Picket Range and eventually to Mt. Baker and the **Northern Unit** of North Cascades National Park. The **Sourdough Mountain** and **Desolation Peak** lookout towers near Ross Lake have eagle's-eye views of the range.

The National Park's **Goodell Creek Campground,** just south of Newhalem, has 22 sites ($3) suitable for tents and trailers, and a launching site for white-water rafting along the Skagit River. (Open year-round. Drinking water and pit toilets.) **Colonial Creek Campground,** 10 miles to the east, is a fully developed, vehicle-accessible campground with flush toilets, a dump station, and campfire programs every evening. (Open mid-May-Nov. Sites $5.)

Diablo Lake is directly to the west of Ross Lake, the foot of Ross Dam acting as its eastern shore and the top of the Diablo Dam stopping it up on the west. The town of **Diablo Lake,** on the north-eastern shore, is the main trailhead for hikes into the southern portion of the North Cascades National Park. The Thunder Creek Trail traverses Park Creek Pass to the Stehekin River Rd. in Lake Chelan National Recreation Area. Diablo Lake has a boathouse and a lodge that sells groceries and gas.

The **Pacific Coast Trail** crosses **Rainy Pass** (alt. 4,860 ft.) 30 miles farther on the **North Cascades Hwy.,** on one of the most scenic and challenging legs of its 2500-mile Canada-to-Mexico span. The trail leads up to **Pasayten Wilderness** in the north and down to **Glacier Peak** (10,541 ft.), which dominates the central portion of the range. (Glacier Peak can also be approached from the secondary roads extending northward from the Lake Wenatchee area near Coles Corner on U.S. 2, or from Rte. 530 to Darrington.) An overlook at Washington Pass rewards a very short hike with an astonishing view of the red rocks of upper Early Winters Creek's Copper Basin. (For information on the eastern slopes of the North Cascades, see Okanogan County in Eastern Washington.)

Despite the Puritan namesake, the town of **Winthrop** now capitalizes on a Wild West theme. The one row of restaurants, stores, and hotels along the main street—all made of weather-beaten wood with corrugated tin roofs, features creaky wooden sidewalks and painted signs. The whole scene is slightly ludicrous, but it'll certainly impress the kids.

The great billows of hickory-scented smoke draw customers to the **Riverside Rib Co. Bar B-Q,** 207 Riverside (996-2001), which serves fantastic ribs in a convertible prairie schooner (i.e. covered wagon); satisfying vegetarian dinners ($7) are also available. (Open daily 11am-9pm.) Across the street is the **Winthrop Information Station** (996-2125), on the corner of Rte. 20 and Riverside. (Open Memorial Day-Labor Day 9am-5pm.)

While in Winthrop, mark time at the **Shafer Museum** 285 Castle Ave. (996-2712), up the hill overlooking the town, 1 block west of Riverside Ave. The museum features all sorts of bizarre pioneer paraphernalia in a log cabin built in 1897. (Open daily 10am-5pm. Free.) You can rent horses at the **Rocking Horse Ranch** (996-2768), 9 miles north of Winthrop on the North Cascade Hwy. (996-2768; $10 per hr.), and mountain bikes at **The Virginian Hotel** just east of town on Rte. 20 ($4.50 for the 1st hr., then $3 per hr. Full day $20).

The **Winthrop Ranger Station,** P.O. Box 158 (996-2266), up a marked dirt road west of town, has information on camping in the National Forest. (Open Mon.-Fri. 7:45am-5pm, Sat. 8:30am-5pm.) North of Winthrop, the **Early Winters Visitor Center,** outside Mazama, is stocked with information about the Pasayten Wilderness, an area whose relatively gentle terrain and mild climate endear it to hikers and equestrians. (996-2534; open Sun.-Thurs. 9am-5pm, Fri.-Sat. 9am-6pm; in off-season weekends only.)

Early Winters has 15 simple campsites ($5) 14 miles west of Winthrop on Rte. 20, and **Klipchuk,** 1 mile further west, has 39 better developed sites ($5). Cool off at **Pearrygin Lake State Park** beach. From Riverside west of town, take Pearrygin Lake Rd. for 4 miles. Sites ($6) by the lake have flush toilets and pay showers. Arrive early, since the campground fills up in the early afternoon.

Leave Winthrop's prohibitively expensive hotel scene and stay in **Twisp,** the town that should have been a breakfast cereal. Nine miles south of Winthrop on Rte. 20, this peaceful town offers low prices and fewer tourists. Stay at **The Sportsman Motel,** 1010 E. Rte. 20 (997-2911), whose barracks-like exterior belies its tasteful rooms, decor, and kitchens. (Singles $26, doubles $30; Oct. 31-June 15 singles $18, doubles $23.) The **Blue Spruce Motel** (997-8852) offers more spartan accommodations just a ½ block away. (Singles $21. Doubles $31.) The **Twisp Ranger Station,** 502 Glover St. (997-2131), has an extremely helpful staff ready to load you down with trail and campground guides. (Open Mon.-Fri. 7:45am-4:30pm, Sat. 10am-2pm.) The **Methow Valley Tourist Information Office,** at the corner of Rte. 20 and 3rd St., has area brochures. (Open Mon.-Fri. 8am-noon and 1-5pm.)

The Methow Valley Farmer's Market sells produce from 9am to noon on Saturdays (Apr.-Oct.) in front of the community center. Join local workers and their families at **Rosey's Branding Iron,** 123 Glover St. (997-3576). Wonderfully droll staff serve all-you-can-keep-down soup and salad for $6. (Open daily 5am-9pm.)

Five miles east of Twisp is a training station for **Smoke Jumpers,** folks who get their kicks by parachuting into the middle of blazing forest fires and taking a more *offensive* approach to firefighting. Occasionally they give tours or have training sessions that the public can watch. Call the base (997-2031) for details.

Gray Line Tours (343-2000) runs buses to North Cascades National Park from Seattle ($20, under 12 $10). Take the 12-hour tour or stay in the park for the week. Buses depart Sundays at 7:45am from the Space Needle (June 5-Sept. 26). **Greyhound** stops in Burlington once per day on its Portland-Seattle route, and **Empire Lines** (affiliated with Greyhound), serves Okanogan, Pateros, and Chelan on the eastern slope. Hitching in this area is not adviseable.

Mount Rainier National Park

Mt. Rainier rises grandly above the tops of the other Cascade mountains, 2 miles taller than many of the surrounding foothills. Residents of Washington refer to it simply as "The Mountain."

Unfortunately, Rainier's meteorological effect is to drench all that lies in its shadow. Warm ocean air condenses when it reaches Rainier and falls on the mountain at least 200 days of the year. When the sun does shine, the effect is dazzling. It isn't difficult to understand why Native Americans called Mt. Rainier "Tahoma" (Mountain of God).

First-time visitors will appreciate Mt. Rainier more from lower elevations than from the 14,410-foot summit. Although an expedition to the summit is exhilarating, many experiences available at slightly lower elevations—midnight views of the mountain silhouetted against the moon, inner-tube rides down the slick sides in winter, romps in alpine meadows full of unparalleled wildflower displays—approach the same intensity at much less cost and personal risk. Nevertheless, 2500 determined climbers ascend to Rainier's peak each year.

For visitor information stop in at the **Longmire Museum and Hiker's Center** (open mid-June to Sept. daily 8am-5:30pm; off-season daily 9am-5pm); **Paradise Visitors Center** (open mid-June to mid-Sept. daily 9am-6pm; off-season hours vary); **Ohanapecosh Visitor Center** (same hours as Paradise); or **Sunrise Visitors Center,** (same hours as Paradise). All centers can be contacted c/o Superintendent, Mt. Rainier National Park, Ashford, WA 98304, or through the park central operator (569-2211). Admission to the park is $5 per car or $2 per hiker. Gates are open 24 hours.

Much of the activity in Rainier occurs here. Each center has displays, a wealth of literature on everything from hiking to natural history, postings on trail and road conditions, and a smiling ranger to fill in any gaps. Naturalist-guided trips and talks, campfire programs, and slide presentations are given at the visitors centers and vehicle campgrounds throughout the park. Check at a visitors center or pick up a copy of the free annual newsletter, *Tahoma,* for details.

A car tour provides a good introduction to the park. All major roads offer scenic views of the mountain and have numerous roadside sites for camera-clicking and general gawking. The roads to Paradise and Sunrise are especially picturesque. **Stevens Canyon Road** connects the southeast corner of the national park with Paradise, Longmire, and the Nisqually entrance, and affords truly spectacular vistas of Rainier and the rugged Tatoosh Range that would put the Swiss Alps to shame. Mt. Adams and Mt. St. Helens can't be seen from the road, but there are good views of these from the mountain trails.

Several less-developed roads provide access to more isolated regions. These roads often abut trailheads that crisscross the park or lead to the summit. Cross-country hiking and camping outside designated campsites is permissible through most regions of the park, but a permit is always required for overnight backpacking trips. The **Hikers Center** at Longmire has information on day and backcountry hikes through the park. You can also obtain permits there. (Open mid-June to Sept. daily 7am-7pm.)

A segment of the **Pacific Crest Trail (PCT),** running between the Columbia River and the Canadian border, crosses through the southeast corner of the park. Geared for both hikers and horse riders, the PCT is maintained by the U.S. Forest Service. Primitive campsites and shelters line the trail; no permit is required for camping, although you should contact the nearest ranger station for information on site and trail conditions. The trail, sometimes overlooking the snow-covered peaks of the Cascades, snakes through delightful scenery where wildlife abounds.

Hardcore campers will be thrilled by **Wonderland Trail,** a 95-mile loop around the entire mountain. Because it includes some brutal ascents and descents, rangers recommend that even experts plan on covering only 7-10 miles per day. Rangers can provide information on weather and trail conditions, and can even help with food caches at stations along the trail. Specific dangers to be aware of along Wonderland include snow-blocked passes in June, muddy trails in July, and early snowstorms in September. Expert climbers can discuss options for reaching the summit itself with rangers.

Less-ambitious, ranger-led **interpretive hikes** feature themes from local wildflowers to area history. Each visitors center (see Practical Information) conducts its own hikes and each has a different schedule. The hikes, lasting anywhere from 20 minutes to all day, are ideal outings for families with young children. These free hikes complement evening campfire programs, also conducted by each visitors center.

The towns of **Packwood** and **Ashford** have a few motels near the park. For general lodging information and reservations at the two inns within the park, call 569-2275. Camping at the auto campsite costs $6 between mid-June and late Sept. Alpine and cross-country camping require free permits year-round, and are subject to certain restrictions. Pick up a copy of the *Backcountry Trip Planner* at any ranger station or hiker's center before you set off. Alpine and cross-country permits are strictly controlled to prevent enviromental damage, but auto camping permits are easy to come by. The best developed campgrounds are at **Sunshine Point** near the Nisqually entrance, at **Cougar Rock** near Longmire, at **Ohanapecosh,** at **White River** in the northeast corner, and at **Carbon River.** Open on a first come-first camp basis, they fill up only on the busiest summer weekends. Sunshine Point, however, is the only campground open throughout the year. With a permit, cross-country hikers can use any of the free, well-established **trailside camps** scattered throughout the park's backcountry. Most camps have toilet facilities and a nearby water source; some have shelters. Fires are prohibited and there are limits on the number of members in a party. Mountain and glacier climbers must always register in person at ranger stations in order to be granted permits.

To reach Mt. Rainier from the west, drive south on I-5 to Tacoma, then go east on Rte. 512, south on Rte. 7, and east on Rte. 706. This scenic road meanders through the town of Ashford and into the park by the Nisqually entrance. Rte. 706 is the only access road kept open throughout the year; snow usually closes all other park roads from November through May. The total distance from Tacoma is 65 miles. The city of Yakima is the eastern gateway to the park. Take I-82 from the center of town to U.S. 12 heading west. At the junction of the Naches and Tieton Rivers, go either left on U.S. 12 or continue straight up Rte. 410. U.S. 12 runs past Rimrock Lake, over White Pass to Rte. 123, where a right turn leads to the Stevens Canyon entrance to Rainier. **Gray Line Bus Service,** 2411 4th Ave., Seattle (343-2000), runs excursions from Seattle to Rainier daily from May 15 to October 15. (Round-trip $20, under 13 $10.) **Hitchhiking** along the mountain roads is exceptionally good.

Mount St. Helens

Once thought to be extinct, Mt. St. Helens started rumbling on May 18, 1980. In the three days that followed, a hole 2 miles long and a mile wide opened in the mountain. Ash from the crater blackened the sky for hundreds of miles and blanketed the streets of towns as far as Yakima, 80 miles away. Debris spewed from the volcano flooded Spirit Lake, choked rivers with mud, and descended to the towns via river and glacier. Entire forests were leveled by the blast, leaving a stubble of trunks on the hills and millions of trees pointing like arrows away from the crater. Because the blast was lateral, not vertical, it was more destructive: No energy was dissipated fighting gravity. Almost a decade later, the Mt. St. Helens National Monument still looks like a disaster area. The vast expanses of downed timber look like nothing more than an immense graveyard, an eternal monument to a blast of an intensity many times greater than that of any manmade atomic detonation. The spectacle of disaster is dotted with signs of returning life: saplings push their way up past their fallen brethren, insects flourish near newly formed waterfalls, a beaver has been spotted in Spirit Lake.

The **Mount St. Helens National Volcanic Monument Visitor Center** (247-5473), on Rte. 504, west of Toutle (take exit 49 off I-5, and follow the signs) is the best place to start a trip to the mountain. The **Gifford Pinochet National Forest Headquarters,** 500 W. 12th St., Vancouver, WA (696-7500), has camping and hiking information. For information on current volcanic activity, call 696-7848.

Gray Line, 400 NW Broadway, Portland, OR (503-226-6755) runs buses from Portland to Mt. St. Helens. (Round-trip $23, under 13 $12.)

Mount St. Helens' **area code** is 206.

Spokane

Originally named Spokan Falls after the Spokan-ee Indians who once inhabited the area, Spokane was the first pioneer settlement in the Pacific Northwest. Though ravaged by the "great fire of 1889," Spokane quickly reestablished the industries spawned by local natural resources. Today, the spunkiest city in Eastern Washington remains one of the Northwest's major trade centers, with an economy still based on lumber, mining, and agriculture.

In its own unwilling way, Spokane achieves urbanity without typical big-city hassles. The downtown thrives, though the pace is slow (not a soul crosses the street until the "Walk" sign flashes). The Expo '74 legacy includes Riverfront Park with its museum and theater, as well as a number of trendy restaurants and hotels. And, in typical Northwest fashion, Spokane takes full advantage of its setting. Arboretums, gardens, abundant outdoor activities, and a spectacular series of bridges spanning the Spokane River and Falls celebrate an environment more ancient than concrete.

Practical Information and Orientation

Visitor Information: Spokane Area Convention and Visitors Bureau, W. 926 Sprague Ave. (747-3230). Open Mon.-Fri. 8:30am-5pm, and most summer weekends 9am-3pm. **Spokane Area Chamber of Commerce,** W. 1020 Riverside, P.O. Box 2147 (624-1393). Open Mon.-Fri. 8am-5pm.

Travelers Aid: W. 1017 1st Ave. (456-7169), near the bus depot. Helps stranded travelers find lodgings. Open Mon.-Fri. 1-5pm.

Spokane International Airport: off I-90 southwest of town.

Amtrak: W. 221 1st Ave. (624-5144), at Bernard St., downtown. To: Chicago (1 per day, $192); Seattle (1 per day, $60); and Portland (1 per day, $60). Depot open Mon.-Fri. 11am-3:30am, Sat.-Sun. 7:15pm-3:30am.

Buses: Greyhound, W. 1125 Sprague (624-5251), at 1st Ave. and Jefferson St., downtown. To Seattle (5 per day, $33). **Empire Lines** and **Gray Lines** (624-4116) share the terminal with Greyhound, serving Eastern Washington, Northern Idaho, and British Columbia. Station open daily 6am-8pm and 1-3am.

Spokane Transit System: W. 1229 Boone Ave. (328-7433). Serves all areas of Spokane, including Eastern Washington University in Cheney. All buses start and finish their runs at Riverside and Howard St. Operates until 12:15am downtown, 9:15pm in the valley along E. Sprague Ave.Fare 60¢, seniors and disabled travelers 30¢. Coupon booklets available at midday, giving discounts in local shops and restaurants.

Taxi: Checker Cab, 624-4171. 24 hours. **Yellow Cab,** 624-4321. **A-1 Taxi,** 534-7768.

Car Rental: U-Save Auto Rental, W. 918 3rd St. (455-8018), at Monroe. From $19 per day, with 100 free miles, 20¢ each additional mile. Open Mon.-Fri. 8am-6pm, Sat. 8am-5pm. Must be 21 with a deposit of $250 or major credit card.

Help Line: Crisis Hotline, 838-4428. 24 hours.

Post Office: W. 904 Riverside (459-0230), at Lincoln. Open Mon.-Fri. 8:30am-5pm. **ZIP code:** 99210.

Area Code: 509.

Spokane lies 280 miles east of Seattle by I-90. Downtown is wedged between I-90 and the Spokane River. Exits 279 to 282 serve the area. Avenues run east-west parallel to the river, streets north-south, and both alternate one-way. The city is divided into north and south by **Sprague Avenue,** east and west by **Division Street. Riverfront Park** abuts Spokane Falls at the heart of the city. Downtown is the area north of Sprague and west of Division. Street addresses are listed with the compass point first, the number second, and the street name third (e.g., W. 1200 Division). No one knows why.

Accommodations and Camping

Let's face it: you have few options. A handful of hotels south of downtown are cheap but sleazy. Most camping areas are at least 20 miles away. Don't try to sleep in Riverfront Park; the police don't appreciate it.

Brown Squirrel Hostel (AYH), W. 1807 Pacific Ave. (838-5968), in Brown's Addition. Near a supermarket and Elks Drug, an old-fashioned pharmacy with real fountain sodas. Cozy rooms, unmatched hospitality. 20 beds. Officially open 8-10am and 5-10pm but stop in just about anytime. Linens, towels, and transportation to the airport or bus station. $8, nonmembers $11.

Eastern Washington University (359-7022), 18 miles from Spokane in Cheney. Take bus #24 from Howard and Riverside St. downtown. By car, take I-90 southwest 8 miles to exit 270, then Rte. 904 south; turn right on Elm St. and continue to 10th. Pleasant dorm rooms. Linen provided. Inquire at Morrison Hall in the summer, or Anderson Hall during the school year. Singles $9.70, students $7. Doubles $19.40, students $14. Rarely full.

Town Centre Motor Inn, W. 901 1st (747-1041), at Lincoln St. Large, comfortable rooms with phones and wonderfully garish oil paintings. Some rooms also have refrigerators at no extra charge. Complimentary coffee served with the morning paper. Singles $28. Doubles $35. Canadian dollars accepted at par. Call for reservations.

El Rancho Motel, W. 3000 Sunset Blvd. (455-9400). Take 2nd Ave. west to Maple St., where Sunset cuts diagonally across the intersection. Follow Sunset approximately 15 blocks. On the edge of town, with easy access to freeway. Rooms have cable, free coffee, A/C, and phones. Equipped with laundromat and pool. Singles $27.50. Doubles $30.50.

Motel 6, S. 1580 Rustle St. (459-6120), at exit 277 on I-90. Far from downtown. TV, phone, and pool. Singles $24. Doubles $30. Call 2-3 weeks in advance for reservations.

Riverside State Park (456-3964), 6 miles northwest of downtown on Rifle Club Rd., off Rte. 291 or Nine Mile Rd. Take Division north and turn left on Francis. 101 standard sites in an urban setting. Kitchen and small museum in the park. Facilities for the disabled. Shower and bath. Sites $7.

Mt. Spokane State Park (456-4169), 30 miles northeast of the city. Take Rte. 395 5 miles north to Rte. 2, then go 7 miles north to Rte. 206, which leads into the park. Popular for its cross-country ski and snowmobiling trails. From the Vista House, views of 4 states and Canada. Flush toilets, cold water only. Twelve sites, $7 each.

Food

For a variety of interesting restaurants downtown, head to **The Atrium,** on Wall St. near 1st. Ave. **Europa Pizzeria,** one of the restaurants in this small brick building, bakes the best pizzas in town. May through October, Wednesdays and Saturdays in Riverfront Park, the **Spokane County Market** (456-5512) sells fresh fruit, vegetables, and baked goods. The **Green Bluff Growers Cooperative** is an organization of 20-odd fruit and vegetable farms, 16 miles northwest of town off Day-Mountain Spokane Rd. Many of the farms have "U-pick" arrangements, and nearby are free picnic areas with panoramic views. Peak season for most crops is from August to October.

Dick's, E. 10 3rd Ave. (747-2481), at Division. Look for the pink panda near I-90. A takeout burger phenomenon whose fame grows as its prices stay the same. Burgers 49¢, fries 37¢, soft drinks 31¢, pies 35¢, sundaes 50¢, pints of ice cream 67¢. The list goes on and on. Always crowded, but lines move quickly. Open daily 9am-1:30am.

Cyrus O'Leary's, W. 516 Main St. (624-9000), in the Bennetts Block complex at Howard St. A Spokane legend. Devour delicious food from a creative 25-page menu. Dress in proper attire—i.e., crazy 1890s Wild West. Costumed staff serves enormous $6-12 meals. Sandwiches $3-5. Happy Hour 4-6pm. Open Mon.-Thurs. 11:30am-11pm, Fri.-Sat. 11:30am-midnight, Sun. 11:30am-10pm.

Thai Cafe, W. 410 Sprague (838-4783). This tiny restaurant adds plenty of spice (or a little, depending upon your preference) to Spokane's otherwise Americanized ethnic fare. Traditional dishes like *pad thai* and *gai pahd* $4-6. Open Mon.-Fri. 11:30am-1:30pm and 5-8:30pm, Sat. 5-8:30pm.

Coyote Cafe, W. 702 3rd Ave. (747-8800). This jazzy Mexican joint has *cerveza* (beer) signs on the walls, cacti in the windows, and serves $2.16 margaritas all day. Specialties include the Coyote Chimichanga ($6) and *fajitas* ($8). Open Sun.-Thurs. 11am-11pm, Fri.-Sat. 11am-midnight.

Sights and Entertainment

Spokane has few aspirations to flashy exhibits or high-flown architecture. The city's best attractions are those concentrating on local history and culture. The unusually shaped **Museum of Native American Cultures (MONAC),** E. 200 Cataldo St. (326-4550), a few blocks east of Riverfront Park, stands on a hill to the northeast of downtown, off Division St. The four-story museum houses a collection of native North and South American art and artifacts. (Open Tues.-Sat. 10am-5pm, Sun. 11am-5pm. Admission $3, seniors and students $2, families $7.)

Local Native American organizations have instituted the **Indian Community Center,** E. 801 2nd (535-0886), as both a social resource for Native Americans and a center for preserving their heritage. It sponsors traditional dances, and is a good source of information on Native American fairs and powwows in the Northwest. The **Cheney Cowles Memorial Museum,** W. 2316 1st Ave. (456-3931), also has exhibits on Native American culture and history. In addition, it offers well-explicated displays on the natural history and pioneer settlement of Eastern Washington, and a gallery devoted to contemporary local art. The **Grace Campbell House** (456-3931) next door is affiliated with the museum. Built in the Tudor revival style with a fortune extracted from the Coeur d'Alene gold mines in Idaho, this elegant Victorian museum describes Spokane's high-society life during the 1890s boom era. (Museum open Tues.-Sat. 10am-5pm, Sun. 2-5pm. Admission $2, seniors and students with ID $1, families $5. House open Tues.-Sat. 10am-4pm, Sun. 2-5pm. Free.) The **Ad Gallery,** E. 502 Boone (328-4220, ext. 3211), showcases rotating exhibits of local and national artists, and a contemporary print collection. (Open Mon.-Fri. 10am-4pm.) For more on the arts, contact the **Spokane Arts Department,** 4th floor, City Hall, W. 808 Spokane Falls Blvd. (456-3857).

Riverfront Park, N. 507 Howard St. (456-5512), just north of downtown, is Spokane's center of gravity. Built for the 1974 World's Fair, here is where the populace strolls on leisurely weekend afternoons. Ride the beautifully hand-carved **Looff Carousel** (open daily 11am-9pm; admission 60¢). The **IMAX Theatre** (456-5511) shows

3D films on a 5½ story screen. (Shows run noon-9pm and start on the hr. Admission Tues.-Sun. $3.75, ages 17 and under $2.75). The **Gondola Skyride Over the Falls** travels from the park over Spokane Falls and over to the north side of the river. (Open in summer daily 11am-9pm. Fare $2.50, children $1.50.)

Hard-core Bingsters will be drawn to the **Crosby Library,** E. 502 Boone St. (328-4220), at Gonzaga University. Here, the faithful display the crooner's relics: gold records, awards, photographs and even a piece of his right index finger bone. (Open Mon.-Thurs. 8am-midnight, Fri. 8am-5pm, Sat. 9am-5pm, Sun. 1pm-midnight. Free.)

Spokane's collection of two dozen parks includes tranquil, well-groomed **Finch Arboretum,** W. 3404 Woodland Blvd. Over 2000 species of trees, flowers, and shrubs are available 24 hours for viewing. **Manito Park,** on S. Grand Ave. between 17th and 25th Ave. (856-4331), south of downtown, features flower gardens, tennis courts, a duck pond, and the Gaiser Conservatory which houses many tropical and local plant species. (Open daily 8am-dusk; off-season daily 8am-3:30pm. Free.) Adjacent to the Manito Park is the **Nishinomiya Garden,** a lush Japanese garden symbolizing the friendship between Spokane and her Japanese sister city, Nishinomiya. (Open 8am-dusk. Free.)

The state runs two parks near Spokane, and both merit a trip. **Riverside State Park** (456-3964 or 456-2499) follows the Spokane River and features 7,655 acres of volcanic outcroppings, rushing water, hiking (especially good in Deep Greek Canyon), and equestrian trails (horse rental $7 per hr. in nearby Trail Town; 456-8249). The park is prime cross-country ski territory in the winter. (Open daily 6:30am-dusk; Nov.-March 8am-dusk.) **Mount Spokane State Park** (456-4169) stands 35 miles to the northeast of the city with a road extending to the summit. Clear days afford views of the Spokane Valley and the distant peaks of the Rockies and Cascades. Mt. Spokane is a skiing center with free cross-country trails and $15-20 downhill ski packages.

Don't leave Spokane without sampling one of the fine Eastern Washington wines. Try **Worden's Washington Winery,** W. 7217 45th St. (455-7835), at exit 276 off I-90 west. Take Grove Rd. to Thorpe Rd., then Thorpe to Westbow Blvd. Free tours are given daily on the hour from noon to 4pm.

Spokane's more traditional tastes are reflected in the large number of bowling alleys and movie theaters gracing the city. However, the variety of live music here keeps the populace boppin' until they're droppin'. The *Spokane Spokesman-Review's* Friday Weekend section and the *Spokesman Chronicle's* Friday Empire section give the low-down on area happenings. During the summer, the city parks present a free **Out-to-Lunch** concert series at noon on weekdays. (Call 624-1393 or check in the Weekend for schedule information.)

Henry's Pub, W. 230 Riverside Ave. (624-9828), is the place for live rock Wed.-Sat. nights. Local favorites New Language, Young Brians, and the Cruizers belt their 50s and 60s rock here. Draft beer $1. (Open Wed.-Sat. 7pm-2am.) Although you'd never guess it from looking at the shabby exterior, you'll find some of Washington's best R&B and rock 'n' roll at the **Red Lion Inn Tavern,** N. 126 Division St. (624-1934). Happy hour 11:30am-6pm. (Open Mon.-Fri. 11am-2am, Sat.-Sun. 4pm-2am. Shows start at 9pm. Tickets $7-10.)

HAWAII

Between 25 and 40 million years ago, molten rock welled up from the depths of the earth and burst through the ocean floor in an isolated sector of the Pacific Ocean. Over millenia, giant shield volcanoes built up to puncture the ocean's surface. As the Pacific Plate shifted to the northwest, the underlying source of the eruptions remained stationary, so that the original island volcanoes moved beyond the active zone of volcanic intrusion while new eruptive fissures progressively surfaced farther southeast. In this conveyer belt fashion, the 1600 mile archipelago known as the Hawaiian Islands formed. The oldest islands in the northwest have been worn away to tiny coral atolls by the erosion of the sea while at the other end of the chain, fiery eruptions reclaim new land from the ocean's depths.

Long before Plate Tectonics became in vogue, the ancient Hawaiians grasped the volcanic mechanism at work. Their legends told of the Fire Goddess, Pele, who fled from island to island, moving southeast down the chain to escape the watery intrusions of her older sister, the ocean. These early Polynesian settlers arrived long after Pele's voyage had brought her to her current abode on the Big Island, but their own odyssey is no less remarkable. Traveling across thousands of miles of unbroken ocean as early as the 6th century C.E., the first inhabitants carried with them roots, seeds, dogs, chickens, and a pig or two in their double-hulled canoes.

In 1778, Captain Cook sailed through Hawaii while searching for the Northwest Passage. He was received as a god but was accidently killed in a skirmish eight months later. His inadvertent discovery propelled Hawaii into the modern world. King Kamehameha I of the Big Island exploited the advent of Western arms and conquered all of the other islands escept Kauai within 20 years of Cook's arrival. He is revered today as the man who united the islands and created modern Hawaii. Yet the European trade ships Kamehameha welcomed brought more than he had bargained for. The washing away of Hawaiian culture by an inexorable tide of Western influence paralleled the physical decimation of the Hawaiian people by an influx of Western disease.

Following the arrival of Calvinist missionaries from Boston in 1820, the *haole* (Caucasian) presence in island life became entrenched. By 1853, 30% of Hawaiians belonged to Christian churches. An expanding sugar (and later pineapple) industry supplanted the original whaling and sandalwood trade. Chinese, Japanese, and Filipinos were brought in as indentured plantation laborers to replace the dying Hawaiians. American sugar magnates, leery of a strong monarchy and desirous of ensuring a market for their product, overthrew King Kalakaua in 1887. In 1898, the U.S., having acquired Spain's interests in the Pacific and desiring Hawaii as a military base, annexed the islands as a formal U.S. territory. The Japanese attack on Pearl Harbor, half a century later, dramatically summoned the U.S. into World War II. In 1959, Hawaii became the fiftieth state.

Although on Hawaii every ethnic group is a minority, there is surprisingly little racial tension. Instead, residents have taken parts of each ethnic heritage and merged them to form a "local" culture—more of a tossed salad than a melting pot. This culture manifests itself everywhere from the menus of the island lunchwagons to the linguistic pot-pourri of Pidgin (the islands' dialect of bastardized English.)

For more comprehensive coverage of Hawaii than we can provide here, consult *Let's Go: California & Hawaii.*

Practical Information

Capital: Honolulu.

Tourist Information: Hawaii Visitors Bureau, 2270 Kalakaua Ave., #801, Honolulu 96815 (923-1811). Open Mon.-Fri. 8am-4:30pm. The prime source. Neighboring islands staff offices at major towns, as listed in the appropriate sections. **Department of Land and Natural Re-**

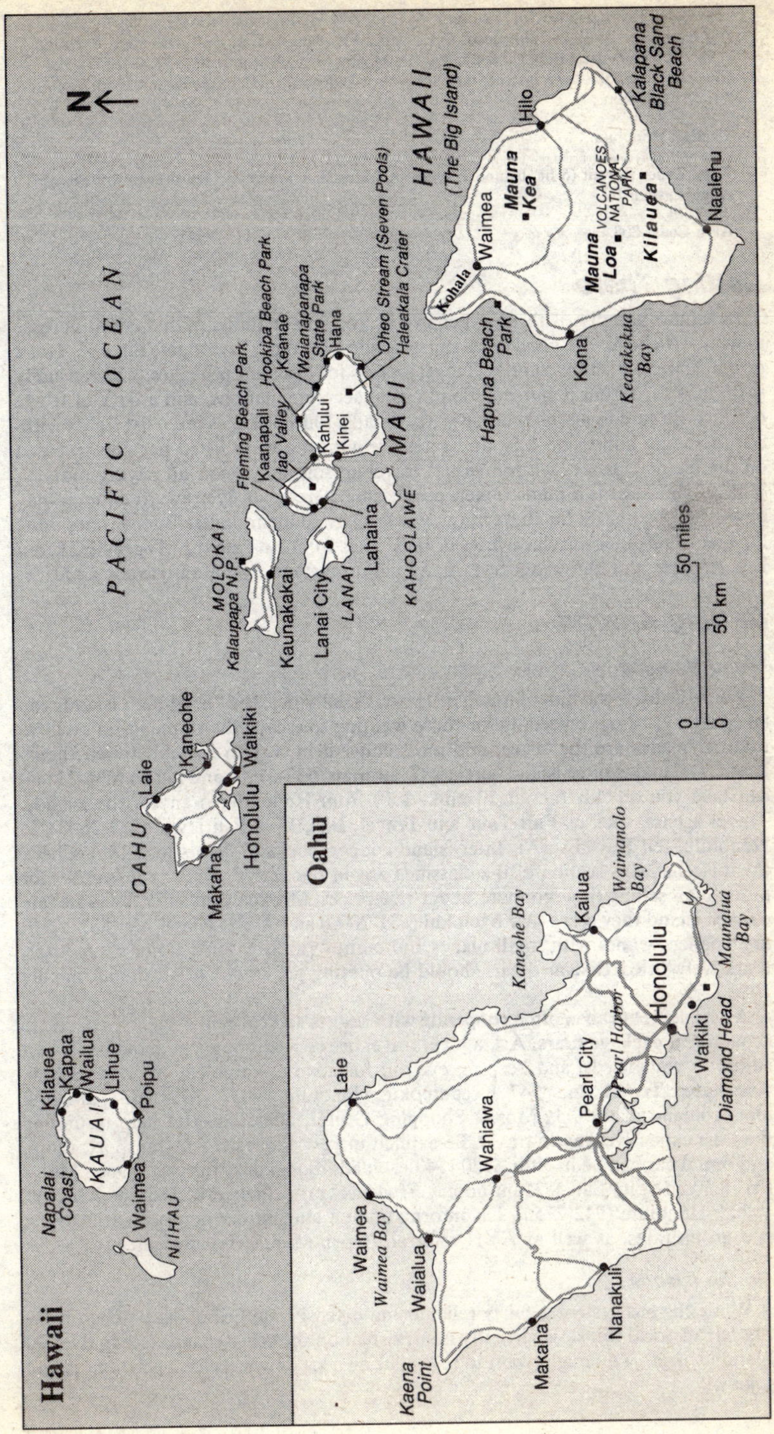
Hawaii
PACIFIC OCEAN
N
NIIHAU
KAUAI
Napalai Coast
Waimea
Kilauea
Kapaa
Wailua
Lihue
Poipu
OAHU
Laie
Kaneohe
Waikiki
Honolulu
Makaha
MOLOKAI
Kalaupapa N.P.
Kaunakakai
LANAI
Lanai City
KAHOOLAWE
Lahaina
Fleming Beach Park
Kaanapali
Iao Valley
Kahului
Kihei
Hookipa Beach Park
Keanae
Waianapanapa State Park
Hana
Oheo Stream (Seven Pools)
Haleakala Crater
MAUI
HAWAII
(The Big Island)
Kohala
Waimea
Hapuna Beach Park
Mauna Kea
Mauna Loa
VOLCANOES NATIONAL PARK
Kilauea
Hilo
Kalapana Black Sand Beach
Naalehu
Kona
Kealakekua Bay
0 50 miles
0 50 km
Oahu
Kaena Point
Makaha
Waialua
Waimea
Waimea Bay
Laie
Wahiawa
Nanakuli
Pearl City
Pearl Harbor
Kaneohe Bay
Kailua
Waimanolo Bay
Honolulu
Waikiki
Diamond Head
Maunalua Bay

sources, 1151 Punchbowl St., Honolulu 96813 (548-7455). Information and permits for camping in state parks, and trail maps. Open Mon.-Fri. 8am-4:15pm. **National Park Service,** Prince Kuhio Federal Bldg., #6305, 300 Ala Moana Blvd., Honolulu 96813 (541-2693). Permits aren't available here; instead, they are given at individual park headquarters. Open Mon.-Fri. 7:30am-4pm.

Capital: Honolulu.

Time Zone: Hawaii (6 hr. behind Eastern in spring and summer; 5 hr. otherwise). **Postal Abbreviation:** HI.

Area Code: 808.

Getting There

Reaching paradise isn't as expensive as you might think. While costs increase in winter (Feb.-April), good deals can be made even then. Investigate the *L.A. Times* or the *New York Times* Sunday Travel section for discount packages, which usually include airfare from major mainland cities, accommodations, and a bevy of fringe benefits. Be sure to learn the nitty gritty details: tour packages often list sights without including admission fees, and rates are almost always listed per person based on double occupancy. An individual traveling solo may wind up paying more.

If all you need is a plane ticket, purchasing a frequent flyer award coupon may be the best bet. Look for these in the newspaper. Along more traditional lines, look for special advance purchase fares or bulk rates from cut-rate travel agencies. From Los Angeles and San Francisco, many major carriers fly round-trip for $200.

Getting Around

Island Hopping

While Oahu is the hub of much of Hawaii's activities, the "neighbor" islands can be equally exciting, especially for those wanting to escape the trappings of civilization. Airplanes are the fastest and most convenient way to travel between the islands. The major inter-island carriers (**Hawaiian** (537-5100) and **Aloha** (836-1111)) can take you quickly (about 30 min., $50) from Honolulu to any of the islands. Travel agents, such as **Pali Tour and Travel, Inc.,** 1304 Pali Hwy. (533-3608), in Honolulu, sell Hawaiian Air inter-island coupon books (6 flights for $185). Check the miscellaneous section of the classified ads in the *Star-Bulletin* or *Advertiser* for individuals selling these coupons at cut-rate prices. Most carriers offer the same fare to each island they serve. **Air Molokai** (831-2000) and **Aloha Island Air** (831-3219) are smaller airlines with small planes and bumpy rides. A third major competitor, tentatively titled Discover Air, should be offering jet service to all the islands by 1990.

Aloha and Hawaiian often cooperate with resorts and car rental agencies to create economical **package tours.** Ask a local travel or reservations agent about deals best suited to your needs, and keep an eye out for ads in pamphlets and newspapers. **Associated Travel, Inc.** 947 Keeaumoku, Honolulu 96813 (949-1033), about 3 blocks inland of the Ala Moana Shopping Center, offers cheerful help in finding the least expensive way to travel. Be explicit in your requests. Air transport, room, and rental car can be had for $120 ($43 each additional day) for two. (Open Mon.-Fri. 8:30am-5pm, Sat. 8:30am-noon.) **Student Travel Network,** 1831 S. King St. #202, Honolulu (942-7755), has information on student discounts, student tours, and group rates, as well as AYH referral. (Open Mon.-Fri. 9am-5pm.)

On the Islands

While the **bus** system is fairly reliable and extensive on Oahu and patchy on the Big Island, local transit is virtually non-existent on the other islands (see individual island listings). You might want to rent your own set of wheels for a neighbor island sojourn.

Car rental agencies fill major island airports and tourist areas in towns. If you have not booked a rental through an airline or other package deal, check local weekly and monthly travel guides for specials and ask about weekly rates. Because car rental agencies are not state-regulated, a day's use of an automatic, air-conditioned compact car can range from $10 to $37. Hawaii is a no-fault insurance state so insurance coverage is *optional,* but most companies do not honor individual coverage even if you already own a car. **Budget** is one of the few agencies that will rent to those ages 18 to 21, but only with a major credit card. Starting your car rental search upon arrival at an airport is a sure way to be stuck with the most expensive rates. Whenever possible, use the phone to hunt down cars, and make reservations at least 24 hours in advance.

Bicycle and **moped rentals,** based in tourist centers, offer competitive rates, and are a great way to see Hawaii in an easy-going, close-up manner. Congestion in Honolulu, however, may be too much for two wheels. They are better used on the other side of Oahu, or on the neighbor islands. If you bring your own bicycle, you should register it (for $3.10) at the **Pawaa Police Station,** 1455 S. Beretania St., Honolulu (943-3324; open Mon.-Fri. 7:45am-4:15pm). You can also pick up the free *Bicycle Regulations Pamphlet* here. More information is available at **The Bike Shop,** 1149 S. King St. (531-7071) in Honolulu (open Mon.-Thurs. and Sat. 9am-5:30pm, Fri. 9am-8pm, Sun. 10am-5pm), or from the **Hawaii Bicycling League,** Box 4403, Honolulu 96813 (732-5806). Inter-island airlines charge about $20 for your bike's flight. Continental flights charge about $15.

Accommodations and Camping

Despite rumors to the contrary, reasonable room rates do exist on the islands. In general, high tourist season runs from mid-December to late April. Look for special deals that often include rental car and air transportation. **Hukilau, Sands** and **Seaside Hotels,** (922-5737 or 922-1228 on Oahu, 800-451-6754 from the outer islands, 800-367-7000 from the mainland), manage some of the cheapest resort hotels ($32-55 per night).

Hostels and the **YMCA** provide cheap shelter on most islands. Another alternative is the growing number of bed and breakfast organizations which offer doubles in private homes for $35 to $55. **B&B Hawaii,** P.O. Box 449, Kapaa 96746 (536-8421 on Oahu, 822-7771 on Kauai, and toll-free on neighboring islands 1-367-8047, ext. 339) and **B&B Honolulu,** 5242 Keehinani Dr., Honolulu 96817 (595-7533), operates statewide.

Camping in state parks is popular and rigidly regulated. Free camping permits are required, and applicants must be at least 18 years old to receive a permit for an individual or group. Camping is limited to five nights per thirty days. Sites are open Friday through Tuesday on Oahu, daily on the other islands. Two sorts of shelters are also available in state parks, but usually require reservations at least a month in advance. **A-Frames** are single rooms with wooden sleeping platforms, cooking facilities, bathroom, and shower facilities ($7 per night, 4-person max.); **housekeeping cabins** come with kitchen, living room, and one or two bedrooms, as well as utensils, linen, and heating or fireplace wood ($15 per night for 1 person, rates decreases as number in group increases, max. 6 persons). For information, reservations, and permits, write or visit one of the **State Parks Division** offices (also called the Department of Land and Natural Resources). (All open Mon.-Fri. 8am-4:15pm.) The **national** and **county parks** on each island also maintain campsites. Free camping outside of designated parks is widely practiced throughout the state by locals, although visitors are more than likely to be harrassed by the police (or locals) if they are too obvious or too permanent (especially on Oahu and Maui). Nevertheless, with some discretion and enough sense to avoid four-wheel drive tire tracks and empty beer cans, consider picking your own quiet beach. Camping on Oahu is not as convenient or as safe as on the other islands, especially the Big Island.

Outdoors

The Hawaiian Islands are punctuated with hidden treasures: rare birds, tropical fish, botanical delights, and sandy beaches with glassy waves. Surfing was invented here, and the 20 footers breaking off Oahu's North Shore continue to beckon a die-hard faithful, while the new hybrid sport of windsurfing dominates Maui beaches. Hiking, snorkeling, swimming, bird- and whale-watching, and fishing also number among the outdoor activities visitors can enjoy with little or no expense. However, inland valleys of Maui, the Big Island, and Oahu—prime spots for illegal marijuana cultivation—can put hikers in danger of trespassing, so stay on defined trails. Even more care should be taken while wandering in sugar cane fields.

Hawaiian Trail and Mountain Club, P.O. Box 2238, Honolulu 96804. Watch for listing of free hikes in the weekly "Pulse of Paradise" column of the *Honolulu Star-Bulletin.*

Sierra Club Hawaii Chapter, 1212 University Ave., Honolulu 96826 (946-8494), behind the Church of the Cross Roads. Phone for recorded message, an update of hikes on Oahu. A major source of hiking information and organized weekend hikes. Open Mon.-Sat. 8-11am.

State Forestry Division, 1179 Punchbowl St., #325, Honolulu 96813 (548-8856). Provides free maps for its 24 trails. Open Mon.-Fri. 7:45am-4:30pm.

Oahu

Since the arrival of missionaries in the 1820s, Oahu and its principal city of Honolulu have constituted the cultural, commercial, and political focal point of modern Hawaii. Tourism is the island's major industry, centered at the famous ¾-mile stretch of Waikiki Beach. The nearby downtown area is a major business and economic center of the Pacific basin.

Oahu can be roughly divided into four sections: **Honolulu,** the **Windward Coast,** the **North Shore,** and the **Leeward Coast.** The slopes of two now-extinct volcanic mountain ridges (to whom the island owes its existence), **Waianae** in the east and **Koolau** in the west make up the bulk of Oahu's 600 square miles. The narrow inlets of **Pearl Harbor** push in from the sea at the southern end of the valley between the two ridges. Honolulu spreads along 6 miles of oceanfront southeast of Pearl Harbor, hemmed in by the Koolau Range in the northeast. **Waikiki Beach** lies near Diamond Head, the island's southernmost extremity; the downtown area clusters 3 miles west. With the exception of the Leeward Coast and Kaena Point, well-maintained highways circle the rest of the coast and navigate the central valley.

Honolulu

Like any other metropolis, Hawaii's capital city of Honolulu is overcrowded and plagued by traffic. Unlike other cities, however, the trade winds keep Honolulu free of stagnant pollution, and the pleasant climate brightens the environment. Further, zoning rules prohibit large, flashy billboards and signs.

Waikiki, Hawaii's famed concrete jungle on the coast, revolves around the high-rise hotels that line Kalakaua and Kuhio Ave. Soak in the tackiness while soaking in the rays or skip this "Las Vegas on the Beach" altogether. Wander through downtown at lunchtime for more (and more tasteful) Aloha shirts than you had ever hoped to see, or tour the ethnic communities of Chinatown, Kalihi, and Kapahulu. Here, away from the tourist towers lining the beach, is the *real* Honolulu—the city that most visitors never see.

Practical Information and Orientation

Emergency: 911.

Visitor Information: Hawaii Visitors Bureau, 2270 Kalakaua Ave., #804, Honolulu 96815 (923-1811). Information on Oahu and the rest of the state. Pick up the member *Accommodation Guide* and the member *Restaurant Guide,* a map of points of interest, and a walking tour of downtown Honolulu. Also has a special travel guide for the disabled. All are free. Open Mon.-Fri. 8am-4:30pm. Information centers located in both the overseas and inter-island air terminals and at the Ala Moana Shopping Center. **Department of Parks and Recreation,** 650 S. King St., Honolulu 96817 (523-4525). Information and permits for county parks. Open Mon.-Fri. 7:45am-4pm. Permits available no earlier than 2 weeks in advance. **Department of State Parks,** 1151 Punchbowl St., Honolulu 96813 (548-7455). Information and permits for camping in state parks, and trail maps. Open Mon.-Fri. 8am-4pm.

Honolulu International Airport, 20 minutes west of downtown, off the Lunalilo Freeway (H-1). Several companies will tote you and your luggage between the airport and Waikiki or downtown for $5. **Grayline** (834-1033) operates from 5am to 11:30pm. **Waikiki Express** (942-2177) operates from 7am to 9pm, and requires reservations; **Airport Motor Coach** (926-4747) operates from 6:30am to 10pm. Reservations required.

Local Transit: 531-1611. Buses cover the entire island, from about 5:30am-midnight, most frequently in downtown Honolulu and Waikiki. Very frequent and reliable. The Bus runs less frequently to North Shore and Waianae than to downtown. Fare 60¢.

Transit for Disabled: Handi-Van, 905 Ahuh St. (833-2222). Curb-to-curb service if reservations are made at least a day in advance. Service runs Mon.-Fri. 8am-4pm. Disabled travelers can obtain a bus pass from the City Department of Transportation Services. Write in advance to **Handicapped Bus Pass,** 650 S. King St., Honolulu 96813 (523-4083). **Handi-Cabs of the Pacific,** P.O. Box 22428 (524-3866), a private taxi company with van ramps for wheelchairs. $28 for airport-to-Waikiki service. Call for reservations.

Taxi: Sida, 439 Kalewa St. (836-0011). All cabs charge 20¢ per 1/6 mile. Base rates are about $1.40. Airport to Waikiki $15-18.

Car Rental: Honolulu Rentacar, 1856 Kalekaua Ave. #105 (941-9099 or 942-7187) or **Maxi Rentals,** 413 Seaside Ave. (923-7381). Both have used cars from $9 per day, $7 insurance mandatory if under 25.

Moped and Bike Rentals: Aloha Funway Rentals, 2025 Kalakaua Ave. (942-9696) and 2976 Koapakapaka St. (834-1016), near the airport. Mopeds $20 per day, $75 per week; bikes $12 per day. Open daily 8am-5pm. **Inter-Island Rentals,** 353 Royal Hawaiian Ave. (946-0013). Mopeds $19 per day, $90-100 per week. Bikes $12 per day. Open daily 8am-6pm. Must be 18 with cash or credit card deposit.

Water Equipment Rentals: Ohana Rentals, near the breakers at Queen's Beach. Boogie boards $8 per day and fins $8 per day. Cash only. Open daily 8am-6pm. **Star Beachboys,** Kuhio Beach, to the left of the pavilion. Canoe rides $3.50, surfboard lessons $10 per hr., boogie boards $3 per hr. **South Sea Aquatics,** 870 Kapahulu (735-0437). Snorkeling gear $8 per day. Open Mon.-Fri. 8am-6pm, Sat.-Sun. 8am-5pm.

Help Lines: Sex Abuse Treatment Center, 524-7237. **Coast Guard Search/Rescue,** 536-4336. **Suicide and Crisis Center,** 521-4555. **Gay Information Services,** 926-2910. Lists gay-supported community programs and businesses.

Post Office: Main office, 3600 Aoleilei Ave. (423-3990). Open daily 8am-4:30pm. **ZIP code:** 96813. **Waikiki Branch,** Royal Hawaiian Shopping Center, 2nd floor, Bldg. B. Open Mon.-Fri. 8:15am-11:45am and 1pm-3:30pm. **ZIP code:** 96815.

Area Code: 808.

The **H-1 Freeway** stretches the length of Honolulu. Downtown Honolulu is about 6 blocks long and 4 blocks wide, wedged between Honolulu Harbor and Punchbowl. In Waikiki, Ala Wai Boulevard, Kuhio Avenue, and Kalakaua Avenue run parallel to the ocean and are the main routes of transportation. **Hitchhiking** is illegal on Oahu.

Besides *mauka* (inland) and *makai* (seaward), you are also likely to hear directions given as *ewa* (west) and *diamondhead* (east).

Accommodations

Finding a reasonably priced room in Honolulu is a surmountable challenge. Page through the *Honolulu Advertiser* for deals if you can't land a spot at a hostel or at a Y.

Manoa Hostel (AYH), 2323A Seaview Ave., Honolulu 96822 (946-0591), 1 block west of University Ave., 1½ miles north of Waikiki, near U. of H. at Manoa. By car, take University Ave. exit off H-1. Bus #6 at Ala Moana Shopping Center, go to Metcalf and University Ave. stop. Clean facilities. Kitchen, bike storage, lockers, recreation room. Hostel locked daily 9:30am-5pm. Office open daily 7:30-9:30am and 5-11pm. $8.50, nonmembers $11.50. Linen $1. All of Aug.-March are busy, so write early and include one night's deposit.

Hale Aloha (AYH), 2417 Prince Edward St. (926-8313), in Waikiki, 2 blocks from the beach. Members only. Spots guaranteed for 3 nights. Open daily 8-10am and 5-9pm. Dorm bunks $10. Studio doubles $22. Reservations required.

Inter-Club Hostel Waikiki, 2413 Kuhio Ave. (942-2636). Standard hostel facilities. Weekend BBQs. Bunks $15. Open 8am-11pm.

YWCA and YMCA: Fernhust Residence, 1566 Wilder Ave. (941-2231), near the university. Take bus #4 to Punahou School. For single women over 18. 2 rooms per bath; 2 persons per room. Office open daily 8:30am-8:30pm. $20, nonmembers $23. 3-day max. stay for non-members. Breakfast and dinner included Mon.-Sat. **Central Branch,** 401 Atkinson Dr. (941-3344), across from Ala Moana Shopping Center downtown. Men over 18 only. Open 24 hours. Singles $25, with bath $30.50. Doubles $35. Key deposit $5. **Nuuanu Branch,** 1441 Pali Hwy. (536-3556), downtown. Singles $23. Key deposit $5.

Edmunds Hotel Apartments, 2411 Ala Wai Blvd. (923-8381), across from the Ala Wai Canal. Plain, printed rooms with fans and good views, but no phone. Laundry facilities, small TV, refrigerator, and ancient stove. Singles $24. Doubles $28. Weekly rates negotiable.

Waikiki Prince, 2431 Prince Edward St. (922-1544). Functional rooms all with A/C $29, with kitchenette $33, with full kitchen $37.

Camping

Camping on Oahu is not as good an idea as on the other islands. The campgrounds are located in the more rural Hawaiian communities, and locals often consider the campgrounds their domain, especially on Oahu's western shore. Four state parks and 13 county parks allow camping. For free required **permits** contact the Department of Parks and Recreation (see Practical Information). In Honolulu, tent camping is available at two state parks, **Sand Island** and **Keaiwa Heiau State Recreation Area.** (5-day max. stay. Check-out 11am.) Apply at the Division of Land and Natural Resources (see Practical Information). Sand Island offers flat camping outside Honolulu Harbor (take Sand Island Access Rd. from Rte. 92). Keaiwa Heiau State Recreation Area, at end of Aiea Heights Dr. (488-6626), has forest sites—hike over to the ruins of the **heiau hoosola** (temple of healing).

Food

Eating in Honolulu can be a truly international dining extravaganza, so "grind (eat) to da max, no shame, just scahf out." Don't miss Ala Moana's **Food Market** for a true cornucopia of cuisines. Small Chinese counters serve excellent lunch snacks downtown; try the area around **Hotel Street,** in the red light district. Be sure to have the *dim sum,* served daily at most counters from 11am to 2pm. A variety of ethnic restaurants, including Hawaiian, Japanese, Thai, and French, are located between the 500 and 1000 blocks of **Kapahulu Avenue** and in the surrounding area. Catch bus #2 going *mauka* up Kapahulu Ave. from the Diamond Head area of Waikiki.

Travelers to Waikiki will be deluged with ads and flyers recommending *luaus.* These Hawaiian-style dinners with Polynesian dancing rake in the tourist bucks and are often pretty cheesy, but some can be fun and belly-filling (and a few are even reasonably priced). The **Queen Kapiolani,** 150 Kapahulu Ave. (922-1941), for example, offers a $9.50 unlimited *luau* luncheon buffet with entertainment, Mon.-Wed. and Fri.-Sat. 11am-2pm.

Grace's Inn, 2227 S. Beretania St. (946-8020), near the university; also at 1296 S. Beretania. Serves the best plate lunch in town, an assortment of rice, macaroni salad, noodles, and an entree. Their specialty is chicken *katsu* (a breaded cutlet). Entrees about $3.50. Open Mon.-Sat. 10am-10:30pm, Sun. 10am-10pm.

Ono Hawaiian Food, 726 Kapahulu Ave., Waikiki (737-2275), next to the Ala Wai golf course. Family-style restaurant that lives up to its name (*ono* means good). Try the *poi* or *opihi* (limpets) if you're adventurous. Go early—the lines often stretch outside. Kalua plate $4.55. Combination plate $6. Open Mon.-Sat. 11am-7:30pm. For desert, head to nearby **Leonard's Bakery,** 933 Kahapulu Ave. (737-5591), which sells hot *malasadas* (an island tradition).

Patti's Kitchen, Ala Moana Shopping Center (946-5002), also in the Windward Mall in Kaneohe. Build your own buffet-style Chinese plate lunches ($3.35-5). An incredible bargain. Open Mon.-Sat. 10am-8pm, Sun. 10am-4:30pm.

Ted's Drive Inn, 2820 S. King St. (946-0364), a block south of University Ave. Tongue-tingling Korean plate lunches $3-5. Open Mon.-Wed. 9:30am-9:30pm, Thurs.-Sat. 9:30am-10pm, Sun. 9:30am-9pm.

New Taste, 3452 Waialae Ave. (732-0778), corner of 9th St. A simple, unadorned eatery with delicious traditional Chinese fare at basement prices. Open Mon.-Tues. and Thurs.-Sun. 10:30am-3pm and 4:30-9pm; Wed. 8:30am-4:30pm.

Sights and Activities

Here in the capital you will find museums, palaces, parks, historic houses, shops and ethnic neighborhoods, some which enhance and some which detract from the surrounding paradise. The one-hour loop around the #14 route provides a colorful cross section of Honolulu's neighborhoods from Waikiki to St. Louis Heights.

In the wake of World War II, the dramatic crescent of Waikiki's white sand beach backdropped by the profile of Diamond Head lured growing crowds of vacationers. Today more savvy visitors spend time on the less crowded neighbor isles; however, as an unrelenting focus of glitzy tourism and rampant commercialism, Waikiki itself provides a spectacle.

Waikiki Beach, actually comprised of several smaller beaches, puts Hawaii's tourists on exhibit. Farthest to the east is the **Sans Souci Beach,** in front of the Kaimona Otani Hotel. Site of an old natatorium built as a war memorial, Sans Souci has shower facilities but no public restrooms. The **Queen's Surf Beach,** closer to downtown, attracts swimmers and roller skaters; local musicians often perform in its large pavilion. The area between the pavilion and the snack bar is a popular tanning spot for gay people. On Sunday evenings, bongo players gather under the banyan tree to cut a tropical tattoo through the serenity of an unforgettable sunset.

When you want a change from the beach, hike the 1 mile into and up to the top of the **Laeahi (Diamond Head) Crater,** at Queen's Surf. To reach Diamond Head, take bus #58 from Waikiki. During the summer, the **Clean Air Team** (944-0804) leads a free two-and-a-half-hour guided hike from the zoo parking lot to the top of the crater every Saturday and Sunday at 9am. (No reservations necessary.) The lookout area along Diamond Head Rd. affords a breathtaking view of the windsurfers below. Conspicuous estates cover the slopes of Diamond Head, some belonging to scions of Hawaii's original missionaries. It has been said that the missionaries came to do good, and did very well indeed.

Several cultural and historical attractions are located around the downtown area. Get a seagull's eye view of all Oahu from the **Aloha Tower** (537-9260) on the 10th floor of Pier 9. (Free.) The **Iolani Palace,** King and Richard St. (538-1471), was first the residence of King Kalakaua and Queen Liliuokalani and later nerve center to *Hawaii Five-0.* Now it's a fabulous museum in the process of multi-million dollar reconstruction, featuring sumptious carved *Koa* furniture and elegant European decor. (45-min. tours by reservation only at the barracks in the palace grounds. Tours $4, ages 5-12 $1, ages under 5 not admitted. Palace open Wed.-Sat. 9am-2:15pm.)

At the corner of Beretania and Richard St. is Hawaii's **State Capitol,** an architectural montage reflecting all facets of the state's geography. The pillars represent palm trees, while the inverted dome of the house chambers stands like a volcano. Reflecting pools recall the blue Pacific nearby. (Open Mon.-Fri. 9am-4pm. Free.)

The collection of Asian art at the **Honolulu Academy of Arts,** 900 S. Beretania St. (538-1006), is one of the finest in the U.S. Thirty galleries and six garden courts also display 17th-century samurai armor, African art, and temporary exhibits. (Tours Tues.-Wed. and Fri.-Sat. at 11am, Thurs. at 2pm, and Sun. at 1pm. Open Tues.-Sat. 10am-4:30pm, Sun. 1-5pm. Free.) Island history comes alive at the **Honolulu Mission House Museum,** 553 S. King St. (531-0481), near the Iolani Palace. Using Hawaii's oldest western buildings as their backdrop, museum actors bring visitors back to the missionary age of the 1830s. (Open daily 9am-4pm. Admission $3.50, ages 6-15 $1, under 6 free.) The **Bishop Museum,** 1525 Bernice St. (848-4129 or 848-4106), in Kalihi, has the best collection of Hawaiiana in the world and offers daily craft demonstrations. (Open Mon.-Sat. 9am-5pm. Admission $4.75, ages 6-16 $2.50. Take bus #2 ("School St.") from Waikiki.)

Over 40 years ago, a stunned nation listened to the reports of the Japanese obliteration of **Pearl Harbor.** The **U.S.S. Arizona National Memorial** is an austere, three-part structure built over the sunken hull in which over a thousand servicemen perished. (422-2771. Free tours 7:45am-3pm, including ½-hr. film. Launches out to the hull every 15 min. No children under 6 years of age or under 45 inches in height will be admitted on the launch.) The **visitors center** is open Tuesday through Sunday 7:30am to 5pm. Take the #20 from Waikiki or the #50, 51, or 52 from Ala Moana or the $2 shuttle from major Waikiki hotels (926-4747).

Looking *mauka* (inland) from downtown you'll see the lush **Nuuanu Valley;** the next valley to the east is the **Manoa Valley.** At the mouth of the Manoa Valley lies the **University of Hawaii,** a sanctuary for those unfortunate academics who must contend with tropical weather 12 months per year. The highlight of the entire valley is a 1-mile trail through tropical plants to **Manoa Falls** leading from the end of Manoa Rd. behind Paradise Park. But don't hike after a hard rainfall or you'll make an unwitting discovery of the popular sport of mudsliding. Bus #5 serves all of Manoa's attractions.

Parallel to the Manoa Valley, the **Pali Highway** (Rte. 61) winds its way through **Nuuanu Valley** and over into Kailua, on the windward side of the island. As you near the top of the Pali, pull into the **Pali Lookout.** The view overlooking the windward side is one of the finest in all of the islands. But hang onto your hat—the wind is powerful. Kamehameha the Great consolidated his kingdom by defeating Oahu's soldiers and driving them over this dramatic cliff.

Entertainment

In Waikiki, you'll find as active a nightlife as your feet and liver can take. There is a symphony and opera season at the N. Blaisdell Center (527-5400); theater is staged at the **Honolulu Community Theater** (734-0274) near Diamond Head, and the **Manoa Valley Theater** (988-6131).

The Wave, 1877 Kalakaua Ave. (941-0424), on the edge of Waikiki. Videos and special events every weekend. Local bands, such as Sonia and Revolución, perform live (Wed.-Sun.). The building sports a huge *ukiyoe* wave. Cover $3, free 9-10pm.

Masquerades, 224 McCully (949-6337), is the place for gold chains and shirts open to the navel. Hey, babe—what's your sign? Cover $5, $3 for residents; ages 18-21 $10, $6 for residents. Open daily 8pm-1am.

Hamburger Mary's, 2109 Kuhio Ave. (922-6722). A popular gay bar, organic and co-ed. No cover. Open daily 11:30am-2am.

Moose McGillycuddy's Pub & Cafe, 1035 University Ave. (944-5525), near the university. A real student hangout serving huge sandwiches for lunch and dinner ($3-6). Special promotion each night. Must be 21 for the disco after 9pm. No cover. Open Mon.-Sat. 11:30am-2am, Sun. 10am-2am. Happy Hour 4-8pm.

Seagull Bar and Restaurant, 2463 Kuhio Ave. (924-7911), in Waikiki. A hostel hang-out. Drink 75¢ beers with the international crowd. Open daily 4:30pm-2am.

The Other Side of the Island

The part of Oahu outside Honolulu is considered "the other side." Windward and Leeward Oahu are walled off by the islands' two mountain chains to the East and West, while Central Oahu and the North Shore lie north of Honolulu. Boundaries have become blurred in recent years as Honolulu has pushed west into the city of Ewa and north into Central Oahu's plantation land. The controversial addition of H-3, a major new highway across the mountains, may further erode the region's geographic autonomy. But for now, these outlying communities cling to their isolation.

Separated from Honolulu by the Koolau Mountains, the **Windward Coast** thrives on the combination of picture postcard scenery and isolated serenity which made Hawaii famous. Miles of beaches and rural towns span the 40-mile coast running from Laie, in the north, to Makapuu Point, in the south, where the highway wraps around a rugged 4-mile stretch to Koko Head. From Waikiki, take **Kalanianaole Highway** (Rte. 72) east to **Koko Head Crater** whose eastern wall has been penetrated by the ocean to form spectacular Hanauma Bay. The bay is a snorkler's Arcadia, as its federally protected waters contain some of the tamest, most beautiful fish in the Pacific. Bring some bread or peas and the fish will eat right out of your hand. If you're lucky, you might attract the small *humuhumunukunukuapuaa* ("fish with a pig-like nose"). Follow the locals around the bay to the left to the wave-flushed **"Toilet Bowl."** Climb into the "bowl" when it's full and get flushed up and down by the natural lava plumbing.

A mile further on, a similar mechanism drives the **Halona Blow Hole** to spout its spray. The secret beach to the right of Halona Blow Hole was the designated site for the famous "kiss in the sand" scene in *From Here to Eternity. Let's Go* couples may feel inclined to indulge in a reenactment in this tiny romantic cove.

Kalanianaole ends by intersecting **Kailua Road.** Follow this road toward **Kailua town** and the **Ulupo Heiau** (1200 Kailua Rd.), next to the YMCA. The temple still stands as a platform of black lava rock overlooking the Keanui swamp. Swimmers and windsurfers will love **Kailua Beach Park** (450 Kawailoa Rd.) and **Lanikai Beach** (Mokulua Dr.)

Further up the coast, the Mormon-dominated city of Laie hosts the **Polynesian Cultural Center,** 55-3700 Kamehameha Hwy. (293-3333), an authentically recreated village representing the indigenous cultures of New Zealand, Samoa, Tonga, Fiji, Hawaii, Tahiti, and the Marquesas. Special performances throughout the center include *hula* dancers on canoes and coconut-husking. Walk through the park at your own leisure or take a guided tour at no extra cost. (Open Mon.-Sat. noon. Dinner served 4:30-7pm, followed by a spectacular evening show at 7:30pm. Admission to the grounds is $25, with dinner and show $35.)

The surfer's mecca on the North Shore is **Haleiwa,** an old plantation town now enlivened by boutiques and art galleries. The central supplier of water sport equipment on Oahu's "other side," Haleiwa is also crammed with surf shops and rental agencies. **Surf-N-Sea, Inc.,** 62-595 Kamehameha Hwy. (637-9887), rents windsurfers ($18 per day), surfboards, boogie boards, scuba and snorkeling equipment ($10.50 per day). They also offer instruction and organize fishing, sailing, and dive charters.

Places to stay on the "other side" include the **Vacation Inn & Hostel,** 59-788 Kamehameha Hwy. (638-7838), ¼ mile north of Waimea Bay (Beachside bunks $15; doubles $30-35; apartments for 4-6 persons on the beach $50-60. Reserve 2 weeks in advance, especially during the winter by writing P.O. Box 716, Haleiwa, HI 96712.), and **Countryside Cabins,** 53-224 Kamehameha Hwy. Panaluu 96717 (237-8169), across the hwy. on the Kanoehe end of Panaluu Beach Park (2-person studios $20, 2-person cottages $30, 4-person houses $45).

The island is ringed with state and county beach parks where camping is possible (permit required, see Practical Information). Unfortunately, escalating violence from locals makes many unsafe. Those on the Windward Coast are probably the best bet.

Malaekahana State Recreation Area, (293-1736), north of Lanea is ranger patrolled for safety. Wade across at low tide to Mokuauia Island, a bird refuge. (Showers, toilets, picnic tables, BBQ pits. Permit required.)

Hawaii (Big Island)

Hawaiian legend has it that the island is the home of Pele, the Polynesian goddess of volcanoes; if so, she has been a busy deity in this last decade. In the spring of 1984, the Kilauea and Mauna Loa volcanoes erupted simultaneously. Geological history is still being made here daily, and you can inspect the steam vents, lava tubes, and the still-bubbling molten mess by visiting Volcanoes National Park.

The island of Hawaii anchors the Hawaiian archipelago on its southeasternmost end. Twice the size of all the other Hawaiian Islands combined, the Big Island encompasses a multitude of climates from the hot, desert-like North Kona coast to the cold 13,000-foot peaks of Mauna Kea and Mauna Loa, to the rain forest valleys and waterfalls of the Hamauka Coast.

Highways circle both Mauna Kea and Mauna Loa along the coast. Both the old Saddle Road (Rte. 200) cutting between the mountains and the Chain of Craters Road in Kilauea Crater offer a closer view of the volcanoes at Volcanoes National Park. The main arrival points for tourists are Hilo on the windward, eastern side and the resort town of Kailua-Kona on the leeward, western side. The sun-drenched white sand beaches of the Kona coast are more suitable for snorkeling and swimming than those in rainier Hilo. The most striking scenery lies in the island's northern Kohala peninsula, highlighted by lush Waipio Valley.

Hilo

After Honolulu, Hilo is the largest city in the state. The center of the Hawaiian orchid and anthurium industry, the city is primarily residential, and travelers will find both hotels and food inexpensive. Hilo itself can be covered in just a day, but provides a convenient base to visit the island's other attractions such as Volcanoes National Park or Kaimu Black Sand Beach (see the Volcano Area).

Hilo and its environs are a nature-lover's dream. Take a morning stroll, or drive, down **Banyan Court,** around **Liliuokalani Garden** (a Japanese-style garden), and out to **Coconut Island** for a view of Mauna Kea before the clouds roll in. From Hilo, take Waianuenue Ave. up to **Rainbow Falls,** the legendary home of the goddess Hina. When Hina's rebuffed suitor trapped her behind Rainbow Falls with dammed-up waters, Hina's demigod son Maui rescued her by breaking the dam with his canoe paddle. One mile farther inland is **Peepee Falls** and the **Boiling Pots;** it's possible to walk down from the observatory to the falls by following the trail which starts at the left of the stone wall. Swimming is prohibited, but locals do anyway. Fifteen miles north on Rte. 220, off Rte. 19, **Akaka Falls** plummets a spectacular 420 feet. Route 130 winds down to **Kaimu Black Sand Beach.** Past **Kalapana,** the daring will want to walk out on the still-warm lava flows which have cut across the highway as they pour into the sea.

Remember that this soggy town averages about 125 inches of rain per year. You'll get discouraged if you try to wait out a storm more than a day or two—the best idea is to go to the sunny Kona-Kohala coast and roast a while.

Be sure to try the island specialties—macadamia nuts and Kona coffee. Get free samples of the nuts at the **Hawaiian Holiday Macadamia Nut Company** in Haina, off Rte. 19 near Honokaa. Downtown Hilo is loaded with cheap restaurants, sushi counters and *okazu-ya.*

Outstanding local cuisine can be had at **Cafe 100,** 969 Kilauea St. (935-8683). Try the *loco mocos,* big island specialties with rice, meat, gravy, and a fried egg ($1-2), and wash it down with guava juice (80¢). (Open Mon.-Thurs. 6:45am-8:30pm, Fri.-Sat. 6:45am-9:30pm.) **Lanky's Pastries and Deli,** at Kilauea and Kekuanaoa in the Hilo Shopping Center (935-2769), under the Mall Entrance sign, is a local favorite. Go back to basics with a Hawaiian twist. (Most items $3-5. Open Mon.-Sat. 7am-10pm, Sun. 7am-10:30pm.) **Tomi Zushi,** 68 Mamo St. (961-6100), has fantastic special *teishoku:* Japanese appetizers, soup, rice, tea, and 2 entrees for $5.50. (Open Mon.-Tues. and Thurs.-Sat. 10:30am-2pm and 4:30-8:30pm, Sun. 4:30-8:30pm.)

Outside of Kona, tourism on the Big Island has never been as expensive and popular as on other islands. Even the hotels clustered on Banyan Dr. by the bay are often quiet and empty. Rooms become scarce only during spectacular volcanic eruptions. Booking rooms locally, rather than from the mainland, can save you $5-10 per day.

Dolphin Bay Hotel, 333 Iliahi St., Hilo 96720 (935-1466), in the Puueo section of town, across the river, has 18 units, some plush. Cool, tropical gardens supply rooms with daily flower arrangements. Has fans, TV, and kitchens. (Singles from $26. Doubles from $36. Pre-payment required; make deposit 10 days prior to stay to confirm reservations.) **Hilo Hotel,** P.O. Box 726, Hilo 96720 (961-3733), at 142 Kinoole St. downtown, across from Kalakaua Park is old, yet neat and clean. It offers A/C, refrigerators, free coffee and sweet rolls in the morning. (Singles and doubles $32.) **Onekahakaha Beach Park** and **Kealoha Beach Park** are both within 3 miles of Hilo. The tentsites feature toilets and showers. ($1 permit required.) **Harry K. Brown County Beach Park** is in the Puna District, across from Kaimu Black Sands Beach. Sites, near the most recent lava flow into the ocean, offer clean restrooms and indoor showers. (Tents and campers only. $1 permit required.)

Visitor information is available from: **Hawaii Visitors Bureau,** 180 Kinoole St. (961-5797; free bus schedules, island guides, and maps; open Mon.-Fri. 8am-noon and 1-4pm); **Wailoa Center,** P.O. Box 936, Hilo 96720, Kamehameha Ave. and Pauahi St., on the seaward side of the State Building (961-7360; open Mon.-Fri. 8am-4:30pm); **State Visitor Information Center,** Hilo Airport (935-1018); and the **Big Island Center for Independent Living,** 1190 Wainuenue (935-3777; assistance for disabled visitors).

For outdoors information, contact: **Department of Parks and Recreation,** 25 Aupuni St., #210, Hilo 96720 (961-8311; information on county parks; open camping permits $1 per night per person; open Mon.-Fri. 7:45am-4:30pm); **Division of State Parks,** 75 Aupuni St., Hilo 96720 (961-7200; information on state parks; free permits with a 5-day maximum; open Mon.-Fri. 7:45am-4pm); **Hawaii District Forester,** 1643 Kilauea Ave., Hilo 96720 (961-7221; open Mon.-Fri. 7:45am-4pm); **Division of Forestry and Wildlife,** Dept. of Enforcement (next to the State Parks Office), P.O. Box 936, Hilo 96720 (961-7291; information on hunting, fishing, hiking, and forest regulations; open Mon.-Fri. 7:45am-4pm).

The airport, **General Lyman Field,** 3 miles from town, is served by inter-island and mainland flights. It's a $5 taxi ride from the hotel district or a $6 ride from downtown. Local transit is provided by **Hele-On-Bus,** 25 Aupuni St. (935-8241). Buses operate Mon.-Sat. 6:30am-6pm, and the fare ranges from 50¢ to $6. Luggage and backpacks are $1, plus an additional charge per piece. Pick up schedules at the office or the Hawaii visitors bureau. The company also runs a bus between Kona and Hilo at least once per day, making a convenient circuit of the island (one way $5.25). Disabled travelers can be accommodated with curb to curb service on a day's notice. (Call 323-2085.) All national and state car rental chains are located at Hilo aiport. **Budget** (800-935-7293) charges $25 per day. You must be 18 with a major credit card. Rent a moped from **Ciao,** 71 Banyan Dr. (969-1717). Mopeds are $20 per day, cruiser bikes $10. (Open daily 8am-7pm.) Water equipment rentals are available from **Nautilus Dive Center,** 382 Kamehameha Ave. (935-6939). Mask and snorkel are $3 per day, an underwater camera $15 per day. The center also offers beginner and certified dive charters for $45. (Open Mon.-Sat. 8:30am-5pm.) Deposit required.

The **post office** is at Waianuenue Ave. (935-6685) in the Federal Bldg. (Open Mon.-Fri. 8:30am-4:30pm, Sat. 9am-noon.) Hilo's **ZIP code** is 96720; the **area code** is 808.

The Volcano Area

The volcanoes of the Big Island are unique in the world for their size, frequency of eruptions, and accessibility. Resting on the current center of the geological hot spot whose volcanic upthrusts fashioned each of the Hawaiian islands in turn, the two mountains in **Volcanoes National Park** continue to heave and grow, adding acres of new land each year. **Kilauea Crater,** with its steaming vents, sulfur fumes, and periodically spectacular "drive-in" eruptions, is the star of the park. However, the less active **Mauna Loa** and its dormant northern neighbor, **Mauna Kea,** are in some respects more amazing fire breathers. Each towers nearly 14,000 feet above sea level and drops 30,000 feet to the ocean floor. Mauna Loa is the largest volcano in the world, while Mauna Kea, if measured from its base on the ocean floor, would be the tallest mountain on earth. (Park entrance $5; good for 7 days.)

An 11-mile scenic drive around the Kilauea Celdera on **Crater Rim Drive** is accessible via Rte. 11 from the east and west, or via the Chain of Craters Rd. from the south. Well-marked trails and lookouts dot the road, so you can stop frequently to explore. You might also hike the 11 miles along the vista-filled **Crater Rim Trail,** which traverses *ohia* and giant fern forests, *aa* (rough) and *pahoehoe* (smooth) lava flows, and smoldering steam and sulfur vents. Walk through the **Thurston Lava Tube,** formed by lava that cooled around a hot core which continued to move, leaving the inside of the flow hollow.

The free **Jaggar Museum,** next to the closed volcano observatory, explains the volcano's history, and contains displays on many Hawaiian legends. (Open daily 8:30am-5pm.)

Four-mile **Kilauea Iki Trail** starts at the Kilauea Iki overlook on Crater Rim Rd. It leads around the north rim of Kilauea Iki, through a forest of tree ferns, down the wall of the little crater, past the vent of the '59 eruption, over steaming lava, and back to Crater Rim Rd. On the way you pass *ohelo* bushes laden with red berries. Legend has it that you must offer some berries to Pele, or you'll incur her wrath. The 3.6-mile **Mauna Iki Trail** begins 9 miles southwest of park headquarters on Rte. 11. It leads to footprints made in 1790 ash. From here you may hike down into the coastal area.

The **Chain of Craters** road leads down the slopes of Kilauea to the Puna Coast, where the current eruption meets the sea. In June 1989, a new phase of the lava flows blocked off the connection to Rte. 130 from the north. Park ranger can inform you of the current status of the eruption, and the safety of lava-watching. The crashing white ocean sprays against black rock provide a spectacle as powerful as its volcanic antithesis nearby. The famous **Kaimu Black Sand Beach** to the north on Rte. 130 was formed in this way, a sparkling gem born of nature's torment.

At the visitors centers at **Kilauea,** Crater Rim Rd. (967-7311; open 7:45am-5pm), you can see 10-minute films shown hourly from 9am to 4pm and catch the bulletins on the latest volcanic activity. Trails of varying difficulty lead around Kilauea and to the summit of Mauna Loa; speak to a ranger before setting out. It's best to picnic in the park, since prices at the only restaurant and snackbar are outrageous.

Volcano House, P.O. Box 53, Hawaii Volcanoes National Park 96718 (967-7321), offers 37 units overlooking Kilauea Crater from a 1220-foot vantage point. (Rooms from $57. 4-person cabins $24.) **Morse Volcano B&B,** P.O. Box 100, Volcano 96785 (967-7216), in Volcano Village just outside the park, offers roomy common areas and single rooms for $25, with bath $30. (Doubles $40, with bath $45.)**Volcanoes National Park** (967-7311) has free sites at **Kipukanene, Namakanipaio** (near Kilauea Crater), and **Kamoamoa** (on the coast)—each with shelters and fireplaces, but no wood. **Kalopa State Recreation Area** is at the end of Kalopa Rd. (775-7114), 3 miles inland from Mamalahoa Hwy. 19. Sites are surrounded by a wonderful *ohia* forest and feature camping, group lodging, picnicking, nature trails.

Kona

Kona, on the western side of Hawaii, is home to the town of Kailua (officially hyphenated as Kailua-Kona), a resort center whose shops, nightlife, and perfect weather cater to tourists. Hot and gorgeous, the white sand beaches of Kona and the coves of the major hotels (all hotels must have public access paths to the beach) are perfect for tanning. The calm deep waters along the entire coast are ideal for novice scuba divers and prized for giant billfish.

Kailua-Kona is small enough to see in a short walk. Historic sites and white sand beaches abound, the latter dotted with cheap fast-food restaurants and some nightclubs. **Hulihee Palace,** 75-5718 Alli Dr. (329-1877), King Kalakaua's summer home, is beautifully restored. (Open daily 9am-4pm. Admission $4, ages 12-18 $1, under 12 50¢.) The nearby **Mokuaikaua** was Hawaii's first church (1820). The building has been lovingly cared for and is still used for sermons and as a museum; the chimes ring every afternoon at 4pm. (Open daily sunrise-sunset.)

To the south on Rte. 11 is **Kealakekua Bay.** From Rte. 11 turn right onto Napoopoo Dr., which leads down to the small bay (about 15 min.). This area is steeped in history. In 1778, Captain Cook tried to restock his ship here during the **Makahiki**—a holy season honoring the god Lono. The Hawaiians thought Cook's white sails and masts signified the return of Lono, and they proclaimed Cook a god at the **Hikiau Heiau** on the bay. A year later Cook was killed on the far side of the bay when he tried to end a fight between his men and the islanders. A white monument marks the site. **Captain Bean's Glass Bottom Cruises** (329-2955) can take you across the bay to the monument where you can see the fish that inhabit this protected marine life preserve. (Tickets $22, under 12 $11. Prices include equiptment and food. Departs Kailua Pier daily at 8:30am.)

The beaches are Kona's main attraction. **Magic Sands** (also called "Disappearing Sands") at the Kona Magic Sands Hotel, 77-6452 Alii Dr. (329-9177), is a good place to park your towel and wade in the surf. Or, travel up Rte. 19 to prime **Hapuna Beach** and **Spencer Beach** parks, 35 miles north. Both parks have disabled access.

Food can be expensive; take advantage of the 24-hour Food-4-Less on Pawai St. and the early bird specials (5-6pm) at most hotels.

For breakfast, try **Stan's,** 75-5646 Palani Rd. (329-2455), in the Kona Hukilau. (All-you-can-eat hotcakes and 1 egg for $4. Complete dinners $6.25-7. Open daily 7-9:30am and 5:30-8:30pm.) The **Ocean View Inn,** 75-5683 Alii Dr. (329-9998), across from the boat dock, is a popular establishment serving seafood, American, Chinese, and Hawaiian fare in diner setting and price range. (Lunch $3-6, dinner $6-9. Open Tues.-Sun. 6:30am-2:45pm and 5:15-9pm.) **Poki's Pasta,** 75-5699F Alli Dr. (329-7888), a traditional Italian place, spotlights delicious pasta made fresh daily. (Lunch $5-6; dinner $8-10. Open daily 11am-3pm and 4-9pm.)

Staying overnight in Kailua-Kona can be an expensive proposition, since its hotels cater to the affluent traveler. Other nearby towns provide more reasonable lodgings. The nearest camping is at Kohala.

Kona Lodge and Hostel, 7 miles south of Kailua-Kona on Rte. 11 (322-9056 or 322-8136), is somewhat shabby but offers a kitchen and fruit from the gardens. (Office open daily 5-9pm. Primitive coed dorm bunks $12, nonmembers $14. Private rooms $24.) **Manago Hotel,** P.O. Box 145, Captain Cook 96704 (323-2642), is comfy and clean, but austere. (Singles $17. Doubles $20.) More spacious rooms with bath and ocean view in newer wing from $26. A darling hotel near a snorkeling beach is the **Kona Tiki Hotel,** P.O. Box 1567, Kailua-Kona 96740 (329-1425), at 75-5968 Alii Dr. on the southern side of town. (Some singles for $33. Doubles $35, with kitchen $40. Reservation deposit $50.)

For visitor information and maps, contact the **Hawaii Visitors Bureau,** 75-5719 Alii Dr. (329-7787), across from the Kona Inn Shopping Center. (Open Mon.-Fri. 8am-noon and 1-4pm.) **Department of Parks and Recreation,** Yano Stall, Captain Cook (323-3046 or 323-3060), by the police station, has information on county parks, camping, and permits. (Open Mon.-Fri. 7:45am-4:30pm.)

Keahole Airport, is 9 miles (15 min.) north of town. Taxi rides into town are about $16, plus 30¢ per bag. The local transit system, **Hele-on-Bus,** (935-8241), provides infrequent service up and down the west coast out of Kona 6:15am-4:30pm, 3 times per day via Alii Dr., once via Hulualoa. **Honolulu Rent-a-Car,** 74-5588 Pawaii Place (329-7328), rents used cars for as little as $14 per day (3-day min. rental). For bikes, check out **B&L Bik&Sports,** 74-5576B Pawaii Place (329-3309), at Kaiwi St. (Open Mon.-Fri. 9am-5:30pm, Sat. 9am-3pm.) For water equipment rentals, stop in at **Big Island Divers,** Kona Market Place (329-6068; open daily 8am-9pm.)

The **post office** is at Palani Rd. (329-1927; open Mon.-Fri. 9am-4pm, Sat. 9am-noon.) The **ZIP code** is 96740; the **area code** is 808.

Maui

Long before college athletes celebrated their slogan, "We're number one," Maui's warlike chieftans sounded its defiant equivalent "Maui No Ka Oi." Even after the islands' consolidation under the Kamehameha dynasty from the Big Island, Maui's transcendence was upheld in its selection for a time as the capital of a new kingdom. Although commercial preeminence of Honolulu eventually forced a royal relocation to Oahu, Maui is still the island most choose to visit. With a recent rise in tourism has come traffic, elevated prices, commercial hype, and crime and drug problems. Increasing resort development also means, however, that rent-a-car outfits, restaurants, and an active nightlife have flourished.

Named for the demi-god Maui, who pulled all the islands from the sea-bottom with his fish hooks, Maui is built around the slopes of two mightly volcanoes and a narrow isthmus in between. "The Valley Island," as it is known, features clapboard cane towns, concrete condos, sunny beaches and a (sometimes) snowcapped volcano. Maui's popularity will seem justified once you've toured mountainous, sleepy West Maui; the windy central isthmus that holds Wailuku, Kahului, and acre upon acre of sugar cane; the spiritual Haleakala volcano, which dominates East Maui; and the remote splendor of the Hana Coast.

Practical Information

Visitor Information: Hawaii Visitors Bureau, 380 Dairy Road, Kahului (871-8691). Information on Molokai and Lanai. Open Mon.-Fri. 8am-4:30pm. **Haleakala National Park,** P.O. Box 369, Makawao 96768 (572-9306). Information and permits for national park camping (572-9177). **Visitors Center,** 65 Hana Hwy., Paia (579-8000). Open Mon.-Sat. 9am-noon and 5-6pm. **Department of Parks and Recreation,** War Memorial Gym, 1580 Kaahumanu Ave., between Kahului and Wailuku (244-9018). Information and permits ($3) for county parks. Open Mon.-Fri. 8-11am and noon-4:15pm. **Division of State Parks,** 54 High St. (244-4354), in Wailuku. Information on state parks on Maui and Molokai. Open Mon.-Fri. 8-11am and noon-4:15pm.

Kahului Airport, on the northern coast of the isthmus. Serves regular flights from the mainland and other islands. The visitors information booth in front of the terminal's entrance provides free maps, information, and directions. A taxi to hotels will cost $5-8, but renting a car here might save you time later (see Car Rental below). Gray Line (from Oahu 833-8000, on Maui 877-5507, from mainland 800-367-2420) runs between Kahului Airport and the Lahaina-Kaanapali area. Fare $8, reservations required.

Tours: Gray Line, (phone above). Tours to Iao Valley, Lahaina $15-25, to Hana $35-48. Operates daily 7am-9pm.

Boats: Maalaea Activities Center, (242-6982) at Maalaea Harbor. Daily ferries to Kaunakakai, Molokai ($30); 4 trips per week to Kaumalapau Harbor, Lanai ($20). From Lahaina, **Expeditions** (661-3756) boats twice daily to Manele Harbor, Lanai ($25), while the **Maui Princess** (661-8397) runs between Molikai, Oahu, and Maui for $21.

Taxi: Yellow Cab, Kahului Airport (877-7000). $5 to ride into town.

Car Rental: Trans Maui, Kahului Airport (877-5222). $20 per day, $115 per week. Insurance is $6 per day. Must be 21 with major credit card. 24-hour advance reservation required. **Avis,** Kahului Airport (871-7575). $78 per week, $10 per day insurance. $5 more per day if you are 18-25; major credit card required. 24 hour advance reservation.

Bike Rental: The Island Biker, Kahului Shopping Center (877-7744). High-quality 18-speed mountain bikes $18 per day. Open Mon.-Fri. 9am-5pm, Sat. 9am-3pm. Discount with student ID. **Gogo Bikes Hawaii,** 30b Halawai Dr. (661-3063), ¼ mile north of Kaanapali off Rte. 30. 1-speeds $10 per day, 12-speeds $20. Open daily 9am-5pm. Discount with student ID.

Moped and Scooter Rentals: Gogo Bikes Hawaii, Kaanapali (661-3063). One-speed mopeds $5 per hr., $20 per day, $95 per week. Scooters for $25 per day, $125 per week. Open daily 9am-5pm. Must be 18 with a cash deposit or major credit card. Free pick-up in the Kaanapali area. 10% discount with student ID. **Paradise Scooters,** 102 Halawai Dr. (661-0300), next to Gogo Bikes. Free snorkeling equipment with each rental. Delivery to Kihei, Wailea, and Kahului $20. Open Mon.-Sat. 8am-5pm, Sun. 8am-noon.

Water Equipment Rentals: Maui Dive Shop, Azeka Place, Kihei (879-3388), and Wakea Ave., Kahalui (661-5388). Free scuba and snorkeling lessons with equipment rental. Mask $2.75, snorkel $1.75, boogie board $7.50, wetsuit $5, underwater camera $20 per day. Open Mon.-Fri. 8am-9pm, Sat.-Sun. 8am-6pm. **Hunt Hawaii,** 120 Hana Hwy. (579-8129), Paia. Surfboards $15 per 2 hr., $25 per day. Windsurfers $30 per day, $150 per week. Surf or sailboard lessons $30 per 2 hr. Open daily 9am-6pm.

Help Lines: Sexual Assault Crisis Center, 242-4357. 24 hours. **Coast Guard:** 244-5256. 24 hours.**Gay and Bi Information,** 572-1884 (serves Maui, Molokai, Lanai). 24 hours.

Post Office: Lahaina. Open Mon.-Fri. 8:15am-4:15pm. **ZIP code:** 96761. In **Paia,** on Baldwin Ave. Open Mon.-Fri. 8am-4:30pm, Sat. 10:30am-12:30pm. Mail collection Mon.-Sat. 1:15-3:45pm. **ZIP code:** 96799. In **Wailuku,** next to the State Office Building, on High St. Open Mon.-Fri. 8:30am-4:30pm, Sat. 9-11am. **ZIP code:** 96793. In **Kihei,** 1254 S. Kihei Rd., in Azeka Market Place. Open Mon.-Fri. 9am-4:30pm, Sat. 9-11am. **ZIP code:** 96753.

Maui is shaped like a bowling pin, around which the highways wind like a broken figure eight. To the west lie **Kahului** and **Wailuku,** business and residential communities offering less expensive food and supplies than the resort towns. From Kahului, Rte. 30 will lead you clockwise around the small, western loop of the figure eight to hot and dry **Lahaina,** the former whaling village, and **Kaanapali,** the major resort area.

Most roads are fairly well-marked but poorly lit. Heed the warnings on roads recommended for four-wheel-drive vehicles only; a passing rainstorm can quickly drain your funds, since most rental car contracts stipulate that dirt road driving is at the driver's risk. **Hitchhiking** is difficult and illegal. People do hitch, however, and as a rule, the farther they are from Kahului and Kaanapali, the better they fare.

Accommodations

Abandon all desire to stay in the resort areas. Stay in Honokowai instead of Kaanapali, or in Kahului instead of Kihei. Groups of two or more can profit from car/room packages. Larger groups should investigate condominium rentals. **Bed and breakfasts** usually run $35-50. In East Maui camping is the watchword.

Maui YMCA (AYH), Keanae (248-8355), about 32 miles and a 2-hr. drive east of Kahului Airport, midway along Hana Hwy. Rte. 36 to Hana. Inaccessible by public transportation. 100 beds, 6-8 persons per room. 3 dormitory cabins, kitchen, public hot showers. Extensive sports facilities. Cafeteria. 3-day max. stay. Curfew 9pm. Check-in 4-6pm. Check-out 9am. $5, nonmembers $6. Call 244-3253 for reservations.

Happy Valley Inn, 310 Market St. (244-4786), Wailuku. No sign, just a green roof camoflaged behind a shower tree, immediately across the bridge. Frequented by an international windsurfing crowd. Fans, TV room, laundry facilities. One-week min. stay. Check-in Mon.-Sat. 4-6pm. Modest singles $20, with shared bath. Four dorm beds $12 each.

Pioneer Inn, 658 Wharf St. (836-1411), Lahaina. Directly in front of the boat harbor and next to the giant banyan tree. 2 buildings make up the hotel, the "original" and the "Mauka." The Old Whaler's Saloon maintains its swashbuckling spirit long into each night, making part of the inn noisy. Pool. Ask for a room with a harbor view. Original building: singles $21, with bath $27; doubles $24, with bath $30. Mauka building: singles $42, doubles $45. Call at least 3 months in advance for reservations.

The Bungalow, 2044 Vineyard St. (244-3294), Wailuku. Primitive quarters with shared bath may be available on a daily basis. Singles $10. Doubles $15.

Nani Kai Hale, 73 N. Kihei Rd. (879-9120 or 800-367-6032 from the mainland), Kihei. Condominium on a sandy beach. Double with bath April 16-Dec. 15 $32.50. 3-day min. stay; Dec. 16-April 15 $42.50, 1-week min. stay. Call in advance for reservations.

Maui Palms Resort, 170 Kaahumanu Ave. (877-0071), Kahalui. Unpretentious hotel by the sea. TV. Singles $40. Doubles $43.

Camping

The county maintains two campsites in Paia, **H.A. Baldwin Park** and **Rainbow Park,** both about 5 miles east of the Kahului Airport. Neither are safe for solitary travelers. (3-day max. stay; tent and permit required. $3, under 18 50¢. The Baldwin offers restrooms, showers, and a beautiful and windy white-sand beach; unfortunately, the fenced-in camping area lies on the edge of busy Hwy. 36. Rainbow Park lies along Baldwin Ave., 3 miles upcountry from Paia. For more information contact the Department of Parks and Recreation (see Practical Information above).

On West Maui, the only recognized camping is at **Camp Pecusa,** ¼ mile north of the 14-mile marker on Hwy. 30. (661-4303). This campground is less than glamorous and offers little shade. (Shower, washbasin, pit toilets, and tables. $3 per person on a walk-in basis.)

You can camp in any of the three state parks (5-day max. stay) after obtaining a permit (free) at the Department of Parks and Recreation. **Waianapanapa State Wayside** in Hana, about 52 miles east of Kahului Airport, offers by far the best state camping facilities on the island. The sites for campers and tents include restrooms, picnic tables, barbecue grills, and outdoor showers. (12 cabins available, $5 per person for groups larger than 6; $10 for a single bed. Reservations recommended.)

Maui's two federal parks require no permit. **Hosmer Grove,** 7000 feet up Haleakalā's slope, is a small campground with drinking water, toilet, grills, and firewood. On a weekend night, you'll have to squeeze your tent in with a crowbar. (Groups limited to 15 people and 3 nights.) **Oheo** is at sea level, about 67 miles from Kahului Airport, ¼ mile south of **Oheo Stream,** near the Seven Pools. (No drinking water or firewood. 3-day max. stay.)

Camping at the **national campsites** within the crater requires a permit and a hike to the site. (2-day max. stay per campground.) Permits are available from the **Haleakala National Park Headquarters,** P.O. Box 369, Makawao, Maui 96768 (572-9306).

Food

Guava trees line the road to Hana. Other fruits are available for a song at stands along the Hana Hwy. and Rte. 35 in Kihei. Maui specialties such as sweet kula onions and Maui potato chips (try them chocolate-covered) are sold in most supermarkets. *Guri Guri,* a local-made sherbet that comes in pineapple and strawberry, has pleased islanders for years from its main outlet **Tasaka Guri Guri,** in the Maui Mall (871-4512; open daily Hawaiian time, i.e. whenever).

Delicious fish can be found everywhere on the island. Restaurants serve seafood fresh from the sea; add some native sauces, and the result is *ono* (delicious). The cheapest places to eat are away from the resorts, especially in Wailuku.

Ichiban the Restaurant, Kahului Shopping Center (871-6977). Japanese cuisine with a local Hawaiian atmosphere. Lunch buffet $3-5. Open Mon.-Sat. 7am-2pm and 5-9pm.

Porttown Deli, Kahului Shopping Center. Daily Hawaiian/Oriental specials, including such staples as *laulau* (pork), lomi salmon, poi, and sukiyaki chicken. Lunch plate $3.50. Open Mon.-Sat. 6am-4:30pm.

The Maui Boy, 2102 Vineyard St. (244-7243), corner of Vineyard and Church St., in Wailuku. Curtains and potted plants give this diner an edge over the competition. The *lau-lau* plate includes poi, lomi salmon, and macaroni salad ($7). Open Tues.-Fri. 10am-2pm and 5-9pm, Sat.-Sun. 7am-2pm and 5-9pm.

Siam Thai Cuisine, 123 N. Market St. (244-3817), Wailuku. Trendy eatery serving vegetarian dishes for $5, other entrees $6-9. Lunch Mon.-Fri. 11am-3pm, dinner daily 5-10pm.

La Vie en Rose, 62 Baldwin Ave. (579-9820), Paia. A bakery with adjoining pink potted plants and white trellis café. Epicurean windsurfers thrive here on Old World cuisine at ludicrous prices. Try the duck confit ($6.25). Open daily 7:30am-2:30pm and 4-9pm.

Sights and Activities

Haleakala Crater, the "House of the Sun," dominates the eastern end of the island from its perch 10,000 feet above the sea. According to Polynesian legend, the demi-god Maui ascended Haleakala to slow the sun's trip across the sky so that his mother would have more of the sun's rays to dry her **tapa** cloth. When the sun arose from his house at the end of the sky, Maui lassoed him by his genitals, and the sun agreed to cruise across the sky more slowly. Ouch! The House of the Sun is still a moving place from which to watch the sun rise. **Haleakala National Park** is open 24 hours. (Park entrance $3 per car.) Be sure to stop at the **park headquarters** (572-9306), about a mile from the Rte. 378 entrance.

Haleakala Visitors Center (572-9172), near the summit, has exhibits on the geology, archeology, and ecology of the region. (Free ranger talks at 9:30am, 10:30am, and 11:30am. Open daily 6:30am-4pm.) The **Puuulaula Center,** at Haleakala's summit, offers shelter to those who forgot a sweater or jacket. (Open 24 hours.) An 11-mile descent into the crater via **Sliding Sands Trail** and out again via **Halemauu Trail** could be the most impressive seven hours of your trip to Hawaii. Along it you'll find the **Kaluuokaoo Pit,** also called the Bottomless Pit, one of several exposed lava tubes in the crater. Early Hawaiians threw the umbilical cords of their newborns into the pit to ensure that the sacred cords would not be eaten by the valley's evil rodents. Drive farther south on Rte. 37 to **Tedeschi Winery** (878-6058), to taste their "Maui Blanc" pineapple wine for free. (Open Mon.-Fri. 9am-5pm, Sat.-Sun. 10am-5pm.)

A full day can be spent touring the **Hana Coast.** The northern route (H-36) through **Paia** and **Keanae** is incredibly torturous and tough on the internal organs, but the scenery is rewarding. Make sure you start out from Paia with a full tank of gas, and don't go if the road is wet—it's a long way down. Paia itself has flourished with nearby **Hookipa Beach Park,** the mecca for international windsurfing.

Wailuku is a tranquil plantation town, worth an afternoon stroll. The government buildings on High St. and vintage shops on Market St. reveal urban life "local style," unaltered by the ravages of resort development to the south.

You can visit a reconstructed ancient native place of worship at the **Hale Kii** (House of Images), atop a nearby hill near Rte. 32 between Wailuku and Iao Valley. The temple affords the islands most idyllic views, and the locals know it well (high school lovers make the trek uphill every Thurs. evening). Follow Main St. (Rte. 32) to the traffic light at Rte. 330. Make a left, pass the macadamia grove, and turn right on Rte. 340. Continue to Kuhio Place, and follow the tortuous route to the right.

Lahaina, an old whaling port, was the capital of the islands during the time of Kamehameha the Great. Whale-watching in spring and fall is still popular today all along the coast. Lahaina itself remains a sunny, dry town that immediately infects everyone with laid-back syndrome. When Mark Twain visited, he planned to stay one week and work; he stayed a month and didn't write a thing. The huge tree in Lahaina's town square is a 114-year-old East Indian **banyan tree.** Obtain a free copy of the *Lahaina Historical Guide* from one of the many tourist activities centers that crowd the town.

Kihei and **Wailea,** on the southwest coast, are beginning to merge into the Kaanapali, Lahaina, Kapalua resort area. Some good swimming beaches and parks cluster around Kihei's condominiums. **Kamaole Sands Beach Parks** (numbered 1 to 3) have the best facilities. Check the *Maui News* to rent unsold units from condos at bargain prices. **Kalama Beach Park,** a 36-acre park with volleyball and basketball courts, is a reliable standby if Kamaole is crowded. Rte. 31 continues past Wailea to some fabulous uncrowded beaches.

West Maui hosts most of the hot spots on Spuds Mackenzie's top-ten list of island party pads. Go dancing at **Partners,** 118 Makawao Ave. (572-6611), in Makawao, **Spats,** in the Hyatt Regency Maui (667-7474), or **Banana Moon,** in the Maui Marriott (667-1200).

The free *Maui Beach Press* provides decent listings of both local and tourist resort happenings.

ALASKA

Called "Alashka" ("The Great Land") by the Aleuts and "The Last Frontier" by adventurous settlers, Alaska is large and unspoiled enough to accommodate even the most rugged individualist. Misty fjords, mountain lakes, forests, glaciers, and tundra complement a population as varied as the Great Land itself. It is hard to say exactly what being "Alaskan" means because the term encompasses everything from Native American to lifetime resident to *cheechako* (outsider) lured by the opportunity to homestead. But Alaskans' sense of community and statehood is strong; ask any local to tell you about the state, and you'll see someone get more excited than a polar bear contemplating a fat seal dinner.

Though broad enough to accommodate England, France, Spain, and Italy within its borders, Alaska did not host a European visitor until 1741 when the czar of Russia hired Dutch navigator Victor Bering to map out the region near the Kenai Peninsula. Bering died in the effort, but his crew brought home such an abundance of valuable furs that Russian traders soon overran Kodiak Island with traps in hand (and rubles in mind). The fur harvest dried up in less than a century, and the czar, dead broke from the Crimean War, decided to sell what he considered to be a territory sucked dry of its natural resources. In 1967 the U.S. bought the vast wasteland for less than 2¢ per acre—quite a bargain until you do some quick multiplication to get the total price of $7,200,000. Alaska soon became known as "Seward's Icebox," a jab at Secretary of State William Seward who negotiated the purchase. But within 20 years, Yankee prospectors unearthed enough gold to turn Seward's folly into a billion-dollar profit.

The modern development of Alaska began with World War II. In response to the 1941 Japanese occupation of the Aleutian islands, the military connected Alaska to the lower 48 with the Alaskan Highway and built ports and airfields. Many GIs liked what they saw, and stayed. The Cold War with Russia led to an increase in military development in Alaska. In the 60s, oil became the catalyst for Alaska's growth when it was discovered on the Kenai Peninsula and on the north slope of the Brooks Range. The Alaska pipeline pumped its first barrel of crude 800 miles from Prudhoe Bay to Valdez in July of 1968.

The recent uproar surrounding the spill of Exxon *Valdez's* oil cargo obscures the fact that only 1% of Alaska's coastline was damaged. The area covered by the leak was just a speck in Alaska's enormity. Despite the pipeline, the Alcan highway, and the still-secret Nucleon Early Warning System access roads, only one-fifth of the land is accessible by roads—the float plane is the primary mode of transportation. Native Alaskans still live with privacy and autonomy unknown to most other Native Americans; Athabascans, Aleuts, Eskimos, Tlingits, and Haidas still subsist on the land's abundant resources. The rivers teem with salmon; the rocky shores harbor water fowl and seals while whales sing offshore; black, brown, grizzly, polar, and Kodiak bears compete with wolves, lynx, and other carnivores for food and territory; magnificent northern species including caribou and walrus abound; and moose, bighorn sheep, and bald eagles coexist in numbers unheard of elsewhere in the United States.

Practical Information

Capital: Juneau.

Tourist Information: Alaska Division of Tourism, Pouch E-101, Juneau 99811 (465-2010). Open Mon.-Fri. 8am-4:30pm. **Alaskan Public Lands Information Center,** Old Federal Building (271-2737), 4th Ave., Anchorage 99510. Tips on all federal, state, and local parks, refuges, and forests. Will refer you to the appropriate office such as: **Alaska State Division of Parks,** Pouch 7-001, Anchorage 99510 (561-2020). Open Mon.-Fri. 8am-4:30pm. **United States Forest Service,** Box 1628-ATD, Juneau 99802 (586-7282). General information regarding national parks and reserves. Open Mon.-Fri. 8am-4:30pm. **National Park Service,** Parks and Forests Information Center, 2525 Gampbell, Anchorage 99503 (261-2643). Open Mon.-Fri. 8am-5pm. **State Department of Fish and Game,** P.O. Box 3-2000, Juneau 99802. Find out about hunting and fishing regulations here.

Time Zones: Alaska (4 hr. behind Eastern); Aleutian-Hawaii (5 hr. behind Eastern). **Postal Abbreviation:** AK.

Travel

Anyone who has ever ventured onto Alaska's roads owns a copy of *The Milepost,* published by the Alaska Northwest Publishing Company, 130 2nd Ave. S., Edmond, WA 98020 (for information, call 907-563-1141, Mon.-Fri. 8:30am-4:30pm). Each thick volume ($14.95) is packed with information about Alaskan and Canadian communities as well as up-to-date ferry schedules and maps of the highways and roads.

Travel in Alaska is easy but expensive. Most Alaskans use air travel, often piloting themselves (one in 36 has a pilot's license). Several airlines run frequent scheduled flights to most places any visitor might be inclined to go: **Alaska Air** (larger towns—contact your local Delta desk); **Markair** (to larger Bush towns, Kodiak, and the Aleutians; 800-426-6784); **ERA Aviation** (southcentral; 243-3300); and **Ryan Air Service** (practically anywhere in the Bush; 248-0695). Many other charters and flight-seeking services are available. Check *The Milepost* (see above) or write **Ketchum Air Service Inc.,** North Shore Lake Hood, Anchorage 99503 (243-5525), to ask about their charters.

Trains along the **Alaskan Highway** connect Seward and Whittier in the south to Fairbanks in the north via Anchorage and Denali. The train itself and the view it affords are beautiful, but may not be entirely worth the fare ($88 from Anchorage to Fairbanks). The train will stop to drop off passengers anywhere with advance notice. It also provides semi-local service from Anchorage to Portage Glacier ($47.50). All trains run daily. Advance reservations are required for all except Whittier trips. Write **Alaska Railroad Corporation,** Passenger Services, P.O. Box 7-2111, Anchorage 99510-7069. (Call 265-2623 for schedules, fares, and reservations.)

Scheduled **bus service** connects Whitehorse, British Columbia, and Haines with Central Alaska, including Anchorage. **Alaska Sightseeing Company,** 327 F St., Anchorage 99510 (276-1305), provides service to Anchorage from Haines, which is on the Alaska Marine Highway. **Whitepass-Yukon Motorcoaches,** P.O. Box 100479, Anchorage 99510 (279-0761), has two buses per week from Whitehorse, YT to Anchorage; service to Haines is also available twice per week. Bus rides to Anchorage from the Lower 48 are expensive. **Greyhound** charges well over $300 from Seattle, slightly less from Vancouver. **Bus tours** that often include meals, lodging, and sights otherwise difficult to get to can be a good deal. For example, **Gray Line Tours** (547 W. 4th Ave., Anchorage 99501; 277-5581) offers a three-day excursion from Whitehorse to Anchorage that includes a sail across Prince William Sound, a train ride from Whittier, and two nights' worth of accommodations, all for under $500.

Driving in Alaska is not for the faint at heart. To the embarrassment of most residents, many major roads in Alaska are still in deplorable condition. Dust and flying rocks are a major hazard in the summer, as are miserable 10- to 30-mile patches of gravel. Radiators and headlights should be protected from flying rocks with a wire screen, and a fully functioning spare tire is essential. Winter can actually offer a smoother ride. Active snow crews keep roads as clear as possible, and the packed surface and thinned traffic permit easy driving without summer's mechanical troubles. At the same time, the danger of avalanches and ice is cause for major concern. Be sure to check the road conditions before traveling; in Anchorage call 333-1013, or simply tune in to local radio stations. Both winter and summer travelers are advised to let a friend or relative know of their position along the highway several times in the course of a trip. Drivers should also take into account the cost of gas, which varies significantly from station to station.

Hitchhiking in Alaska is easier, safer, and more culturally accepted than in the lower 48. Campgrounds, service stations, and the old standby—on-ramps—are good places to try. Catching a ride into Alaska on the Alaska Highway involves passing the Alaska/Yukon border check—it's common procedure for hitchhikers to walk across the border to avoid hassles. A popular alternative to hitching the entire length of the Alaska Hwy. is to take the Marine Hwy. to Haines and hitch a ride from there with cars off the ferry. All long-range hitchhikers should carry a sleeping bag, food, and warm clothing—everything necessary for a few days out on the lonely Alcan. While this happens infrequently, be prepared. Hitching within towns is common, even among locals.

Physical Characteristics and Climate

Alaska spans 586,412 square miles, one-fifth the area of the continental United States, stretching west to a longitude that coincides with New Zealand. It has 33,904 miles of shoreline (about 1½ times the combined coastlines of the Lower 48), and the highest mountain in North America (20,320-ft. Mt. Denali). No single temperate zone covers the whole region; Prudhoe Bay differs from Ketchikan as much as Minneapolis does from Atlanta. In general, summer and early fall (June-Sept.) are the best times to visit. Visitors can expect daylight from 6am to 2am in many areas during these months.

Fairbanks, Tok, and the Bush frequently enjoy 95°F hot spells, receiving less than eight inches of precipitation annually. The Interior freezes in its −60° to −80°F temperatures. Farther south, the climate is milder, but also rainier. Sitka "rusts" with 82 inches of precipitation annually. Anchorage and other coastal towns in the southcentral are blessed with the Japanese Current, which has a moderating effect on the climate. Average temperatures for Anchorage are 13°F in January (the coldest month) to 57°F in July (the warmest).

Travelers should be prepared for wet, wind, and cold year-round. In summer, those staying below the Arctic Circle probably won't need anything heavier than a light parka or jacket and sweater. For forays into the "Bush" (Alaskans' term for the wilderness), be absolutely certain to bring waterproof boots and sturdy raingear. Wool and polypropylene are staples for socks, underwear, pants, shirts, and hats. The warmest coats and snowsuits are hollofil, not down-filled, garments.

Winter travelers should always expect the chilly unexpected. The National Park Service advises that visitors learn to recognize the symptoms of hypothermia, the gradual lowering of the body temperature; also be sure to carry extra dry clothing, blankets, and food. Read Jack London's *To Build a Fire* to learn what a drag it can be to freeze to death.

Camping

Just setting up a tent or igloo in a scenic spot is an ancient Alaskan tradition kept up by land-bridging, roving Athabascans to homesteading ex-GIs. "Squatting" has long been an Alaskan right—and now institutions have stepped in to make it possible for tourists.

The U.S. Forest Service maintains more than 178 wilderness log cabins for public use: 142 in Tongass National Forest in Southeastern Alaska and 36 in Chugach National Forest in Southcentral Alaska. The cabins are beautifully located and well maintained. User permits are required along with a fee of $10 per party per night. Reserve several months in advance. Most cabins have seven-day use limits, except hike-in cabins (3-day max. stay May-Aug.). Cabins sleep six, and are usually accessible only by air, boat, or hiking trail. Facilities at these sites rarely include more than a wood stove and pit toilets. Some cabins provide skiffs (small boats). For maps or further information write to the U.S. Forest Service. For information about free cabins within wildlife ranges, contact the U.S. Fish and Wildlife Service (see Practical Information above).

Alaskan state-run campgrounds are always free. Often they have toilets and drinking water, but no showers. For information on state campgrounds and waysides, contact the Alaska State Division of Parks (see Practical Information above). Four federal agencies control and manage park lands in Alaska: the U.S. Forest Service (USFS), the Bureau of Land Management (BLM), the National Park Service, and the U.S. Fish and Wildlife Service (see Practical Information above). The USFS maintains numerous campgrounds within the Chugach and Tongass National Forests (sites $4-5; 14-day max. stay). The BLM runs about 20 campgrounds throughout the state, all free except the Delta BLM campground on the Alaska Highway. The National Park Service maintains campgrounds in Mt. Denali National Park, Glacier Bay National Park, and Katmai National Park and Preserve. (Sites $4-6.) The several campgrounds managed by the U.S. Fish and Wildlife Service are confined to the Kenai National Wildlife Refuge, Box 2139, Soldotna 99669. Government campgrounds in Alaska rarely have dump stations or electrical hookups.

Most towns, and all those with canneries, have tent cities for seasonal workers. These will cost you a few dollars a night to bunk down, and generally have poor facilities but interesting, if fish-smelling, communities of students and workers.

Remember to leave an itinerary at the offices of parks, hotels, state troopers, guides, etc. This is an important safety measure that takes little time to execute. Alaska is bigger and more rugged than you can possibly imagine and the weather is unpredictable.

For additional information about hiking and camping in Alaska, consult one of the following books: *55 Ways of Wilderness* or *Alaska's Parklands,* both published by the Mountaineer Press, or *Adventuring in Alaska,* published by the Sierra Club.

Southeastern Alaska (The Panhandle)

The Panhandle is flung 500 miles from the Gulf of Alaska to Prince Rupert, B.C. The Tlingit (pronounced KLING-kit) and Haida (pronounced HI-duh) tribes have left a deep mark on the region, which forms a loose network of islands, inlets, and deep saltwater fjords, surrounded by deep valleys and rugged mountains. Temperate rain forest conditions, 60-odd major glaciers, and 15,000 bald eagles distinguish the Panhandle.

Southeastern Alaska is one of the few places in the world where the blast of a ferry boat heralds the day's important event. The 1000 islands and 10,000 miles of coastline in the Alexander Archipelago are connected to each other and to Seattle by ferries run by the Alaska Marine Highway. While the Interior and the Southcentral regions of Alaska have experienced great urban sprawl (by Alaskan standards), the communities of Southeastern Alaska cling to the coast. While Gold Rush days haunt such towns as Juneau, others like Sitka hearken back to the era of the Russian occupation.

The cheapest, most exciting way to explore the area is on the Alaska Marine Highway system. The state-run ferries connect Seattle, Ketchikan, Sitka, Juneau, and Haines, as well as some smaller Native and fishing communities. You can avoid the high price of accommodations in smaller communities by planning your ferry trip at night and sleeping on the deck.

Ketchikan

According to a Ketchikan proverb, "if you can't see the top of Deer Mountain, it's raining; if you *can* see the top, it's about to rain." About 164 inches per year pour down upon this working community of 14,600, cradled at the watery base of the mountain; locals have to ignore the rain, or nothing would ever get done. The southernmost city in Alaska, Ketchikan is also the first port for ferries and cruise ships visiting the state, and maintains elevated walkways and numerous staircases between multi-leveled streets to keep tourists—the most important source of the town's income—high and dry.

The **Ketchikan Visitors Bureau,** 131 Front St. (225-6166), across from the cruise ship docks downtown, offers maps of a good walking tour. (Open daily 9am-6pm.) Ketchikan's history as a mining boomtown settled by fortune-hunting prospectors is preserved on **Creek Street,** the Red Light District that thrived until 1954. At #24 you can revel in the nebulous history of **Dolly's House** (225-6329), a brothel-turned-museum. Hours vary, so call ahead if you want to visit. (Admission $2.) Also on the walking tour is the **Totem Heritage Center,** 601 Deermount St., housing 33 well-preserved totem poles from Tlingit and Haida villages. (Open Mon.-Sat. 8am-5pm, Sun. 9am-5pm. Admission $1.50, under 18 free; Sun. afternoon free.) The **Tongass Historical Society Museum,** on Dock St., explains the strange interaction between Natives, rain, salmon, and prostitutes. (Open mid-May to Sept. Mon.-Sat. 8:30am-5pm, Sun. 1-5pm. Admission $1, under 18 free; free Sun.) Ketchikan currently has the highest population of Native Alaskans in the southeastern portion of the state; consequently, the town and its environs are blessed with many other fine totem pole collections. **Saxman Native Village,** 2½ miles south of town, displays 24 totems from original sites at villages in the Inland Passage. (Open daily 9am-5pm and on weekends when a cruise ship is in.) Thirteen-and-a-half miles north of town lies the reconstructed Tlinget community house and the 13 totems of the **Totem Bight.** Without wheels it is difficult to reach the park other than by hitching; taxis charge $7 each way to Saxman. Tour buses leave in front of the Ingersoll Hotel across from the visitors bureau ($18); call **Alaska Tours** (225-2240) or drop in the lobby to check on the schedule.

The **Ketchikan Youth Hostel (AYH),** P.O. Box 8515, Ketchikan 99901 (225-3319), is in the United Methodist Church on the corner of Grant and Main St. (Kitchen available; no beds, just mats on the floor. Lockout 8:30am-6pm. Lights out 11pm. $4, nonmembers $7. Open June 1-Sept. 1.) The **Rain Forest Inn,** 2311

Hemlock St., Ketchikan 99901 (225-9500), offers dorm rooms. Take Tongass Ave. about 6 blocks into town from the ferry terminal, then follow Jefferson St. left for ½ block. Kitchen and laundromat are available. (Bunks $17. Singles $39.) Anne Rothrock, at the **Ketchikan Bed and Breakfast Network,** Box 3213, Ketchikan 99901 (225-8550) can find you slightly more glamorous accommodations. (Singles $30-65.) Camp on the shores of Ward Lake at the **Signal Creek Campground,** 6 miles north on Tongass Hwy. from the ferry terminal. (Water and pit toilets. Open in summer. 25 sites $5 each.) The **Last Chance Campground,** 2.2 miles from Signal Creek down Ward Lake, is privately run and caters mostly to RVs. (23 sites, water, pit toilets. Sites $5.)

The most convenient supermarket to downtown is **Tatsuda's,** 633 Stedman, at Deermount St. just beyond the Thomas Basin. (Open daily 7am-11pm.) **Pioneer Pantry,** 124 Front St. (225-3337), across from the visitors bureau offers clean-cut decor with a few tables and a long bar. Sandwiches include salad, fries, or soup ($4.25-7). (Open daily 8am-6pm.) **Kay's Kitchen,** 2813 Tongass Ave. (225-5860), 600m toward town from the ferry terminal, is a busy little café with homemade everything. (Open June-Sept. Tues.-Sat. 11am-4pm.)

Ketchikan sits on an island 235 miles south of Juneau, 90 miles north of Prince Rupert, BC, and 600 miles north of Seattle, WA. The town stretches for 12 miles but rarely exceeds 7 blocks in width.

The magical **Misty Fjords National Monument** lies 30 miles east of Ketchikan and is accessible by boat or float plane. This 2.2-million-acre park offers great camping, guided tours in summer, and workshops year round. Call the Ketchikan Visitors Bureau or the **Misty Fjords Visitor Center,** on Mill St., for information about tours to the park (over $100). In town, the **Frontier Saloon,** 127 Main St. (225-4707), has live music Tuesday though Sunday in summer. (Open daily 10am-2am.) The **Arctic Bar,** (225-4709), on the other side of the tunnel, is a more earthy fishers' haunt. (Open Sun.-Wed. 9am-midnight, Thurs.-Sat. 9am-2am.)

Ketchikan **buses** run about every ½ hour from Mon.-Sat. 6:45am-6:45pm. (Fare $1, seniors and under 11 75¢.) Ketchikan's **ZIP code** is 99901; the **area code** is 907.

Sitka

Dominated by the snow-capped volcano of Mt. Edgecumbe, Sitka was the center of Alaskan history until the early twentieth century. Alexander Baranof, the manager of the Russian-American company, quelled the bloody uprisings of the native Tlingits by establishing "New Archangel" as the capital of Russian Alaska in 1804. The settlement was Russia's "Paris of the Pacific" for the next 63 years, larger than either San Francisco or Seattle; visitors from all nations came here for the lure of money from sea otter pelts and the trappings of glittering society life. After the transferral of Alaska to American hands in 1867, Sitka remained the territory's capital from 1884 until 1906.

The Slavic influence in this Tlingit village is particularly evident in the beautiful, onion-domed **Saint Michael's Cathedral.** This Russian Orthodox Church still holds services for the many half-Russian, half-native residents. The church is a replica of the original, decimated by fire in 1964. Its precious icons and vestments from Russian colonial days were saved, and are now back in place. (Open daily noon-4pm; 9am-4pm if a cruise ship is in. Donation required.) Historic **Castle Hill,** site of Baranof's Castle and Tlingit forts, offers an incredible view of Mt. Edgecumbe, an inactive volcano known as the "Mt. Fuji of Alaska." It was on Castle Hill that Alaska was sold to the United States in 1867.

Stroll down the enchanting, manicured trails of the **Sitka National Historic Park** (Totem Park, as locals call it), at the end of Lincoln St. (747-6281), 1 mile east of St. Michael's. The trails pass by many restored totems on the way to the side of the **Tlingit fort,** where hammer-wielding chieftain Katlian almost held off the Russians in the battle for Alaska in 1804. The park **visitors center** offers audiovisual presentations and the opportunity to watch native artists in action in the Native American Cultural Center. (Open daily 8am-5pm.) The **Russian Bishop's House,** across from Crescent Boat Harbor, was recently restored by the park service to approximate its appearance when built in 1842 for its first resident, Bishop Ivan Veniaminor. The small museum displays Russian artifacts from New Archangel. (Open daily 8am-5pm; tours of the upstairs 8am-noon and 2-4pm.)

There are excellent **hiking** opportunities in the Sitka area—make sure to pick up the thick booklet *Sitka Trails* at the **USFS information booth,** in front of the Centennial Bldg. at Lincoln St. Several outstanding trails include the **Indian River Trail,** an easy 5.5-mile trek up the valley to the base of **Indian River Falls,** and the 3-mile uphill trail to the top of **Gavan Hill.** There is also a fine 3-mile trek from downtown across the runway at the Japonski Island airport to the old WWII causeway that heads past abandoned fortifications all the way to **Makhanati Island.**

Sitka has about eight bed-and-breakfast homes, all priced from $30 to $50 per person. The **visitors bureau,** Centennial Bldg., 330 Harbor Dr. (747-8601 or 747-5940; open Mon.-Sat. 9am-5pm), has a complete list. The **Sitka Youth Hostel (AYH),** Box 2645, Sitka 99835 (747-8356), is a small hostel with army cots in the United Methodist Church on Edgecumbe and Kimsham St. Find the McDonald's, a mile out of town on Halibut Pt. Rd., and walk 25m up Peterson St. to Kimsham. (No kitchen facilities; 1 chore required. Lockout 8am-6pm. Curfew 11pm. $5, non-members $8.) **Potlatch House,** 713 Katlian St. (747-8611), Box 58, Sitka 99835, is clean and modern. (Singles $52.30. Doubles $64.50.) The USFS runs the **Starrigaven Creek Campground,** at the end of Halibut Point Rd., 1 mile from the ferry terminal, 8 miles from town. (23 sites, pit toilets. 14-day max. stay. Sites $5.)

Pick up your groceries at the **Market Center Grocery** at Sawmill Creek and Baranof St., uphill from the Bishop's House (open Mon.-Sat. 10am-8pm, Sun. noon-6pm), or close to the hostel at **Lakeside Grocery,** 705 Halibut Pt. Rd. (Open Mon.-Sat. 9am-9pm, Sun. 11am-7pm.) Fresh seafood is available from fishers along the docks or at **Sitka Sound Seafood** on Katlian St., which occasionally offers fish for retail sale. **The Bayview Restaurant,** upstairs in the Bayview Trading Company at 407 Lincoln St. (747-5440), cooks up everything from *russkia ribnia blyood* ($6.50) to a Mousetrap sandwich (grilled cheese, $3.25), as well as great burgers. (Open Mon.-Fri. 11am-7pm.) The **Channel Club,** 2906 Halibut Point Rd. (747-9916), 3 miles from downtown, is frequented by locals for fantastic salad bar with over 30 toppings. (Open Sun.-Thurs. 6-11pm, Fri.-Sat. 6pm-midnight.)

Sitka sits on the western side of Baranof Island, 95 miles southwest of Juneau and 185 miles northwest of Ketchikan. The O'Connell Bridge connects downtown to Japonski Island and the airport.

Sitka Tours offers a shuttle bus and tour guide service from the ferry terminal (ride into town $2.50; tours $8). Sitka's **post office** is at 1207 Sawmill Creek Rd./ outside of downtown. (Open Mon.-Fri. 9am-6pm.) **ZIP code:** 99835. The **area code** is 907.

Juneau

Built on a tiny strip of land at the base of noble Mt. Juneau, Alaska's capital city is the only one in the nation inaccessible by highway. Juneau mixes and matches Victorian mansions, log cabins, Russian Orthodox churches, "Federal" style *quonset* huts, and simple frame houses with shutters painted in Norwegian *rosemaling.* The potpourri of styles only hints at the richness of Juneau's history.

Tlingit Chief Kowee led Joe Juneau and Richard Harris to the "mother lode" of gold in the hills up Gold Creek in October, 1880. By the next summer, boatloads of would-be prospectors had found themselves at work in the already claimed mines. Twenty-five years later Juneau superseded Sitka as capital of the territory of Alaska. Mining ended in Juneau in 1941, but by then fishing, lumber, and the government had filled in to support Juneau's economy. Today, Juneau exists for the government and tourists. It remains a city of energy and beauty.

Practical Information

Emergency: 911.

Juneau Visitors Information Centers: Davis Log Cabin, 134 3rd St. (586-2284), at Seward St. Open Mon.-Fri. 8:30am-5pm, Sat.-Sun. 10am-4pm; Oct.-May Mon.-Fri. 8:30am-4pm. **Marine Park Kiosk,** Marine Way at Ferry Way, right by the cruise ship unloading dock. Open May-Sept. daily 9am-6pm. **U.S. Forest and National Park Services:** 101 Egan Dr. (586-8751), in Centennial Hall. Make reservations for USFS cabins in Tongass Forest here. Write for application packet (see Camping under Ketchikan). Open daily 9am-6pm; Labor Day-Memorial Day Mon.-Fri. 9am-6pm.

Juneau International Airport: 9 miles north of town on Glacier Hwy. **Alaska Air,** in the Baranof Hotel, Franklin St. at 2nd St. (789-0600 or 800-926-0333). One way to Anchorage ($122), Sitka ($65), and Ketchican ($65).

Buses: Capital Transit (789-6901). Runs from downtown to Douglas, the airport, and Mendenhall Glacier. Leaves Marine Park for aiport and glacier 5 min. after the hr. every hr. 7am-3pm. From 3-10pm, leaves Marine Park 35 min. after the hr. The fare is 75¢ to all points. **Mendenhall Glacier Transport** (789-5460) runs vans to the airport ($3) and has an excellent, cheap tour of Juneau and Mendenhall Glacier (2½ hr., $7). Departs 10:30am and 2:30pm from the Marine Park.

Alaska Marine Highway: P.O. Box R, Juneau 99811 (465-3941 or 800-642-0066). Ferries dock at the Auke Bay terminal at Mile 13.8 Glacier Hwy. To Seattle, WA ($190, car and driver $464), Ketchikan ($60, car and driver $150), and Sitka ($20, car and driver $44).

Taxis: Capital Cab, 586-2772. **Taku Taxi,** 586-2121. Both conduct city tours as well as runs to Mendenhall ($50 per 1½ hr.)

Car Rental: Ugly Duckling, 287 S. Franklin St. (586-3825), across from the parking garage. $25 per day, 10¢ per mile. **Rent-a-Dent,** 789-9000. At the airport, with free courtesy van pickup. $30 per day with 100 free miles.

Help Lines: Crisis Line, 586-4337. 7-11pm. **Gay-Lesbian Switchboard,** 586-4297.

Post Office: 709 W. 9th St. (586-7138). Open Mon.-Fri. 9am-5:30pm. General Delivery ZIP Code: 99801.

Area Code: 907.

Juneau stands on the Gastineau Channel opposite Douglas Island, 650 miles southeast of Anchorage and 900 miles north of Seattle. The **Glacier Highway** connects downtown, the airport, the residential area of the Mendenhall Valley, and the ferry terminal.

Accommodations, Camping, and Food

If you can't get into Juneau's wonderful hostel, the **Alaska Bed and Breakfast Association,** P.O. Box 3/6500, #169 Juneau 99802 (586-2959), will provide information on rooms in local homes year-round. Most Juneau B&Bs are uphill, beyond 6th St., and offer singles from $40 and doubles from $45. Reservations recommended.

Juneau Youth Hostel, 614 Harris St. (586-9559), corner of 6th and Harris. A glorious hostel: clean, friendly, and well-managed. 24 bunk beds. Showers, laundry, and kitchen facilities available. Lockout 9am-5pm. $7.50, nonmembers $9.50. Make reservations well in advance.

Alaska Hotel, 167 S. Franklin St. (586-1000). A beautiful hotel made all of dark wood, right in the center of downtown. Has been restored to its original 1913 Victorian decor. Singles $40, with bath $50. Doubles $45, with bath $55. Hot tubs 8am-4pm $10.40, after 4pm $20.80.

Driftwood Lodge, 435 Willoughby Ave., Juneau 99801 (586-2280). Behind the State Office Building. Courtesy van will whisk you to and from the airport, and sometimes out to Mendenhall Glacier. Singles $49. Doubles $56. Kitchenette units $56-63.

Campgrounds: Mendenhall Lake Campground, Montana Creek Rd. Take Glacier Hwy. north 9 miles to Mendenhall Loop Rd.; continue 3½ miles and take the right fork. A nice view of the glacier, with trails that can take you even closer. 61 sites. Fireplaces, water, pit toilets. Sites $5. **Auke Village Campground,** on Glacier Hwy., 15 miles from Juneau. 11 sites. Fireplaces, water, pit toilets. Sites $5. Both campgrounds have a 14-day max. stay. Contact the forest service (see Practical Information) for further details.

Travelers on a shoestring should head to the **Foodland Supermarket,** 631 Willoughby Ave., past the Federal Building and near Gold Creek. (Open Mon.-Sat. 9am-7pm, Sun. 10am-6pm.) Seafood lovers should haunt **Merchants Wharf,** next to Marine Park.

Fiddlehead Restaurant and Bakery, 429 W. Willoughby Ave. (586-3150), ½ block from the State Museum. Caters to the sprouts set. Lures mobs of local residents with beef, salads, seafood, exquisite desserts, and fresh Alaskan sourdough. Great sandwiches and burgers on Fiddlehead buns ($3-6). Dinner $7-18. Open Mon.-Sat. 7am-9pm, Sun. 9am-9pm.

Heritage Cafe And Coffee Co., Franklin St. (586-1088), across from the Senate Bldg. An upscale espresso bar, complete with ferns and formica. Best place in town for vegetarians. Excellent coffee $1. Soup du jour and ½-a-deli sandwich $5.25. Open daily 7:30am-6pm.

Silverbow Inn, 120 2nd St. (586-4146), downtown. This is the place to bust your budget. French and American cuisine served on antique oak tables in a country-inn atmosphere. Rotating menu. Lunchc $7-13, dinner $12-24. Reservations recommended. Open daily 9am-9pm; off-season Mon.-Fri. 9am-9pm, Sat. 5:30-9pm.

Sights

Juneau's greatest attraction is undoubtedly the **Mendenhall Glacier,** about 10 miles north of downtown. The glacier, descending from the thousands of square miles of the Juneau Ice Field to the east, glowers over the valley where most downtown workers reside. At the glacier **visitors center,** rangers explain the relation of the glacier to the ice field, how the moving ice carves out a valley, and why the glacier is now retreating. (Open daily 9am-6:30pm.) The rangers give a good ecology walk everyday at 10:30am. THe best view of the glacier without a helicopter is from the 3-mile-long East Trail. To reach the glacier, you can either hitchhike or take the local public bus down Glacier Hwy, and up Mendenhall Loop Rd. until it connects with Glacier Spur Rd. From here it's less than a half-hour walk to the visitors center. **Mendenhall Glacier Transport's** two-and-a-half-hour Juneau tour spends almost an hour at the glacier—a bargain at $7 (see Practical Information). Call for arrangements at 789-5460.

In Juneau itself, the **Alaska State Museum,** 395 Whittier St. (495-2901), is a good introduction to the history, ecology, and native cultures of "The Great Land." The museum's exhibits are unusually informative on the differences among Alaska's four main native groups: Tlingit, Athabaskan, Eskimo, and Aleut. (Open May 15-Sept. 15 Mon.-Fri. 9am-6pm, Sat.-Sun. 10am-6pm; off-season Tues.-Sat. 10am-4pm. Admission $1, students free.)

The unimpressive **state capitol** building is located at 4th and Main. Tours are offered daily from 9am to 5pm in the summer, but your time is better spent wandering uphill to check out the **St. Nicholas Russian Orthodox Church** on 5th St. between North Franklin and Gold Streets. Built in 1894, the church is the oldest of its kind in southeastern Alaska. Services, conducted in English, Slavonic, and Tlingit are open to the public. One block farther uphill on 6th St. is a 45-foot **totem pole** carved in 1940.

Finding the best view of downtown is simply a matter of walking to the end of 6th St. and then up a trail to the summit of **Mt. Roberts** (3576 ft.)—a steep 4-mile climb. Miners flocked to "them thar hills" in the 1880s after Joe Juneau and Dick Harris found treasure in Gold Creek. Mining is no longer an active industry in Juneau, but the mines are active tourist sights and frequently host salmon bakes. The **Alaska-Juneau Mine** was the largest in its heyday. **Last Chance Basin,** at the end of Basin Rd., is now Gold Creek's mining museum.

Juneau is one of the best hiking centers in the southeast. In addition to the ascent of Mt. Roberts, one popular daytrek is along the first section of the **Perseverance Trail,** which leads past the ruins of the historic **Silverbowl Basin Mine** behind Mt. Roberts. For more details on this as well as several other area hikes, drop by the state museum bookstore, the park service center, or any local bookstore to pick up

Juneau Trails, published by the Alaska Natural History Association ($2). The rangers will provide copies of particular maps in this book at the park service center. (See U.S. Forest and National Park Service under Practical Information.)

During winter the slopes of the **Eaglecrest Ski Area** on Douglas Island (contact 155 S. Seward St., Juneau 99801, 586-5284), offer good skiing. ($19 per day, ages 12-18 $14, under 12 $10. In summer, the Eaglecrest "Alpine Summer" self-guided nature trail is a good way to soak in the mountain scenery.

At night, tourists head to the **Red Dog Saloon** 9463-3777) on S. Franklin. This bar, with imported sawdust on the floor and folksy frontier sayings on the wall, tries hard to be authentic but winds up as kitsch. It does have live music on weekends, though. Locals hang out farther up Franklin: the **Triangle Club** (586-3140), at Front St., attracts the more hard-drinking set, while young people (as well as the cruise ship crowd) congregate at the **Penthouse,** on the fourth floor of the Senate Building. The **Lady Lou Revue** (586-3686), a revival of Gold Rush days, plays multiple shows daily at the Elks Lodge on Franklin. (Admission $8.)

Northern Panhandle

North of Juneau, the inside passage grows in magnificence; the mountains become bigger and snowier, the whales and eagles friendlier and more plentiful. THe **Alaska Marine Highway** can take you up to Haines ($14 from Juneau, ages 6-11 $8; vehicle up to 15 ft. $35). Sleep on the ferry or stay up all night traveling through this land of many glaciers and soaring peaks.

Haines and the Haines Highway

In the early 1890s, adventurer Jack Dalton improved an old Indian Trail from Pyramid Harbor up to the Yukon. During the Gold Rush from 1897 to 1899, thousands of stampeders paid outlandish rates for a quick trip into the Klondike. Thanks to the army's improvements on the road during World War II, the **Haines Highway** is now the most traveled overland route into the Yukon and the Interior from southeastern Alaska.

The area's main attraction is the convergence of over 3000 bald eagles (almost double the town's population) on the "Council Grounds" on the Chilkat Peninsula from November to January each year. Although both the federal and state government protect our national bird here in its national preserve, the land originally belonged to the Tlingit tribes, whose contemporary solvency relies on a mass production of winged totem poles. White trolling boats from the local harbor now take the place of talons or spears in capturing salmon from the frigid waters. The town of Haines itself is not particularly thrilling, but as one of the only two southeastern ports that connect with the Interior, it may be worth a stop.

The town of **Haines** is not exactly a thrill a minute, but it provides shelter and sustenance. Backpackers should consider staying at the exquisitely trimmed **Portage Cove State Park,** a ½ mile outside of town along Beach Rd., behind the clump of trees (9 sites, pit toilets, water. Sites $5). If you prefer indoor accommodations, the **Hotel Halsingland,** Box 1589 MP, Haines 99827 (766-2000), on the parade grounds south of town, is Haines's luxury hotel. (Singles from $31.50. Doubles from $35.50.) Less luxurious, the **Bear Creek Camp & Hostel (AYH),** Box 1158, Haines 99827 (907-766-2202), on Small Tract Rd. almost 3 miles outside of town. From downtown, follow 3rd Ave. out Mud Bay Rd. to Small Tract Rd., is not exactly a family place, and not exactly clean, either. There is a layer of oily dirt on the thin mattresses, and the showers are broken, but ongoing construction might improve the primitive rusticity. (Kitchen facilities. No curfew. Call ahead for ferry pickup. $7, nonmembers $12. Cabins $30. Showers $2.)

Those wishing to forgo restaurant fare can hit **Howser's Supermarket** on Main St. (open Mon.-Sat. 9am-8pm, Sun. 10am-7pm). The store has a great salad bar with a large pasta selection ($2.49 per lb.). **Porcupine Pete's,** Main and 2nd Ave.

(766-9199), has good sandwiches from $2.90, and the pita pockets ($6.90) make a decent meal. The **Bamboo Room,** Second Ave. near Main St., next to the Pioneer Bar (776-9109), is a great breakfast spot, always crowded with fishermen on their way out to the nets. (Hot cakes and coffee $3.75, omelettes $4.

The town maintains a **visitor information center,** 2nd Ave. near Willard St. (766-2234), with information on accommodations and hiking. Pick up the *Haines is for Hikers* pamphlet. (Open June-Sept. daily 8am-8pm.) The **Alaska Marine Highway Terminal,** 5 Mile Lutake Rd. (766-2111), is 3½ miles from downtown. Hitch or take the Haines Street Car ($4.25).

The **Haines Highway,** one of the most beautiful in the state, winds 40 miles from Haines through the **Chilkat Range** and up through the Yukon Territory in Canada. **Chilkat State Park,** a 19-mile drive up the highway, protects the largest population of bald eagles in North America—3500 of these beauties all told. From November through January, travelers can see great numbers of eagles perched on birchwoods in the rivers or flying overhead. **Chilkat Guides** (766-2409), P.O. Box 170, leads four hour raft trips down the Chilkat River when the eagles are flocking. ($55, rubber boots and ponchos provided.)

Anchorage

Anchorage, or "Los Anchorage," as some rural residents prefer to call it, is "big city" Alaska. Only 70 years ago, it was a wilderness area. But in 1914, the railroads began to bring a steady flow of trains, pioneers, and oil, transforming Anchorage into the state's commercial center. Today more than 250,000 people, half the state's population, live here. Anchorage boasts two daily newspapers, semi-professional baseball and basketball teams, frequent performances by internationally known orchestras and pop stars, dramatic theater, and opera. Its international airport is among the world's busiest, serving passengers en route to East Asia. Perhaps the most remarkable fact about Anchorage is that everything—the glass and steel of the buildings, the food and merchandise of the supermarkets and department stores—arrives here the same way people do: via 1500 miles of tortuous road or an expensive air journey, or by barge or container ship across one of the roughest seas in the world.

Practical Information and Orientation

Visitor Information: Anchorage Convention and Visitors Bureau, 201 E. 3rd Ave. (276-4118). **Log Cabin Visitor Information Center,** W. 4th Ave. at F St. (274-3531). Open May-Sept. daily 7:30am-7pm; Oct.-April daily 8:30am-6pm. The **All About Anchorage Line** (276-3200) runs a recorded listing of each day's events. For information on fine arts and dramatic performances, call the **Artsline** (276-2787). Smaller visitor information outlets are located in the airport near the baggage claim in the domestic terminal; in the overseas terminal in the central atrium; and in the Valley River Mall, first level.

Alaska Public Lands Information Center, Old Federal Building (271-2737), 4th Ave. between F and G. An astounding conglomeration of 8 state and federal offices (including the **National Park Service, U.S. Forest Service, Division of State Parks,** and the **U.S. Fish and Wildlife Service**) under one roof providing the latest information on the entire state. Open daily 9am-8pm.

Anchorage International Airport: a few miles southwest of downtown off International Airport Rd. The People Mover Bus runs 3 times a day from the airport to downtown, but the visitors center near the baggage claim can direct you to more frequent routes. Airporter vans run constantly to downtown for $5; a cab will set you back about $13.

Alaska Railroad: 2nd Ave. (265-2494) at the head of town. To Denali ($62), Fairbanks ($88), Seward ($35), and Whittier ($27.50). For more information write to Passenger Service, P.O. Box 107500, Anchorage 99510. Office open daily 8am-8pm; may be closed if no trains are arriving.

Local Transit: People Mover Bus: 343-6543, headquartered in the Transit Center, on 6th St. between G and H St. Most buses leave from here to all points in the Anchorage Bowl.

Buses run from 5am-midnight. Fare is 85¢, but tokens cost 75¢ from a machine and are sold by the hostel for 60¢. The Transit Center office is open Mon.-Fri. 9am-5pm.

Alaska Marine Highway: 333 W. 4th St. (272-4482), in the Post Office Mall. No terminal, but ferry tickets and reservations. Open Mon.-Fri. 8am-5pm.

Taxi: Yellow Cab, 272-2422. **Checker Cab,** 276-1234.

Car Rental: Rent-a-Dent, 512 W. International Airport Rd. (561-0350), at the airport. $25 per day with 50 free miles, 20¢ each additional mile. Open daily 7am-11pm.

Time Zone: Alaska (4 hr. behind Eastern).

Post Office: W. 4th Ave. and C St. (277-6568) on the lower level in the mall. Open Mon.-Fri. 10:30am-5pm, Sat. 9am-3pm. **ZIP Code:** 99510.

Area Code: 907.

Anchorage dominates the southcentral region of Alaska, 114 miles north of Seward on the Seward Hwy., 304 miles west of Valdez on the Glenn and Richardson Hwy., and 358 miles south of Fairbanks on the George Parks Hwy. It is due north of Honolulu, and equidistant from Atlanta and Tokyo. Anchorage can be reached by road, rail, or air.

The downtown area of Anchorage follows a grid. Numbered avenues run east-west, with addresses designated East or West from **C Street.** North-south streets are lettered alphabetically west of **A Street,** and named alphabetically east of A Street. The rest of Anchorage is spread out along the major highways. The **University of Alaska-Anchorage** campus lies on 36th Ave. off Northern Lights Blvd.

Accommodations and Camping

Several bed and breakfast referral agencies operate out of Anchorage. Try **Alaska Private Lodgings,** 1236 W. 10th Ave., Anchorage 99511 (258-1717), or **Stay With a Friend,** Box 173, 3605 Arctic Blvd., Anchorage 99503 (344-4006). Both can refer you to singles from $45 and doubles from $55.

There are several free campgrounds outside the city limits; for information contact the **Alaska Division of Parks,** 3601 C St., 10th Floor, Pouch 7-001 Anchorage 99510 or the **Anchorage Parks and Recreation Dept.,** 2525 Campbell St. #404 (271-2500).

Anchorage Youth Hostel (AYH), 700 H St., (276-3635), 1 block south of the Transit Center downtown. Excellent location. Clean rooms with common areas, kitchens, showers, and laundry. Often offers family rooms. Lockout 9am-5pm. $10, nonmembers $13. Hardly ever full.

Green Bough Bed and Breakfast, 3832 Young St. (562-4636). Take bus #93 from the airport. An independent B&B with clean rooms and a casual atmosphere. Three rooms share 2 baths. Singles $40, with king-sized bed $50.

Heart of Anchorage Bed and Breakfast, 725 K St. (279-7066 or 279-7703), at 8th. Intimate house with amusing decor. Dorm beds $15. Singles $35. Doubles $40. Call ahead for reservations.

Northern Lights Thrift Apartments, 606 Northern Lights (561-3005). Rooms clean, but not much bigger than the queen-sized bed. Singles $27.90.

Centennial Park, 8300 Glenn Hwy. (333-9711), north of town off Muldoon Rd.; look for the park sign. Take bus #3 or 75 from downtown. Facilities for tents and RVs. Showers, dumpsters, fireplaces, pay phones, and water. 7-day max. stay. Check-in before 6pm in summer. Sites $12, seniors $8.

Lions' Camper Park, 5800 Boniface Pkwy. (333-1495), south of the Glenn Hwy. In Russian Jack Springs Park next to the Municipal Greenhouse; 4 blocks from the Boniface Mall. Take bus #12 or 45 to the mall and walk. Connected to the city's bike trail system. 10 primitive campsites with water station, fire rings, and showers. Self-contained vehicles only. 7-day max. stay. Open daily 10am-10pm. Sites $12. Open May-Sept.

Food

By virtue of its size and largely imported population, Anchorage's culinary fare is extraordinarily diverse. Within blocks of each other stand greasy spoons, Chinese restaurants, and classy hotel-top French eateries. Alaskan sourdough and seafood—halibut, salmon, clams, crab, and snapper—are often served in huge portions, typical of Alaskan hospitality. The city's finer restaurants line the hills overlooking Cook Inlet and the Alaska Range.

Skipper's, at 5 locations: 3960 W. Dimond Blvd. (248-3165), 702 E. Benson Blvd. (276-1181), 5668 DeBarr Rd. (333-4832), 601 E. Dimond Blvd. (349-8214), and 3611 Minnesota Dr. (563-3656). Only $5.29 for all the fishfries, chowder, and cole slaw you can fit (with shrimp $8). Open daily 11am-11pm.

The White Spot, at A St. and 4th Ave. Lenore's been singlehandedly slinging the hash and burgers since 1959. Eggs, hashbrowns, toast, and coffee, $2.25. Open daily 7am-7pm.

Wing and Things, 529 I St. (277-9464), at I and 5th. Unbelievably delicious BBQ chicken wings. Decorated with wing memorabilia and inspirational poetry. 10 wings, celery, and sauce $6. Open daily 10am-9pm.

Sack's Café, 625 5th Ave. (274-3546). Best vegetarian food in the state, though slightly expensive, as is its New York counterpart. Avocado, marinated swiss, and red onion sandwich with soup $8.

Sights and Entertainment

Mount Susitna, known to locals as the "Sleeping Lady," watches over Anchorage from **Cook Inlet.** For a fabulous view of Susitna, as well as the rest of the mountains that form a magnificent backdrop for Anchorage's ever-growing skyline, drive out to **Earthquake Park** at the end of Northern Lights Blvd. Once a fashionable neighborhood, the park now memorializes the disastrous effects of the Good Friday earthquake in 1964, a day Alaskans refer to as "Black Friday." Registering at 9.2 on the current Richter scale, it was the strongest earthquake ever recorded in North America. On a clear day, you'll even be able to see **Mount McKinley** far to the north.

The visitors center can set you up with a 3-4 hour self-guided walking tour of downtown. For guided walking tours, contact **Historic Anchorage Inc.,** 542 W. 4th Ave. (562-6100, ext. 338), on the second floor of the Old City Hall. Tours leave Monday through Friday at 10am ($2, seniors $1.) The People Mover sponsors less strenuous jaunts. Hop on one of the double-decker buses downtown for a $1 ride through the area. Alaska City Tours (276-7431) offers thorough bus tours of the Anchorage bowl, leaving daily at 9am, 1pm, and 4pm. (3-hr. tours $14.50, seniors $14, children—4pm tour only—$7.) Look for the booth next to the visitors center.

The **Anchorage Museum of History and Art,** 121 W. 7th Ave. (264-4326), on the corner of 7th Ave. and A St., features permanent exhibits of Alaskan native artifacts and art, as well as a Thursday night Alaska wilderness film series (7pm). (Open June-Aug. Mon.-Sat. 10am-6pm, Sun. 1-5pm; Sept.-May Tues.-Sat. 10am-6pm, Sun. 1-5pm. Admission $3.) If you wish to see real, honest-to-goodness Alaskan wildlife, visit the **Alaska Zoo,** Mile 2 on O'Malley Rd. (346-3242. Open daily 10am-6pm. Admission $3.50, seniors and ages 13-18 $2.50, under 13 $1.50.)

If you want to shop where the air literally reeks of authenticity, head to the close confines of the nonprofit gift shop at the **Alaska Native Medical Center** at 3rd and Campbell. Because many natives pay for medical services with their own arts and handicrafts, the Alaska State Museum in Juneau sent its buyers here last year to outfit its exhibitions. Walrus bone ulus ($15-60), fur moccasins and Eskimo parkas, and dolls highlight the selection. (Open Mon.-Fri. 10am-2pm.) Craftworks from Alaska's bush country, similar to those on display at the Museum of History and Art, are sold at the **Alaska Native Arts and Crafts Showroom,** 333 W. 4th Ave. (274-2932; open Mon.-Fri. 10am-6pm, Sat. 10am-5pm).

Anchorageans of all types and incomes party at **Chilkoot Charlie's,** 2435 Spenard Rd. (272-1010) at Spenard and Fireweed. The bar has a rocking dance floor and a quiet, "share-my-space" lounge. Regular patrons always ask about the nightly drink specials. Take bus #7 or 60. Less crowded and more interesting is **Mr. Whitekey's Fly-by-Night Club,** 3300 Spenard Rd. (279-7726), a "sleazy bar serving everything from the world's finest champagnes to a damn fine plate of Spam." The house special gives you anything with Spam at half-price when you order champagne (free with Dom Perignon). Try Spam nachos or Spam and cream cheese on a bagel ($2-6). Nightly entertainment ranges from rock to jazz to blues. (Open 3pm-2:30am.)

Denali National Park

Established in 1917 to protect its abundant wildlife, Denali National Park just happened to include Mt. Denali, "The Great One" in Athabascan, the tallest mountain in North America and base to summit the greatest vertical relief in the world. 20,320 ft. above sea level and 18,000 ft. above the meadows below, Denali is so big it makes its own weather, so it is only visible about 20% of the summer. Missing the mountain doesn't ruin a Denali trip—the park's tundra, taiga, wildlife and lesser mountains are also worthwhile.

The park is accessible by **Alaska Railroad** (see Anchorage Practical Information) or by car. Some vans and buses run from Anchorage to the park. Try **Denali Express Van** (274-3234) for $35. All visitors should check in at the **Riley Creek Visitor Information Center** (683-2686 or 683-2294). Permits are issued here to stay in the park's **campgrounds** ($10), ride the park's **shuttles** ($3), and for **backcountry camping** (free).

Kenai Peninsula

The Kenai (KEE-ny) Peninsula is Alaska in miniature. Like parts of Alaska's interior, Kenai's interior is flat; like the state itself, the peninsula is ringed with mountains. Kenai relies on all three big sectors of Alaska's economy: oil, tourism, and fishing. The Russian influence on the Panhandle can be seen on the town of Kenai, the first Russian settlement in Alaska, and the urban sprawl of Anchorage and Fairbanks is mimicked by such road-side towns as Soldotna.

The Peninsula is the place Alaskans, especially those from Anchorage and Fairbanks, go to vacation, and they don't go to the towns. Take a hint from the natives: find an isolated campsite and fish. Every town can set you up cheaply with the requisite permits and gear. Stay in **USFS Campgrounds,** located every 8 or 10 miles on Seward and Sterling Highways. There are also great spots in between—ask the locals. For more information on hiking, hunting, fishing, camping, and other recreational opportunities as well as regulations, contact the following: **Kenai Fjords National Park** (see Seward); **Alaska Maritime national Wildlife Refuge** (see Homer); **Kenai National Wildlife Refuge** (see Soldotna); **Chugach National Forest,** 201 E. 9th Ave., #206, Anchorage 99501 (261-2500); **State of Alaska, Division of Parks and Outdoor Recreations,** P.O. Box 1247, Soldotna 99669 (262-5581); and **State of Alaska, Department of Fish & Game,** P.O. Box 3150, Soldotna 99669 (262-9368). If you're unclear about which of these offices to contact, check out the **Alaska Public Lands Information Center** (see Anchorage, Practical Information) for a referral.

The Kenai Peninsula is serviced by the **Seward** and **Sterling Highways,** as well as the **Alaska Marine Highway,** which runs between Homer, Seward, and Whittier, and extends out to Kodiak Island and Prince William Sound. To reach the peninsula from Anchorage, simply take any of the buses that run onto the New Seward Highway (such as the #2 or #9) as far south as possible and hitch. Hitching is common, safe, and easy.

Kenai

Kenai (KEE-ny) is the second-oldest white settlement in Alaska, and the peninsula's largest city (pop. 6546). First a native community, it became a Russian village when Fort Saint Nicholas was built in 1791, then was established as an American settlement in 1889 when the U.S. Army built Fort Kenay. Kenai finally became known as the "Oil Capital of Alaska" with the 1957 discovery of oil in Cook Inlet. Vestiges of each era are scattered throughout town: native artifacts, a Russian Orthodox church, an American military installation, and oil rigs stationed in the inlet. Kenai remains one of the most beautiful cities on the Kenai Peninsula, with imperial Mt. Iliamna and the still-active volcano of Mt. Augustine looming nearby.

In the spring and early summer, be on the lookout for migrating white beluga whales in **Cook Inlet,** where they feed on sockeye salmon. The top of the bluff at Alaska and Mission Ave. and the overlook at the end of Forest Dr. are good spots to see these beauties, as well as Mt. Augustine and Mt. Iliamna, which are visible on clear days.

The sights in town are comparatively uninspiring. The **Kenai Historical Museum** and **Fort Kenai** lie next to one another on Overland and Mission St. The museum is threadbare and the fort a cheap replica of the 1868 original. (Museum and fort: 283-7294; open Mon.-Sat. 10am-5pm.) Across from the fort is the **Holy Assumption Russian Orthodox Church,** the oldest building in Kenai and the oldest church still standing in Alaska (1896). This national historic landmark contains a 200-year-old Bible. Call the priest at the rectory (283-4122) for a tour.

Recreational opportunities in the Kenai area abound. Check at the chamber of commerce for fishing charter information (prices are comparable to those in Soldotna); check with the forest service for canoeing and hiking opportunities. The **Captain Cook State Recreation Area,** 30 miles north of Nikiski at the end of Kenai Spur Rd., offers swimming, canoe landing points on the Swanson River, fishing, and free camping. Contact the Kenai Chamber of Commerce for rules and regulations.

To save money, head for the city **campground** on Forest Dr. off Kenai Spur Rd., where you can spend three happy days camping for free. Near the beach not far from the center of town, the campground has fireplaces and covered picnic tables. Unfortunately, the noise from motorcycling patrons and other campers may be a bit much at night. Hard-sided campers can head for the **Kenai Riverbend Campground,** Porter Rd. (283-9489, 262-5715, or 262-1068); take Kalifonsy Beach Rd. off Spur Hwy. Every summer fishers descend to the Kenai Riverbend, one of the best salmon fishing holes in the world. The campground has everything you need: boat launching and rentals, rods and tackle, bait, laundry, and showers. Reservations often necessary, though not required. (Singles $60. Doubles $65. Camping sites $12, RVs $18, with hookup $20.) The town itself also has two RV parks with full hookups: **Overland RV Park** (283-4227) and **Kenai RV Park** (283-4646), both in Old Kenai near Overland St.

Kenai, on the western Kenai Peninsula, is about 160 miles from Anchorage and 144 miles north of Homer. It can be reached via Kalifonsky Beach Rd., which joins Sterling Hwy. from Anchorage just south of Soldotna, or Kenai Spur Rd., which runs north through the Nikishka area and east to Soldotna. Both roads boast superb views of the peninsula's lakes and snow-capped peaks.

The town's **chamber of commerce** and **visitors center** (283-7989), are in the log cabin on Main St. and Kenai Spur Hwy. (Open Mon.-Fri. 9am-5pm, Sat. 10am-4pm; in winter Mon.-Fri. 9am-5pm.) Write to Box 497. Kenai's **ZIP code** is 99611; the **area code** is 907.

Soldotna

Soldotna, once merely a fork in the road which people passed on their way to Homer, Kenai, or Seward, has now become the center of the Kenai Peninsula's government and recreation. Soldotna leads its neighbors on Kenai as the peninsula's premier fishing spot. World record salmon are consistently caught in the Kenai River, a few minutes from downtown. Kenai Riverbend Campground, halfway between Soldotna and Kenai (see Kenai) is offering a $10,000 reward to the person who catches a salmon over the record 97 pounds. Ten thousand dollars will go a long way toward paying for a budget vacation.

Visitors to Soldotna come to fish. Pink, silver, and king salmon, as well as steelhead and dolly varden, are found in the waters all summer long. Numerous **fishing charters** run the river, usually $100-125 for a half-day of halibut or salmon fishing, or $150 for both (contact the visitors center for more information). There is no reason to spend so much, however. The downtown area is loaded with equipment rental shops that will fully outfit you with everything from bait to licenses for under $25 per day. Just wade into the Kenai and plunk in your line.

If fishing is too slow-paced for you, you might participate in river sports at the **Kenai National Wildlife Refuge.** Dozens of **canoe routes** wind their way through the forest on one- to four-day journeys. A few places in town, including the Riverbend Campground, will rent you boats. Otherwise, a drive along the highway from downtown will bring you into the wild depths just as quickly; more than one resident puts their boat in the front yard and hangs a "for rent" sign on it. Boat rentals are far from inexpensive, but the experience of gliding through some of the nation's most remote waterways is well worth the dip into your wallet. For free canoe route maps, write the Refuge Manager, Kenai National Wildlife Refuge, P.O. Box 2139, Soldotna 99669 (262-7021).

You didn't come just for the fish? The **Damon Memorial Historical Museum,** at Mile 3 on Kalifonsky Beach Rd., holds artifacts from native burial grounds and a large diorama. The **Kenai National Wildlife Refuge Visitors Center** (262-7021), off Funny River Rd. at the top of Ski Hill Rd., directly across from the visitors center, is a great source of information on the 197-million-acre refuge for moose, Dall sheep, and other wild game. It also has dioramas and victims of taxidermy (though it's better to see their living counterparts), and a ½-mile nature trail nearby. (Open Mon.-Fri. 8am-6pm, Sat.-Sun. 10am-6pm; Labor Day-Memorial Day Mon.-Fri. 8am-4pm, Sun.-Sat. 10am-5:30pm.)

Soldotna arose as a highway crossroads, so there's plenty of fast food along the road downtown. Burger-chain prices are slightly higher than in the Lower 48, but budget-oriented visitors may still have to opt for the Big Mac over sit-down dining. **Sal's Klondike Diner,** Sterling Hwy. a ½-mile from the river (262-2220), cooks the best dinner in town. "Local Yocals" specials include the $4 Sourdough special (French toast, 2 eggs, bacon). Burgers from $3.25. Caffeine addicts will appreciate $1-per-hour unlimited coffee. (Open Mon.-Sat. 7am-9pm, Sun. 9am-6pm.) The **China Sea Restaurant,** on the upper level of the Blazy Mall (262-5033), ¼ mile from the river, offers Chinese and American food. An all-you-can-eat buffet is served daily 11:30am-1:30pm and 5-8pm ($7). (Open daily 11am-9pm.)

Backpackers can stay at nearby campgrounds and shell out $2 for hot, clean showers at the **River Terrace RV Park** at the river. **Swiftwater Park Municipal Campground** south of Sterling Hwy. at mile 94, and **Centennial Park Municipal Campground,** off Kalifonsky Beach Rd. near the visitors center, are in the woods and have boat launches. Conveniently located on the river, the campgrounds have excellent fishing. There are even tables set aside for cleaning fish. 1-week maximum stay. (Sites $6.) Indoor accommodations are available at **Skip's Idle Hour Inn,** Mile 3 on Kalifonsky Beach Rd. (262-5041; write Box 3634, Soldotna 99669). All rooms have a private bath. (No reservations. Singles $30.75. Doubles $35.75.)

Soldotna has a sizeable **Visitor's Center** (262-1337), on the Sterling Hwy. and Kalifonsky Beach Rd., which serves Soldotna and the less-inhabited regions of the peninsula, such as Winilchik, Clam Gulch, and the interior.

Homer

While other towns on the peninsula are highway-crossed pitstops, Homer is a beautiful artists' enclave with a deep sense of community. It's the kind of place where the natural food store is the town hearth.

Homer has the best museum and art gallery on the peninsula. **Pratt Museum,** at 3779 Bartlett St. (235-8635), has exhibits by local artists and a feature on the Valdez oil spill. (Open 10am-5pm daily. Admission $3.)

Colorful, 4½-mile-long **Homer Spit,** a long walk or a short drive from downtown, is the second-longest spit in the world. Boardwalks line its beaches, and shops perched on pilings hawk souvenirs and snacks.

Townsfolk gather at **Homer Natural Foods,** at 248 Pioneer Ave., (235-7242). Getting groceries there is a good excuse to hear town news and gossip. Open 7am-9pm daily. Those desiring less granola fare can shop at the **Irachemak Food Cache** (235-8618) on the corner of Pioneer and Lake. Fresh seafood is available at **Icicle Seafood Market,** 842 Fish Dock Rd. at the base of the spit in front of the Harbor.

The name of the **Sourdough Express Bakery and Coffee Shop,** 1316 Ocean Dr. (235-7571), says it all, except for the "delicious" added by the clientele. (Open Tues.-Sun. 6:30am-10pm.) **Boardwalk Fish & Chips,** at the end of Cannery Row Boardwalk across from the harbor master's office (235-7749), is a local favorite. (Big hunk of halibut with chips $5.25. Open daily 11:30am-6pm.) **Wallace's Cafe and Icecreamery,** Lake St. (235-7484), between Homer Bypass and Pioneer Ave., offers home-baked bread, gourmet sandwiches, and charbroiled burgers. The "Swine's Pride" bacon burger on a sourdough bun with fries costs $5.29; fish and chips are $6.09. (Open Mon.-Sat. 7am-9:30pm.)

Nightlife in Homer ranges from beachcombing at low tide in the midnight sun to discovering whether the **Salty Dawg Saloon,** under the log lighthouse at the end of the spit, ever really closes (open 11am-whenever, as the sign says). For country fare head to **Alice's Champagne Palace,** 196 Pioneer Ave. (235-7650), a wooden barn with honkytonk music as well as nickel beers and dollar tacos on Monday nights. For the more cultured types, the **Pier One Theater,** Box 894, Homer 99603 (235-7333 or 235-7951), performs classic plays on weekend nights from Memorial Day to Labor Day at their theater halfway down the spit. (Admission $7, seniors and children $5, families $20.)

Homer has two **municipal campgrounds,** one in town, one on the spit. In town, take Pioneer to Bartlett St., go uphill and take a left onto Fairview. The city allows camping on the edges of the spit, two miles out. Sites have neither showers nor hookups ($5). For these amenities, head to the **Homer Spit Campground** (275-8206), at the spit's tip (tent sites $6, full hookups $113).

The visitor's center has a list of **Bed and Breakfasts,** with rooms starting at $40. **Homer Cabins,** at 3601 Main St. (275-6768), come at a flat rate of $55 but sleep at least two. The **Ocean Shores Motel,** 300 TAB Crittendon (235-7775), is close to downtown, and has excellent views of the ocean on one side. Singles from $39.

Half-way down the spit is Homer's **Visitors Center** (235-7740), open 7am-10pm. Beverly Wood literally wrote the book on Homer—*250 Ways to Enjoy Homer.* She can set you up with everything from walking tours to expensive halibut charters.

Homer sits cozily on the southwestern Kenai Peninsula on the north shore of Kachemak Bay. The Sterling Hwy. links it to Anchorage (225.8 miles away) and the rest of the Kenai Peninsula. To reach the downtown area, bear left off the highway onto Pioneer Ave.; bear right onto Homer Bypass to venture onto the spit via the imaginatively named Spit Road. The town and the spit are small enough to be crossed on foot, but the walk from the far end of the spit to downtown is a long 6 miles. Take a $2 bus ride if you have to, but hitching between the town and the spit is common practice.

To reach Homer from Anchorage, either hitch or drive along Seward Hwy. to Sterling Hwy. south. **Alaska Intercity Line** (800-478-2877) will take you from one to the other for $37.50. The **Alaska Marine Highway** serves Homer from Valdez or Cordova ($104), Seward ($74) and Kodiak ($36).

Seward

Russians first established a small shipyard in what is now Seward during the late 18th century. The village soon disbanded. Not until 1903 was a new town built by

U.S. railway workers as a supply center and shipping terminal. Today, the two blocks that comprise most of downtown Seward are strictly middle American, with souvenir shops, gas stations, and pleasant, homey cafes. But only one glance up toward the peaks of Mt. Alice and Mt. Marathon or over to lovely Resurrection Bay will remind you that you're still in Alaska, with its untamed and astonishing natural beauty. Recently Seward has become enshrined in state consciousness as the beginning of the Iditarod dog-sled trail.

The walking tour of Seward printed on the map available at the chamber of commerce passes many homes and businesses that date back to the early 1900s. A complete tour takes two to three hours. The **Resurrection Bay Historical Society Museum,** in the basement of City Hall (corner of 5th and Adams), features exhibits of Native artifacts and implements used by pioneers. (Open June 15-Labor Day daily 11am-4pm. Admission 50¢, children 25¢.) The **K.M. Rae Educational Building,** on 3rd Ave. between Washington and Railway, part of the Seward Marine Science Institute, contains marine life displays and results of institute research. (Open May 25-Aug. Mon.-Fri. 1-5pm, Sat. 9am-5pm. Movie daily at 4pm. Free.)

Seward is a great place for day hikes. Nearby **Mt. Marathon,** up which locals run each fall, offers a great view of the city and ocean. The trail begins at the end of Cowell St. **Exit Glacier,** billed as Alaska's most accessible glacier, is located nine miles west on the road that starts at Seward Hwy. mile 3.7. From the **ranger station** (no phone, open Mon.-Fri. 9am-5pm) take the 4-mile steep and slippery trail to the magnificent **Harding Ice Field.** Only for the intrepid.

Known as the gateway to Alaska because of its position as the southern terminus of the railroad, Seward is also the point of entry to the **Kenai Fjords National Park.** Much of the park consists of a coastal-mountain system with an abundance of wildlife. The best way to see this area is from a boat on the bay; pick up the list of charters at the Park Service visitors center or from companies along the boardwalk next to the harbor master's office. Most run $70-100 per day, $45-50 per half-day. For more information, contact **Kenai Fjord Tours** (224-8068 or 224-8069), **Mariah Charters** (243-1238), or **Quest Charters** (224-3025; open in summer 6am-10pm).

Fishing is heavenly in the Seward area. Salmon and halibut can be caught in the bay, grayling and dolly varden right outside of town. Some people just fish off the docks. For a less luck-oriented approach, try a fishing charter. **Charters** are available for both halibut and salmon throughout the summer; prices run from $90-100, with all gear provided. Call Quest Charters or Mariah Charters.

Downtown Seward has seafood restaurants, hamburger joints, and pizza parlors galore. Pick up groceries at **Bob's Market,** 207 4th Ave. (Open Mon.-Sat. 9am-7pm, Sun. noon-6pm.) **The Depot,** Mile 1 on Seward Hwy. (224-5500), cooks up big burgers with the works for $3 and whips up eight flavors of shakes ($1.50). (Open daily 11am-9pm.) The **Breeze Inn,** Small Boat Harbor (224-5237), is not your average hotel restaurant. Breeze in for the huge all-you-can-eat buffet ($8). Breakfasts include the "2-2-2" (2 eggs, 2 strips bacon, 2 pancakes, $5). (Open Mon.-Fri. 7am-10pm, Sat.-Sun. 8am-10pm.) The **Fairweather Cafe,** 106 4th Ave. (224-3907), serves croissants for breakfast; homemade soups and sandwiches for lunch; and mushroom schnitzel and chicken *cordon bleu,* along with other dishes uncommon to Alaska, for dinner. (Lunches $4-7, dinners $12-17. Open daily 7am-2pm and 5-10pm.)

Seward's three municipal campgrounds are typical: no showers, pleasant view, grassy sites. The best is **City Greenbelt Camping Area,** off 7th Ave. (Sites $4.25). The nearest full-hookup RV Park is **Kenai Fjords** on 4th Ave. (Sites $9, with full hookup $13.50.) Seward boasts a beautifully restored hotel, the **Van Gilder,** at 308 Adams St. (224-3525), which has dorm bunks for $30 and singles from $40. Reservations are a must. One step down in price and quality is **Tony's Hotel and Bar** (224-3045) on Railway and 4th St. Above the bar are surprisingly clean rooms for $25 per night.

Seward is 125 miles south of Anchorage along the Seward Hwy. Downtown cross streets are numbered, while the longer north-south avenues are named after U.S. presidents, sequentially, starting with Washington. **Visitor Information,** in the streetcar Seward, on 3rd and Jefferson, offers an interesting walking tour. (Open

Mon.-Fri., 9am-5pm). The **Seward Ranger Station** on 334 4th Ave. has information on local hikes and trails, while the **National Park Visitor's Center,** at 1212 4th Ave. (224-3395) near the harbor, has information, films, and exhibits on the Kenai Fjords and western Prince William Sound. (Open daily 9am-5pm.)

Seward's **post office** is at 5th and Madison. (Open Mon.-Fri. 9:30am-4:30pm, Sat. 10am-2pm.) The **ZIP Code** is 99664. The **area code** is 907.

CANADA

Canada is the second largest country in the world (after the USSR), and one of the most sparsely populated. Ten provinces and two territories sprawl over more than 9,000,000 square kilometers of land and span seven time zones. Framed by the rugged Atlantic coastline to the east and the Rockies to the west, Canada spreads north from fertile farmland and urbanized lakeshores to barren, frozen tundra. Cities range from cosmopolitan Montréal and Toronto to the leisurely, Old-World Québec City, to bold and youthful Calgary.

The name Canada is thought to derive from the Huron-Iroquois world "kanata," meaning "village" or "community." A national unity, however, is made difficult by the diversity of backgrounds of Canadians, and the geographic segregation of the French- and English-speaking peoples. Both French and English are the offical languages of Canada, and have equal status in federal government; nonetheless, only about 15% of Canadians are bilingual French-English. In contrast to the American ideal of a "melting pot," Canadians see their country as a mosaic, a pattern of integrated yet unadulterated cultures. The mosaic includes the Inuit of northern Canada and other native peoples, the French of Québec province, and the very-British British Columbia. A recent influx of immigrants from Third World countries proves that Canada's attraction as a place of freedom and opportunity still endures.

Travel

Canada's only international border is with the U.S., and this border is easily accessible from Boston, New York City, Detroit, Chicago, Minneapolis/St. Paul, and Seattle. For the budget traveler, Canada is both exciting and inexpensive. Its extensive youth hostel network, fine public transportation system, and helpful visitor information centers make budget trips throughout Canada easy and educational.

Student Travel

The **Canadian Federation of Student Services** sponsors a number of student travel assistance organizations, including the **Studentsaver National Student Discount Program,** which provides discounts for students on admissions and fares throughout Canada, and **Travel CUTS** (Canadian Universities Travel Service Ltd.), which will also assist non-students. The Studentsaver Program allows International Student Identity Card (ISIC) holders to receive 10-25% discounts on food, clothing, books, and other goods in Canada. CUTS, a fully licensed nationwide travel agency, offers discounts to students planning international trips.

The Canadian Federation of Student Services publishes *Canadian Student Traveler,* a free magazine distributed at universities across Canada. The main CFS Services and CUTS offices are at 187 College St., Toronto, Ont. M5T 1P7 (416-979-2406). Other Travel CUTS offices include:

Montréal: Université McGill, 3480 McTavish, Montréal, Québec H3A 1X9 (514-398-0647).

Toronto: 74 Gerrard St. E., Toronto, Ont. M5B 1G6 (416-977-0441).

Vancouver: Student Union Building, University of British Columbia, Vancouver, British Columbia V6T 1W5 (604-228-6890).

Victoria: Student Union Building, University of Victoria, Victoria, British Columbia V8W 2Y2 (604-721-8352).

Customs

To cross the U.S.-Canadian border, the longest undefended border in the world, U.S. visitors need only proof of citizenship. If you are under 18 and unaccompanied by an adult, you must have written consent of your parent or guardian. Non-U.S. citizens must have a Canadian visa for entry. Visitors from other countries should be sure to have their papers in good order, as customs officials on both sides of the border are often tough on anyone with a foreign accent. Those wishing to bring pets with them into Canada must bring certification of the animals' vaccination against rabies. Visitors who spend at least 48 hours in Canada may take back to the U.S. up to CDN$400 worth of goods duty-free, including up to 100 non-Cuban cigars and one carton of cigarettes. Only one liter of liquor can be exported duty-free. U.S. residents who stay in Canada for less than 48 hours may return with CDN$25 worth of duty-free merchandise, including 50 cigarettes, 10 non-Cuban cigars, and four ounces of alcohol or perfume. There are several helpful Customs offices located throughout Canada. Write for their helpful pamphlet *I declare/Je declare* to Revenue Canada Customs and Excise Department, Communications Branch, Mackenzie Ave., Ottawa, Ont. K1A UL5 (613-957-0275).

Money

During the past several years, the Canadian dollar has run about 30-35% less than the American dollar. In order to take full advantage of the current exchange rate, visitors should trade in their cash at banks or exchange houses. (Most Canadian banks open Mon.-Thurs. 10am-3pm, Fri. 10am-6pm. Some open Sat. 10am-3pm. Trust companies open Mon.-Thurs. 9am-5pm, Sat. 9am-noon.) Although Canadian businesses may accept or exchange American currency, they are under no legal obligation to give you any, let alone all of the difference.

Telephones and Mail

As in the U.S, telephone numbers have seven digits, and are preceded by a three-digit area code. Direct phone calls may be made from one country to the other without the need for operator assistance. As in the U.S., long-distance calls within Canada and to the U.S. are 35-65% cheaper in the evening or on weekends. Local calls cost 25¢ throughout Canada. **Canada Post** requires a 37¢ Canadian postage stamp for all domestic first class mail within the country. Letters or postcards sent to the U.S. cost 43¢. Since postage prices increase yearly, expect to pay a bit more in 1990. When sending mail to destinations within Canada, be sure to note the six-character **postal code.** Even with the postal code, expect items passing through the Canadian mail system to take longer than they would south of the border.

Holidays

Canadians enjoy both national and provincial holidays. All government offices and most businesses close on national holidays, except on Easter Monday and Remembrance Day. Check in local newspapers for a list of what is and isn't open. The following is a list of the major national holidays in 1990: New Year's Day (Jan. 1); Good Friday (April 13); Easter Monday (April 16); Victoria Day (May 21); Canada Day (July 1); Labor Day (Sept. 3); Thanksgiving (Oct. 8); Remembrance Day (Nov. 11); Christmas Day (Dec. 25); and Boxing Day (Dec. 26).

Accommodations

Hotels, especially those at resorts, have three price options. The American Plan charges for a room and three meals; the Modified American Plan includes a room, breakfast, and dinner; the European Plan offers just a room. The price of any hotel, though, combined with the lack of budget motel chains in Canada, should steer budget travelers away. Less expensive lodgings can be found at one of the multiplying **bed and breakfasts,** ($25-60). A similar yet more structured lodging option is the **farm vacation.** With a minimum duration of one week (average rate about $250 per person), the family-oriented farm vacation system integrates guests into the daily life of farm families in the Maritimes (New Brunswick, Nova Scotia, and Prince Edward Island), Québec, and Ontario. Guests eat with the family and are encouraged to help with the chores. For travelers who prefer urban lodgings, the network of **YMCAs** and **YWCAs** stretching through the larger cities offers clean and affordable rooms, generally in downtown areas. In summer, other budget choices include university dorms, some of which open for travelers as early as mid-May, and close in mid-August.

The **Canadian Hostelling Association (CHA),** founded in 1933, maintains over 70 hostels nationwide. Graded "basic," "simple," "standard," or "superior," hostels have kitchens, laundries, and often meal service ($4-14). Open to members and non-members, most hostels allow a maximum stay of three nights. For hostels in busy locations, reservations are recommended. In addition, hostelers must have a sleeping bag or "sleepsheet;" rentals are usually available for $1. The Canadian Hostelling Association, affiliated with the International Youth Hostel Federation, upholds generally the same rules and rates as American Youth Hostels. For information, write Canadian Hostelling Association, 1600 James Naismith Dr., Gloucester, Ont. K1B 5N4 (613-748-5638).

Members of CHA receive a $1-2 reduction in room rates and the opportunity to take advantage of concessions at many local businesses. Furthermore, CHA membership includes membership in IYHF, which allows for discounts in the use of hostels around the world. Memberships are valid from October 1 of the year purchased until December 31 of the following year.

Canada's **national** and **provincial parks** entice travelers with acres upon acres of excellent campgrounds. National parks are sprinkled throughout Canada: There are 12 in western Canada, six in the central provinces, seven in the Atlantic Provinces, and four in the Yukon and Northwest Territories (all free). Both provincial and national parks prohibit campfires on the beach, and no camping is allowed in picnic parks.

Transportation

Train Travel

VIA Rail handles all of Canada's passenger rail service. VIA Rail's routes are as scenic as Amtrak's and its fares are often more affordable. Fares vary according to season: In off-season, from September 15 to June 15, **Advance Purchase Excursion (APEX)** tickets, purchased two weeks in advance, may shave as much as 40% off the fare. However, APEX fares only cover round-trip travel from one point to another and do not allow for stops on the way. Best for transcontinental travel in summer is the **Canrailpass,** which is good for 15 days and allows unlimited travel and unlimited stops. Travelers who know ahead of time that they will be staying for more than 15 days can pay an additional fee to extend the pass to a maximum of 30 days. Canrailpasses cost CDN$299, with $9 for each additional day; for students with ID CDN$239, $5 each additional day. **Amtrak** links with VIA Rail in Toronto and Montréal. For more information, contact VIA Rail Canada, P.O. Box 8116, Montréal, PQ H3C 3N3 (in Québec 800-361-5390; in Ontario 800-665-8630; outside Canada 800-561-3949).

Bus and Car Travel

The major inter-provincial carriers are Gray Coach, Greyhound, Voyageur, and Charterways. Greyhound makes the most convenient links between the Canadian and American bus networks. The Trans-Canada Highway, the world's longest national highway, stretches 8000 miles from St. John's, Newfoundland, to Victoria, British Columbia. Drivers in Canada must have proof of insurance coverage; the minimum required coverage is higher than that in the U.S.; check with your insurance company to ensure sufficient coverage. Drivers entering Canada from the U.S. must also carry the vehicle registration certificate. If the car is borrowed, have on hand a letter of permission from the owner; if rented, keep a copy of the rental contract for use when crossing the border. In addition, radar detectors are illegal in Canada. The law in British Columbia, Ontario, and Québec requires auto travelers to wear seatbelts.

A valid driver's license from any country (including the U.S.) is good in Canada for three months. Although international bridges, tunnels, and ferries charge a fee, highways are toll-free. Along the Trans-Canada Highway, some toll-free ferries are part of the highway system and operate during daylight hours. In summer, cross early in the morning or late in the afternoon to avoid traffic.

If you plan to rent a car in Canada, investigate the discount White-Corp rate, offered to Canadian Hostelling Association members over 21. In addition, agencies dealing in late-model automobiles rent cars throughout Canada for significantly less than their American counterparts. Finally, you can contact one of the numerous auto-transport agencies. If you are 21, have a valid driver's license, and agree to travel at least 400 miles per day on a reasonably direct route to the destination, you could have a whole car for the price of the gasoline.

Québec

If you can't sleep together, you might as well have separate beds.
—René Lévesque (Leader of the Parti Québécois, 1968-1985, and Premier of Québec, 1976-1985)

Québec and the rest of Canada have always had an unhappy marriage, not arranged for love or even convenience, but forced by conquest. Most *Québécois* feel a primary allegiance and sense of identity with their province rather than with their country.

Language is not all that divides Canada's two main cultures; French-Canadians have struggled to maintain their separate customs, traditions, law code, educational system, and religion. The political impulse to separatism peaked in the 1970s, but had begun to wane by the 1980 referendum on Sovereignty-Association, in which the country voted 60-40 to keep Qubec as a Canadian province. Economic difficulties, brought on by a rapid flight of capital from Québec to the neighboring anglophone province of Ontario produced rifts within the Parti Québécois (PQ), the separatist actors of the Québec Nationalist government. The resignation of the PQ's fiery leader, René Lévesque, in the summer of 1985, virtually sealed the party's defeat by the rival and more conservative Liberal Party of the Québec province.

The Québécois nurture a strong sense of their past. Generally much more aware of Canadian history than their anglophone counterparts, French-Canadians have vowed not to forget the British take-over in 1763—hence the provincial motto, seen on Québec license plates: *Je me souviens* ("I remember"). French-Canadian culture thrives; the province's "national" holiday (called **La Fête Nationale**) is celebrated on Saint-Jean-Baptiste Day, in late June. Singing, dancing, drinking, and fireworks mark the holiday.

Practical Information

Capital: Québec City.

Tourist Information: Tourisme Québec, c.p. 20,000, Québec G1K 7X2 (800-361-5405 in Québec province, 800-443-7000 in eastern USA, 800-361-6490 in Ontario and the Maritimes).

Time Zone: Eastern.

Alcohol: Legal drinking age 18.

Québec is the largest Canadian province, covering almost 600,000 square miles of land and water. Its six million inhabitants make it the second most populated province in Canada, behind Ontario.

Tourist information is easily located in almost every town. Look for the square brown signs with a question mark. Transportation by train or bus covers the entire province and is excellent. The one bus line in Québec, **Voyageur,** also serves Ontario.

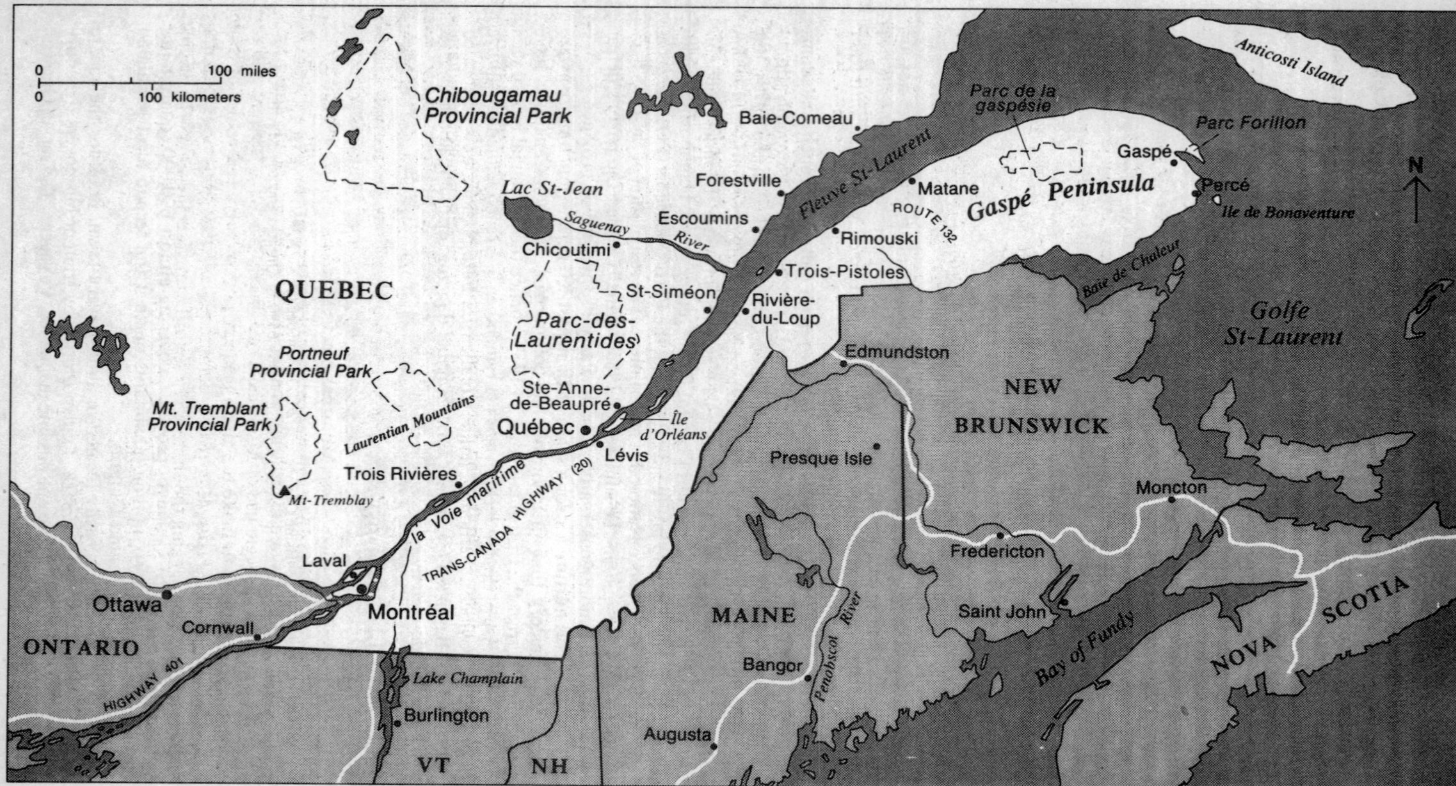
0 100 miles
0 100 kilometers
Chibougamau Provincial Park
QUEBEC
Lac St-Jean
Saguenay River
Chicoutimi
Baie-Comeau
Forestville
Escoumins
Fleuve St-Laurent
Parc de la gaspésie
Matane
ROUTE 132
Gaspé Peninsula
Gaspé
Parc Forillon
Percé
Ile de Bonaventure
Anticosti Island
N
Rimouski
Trois-Pistoles
Baie de Chaleur
Golfe St-Laurent
St-Siméon
Rivière-du-Loup
Parc-des-Laurentides
Edmundston
Portneuf Provincial Park
Mt. Tremblant Provincial Park
Laurentian Mountains
Ste-Anne-de-Beaupré
Québec
Île d'Orléans
Lévis
NEW BRUNSWICK
Presque Isle
Trois Rivières
Mt-Tremblay
la Voie maritime
TRANS-CANADA HIGHWAY (20)
Moncton
Fredericton
Laval
Ottawa
Montréal
Cornwall
ONTARIO
HIGHWAY 401
MAINE
Penobscot River
Saint John
Bay of Fundy
NOVA SCOTIA
Bangor
Lake Champlain
Burlington
Augusta
VT
NH

Besides its regular fares, Voyageur offers a **Tour Pass** in summer for unlimited travel. Call for dates and rates. **VIA Rail** of Canada is the main railroad for passenger and tourist service, with frequent service between major urban centers. VIA Rail also offers a fixed-cost travel card for unlimited travel (8 days $170, 15 days $198; under 12 ½-price).

Traveling by **car** in Québec can be expensive, since gas is heavily taxed. Remember that gas is sold by the liter (3.8 liters = 1 gallon). When you travel on Québec's roads you must have liability coverage ($50,000 minimum). For more information, call the *Régie de l'assurance automobile du Québec* (Québec Automobile Insurance Board, 418-643-7620). Parking and traffic violation fines begin at $30.

Most of Québec is rural and sparsely populated. Just outside the major cities you can visit magnificent lakes, mountains, forests, cliffs, waterfalls, and beaches in such regions as la Gaspésie and les Laurentides. The province is famous for its fishing, canoeing, hunting, and skiing. Sun-kissed summer and brilliant fall encourage people to bike, camp, windsurf, and waterski. (Fishers and hunters must obtain a Québec permit. Contact the Ministère du Loisir, de la Chasse et de la Pêche, Service de la Réglementation et des Permis, 150, blvd. St-Cyrille E., Québec G1R 4Y3 (418-890-5349).)

In addition to the many private campgrounds, camping is available in the **Provincial Parks** and **forest reserves** (418-890-5349 or 514-790-0241; sites $5-12). The latter are primarily wilderness areas but some offer primitive camping. More typical campgrounds are abundant in the provincial parks. The Québec government also arranges **farm accommodations** ($30 per night, under 18 $25; meals included.) Experience rural Québec hospitality first-hand and practice your French in a family setting by writing about a month in advance to Fédération des Agricoteurs du Québec/Vacances-Familles, Stade Olympique, 4545, ave. Pierre-de-Coubertin, c.p. 1000, Succursale "M", Montréal, P.Q., H1V 3R2 (514-252-3138 or 282-9580). Québec has at least 26 youth hostels. Many provide access to excellent recreational facilities. For information, contact **La Fédération Québécoise de l'Ajisme** (Québec Hostelling Federation), 3541 Aylmer St., Montréal H2X 2B9 (514-843-3317). For short stays try one of the many **Gîtes du Passant** (bed and breakfasts) throughout the province. Make reservations one day in advance. For information, contact Vacances-Familles, 1661, ave. du Parc, Ste-Foy, Qc. G1W 3Z3 (418-658-0576).

Montréal

Montréal is the second-largest city in Canada and the second-largest French speaking city in the world (behind Paris). Montréalers (*les Montréalais*) take tremendous pride in their city, and have worked to maintain its cosmopolitan character. In the past 20 years, the **Vieux Montréal** (Old Montréal) historic district has been restored, the **Place des Arts** has opened, and the "underground city" of Montréal has flourished. A constant inflow of international exhibits and festivals and the natural beauty of the city add to the general *joie de vivre* of Montréal residents.

The first French settlement in Montréal was founded in order to evangelize the indigenous population in 1642 and was called Ville-Marie. By the 19th century, the influx of rich Scottish and British merchants, the development of the continent's railroad, and the strategic use of Montréal's two rivers, the Saint Laurent and the Ottawa, all combined to make the city a primary port of entry and center of trade for the New World. *Vieux Montréal,* a community of stern gray stone buildings and sidewalk cafés hugging the shore of the Saint Laurent, is the site of the original Ville-Marie and offers one of the greatest concentrations of 17th-, 18th-, and 19th-century buildings in North America.

Practical Information

Emergency: 911.

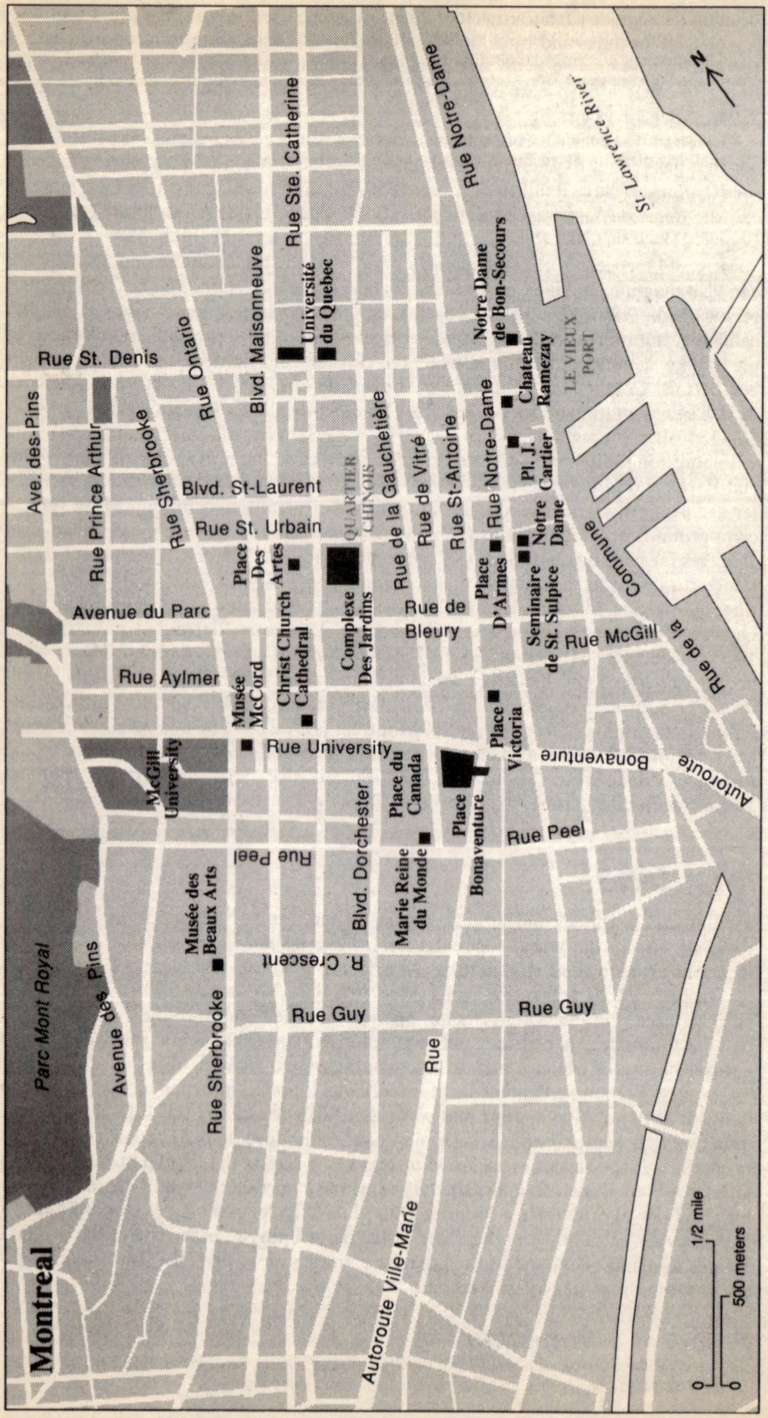
Montreal
Parc Mont Royal
Avenue des Pins
Ave. des-Pins
Rue St. Denis
Rue Prince Arthur
Rue Sherbrooke
Rue Ontario
Blvd. Maisonneuve
Rue Ste. Catherine
Université du Quebec
Rue Notre-Dame
St. Lawrence River
N
Notre Dame de Bon-Secours
LE VIEUX PORT
Chateau Ramezay
Pl. J. Cartier
Rue Notre-Dame
Rue St-Antoine
Rue de Vitré
Rue de la Gauchetière
QUARTIER CHINOIS
Blvd. St-Laurent
Rue St. Urbain
Place Des Artes
Complexe Des Jardins
Place D'Armes
Notre Dame
Seminaire de St. Sulpice
Rue de Bleury
Avenue du Parc
Rue McGill
Rue de la Commune
Rue Aylmer
Musée McCord
Christ Church Cathedral
Rue University
McGill University
Place Victoria
Autoroute Bonaventure
Place du Canada
Place Bonaventure
Rue Peel
Rue Peel
Blvd. Dorchester
Marie Reine du Monde
Musée des Beaux Arts
R. Crescent
Rue Guy
Rue Guy
Rue Sherbrooke
Rue
Autoroute Ville-Marie
1/2 mile
500 meters
0

Visitor Information: Infotouriste, 1001, rue du Square-Dorchester (871-1595), on Dorchester Sq. between Peel and Metcalfe St. Métro: Peel. Free city maps and guides, plus extensive restaurant and accommodations listings. Open daily May 21-June 11 8am-6pm; June 12-Sept. 4 8am-7:30pm; Sept. 5-Oct. 31 8am-6pm; Nov. 1-May 20 9am-5pm. Branch office of Infotouriste at 174 Notre-Dame St. E. Same hours as main office.

Language: The population of Montréal is 80-85% French-speaking. Most people are bilingual, but prefer to avoid English. If you know French, speak it.

Consulates: American, place Desjardins (281-1886). Open Mon.-Fri 8:30am-2pm. **British,** 635, Dorchester ouest (866-5863). Open Mon.-Fri. 9am-12:30pm and 2-4:30pm. **German,** 3455, Mountain (286-1820). Open Mon.-Fri. 9am-noon.

Québec Student Tourist Office, "L'OTEQ": 4545, Pierre de Coubertin (252-3119). Métro: Pie-IX. Right on the Olympic site, in a large and confusing building. Free maps and youth hostel information. Open Mon.-Fri. 9am-4:30pm. Mailing address: C.P. 1000, Succursale "M," Montréal P.Q., H1V 3R2. More convenient to the center of town is **Travel CUTS,** at the McGill Student Union, 3480, rue McTavish (849-9201). Métro: McGill. They also sell the ISIC and provide budget travel information. Open Mon.-Fri. 9am-5pm.

Currency Exchange: Exchange bureaus at 1240, rue Peel and 390, rue St. Jacques ouest 18 (open Mon.-Fri. 8am-5pm and Sat. 8am-3pm); at 1218, rue McGill (open Sat.-Sun. 10am-5pm). **Deak International Exchange,** 625 blvd. Dorchester W. (397-4029). Open daily 9am-5pm. Most cafés will take U.S. dollars and give you Canadian change, but at a worse exchange rate than the banks.

American Express: 1141, blvd. de Maisonneuve ouest (284-3300). Métro: Peel. Open Mon.-Fri. 9am-5pm.

Airports: Dorval Airport (636-5921), 10 miles from downtown. From the Lionel Grioulx Métro stop, take bus #211 to Dorval Shopping Center, then transfer to bus #204. **Aerocar** (397-9999) runs buses from the airport to the Queen Elizabeth Hotel, the Sheraton Center, Terminus Voyageur (the stop closest to St-Denis), and the Bonaventure Hotel (Mon.-Fri. every 20 min,. Sat.-Sun. every ½ hr., $10). **Mirabel International Airport** (476-3010), 35 miles from downtown. **Aerocar** buses connect this airport to the city's central train station (daily 11am-11pm departures from Mirabel, 11am-10pm departures from Montréal $12).

Trains: Central Station, 800, rue de la Gauchetière and **Windsor Station,** 1170, rue de la Gauchetière (871-6000). Métro: Bonaventure. Served by **VIA Rail** (871-1331) and **Amtrak** (800-426-8725). Direct service to: Québec City (3 per day, 3 hr., $32); Toronto (5 per day, 5 hr., $60); Vancouver (1 per day, $319); New York City (2 per day, US$72); and inconvenient connections to Boston (US$89, change trains in New Haven). Ticket counters open daily 7am-11:30pm.

Bus Station: Terminus Voyageur, 505, blvd. de Maisonneuve est (842-2281). Métro: Berri de Montigny. Voyageur offers 10-day unlimited tour passes for $99 in summer, which will take you all over Québec and Ontario. **Greyhound** serves New York City (5 per day, US$81.75). **Vermont Transit** serves Boston (2 per day, US$73.20); Burlington, VT (3 per day, US$18.30); and Québec (US$26.20). Open 24 hours.

CTCUM, Métro and Bus: 288-6287. A safe and efficient network, with Métro subway service to the city core only. The 4 Métro lines operate 5:30am-1:30am; buses usually run 5am-1:30am, with some 24-hour schedules. Network maps at the tourist office, or at any Métro station toll booth. Fare for Métro or bus $1.05, 6 tickets $5.50.

Car Rental: Beau Bazou, 295, rue de la Montagne (939-2330). Métro: Lucien l'Allier. $22.70 per day plus 9¢ per km; insurance included. Open Mon.-Fri. 9am-9pm. Must be 25 with credit card. Reserve in advance. **Rent-a-Wreck,** 1444, René Lévesque ouest (871-1166). $30 per day plus 9¢ per km; insurance $9 per day. Open Mon.-Fri. 8am-6pm. Must have credit card. Reserve at least 3 days ahead. **Budget Rent-a-Car,** 1460, rue Guy (937-9121). Métro: Guy-Concordia. **Hertz** (842-8537), at the airport, at Central Station, and at 1475, rue Aylmer. Métro: McGill. $54 per day; insurance $12.

Bike Rental: Cycle Peel, 6665, St-Jacques (486-1148). Take bus #90 W. from Vendome Métro stop. First day $13, $7 thereafter. $40 per week. Open Mon.-Wed. 9:30am-6pm, Thurs.-Fri. 9:30am-9pm, Sat.-Sun. 9:30am-5pm. Must have credit card or a $200 cash deposit.

Driver/Rider Service: Allo Stop, 4317, rue St-Denis (282-0121). Will match you with a driver for destinations in Québec and the eastern U.S. To Québec City $11.

Help Lines: Medical Aid, 842-4242. 24 hours. **Distress Centre,** 935-1101. 24 hours. **Gay Switchboard,** 933-2395, Thurs.-Sat. 7-10:30pm.

Post Office: Succursale "A," 1025, St-Jacques (283-2567). Open Mon.-Fri. 8am-5:45pm, Sat. 8am-noon for all services, including Poste Restante. **Postal code:** H3C 1T1.

Area Code: 514.

Montréal lies 554km (334 miles) down Rte. 401 and the St-Laurent from Toronto, 250km upstream (southwest) of Québec City, 615km (382 miles) north of New York City, and 500km (310 miles) northwest of Boston. Québec autoroutes link directly with I-87 in New York and I-91 in Vermont.

Two major streets divide the city and are convenient for orientation. The **boulevard St-Laurent** (also called "The Main") runs north-south, dividing the city and streets east-west. The boulevard is also the unofficial French/English divider: English **McGill University** lies to the west of St-Laurent, while St-Denis, the **French student quarter** (also called the "*Quartier Latin*") is slightly east. **Rue Sherbrooke** runs almost the entire length of Montréal, perpendicular to boulevard St-Laurent and parallel to the St. Laurent River.

Parking is often difficult in the city, particularly in winter when snowbanks narrow the streets and slow down traffic. Take the **Métro** instead.

Accommodations and Camping

The Québec Tourist Office is the best resource for information about hostels, hotels, and **chambres touristiques** (rooms in private homes or small guest houses). Universities offer inexpensive accommodations, although availability during the school term is unlikely. Bed and breakfast singles cost $25-40, doubles $35-75. The most extensive B&B network is **Bed & Breakfast à Montréal,** 4912, ave. Victoria, H3W 2N1 (738-9410). They list about 50 homes, but recommend that you reserve by mail ($25-40 deposit required for reservations). B&B à Montréal also provides 15% discounts on Gray Line city tours and some restaurant coupons. (Singles $30-45. Doubles $45-70. Open daily 9am-7pm). The **Downtown Bed and Breakfast Network,** 3458, ave. Laval, Montréal H2X 3C8 (289-9749), at Sherbrooke, works with 15 to 20 homes. (Singles $25-40. Doubles $35-55. Open in spring and summer daily 8:30am-8:30pm; in fall and winter 8:30am-6pm). The cheapest B&B service may come from **Mont-Royal Chez Soi,** 101, ave. Northview, H4X 1C9 (486-6910. Credit cards not accepted). Many of the least expensive tourist homes *(maisons touristiques)* and hotels are around rue St-Denis, which ranges from quaint to seedy. The area is convenient to the bus station, boasts lively nightclubs, and abuts Vieux Montréal.

Schools: Concordia University, 1455, blvd. de Maisonneve ouest, Montréal H3G 1MB. Métro: Guy. Excellent location. 145 beds. Singles $15, nonstudents $21. Doubles $30, nonstudents $32. Linen and towels included. Discounts for extended stays. Must reserve with 1 night's deposit. Open May 11-Aug. 27. **McGill University,** 3935, rue de l'Université, Montréal H3A 2B4 (398-6367). Métro: McGill. 1000 beds. Students $21, nonstudents $28.50. Linen and towels included. Discounts for extended stays. Reservations recommended (1 night deposit). Open May 15-Aug. 2Q. **Université de Montréal,** Résidences, 2350, Edouard-Montpetit Montréal H2X 2B9 (343-6531), further from downtown. Métro: Côte des Neiges, or bus #51. 1170 beds. Students $17, nonstudents $27. Linen and towels included. Reserve a week ahead (1 night deposit). Mailing address: C.P. 6128 Station "A," Montréal, H3C 3J7. Open May 1-Aug. 23.

International Youth Hostel (IYHF), 3541, rue Aylmer, Montréal H3A 2W6 (843-3317), in the McGill campus area, 10 min. from downtown. Métro: McGill. Bunk beds in dorms. 108 beds. Kitchen available. Open daily 8am-2pm. $9.50, nonmembers $12.50. Deposit $5. Hot showers and linen included. Reservations (1 night deposit) preferred. Fills up quickly. Overflow youth hostel at **Collège Français,** 5155, de Gaspé, Montréal H3G 1M8 (no phone). Métro: Laurier, then walk west and north. Over 1000 beds. Reservations not needed. $9.50. Open daily 8am-2am.

YWCA, 1355, rue René-Lévesque ouest, Montréal H3G 1T3 (866-9941). Métro: Lucien l'Allier. Women only. Clean, safe rooms. Singles $30-46. Doubles $41-57.

Maison André Tourist Rooms, 3511, rue Université (849-4729). Each room has a sink, with one bath per floor. Small, quiet and clean. No smoking. Singles $25-35. Doubles $35-40.

Hôtel Viger Centre-ville, 1001-1005, rue St. Hubert (845-6058). Most rooms have A/C, TV, and private bath. Singles $29-35. Doubles $32-40.

Hôtel Amor, 151, rue Sherbrooke est (285-0894). Adequate singles and doubles with shared bath both from $25. Most have A/C and TV.

Hôtel The Vines Tourist Rooms, 1208, rue Drummond (861-8748). Right next to the fire station. Singles $27. Doubles $36.

Camp at **Camping Henri,** 14678, rue Notre-Dame est Montréal H1A 1W1 (642-5477), in an old farmhouse setting in Pointe-Aux Trembles, near the St. Lawrence. From Hwy. 40, take exit 85, then drive 7.5km (4.6 miles) southeast via St-Jean Baptiste sud to Notre-Dame est. 70 sites. $15 for 2, with hookup $18. **KOA Montréal-South,** 130, blvd. Monette, St-Phillipe JOL 2KO (659-8626), a 15-minute drive from the city. Follow Rte. 15 south, take exit 38, turn left at the stop sign, and go straight about 1 mile—it's on your left. (180 sites. $15, with electricity $21.)

Food

French Canadian cuisine is unique but generally expensive. If you're on a tight budget, look for *tourtière,* a traditional meat pie with vegetables and a thick crust, or *Québecois crêpes,* which are stuffed with everything from scrambled eggs to asparagus with *béchamel* and make a filling meal. Wash it down with *cidre* (hard cider) and *caribou* (a heady combination of Bordeaux and hard stuff). The drinking age in Montréal is 18. Other specialties of Montréal cuisine include French bread (the best on the continent), smoked meat, Gaspé salmon, Matane shrimp, and lobster from the Maydalen Islands.

Montréal's ethnic restaurants offer a variety of cuisine from curry to pirogi at reasonable prices. Look for Greek *souvlaki* or the Vietnamese asparagus and crab soup. A small **Chinatown** lies along rue de la Gauchetière, near old Montréal's Place d'Armes. See boiled bread baked on a fire 'round the clock at the **Bagel Bakery,** 263, St-Viateur ouest (276-8044), or at the **Bagel Factory,** 74, Fairmount ouest (272-0667). From St-Laurent Métro stop, take bus #55 north to Fairmount or St-Viateur and turn left.

You can save money by buying your own wine and bringing it to **unlicensed restaurants.** These are concentrated on the **boulevard St-Laurent,** north of Sherbrooke, and on the pedestrian precincts of **rue Prince Arthur** and **rue Duluth.** If you're preparing your own grub, poke around. The produce at the **Atwater Market** (872-2009; Métro: Lionel-Groulx); the **Marché Maisonneuve,** 4375, rue Ontario est (256-4974); or the **Marché Jean-Talon** (Métro: Jean Talon). (All open Mon.-Wed. 7am-6pm, Thurs.-Fri. 7am-9pm.)

Rue St-Denis, the main thoroughfare in the French student quarter, has many small restaurants and cafés, most of which cater to student pocketbooks. **Da Giovanni,** 572, Ste-Catherine est, serves generous portions of fine Italian food; don't be put off by the lines or the diner atmosphere.

For more information, consult the "Shopping, Restaurant, and Nightlife" guide, available free from the Greater Montréal Convention and Tourism Bureau (see Practical Information above).

McGill Student Union, 3480, rue McTavish, Métro: McGill. Cheap cafeteria food (meals $2-6) Mon.-Thurs. 8am-6pm, Fri. 8am-4pm. There are also a couple of hopping bars; open Sept.-May only.

Café Santropol, 3990, St-Urbain at Duluth, slightly northwest of the McGill campus downtown. The best sandwiches, desserts, and student atmosphere in town, with an eclectic clientele. Satisfying meals with huge portions $5-7. Open Tues.-Thurs. 11:30am-midnight, Fri.-Sun. noon-midnight.

Kam Fung, 1008, ave. Clark, (866-4016), in Chinatown. Métro: Place d'Armes. The huge dining room is more suited to a banquet than an intimate meal, but the inexpensive *dim sum* dishes are excellent ($2-6; served daily 11am-3pm). Regular Cantonese entrees more expensive ($9-15). Open Mon.-Thurs. 11am-midnight, Fri.-Sat. 11am-1am, Sun. 10am-midnight.

Wilensky's, 5167, ave. Clark (271-0247). Take bus #51 from the Laurier Métro stop to the corner of St-Urbain and Laurier, then go 1 block north and 1 block east. A great place for quick lunch in the heart of the old Jewish neighborhood. Lunch $2.50-5. Open Mon.-Fri. 9am-4pm.

Schwartz's Montréal Hebrew Deli, 3895, St-Laurent (842-4813), near Napoléon and St-Laurent. Métro: St-Laurent. Best smoked meat in town; they pile it on thick ($3-5). Open daily 9am-12:45am.

Restaurant Jam-Can, 5518 Sherbrooke ouest (484-9824). This casual and unpretentious establishment serves Caribbean cuisine which, while not gourmet, is spicy and filling. Curried goat $6, meat or vegetable patty $1. Open daily 11am-10pm.

Terasse Lafayette, Jeanne Mance and Villeneuve, west of the Mont-Royal Métro. The name is misleading; one of the better Greek restaurants in this neighborhood. *Brasserie* atmosphere. Pizza, pastas, *souvlaki,* and salad $6-10. Open Mon.-Sat. 11am-3pm, 6pm-midnight.

Etoile des Indes, 1806, Ste-Catherine ouest (932-8330). Métro: Guy. The best Indian fare in town. The very brave should try their spicy *bangalore phal* preparations. Lunch $4-5, dinner $6-8. Open Mon.-Fri. 11:30am-2:30pm and 5-11pm; Sat. noon-3pm and 5-11pm; Sun. 5-11pm.

Sights

Montréal at its most futuristic does not rise 40 stories above ground—it tunnels beneath the skyscrapers. Victims of a brutally cold climate, Montréalers have constructed an attractive option to going outdoors in February; you'll find shops, movies, discos, and art exhibits sheltered below ground. Start your exploration at the **Place Bonaventure** (Métro: Bonaventure), with its exhibition hall and **Le Viaduc** shopping center, a cluster of shops each selling products of a different country. The tunnels wind around to **Windsor Station** and the **Place du Canada. Les Terrasses,** a subterranean garden and multi-level shopping complex, graces the McGill Métro stop and adds a welcome spot of green. Altogether the underground city has 13km of passageways connecting 8 hotels, 1000 shops, 130 restaurants, and 25 cinemas. The tourist office's *Montréal* guide contains maps of the tunnels and underground attractions. (Underground shops open Mon.-Wed. 9am-6pm, Thurs.-Fri. 9am-9pm, Sat. 9am-5pm.)

Students will feel at home on the **McGill University** campus (main gate at the corner of McGill and Sherbrooke St.; Métro: McGill). The campus stretches up Mont-Royal, offering Victorian buildings and a pleasant spot of green grass and oak trees in the midst of downtown. The oldest university in Québec, it was founded in 1821 by the estate of James McGill, a Canadian merchant and politician. McGill, more than any other sight in Montréal, exemplifies the British tradition and continuing English presence in the city.

Parks and Museums

The finest of Montréal's parks, **Parc du Mont-Royal** (872-6211), is a vast expanse of green swirling up the mountain from which the city took its name. Visitors from New York may recognize the hand of Frederick Law Olmstead, the architect who planned Central Park. From rue Peel, hardy hikers can take a foot path and stairs to the top, where a fantastic view of the city awaits. In 1643, De Maisonneuve promised to climb Mont-Royal bearing a cross if the flood waters of the St-Laurent would recede. The existing 30-foot cross, built in 1924, commemorates this climb. When illuminated at night, the cross is visible for miles. In winter, *Montréalais* congregate here to ice-skate and cross-country ski.

Parc Lafontaine contains the **Jardin de Merveilles** (Garden of Wonders), and a **children's zoo** (872-2815; Métro: Sherbrooke). There are also picnic facilities, an outdoor puppet theater, 17 public tennis courts, ice-skating in the winter, and an international festival of public theater in June. (Zoo open mid-May to end of Sept.

daily 10am-7pm; Sept.-June daily 10am-6pm. Admission $2.50, under 18 $1.50. Free parking.)

For a beautiful view of Montréal and the St-Laurent, head up rue Belvedere to **Westmount Summit.** This small wooded park crowns **Westmount,** one of the wealthiest neighborhoods in the city. Subdued, green, and very Anglo, Westmount is an enclave of stately mansions. (Take bus #66.) On the northern edge of Westmount stands **Oratoire St-Joseph** (St. Joseph's Oratory), 3800, rue Queen Mary (Métro: Snowdon, Guy, and bus #165.) This mammoth monument of *québécois* Catholicism was built in honor of the monk Frère André, famous at the turn of the century for his curative powers. Aside from an impressive basilica, the complex includes the **Musée de Frère André** and the **Musée de l'Oratoire** (a spacious art gallery). (Oratory open daily 6am-10pm. Museums (733-8211) open daily 10am-5pm. Donation.)

Musée des beaux-arts de Montréal (Montréal Fine Arts Museum), 1379, Sherbrooke ouest (285-1600, Métro: Guy), houses a small permanent collection that touches upon all major historical periods, and includes Canadian and Inuit (Eskimo) work. (Open Tues.-Wed. and Fri.-Sun. 10am-5pm, Thurs. 11am-9pm. $4, families $6, seniors, handicapped and under 12 free, students $2, ages 12-15 $1.) **Musée d'art Contemporain** (Museum of Contemporary Art), Cité du Havre (873-2878), has the latest by *québécois* artists, as well as textile, photography, and avant-garde exhibits. (Open Tues.-Sun. 10am-6pm. Free. Métro: McGill, then bus #168. Tues.-Fri. The museum provides a bus from noon Sat.-Sun. every ½-hr. from McGill and the Bonaventure Métro.)

The **Centre Canadien d'Architecture,** 1920 Baile St. (939-7000; Métro: Guy.), just opened in May 1989, and houses one of the most important collections of architectural prints, drawings, photographs and books in the world. (Open Wed. 11am-6pm, Thurs. 11am-8pm, Fri. 11am-6pm, Sat. and Sun. 11am-5pm. Admission $3, students $2, under 13 free.) The **Olympic Park,** 4545, ave. Pierre-De-Coubertin (252-4737; Métro: Pie-ix or Viau), was the home of the 1976 Summer Olympic Games. Its daring architecture includes the world's tallest inclined tower and a stadium with one of the world's only fully retractable roofs. (Guided tours daily every hour 9am-5pm, Sept.-May 12:30 and 3:30pm. Admission $4, children $2.50.)

Vieux Montréal

An exploration of Montréal's French heritage should begin on the stretch of riverbank between rue McGill, Notre-Dame, and Berri. This is Vieux-Montréal (Old Montréal), site of the first settlement on the island. While the fortified walls that once protected the quarter have crumbled, the beautiful 17th- and 18th-century mansions of politicos and merchants are preserved in full splendor. (Métro: Place d'Armes.)

The 19th-century church **Notre-Dame-de-Montréal** towers above the Place d'Armes and the memorial to de Maisonneuve, Montréal's founder. A historic center for the city's Catholic population, the neo-Gothic church was the site of French Canadian separatist rallies, and, more recently, a tradition-breaking ecumenical gathering. Seating 4000, Notre-Dame is one of the most magnificent and also one of the largest churches in North America. Don't miss the Wedding Chapel behind the altar. Destroyed in a fire eight years ago, the chapel was re-opened in 1982 with a tremendous bronze altar.

Walk next door from Notre-Dame to the **Sulpician Seminary,** Montréal's oldest remaining building (built in 1685) and still a functioning seminary. The clock over the facade (built in 1700) is the oldest public timepiece in North America. A stroll down rue Saint-Sulpice will bring you to **rue de la Commune** on the banks of the St. Lawrence River. Here the old docks of the city compete with the new. Proceed east along rue de la Commune to **rue Bonsecours.** At the corner of Bonsecours and **rue St-Paul** (the busiest and most commercial street in Old Montréal) stands the 18th-century **Notre-Dame-de-Bonsecours.** Older and less ornate than Notre-Dame-de-Montréal, the church on the port was a sailor's refuge, founded by Marguerite Bourgeoys (1620-1700), leader of the first congregation of non-cloistered nuns.

Look closely at the ceiling lamps. Climb the tower for a view of Vieux Montréal. (Open Tues.-Sat. 9-11am and 1-4:15pm. Admission to tower 75¢.)

Opening onto rue St-Paul is **Place Jacques Cartier,** site of Montréal's oldest market. Here the modern European character of Montréal is most evident; in summer, street artists display their work, and cafés line the square. Visit the grand **Château Ramezay,** 280, Notre-Dame est (861-3708), built in 1705 to house the French viceroy, and its museum of québécois, British, and American 18th-century artifacts. (Open Tues.-Sun. 10am-4:30pm. Admission $3, students 50¢.) Nearby, in the square of Place Vauquelin, is the Vieux Palais de Justice, built in 1856, and across from it stands City Hall. **Rue St-Jacques** in the Old City, inaugurated in 1687, is Montréal's answer to Wall Street.

There are three good reasons to venture out to **Ile Ste-Hélène,** an island in the St. Lawrence River, just off the coast of Vieux Montréal. The first is **La Ronde** (872-6222), Montréal's popular amusement park. Since La Ronde fills at night, it's best to go in the afternoon, buy an unlimited pass ($17, children $10), and stay until the evening crowds overtake the place. (Open June 20-Labor Day daily noon-2am.) The second reason is the **Terre des Hommes** (World of People) exhibit, from the 1967 World's Fair. A few pavilions are still open, and outdoor concerts, educational exhibits, and films are featured here in summer. (Open June 22-Sept. 8am-midnight. Buildings open 11am-8pm.) Finally, there's **Le Vieux Fort** (The Old Fort; 861-6701), built in the 1820's to defend Canada's inland waterways. Now primarily a military museum, the fort displays artifacts and costumes detailing Canadian colonial history. Military parades take place daily 11am-4:30pm. (Museum open May-Labor Day daily 10am-5pm; Sept.-April Tues.-Sun. only. Admission $3, seniors and under 18 $2.) Take the Métro under the St. Lawrence to the Ile Ste-Hélène stop.

Whether swollen with spring run-off or frozen over during the winter, the **St. Lawrence River** can be one of Montréal's most thrilling attractions. The whirlpools and 15-foot waves of the **Lachine Rapids** were once a barrier to river travelers. St. Lawrence and Montréal harbor cruises depart from Victoria Pier (842-3871) in Vieux Montréal (May 15-Sept. 30, 4 per day, 1½ hr., $7.50, seniors $6, children $4).

Nightlife and Entertainment

Montréal steps out at night. Nightclubs, discos, and café-théâtres will set you back quite a few dollars; *brasseries,* pubs, and *tavernes* are just as typical and much cheaper. **Tavernes** are a *québécois* male institution, usually frequented by TV-watching locals. The taboo against women is seldom enforced. **Brasseries** serve food, while **pubs** are places to relax and quaff a few in the best Canadian tradition.

Rue Ste-Catherine ouest is a glitzy show of neon lights and not much else. The real action is to be found on smaller side streets off Ste-Catherine. The English stronghold is around **rue Crescent** and **rue Bishop** (Métro: Guy). Bar-hopping is a must here. Try the **Déjà-Vu,** 1224, Bishop (866-0512), or **D.J.'s Pub,** 1433, Crescent (845-1813). (Both open daily 11am-3am.) Jazz enthusiasts will enjoy **Biddles,** 2060, rue Aylmer (842-8656; Métro: McGill; open Mon.-Fri. 11:30am-3am, Sat.-Sun. 6pm-3am.; cover Sat.-Sun. $6). You can boogie at **Tangerine,** 2125, rue de la Montagne (845-3607; no jeans; open daily 6pm-3am. Cover $8.), the **Club Scaramouche** across the street, or at countless other dancing places in this area. Reggae fans must go to **Rising Sun,** 286, Ste-Catherine ouest (861-0657; Métro: Place des Arts or McGill; open daily 8pm-3am; no cover).

French nightlife is concentrated on **rue St-Denis** (Métro: Berri de Montigny). Stop in for live jazz at **Le Grand Café,** 1720, rue St-Denis (849-6955; open daily 11am-2:30am. Cover in the evening $4). Also in the Latin Quarter is young, lively rue Prince Arthur, densely packed with Greek, Polish, and Italian restaurants. Street performers and colorful wall murals further enliven this ethnic neighborhood. The accent changes slightly at ave. Duluth, where Greek and Vietnamese establishments prevail. Vieux Montréal, too, is best seen at night. Street performers, artists, and *chansonniers* in various *brasseries* set the tone for lively summer evenings of clapping, stomping, and singing along. Walk down St-Paul, and try the *brasseries* near the corner of St-Vincent.

Montréal has long been the cultural capital of Québec. The city bubbles with a wide variety of theatrical groups: The **Théâtre du Nouveau Monde,** 84, Ste-Catherine ouest (861-0563), and the **Rideau Vert,** 4664, St-Denis (844-1793), stage québécois works. For English language plays, try the **Centaur Theatre,** 453, rue St-François-Xavier (288-3161). The city's exciting **Place des Arts,** 175, Ste-Catherine ouest (842-2112 for tickets; 285-4200 for information), is home to the **Opéra de Montréal,** the **Montréal Symphony Orchestra,** and **Les Grandes Ballets Canadiens.** Check the *Calendar of Events* (available at the Québec tourist office and reprinted in daily newspapers), and call **Ticketron** (288-3651) for tickets.

Québec City

Québec City, the capital of Québec province, is Canada's oldest city, and has been the country's capital under both French and English regimes. Built on the rocky heights of Cape Diamond, where the St. Lawrence River narrows and joins the St. Charles River in northeast Canada, it's been called the "Gibraltar of America" because of the stone walls and military fortifications protecting the port.

The Algonquin village of Stadcona was visited in 1535 by the French explorer Jacques Cartier, and on July 3, 1608, Samuel de Champlain founded Québec City on the same site. It was the capital of French North America until September 1759, when the British scaled the city's cliffs. Fighting between the French and British forces continued until 1763, when Canada became a British colony under the Treaty of Paris. But, despite the past British control of the area, the French have proved unwilling to relinquish their heritage or their language. Québec City is at least 95% French-speaking and offers traditional French-Canadian cuisine, music, and ambiance. Visitors who speak French should certainly do so, but enough of the population is bilingual that Anglophones will have little difficulty getting around. The city is lovely by day and by night; in summer, tourists and students crowd the narrow streets and the warm air fills with music from the rows of nightclubs and cafés. For those who can't afford a trip to Europe, Québec City offers an old-world charm nearly unparalleled in North America. The best times to visit are during the summer arts festival in mid-July and February's winter carnival, a raucous Canadian-style Mardi Gras.

Practical Information

Emergency: Police, 691-6123 (city); 623-6262 (provincial). **Télémedic:** 687-9915. 24 hours.

Visitor Information: Maison du Tourisme de Québec (Québec Province Information), 12, rue Ste-Anne (800-443-7000; 800-361-5405 in Québec; 800-361-6490 in Ontario). Visit here before touring Québec City or if you plan forays into the Québec countryside, where information centers are rare. Accommodation listings for the entire province and free road and city maps. Open daily 8:30am-8:30pm; Sept.-May 9am-5pm. **Ste-Foy Tourist Information Office:** Ministère de l'Industrie, du Commerce et du Tourisme et Communauté Urbaine de Québec 3005, blvd. Laurier, Ste-Foy (651-2882), at rue Lavigerie, 4 miles southwest of the old city. Open daily 8:30am-8pm; Sept. to mid-May daily 8:30am-6pm.

U.S. Consulate: 1, Ste-Geneviève (692-2095). Open Mon.-Fri. 8:30am-5pm.

Airlines: Air Canada (692-0770) and **Québecair** (692-1031). To: Montréal ($97, if under 22 years standby $49) and New York City ($209, standby $105). Ask the airline about special deals.

Trains: Via Rail Canada, 3255, chemin de la Gare (692-3940), in Ste-Foy (658-8792), and 1, ave. Laurier, in Lévis (833-8056). To Montréal (5 per day, 2½ hr., $27).

Buses: Voyageur Bus, 225, blvd. Charest est (524-4692). Open daily 5:20am-1:20am. Also outlying stations at 2700, blvd. Laurier, in Ste-Foy (651-7015; open daily 5:45am-1:15am) and 63, rte. Trans-Canada ouest (Rte. 132), in Lévis (837-5805; open 24 hours). To: Montréal

(6am-1am every hr., 3 hr., $26.20) and Ste-Anne-de-Beaupré (10 per day, $2.50). Connections to U.S. cities via Montréal or Sherbrooke.

Local Transit: Commission de transport de la Communauté Urbaine de Québec (CTCUQ), 270 rue des Rocailles (627-2511). Buses run 5:30am-midnight. Fare $1.20, seniors free.

Taxis: Taxi Québec: 525-8123.

Car Rental: Rent-a-Wreck, 265, blvd. Hamel (683-2333). $16 per day plus 9¢ per km, insurance $7 per day, under 25 $9. Open Mon.-Fri. 7:30am-6pm, Sat. 8am-noon. Must be 21 with credit card or a $500 deposit; 25 with credit card or $200 deposit.

Help Lines: Tel Aide, 683-2153.

Canada Post: 3, rue Buade (648-4682). Open Mon.-Fri. 8am-5:45pm. **Postal Code:** G1R 2J0.

Area Code: 418.

Québec is 253km (160 miles) from Montréal, 700km (426 miles) from Gaspé, and 620km (400 miles) from Boston. From Montréal, take Autoroute 20. Autoroute 23 and Rte. 173 join U.S. 201 in a deserted corner of northwestern Maine.

Accommodations and Camping

Québec City now has two bed and breakfast referral services. Try **B&B Bonjour Québec,** 3765, blvd. Monaco, Québec G1P 3J3 (527-1465; best to call 7:30-11:30am or 7-8pm) for listings throughout the city. Singles are usually $30-40, while doubles go for $45-60. **Gîte Québec** offers similar services. Contact Thérèse Tellier, 3729, ave. Le Corbusier, Ste-Foy, Québec, G1W 4R8 (651-1860). (Singles $30. Doubles $50-60.)

You can obtain a list of nearby campgrounds from the Maison du Tourisme de Québec, or by writing Ministère du Tourisme, Direction de l'hôtellerie, 710, place D'Youville, 3e étage, Québec G1R 4Y4 (643-2230 or 800-463-5009).

Centre international de séjour, 19, Ste-Ursale (694-0755), between rue Ste-Jean and Dauphine. A renovated convent in the heart of the old city. No kitchen, but an inexpensive cafeteria is open for breakfast and lunch in the basement, and a microwave is always accessible. Desk open 7am-2am. Lights out 11pm-7am. 4-person rooms $12 (key deposit $5), dorms $6.50 (no key). Reservations accepted.

Auberge de la Paix, 31, rue Couillard (694-0735), in the heart of the old city. Small and cramped, but clean. Predominately 8-10 bed dorms, some doubles. Curfew 2am. $11. Breakfast included.

CEGEP de Ste-Foy, chemin Ste-Foy, Pavillion Lasalle (659-6600), Ste-Foy. Adequate singles with shared bath $10. Open May 10-Sept.

Campus de l'université Laval, Pavillion Parent (656-2921), Ste-Foy. Take bus #11. Modern building with dorm rooms available in summer. Singles $11.50. Doubles $19. Nonstudents $19 and $25, respectively. Discounts for longer stays.

Montmartre canadien, 1679, chemin St-Louis, Sillery (681-7357), on the outskirts of the city. Take bus #25. Run by friendly monks. Dorm-style singles $12. Doubles $20.

Manoir La Salle, 18, rue Ste-Ursale (647-9361), opposite the youth hostel. Private rooms in a nice atmosphere. Singles $23. Doubles $37-42. Fills up in summer by evening.

Camping Canadien, Ancienne-Lorette (872-7801). Open May 11-Oct. 27. Go out Rte. 360—it's only 4-5km east of town. Ask at the tourist office for the municipal bus to nearby Beauport. 50 sites. The site on the Riviere Montmorency, just above the falls, is worth paying for. Sites $14, with hookup $17.

Municipal de Beauport, Beauport (666-2228). Take Autoroute 40 east, exit at rue Labelle onto 369, turn left and follow signs marked "camping". 137 sites. $10, hookups $15.

Food and Nightlife

In general, **rue Buade** and **Ste-Jean** and **avenue Grande Allée** and **Cartier,** as well as the **Place Royale** and **Petit Champlain** areas offer the widest selection of food. One of the most filling yet inexpensive meals is a *croque monsieur,* a large, open-faced sandwich with ham and melted cheese ($5), usually served with salad. Québécois French onion soup is always substantial, loaded with onions, slathered with melted cheese, and usually served with lots of French bread. Other specialties include the French crêpe, stuffed differently for either main course or dessert, and the French-Canadian "sugar pie," made with brown sugar and butter. For home-cooked basic meals, eat at the clean and cheap cafeteria in the basement of the Centre internationale de séjour (see Accommodations above).

Cochon Dingue, 46, blvd. Champlain (692-2013). Popular outdoor café serving light fare (salads, sandwiches, *grignotines*—finger food) under $5. More substantial entrees $6-9. Open daily 8am-1am.

Casse Crêpe Breton, 1136, rue Ste-Jean (692-0483). Great, inexpensive crêpes come with friendly (if slow) service in a bohemian-chic atmosphere. Crêpes $2.60-4.50; breakfast special (2 eggs, bacon, toast, and coffee) $2.50; lunch specials (served 11am-2pm) an even better bargain. Open Sun.-Thurs. 8am-1am, Fri.-Sat. 8am-2am.

Les Couventines, 1124, rue Ste-Jean (692-4850). Buckwheat crêpes in a quiet, earthy atmosphere. Quiche and soup also available. Full meal with wine $10-12.

La Fleur de Lotus, 50, Côte de las Fabrique (692-4286), across from the Hôtel de Ville. Cheerful and unpretentious. A local favorite. Thai dishes $3-7. Open Mon.-Wed. 11:30am-10:30pm, Thurs.-Fri. 11:30am-11:30pm, Sat. 5-11:30pm, Sun. 5-10:30pm.

Restaurant Liban, 23½, rue d'Auteuil (694-1888). Good *baba ghanoush* (spiced eggplant dip) plates $2.75, tabouli and hummus plates $2, both with pita bread. Open daily 11am-4am.

L'Entrecôte St-Jean, 23, rue d'Auteuil. Pleasant garden terrace with live music. Salads and sandwiches $4-6, grilled chicken or steak $8-10. Open daily 11am-2am.

Numerous boisterous nightspots line rue Ste-Jean. Duck into any of these establishments and linger over a glass of wine or listen to some *québécois* folk music. Most have no cover charge and close around 3am. **L'Apropo,** 596, rue Ste-Jean, frequently has live music. (Open noon-whenever.) The **Bar en Bar,** 58, Côte du Palair is full of locals and has a pool table. (Half-price drinks daily noon-8pm.) In summer, musicians, magicians, and other performers take their act to the street. Call 529-5511 for a recorded message (in French) of cultural events.

Sights

Confined within walls built by the English, *le vieux Québec* (old Québec City) holds most of the city's historic attractions. Monuments are clearly marked and explained, but you'll get more out of the town with the tourist office's *Québec Walking Tour Guide,* available from the **Maison du Tourisme** (see Practical Information above). It takes one or two days to explore old Québec by foot, and you are likely to discover more that way than with the many guided bus tours.

La Haute-Ville

Begin your walking tour of Québec City by climbing uphill, to the top of **Cap Diamont** (Cape Diamond), just south of the **Citadelle.** From here take **Promenade des Gouveneurs** downhill to **Terrasse Dufferin.** Built in 1838 by Lord Durham, this popular promenade offers excellent views of the St. Lawrence River, of the Côte de Beaupré (the "Avenue Royale" Highway), and of Ile d'Orléans across the Channel. The promenade passes the landing spot of the European settlers, marked by the **Samuel de Champlain Monument,** where Champlain built Fort St-Louis in 1620, securing the new French settlement. A *funiculaire* (cable car) (692-1132; daily 7:20am-11:30pm; 60¢) connects Lower Town and Place Royale. The western end of the terrace has **la grande glissade** (a long public toboggan run) in winter, frequented by drunk revelers during the Winter Carnival.

At the bottom of the promenade, towering above the terrasse, near rue St-Louis, you'll find **le Château Frontenac,** built on the ruins of two previous *châteaux.* The immense, baroque Frontenac was built in 1893 by the Canadian Pacific Company and has become a world renowned luxury hotel. Although budget travelers will have to forgo staying here, the grand hall is open to the public and contains a small shopping mall.

Near Château Frontenac, between rue St-Louis and rue Buade, is the **Place d'Armes.** The *calèches* (horse-drawn buggies) that congregate here in summer provide a nice atmosphere, but the smells can be strong in muggy weather. Tours by carriage are expensive ($35). Also on rue Buade, right next to Place d'Armes, is the **Notre-Dame Basilica.** The clock and outer walls date back to 1647; the rest of the church has been rebuilt twice (most recently after a fire in 1922). Notre-Dame, with its odd mix of architectural styles, contrasts sharply with the adjacent **Seminary of Québec.** The seminary, founded in 1663, is an excellent example of 17th-century *québecois* architecture. At first it was a Jesuit training school; it became the University of Laval in 1852. The **Musée du Séminaire,** 6, rue de l'Université (692-3981), is nearby. (Open daily 10:30am-5pm. Admission $2, seniors and students $1, children 50¢.)

The **Musée du Fort,** 10, rue Ste-Anne (692-2175), presents a sound-and-light show that narrates (in French and English) the history of Quebec City and the series of six battles fought for control of the city. (Open in spring and summer Mon.-Fri. 10am-6pm, Sat.-Sun. 10am-5pm; in fall Mon.-Fri. 10am-5pm; in winter Mon.-Fri. 11am-5pm, Sat. 10am-5pm, Sun. 1-5pm; closed Dec. 1-20. Admission $3.50, seniors and students $2.)

Walk along rue St-Louis to see its 17th and 18th century homes. Of historic note is the **Maison Kent,** 25, rue St-Louis, built in 1648, where the surrender of Québec to the British was signed in 1759. The house is now used and operated by the Québec government. At the end of rue St-Louis is **porte St-Louis,** one of the oldest entrances to the fortified city.

La Basse-Ville

You can take a *funiculaire* (60¢) from Terrase Dufferin to **La Basse-Ville,** the oldest section of Québec, or walk down the steps from Côte de la Montagne. Either way leads to **rue Petit-Champlain,** the oldest road in North America. Many of its old buildings have been restored or renovated and now house cutesy craft shops, boutiques, cafés, and restaurants. The **Café-Théâtre Le Petit Champlain,** 68, rue Petit-Champlain (692-3094), presents québécois music, singing, and theater. The **Poste de taite,** at 79, rue Petit-Champlain, sells and displays high-quality native art.

From the bottom of the *funiculaire* you can also take rue Sous-le-Fort and then turn left to reach **Place Royale,** built in 1608, where you'll find the small but beautiful **l'Eglise Notre-Dames-des-Victoires** (692-1650), built in 1688, the oldest church in Canada. (Open daily 8:30am-5pm; Oct.-May Mon.-Sat. 8:30am-noon and 2-3:30pm, Sun. 8am-1pm.) The houses surrounding the square have been restored to late 18th-century styles. Considered the cradle of French civilization in North America, the Place Royale is now one of the best spots in the city to see outdoor summer theater and concerts.

The boardwalk on the shore of the St. Lawrence River provides access to Québec's active marina. The "lock" is still used to maintain the safety of the boats docked in the city's Bassin Louise.

Outside the Walls

From the old city, the **promenade des Gouverneurs** leads to the **Plains of Abraham** (otherwise known as the **Parc des Champs-de-Bataille**) and the **Citadelle** (694-3563). On the Plains of Abraham you'll find the **Musée du Québec,** 1, ave. Wolfe-Montcalm, parc des Champs-de-Bataille (643-4103). The museum contains a collection of *québécois* paintings, sculptures, decorative arts, and prints. (Open daily 9:15am-9pm. Free.) The park was the site of the final battle between French and British troops in 1759 before the French surrendered. The Citadelle is a magnificent fortification overlooking and still protecting Québec City. Visitors can witness the

changing of the guard daily at 10am from mid-June through Labor Day. (Tours daily every 50 minutes from 9am-7pm. Admission $3, children $1.)

Exit the Citadelle along Côte de la Citadelle, which leads back to Porte St-Louis and the Grande Allée. At the corner of la Grande Allée and rue Georges VI, right outside Porte St-Louis, stands **l'Assemblée Nationale** (643-7239). Completed in 1886 and built in the style of French King Louis XIII, it is well worth a visit. You can view debates from the visitors gallery; anglophones have recourse to simultaneous translation earphones. (Guided tours Mon.-Fri. 9am-9pm, Sat.-Sun. 9am-5pm; Sept.-May Mon.-Fri. 9am-5pm. Free.)

The **Nordiques,** Québec's hockey team, are followed here with near-religious fanaticism; they play from October through April in the Coliseum (691-7211). The raucous **winter carnival** is in the second week in February; call 626-3716 for more information. Québec's **summer festival** (692-4540), in the second week in July, is also spectacular.

Near Québec City

Québec City's public transportation system leaves St. Lawrence's **Ile-d'Orléans** untouched. Its proximity to Québec (about 10km downstream), however, makes it ideal for a short side trip by car or bicycle; take Autoroute Montmorency (440 est), and cross over at the only bridge leading to the island (Pont de l'Ile). Originally called *Ile de Bacchus* because of the number of wild grapes growing here, the Ile-d'Orléans is a sparsely populated retreat of several small villages, and strawberries are now its main crop. Check out the Chabot family crest emblazoned on the stained glass window of the cathedral. The **Manoir Mauvide-Genest,** 1451, chemin Royal (829-2915), dates from 1734. A private museum inside has a collection of crafts as well as traditional French and Anglo-Saxon furniture. (Open daily 10am-5pm; Oct.-May Sat.-Sun. 10am-5pm. Admission $1.50.)

Exiting l'Ile-d'Orléans, turn right (east) onto Rte. 138 (blvd. Ste-Anne) to view the splendid **Chute Montmorency** (Montmorency Falls), one and a half times as high as Niagara Falls. In winter the falls freeze completely and are even more beautiful. About 20km (13 miles) along 138 lies **Ste-Anne-de-Beaupré** (Voyageur buses link it to Québec City, $2.15 one-way). This small town's entire *raison d'être* is the famous **Basilique Ste-Anne-de Beaupré,** 10,018 ave. Royale (827-3781). Since 1658, this double-spired basilica containing the Miraculous Statue and the forearm bone of Ste-Anne, the mother of the Virgin Mary, has been associated with miraculous cures. Every year over a million pilgrims come here to pray. (Open daily June-Sept. 7am-10:30pm; Oct.-May 7am-5pm.)

Ontario

To the visitor who knows Canada only through hockey games and lumberjack movies, Ontario's cosmopolitan cities and varied terrain will come as a surprise. Ottawa, the national capital, perches on the province's eastern edge, and Toronto, the sophisticated provincial capital, is bathed by the waters of Lake Ontario. Abundant in ski resorts during the winter months, Ontario also encompasses miles of parkland and lakes, dotted with summmer cottages and campsites.

Practical Information

Capital: Toronto.

Tourist Information: Ontario Travel, 77 Bloor St. W., 9th floor, Toronto M7A 2R9 (800-268-3735). Free maps. Walk-in center at **Toronto's Eaton Centre,** Level 1 at the north end, near Yonge and Dundas St.

Time Zone: Eastern. **Postal Abbreviation:** Ont.

Toronto

Until the late 1950s, Toronto was a city of well under a million, known as "Toronto the Good." Charles Dickens commented that the townspeople's idea of Saturday night revelry was wrapping themselves in a Union Jack and singing "God Save the Queen." Today, the city's residents have developed other ways to amuse themselves. Waves of European and Asian immigrants since World War II have transformed Toronto into a thriving, cosmopolitan city with diverse ethnic neighborhoods. Since the late 70s, when a number of companies' head offices moved from Montréal to Toronto (perceiving *Québécois* nationalism as a threat), the city has become Canada's unrivaled financial leader. Toronto's economy has prospered, escaping the double-digit unemployment rates that have plagued many other parts of Canada. Gleaming office towers in the downtown core and the striking absence of seedy areas testify to economic success. Now home to more than 2.3 million residents, and half as many again in its sprawling suburbs, Toronto has surpassed Montréal as the largest urban center in the country. Despite its rapid growth, the city remains clean, safe, and well-organized. (The subways are efficient and graffiti-free, a fact which amazes many American tourists.) Excellent cultural events abound, especially during open-air festivals in summer.

Practical Information

Emergency: 9ll.

Visitor Information: Toronto Tourist and Convention Information, on the bottom floor of the Eaton Centre Galleria, #110, 220 Yonge St. (979-3143), just south of the Dundas subway stop. Free city maps and accommodation and entertainment listings. Open Mon.-Fri. 9am-5pm. **Tourist Information,** 800-268-3735.

Consulates: U.S., 360 University Ave. (595-1700; 595-1708 for a recording about visas; 368-3775 for emergencies). Subway: St. Patrick. Open Mon.-Fri. 9am-2:30pm. **Australian,** 25 King St. W., 22nd floor, in the Commerce Court North building (367-0783), located at the corner of King and Bay St. Subway: King. Open Mon.-Thurs. 9am-4:15pm, Fri. 9am-3:30pm. **British,** 777 Bay St., #1910 (593-1267 or 593-1290). Open Mon.-Fri. 9am-5pm. **German,** 77 Admiral St. (925-2813). Subway: St. George. Open Mon.-Tues. and Thurs.-Fri. 9am-noon.

Canada Customs: 55 Bloor St. W., 10th floor of Manulife Centre (973-8022 Mon.-Fri. 8:30am-4:30pm; 676-3643 Sat.-Sun. and holidays).

Student Travel Agency: Travel CUTS, 187 College St. (979-2406), just west of University Ave. Subway: Queen's Park. Helpful staff sells ISIC ($8.50) and IYHF cards ($20). Open Mon.-Fri. 9am-5pm. **YHA Travel** (862-0226), in the Toronto International Youth Hostel (see Accommodations below), is excellent for advice and cheap flights. Open Mon.-Fri. 9:30am-4:30pm.

American Express: 50 Bloor St. W. M4W 1A1 (967-3411; 477-8747 24-hour travel assistance). Subway: Bloor-Yonge. Open Mon.-Wed. and Sat. 10am-6pm, Thurs.-Fri. 10am-7pm.

Lester B. Pearson International Airport: 676-3506. About 20km west of Toronto, via Hwy. 401 or 409. Take one of the two special airport bus services (979-3511) to get downtown. **TTC** airport buses connect to the Islington ($4), York Mills ($5), and Yorkdale ($4.50) subway stops. Faster **Gray Coach Airport Express** bus service runs directly to downtown hotels (Royal York Hotel, Hilton Harbour Castle, Holiday Inn Downtown, Delta Chelsea Inn, and Sheraton Centre) every 20 minutes from about 5:30am-11pm. ($8, under 12 $5. Child with parent travels free.) **Air Canada,** 925-2311. To: Montréal ($167); Calgary ($471); and Vancouver ($564). All flights 50% less for "student standby"; maximum age 21.

Trains: Via Rail Union Station, 48 Front St. W. (366-8411), at the Union subway stop. To: Montréal ($60); Windsor ($45); Calgary ($250); Vancouver ($302); Chicago ($105); and New York City ($121). 33% discount for seniors on all fares. Ticket office open Mon.-Sat. 6:45am-11:35pm, Sun. 7am-ll:35pm.

Buses: Voyageur/Greyhound Bus Terminal, 610 Bay St. (393-7911), just north of Dundas. Subway: St. Patrick or Dundas. Service to: Montréal ($36); Calgary ($99); Vancouver ($99); Chicago ($133.30); and New York City ($126.15). 10% discount for seniors. Ticket office open daily 5:30am-1:30am.

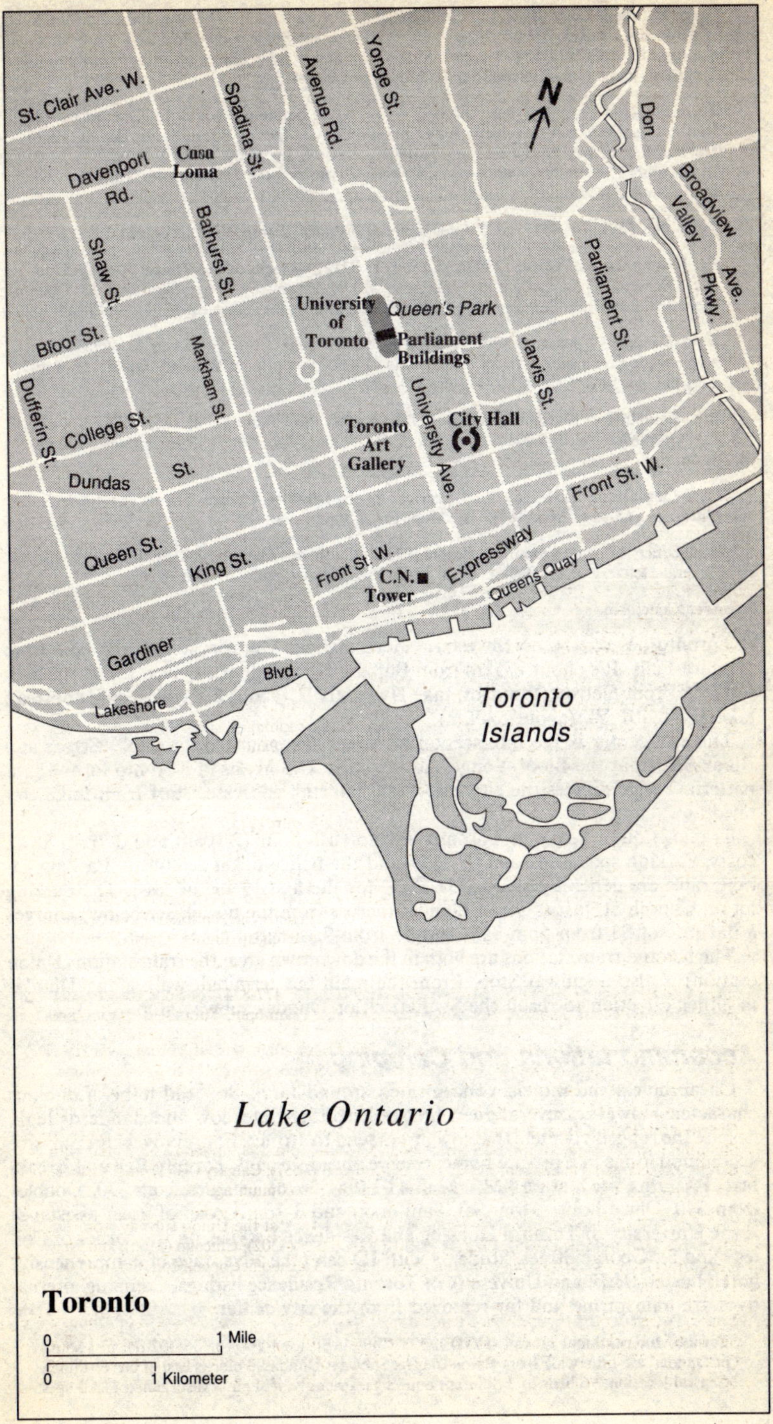
St. Clair Ave. W.
Spadina St.
Avenue Rd.
Yonge St.
N
Don
Casa Loma
Davenport Rd.
Broadview Ave.
Valley Pkwy.
Bathurst St.
Shaw St.
Parliament St.
University of Toronto
Queen's Park
Parliament Buildings
Bloor St.
Markham St.
Jarvis St.
Dufferin St.
College St.
University Ave.
Toronto Art Gallery
City Hall
Dundas St.
Front St. W.
Queen St.
King St.
Front St. W.
C.N. Tower
Expressway
Queens Quay
Gardiner
Blvd.
Lakeshore
Toronto Islands
Lake Ontario
Toronto
0
1 Mile
0
1 Kilometer

Toronto Transit Commission (TTC): 393-4636. Network includes 2 subway lines and numerous bus and streetcar routes. Free maps at all stations. Some routes 24 hours. Fare $1.10, 8 tokens $7; ages 2-12 50¢, 4 tokens $1.05. Sun. and holiday passes $3.50 per family of 1-5 persons (maximum 2 adults) for unlimited travel that day.

Toronto Island Ferry Service: 392-8193 or 392-8194. Numerous ferries to Toronto Islands Park on Centre Island leave daily from Queen's Quay at foot of Yonge St., or Bay St. Ferry Dock at foot of Bay St. Service approximately every ½ hr. (during daytime); $2.10 round-trip, seniors 75¢, under 14 40¢. A 1½ hr. harbor cruise on the *Trillium* runs Tues.-Sat., $5, seniors and children $3.

Taxi: Ace Taxi, 449-6911. $1.25 plus metered distance charge. Visa accepted.

Car Rental: Rent-a-Wreck, 123 Dundas E. (947-0212), 4 blocks east of Yonge. Subway: Dundas. $31 per day plus 12¢ per km. Insurance $13.94 per day, $9.50 per day if over 25. Open Mon.-Fri. 8am-6pm, Sat. 9am-5pm. Must be 21 with major credit card.

Auto Transport Company: Auto Driveaway, 5803 Yonge St. (225-7754 or 225-7759), just north of the Finch subway stop, north of Hwy. 401. Most rides to Western Canada. In summer, pay gas plus $50-100 to Western Canada.

Bike Rental: Brown's Sports and Cycle Bike Rental, 2447 Bloor St. W. (763-4176). $14 per day. Open Mon.-Wed. 9:30am-6pm, Thurs.-Fri. 9:30am-8pm, Sat. 9:30am-5:30pm. $100 deposit.

Help Lines: Rape Crisis, 964-8080. **Services for the Disabled,** Ontario Travel, 965-4008. **Toronto Area Gays (TAG),** 964-6600. Mon.-Fri. 7-10pm.

Post Office: Toronto Dominion Centre (973-3120), at the junction of King St. and Bay St. General Delivery at 40 Bay St. Open Mon.-Fri. 8am-5:45pm, Sat. 10am-2pm.

Area Code: 416.

Toronto lies on the northwestern shore of Lake Ontario, across the lake from Niagara Falls. It's about 175km from Buffalo, NY, along the Queen Elizabeth Way (QEW). From Detroit/Windsor, take Hwy. 401 E. (about 380km); from Montréal, take Hwy. 401 W. (about 540km).

The city center is the intersection of **Yonge** (pronounced "young") **Street** and **Bloor Street,** at the Bloor-Yonge subway stop. The streets of Toronto form a grid pattern. Yonge divides the city east-west. "North" addresses start from Lake Ontario.

Traffic is quite heavy in Toronto—avoid rush hour (7-10am and 3-7pm) at all costs. Parking spots are hard to find—and the police ticket zealously. Parking garage rates are generally steep (75¢-$2.50 for the first ½ hr. or less). The parking lot on Church St. just south of Dundas (across from the hostel, see below) charges a flat rate of $3 from 6pm-7am and $7 from 7am-6pm.

The bus and train stations are both in the downtown area; the train station (Union Station) is also a subway stop. From the main bus terminal, walk along Dundas in either direction to reach the St. Patrick or Dundas subway stop.

Accommodations and Camping

Cheap hotels and motels, concentrated around Jarvis St., tend to be of dubious character. However, several guest houses keep their rates low and standards high, despite the rugged clientele that low prices tend to attract. For relatively inexpensive accommodations in a private home, reserve ahead through **Toronto Bed and Breakfast,** P.O. Box 74, Station "M," M6S 4T2 (961-3676). (Singles from $30. Doubles from $40. Office hours Mon.-Sat. 9am-noon and 3-7pm.) Also of great assistance is the **University of Toronto Housing and Residence Service,** on the corner of College and St. George Street. Students with ID can take advantage of comprehensive hotel, hostel, B&B, and University of Toronto Residence listings. Camping alternatives are uninspiring and far-removed from the city center.

Toronto International Hostel (IYHF), 223 Church St. (368-1848 or 368-0207), just south of Dundas, a 5-min. walk from Eaton Centre. Subway: Dundas. 3 blocks east of bus terminal. Central location. 96 beds in 3 different buildings. Friendly, if slightly disorganized. All ages welcome. Check-in 7-10am and 3pm-midnight. Curfew Sun.-Mon. 12:30pm, Tues.-Sat. 2am. $11, nonmembers $14. Coffee 55¢. Linen $1.

Neill-Wycik College Hotel, 96 Gerrard St. E. (977-2320). Subway: College. From subway, walk 1 block east on Carleton to Church St., turn right, walk to Gerrard and make a left. Ryerson College residence. Rooms are small, but clean. Singles $34, breakfast included. Doubles $40. Extra bed $7. Up to 2 children under 18, with family, free. Weekly discount $10. 20% discount for IYHF members. Open mid-May to Aug.

Victoria College Residence, 140 Charles St. W. (585-4524), just east of Avenue Rd., 1 block south of Bloor St. Subway: Museum. 150 University of Toronto dorms with shared baths. Great location near trendy shopping areas and Museum. Limited kitchen space also available. Singles $24, seniors and students $21. Doubles $42, seniors and students $20. Members $18.50. Huge breakfast included.

Trinity College Residence, 6 Hoskin Ave. (978-2523), on Queen's Park Crescent, close to the Royale Ontario Museum and shopping on Bloor St. Subway: Museum. University of Toronto dorms with shared baths. Shared doubles $21. Singles $32. Doubles $42. Open May 22-Aug. 27.

Karabanow Guest House and Tourist Home, 9 Spadina Rd. (923-4004), at Bloor St., 6 blocks west of Yonge. Subway: Spadina. Centrally located. Small and intimate. The 18 rooms are a mixture of old-fashioned and renovated modern styles. TV and parking. Singles from $30. Doubles from $45. Rates lower off-season. Reservations accepted.

Janvary Guest House, 314 St. George St. (923-8186), located in the University student district. Subway: St. George. 2-day min. stay. Singles $25. Doubles $40. Reservations recommended.

Indian Line Tourist Campground, Finch Ave. W. (678-1233), at Darcel Ave. Follow Hwy. 427 north to Finch and go west on Finch. 186 sites; $10-15. Open mid-May to mid-Oct.

Food

The best and least expensive food in Toronto is found in ethnic restaurants and open-air markets. You can find just about any kind of food here; check the yellow pages, where restaurants are listed by ethnic category. The best way to sample the numerous cuisines of Toronto is to walk all of the ethnic neighborhoods of the city. These include an immense China and Vietnam Town, Little Italy, Greek Island, Hungarian Village, and Little India.

In **Chinatown,** around Dundas St. east and west of University Ave. You'll find delicious and cheap Chinese food of every variety. In recent years Chinatown has been expanding north onto Spadina Ave. (Subway: St. Patrick.)

From the heart of Chinatown, walk across Spadina Ave. and up 1 block for the freshest and cheapest meat, produce, and cheese in **Kensington Market,** at Augusta and Baldwin St. west of Spadina, south of College St. Kensington Market, originally the old Jewish ghetto of the city, is now predominantly Portuguese, Chinese, and West Indian. Be sure to visit the Portuguese bakeries on Augusta St. for sweet bread and pastries and the West Indian shops for *roti* and spicy meat patties. The **St. Lawrence Market,** 95 Front St. E., at Jarvis, a few blocks east of King subway stop, is a huge two-story warehouse where farmers, fishers, and butchers sell their produce.

Little Italy, mostly on St. Clair Ave. W. (take St. Clair streetcar west from Yonge subway), but also west of University Ave. on College St. (College streetcar), is one of the neighborhoods that gives Toronto its distinctly European flavor. Cafés, social clubs, bakeries, and sandwich shops are open until very late and the *gelati* and espresso rival Italy's best.

Greek Island, on Danforth Ave. E. (take Bloor subway eastbound), has miles of shish-kebab houses and bakeries brimming with flaky *baklava* and sugary *Turkish delight.* This neighborhood has recently become more popular with tourists, and prices are rising.

Little India is concentrated in a 2-block area on Gerrard St. E. (Take the Gerrard or College St. streetcar.) Many cheap *tandoori* places provide buffets for under $6, and shops selling *paan* (dessert of nuts, seeds, and honey wrapped in paan leaf) delicacies line the streets.

Blue Cellar Room, 469 Bloor St. W. (921-6269), west of Spadina near Brunswick Ave., part of L'Europa Restaurant. Subway: Spadina. If you're a student you'll have lots of company in this Hungarian haunt. Heaps of *goulash* or a plateful of *wienerschnitzel* less than $6. Open Mon.-Sat. 11am-1am, Sun. 11am-midnight.

Cafe Mariko, 298 Brunswick Ave. (968-0883), just south of Bloor St. Subway: Spadina. Tasty Japanese cuisine and a pleasant, relaxed atmosphere—at half the competitors' prices. Entrees about $6, sushi plate $9. Open daily 5:30-10pm; off-season 5-9:30pm.

House of Noodles, 457 Dundas St. W. (597-8878). Subway: St. Patrick. Enormous mounds of noodles cooked in every conceivable Asian way, topped with the meats and vegetables of your choice. Right at the center of bustling Chinatown. Entrees $4-6. Open daily 11am-midnight.

Astoria Shish Kebab House, 400 Danforth Ave. (463-2838). Subway: Chester Ave. Traditional Greek cuisine—tasty shish kebab and *baklava.* Full meal under $10. Comfortable patio in summer. Open daily 11:30am-midnight.

Café Diplomatic and Restaurant, 594 College St. (534-4637). Take the College streetcar west from Yonge. Wonderful European-style café, with colorful clientele and relaxed outdoor seating. Excellent *gelati,* espresso, cappuccino, and San Pelligrino. Open daily 9am-2am.

Renaissance Café, 501 Bloor St. W. (923-4346). Subway: Spadina. Fun for oat bran groupies. Moon burger (tofu, spices and *tahini* sauce) $6. Open Mon.-Thurs. noon-midnight, Fri. and Sat. noon-1am, Sun. noon-midnight.

Yung Sing Pastry Shop, 22 Baldwin St. (979-2832). Take the Dundas streetcar to McCaul St. and walk 2 blocks north. Serves the best barbequed pork *bao* and *don tart* in the city. Small, family business that always has freshly baked sweets, *dim sum* specialties, and friendly service. Located on an exciting street of student-filled cafés and bars. Most delicacies under $1. Open daily 10am-10pm.

Bahamian Kitchen, 14 Baldwin St. (595-0994), 2 blocks north of Dundas, off McCaul St. Take the Dundas streetcar. Lively café/restaurant with cheap and spicy Bahamian treats. Try the *conch* shells. Lunch $5-10. Dinners more expensive. Open Mon.-Sat. 11am-1am.

Sights

Urban **Yonge Street** is Toronto's main shopping street, intersecting with Bloor in the ritzy, 3-piece-suit-filled city center. Bloor Street West, between Yonge St. and Avenue Rd., will remind you of New York's Fifth Avenue. Just north of this area is **Yorkville,** which attracted the hippie counterculture during the 60s (Joni Mitchell and James Taylor used to play here). Today it's a *très* chic shopping and dining neighborhood. The prices are outrageous, but it's fun to window-shop, people-watch from outdoor cafés, or have your fortune told.

The vast, ultra-modern **Eaton Centre,** a glass-domed, 4-tiered shopping mall, preens on Yonge St., spanning the distance between Queen and Dundas St., several blocks north. While you're in the area, visit the trendy strip of **Queen Street West,** at its funkiest between University Ave. and Spadina Rd. (Subway: Osgoode.) You'll see Bohemian, punk, and new wave clubs and bizarre second-hand clothing stores. The newest fads start here, at the "cutting edge of the wedge" hangouts.

Slightly north of the Queen St. W. strip lies Canada's largest and most exciting **Chinatown.** Centered at Dundas and Spadina, this neighborhood offers authentic Chinese cuisine, grocery stores, bakeries, boutiques, and theater. Visit the famous **China Court,** 208 Spadina, just south of Dundas, a colorful Chinese shopping plaza modeled after the Imperial Palace in Peking. Reach Chinatown on a streetcar going west from Dundas subway stop. The bilingual streetsigns let you know when you're there.

Members of Toronto's various ethnic groups meet and sell their wares at famous **Kensington Market.** This frenetic multilingual bazaar is located south of College on Baldwin, Augusta, and Kensington St. Friday afternoons and Saturdays see the most activity. Other neighborhoods worth visiting include **Greek Town** on Danforth, east of the Don Valley Pkwy. (extension of Bloor St. E., Subway: Broadview), and **Little Italy** on College, west of Bathurst, and along St. Clair Ave. W. The **Harbourfront** development, 2½ miles of renovated lakeshore piers, encompasses malls, craft shops, and stages for cultural events. (Take the subway to Union, then the streetcar south.) The extensive **underground** system of shops is considered an architectural coup, and enjoys temperature-controlled tunnels for the benefit of chic shoppers and anyone besieged by the elements.

The neighborhood of Bloor St. W., next to the University, features the *Hungarian Village*, Peruvian craft shops, bookstores, student bars, and various lively cafés.

Famous landmarks figure prominently in Toronto. You'll need more than a weekend to explore and appreciate them thoroughly. Since the city is so large and sprawling, it's impossible to construct a single walking tour to cover the important spots. If you'll only be in Toronto briefly, a bus tour is a good idea. **Gray Line Sight-seeing** (979-3511) offers tours of the principal sights (2½-hr. tour of Toronto and Casa Loma or Toronto and CN Tower $16. Buses leave from Bay and Queen St. on the west (City Hall) side at 4:30am and 2pm. 2-hr. "Inside Toronto" tour also departs from here at 10am, noon, and 3pm.)

The building that folks back home will ask if you've seen is the **CN Tower,** at 301 Front St. W. (360-8500). Visible from almost everywhere in the city, it's the tallest free-standing structure in the world (553m). The tower contains three observation decks offering panoramic views of the vast metropolitan area. Choose a clear, dry day and you might even see Niagara Falls, 100 miles distant. Unfortunately, the view isn't free—you'll have to shell out $8 to take the glass-fronted elevator to the first observation deck, 346m up (seniors and ages 13-17 $5, under 13 $3.50). Traveling farther up to the "space pod," the highest observation level, costs an extra $1. This is not really necessary—but who would stop three-fourths of the way up Everest? (Open Mon.-Sat. 9am-midnight, Sun. 9am-11pm; Sept. 8-June Mon.-Fri. 10am-10pm, Sat. 9:30am-11pm, Sun. 9:30am-10pm.)

Another classic tourist attraction is the 98-room **Casa Loma,** Davenport Rd. (923-1172), at 1 Austin Terrace, near Spadina, a few blocks north of the Dupont subway stop. The outside of the only real turreted castle in North America belongs in a fairy tale but the inside's dusty old exhibits can be skipped. (Open daily 9:30am-4pm. Admission $6, seniors $1, ages 4-18 $3.)

The pink sandstone **Provincial Parliament Buildings** of the Ontario government are located in beautiful **Queen's Park** right in the city's center. (Subway: Queen's Park.) Begin a tour of the area with these Romanesque 19th-century edifices. Stroll through the marble halls, or take a free guided tour (965-4028; daily 9am-4pm every hr. on the hr. or ½ hr., Sept. 8 to mid-May Mon.-Fri. only). To see the legislative assembly in action, line up for admission passes to the visitors gallery one hour prior to parliamentary sittings (approximately Oct.-Dec. and Feb.-June Mon.-Wed. 2-6:30pm, Thurs. 10am-noon and 2-6:30pm). Just west of Queen's Park is **King's College Circle,** the focal point of the **University of Toronto,** established in 1827. The University of Toronto (or U of T) stretches miles across the city, but most of the older buildings are near this circular grass playing field. The university is divided into colleges; each college has a distinctive architectural style. Look for Romanesque **University College** (1859) and the adjacent Gothic **Hart House** (1919). Student guides conduct free hour-long walking tours of the campus in English and French, beginning in the Map Room of Hart House. (June-Aug.; 978-5000 Mon.-Fri. at 10:30am, 12:30pm, and 2:30pm; Sept.-May 978-2103.)

From here, head back toward Queen's Park and walk north to visit the **McLaughlin Planetarium,** 100 Queen's Park Crescent (586-5736; call for specific programs), the neighboring **Royal Ontario Museum (ROM),** just south of Bloor (586-5549), and the **George M. Gardiner Museum of Ceramic Art,** 111 Queen's Park (593-9300), opposite the ROM. The planetarium's cozy reclining seats allow you to lie back as you take in the excellent evening laser light shows projected on the domed ceiling. You can see an audiovisual presentation on astronomy in the afternoon or evening. (Open Tues.-Sun.; laser shows $6, regular shows $4, seniors, students, and children $2.25.) The ROM is one of the best natural history museums on the continent, and also contains a superb collection of Chinese art and archeology. (Open Fri.-Mon. and Wed. 10am-6pm, Tues. and Thurs. 10am-8pm. Admission $5, seniors, students, and children $2.50, family $10. Free Thurs. after 4:30.)

The **Art Gallery of Ontario (AGO),** 317 Dundas St. W. (977-0414), 2 blocks west of University Ave., in the heart of Chinatown, houses an enormous collection of Western art from the Renaissance up through the past decade, with particular concentration on Canadian masters. (Open Tues. and Thurs.-Sun. 11am-5:30pm, Wed. 11am-9pm; June 16-Sept. 15 11am-5:30pm. Admission $3.50, seniors and students $1.50, under 12 free, families $7. Free Wed. 5-9pm for all and Fri. for seniors. Subway: St. Patrick.) The **Ontario Science Centre,** 770 Don Mills Rd. at Eglinton Ave. E. (429-0193 or 429-4100), is one hour from downtown; take the subway to Eglinton, then eastbound bus to Don Mills Rd. It's partly a museum, and partly a hands-on fun-fair with great gadgets and displays. (Open Sun.-Wed. 10am-6pm, Thurs.-Sat. 10am-9pm; Sept.-June daily 10am-6pm. Admission $4, seniors free, ages 13-17 $3, under 13 $1.50, families $9.)

Modern architecture fans should visit the **City Hall,** at the corner of Queen and Bay St. (947-7341), between the Osgoode and Queen subway stops. The twin, curved towers and rotunda were considered quite avant-garde when completed in 1965. **Nathan Phillips Square,** in front of City Hall, is a forum for art shows, rock concerts, and multi-cultural festivals; it's also a great place to soak some sun, picnic, and people-watch.

Metro Toronto Zoo (284-8181), about 25km northeast of downtown, 5km north of Hwy. 401 on Meadowvale Rd., has 700 acres of huge, climate-controlled pavilions representing the world's geographic regions. (Open daily May-Labor Day 9:30am-7pm, ticket office closes 6pm; Labor Day-April 9:30am-4:30pm, ticket office closes 3:30pm. Admission $6, seniors and ages 12-17 $3, ages 5-11 $1.50. Cheaper off-season. Take subway to Kennedy station, then take Bus 86A.) **Canada's Wonderland** (832-2205 April-Oct.; 832-7000 Nov.-March; toll-free 800-268-3735), 30km north of downtown, has 33 rides and seven theme areas, including five roller-coasters. Picnics are not permitted. (Open mid-June to Labor Day daily 10am-10pm; May 4 to mid-June and Sept. 8-Oct. 12 Sat.-Sun. 10am-8pm. One-day pass $19, ages 3-6 $9.50.) **Toronto Islands Park** (392-8193; 392-8194 for ferry information), a 4-mile strip of connected islands just opposite the downtown area (15-min. ferry trip), is a popular "vacationland," with a boardwalk, bathing beaches, canoe and bike rentals, a Frisbee golf course, and a children's farm and amusement park. Ferries leave from the **Bay Street Ferry Dock,** at the foot of Bay St. (Bay St. bus stops there), and **Queen's Quay,** at the foot of Yonge St.

Entertainment

Nightlife

Many of Toronto's clubs and pubs remain closed on Sundays because of antiquated liquor laws. Otherwise, the city's Victorian stiffness has vanished, though dress codes are upheld. There are bars and nightclubs to suit every mood and lifestyle, from mellow to boisterous. Infiltrating the university crowd can be somewhat difficult since most campus pubs restrict admission to their own students. But you can mingle with students dedicated to several classic bars near U of T, Ryerson, and York including **The Brunswick House** (see below); **Lee's Palace,** 529 Bloor St. W. (532-7383), just east of the Bathurst subway; and the **All-Star Eatery,** 277 Victoria (977-7619), at Dundas, 1 block east of the Dundas subway. The most interesting new clubs are on trendy **Queen Street West;** most have a cover charge that's worth paying. The gay scene centers around Wellesley and Church, although there's also some gay activity on Queen and Yonge St. *Now* magazine, published every Thursday, is the city's comprehensive entertainment guide, available in restaurants and record stores all over the city. The Friday edition of the *Toronto Star* has a section called "What's On," which is filled with information on clubs, dance-places, pubs, restaurants, concerts and movies.

Bamboo, 312 Queen St. W. (593-5771), 3 blocks west of Osgoode subway stop. Popular with students. Reggae, jazz, and rock, and Afro-funk. Great dancing and atmosphere. Caribbean/Thai menu. Patio upstairs. Open Mon.-Sat. noon-1am. Cover up to $6.

The Copa, Yorkville Ave. and Yonge St. (922-5107), entrance off Yorkville. Subway: Bloor. Huge warehouse dance club. Great hot/cold buffet included with cover: Wed.-Thurs. $5.50, Fri. Sat. $6, Sun. $5. Open Wed.-Thurs. 7pm-1am, Fri.-Sat. 6pm-4am, Sun. 6:30pm-1am.

El Mocambo, 464 Spadina Ave. at College St. (961-8991; 961-2558 recording), at the edge of the U of T campus. Neon palm tree facade. Loud rock & roll club, with dancing and live performances. The Rolling Stones recorded "Love You Live" here in 1977 before an audience that included Margaret Trudeau. Doors open at 8pm. The music upstairs and the show downstairs start at 9:30pm. Open Mon.-Sat. 11am-1am.

Brunswick House, 481 Bloor St. W. (964-2242), at corner of Brunswick, between the Bathurst and Spadina subway. Rowdy dive full of students. Beer 85¢. Upstairs is **Albert's Hall,** famous for blues music. Open Mon.-Sat. 8pm-1am.

Nuts and Bolts, 277 Victoria St. (977-1356), at Dundas. Underground dance club and bar popular with Ryerson students. Tri-level dance floor packed on weekends. Open Mon.-Wed. and Sun. 9pm-1am, Thurs. 9pm-3am, Fri.-Sat. 9pm-4am. Cover: Thurs. $2, Fri.-Sat. $5.

George's Spaghetti House, 290 Dundas St. E. at Sherbourne St. (923-9887). Subway: Dundas; take the streetcar east to Sherbourne. The city's best jazz club has the nation's top ensembles. Complete dinner $7.50-15. Open Mon.-Sat. 6:30pm-1am. Cover Tues.-Sat. $4.

Second City, in The Old Firehall, 110 Lombard St. at Jarvis (863-1111), 2 blocks east and 2 short blocks south of Queen subway station. One of North America's craziest and most creative comedy clubs. Spawned comics Dan Aykroyd, John Candy, Gilda Radner, and Dave Thomas; a hit TV show (SCTV); and the legendary "Great White North." Dinner and theater ($23-25). Theater without dinner $10.50-12, students $6.50. Improv sessions (Mon.-Thurs. at 10:30pm) free—students welcome. Shows Mon.-Thurs. 8:30pm, Fri.-Sat. 8pm and 11pm. Reservations recommended, especially for weekends.

Festivals and Cultural Events

Toronto boasts some lively ethnic festivals and special events. If you're in town in late June, don't miss the **Metro International Caravan** (977-0466). Dancers, singers, musicians, and chefs representing more than 50 nations and cultures demonstrate their skills in pavilions dotted around the city (single day $5, 9-day passes $10). **Caribana,** an enormous celebration led in early August by Canada's West Indian community, is an excuse for a massive open-air party in the streets with a parade and plenty of *soca* music. Devotees of the big screen should catch the **Festival of Festivals** (961-3673), a movie marathon offering 300 screenings of 250 innovative new films over 10 days in early September.

Toronto offers a few first-class freebies. The **Harbourfront's York Quay Centre** (364-5665) hosts free, open-air jazz and classical concerts throughout the summer on the shipdeck stage. You can enjoy superb performances of Shakespeare by **Toronto Free Theater** (392-7251) amid the greenery of **High Park,** Bloor St. W. at Parkside Dr. (Subway: High Park. Bring something to sit on or wedge yourself on the 45° slope to the stage. Performances mid-July to mid-Aug. Tues.-Sun. at 8:15pm.) Every Thursday night in July and August between 7:30 and 9:30pm, the **Toronto Summer Music Festival** presents free jazz concerts on the grounds of **Queen's Park** (Subway: Queen's Park).

Several free guides are useful: Monthly *Key to Toronto* and *Toronto Life* magazines list current cultural events and restaurants; *Now* magazine provides comprehensive theater listings. You can often beat the high cost of culture by seeking out standby or student discount options. **Five Star Tickets** (596-8211) has two booths that sell half-price tickets for theater, music, dance, and opera on the day of performance. The first is at Dundas and Yonge right in front of the Eaton Centre. (Subway: Dundas. Open Mon.-Sat. noon-7pm, Sun. 11am-3pm.) The second, newer location is inside the **Royal Ontario Museum,** Bloor and Avenue Rd. (Subway: Museum. Open Tues.-Sat. 11am-6pm, Sun. 11am-2pm.)

Ontario Place, 955 Lakeshore Blvd. W. (965-7711), features cheap first-class entertainment in summer—the Toronto Symphony, National Ballet Company, Ontario Place Pops, and top jazz, pop, and rock artists perform here free with admission to the park. Kids will love the slides and water games of Children's Village (waterslide and log ride $3). It also houses a six-story Cinesphere: Experience a simulation of flight or free-fall. (Open mid-May to early Sept. Mon.-Sat. 10am-1am, Sun. 10am-11pm. Admission $6, seniors free before 1pm, afterwards $2, under 14 $2.) **Roy Thomson Hall,** 60 Simcoe St. at King St. W (593-4828 or 872-2233), is the home of the Toronto Symphony Orchestra. Tickets are expensive ($15-30), but $7.50 rush tickets go on sale at 6pm the day of the concert at the box office (598-3375; open Mon.-Fri. 10am-6pm, Sat. noon-5pm). The opera and ballet companies perform at **O'Keefe Centre,** 1 Front St. E. at Yonge (365-9744). Ordinarily, tickets are $8.50-60, but ballet rush tickets ($6-7) go on sale at 11am and senior and student standby tickets ($5-6) an hour prior to performance. Opera standby tickets ($7) are available a half-hour before curtain. (Box office open Mon.-Sat. 11am-8pm.) **St. Lawrence Centre,** 27 Front St. E. (366-7723 or 366-1656), next door to the O'Keefe Centre, presents excellent classic and Canadian drama ($13-20) and chamber music recitals ($17). Student rush tickets for theater are available half-hour before showtime ($6). **Massey Hall,** 178 Victoria St. (593-4828), near the Dundas subway stop, is great for rock and folk concerts, and cheaper than the main stages. (Box office open Mon.-Fri. 10am-6pm, Sat. noon-5pm.)

Near Toronto: Algonquin Park

The wilder Canada of endless rushing rivers and shimmering lakes awaits the visitor in Algonquin Provincial Park, about 300km north of Toronto. There are two ways to experience Algonquin: the Highway 60 Corridor, where tents and trailers crowd the roadside; and the park interior, the "essence of Algonquin." You can rent gear for a backcountry adventure at several outfitting stores around and inside the park; one of the best is **Algonquin Outfitters,** RR#1-Oxtongue Lake, Dwight POA 1HO (April-Nov. 705-635-2243), just off Hwy. 60, about 10km west of the park's West Gate. To enter the park, you need an Interior Camping Permit ($2.50 per person per night), available at the main gate or from any outfitter.

Ottawa

Sir Wilfred Laurier, Canada's Prime Minister at the turn of the century, lamented the unsavory appearance of the booming logging and railroad town and called for its transformation into a "Washington of the North." Urban planners and officials have since made Ottawa a capital of which Canadians can be proud. Its museums, artistic community, and parks system are now highlights of the city.

Ottawa's "designer" development cannot hide the fact that it remains a small, young city that owes its existence to the presence of the federal government. Queen Victoria chose the remote lumbering settlement of 7000 as the national capital not for its prominence but for its location. On the border of Upper and Lower Canada, it provided a suitable compromise between French and English interests. Ottawa still retains the somewhat artificial character of a city implanted in the wilderness.

Practical Information

Emergency: 0. Ask for Zenith 5000. **Ambulance:** 0. Ask for Zenith 9000.

Visitor Information: Canada's Capital Visitor Information Centre, 14 Metcalfe St., at Wellington, opposite Parliament Buildings. Extraordinarily helpful (and free) visitor guide and map. Open May 2-Sept. 4 daily 8:30am-9pm; Sept. 5-May 1 Mon.-Sat. 9am-5pm.

Embassies: U.S., 100 Wellington St. (238-5335). Open Mon.-Fri. 8:30am-5pm. **British,** 80 Elgin St. (237-1530). Open Mon.-Fri. 8:30am-5pm.

Student Travel Agency: Travel CUTS, 60 Laurier St. E. (238-8222), just west of Nicholas. Experts in student travel—youth hostel cards, cheap flights. Open Mon.-Fri. 9am-5pm.

American Express: 220 Laurier W. (563-0231), between Metcalfe and O'Connor in the heart of the business district. Open Mon.-Fri. 8:30am-5:30pm.

Airport: Ottawa International Airport, 20 min. south of the city off Bronson Ave. Accessible by OC Transpo buses from downtown (741-4390) or by special airport buses to and from the major hotels in the city core. Buses leave Lord Elgin Hotel every ½ hr. from 6:30am-10pm (fare $5). Taxi fare is approximately $18.

Via Rail Station: 200 Tremblay Rd. (238-4720), just off Alta Vista Rd. To Montréal (2 hr., $24) and Toronto (4 hr., $53.36). Poor connections to U.S. Discounts available for 1-day and 2 to 5-day excursions.

Voyageur Bus: 265 Catherine St. (238-5900), between Kent and Lyon. Service throughout Canada and the U.S. To: Montréal ($16.50); Toronto ($34); and New York ($98.35). Open daily 6am-12:30am.

OC Transpo: 294 Albert St. (741-4390), at Kent. Excellent, but somewhat complex bus system. Buses congregate at Rideau Centre, corner of Rideau and Nicholas. Operates daily 6am-12:30am. Fare 85¢. You can also buy a **Visibus** pass which allows you unlimited travel for 1 day on the green buses that tour the major points of interest in Ottowa and Hull, as well as travel during off-peak hours on the regular buses. ($2, children under 6 free, $5 for 5-person family.)

Car Rental: Rent-A-Wreck, 449 Gladstone (238-5595), at Kent. Cars from $19 per day, plus 9¢ per km. Insurance $8 for ages 21-24, $7 for ages 25 and up. Open Mon.-Fri. 8:30am-5:30pm, Sat. 8:30am-1pm. Must have major credit card.

Bike Rental: Rent-A-Bike-Location Velo, 1 Rideau St. (233-0268), behind the Château Laurier Hotel. Bikes from $9 per day. Tandem $20 per day. Open May to mid-Oct. daily 9am-7pm. Closed when raining.

Rider-Driver Matching Agency: Telelift, 402 Bank St. (234-9927). Open Tues.-Fri. 11am-6pm.

Help Line: Gayline-Telegai, 238-1717. Information and special events and meetings, as well as counseling services. Mon.-Fri. 7:30am-10:30pm.

Alcohol: Legal ages 19 (Ottawa) and 18 (Hull). Bars stay open in Ottawa until 1am, in Hull until 3am.

Post Office: Postal Station "A," 347 Dalhousie St. at George St. (992-4760). Open Mon.-Fri. 8am-6pm.

Area Codes: 613 (Ottawa); 819 (Hull).

Ottawa is 195km west of Montreal, 170km north of Kingston, and 395km north-east of Toronto. Driving from Montréal, take Hwy. 40 west to Hwy. 417, which leads to Ottawa. Drivers with an extra half-hour to spare might prefer to take scenic Hwy. 17 or Hwy. 148, which follow the banks of the Ottawa River. Highway 17 is accessible from Hwy. 417 just after the end of Hwy. 40 from Québec. Drivers from Toronto and Kingston should take Hwy. 401 east to Hwy. 16 north, and then follow Hwy. 16 to Ottawa.

The **Rideau Canal** divides Ontario into eastern and western sections. West of the canal, the main east-west artery, **Wellington Street,** is lined by Parliament buildings and many other government offices. East of the canal, Wellington St. becomes Rideau St., which is surrounded by a new fashionable shopping district. To the north of Rideau St. lies the **Byward Market,** a recently renovated shopping area and the focus for Ottawa's nightlife. **Bank Street,** which traverses the entire city and services the other, older shopping area, is the primary north-south street. **Elgin Street,** the other major north-south artery, stretches from the **Queensway (Highway #417)** to the War Memorial in the heart of the city in front of **Parliament Hill.** The canal is itself a major access route: in winter, thousands of Ottawa residents skate to work on the world's longest skating rink; in summer, power boats breeze by. The canal is lined by bike paths and pedestrian walkways that allow a pleasant alternative to transit by car or bus.

Across the Ottawa River lies **Hull,** Québec, most notable for its proximity to Gatineau Provincial Park and its many bars and discos that rock until 3am seven days per week. Hull is accessible by several bridges and the blue Hull buses from downtown Ottawa.

Accommodations and Camping

Clean, inexpensive rooms are not difficult to find in Ottawa, except during May and early June, when droves of high school students studying politics make a pilgrimage to the capital and fill budget lodgings to the brim.

Nicholas Gaol International Hostel (IYHF), 75 Nicholas St. (235-2595), near Daly St. in the heart of downtown Ottawa. Take bus #4 from the inter-city bus terminal or bus #95 west from the train station. Site of Canada's last hanging, this intriguing hostel now houses 4-8 guests in each of what were once Carleton County jail's cells. 160 rooms. Hot showers and kitchen, as well as extensive lounge facilities. Open daily 7am-midnight. Curfew 1am. $10, nonmembers $14.

University of Ottawa Residences, 100 Hastey St.(564-5400), at the end of College Lane. Contact University Housing Office at 100 Thomas More, on campus. Walking distance to downtown. 650 clean and indestructible modern rooms in a huge university dorm. Clean and indestructible modern rooms. Showers in shared bathrooms on each level. Singles $26.50. Doubles $35.50. Students with ID $12. Open May 5-Aug. 25.

Centre Town Guest House Ltd., 502 Kent St. (233-0681), just north of the bus station. Impeccably clean, if excessively perfumed. Singles $25. Doubles $35. For stays of a week or more, rooms are available in nearby houses at lower rates. Dec. 21-April $5 less. Breakfast and hot showers included. Reservations recommended. Walk-ins until 11pm.

Camp Lebreton, a field at the corner of Fleet and Booth. Urban camping within sight of the Parliament Buildings. Tent sites only. Washrooms, showers, and drinking water. 5-day max. stay. Open daily 8:30am-10:30pm, but you can return to camp after 10:30pm. Sites $5 per person.

Gatineau Park, northwest of Hull. Map available at visitors center. 3 rustic campgrounds within ½ hr. of Ottawa: Lac Philippe Campground, with facilities for family camping, trailers, and campers; Lac Taylor Campground, with 35 "semi-wilderness" sites; and Lac la Pêche, with 39 campsites accessible only by canoe. (Canoeing equipment $18 per day.) Each campground off Hwy. 366 northwest of Hull—look for signs. From Ottawa, take the Cartier-MacDonald bridge, follow Hwy. 5 north to Scott Rd., turn right to Hwy. 105 and follow it to 366. Camping permits ($12 per night) available at the information center just off Hwy. 366 on the road to Lac Philippe.

Food

Ottawa has little in the way of unique eats, save the **Beaver Tail,** a glorified piece of fried dough with toppings. Restaurants cluster in the **Byward Market** area centering around York and William; on Rideau, east of the canal; and on Bank and Elgin Streets west of the canal.

Nate's Deli, 316 Rideau St. (236-9696), a short walk east of the canal. Cooks up the best breakfast special in town—2 eggs, toast, sausage, bacon or ham, and coffee $1.75 (served Mon.-Fri. 7-11am, Sat.-Sun. 8-11am). Tasty deli sandwiches and express service. Open Mon.-Wed. 8am-2am, Thurs.-Sat. 7am-3am, Sun. 8am-3am.

Mexicali Rosa's, 207 Rideau St. (234-7044), at Waller St. A colorful Mexican restaurant boasting Ottawa's only "Texas wood-burning smoker." Entrees $4-9. 20% discount for youth hostel members. Open Mon.-Tues. 11:30am-10:30pm, Wed.-Thurs. 11:30am-11pm, Fri.-Sat. 11:30am-midnight, Sun. 4-10pm.

Malibu Jack's, 47 Clarence St. (594-9033), at Parent St. in the Byward Market area. In this self-proclaimed "California Food Epic," you may feel out of place without surfboard and Ray-bans. A jazzed-up burger and barbeque joint. Haight Ashbury pizza (sprouts, guacamole, cheese and tomato) $6. Open Mon.-Sat. 11:30am-1am.

Hitsman's Restaurant and Bakery, 1242 Bank (731-6111), at Chesley St. south of 417. Take one of the several buses that travel down Bank from downtown. An incredibly cheap sandwich shop and bakery. Sandwiches $2-3. Chocolate lovers should sample the 50¢ rumballs. Open Mon.-Thurs. 7:30am-5:30pm, Fri. 7:30am-7pm, Sat. 7:30am-5pm, Sun. 7:30am-3pm.

Café Crêpe de France, 76 Murray St. (235-2858). A cozy spot in the heart of the market area. Meat, vegetable and fruit crêpes, salads and omelettes, $7-10. Open Mon. 5:30-10pm, Tues.-Thurs. 11:30am-11pm, Fri.-Sat. 11:30am-midnight, Sun. 11am-10pm.

Mother Tucker's, 61 York St. (238-6525), by the Byward Market. Dimly-lit restaurant with glorious 60-item salad bar and huge entrees. Well worth saving both your money and appetite for a feast here. Lunch $4-6. Dinner $8-16. Open Mon.-Thurs. 11:30am-2:30pm and 4:30-10pm, Fri. 11:30am-2:30pm and 4:30-11pm, Sat. 11:30am-2pm and 4-11pm, Sun. 10:30am-2pm and 4-9:30pm.

Sights

Although Ottawa is the nation's capital, it remains a small city, so most major attractions can be reached on foot. **Parliament Hill** (992-6656), at the corner of Wellington and Metcalfe, is the focal point of the city and its primary tourist attraction. On these lush and spacious grounds stand the majestic **Parliament Buildings,** the nation's political nerve center. **Centre Block,** the main structure, is home to the **House of Commons,** the **Senate,** and the **Library of Parliament.** The **Peace Tower,** Canada's most visible political symbol, rises high above Centre Block (214 ft.) and offers visitors a panoramic view of the city. Free and worthwhile tours of the Parliament buildings, in both English and French, depart every 10 minutes from the Info-tent to the rear of Centre Block on the right. (Tours July-Sept. 9am-dusk; Sept.-June 9am-4:30pm.) Lovers of pageantry will adore the **Changing of the Guard,** ceremoniously presented on the broad lawns in front of Centre Block (June 23-Aug. 27 daily at 10am). At dusk, Centre Block and lawns are transformed into the set for *Sound and Light,* which relates the history of the Parliament buildings and the development of the nation. A five-minute walk west along Wellington St. is the **Supreme Court of Canada** (995-4330, ext. 220), where nine justices preside. One block south of Wellington, Sparks St. is home to one of North America's first pedestrian malls, hailed as an innovative experiment in 1960. The **Sparks Street Mall** was recently given a $5-million facelift.

East of the Parliament buildings at the junction of Sparks, Wellington, and Elgin stands **Confederation Square** and in its center the enormous **National War Memorial,** dedicated by King George VI in 1939. The towering structure symbolizes the triumph of peace over war, a somewhat ironic message considering the state of world affairs in 1939. The **Rideau Centre,** south of Rideau St. at Sussex Dr., is the city's primary shopping mall as well as the main bus depot.

The **Byward Market,** 2 blocks north of the Rideau Centre, is a bustling farmers market where artisans congregate to sell arts and crafts. **Nepean Point,** several blocks northwest of the Market by the Alexandra Bridge, provides a panoramic view of the capital. An open-air theater was constructed on Nepean Point in 1967.

Parks and Museums

Ottawa boasts a multitude of parks and recreational areas. The green spaces, walkways, and bike paths surrounding the canal are the city's largest and longest parklands. Those near the mouth of the canal, near the Parliament Buildings, provide incredible views. **Major Hill's Park,** behind the Château Laurier Hotel on the banks of the Ottawa, is the city's oldest park. Within it stands the **Noon Day Gun,** a relic from the Crimean War. The gun is fired daily at noon (except on Sun. when it resounds at 10am). **Dow's Lake** (232-1001), accessible by means of the Queen Elizabeth Driveway, is an artificial lake on the Rideau Canal, 15 minutes south of Ottawa. A popular recreation area year-round, Dow's Lake is ablaze with color in spring when 150,000 tulips bloom along its shore. Pedal boats, canoes, and bikes are available at the **Dow's Lake Pavilion,** just off Queen Elizabeth Driveway.

Ottawa is the headquarters of many of Canada's huge national museums. **The National Gallery** (990-1985) is in a spectacular glass-towered building at 380 Sussex Drive, adjacent to Nepean Point. Its exterior echoes in postmodern form the facing neo-Gothic buttresses of the Parliament Library. Inside, you'll find the world's most comprehensive collection of Canadian art, as well as outstanding European, American and Asian works. (Open May 1-Sept. 4 Tues.-Sun. 10am-6pm; Sept. 5-April

30 Tues.-Wed. and Fri.-Sun. 10am-5pm, Thurs. 10am-8pm. Admission $4, seniors and students $3, Thurs. free.) The **Canadian Museum of Civilization** is housed in a spaceship-like structure across the river in Hull, at 100 Laurier St. (994-0840). Exhibits from totem poles to the **Ciné Plus,** the first cinema in the world capable of projecting both Imax and Omnimax, offer a perspective on 10,000 years of human history in Canada. (Open June 29-Sept. 4 daily 10am-8pm; Sept. 5-May 18 Tues.-Sun. 10am-5pm; call for hours May 18-June 29. Admission $4, seniors and students $3, under 15 free.) The **National Museum of Natural Sciences** (996-3102) introduces visitors to the natural world with multi-media displays. (Open daily 9:30am-5pm; Sept. 5-April 30 daily 10am-5pm. Admission $2, seniors and students $1.50, ages 6-16 $1, under 6 free.)

The **Canadian War Museum,** 330 Sussex Dr. (992-2774), just north of St. Patrick, houses a fine collection of war art, medals, weaponry, and artifacts. (Open daily 10am-5pm. Admission $2, seniors and students $1, under 15 free.) The **Royal Canadian Mint,** 320 Sussex Dr. (992-2348), beside the War Museum, gives guided tours of the plant that manufactures Canada's currency. (Open Mon.-Fri. 8:30-11am and 12:30-3pm. Reservations recommended.) History enthusiasts could easily disappear in the **National Library and Public Archives,** 395 Wellington St. (995-7969 or 995-5138). The building houses enormous quantities of Canadian publications, old maps, photographs, and letters, as well as historical exhibits. (Library open Mon.-Fri. 8:30am-5pm. Exhibit area open daily 9am-9pm.)

Farther out of town, the **National Museum of Science and Technology,** 1867 St. Laurent Blvd. (998-4566), lets visitors explore the developing world of mechanics, transportation, and high technology with hands-on exhibits. Huge locomotives and train cars enliven the transportation exhibits. (Open May-Labor Day daily 10am-8pm; Sept.-April Tues.-Sun. 9am-5pm.) The **National Aviation Museum** (998-4566), at the Rockcliffe Airport off St. Laurent Boulevard north of Montreal St., illustrates the history of flying with more than 100 aircraft. (Open daily 10am-8pm.)

Entertainment

Ottawa's government fuels the "serious" artistic community with large grants, and visitors can reap the reward. The **National Arts Centre,** 65 Elgin St. (996-5051), home of an excellent small orchestra and theater company, frequently hosts international soloists and performing groups. **Odyssey Theatre** (232-8407) holds open-air shows at **Strathcona Park,** at the intersection of Laurier Ave. and Range Rd. well east of the canal. (Tickets $5, students $3, Sun. "pay what you can.") Dancers, musicians, and actors often add flair to Parliament Hill in summer. Also on Parliament Hill, roving groups of actors present historical vignettes at fairly random times and locations. Don't be surprised if you suddenly find yourself entangled in a wild political rally or an emotional legal case—you've merely stumbled into one of these intriguing skits.

Nightlife

The determined bar-hopper or disco-devotee heads across the river to Hull, where most establishments grind until 3am every day of the week, and the legal drinking age is 18. In Ottowa, the Byward Market area has most of the action. Ottawa clubs close at 1am (and on Sun.), but most, in an effort to keep people from going to Hull, offer free admission. **Stoney Monday's,** 62 York St. (236-5548), just west of William, is a trendy bar for people in their early to mid-20s. **Chateau Lafayette,** 42 York St. (236-5548), caters to an older, tougher clientele, but lures the budgeteer with $1 draft beer.

There are over 20 popular nightspots on *promenade du Portage* in Hull, just west of Place Portage, the huge government office complex. **Helium,** 75 promenade du Portage (771-0396), has it all: huge video screens, lights, a balcony for surveying the scene, good loud dance music, and plenty of people. **Chez Henri,** 179 promenade du Portage (777-2741), is a classier dance club with six bars and an older clientele. A tougher crowd congregates at **Le Zinc,** 191 promenade du Portage, and enjoys the large dance floor, loud music, and $2 schnapps, the house special. For something more peaceful, **Le Coquetier,** 147 Promenade du Portage (771-6560), is a great place to treat a friend to a glass of wine or beer.

Alberta

The icy peaks and torquoise lakes of Banff and Jasper National Parks preside as Alberta's most sought-after landscapes. But there is more to Alberta—plenty more farmlands, prairie, and oil fields, that is. Rural Alberta features kilometer after kilometer of untraveled roads, thousands of prime fishing holes, world-renowned dinosaur fossil fields, and intriguing remnants of Native American culture.

Practical Information

Emergency: 911.

Capital: Edmonton.

Visitor Information: Travel Alberta, 15th floor, 10025 Jasper Ave., Edmonton T5J 3Z3 (800-661-8888, in AB 800-222-6501). Information on Alberta's provincial parks can be obtained from **Recreation and Parks,** #1660, Standard Life Centre, 10405 Jasper Ave., Edmonton T5J 3N4 (427-9429). For information on the province's national parks (Waterton Lakes, Jasper, Banff, and Wood Buffalo), contact **Parks Canada,** Box 2989, Station M, Calgary T2P 3H8 (292-4440). The **Alberta Wilderness Association,** P.O. Box 6389, Station D, Calgary T2P 2E1, carries information on off-highway adventures.

Time Zone: Mountain (2 hr. behind Eastern). **Postal Abbreviation:** AB.

Area Code: 403.

Highway 16 connects Jasper with Edmonton, while the **Trans-Canada Highway** (Hwy. 1) runs right through Banff and then continues 120km (75 miles) east to Calgary. The extensive highway system facilitates bus connections. Use Calgary as a travel hub. **Greyhound** and **VIA Rail** run from Calgary to Edmonton to Jasper, as well as from Calgary to Banff. **Brewster** has an express bus running between Banff and Jasper. Calgary and Edmonton are home to Alberta's two major airports. You must leave the Trans-Canada Hwy. to explore rural Alberta—a feat easier said than done. **Hitchhiking** in rural Alberta is a hit-or-miss proposition. If you can get a lift, it'll probably last a long time, but you might have to wait an eternity between lifts. To reach out-of-the-way sights, consider renting a car from **Rent-A-Wreck,** a Canadian-based company that rents cars that aren't really wrecks for very reasonable rates.

From the glaciers of Jasper National Park to the huge lakes of northern Alberta, the Ice Age designed the province with the hiker, ice climber, canoeist, and bicyclist firmly in mind. Virtually every region of Alberta provides the setting for any outdoor activity; however, there are some "hot spots" for each. Hikers, mountaineers, and ice climbers will find the most, and the best, terrain in the mountains surrounding Banff and in Jasper National Park. Canoeing centers dot the lakes of northern Alberta and the Milk River in the south. Bicyclists love the Icefields Parkway, as well as the wide shoulders of most other Alberta highways. Consider bringing a mountain bike instead of the usual 10-speed. Some highway segments, such as the Trans-Canada between Banff and Calgary, have special bike routes marked on the right-hand shoulder of the road. The national parks have made an effort to improve the situation by setting up hostels between Banff and Jasper and by establishing campsites that accept only hikers and bicyclists. **Lone Pine Publishing,** 9704 106 St., Edmonton T5K 1B6, prints an extensive array of guides to exploring Alberta.

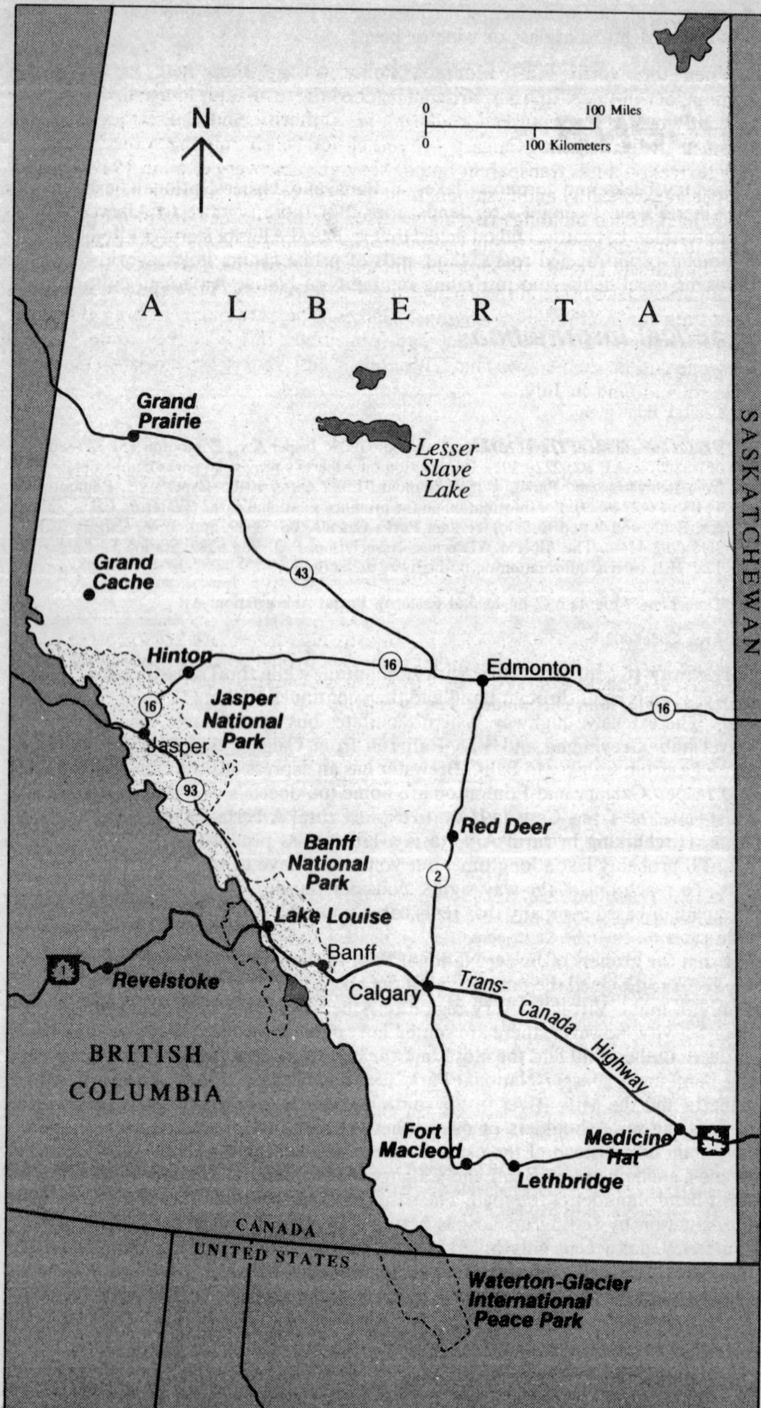
N
0
100 Miles
0
100 Kilometers
ALBERTA
SASKATCHEWAN
Grand Prairie
Lesser Slave Lake
Grand Cache
43
Hinton
16
Edmonton
16
16
Jasper National Park
Jasper
93
Red Deer
Banff National Park
2
Lake Louise
Banff
Revelstoke
Calgary
Trans-Canada Highway
BRITISH COLUMBIA
Fort Macleod
Medicine Hat
Lethbridge
CANADA
UNITED STATES
Waterton-Glacier International Peace Park

Calgary

When the North West Mounted Police set up shop here in the 1860s, Commander-in-Chief Ephrem Brisebois named the town after himself. He was subsequently ousted from power for abusing his authority, and Col. James MacLeod renamed the settlement "Calgary"—Scottish for "clear running water." The city now thrives on a less transparent liquid. Since the discovery of oil in 1947, Calgary has become a wealthy and cosmopolitan city—the oil may be crude, but the people are refined. Office buildings rise higher than the oil derricks, businessmen scurry about in three-piece suits toting leather briefcases, and a newly built transport system soundlessly threads through the immaculate downtown streets.

Calgarians take pride in their petroleum-subsidized city. They cling to memories of hosting the XVth Winter Olympic Games. They are quick to brag that their Flames captured the 1989 Stanley Cup (remember, this is hockey country). And everyone puts on their cowboy hats, Wranglers, and western accents when the Stampede rolls around in July.

Practical Information

Visitor Information: Calgary Tourist and Convention Bureau, 237 8th Ave. SE (263-8510), on the 2nd floor. Will help locate accommodations, especially around Stampede time. Open daily 8:30am-4:30pm. **Information booth** at the same address open June-Sept. daily 8am-7pm; Sept.-June Mon.-Fri. 8:30am-4:30pm. **Travel Alberta:** 455 6th St. SW (297-6574; in AB 800-661-8888), on the main floor. Open Mon.-Fri. 8:15am-4:30pm. **Trans-Canada Highway Office,** 6220 16th St. NE. Open daily 8am-9pm; Sept.-June 10am-5pm.

Calgary International Airport: (292-8400), is about 5km from the city center. Free shuttle buses service to the city is infrequent. The **Airporter Bus** offers frequent and friendly service for $6. Greyhound drops off close to the city center (about ½-hr. walk from downtown) and offers free shuttle buses to the C-Train. VIA Rail unloads passengers next door to the Calgary Tower, in the heart of downtown. Taxi fare is $19.

VIA Rail: 131 9th Ave. SW (265-8033, in AB 800-665-8630), at Centre St. Trains to Banff (1 per day, $16); and Vancouver (1 per day, $86). Tickets sold daily 9am-5pm. Full time students receive 1/3 off fares. Some restrictions apply.

Greyhound: 850 16th St. SW (260-0877 or 800-332-1016; reservations 265-9111). To Edmonton (8 per day, $20); frequent service to Banff ($9.25). Free shuttle bus from C-train at 7th Ave. and 10th St. to bus depot. 10% seniors discount.

Calgary Transit: Information and Downtown Sales Centre, 206 7th Ave. SW. Bus schedules, passes, and maps. Open Mon.-Fri. 8:30am-5pm. Buses and streetcars (C-Trains). Buses run all over the city (fare $1.25, ages 6-14 75¢, under 6 free; exact change required). C-Trains cover less territory, but you can ride them free in the downtown area (along 7th Ave. S.; between 10th St. SW and City Hall). Day pass $3.50, children $2. Book of 10 tickets $10, children $6.50. **Information line** (276-7801) open Mon.-Fri. 6am-11pm, Sat.-Sun. 8am-9:30pm.

Taxi: Checker Cab, 272-1111. **Red Top Taxi,** 250-9222. **Yellow Cab,** 250-8311.

Car Rental: Rent-a-Wreck, 2339 Macleod Trail (237-7093). Cars start at $30 per day with 100 free km, plus 11¢ each additional km. Open Mon.-Fri. 8am-7:30pm, Sat. 9am-5:30pm, Sun. 10am-5:30pm. Must be 21 with major credit card.

Bike Rental: Sports Rent, 7218 Macleod Trail SW (252-2055). 12-speeds $12 per day; mountain bikes $20 per day. **Abominable Sports,** 640 11th Ave. SW (266-0899). Mountain bikes $15 per day; mopeds $20 per day.

Help Line: Gay Lines Calgary, 223 12th Ave. SW (234-8973), on the 3rd floor. Recorded phone message provides gay community information; peer counseling available at the office. Phone and office open Mon.-Fri. 7am-10pm.

Post Office: 220 4th Ave. SE (292-5512). Label mail General Delivery, Station M, Calgary, AB T2P 2G8. Open Mon.-Fri. 8am-5:45pm. Postal Code: T2P 2G8.

Area Code: 403.

Calgary is an extremely well-planned city and a cinch for back-seat navigators. The city is partitioned into quadrants. **Centre Street** divides it east-west, and the **Bow River** (with the adjacent Memorial Drive, where the Bow starts bowing) divides the north from the south. Address numbers increase as you move away from these thoroughfares. You can always determine the cross-street from an avenue address by disregarding the last 2 digits: thus 206 7th Ave. is at 2nd St., and 2339 Macleod Trail is at 23rd St. Avenues run east-west, streets north-south.

Hitchhiking is illegal within the Calgary city limits; the law is enforced and punishable by a cruel $500 fine.

Accommodations

Cheap rooms in Calgary are plentiful except during the Stampede. While most of the places listed below don't raise their prices seasonally, reserve ahead for July.

Calgary International Hostel (IYHF), 520 7th Ave. SE (269-8239). Conveniently located several blocks south of downtown with access to C-Train and public buses. Complete with snack bar, meeting rooms, cooking and barbecue facilities, laundry, and a cycle workshop. Disabled access. Lockout 10am-5pm. Curfew midnight. Members $7, nonmembers $10.

University of Calgary, 3330 24th Ave. (220-3203), in the NW quadrant of the city. A little out of the way, but very accessible via bus #9 or the C-Train. Olympian-sized (literally) rooms for competitive prices. There's also a cafeteria and a pub on campus. Room rental office, in the Kananaskis Building, open 24 hours. Singles $22, doubles $30. Student rate: singles $15.75; shared rooms $10.50. Fewer rooms available in winter.

YWCA, 320 5th Ave. SE (263-1550). A deluxe place for women only, in a fine quiet neighborhood. A range of rooms. The security makes for a somewhat lifeless lodging. Cafeteria. Dorm beds $10. Singles $22, with bath $29.50. Sleeping bag space (summer only) $7.

St. Louis Hotel, 430 8th Ave. SE (262-6341), above the St. Louis Tavern. Depending on your point of view, the location means either excitement or danger. Not suggested for women. The few grim-looking long-term residents generally keep to themselves. Friendly management. Singles $15.75, with TV and bath $21. Doubles with bath and TV $26.25.

York Hotel, 636 Centre St. SE (262-5581). More central location and larger rooms than the St. Louis. Bath and cable TV included. Singles and doubles regularly cost over $40, but with a Greyhound ticket or receipt your first night's lodging is only $26. 20% discount for seniors.

Food

Finding a good, inexpensive place to eat is relatively easy in Calgary. Ethnic and cafeteria-style dining spots line the **Stephen Ave. Mall,** 8th Ave. S. between 1st St. SE and 3rd St. SW, and the indoor mini-malls nearby. Good, cheap food is also readily available in the **"Plus 15" skyway system.** Desinged to provide indoor passageways during bitter winter days, this bizarre mall connects the second floors of dozens of buildings throughout the city. You can join the system at any "participating" building; just look for the blue-and-white "Plus 15" signs on street level. For more expensive, trendy restaurants, go to the **Kensington District,** along Kensington Rd. between 10th and 11th St. NW.

Hang Fung Foods Ltd., 119 3rd Ave. SE (269-5853), located in the rear of a Chinese market with the same name. Enormous bowl of plain *congee* (rice broth) $1, with abalone and chicken $3. A heaping plateful of BBQ duck and steamed chicken on rice is $4. Bring your own silverware if you haven't mastered chopsticks. Open Mon.-Fri. 8:30am-9pm.

4th Street Rose, 2116 4th St. SW (228-5377). California cool pervades this fashionable restaurant on the outskirts of town: high ceilings, tile floors, and servers sporting jeans and short-sleeved shirts. Gourmet pizzas, homemade pasta, and fresh salads ($2.75-8). Take bus #3 or 53 and avoid the hike. Open Mon.-Thurs. 8am-midnight, Fri.-Sat. 10am-1am, Sun. 10am-1am.

Take Ten Cafe, 304 10th St. NW (270-7010). Light dining in Kensington with a German accent. The wiener schnitzel ($4.45) includes gravy, vegetable, and fries. Hungarian ghoulash $4. Homemade cakes and muffins. Open Mon.-Wed. 8am-5:30pm, Thurs.-Fri. 8am-7pm, Sat. 10am-4pm.

Bohemia Bistro, 124 10th St. NW (270-3116), near Kensington Rd. (on the 2nd floor). Bohemia in the original sense of the word—the region around Prague. Perhaps the most unusual of the Kensington district restaurants. An eclectic menu features unkosher kosher sandwiches ($6-7) and pastas ($7-8.50). Pick up a chocolate truffle on the way out $1. Open Tues.-Thurs. 11:30am-midnight, Fri.-Sat. 11:30am-1am.

Sights

The **Calgary Tower** (266-7171), 101 9th Ave. SW, presides over the city. Rather than simply gaze up at the spire, ride an elevator to the top ($2.75 round-trip, children $1) for a spectacular view of the Rockies on clear days. The 190m tower also affords a 360° view of the city.

The **Glenbow Museum,** 130 9th Ave. SE (264-8300), just across the street from the tower, is a nexus of cultural pride in this boomtown and an odd mix of modern art, military artifacts, and mineral samples. At the entrance are five cases of Olympic pins, the most extensive collection in town. (Open daily 10am-6pm. Admission $2, seniors 50¢, students and children $1; free on Sat.) Less than a block northeast of the museum, the **Olympic Plaza** still attracts crowds on sunny days. The site of the medal presentations during the Winter Games, this open-air park now hosts a variety of special events including Kids' Fest and the Calgary Jazz Festival (both in June). For an update on Olympic Plaza programming, call 268-4776 during business hours.

A short walk down 8th Ave. to the west will bring you to the home of **Devonian Gardens,** 4th floor Toronto Dominion Sq., 8th Ave. and 3rd St. SW. This 2.5-acre indoor garden contains fountains, waterfalls, bridges, and over 20,000 plants, including 138 different local and tropical varieties. (Open daily 9am-9pm. Free.) A few blocks to the northwest, the **Energeum,** 640 5th Av. SW (297-4293), in the lobby of the Energy Resources Building, is Calgary's shrine to fossil fuel. A film in the upstairs theater of this small but informative oil museum recreates the mania of Alberta's first oil find 1947. In a hands-on display, you can run your gloved hand through a pile of the oozing glop. (Open Sun.-Fri 10:30am-4:30pm; Sept.-May Mon.-Fri. 10:30am-4:30pm. Free.)

Farther west, about 4.3 light-years from Alpha Centauri, is the **Alberta Science Centre and Centennial Planetarium,** 11 St. and 7th Ave. SW. (Open Wed.-Sun. 1-9pm. Hands-on experiments here test the law of physics, and planetarium shows give you a close look at Jupiter (Open Wed.-Sun. 1-9pm. Most planetarium shows after 6pm. Admission to both planetarium and Science Centre $4, children $2; Science Centre only $2, children $1.)

St. George's Island is accessible by the river walkway to the east. The island is home to the **Calgary Zoo.** Try to visit in the late spring when many of the animals give birth to new attractions—the Australian mothers seem to be especially prolific. The zoo also features a **prehistoric park,** which takes you back in time some 65 million years, a **botanical garden,** and a **children's zoo.** (Open daily at 9am; closing time is seasonally adjusted. For more information, call Zooline, 262-8144. (Admission $5.50, seniors and ages 12-17 $3, under 12 $2. On Tues. $2.75, seniors free.)

The nearby **Fort Calgary Interpretive Centre** (290-1875) maps out Calgary's evolution from cowtown to oiltown with an exhibit hall and a comprehensive film. (Open year-round Wed.-Sun. 10am-6pm. Free.) The center is on 9th Ave. SE, just east of downtown; grab bus #1 ("Forest Lawn") eastbound.

Although the actual Olympic flame has long since extinguished in Calgary, retailers still carry the torch, offering hundreds of different forms of official Olympic merchandise at reduced prices. The more substantial and important legacies of the Games are several newly built, world-class athletic facilities—not only great arenas for recreation but also fascinating architectural sights. The two most impressive are the **Olympic Oval,** an indoor speed-skating track on the University of Calgary campus (hours vary from season to season; call 220-7890 for more information), and **Canada Olympic Park,** the site of the bobsled, luge, and ski jumping competitions. A guided tour of Olympic Park will cost you $5 (seniors and children $2), but take the plunge—the one-hour trip around includes a chance to stand in the bobsled track and to glance down the slope from atop the 90km ski jump tower. The **Olympic Hall of Fame,** (268-2632), also located in Olympic Park, reinforces the Olympic ideology with displays, artifacts, and videos. (Open daily 10am-5pm. Admission $6, seniors, students, and children $3.)

The Stampede

Even people who think that rodeo is grotesque and silly have trouble saying "Calgary" without letting a quick "Stampede" slip out. Somehow, it seems as though everyone envisions the city as wedded to "The Greatest Outdoor Show On Earth." Calgarians themselves are perhaps the most guilty of perpetuating this relationship. Every year around Stampede time, the locals throw free pancake breakfasts and paint every ground-level window downtown with cartoon cowboy figures offering misspelled greetings ("Welcum, y'all"). Capped by ten-gallons, locals command tour groups to yell "Yahoo" in the least likely of circumstances. Simply put, at Stampede time the entire city of Calgary wigs out.

And why not? Any event that draws millions from across the province, the country, and the world deserves the hoopla. Make the short trip out to **Stampede Park,** just southeast of downtown; those smart enough to arrive in July will get a glimpse of steer wrestling, bull riding, wild cow milking, and the famous chuckwagon races, where canvas-covered, box-shaped buggies whiz by in a chariot race that defies the laws of aerodynamics. (Tickets $9-31.) The Stampede also features a **midway,** where you can perch yourself atop the wild, thrashing back of a roller coaster.

Parking is ample, but the crowd is always more than ample in July, so take the C-Train from downtown to the Stampede stop. In 1990, the Stampede will run from July 6-15; in 1991, from July 5-14. For official information and ticket order forms, write Calgary Exhibition and Stampede, Box 1860, Calgary T2P 2K8, or call 800-661-1260. If you're in Calgary, visit **Stampede Headquarters,** 1410 Olympic Way, or call 261-0101 for more information.

Entertainment

After a long, hard day of counting barrels of crude, Calgarians knock down bottles of local brew along **"Electric Avenue,"** the stretch of 11th Ave. SW between 5th and 6th St. SW. Here several look-alike clubs swimm in neon, all spinning the same Top-40 music. Last call in Calgary is at 1:45am.

Bandito's, 620 11th Ave. (266-6441). The current favorite, but any of the joints along 11th Ave. will do. Drinks $3-4. Most open for lunch around 11am and stay open until somewhere past 2am.

Ranchman's Steak House, 9615 Macleod Trail S. (253-1100). One of Canada's greatest honkytonks. Experience Calgary's Wild West tradition firsthand, on the dance floor to the tune of live C&W tunes or in the not-so-subtle flavor of Calgary Stampede beer. Open Mon.-Sat. 7pm-2am.

The Stadium Keg, 1923 Uxbridge Dr. NW (282-0020). Where the "Dinos" from nearby University of Calgary eat, drink, and be merry. On Thurs. nights from 6-10pm, devour chicken wings (25¢ each) and wash them down with a mug of Big Rock ($1.25), the dark, delicious local brew. Open daily 4:30pm-1am or 2am.

Banff National Park

For natural splendor, you really can't do better than Banff. Snowcapped mountains and turquoise lakes are only two of the park's gorgeous physical features. Free-roaming wildlife are another attraction; moose rule the marshes of Bow River Valley and bighorn sheep reign on the rocky slopes.

Unfortunately, scores of tourists seem to have discovered this national treasure and overrun the park. The townsite is similar to resort towns such as Vail or St. Moritz; a deluxe suite at the Banff Springs Hotel costs $735 per night, plus $15 per pet. This is not to say that a less jet-set crowd doesn't exist as well. Bicyclists from around the world come to enjoy Banff's facilities. The Trans-Canada Hwy. has a large shoulder built as a bike path, while the older Hwy. 1A has less traffic and better access to campgrounds and hostels.

Practical Information and Orientation

Emergency: in Banff 762-2226, at Lake Louise 522-3811.

Visitor Information: Banff Information Centre, 224 Banff Ave. (762-4256). Open mid-May to mid-June 10am-6pm; mid-June to Sept. 8am-10pm; Sept.-Oct. 10am-6pm. **Lake Louise Information Centre** (522-3833). Open mid-June to Aug. daily 8am-10pm; mid-May to mid-June and Sept.-early Oct. 10am-6pm. **Park Headquarters:** Superintendent, Banff National Park, Box 900, Banff T0L 0C0 (762-3324).

VIA Rail: At the intersection of Lynx and Elk St. (800-665-8630 or 762-3255), in the northwest corner of Banff Townsite. To: Lake Louise (4:25pm, 45 min., $8); Calgary (12:15pm, 2 hr., $14); Vancouver (20½ hr., $65); and Montreal (2 days, $238). No trains to Jasper.

Greyhound: operates out of the Brewster terminal. To: Lake Louise (5 per day, $6.15) and Calgary (6 per day, $9.20). The Lake Louise buses continue to Vancouver ($55).

Brewster Transportation: 100 Gopher St. (762-2286), near the train depot. Specializes in tours of the area, but runs 1 express daily to Jasper ($24). Depot open daily 7am-midnight.

Car Rental: Banff Used Car Rentals, corner of Wolf and Lynx (726-3352). $34 per day. 100km free, 10¢ each additional km. Must be over 21 with a credit card. Also, **Avis,** 209 Bear St. (762-3222). $44 per day. 100km free, 19¢ each additional km. Ask about IYHF member discount.

Other Rentals: Mountain Mopeds, in the Sundance Mall (762-5611). $8.50 per hr., $30 per ½ day, $45 per day. Open daily 10am-8pm. Must have ID. **Spoke 'n' Edge,** 315 Banff Ave. (762-2854). 3-, 5-, and 10-speed bicycles. $2.50 per hr., $10 per day; mountain bikes $4 per hr., $16 per day.

Post Office: Buffalo and Bear St. (762-2586). Open Mon.-Fri. 9am-5:30pm. **Postal Code:** T0L 0C0.

Area Code: 403.

Banff National Park adjoins the Alberta-British Columbia border, 120km west of Calgary. The **Trans-Canada Highway** (Hwy. 1) runs east-west through the park. Both Greyhound and VIA Rail connect the park with major points in British Columbia and Alberta. Civilization in the park centers around the twin townsites of Lake Louise and Banff, 55km to the southeast. Buses and the daily train are expensive; if you're hitching, expect plenty of competition.

Accommodations, Camping, and Food

Over 20 residents of the townsite offer rooms in their own homes—many year-round, and the majority in the $20-40 range. Just ask for the *Banff Private Home Accommodation* list at the Banff Townsite Information Centre. The local **YWCA,** (762-3560) also opens its doors to travelers, both male and female. Although not well-decorated, their rooms are spacious and affordable. (Singles $18. Doubles $24-32. Bunk rooms from $10.)

Banff International Hostel (IYHF), Box 1358, Banff T0L 0C0 (762-4122), 2 miles from Banff Townsite on Tunnel Mountain Rd., among a nest of condominiums and lodges. The look and setting of a chalet, but when full, the feel of an overstuffed warehouse. A hike from the center of the townsite, but worth it for the modern amenities and friendly staff. Ski and cycle workshop, laundry facilities, disabled access. Clean quads with 2 bunk beds; linen provided. $9, nonmembers $14. Open 6-10am and 4pm-midnight.

Hilda Creek Hostel (IYHF), 8.5km south of the Icefield Centre on the Icefields Parkway. Features a tiny primitive sauna. In the morning, guests must replenish the water supply with a shoulder-bucket contraption that will give you an appreciation for the agility of the peasant farmer. Accommodates 21. $5, nonmembers $6. Closed Thurs. night.

Rampart Creek Hostel (IYHF), 34km south of the Icefield Centre. Wood-heated sauna. Accommodates 30. $5, nonmembers $6. Closed Wed. night.

Mosquito Creek Hostel (IYHF), 103km south of the Icefield Centre and 26km north of Lake Louise. Fireplace and sauna. Accommodates 38. $5.50, nonmembers $6.50. Closed Tues. night.

Corral Creek Hostel (IYHF), 5km east of Lake Louise on Hwy. 1A. The hostel nearest Lake Louise. Accommodates 50. $5, nonmembers $6. Closed Mon. night.

Castle Mountain Hostel (IYHF,) on Hwy. 1A (762-2637), 1.5km east of the junction of Hwy. 1 and Hwy. 93. Recently renovated. Accommodates 36. $6, nonmembers $8. Closed Wed. night.

Banff's popularity keeps "campgrounds full" signs up, and none of the park sites accept reservations, so arrive early. Many campgrounds reserve sites for bicyclists and hikers; inquire at the office. Some campgrounds raise rates during the "premium period" (late June-Labor Day); rates range from $7.50 to $11.50. Park facilities include (listed from north to south): Waterfowl Lake (116 sites), Lake Louise (221 sites), Protection Mountain (89 sites), Two Jack Main (381 sites), Two Jack Lakeside (80 sites), and Tunnel Mountain Village (622 sites).

Bring along your favorite recipes for campfire cooking, and you'll eat well here. Otherwise, you'll pay high prices for mediocre food. The International Hostel and the YWCA, however, serve affordable meals. The hostel's cafeteria serves up a great breakfast special (egg, cheese, and bacon on a kaiser roll with coffee, $1.75; served 7-9am), as well as decent dinners (5-7pm). The **Spray Cafe,** at the Y, boasts an even bigger breakfast deal: two eggs, bacon, hashbrowns, and toast for $2.75. Burgers served at lunch. (Open 8am-3pm Thurs.-Tues.)

Coriander Nature Food, in the Sundance Mall, upper level, on Banff Ave. (762-2878). This place even smells healthful thanks to freshly-cut lilacs at each table. Take a break from that burger diet with Mexican beans and rice in a pita ($3, with tofu $4.50). Pick up some vitamins and trail mix on your way out. Open Mon.-Sat. 10am-6pm, Sun. 11:30am-5:30pm.

Joe Btfsplk's Diner, 221 Banff Ave. (762-5529). Dubbed after a *L'il Abner* character, the name of this diner may be hard to pronounce (bi-TIF-spliks), but you'll be speechless when you see the sandwiches on fresh-baked bread ($5-7). The meatloaf blue plate special with all the fixin's ($8.50) will keep your stomach happy well into tomorrow. Open daily 8am-11pm.

Sights and Activities

Hike to the **backcountry** for privacy, beauty, and trout that bite anything. The pamphlet *Drives and Walks* covers both the Lake Louise and Banff areas, describing both day and overnight hikes. In order to stay overnight in the backcountry, you need a permit, available free from park information centers and park warden offices. All litter must be taken out of the backcountry with you; in addition, no wood may be chopped in the parks. Both the International Hostel and the Park Information Centre have copies of the *Canadian Rockies Trail Guide,* an excellent, in-depth source of information and maps.

Canada's first national park (and the world's third), Banff was founded in 1885 as Hot Springs Reserve, featuring the **Cave and Basin Hot Springs** nearby. In 1914, a resort was built at the springs. The refurbished resort, now called the **Cave and Basin Centennial Centre** (762-4900), screens documentaries and stages exhibits. Relax in the hot springs pool, watched over by lifeguards in pre-World War I bathing costumes, or explore the original cave. The center is southwest of the city on Cave and Basin Rd. (Center open daily early June-Sept. 10am-8pm; Sept.-early June 9am-5pm. Pool open early June-Sept. only. Admission to pool $2, ages 3-16 $1.25.) If you find Cave and Basin's 90°F (32°C) water too cool, try the **Upper Hot Springs pool,** a 104°F (40°C) cauldron up the hill on Mountain Ave. (Cooler in spring during snow run-off. Open June-Sept. daily 8:30am-11pm. Admission $2, under 12 $1.25.) Bathing suit rental at either spring is $1, towel rental and locker rental 25¢.

Taking a gondola to the top of a peak saves your legs for hiking at the summit. The **Sulphur Mountain Gondola** (762-2523), located right next to the Upper Hot Springs pool, affords a good view of Banff Townsite, and offers a $3 "early bird" breakfast special. (Open Nov. 15-Dec. 15 and in summer daily 9am-8pm. Fare $8, under 12 $4.) The **Sunshine Village Gondola** (762-6555) climbs to the resort village, at 7200 feet. (Open June 27-Sept. 7 Mon.-Thurs. 8:30am-7:30pm, Fri.-Sun. 8:30am-10:30pm. Fare $6, under 12 $3.) If that's not high enough for you, jump on the **Standish Chairlift,** which will carry you to the peak, almost 7900 feet up.

If you'd prefer to look up at the mountains rather than down from them, all the nearby lakes will provide a serene vantage point. **Moraine** (near Lake Louise) and **Two Jack** (near Banff) Lakes can be explored by boat and canoe. On Two Jack Lake, rowboats cost $8.50 per hour, $42.50 per day; canoes $8 per hour, $40 per day, with a $20 deposit. (Open July-Aug. daily; June Sat.-Sun. only.) On Moraine Lake, rent a canoe for $10 per hour with a $20 deposit. (522-3733. Open daily in summer 9am-sundown.) **Fishing** is legal virtually anywhere you can find water, but you must hold a national parks fishing permit, available at the information center ($5 for a 7-day permit, $10 for an annual one). And after you catch your 10-pound trout, bring it to a restaurant and ask them to cook it up for you; many restaurants will provide this service for about $10.

The hilly road leading to Lake Minnewanka provides **cyclists** with an exhilarating trip, as do many other small paths throughout the park. Bicycling is also allowed on most trails in the Banff Townsite areas. Remember, however, to dismount your bike and stand to the downhill side if a horse approaches. Also be forewarned that the quick and quiet bicycle is more likely to surprise bears than hikers' tromping.

Horseback riding is the true grit of the Wild West, sure 'nough. Rates are almost identical throughout the park, so pick your favorite location, pardner.

North American filmmakers often use **Lake Louise's** crystal waters framed by snow-capped peaks as a substitute for Swiss alpine scenes. Rent a canoe from **Chateau Lake Louise Boat House** (522-3511) for $12 per hour; binoculars to scan the hills for wildlife cost $3. Several hiking trails begin at the lake. If you aim for one of the two teahouses (at the end of the 3.4km Lake Agnes Trail and the 5.3km Plain of Six Glaciers Trail), be prepared to pay dearly for your meal, since all the food must be brought up on horseback. (Teahouses open in summer daily 9am-6pm.) The **Lake Louise Gondola** (522-3555), which runs up Mt. Whitehorn across the Trans-Canada Hwy. from the lake, provides another chance to ooh and aah at the landscape. (Open mid-June to late Sept. daily 9am-6pm. Fare $6.50, ages 5-11 $3.25. "One-way hiker's special" $4.)

After a long day of hiking and biking, knock back a few at one of Banff's rocking bars. Each night, a different place hosts "Locals Night" with drinks for $1.75. For culture afficianados, Banff offers the **Banff Festival of the Arts,** a summer-long event featuring drama, ballet, opera, and jazz. Pick up a brochure at the Visitor Information Center or call 762-6300 for details.

Icefields Parkway

A glacier-lined, 230-kilometer road connecting Lake Louise with Jasper Townsite, the Icefields Parkway (Hwy. 93) snakes past dozens of ominous peaks and glacial lakes. Wise drivers and cyclists set aside at least three days for the parkway. The challenging hikes and endless vistas just get better and better. All points on the parkway are within 30km of at least one place where you can roll out your sleeping bag.

Before setting your wheels (2 or 4) on the road, pick up a free map of the Parkway, available at park information centers in Jasper and Banff. The pamphlet is also available at the **Icefield Centre,** to the side of the parkway at the boundary between the two parks. The center sits in sight of the **Athabasca Glacier,** the most prominent of the eight glaciers that stem from the 325-square-kilometer Columbia Icefield.

Jasper National Park

Jasper boasts the same natural wonders and outdoor opportunities as Banff, minus the ritz and glitz of its southern neighbor. The town is small, the locals are friendly and down-to-earth, and the surroundings consist of 10,000 square kilometers of breathtaking nature.

Practical Information and Orientation

Emergency: 852-4848.

Visitor Information: Park Information Centre, 500 Connaught Dr. (852-6176). Trail maps and information on all aspects of the park. Open June 14-Labor Day daily 8am-6pm; in spring and fall daily 9am-5pm. **Travel Alberta,** 632 Connaught Dr. (in AB 800-222-6501). Open May-Oct. daily 8am-7:30pm. **Jasper Chamber of Commerce,** 634 Connaught Dr. (852-3858). Open Mon.-Fri. 9am-5pm. **Park Headquarters,** Superintendent, Jasper National Park, Box 10, Jasper T0E 1E0 (852-6161).

VIA Rail: 314 Connaught Dr. (800-665-8630 or 852-4102). To: Vancouver (1 per day, 16 hr., $70); Edmonton ($39); and Winnipeg ($141). Seniors and students with ID 1/3 off. Station open Mon.-Sat. 7:30am-10:30pm, Sun. 7:30-11am and 6:30-10:30pm.

Greyhound:314 Connaught Dr. (852-3926), in the VIA station. To: Edmonton (3 per day, $24.80) and Kamloops ($34.90).

Brewster Transportation and Tours: Also in the VIA station CNR depot (852-3901). To Banff (full-day tour $42, daily 5½-hr. express $24) and Calgary (1 per day, 8 hr., $31).

Car Rental: Jasper Car Rental, 626 Connaught Dr. (852-3373). $50 per day, seniors and students $40. 100 free km, 19¢ each additional km. Reduced rates for multi-day rental. Must be 21 with credit card.

Bike Rental: Free Wheel Cycle, 600 Patricia St. (852-5380). Enter through the alley behind Patricia St. Mountain bikes (preferable for this terrain) $4 per hr., $10 per ½ day, $17 per day. Also 10- and 15-speeds. Open July 1-Labor Day Mon.-Sat. 9am-8pm, Sun. 10am-8pm; April-July 1 and Labor Day-Oct. 9am-6pm. Must have valid ID, and place a deposit. **Whistler's Youth Hostel** also rents mountain bikes. IYHF members $8 per ½ day, $14 per day. Nonmembers $10 per ½ day, $16 per day.

Post Office: 502 Patricia St. (852-3041), across Patricia St. from the townsite green. Open July-Aug. Mon.-Fri. 9am-5pm, Sat. 9am-3pm; Sept.-June Mon.-Fri. 9am-5pm. **Postal Code:** T0E 1E0.

Area Code: 403.

All of the above addresses are in Jasper Townsite, which sits near the middle of the park, 362km southwest of Edmonton and 287km north of Banff. **Highway 16** shuttles travelers through the park north of the townsite, while the **Icefields Parkway** (Hwy. 93) connects to Banff National Park in the south. Buses run to the townsite daily from Edmonton, Calgary, and Vancouver. Trains arrive from Edmonton and Vancouver. Arrange a ride between Banff and Jasper if you are hitching, as most cars traveling between the two parks are jammed with tourists and backpacks. Renting a bike is the most practical option for short jaunts within the park.

Accommodations, Camping, and Food

Ask for the **Approved Accommodations List** at the Park Information Center if you wish to sleep cheaply in Jasper (singles $20-25, doubles $25-35, triples $35-40, quads $30-55). If you prefer mingling with the youthful set, head to a hostel (listed below from north to south). Reservations, as well as information on closing days and on the winter "key system," are channeled through the Edmonton-based Southern Alberta Hostel Association (439-3089).

Maligne Canyon Hostel (IYHF), on Maligne Canyon Rd., 15km northeast of the townsite. Accommodates 24. $4, nonmembers $6. Closed Wed.

Whistlers Mountain Hostel (IYHF), on Sky Tram Rd.(852-3215), 7km south of the townsite. Closest to the townsite, this is the park's most modern (and crowded) hostel. A hike from town, mostly uphill. The management shuts off the lights at 11pm sharp and flicks them on again at 7am. You may have to sweep out the fireplace before you leave in the morning, but at least it works. Accommodates 50. $6, nonmembers $9.

Mount Edith Cavell Hostel (IYHF), on Edith Cavell Rd., off Hwy. 93A. Accommodates 32. The road is closed in winter, but the hostel welcomes anyone willing to ski or snowmobile the 11km from Hwy. 93A. $4, nonmembers $6. Open mid-June to mid-Sept. Fri.-Wed.; mid-Dec. to mid-April Fri.-Tues.

Athabasca Falls Hostel (IYHF), on Hwy. 93, 30km south of Jasper Townsite, near the namesake Falls. $4.50, nonmembers $7. Closed Tues.

Beauty Creek Hostel (IYHF), on Hwy. 93, 78km south of Jasper Townsite. Beautifully located next to a brook. Accommodates 20. Accessible through a "key system" in winter. $4, nonmembers $6. Open May to mid-Sept. Thurs.-Tues.

For campground updates, tune in to 1450 AM on your radio near Jasper Townsite. The park maintains sites at 10 campgrounds, including (north to south): Whistlers (781 sites), Wapiti (345 sites), Wabasso (238 sites), Columbia Icefield (22 sites), and Wilcox Creek (46 sites). Rates range from $6 to $14.

Your best bet for cheap eats is to stock up at a local market or bulk foods store and head for the backcountry. For around-the-clock grocery supplies, stop at the **Red Rooster Food Store,** 605 Patricia St. **Nutter's,** also on Patricia St., offers grains, nuts, dried fruits, and (if you're sick of healthful food) candy, all in bulk form. They also sell deli meats, canned goods, and fresh-ground coffee. (Open Mon.-Sat. 9am-10pm, Sun. 10am-9pm.) For a sit-down meal, try **Mountain Foods and Cafe,** 606 Connaught Dr. (852-4050). The menu features sandwiches, soups, and desserts. (Open daily 8am-10pm.) **The Red Dragon** (852-3171), in the Athabasca Hotel, has the cheapest Chinese cuisine in town. Eat in or take out an order of egg foo yung or shrimp chow mein (either $6). (Open daily 7am-midnight for breakfast, lunch, and dinner. Winter hours daily 8am-10pm.)

Sights and Activities

An extensive trail network connects most parts of Jasper, with many paths starting at the townsite. Information centers distribute free copies of *Day Hikes in Jasper National Park* and a summary of the longer hikes.

Mt. Edith Cavell, named after a WWI hero, often thunders with the sound of avalanches off the Angel Glacier. Take the 1-mile loop trail or the 5-mile return **Path of the Glacier.** Mt. Edith Cavell is 18 miles south of the townsite on Cavell Rd. **Maligne Lake,** the largest glacier-fed lake in the Canadian Rockies, has vivid turquoise water. One special feature of Jasper National Park is **Medicine Lake,** 18 miles east of Jasper Townsite. Water flows into the lake, but there is no visible outlet. The trick? The water flows out through a series of underground caves, and emerges in such areas as **Maligne Canyon,** 7 miles east of the townsite on Maligne Canyon Rd. Another natural phenomenon, this canyon is over 150 feet deep, and squirrels can jump across the narrow gorge. Humans cannot, though; several squirrel-wannabees have proven this by falling to their deaths.

Joining the Banff tradition, Jasper has a **gondola** of its own. Rising 1½ miles up the side of Whistlers Mountain, the Jasper Tramway affords majestic views of the park, as well as an opportunity to spend money at its gift shops and restaurant. (Fare $7, under 12 $3.50. Open mid-June to mid-Aug. daily 8am-10pm; mid-Aug. to Labor Day daily 8am-9pm; mid-April to mid-June daily 9am-5pm. Call 852-3093 for more information.) A trail starting from the Whistlers Mountain Hostel also leads up the slope, but it's a steep 10km, and to spare your quadriceps you'll want to take the tram ride down ($3.50). But no matter which way you go, be sure to bring along a warm coat and sunglasses to combat the rapidly-changing climate at the peak.

Guided trail rides are available for high prices. One-and-a-half-hour rides cost $20 at the Jasper Park Lodge (852-5794), 3 miles north of the townsite on Hwy. 16. Guided rides at Pyramid Lake are $9 per hour (852-3562).

British Columbia

Larger than California, Oregon, and Washington combined, British Columbia attracts so many visitors year-round that tourism is ranked as the province's second largest industry (after timber). The million flowers of Victoria and the million people of Vancouver draw city slickers, while the graceful lakes of the nearby Okanagan Valley lure those intent on escaping civilization. B.C., Canada's westernmost province, covers over 350,000 square miles, bordering four U.S. states (Washington, Idaho, Montana, and Alaska) and three other Canadian provinces (Alberta, the Yukon, and the Northwest Territories). The difficulty of road travel throughout the province varies with the immensely diverse terrain. If you decide to take your own vehicle, be sure to avoid potential hassles by obtaining a Canadian non-resident Interprovince motor vehicle **liability card** from your insurance company before leaving. (Border police may turn you away for not being properly insured.) In the south, roads are plentiful and well paved, but further north, the asphalt (and the towns) seems to have been blown away by the arctic winds.

Practical Information

Capital: Victoria.

Visitor Information: Ministry of Tourism and Provincial Secretary, Parliament Buildings, Victoria V8V 1X4 (604-387-1642). Write for the accommodations guide, which lists prices and services for virtually every hotel, motel, and campground in the province. In the U.S., write **Tourism BC,** P.O. Box C-34971, Seattle, WA 98124-1971. Branches also in **San Francisco,** 100 Bush St., #400, San Francisco, CA 94104 (415-981-4780); and **Irvine,** 2600 Michelson Dr. #1050, Irvine, CA 92715 (714-852-1054). **Canadian Parks Service,** Senior Communications Officer, 220 4th Ave. SE, P.O. Box 2989, Station M, Calgary AB T2P 3H8, or call **BC Parks** at 387-5002.

Time Zone: Pacific (3 hr. behind Eastern) and Mountain (2 hr. behind Eastern). **Postal Abbreviation:** B.C.

Alcohol: Drinking age 19.

Vancouver

Canada's third largest city comes as a pleasant surprise to the jaded, metropolis-hopping traveler. Its 1.4 million residents display big-city sophistication but small-town friendliness and courtesy. The city's transit system is fast and efficient, the streets are clean and well planned, and even the seediest-looking areas are generally safe. Nearby, towering mountains, vast expanses of rocky beach, and a profusion of parks provide plenty of excitement for the outdoorsy types. In short, Vancouver is an extraordinarily "livable" combination of big city action and small town attitudes.

Practical Information

Visitor Information: Travel Infocentre, 1055 Dunsmuir (683-2000), near Burrard, in the West End. Includes currency exchange. Open daily 8:30am-6:30pm. **B.C. Transit Information Centre:** 261-5100.

Vancouver International Airport: on Sea Island 7 miles south of the city center. Connections to major cities. To reach downtown from the airport, take Metro Transit bus #100 to 70th

ALASKA
UNITED STATES
CANADA
0 100 200 Miles
0 100 200 Kilometers
Dawson City
Yukon
Territory
1
Kluane
National
Park
NORTHWEST
TERRITORIES
Whitehorse
1
Alaska
Watson
Lake
Highway
Juneau
Cassiar
ALASKA PANHANDLE
Cassiar Highway
Fort
Nelson
97
37
British
Columbia
Ketchikan
97
16
Dawson
Creek
Queen
Charlotte
Islands
Prince
Rupert
Fort
McLeod
ALBERTA
Prince
George
16
Jasper
National
Park
Wells Gray
Provincial
Park
Banff
National
Park
Revelstoke
Cache
Creek
Salmon
Arm
N
Vancouver
Island
Kamloops
1
Glacier
National
Park
Trans-
Canada
Highway
Okanagan Lake
Vancouver
Victoria
Penticton
UNITED STATES
CANADA

Ave. Transfer there to bus #20, which arrives downtown heading north on the Granville Mall.

Trains: VIA Rail Canada, 1150 Station St. (800-665-8630), off Rte. 99 (Main St.) at 1st Ave. To: Banff (1 per day, $75); Calgary (1 per day, $86); and Jasper (1 per day, $70). Open daily 9am-6pm. **B.C. Rail,** 1311 W. 1st St. (984-5246), just over the Lions Gate Bridge in North Vancouver. Take the SeaBus downtown to North Vancouver, then bus #239 west. To: Garibaldi ($9), Williams Lake ($44.50), Prince George ($61), Whistler ($11), and Squamish and points north daily. Open daily 7am-9pm.

Buses: Greyhound, 150 Dunsmuir (662-3222), downtown at Beatty St. Service to the south and across Canada. To: Calgary (4 per day, $65); Banff (4 per day, $62); Jasper (3 per day, $61); and Seattle (7 per day, $24). Open daily 5:30am-midnight. **Pacific Coach Lines:** 150 Dunsmuir (662-3222). In cooperation with Greyhound, serves southern B.C., including Vancouver Island. To Victoria ($16.50, including ferry).

B.C. Ferries: Ferries to Victoria, the Gulf Islands, Sunshine Coast, Inside Passage, Prince Rupert, and the Queen Charlotte Islands. Vancouver general information 669-1211; recorded information 685-1021; Tsawwassen ferry terminal 943-9331. Mainland to Vancouver Island ($4.75, car and driver $22, motorcycle and driver $12.75, bicycle and rider $6.85; ages 5-11 ½-price). The terminal serving Victoria is actually located in Swartz Bay, north of Victoria. (See Victoria Getting There for more information.)

Gray Line Tours: 900 W. Georgia St. (681-8687), in Hotel Vancouver. Expensive but worthwhile city tours with a number of package options. Basic tours leave daily and last 3½ hr. (fare $27.50, children $14). Call for reservations.

Local Transit: see below.

Car Rental: Rent-A-Wreck, 1015 Burrard St. (688-0001), in the West End, or 1085 Kingsway (876-5629) at Glen. From $17 per day plus 10¢ per km. (Open Mon.-Fri. 8am-9pm, Sat. 8am-6pm, Sun. 9am-5pm. Kingsway location open Mon.-Fri. 8am-7pm, Sat. 9am-5pm.) Must be 25 with credit card.

Help Lines: Vancouver Crisis Center, 733-4111. 24 hours. **Rape Crisis Center,** 875-6011. 24 hours. **Gay and Lesbian Switchboard,** 1-1170 Bute St. (684-6869). Open Mon.-Fri. 7-10pm, Sat.-Sun. 4-10pm. **Seniors Information and Support,** 531-2320 or 531-2425.

Time Zone: Pacific (3 hr. behind Eastern).

Post Office: 349 W. Georgia St. (662-5725). Open Mon.-Fri. 8am-5:30pm. **Postal Code:** V6B 3P7.

Area Code: 604.

Vancouver is located in the southwestern corner of mainland British Columbia, across the Georgia Strait from Vancouver Island and the city of Victoria. Vancouver is divided into regions and neighborhoods by rivers, inlets, and bays. Bridges and boats abound and the profusion of waterways can confuse even the most diligent map-reader. Most of the city's attractions are concentrated on the city center peninsula and the larger rhino snout to the south. Many neighborhoods, as the residents perceive them, are not labeled on the city maps issued by Tourism B.C. The residential area of the city center peninsula, bounded by downtown to the east and Stanley Park to the west, is referred to as the **West End.** The western portion of the southern peninsula from around Alma Ave. to the University of British Columbia campus is **Point Grey,** while the central area on the same peninsula, from the Granville Bridge roughly to Alma Ave., is the Kitsilano, (familiarly known as **"Kits"**).

There is no rhyme or reason to the distinction between streets and avenues. The one exception to this madness is the numbered streets, which are always avenues in Vancouver proper (running east-west), and always streets in North Vancouver (running whichever way they choose). Downtown, private vehicles are not allowed on the **Granville Mall,**between Nelson and W. Pender. Both **Chinatown,** running east-west between Hastings and East Pender, from Garrel Ave. to Gore Ave., and **Gastown,** on Alexander as it runs into Water St., are easily reached on foot from the Granville Mall.

Vancouver's **Metro Transit** covers most of the city and suburbs, with direct transport or easy connecting transit to the city's points of departure: Tsawwassen, Horseshoe Bay, and the airport. You can ride in Metro Transit's central zone one way for $1.25 (seniors and ages 5-11 65¢) at all times. During peak hours (6:30-9:30am and 3-6:30pm), it costs $1.75 (seniors and ages 5-11 90¢) to travel through two zones. During off-peak hours, passengers pay only the one-zone price. Day-passes are $3.50, and transfers are free. Single fares, passes, and transfers are good for the SeaBus and SkyTrain, as well as the bus. Schedules are available at 7-11 stores, public libraries, city halls, community centers, and the Vancouver Travel Infocentre (see Practical Information). Metro Transit's **SeaBus** runs from the Granville Waterfront Station, at the foot of Granville St. in downtown Vancouver, to the Lonsdale Quay at the foot of Lonsdale Ave. in North Vancouver. The fares are the same as one-zone bus fares, and all transfers and passes are accepted.

Driving in Vancouver is a serious hassle, and finding parking spaces downtown is next to impossible. Consider leaving your car at the **Park'n'Ride** in New Westminster. (Exit Hwy. 1 and follow signs for the Pattullo Bridge; watch for signs just over the bridge.) Rush hour begins at dawn and ends at sunset. Beware of the 3pm to 6pm restrictions on left turns and parking on the streets. If you can't find parking at street level, look for underground lots, but be prepared to pay exorbitant prices. Try the lot below Pacific Centre at Howe and W. Georgia.

Accommodations and Camping

Greater Vancouver has a well-developed network of bed and breakfast accommodations; average rates are about $25 for singles and $35 for doubles. The visitors bureau has a long list of B&Bs in Vancouver. Several private agencies also match travelers with B&Bs, usually for a fee; get in touch with **Town and Country Bed and Breakfast** at 731-5942 or **Best Canadian** at 738-7207. Always call for reservations at least two days in advance.

Vancouver International Hostel (IYHF), 1515 Discovery St. (224-3208), in Point Grey on Jericho Beach. Turn north off 4th Ave. and follow signs for Marine Dr. Take bus #4 from Granville St. downtown. Beautiful location on beach and park, with a superb view of the city from False Creek. Over 350 beds, massive dorm rooms, small but well-equipped cooking facilities, and TV room. 8 family rooms. In summer, 3-day max. stay. Midnight curfew strictly enforced. Open daily 7-10am and 4pm-midnight. $10, nonmembers $12. Linen $10 (sleeping bags permitted).

Vincent's Backpackers Hostel, 927 Main St. (682-2441 or 254-7462), right next to the VIA train station, 2 blocks from the Main St. SkyTrain station. Not quite as clean or as structured as the IYHF hostel, but has more atmosphere, is cheaper, and is walking distance from downtown. Kitchen, fridge, TV, stereo, and the lulling sounds of revving Greyhound engines. Office open 8am-midnight. Check-in before noon for the best chance at a bed. Shared rooms $8. Singles with shared bath $16. Doubles with shared bath $20.

YWCA, 580 Burrard St. (662-8188), downtown at Dunsmuir, 7 blocks from the bus depot. Women, couples, and families only; no male visitors allowed upstairs. Recently remodeled and clean. High-quality sports facilities for female guests over 15 (free). Kitchens on every other floor, and cafeteria in basement. 4-week max. stay. Staff on duty 24 hours, but building locked at midnight; buzz for entry. Some singles smaller than others, so ask to see a few before choosing. Singles $31. Doubles $46. Additional bed $10. 10% discount for YWCA members, seniors, and groups. Weekly and monthly rates available from Sept.-June.

YMCA, 955 Burrard (681-0221), between Smithe and Nelson, 4 blocks south of the YWCA. Newly renovated, with a friendly staff, on duty 24 hours. Shared washrooms and showers. Pool, gymnasiums, ball courts, and weight rooms (free). Cafeteria open Mon.-Fri. 7am-4pm, Sat. 8am-2pm. Singles $27. Doubles $46. Additional cot $7. Weekly and monthly rates available Oct.-April.

Sylvia Hotel, 1154 Gilford St. (681-9321), 2 blocks from Stanley Park in a quiet residential neighborhood. Magnificent singles $40. Doubles $48. Additional cots $8. Reservations recommended.

Richmond RV Park, 6200 River Rd. (270-7878), near Holly Bridge in Richmond. Take Hwy. 99 to Westminster Hwy., then follow the signs. Sites offer little privacy, but the great showers and friendly staff are sure to soothe your woes. Sites $13, with hookup $13-20. Open April-Oct.

ParkCanada 4799 Hwy. 17 (943-5811), in Delta, about 20 miles south of downtown Vancouver. Take Rte. 99 south to Tsawwassen Ferry Terminal Rd., then go east for 1½ miles. The campground, located next to a giant waterslide park, has flush toilets and free showers, though the lines may be long. Sites $11.50.

Food

Steer clear of places specializing in "authentic Canadian cuisine," as nobody really knows what Canadian cuisine is. The city's best offerings are the diverse ethnic restaurants and the older natural-foods eateries. The East Indian neighborhoods along Main and Fraser and 49th St. offer spicy dishes of the subcontinent. Vancouver's **Chinatown** is the second largest in North America, after San Francisco's. Here groceries, shops, and restaurants cluster around East Pender and Gore St. The **Granville Island Market,** under the Granville Bridge, off W. 4th Ave. and across False Creek from downtown, intersperses trendy shops, art galleries, and restaurants with produce stands that sell local and imported fruits and vegetables. Take one of the many buses that run south on Granville and cross the Granville Bridge; get off at W. 4th St. and walk back 6 blocks down the hill. Otherwise, stay on the bus to Broadway and Granville Exchange and change to bus #51; it will take you directly to the island. (Market open daily 9am-6pm, Labour Day-Victoria Day (late May) Tues.-Sun. 9am-6pm.)

The Naam, 2724 W. 4th Ave. (738-7151) in the Kits area. Take bus #4 or 7 from Granville. Vancouver's oldest natural-foods restaurant, the Naam is a delight for both the fanatic and the indifferent. Very good tofu-nut-beet burgers ($4.25), spinach enchiladas ($8), and salad bar ($1.10 per 100 grams). Open 24 hours.

Isadora's Cooperative Restaurant, 1540 Old Bridge Rd. (681-8816), on Granville Island, 1 block to your right immediately after entering the shopping area. This natural-foods restaurant sends surplus funds to community service organizations. Sandwiches $7, dinner entrees $10, Bamfield burger made with filet of rock sole $6.25. Open Mon.-Thurs. 7am-10pm, Fri. 7am-11pm, Sat. 9am-10pm. Closed Mon. evenings in winter.

Did's Pizza, 622 Davie St. (681-7368), near Seymour. The graffiti and loud music belie the tame clientele. The east-coast style pizza is excellent, with just the right amount of semi-coagulated grease. $2.75 per slice regardless of toppings. Open Mon.-Sat. 11am-3:30am, Sun. 5pm-1am.

The Souvlaki Place, 1807 Mortan St. (689-3064), at Denman, near Stanley Park. Genuine Greek establishment with an inspiring view of English Bay. *Souvlaki* $4.25, yogurt, honey and pita $2.75. Open daily 11:30am-11pm.

The Only Seafood Cafe, 20 E. Hastings St. (681-6546), at Carrall St. on the edge of Chinatown, within walking distance of downtown. Large portions of great seafood at decent prices. They've been around since 1912, and they *still* don't have a rest room. Fried halibut steak $8. Open Mon.-Thurs. 11am-9:30pm, Fri.-Sat. 11am-10pm.

The Green Door, 111 E. Pender (685-4194), in central Chinatown, 3 blocks from The Only. Follow the alley off Columbia St. to find the hidden entrance. This wildly green establishment plays a prominent role in the annals of Vancouver hippie lore. Huge, slightly greasy servings of Chinese seafood $5.50. Open daily noon-10:30pm, Oct.-May Wed.-Mon. noon-10pm.

A Taste of Jamaica, 941 Davie St. (683-3464), downtown. Reggae, Jamaica posters, and red, green, and yellow seat covers. Filling and authentic food. Oxtail stew $6, goat or lamb curry $6, blended banana/carrot drink $2.50. Open Mon.-Sat. 11am-11pm, Sun. 5-11pm.

Nick's Spaghetti House, 631 Commercial Dr. (254-5633), on the main drag of the Italian district. Take bus #20. An old restaurant with new management. Standard Italian food in a traditional atmosphere. Great spaghetti $8.50. Open Mon.-Thurs. 11:30am-11pm, Fri. 11:30am-midnight, Sat. 4pm-midnight, Sun. 4-10pm.

Sights

The landmark of the Expo '86 World's Fair is a 17-story, metallic, geodesic sphere in the former main Expo grounds, which houses **Science World,** 1455 Quebec St. (687-7832), at Terminal Ave. Science World features hands-on exhibits for children and the **Omnimax Theatre** (875-6664), a high-tech hemispheric screen-house. Featured film subjects range from dinosaurs to asteroids. (Admission to the museum *or* to Omnimax movies is $6, seniors and under 18 $4.50. Open daily 10am-6pm.) The second expo site is the Canada Pavilion, now called **Canada Place,** about 1 mile away. It can be reached by SkyTrain from the main Expo site. Visitors who make this four-minute journey are treated to Canadian arts and crafts as well as films in the CN IMAX Theatre (682-4629). Ranging in price from $5.50 to $8, the not-so-cheap thrills in these movies are certainly impressive on the 5-story flat screen, but not quite so stunning as the domed screens of other IMAX theatres. (Open daily noon-9pm.)

Downtown, the **Harbour Centre Observation Deck,** 555 W. Hastings St. (683-5684), is actually worth the admission price for the 360° view of the city and surrounding areas. Plaques point out the world's narrowest building (6 ft. thin) and historic or unusual skyscrapers. To reach the tower, take Hastings St. 2 blocks west from Gastown. (Admission $3, seniors and students $2.50. Open daily 9am-10pm.) The **Vancouver Art Gallery,** 750 Hornby St. (682-5621), in Robson Square, has a small but well-presented collection of classical and contemporary art and photography. Free tours for large groups are frequently given; just tag along. (Open Mon.-Wed. and Fri.-Sat. 10am-5pm, Thurs. 10am-9pm, Sun. noon-5pm. Admission $2.75, seniors and students $1.25. Free Thurs. 5-9pm.)

Gastown is a revitalized turn-of-the-century district viewed with disdain by most Vancouverites as an expensive tourist trap. The area is named for "Gassy Jack" Deighton, the glib con man who opened Vancouver's first saloon here in 1867. It's jam-packed with craft shops, boutiques, nightclubs, and restaurants. Many cater exclusively to tourists, but the whole area is still enjoyable, especially along **Water Street.** Listen for the continent's only steam-powered clock on the corner of Cambie and Water St.—it chimes every 15 minutes. Gastown is a fair walk from downtown or a short ride on bus #22 along Burrard St. to Carrall St. It is bordered by Richards St. to the west, Columbia St. to the east, Hastings St. to the south, and the waterfront to the north.

Just east of Gastown, **Chinatown** is within walking distance of downtown. You can also take bus #22 on Burrard St. northbound to Pender St. at Carrall St., and return by bus #22 westbound on Pender St. Vancouver's Chinatown spreads out along Pender St. and both sides of Main St., replete with restaurants and shops. The area is rundown and some consider it unsafe. At night, women traveling alone should exercise caution. A safer (albeit more expensive) way to see Chinatown is through Gray Line Tours (see Practical Information).

Probably the most popular of the city's attractions, **Stanley Park** (681-1141) is on the westernmost end of the city center peninsula. (Take bus #19.) The watery perimeter is followed by a **seawall promenade,** with more views, and more company to the walker or cyclist. Within the park's boundaries lie various restaurants and tennis courts, the Malkin Bowl (an outdoor theater), and equipped beaches. Nature walks are given daily in the summer. Call the park for times and departure points. **Bike rentals** are available at the park entrance across from the bus stop (676 Chilco St.; 661-5581). 5-speeds cost $5 per hour or $20 per day, while mountain bikes cost $6 per hour or $25 per day. (ID and $20-30 deposit required.) Strange aquatic species lurk at the **Vancouver Aquarium** (682-1118), on the eastern side of the park, not far from the entrance. (Open daily 9:30am-8pm; in off-season 10am-5:30pm. Admission $5.75, seniors and ages 13-18 $4.75, under 12 $3.25.) Stanley Park's small, free **zoo** next door is worth visiting just to see the green monkeys pelt the neighboring harbor seals with apple cores. (Open daily 10am-5pm.)

Follow the western side of the seawall south to **Sunset Beach Park** (738-8535), a strip of grass and beach that extends south all the way to the Burrard Bridge. All of Vancouver's beaches have lifeguards from Victoria Day to Labor Day daily from 11:30am to 9pm. At the southern end of Sunset Beach is the **Aquatic Centre,** 1050 Beach Ave. (689-7156), a public facility with a 50m indoor saltwater pool, sauna, gymnasium, and diving tank. (Open Mon.-Thurs. 6:30am-10pm, Sat. 8am-9pm, Sun. 10am-9pm; pool opens Mon.-Thurs. at 7am. Gym use $3, pool use $2.15.)

Kitsilano Beach, known to locals as **"Kits,"** on the other side of Arbutus Ave. from Vanier, is a favorite beach among Vancouverites. It is equipped with a heated salt water outdoor pool (731-0011; open in summer only). The pool has changing rooms, lockers, and a snack bar. (Beach open daily 7am-8:45pm; Oct.-May Mon.-Fri. noon-8:45pm, Sat.-Sun. and holidays 10am-8:45pm. Admission to the pool $1.35, seniors and children 70¢, families $2.70.)

Jericho Beach, to the west, tends to be less heavily used than Kits Beach. Jericho begins a border of beaches and park lands that lines Point Grey and the University of British Columbia. Old-growth forest covers much of the extensive UBC campus in a delightfully untailored fashion. Bike and hiking trails cut through the campus and around the edges. The university rests on a hill, providing lovely views of the city and the surrounding mountains.

Scrambling down the cliffs to the southwest of the campus will take you to **Wreck Beach,** an unofficial, unsanctioned, unlifeguarded beach for folks who will stop at nothing to achieve that all-over body tan. Any UBC student can point you toward one of the semi-hidden access paths.

Entertainment

To keep abreast of the entertainment scene, pick up a copy of the weekly *Georgia Straight* (an allusion to the body of water between mainland B.C. and Vancouver Island), free at newsstands and record stores. The 25¢ *Westender* lists entertainment in that lively neighborhood and also reports on community issues, while the free *Angles* serves the city's gay community.

Blarney Stone Inn, 216 Carrall St. (687-4322). Live Irish music, restaurant, and dance floor. Lunch $5, dinner around $12. Open Mon. 11:30am-5pm, Tues.-Fri. 11:30am-2am, and Sat. 5pm-2am. Cover $3.

Town Pump, 66 Water St. (683-6695), a few blocks away from the Blarney Stone in the center of Gastown. Nightly live music from jazz to reggae. Clientele ranges from college students to business people. Snack menu available all day, burgers $6. Open Mon.-Sat. 11:30am-2am, Sun. 11:30am-midnight.

The Railway Club, 579 Dunsmuir St. (681-1625). Lively jazz sessions Sat. 3-7pm. Get there before the band in the evening and avoid the cover charge. Open Mon.-Sat. noon-2am, Sun. 7pm-midnight.

Castle Pub, 750 Granville St. (682-2661). Quieter than many of the other gay and lesbian pubs. Frequently sponsors benefit receptions for local charities. Open Mon.-Sat 10am-midnight.

Robson Square Media Centre, 800 Robson St. (660-2487), sponsors events almost daily during the summer and weekly the rest of the year, either on the plaza at the square or in the center itself. Their concerts, theater productions, exhibits, lectures, symposia, and films are all free or at low cost. The center's monthly brochure *What's Happening at Robson Square* is available from the visitors bureau or businesses in the square.

Vancouver also has an active theater community. The **Arts Club Theatre,** Granville Island (687-1644), hosts big-name theater and musicals, and the **Theatre in the Park program,** in Stanley Park's Malkin Bowl, has a summer season of musical comedy. Call 687-0174 for ticket information. The annual **Vancouver Shakespeare Festival** (June-Aug. in Vanier Park) often needs volunteer ushers and program-sellers, who may then watch the critically acclaimed shows for free. Call 734-0194 for details.

Both the **University of British Columbia (UBC)** and the **Simon Fraser University (SFU)** have full schedules of cultural activities. The **SFU Centre for the Arts** (291-3514) offers both student and guest-professional theater, primarily from September to May. For **UBC's** activities, call Public Events Information at 228-3131 or pick up a free copy of *Ubissey.* UBC's film series screens high-quality movies Thursday and Friday nights for $1.50.

Vancouver's Chinese community celebrates its heritage on **Chinese New Year** (usually in early Feb.). Fireworks, music, parades, and dragons highlight the celebration. The famed **Vancouver Folk Music Festival** is held in mid-July in Jericho Park, where for three days North America's best big- and little-name performers give concerts and workshops. Tickets can be purchased by the event, or for the whole weekend. Buy a whole-weekend ticket before June 1 to receive a $5 discount. For more details, contact the festival at 3271 Main St., Vancouver V6V 3M6 (879-2931).

Also in mid-July, the **Vancouver Sea Festival** (684-3378), schedules four days of parades, concerts, sporting events, fireworks, and salmon barbecues in English Bay.

Near Vancouver

Puff along on the **Royal Hudson Steam Locomotive,** operated by 1st Tours (688-7246). After a two-hour tour along the coast from Vancouver to Squamish (the gateway to Garibaldi Provincial Park), passengers are granted 1½ hours to browse in town before they head back. (Excursions May 21-July 16 Wed.-Sun.; July 19-Sept. 4 daily; Sept. 6-Sept. 24 Wed.-Sun. Fare is $24, seniors and youths $20, children $14.) The train departs from the B.C. Rail terminal, 1311 W. 1st St., across the Lions Gate Bridge in North Vancouver. Call 1st Tours for required reservations.

To the east, the town of **Deep Cove** has the atmosphere of a fishing village. Sea otters and seals gather on the pleasant Indian Arm beaches. Take bus #210 from Pender to the Phibbs Exchange on the north side of Second Narrows Bridge. From there, take bus #211 or 212. **Cates Park,** at the end of Dollarton Hwy. on the way to Deep Cove, has popular swimming and scuba waters and is a good destination for a day bike trip out of Vancouver. Bus #211 also leads to beautiful **Mount Seymour Provincial Park.** Trails leave from Mt. Seymour Rd., and a paved road winds the 5 miles to the top. One hundred campsites (sites $7) are available, and the skiing is superb.

For a less vigorous hike that still offers fantastic views of the city, head for **Lynn Canyon Park.** The suspension bridge here is free and uncrowded, unlike its more publicized look-alike in Capilano Canyon. Take bus #228 from the North Vancouver Seabus terminal and walk the ¼ mile to the bridge.

A classic trip farther outside Vancouver is the two-hour drive up Rte. 99 to the town of **Whistler** and nearby **Garibaldi Provincial Park.** Follow Rte. 99 north from Horseshoe Bay, or take local **Maverick Coach Lines** (255-1171). **B.C. Rail** (see Getting There) also serves Whistler from Vancouver; their run stops directly behind the local youth hostel (see below). Check the ride board at the International Youth Hostel in Vancouver, as trekkers frequently travel between the two. Whistler Mountain is considered top skiing, with the highest accessible vertical drop in North America. Slopes for the beginner and intermediate are also available. For more information contact Whistler Resort Association, Whistler V0N 1B0 (932-4222). The park also offers some fine wilderness hiking but vehicle access is out of the question. On Alta Lake in Whistler is a pleasant **IYHF youth hostel** (932-5492), which has 35 beds, a living room, cafeteria, but unfortunately no kitchen. ($8, nonmembers $10.50; in off-season $10.50, nonmembers $25.)There is also a **backpackers hostel** (associated with Vincent's in Vancouver) at 2124 Lake Placid Rd. (932-1177), near the train station. Shared rooms start at $15, and the hostel has kitchen and laundry facilities.

Victoria

British Columbia's capital will remind you of its imperial and imperious namesake. The one-and-a-half hour ferry trip between Vancouver and Victoria imitates an English Channel crossing; as you step ashore in the Inner Harbour, you will be greeted by double-decker buses, many adorned with British flags. In kilt and sporran, a bagpiper plies his street trade at the corner of the Parliament Buildings, stately stone edifices worthy of the English Assembly, not some "bloody colonial government." The ivy-shawled Empress Hotel, also named for Queen Victoria, gazes regally at its own image reflected by the waterside. Tea shoppes are more prevalent than hockey pucks in Victoria; on warm summer days, residents sip their noon teas on the lawns of Tudor-style homes in the suburbs, while downtown, horse-drawn carriages clatter through Bastion Square.

The first stop for every visitor should be the **Royal British Columbian Museum,** 675 Belleville St. (387-3701; recorded message 387-3014). Considered by most to be the best museum in Canada, it chronicles the geological, cultural and economic histories of the province. The displays on Native American cultures are especially good. In the summer, fascinating free films aobut British Columbia's heritage run in the museum's Newcombe Theatre. (Open May-Sept. daily 9:30am-7pm; Oct.-April daily 10am-5:30 pm. Admission $5, seniors, disabled persons, students with ID, and ages 13-18 $3, children 6-12 $1. Films run 11am-3:30pm.) Behind the museum, **Thunderbird Park** is a striking collection of totems and longhouses, backed by the intricate towers of the Empress Hotel. Also on the museum grounds, **Helmcken House**, a Heritage Conservation building, dates from 1852. Originally the home of Dr. John Helmcken, the medic for Fort Victoria, the house still displays many of the family's furnishings and some of the doctor's medical instruments. (Open Wed.-Sun. 10am-4pm. Free.)

Across the street from the front of the museum are the imposing **Parliament Buildings,** 501 Belleville St. (387-6121), home of British Columbia's government since 1859. The buildings feature several obsolete (and, for various reasons, illegal) provincial seals. Free tours every 20 minutes (off-season every hour) daily 9am-5pm.

South of the Inner Harbour, **Beacon Hill Park** has beautiful views over the Strait of Juan de Fuca. Take bus #5. The park, with flower gardens, 350-year-old garry oaks, and a network of paths, is a perfect picnic spot. One mile east of the Inner Harbour, **Craigdarroch Castle,** 1050 Joan Crescent (592-5323), is a product of Victorian wealth. (Take bus #11 or 14.) The house was built in 1890 by Robert Dunsmuir, a B.C. coal and railroad tycoon, in fulfillment of the promise that tempted his wife away from their native Scotland. His former home is packed with Victoriana, and the interior detail is impressive. (Open in summer daily 9am-7:30pm; in winter daily 10am-5pm. Admission $3, seniors and students $2.50.)

Nearby, the **Art Gallery of Greater Victoria,** 1040 Moss St. (384-4101), has a fine contemporary collection, including the works of many Asian-Canadian artists. Take bus #10, 11, or 14. (Open Mon.-Sat. 10am-5pm, Thurs. 10am-9pm, Sun. 1-5pm. Admission $3, seniors and students $2.) Stay on bus #11 out to Oak Bay Ave. and stop at the Blethering Place for tea (see below) or continue out to **Willow's Beach,** along Beach Dr., a somewhat rocky but otherwise pleasant spot. Windsurfing is popular in the protected bay; equipment can usually be rented from trucks along the beach for about $10 per hour.

The stunning **Butchart Gardens,** 14 miles north of Victoria (652-4422 9am-5pm; recorded message 652-5256), were begun by Jennie Butchart in 1904 in an attempt to reclaim the wasteland that was her husband's quarry and cement plant. The gardens are a maze of pools and fountains. (Gardens open May-June and Sept. daily 9am-9pm; July-Aug. daily 9am-11pm, March-April and Oct. daily 9am-5pm, Jan.-Feb. and Nov. daily 9am-4pm; Dec. daily 9am-8pm. Admission $8.50, ages 13-17 $4, ages 5-12 $1; off-season prices vary—the more flowers, the more bucks. Take bus #74. Motorists should consider an approach to Butchart Gardens via the **Scenic Marine Drive,** following the coastline along Dalles and other roads for a total of 45 minutes. The route passes through pleasant suburban neighborhoods and offers a memorable view of the Olympic Mountains across the Strait of Juan de Fuca.)

Pick up a copy of *Monday Magazine,* the free news and entertainment weekly, for a complete listing of Victoria's evening activities. Jazz, blues, country, rock, and folk all get playtime. The **Victoria Symphony Society,** 846 Broughton St. (385-6515), performs regularly under conductor Peter McCoppin, and the **University of Victoria Auditorium,** Finnerty Rd. (721-8480), houses a variety of student productions. The **Pacific Opera** performs at the McPherson Playhouse, 3 Centennial Sq. (386-6121), at the corner of Pandora and Government St. During the summer, they undertake a popular musical comedy series. Keep in mind, as well, that on Tuesdays movies throughout Victoria cost a mere $3.50 (rather than the usual $7).

Victoria's predilection for the old ways is perhaps best evidenced by the way it eats. Victorians actually do take tea some only on occasion, others every day. Other foods exist, of course, but to indulge in the romanticism of the city, you must participate in the ceremony at least once. **The Blethering Place,** 2250 Oak Bay Ave. (598-1413), in upright Oak Bay at Monterey St., is a superb tearoom frequented by sensible, elderly Oak Bay residents. Afternoon tea, served with scones, Devonshire cream tarts, English trifle, muffins, and sandwiches baked on the premises, is yours for $5.50. Coffee is served in the morning, of course. For another taste of Old England, try the steak and kidney pie at lunch for $6. (Dinners $10. Open daily 8am-10pm.)

Contrasting with the old-world charm of tea shoppes is a Californian wave of chic sidewalk cafes, bagel delis, and frozen yogurt parlors between Wharf and Government St. If you have kitchen facilities and don't feel like brewing tea, head down to **Fisherman's Wharf,** at Superior and St. Lawrence St. On summer mornings, you can buy the day's catch straight off the boats. The **Green Machine,** at Douglas and 4th St. (382-5108), has fresh produce. **Floyd and Floyd's Flying Rhino Diner,** 1219 Wharf St. (381-5331), just down the street from Tourism B.C. and Bastion Sq., offers vegetarian sandwiches ($4-6), homemade soups, and if you're lucky, special nutburgers ($6). (Open Mon.-Fri. 8am-8pm, Sat. 10am-6pm, Sun. 10am-4pm.) At **Lin Heung,** 626 Fisgard St. (385-1632), in Chinatown, just across from the police station, Victorians wait in line for pork buns straight from the oven. The seafood is fresh and plentiful. (Open Wed.-Mon. 11am-9pm.) **Las Flores,** 536 Yates St. (386-6313), is a Mexican jumping bean's hop from the hostel. Filling and authentic burrito/enchilada combos for $8.

The cheapest bed in Victoria is the **Victoria Youth Hostel (IYHF),** 516 Yates St. (385-4511), at Wharf St. downtown. (Kitchen facilities. 102 beds. 2 family rooms with 4 beds each. Open 7:30-10am and 4pm-midnight. $10, nonmembers $15.) The **Salvation Army Men's Hostel,** 525 Johnson St. (384-3396), at Wharf St., is modern, immaculate, and well run. (Men only. Dorms open daily at 4pm on a first come-first serve basis. Strict 11pm curfew; ask for a late pass. Dorm beds $6, with meals $13.50.) The **YWCA,** 880 Courtney St. (386-7511), is within easy walking distance of downtown. (Women only. Heated pool and private rooms with shared baths. Check-in 11am-6pm. Check-out 6-11am. Singles $21. Doubles $34.) The **Battery Street Guest House,** 670 Battery St. (385-4632), 1 block in from the ocean between Douglas and Government St. has singles from $25 and doubles from $40. The **James Bay Inn,** 270 Government St. (384-7151), at Toronto St., is near everything, but quiet and relatively inexpensive nonetheless. Light and airy rooms have phone, TV, and soft beds. (Reservations necessary July-Sept. Singles $31, with shared bath. Doubles $40, with private bath $52.)

The few campgrounds on the city perimeter cater largely to RV drivers who are willing to pay dearly. Be forewarned that many campgrounds fill up in July and August, so make reservations if you want a site then. **McDonald Park** (655-9020), less than 2 miles south of the Swartz Bay Ferry Terminal, 18 miles north of downtown on Rte. 17, is not even slightly rural. (No showers. Sites $6.) **Thetis Lake Campground,** 1938 Trans-Canada Hwy. (478-3845), 6 miles north of the city center, serves traffic entering Victoria from northern Vancouver Island. The sites are peaceful and removed, maybe too removed—it's a long walk to the bathroom. (Sites $9, with hookup $12. 50¢ each additional person.)

Before you set out to explore, you might want to stop by the visitors center, **Tourism Victoria,** 812 Wharf St. (382-2127), in the Inner Harbour. There you can also pick up transit maps and the *Rider's Guide,* which lists bus routes to major tourist spots. **Victoria Regional Transit** (382-6161) serves the whole city, with major bus connections at the corner of Douglas and Yates St. downtown. Travel in the single-zone area for 85¢, in the multi-zone (north to Sidney and the Butchart Gardens) for $2. Daily passes for unlimited single-zone travel are available at the visitors center and at 7-11 convenience stores for $3 seniors and under 12 $2).

The city of Victoria is centered on the Inner Harbour; **Government Street** and **Douglas Street** are the main north/south thoroughfares. Traditional tourist attractions crowd this area, and locals are few and far between. Residential neighborhoods form a semicircle around the Inner Harbour, the more desirable and moneyed toward the beaches to the east.

On Vancouver Island's southern tip, Victoria is connected by ferry and bus to many cities in British Columbia and Washington State. **B.C. Ferry** (386-3431) runs between the Tsawwassen terminal, south of Vancouver, and Swartz Bay, 20 miles north of Victoria. (Ferry runs 7am-9pm. 14 per day. Fare $4.75.) Ferries also operate between Horseshoe Bay, just above Vancouver, and the town of Nanaimo, 72 miles north of Victoria. (Ferry runs 7am-9pm. 10 per day. $4.75.) Pacific Coach Lines and VIA Rail both serve Victoria from Nanaimo. **Washington State Ferries** (381-1551 or 656-1531) connect Victoria to the San Juan Islands and Anacortes, WA. Their pier is in Sidney, 3 miles south of Swartz Bay. (2 per day, 1 in winter. Fare $7.50, car and driver $35.) **Black Ball Transport,** 430 Belleville St. (386-2202), runs from Port Angeles, WA, on the Olympic Peninsula, to Victoria's Inner Harbour. ($6.80, car and driver $27.80, children 5-11 $3.40.) **B.C. Stena Line,** 390 Belleville St. (386-1124), runs cruise ships (either *Princess Marguerite* or *Vancouver Island Princess*) daily between the Inner Harbour and Seattle, WA. (2 per day, 1 in winter. $29 one way, $39 round-trip.) Victoria's **bus depot** is at 710 Douglas St., at Belleville, behind the Empress Hotel. **Pacific Coast Lines** (385-4411) goes to Vancouver (16 per day, $16.50), Seattle (1 per day, $25), and Nanaimo (7 per day, $10.50). **Greyhound** (385-5248) serves northern B.C.

Victoria's **time zone** is Pacific (3 hr. behind Eastern). The **post office** is at 1230 Government St. at Yates St. (Open Mon.-Fri. 8:30am-5pm.) The **postal code** is V8W 2L9; the **area code** is 604.

Okanagan Valley

Known throughout Canada for its bountiful fruit harvests, the Okanagan Valley lures visitors with summer blossoms, sleepy towns, and tranquil lakes. The cities' Native American names bespeak the Okanagan's quiet heritage. Although high-powered tourists will be bored by the long stretches of empty road and the slow Okanagan pace, the valley is the place for the subtler pleasures of camping, driving along lake-lined highways, buying fruit at a family stand, sampling wines at a local winery, or fishing in one of the bountiful lakes.

Penticton

Native American settlers named the area wedged between the Okanagan and Skaha Lakes *Pen-tak-tin,* "a place to stay forever." Today, budget travelers may find it a strain to spend a weekend in Penticton, let alone forever. But beyond all the glitz, commercialization, and high prices, it is Penticton's natural beauty that attracts so many to its shores. The warm, clean water and sprawling beaches of the Okanagan and Skaha Lakes are ideal for sunning, swimming, sailing and fishing.

Sail Inland (492-2628 or 493-8221) arranges cruises, charters, and lessons. **The Marina,** 293 Front St., Box 460 (492-2628), offers rentals of ski boats and fishing equipment. **Roli's** (493-0244), rents windsurfers next to the Penticton Lodge for $11 per hour. The **Casabella Princess,** 45 E. Lakeshore Dr. (493-5551), gives pleasant paddlewheel cruises on the Okanagan for less active water-worshipers.

Although hard-core budget travelers to Penticton may have to swallow their pride and settle for McDonald's or Burger King, the **Sunshine Sandwich Shop,** 410 Main St. (493-2400) serves soups, salads, and sandwiches in a variety of combinations for $3. (Open Mon.-Fri. 8:30am-4:30pm.)

Because it is a major resort city, Penticton allows the hotels to charge prices higher than those in the surrounding towns. Singles do not come much cheaper than $35, especially after Canada Day on July 1. And even worse, campgrounds convenient to town are scarce; you may easily wind up having to grit your teeth in a hotel lobby and open your wallet wide. The **Kozy Guest House,** 1000 Lakeshore Dr. (493-8400), has singles for $35 and doubles for $45; in off season $25 and $35, respectively. The **Three Gables Hotel,** 353 Main St. (492-3933), has large air-conditioned rooms in a central location. (Singles $30. Doubles $32.) **Wright's Beach Camp,** Site 40, Comp. 4, R.R. 2 (492-7120), is directly off Hwy. 97 on the shores of Skaha Lake at the south end of town. (Sites $16, with full hookup $2.)

Penticton's **chamber of commerce** is at 185 Lakeshore Dr. (492-4103; open daily 8am-8pm; Sept.-mid-June Mon.-Fri. 9am-5pm, Sat.-Sun. 10am-4pm.) In summer, the city also sets up **North** and **South Information Centers** along Hwy. 97. (Open mid-June to Sept. daily 8am-8pm.) Penticton lies in south-central British Columbia, 245 miles east of Vancouver on Hwy. 97. Lake Okanagan borders the north end of downtown, with Penticton Airport and the smaller Skaha Lake lying to the south. Main Street (Hwy. 97) bisects the city from north to south. **Greyhound** serves Vancouver five times per day ($26.90). **Penticton Transit Service,** 301 E. Warren Ave. (492-5602), provides local transport (65¢) and a lake-to-lake shuttle between Skaha and Okanagan in July and August.

Penticton's **postal code** is V2A 6J8; the **area code** is 604.

INDEX